THE OXFORD HANDBOOK OF

CHILDREN'S FILM

THE OXFORD HANDBOOK OF

CHILDREN'S FILM

Edited by

NOEL BROWN

OXFORD

UNIVERSITY PRESS

OXFORD

UNIVERSITY PRESS

Oxford University Press is a department of the University of Oxford. It furthers
the University's objective of excellence in research, scholarship, and education
by publishing worldwide. Oxford is a registered trade mark of Oxford University
Press in the UK and certain other countries.

Published in the United States of America by Oxford University Press
198 Madison Avenue, New York, NY 10016, United States of America.

© Oxford University Press 2022

CIP data is on file at the Library of Congress
ISBN 978–0–19–093935–9

1 3 5 7 9 8 6 4 2

DOI: 10.1093/oxfordhb/9780190939359.001.0001

Printed by Sheridan Books, Inc., United States of America

Contents

PART III CHILDREN'S FILM AND PERFORMANCE

PART IV CHILDREN'S CINEMA, SOCIETY, AND NATIONAL IDENTITY

PART V HOLLYWOOD AND FAMILY AUDIENCES

PART VI AUDIENCES, ENGAGEMENT, AND PARTICIPATORY CULTURE

LIST OF ILLUSTRATIONS

LIST OF TABLES

ABOUT THE CONTRIBUTORS

Claudia Alonso-Recarte is Senior Lecturer in English at the University of Valencia (Spain). Her research is in the field of (Critical) Animal Studies, with a particular focus on the cultural history and manifestation of nonhuman others in literature and the performing arts. She has published in the journals *Men and Masculinities*; *Critical Studies on Terrorism*; *Gender, Place and Culture*; *Atlantis*; *Studies in Theatre and Performance*; *Cahiers victoriens et édouardiens*; and *Journal for Critical Animal Studies*, among others.

Filipa Antunes is Lecturer in Humanities at the University of East Anglia. She researches childhood, horror, and popular culture, with a special focus on children's media. Her first monograph, *Children Beware! Childhood, Horror and the PG-13 Rating* (McFarland 2020), charts the children's horror media trend (1980–1999) to explore critical shifts in American cultural attitudes toward childhood and horror. Filipa has also published on genre, the PG-13 rating, and the Hollywood family film.

Bruce Babington is Emeritus Professor of Film at Newcastle University. His eleven books and many articles cover such topics as the musical, classical British film, star studies, New Zealand cinema, the sports film, romantic comedy, the Biblical Epic, and opera on film. He is co-editor (with Noel Brown) of *Family Films in Global Cinema: The World beyond Disney* (2015) and (with Charles Barr) *The Call of the Heart: John M. Stahl and Hollywood Melodrama* (2018). He enjoys running his website, ProfBruce (https://www.profbruce.co.uk), which includes his later work on Stahl and New Zealand cinema.

Koel Banerjee is a Visiting Postdoctoral Fellow at Carnegie Mellon University. Her research interests include South Asian cinema, transnational melodrama, neoliberalism, and consumer culture. She has published in the journals *Cultural Critique, Studies in South Asian Film and Media, Film Quarterly*, and *Screen* (forthcoming), and her work has appeared in several anthologies, including *Third Cinema, World Cinema and Marxism*, and *Bollywood's New Woman: Liberalization, Liberation, and Contested Bodies*.

Martin Barker is Emeritus Professor at Aberystwyth University. He is the author of fifteen books and many essays. In the latter years of his research career, he particularly focused on the field of media audience research, leading a number of international projects, and also conducting commissioned research for the British Board of Film Classification. He was founder and is now co-editor of the online journal *Participations*.

Daniel Batchelder is a Musicologist specializing in the study of Hollywood and Broadway musicals, with a particular emphasis on the animated musicals of the Walt

Disney Studios. He has contributed work on Disney music to *Paris in the Musical: The City of Light on Stage and Screen*, edited by Olaf Jubin, (Routledge, 2021) and on music and sound in Disney media to a special issue of the journal *American Music*, of which he also served as guest editor.

Cary Bazalgette taught English in London schools in the 1960s and 1970s before joining the British Film Institute in 1979. As Head of Education at the British Film Institute from 1999 to 2006 she led the development of new approaches to education about moving-image media for the three-to-fourteen age group. In 2018 she completed her PhD at University College London Institute of Education, investigating how two-year-olds learn to understand moving-image media. She continues to research and write on this subject.

Daniël Biltereyst is Professor in Film and Media History and director of the Cinema and Media Studies (CIMS) research centre at Ghent University (Belgium). He explores new approaches to historical screen cultures and controversy. He is the co-editor (with Richard Maltby and Philippe Meers) of several volumes, including *Explorations in New Cinema History* (2011); *Cinema, Audiences and Modernity* (2012); and *The Routledge Companion to New Cinema History* (2019); as well as *Moralizing Cinema* (2015, with Daniela Treveri-Gennari); and *Mapping Movie Magazines* (2020, with Lies Van de Vijver).

Noel Brown is Senior Lecturer in Film at Liverpool Hope University. He has written several books on aspects of children's film, family entertainment, and animation, including *Contemporary Hollywood Animation* (Edinburgh University Press, 2021); *The Children's Film: Genre, Nation and Narrative* (Columbia University Press, 2017); *British Children's Cinema* (I.B. Tauris, 2016); and *The Hollywood Family Film* (I.B. Tauris, 2012). He is also co-editor of *Toy Story: How Pixar Reinvented the Animated Feature* (Bloomsbury, 2018) and *Family Films in Global Cinema: The World beyond Disney* (I.B. Tauris, 2015).

David Buckingham is an Emeritus Professor at Loughborough University, and a Visiting Professor at Kings College, University of London. His work focuses on children's and young people's interactions with media and on media education. He has published over thirty books and over 250 articles and book chapters in these areas. His latest publication is *Youth on Screen: Representing Young People in Film and Television Drama* (Polity). More information, as well as a blog and numerous essays and articles, can be found at his website, https://www.davidbuckingham.net.

Ryan Bunch is a Ph.D. candidate in the Department of Childhood Studies at Rutgers University Camden. His book *Oz and the Musical: Performing the American Fairy Tale* is forthcoming from Oxford University Press. Vice president of the International Wizard of Oz Club, he has spoken about Oz at the club's conventions, at academic conferences, at libraries, and in media. His writing about Oz has appeared in *The Baum Bugle*, *Studies in Musical Theatre*, and *Adapting the Wizard of Oz: From Baum to MGM and Beyond*.

Amy M. Davis is a Lecturer in Film History at the University of Hull. She is the author of numerous books and papers on Disney and animation, including *Good Girls and Wicked Witches: Changing Representations of Women in Disney's Feature Animation, 1937–2001* (2006) and *Handsome Heroes and Vile Villains: Masculinity in Disney's Feature Films* (2013), and is the editor of the book *Discussing Disney* (2019). Her primary research interests are Disney studies, US animation history, gender studies, and Hollywood horror.

Stephanie Hemelryk Donald is Professor of Film and Head of the School of Arts and Social Sciences at Monash Malaysia. Recent publications include "Refugee Filmmaking" (2019) in *Alphaville: Journal of Film and Screen Media* (http://www.alphavillejournal.com/Issue18.html); *There's No Place like Home: The Migrant Child in World Cinema* (2018); and, as co-editor, *Childhood and Nation in Contemporary World Cinema: Borders and Encounters* (2017). She has had a long-term interest and a record of publication and media research with children and young people, particularly but not solely in China and Australia.

Lincoln Geraghty is Professor of Media Cultures in the School of Film, Media and Communication at the University of Portsmouth. He serves as editorial adviser for the journals *Journal of Popular Culture, Transformative Works and Culture* (online), *Journal of Fandom Studies*, and *Journal of Popular Television*. Major publications include *Living with Star Trek: American Culture and the Star Trek Universe* (I.B. Tauris 2007), *American Science Fiction Film and Television* (Berg 2009), and *Cult Collectors: Nostalgia, Fandom and Collecting Popular Culture* (Routledge 2014).

Gábor Gergely is Senior Lecturer in film studies at the University of Lincoln's School of Film and Media. His research focuses on national cinemas and the discourse of exclusion. His publications include books on émigré actors in Hollywood (*Foreign Devils*, 2012), on Hungarian cinema and anti-Semitism (*Hungarian Film 1929–1947: National Identity, Anti-semitism and Popular Cinema*, 2017), and journal articles and book chapters on French, Italian, British, Hungarian, and American cinema. He is co-editor of *The Routledge Companion to European Cinema* (2021).

Yuhan Huang is an Assistant Professor in modern languages and cultures at Rochester Institute of Technology. She earned her Ph.D. in comparative literature at Purdue University with a focus on film studies, women's studies, and Chinese studies. Her dissertation project, "Remembrance and Rumination: The 1.5 Generation of the Chinese Cultural Revolution," examines the poetics and politics of reviving and representing childhood and adolescent memories of the Cultural Revolution by writers, filmmakers, and painters. Yuhan is the co-editor of *Mo Yan in Context* (Purdue University Press, 2014), and a recipient of a Purdue Research Foundation dissertation grant (2016–2017) and a Lynn Fellowship (2013–2014).

Peter Krämer is a Senior Research Fellow in Cinema and TV in the Leicester Media School at De Montfort University (Leicester, UK). He also is a Senior Fellow in the

School of Art, Media and American Studies at the University of East Anglia (Norwich, UK). He is the author or editor of eleven academic books, including the BFI Film Classics *2001: A Space Odyssey* (2nd ed., 2020) and *The General* (2016), as well as *"Grease Is the Word": Exploring a Cultural Phenomenon*, co-edited with Oliver Gruner (Anthem, 2020), and *United Artists*, co-edited with Gary Needham, Yannis Tzioumakis, and Tino Balio (Routledge, 2020).

Bettina Kümmerling-Meibauer is Professor in the German Department at the University of Tübingen, Germany. Writ large, her research focuses on international children's literature, picture-book studies, children's films, and the relationship between children's literature and the avant-garde. She has written four books and edited more than fifteen volumes. Her recent studies are *Canon Constitution and Canon Change in Children's Literature*, co-edited with Anja Müller (Routledge, 2017) and *The Routledge Companion to Picturebooks* (2018).

Peter C. Kunze sits on the boards of the Literature/Film Association and the journals *Studies in American Humor* and *Studies in Musical Theatre*, and he cofounded the Society for Cinema and Media Studies (SCMS) special interest group for children's and youth media and culture. He edited *The Films of Wes Anderson: Critical Essays on an Indiewood Icon*, and *Conversations with Maurice Sendak*, and co-edited *American-Australian Cinema: Transnational Connections*. His current book project, *Staging a Comeback: Broadway, Hollywood, and the Disney Renaissance*, examines the creative and industrial relationships between Hollywood and Broadway.

Sung-Ae Lee is a Lecturer at Macquarie University. Her research centres on relationships between cultural ideologies in Asian societies and representational strategies. She is interested in cognitive and imagological approaches to adaptation studies, Asian popular culture, Asian cinema, the impact of colonization in Asia, trauma studies, fiction and film produced in the aftermath of the Korean War, and the literature and popular media of the Korean diaspora.

Anders Lysne is Assistant Professor of media studies at the University of Bergen. His teaching and research interests include youth media, film history, and media aesthetics. He has published several journal articles and book chapters on youth in Nordic screen media.

James R. Mason earned his Ph.D. at the School of Media and Communication, University of Leeds, and his research on Disney films and their adult audiences was the basis of his chapter in this volume. He has since written the nonacademic reference books *Disney Connections and Collections*, Vols. 1 and 2, published by Theme Park Press.

Philippe Meers is Professor in Film and Media Studies and deputy director of the Visual and Digital Cultures Research Center (ViDi) at the University of Antwerp (Belgium). He publishes mainly on historical and contemporary film cultures. With Richard Maltby and Daniël Biltereyst, he edited *Explorations in New Cinema History* (2011), *Cinema, Audiences and Modernity* (2012), and *The Routledge Companion to New Cinema*

History (2019). With Annette Kuhn and Daniël Biltereyst, he co-edited a special issue of *Memory Studies* (2017).

Debbie Olson, Ph.D., is Associate Professor of English at Missouri Valley College. She is editor-in-chief of *Red Feather Journal: An International Journal of Children in Popular Culture* (www.redfeatherjournal.org). Her research interests include images of children in film and media, race politics, and cultural studies. She is the author of *Black Children in Hollywood Cinema* (2017), and editor of *The Child in World Cinema* (2018), among others. She is the editor of the Lexington Books Children and Youth in Popular Culture series. Olson is currently at work on her next book, *Youth in Transition: The Child in New Hollywood Cinema*.

Becky Parry is the Programme Director for the MA Digital Literacies, Culture and Education in the School of Education at the University of Sheffield, and a leading scholar in the emerging field of children's film scholarship, focusing on gender and the representation of children and childhood in international films for children, as well as film and media literacy, She is a board member of the European Children's Film Association (ECFA), the international professional body for the children's film industry. Prior to her academic career, she was the director of a children's film festival and a film and media educator.

Ignacio Ramos-Gay is Professor of French and Comparative Literature at the University of Valencia in Spain. His research focuses on contemporary European drama and animal studies. A Fulbright visiting scholar at the Martin E. Seagal Theatre Center at the City University of New York, he is currently the team leader of the research project Live Animals on the Contemporary French Stage (1979–2016), funded by the Spanish Ministry of Economy and Industry.

Caroline Ruddell is Reader in Film and TV and Divisional Lead for Production and Performance at Brunel University London. She specializes in animation and representation on-screen and has published widely in these areas. She is currently researching craft-based, handmade animation. She is the co-editor, with Paul Ward, of *The Crafty Animator: Handmade, Craft-Based Animation and Cultural Value* (2019), and, with Nichola Dobson, Annabelle Honess Roe, and Amy Ratelle, of *The Animation Studies Reader* (2018). She is Associate Editor for the *animation: an interdisciplinary journal*, and co-editor (with Paul Ward) of the Palgrave Animation book series.

James Russell is head of the Leicester Media School at De Montfort University. His research looks at the intersection of cinema, social history, and economics. His most recent monograph, written with Dr Jim Whalley, is *Hollywood and the Baby Boom: A Social History*.

Adrian Schober has a Ph.D. in English from Monash University, Australia. He is the author of *Possessed Child Narratives in Literature and Film: Contrary States* (Palgrave 2004) and co-editor (with Debbie Olson) of *Children in the Films of Steven Spielberg* (Lexington 2016) and *Children, Youth, and American Television* (Routledge 2018). He is currently writing the monograph *The Omen* for the Devil's Advocates series (Auteur/ Liverpool University Press, 2022) and is researching the relationship between Steven Spielberg and Romanticism at the University of Melbourne under an Australian Commonwealth Scholarship.

Robert Shail is Professor of Film in the Northern Film School at Leeds Beckett University, UK, and former Head of Film and Media at the University of Wales, Lampeter. He has published widely on British cinema, gender identity in film, comic books, and children's film. His study of the Children's Film Foundation, which was supported by a Leverhulme Fellowship, was published by Palgrave Macmillan/BFI in 2015.

Timothy Shary has published extensively on ageing representation in cinema. His studies of youth include *Generation Multiplex: The Image of Youth in Contemporary American Cinema* (University of Texas Press, 2002; rev. ed. 2014) and *Teen Movies: American Youth on Screen* (Wallflower 2005); and he edited *Youth Culture in Global Cinema* (University of Texas Press 2007) with Alexandra Seibel. He recently authored *Boyhood: A Young Life on Screen* (Routledge 2017), about the 2014 Richard Linklater film *Boyhood*, and edited the collection *Cinemas of Boyhood: Masculinity, Sexuality, Nationality* (Berghahn 2021). He teaches at Eastern Florida State College in Palm Bay, Florida.

Matthew Smith is an independent scholar with an interest in British cinema, children's cinema, and representations of childhood on screen. He recently completed a Ph.D. thesis entitled "The Figure of the Child in British Cinema" at Lancaster University. A revised version of this thesis is forthcoming from Palgrave Macmillan in 2022.

Susan Smith is an independent scholar, previously Associate Professor of Film Studies at the University of Sunderland, UK. She is author of *Elizabeth Taylor* (2012); *Voices in Film* (2007); *The Musical: Race, Gender and Performance* (2005); and *Hitchcock: Suspense, Humour and Tone* (2000). She is the co-editor of *Toy Story: How Pixar Reinvented the Animated Feature* (2018), and co-edited a Child Performance Dossier for *Screen* (2012). She is co-editor of the British Film Institute's Film Stars book series, published by Bloomsbury..

Ingvild Kvale Sørenssen is an Associate Professor at the Department of Education and life-long learning, NTNU, Trondheim. With a Ph.D. in Interdisciplinary Studies of Culture and a background in childhood studies, she has previously researched and published on the tweens age group in relation to media and consumption, and on digital tools in early Childhood Education and Care settings. Her theoretical focus is on the relationality of human and nonhuman actors in different sociomaterial assemblages, especially children and media.

John Stephens is Emeritus Professor in the Department of English at Macquarie University. Founding editor of the journal *International Research in Children's Literature*, he was a recipient of the International Brothers Grimm Award in 2007 and the Anne

Devereaux Jordan Award in 2014. His books include *Language and Ideology in Children's Fiction* (1992); and, as editor, *Ways of Being Male: Representing Masculinities in Children's Literature and Film* (2002); *Subjectivity in Asian Children's Literature and Film* (2013); and *The Routledge Companion to International Children's Literature* (2017).

Sam Summers lectures in animation history and theory at Middlesex University, specializing in computer animation, aesthetics, intertextuality, and the Hollywood animation industry. As well as publishing several articles and book chapters on these topics, he is the co-editor of *Toy Story: How Pixar Reinvented the Animated Feature* (2018) and the author of *DreamWorks Animation: Intertextuality and Aesthetics in Shrek and Beyond* (2020).

Aleit Veenstra is Senior Media Researcher at GfK in The Netherlands. She obtained a Ph.D. in communication studies (2017) at the University of Antwerp, Belgium, on the project "Screen(ing) Audiences." She published on young film audiences in *Communications* (2020) and *Tripodos* (2017, with Philippe Meers and Daniël Biltereyst), fan audiences in *Participations* (2016, with Tonny Krijnen, Annemarie Kersten, Philippe Meers, and Daniël Biltereyst) and popular culture and consumption in *Sociology Compass* (2013, with Giselinde Kuipers).

Katherine Whitehurst is a Lecturer in Media and Cultural Studies at the University of Liverpool. Her current research focuses on the adaptation of literary works across film, television, and comic books. More specifically, she writes and publishes on representations of female youth, development, and ageing in contemporary fairy-tale adaptations and youth films.

Anders Wilhelm Åberg is a Senior Lecturer at Linnaeus University. He has published a book on the Swedish filmmaker Vilgot Sjöman and articles on televised fiction, film criticism, and Swedish children's films.

Pamela Robertson Wojcik is Professor and Chair of the Department of Film, TV and Theatre at the University of Notre Dame. She is most recently author of *Gidget: Origins of a Teen Girl Media Franchise* (Routledge 2021) and *Fantasies of Neglect: Imagining the Urban Child in American Film and Fiction* (Rutgers University Press 2016) and co-editor of *Media Crossroads: Intersections of Space and Identity* (Duke University Press 2021).

Ian Wojcik-Andrews is Professor of Children's Literature at Eastern Michigan University (USA). His publications include *Children's Films: History, Ideology, Pedagogy, Theory* (Garland 2000) and chapters in *Kidding Around: The Child in Film and Media* (Bloomsbury Academic 2014), *Little Red Readings: Historical Materialist Perspectives on Children's Literature* (University Press of Mississippi 2014), *Children's Play in Literature: Investigating the Strengths and the Subversions of the Playing Child* (Routledge 2018), and *The Palgrave Handbook of Children's Film and Television* (Palgrave Macmillan 2019).

INTRODUCTION: COMING TO TERMS WITH CHILDREN'S FILM

NOEL BROWN

ON December 28, 1895, the Lumière brothers, Auguste and Louis, held their first public screening of projected motion pictures for a paying public at the Grand Café, Paris. This event marked the beginning of commercial cinema. One of the ten shorts on display was *L'Arroseur arrosé* (*The Sprinkler Sprinkled*, 1895), a 49-second film in which a young boy tricks a grown-up gardener into spraying himself with water from his own hose pipe and is rewarded for his impertinence with a smacked bottom. According to one of the first substantial works on the subject, this unassuming short—which presents a familiar image of the child as both innocent and as a mischievous, trickster figure—can be seen as the first children's film.[1]

The earliest commercial productions were examples of what Tom Gunning calls the "cinema of attraction," designed to showcase the aesthetic potentiality of the film medium; they were intended for the consumption of a general public that was not differentiated by age or background.[2] However, exhibitors soon began programming separate screenings for children. The first commercial film screening in the United States took place at Koster & Bial's Music Hall in New York (on the site of what would later become Macy's department store) in April 1896. A variation of the same programme subsequently toured the country. In March 1897, the Opera House in Calumet, Michigan, offered a children's programme composed of various non-fiction short subjects including "The Rescue of Four Horses from a Burning Building," "Athletic Performances," "Dances," and, perhaps most intriguingly, "The New York Fire Department Answering Alarm."[3]

The Eden Musée in Manhattan, New York, also held special yuletide film shows for children from 1898 onwards, advertising a "Children's Christmas Pantomime Cinematograph."[4] Adults and children paid different admission fees (evening shows cost 35 cents for adults and 15 cents for children), and the theatre also offered a Saturday "School children's matinee" for 10 cents. Another early example was a tour by the Great

American Bioscope, which presented a film show in Mickleover, Great Britain, in February 1900. The screening was promoted as "free from vulgarity throughout" and the admission fee for children was 1 penny, as opposed to 3 pence for adult patrons.[5] The practice of separating child and adult audiences by offering specialized children's film performances (typically charged at half-price) was later adopted by commercial exhibitors in many countries. More importantly, specialized children's film shows of this type (even at this early stage) were based on a presumption that has underpinned the larger history of children's film: that young people have different aesthetic and moral requirements to those of adults.

But while children's film may be as old as cinema itself (or very nearly), a consistent body of scholarship on the subject did not emerge until much later. Many early works were sociological studies of children's engagement with movies, either examining their consumption habits or exploring the behavioural effects of cinemagoing on young minds. Studies of this type include *The Cinema: Its Present Position and Future Possibilities*, commissioned by the National Council of Public Morals (1917),[6] Alice Miller Mitchell's *Children and Movies* (1929),[7] and the Payne Fund Studies, a comprehensive series of sociological and theoretical works published between 1933 and 1935, organized by an anti-movie lobby, the Motion Picture Research Council.[8] In these works, the primary interest was in children as audiences, and this remains a fertile subject to this day. However, more analytical works on children's cinema did not appear until the 1980s, by which point academic disciplines such as cultural studies, film studies, education studies, and children's literary studies were well-established in university and college courses internationally.

In the absence of a disciplinary framework of its own, much of the foundational scholarship on children's film emerged from these fields. Important works that considered the representation of children on film included Ruth M. Goldstein and Edith Zornow's *The Screen Image of Youth: Movies about Children and Adolescents* (1980), Kathy Merlock Jackson's *Images of Children in American Film: A Sociocultural Analysis* (1986), and Neil Sinyard's *Children in the Movies* (1992).[9] Ian Wojcik-Andrews's *Children's Films: History, Ideology, Pedagogy, Theory* (2000) was the first monograph to explore the genre in its international manifestations. Nevertheless, until recent years there was comparatively little interest in children's cinema in the arena of film studies, a fact that Peter Krämer, author of several ground-breaking articles on Hollywood children's films, attributed to a combination of aesthetic prejudice against what has often been perceived as a "low" cultural practice, and the difficulties of conceptualizing such a diverse format.[10] Valuable research on children's film has also emerged from children's literary studies (often exploring issues of adaptation between films and their literary pre-texts);[11] children's education (including the role of films in developing media literacy in children);[12] and animation studies (particularly auteurist accounts of key filmmakers and studios, most notably, Disney).[13]

Children's film studies has emerged as a vibrant and diverse field of critical enquiry. Nevertheless, until recently very few scholars would have regarded children's film as their exclusive (or even primary) scholarly pursuit. Indeed, children's film studies remains an inherently interdisciplinary field, one positioned at the intersection of several larger disciplines. Text-focused research on children's film has its methodological origins in literary (and later film) studies, with a particular emphasis on history, poetics, and ideological meanings; audience-focused research on children's film has used the tools of sociology, anthropology, and psychology. Some works combine elements of both traditions, approaching the subject from the perspectives of media industries, reception studies, and fandom.

This volume serves as an in-depth introduction to children's film. It is unapologetically broad in its historical and geographic scope, encompassing the entire history of children's film from the silent era to the present and exploring children's film as an international phenomenon, both in terms of production and consumption practices. There are no pretentions to be a complete account of children's film (which would be impossible in any single work). Nonetheless, this handbook does acknowledge that scholarship on children's cinema has focused its attentions primarily on Western nations, particularly Hollywood, thereby obscuring the wider field of international children's films. It seeks to redress the balance, building on a series of recent publications that explore children's films in their global, multicultural, and regional diversity.[14]

The intention here is twofold: to capture a cross-section of ground-breaking, interdisciplinary research in the field, and to establish—or, in some cases, cement—foundations for subsequent scholarship. The book is divided into six parts, each of which represents a major avenue of current research: (i) Genre and Form; (ii) Children, Childhood, and Growing Up; (iii) Children's Film and Performance; (iv) Children's Cinema, Society, and National Identity; (v) Hollywood and Family Entertainment; and (vi) Audiences, Engagement, and Participatory Culture. As editor, I devised the basic layout of the book and commissioned the majority of the contributors to write on specific topics. However, the result is very much a collaborative effort, and many authors took their chapters in quite different directions to those initially envisaged. Where possible, I encouraged creative deviations from the initial plan, preferring to avoid an overly schematic, "top-down" editorial model. Instead, the focus on is promoting new theoretical approaches and original case studies of neglected films, filmmakers, performers, cinematic trends, and consumption habits, as well as original perspectives on topics (such as Disney and Hollywood) that have already been the subject of considerable scholarship.

QUESTIONS OF DEFINITION

It has become something of a tradition that a book about children's film opens with a lengthy preamble that attempts to unpick the problems, or at least the ambiguities, of definition. By necessity, this introduction follows a similar pattern. Kimberley Reynolds's observation that there is "no single, coherent, fixed body of work that makes up children's literature" applies equally well to children's film.[15] Instead, there are many kinds of children's film, "produced at different times in different ways for different purposes produced by different kinds of people."[16] We must therefore begin by acknowledging the inherent plurality of children's film, which reaches across different historical periods and nations, languages and cultures, genres and media. Unsurprisingly, there is no absolute consensus on how it should be defined, and even whether it is possible to define it. Broadly speaking, scholarship on the subject falls into one of two camps. The first actively resists critical definition, often admitting any film that (i) features children or (ii) is viewed by children. Such a position is championed by Wojcik-Andrews, whose broadly encompassing approach to the field has been adopted by several subsequent works, including the recent volume *The Palgrave Handbook of Children's Film and Television* (2019).[17] The second position argues in favour of a narrower understanding of children's film, encompassing films that are produced and marketed for children (or for a wider audience that substantially includes children) and popularly received as such.[18] While scholars in the former camp might regard tighter conceptualizations of this kind as unnecessarily restrictive, adherents of the latter camp tend to view broader definitions as counterproductive, since many films that feature children, such as *The Exorcist* (William Friedkin, 1973), are intended for adults, and therefore are likely to have very little in common with films that specifically *address* children, such as *The Wizard of Oz* (Victor Fleming, 1939).

Generally speaking, this handbook adopts the narrower conceptualization of children's film.[19] In so doing, it follows Stephanie Hemelryk Donald's helpful distinction between "childhood films" (which explore the condition of childhood and centre on children but may be unsuitable for their consumption) and "children's films" (which are intended for and actively consumed by child audiences).[20] It must be noted that this distinction is not always clear-cut. François Truffaut's *The 400 Blows* (*Les quatre cents coups*, 1959), described by Vicky Lebeau as "*the* definitive film about childhood," might be considered morally "suitable" for children but probably appeals primarily to adults.[21] Conversely, action-adventure movies such as *Jaws* (Steven Spielberg, 1975) and the *James Bond* series (1962–) often appeal to (and are widely consumed by) children. However, it is important to remember that a film's generic identity is not just determined by what takes place on screen: it is also manufactured through a wide range of non-textual discourses, and negotiated by audiences.[22] For example, even without having watched the film, audiences might recognize *Frozen* (Chris Buck and Jennifer Lee, 2013) as a film for children solely through contextual discourses such as (i) its marketing and distribution strategies (such as movie posters and trailers); (ii) its suitability rating (PG in the United States); (iii) reviews and word-of-mouth reception to the film; (iv) the merchandizing that surrounds it (helped by its association with Disney, the quintessential purveyor of children's media); and (v) the child-friendly exhibition strategies that have accompanied it (e.g.,, daytime or early evening scheduling in cinemas, festivals, and television, and categorizations on video-on-demand platforms).

By the same token, contextual discourses are shaped by recognition of the *textual* elements that place films within an interpretive framework. In very simple terms, most people (and not just children) seem to recognize children's films when they see them. This suggests that children's film possesses a set of textual and associative significations that differentiates it from cinema intended primarily for adult audiences. Brown suggests five broad, overarching conventions: (i) the reaffirmation of family, kinship, and community; (ii) the foregrounding of child or childlike figures—including symbolic children, such as animals and immature adults—and their experiences; (iii) the exclusion and/or eventual defeat of disruptive social elements, such as criminals or other wrong-doers; (iv) the minimization of "adult" representational aspects, such as sex, strong violence, or extreme suffering; and (v) predominantly optimistic, emotionally uplifting endings.[23] Other fairly common story elements include the foregrounding of animals, magic, adventure, and play, and an emphasis on children's coming to terms with their place in the world, learning responsibility, and coming-of-age. Wojcik-Andrews also comments on the frequency with which "alternative worlds" are utilized as settings and on the use of "metafilmic" strategies that acknowledge and emphasize the artifice of the medium.[24]

As we will see, these conventions are far from inviolable. However, they do raise important questions regarding the boundaries of children's film. Several scholars, including Bazalgette and Staples,[25] Krämer,[26] Brown and Babington,[27] and Rössler et al.,[28] suggest that children's films are those produced primarily (but not exclusively) for children under the age of about twelve. As Krämer points out, young people aged thirteen to nineteen are usually targeted with "teen films," a genre that film scholars have tended to regard as distinct from children's film. This is not just because teen films attempt to mobilize a different audience demographic, but also because they emphasize taboo themes and representations of sex, violence, and other issues that are considered off-limits in the more protected realm of children's film. As such, the children's film conventions outlined here are most visible in films intended for younger children, and progressively less so in films made for young adults. Nevertheless, "children's film" is, to some degree, a contested site. *My Life as a Courgette* (*Ma vie de Courgette*, Claude Barras, 2016), an acclaimed French-Swiss stop-motion animated feature, was promoted and widely received as a children's film on the European continent, yet was viewed by several critics in the United States as a childhood-themed adult film.[29] Indeed, it was rated PG-13 in North America; it has a PG rating in Britain, Australia, and New Zealand; it was rated 10 in Brazil, 7+ in Turkey, and 6 in Switzerland; and it was not age restricted at all in France, Germany, and many other European markets. This absence of consensus points to a degree of cultural variance in perceptions of children's film.

While everyone has an idea of children's film, not everyone understands it in quite the same way. Differences in perception are not just a matter of individual subjectivity, but are determined by larger social, cultural, and political contexts. There are films produced for children that were not widely taken up by child audiences, and films that were once popular but have fallen out of fashion or into obscurity. There are also films originally intended primarily for grown-ups that have been appropriated by children, and children's films that are only recognized as such within specific national or cultural contexts.[30] Children's films may be a constant in the history of international cinema, but ideas of what they represent are dialogic. Several older accounts of children's film, such as Henri Storck's UNESCO report on children's entertainment films, published in

1950, argues that cinema for children should be "simple" and avoid "artistic direction." Yet some productions (especially in more recent years) blur the traditional boundaries between children's and adult films, addressing complex themes with greater degrees of aestheticization.[31] Any conceptualization of children's film, no matter how broad, must take these ongoing developments into account and consider sub-genres and cycles of film at the national and local level.

We must also explore the relationship between children's film production and consumption habits. The term "children's film" implies ownership by children—*their* cinema—but films supposedly made for children have always been consumed by audiences of all ages, particularly in commercial cinemas. The considerable crossover in audience composition for children's films can be gauged by the face that, in 2007, eleven Danish children's and youth films attracted 59 per cent of theatrical admissions, and in 2014, German children's films comprised seven out of the top twenty films at the national box office.[32] This phenomenon corresponds with a broader, international embrace of what is ostensibly children's culture among a multi-demographic audience. The old prejudice that children's film is some other realm, separate from (and forever subordinate to) a more legitimate cinema for adults is not borne out by the realities of consumption: children's film is at the heart of contemporary popular culture. However, this is a two-way process: just as popular culture is more "juvenilized" than it used to be (say, in the middle part of the twentieth century), so children's media has gradually become more identifiably "adult." Céline Sciamma, the screenwriter of *My Life as a Courgette*, has spoken of her intention to treat the film's characters "as grown ups," and of her conception of child audiences as "people looking for being consumed by an intense narrative."[33]

Examples such as this, as well as so-called tween franchises, such as *High School Musical* (2006–2008), *The Hunger Games* (2012–2015), and the superhero films released under the banner of the Marvel Cinematic Universe (2008–), speak to the increasing fluidity between everyday categories like "children's film," "youth film," and "teen film." Disney's *High School Musical* series, for instance, has generic similarities both to children's film (the avoidance of strongly "adult" representational elements, the narrative focalization on children, the happy ending) and to teen film (the emphasis on sexual awakenings and emotional maturation). The emergence of the "tween film" as an intermediate stage between children's and teen cinema responds to changing definitions of childhood in Western societies, in which the *non-biological* onset of "adulthood" is seen to occur at an earlier age than in previous generations. In most countries, however, more liberal conceptions of children's film (such as those in Scandinavia) have failed to gain traction. Internationally, the protectionist ethos that children's films should avoid representations of extremely unpleasant, traumatic, or potentially corrupting issues and forms of representation is still dominant; this is especially true of Hollywood, where there is a compelling commercial imperative in ensuring that child-oriented films can play to the widest cross-section of audiences. Still, it is important to acknowledge that children's film is (and will remain) a fluid and richly complicated phenomenon. This volume does not attempt to resolve the ambiguities identified here, but it does not deny them, and several chapters address films that blur the lines between children's, youth, and adult cinema.

Childhood itself, of course, is equally contested. Variously, the child figure in film has come to represent a broad number of states, ranging from innocence, freedom, naturalness, receptivity, playfulness, purity, spontaneity, and perceptiveness to know-ingness, anarchism, wickedness, filth, corruption, and degradation. By the same token, as Karen Lury observes, "The child and childhood, and indeed children them-selves, occupy a situation in which they are 'other': other to the supposedly rational, civilized, 'grown up' human animal that is the adult."[34] This "othering" of the child as a not-yet-competent person is reflected in popular perceptions of children's cinema as something that is distinct from films/cultural forms intended primarily for adult con-sumption.   Although this volume often problematizes conventional binaries between "children's film" and "adult film," it is true that some of the specificity of the former lies in its attempt to inculcate within young audiences a preferred worldview, one that is already held by the producers—and, in many cases, by society-at-large. A dominant metanarrative of children's film is the child figure's learning of responsibility and "cor-rect" codes of behaviour. This educative function is paralleled, in the overwhelming ma-jority of children's films, by the tendency to insulate child audiences from exposure to the atrocities of the "adult" world. The fact that, all too often, real children are victims of abuse, exploitation, slavery, war, forced displacement, and ethnic cleansing is elided in fictional representations, ostensibly to "protect" them. This kind of dishonesty (or, more charitably, benevolent selective honesty) is common to children's fiction—and, indeed, to popular culture more broadly.

All of this is underpinned by the fact that children's film is an invention of adult so-ciety. The genre does not just respond to children's preferred patterns of fantasy, or even to what producers believe children desire in their screen entertainment. Instead, it is prescribed by what society believes children *should* see. Determinations of this kind are based on cultural, psychological, and ethical considerations. Children's films, no doubt, also offer up images and situations that adults wish to see. Lury, following Andre Bazin, suggests that the cinematic construction of childhood as "a blank screen" upon which "adult emotions and fears" are projected is akin to the way that humans anthropomorphize animals.[35] This use of children as a blank signifier is perhaps more prevalent in adult-oriented films in which children are "perfect victims" of adult con-flict and brutality (a kind of representation that, as Lury points out, is calculated to arouse in adults complex feelings of sorrow and moral satisfaction) than in films in-tended for the consumption of children.[36] But as Sarah Wright points out, "cinema has revealed the potential of the child to act as a motif not just for the "other," but also for the self."[37] Childhood is a universal experience, and children's film shows us who we are, how we were, and what we could become. In its more nostalgic (and thus adult-driven) configurations, it also offers up visions of how were imagine we were, and who we wish we had been. Perhaps for this reason, Walt Disney repeatedly denied that his productions were children's films, instead claiming that they aimed to recuperate "that fine, clean, unspoiled spot down deep in every one of us that maybe the world has made us forget and that maybe our pictures can help us recall."[38]

Although discussions of children's film inevitably often focus on their pedagogic dimensions, Walt Disney's characterization of his films reminds us that the genre is also a medium of pleasure. Some of these pleasures are predicated on the celebration of the most appealing cultural associations of childhood: a sense of freedom and timelessness, the absence of burdensome adult concerns and affectations, the possibilities for pre-sexual adventure liberated from the pressures and responsibilities of "real life." Writing in the 1940s, the Soviet filmmaker and theorist, Sergei Eisenstein, postulated that the attraction of the early Disney features rested on their capacity to arouse "pure ecstasy," deriving from animation's "pre-logical attractiveness" which is "not yet shackled by logic, reason or experience."[39] The inherent mutability of the form, he argued, opened up a space "from which *everything* can arise."[40] Animation, of course, is a prevalent tradition of children's film, one predicated on bringing the inanimate to life in ways that evoke (and mirror) children's play. Its cross-demographic appeal can be seen in the popularity of traditional cel animation (e.g., classic Disney) and modern computer animation (e.g., Pixar, DreamWorks), puppet animation (e.g., Soviet fairy tales), and monster movies (e.g., Ray Harryhausen, Japanese *kaiju* films) alike.[41] Indeed, pleasurable depictions of play—or playful anarchy—are foregrounded in many children's films, as well as in productions with multi-demographic appeal, including Laurel and Hardy and Tom and Jerry. We might speculate that the guilt-free violations of decorum and appeals to unfettered physicality and absurdity at the heart of such films capture some of the pre-social attractions of animation identified by Eisenstein, and are undergirded by what Stephen Klein refers to as a quintessentially twentieth-century reconstitution of play as not mere idleness or irresponsible levity, but as the very "work of childhood."[42]

Of course, as the chapters in this handbook show, historical and cultural variations in children's film reflect the wider mutability of children's culture and childhood, as well as considerations of commerce and morality. While it may be governed by broad, structuring conventions, children's film remains pluralistic in the themes and ideologies it explores, in its stylistic and aesthetic range, and in the audiences it mobilizes. Children's films can be radical or conservative, escapist or didactic, formally conventional or stylistically innovative. They also encompass a broad array of media, including fiction and documentary formats; live-action shorts and feature films; and cel, puppet, stop-motion, and computer animation. Furthermore, just as Aristotelian modes such as "comedy" or "tragedy" may be channelled into a wide array of generic forms, children's films and family films are generically diverse. The following Hollywood child-oriented films all possess distinct multi-generic identities: *Snow White* (fairy tale), *National Velvet* (animal film), *Mary Poppins* (musical), *E.T.* (sci-fi), *Back to the Future III* (western), *Who Framed Roger Rabbit* (film noir), *Mrs Doubtfire* (comedy), *Toy Story* (buddy movie), *Coraline* (horror), and *Harry Potter* (fantasy). But while they may be approached from multiple standpoints, each of them can be located within—and, to a degree, are bound by—the broader conventions of children's cinema.

SURVEYING THE FIELD

In the early twentieth century, children's cinema developed in two partly intersecting, partly discrete traditions. The first was primarily non-commercial and intended for the near-exclusive consumption of children; the second was primarily commercial and usually intended for multi-demographic "family audiences."[43] Non-commercial children's films have typically been made under pedagogic principles, aimed at inculcating certain moral and behavioural practices. There is a long history of films aimed at children made for explicitly didactic purposes within systems of state-regulated propaganda. These include the fairy-tale and animated films produced by the internationally renowned Soviet studios, *Soiuzmul'tfilm* and *Soiuzdetfilm*; children's films produced by the state-run, socialist production company DEFA (*Deutsche Film-Aktiengesellschaft*) in the German Democratic Republic (GDR, or East Germany); post-war Czech puppet films, such as those produced by the likes of Jiří Trnka (the so-called "Walt Disney of Eastern Europe") under the auspices of the Czechoslovak Film Institute (*Československý filmový ústav*, ČSFÚ); and the more formally diverse productions of the Beijing-based China Children's Film Studio (CCFS), founded by the Chinese Ministry of Culture in 1981.

Non-commercial children's films have also been produced for largely non-political purposes. Britain's Children's Film Foundation (1951–1985) and the Children's Film Society, India (1955–) were borne out of a paternalistic governmental conviction that children should be offered films that meet their specific psychological and ethical needs, as well as their aesthetic sensibilities. While the creation and development of the Russian *Soiuzmul'tfilm*, the British CFF, and the Indian CFSI reflected an explicitly interventionist programme of cultural policy, state support of specialized children's films on a more modest, partly commercial footing remains commonplace in continental Europe, particularly in Scandinavia. In such cases, children's films are perceived as expressions of cultural identity, and as antidotes to the international commercialization of children's culture.

On the other hand, all but the most inexpensive commercial films are predicated on the economic necessity of attracting as large an audience as possible. As such, their producers almost invariably attempt to transcend their base audience of children. In mainstream commercial cinema, the perceived unprofitability of the "child audience," and the need to appeal to parents (who are usually required to accompany children to the cinema) has led to multi-layered modes of address. Films capable of appealing to multiple demographics—"family films," as they are usually called—are widely associated with (but not limited to) mainstream Hollywood cinema. Their appeal to older audiences is typically underpinned by the addition of adult stars, as well as material such as jokes, intertextual allusions, subtexts, subplots, and double-coded humour (e.g., wordplay or innuendo). It is also worth noting that commercial family films are far less likely to be explicitly moralistic or educational than non-commercial and state-funded children's films.[44]

During cinema's silent era (c. 1895–1930), the production of children's films was largely confined to North America and Western Europe, particularly France, Germany, and Britain. Cinema's silent era was, in some ways, inherently child-friendly, in that the films contained no dialogue and were often short and built around action and physical comedy. Some films focused on child stars or animals (such as Rin Tin Tin); others were adapted from family-friendly literary classics. Although children were among the most enthusiastic early cinemagoers, most films were intended for a "mixed" clientele comprising both children and adults. However, in the years after the coming of sound in the early 1930s, the proportion of films thought to be suitable *only* for adults increased dramatically. As tighter censorship restrictions were brought in, there was greater recognition in many countries that children and adults required their own distinct entertainment spaces. The two most important consequences were an increase in the provision of separate children's cinema shows ("matinees"), and the rise of purpose-made children's films.

While children's film was part of the fabric of commercial cinema from an early date in the United States, Britain, and much of continental Europe, not all national cinemas have an extensive history of producing child-oriented films. In general, a flourishing tradition of children's cinema is dependent on a cultural consensus that (indigenous) children's film is desirable, an industrial manufacturing and distribution base, the availability of creative talent, and a ready-made market. In commercial cinema, this market is usually a paying audience; in non-commercial cinema, it generally takes the form of organized performances for children (e.g., matinees, festival exhibitions, or screenings in schools). A further requirement is a political will to permit or facilitate such production. In state-supported systems, this typically rests on recognition of the potential ideological value of children's films, or a paternalistic desire to meet children's particular ethical, behavioural, and entertainment needs.

However, Hollywood family films have dominated the field of global children's film since the 1930s. Hollywood films are exported internationally, and account for approximately 60 per cent of the global box office. Moreover, much of Hollywood's ongoing global success is underpinned by blockbuster family films that target an all-inclusive audience composed of children, teenagers, and adults. Since the late 1970s, as Krämer observes, "most of Hollywood's superhits" have been "children's films for the whole family and for teenagers, too."[45] In the wake of huge, cross-generational hits such as *Star Wars* (George Lucas, 1977) and *E.T. The Extra-Terrestrial* (Steven Spielberg, 1982), Hollywood studios began to realise that blockbuster family films, besides their considerable box office potential, also represent the best opportunities for exploiting their brands synergistically across multiple platforms. Consequently, blockbuster family films are not stand-alone entities, but part of larger franchises that are realised across multiple platforms, including theme parks, TV shows, books, comics, games, and merchandise of many kinds.

At the time of writing, the list of the top fifty highest-grossing films of all time globally includes forty-nine productions classified (under the US rating system) as suitable for the consumption of children.[46] This list includes three "G"-rated films ("General audiences—all ages admitted"), 12 "PG"-rated films ("parental guidance suggested—some material may not be suitable for children"), 34 "PG-13"-rated films ("Parents strongly cautioned—Some material may be unsuitable for children under 13"), and only one "R"-rated film ("restricted—under 17 requires accompanying parent or adult guardian"). Since the 1990s, PG-13 has emerged as the preferred rating for films that target an all-inclusive mass audience. Despite the implicit warning of "adult" content, a high proportion of PG-13 films are marketed at children under the age of twelve, including *The Simpsons Movie* (David Silverman, 2007) and the last five instalments in the *Harry Potter* series (2001–2011). Consequently, just one of the top fifty highest-grossing films of all time is explicitly "not for children." On the other hand, several of them—including *Frozen*, with $1.2 billion, *Minions* (Pierre Coffin and Kyle Balda, 2015), with $1.1 billion, and *The Lion King* (Roger Allers and Rob Minkoff, 1994) and *Harry Potter and the Sorcerer's Stone* (Chris Columbus, 2001), with just under $1 billion each—are very much part of the landscape of contemporary children's multimedia culture.[47]

Again, the huge popularity of these films raises important questions regarding their audience, particularly in light of box office statistics revealing that children under the age of twelve accounted for just 10 per cent of all tickets sold in the United States in 2017 and 2018.[48] Although comprehensive data on the demographic breakdown of children's film audiences is not available, ComScore's PostTrak exit polling service provides valuable insights on the composition of audiences during films' initial theatrical run in North America. PostTrak data consistently registers that adults—people over the age of eighteen—make up around half of all attendees during the opening weekend of major animated features in the United States. Even accounting for the fact that parents are often required to accompany young children to theatres, this is a striking statistic, showing that adult audiences play a major role in sustaining Hollywood's industry of "children's films."[49]

Currently, the only major challenge to Hollywood's dominance of the global market in children's film comes from China, where the state has invested significant capital in building the infrastructure for a commercially autonomous national film industry. With its population of 1.4 billion, there is a huge, ready-made domestic market. According to Motion Picture Association statistics, China is now the second most profitable film market in the world (worth approximately $9 billion per year), behind North America (worth just over $11 billion).[50] Although state-funded children's cinema still exists in China, the biggest hits are products of commercial studios made for a broad, cross-demographic audience, many of them animated features that draw on aspects of Chinese folklore. Until the mid-1990s, animation in China was produced by a handful of state-owned studios. The turning point, as Shaopeng Chen observes, was the re-designation of animation as an industry; in 2001, "the state decided to develop it in the long term as a part of the national economy."[51] By 2006, there were more than 5,000 animation studios in China, with almost 500 universities running animation programmes.[52] The increasing importance of the Chinese film market is underlined by the fact that the only non-Hollywood film in the top 100 all-time box office hits is the Mandarin-language action film, *Zhan Lang II* (Wu Jing, 2017), and the highest-grossing non-Hollywood children's film (with a gross of over $700 million) is the Chinese animated feature, *Ne Zha* (Jiaozi, 2019). Both films earned almost all their money domestically. This adds weight to the observation that, while mainstream Hollywood films are transnational (typically grossing in the region of 50–70 per cent of total receipts outside the United States), non-Hollywood films are often largely restricted to their own national or regional territories.

Of course, by far the largest presence in the international children's film market is Disney. Indeed, the products of this single studio are almost synonymous in the minds of many people with the genre of children's film. In addition to the graphic richness of its animated features (and its huge commercial clout), Disney's international success has rested partially on its projection of universalist values. The Global Disney Audiences Project (GDAP), which around the turn of the millennium sampled over 1,200 responses to Disney films in several countries, found that the overwhelming majority of respondents associated Disney with universal qualities such as "fun and fantasy," "magic," "good over evil," "family," "imagination," and "love/romance."[53] The company has zealously protected its brand identity as a purveyor of such values, and in recent years has focused its energies almost exclusively on family entertainment, divesting itself of Miramax, its "indie" subsidiary, in 2010, and acquiring Pixar in 2006 (for $7.4 billion), Marvel in 2009 (for $4 billion), and Lucasfilm in 2012 (for $4 billion). In the aftermath of the Pixar deal, Disney executive Dick Cook enthused: "You can't come close to calculating what [this acquisition] means in the long term for the company in terms of new characters, stories, and lands for films and parks and publishing and more."[54] Disney CEO Bob Iger made similar remarks after the Lucasfilm acquisition, predicting that the ownership of *Star Wars*, "one of the greatest family entertainment franchises of all time," would "give us a great footprint in consumer products globally."[55] In 2019, Disney films accounted for 26 per cent of the global box office—an extraordinary statistic given that the company is almost wholly oriented to the production of family entertainment.[56]

This dominance is not just commercial; it is also cultural. With their high production values, international casts, and transnational appeal, Hollywood family films have had a major impact on children's films at the national level. Many countries have never developed a strong local tradition of children's cinema for the simple reason that Hollywood (and, particularly, Disney) films are so widely consumed. The GDAP found that,

> of those responding, 98 percent have viewed a Disney film; 79 percent have seen a Disney television programme (not including the Disney Channel); 50 percent have seen the Disney Channel; 72 percent have rented a video and 44 percent have purchased a video; 82 percent have read a Disney book; 53 percent have read a Disney comic book and 46 percent have read a Disney magazine; 72 percent have received Disney merchandise as a gift, while 60 percent have given a Disney gift; 64 percent have been in a Disney store; 73 percent have owned a Disney toy, 61 percent own Disney clothing; 30 percent have owned a Mickey Mouse watch and 26 percent have had Mickey Mouse ears; 54 percent of respondents have visited one of the four Disney theme parks in France, Japan or the USA—either California or Florida.[57]

The survey also found widespread willingness among respondents not only to introduce their own children to Disney products, but also to use them in an educational setting in order to help teach children "positive" values. Although critics have often viewed Disney with great suspicion on account of its supposed ideological conservatism and cultural imperialist practices, most consumers of Disney products across the world have over-whelmingly positive impressions of the company.

Disney's aim to be the world's leading multimedia organization for decades to come requires not just sensitivity to the needs and beliefs of different demographic groups in the United States and the Western world, but also the cultivation of stories and modes of representation that are capable of transcending borders, such as culture, language, and ethnic background. In its 1999 annual report, Disney described itself as having "underpenetrated overseas," and the company has since emphasized the necessity to "move with agility" in foreign markets by "exploiting international opportunities."[58] One of the great confidence tricks of corporate marketing is the ability to make the con-sumer believe that the product belongs to them, intimately and uniquely. Hollywood studios foster this perception through strategies of localism and individualization. Since its beginnings, Disney has taken its stories from international traditions of folk tale and fairy tale, and subtitling, dubbing, and local marketing and release strategies are all familiar ways of retailoring North American media to local markets. These strategies have intensified since the 1990s. For example, the dubbing of songs as well as dialogue has become more widespread, allowing Disney—as one executive put it—to "take our movies around the world and make them sound like local movies."[59] Perhaps the most important trend in contemporary Disney animation is the explicit, carefully signalled foregrounding of values of "diversity," "multiculturalism," and "authenticity" in productions such as *Moana* (Ron Clements and John Musker, 2016), *Coco* (Lee Unkrich, 2017), and *Mulan* (Niki Caro, 2020).[60]

To some degree, the antithesis between "Hollywood" and "world" cinema is mis-leading. Post-1980s multimedia conglomeration has decentralized film production. While Hollywood remains the nominal centre of the US film industry, a large per-centage of its films are produced in other countries, making use of cheaper labour (e.g., in Prague), or specialist technical facilities: the *Harry Potter* movies were shot at Leavesden Studios in England, and WETA Digital in Wellington, New Zealand, produces digital special effects for many "Hollywood" films. With the exception of Disney, none of the parent companies of the major studios are based in Hollywood (Sony's headquarters, for instance, are in Tokyo). Moreover, conglomerates such as Disney now favour a multi-layered production policy. While continuing to produce recognizably "Hollywood" films made in the "classical" style, they also invest heavily in family-oriented films produced by non-Hollywood studios felt to possess interna-tional box office appeal. Examples include Disney's distribution deal (since 1996) with the renowned Japanese anime production company, Studio Ghibli; Warner Bros.' in-vestment and distribution deal with Heyday Films, the British company that produced the *Harry Potter* series; and British animation studio Aardman's funding and distribu-tion deals with DreamWorks and Sony. Another trend is investment in "national" films produced in the local idiom (language, style) by companies in which Hollywood studios hold a financial stake or a controlling interest. In 2011, Disney acquired the Indian media company, UTV, and promptly announced a programme of Indian films "that embody Disney brand values—optimistic, fun, meaningful and emotional entertainment for the entire family."[61] Similarly, in 2012, DreamWorks entered the Chinese animation industry by co-founding Oriental DreamWorks with a consortium of Chinese investment companies.

Such initiatives tend to obscure the decline of small-scale, independent, and state-supported children's film. In particular, Hollywood's near hegemony has had a major impact on state-supported children's cinema, particularly since the 1980s, when the state-backed children's cinemas of Britain and the Soviet Union faltered in the international climate of economic liberalism. Although national initiatives such as the Indian CFSI and the Danish Children and Youth department still produce films, their subsidies are extremely low. There is still a widespread acceptance in many countries that films for children remain socially desirable, but the less active role of the state reflects a shift away from interventionist models of governance. It may be that mindfulness of the historical (mis)uses of state propaganda in regimes such as Nazi Germany and Soviet Russia has contributed to the conviction that the state has no business inculcating moral and behavioural values in young children in this way. Another factor is the so-called "soft power" exerted by Hollywood. Arguing that "the trend towards US dominance [of global cinema] is indubitable," Toby Miller and his co-authors in *Global Hollywood 2* point to aggressive strategies of protectionism, supported by the federal government and linked to broader expansionist agendas. Via government intervention, Hollywood studios have legally opposed attempts on the part of foreign markets to establish import barriers and other methods of sustaining local film production, arguing that such practices contravene established trade agreements.[62]

Outside the institutionalized structures of the multinational media conglomerates, producers of children's films since the turn of the millennium have encountered several seemingly intractable obstacles. Firstly, the dominance of Hollywood blockbuster family-oriented films has made virtually everything else look like a poor relation. Secondly, and relatedly, Hollywood's ubiquity has eroded the political will for state involvement in children's media culture in many countries, not least because Disney films fulfil several—though not all—of the instrumental functions of children's cinema. Thirdly, there are long-term difficulties surrounding funding and distribution. A 2008 article published in the European Children's Film Association's *ECFA Journal* addressed the issue of the "visibility" of home-grown child-oriented productions in a market dominated by Hollywood blockbusters, noting a "lack of money and a lack of screens," as public broadcasters injected fewer funds and multiplexes gravitated towards blockbusters.[63] Surveys commissioned by the ECFA reveal the extent to which European children's films struggle even to secure regional distribution. Of ninety European children's films produced in 2000–2004, almost half were shown in only one other European country.[64] Similarly, of 161 films released in 2004–2007, only fifteen were screened in more than ten countries in Europe, and less than half of these were distributed by independent companies. Overall, the survey found that approximately 80 per cent of admissions for European children's films occur in the domestic market.[65]

Despite these issues, children's cinema persists because of a deeply held conviction, in many countries, that it is a vital expression of local, regional, and national identity. Prior to the foundation of the Indian Children's Film Society, the country's prime minister, Jawaharlal Nehru, announced:

> There is one thing, I feel, India has been lacking in, and that is children's films. Films which are really children's films are of high importance... Good children's films can be a very powerful instrument in developing the child.[66]

In more recent years, the importance of a sustainable, indigenous children's cinema has also been highlighted by leading industry figures in Denmark,[67] Brazil,[68] and India.[69] The general sentiment here is aptly summed up by Charlotte Giese, head of the Danish Film Institute's Children and Youth department: "It means a lot to us that Danish children are watching Danish films."[70]

The most common avenue for international distribution of low-budget children's films is via the hundreds of festivals that take place every year. Although Peter Bosma describes film festivals as "the first curatorial phase in the process of global film circulation," the majority of films screened in children's festivals never receive widespread commercial distribution.[71] Instead, they may be seen via schools, clubs, and, in fortunate cases, television broadcasts. While film festivals remain vital to the distribution of children's films worldwide, their limitations as a forum for transnational cultural exchange are clear: in 2007, Günther Kinstler, a former organizer of the Frankfurt International Film Festival, claimed that even though more children's film festivals exist than ever before, "the chances for [a film] to find its way to young audiences in cinemas or on TV screens have decreased to a remarkable degree."[72] The continued importance of festivals, most of which primarily serve local communities, reflects the oligopolistic nature of international multimedia distribution—an oligopoly that global digital connectivity has, so far, failed to break.

Children's film festivals serve a crucial role in disseminating films that would not otherwise be seen. They also serve as institutional gatekeepers. While they do have a cultural (rather than merely commercial) mandate and often promote films that challenge genre conventions, festival programmers also have to consider the perceived requirements of their visitors (i.e., children, parents, and local schools) as well as the social and political considerations of sponsors—usually corporate entities and branches of regional or national government. Put another way, even though film festivals may be considered champions of independent-minded artistry, the content they screen is circumscribed by broader ideologies. Inevitably, of course, their selection is also limited by the films that are submitted for consideration; but since festivals are a vital outlet for many small-scale commercial children's films, it is easy to see how producers might self-censor more radical inclinations in order to conform to accepted standards. Furthermore, although children's film festivals are ostensibly for children, in some ways they are heavily mediated, "adult" spaces. Almost without exception, adults produce the films screened at these festivals, curate the programmes, and usually judge the prize-winners (although some festivals do have children as jury members).

Indeed, a frequently remarked-upon paradox of children's film is that it is a form that "belongs" to children, but is almost always produced by adults, and is often consumed by adults too. It has become *de rigueur* to reference Jacqueline Rose's claim to the "impossibility" of children's literature.[73] At its simplest, Rose's argument is that children's fiction does not address real children, but only constructs an imaginary audience from adult fantasies of childhood as a site of innocence and purity. As such, she contends that such fictions have little to do with "real" children, and merely reproduce adult desires of what childhood should represent. If, on its initial publication, Rose's argument might have appeared to invalidate the entire project of children's fiction, subsequent criticism has exposed several flaws in it: her extremely narrow terms of reference; her refusal to acknowledge the ways in which children's fiction can challenge (not just reproduce) ideological structures; and her under-appreciation of the complex, often dialogic mechanisms of consumption and participation, in which young people are able to "colonize" adult-produced media texts. As Joe L. Kincheloe points out (too optimistically, perhaps), "children's culture... takes shape in shadows far away from the adult gaze—as well it should."[74] Nonetheless, the enduring legacy of Rose's argument is a broader awareness of the near-inevitable imposition of adult preoccupations on children's fictions.

A lesser-spotted flaw in Rose's claim to the "impossibility" of children's fiction is that it presupposes that children cannot, and do not, produce it themselves. In the pre-internet age, this was not far off the mark; it was virtually impossible for children to produce and distribute a film (and much harder than, say, writing and disseminating a short story). At the very least, such initiatives were usually possible only with the involvement—and possibly the oversight—of adults. Perhaps the most notable example of children producing films in the age of "old media" is the work of the British Children's Film Unit (CFU), which was formally established in 1981 as a registered charity overseen by schoolteacher Colin Finbow, who solicited involvement from school children aged ten to sixteen. Volunteer children participated both as on-screen performers and behind-the-camera technicians. Films were shot during school holidays, largely on location, with Finbow writing the scripts, directing, and overseeing post-production work, and the resulting films were screened on British national television. While it is impossible to tell which narrative and stylistic elements are present at the behest of the young filmmakers, as opposed to Finbow, the work of the CFU remains notable at least in its *attempt* to capture the aesthetic and political interests of children.[75]

There are various subsequent examples of similar practices. Seven-year-old Saugat Bista is the current Guinness world record holder as the youngest director of a professionally distributed feature film (the Nepali production, *Love You Baba* [2014], although Saugat's father, Gajit, who wrote the screenplay and starred in the film, guided him through the process). Similarly, Brooklynn Prince, who wrote, directed, and starred in the short film *Colours* (2019), was "assisted" in these roles by Sean Baker, who had directed Prince in his recent film *The Florida Project* (2017). Perhaps more significantly, the film was distributed via the "Curated by Facebook" platform, highlighting (once again) the role that global corporations hold in mediating and disseminating children's culture. To date, the most famous example of a child making a feature-length film is Emily Hagins, who wrote, directed, and produced the independent zombie horror film, *Pathogen* (2006), as a twelve-year-old. Tellingly, perhaps, *Pathogen* is not intended for the consumption of children, but rather utilizes conventions of adult-oriented horror cinema, reflecting a broader tendency for older children to repudiate media content associated with younger children. A much more recent sphere of activity—one that film scholars have not yet caught up with—is children shooting, editing, and disseminating films using smartphones and free online-distribution platforms.[76] The Critics Company, a group of Nigerian teen filmmakers, have produced a number of micro-budget sci-fi films in this way. The relative ease with which children can undertake these activities has the potential to open up an entirely new sphere of cultural activity (although the high concentration of ownership in the global children's media industries demands a degree of caution in raising such a possibility).[77]

THIS VOLUME

Part I of this volume, "Genre and Form," is concerned with exploring the boundaries, the possibilities, and the constraints of children's film. Building on the debates outlined earlier in this introduction regarding the complexities of definition, Becky Parry's opening chapter examines similarities and differences in how children's films are defined internationally. Analysing a range of films, including the Kenyan production *Supa Modo* (Likarion Wainaina, 2018), she also interviews a number of children's film festival programmers based in Europe in an attempt to discern the criteria they use in selecting films for children's consumption. In so doing, Parry stresses the need to view children's film as a global phenomenon, arguing that the tendency to focus on Western (and particularly North American) attitudes to children's film—and to childhood more broadly—has stunted the discipline, and she points to a number of non-Hollywood films released in recent years that problematize the traditional boundaries between childhood and adulthood.

In chapter 2, Debbie Olson explores the ways that children's films "perform" innocence. Widely regarded as one of the fundamental tenets of children's fiction, the prelapsarian association between childhood and innocence is actually, Olson argues, primarily an invention of White, middle-class Western society. With reference to a wide range of films, she shows how Hollywood's sentimentalized representations of innocent childhood consistently exclude children from ethnic minority backgrounds and contrasts a range of Hollywood films with international productions that challenge this model. Ultimately, Olson argues for the constructedness, and the cultural variance, of cinematic performances of innocence; far from being "natural," such representations are heavily politicized.

Ryan Bunch, in chapter 3, turns his attentions to Hollywood adaptations of L. Frank Baum's *The Wonderful Wizard of Oz* (1900). In addition to MGM's famous 1939 version, Bunch discusses a range of other adaptations, from Baum's own silent-era shorts to more recent Disney reworkings of the source material. Drawing on Ian Wojcik-Andrews's contention that a playful, "metafilmic" dimension is a common feature of the genre, Bunch argues that Oz films consistently signal their identity as children's films by self-consciously invoking familiar tropes from fairy tales and other children's literary forms, and invite children to engage with them on this basis. By examining a sample of reviews of Oz films written by children, Bunch goes on to explore the ways these films have been received and utilized by young viewers. In the process, he shows how these adaptations respond to changing attitudes towards childhood and children's film in the United States.

In chapter 4, Bettina Kümmerling-Meibauer takes issue with the common presumption that children's films are inherently formally conservative. In fact, as she convincingly demonstrates, a wide range of international children's films have employed avant-garde cinematic techniques, ranging from the silhouette animation of Lotte Reiniger to the German expressionist influences in Disney's *Snow White and the Seven Dwarfs* (David Hand et al., 1937) and the French poetic realism of *The Red Balloon* (*Le ballon rouge*, Albert Lamorisse, 1956). Given that the supposed visual and narrative simplicity of children's film is often regarded as a primary point of difference from cinema intended for general audiences, Kümmerling-Meibauer argues that such examples of avant-garde stylization complicate binary distinctions between "children's film" and "adult film."

In chapter 5, Sam Summers shows how many contemporary children's films use intertextuality as a deliberate textual strategy, mostly in an attempt to broaden the appeal to adult audiences. With close reference to a range of post-1990s Hollywood animated features, he argues that the use of "authorial intertextuality," as he calls it, became part of the grammar of post-1980s children's cinema to tap the perceived profitability of the cross-demographic family audience. Focusing on the insertion of "adult" humour, Summers argues that many of the jokes programmed into such films as *Aladdin* (Ron Clements and John Musker, 1992) and *Space Jam* (Joe Pytka, 1996) address a more culturally literate audience (usually, but not necessarily, primarily made up of older spectators). These jokes are intended to be invisible to people—mostly younger children—who do not recognize what is being referenced. Intertextual strategies of this kind therefore reaffirm the sometimes arbitrary segregation of "child" and "adult" audiences.

In the final chapter of the opening section, Noel Brown examines one of the most widely observed narrative characteristics of the children's film—the so-called "happy ending". According to Brown, the vast majority of films for children do, indeed, possess a broadly optimistic resolution and attempt to arouse emotional uplift in their audiences. However, Brown problematizes the happy ending by pointing to the inherent ambiguities in many films—such as *The Wizard of Oz* (1939)—that might appear, on the surface, to exhibit unalloyed utopianism. He goes on to explore counter-tendencies that deliberately subvert the convention, while arguing that the subjectivities of viewers play a major role in making meaning even in the most apparently straightforward resolutions.

In Part II, "Children, Childhood, and Growing Up," contributors examine how cinema constructs childhood (and adulthood) across different historical periods and sociocultural contexts. In chapter 7, Pamela Robertson Wojcik examines the dual representations of children and the police in 1930s Hollywood films. Against the prevailing tendency in 1930s Hollywood child-centred films, such as those starring Shirley Temple or Deanna Durbin, the films Wojcik explores, which include Chaplin's *The Kid* (1921) and the vehicles of Jane Withers, Jackie Cooper, and the Dead End Kids, present children as tough, knowing inhabitants of urban spaces; equally, cops are shown as vaguely benevolent, ineffectual figures. Wojcik contrasts these portrayals of self-sufficient children outmanoeuvring unthreatening representatives of authority with more contemporary discourses in the United States that tend to construe children as unknowing victims of adult authority.

In chapter 8, Ian Wojcik-Andrews explores children's film as a site of tension between play and trauma. Pointing to a wide range of child-centred films that focus on war and human suffering, he focuses his analysis on the classic French post-war drama, *Forbidden Games* (*Jeux interdits*, René Clément, 1952). He shows how the film uses the perspective of its two child protagonists to emphasize the horror and brutality of war, and how their use of play when attempting to cope with suffering and loss subverts normative depictions of children's play as part of an arcadian realm of unfettered innocence. More broadly, Wojcik-Andrews suggests that a film like *Forbidden Games* resists categorization either as a "children's film" or an "adult film," thereby complicating critical attempts to impose genre labels.

In chapter 9, Robert Shail discusses the shifting representations of childhood in the work of the British Children's Film Foundation, which made non-commercial films for children's Saturday morning cinema shows between 1951 and 1985. Shail traces the development of the CFF films from their early middle-class paternalism to the much grittier, more complex portrayals of contemporary childhood in the later productions of the 1970s and 1980s. Drawing on a series of small-scale audience surveys of adults recalling their childhood participation in Saturday morning clubs, Shail also emphasizes children's cinemagoing as a social activity in which the relatively unmediated space of the Saturday morning children's clubs offered both a pleasurable viewing experience and a respite from adult supervision and parental authority.

In chapter 10, Stephanie Hemelryk Donald explores how the child-centred films of the Greek auteur filmmaker, Theo Angelopoulos, use what French cinematography refers to as *l'intervalle* ("the space between") to represent the subjectivities of migrant children and their often fractious, occasionally intimate interactions with adults. Donald's argument, like that of Olson, shows how adult ideas about the need to protect children and preserve their innocence are contingent on social and biological factors such as ethnicity, class, nationality, appearance, and—by extension—the child's ability to "perform" as children are expected to. As with *Forbidden Games*, Angelopoulos's films complicate our preconceptions of what children's film is or may be.

John Stephens, in chapter 11, turns his attention to visions of childhood and young adulthood in Iranian cinema since the 1970s. Stephens argues that Iranian child-centred films since the Islamic Revolution of 1979 have often foregrounded the child's point-out-view on the world-at-large, emphasizing young people's emotional and moral responses to the sometimes unfathomable adult world that surrounds them. As Stephens observes, many of these films are part of a larger tradition (critically referred to as the "New Iranian Cinema") that engage in social commentary under the guise of non-political children's cinema. Major Iranian filmmakers, such as Abbas Kiarostami, have recognized this relatively unmonitored space as an opportunity to confront pressing social issues while avoiding censorship by using strategies of metonymy and ellipsis. In discussing these tendencies, Stephens explores three distinct but interrelated traditions in post-1980s Iranian cinema: films for young children, films about children, and Young Adult films.

In chapter 12, Timothy Shary presents an in-depth generic examination of the under-addressed Hollywood "tween film"—defined here as productions that focus on, and are intended to appeal to, children roughly between the ages of eleven and thirteen. As Shary rightly points out, much of the existing scholarship has focused either on films for younger (generally pre-teen) children, or on older teenagers, thus overlooking the tween both as an audience and as an on-screen figure. He suggests that the tween film is primarily a post-1980s phenomenon that intersects with the advent of the PG-13 rating in the United States. He views the tween film as representing something of a midpoint between more traditional children's films and the increasingly mature content of the teen film, with an increased focus on the complexities of growing up, particularly sexual awakenings.

Anders Lysne rounds off this section by exploring representations of youth and maturation in Scandinavian cinema. He contends that Scandinavian youth films are typically concerned with issues of adolescence and engage with more "adult" subject matter than is usually considered permissible in films for younger children in most countries, including explicit violence and sexual frankness. Such films have often blurred the boundaries between films *for* children and films *about* children—partly a consequence, Lysne argues, of the collective status of Scandinavian cinemas as "minor cinemas" intended mostly for local consumption, and without the same commercial imperative to address cross-demographic audiences that exists in larger, transnational traditions of cinema. Equally, the films' less popularist modes of address and realist aesthetic have allowed them considerable success on international art house circuits as they continue to find popular acclaim in the domestic markets.

Part III, "Children's Film and Performance," engages with several interrelated areas of current research, including child and adult stardom in children's films, the use of real animals as on-screen performers, the behind-the-scenes work of animators, and musical performance. In chapter 14, Matthew Smith explores female stardom in early British and Hollywood silent-era cinema, focusing specifically on the films of Alma

Taylor and Mary Pickford. Smith argues that these representations of adolescent girls, which oscillated between tomboyish agency and innocent vulnerability, negotiated complex social changes during the early twentieth century (such as the suffragist movement), reconciling tensions between tradition and modernity. As such, these visions of girlhood engaged in much wider and historically important debates about the role of women in Britain and America.

In chapter 15, Caroline Ruddell explores the fairy-tale films of the pioneering German filmmaker Lotte Reiniger, whose meticulous silhouette paper cut-out animation occupies an ambivalent position in relation to the wider field of children's animation. According to Ruddell, Reiniger's work is quintessentially "crafty," predating (and, in some senses, disavowing) the methods of industrial manufacture that characterize subsequent examples of mainstream animation, including those of Disney. Although Ruddell is uncertain of Reiniger's placement within the category of children's film, noting that her productions have often been associated with an adult "art" crowd, she does argue that Reiniger's films embody values of "play" and aspects of moral instruction, both of which are familiar components of films for children. Furthermore, she points out that the "craftiness" at the heart of Reiniger's films, which result in a "handmade" aesthetic, affiliates them with the craft-like activities often undertaken by children. As with several other chapters in this handbook, Ruddell emphasizes the way that straightforward definitions of children's (and, by extension, adult) culture are problematized by figures like Reiniger.

In chapter 16, Daniel Batchelder explores the synchronization between animation and the musical structures of the early Disney shorts and feature films, ranging from *Steamboat Willie* (Ub Iwerks, 1928) to *Bambi* (David Hand et al., 1942). With close analysis of a range of films, he argues that these animated musicals utilize music not merely as a tonal counterpoint to the visual performance, but as a form of "synaesthetic presentation," actively working to create a utopian diegetic world that foregrounds a sense of harmony between its characters and the landscapes they inhabit; in the process, the boundaries between sound and image are collapsed. Part of the impact of this synchronization lies in the specificity of the animated medium, which—as Batchelder notes—extends the limits of diegetic space far beyond that of live-action cinema.

In chapter 17, David Buckingham considers the phenomenon of child stardom. Focusing on the early films of Hayley Mills, who began her career in Britain but who later became one of Disney's most bankable performers, he argues that child stars function in two primary ways, as *commodities* and as *representations*. Buckingham contrasts the realist spontaneity of Mills's performances in her British films, *Tiger Bay* (J. Lee Thompson, 1959) and *Whistle Down the Wind* (Bryan Forbes, 1961), with her Disney vehicles, *Pollyanna* (David Swift, 1960) and *The Parent Trap* (David Swift, 1961), in which her attributes of naturalness are transformed into a more conventional, cutesy image of ideal childhood. Mills's trajectory as a child performer is seen in context of a broader trend towards what Buckingham calls "Disneyfiction," in which childhood is sentimentalized and commodified, usually within films that tend to moral simplification and a right-wing social agenda, particularly in relation to gender norms.

In chapter 18, Bruce Babington approaches the topic of stardom in children's film from the often-overlooked perspective of adult performance, focusing on Danny Kaye's long career as a children's film star. As Babington points out, Kaye is one of the few major Hollywood comedians who interacts with children in his films in any significant way, perhaps because such comedians often embody childlike attributes themselves. Beginning with a thorough analysis of the way that Kaye's star persona—a combination of gentleness and vulnerability mixed with anarchic physicality—appeals to child audiences, Babington then turns his attention to Kaye's most famous and enduring vehicle, *Hans Christian Andersen* (Charles Vidor, 1952). He pays particular consideration to Kaye's performance in four musical numbers written by Frank Loesser that collectively, in Babington's estimation, encapsulate the actor's considerable appeal to children.

Rounding off the section, in chapter 19 Claudia Alonso-Recarte and Ignacio Ramos-Gay explore the anthropomorphizing of real animals in a range of children's films, and the ethical implications of this practice. Although there is a fairly extensive body of scholarship that explores the representation of animals in film (including humanlike animals in animation), real animal performativity in children's cinema has been comparatively under-addressed. Alonso-Recarte and Ramos-Gay argue that children's films almost invariably impose ideas about childhood on its representation of animals, thereby forcing them to conform to our desires and expectations. Like Buckingham, they also examine the ways that Disney's (mis)representations "bend[s]" the performer to the will of the presumed audience, and, more perniciously, the various ways in which animals have been physically abused during production processes. Considering the ethical repercussions of such treatments, Alonso-Recarte and Ramos-Gay conclude with a discussion of whether the substitution of real animals for CGI ones in the age of digital cinema should be welcomed.

Part IV, "Children's Cinema, Society, and National Identity," explores children's film as a site on to which national (and sometimes nationalist) ideologies are inscribed. As we have seen, there is a long history of children's film being used as a vehicle for state propaganda, but the chapters in this section are also concerned with the ways that children's film can challenge dominant ideologies, and, less polemically, how the genre often reflects aspects of local and national identity. A prime example of the latter is Adrian Schober's exploration, in the opening chapter of this section, of the "larrikin streak" in Australian children's cinema. As Schober demonstrates, larrikinism is a peculiarly Australian concept, denoting—very basically—the intersection of youth, anti-authoritarianism, self-sufficiency, and class consciousness. It formed an integral part of the national identity from the beginnings of the twentieth century onwards. In particular, the figure of the larrikin child can be seen as a conscious subversion of Romantic conceptions of childhood innocence and moral purity. Analysing a range of films that focus on larrikin children from the 1920s to the 1980s, Schober also reflects on the apparent demise of this archetype from more recent Australian children's and family films, perhaps reflecting a more diverse, multicultural social context, coupled with the commercial need in contemporary Australian cinema to downplay strong cultural specificities in the pursuit of transnational audiences.

In a similar vein, in chapter 21, Anders Wilhelm Åberg discusses the markers of national culture in Swedish children's cinema, focusing particularly on adaptations of the
children's books of Astrid Lindgren. Whereas children's cinema in Australia was primarily a commercial operation, in Sweden it developed in the 1940s as part of a national film policy. As Åberg shows, Swedish children's cinema has traditionally been
concerned with instilling good civic values and promoting aspects of cultural identity
believed to be intrinsic to the national character. The political discourse advanced an
idea of Swedish identity that is encapsulated by the word *Folkhem*. Such values are especially pronounced in the work of Lindgren, an internationally successful author whose
books are nonetheless felt to typify many of the fundamentals of Swedish national identity, often invoking an idyllic, pastoral community life that disavows modernity and
urban living and, instead, emphasizes security and mutual cooperation. Åberg points
out that, as with recent Australian cinema, such visions no longer seem to reflect the
realities of contemporary, multicultural Sweden, yet they still exert a considerable nostalgic pull in the twenty-first century.

In chapter 22, Koel Banerjee explores children's film as a possible site of resistance to
dominant ideologies. With close reference to *Hirak Rajar Deshe* (*Kingdom of Diamonds*,
1980), a children's film written and directed by the celebrated Indian filmmaker, Satyajit
Ray, Banerjee explores how Ray utilizes the allegorical potential of the fantastic mode
to articulate surprisingly direct criticisms of Indira Gandhi's notorious, unilaterally
imposed "Emergency" government of the 1970s, a period in which civil liberties were
savagely curtailed. In the film, its childlike adult protagonists, Goopy and Bagha, rise up
to oppose the ruler of a rival kingdom who controls all aspects of his subjects' lives with
a brainwashing machine. This allegory of proletarian revolt against fascist oppression,
Banerjee argues, also serves as a repudiation of any and all systems of oppressive government, including the current rise of Hindu fascism in modern-day India.

In contrast, in chapter 23, Yuhan Huang considers the history of children's cinema in
China as an instrument of nationalist ideology. Although children's films (and child-
centred films not specifically for children) existed prior to the establishment of the
People's Republic of China (PRC, 1949–), many of the most notable PRC-era children's
films, such as *Sparkling Red Star* (Li Jun and Li Ang, 1974), are revolutionary narratives
in which heroic child soldiers and workers fight for the creation or the maintenance of
a socialist utopia. Orphans are recurrent figures in such narratives, and the state serves
as benign symbolic parents. Narratives often present these orphan figures undertaking
heroic deeds that serve as a model for conduct to be emulated by viewers. Huang goes on
to explore the more liberal, Western-influenced individualist tendencies of some 1980s
films, such as *The Girl in Red* (Lu Xiaoya, 1985), before concluding with a discussion of
the "postsocialist" period of marketization in Chinese children's cinema since the 1990s,
which combines a mainstream aesthetic with relatively strict political censorship.

In chapter 24, Gábor Gergely turns his attentions to *Cat City* (József Nepp and Béla
Ternovszky, 1986), one of the most iconic Hungarian animated children's films, and its
belated sequel, *Cat City 2: Cat of Satan* (Béla Ternovszky, 2007). Noting the first film's
ideological placement within the state socialist system of the period, Gergely argues

that *Cat City*—in its allegory of a peaceful mouse society attempting to overturn a sadistic and tyrannical ruling order comprised of cats—exhibits racist and anti-Semitic undertones. With its story of greedy, brutal, racketeering cats attempting to destroy the benevolent mouse society, *Cat City 2*, Gergely notes, is even more overt in its anti-Semitic subtext, identifying the cat culture as an irredeemable racial enemy of a victimized nation. Although he stops short of ascribing racist and anti-Semitic intent to the filmmakers, he nonetheless draws compelling parallels between the historical treatment of Jews in Hungary and the films' representation of the cat society.

In chapter 25, Katherine Whitehurst considers how the representation of childhood in Hayao Miyazaki's acclaimed anime film, *Spirited Away* (2001), reflects aspects of Japanese history and culture. In particular, she shows how the film negotiates a tension between two contrary impulses in contemporary Japanese society: *kokusaika* (internationalization, particularly associated with Western individualism) and *furusato* (native place, associated with collectivism). Through the journey undertaken by the film's child protagonist, Chihiro, Whitehurst suggests that *Spirited Away* disavows the strong form of individualism, which is seen in the film to result in greed and ecological destruction. Instead, it advances a milder form of individualism that can be contained within a larger collectivist structure (manifested in the film's primary location, the fantastical bathhouse). As such, this deceptively simple film, Whitehouse argues, explores the ways in which Japanese tradition and neoliberal globalizing currents might be reconciled.

Sung-Ae Lee, in the section's final chapter, examines coming-of-age stories in South Korean cinema. Lee argues that Korean coming-of-age films, which are generally intended for a young adult audience, can be divided into two basic narrative patterns, or "scripts." In the first of these, which Lee terms the "well-being script," the young adult protagonist is typically an outsider, alienated from family and other social structures. Over the course of the narrative, they forge an emotional connection with another person (or persons), achieves a sense of growth, realisation, and well-being as they are finally reintegrated into civilization. The second recurrent narrative form, Lee suggests, is the "dysphoria script," in which the alienation of the protagonist is absolute, and which often ends in their death (typically by suicide). Lee concentrates particularly on these films' representations of female characters who seek agency, but are constrained by conservative social norms; in these cases, the narrative trajectory is resolved by a seemingly inevitable dysphoric ending, or the deus ex machina "well-being" ending that either attempts to reassert ideological reassurance—or, in some cases, self-consciously draws the viewer's attention to the improbability of a positive ending for female characters who strive for autonomy in contemporary South Korean society.

Part V of this handbook, "Hollywood and Family Audiences," delves more deeply into the commercial and cultural dominance of Hollywood films for an all-inclusive mass audience. As suggested earlier in this introduction, Hollywood children's and family films warrant particular consideration because they have attained a position of near-ubiquity in the global arena. Fittingly, then, the section's opening chapter, by Peter Krämer, examines the extent of Disney films' commercial dominance of the international market. Krämer begins by analysing the box office performance of Disney's hit films from the 1930s to the present in North America, contextualizing this data with evidence of the films' popularity on home video. In the second part of the chapter, Krämer goes on to discuss Disney's global industry position over the same period and considers production trends on a broader level. Until the 1970s, he suggests, Disney's films—then mostly musicals and adaptations of fairy tales—stood out from the biggest hits produced by rival studios, many of which were historical epics and live-action musicals. Since the late 1970s, however, most of Hollywood's biggest hits are family films intended for a broad cross-section of audiences. A recurring theme in many such films, as Krämer notes, is that they combine the threat (and sometimes the vision) of large-scale destruction with smaller, more intimate narratives about human relationships, particularly between parents and their children.

In chapter 28, Susan Smith takes a close look at *Jason and the Argonauts* (Don Chaffey, 1963), perhaps the quintessential film by the great stop-motion animator, Ray Harryhausen. With close textual analysis, Smith discusses the degree to which the film conforms to the broader conventions of children's cinema, and the features that might appeal particularly to young audiences. In the first part of the chapter, she highlights the childlike allure of the Talos episode, in which the huge bronze statue slowly comes to life, and which represents an animism (at the heart of all forms of animation) that captures something of children's fascination with investing inanimate objects with "life." Smith goes on to liken Jason's alternately dependent and fractious relationship with the all-powerful but capricious gods of Greek mythology, who watch over his search for the Golden Fleece, to the maturing child's attitude towards parental authority, arguing that—through Jason's narrative journey—the film ultimately balances its representations of quasi-parental censoring with a more empowering potential for rebellion.

In chapter 29, James Russell looks at the relationship between Hollywood and the baby boomers in the 1950s and 1960s. Usually seen as beginning in 1946 and continuing until the mid-1960s, the baby boom was a huge, unprecedented surge in the birth-rate in the United States. By the late 1950s, the US population included more children than at any point before and since, and—as Russell shows—this demographic trend had a substantial impact on popular cinema in the decades that followed. Initially, though, Hollywood was slow to realise the box office potential of the baby boom audience, continuing to make comparatively old-fashioned films for an all-encompassing family market rather than catering to the youth demographics. The incipient medium of television took advantage, with a large number of series aimed directly at adolescent children and teenagers during the 1950s and 1960s. In this period, the only major Hollywood studio that produced a consistent roster of films for a primary audience of children was Disney; as Russell points out, the company had almost uncontested access to child audiences during this period. Although the best-remembered Disney films of the period are its animated features, the studio was most prolific in the genres of live-action adventure stories. It was not until the 1970s (as Krämer shows in chapter 27) that the Hollywood film industry reoriented itself to the youth demographics.

In chapter 30, Peter C. Kunze looks at the under-appreciated role played by Hollywood animator Don Bluth in guiding Disney towards its resurgence in the 1990s, a period now widely known as the "Disney Renaissance." Bluth started has career as an animator at Disney and became one of the animation division's key figures before his high-profile departure in 1979 to form his own studio. With in-depth discussion of Bluth's key films during the 1980s, including *The Secret of NIMH* (1982) and *An American Tail* (1986), Kunze argues that Bluth's success (and the high-profile nature of his "defection") provided the impetus for Disney's reorientation to feature animation in the late 1980s after a long period in which its live-action productions and non-filmic activities (such as its theme parks and hotels) had taken precedence. In Kunze's estimation, the subsequent neglect of Bluth's films, and of his broader significance in the larger histories of Hollywood animation, testify to Disney's unparalleled ability to self-mythologize.

In chapter 31, Amy M. Davis looks closely at Disney's *Frozen* franchise (2013–), showing how the films, besides their colossal popularity, reinterpret the classical Disney formula in sometimes radical ways. As she observes, the *Frozen* films form part of a larger cycle of female-centric Disney narratives that de-emphasize the premium placed on heterosexual romantic love. More broadly, however, Davis argues that they place emphasis on female agency and self-actualization to an extent hitherto unseen in the Disney oeuvre. Drawing on Maureen Murdock's idea of the "heroine's journey" (a female variant of Joseph Campbell's "hero's journey"), she demonstrates that the films follow a narrative structure that culminates with the self-discovery of the films' co-protagonist, Elsa. Finally, addressing the controversy in media discourses over whether Elsa would be given a girlfriend in *Frozen II* (Chris Buck and Jennifer Lee, 2019)—thus becoming the first unambiguously queer major character in a Disney feature—Davis argues that the more radical move was to retain the character's apparent lack of interest in romance, thereby liberating the character (and audiences) from the conventional reaffirmation of romantic union as the truest form of happiness and fulfilment.

In the final chapter in this section, Filipa Antunes explores the catastrophizing discourses that surround contemporary Hollywood children's film that insist on its imminent demise due to a perceived surge in "adult" content. Much of this controversy, Antunes suggests, can be sourced to Hollywood's ambivalent identity, simultaneously a commercial enterprise and a culture industry. Antunes highlights three key moments that highlight the nature of this ambivalence: the replacing of the Production Code (Hollywood's system of self-censorship that existed between 1930 and 1966) with the present-day ratings system in the United States in 1968; the advent of the PG-13 rating in 1984; and the subsequent emergence in the 2010s of PG-13 as the de facto rating for family entertainment franchises. Ultimately, Antunes suggests, there is a perhaps irresolvable tension between social expectations for a discrete tradition of "children's films" in Hollywood and the industry's commercially motivated tendency to produce films for an all-inclusive, global mass audience.

Part VI, the final section of the handbook, "Audiences, Engagement, and Participatory Culture," focuses on what audiences—both children and adults—make of their experiences of film consumption. It opens with Cary Bazalgette's ground-breaking analysis of how young children—between the ages of 17 and 42 months—learn to "read" films. As Bazalgette points out, it is obvious that young children must actively learn to follow and interpret film narrative, as babies cannot, and three-year-old children usually can. However, it is not altogether clear *how* this process occurs. In response to these questions, Bazalgette finds that young children's acquisition of these skills is mostly self-directed, and that very young children invest considerable attention and energy to their movie-viewing activities. Although she argues that the social context (usually family viewing) has an important influence on children's engagement with movies, Bazalgette rejects the common presumption that media consumption at this early age is a passive spectatorial experience. Rather, even at this young age, the experience is one of intense, self-directed learning.

In chapter 34, Lincoln Geraghty examines children's film culture through the lens of fandom and paratexts. Traditionally, film studies approaches have been primarily text-based, analysing films for their thematic patterns, ideological orientation, and philosophical meanings. In recent years, however, a substantial body of scholarship has emerged surrounding the broader issues of how films are received by audiences, the meanings they make from their viewing experience, and the communities of fandom and production they participate in. Using *Star Wars* as his case study, Geraghty shows how a transmedia franchise of this kind exists alongside a semi-autonomous fan culture that invests in the diverse range of multimedia and paratextual materials (ranging from the film and TV spin-offs to merchandise of many kinds) and thereby extends and perpetuates the franchise. However, Geraghty argues that these paratexts are not merely an exploitative commodification of the source material, but part of a process of personalization undertaken by fans/consumers. These activities are often part of a life-long, nostalgic engagement with media texts that extends well beyond childhood.

In chapter 35, Ingvild Kvale Sørenssen draws on ethnographic research to explore how tween girls in Norway aged nine to eleven incorporate the Disney franchises *High School Musical* and *Hannah Montana* (2006–2011) into their everyday lives. As Sørenssen demonstrates, Disney is almost ubiquitous in contemporary Norwegian culture. Several of the girls interviewed for the project express the feeling that the Disney Channel is *their channel*, reflecting Geraghty's observation that fans not only partake of multimedia products, but also domesticate and assume ownership of them too. Furthermore, the girls' consumption of Disney products does not appear to be a result of institutional or peer pressure, but rather a pleasurable activity entered into voluntarily. Sørenssen concludes that Disney's role in the everyday lives of these girls is as a form of "social currency" that underpins friendships groups and informs other kinds of regular interaction.

In chapter 36, Aleit Veenstra, Philippe Meers, and Daniël Biltereyst draw on the results of an audience survey investigating how sixteen- to eighteen-year-olds engage with cinema in Flanders, Belgium. Veenstra, Meers, and Biltereyst address two overarching questions. First, they investigate whether film is still a central part of the media consumption habits of young people. Secondly, and more broadly, they seek to uncover the extent to which the assumption that multimedia convergence has inaugurated an age of widespread participatory culture is valid. The evidence of the survey suggests that film is still a major part in the everyday lives of young people, but Veenstra, Meers, and Biltereyst argue that active audience participation—beyond the act of watching films—is not a widespread phenomenon; nor is the claim that young people are entirely autonomous in their film consumption habits borne out. Rather, their choices are still largely circumscribed by the media that is made available to them in cinemas, on television, and on video-on-demand platforms.

In chapter 37, Martin Barker draws on two large-scale audience surveys that explore the reception of *The Lord of the Rings* (2001–2003) and *The Hobbit* (2012–2014) franchises. Although most of the respondents in these surveys were adults, Barker here delves into the reactions to these franchises from children aged eight to fifteen. As Barker points out, the films in these series reside on the boundaries of suitability for children, and may, indeed, be regarded as "adult" texts. Yet, as the data shows, they possess considerable appeal for children, even though many young respondents vocally disavow the suggestion that they are "children's films"—a genre that older children, in particular, tend to equate with simplicity and sentimentality. Moreover, many of the children interviewed as part of these projects emphasize the franchises' *transformative* potential—the sense that the films are not merely pleasurable objects but offer cinematic experiences that have substantively altered their perception of the world. Barker concludes with the cautious, but optimistic, proposition that the rise of fantastic literature and film is making a small but perceptible contribution to young people's sense of the potential mutability of the world at large.

Finally, in the last chapter in this volume, James R. Mason explores an important but still hugely under-addressed avenue of research: adults' consumption of children's films. As Mason points out, Disney films are watched by adults in huge numbers. Drawing on a survey of approximately 3,500 adults, Mason finds that the principal reasons for Disney's popularity among adults include appreciation of the films' "hidden jokes" (the intertextual humour that Summers discusses in chapter 5), the perceived quality and artistry of the productions; and the films' ability to elicit a sense of comfort and nostalgia. Conversely, the minority of respondents who dislike Disney highlighted the company's problematic representations (or non-representations) of race, gender, sexuality, disability, and body image; the impression that Disney's films were only for children and that they had outgrown them; and the company's excessive commercialization. Mason points out, however, that people may hold apparently conflicting or ambivalent views in relation to such issues. He concludes by noting that consumers' perception of Disney as primarily a purveyor of children's animation lags behind the company's current identity as a producer of all-inclusive family entertainment across multiple media platforms. Mason's observation that the Global Disney Audience Project, the last large-scale audience survey of responses to Disney products, is outdated in several regards serves as an important reminder of the ongoing need for timely and thorough investigations of how consumers—both children and adults—experience children's films (and the culture that surrounds them), and what they do with these experiences.

Collectively, the chapters in this volume represent a substantial addition to the existing scholarship on children's film. They address a broad range of questions that are fundamental to the study of the form: What is children's film? What are its boundaries, its possibilities, and its limitations as a form of cultural expression? For what purposes are children's films produced, and whose agenda do they serve? Who consumes children's films? And to what ideological, practical, creative, and imaginative uses are children's films put? However, although these chapters are authoritative, they are far from a definitive account. This volume is intended not as a comprehensive survey of the field, but as a basis for further enquiry and a resource for future scholars. The task of exploring the theoretical, historical, cultural, and political aspects of children's film has only just begun.

Notes

1. Kathy Merlock Jackson, *Images of Children in American Film: A Sociocultural Analysis* (London: Scarecrow Press, 1986), pp. 31, 35.
2. Tom Gunning, "The Cinema of Attractions: Early Cinema, Its Spectator, and the Avant Garde," in Thomas Elsaesser (ed.), *Early Cinema: Space, Frame Narrative* (London: BFI Publishing, 1990), pp. 56–62.
3. "Opera House," *Copper Country Evening News*, March 1, 1897, n.p.
4. "The World in Wax," *New York Tribune*, December 29, 1898, p. 10.
5. Terry Staples, *All Pals Together: The Story of Children's Cinema* (Edinburgh: Edinburgh University Press, 1997), pp. 2–3.
6. *The Cinema: Its Present Position and Future Possibilities—being the Report and Chief Evidence Taken by the Cinema Commission of Inquiry Instituted by the National Council of Public Morals* (London: Williams and Norgate, 1917).
7. Alice Miller Mitchell, *Children and Movies* (Chicago: University of Chicago Press, 1929).
8. For an in-depth discussion of the Payne Fund Studies, see Garth S. Jowett, Ian C. Jarvie, and Kathryn H. Fuller, *Children and the Movies: Media Influence and the Payne Fund Controversy* (Cambridge, UK: Cambridge University Press, 1996).
9. Ruth M. Goldstein and Edith Zornow, *The Screen Image of Youth: Movies about Children and Adolescents* (Metuchen, NJ: Scarecrow, 1980); Jackson, *Images of Children in American Film*; Neil Sinyard, *Children in the Movies* (London: B. T. Batsford, 1992).
10. Peter Krämer, " 'The Best Disney Film Disney Never Made': Children's Films and the Family Audience in American Cinema since the 1960s," in Steve Neale (ed.), *Genre and Contemporary Hollywood* (London: BFI Publishing, 2002), pp. 185–200, at 186.
11. In particular, see Fiona M. Collins and Jeremy Ridgman (eds.), *Turning the Page: Children's Literature in Performance and the Media* (Bern: Peter Lang, 2004); Robyn McCallum, *Screen Adaptations and the Politics of Childhood: Transforming Children's Literature into Film* (London: Palgrave Macmillan, 2018); Casie Hermansson, *Filming the Children's Book: Adapting Metafiction* (Edinburgh: Edinburgh University Press, 2019); and Meghann Meeusen, *Children's Books on the Big Screen* (Jackson: University Press of Mississippi, 2020).
12. See David Buckingham, *Media Education: Literacy, Learning and Contemporary Culture* (Cambridge, UK: Polity, 2003); Cary Bazalgette, *Teaching Media in Primary Schools*

(London: Sage, 2010); Becky Parry, *Children, Film and Literacy* (Basingstoke, UK: Palgrave Macmillan, 2013); and Jeannie Hill Bulman, *Children's Reading of Film and Visual Literacy in the Primary Curriculum* (Cham, Switzerland: Palgrave Macmillan, 2017).

13. There is a particularly rich tradition of scholarship on Disney; a thorough survey is beyond the scope of this introduction, but a very select list of key works in the field includes Richard Schickel, *The Disney Version* (1968; repr. Chicago: Elephant Paperback, 1997); Donald Crafton, *Before Mickey: The Animated Film, 1898–1928* (Chicago: University of Chicago Press, 1993); Steven Watts, *The Magic Kingdom: Walt Disney and the American Way of Life* (Columbia: University of Missouri Press, 1997); Janet Wasko, *Understanding Disney: The Manufacture of Fantasy* (Cambridge, UK: Polity Press, 2001); Nicholas Sammond, *Babes in Tomorrowland: Walt Disney and the Making of the American Child, 1930–1960* (Durham, NC: Duke University Press, 2005); and Chris Pallant, *Demystifying Disney: A History of Disney Feature Animation* (London: Continuum, 2011).

14. See, for instance, Noel Brown and Bruce Babington (eds.), *Family Films in Global Cinema: The World beyond Disney* (London: I.B. Tauris, 2015); Stephanie Hemelryk Donald, Emma Wilson, and Sarah Wright (eds.), *Childhood and Nation in Contemporary World Cinema: Borders and Encounters* (London: Bloomsbury, 2017); Noel Brown, *The Children's Film: Genre, Nation and Narrative* (New York: Columbia University Press, 2017); Stephanie Hemelryk Donald, *There's No Place Like Home: The Migrant Child in World Cinema* (London: I.B. Tauris, 2018)); Debbie Olson (ed.), *The Child in World Cinema* (Lanham, MD: Rowman and Littlefield, 2018); Casie Hermansson and Janet Zepernick (eds.), *The Palgrave Handbook of Children's Film and Television* (Cham, Switzerland: Palgrave Macmillan, 2019).

15. Kimberley Reynolds, *Children's Literature: A Very Short Introduction* (Oxford: Oxford University Press, 2011), pp. 2–3.

16. Reynolds, *Children's Literature*, pp. 2–3.

17. Ian Wojcik-Andrews, *Children's Films: History, Ideology, Pedagogy, Theory* (New York: Garland, 2000); Hermansson and Zepernick, *Palgrave Handbook of Children's Film and Television*; also Bettina Kümmerling-Meibauer, "Introduction: New Perspectives in Children's Film Studies," *Journal of Educational Media, Memory, and Society* 8:2 (2013), pp. 39–44. M. Keith Booker does not even see definition as being an important issue and adopts a "common sense" approach to identifying the films he examines. See M. Keith Booker, *Disney, Pixar, and the Hidden Messages of Children's Films* (Santa Barbara, CA: Praeger, 2010).

18. For example, Stephanie Hemelryk Donald and Kirsten Seale argue that "a children's film is a film produced for a primary audience of children." Stephanie Hemelryk Donald and Kirsten Seale, "Children's Film Culture," in Dafna Lemish (ed.), *The Routledge International Handbook of Children, Adolescents, and Media* (London: Routledge, 2013), pp. 95–102, at 98. Also see Cary Bazalgette and Terry Staples, "Unshrinking the Kids: Children's Cinema and the Family Film," in Cary Bazalgette and David Buckingham (eds.), *In Front of the Children* (London: BFI Publishing, 1995), 92–108; Krämer, "Best Disney Film Disney Never Made," p. 186.

19. It does, however, explore "grey areas" in several chapters, such as those by Wojcik-Andrews, Hemelryk Donald, Lysne, and Lee.

20. Stephanie Donald, *Public Secrets, Public Spaces: Cinema and Civility in China* (Lanham, MD: Rowman and Littlefield, 2000), p.48.

21. Vicky Lebeau, *Childhood and Cinema* (London: Reaktion Books, 2008), p. 73.

22. For a deeper discussion of contextual approaches to genre in relation to children's cinema, see Brown, *Children's Film*, p. 5.

23. Ibid., pp. 12–15.

24. Wojcik-Andrews, *Children's Films*, pp. 10–11.

25. Ibid., pp. 10–11.

26. Krämer, "Best Disney Film Disney Never Made," p. 186.

27. Noel Brown and Bruce Babington, "Introduction: Children's Films and Family Films," in Brown and Babington *Family Films in Global Cinema*, pp. 1–16, at 2.

28. Patrick Rössler, Kathleen Arendt, Anja Kalch, and Franziska Spitzner, "Children's Film in Europe: A Literature Review" (Erfurt: University of Erfurt, 2009), p. 2.

29. See Noel Brown, "Change and Continuity in Contemporary Children's Cinema," in Hermansson and Zepernick (eds.), *Palgrave Handbook of Children's Film and Television*, pp. 225–244.

30. The occasional disjuncture between presumed/intended audience and patterns of spectatorship is aptly summed up by Aaron Gerew's study of the "childish" aspects of monstrosity in 1950s Japanese *kaiju* films and manga, which "offer a window onto what we could call the dual monsters of textuality and spectatorship." See Aaron Gerew, "Wrestling with Godzilla: Intertextuality, Childish Spectatorship, and the National Body," in William M. Tsutsui and Michiko Ito (eds.), *In Godzilla's Footsteps: Japanese Pop Culture Icons on the Global Stage* (New York: Palgrave Macmillan, 2006), pp. 63–81, at 63.

31. Henri Storck, *The Entertainment Film for Juvenile Audiences* (Paris: UNESCO, 1950), pp. 73–74.

32. Rössler et al., "Children's Film in Europe," p. 64; Reinhard Kleber, "Original Children's Films Urgently Wanted," Goethe-Institut, January 2016, unpaginated.

33. Demetrious Matheou, "Claude Barras and Céline Sciamma on My Life as a Courgette," The Arts Desk, June 3, 2017. http://www.theartsdesk.com/film/theartsdesk-qa-claude-barras-and-c%C3%A9line-sciamma-my-life-courgette [accessed August 27, 2020].

34. Karen Lury, *The Child in Film: Tears, Fears and Fairytales* (London: I.B. Tauris, 2010), p. 1.

35. Lury, *Child in Film*, p. 106.

36. Ibid., p. 105.

37. Sarah Wright, *The Child in Spanish Cinema* (Manchester, UK: Manchester University Press, 2013), pp. 15–16.

38. "Interview of Walt Disney by Cecil B. DeMille," in Kathy Merlock Jackson (ed.), *Walt Disney: Conversations* (Jackson: University Press of Mississippi, 2006), pp. 13–14.

39. Sergei Eisenstein, *Eisenstein on Disney* (London: Methuen, 1988), p. 42.

40. Eisenstein, *Eisenstein on Disney*, pp. 41, 2, 46.

41. Monster movies, obviously, also cater to children's interest in monstrosity, reflected in the enduring appeal of horror films amongst young audiences. On the subject of children's horror films, see Sarah J. Smith, *Children, Cinema and Censorship: From Dracula to the Dead End Kids* (London: I.B. Tauris, 2005); Filipa Antunes, *Children Beware! Childhood, Horror, and the PG-13 Rating* (Jefferson, NC: McFarland, 2020); and Catherine Lester, *Horror Films for Children: Fear and Pleasure in American Cinema* (New York: Bloomsbury, 2021).

42. Stephen Klein, "The Making of Children's Culture," in Henry Jenkins (ed.), *The Children's Culture Reader* (New York: New York University Press, 1998), pp. 95–109, at 100.

43. Bazalgette and Staples, "Unshrinking the Kids," pp. 94–95.

44. For a much more in-depth consideration of family films, see Noel Brown, *The Hollywood Family Film: A History, from Shirley Temple to Harry Potter* (London: I.B. Tauris, 2012).

45. Peter Krämer, "'It's Aimed at Kids—the Kid in Everybody': George Lucas, *Star Wars* and Children's Entertainment," in Yvonne Tasker (ed.), *Action and Adventure Cinema* (London: Routledge, 2004), 358–370, at 366–367.

46. Statistics are taken from "All Time Worldwide Box Office," *The Numbers*, https://www.the-numbers.com/box-office-records/worldwide/all-movies/cumulative/all-time [accessed August 20, 2020].

47. It should be noted, of course, that the US censorship system is just one of many, and ratings classifications vary somewhat internationally.

48. "2017 THEME Report" (New York: Motion Picture Association of America, 2018), p. 19; "2018 THEME Report" (New York: Motion Picture Association of America, 2019), p. 26. The proportion of under-12s in the US cinemagoing audience rose slightly to 15 per cent in 2020, but this may be due to the parallel decline in cinema-going among audiences over the age of fifty during the Covid-19 pandemic. See "2020 Theme Report" (New York: Motion Picture Association of America, 2021), p. 50.

49. See Noel Brown, *Contemporary Hollywood Animation: Style, Storytelling, Culture and Ideology Since the 1990s* (Edinburgh: Edinburgh University Press, 2021), pp. 46–47.

50. 'Theme Report 2019" (New York: Motion Picture Association, 2020), pp. 11–12. These figures were published prior to the Covid-19 pandemic. At the time of writing, it is unclear the extent to which the international theatrical box office will rebound in the longer term.

51. Shaopeng Chen, "Industrial Transformation and Aesthetic Exploration: China's New Generation Cinema Animation" (unpublished paper presented at the Theorising the Popular conference, Liverpool Hope University, June 2016).

52. John A. Lent and Ying Xu, "Chinese Animation Film: From Experimentation to Digitalisation," in Ying Zhu and Stanley Rossen (eds.), *Art, Politics and Commerce in Chinese Cinema* (Hong Kong: Hong Kong University Press, 2010), 111–125, at 121–122.

53. Janet Wasko and Eileen R. Meehan, "Dazzled by Disney? Ambiguity in Ubiquity," in Janet Wasko, Mark Phillips, and Eileen R. Meehan (eds.), *Dazzled by Disney? The Global Disney Audiences Project* (London: Leicester University Press, 2001), pp. 329–343, at 334.

54. Ben Fritz, "Disney Animation Gets Pixar-ization: Catmull Thinks a Radical Shift Is Needed," *Variety*, February 24, 2007, n.p.

55. Marc Graser, "Disney Buys Lucasfilm, New 'Star Wars' Planned," *Variety*, October 30, 2012, n.p.

56. Pamela McClintock, "2019 Global Box Office Revenue Hit Record $42.5B Despite 4 Percent Dip in U.S.," *Hollywood Reporter*, January 10, 2020. https://www.hollywoodreporter.com/news/2019-global-box-office-hit-record-425b-4-percent-plunge-us-1268600 [accessed August 20, 2020]. This figure does not include the collective box office of 20th Century Fox, which Disney acquired in 2019.

57. Mark Phillips, "The Global Disney Audiences Project: Disney Across Cultures," in Wasko, Phillips, and Meehan, *Dazzled by Disney?*, pp. 31–61, at 42.

58. Wasko, *Understanding Disney*, pp. 63, 99–101.

59. Don Groves, "Disney Goes Ape on Tarzan Dubs," *Variety*, June 14, 1999, p. 12.

60. See Brown, *Contemporary Hollywood Animation*, chap. 4; also Michelle Anya Anjirbag, "Mulan and Moana: Embedded Coloniality and the Search for Authenticity in Disney Animated Film," *Social Sciences* 7, no. 11 (2018), pp. 1–15.

61. "Walt Disney, UTV to Co-produce Family Films," *Economic Times*, May 19, 2011, n.p.

62. Toby Miller, Nitin Govil, John McMurria, Richard Maxwell, and Ting Wang, *Global Hollywood 2* (London: BFI Publishing, 2005), pp. 17, 28.

63. Gert Hermans, Wendy Koops, and Nina Cetinic, "It Is Time for a New Approach," *ECFA Journal* 4 (December 2008), pp. 1–3.
64. Felix Vanginderhuysen, "Focus on the Distribution of Films for Children in Europe," *ECFA Journal* 4 (December 2005), https://www.ecfaweb.org/wp-content/uploads/2013/11/survey_distribution.pdf [accessed August 21, 2020].
65. Vanginderhuysen, "Focus on the Distribution of Films."
66. S. P. Agrawal and J. C. Aggarwal (eds., *Nehru on Social Issues* (New Delhi: Askok Kumar Mittal, 1989), p. 188.
67. Nick Vivarelli, "Scandi Markets Drive Kidpic Biz: Laws Set Aside Coin for Children's Films," *Variety*, February 5, 2007, p. 60.
68. José Mário Ortiz Ramos, *Cinema, Televisão e Publicidade: Cultura Popular de Massa no Brasil dos Anos 1970–1980* (São Paulo: Annablume, 2004), p. 132.
69. "Clean Films Necessary to Promote Family Values: CM," *Times of India*, March 24, 2012, n.p.
70. Vivarelli, "Scandi Markets Drive Kidpic Biz."
71. Peter Bosma, *Film Programming: Curating for Cinemas, Festivals, Archives* (New York: Columbia University Press, 2015), p. 69.
72. Rössler et al., "Children's Film in Europe," p. 22.
73. Jacqueline Rose, *The Case of Peter Pan; or the Impossibility of Children's Fiction* (Basingstoke, UK: Macmillan, 1984).
74. Joe L. Kincheloe, "The New Childhood: Home Alone as a Way of Life," in Henry Jenkins (ed.), *The Children's Culture Reader* (New York: New York University Press, 1998), pp. 159–177, at 163.
75. For more on the Children's Film Unit, see Noel Brown, *British Children's Cinema: From The Thief of Bagdad to Wallace and Gromit* (London: I.B. Tauris, 2016), pp. 213–217.
76. Nevertheless, see Mary Celeste Kearney, *Girls Make Media* (London: Routledge, 2006); and Andrew Zolides, "Created by Children: Conceptualising the Child as Media Producer," in Jane O'Connor and John Mercer (eds.), *Childhood and Celebrity* (New York: Routledge, 2017), pp. 147–158, for useful primers on children's production of media texts more broadly.
77. I am indebted to Dr. Catherine Lester, who generously pointed me in the direction of some of the young filmmakers discussed here.

BIBLIOGRAPHY

Bazalgette, Cary, and David Buckingham, eds. *In Front of the Children: Screen Entertainment and Young Audiences*. London: BFI Publishing, 1995.
Beeler, Karin, and Stan Beeler, eds. *Children's Film in the Digital Age: Essays on Audience, Adaptation and Consumer Culture* (Jefferson, NC: McFarland, 2015.
Brown, Noel. *The Children's Film: Genre, Nation and Narrative* (New York: Columbia University Press, 2017.
Brown, Noel. *The Hollywood Family Film: A History, from Shirley Temple to Harry Potter* (London: I.B. Tauris, 2012.
Brown, Noel, and Bruce Babington, eds. *Family Films in Global Cinema: The World beyond Disney*. London: I.B. Tauris, 2015.
Donald, Stephanie Hemelryk. *There's No Place Like Home: The Migrant Child in World Cinema*. London: I.B. Tauris, 2018.

Donald, Stephanie Hemelryk, Emma Wilson, and Sarah Wright, eds. *Childhood and Nation in Contemporary World Cinema: Borders and Encounters*. London: Bloomsbury, 2017.

Goldstein, Ruth M., and Edith Zornow. *The Screen Image of Youth: Movies about Children and Adolescents*. Metuchen, NJ: Scarecrow, 1980.

Hermansson, Casie, and Janet Zepernick, eds. *The Palgrave Handbook of Children's Film and Television*. Cham, Switzerland: Palgrave Macmillan, 2019.

Jackson, Kathy Merlock. *Images of Children in American Film: A Sociocultural Analysis*. London: Scarecrow Press, 1986.

Krämer, Peter. "'The Best Disney Film Disney Never Made': Children's Films and the Family Audience in American Cinema since the 1960s." In Steve Neale (ed.), *Genre and Contemporary Hollywood*. London: BFI Publishing, 2002, pp. 185–200.

Lury, Karen. *The Child in Film: Tears, Fears and Fairytales*. London: I.B. Tauris, 2010.

Olson, Debbie, ed. *The Child in World Cinema*. Lanham, MD: Rowman and Littlefield, 2018.

Parry, Becky. *Children, Film and Literacy*. Basingstoke, UK: Palgrave Macmillan, 2013.

Sinyard, Neil. *Children in the Movies*. London: B. T. Batsford, 1992.

Wojcik-Andrews, Ian. *Children's Films: History, Ideology, Pedagogy, Theory*. New York: Garland, 2000.

Zipes, Jack. *The Enchanted Screen: The Unknown History of Fairy-Tale Films*. New York: Routledge, 2011.

PART I

GENRE AND FORM

CHAPTER 1

....

EXPLORING CULTURAL AND SOCIAL DIFFERENCES IN DEFINING FILMS FOR CHILDREN

....

BECKY PARRY

THE film *Good Boys* (Gene Stupnitsky, 2019) provides a timely provocation regarding the way that children's films are defined and understood. The R-rated US film is the directorial debut of Gene Stupnitsky, a Ukrainian-born North American film and television writer and producer best known for writing and directing episodes of the United States NBC series, *The Office* (2005–2013). The film is produced by Seth Rogan and Evan Goldberg, whose particular brand of "stoner" humour has surfaced in films such as *Pineapple Express* (David Gordon Green, 2008) and *Superbad* (Greg Mottola, 2007), and the TV series *Freaks and Geeks* (1999–2000).[1] Stoner films are a subgenre of comedy films and involve predominantly male protagonists trying to find cannabis and being comically inept at doing so. The trailer for *Good Boys* begins in the office of the producer, Rogan, who has to tell the three young male leads that they cannot go to see the movie they act in, because it "isn't suitable." A montage sequence follows that show what exactly is unsuitable, viscerally depicting the very same qualities that establish the film's appeal to the adult male audience. On the surface, the film appears to be a rather formulaic coming-of-age children's film, featuring three boys, complete with the ubiquitous nicknames, crushes on girls and scenes of riding bikes. These are common tropes in Hollywood live-action children's cinema, and the film even features a self-conscious recognition of this as a cliché, when the boys are caught spying on a couple kissing and are collectively described as "Stranger Things," a reference to the boys on bikes in the highly successful Netflix series.

While the vibrant mise-en-scène, the generic plot, and the male characters suggest that the film is for children, the use of expletives, encounters with sex toys and drugs, and an attempt to cross a busy highway take it well out of the reach of the PG or even the PG-13 certificate. The paradox of the film is that what creates the humour is the juxtaposition of the generic conventions of a children's film with the stock characters' unknowing encounters with anal beads, vibrators, a sex doll, and, finally, a sex swing. The film is almost a parody, yet the "Bean Bag Boys" (Max, Thor, and Lucas) also represent the childhood selves of male audiences who laugh, sometimes despite themselves, at recognizing emerging adolescent interest in sex, alcohol, and new friends referred to in such a transgressive way. *Good Boys* is self-conscious in looking like a children's film, but its appeal lies in the way it offers male viewers a vicarious return to being "good" (or rather bad) boys. This blurring of the edges of what conventionally makes a film suitable for children is nothing new; the use of irony, romantic side narratives, and intertextuality are now accepted as necessary to broaden the appeal of children's films.

However, *Good Boys* is a departure because it is *not* for children. It is a film for adults that subverts the narrative and stylistic conventions of children's film. That these conventions are so common and so available for parody perhaps signals that children's films have reached a generic maturity—a "coming of age" that merits critical attention. However, the films it parodies are largely the cultural offerings of one country and one film industry that is underpinned by structural inequalities and dominated by White men. It is imperative that emerging children's film scholarship take account of films for children that are made outside Hollywood. This is not simply a matter of valuing diverse cultural content; rather, it is a recognition that childhood is not a universal experience, and that outside Hollywood, children's films are an important site for contesting and negotiating the understanding of what it means to be a child.

In this chapter, I attempt to look beyond the "long shadow of Hollywood"—which not only dominates the international field of cultural production but has also dominated scholarship in this area—to understand how children's films are defined and understood internationally.[2] To this end, I undertook a series of interviews with European Children's Film Association members in order to demonstrate how those working in the exhibition and education sectors of the children's film industry decide which children's films to screen in festivals and events.[3] I aimed to identify cultural and social differences in their understandings of what a children's film is. Collectively, the participants' responses contribute to the contemporary study of children's films by highlighting differences in the definitions of films for children even among closely aligned European countries. Far from being universal, then, childhood is usefully understood as a dynamic and contingent construct; and childhood is experienced very differently.[4] Considering these examples of differing professional understandings of what constitutes a children's film help us to recognize that there is a greater diversity of ideas about childhood in international children's films. What is more, they highlight the ways in which different assumptions and ideas about childhood and the needs of children are enacted in the decisions made about creating and sharing these films with children. Before presenting the interviews, I will reflect on the some of the ways the issue of defining children's film has been addressed in literature, predominantly in the global north.

In the context of the study of film, children's films are inherently a conundrum, with a number of contradictory dimensions, all of which hinge on the relationship between the adult and the child. Ian Wojcik-Andrews and Bettina Kümmerling-Meibauer offer broad definitions of children's film, including within their scope films about children, films for children, and films children choose to watch.[5] However, as Noel Brown argues, these broad parameters do not acknowledge that children's film exists as a genre distinct from other forms.[6] The tendency to blur distinctions is also frequently found in reviews, where children's films are predominantly valued for what they offer adults. As Catharine Des Forges of the Independent Cinema Office suggested in 2005:

> The great children's films are the ones that adults love too, that everybody loves. It's something that really engages you—makes you laugh, makes you cry, takes you into its world and you come out thinking differently.[7]

Similarly, in the context of children's literature scholarship, Perry Nodelman highlights the dominance of the idea that a good book for children is also a good book for adults— the appeal to adults being seen as an indication of quality.[8] This is an assumption he challenges as an underestimation of children and a misunderstanding of the complexity and specialism of children's fiction, a point I will return to.

The duality of the audience of children's films is acknowledged by Brown, who suggests that a useful distinction can be made between a *children's film* and a *family film*. Cary Bazalgette and Terry Staples also define children's films as distinct from more commercial family films, often in style, budget, and themes, but most importantly in point of view:

> Children's films can be defined as offering mainly or entirely a child's point of view. They deal with the fears, misapprehensions and concerns of children in their own terms. They foreground the problems of coping with adults, or of coping without them.[9]

By contrast, according to Brown, family films are those that appeal to audiences of all ages, such as *Star Wars* (George Lucas, 1977) and *E.T. The Extra-Terrestrial* (Steven Spielberg, 1982).[10] However, family film as s separate category is problematic because many of the features of children's films are also typically found in family films. What is more, it is not possible to define children's film entirely according to the absence or minimal presence of adults or adult perspectives, as this, too, is a common feature of children's fiction. Films such as *The Adventures of Robin Hood* (Michael Curtiz and William Keighley, 1938), *The Princess Bride* (Rob Reiner, 1987), and *Shrek* (Andrew Adamson and Vicky Jensen, 2001) do not feature children or children's life experiences but are usually understood to be for children. The adult and the child also coexist in films such as *Heidi* (Allan Dwan, 1937), *Pollyanna* (David Swift, 1960), and *Anne of Green Gables* (Kevin Sullivan, 1985), where a child (a girl) enriches the life of an older adult, providing hope and resilience in the face of adversity. The relationship of the adult and child in these stories is key to the development of the narrative, which is told from different points of view at different moments.

Furthermore, despite the ubiquity of orphans in children's stories, the relationship between adults and children is important to children's films. In *Matilda* (Danny DeVito, 1996), Matilda liberates Miss Honey's class from tyranny, but Miss Honey also liberates Matilda from her dreadful parents. In *Hunt for the Wilderpeople* (Taika Waititi, 2016), Ricky Baker wins the affection of grumpy widower Hec, but Hec also wins Ricky's trust and finds hope. Adults are often "baddies" in children's films, but they are also sources of information, comfort, safety, and love. The narrative of children's films is often driven by conflict between adults and children, but adults also serve to enable resolution and "homecoming." The inclusion of adult perspectives in children's stories is not, therefore, only for the purpose of reaching a wider family market but, rather, has a long history in children's culture that must be acknowledged.[11]

Those who make global, commercially successful children's films are not only focused on the commercial imperative to appeal to large audiences, but often reflect on wider societal debates about that relationship. It is noticeable that a number of popular animated films explore contemporary concerns about parenting. In *Toy Story 3* (Lee Unkrich, 2010), the mother's sense of loss when her son, Andy, the toys' owner, grows up and leaves home is an underlying theme throughout the film. In *Finding Nemo* (Andrew Stanton, 2003), the impact of the over-anxious, over-controlling father who restricts the actions of the child (fish) Nemo, is more prominent than the time spent following the child's point of view. In *Inside Out* (Pete Docter, 2015), both parents try to understand and control the emotional complexity of their daughter's response to moving to a new city, school, and home.

In Bazalgette and Staples's and Brown's work, it is clear that the distinction between children's films and family films also relates to distinguishing between Hollywood productions and those made elsewhere. Given the continued global prominence and popularity of children's films made in the United States, it is important to combine them in discussions of the corpus of "children's films," particularly if we are to look to formal or genre elements to help establish defining features of films for children. Brown utilizes the concept of "genre" from film studies to argue that children's films have discernible features that make them distinctive. He argues that children's films are often constructed through contextual and paratextual processes that include "marketing and distribution, censorship and suitability ratings, critical reception, merchandising and exhibition strategies."[12] Brown goes on to suggest five characteristics that are recognizable narrative elements of children's films, including the "foregrounding of the child," "the reaffirmation of family," and the uplifting ending.[13]

Recognizing that children's films make up a dynamic and contingent but distinct category (or genre) helps to move our emerging discipline forward, making explicit as it does that we are describing films *made for children by adults*. This definition enables attention to be paid to a particular body of work in a generative way, while acknowledging that there are features that can be debated in interdisciplinary contexts. This definition also enables us to navigate a path through the assertion that children's films are "impossible," a claim made by Jacqueline Rose in relation to children's literature, where she suggests that such texts always serve the purposes of adults, colonizing, controlling, or even reifying childhood.[14] Although clearly many children's films serve adult interests in relation to didacticism and morality, and these should be scrutinized, there are equally examples of children resisting and challenging adults. In the Danish children's film, *We Shall Overcome* (Niels Arden Oplev, 2006), a young boy rebels against the cruelty of a schoolteacher and gains the support of his peers. Films that represent children disrupting authority become sites for negotiation about what it means to be a child and how childhood is understood. In the context of the new sociology of childhood, childhood has been described as a socially and culturally constructed and reconstructed concept.[15] This theory acknowledges that, far from being universal, childhood is experienced differently from country to country, context to context, and even within families on the same street or in the same house or school. Constructions and reconstructions of children and childhood proliferate in children's media, including film. Recognizing the child and childhood as constructed is useful to the study of children's films and the role of the adult. Calvert argues:

> Members of any society carry within themselves a working definition of childhood, its nature, limitations and duration. They may not explicitly discuss this definition, write about it, or even consciously conceive of it as an issue, but they act upon their assumptions in all their dealings with, fears for, and expectations of their children.[16]

This implies that it is adults who carry these definitions; but children, too, have emerging ideas and experiences about childhood that they draw on in their engagements with children's film, and which subsequently influence scriptwriters and filmmakers. Negotiations about what childhood is perceived to be, what is suitable for children, children's relationships with adults, and what children will enjoy are explicitly played out in cultural texts. For example, the idea that some films are "just" for children (which is found in many reviews) implies their inferiority and that children's films that are also for adults are superior. This idea can usefully be problematized from the perspective of the new sociology of childhood, suggesting that children have expertise in their own lives, and a desire for agency. Those working in the screen industries recognize the appeal of challenging the authority of adults and often represent children disobeying adults. Drawing on Bahktin's theories of the carnivalesque, Grace and Tobin suggest that popular culture is often a site in which children establish a distance between themselves and adults.[17] James argues that

> children, by the very nature of their position as a group outside adult society, have sought out an alternative system of meanings through which they can establish their own integrity. Adult order is manipulated so that what adults esteem is made to appear ridiculous; what adults despise is invested with prestige.[18]

It would sometimes seem that children choose to love the things that are the antithesis of what parents and the wider society might think is "good" or "suitable" for them, The huge popularity of brands such as *Pokemon: The Movie 2000* (Kunihiko Yuyama, 2000),

Power Rangers (Dean Israelite, 2017), and *The Teenage Mutant Ninja Turtles* (Jonathan Liebesman, 2014) make them sites of controversy about what is suitable for children.

We might want to argue, therefore, that transgression against authority is an important narrative element in many children's films. Yet adults make these transgressive texts for children—as authors, directors, toymakers, or comic-strip artists. What is more, adults buy or enable children to buy and access popular culture. Adults do not always adopt the role of moral guardian or protector of childhood. Many adults also play *Pokemon Go*, read and watch J. K. Rowling's *Harry Potter* series (1997–2007), and continue to enjoy *Star Wars* (1977–). I have argued elsewhere that children's culture has two parallel manifestations: that which children engage with as part of social activity with friends, and that which adults create for them in the form of books, films, television series, food, sweets, cards, and games.[19] These two worlds coexist and often collide, and both children and adults can take up various adult- or childlike positions in relation to texts, practices, and phenomena.[20] Childlike adults and adult-like children are regular features in children's films. Children's films have the potential to provide spaces in which playful and sometimes transgressive responses develop as part of a wider meaning-making process. Those who make cultural texts for children must navigate public discourses about childhood, but they also must make texts that offer rich, imaginative fictional spaces for children.

In making this argument, I am conscious of the need to acknowledge the financial imperative in the children's film industry, which has an undeniably important role in the development of ideas. The most successful Hollywood films since the turn of the millennium have almost all been children's films, and their international distribution has been accompanied by numerous multimedia and transmedia products through which children can further experience a preferred narrative, and more profit can be made. This shapes choices about characters and how they are adaptable in different forms. It also leads to risk aversion and an adherence to certain schemas about what will be popular with boys and with girls. However, success is not formulaic and is not guaranteed by marketing. Children also do not always participate in children's culture in the way adults might have expected, and ways in which children take up film and media narratives can be seen as a dialogue between audience and maker.[21] What Rose describes as an impossibility is actually a complex and contradictory problem that stretches the creative abilities of authors, illustrators, and filmmakers, leading to the production of contemporary texts that use visual, audio, spatial, and linguistic modes in quite distinct ways, not solely to serve adults, but to provide imaginative fictional spaces for children to inhabit.[22]

Perry Nodelman suggests that what is distinctive about children's fiction is the ability to imply more complexity visually than in what is said, highlighting the role of images in "providing the visual and emotional information about which the text remains silent."[23] This observation is relevant to the study of children's films, enabling a focus on *how* stories are told for children in film form. There is an urgent need for further interdisciplinary and empirical research of the broader corpus of international and archive films for children, in addition to Hollywood children's film, paying attention to its narrative or genre conventions while also paying attention to style, mise-en-scène, and form. This chapter contributes to this relatively new programme of research, emerging in different disciplines, by considering the ways in which those who currently work in the children's film exhibition sector "carry with them" ideas or constructions of children and childhood, and how this orients them to making choices of films for screenings for children.

RESEARCH APPROACH

I approached over twenty members of the European Children's Film Association and received five responses from individuals who were both willing and able to take part over a six-week period.[24] All of those interviewed had currently or recently programmed or selected films for children for film festivals in Europe. These festivals have a mandate to enable children to see films (outside the Hollywood mainstream) in their own languages set in their own countries. A further priority is to screen international films to local audiences which otherwise remain largely unseen outside their own national boundaries. Unlike many commercial film festivals, which function as marketplaces for the buying and selling of new films, children's films festivals are usually more concerned with meeting the needs of local children and their families and teachers, providing film education and creative production activities.

This was a small-scale, qualitative, and interpretive approach, providing findings that are potentially transferable to other settings (that is to say, that those who engage with this research recognize and relate the issues raised in the data with their own contexts).[25] As Egan suggests, conducting email interviews overcomes geographical barriers and offers participants the time to think about their responses and articulate them in their own way.[26] This is also compatible with the aspiration to provide direct testimony which, as Tracey suggests, facilitates the generation of transferable findings.[27] The respondents were eager to highlight key issues for use in their professional contexts and to share their perspectives with one another, so they have not been anonymized. Indeed, given the relatively small professional context of the children's film industry, anonymity would have been challenging to guarantee. I have therefore presented the interview data in a manner that is sensitive to the need to maintain individuals' professional reputations and gave them the opportunity to review the chapter. One set of responses was provided by three members of one team but has been presented as a collective response. The names of the respondents are listed below, and there is a brief biography of each in "Notes" at the end of the chapter:

- Gloria Morano: Head of the Young Audiences Programme at the Luxembourg City Film Festival[28]
- Martin Grund (producer), Debbie Maturi (head), and Gage Oxley (youth engagement coordinator) at Leeds Young Film (LYF)[29]
- Eva Schwarzwald: member of the European Children's Film Association[30]

- Dimitris Spyrou: artistic director, Olympia International Film Festival for Children and Young People[31]
- Katri Tenhola: Film programmer at National Audiovisual Institute of Finland.[32]

I used a first- and second-cycle data-coding process, first deconstructing each interview to identify participant perspective codes, and then comparing the similarities and differences in relation to constructions of childhood.[33] I drew on Harry Hendrick's useful chronology of changing constructions of childhood in the United Kingdom to identify traces of shared constructions, such as the "romantic," "innocent," or "delinquent" child in need of protection and moral guidance.[34]

RESPONSES AND INTERPRETATION

I asked the interviewees a variety of questions related to the qualities they believe make films appropriate and enjoyable to children. Their responses were based on many combined years of experience programming festivals and viewing and screening films for and with children. Following a process of thematic coding, I divided their responses into five categories, which relate to the ideas they "carry with them" about children and childhood when performing their professional roles. These five categories emerged from what the respondents identified as key decisions about curating their film programmes and making active decisions about what they think constitutes a "good, appropriate or engaging" children's film, which is also inflected by a consideration of the ideas of others.

COMPLEXITY

In contrast to the common view that children watch media passively, my respondents perceived children as actively "reading" film. They all felt that the level of complexity of a film should be considered, as would be the case with children's books. For example, Eva, based in Italy, expressed her view that children's films should be intelligent but not ironic. Given that the irony in children's film often relies on shared understandings outside the text, this suggestion constructs children as competent but as having less experience of texts than adults. Dimitris, from the Greek context, similarly challenges the idea that films can operate at different perceptual levels for adults and children, arguing that "the content should be compatible with the perceptive skills of children" and "that films for children do not only create "the smart audience of the future," as many people wrongly claim." This proposal recognizes that in children's films there are levels of complexity, not just to do with the familiar adult-oriented quips in many mainstream

Hollywood films, but to do with the way the narrative is edited, or the inclusion of ambiguity, which younger children may not have previously encountered. This is not to underestimate children's capacity to deal with complex modes of storytelling, but to recognize that they may need to learn these aspects of film language just as they learn to read by reading gradually more challenging books (for more on the processes by which children learn to "read" films, see Cary Bazalgette, this volume).

Katri, working in Finland, associates the need for different levels of complexity in children's films in terms of theme or issues (as there are with books) with age. She suggests "that the films' topics are understandable and suitable for each age group and that, for example, the protagonists are in some way relatable to young audiences." Subtitled films add a layer of complexity, as the LYF team note:

> This means that we take the curation responsibility very seriously; for younger children we look for films with an easier-to-follow narrative and generally in English (if they are under 7) as we find that often films with complex narratives rely on subtitles, which an under 7 audience would struggle with.

Drawing on the work of Spencer Meek, I have argued elsewhere in relation to film that "texts teach texts," and this accords with the participants' view that children are not homogenous in terms of levels of understanding or range of experiences, and, consequently, the need for films that range in complexity.[35] The LYF team also suggest:

> We would really like children's filmmakers to have a way to talk to young audiences more in the development stage. Many rely (of course) on their own experiences of childhood and we often are presented with films "for children" that are actual[ly] adult films with children in them. These are very hard to place for an audience!

They go on to say that if children have previously only experienced "anodyne" children's films, it can be a challenge to introduce them to more complex or unconventional films. There is also a perception that children read film texts in different ways. For example, Eva highlights children's embodied engagement with film ("You may feel it in your physical body!!!!"), and LYF suggest that children have a deeper immersion in the fictional world of the film:

> We are excited by the fact that children watch films in a different way to adults, often feeling that they "are" the character they see, such is their absorption and level of empathy (hence watching the same film or clip of a film, over and over again and acting out the character in their play).

The need for variety in levels of complexity should not, then, be conflated with the idea that children's films should be simple. As Gloria, in Luxembourg, comments, I would suggest the filmmakers "consider the intelligence of children, their capacity to understand a 'difficult' film." Eva urges filmmakers not to "underestimate the audience."

However, this is a complex issue, and as the LYF respondents suggest, there are clearly considerable international differences in this respect:

> Many Eastern European films that are submitted as children's films often have a much more mature adult storyline than what we would consider suitable for children. Many often include themes of prostitution, trafficking, addiction, destitution etc., and are generally much more sombre.

This is a useful example of the way in which film becomes a site for the construction of childhood. In some national contexts, issues of poverty or drug use would move films from being *for* children to being *about* them. British films such as *The Selfish Giant* (Clio Barnard, 2013) and *Ratcatcher* (Lynne Ramsay, 1999) are about children, but would be considered too distressing to be screened for them, featuring as they do scenes that include violent death and no "uplifting" ending. However, it is clear that there are children who do have experiences of what are described here as "adult" issues, and not representing them denies these experiences; more importantly, it does not offer any opportunity for those children to see their own lives reflected on-screen. Having worked in two distinct national contexts, Gloria notices an interesting difference related to the way the adult or child point of view is taken in a children's film:

> I also have the impression in several international young audience film festivals, films chosen for children's programmes keep focusing on the children's point of view in the story, but sometimes a film about children with an adult's point of view (or a film without children characters) can also be absolutely interesting for young audiences. In other international contexts the borders between films for children and films for an adult audience seem to me more liquid.

In a professional context, then, this "border" can be difficult to pin down and may function as a barrier to some films being shown. Where traumatic life events are represented, LYF expresses concern and suggests that children watching films about abuse or death need adult support:

> We know that when children watch films with their peers, they sometimes feel they are not as able to express their real emotional responses as they are with adults that they trust. We do, however, know that dealing with these issues in an age appropriate, honest way is often enormously beneficial for young people, particularly if the lead character resonates with them.

LYF also suggests that screenings should be accompanied by opportunities to discuss issues shown in films:

> Having worked with the Young Jury for the past three years at Leeds Young Film Festival, I have experienced deep conversations from young children about

challenging topics and difficult narratives presented in the film. I suppose children are a lot more aware of complex narratives than we think—and that critical break-down and understanding, which is then translated into a critique to their peers is absolutely monumental.

Katri similarly suggests that the context and educational materials that support screenings enable "a challenging subject matter" to be dealt with. Each of these responses make it clear that the respondents recognize that childhood is not a universal experience and that children have diverse experiences which orient them differently to texts. There is also a shared commitment to making films for children that do not under-estimate or patronize them that runs counter to the idea that protecting the "innocent" child is paramount. However, as we will see in the next section, the respondents also make judgements about the suitability of children's films in moral terms.[36]

Morality

I have opted to use the term "morality" with some caution, as it represents such a broad spectrum of ideas. I use it to group together ideas about what is considered suitable for children in terms that relate to certification (such as swearing, sex, drugs, and dangerous behaviour), but also to discuss a broader moral position that children's films are expected to sustain. These ideas all relate to a highly preva-lent construction of childhood as in need of protection, and though this is a highly contested historical construct, these are some of the dominant features of children's film that are subject to classification, parental guidance, or age ratings. There are far more detailed accounts of morality and censorship in relation to children's films; however, it is useful to reflect on key cultural differences that impact the respondents in relation to their own work. The LYF highlights the sensitivity in the United Kingdom to swearing and the way different attitudes to swearing may deter-mine whether a film can be shown:

> One film from a few years ago that we had to reject was a children's animated comedy called Kurt Turns Evil [Rasmus A. Sivertsen, 2008; Norway/Denmark] which was aimed at very young children and would have been classified a U in the UK had it not been for the fact that the main character's nickname, repeated frequently throughout the film, was 'motherf**ker.' "

The film's humour might well be contingent on the name of the character, so the filmmakers might be keen to retain it, but because this normalizes language that chil-dren would be severely reprimanded for using in UK schools, the film can no longer be considered to be *for* children in the UK context.

Eva highlights the issue of vulgarity and points out the cultural differences between countries she found regarding representations of sex in children's films:

> The northern countries have always had a different, more open approach to sexuality and gender issues. I would never suggest some films to Italian schools where a little girl of 8 years old plays with a friend to explore what is an orgasm. Or drugs or alcohol. I do not say that here we don't have to approach or consider these kinds of issues, but we arrived later.

Different attitudes to children and sex were also noted by Katri:

> When I saw Michel Gondry's film *Microbe et Gasoil* [2015; France] I remember thinking that in [a] Finnish youngsters' film we would not necessarily talk about sex in the same way as this French film.

In a follow-up exchange, Katri suggested that the film's exaggerated, almost caricatured, talk about sex, coming from an adult character (the mum), seemed like something a Finnish film would not have:

> Instead, I could imagine a Finnish film where teenagers talk about sex with other teenagers, and in a more down to earth way—without the weird comical tones of Microbe's mother.

Interestingly, the UK team in Leeds indicated that they found a more relaxed attitude to nudity and swearing in films from Denmark, Sweden, Finland, and Norway.

Dimitris articulates his perspective slightly differently, focusing on the director and whether they maintain "an acceptable moral and ideological position in the representation of violence, fear, premature eroticism etc." Katri, however, highlights a broader organizational policy to "consider the moral message of the film—what is its view on the world and humanity." Here, Katri is expanding the notion of morality to focus on the overall theme of the film, and this relates to how characters, places, and ideas are represented. What is most significant about morality is the contradictory role of adults. Adults must act as moral guardians for children, but the morality that children are being protected from is that which emerges from the adult world. It is not in the scope of this chapter to unravel this conundrum, but it is important to ask questions about which children we are most concerned about protecting, in this context, and whether the protection we afford them in screen representation is parallel to that which they might experience in their everyday life. This criterion is one in which the adult—as gatekeeper or mediator— is in a powerful role, and in practice any ambiguity in the overall moral position of the film may make film distributors cautious of taking a risk. Even where children's films include what might be considered transgressive behaviour by a child, they often have an uplifting ending with moral closure that brings them back within the domain of home and family. This moral closure often chimes with hegemonic and patriarchal ideas at the time of production and undermines the potential for children's films to be radical or experimental. And although simplistic causal accounts of media effects on children have been discredited, Casie Hermansson and Janet Zepernick rightly point out that "the reality of film and television as expounding one ideology or another is unarguable."[37]

I would argue, however, that there are many cases where children's films attempt to explore counter-hegemonic values. Even the most branded and commercial children's films question contemporary values, as is the case in *The Lego Movie* (Phil Lord and Chris Miller, 2014), where Emmet, the central character, realises that "everything is certainly not awesome" and that an evil money-grabbing tyrant needs to be thwarted. This is not to say that the film can be read as a challenge to capitalism, but it serves as an interesting example of the way we simultaneously invite children to condemn greed while actively grooming them for consumerism. A similar theme is taken up in the Tamil film *Kaaka Muttai* (M. Manikandan, 2015), where two boys realise that their desire for pizza is wholly unsatisfying, both in terms of taste and in terms of their self-respect and family and cultural identity. The respondents highlighted the potential of children's films to challenge normative ideas, even if often only on an interpersonal level. In terms of the moral stance they take, the stories adults tell children reflect a desire for them to *be* a better future. This is reflected in a focus of children's films on issues such as discrimination and the depletion of the environment and immigration. I suggest that a new construction is emerging in children's films and film programming so that the child, both as character and audience member, is constructed as a potential "moral saviour" who—like Greta Thunberg or Malala Yousafzai—might inspire others into civic action. This construction also relates to the way in which children's film is seen to have a responsibility to represent children and childhood, ethnicity, gender, disability, and class in particular ideological ways.

REPRESENTATION

In the professional context of film festivals for children, it appears to be a strong shared priority to question stereotypical or problematic representations based on gender, ethnicity, disability, or sexuality. This constructs the child as needing guidance or support, but also as having potential to be emancipated or emancipator. As Eva suggests, "You must go out from the screening with some good feelings, not depressed, with hopes, suggestions for your daily life, opening your mind." Dimitris suggests that "there should be no reproduction of stereotypes and there should be a certain way to deal with the Other and the Different etc." Similarly, Katri highlights the need to select films which do not "reinforce conventional gaps and stereotypes for example between female/male characters, especially if they are not dealt with in the film." According to Katri, in Finland this emerges from the shared national values of the country:

Finland is quite an egalitarian country when it comes to gender and class issues, and teachers are well aware of gender roles and equal starting points. So very conservative worldviews are not necessarily welcomed well from the side of parents and teachers, or kids.

Children's films are also seen as providing role models both in terms of who makes them and whose stories are told. LYF suggest:

> We would love to screen more children's films directed by women—the majority of children's films are still directed by men (no different to the rest of the industry). More live action films that reflect the diversity of society (i.e., not all middle-class White kids).

The dominance of White men in the screen industries for children is well documented, but as the LYF team point out, this has implications for the stories that are told, regardless of benign intentions.[38] Dimitris suggests that his "selections are defined by the originality of the topic, the personal angle of the director and the 'locality' of a topic which can break national borders." However, if these films are predominantly made by White men, the "personal angle" being presented is also predominantly male. However, when I asked the respondents to reflect on a film they would like to make for children, their ideas indicated concerns that are less told, as this LYF response reveals:

> So, I would make a film with a young protagonist at the forefront which tackles difficult or challenging topics that can engage this generation. Issues such as the environment, different cultures, sexism or gender disparity, homophobia and transphobia are all very prominent topics for a young generation in understanding and being able to navigate the world they are growing up in.

Here, children and young people are constructed as in need of films that address challenging issues they might be facing. Eva also highlights the need for stories "of solidarity between humans, a story which destroys stereotypes," adding "I would say give small children new dreams, new hopes, something positive, teach them respect of the other, teach boys to respect girls and women." Children, here, are constructed as a new generation that can be taught ideas that challenge traditional values (in relation to gender, for example). Each respondent highlighted the potential of film to "emancipate" children. Dimitris observes that

> Films that contribute to the mutual understanding of people with different cultures, develop critical thought, undermine violence, racism and all kinds of discrimination are in demand if they are not dominated by didacticism.

Children are seen here as in need of a particular form of "emancipation." There is a tension between a perception of children as potentially in need of support in dealing with their own "otherness" and a perception of children as having prejudices that need to be addressed, children as both the bullied and the bullies. The role of the central protagonist that children can connect to and empathize with in children's film in this discourse of childhood is one of "conscientization," in Freirian terms, or to be "woke" in the vernacular of young people in the United Kingdom.[39] This construction of childhood is especially common in children's film outside Hollywood and is consistent with the notion that children's films are often essentially "pedagogic," viewing the child in terms of their future selves as global citizens. As Dimitris observes:

> There are many films that had some success at home but didn't manage to provoke some international interest. They are films that reproduce various commercial clichés, they are not original, they don't have an educational aspect, they are superficial, they want to overfeed the children audience with optimism. As such, they are not interesting to children film festivals, through which children films get a passport for an international course.

LITERACY

Children are consistently constructed as in need of education. This is something that is almost unquestioned in contemporary society, although compulsory education for all children is a relatively recent initiative. All the respondents took a particular stance in relation to learning about film or film literacy:

> After the Renaissance, the child is not considered a ring between generations, but an independent personality. So the challenge is to cultivate children's aesthetics, to develop their critical thought, to help them acquire social consciousness and empathy. (Dimitris)

All the respondents focused on the need to teach children about film, instead of using to film to teach other topics. Gloria highlights a need to

> work on film literacy with the children through the film as well as the thematic aspects in order to make the children think about the link between subjects and forms.

The respondents all seem to agree that developing an understanding of film language is especially important in relation to contemporary visual culture:

> Image is dominant in our lives and children should be able to decode the language of images. (Dimitris)

The respondents refer to the need to focus on aesthetic aspects of both fiction and documentary films with exchange of opinions, screenings, and analyses of films. Gloria also suggests that children need to see "rarer forms of films, they're already used to stories and fiction through theatre, films and TV series."

However, each country has different infrastructures to support this work, and though programmes of work are growing in some countries (such as Finland), in others they are in decline. The respondents perceive their own work to be important in sustaining interest in media literacy, even where it is absent in policy:

> As there's no extensive media literacy plan in Luxembourg (as the CNC [Centre National du Cinéma] ones in France), our festival is the main way for teachers to add films in their education program. Very often teachers are not used to work with films in their classes, but we're having very good surprises: teachers are more and more enthusiastic about the pedagogical documents we send them when we publish our film program, children's screenings and the work of specialists during the screenings (introductions, discussions and/or Q&A with guests). (Gloria)

The participants also referred to a need to respond to changes in children's use of digital technologies, which have increased their access not only to a wider variety of moving-image content, but also to software to make and share their own media content. Here a common contemporary discourse about children as creative users of technology was in evidence:

> Children should make creative use of new technologies and not be their passive users. (Dimitris)

LYF highlighted what they see as an important need to "understand the modern landscape" more in relation to what children were able to access:

> Children's access to moving-image content has changed dramatically in recent years, and continues to develop. (LYF)

The idea that children need to be competent in digital skills is a strong twenty-first-century discourse, but this focus on the increasing range of content that is available to children is an aspect of the digital landscape that is sometimes overlooked. LYF suggest that, by engaging with tablets, in particular, children and young people are able to exercise agency, making their own selections of content they wish to engage with:

> Young children are now very proficient in understanding technology such as iPads to access YouTube, and so, a great deal of content young people access is independent and self-scheduled.

However, respondents were also concerned about negative media content impacting on mental health:

> Children are bombarded with sexual images, wars, global warming problems, they are anxious and the context of technologies surrounding them is terrible. (Eva)

This more protective discourse of children at risk and in need of protection from the media has been a prevalent discourse in relation to media in the twentieth century. Cinema education and media literacy programmes are often seen as a means of enabling children to become more critical citizens in relation to popular culture. The ability to "read" or "decode" film is seen as key to enabling children to engage with films outside their own experiences:

> Comparing with the French context, I have the impression in Luxembourg we dare less to show arthouse films for the young audience judging them 'difficult films' because the media literacy is still developing here. (Gloria)

What Gloria describes as "art house" films here are often low-budget, live-action films made outside Hollywood. In some non-English-speaking countries, there are even subsidies for children's film production and a growing oeuvre of work with a distinct style. For example, some films from Iran, influenced by the work of Abbas Kiarostami, evidence a well-defined style and represent quite distinct ideas about children and childhood. These films are shown at festivals, using the differences between the familiar and the unfamiliar as pedagogic tools in relation to film literacy. By contrast, there are also some films that the respondents felt children recognized as adhering to universal aesthetics of children's films, also expressed by Nodelman as a characteristic of children's texts where sound and images convey greater complexity than spoken or written language.[40] These films had been successful internationally:

> A film for children that recently had a very good course, was " 'Supa Modo,' " by Likarion Wainaina [2018; Kenya/Germany]. I believe that its success was based on the very elaborate script and the originality of film direction. It combines optimism and grief in an exemplary simple modern fairy tale. It does not restrict the notion of "superhero" on the individual level, but it raises it to the superpower of the community. Drama is in a dialectic relationship with magic realism. Local culture is present through the whole film, but we can find connections with our own cultures. (Dimitris)
> *My Life as a Courgette* [Claude Barras, 2016; France/Switzerland] is an excellent stop-motion film about a young boy who finds himself in care after the death of his mother. Although it is a challenging story, the references and humour work across cultures and languages and all children are able to identify with the character and the challenges he faces. (LYF)

Both films are shown outside their country of origin with subtitles and, as a result, much of the meaning relies on music and images. The Kenyan film *Supa Modo* mentioned by Dimitris was internationally co-funded and directed by Wainaina as part of the One Fine Day Films workshop project, which links African filmmakers with mentors who can help them to realise their stories for an international audience. It is a film about death, and it breaks a strong convention of children's films in which central characters survive. The film is innovative in both its production and the way it enables a profoundly

FIGURE 1.1. The loss of Jo is sad, but her life is full of hope. *Supa Modo* (2018, Ginger Ink Films).

sad story to be told in a way that keeps the contract with the child viewer to be hopeful—or, at least, not unremittingly bleak (Figure 1.1).

CONCLUSION

According to the respondents in this study, access to children's films not made in Hollywood is a matter of social justice; diverse children's films enable children to see themselves represented on screen, empathize with others, encounter countercultural ideas about the world, and develop as critically engaged and creative citizens. Indeed, in the context of a festival or film-education project, cinema is seen not as a commercial medium but as a cultural form that can "make a difference" in the lives of children and young people. This is a lot to expect of cultural texts, especially as most children (and adults) would say the primary function of film is to entertain.

The interview testimonies demonstrate that there are nationally distinct ideas about childhood and that childhood is far from being a universal experience, as is often assumed. Providing a diversity of ideas and representations about childhood is clearly something that children's film-festival professionals value. In both film programming and scholarship it is critical that films for children, beyond those of Hollywood, inform the way the genre is understood.

Alongside the differences identified in the way children's films are defined and understood, there is an acknowledgement that children's films articulate complexity through visual and aural but not necessarily verbal modes. This may account for the way in which some films transcend international boundaries, and it is this element of films for children that now demands attention. *Supa Modo* pushes the boundaries of definition and helps us think about how we define both childhood and children's films. The film demonstrates the importance of cinema in the lives of children, and we see the Kenyan practice of audio performance as superhero films are screened. In *Supa Modo*, every adult in the village is involved in first "pretending" that the child protagonist, Jo, has superpowers, and then in making a film with her as the star. Jo's mother has to reach an understanding of what her daughters need rather than assuming she knows what is best. Neither film contains lead protagonists that are functionally heroic or emancipated; instead, they are well-developed, complex characters who do more than simply drive the narrative. Jo is at once a child frustrated by medical treatment and a lack of choices, but in another moment, she is the "grown up" who knowingly goes along with the pretence that the village is maintaining that she has superpowers. All the adults in the village embrace the idea of playing goodies and baddies like children in the film, but also take shared responsibility for supporting Jo's family (Figure 1.2).

There is a moment in *Supa Modo* when the child protagonist is shown lying on a backdrop on the ground in the posture of a superhero, with two adults running around her fanning her to give the impression of the movement of the wind. Later, we see this scene in the film creating an illusion that Jo (or, rather, Supa Modo) is flying. Adults and children playfully collude with the film within a film, showing the action in front and behind the camera. The audience learns how films are made, and how characters are shown to

FIGURE 1.2. The adults play the baddies who will be conquered by Supa Modo as played by Jo. *Supa Modo* (2018, Ginger Ink Films).

FIGURE 1.3. In *Supa Modo*, the boundaries of adulthood and childhood are blurred (2018, Ginger Ink Films).

fly, and it is this that, in the end, reminds the audience that it is fiction and that the loss of Jo is fictional. There is a great deal of suspending of disbelief for the characters, but also for the *audience*.

In contrast to *Good Boys*, a parody of the tired clichés of many Hollywood movies, *Supa Modo* and *My Life as a Courgette* take films for children into new realms, blurring the boundaries of adulthood and childhood (Figure 1.3). What makes them distinct as films for children is not only which or whose story is told, but the way in which children are invited to make meaning from the images, the editing, and the music. So much of the media made for children is overtly and, at times, clumsily pedagogic, whether it is confirming normative values or raising awareness of ideas that may challenge them. It is of particular interest, therefore, to focus on films that rise to the surface in festivals as audience or jury favourites, and to pay attention to the characteristics of these films that result in strong affective responses from children. In doing so, we may have a better understanding not only of children's films, but also of children.

NOTES

1. The category "stoner" is commonly used in popular film reviewing. See, for example, https://www.esquire.com/entertainment/g27185365/best-stoner-movies/ [accessed April 14, 2020].
2. Casie Hermansson and Janet Zepernick (eds.), *The Palgrave Handbook of Children's Film and Television* (Cham, Switzerland: Palgrave Macmillan, 2019).

3. The European Children's Film Association website is accessible here: https://www.ecfa web.org/.

4. Alison James and Alan Prout, *Constructing and Reconstructing Childhood: Contemporary Issues in the Sociological Study of Childhood* (New York: Routledge, 2015).

5. Bettina Kümmerling-Meibauer, "Introduction: New Perspectives in Children's Film Studies," *Journal of Educational Media, Memory, and Society* 5:2 (2013), pp. 39–44; Ian Wojcik-Andrews, *Children's Films: History, Ideology, Pedagogy, Theory* (New York: Garland, 2000).

6. Noel Brown, *The Children's Film: Genre, Nation and Narrative* (New York: Columbia University Press, 2017).

7. S. F. Said, "What Makes a Children's Film Great?," *The Telegraph*, October 29 2005.

8. Perry Nodelman, *The Hidden Adult: Defining Children's Literature* (Baltimore, MD: Johns Hopkins University Press, 2008).

9. Cary Bazalgette and Terry Staples, "Unshrinking the Kids: Children's Cinema and the Family Film," in David Buckingham and Cary Bazalgette (eds.), *In Front of the Children: Screen Entertainment and Young Audiences* (London: BFI Publishing, 1995), pp. 92–108.

10. Brown, *Children's Film*.

11. Bazalgette and Staples, "Unshrinking the Kids."

12. Brown, *Children's Film*, pp. 5–10.

13. Ibid., pp. 13–15.

14. Jacqueline Rose, *The Case of Peter Pan, or the Impossibility of Children's Fiction* (London: Macmillan, 1984).

15. James and Prout, *Constructing and Reconstructing Childhood*.

16. Karin Calvert, "Children in the House: The Material Culture of Early Childhood," in Henry Jenkins (ed.), *The Children's Culture Reader* (New York: New York University Press, 1998), pp. 67–80.

17. Donna J. Grace and Joseph Tobin, "Carnival in the Classroom: Elementary Students Making Videos," in Joseph Tobin, *Making a Place for Pleasure in Early Childhood Education* (New York: Yale University Press, 1997), pp. 159–187.

18. Allison James, "Confections, Concoctions, and Conceptions," in Henry Jenkins (ed.), *The Children's Culture Reader* (New York: New York University Press, 1998), pp. 394–405.

19. Becky Parry, *Children, Film and Literacy* (Basingstoke, UK: Palgrave Macmillan, 2013).

20. Becky Parry, "Reading and Re-reading 'Shrek,'" *English in Education* 43:2 (2009), pp. 148–161.

21. James, "Confections, Concoctions, and Conceptions."

22. Rose, *Case of Peter Pan*.

23. Nodelman, *Hidden Adult*, p. 77.

24. Prior to commencing this research, I gained ethical approval from the University of Sheffield to undertake interviews with those working in film education or film exhibition.

25. Brett Smith, "Generalizability in Qualitative Research: Misunderstandings, Opportunities and Recommendations for the Sport and Exercise Sciences, *Qualitative Research in Sport, Exercise and Health* 10:1 (2018), pp. 137–149.

26. Jennifer Egan, Lesley Chenoweth, and Donna McAuliffe, "Email-Facilitated Qualitative Interviews with Traumatic Brain Injury Survivors: A New and Accessible Method," *Brain Injury* 20:12 (2006), pp. 1283–1294.

27. Sarah J. Tracy, "Qualitative Quality: Eight 'Big-Tent' Criteria for Excellent Qualitative Research," *Qualitative Inquiry* 16:10 (2010), pp. 837–851.

28. Gloria worked for several years on different experimental cinema projects for, among others, a DVD publishing house and a filmmakers' co-operative in Paris, France.

29. Martin Grund worked as a volunteer at Leeds International Film Festival before joining the Leeds Young Film team in 2006. Debbie Maturi has worked in children's cinema for over twenty-five years, starting out as a volunteer at Bradford Playhouse and Film Theatre. Now the head of Leeds Young Film, she is the director of INDIs (Independent Directions) Film Festival and Leeds Young Film Festival. Gage Oxley is a writer/director, and the managing director of Oxygen Films, a multi-award-winning, non-profit, community-interest production company based in Leeds. Gage's role at LYF involves supporting access to the industry for young people, engaging them to see film as a potential career.

30. Eva Schwarzwald worked was director of the Cinematographic and Audiovisual Activities Bureau at the Lombardy Region Culture, for twenty years and is a specialist in audiovisual projects for schools and children in Italy. She is a past president and member of the board of the European Children's Film Association and artistic director of the Italian project *Cinema senza barriere* (Cinema without barriers) and has coordinated four seminars on various issues associated with disabilities, cinema, art, and culture. See http://www.mostra invideo.com.

31. Dimitris Spyrou created the Olympia International Film Festival for Children and Young people. Since 2018, the Olympia International Film Festival for Children and Young People has been organized by a social co-operative enterprise under a programme contract with the Ministry of Culture and the Region of Western Greece.

32. Katri Tenhola is a film programmer at National Audiovisual Institute of Finland. Katri's work includes organizing and curating the National Audiovisual Institute's school screenings.

33. Mojtaba Vaismoradi et al., "Theme Development in Qualitative Content Analysis and Thematic Analysis," *Journal of Nursing Education and Practice* 6:5 (2016), pp. 100–110.

34. Harry Hendrick, "Constructions and Reconstructions of British Childhood: An Interpretative Survey, 1800 to the Present," in Alison James and Alan Prout (eds.), *Constructing and Reconstructing Childhood: Contemporary issues in the Sociological Study of Childhood* (New York: Routledge, 2015), pp. 29–53.

35. Margaret Spencer Meek, *How Texts Teach What Readers Learn* (Stroud: Thimble Press, 1988); Parry, *Children, Film and Literacy*.

36. There are a number of studies of children's film in relation to censorship, including Marjorie Heins, *Not in Front of the Children: "Indecency," Censorship, and the Innocence of Youth* (New Brunswick, NJ: Rutgers University Press, 2007).

37. Hermansson and Zepernick, *Palgrave Handbook of Children's Film and Television*.

38. Dafna Lemish, *Screening Gender on Children's Television: The Views of Producers around the World* (New York: Routledge, 2010).

39. Paulo Freire, *Pedagogy of the Oppressed* (Freiberg: Herder and Herdher, 1970).

40. Nodelman, *Hidden Adult*.

BIBLIOGRAPHY

Bazalgette, Cary, and Terry Staples. "Unshrinking the Kids: Children's Cinema and the Family Film." In David Buckingham and Cary Bazalgette (eds.), *In Front of the Children: Screen Entertainment and Young Audiences*, London, BFI Publishing, 1995, pp. 92–108.

Brown, Noel. *The Hollywood Family Film: A History, from Shirley Temple to Harry Potter*. London: I.B. Tauris, 2012.

Brown, Noel. *The Children's Film: Genre, Nation and Narrative*. New York: Columbia University Press, 2017.

Calvert, Karin. "Children in the House: The Material Culture of Early Childhood." In Henry Jenkins (ed.), *The Children's Culture Reader*. New York: New York University Press, 1998, pp. 67–80.

Lemish, Dafna. *Screening Gender on Children's Television: The Views of Producers Around the World*. New York: Routledge, 2010.

....

CHAPTER 2

SCREENING INNOCENCE IN CHILDREN'S FILM

....

DEBBIE OLSON

There is no aphrodisiac like innocence.

—Jean Baudrillard[1]

IN his classic film *Sabotage* (1936), Alfred Hitchcock blew up a child named Stevie. Even more traumatizing, he put a puppy on the bus next to the child! Mark Osteen believes that audiences at the time didn't "really believe that the boy and dog will be blown to bits...Surely these two adorable innocents won't die horribly!"[2] And yet that is exactly what happened. Young Stevie had unknowingly transported a bomb on to the bus, killing himself, the puppy, the sweet old lady holding the puppy, and everyone else nearby. Viewers were aghast at such a shocking occurrence. The scene's violence and its child (and puppy) victim compelled film audiences to face their unconscious expectations about innocence. Actress Sylvia Sydney, who played Mrs Verloc, Stevie's sister, "took great offense with the 'innocents' death...especially the "unnecessary death of the darling dog.'"[3] Why was she so bothered by the death of a child and a puppy? Because the child and puppy are visual representations of innocence, and innocence must never be contaminated by violence or other adult things. Filmmakers like Hitchcock cleverly understand that film audiences are susceptible to images of "sentimentalized innocence" or innocent victims of outside forces, a feature Hitchcock continued to use masterfully throughout his career.[4] Innocence on film is a powerful but rarely explored phenomenon, regularly exploited with images of children.

One of the defining features of childhood in Western popular culture is innocence, that state of purity or unknowing that forms the foundation for concepts like nostalgia. Such notions of childhood innocence are rooted in the Romantic-era philosophies of John Locke and Jean-Jacques Rousseau; both argued for an inherently innocent child from birth who is eventually corrupted by experience and culture.[5] Parents go to great lengths in the West to protect a child's innocence until an age when the outside world and the child's growing awareness begin to encroach on, and eventually corrupt, the innocence that parents worked so hard to maintain. Neil Postman famously bemoaned what he viewed as the loss of childhood in postmodern society: "Everywhere one looks, it may be seen that the behaviour, language, attitudes, and desires—even the physical appearance—of adults and children are becoming increasingly indistinguishable."[6] His book, *The Disappearance of Childhood* (1982) became a treatise on the evils of modern society that corrupt the innocence and purity of children and childhood.

In cinema, however, innocence is a reliable *accoutrement* to images of children and childhood. The camera caresses innocence, embraces and nurtures it, and sometimes purposely fractures it, so that a wave of nostalgia for that lost innocence bubbles up and lingers throughout the rest of the film (*Hook* [Steven Spielberg, 1991] or *Ender's Game* [Gavin Hood, 2013], for instance). As Vicky Lebeau states, childhood innocence inhabits a "space and time that we have all known without knowing it."[7] Elizabeth Wolgast perhaps best describes the complexities of innocence: "The conception of innocence does not require a context or a background of specific events to be understood. It has the simple form of an enviable condition of character, one for others to wonder at, even revere, to wish for and protect."[8] The notion of innocence is disseminated in a variety of ways throughout material culture. Through the magic of cinema, adults can re-inhabit the space of childhood innocence, and children can experience what Postman would consider to be a much-needed model for the idealized childhood that children themselves should also desire.

Innocence is an integral part of the cinematic geography of children's films. In what ways does cinema for children visualize innocence, and to what purpose? How is innocence framed? What cinematographic techniques create innocence on screen? This chapter will examine the ways cinema manufactures, privileges, and interrogates notions of innocence in film. While there are numerous films made *for* children that do not feature children (including many animated features), this chapter will focus the discussion of innocence on select case studies of live-action films for children and families that *star* children. Although innocence is key to any depiction of the child—whether it is being challenged or reinforced—many of the films examined here rely on a central belief in the innocence of the child as an ontological condition, one that either stays intact, is unsettled, or is lost completely.

THE PRIVILEGE OF INNOCENCE

Joanne Faulkner, in *The Importance of Being Innocent*, defines innocence as a "rigid understanding of childhood as unworldly, incapable, and pure" that reinforces sentimental notions of an idealized state of being and a purity of the soul.[9] The concept of innocence is much more complex, however. To have innocence is often considered to be spiritual, to be closer to God, to be untainted by the sin of Eve. To be innocent assumes freedom from its opposite, guilt. Innocence suggests a lack of knowledge—particularly carnal knowledge—an immaturity of thought, a deficit in reason. Norvin Richards argues that innocence is conceptual, an "unawareness deriving from inexperience."[10] In Lacanian terms, innocence functions as a Lack, which fuels powerful nostalgic desire in adults to return to a state of being before knowledge. Stephen R. Munzer's discussion of innocence suggests it is a lack of moral knowledge and a lack of "evil" behaviour.[11] Elizabeth Wolgast views innocence as the best of all moral conditions, one that holds a "complete absence of error and regret." She finds the state of innocence to be one that features "unalloyed trust, of virtue unconscious of the existence of wrong" and which presents a "rare kind of beauty."[12]

In a legal context, ethics scholar Jacqueline A. Laing equates innocence as "central to right conduct" and argues that a key part of the "very concept of innocence [is] that it is not susceptible to variation by the desires or consent of others."[13] In "The Innocence of Victimhood Versus the Innocence of Becoming," Joanne Faulkner suggests that innocence "is integral to the skilful exercise of agency . . . [innocence] suggest[s] a resistance to passivity and victimhood and a choice to take part in the inevitability of the moment."[14] In her discussion of the "cultural value of innocence," Faulkner describes the state of innocence as a "privileged site" from which adults in the West construct childhood for children.[15] However, in *The Child in Film*, Karen Lury argues that the "privileged site" of innocence functions as an "othering" of children against the norm of adulthood.[16] All these scholars recognize that innocence is integral to right conduct and childhood; but not all agree on what or who constitutes an "acceptable" innocent childhood.

Many of these conceptions of innocence are repeatedly applied to children in ways that create cultural expectations for children's behaviour and shape political policies that attempt to protect childhood innocence. In the West, "life begins innocent and wants to return to innocence, which thereby summarizes all that is culturally valuable."[17] In Western culture, children occupy a "sacred" position; one that must be preserved at all costs.[18] Cinema for children endeavours to capture and unfold innocence for the viewer as a way to reinforce the desire to be innocent, as well as to promote film-inspired products in order to relive the adventure and fuel nostalgia. As Gary Cross argues, children are encouraged to "want objects that ma[k]e them feel connected to imaginative stories."[19] Indeed, innocence, particularly in modern consumer culture, is "understood to hold the secret to the self [in] the nostalgic construction of a simpler past," which can only be accessed through our children, or through the *viewing* of our children and their childhood in popular visual media.[20] Film functions to "socially circulate" this desire for innocence, even to the children themselves.[21] Children are regularly "positioned as desire-free objects of desire" in cinema, constantly under threat of corruption by adults.[22] As we will see, film children *perform* innocence in all of its richly textured moral, ideological, sociological, and cultural intricacies, regularly leaving viewers (both adult and child) nostalgic for the idealized childhood depicted on screen.

INNOCENCE IN THE GARDEN

Like the mythical Garden of Eden, where adult knowledge does not exist, innocence is a cultural construct that represents an unachievable state of purity. Children have become the embodiment of the notion of innocence and purity by virtue of their lack of worldly experience (although, as we will see, not all children are included in the realm of innocence). The most common depiction of innocence in film is the whimsical, sinless, carefree, wholesome state of happiness that allows middle-class children to spend their days in culturally approved childhood pursuits. These children are almost always White, often with large eyes (preferably blue), plump cheeks (preferably dimpled), and usually blonde or light-coloured hair, and the girls have curls or pigtails. The largest purveyor of prelapsarian innocence on screen is the Walt Disney Company. The Disney image of innocence, firmly rooted in Victorian culture, underscores the fairy tale accoutrement surrounding Disney characters, which adds to the pastoral purity of the child character—colours are soft pastels or earth tones, the child wears traditional, gender-norm clothing, locations are garden-like or pristine and often "cosy," evoking warmth and happiness. And though Disney's more recent films are more diverse, the Disneyfication of innocence still embodies much the same patterns.[23] Beginning in 1923 with the silent, part-animated short *Alice's Wonderland* (Walt Disney, 1923), starring five-year-old Virginia Davis, Disney visually manufactured the very essence of childhood innocence, a style that has become the studio's trademark, particularly in its animated films.[24] The film highlights Virginia's youthful innocence with high-key lighting and close-ups that emphasize her large expressive eyes, pointed chin, button nose, and her curiosity alongside the animated animals dancing around her. The camera often films her from a slightly high angle, and she is positioned looking up in close-ups to accentuate her vulnerability. This chin down, eyes-up movement is a standard shot to underscore a child's innocence, particularly for girls, who must also model submissiveness or coquetry.

Disney idealized the look of innocence in 1928 with the invention of Mickey Mouse. According to Tony Campolo:

> Mickey is a purely innocent creature.... There is no guile in him. He is the unfallen creature. And he's never done anything sinful in his life. He's Adam before the Fall. There's a naiveté about him. And all of us are attracted to him. And we all cheer for him because he is "so good"... Mickey is a wonderful, wonderful creature. He is innocence.[25]

Even though he is an animated character, the influence of Mickey Mouse's innocence has continued in the ongoing and substantial body of children's films produced by Disney. Notable films include *Mary Poppins* (Robert Stevenson, 1964), which featured a slightly dysfunctional family that comes together under the firm but gentle guidance of the nanny Mary Poppins (Julie Andrews). The children, Jane and Michael Banks (played, respectively, by Karen Dotrice and Matthew Garber) underscore the importance of the film's project—to restore the traditional family and reform two misbehaving, though far from sinful, children. The film features many close-ups of Matthew Garber, particularly, whose very expressive face captures his transition from naughty to nice, from miscreant to innocent once again. The two starred together in two other classic Disney films, *The Three Lives of Thomasina* (Don Chaffey, 1963) and *The Gnome-Mobile* (Robert Stevenson, 1967). And there is no scene that highlights the Disney version of a child's innocence more than when veterinarian and father Andrew McDhui (Patrick McGoohan) has to tell his daughter, Mary (Karen Dotrice), that he could not save her beloved cat, Thomasina. The camera's shot-reverse-shot of their dialogue freezes on young Mary's face the moment her father tells her he put her cat to sleep. Innocence dies for her in that lingering close-up as she is confronted with the reality of death.

The Disney canon is filled with children that embody a particular brand of innocence: tow-headed, White, freckled, blue-eyed boys; and White, blonde, large-eyed, curly haired or pigtailed girls. Both are smart, but not corrupted by adult knowledge. We often find Disney children in nature, which highlights their innocence as a natural condition, in films such as *Treasure Island* (Byron Haskin, 1950), *Old Yeller* (Robert Stevenson, 1957), *Darby O'Gill and the Little People* (Robert Stevenson, 1959), and *Swiss Family Robinson* (Ken Annakin, 1960). Other notable films that align innocence with nature are *Bedknobs and Broomsticks* (Robert Stevenson, 1971), set in small-town England with a romp on the tropical island of Naboombu; *Pollyanna* (David Swift, 1960), set in small-town America, with all of its pastoral markers, and featuring Hayley Mills, who went on to star in one of the most popular Disney films, *The Parent Trap* (David Swift, 1961); *The Love Bug* (Robert Stevenson, 1968), set in San Francisco and the Sierra Nevada Mountains, in which a Volkswagen bug plays the "innocent," with its softly rounded body and large headlight eyes; and *Escape to Witch Mountain* (John Hough, 1975), set in the US Blue Ridge Mountains, starring Ike Eisenmann as Tony Malone, and blonde, dimpled, cute-as-a-button Kim Richards as his sister, Tia Malone.

Indeed, innocence in Disney is most often the visual realm for girl protagonists, even though—according to a comprehensive study by Carmen Fought and Karen Eisenhauer—the male characters in Disney films have more speaking roles than female characters, even in films with a female lead.[26] And the Disney innocence-image carries across all the princess films. According to Olga Khazan, the Disney princesses have a familiar facial pattern, and their "enlarged eyes, tiny chins, and short noses make them look more like babies, which creates an air of innocence and vulnerability."[27] Henry Giroux argues that innocence in Disney is "carefully constructed" to rationalize the dominant culture. For Giroux, innocence in Disney is a performance of ideology, a particularly Western ideology of consumption, individualism, and clear gender roles.[28] And for children who view Disney films, the innocence of time, character, and place in some ways works to create nostalgia for the idealized childhood that frames the adventure. This nostalgia for the filmic universe is satisfied by a cacophony of film-related products available to help kids relive the adventure; or, as Jyotsna Kapur argues, "Disney's production of commodities and of culture reinforce each other."[29]

In Disney films, innocence is often character-driven, in that characters are created in such a way as to reinforce the visual determinants of what innocence should look like. Director and producer Steven Spielberg is another leading purveyor of cinematic innocence who combines elements of character and place to create a totality of innocence on screen. Spielberg's oeuvre is filled with family films that highlight innocence and the magic of youthful wonder. One of Spielberg's best-known films, his sci-fi adventure, *E. T. The Extra-Terrestrial* (1982), stars Henry Thomas as Elliot, a boy who befriends an alien that was inadvertently left behind when his ship departed. Elliot, his siblings, and friends work together to help E.T. find his way home. Innocence in a Spielberg film often undergirds the adventure and usually emerges unscathed. According to Gary Arms and Thomas Riley, "The formula for many of Spielberg's most famous films is innocence in great jeopardy."[30] In *E. T.*, innocence presents itself in new and unique ways. For Spielberg, innocence "is to be harmless, simple, naive, pure, open, and [most importantly] filled with wonder."

Spielberg is masterful at weaving characters together in a narrative that challenges the notion of childlike wonder to reinforce the importance of that wonder. According to James Kendrick, Spielberg films also harbour an underlying darkness that can reveal uncomfortable complexities, even ugliness, particularly regarding the family. He argues that in many films Spielberg "visually reinforce[s] the fractured, fragmented, and stressed nature of the traditional nuclear famil[y]," which exists in a pervasive "suburban malaise."[31] And in one particular film, *Empire of the Sun* (1987), Spielberg documents in disturbing detail, and cinematic beauty, the complete destruction of a young boy's childhood and innocence.[32] But Spielberg creates characters "worthy of our preferential attention just by virtue of their being pure and without guile, incapable of dissembling or dishonesty... We are drawn in... to believe that innocence is something to be preserved in itself," and especially, indeed almost desperately, within settings that are anything but innocent and pure.[33] Spielberg films, then, address both child and adult to create a "double nostalgia" that captures "a memory trace of childhood" for adults and for children, the hope of an adult world in which the inner child survives, a sentiment that is at the heart of *E. T.*[34]

E. T. opens at night; the camera tilts up from a silhouette of trees to view the wide expanse of stars, and then zooms in on a spaceship and alien beings moving around it. The music here is non-threatening, vaguely playful, but slightly edgy; there is tension, but no fear. The aliens are collecting plants; the camera focuses briefly on a rabbit calmly resting near them, suggesting there is little to fear. The camera cuts to a long shot of E.T. alone and small in the forest, establishing his vulnerability. But the ship is almost discovered and abruptly departs, leaving E.T. to fend for himself. Men with flashlights almost find him as he scrambles to get away. His breathing is childlike and high-pitched, and as the men chase him, he makes mewling "baby cries." So, while E.T. is an alien Other, his innocence as an outsider is firmly established as he runs and hides from the adult men chasing him.

Elliot's mother's reaction to E.T. highlights the division between innocence and knowledge, but in a negative way. Adult knowledge breeds fear—fear of the Other, in this case, of an alien Other. Here, innocence and the sense of wonder at difference are privileged. For the children, believing in and empathizing with E.T. is a natural thing, but for the adult characters, the fear of difference outweighs wonder. As E.T. becomes ill, he loses his healthy, earthy-brown glow and turns a sickly grey. E.T. here is even *more* innocent as the outsider, alone in a strange land, fearing the evils of science (knowledge) and relying on Elliot to save him.

Innocence in *E.T.* resides mostly in the dark. *E.T.* is one of Spielberg's darkest films in terms of cinematography. Much of the action takes place at night and Spielberg's play with light and shadow—numerous moving flashlights, light coming through the slats in the closet door, lights through the forest trees—suggests the light-dark emotional texture of coming of age. This play of light and shadow culminate in Spielberg's most famous silhouette shot of Elliot and E.T. riding the flying bike in front of the moon. The magic of this one shot has become a cultural, even global, icon for innocence. The film positions the children and E.T. in opposition to the adults in their unfettered acceptance of E.T. Interestingly, E.T., as a dark-brown and wrinkled alien, is uniquely an innocent Other. It is no small thing that E.T. is dark-brown with blue eyes—a merging of blackness and whiteness into one character. That E.T. is brown *and* innocent is a rarity in film, even today. Helen Addison-Smith argues that E.T. must return home to "keep both the family and the nation safely 'white.'"[35] But Spielberg's project here emphasizes acceptance and empathy for the Other. Elliot sacrifices everything to help E.T. Innocence here undergirds Elliot's motives—a lack of predetermined and fear-laced beliefs about "alien others."

For Spielberg, Elliot's friendship with E.T. is the fulfilment of the promise set out in *Close Encounters of the Third Kind* (1977), Spielberg's earlier film about a man, Roy Neary (Richard Dreyfus), who is obsessed with aliens. For Roy, leaving with the very childlike aliens at the end of *Close Encounters* allows him to return to a state of innocence and wonder, even giving up his family and his home to do so. But for Elliot, innocence is located not with E.T., but at home with his family, where he chooses to stay.[36] Elliot is confident that he can hold onto his sense of wonder, his childness, as E.T. tells him "I'll be right here," touching Elliot's forehead. In *E.T.*, innocence resides in empathy and trust, in acceptance of the Other, and a simple belief in human, and alien, goodness.

In *Pictures of Innocence*, Anne Higonnet observes that images of children "belong to the past, or else belong to forever, not to real time, but to a timeless utopia (no place)."[37] Many films for children frame the narrative with unstated affirmations of innocence. Films like *The Red Balloon* (Albert Lamorisse, 1956), *The NeverEnding Story* (Wolfgang Petersen, 1984), *The Goonies* (Richard Donner, 1985), *Whale Rider* (Niki Caro, 2002), *The Chronicles of Narnia: The Lion, The Witch and the Wardrobe* (Andrew Adamson, 2005), and *The Cave of the Yellow Dog* (Byambasuren Davaa, 2005) articulate innocence through visual simplicity—a balloon, a book, a map, a fish, a wardrobe, and a dog—items that in these films perform the cultural work of anchoring innocence to childhood, to "secure meanings" about idealized childhood and its reliance on innocence within the film's diegetic space.[38] Yet much of the scholarship about children and film limits such discussions to White, middle class children. Children that are not framed in the idealized child space—per the West's narrow definition—challenge dominant cinema's hold on the artifice of innocence.

THE COLOUR OF INNOCENCE

Idealized Western childhood is dependent upon notions of innocence to continue its privileged status. The concept of innocence often functions as an unspoken framework for judgements about human value. People who are deemed not innocent are often people of colour or those who are from historically marginalized groups, such as the Romani. Adults manufacture and reaffirm idealized childhood innocence in ways that are deeply entrenched throughout popular culture to help alleviate adult fears. Images of innocence are replicated daily through such things as food labels, clothing, books, toys, television, digital images (especially memes), and film, offering a "vision of time-less edenic bliss as an escape from the vicissitudes of adult life."[39] But the image of the romantic child is firmly rooted in the West. As Higonnet argues, "oblivious innocence confirms a long-standing western tradition of seeing anyone who isn't western as an innocent savage, a savage who remains perpetually a dependent child."[40] The West's belief that some children inherently lack innocence has had serious and sometimes deadly consequences in places like the United States, where Black children—most often boys—are routinely treated as adults, even at very young ages.[41] According to the CDC (Center for Disease Control and Prevention), gun violence is the leading cause of death for Black children in the United States, underscoring the notion that Black children are rarely protected like White children.[42]

As I have argued elsewhere, part of the social construct of innocence depends on the discourse that shapes who is and who is not considered innocent. In order for the West to maintain its dogma of idealized innocence, children of colour must remain outside that sphere of purity. Hollywood film plays a key role in the way some children are seen as innocent while others are not.[43] Disney, for all of the hundreds of films it has released, has produced only a handful with a child of colour as the protagonist and mostly in ani-mated films: Mowgli from *The Jungle Book* (Wolfgang Reitherman, 1967), Jasmine from *Aladdin* (Ron Clements and John Musker, 1992), *Pocahontas* (Eric Goldberg and Mike Gabriel, 1995), *Mulan* (Tony Bancroft and Barry Cook, 1998), Tiana (the only African American) from *The Princess and the Frog* (Ron Clements and John Musker, 2009), *Moana* (Ron Clements and John Musker, 2016), and Miguel from *Coco* (Lee Unkrich, 2017). Most recently, Disney announced the casting of Black actor Halle Bailey to play Ariel in a live-action version of *The Little Mermaid*. The announcement sparked a volley of racist backlash across social media by Whites who believe Ariel should stay White. But Disney is not the only White-centred family film producer—Spielberg's family films also lack child protagonists of colour. Even major animated films (such as those by Pixar) tend to favour the White child as the visual icon of innocence.

The few films that do feature children of colour as protagonists tend to construct that child as not innocent from the beginning. One such film is Cary Fukunaga's adaptation *Beasts of No Nation* (2015), from Uzodinma Iweala's novel of the same name. It is a coming-of-age film (not rated) about a child soldier set in an unnamed African country. In the novel, a young Black boy named Agu is conscripted into a rebel gang after a raid on his village that killed his father and brother. Agu is forced to become a child soldier. His struggle throughout the book is somehow to stay a "good boy" and hold on to his innocence despite the horrific things he witnesses and eventually must do. He is an innocent victim of circumstance throughout. Yet Fukunaga's film version opens with Agu and his friends trying to sell a stolen TV box. They play cruel pranks on people, try to scam drivers out of money, and are quite mischievous—all in the film's first ten minutes. The film positions Agu (and his friends) from the outset as *not* innocent and in fact *deserving* of what later happens to him *because* he was not innocent.[44] The changes Fukunaga made to Agu's character specifically locate him outside the West's code of childhood innocence, a move that happens often to children of colour in Hollywood films (such as *Beasts of the Southern Wild* [Benh Zeitlin, 2012] or *Fresh* [Boaz Yakin, 1994]). As Joanne Faulkner astutely argues, Western media, particularly Hollywood, must "maintain the ideal of childhood innocence that sanctifies the Western way of life."[45] In popular Hollywood family films, children of colour call into question the fantasy of childhood innocence reserved for Whites, and they are startlingly absent from big-budget films for children. That absence in film is sadly offset by a daily barrage of images in television and news media that offer images of children of colour as dangerous or adultified—decidedly *not* innocent.

One of the ways film is used to reaffirm innocence and idealized childhood is by positioning a Western child in a non-Western context, a practice of "Orientalizing" non-Western childhoods. The remake of *The Karate Kid* (Harald Zwart, 2010) is one such film. Dre (Jaden Smith) and his mom, Sherry (Taraji P. Hanson), move from Detroit, Michigan, to Beijing, China, for her new job. The film follows Dre's experience in a culture that is completely unfamiliar to him. Like the original *Karate Kid* (John G. Avildsen, 1984), this version is about a boy learning to deal with bullies, particularly the sadistic Chen (Zhenwei Wang), and stand on his own. But in the 2010 version, the camera spends significant time in slow-motion, almost sensual, close-ups of Dre's face contorted with pain. During the first fight scene, which happens on the day they arrive in China, the close-up shots reveal the pain of each punch, kick, and slam to Dre's small and defenceless body by the older Chinese boys, who are depicted as violent and dangerous "oriental" Others. The boys warn Dre to "stay away from us—ALL of us" referring to the Chinese girl, Mei Ying (Wenwen Han), who befriended Dre. The first fight scene ends with an overhead shot of Dre lying motionless on the playground, the camera slowly circles downward, emphasizing both Dre's Otherness and vulnerability.

The film tends to orientalise Chinese cultural differences in ways that privilege Western childhood and notions of innocence, though with subtle reminders of Dre's race. When Dre first meets Han (Jackie Chan) he is eating his lunch and refuses to acknowledge Dre, who is trying to get Han's attention. Dre watches Han kill a fly on the wall and remove it from the flyswatter with his chopsticks. Han drops the fly in the trash, wipes the sticks on his pants, and continues to eat.[46] Dre exclaims that was so "gross," suggesting Chinese food practices are beneath those of the West, an orientalising strategy that rests on the long-standing comic trope of Westerners trying to use chopsticks, which also occurs at various places in the film. *The Karate Kid* also highlights African American difference with a specific motif historically rooted in White racism—characters throughout the film ask to "touch" Dre's and his mom's hair. This is one of those rare films that star a Black child as an innocent, though only amongst non-White foreigners. Dre can be innocent, but only outside the West, where he functions as the superior in a binary opposite the Chinese. Yet the film stubbornly reminds us of Dre's difference in scenes that underscore his race, such as the hair scenes (no one asks to touch the White boy Henry's hair). The film is brutally violent, the camera seeming to linger on and caress Dre's pain-filled face during the fight scenes, which hearken back to the historical abuse and lynching of Black children during slavery and Jim Crow. Reviewer Colin Colvert claims that the remake "lacks the innocence" of the original, in part because of the way Dre's pain filled body is fetishized by the camera, which is evident in the final fight scene when Dre's little body endures a brutal beating. Most disturbingly, the camera cuts to his mother cheering him on, encouraging him to *keep going* despite his broken bones and extreme pain resulting from Chen's vicious attack.

Jordan Roberts's *Burn Your Maps* (2016) centres on a young, affluent White boy named Wes (Jacob Tremblay). His parents are struggling with the death of their infant daughter and in response, Wes, who is very imaginative, has convinced himself that he is really a Mongolian goat herder. He dresses in traditional Mongolian garb, makes toilet paper goats, works to learn the language, and even learns about taking care of goats via YouTube. The film excuses its cultural appropriation by framing it through Wes's innocence of such things. In fact, one of the themes in the film is the danger of the Internet as a place for knowledge about other cultures, as Wes discovers when he and his mother travel to Mongolia. The film views Mongolia and its people and culture through the lens of privileged White America. Jordan Hoffman claims the film is "as orientalist as it comes" and although it does not disrespect Mongolian culture, it "uses it to help a group of well-off White people get their groove back."[47] Tomris Laffly argues that while the film's "cringe-worthy cultural exploitation" borders on offensive, the whimsical cinematography and the undeniable innocence of Wes's joy at being able to experience being a Mongolian goat-herder provide an acceptable childish gloss over the film's orientalist leanings.[48] *Burn Your Maps* is like the adult version of the "White Pilgrimage" films, where White people travel to an "exotic" land to heal or rediscover themselves.[49] In this film, the Mongolian children are depicted as exotic others against which Wes's innocence is affirmed.

In contrast, *Cave of the Yellow Dog* is a Mongolian/German film directed by Byambasuren Davaa that follows six-year-old Nansal (Nansal Batchuluun), the oldest daughter of a nomadic family who finds a dog in a cave. She names it Zochor (Spot), but her father is worried that wolves will follow the scent of the dog and find their sheep. He tells Nansal she cannot keep the dog when they move, and she is forced to leave him behind. But in the end, the dog saves Nansal's baby brother from vultures and her fa- ther then accepts the dog into the family. The film contrasts Nansal's innocence with the adult fears of wolves destroying their livelihood. She is often presented in long shots with her small body surrounded by stunning meadows and mountains. She is playful, precocious, and very cherub-like as she tries to help her parents in their day to day tasks; for instance, there is a beautiful and comical scene where Nansal is trying to collect dung for her mother, but the tool she's using (which is like a shovel-rake) is too long and when she scoops the dung and tosses it behind her it misses the basket almost every time. No matter, she is happy and singing with that joyful, innocent abandon unique to children.

Davaa shoots the film with little editing, many medium and long shots, some hand- held shots, and an often-stationary camera that quietly reveals the oft-hidden world of childhood. The film does not dramatize or exploit Mongolian life like *Burn Your Maps*; rather, it draws us into its gentle rhythm. Nansal's play is equally balanced by her responsibilities, even at such a young age (she is tasked with minding the herd for a day when her father is gone). And while Western audiences may cringe watching a six-year- old mount a horse and herd the sheep up a mountain, Nansal is fully confident in her ability to do the job. Innocence for the children here is not connected to a lack of know- ledge, but instead to the honesty and wonder with which they perceive the world around them. The children here learn lessons about life and faith like all other children, but they do so without idealized parameters of acceptability. Nansal does not understand her father's fear that the dog will draw wolves to kill the sheep; she just sees a puppy that was given to her by fate. While the film does not have the Hollywood polish and scriptedness of *Burn Your Maps*, it offers a non-exploitive, non-Western, and richer portrayal of Mongolian childhood innocence and the universal love of a little girl and her dog.

While Western media romanticizes the White child, its depictions of brown and Black children are often limited to locations of extreme poverty, urban jungles (also in poverty), or abuse. NGOs (non-governmental organizations) are famous for utilizing the image of the starving, big-bellied, fly-covered Black or Brown child as a draw for Westerners to donate money and alleviate such suffering. In these conditions, inno- cence functions as a visual cue that this is a child and therefore worthy of donations, but the raw reality of suffering tends to disassociate innocence from that brown child so that she or he remains Other to the Western idea of childhood. As Faulkner observes, "The material conditions of these children cannot support the rarefied fantasy of [Western] childhood innocence...because their existence gives the lie to the myth."[50] One such film that complicates the West's notion of innocence is British director Danny Boyle's award-winning *Slumdog Millionaire* (2008). The film is a Dickensian rags-to-riches story that follows Jamal (Dev Patel), a boy growing up in the Dharavi slum in Mumbai, India. The film was dubbed "poverty porn" for its voyeuristic and exploitive representa- tion of India's poor. Films like *Slumdog Millionaire* have inspired a new growing industry of "poverty tours," or "poorism," in which people, usually from the global north, pay to tour slums and areas of extreme poverty. The film orientalises its young stars so that they appear to "[thrive] via the same fantasies that bolster Western civilization, illuminating new ways in which dominant Western society perceives "other" cultures."[51]

The film revels in images of brown children in pain, particularly the close-ups of the police torture of Jamal (which is the film's opening scene), the burning out of a young boy's eyes with acid, and the constant threat of child rape. All this happens within the framework of a Western-style game show, "Who Wants to Be a Millionaire?" We learn of Jamal's difficult childhood via the answers he gives to a policeman after he is arrested under suspicion of cheating when he unexpectedly wins the show. And while there is a great deal of violence against the children in *Slumdog Millionaire*, there is also an innocence that transcends that violence, and Western constructions of childhood. For instance, when a helicopter brings Bollywood star Amitabh Bachchan to see fans, Salim locks Jamal in the public toilet so he cannot see his hero. Jamal decides to escape by jumping through the toilet hole into a lake of faeces—a scene the camera captures in all its gory details, particularly the moment Jamal's face sinks beneath the sludge and then resurfaces. Undeterred, Jamal runs to the gathering, covered in sewage, and easily pushes through the crowd to secure an autograph from his favourite actor. The scene highlights the abject poverty, lack of sanitation, and horrific conditions in the Mumbai slum yet, despite its visual filth, rearticulates Jamal's innocence so that it transcends the sewage and shines through as pure childlike abandon, whimsical and magical. Jamal gets his coveted autograph, like any child seeking an autograph from an admired celebrity (Figure 2.1).

FIGURE 2.1. Jamal gets the autograph. *Slumdog* Millionaire (2008, Celador Films). Frame-grab.

What films like *Slumdog Millionaire* challenge is the West's limited notion of innocence as pure and free of violence, sex, or knowledge. Throughout the film, the street children are left alone to negotiate the dangers surrounding them, and their innocence—"adorably dirty yet perpetually wide-eyed"—often works against them. At the same time, however, it is at the heart of their experiences and their understanding of the world. And despite the unrealistic, Hollywood-style ending (Jamal wins the game and gets the girl), the children in the film represent hope in a place of death, "simultaneously as promise and object...as proxy and metaphor,"[52] for an innocence that is aesthetically transformed and recycled on screen beyond the narrow Western framework of "cute wondrous [White] innocence."[53] Above all, even covered in literal excrement, the childlike wonder of the children in *Slumdog Millionaire* shines through, reinforcing a broader, more realistic concept of innocence that breaks through, despite adult knowledge and violence.

INNOCENCE AWRY

Innocence on screen occupies an interesting interstitial space between purity and its opposite, contamination, or evil. In many ways, childhood innocence is an aesthetic performance that is interpreted by adults in ways that comfort and reaffirm their idealistic notions of what children are or should be. But this performance is fragile and easily polluted by knowledge, sex, violence, or worse. Adults *expect* innocence from children and fetishistically revel in films that feature the idealistic portrayal of childhood that fits that narrative. Parents flock to surround their children with the fantasy childhood they themselves embrace, hence the almost universal popularity of Disney films, which is the largest purveyor of idealized childhood images. As Higonnet argues, the innocent child is the "most powerful contradictory image in Western...culture. Promising the future but also turned nostalgically to the past, trading on innocence but implying sexuality, simultaneously denying and arousing desire, intimate on a mass scale, media spectacles of children are bound to be ambiguous," and that contradiction is nowhere more apparent than in movies starring deadly, dangerous, and corrupt children.[54]

One of the most psychologically challenging notions is that of an innocent child knowingly committing a heinous act. According to Susan Neiman, evil, and the notion of evil, are rooted in three main categories: natural, metaphysical, or moral. She argues that while evil in the modern sense is less rooted in the supernatural, the use of the word "evil" today functions as a discursive code that identifies something that "threatens the trust in the world."[55] And the one constant trust adults, and children, have is in childhood innocence. On screen, no visual image is more disconcerting than a child who has committed an adult crime. And some of the most famous screen children are those who lost their innocence to something much more sinister: the possessed (*Audrey Rose* [Robert Wise, 1977]; Regan in *The Exorcist* [William Friedkin, 1973]), sons or daughters of Satan (Damien in *The Omen* [Richard Donner, 1976]; Rhoda from *The Bad*

Seed [Mervyn LeRoy, 1956]; an evil infant in *Rosemary's Baby* [Roman Polanski, 1968), murderers (Gage in *Pet Sematary* [Mary Lambert, 1989]; Esther from *Orphan* [Jaume Collet-Serra, 2009]), or who weren't human at all (Brahms in *The Boy* [William Brent Bell, 2016]; *Children of the Damned* [Anton Leader, 1964]; Lilith in *Case 39* [Christian Alvart, 2010]).

All these evil children challenge the idealized image of innocence embraced by the West. But are they evil children playing at innocence? Or are they innocent victims of evil? Karen Renner argues that evil children are more "'infected' than inherently evil"[56] and Terry Eagleton suggests that "there are always those who believe in bad blood or malevolent genes. If some people really are born evil, however, they are no more re-sponsible for this condition than being born with cystic fibrosis. The condition which is supposed to damn them succeeds only in redeeming them."[57] Where children are con-cerned however, "'Evil' has become the word we apply to perpetrators who we're both unable and unwilling to do anything to repair, and for whom all of our mechanisms of justice seem unequal: it describes the limits of what malevolence we're able to bear. In the end, it's a word that says more about the helplessness of the accuser than it does the transgressor."[58] Evil children in popular imagery tend to belong to marginalized groups such as the poor or children of colour who are accompanied by narratives that demonize non-Western children as tainted by their lack of innocence. And while the evil child is a persistent part of popular visual culture, particularly in horror films, evil children are not often a part of children's visual culture. Yet evil does present itself in children's films in ways that challenge a child viewer's notion of innocence and safety the same way evil children in film challenge these things for adults. Evil in children's films tends to come in the form of adults they normally, and innocently, would trust. So, just as adults are discombobulated by images of evil children, the child viewer is unsettled by images of adults with evil intent.

One of the most disturbing evil characters in children's film is Judge Claude Frollo from the Disney version of *The Hunchback of Notre Dame* (Gary Trousdale and Kirk Wise, 1996) who is so beset by lust for Esmeralda that he threatens to burn her alive if she will not sleep with him. Rasputin from *Anastasia* (Don Bluth and Gary Goldman, 1997) makes a deal with the devil, and with the help of the "dark forces" kills Anastasia's entire family. And the film *Gremlins* (Joe Dante, 1984), which was not intended for young chil-dren, was marketed in such a way that families flocked to see the fluffy "Gizmo," who turned into a murderous, evil monster when he got wet, challenging the innocence of a child's stuffed toy. Henry Selick's disturbing stop-motion animated feature, *Coraline* (2009), features the evil Other Mother who intends to keep Coraline with her forever, whether Coraline wants to be there or not. *Harry Potter*'s Voldemort is a particularly evil character that tortures, murders, and inspires the "Death Eaters" to follow him. Disney's *Snow White and the Seven Dwarfs* (David Hand et al., 1937) features an old, grandmotherly witch who, at the behest of Snow White's stepmother, attempts to kill Snow White with a poisoned apple. And Ursula, the sea witch in *The Little Mermaid* (Ron Clements and John Musker, 2009), in exchange for giving Ariel legs, takes away her voice and tries to destroy her. Witches who turn into mice then get hacked to pieces by the kitchen workers is only one of the disturbing scenes in *The Witches* (Nicolas Roeg, 1990), based on the book by celebrated children's book author, Roald Dahl. But the oddest film for children may be Disney's *Maleficent* (Robert Stromberg, 2014), which highlights an innocent young woman's journey into evil. Maleficent is made sympathetic, but loses her innocence and becomes pure evil, creating—for the young viewer—a fragmented oscillation between empathy and fear. The film was so popular it spawned a sequel, *Maleficent: Mistress of Evil* (Joachim Rønning, 2019). And so, children are not introduced to visual images of evil via images of themselves, but rather of what they could become. In children's films, innocence goes awry in adults who seem trustworthy, suggesting that the "potential for evil that resides in every child" as they mature. In film, however, such evil is soundly defeated by each film's end with the triumph of the innocent child protagonist.[59]

Conclusion

In "The Politics of Innocence," Angela West argues that the belief in an inherent innocence is "a kind of doctrine" that has spawned a particular narrative that holds those suffering in "poverty or disability… [as] being morally responsible for their condition. Thus their condition is not seen as the proper concern of the "unafflicted" parts of society."[60] We see this type of narrative quite often in Western news media, where people of colour, the poor, or people from the global South are often framed by the social ills that affect them but should not define their humanity or their dignity. Rather, film and visual media tend to depict Othered children as somehow deserving of their fate, as if innocence and morality are mutually exclusive and reserved for those who meet Western standards. Adult expectations of innocence, though unspoken, become a key element in shaping public, political, and visual discourses that, in turn, affect attitudes and national policies that directly affect children. The concept of innocence in the visual depiction of childhood in film often has the same function: to elevate and naturalize the innocence of some children while questioning or negating the innocence of others. Such notions of a universalized innocence are particularly reinforced via the global reach of Disney films and their continuing supply of film-based products. The narrow and limiting Disney image of innocence—wide eyed, dimpled, blonde or brown haired, and White—continues to be part of the one-way media flow of children's films from the West. These idealized images conflict with both children's and adult's lived reality.

But if Western films tend to dominate the global digital flow, there is a growing counter-flow from non-Western films that challenge the classic Disneyfied images of childhood innocence, as we see in *Cave of the Yellow Dog* and *Slumdog Millionaire*. Although childhood itself is common to all children around the world, culture and lived conditions are not. Social structures and dominant power relationships among adults affect how much agency children may have, what their play entails, and how their worlds are depicted on screen. As a concept, innocence is also affected by these same social structures and adult relationships and can vary by society. All children have, at some point, "innocence," but in quite different forms. Contrary to Western popular culture, there is no one type of innocence, and stories about non-Western innocence are as magically compelling and as richly textured as any Western film. Animated films like Hayao Miyazaki's *Ponyo* (2009), a Japanese version of Hans Christian Andersen's "The Little Mermaid," offers a counter-narrative, sans patriarchal romance, to the Disney version of the same tale. For instance, *Like Stars on Earth* (*Taare Zameen Par*, Aamir Khan, 2007) is a delightful tale of an Indian boy with dyslexia who is rejected and bullied, but eventually finds his way through the efforts of a dedicated teacher (Figure 2.2). *Like Stars on Earth* depicts innocence in the face of adversity, yet with the stubborn magic of a child who overlooks the world's ugliness with a captivating wonder.

Despite Disney's global influence on notions of innocence and childhood, there is also a growing ambiguity in some contemporary cinematic depictions of innocence that reflect changes in childhood in the digital age. Some film children have adult knowledge but are still portrayed as innocent despite such knowledge. For instance, in Stephen King's *It* (both the 1990 TV miniseries directed by Tommy Lee Wallace and the 2017 film directed by Andrés Muschietti), the children are imbued with knowledge that adults do not have about a horrific and deadly entity that kills. The children also have sexual knowledge, which works in tandem with their innocence, not contrary to it. In fact, the strength of the Losers Club comes from their belief in innocence (especially a sexual innocence) despite their adult knowledge.[61] Similarly, *Ender's Game* (Gavin Hood,

FIGURE 2.2. Ishaan gets some guppies. *Like Stars on Earth* (2007, Aamir Khan Productions). Frame-grab.

2013) features a very knowing boy, who is placed in a very adult role, but who holds onto his belief in innocence and goodness, despite his military training and upbringing. It is Ender's innocent (perhaps naive) belief that he alone can repopulate the species he was tricked into destroying, a childish insistence that he can make it "right," that re-orients him back to a childhood of sorts. And in *Beasts of No Nation* (Cary Fukunaga), young Agu is conscripted into a rebel group, becomes a child soldier, and commits horrible acts of violence. Yet throughout his trauma, Agu, just wants to be "a good boy" and go to school. Agu's hold on his own innocence helps him survive. In contemporary films for children then, child characters can accommodate adult knowledge as long as their ontology and motivation remains without malice and rooted in classic notions of innocence.

According to Anne Higonnet, "The modern child is always the sign of a bygone era, of a past which is necessarily the past of adults, yet which, being so distinct, so sheltered, so innocent, is also inevitably a lost past, and therefore understood through the kind of memory we call nostalgia."[62] Film images of innocence play a key role in creating that kind of nostalgia for both adults and children. But cinematic images of innocence also reinforce a "rare kind of beauty" found in all children everywhere that defies adult control or corruption.[63] For Tito and Ossie in Mike Newell's Irish film, *Into the West* (1994), their innocence and belief in magic helps them save the beautiful mythical horse Tír na nÓg, and in the process they save their father too. Despite the trauma of an abusive stepfather, brothers Mike and Bobby in *Radio Flyer* (Richard Donner, 1992) demonstrate the power of their innocent belief in an urban legend when they convert their Radio Flyer wagon into an airplane allowing Bobby to escape. And innocence plays a key role that helps little Doggie convince her adoptive father, Wang, that girls can be just as good as boys in the charmingly lyrical *King of Masks* (Wu Tianming, 1996). Cinematic depictions of innocence remind us of the "endurance and transformative power" of childhood in the modern world. Children are a "source of human feeling that opposes [adult] limits." These limits are overcome by the child's "assertion of authentic and humanizing ideals consistent [with] the...appetites of childhood itself."[64] For adults, the depiction of childhood innocence in film reminds them of hope, worry-free play, and the whimsical belief—if even momentarily—in the essential goodness of humanity. On film, the depiction of childhood appetites for love, adventure, magic, and the wonder of discovery affirm the seductive and transcendent power of Innocence.

NOTES

1. Jean Baudrillard, *Cool Memories* (London: Verso, 1990), p. 185.
2. Mark Osteen, "'It Doesn't Pay to Antagonize the Public': *Sabotage* and Hitchcock's Audience," *Film/Literature Quarterly* 28:4 (2000), pp. 259–268, at 268.
3. Peter W. Lee, "No Laughing Matter: Imperiling Kids and Country in Alfred Hitchcock's *Sabotage*," in Debbie Olson (ed.), *Children in the Films of Alfred Hitchcock* (New York: Palgrave, 2014), pp. 67–85, at 81.

4. Mark A. Wollaeger, "Killing Stevie: Modernity, Modernism, and Mastery in Conrad and Hitchcock," *Modern Language Quarterly* 58:3 (1997), pp. 323–350, at 337.

5. John Locke, *An Essay Concerning Human Understanding* (1690), ed. Roger Woolhouse (New York: Penguin Classics, 1989); Jean-Jacques Rousseau, *Emile* (1762), trans. Allan Bloom (New York: Basic Books, 1979).

6. Neil Postman, *The Disappearance of Childhood* (New York: Vintage, 1982), p. 4.

7. Vicky Lebeau, *Childhood and Cinema* (London: Reaktion Books, 2008), p. 84.

8. Elizabeth Wolgast, "Innocence," *Philosophy* 68 (1993), pp. 297–307, at 298.

9. Joanne Faulkner, *The Importance of Being Innocent* (Cambridge, MA: Cambridge University Press, 2011), p. 2.

10. Norvin Richards, "Innocence," *American Philosophical Quarterly* 31:2 (1994), pp. 157–167, at 158.

11. Stephen R. Munzer, "Innocence," *Faith and Philosophy* 29:2 (2012), pp. 125–143.

12. Elizabeth Wolgast, "Innocence," *Philosophy* 68:265 (1993), pp. 297–307.

13. Jacqueline A. Laing, "Innocence and Consequentialism: Inconsistency, Equivocation and Contradiction in the Philosophy of Peter Singer," in David S. Oderberg and Jacqueline A. Laing (eds.), *Human Lives: Critical Essays on Consequentialist Bioethics* (Basingstoke, UK: Macmillan, 1997), pp. 196–224.

14. Joanne Faulkner, "The Innocence of Victimhood versus the 'Innocence of Becoming': Nietzsche, 9/11, and the 'Falling Man,'" *Journal of Nietzsche Studies* 35:36 (2008), pp. 67–85.

15. Joanne Faulkner, "Vulnerability of 'Virtual' Subjects: Childhood, Memory, and Crisis in the Cultural Value of Innocence," *SubStance* 42:3 (2013), pp 127–147.

16. Karen Lury, *The Child in Film: Tears, Fears and Fairy Tales* (London: I.B. Tauris, 2010).

17. Faulkner, *Importance of Being Innocent*, p. 7.

18. See Viviana A. Zelizer, *Pricing the Priceless Child: The Changing Social Value of Children* (New York: Basic Books, 1985).

19. Gary Cross, *The Cute and the Cool* (New York: Oxford University Press, 2004), p. 128.

20. Joanne Faulkner, "The Innocence Fetish: The Commodification and Sexualisation of Children in the Media and Popular Culture," *Media International Australia*, 135 (2010), pp. 106–117, at 109.

21. Jacqueline Rose, *The Case of Peter Pan, or the Impossibility of Children's Fiction* (Philadelphia: University of Pennsylvania Press, 1993), p. xv.

22. Faulkner, "Innocence Fetish," p. 110.

23. Cross, *The Cute and the Cool*, p. 6. See also Zelizer, *Pricing the Priceless Child*; Karen Sanchez-Eppler, *Dependent States* (Chicago: University of Chicago Press, 2005); and Anne Higonnet, *Pictures of Innocence* (London: Thames and Hudson, 1998).

24. Virginia Davis would go on to star in the *Alice Comedies*, or *Alice in Cartoonland*. Disney produced fifty-seven films in this series from 1925 to 1928; Davis starred in fifteen of them.

25. Tony Compolo, quoted in Mark L. Pinsky's *The Gospel according to Disney: Faith, Trust, and Pixie Dust* (Westminster: John Knox Press, 2004), p. 9.

26. Jeff Guo, "Researchers Have Found a Major Problem with 'The Little Mermaid' and other Disney Princess Movies," *Washington Post*, January 26, 2016, https://www.washingtonp ost.com/news/wonk/wp/2016/01/25/researchers-have-discovered-a-major-problem-with-the-little-mermaid-and-other-disney-movies/?ref=yfp&utm_term=.eda71afbaa58 [accessed October 16, 2019].

27. Olga Khazan, "The Psychology of Giant Princess Eyes," *The Atlantic*, November 7, 2013, n.p.,

28. Henry Giroux. "Innocence and Pedagogy in Disney's World," *International Journal of Educational Reform* 2:4 (1993), pp. 425–428.

29. Jyotsna Kapur, *Coining for Capital: Movies, Marketing, and the Transformation of Childhood* (New Brunswick, NJ: Rutgers University Press, 2005), p. 34.

30. Gary Arms and Thomas Riley, "The 'Big-Little' Film and Philosophy: Two Takes on Spielbergian Innocence," in Dean A. Kowalski (ed.), *Steven Spielberg and Philosophy* (Louisville: University of Kentucky Press, 2008), pp. 7–37, at 8.

31. James Kendrick, *Darkness in the Bliss-Out* (New York: Bloomsbury Academic, 2014), pp. 46; 4.

32. See Tamás Bényei, "White Light: J. G. Ballard's *Empire of the Sun* as a War Story," *The AnaChronisT: The Literary Journal of the Department of English Studies* 6 (2000) available at https://www.jgballard.ca/criticism/white_light_empire_war_story.html.

33. Bényei, "White Light,".

34. Michael Richardson, *Otherness in Hollywood Cinema* (New York: Continuum, 2010), p. 177.

35. Helen Addison-Smith, "E.T. Go Home: Indegeniety, Multiculturalism, and 'Homeland' in Contemporary Science Fiction Cinema," *Papers: Explorations into Children's Literature* 15:1 (2005), pp. 27–35, at 30.

36. Peter Kramer, "'I'll Be Right Here!': Dealing with Emotional Trauma in and through *E.T. The Extra-Terrestrial*," in Adrian Schober and Debbie Olson (eds.), *Children in the Films of Stephen Spielberg* (Lanham, MD: Lexington Books, 2016), pp. 91–119, at 102–104.

37. Higonnet, *Pictures of Innocence*, p. 77.

38. Patricia Holland, *Picturing Childhood: The Myth of the Child in Popular Imagery* (London: I.B. Tauris, 2004), p. 5.

39. Higonnet, *Pictures of Innocence*, p. 216.

40. Ibid., p. 120.

41. In 2014, twelve-year-old Tamir Rice was shot and killed while playing with a toy gun in a park in Cleveland, Ohio. The officers shot him within two seconds of arriving on the scene.

42. "Centers for Disease Control and Prevention, National Center for Injury Prevention and Control, Web-based Injury Statistics Query and Reporting System (WISQARS) Fatal Injury Reports. Data from 2017. Children and teenagers aged 1 to 19, Black defined as non-Hispanic, number of deaths by known intent (homicide, suicide, unintentional deaths). Age 0 to 1 calculated separately by the CDC because leading causes of death for newborns and infants are specific to the age group." https://everytownresearch.org/gun-violence-america/#foot_note_21 [accessed October 16, 2019]. See also T. Rees Shapiro, "Study: Black Girls Viewed as 'Less Innocent, than White Girls," *Washington Post*, June 27, 2017.].

43. Debbie Olson, *Black Children in Hollywood Cinema* (New York: Palgrave Macmillan, 2017).

44. Debbie Olson, "On the Innocence of Beasts," in De-Valera N. Y. M. Botchway, Awo Sarpong, and Charles Quist-Adade (eds.), *New Perspectives on African Childhood* (Wilmington, DE: Vernon Press, 2018), pp. 83–107.

45. Faulkner, *Importance of Being Innocent*, p. 105.

46. The chopsticks and fly scene here is a tongue-in-cheek reference to the same scene in the original *The Karate Kid* where Daniel-san asks Mr. Miyagi why he doesn't just use a fly swatter.

47. Jordan Hoffman, "*Burn Your Maps* review: If the Kid from Room Wants to Be Mongolian, Let Him," *The Guardian*, September 9, 2016. https://www.theguardian.com/film/2016/sep/09/burn-your-maps-review-jacob-tremblay-vera-farmiga-toronto-tiff [accessed October 16, 2019].

48. Tomris Laffly, "Burn Your Maps," Rogerebert.com, June 19, 2019. https://www.rogerebert.com/reviews/burn-your-maps-2019 [accessed October 16, 2019].
49. Such films include The World of Suzy Wong (Richard Quine, 1960), Seven Years in Tibet (Jean-Jacques Annaud, 1997), and Beyond Rangoon (John Boorman, 1995).
50. Faulkner, Importance of Being Innocent, p. 101.
51. Anjana Mudambi, "Another Look at Orientalism: (An)Othering in Slumdog Millionaire," Howard Journal of Communications 24:3 (2013), pp. 275–292, at 277.
52. Heather Snell, "Uses and Abuses of the Child Figure in Slumdog Millionaire and Vikus Swarup's Q&A," Adaptation 9:2 (2016), pp. 234–248, at 248.
53. Cross, The Cute and the Cool.
54. Higonnet, Pictures of Innocence, p. 153.
55. Susan Neiman, Evil in Modern Thought: An Alternative History (Princeton, NJ: Princeton University Press, 2002), p. 9.
56. Karen J. Renner (ed.), introduction to The Evil Child in Literature, Film, and Popular Culture (New York: Routledge, 2013), pp. 1–27, at 5.
57. Terry Eagleton, On Evil (New Haven, CT: Yale University Press, 2010), p. 7.
58. Rollo Romig, "What Do We Mean by Evil?," New Yorker, July 25, 2012. https://www.newyorker.com/books/page-turner/what-do-we-mean-by-evil [accessed October 16, 2019].
59. William Wandless, "Spoil the Child: Unsettling Ethics and the Representation of Evil," Literature Interpretation Theory 22:2 (2011), pp. 134–154, at 151.
60. Angela West, "The Politics of Innocence," New Blackfriars 78:919 (September 1997), pp. 383–385.
61. See Kerry H. Robinson, Innocence, Knowledge and the Construction of Childhood: The Contradictory Nature of Sexuality and Censorship in Children's Contemporary Lives (New York, Routledge, 2012).
62. Higonnet, Pictures of Innocence, p. 27.
63. Wolgast, "Innocence," p. 300.
64. Robert A. Davis, "Brilliance of a Fire: Innocence, Experience and the Theory of Childhood," Journal of Philosophy of Education 45:2 (2011), pp. 379–397, at 390.

BIBLIOGRAPHY

Bernstein, Robin. Racial Innocence: Performing American Childhood from Slavery to Civil Rights. New York: New York University Press, 2011.
Bruhm, Steven, and Natasha Hurley, eds. Curiouser: on the Queerness of Children. Minneapolis: University of Minnesota Press, 2004.
Cross, Gary. The Cute and the Cool. New York: Oxford University Press, 2004.
Cunningham, Hugh. The Invention of Childhood. London: BBC Books, 2006.
Edelman, Lee. No Future: Queer Theory and the Death Drive. Durham, NC: Duke University Press, 2004.
Faulkner, Joanne. The Importance of Being Innocent. Cambridge, UK: Cambridge University Press, 2011.
Giroux, Henry. The Mouse That Roared. Lanham, MD: Rowman and Littlefield, 1999.
Higonnet, Anne. Pictures of Innocence. London: Thames and Hudson, 1998.
Holland, Patricia. Picturing Childhood: The Myth of the Child in Popular Imagery. London: I.B. Tauris, 2004.

Kapur, Jyotsna. *Coining for Capital: Movies, Marketing, and the Transformation of Childhood.* New Brunswick, NJ: Rutgers University Press, 2005.

Kincaid, James R. *Erotic Innocence: The Culture of Child Molesting.* Durham, NC: Duke University Press, 1998.

Lury, Karen. *The Child in Film: Tears, Fears and Fairy Tales.* London: I.B. Tauris, 2010.

Mintz, Steven. *Huck's Raft: A History of American Childhood.* Cambridge, MA: Belknap Press of Harvard University Press, 2004.

Postman, Neil. *The Disappearance of Childhood.* New York: Vintage, 1982.

Stearns, Peter N. *Childhood in World History.* New York: Routledge, 2011.

CHAPTER 3

SCREEN ADAPTATIONS OF *THE WIZARD OF OZ* AND METAFILMICITY IN CHILDREN'S FILM

RYAN BUNCH

THE *Wizard of Oz* and its wider fictional universe occupy a central position in childhood and children's film. Yet, while MGM's *The Wizard of Oz* (Victor Fleming, 1939) is recognized as an important film for children, its treatment *as* a children's film has been uneven in scholarly literature. Possibly reflecting the marginalization of children's culture in the academy, studies treating it as a fantasy film, a queer film, or a musical may touch on, but not make central, its fundamental association with childhood.[1] For more than a century, films based on L. Frank Baum's children's book *The Wonderful Wizard of Oz* (1900) and its numerous sequels, from the silent era to Disney's *Oz the Great and Powerful* (Sam Raimi, 2013), have addressed children as their core, if not exclusive, audience. Recentring this child audience in the assessment of these films not only repositions them as children's films, but also foregrounds the active role children themselves play in the negotiated meanings of the children's film as a genre. Expanding on the "negotiated identities" of children's film proposed by Noel Brown based on contextual evidence such as marketing, distribution, ratings, reviews, merchandising, content, and exhibition strategies, I propose that Oz films' metafilmic, material, and transmedia affordances promote an understanding of children's film that involves what kids might *do* with a movie, rather than strictly on the basis of formal characteristics.[2]

As a repertoire of media texts, Oz films display their narrative artifice, inviting children to become co-authors in the definition of children's film. These films have what Ian Wojcik-Andrews identifies as a characteristic metafilmicity in children's movies. Oz films are often framed by images of opening books or dream sequences, and they necessarily reference each other and other children's films.[3] They are consciously theatrical, influenced from the beginning by the popular 1903 Broadway stage musical *The Wizard of Oz*, which helped establish the public's early experience of Oz. The influence of musical theatre conventions is felt even in the silent films and non-musical adaptations.[4] An early case of transmedia world-building, Oz films are networked with Baum's book, its sequels, and adaptations to the stage, comic books, and other media.[5] Because of these disparate sources, their diverging generic conventions, and their market relationship to ancillary toys and material culture, Oz films are often carnivalesque, inviting audiences into their playful world-building.[6]

Oz films signal their status as children's films through modes of audience address. As outlined by Noel Brown and Bruce Babington, these modes include single address to children, dual address to children and adults on separate levels, and undifferentiated address.[7] In the last case, kids and adults may have multivalent engagements with satire, mixed forms of humour, and intertextuality, as suggested by Adrian Schober.[8] I propose that, concurrently with these modes, a children's film also employs a mode of metafilmic address, in which it signals that it is indeed addressing its audience in purposive ways. This metafilmic mode invites kids to recognize that they are being addressed and to assess how successfully a film is addressing them as children. Much as Dorothy's friends continue to believe in the Wizard's powers after he has been exposed as a humbug, children may enjoy films while participating in the discourses that position such films as intended for them. This metafilmic relationship is most obvious in films that signal their "filmness" through metatheatrical techniques, such as story frames and playful artifice. More generally, metafilmicity is available in any film by virtue of its being recognizable as a film.

In response to these metafilmic texts, children become active participants in the definition of children's film through their critical engagements. Kids' film reviews on family viewing guide websites like *Common Sense Media* may represent something of a self-selected sample of child viewers, but they are one piece of evidence that young people consciously engage with discourses of children's film, which they co-construct with parents, industry, and other adults. In addition to more traditional criteria involving judgements about sex, violence, and frightening or disturbing material, contemporary child reviewers may assess gender, race, and other representations by current standards.[9] Based on these judgements, kids advise other kids on what to see. Attention to the dialogical construction of children's film between adults and children can challenge assumptions about the adult-child binary and reduce the temptation to exclude cross-generational "family films" from the definition of children's film. Children's literature scholars have recently emphasized that rather than simply being written for children by adults with adult ideas about childhood, as famously argued by Jacqueline Rose, children's literature involves collaborative reading and writing between adults and children.[10] Similarly, the co-presence of adults in the film audience does not diminish children's full participation in the creative consumption of films that are addressed to them.

Metafilmic and material affordances enable children to re-use, reinterpret, and transform film repertoires. As Becky Parry notes, kids draw on repertoires of media texts when engaging with films.[11] These repertoires are the schemata in which children amass their cultivated knowledge and expectations about children's films, media conventions, and fairy tale tropes. Each new film has the challenge of negotiating the memory of previous films, especially after MGM's version. Material play is an indispensable part of children's negotiations of these texts. As Robin Bernstein notes, children's literature and cultures have always been closely related to material objects.[12] With children's books historically being sold with or as toys, children's active performances foreground their relationships to literature. Similarly, children's films are not abstract texts but material ones, with which children interact directly as well as through associated ancillary items. Like the toys that are marketed with them, children's films are things to be played with. This relationship between film, toys, and play has particular resonances with Oz, whose Scarecrow, Tin Man, Lion, and other non-human characters raise questions about what it means to be a person, animal, or animated object.

Oz films provide one avenue for tracing varied dynamics of children's films in the United States from the silent era to the age of the contemporary global blockbuster. Even when Oz films fail, as they often have, the reasons for their failure may prove instructive, as in the case of the early silent films.

Oz before MGM: Children's Film in the Silent Era

Early Oz films established a metafilmic repertoire with playful material extensions. Their staginess, storybook visuals, and obvious trick photography are reminiscent of the theatrical fantasies of Georges Méliès, the special effects of Edwin S. Porter, and the metacinematic techniques of early animators like J. Stuart Blackton and Winsor McCay, in which live actors interacted with filmed or animated elements. Marketing and distribution challenges prevented these films from reaching a wide audience, but they are important for what they suggest about audiences for children's film in the silent era and for their influence on later films, especially MGM's *The Wizard of Oz*.

Baum's own *Fairylogue and Radio-Plays* (1909) was innovative in its use of multiple media, metafilmic effects, and synergy as an advertisement for the Oz books. A touring show, it was presented as a travelogue hosted live by Baum in the tradition of nineteenth-century slide lectures. Recounting a visit to the Land of Oz, Baum provided narration for a series of still images interspersed with short, filmed episodes from the Oz books.[13] In alternation with his live presence, Baum appeared in the films as well, so that he so that he seemed to move between the stage and the screen worlds. He introduced the characters, each a black and white illustration in a giant book, who stepped off the page, transforming into an actor in hand colouring. Literature, film, and live performance interacted fluidly in Baum's demonstration of how these modes of storytelling could be mastered. In interviews, Baum spoke of the fairy realm as though he believed in it, but he also delighted in explaining how the film's magical effects were achieved through camera tricks and other techniques.[14] The mixing of media may have been both absorbing and distancing, allowing audiences to marvel at the technological ingenuity of the illusions while being taken in by them. All the *Fairylogue* actors were children, modelling make-believe play and affording children in the audience the opportunity to see themselves in this manifestly theatrical Oz universe.[15] During intermission, slides promoted the newest Oz books, which were sold in the lobby. Despite critical praise, the *Fairylogue and Radio Plays* was unprofitable due to its expense, but it set the tone for combining wonderment and humbug in the Oz film repertoire.

The next Oz films were more conventional but retained metafilmic aesthetics. Four one-reel films were produced by the Selig Polyscope Company, which had produced the filmed segments of the *Fairylogue and Radio Plays*. *The Wonderful Wizard of Oz* (Otis Turner, 1910) is the only one to survive. These were followed in 1914 by three films from Baum's own Oz Film Manufacturing Company: *The Patchwork Girl of Oz*, *The Magic Cloak of Oz*, and *His Majesty the Scarecrow of Oz* (all directed by J. Farrell MacDonald).[16] These playful, carnivalesque, almost nonsensical films diverge significantly from their source material. *His Majesty, the Scarecrow of Oz* exemplifies their complex relationship to other texts in the Oz repertoire. Loosely adapted from the first Oz book, *The Wonderful Wizard of Oz*, it adds a romantic plot about a princess in love with the palace gardener's son, reflecting the influence of the stage musical. It was subsequently re-adapted as the ninth Oz book, *The Scarecrow of Oz* (1915).

These films drew on the legacies of live theatre, as many silent films did, and film itself was part of the technology on display. The trick photography was notable for its reflexive cleverness. In a typical effect drawing attention to the film apparatus, the camera was turned sideways so that characters could appear to walk up a wall. Theatrical staging, scenery, makeup, and pantomime animal costumes were reminiscent of the *Wizard of Oz* musical extravaganza. Characters spontaneously sang, danced, and made music (Figure 3.1), making these appear almost as "silent" film musicals, and indeed they were often promoted as adaptations or sequels of the stage version.[17] Following a common theatrical practice, boys were sometimes played by young actresses, and many elements resemble children's outdoor, fantasy, and non-linear play. The title character of *The Patchwork Girl of Oz* is made of a quilt pulled out of an attic trunk and animated with the magic Powder of Life, suggesting the ways in which children bring their toys and stuffed animals to life. The amusing antics of the pantomime animals, many performed by master animal imitator Fred Woodward, are eccentric diversions incorporating slapstick comedy and chase scenes. Recurring animal characters, such as the Muwell the mule and a mysterious, randy creature called the Lonesome Zoop, seem designed to appeal to young audiences as forerunners of the casts of popular characters developed for cartoons such as those by Disney and Warner Brothers and comedy shorts such as the *Our Gang* films.

Some uncertainty about what audience these films were meant to address may have contributed to their commercial failure. Baum claimed that they were for a mixed audience of children and those who enjoyed musical comedy.[18] The inclusion of romantic subplots for adults, against Baum's own philosophy of sex-free children's literature, had

FIGURE 3.1. Dorothy taking a solo in a dance number with Scarecrow, Tin Woodman, Cowardly Lion, Toto, and other animals in the Selig Polyscope Company's *The Wizard of Oz* (1910). Frame-grab.

worked well for the stage show but seemed to falter in the films, which were seen by critics and audiences as exclusively for children.[19] Media scholar Anne Morey suggests that the films' excessive use of "exhibitionistic" metafilmic gestures associated with fairy tale films and the cinema of attractions were intended to appeal to adults but were regarded as juvenile because the vogue for such entertainments had passed. Cary Elza adds that the multifocal spectacle of the films took focus away from Dorothy, whose crossing from the real world to the fantasy world of Oz is a point of identification for the audience in the book and other adaptations.[20] During the silent era, a "balanced programme" of offerings addressed adults and children in the course of the evening, with material appealing to young audiences emphasized in the short subjects that preceded the feature.[21] Audiences at the time may not have been accustomed to children's features, and while contemporary accounts suggest that children often enjoyed the Oz films, adults reportedly demanded their money back after seeing *Patchwork Girl*.[22]

The profitability of Baum's Oz films seems to have suffered from ambivalent or negative reception, along with difficulty securing national exhibition after poor receipts for *Patchwork Girl* scared off distributors.[23] In a press interview, Baum extolled the affordability of his films for children who could not buy Oz books, which were relatively expensive because of their colour illustrations: "I will put all my books into the film that every child in the whole country may see them. A whole book for a nickel. That is the reason for the Oz Film Company."[24] However, Morey suggests that the films' incoherence made them accessible only to middle-class family audiences already familiar with the books and disinclined toward the lowbrow and outmoded spectacle of the films. If this is the case, a mismatch between audience address and economic realities related to their accessibility as works referring to other texts may have been a factor in the films' limited performance.

After Baum's death in 1919, his son, Frank J. Baum, approached filmmakers to continue adapting Oz properties. One result was *The Wizard of Oz* (1925), directed by Larry Semon, who also starred as the Scarecrow. Showcasing Semon's slapstick specialties and comedic routines, the movie eschews magic in favour of adult situations and racial stereotypes.[25] Dorothy, a flapper, is the long-lost princess of Oz, destined to become queen on her eighteenth birthday. Semon and Oliver Hardy (pre–Stan Laurel) play farmhands who vie for Dorothy's affections. Scheming villains from Oz show up in Kansas to prevent Dorothy's ascent to the throne, and in the shenanigans and trip to Oz that follow, Semon and Hardy briefly wind up in disguise as the Tin Man and Scarecrow, while the stereotyped Black farmhand, Snowball (Spencer Bell, credited as G. Howe Black), briefly appears in the disguise of a Lion. These performances draw on theatrical legacies of pantomime, minstrelsy, and vaudeville, while providing a precedent for the MGM film in the use of extended Kansas scenes with "real" counterparts to the theatrically costumed Scarecrow, Tin Man, and Cowardly Lion.[26]

Semon's *Wizard of Oz* was also the first to frame Oz as a dream, conflated here with children's literature, bedtime stories, and doll play. The film opens with an old toymaker (also played by Semon), completing dolls of the Scarecrow, Tin Woodman, and Dorothy (Figure 3.2). A little girl trounces downstairs and asks him to read her the story of *The Wizard of Oz*. As the old man begins to read, the book opens to show the film's credits. The girl interrupts the story twice to say she doesn't like the adult parts and to urge the toymaker to get to the parts about Dorothy. By portraying adult-child co-reading, the film acknowledges the co-presence of adults and children in the theatre. The story itself, rather than resolving, simply ends in the middle of a climactic action scene in which the Scarecrow falls from an aeroplane. At this moment, the Scarecrow doll falls to the floor, rousing the girl from what has been a dream induced by the bedtime story. The film is ambiguous about whether the story is taking place in the book or in the girl's dream. The dolls may be an instance of subtle product placement, as Frank J. Baum owned a company that manufactured oilcloth Oz dolls, which had been sold in conjunction with the books and were also marketed with the film. In addition, a "photoplay" edition of the book including photographic stills from the movie was issued. The relationship among books, film, play, and material culture is explicit in the possibility of recalling the film while reading the book, playing with dolls, and using all of these materials to construct one's own playful version of Oz.

Semon's *Wizard of Oz* includes romance and political intrigue for adults and comedy for all ages but had limited success. The story follows something more akin to the

FIGURE 3.2. The little girl and the toymaker read *The Wizard of Oz* together with Oz dolls beside them in *The Wizard of Oz* (1925, Chadwick Pictures). Frame-grab.

European fairy tradition than Baum's romance-free tale of American self-reliance and implicit feminism. Semon was aware that his slapstick style was an important draw for the juvenile audience, and the melodramatic damsel-in-distress scenarios Dorothy undergoes, such as dangling from a tower by a rope, supplemented his own slapstick routines. Attendance was better at the matinees than the evening showings at the New York premiere, suggesting that the film successfully drew a child audience, but made less money from adults, who paid full ticket prices.[27] The independent production company, Chadwick Pictures, was unable to contract with a national distributor, posing a challenge to wide exhibition.[28]

Exhibition challenges struck once again with the 1933 animated short, *The Wizard of Oz*, directed by Ted Eshbaugh, which was also produced in association with Frank J. Baum. Like the stage extravaganza before it, it featured the Scarecrow and Tin Woodman prominently, and like the MGM film after it, it used black-and-white for the Kansas scenes and Technicolor for Oz. However, it was blocked from theatrical release because Disney held the exclusive rights to Technicolor in animation.

On the whole, the early Oz films fared poorly, possibly because they failed to appeal to adults in a market that required feature-length films to address audiences of all ages. However, they established the metafilmic and cross-media conventions that future films, including MGM's *The Wizard of Oz*, would leverage to reach wide audiences while maintaining their essential appeal to children.

MGM's Oz and the Family Film in Classical Hollywood

The MGM film belongs to a generation of family films that flourished in classical Hollywood under the Motion Picture Production Code. As Noel Brown notes, it is regarded as "the quintessential family film" of the era.[29] Although, as one of MGM's expensive "prestige" films, it did not turn a profit in its first release, it was far from the theatrical flop that popular myth has portrayed, and its later success on television cemented its legacy.[30] Drawing on precedents in the Oz theatre and film repertoires, it incorporated a dream frame, Kansas counterparts to Dorothy's Oz friends, and a switch from black-and-white to colour. Marketing materials invoked the repertoires of Oz, children's film, and fairy tale to compare the new film favourably to Disney's *Snow White and the Seven Dwarfs* (David Hand et al., 1937), Baum's book, and the still-remembered stage musical.[31]

The metafilmic style of *The Wizard of Oz*, particularly its framing of Oz as Dorothy's dream, arises in part from ambivalence about its audience. *Snow White* had demonstrated that children and adults would embrace an animated fairy tale, but MGM was uncertain that audiences would accept its live-action fantasy.[32] Perhaps reflecting anxiety about appealing to adults, early script drafts resembled contemporary musical comedy with stock characters, romantic subplots, and a comedic Wicked Witch. Ultimately, the film took a more earnest approach, sticking closer to Baum's book than any film adaptation ever had. As Noel Brown has shown, discourses in the marketing and reception of *The Wizard of Oz* constructed its "ambivalent generic identity" between children's film and family film. Along with advertising in adult and juvenile periodicals, licensing agreements for children's products, and evidence of ticket sales, the press book distributed to exhibitors promoted the film's sophistication and unprecedented combination of "adult and juvenile appeal in a motion picture" through the use of singable songs and clever lyrics.[33]

The fairy tale tradition combined with metafilmic techniques in the MGM film to enable participation by adults and children in a surreal Oz where age norms are de centred. This dreamscape is synonymous with Hollywood itself, which has been described as a dream factory and with film, which has been analysed as dream work. Unencumbered by cinematic realism, like the silent films, it resembled a filmed theatrical production with painted backgrounds, plastic flora, whimsical costumes, and sparking ruby slippers whose Technicolor splendour outshine the silver shoes of Baum's book. Adult critics in 1939 mostly praised the film for its equal appeal to children and adults, though a prominent minority dismissed it as excessive and childish.[34]

As a consequence of its dream frame and exaggerated style, MGM's *Wizard of Oz* is a playful, make-believe performance of the magical world of childhood that adults and children can embrace on their own terms. As musicologist Raymond Knapp observes, the actors, recognizable as the Kansas farmhands in their costumes, seem to be grown men playing dress-up with Dorothy.[35] Quotable lines like "Lions, and Tigers, and Bears, Oh, My!" singable songs like "We're Off to See the Wizard," and simple choreography, such as the skipping dance down the yellow brick road, are easily imitated by kids "playing Oz." Vaudevillian humour and musical comedy foreground performance. The film's famous camp style employs an exaggerated innocence, most evident in Judy Garland's wide-eyed affect and Tin Man actor Jack Haley's suggestion that everyone recite their lines in the same wonder-struck tone that he used to read to his children and bedtime.[36]

Many critics praised Bert Lahr for his performance as the Cowardly Lion, but some faulted him for breaking the spell of fantasy by injecting too much of his own comedic personality.[37] However, Lahr's comedic turn as the child-like Cowardly Lion may be a significant component of how children see the film as appealing to them. At least two children who saw the movie in 1939 appreciated Lahr's performance. Mary Diane Seibel, the nine-year-old daughter of a theatrical press agent, reported that the Lion was the part she liked best.[38] An eight-year-old guest reviewer for the Associated Press, identified only as Tim, agreed: "I guess the best part of it was the Cowardly Lion…The lion was even afraid of his shadow. He said he was afraid to go to sleep even and somebody said why don't you count sheep and he said, 'I'm afraid of them!' "[39]

The MGM film addresses its audience not on separate knowing and naïve levels for adults and children, but through complex performances that can be decoded by people of all ages. In "If I Were King of the Forest," Lahr's Cowardly Lion sends up gender and class pretensions in an operatic parody, alternately bellowing with bravura and flouncing daintily through the song. His protean performance, growling and threatening one minute and bursting into tears in the next, disrupts the distinction between adulthood and childhood. Kids performing this role in school and community theatre productions of *The Wizard of Oz* add their own spins to the character, alternating between posh accents and street slang while performing the character's classed and gendered mannerisms.

For her own part, Judy Garland's Dorothy is a complex performance of American girlhood. A teenager costumed, somewhat unconvincingly, as a pre-adolescent girl, Garland participates in a long tradition of age transvestism in the theatre, destabilizing adult-child categories.[40] Garland's wide-eyed innocence allows adults to watch as through the eyes of a child who believes in fairy tales. At the same time, her mature singing and confident acting imply a good deal of agency for the child protagonist in the film's world as well as the child in the audience who identifies with her. On the other hand, contemporary child reviewers sometimes find fault with her sweetness (and tendency to burst into tears), observing that Dorothy is a bit of a damsel in distress compared to the character in the book or more recent films like *Return to Oz*.

Kids assess the MGM film in conversation with repertoires and discourses of children's film. In his review, Tim said the film "was just like the book, only better," and Mary Diane Seibel remarked, "*Snow White* was my favorite till now."[41] While the MGM film was the first experience of Oz for many in the twentieth century, children today may encounter it only after discovering Oz in other iterations. Some find their way to it out of interest in the origins of new versions such as *The Wiz* (Sidney Lumet, 1978), *Oz the Great and Powerful*, or the stage musical *Wicked* (2003). Others watch it as research for participation in school or community theatre productions of *The Wizard of Oz*.[42] Using their knowledge of Oz and children's films, kids reviewing the movie on *Common Sense Media* mostly judge it as good for all ages, but older kids warn that younger children might be frightened by the Wicked Witch and the Winged Monkeys (or confess to being frightened themselves). Kids identify themes sometimes overlooked by adult critics, such as friendship and perseverance. A nine-year-old commented, "I love this movie because it has a lot of singing and friendship in it."[43]

Kids may cultivate their relationship to the film through its material, sensorial and metafilmic properties. Tim described negotiating his contact with the film as a sonic and visual object by closing his eyes and covering his ears during the scary parts:

> I liked everything about it except the tornado and the witch. I didn't want to look at the picture when the witch was getting after Dorothy. She was mean. I mean the witch was. And she had a green face. When she sent her flying monkeys to catch Dorothy's dog, I cried. I didn't like the flying monkeys, either.... That bad witch came back but I didn't hear what she said because I shut my eyes and put my fingers in my ears. Pretty soon I peeked and Dorothy was dancing with the Scarecrow.[44]

Playful practices, such as dressing up, can be therapeutic. In a May 1975 episode of *Mister Rogers' Neighborhood* (1968–2001), Margaret Hamilton put on her witch costume in front of the television audience so kids could see it was make-believe.[45] Tim recognized this aspect of the film as well, describing the Witch's makeup and the Scarecrow's straw body. He mused, "I wonder if that really was a tin suit the tin woodman had on?" Tim ultimately was comforted by the revelation of the film as a dream: "It was all a dream. Really it was. I was glad everything ended all right."[46] Mary Diane Seibel, however, was ambivalent about whether Oz was real or a dream: "Everybody but Dorothy and Toto thought it was a dream. I don't know what to think."[47] The film's dream frame may have been employed to counter a bias against fantasy as infantile, but children seem to find their own considered reasons to decide whether Oz is real or a dream, or to keep both possibilities tantalizingly open.[48]

MGM AND ITS LEGACIES: CHILDREN'S FILM ON TV AND HOME MEDIA

The MGM film found its greatest success in regular television broadcasts beginning in the 1950s, which brought it into the everyday space of the home and made it all the more available for playful repurposing.[49] For a cohort of American children, Oz on television was a holiday-like annual ritual, and many people have memories of playing Oz in the backyard or in the neighbourhood with other kids on the day after the broadcast.[50] Early broadcasts were metafilmically framed by segments hosted by celebrities and children, beginning with Bert Lahr, ten-year old Liza Minnelli, and thirteen-year-old Oz collector Justin Schiller in 1956. Two other important events occurred during this year. The soundtrack album was released for the first time, making it possible for kids to sing and play along between broadcasts, and the copyright expired on Baum's book, leading to an explosion of new Oz films, television programmes, and merchandise.[51] MGM's Oz became the exclusive version for many, but other versions did exist, and they had to carefully negotiate their adaptations of Baum's books in line with audience expectations from the MGM film.

Many of the Oz films made their way to television and home media after less than stellar engagements in the cinema. With MGM always in the background, they often involve nostalgia or parody. After the animated musical *Journey Back to Oz* (Hal Sutherland, 1972) had a disappointing theatrical run, it was televised as a Christmas special in 1976, remained in syndication until 1983, and was later released on home video. Like the early MGM broadcasts, it was hosted by celebrities in a storytelling frame addressing the child audience. Based on the second Oz book, *The Marvelous Land of Oz* (1904), it comes across rather as a sequel to the MGM film, for which it is nostalgic, along with classic Hollywood and Broadway. Whereas Dorothy does not appear in the second Oz book, here she returns, once again by cyclone, as if to satisfy a desire for repetition of familiar story. She is voiced by Judy Garland's daughter, Liza Minnelli, evoking the memory of the iconic Dorothy, who had died in 1969. Margaret Hamilton, who played the Wicked Witch in the MGM film, voices Aunt Em, and Garland's juvenile co-star Mickey Rooney plays the Scarecrow, while Milton Berle, Ethel Merman, and Paul Lynde add to the film's showbiz pedigree. *The Wiz*, a Black retelling adapted from the 1975 Broadway musical, struggled at the box office, and the scarcity of ancillary products suggests that kids were not a significant intended audience for the film. Nonetheless, children and families emerged as its core fan base when it became traditional television viewing and an icon of cultural identity in the Black community. Furthering *The Wiz*'s relationship to television, the 2015 NBC production *The Wiz Live!* was a ratings success, particularly in a cross-platform environment of live tweeting.[52]

Oz films made specifically for television or home video more unambiguously address kids as part of their audience and may bring a strong ethos of playful metafilmicity to their nostalgic and parodic approaches. Nostalgia for legendary entertainers of the kind found in *Journey Back to Oz* also operates in an episode of *The Shirley Temple Show* (1960) adapting the second Oz book, *The Marvelous Land of Oz*. An adult Shirley Temple both hosts the episode and takes the role of Ozma, queen of Oz, playing make-believe and dress-up with co-stars like Sterling Holloway.

On the parodic end of the scale, *The Muppets' Wizard of Oz* (Kirk Thatcher, 2005) is meant to appeal to a mixed audience, using double address (and double entendre) while acknowledging kids' play with mixed repertoires. Online reviews by kids reveal that adult jokes don't necessarily go over their heads, and references to clearly child-inappropriate material like the *Girls Gone Wild* franchise (Joe Francis, 1997–) may be criticized by children who find them inappropriate and unappealing in a film for them.[53] Metafilmic references to the Muppets' universe and to narrative gaps in the MGM film encourage an irreverent posture toward the film and the fairy tale. The Good Witch, played by Miss Piggy, addresses a question many viewers have asked about the MGM film: Why doesn't Glinda tell Dorothy the magic shoes can take her home to begin with? Piggy justifies her actions with reference to the conventions of fairy tale films, saying to Dorothy, "Listen, highpockets, here's how things work in enchanted lands. Shoes have magical powers. If you have the shoes, you get the powers. But if you're going to question every little detail, the whole thing's gonna fall apart." At the end of the film, she adds "Look, this is how things work in enchanted lands. The thing you were looking for was there all along!" Muppet films operate on the metafilmic conceit that the familiar Muppet characters know they are playing roles in a movie, encouraging a playful relationship to the film.[54]

Home media and ancillary products are subject to kids' playful practices and viewing habits. VHS, DVD, and streaming videos can be fast-forwarded through boring, disturbing, or annoying parts. With musicals, one can skip ahead to the songs for singing and dancing along. Toys and other playthings may either be official ones depicting the characters in the movie or other toys kids have on hand to play the roles. In the former category are puppets based on the characters in the *Off to See the Wizard* (1967–1968) anthology series, and the Dorothy doll that came with a home video release of *Journey Back to Oz*.[55] The use of Puppetry in *The Muppets' Wizard of Oz* suggests how play with toys, dolls, and stuffed animals can introduce characters from one media universe into another. A child may use a Kermit the Frog doll or puppet as the Scarecrow, much as Kermit plays the Scarecrow in the film. *Tom and Jerry and the Wizard of Oz* (Spike Brandt and Tony Cervone, 2011) mimics children's playful insertion of themselves into the Oz universe, as the title characters follow Dorothy on her journey. The "fractured fairy tale" approach exemplified by *The Muppets' Wizard of Oz* and *Tom and Jerry and the Wizard of Oz* both reflects and encourages practices in which kids may combine elements of Oz books and films they are familiar with for their own purposes and storytelling preferences.

DISNEY'S OZ: CHILDREN'S FILM IN THE NEW HOLLYWOOD AND BEYOND

For decades, Oz seemed to escape Disneyfication, with MGM having beaten Disney to making the definitive version. It could be said, on the other hand, that Oz was MGM-ified. It was difficult for most people to conceive of Oz without Judy Garland and the ruby slippers. The dominance of the MGM film may be one reason Disney opted not to follow through on its planned live-action Oz musical, *The Rainbow Road to Oz*, in the

1950s. Ironically, whereas the MGM film relies heavily on the image of sentimentalized childhood usually promoted by Disney, Disney's recent attempts to adapt Oz take a generally darker approach seen by many as lacking the Disney "magic."

Return to Oz aspired to be a family blockbuster, and critics compared its world-building, undifferentiated adult–child address, and marketing strategies to the *Star Wars* franchise (1977–), whose success it failed to duplicate despite significant merchandising.[56] Its dark, psychological mood was considered joyless in comparison with the MGM film, and some commentators were incredulous that it wasn't even a musical.[57] In the story, Dorothy has been unable to sleep since returning from her first trip to Oz, which the adults in the film attribute to a pathological "imagination" and "bad waking dreams," so she is taken to a nightmarish electrotherapy clinic. Escaping, she falls into a turbulent stream which, ambiguously, either takes her to Oz or leaves her unconscious to dream again. This time, she finds herself on a journey to save Oz from the Nome King, who has destroyed the Emerald City and turned her friends to stone.

The possibility that Dorothy is dreaming evokes the relationship among dreams, film, and literature in children's entertainment cultures. Possibly implying a comparison between Dorothy and Lewis Carroll's Alice, Dorothy encounters Ozma, the enchanted young Princess of Oz, in mirrors and reflections, suggesting the ways films reflect and refract reality and identity. At the end of the film, Ozma appears in Dorothy's bedroom mirror, ambiguously affirming that Oz is real, but since mirror images, like movies, are illusions, it's hard to be sure. The film's stark realism is in contrast to MGM's artifice but is broken by moments of humour and references to the Oz and Disney repertoires. The ruby slippers appear under a licensing agreement with MGM, and Dorothy's fall into the Nome King's lair is visually reminiscent of Disney's Alice slowly falling down the rabbit hole. Ten-year-old Fairuza Balk's Dorothy is more sober than Judy Garland's. Her prior experience with Oz leaves her unsurprised by her new encounters, although, as if to echo the thoughts of the audience when characters not in the MGM film appear, she remarks, "I don't remember *them*." One child felt that Balk was too young for the role formerly played by Garland, while another compared her and the books' Dorothy favourably to MGM's meeker heroine.[58]

Characters and objects evince the potential of material play. When Dorothy finds a key from the old house in Kansas, she believes it is from Oz, in much the way objects found at home form links between the primary world and the world of imagination during play. The thing-like characters, faithfully recreated from the book illustrations, resemble life-size dolls and puppets. The Gump, a flying creature made of the animal head of a hunting trophy tied to two couches for a body and palm fronds for wings recalls some plaything built by kids out the materials at hand (Figure 3.3).

These characters pose profound questions of what it means to be a person or thing, living or not, child or adult, with agency and limits. Dorothy's non-human companions—Billina (a hen from the farm, who can talk in Oz), Tik-Tok (a life-size wind-up toy of a man), Jack Pumpkinhead (a large wooden doll with a jack-o-lantern head), and the aforementioned Gump (as Dorothy notes, just "a *thing* with a Gump's head on it"), are loose analogues to the thing-like and animal companions who accompanied

FIGURE 3.3. Dorothy, Jack Pumpkinhead, and Tik-Tok repair the Gump after a crash in *Return to Oz* (1985, Disney). Frame-grab.

her on the first trip. While the Gump expresses ambivalence about what kind of creature he is, Tik-Tok boasts, "I am not alive and never will be, thank goodness," an assertion that does not prevent him from shedding a tiny stream of emerald-green tears by the film's end. Occasionally assisted by Ozma from behind the mirror, this alliance of assorted children and things prove capable of saving the world by pulling together.[59] With its dark mood and existential questions, *Return to Oz* resonates with late-twentieth century perceptions of a loss of childhood innocence and threat of molestation.[60] Whereas in the MGM version, positioned between depression and looming war, adults are well-meaning but momentarily helpless, adults in *Return to Oz* are simply not to be trusted, whether they are grim Kansas nurses or Oz's Princess Mombi, who wants to remove Dorothy's head and add it to her collection. It seems fitting that this film's Dorothy later went on to play a witch in *The Craft* (Andrew Fleming, 1996).[61]

The conventional wisdom is that *Return to Oz* missed the mark by failing to appeal to either childlike wonder or adult nostalgia, but it has a cult following among people who became obsessed with it during childhood. Kids have a variety of responses to the film according to their expectations based on the larger corpus of Oz, Disney films, and children's films. Many reject it as a kids' film because of its frightening content, but one young reviewer said that "it was so cool!" despite (maybe because of) the nightmares it gave her.[62] One adult reviewer recalls it as a good horror film for kids.[63]

Disney's most recent Oz feature, *Oz the Great and Powerful*, had a modest reception perhaps resulting from its own failures to meet expectations.[64] A prequel telling the story of how the Wizard, Oscar Diggs, first came to Oz, it abounds in references to the repertoires of Oz, Disney, theatre, and cinema. The opening credits take place inside a toy theatre evoking both the stage and the aesthetics of early cinema. The opening scenes in Kansas are in sepia and classic Hollywood aspect ratio, expanding to wide-screen, colour, and CGI animation in Oz. References to MGM include a swirling yellow brick road and Glinda's use of bubbles for travel. These images avoid direct copyright infringement by referring to memories of the MGM film without quoting the designs exactly. A tribute to Disney's *Snow White* appears when the Wicked Witch is cursed by the bite of an enchanted apple.

The pleasurable effect of these recognizable tropes is in counterpoint to the film's forsaking of a traditionally feminist, queer, and "musical" repertoire in pursuit of pro-ducer Joe Roth's objective to make "a fairy tale with a good strong male protagonist."[65] Oscar, played by James Franco, is less than admirable in this role. He seduces Theodora, one of Oz's witches, who then becomes jealous when he falls in love with Glinda. Her subsequent hysterical rage is the reason she becomes the Wicked Witch of the West. Evanora, the Witch of the East, is at first young and beautiful, but her wickedness is con-firmed when her magic is revealed as deceitful and her actual age and appearance those of an old woman. Oscar adopts a china doll and a winged monkey, forming a family whose potential queerness is overwhelmed by the paternalistic force of its consumma-tion in Oscar's romantic pairing with the mother figure Glinda. China Girl is a fragile and sentimentalized object, despite occasional flashes of bossiness. She is literally broken so that the Wizard can fix her in completion of an ableist cure fantasy involving her Kansas counterpart, a girl in a wheelchair.[66] Her ultimate purpose is to make Oscar accept the role of protective father. Not only is the film not a musical, it ridicules the genre when the Wizard reacts to the Munchkin's singing by begging them to stop. Gothilocks, a ten-year-old reviewer on *Common Sense Media*, assessed the film in terms of her understanding of Oz as a repertoire with strong heroines:

> I had truck-loads of hope for Theodora, but they had to put a wicked spin on things and make her the evil witch just because some idiotic con-man lied to her? The fem-inine power that should have been there was washed away by their waterfall of doubt for female characters. With a name like Oz 'the great and powerful' you would expect him to be, oh, I don't know, great and powerful. I just wish they could have added at least a hint of Dorothy into one of the characters.[67]

Many child reviewers like the film, but others feel that it is for adults or is not a good children's film because of violence, sex, or incredible scenarios. One of the suggested criteria by which posters to *Common Sense Media*'s review section evaluate movies is the presence of good role models, and many kids identify Oscar as what one young reviewer calls a "player."[68] Child reviewers also complain of too much flirting and cleavage, which might be self-policing according to the dominant discourses of appropriate content in children's film or a genuine distaste for adult content in a movie that doesn't seem to be addressing them. Good acting and believable writing are criteria for a good kids' film as they would be for any other. Some kids criticize the acting as melodramatic and find Theodora's transformation into the Wicked Witch out of rage and jealousy simply dram-aturgically and psychologically unconvincing.

Oz the Great and Powerful's box office performance was sufficiently modest to prevent any rumoured sequels, but it has entered the home video repertoire, where its status as children's film is likely to be assured. In the climax of the film, Oscar uses creativity and ingenuity to defeat Evanora with fireworks and smokescreen projections, emulating the entrepreneurship of his hero Thomas Edison—a inventor and maker of the American kind of magic for which Baum was also known. This is the most playful and Oz-like part of the movie. Kids engaging in play with the film and any of its toys will undoubtedly have found their own creative ways of making it their own, on their own terms.

The Expanding Worlds of Oz and Children's Film

This survey of Oz films represents only some highlights, leaving out recent streaming series for children, such as Amazon's *Lost in Oz* (2017) and Boomerang's *Dorothy and the Wizard of Oz* (2017), foreign adaptations, and adult versions of Oz, such Australia's *20th Century Oz* (Chris Löfvén, 1976), Sci-Fi Channel's *Tin Man* (2007), and NBC's *Emerald City* (2017). These Oz films in turn are just one segment of the vast repertoire of movies with something to say about how films are understood as for children, or not, and how changing media forms enter into the process. When the Wizard of Oz is revealed as a humbug, in the book he has been hiding behind a screen, while in the MGM film he is hidden by a curtain. Both images evoke cinema and its theatrical legacies. As fairy tale scholar Maria Tatar has suggested, what makes Oz a modern fairy tale is that it acknowledges its humbug, the revelation of magic and belief as performed.[69] Our concepts of children's film might usefully be seen as a kind of humbug too—manifestly make-believe, provisional, and negotiated by people of all ages.

Notes

1. Katherine A. Fowkes, *The Fantasy Film* (Hoboken, NJ: John Wiley & Sons, 2010); Alexander Doty, *Flaming Classics: Queering the Film Canon* (New York: Routledge, 2000); Salman Rushdie, *The Wizard of Oz* (London: British Film Institute, 1992); Raymond Knapp, *The American Musical and the Performance of Personal Identity* (Princeton, NJ: Princeton University Press, 2006); Danielle Birkett and Dominic McHugh, *Adapting the Wizard of Oz: Musical Versions from Baum to MGM and Beyond* (New York: Oxford University Press, 2018). Works that do discuss the MGM film in the context of children's film and culture include Joel Chaston, "The 'Ozification' of American Children's Fantasy Films: *The Blue Bird, Alice in Wonderland*, and *Jumanji*," *Children's Literature Association Quarterly* 22:2 (Spring 1997), pp. 13–20; Suzanne Rahn, *The Wizard of Oz: Shaping an Imaginary World* (New York: Twayne, 1998), pp. 109–128; and Pamela Robertson Wojcik, *Fantasies of Neglect: Imagining the Urban Child in American Film and Fiction* (New

Brunswick, NJ: Rutgers University Press, 2016), pp. 97–98; Meghann Meeusen, "The Difficulty in Deciphering the 'Dreams That You Dare to Dream': Adaptive Dissonance in Wizard of Oz Films," *Children's Literature Association Quarterly* 42:2 (2017), pp. 185–204; and Noel Brown, *The Children's Film: Genre, Nation and Narrative* (New York: Columbia University Press, 2017), pp. 15, 42–44.

2. Brown, *Children's Film*, p. 5.

3. Ian Wojcik-Andrews, *Children's Films: History, Ideology, Pedagogy, Theory* (New York: Garland, 2000), p. 11.

4. Mark Evan Swartz, *Oz Before the Rainbow: L. Frank Baum's "The Wonderful Wizard of Oz" on Stage and Screen to 1939* (Baltimore, MD: Johns Hopkins University Press, 2000), 1–3. On Baum's stage and screen adaptations, see Michael Patrick Hearn, introduction to L. Frank Baum, *The Annotated Wizard of Oz, Centennial Edition* (New York: W. W. Norton, 2000), esp. pp. lvi–lxxii.

5. On Oz as transmedia, commercial, and adaptive, see Matthew Freeman, "Advertising the Yellow Brick Road: Historicizing the Industrial Emergence of Transmedia Storytelling," *International Journal of Communication* 8 (2014): 2362–2381; Henry Jenkins, "'All Over the Map': Building (and Rebuilding)," *Acta Universitatis Sapientiae, Film and Media Studies* 9:1 (2014), pp. 7–29; Kelleter, "Toto, I Think We're in Oz Again"; and Richard Flynn, "Imitation Oz: The Sequel as Commodity," *Lion and the Unicorn* 20:1 (June 1996), pp. 121–131.

6. Joel Chaston, "Baum, Bakhtin, and Broadway: A Centennial Look at the Carnival of Oz," *Lion and the Unicorn* 25:1 (January 2001), pp. 128–149.

7. Noel Brown and Bruce Babington (eds.), *Family Films in Global Cinema: The World beyond Disney* (London: I.B. Tauris, 2015), Kindle edition.

8. Adrian Schober, "'Why Can't They Make Kids' Flicks Anymore?': *Willy Wonka and the Chocolate Factory* and the Dual-Addressed Family Film," in Noel Brown and Bruce Babington (eds.), *Family Films in Global Cinema: The World Beyond Disney* (London: I.B. Tauris, 2015), pp. 53–68.

9. On the more traditional criteria mentioned, see Brown, *Children's Film*, p. 14; and Brown and Babington, *Family Films in Global Cinema*, locations 226–281.

10. Jacqueline Rose, *The Case of Peter Pan, or the Impossibility of Children's Fiction* (Philadelphia: University of Pennsylvania Press, 1984); Marah Gubar, *Artful Dodgers: Reconceiving the Golden Age of Children's Literature* (New York: Oxford University Press, 2010), pp.7–8; Victoria Ford Smith, *Between Generations: Collaborative Authorship in the Golden Age of Children's Literature* (Jackson: University Press of Mississippi, 2017).

11. Becky Parry, "Reading and Rereading *Shrek*," *English in Education* 43:2 (2009), pp. 148–161.

12. Robin Bernstein, "Toys Are Good for Us: Why We Should Embrace the Historical Integration of Children's Literature, Material Culture, and Play," *Children's Literature Association Quarterly* 38:4 (2013), pp. 458–463.

13. Swartz, *Oz before the Rainbow*, pp. 161–172.

14. "In the Fairyland of Motion Pictures: L. Frank Baum Explains How His Modern Fairies Work, Aided by Ingenuity and the Camera," condensed from an article in *New York Herald*, September 26, 1909; *Baum Bugle*, August 1962, pp. 39–40.

15. Richard A. Mills, "The *Fairylogue and Radio-Plays* of L. Frank Baum," *Baum Bugle*, Christmas 1970, p. 101.

16. Swartz, *Oz before the Rainbow*, pp. 173–196.

17. Ibid., pp. 161–238.

18. David L. Greene, "L. Frank Baum on His Films," *Baum Bugle* 17:2 (Autumn 1973), pp. 14–15.

19. Baum spoke of his objection to romantic love in children's books in an interview in *The Advance*, July 22, 1909, reprinted in *Baum Bugle* 30 (Autumn 1986), p. 9.

20. Anne Morey, "'A Whole Book for a Nickel?': L. Frank Baum as Filmmaker," *Children's Literature Association Quarterly* 29:4 (Winter 1995), pp. 155–160; Cary Elza, "Boundary-Crossing Girls and Imaginary Worlds: Gender, Childhood, and the Cinematic Spaces of Modernity," (PhD diss., Northwestern University, 2001), pp. 249–319.

21. Noel Brown, *The Hollywood Family Film: A History, from Shirley Temple to Harry Potter* (London: I.B. Tauris, 2012), p. 22.

22. Frank Joslyn Baum and Russell P. MacFall, *To Please a Child: A Biography of L. Frank Baum, Royal Historian of Oz* (Chicago: Reilly and Lee, 1961), p. 261.

23. Swartz, *Oz before the Rainbow*, pp. 192–196; Sean P. Duffly, "Oz under Scrutiny: Early Reviews of the Oz Film Manufacturing Company's *The Patchwork Girl of Oz* and *The New Wizard of Oz*," *Baum Bugle* (Winter 2005), pp. 25–32.

24. Quoted in W. E. Wing, "From 'Oz to the Magic City,' " *New York Dramatic Mirror*, October 7, 1914, reprinted in *Baum Bugle* 17:2 (Autumn 1973), p. 10.

25. On Semon's *Wizard of Oz*, see Swartz, *Oz before the Rainbow*, pp. 197–238.

26. On influences of minstrelsy on the Oz repertoire, see Robin Bernstein, *Racial Innocence: Performing American Childhood and Race from Slavery to Civil Rights* (New York: New York University Press, 2011), pp. 159–166.

27. Swartz, *Oz before the Rainbow*, p. 205.

28. Ibid., pp. 236–238.

29. Brown, *Children's Film*, p. 42.

30. On the MGM film, see John Fricke, Jay Scarfone, and William Stillman, *The Wizard of Oz: The Official 50th Anniversary Pictorial History* (New York: Warner Books, 1989).

31. Rick Payne, "1939 Wizard of Oz Pressbook: The Snow White Pages," *Filmic Light Snow White Archive*, March 13, 2013, http://filmic-light.blogspot.com/2013/03/1939-wizard-of-oz-pressbook-snow-white.html [accessed August 11, 2019].

32. Fricke, Scarfone, and Stillman, *Wizard of Oz*, p. 45.

33. Brown, *Children's Film*, pp. 5, 42.

34. Fricke, Scarfone, and Stillman, *Wizard of Oz*, pp. 172–187.

35. Knapp, *American Musical*, p. 133.

36. Aljean Harmetz, *The Making of "The Wizard of Oz"* (1977; reprinted New York: Hyperion, 1998), pp. 160–161.

37. For critical reception of the MGM film, see Fricke, Scarfone, and Stillman, *Wizard of Oz*, 172–187; and Danielle Birkett, "'The Merry Old Land of Oz?' The Reception of the MGM Film," in Birkett and McHugh, Adapting the Wizard of Oz, pp. 121–142.

38. Fricke, Scarfone, and Stillman, *Wizard of Oz*, p. 186.

39. "Eight-Year-Old Previews *Wizard of Oz*," *Washington Post*, August 20, 1939.

40. Marah Gubar, "Who Watched *The Children's Pinafore*? Age Transvestism on the Nineteenth-Century Stage," *Victorian Studies* 54:3 (2012), pp. 410–426.

41. "Eight-Year-Old Previews *Wizard of Oz*."

42. "Kid Reviews for *The Wizard of Oz*," *Common Sense Media*, [accessed August 11, 2019].

43. Kid, nine years old, "Best movie EVER!!!," "Kid Reviews for *The Wizard of Oz*," *Common Sense Media*, December 24, 2016, https://www.commonsensemedia.org/movie-reviews/the-wizard-of-oz/user-reviews/child?page=1 [accessed March 17, 2020].

44. "Eight-Year-Old Previews *Wizard of Oz*."

45. *Mister Rogers' Neighborhood*, episode 1453, May 14, 1975.

46. "Eight-Year-Old Previews *Wizard of Oz.*"

47. Fricke, Scarfone, and Stillman, *Wizard of Oz*, p. 186.

48. See also Noel Brown, this volume, on endings in children's films.

49. On Oz, television, and the home, see Annah E. MacKenzie, "From Screen to Shining Screen," in Matthew Wilhelm Kapell and Ace G. Pilkington (eds.), *The Fantastic Made Visible: Essays on the Adaptation of Science Fiction and Fantasy from Page to Screen* (Jefferson, NC: McFarland, 2015), pp. 180–187.

50. Doty, *Flaming Classics*, 54–55; Dee Michel, *Friends of Dorothy: Why Gay Boys and Gay Men Love "The Wizard of Oz"* (n.p.: Dark Ink Press, 2018), Kindle edition, location 1325.

51. Fricke, Scarfone, and Stillman, *Wizard of Oz*, pp. 234, 235.

52. Ryan Bunch, "You Can't Stop the Tweet: Social Media and Networks of Participation in the Live Television Musical," in Jessica Hillman-McCord (ed.), *Broadway: Musical Theatre in the Digital Age* (New York: Palgrave Macmillan, 2017), pp. 173–205; Tommy J. Curry, "When *The Wiz* Goes Black, Does It Ever Go Back?," in Randall E. Auxier and Phillip S. Seng (eds.), *The Wizard of Oz and Philosophy: Wicked Wisdom of the West* (Chicago: Open Court, 2008), pp. 63–78; La Donna L. Forsgren, "The Wiz Redux; or, Why Queer Black Feminist Spectatorship and Politically Engaged Popular Entertainment Continue to Matter," *Theatre Survey* 60:3 (2019), pp. 325–354.

53. "Kid Reviews for *The Muppets' Wizard of Oz*," *Common Sense Media*, https://www.commonsensemedia.org/movie-reviews/the-muppets-wizard-of-oz/user-reviews/child [accessed August 11, 2019].

54. Ginger Stelle, "'Starring Kermit the Frog as Bob Cratchit': Muppets as Actors" in Jennifer C. Garlen and Anissa M. Graham (eds.), *Kermit Culture* (Jefferson, NC: McFarland, 2009), Kindle edition, location 1353–1517; and Alissa Burger, "A Rainbow for the 21st Century: *The Muppets' Wizard of Oz* and the Reimagination of the American Myth," in Garlen and Graham, *Kermit Culture*, Kindle edition, location 1517–1715.

55. For these and other Oz objects, see Jay Scarfone and William Stillman, *The Wizard of Oz Collector's Treasury* (Atglen, PA: Schiffer, 1992).

56. *Return to Oz* reviews include Janet Maslin, "A New *Oz* Gives Dorothy New Friends," *New York Times*, June 21, 1985; "Return to Oz," *TV Guide*, https://www.tvguide.com/movies/return-to-oz/review/115840/ [accessed August 11, 2019]; Sheila Benson, "Breathing a New Life into Baum's Land of Oz," *Los Angeles Times*, June 21, 1985; Gene Siskel, "*Return to Oz* Is Missing a Welcome Mat," *Chicago Tribune*, June 21, 1985; Dolores Barclay, "New Oz Characters Interesting Enough," *Desert Sun*, July 8, 1985; Jay Boyar, "Return Trip to Land of Oz Is Grim Going," *Orlando Sentinel*, June 22, 1985; and Lawrence O'Toole, "Farther Down the Yellow-Brick Road," *Maclean's*, July 8, 1985.

57. Siskel, "*Return to Oz* Is Missing a Welcome Mat."

58. Someone You Don't Know, 'Very Creepy but Fun Sequel Actually Improves upon the First," Kid Reviews for *Return to Oz*, *Common Sense Media*, March 27, 2013, https://www.commonsensemedia.org/movie-reviews/return-to-oz/user-reviews/child [accessed June 14, 2020]; Susieboo, "Talk about Not Being in Kansas Anymore!," Kid Reviews for *Return to Oz*, *Common Sense Media*, June 27, 2011, https://www.commonsensemedia.org/movie-reviews/return-to-oz/user-reviews/child [accessed August 11, 2019].

59. On disability in Oz, see Joshua Eyler, "Disability and Prosthesis in L. Frank Baum's *The Wonderful Wizard of Oz*," *Children's Literature Association Quarterly* 38:3 (2013), pp. 319–334.

60. Steven Mintz, *Huck's Raft: A History of American Childhood* (Cambridge, MA: Harvard University Press, 2004), pp. 335–384.

61. For a discussion of *Return to Oz*, see Kelleter, "Toto, I Think We're in Oz Again," pp. 30–32.
62. Susieboo, "Talk About Not Being in Kansas Anymore!"
63. Louisa Mellor, "*Return to Oz*: A Disturbing '80s Fantasy Classic," *Den of Geek*, June 21, 2018, https://www.denofgeek.com/us/movies/return-to-oz/17676/return-to-oz-a-disturbing-80s-fantasy-classic [accessed August 11, 2019].
64. For critical analyses of *Oz the Great and* Powerful, see Jenkins, "All Over the Map"; Meeusen, "Dreams," pp. 195–202; and Mackenzie, "From Screen to Shining Screen," pp. 187–189.
65. Jim Hill, "Joe Roth Reflects on *Oz the Great and Powerful*, Looks Forward to *Maleficent* in 2014," *Huffington Post*, March 4, 2013, https://www.huffpost.com/entry/joe-roth-reflects-on-oz-t_b_2806542 [accessed August 11, 2019]. On the queerness of Oz, see, for example, Pamela Robertson (Wojcik), "Home and Away: Friends of Dorothy on the Road in Oz," in Steven Cohen and Ina Rae Hark (eds), *The Road Movie Book* (London and New York: Routledge, 1997), pp. 271–286; Hannah Robbins, "'Friends of Dorothy': Queerness in and Beyond the MGM Film" in Danielle Birkett and Dominic McHugh (eds), *Adapting The Wizard of Oz: Musical Versions from Baum to MGM and Beyond* (New York: Oxford University Press, 2019), pp. 143–160; Tison Pugh, "'There Lived in the Land of Oz Two Queerly Made Men': Queer Utopianism and Antisocial Eroticism in L. Frank Baum's Oz Series," *Marvels & Tales*, 22:2 (2008): pp. 217–239; and Michel, *Friends of Dorothy*.
66. On disability narratives, see David T. Mitchell and Sharon L. Snyder, *Narrative Prosthesis: Disability and the Dependencies of Discourse* (Ann Arbor: University of Michigan Press, 2014).
67. Gothilocks, "Great and Powerful, Indeed!," Kid Reviews for *Oz The Great and Powerful*, *Common Sense Media*, April 25, 2014, https://www.commonsensemedia.org/movie-reviews/oz-the-great-and-powerful/user-reviews/child [accessed August 11, 2019].
68. "The main character is a player among women": Kid, 12 years old, "Worth Seeing Once Maybe. .. ," "Kid Reviews for *Oz The Great and Powerful*, *Common Sense Media*, June 24, 2013, <https://www.commonsensemedia.org/movie-reviews/oz-the-great-and-powerful/user-reviews/child> [accessed August 11, 2019].
69. Maria Tatar, "Why Fairy Tales Matter: The Performative and the Transformative," *Western Folklore* 69:1 (2010), pp. 55–64.

BIBLIOGRAPHY

Birkett, Danielle, and Dominic McHugh. *Adapting the Wizard of Oz: Musical Versions from Baum to MGM and Beyond*. New York: Oxford University Press, 2018.

Brown, Noel. *The Children's Film: Genre, Nation and Narrative*. New York: Columbia University Press, 2017.

Kelleter, Frank. "'Toto, I Think We're in Oz Again' (and Again and Again): Remakes and Popular Seriality." In Kathleen Loock and Constantine Verevis (eds.), *Film Remakes, Adaptations and Fan Productions*. London: Palgrave Macmillan, 2012, pp. 19–44.

Knapp, Raymond. *The American Musical and the Performance of Personal Identity*. Princeton, NJ: Princeton University Press, 2006.

MacKenzie, Annah E. "From Screen to Shining Screen." In Matthew Wilhelm Kapell and Ace G. Pilkington (eds.), *The Fantastic Made Visible: Essays on the Adaptation of Science Fiction and Fantasy from Page to Screen*. Jefferson, NC: McFarland, 2015, pp. 175–191.

Meeusen, Meghann. "The Difficulty in Deciphering the 'Dreams That You Dare to Dream': Adaptive Dissonance in Wizard of Oz Films." *Children's Literature Association Quarterly* 42:2 (2017), pp. 185–204.

Morey, Anne. "'A Whole Book for a Nickel'? L. Frank Baum as Filmmaker." *Children's Literature Association Quarterly* 20:4 (Winter 1995), pp. 155–160.

Parry, Becky. "Reading and Rereading *Shrek*." *English in Education* 43:2 (2009), pp. 148–161.

Rahn, Suzanne. *The Wizard of Oz: Shaping an Imaginary World*. New York: Twayne, 1998.

Rushdie, Salman. *The Wizard of Oz*. London: British Film Institute, 1992.

Swartz, Mark Evan. *Oz before the Rainbow: L. Frank Baum's "The Wonderful Wizard of Oz" on Stage and Screen to 1939*. Baltimore, MD: Johns Hopkins University Press, 2000.

Wojcik-Andrews, Ian. *Children's Films: History, Ideology, Pedagogy, Theory*. New York: Garland, 2000.

CHAPTER 4

CHILDREN'S FILMS AND THE AVANT-GARDE

BETTINA KÜMMERLING-MEIBAUER

THE notion of "avant-garde film" spontaneously evokes the impression of famous films produced in the first half of the twentieth century, such as the German silent movies inspired by expressionism; the constructivist movies by Sergei Eisenstein, which made ample use of the technique of montage; and the surrealist films by Luis Buñuel. These films are regarded as significant parts of our cultural heritage and therefore are regularly shown at film festivals and in art-house cinemas.[1] Moreover, films of this kind are distinguished by a sophisticated film language that includes highly abstract form experiments, non-linear stories, an unusual manner of representation, and a mixing of styles or genres. As a result, they challenge the viewers in multiple respects, because they oppose usual spectatorial expectations to the extent of presenting ambiguous narratives and characters whose ambiguity cannot be completely dissolved. Considering this, one may assume that children's films have no relation to avant-garde films. Children's films usually address an audience that has not yet acquired a fully developed film literacy—that is, the ability to understand and interpret the filmic codes of this multimodal medium—and vanguard styles and techniques would certainly overstrain the competencies of this target group.

Despite these reservations, vanguard styles and experiments emerged in children's films early. The first feature-length animated film, Lotte Reiniger's *Die Abenteuer des Prinzen Ahmed* (*The Adventures of Prince Ahmed*, 1926), and the first feature-length live-action movie for children, *Emil und die Detektive* (*Emil and the Detectives*, 1931), directed by Gerhard Lamprecht, are both influenced by vanguard techniques and references to avant-garde styles of their times. These two films are two prime examples of children's films inspired by the avant-garde. This chapter therefore strives to demonstrate the impact of the avant-garde on children's films from the 1920s to the present. The selection of films considers different genres and films from four countries: France, Germany, Russia, and the United States. The films presented here are particularly innovative in their use of avant-garde techniques and had a great deal of influence on subsequent children's films.

First, this chapter will define and contextualize the notion of "avant-garde film." Second, it will elaborate on the significance of early animated films and their connection to vanguard tendencies. Third, it will focus on the impact of the avant-garde on children's films released in the interwar period before going on to examine the influence of the avant-garde on children's films after 1945. Finally, it will demonstrate that references to the avant-garde still appear in contemporary children's films.

WHAT IS AN AVANT-GARDE FILM?

The French term "avant-garde" originates from military jargon and means the "advance guard" or spearhead of an army. At the end of the nineteenth century, its original meaning changed, and it began being used to describe progressive and politically engaged art and literature. Seen in this light, the original association of the avant-garde with social revolution and historical progress had been conferred on histories of art and literature studies. Since the beginning of the twentieth century, this notion had been used to describe art movements that are considered to be ahead of their times. Accordingly, the term is now widely employed to designate those artists, authors, publishers, and directors who aspire to push the boundaries of what is regarded as a norm.

Strictly speaking, *avant-garde* is an umbrella term for diverse European and non-European art movements that flourished between 1910 and 1940, such as Dadaism, expressionism, futurism, surrealism, and New Objectivity (*Neue Sachlichkeit*). In addition, the Soviets introduced the paradigm of montage, which engaged the viewer in a radically new view of reality, while the post-war period emphasized the subjectivity of characters.[2] Two salient tendencies in interwar avant-garde filmmaking are abstraction and surrealism, which resulted in films that inspired post-war cinema in Europe, North America, South America, and elsewhere.[3]

These artistic movements were conceptualized as counter-projects to established and traditional culture and art, and they impacted the visual arts, literature, music, and film—the silent movies of the 1910s and 1920s, and the sound films since the late 1920s. These avant-garde movements expressed a general belief in the historical progress of art, and therefore questioned the idea of the unified organic artwork. The avant-garde artists focused on the material aspects of art and aimed at merging disparate materials, which boosted artistic strategies such as montage and collage.

The Second World War marked a significant shift in the avant-garde. Despite this recess, avant-garde artists of the interwar period continued to work in the avant-garde styles of the 1920s and 1930s in the post-war period. For this reason, scholarly studies distinguish between a historical avant-garde and a neo-avant-garde or post-avant-garde.[4] This differentiation implies that the avant-garde is subject to historical processes. Seen in this light, one may presume that artworks that were once regarded as provocative and innovative lost their provoking effects over time. Yet contemporary artists have continuously tried to renew pivotal avant-garde concepts and ideas of the first half of the twentieth century by developing new art programmes and neo-avant-garde art movements, such as COBRA and Pop Art.

These considerations notwithstanding, *avant-garde* is still hard to define precisely because its meaning has changed over time. Moreover, in certain contexts and countries, scholars often assigned avant-garde movements to the category of modernism. Early avant-garde artists and theoreticians stressed that the concept of avant-garde cannot distinctly be separated from any contemporary political and social discussion, thus underlining the close relationship between aesthetic and political issues in relation to the avant-garde as an umbrella term for any radical art movement. Consequently, scholars such as Rosalind Krauss and Paul Mann have argued that the notion and conceptualization of avant-garde have become diluted to the extent of becoming obsolete.[5] However, Peter Bürger's seminal study, *Theory of the Avant-garde* (1984), contributed to the rehabilitation of the (historical) avant-garde.[6] He claimed that the avant-garde touches on all art forms and represents a break from academic and artistic institutions that tend to preserve traditional opinions rather than supporting innovative artistic tendencies.[7] Despite this justifiable criticism, scholars have increasingly shown an interest in the investigation of the (historical) avant-garde since the end of the twentieth century, advocating the emergence of avant-garde studies. Within this newly developed field, the avant-garde film plays a minor yet significant role.

There is a close relationship between avant-garde films and avant-garde tendencies in literature and the visual arts due to the interest in abstract form experiments, visual effects, montage, and the synchronization of cinematic movements and sounds. The avant-garde film can be distinguished by its taboo-breaking topics, formal experimentality, and an opposition to commercial mainstream cinema. Moreover, avant-garde films often emphasize the specificity of the film medium through self-referentiality or by the inclusion of metafilmic references, as they are already discernible in the early Cinema of Attraction, whose main representative is French director Georges Méliès.[8] In the 1920s, critics in Western European countries applied the notion of "avant-garde" particularly to those films that consciously distanced themselves from mainstream cinema. In Germany, however, this notion was initially confined to abstract and what were called "absolute" films. These films mostly show abstract compositions of forms and colours in rhythmic movements. They were quite short, not longer than seven to fifteen minutes. Moreover, these abstract films refrained from any traditional narration or storyline and were addressed to audiences of the elite, which showed an interest into these novel forms and motion studies.

Outside Germany, critics and theoreticians used the notion of "avant-garde film" in a broader sense, as a reference to all those films whose design shows the influence of avant-garde art movements, borrowing from paintings, sculpture, and other art forms. Directors of avant-garde films advocated new ways of seeing by pointing to the close relation between the human eye and the camera, the mechanical nature of machines, and the interdependence of light, movement, time, and perspective as key issues in filmmaking. One frequent aim of avant-garde films consists in deliberately provoking the spectator, thus disrupting conventional principles of perception.[9] Moreover, avant-garde films are expected to constantly challenge expectations and to offer complex thematic and formal innovations, which promote multiple interpretations.[10]

Scholars Michael O'Pray and William Verrone, both experts in the history of avant-garde films, rightly point out that "avant-garde film" is a contested concept, and is marginal to commercial cinema.[11] Despite this attitude, avant-garde films paved the way for the modernization of film in general, whether full-length feature films, short films, animation films, or documentaries. Regarded as antithetical to mainstream cinema, avant-garde films display multiple features. They typically have an experimental style or form. As for the plot construction, they tend to non-linear, even achronological stories. Furthermore, they stand out due to their unusual representations of reality, contributing to a destabilization of fixed and conventional ideas on the condition of reality. Avant-garde films are characterized by a mixture of genres and styles. Finally, they are provocative, since they represent highly ambiguous characters and plots.[12] In spite of these efforts, there is no general definition of the avant-garde film, or as Verrone puts it, "there is no one particular way of defining an avant-garde film."[13] This assertion notwithstanding, there is a consensus that avant-garde films represent a significant corpus of film history. Regarded as a counterculture to dominant cinema, avant-garde filmmakers eschew the commercial field and are inspired by the vanguard debate of their times, which transgresses the boundaries of art, popular culture, and academic discourse.

While there are ample studies that investigate the history and theory of the avant-garde film from a national or international perspective, studies on the relationship between avant-garde and children's films are virtually nonexistent. An exception to this rule is *Die Abenteuer des Prinzen Ahmed* by Lotte Reiniger, which is often mentioned as an early and exceptional example of an avant-garde animation film.

AVANT-GARDE ANIMATION FOR CHILDREN

The 1920s represent the heyday of avant-garde film in Europe, as filmmakers in France, Germany, Russia, and elsewhere experimented with the technical, aesthetic, and narratological aspects of filmmaking. While the German filmmakers Hans Richter, Oskar Fischinger, and Walter Ruttmann focused on abstraction and animation, the Russians Sergei Eisenstein and Dziga Vertov exploited the aesthetic and ideological potentialities of montage. Fernand Léger and Man Ray from France created abstract avant-garde films inspired by photography and constructivism, whereas the Spanish director Luis Buñuel created a couple of avant-garde films in close cooperation with Salvador Dalí, whose surrealist episodes shocked the contemporary audience.

This fruitful decade of avant-garde filmmaking, which points to the cross-fertilization of the arts and different art movements, was also a highly productive period for Lotte Reiniger. Nowadays film scholars regard Reiniger as a pioneer of animation film. She started as a book illustrator, creating delicate paper cuttings for children's books.

The actor and director Paul Wegener, famous for his silent movies, *Der Student von Prag* (*The Student of Prague*, 1913) and *Der Golem* (*The Golem*, 1920), called her attention to the artistic potential of filmmaking. The technical achievement to make single images with the help of a specific camera and to mount them into a film inspired Reiniger to create short, animated silhouette films, beginning with Wegener's fairy-tale films, *Rübezahl's Hochzeit* (*The Wedding of Rübezahl*, 1916) and *Der Rattenfänger* (*The Pied Piper of Hamelin*, 1918).[14]

In close cooperation with her husband, the camera operator Carl Koch, and the avant-garde filmmakers Bertold Bartosch and Walter Ruttmann, Reiniger produced the first feature-length animated film, *Die Abenteuer des Prinzen Ahmed* (1926). She drafted the script which consists of a compilation of fairy tales taken from the collection *The Arabian Nights*. The adventurous story focuses on two love affairs: Prince Ahmed falls in love with the fairy queen Peri Banu, while his fellow, Aladdin, is in love with Ahmed's sister, Dinarsade. The lovers must face a wicked sorcerer and a cruel witch who threaten their lives and are responsible for the separation of the couples. The setting evokes an oriental atmosphere, with multiple changes of locations and numerous fairy-tale characters, such as demons, ghosts, fairies, and witches. The silent film has 120 intertitles that provide relevant information about the characters and the storyline.

Reiniger created 250,000 single images, of which 96,000 were used for the sixty-six-minute silhouette film. The limbs of the cut-out figures were connected to tiny wires to generate their movement. Inspiration sources for this artistic technique and the depiction of the figures were the South Asian shadow theatre, ancient Egyptian art, and Greek vase painting. These art styles have one feature in common: they present figures in profile only. Reiniger used two strategies to individualize the figures: as in Asian shadow theatre, the bodies are partially pierced with patterns. Moreover, the cut-out eyes consist of white surfaces with inserted pupils, simulating liveliness. By minimally changing the position of figures from image to image, Reiniger applied the stop-motion technique to generate movement.[15]

She captured the oriental mood by mixing references to different artistic movements, romanticism, art nouveau, and expressionism. Since paper cutting reached a peak in the beginning of the nineteenth century, when silhouette illustrations featured in books for children and adults, Reiniger's silhouettes point to the delicate paper cuttings of the Romantic period and the Biedermeier. The ornamental design with an emphasis on floral patterns, arabesques, and wavy lines clearly refers to art nouveau style, while the exaggerated bodily movements and gestures show the impact of expressionism. By doing this, Reiniger varied the outlines and ornaments in her silhouettes to the extent of creating vibrant sceneries with abundant objects and figures.[16] Reiniger photographed these figures and the cut-out buildings, objects, animals, and plants against multiple layers of transparent paper to create the impression of a landscape or city. These sceneries are visible in establishing long-shots that give the viewer an overview on the setting. These panoramic views, interspersed with a few close-ups, evoke intimacy but also create tension. Finally, the individual action sequences are tinted blue, green, yellow, and red.

The avant-garde director Walter Ruttmann created the background design and the abstract form and colour compositions, which protrude in the beginning and the battle scenes. As in "absolute films," the viewer sees moving geometrical forms in different colours in which there are no figures and "real" settings. In addition, the filmmaker Bertold Bartosch experimented with lighted glass plates to achieve the impression of depth. This procedure anticipated the technical achievement of the multiplane camera. In contrast to traditional music for silent movies (which usually consisted of a piano accompaniment), the composer Wolfgang Zeller drafted a symphonic music whose individual instruments serve as guiding principles for the main characters.

Die Abenteuer des Prinzen Ahmed is assigned to avant-garde cinema for different reasons. First, Reiniger refined the silhouette technique to adjust it to the requirements of animated film. Second, the musical score matches perfectly with the figures' movements, preceding a technique further developed by Walt Disney Studios. Third, the film is distinguished by abstract film sequences which are inspired by German "absolute films," thus creating a tension between abstract and figural scenes. Finally, Reiniger and her team applied new film techniques, stop-motion and the multiplane camera.

Although contemporary critics, such as Bela Balász,[17] praised the film's artistic performance, the film was not a great success, at least in Germany. The political situation following the seizure of power by the Nazis in 1933 were unfavourable, and Reiniger's masterpiece fell into oblivion. Reiniger and her husband emigrated to England in 1935, where she produced further silhouette films (her estate encompasses about forty films).[18] During a bombing attack on Berlin, the original version and the negative copies of *Die Abenteuer des Prinzen Ahmed* were completely destroyed. In the 1990s, however, staff members of the British Film Institute accidentally discovered backup copies with English intertitles in the archive. By means of these copies and the German censor's certificate, experts of the German Film Museum in Frankfurt reconstructed the original version, which premiered in 1999. This restored version contributed to Reiniger's retrospective fame as a pioneer of animation film.

With Reiniger's silhouette film long presumed lost, Walt Disney's *Snow White and the Seven Dwarfs* (David Hand et al., 1937) was deemed the first feature-length animation film. Disney films are usually not seen considering vanguard aspirations. However, even the popular early animated films reveal the influence of the European avant-garde cinema. A case in point is *Snow White and the Seven Dwarfs*, whose film language clearly refers to German expressionist films. This comes to the fore in the forest scenes and the episodes that focus on Snow White's wicked stepmother, which are dominated by a play of light and shadow. The nightly scene of Snow White's flight creates a nightmarish atmosphere, since the wood seems to become alive as the branches of trees entangle the frightened girl and impede her forward movement. At the same time, bright eyes of unseen animals observe Snow White, additionally inciting the girl's panic.[19]

While this animated film occasionally alludes to avant-garde films of the 1920s, *Fantasia* (Ben Sharpsteen et al., 1940) is replete with references to avant-garde art and film. This film presents a stand-alone work among Disney's comprehensive oeuvre. Instigated by the incredible success of *Snow White and the Seven Dwarfs*, Disney had the vision to create a unique artwork that met the highest aesthetic standards and should even convince sceptical critics of the artistic potential of animation. The Disney studio already had gathered a considerable amount of experience in the transposition of music in animation with the short animation film series *Silly Symphonies* (1929–1939). For the new feature-length project, Disney engaged the prestigious conductor Leopold Stokowski and his Philadelphia Orchestra to orchestrate the musical score. Furthermore, he convinced composer Igor Stravinsky to adapt the ballet "Le Sacre du Printemps" to a shorter orchestral piece.

The two-hour animation *Fantasia* consists of seven separate musical pieces which are connected by a frame story, in which the conductor, the orchestra, and Mickey Mouse appear.[20] The first episode, "Toccata and Fugue in D Minor," by Johann Sebastian Bach, is a mixture of silhouette film and abstract film. The German Oskar Fischer, one of the pioneers of the abstract film, was actively involved in the creation of this sequence.[21] The very beginning with the silhouette figures pays tribute to Reiniger's work. "The Nutcracker Suite," by Piotr Tchaikovsky; *The Pastoral Symphony*, by Ludwig van Beethoven; and "Dance of the Hours," by Amilcare Ponchieli are dominated by the typical Disney style. The most famous episode, "The Sorcerer's Apprentice" by Paul Dukas, based on a ballad by Johann Wolfgang von Goethe, as well as "Night on Bald Mountain" by Modest Mussorgsky, which concludes the film together with the ensuing "Ave Maria" by Franz Schubert, demonstrate the impact of German expressionist cinema. Disney especially admired the silent films by Friedrich Wilhelm Murnau, whose film language he applied to selected animated sequences.[22] Finally, "Rite of Spring" by Stravinsky chronicles the Earth's beginning and progresses to the first living creatures, which culminates in the reign and extinction of the dinosaurs. This episode, which followed "The Sorcerer's Apprentice," is a deep bow to the Cinema of Attraction and its great master, Georges Méliès. Hence, *Fantasia* reveals itself to be a typical product of the Disney Studios, as this film uses different models to create a hybrid, yet eclectic artwork. What distinguishes *Fantasia*, though, is the genuine attempt to employ a vanguard film language inspired by European avant-garde film and art.

THE AVANT-GARDE IN EARLY CHILDREN'S FILMS

The first feature-length live-action movie for children was the 1931 adaptation of Erich Kästner's famous novel *Emil und die Detektive* (*Emil and the Detectives*, 1929). Based on a script written by Billy Wilder, Emeric Pressburger, and Erich Kästner, it is the story of the boy, Emil Tischbein (Rolf Wenkhaus), who takes the train to Berlin to visit his grandmother. His hard-working mother entrusts him with 140 marks. During the train trip Emil falls asleep. A thief called Grundeis (Fritz Rasp) seizes the opportunity and steals the money. Emil secretly follows the thief when he exits the train in Berlin.

Luckily, Emil gets to know the boy Gustav and his gang, who support him in the pursuit of the thief. It turns out that Grundeis is a wanted bank robber and will be arrested by the police. Consequently, Emil gets the stolen money back and a reward.

The book by Kästner is regarded as a prototypical novel for children, one that follows the programme of New Objectivity (*Neue Sachlichkeit*), a German avant-garde movement of the late 1920s and early 1930s. Essential features of New Objectivity emerge in *Emil and the Detectives*: the focus on urban life, the matter-of-fact depiction of the life conditions of people belonging to different social classes, the mixture of various linguistic registers, and a close relation to film language. Moreover, the book popularized the genre of the detective novel for children; it follows a group of children who interact without any support by adults. Apart from that, *Emil and the Detectives* includes references to expressionism, surrealism and the Bauhaus as three further avant-garde movements of that time. The exaggerated description of Berlin by Grundeis, Emil's strange dream in the train compartment, and his first impression of Berlin when he entered the main station evidently show the influence of expressionist literature and film, as these scenes pinpoint the main character's emotional condition, which is contrasted with the factual and objective style prevalent throughout the novel. Additionally, Emil's dream recalls surrealist art, as the dream combines elements and episodes in an unforeseeable manner. On closer consideration, the double preface and the ten illustrations that anticipate the story evince modernist ideas, as they refer to surrealist film, the technique of montage, and the aesthetic of New Objectivity. Here the concept of play with geometrical forms comes to the fore, as an idea inspired by Reform pedagogy. Like in a game with toy blocks, the reader is invited to arrange the illustrations and the information provided in the prefaces to speculate on the potential storyline of the subsequent text.[23]

Although the film script omits the prefaces and altered parts of the storyline, it still includes multiple references to the avant-garde. *Emil and the Detectives* is the first children's film that presents urban life in the Berlin metropolis. As in a documentary, the camera follows Emil's (and later the children's gang's) way through the streets and quarters of Berlin, showing the city's traffic, neon signs, crowds of people, advertising column, and landmarks such as the Emperor William Memorial Church, Friedrichstraße railway station, and the Kudamm. The film thus takes up the design of German documentaries of the late 1920s, which focused on the depiction of everyday reality in Berlin. In this regard, Lamprecht's film version has similarities with the avant-garde film *Berlin—Die Symphonie der Großstadt* (*Berlin—Symphonie of a Metropolis*, 1927) by Walter Ruttmann. Like in Ruttmann's silent movie, the sound design plays a significant role in *Emil and the Detectives*. Although the latter is a sound film, several sequences are only accompanied by music without any dialogue, including the episodes in the streets and the very beginning of the film, when Emil and two fellows are disguised with eye masks—a reference to the then popular Zorro movies—and play a prank on the constable. No human voice is audible, just a whistle.

A central passage is the dream sequence. Instead of a wild chase, as in the novel, the first part of the dream happens in the train compartment. Emil's previously indicated fear of Grundeis's staring glance leads from reality to the dream world. Grundeis is reading a newspaper, but his shining eyes seem to percolate the paper, staring at the frightened boy (Figure 4.1). This moment recalls surrealist photographs by Herbert Bayer and Man Ray. In a next step, the proportions become increasingly distorted as Emil shrinks to dwarf-like size in comparison to Grundeis's giant shoes. The menacing situation gains momentum as Emil suddenly hangs on the emergency brake, which seems to be five metres above the ground, while Grundeis eats up the brim of his hat and threatens Emil with an oversized glowing cigar. The dream sequence then fades into street scenery. Emil is holding an umbrella and flies toward a cockpit on a crossroad. The constable in the cockpit unsuccessfully attempts to capture Emil. Losing hold of the umbrella, Emil's fall to the street dissolves into his fall from the bench in the train compartment.

The distorted proportions are reminiscent of German expressionist silent movies, as in *Das Kabinett des Dr. Caligari* (*The Cabinet of Dr Caligari*, Robert Wiene, 1920), where dream sequences and specific emotional conditions are conveyed by means of contorted perspectives and unusual proportions. A clear reference to expressionist film is the play of light and shade. Grundeis is always placed in dark or in shadowy spaces, while Emil and the children's gang are situated in bright areas. These episodes (and there are others)

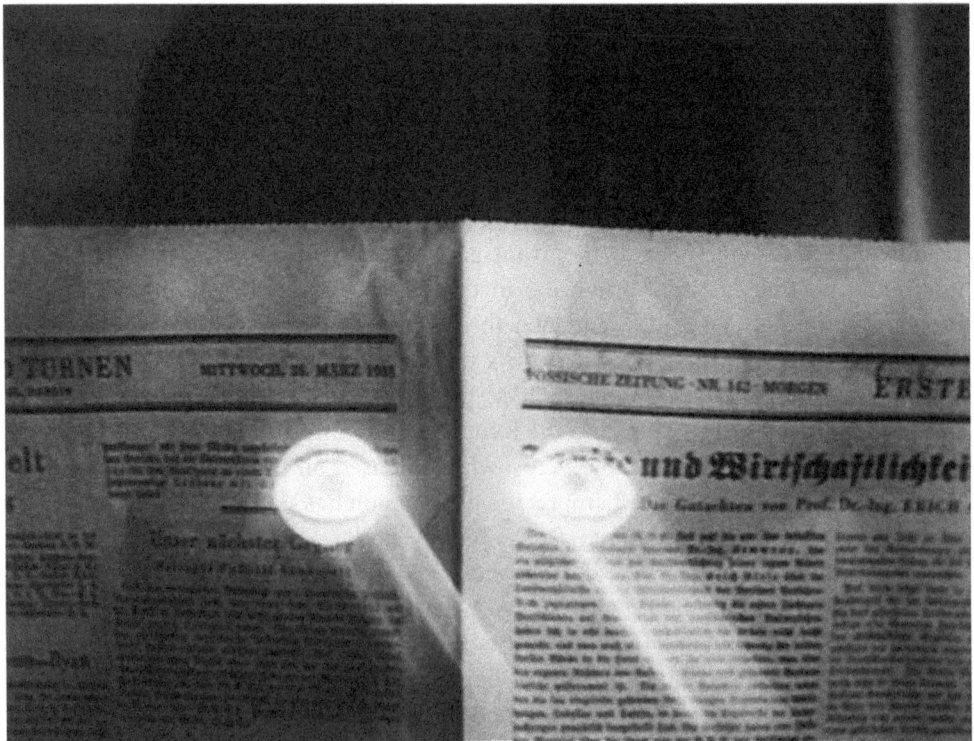

FIGURE 4.1. Grundeis in the train, reading a newspaper. *Emil und die Detektive* (1931, UFA). Frame-grab.

show Lamprecht's use of intermedial references to silent movies, in general, and to expressionist films, in particular, thus pointing to the transition from silent movie to sound movie, on the one hand, and the interfaces between expressionism and New Objectivity on the other hand. The scenes in Berlin and the representation of the children's gang and their actions are inspired by realist documentaries, while the dream sequence and the nightly scenes with the interplay of light and shadow are unequivocal references to expressionist movies and photographs.

The movie was an immense national and international success. Although Kästner's works were destroyed at the book burning in 1933, and most of his children's books were banned from libraries, the Nazis could not do anything about the movie adaptation of *Emil and the Detectives* because of its popularity. Therefore, the film was shown in German cinemas until 1937. After the Second World War, more than ten adaptations of Kästner's children's novel were produced, inter alia in Brazil, Japan, the United Kingdom, and the United States.[24] Two further German adaptations were released in 1954 and 2001. Both versions include intermedial references to Lamprecht's film; however, they deliberately omitted the vanguard episodes.[25]

Two years later, the French vanguard director Jean Vigo released the film *Zéro de conduite* (*Zero for Conduct*, 1933). The status of this film is somewhat questioned, as film historians usually regard it as a film about childhood rather than a children's film. However, in light of the discussion on films that either cross the borders between films for adults and films for children, or whose audience seem to encompass all ages, some critics have argued that *Zéro de conduite* can be seen as a film for children.[26] The film starts with a train trip, which takes the two students Caussat (Louis Lefebvre) and Bruel (Coco Golstein) to a new boarding school. Since they are unable to adjust to the strict rules, they get a "zero for conduct" and therefore develop an escape plan. Other students join in and read out a "declaration of war" against the teachers and supervisors. They cause mayhem in the dormitory which ends in a wild pillow fight. The next morning, there is a school jubilee. After the guests of honour have arrived, four students drop down rubble from the roof of the school building and raise a pirate flag. Afterwards, they climb over the roofs to freedom before the supervisors can catch them. This film consists of a compilation of loosely connected episodes because of the director's small budget. Vigo recruited most of the actors on the streets in Paris, as he wished this film to be populated by non-professionals. What makes this film—besides the critique of the school system—so exceptional is Vigo's playful approach to the technical potential the film medium offered at that time. Moreover, the film sways between sequences that follow the aesthetic of silent movies with episodes that refer to vanguard cinema.

Already the first scene shows the visual language of silent film: the boys are sitting in the train compartment, joyfully interacting without speaking. The smoke of their cigarettes is parallelized with the smoke of the locomotive. The first spoken utterance, "Il est mort" (He is dead), is expressed when a sleeping man slides down the bench. It turns out that he is the new supervisor, who stands on the side of the students. In a later scene, he imitates the performance of Charlie Chaplin in the silent movie *Easy Street* (Charlie Chaplin, 1917). He even demonstrates his acting performance when he does a handstand while drafting a caricature of a dreaded teacher with one hand. When this teacher later bends over the illustration, the drawn figure becomes alive by means of animation and changes into Napoleon—a satirical point against the teacher's presumption.

The key scene, however, is the sequence in the dormitory, which begins with drums and trumpet music and leads to a fierce pillow fight. When the peak seems to be reached and feathers fly around like snowflakes, the tempo suddenly changes. For some seconds everybody and everything stands still, as if frozen, and no sound is heard. Then the students form a procession, which is filmed in slow motion, underlaid with string music whose score plays in reverse. These surreal effects underline the anarchic character of the pillow fight and the students' revolt.

Despite the serious topic—the misuse of power and suppression of students within the boarding school system—Vigo created a funny film whose criticism shines through the playful episodes.[27] The somewhat loosely connected scenes reveal that Vigo was more interested in technical experiments with the film medium than in telling a coherent story. In addition, he contrasts the stiff behaviour of the teachers and supervisors with the anarchy put forward by the rebellious students. The animated episode, the surreal pillow fight, the intermedial references to Charlie Chaplin and the expressionist silent movie evidently show Vigo's interest in vanguard cinema.

The critical stance of *Zero for Conduct* met with strong criticism after the first performance. Pedagogues and parent representatives expressed reservations about the students' revolt and the boys' mischievous behaviour. The famous expression of the student Tabard (Gérard de Bédarieux), "Je vous dis merde" (I tell you shit), in the face of a teacher who repeatedly caresses the boy's curly hair, led to the banning of the movie. After the Second World War, the ban was lifted and the film experienced a revival in the post-war years.[28] Numerous directors, such as François Truffaut and Lindsay Anderson, invoked Vigo's film as an inspiration source for their own filmmaking, particularly in relation to the representation of troubled childhood.

Avant-Garde in Children's Films after 1945

The 1950s and 1960s were fruitful periods with regards to the modernization of children's film. Multiple children's films either took up vanguard tendencies of the interwar period or integrated novel contemporary aesthetic concepts. One notable example is *Le ballon rouge* (*The Red Balloon*, 1956), by Albert Lamorisse, a 30-minute short that follows the adventures of a young boy named Pascal (Pascal Lamorisse). On his way to school, Pascal finds a red balloon that is attached to a lamp post. He unties the balloon and takes it, keeping it with him the whole day, and attracting a lot of attention. The balloon seems to develop a life of its own. It plays hide-and-seek with Pascal, follows a blue balloon that a little girl is carrying, and waits outside the school building until Pascal comes out again. On the run from the children who are envious of the balloon, Pascal hurries through the narrow streets of Paris. Finally encircled by a gang of older boys, Pascal lets the balloon go. Hit by a slingshot, the balloon falls and slowly deflates. Pascal sits sadly on the ground, holding the remnants of the balloon. Suddenly, innumerable coloured balloons break away in town and gather around Pascal. He clutches their strings and floats away above the city (Figure 4.2).

The film's aesthetic was influenced by French cinema of the 1940s, of which the dominant aesthetic was poetic realism. As in those films, the dark and grey cityscape is the backdrop for a poetic story about human relationships and people's longing for friendship and love. The poetic nature of the film is heightened by the loosely connected scenes that highlight certain moments of the boy's adventures and his emotions over the course of one day. *Le ballon rouge*, however, opposes the lack of understanding of adults and the envy of older children with the friendship between a sensitive and lonely boy and a toy. The balloon has a mind and will of its own, and serves as substitute for a "human" friend.

The film was filmed in the Belleville area of Paris, which was demolished in the 1960s to make room for new housing. The shabby streets and grey houses with narrow entrances create a gloomy atmosphere, visualizing Paris as a grey post-war city. This depressing quality contrasts with the bright colour of the balloon, which is a symbol of light and hope. Through a child's gaze, a bleak world changes into a magical one,

FIGURE 4.2. Pascal flies over Paris. *Le ballon rouge* (1956, Lopert Films). Frame-grab.

emphasizing the child's imagination. The final scene, with the multi-coloured balloons against a blue sky and the grey cityscape below, show us that the child's dreamworld has temporarily overcome the harsh reality.

Apart from the influence of poetic realism, the film is deftly interwoven with references to silent movies and expressionism. As in a silent movie, most of the interactions happen without words. The sound design consists of a musical score and the sounds of street noises, running footsteps, or the hard slaps of the slingshot. Additionally, although in a few episodes there is talking, it is not understandable; instead, the words are spoken as if in an unknown language or distorted to imitate the croaks and quacks of poor-quality loudspeakers. But though the viewer cannot understand what Pascal tells the balloon, his gestures and facial expressions indicate a friendly and confident manner.

As the balloon is in a permanent movement, it encourages Pascal to enter new areas of the city. On his tour, Pascal discovers unfamiliar parts of the neighbourhood. Driven by curiosity, the boy is nevertheless aware of the suburb's sombre atmosphere. This situation reached a peak when he is chased by the older boys. The narrow streets seem to constrict Pascal to the extent that he can hardly pass through the alleyways. Since he cannot find a way out, he gets lost as in a labyrinth, confronted with dead ends and locked doors. Dark corners and sharp shadows create an eerie mood. The one ray of light in this surrounding is the red balloon. As in expressionist films, the interplay of light and shadow is used to convey Pascal's emotional state, which changes from sheer joy and feelings of responsibility to fear, confusion, and sadness.

Le ballon rouge was a huge success. It won several prestigious awards, including an Oscar for the best original screenplay and the Palme d'Or for the best short film at Cannes, both in 1956. Although Lamorisse's film reflects past vanguard tendencies derived from silent movies, expressionist films and the poetic realism of French cinema of the 1940s, other children's films produced in the 1950s refer to contemporary cinematic trends. Examples include several of the children's films produced by the DEFA (Deutsche Film AG, German Film Share Cooperative) studios in the German Democratic Republic (GDR). During the 1950s, filmmakers experimented with various subjects and film techniques.[29] A remarkable film is *Die Geschichte vom armen Hassan* (*The Story of Poor Hassan*, 1958), directed by Gerhard Klein. He collaborated closely with the famous Berliner Ensemble established by Bertolt Brecht. Klein could recruit most of the actors of this film from this theatre company. Inspired by Brecht's theory of estrangement, Klein transformed the eponymous Uyghur fairy tale into a parable.

The character of a didactic play already shines though in the opening sequence. The illusion of a fairy tale is shaken, as this sequence openly points to the production of the film. First, the camera team and the director are shown; silence is requested, since shooting is about to begin. The camera then pans to the main protagonist, who turns his gaze towards the viewers, introduces himself with his real name, and then explains the role he will play in the film. Next, he slowly turns the pages of a book. The camera zooms on to these pages, which show photos of the actors and their names as well as the names of the production team. Afterwards, the scenery smoothly changes into a fairy-tale setting. This transition is marked by the change from a black-and-white film to a full-colour film.

Although the story takes place in an oriental setting, Klein strips the film of any exoticism. The stage set is barren. A few buildings and objects indicate the respective setting. From the beginning, the viewer has the impression of watching a theatre performance rather than a detailed fairy-tale film. Since no fantastical events happen, the original fairy-tale script changes into a didactic play on the suppression of the poor by the mighty. Hassan (Ekkehard Schall) is a poor load carrier who kills a dog, since the animal has attacked his parrot. For this reason, he is sentenced to serve as a guard dog for the wealthy owner of the killed dog, Machmud (Erwin Geschonnek). Later, he is even forced to bear a yoke instead of a horse. The sad fate of the slave woman Fatima (Georgetta Sager) and his own sufferings finally serve as an eye-opener. Hassan recognizes that he can only change the situation if he defends himself. He knocks the carriage over and gains the poor people access to the garden and well of the rich businessman.

The inserted songs and the refrain of the final recitative, "Nur der, der keine Kette hält, erkennt die Welt" (Only the one who does not hold a chain recognizes the world), emphasize the critical character of the film. By doing this, Klein pays homage to Brecht's theatre theory as well as to the social-critical films of the Weimar Republic. These films, for instance *Kuhle Wampe, oder: Wem gehört die Welt* (*Kuhle Wampe or Who Owns the World?*, Slatan Dudow, 1933), uses avant-garde techniques, such as montage, crossfade, and break of illusion, to encourage the viewers to actively participate in political changes of society. Comparable to these social-critical films, *Die Geschichte vom armen Hassan* represents the learning process of the main protagonist, who finally overcomes all obstacles.

Another source of inspiration for Klein's work is Italian neorealism, which played a major role in the early DEFA productions. As is typical of neorealist films, the fairy-tale story is set amongst the poor, highlighting the significant part of the working class. The meagre furnishings and the plain dresses contradict usual expectations in relation to a fairy-tale setting. Klein wanted to make the audience reflect on the causes of poverty and misuse of power. Due to the sophisticated structure—with a frame story, which serves as a meta-level and substitutes the opening credits, and an inner story that focuses on the fairy tale and the multiple references to different avant-garde film movements—Klein's film can be regarded as the most radical fairy-tale film produced by the DEFA studios.

Nevertheless, other fairy-tale films followed, such as the popular *König Drosselbart* (*King Thrushbeard*, Walter Beck, 1965). The significance of Brecht's theory of estrangement, as well as the impact of vanguard tendencies on GDR children's films has not yet been explored in all its facets, which probably has to do with the films' supposed adherence to social realism, which implies that their avant-garde aspects were hardly noticed. This demand hampered the reception of the Russian filmmaker Elem Klimov's debut film, *Dobro požalovat', ili postoronnim vhod vospreščjon* (*Welcome, or No Trespassing*, 1964; in the United Kingdom, the film had the title *No Holiday for Inochkin*). Shortly after its completion, this children's film was deemed "anti-Soviet" and was banned as a result. The title refers to a banner above the entrance of a summer pioneer camp.

Children from all over the country are invited to spend their summer holidays in an idyllic river landscape. Ten-year-old Kostya Inochkin (Viktor Kosykh) comes into conflict with the authoritarian camp leader, Dynin (Yevgeni Yevstigneyev), because he opposes to the latter's disciplinary measures. When Kostya breaks one of the cardinal rules, by swimming out alone to an island, he is expelled from camp. Since Kostya is afraid that his grandmother will die from sorrow, he hides in the camp, covertly supported by his fellows. Shortly before the beginning of a summer festival, the children rebel against Dynin's strict regime. He is removed from office, while a popular female teacher becomes the new administrator. The final scenes visualize the joy of freedom, when children and adults swim together and, unrealistically, even jump over the river—which could be interpreted as a symbol of liberation.

Klimov deliberately used montage and other aesthetic means that recall early Russian avant-garde movies. Several film sequences are obviously inspired by Sergei Eisenstein's *Bronenossez Potyomkin* (*Battleship Potemkin*, 1925). In one passage, Kostya is sitting on his suitcase at the train station, awaiting the train which should carry him home. This scene fades into Kostya's world of imagination, as he envisages the sudden death of his grandmother, her funeral, and the eulogy of the mayor. The camera shows the funeral procession from a bird's eye perspective. The coffin bearers and the mourners that follow form a question mark, surrounded by a ring of bystanders (Figure 4.3). Kostya, who is feeling guilty, is situated outside the group, emphasizing his outsider position.

FIGURE 4.3. Kostya at his grandmother's funeral (*Dobro požalovat', ili postoronnim vhod vospreščjon*, 1964, Mosfilm). Frame-grab.

This scene is an ironic allusion to the funeral procession in *Battleship Potemkin*, when a huge crowd of mourners follows the coffin of the shot sailor.

Another scene is set at night: Kostya secretly sneaks into the pioneer camp and walks along a path which is lined by huge stone figures. In the boy's imagination, these figures become alive: a drummer beats the drum, another figure plays the trumpet, and a third figure stretches an arc. This scene is reminiscent of the famous episode in Eisenstein's movie when the stone lions placed at the staircase of Odessa begin to move, serving as a symbol for the revolution. Afraid of the stone figures, Kostya hides in a wooden pedestal beneath a monument. When he closes the door, an arrow penetrates it. This surprising occurrence points to the ambiguity of the stone figures: it is not clear whether they are merely a part of Kostya's fearful vision or actually become alive. The arrow in the wooden door, which is still visible the next morning, seems to indicate the second interpretation.

References to Russian cinema and culture of the 1920s and 1930s infuse Klimov's film throughout. In one scene, for instance, the young pioneers recite a poem by Vladimir Majakovsky. After committing suicide in 1930, Mayakovsky was persona non grata in the Soviet Union. For this reason, the recital of one of his famous poems could be interpreted as a provocation. Consequently, the camp leader immediately prohibits the intended performance of the poem at the summer festival and demands the recital of a pioneer song instead. This is not the only reason the film was banned in 1964. The sharp criticism of Soviet bureaucracy and of the authoritarian—and even fanatic behaviour— of Dynin were a thorn in the side of sceptical critics. The film officially premiered in 1986 within the context of the *Perestroika* movement and was acclaimed. It is said that more than thirteen million viewers saw the movie in the Soviet Union.

The three films discussed here are representatives of the heyday of post-war children's films that aspired to renew the image of childhood as well as to introduce new ways of seeing. They achieved this by implementing a film language influenced by pre-war avant-garde movements. Moreover, they combined this film aesthetic with novel ideas on childhood and the role of the child audience. The filmmakers wanted to ignite the child's imagination but also to take the role of children seriously. While Lamorisse emphasizes the significance of the child's imagination as a counterpoint to rationality and a world dominated by grey colours and a sombre mood, Klein und Klimov encourage the child audience to reflect on the political and societal aspects associated with the content of the films. They use vanguard techniques and aesthetic strategies to call the viewers' attention to the critical aspects of their films.

References to the Avant-Garde in Contemporary Children's Films

The production of children's films in the twenty-first century can hardly be overlooked due to the sheer amount of constantly released new films. Aside from the increasing tendency to create films that cross the boundaries between children's films and films produced for an adult audience in relation to the content and the style—often termed as family films—some prestigious filmmakers show a deep interest in the early history of film and the achievements of avant-garde films. How this trend flows into contemporary children's films can be seen in two case studies: a short, animated interlude in *Harry Potter and the Deathly Hallows—Part 1* (David Yates, 2010) and the live-action movie, *Hugo* (Martin Scorsese, 2011). Both films were extremely successful at the box office. Despite their supposed mainstream aesthetics, on closer inspection, they reveal numerous references to early avant-garde cinema. While the animation film is inspired by Lotte Reiniger's silhouette films, Scorsese's movie pays tribute to the early films created by Georges Méliès.

The *Harry Potter* franchise demonstrates how hugely profitable a successful children's media franchise could be. The seven *Harry Potter* novels by J. K. Rowling—as well as the eight film adaptations (2001–2011)—influenced at least one generation of young readers and viewers. The *Harry Potter* books and films are distinguished by a hybrid mixture of genres—which is one of the main reasons for their overwhelming success.[30] Any reference to avant-garde trends seems to be out of the question, with one notable exception. The penultimate film in the series, *Harry Potter and the Deathly Hallows—Part 1*, includes a three-minute animated sequence created by Ben Hibon. It tells a story within a story: "The Tale of the Three Brothers." This tale plays a significant role because it anticipates the final battle with Voldemort. The story is about three wizard brothers who attempt to outwit Death, to no avail. The first brother gets a powerful wand but is killed by a jealous wizard. The second brother obtains a stone which can call dead people from the grave, but his beloved bride is still cold and emotionless, and he dies of despair. The youngest brother receives the cloak of invisibility because he had asked to go forth without being seen by Death. When he gets old, he bequeaths the cloak to his son and happily accepts being led away by Death.

In the eponymous novel, this tale is part of a book bequeathed to Hermione by Dumbledore. Because Hermione reads the story aloud to her audience, director David Yates wanted to visualize the content of the tale, but in a different film language. Ben Hibon suggested creating an animated film sequence that would combine traditional oriental shadow theatre with the aesthetic of the silhouette films by Lotte Reiniger.[31] As Hibon has pointed out, he intended to imitate the "graphical and naïve" style of Reiniger.[32] The characters are silhouette figures placed against a sepia-toned landscape. Following the tradition of shadow theatre and the silhouette film, the figures express their emotions by means of gestures and bodily postures (Figure 4.4). What distinguishes Hibon's animated sequence from these role models is the usage of a 3-D camera. Hence, the animation has an enhanced depth effect that intensifies the uncanny atmosphere. The artistry of this inserted sequence has been praised by several critics, more so because it perfectly captures the gloomy mood of the tale and foreshadows the perils Harry Potter and his companions will face in the story. The connection between the Technicolor live-action film and the sepia-toned animation not only contrasts two film aesthetic traditions, but also points to the significance of fantasy: the animated sequence illustrates the listeners' power of imagination: they can (mentally) visualize what

FIGURE 4.4. The death of the first brother, indicated by blown-out candle. *Harry Potter and the Deathly Hallows: Part 1* (2010, Warner Bros.). Frame-grab.

Hermione is reading to them. Moreover, the animated sequence demonstrates that a conscious reference to avant-garde film within a mainstream film does not necessarily have to be contradictory. Quite the contrary: this strategy adds new layers of meaning in relation to the role of imagination and the predictability of future events.

It seems to be the case that an avant-garde aesthetic is permissible in mainstream transnational films only if used in brief interludes; a Hollywood-style film could not all be in an avant-garde style, mostly for marketing reasons and for fear of alienating the mass audience. Instead, Hollywood movies quote from avant-garde films, commodifying the avant-garde cinema rather than practicing it. A case in point is the feature film *Hugo* (2011), directed by Martin Scorsese. The film received numerous accolades and awards, including five Oscars and the Golden Globe for Best Directing for Scorsese in 2012.

Based on the picture novel *The Invention of Hugo Cabret* (2007) by Brian Selznick, the film is a homage to Georges Méliès, particularly his silent movie *Le Voyage dans la Lune* (*A Trip to the Moon*, 1902).[33] It is replete with references to the early history of cinema, with an emphasis on Méliès's significance as the initiator of the "Cinema of Attraction" and the inventor of stop motion.[34] *Hugo* is a nostalgic look back at early film history, with quotations from famous films of the silent film era. Film connoisseurs will recognize references to films by the Brothers Lumière, Charlie Chaplin, Buster Keaton, Fritz Lang, Harold Lloyd, and Jean Vigo. While the opening credits impressively demonstrate the achievements of modern technology in filmmaking (Scorsese used stereoscopy in a breathtaking tracking shot of the Place d'Étoile), the closing credits are a kind of throwback, as they render the crew and actors visually, in framed inserts in the manner of early silent movies. Thus the credits span the history of film from its beginning to present time.[35] As such, they emphasize the close connection between the history of avant-garde films and Scorsese's demand to continue the filmic heritage through a children's film, albeit in a nostalgic, and sometimes even eclectic, manner.[36] Seen in this light,

Hugo testifies that avant-garde styles can lose their iconoclasm through repeated use, and that formerly radical stylistic techniques can be assimilated into the mainstream and co-opted for commercial purposes.

CONCLUSION: AVANT-GARDE AND CHILDREN'S FILM STUDIES

Most of the films presented in this chapter are now considered classics. They are available on DVD and regularly shown on TV or on film festivals. Moreover, these films were sources of inspiration for younger generations of filmmakers. In contrast to most mainstream films for children, children's films influenced by avant-garde movements are quite sophisticated, confronting the viewers with complex artistic strategies, such as montage and mixing of genres, to instigate a new way of seeing. Moreover, they make ample use of references to the history of film, with an emphasis on silent movies and avant-garde films, thus forming part of that very film tradition. A history of children's films and the avant-garde still represents a lacuna in film studies; it is one of the most under-addressed topics in international research in children's films. Addressing this neglect would broaden our knowledge of the potentiality of children's film. It would also show that a clear-cut border between films for children and films for adults cannot always be drawn, because both realms profit from the advancements in film technologies and film aesthetics, which were often developed and designed by avant-garde filmmakers. One can assume that children's films which make ample use of avant-garde techniques and references to avant-garde cinema pave the way for the renewal and further development of children's films in the long run. This is another topic that needs greater attention. The same applies to the crucial question whether children as the intended audience may understand the complex strategies and intermedial references used in the respective children's films—an issue that is connected to film literacy. Finally, because many children's films are adaptations of previously published children's books, a question arises about how the avant-garde techniques advanced in the books will re-appear in the film adaptations, or whether they have to be altered to fit the new technological affordances of the film medium. These are subjects worthy of academic investigation, particularly in relation to the connection between avant-garde aesthetics, film literacy, and novel film technologies in children's films.

NOTES

1. Malcolm Turvey, *The Filming of Modern Life: European Avant-Garde Film of the 1920s* (Cambridge, MA: MIT Press, 2011).
2. Bill Nichols, *Engaging Cinema: An Introduction to Film Studies* (New York: W. W. Norton, 2010), p. 190.

3. Scott MacDonald, *Avant-Garde Film: Motion Studies* (Cambridge, UK: Cambridge University Press, 1993), p. 2.

4. Hubert van den Berg, "Mapping Old Traces of the New: For a Historical Typography of 20th Century Avant-Garde(s) in the European Cultural Fields," *Arcadia* 41 (2006), pp. 331-351.

5. Rosalind E. Krauss, *The Originality of the Avant-Garde and Other Modernist Myths* (1986; repr. Cambridge, MA: MIT Press, 1999); Paul Mann, *The Theory-Death of the Avant-Garde* (Bloomington: Indiana University Press, 1991).

6. Peter Bürger, *Theory of the Avant-Garde* (1974; repr. Minneapolis: University of Minnesota Press, 1984).

7. Elina Druker and Bettina Kümmerling-Meibauer (eds.), *Children's Literature and the Avant-Garde* (Amsterdam: John Benjamins, 2015), p. 3.

8. Tom Gunning, "The Cinema of Attractions: Early Film, Its Spectator and the Avant-Garde," in Thomas Elsaesser (ed.), *Early Cinema: Space, Frame, Narrative* (London: BFI Publishing, 1990), pp. 56-62.

9. William Verrone, *The Avant-Garde Feature Film: A Critical History* (Jefferson, NC: McFarland, 2011), p. 24.

10. Turvey, *Filming of Modern Life*, p. 56.

11. Michael O'Pray, *Avant-Garde Film: Forms, Themes, and Passion* (London: Wallflower, 2007).

12. Verrone, *Avant-Garde Feature Film*, p. 18.

13. Ibid., p. 27.

14. Annika Schoemann, *Der deutsche Animationsfilm: Von den Anfängen bis zur Gegenwart 1909–2001* (Sankt Augustin, Germany: Gardez!, 2003), p. 134.

15. Giannalberto Bendazzi, *Animation: A World History*, vol. 1: *Foundations: The Golden Age* (New York: Routledge, 2017), p. 59.

16. Lotte Reiniger, *Shadow Puppets, Shadow Theatre and Shadow Films* (Boston: Plays, 1975).

17. Belá Balász, *Der Geist des Films* (Frankfurt: Suhrkamp, 2001), p. 85.

18. Evamarie Blattner et al. (eds.), *Animation und Avantgarde: Lotte Reiniger und der absolute Film*, exhibition catalogue (Tübingen: Stadtmuseum, 2015).

19. Kristina Moen, *Film and Fairy Tales: The Birth of Modern Fantasy from The Blue Bird to Harry Potter* (London: I.B. Tauris, 2013); Bruno Girveau and Roger Diederen (eds.), *Walt Disneys wunderbare Welt und ihre Wurzeln in der europäischen Kunst* (Munich: Hirmer Verlag, 2008).

20. On the music in *Fantasia*, see Irene Kletschke, *Klangbilder: Walt Disneys "Fantasia" (1940)* (Stuttgart: Franz Steiner Verlag, 2011).

21. Amy M. Davis, "The Fall and Rise of *Fantasia*," in Melvyn Stokes and Richard Maltby (eds.), *Hollywood Spectatorship: Changing Perceptions of Cinema Audiences* (London: BFI Publishing, 2001), p. 63.

22. Girveau and Diederen, *Walt Disneys wunderbare Welt*, p. 57.

23. Bettina Kümmerling-Meibauer, "Erich Kästner: Emil und die Detektive (1929)," in Bettina Kümmerling-Meibauer, *Kinder- und Jugendliteratur: Eine Einführung* (Darmstadt: Wissenschaftliche Buchgesellschaft, 2012), pp. 101-109.

24. *Pega Ladrão* (Brazil: Alberto Pieralisi, 1957); *Emil to tantei-tachi* (Japan: Mitsuo Wakasugi, 1951); *Emil and the Detectives* (Milton Rosmer: UK, 1935); *Emil and the Detectives* (USA: Peter Tewksbury, , 1964).

25. Tao Zhang, *Vom Premake zum Remake: Gender-Diskurse und intermediale Bezüge in den deutschen Verfilmungen der Kinderromane Erich Kästners* (Heidelberg: Universitätsverlag Winter, 2018).

26. Bettina Kümmerling-Meibauer and Thomas Koebner (eds.), *Kinder- und Jugendfilm* (Stuttgart: Reclam, 2010).

27. Inés Dussel, "Iconoclastic Images in the History of Education: Another Look at Children in Revolt in Two Children's Films from the 1930s," *Pedagogica Historica: International Journal of the History of Education* 53 (2017), pp. 668-682.

28. Paulo Emilio Salles, Gomes, *Jean Vigo* (Berkeley: University of California Press, 1971).

29. Qinna Shen, *The Politics of Magic: DEFA Fairy-Tale Films* (Detroit, MI: Wayne State University Press, 2015).

30. Bettina Kümmerling-Meibauer, "Never-Ending Sequels? Seriality in Children's Films," in Casie Hermansson and Janet Zepernick (eds.), *The Palgrave Handbook of Children's Film and Television* (Cham, Switzerland: Palgrave Macmillan, 2019), pp. 533-548.

31. Hannes Rall, "Lange Schatten einer Pionierin: Der Einfluss von Lotte Reiniger auf nachfolgende Trickfilmergenerationen," in Ute Dettmar, Claudia Maria Pecher, and Ron Schlesinger (eds.), *Märchen im Medienwechsel* (Stuttgart: Metzler, 2017), pp. 101-120.

32. Bill Desowitz, "Shadow Play with Potter's Tale of Three Brothers: Ben Hibon Discusses His Acclaimed Animated Sequence in *The Deathly Hallows, Part 1*," *Animation World Network*, December 3, 2010, https://www.awn.com/animationworld/shadow-play-potters-tale-three-brothers [accessed December 15, 2019]; Ben Hibon, "How the First Animated Sequence in a Harry Potter Movie Came About," *Los Angeles Times*, January 28, 2011, http://latimesblogs.latimes.com/awards/2011/01/how-the-first-animated-sequence-in-a-Harry-Potter-movie-came-about.html [accessed December 15, 2019].

33. On the significance of this film on international film history, see Matthew Solomon, *Fantastic Voyages of the Cinematic Imagination: Georges Méliès's Trip to the Moon* (New York: State University of New York Press, 2011).

34. Jacques Malthête (ed.), *Méliès, magie et cinema* (Paris: Paris-musées, 2002); Elizabeth Ezra, *Georges Méliès: The Birth of the Author* (Manchester, UK: Manchester University Press, 2002).

35. On the impact of the credits on the main film, see Bettina Kümmerling-Meibauer, "Paratexts in Children's Films and the Concept of Meta-filmic Awareness," *Journal of Educational Media, Memory, and Society* 5:2 (2013), pp. 108-123.

36. David Bordwell, *On the History of Film Style* (Cambridge, MA: Harvard University Press, 1997), p. 253.

BIBLIOGRAPHY

Bendazzi, Giannalberto. *Animation: A World History*. Vol. 1. *Foundations: The Golden Age*. New York: Routledge, 2017.

Blattner, Evamarie, Bernd Desinger, Matthias Knop, and Wiebke Ratzeburg, eds. *Animation und Avantgarde: Lotte Reiniger und der absolute Film*. Exhibition catalogue. Tübingen: Stadtmuseum, 2015.

Davis, Amy M. "The Fall and Rise of *Fantasia*." In Melvyn Stokes and Richard Maltby (eds.), *Hollywood Spectatorship: Changing Perceptions of Cinema Audiences*. London: BFI Publishing, 2001, pp. 63–78.

Druker, Elina, and Bettina Kümmerling-Meibauer, eds. *Children's Literature and the Avant-Garde*. Amsterdam: John Benjamins, 2015.

Gee, Felicity. *Magic Realism in World Cinema: The Avant-Garde in Exile*. New York: Routledge, 2019.

Girveau, Bruno, and Roger Diederen, eds. *Walt Disneys wunderbare Welt und ihre Wurzeln in der europäischen Kunst*. Munich: Hirmer Verlag, 2008.

Graf, Alexander, and Dietrich Scheunermann. *Avant-Garde Film*. Amsterdam: Rodopi, 2007.

MacDonald, Scott. *Avant-Garde Film: Motion Studies*. Cambridge, UK: Cambridge University Press, 1993.

Malthête, Jacques, ed. *Méliès, magie et cinema*. Paris: Paris-musées, 2002.

O'Pray, Michael. *Avant-Garde Film: Forms, Themes, and Passion*. London: Wallflower, 2007.

Rall, Hannes. "Lange Schatten einer Pionierin: Der Einfluss von Lotte Reiniger auf nachfolgende Trickfilmergenerationen." In Ute Dettmar, Claudia Maria Pecher, and Ron Schlesinger (eds.), *Märchen im Medienwechsel*. Stuttgart: Metzler, 2017, pp. 101–120.

Reiniger, Lotte. *Shadow Puppets, Shadow Theatre and Shadow Films*. Boston: Plays, 1975.

Schoemann, Annika. *Der deutsche Animationsfilm: Von den Anfängen bis zur Gegenwart 1909–2001*. Sankt Augustin, Germany: Gardez!, 2003.

Turvey, Malcolm. *The Filming of Modern Life: European Avant-Garde Film of the 1920s*. Cambridge, MA: MIT Press, 2011.

Verrone, William. *The Avant-Garde Feature Film: A Critical History*. Jefferson, NC: McFarland, 2011.

CHAPTER 5

··

INTERTEXTUALITY AND "ADULT" HUMOUR IN CHILDREN'S FILM

··

SAM SUMMERS

ABOUT twenty minutes into DreamWorks Animation's *The Boss Baby* (Tom McGrath, 2017), the titular Boss Baby, voiced by Alec Baldwin, is holding an important meeting. The besuited infant has been sent from the clandestine Baby Corp to organize the neighbourhood children for a secret mission. Sophisticated and business-like, Boss Baby struggles to get the regular, childlike babies to focus on the task, and their lack of intelligence and short attention spans cause tensions to escalate. Eventually, Boss Baby explodes, hurling a string of insults at his "employees." One oblivious child grabs a cookie from the table. "Put that cookie down!" the Boss exclaims. "Cookies are for closers!"

The children in the audience—and, indeed, many adults—will likely pay little attention to this line, coming as it does amid a fast-paced rant by the Boss Baby, accompanied by up-tempo strings and followed immediately by a quick comic set piece in which a talking teddy bear malfunctions. Sufficiently informed adult viewers, though, may take notice, and even laugh at the inconspicuous rebuke—to those in the know, it is an obvious reference to one of Baldwin's most iconic roles, that of the sharp-tongued executive Blake in *Glengarry Glen Ross* (James Foley, 1992). In that film, Blake has been sent from corporate to motivate the protagonists, a group of real estate salesmen, which he does through verbal abuse and a promise that the two men who close the fewest deals that month will be fired. "Put the coffee down!," Blake memorably shouts at one employee. "Coffee's for closers only!"

Though the reference to Baldwin's earlier film might elicit a chuckle from savvy viewers, it serves no other apparent purpose in the animated film. There are, of course, parallels between the two scenes: in each a slick, aggressive operator arrives from the head office to wrangle a group of oblivious employees, but in the wider context of *The Boss Baby* the line has little relevance—none of the children are being asked to "close" anything, per se. Accordingly, formally speaking, the film does not encourage the audience to dwell on the line. It passes quickly, instantly interrupted by the abrupt shouting of the talking teddy bear and the babies' bursting into tears as the Boss tackles the toy. The reference is afforded just enough breathing space to register with the informed, but not enough for the "closers" non sequitur to appear incongruent to everyone else. Seemingly aware of the potential obtrusiveness of the reference and not wanting to jeopardize any long-term suspension of disbelief in its world-building, the film endeavours through the pace of its editing to bury the line in the action, leaving it visible to only a select few.

Intriguingly, the film's trailer takes an oppositional approach in deploying the line. That it was included in the trailer at all is noteworthy, given the amount of material from the ninety-minute film that was presumably available to the editors of the two-minute commercial. However, this gag—the only reference to an explicitly adult-oriented text in the film—is given a prime spot at the end of the trailer. Since continuity and suspension of disbelief are less of a concern in the nonnarrative advertisement, the incongruous joke can be placed out of context as a "stinger," reaching out directly to informed adult viewers. Here, rather than being couched in frantic action and dialogue, it is preceded only by the reveal of the film's title and followed only by its release date. The line itself is even extended, with a tiny but perceptible gap added between "Put" and "that cookie down!." This unusual emphasis, particularly in a trailer for a film that, given its subject matter, can easily appear to skew younger than many other modern animated family films, indicates a studio eager to position its latest effort as having added appeal for an adult audience.

This brief example illustrates a conflict that is inherent in the use of intertextual jokes directed to an adult audience in children's films. The different ways in which this line is framed in the film and trailer —glossed over in the former to preserve continuity for the general audience, but highlighted in the latter to advertise the film's potential adult appeal—each reflect different strategies that have been deployed to prioritize different segments of the audience. Presenting a number of case studies from the recent history of children's cinema, the chapter will explore the ways in which the push and pull between a film's deference to a general audience of children or to an audience of informed adults in such instances plays out on screen. Looking closely at the formal aspects of these jokes, as well as their positioning in their movies' narratives, it will illustrate how filmmaking techniques participate in and facilitate this double coding.

WHY REFERENCES?

Including humour aimed at adults in film texts targeted, at least in part, toward children is nothing new, of course. Many Golden Age animation houses, whose shorts were originally created to prefigure live-action features in diverse programmes of entertainment, were aware that they had to accommodate and entertain audiences of all ages. The animator Tex Avery was among the first to build adult humour into films that were ostensibly suitable for children. As Paul Wells puts it, Avery "clearly understood that children would be appeased by physical slapstick while adults required a more knowing, *self-conscious* approach," which typically manifested itself in jokes revolving around violent, morbid, or sexual themes, as well as Brechtian metareference.[1] This same commitment to dual appeal is present in a trend that experienced a significant upswing around the turn of the millennium. As Julian Cornell notes, "Since the 1990s in particular, children's films have seen a deployment of the divergent mode of address, but one that acknowledges the presence of adult spectators," crucially typified by "intertextual references to popular culture and to cinema history, often ancillary to plot and character development, [which] are meant to appeal to adults' superior cultural knowledge."[2] Meanwhile, Noel Brown suggests that "since *Toy Story*, 'postmodern' narrative strategies"—of which intertextuality is a prime example—"have become closely associated with family-orientated animation, being viewed as integral to the medium's cachet with teenagers and adults."[3] This is primarily a commercial strategy aimed at appeasing as wide a demographic as possible. Brown argues that intertextuality "also functions to strengthen appeal to older children who (generally) are seeking to graduate from the fantasies of the child's world that continue to be linked with the 'children's film' in its simplest iterations."[4] It is clear and well-documented, then, that contemporary children's films are wont to employ adult intertextual references as a means of appealing to audiences across a broad range of demographics, and to exploit the various effects resulting from this blurring of boundaries, both between texts and between the child-adult dichotomy. This chapter focuses on the techniques involved in implementing this strategy.

It should be noted that this is largely a post-1990 phenomenon in feature films, with the likes of *Toy Story* (John Lasseter, 1995), *Aladdin* (Ron Clements and John Musker, 1992), and *Shrek* (Andrew Adamson and Vicky Jenson, 2001) serving as key milestones in advancing the technique's popularity. Given that financial concerns are a key motivator for including these adult-oriented references, the technique is less common outside the commercial mainstream. It is also most evident in North American films, though it is present in other commercial Western cinemas as well, including the output of the United Kingdom's Aardman studio and France's live-action *Asterix* series (1999–2012). As such, while the approaches developed in this chapter can be applied to any children's film regardless of time and place, I will focus on commercial Hollywood films from the 1990s onward, as they best exemplify the range of the technique's permutations, and are representative of a broad industrial trend.

As for what constitutes an "adult" intertext, it would, of course, be naive to suggest that there are referents that no children will be familiar with or that all adults will recognize. This chapter aims to avoid this implication wherever possible, using the phrase "adult-oriented" to describe certain intertexts that can reasonably be *presumed* to be inaccessible to most children, either because they are considered unsuitable (carrying an R rating in North America, for example) or because their cultural prominence has faded by the time of the hypertextual film's release. To elaborate, adult-oriented intertextual referents in children's films can be broadly grouped into two overlapping categories based on what constitutes their "adultness." The first and most obvious category includes intertexts that are explicitly and exclusively aimed at adult audiences, owing to their lewd, violent, or otherwise "mature" nature. Rarely, if ever, are any of these aspects directly replicated in the children's hypertext; rather, the quoted elements serve as a synecdoche for the film as a whole, *evoking* the "inappropriate" content without *invoking* it. The second category includes those intertexts that are not necessarily inappropriate but that children are unlikely to be familiar with or, at least, *as familiar* with because of the passage of time. Stan Beeler has commented on the effects of this latter category with reference to music, noting the preponderance of songs, or covers of songs, from the 1960s and 1970s in the children's films of the 2000s. For Beeler, the likes of the Bee Gees's "Night Fever" in *Madagascar* (Eric Darnell and Tom McGrath, 2005) or the Monkees's "I'm a Believer," as performed by Smash Mouth in *Shrek*, are particularly potent tools for "enhanc[ing] the viewing experience for adults without directly presenting material that would be disturbing for the primary audience of young children,"[5] given that their "familiarity to the older generation certainly sends a welcome to certain members of the audience."[6] This can also be applied to innocuous-but-dated reference points from other forms of media, such as the extended *Dating Game* skit in *Shrek* replicating the presentation and iconography of a television show that hadn't been produced in its original format since the 1980s. This appeal to familiarity is only one function of such references, however; the other, of course, being comedy.

Turning to existing theories of comedy and laughter and their associated frameworks, we can begin to elucidate the comic potential of references to adult-oriented texts in children's films. Jerry Palmer offers one comprehensive summary of comedic processes. Drawing on the earlier work of John Morreall,[7] Palmer identifies three major sources of humour:

(1) Where Humour is derived from a sensation of superiority over what is laughed at; (2) where humour derives from a sensation of psychological relief; (3) where humour derives from the perception of incongruity in what is laughed at.[8]

In our context here, the superiority theory would at least seem to account for references that are deployed to *parodic* effect, a *parody* being, in Gérard Genette's terms, "an imitation that is more heavily loaded with *satirical or caricatural* effect."[9] In cases in which the hypotext is somehow mocked or belittled via its re-presentation within the hypertext, the humour can be seen to derive from the audience's "sensation of superiority" over the referent and, indeed, from the hypertext itself. This plainly the case in the films in the *Shrek* franchise, whose raison d'être is the subversion and ridicule of the tropes and conventions of fairy-tale stories and films. When it comes to more adult-oriented source texts, however, any satiric effect encoded in such references is often more difficult to discern, where it exists at all. When *Shrek* movies invoke the likes of *The Matrix* (*Shrek*), *Cops* (*Shrek 2*, Andrew Adamson, Kelly Asbury, and Conrad Vernon, 2004), and *The Untouchables* (*Shrek Forever After*, Mike Mitchell, 2010), it doesn't mock them directly by revealing their flaws or absurdities, but simply re-presents them in the film's animated fairy-tale setting. Indeed, this is also the approach taken with the *Glengarry Glen Ross* quote in *The Boss Baby*; the line, along with the movie from which it is derived, is in a sense rendered ridiculous by being delivered by a diminutive infant as opposed to the imposing character portrayed by the live-action Baldwin, but there is no joke here with anything to say *about* the 1992 film. In fact, the quote is the *form* of the joke rather than its *object*. The humour is derived from this contextual discrepancy, yes; but *The Boss Baby* itself, and its ostensible innocence as a children's animated film, is the target of the gag. In this way, it is incongruity, not superiority, that is chiefly being invoked.

Incongruous comedy, as summarized by Andrew Stott, consists of "the inventive drawing together of apparently distant ideas for the amusement and intellectual thrill of the listener," as well as a "crossing [of] ideational boundaries and the bringing of one thing into a taxonomy to which it is not considered to belong" and "a displacement of order that simultaneously acknowledges order and reveals its absurdity."[10] In the case of *Boss Baby*'s *Glengarry* joke and, indeed, in any explicit reference to an overtly adult-oriented text in a children's film, two distant ideas are effectively drawn together, then, these being the audience's conceptions of "adult" media and "children's" media and the attendant connotations. Most prominently, the presumed innocence of children's media is contrasted with the various "inappropriate" attributes of adult media, even if these are not directly quoted. For example, the "coffee is for closers" line that *Boss Baby* paraphrases is innocuous in and of itself, but anyone familiar with its original context will be aware of the profanities littering the rest of Baldwin's monologue. By the same token, such adult intertexts are brought into a taxonomy to which they are not considered to belong, fulfilling the first two aspects of Stott's definition and gesturing toward the third. This—the "displacement of order" that "reveals its absurdity"—highlights the true object of incongruous humour, that being the strictures of the hypertext into which the incongruous element is placed. Indeed, going into more detail regarding the kinds of "established taxonomies" that can be disrupted by playing host to comic incongruities, Stott gives "the collision or juxtaposition of the great with the low, or the humble adopting the airs of the elite" as examples.[11]

The contrast between childhood innocence and "adult" themes that is drawn by these kinds of intertextual references slots neatly alongside these boundaries. Citing Jacqueline Rose's argument regarding the binary opposition between the roles of adult and child in children's fiction—"a world in which the adult comes first (author, maker, giver) and the child comes after (reader, product, receiver), but where neither of them enter the space in between"[12]—Cornell suggests that adult-oriented intertextual referents have the effect of "reinforcing childhood innocence for adult spectators, of separating them from children through jokes young viewers are not expected to fathom."[13] The references, then, work to support this binary while also drawing attention to it; but equally, part of their function is to suggest a clear disregard for that very same boundary, evinced by their very inclusion. An allusion to an R-rated film may be, by its nature, a joke reserved for adult viewers who are set apart by what Cornell terms their "specific, learned cultural knowledge," but by exposing the vulnerability of the children's film to incursion from corruptive outside elements, it calls childhood innocence into question as much as it reinforces it.[14] In perforating the accepted, yet ultimately arbitrary, boundaries of what constitutes "children's cinema," these referential gags reveal, and revel in, their absurdity, drawing humour—for the adult viewer, at least—from the presumption that there was a boundary in the first place.

The "space between" spoken of by Rose is, in this case, the knowledge gap separating the idealized child viewer from the idealized adult viewer. This is not to suggest that each of the films discussed in this chapter exists as two versions, the "adult" version and the "child" version, depending on who is watching. In fact, there are numerous potential versions, owing to the fact that most viewers, regardless of age, will be able to decode some allusions but not others. And yet, as Cornell has suggested, by including references to unambiguously adult-oriented intertexts, certain children's films implicitly construct their ideal consumers: the child wholly ignorant, the adult wholly informed. It is important, then, to look at the ways in which films work not to bridge the knowledge gap, but to obfuscate it, affording prominence to intertextual adult humour while ensuring continuity of narrative and tone for the large portion of their audience who, it must be presumed, lack the knowledge necessary to interpret them. Three common "strategies" can be identified by analysing the corpus of contemporary children's films that attempt to integrate comic references to adult-oriented hypotexts—that is, three approaches to orienting these allusions in the context of each film and its diegetic story world to account for the disparities in its audience's knowledge base. These are *embedding, segmentation*, and *normalization*, and they differ from one another in terms of the relationship they depict between the adult-oriented intertextual gag and the film as a whole, modulating the obtrusiveness and specificity of the reference as well as its positioning in the film. The remainder of this chapter will illustrate these strategies and explain their unique functions and the ways in which they can affect the reception of this particular form of incongruous humour on the part of their blended audience.

EMBEDDING INTERTEXTUALITY

I have already touched upon the first of these strategies, *embedding*. This is when the site of the intertextual reference—the sign in the film that directs informed viewers toward the intertext—is couched within the formal and semiotic orthodoxy of the scene in such a way as to render it unnoticeable to the uninformed, as exemplified by the *Glengarry Glen Ross* joke in *The Boss Baby*. As we have seen, the "cookies are for closers" line in *Boss Baby* is utterly benign in its presentation: its business-like tone and corporate-sounding jargon fit with what we understand of the Boss's character and with the context of the scene. Further, the editing of the scene subsumes the line as part of a wider sequence, obscuring the fact that it is a joke. Isolating the line—whether through pacing and editing, as was done in the film's trailer, or by having it contrast jarringly with the film's established narrative logic and tone—would have called attention to it and, potentially, given *Boss Baby*'s overall comedic bent, encourage its interpretation as a joke. However, this joke will be understood only by a select few and exclude the vast majority of the film's child audience, and so the film opts for the less disruptive approach of embedding it within the scene, preserving continuity for the audience as a whole. This is a common strategy. As Brown writes, with particular reference to *Toy Story*, "It is important to emphasize that while the film's 'adult' modes of address require close analysis, they are never vital components of the scenes in which they are placed." But not all examples of embedding work by making the joke invisible to the uninformed.[15] Others, such as the *Toy Story* jokes Brown highlights, present adult-oriented intertextual jokes synchronized with broader gags that are accessible to anyone. For instance, when Mr. Potato Head's face is muddled up, causing him to explain "I'm Picasso!", "the incongruity of the misaligned face still works as a sight gag," effectively drawing attention away from the Picasso comment for those who may find it confusing, and providing an analogous moment of levity that caters to the uninformed.[16]

Regardless of whether the site of the reference can be considered incongruous, in the case of embedded references, the comic incongruity of the adult-oriented intertextual reference takes place in a different space altogether. For instance, the "cookies are for closers" line may be considered incongruous insofar as all of the Boss's behaviour and dialogue is incongruous coming from a baby, but this is not the subject of the adult-oriented joke. The unique incongruity of the quotation exists not in the line of dialogue itself, but in what it connotes—that is, the decidedly adult-oriented film *Glengarry Glen Ross*. As a further example, consider the following sequence from *Madagascar*: Stranded on the titular island having unwittingly escaped from his home at the Central Park Zoo, the pampered lion Alex is craving his favourite food, steak. He's used to being fed regularly by the zookeepers, never considering where steaks come from, despite the fact that his best friends are prey animals. The film's core conflict revolves around Alex slowly being taken by the urge to eat his friends, illustrated through dream sequences and hallucinations involving steaks. In one such sequence Alex falls asleep beneath the stars, the "camera" tilting up toward the sky, as hundreds of steaks begin to fade into view, raining down in slow motion. We cut between shots of the falling steaks and shots of Alex lying on his back on a bed of steaks, staring up at the sky as the meat drifts toward him. We watch him catch a steak and begin licking it, only to have a sharp cut bring us out of Alex's dream and into the real world, where he is revealed to be licking the behind of his friend, Marty the zebra. On its face, the dream sequence serves an important narrative purpose, highlighting Alex's growing craving for meat and seeding the threat that he might turn to eating his friends. Clearly operating on dream logic, implied through the use of fades and slow motion even before the eventual unambiguous reveal that Alex has been asleep this whole time, the scene does not present as incongruous because it is in keeping with what the audience already knows of the characters' thoughts and desires.

For the informed viewer, however, the scene is a clear allusion to the R-rated adult drama *American Beauty* (Sam Mendes, 1999) and the iconic scene in which Lester, the film's middle-aged protagonist, fantasizes about Angela, the teenage girl with whom he has become sexually obsessed. Lying in his bed, he envisions rose petals falling from the sky and Angela lying naked on a bed of them. In *Madagascar*'s version of the fantasy, Alex takes on both of these roles. In addition to the red steaks in Alex's dream that resemble the rose petals, *Madagascar* takes great pains to highlight the similarities. Both scenes use the same three shots: one is a close-up Lester/Alex staring toward the sky; another shows the petals/steaks falling downward toward the camera from the characters' point of view; and the third is a full-body shot of Angela/Alex lying among the petals/steaks. *American Beauty*'s opening theme music is also heard in *Madagascar*, particularly significant in that this is *not* the music that plays during Lester's fantasy sequence; the filmmakers have opted to use the more recognizable piece, with the effect of more clearly signifying the link between the two texts. Using these techniques, *Madagascar* invokes *American Beauty* in a manner that is completely unambiguous to anyone familiar with the latter film, without importing any lexical elements from the R-rated picture that might read as overtly foreign to the context of *Madagascar*. Had Alex's version of the fantasy involved rose petals or, indeed, a naked girl, the scene would have read as nonsensical, disruptive, and potentially alienating for uninformed viewers, because these elements have no basis in what we know of the world or narrative of the film to this point.

Instead, references like this one and *The Boss Baby*'s *Glengarry* quotation rearrange components of their own established language and iconography, composing an allusion from a collage of familiar signs. The "cookies are for closers" line is more straightforward in this regard because it's entirely verbal, using, as noted, language drawn from the lexicon of corporate jargon in which the Boss Baby has already proven himself fluent. Meanwhile, in *Madagascar*, the steak—rendered in an iconic, simplified design—is shown to be Alex's favourite food from early in the film. He is frequently seen eating or discussing steaks throughout the first act, which come to represent his attachment to the zoo and the easy-going, pampered lifestyle it afforded him. Despite its specificity, then, little about the *American Beauty* sequence is overtly incongruous, operating as it does from within the confines of what *Madagascar* has conditioned audiences to expect. The incongruity comes instead from the contrast between the child-friendly nature of *Madagascar* and the seediness and sexuality that the steak-based fantasy connotes for anyone familiar with the scene to which it refers. This recourse to double coding, facilitated by rendering the sites of the references innocuous to the uninformed viewer, is what characterizes embedding as a strategy for integrating adult-oriented intertextual humour into children's films.

SEGMENTING INCONGRUITY

Disney's *Aladdin*, itself a watershed moment in the foregrounding of intertextual adult humour in a major children's film, employs a different strategy: that of segmentation. Paul Wells identifies the film as a "clear exception" in Disney's filmography, ground zero for what he terms the "'loosening' of the Disney text" in the 1990s.[17] This is defined as "the increasing prominence of the cartoonal form," the renewed visibility in mainstream feature animation of the postmodern tropes and techniques associated with Golden Age comic animation such as that of Tex Avery and the Warner Bros. studio.[18] Among these techniques is the use of double-coded humour aimed at accommodating adult audiences, which is indeed a key component of *Aladdin*. In fact, Cornell writes that "perhaps no children's film was as pivotal in this regard as Disney's *Aladdin*," highlighting its "playful semiotic mixing," which "reconstitutes popular culture in terms of its very inappropriateness to the children's movie as one source of humour for the adult audience."[19] The primary (indeed, virtually the *sole*) source of these intertextual incongruities is the character of the genie, played by Robin Williams, who reprises the fluid vocal bricolage and—in tandem with animator Eric Goldberg—breathless kineticism of his stand-up comedy routines. Together the two artists weave verbal and visual intertextual references through all of Genie's most memorable scenes, as he transforms both his body and voice to mimic celebrities, from the contemporary (Arnold Schwarzenegger, Rodney Dangerfield, Arsenio Hall) to the historical (Ed Sullivan, Groucho Marx, Cab Calloway). Some of these impressions may have been appreciable by a child audience—by the early 1990s, Schwarzenegger, for example, had begun his transition to family films with *Kindergarten Cop* (Ivan Reitman, 1990)—but others, such as of the conservative intellectual William F. Buckley Jr., were clearly aimed solely at adults. In effect, Goldberg and Williams turn in a consummately postmodern and double-coded performance unlike anything seen to that point in Disney's canon of animated features—including, crucially, in *Aladdin* itself prior to Genie's appearance.

When considering *Aladdin*'s intertextual gags as sources of incongruous humour, it is important to acknowledge how those incongruities are presented in the context of both the film's story world and its status as a children's film, and a Disney one at that. Specifically, these gags are completely segmented from the rest of the film, sequestered in the Genie character. The world of Agrabah, the fictional medieval Arabian kingdom in which *Aladdin* is set, is not unlike that of any Disney film, save for its novel (for Disney) geographical location. It is not a world in which all of the characters are seemingly aware of the popular culture of a society that postdates their own by centuries, like that of *Shrek*, for instance, or one of the many *Looney Tunes* (1930–1969) cartoons set in historical periods. Genie aside, the denizens of Agrabah are depicted realistically; their appearance, words, and actions fit unproblematically into the established fictional world. And, of course, Genie is *not* like the other characters. He is fundamentally unique in his nature, as any viewer can easily understand. He's not a mortal being like *Aladdin*'s other characters but an almost omnipotent spirit, unbound by earthly laws. This explains his frequent physical metamorphoses and, implicitly, his awareness of contemporary culture: as a being of "phenomenal cosmic power," the strictures of time and space simply don't apply to him. As Wells writes, "The genie is located in the contemporary era and directly addresses a contemporary culture aware of the terms of reference Williams brings to the character—the "laughs," as it were, often occur outside the context of the narrative."[20] His anachronistic behaviour is thus reconciled with the film's otherwise consistent setting, as the comic incongruity of the genie's references does not extend to the actual diegesis of the story. Instead, he is cast as an interloper, an unpredictable outside force not only unbound by but also frequently directly at odds with the both the presumed rules of the world of Agrabah and those of the children's film, of which the Disney canon is typically held to be the apotheosis.

Segmentation is thus the second of the three common strategies for integrating adult-oriented intertextual humour into children's films. Unlike the embedding on display in *Boss Baby* and *Madagascar*, segmentation does not necessarily seek to obscure the site of the reference; in fact, this strategy often brazenly foregrounds it. What it does instead is restrict these sites to particular characters or sequences that are coded as separate or distinct from the film's presiding tonal or narrative logic. The intertextual gags, though still presumed to be impenetrable to children, are part of a discrete package of illogical cartoonal qualities; this allows the resulting incongruities to be more explicit without compromising continuity of narrative or tone. The clear and definitive segmentation of the Genie is one particularly overt example, but this technique manifests itself again and again in the 1990s, the period known as the "Disney Renaissance". Beyond *Aladdin* and Genie, we see it with similar comic sidekick characters, such as Timon and Pumbaa in *The Lion King* (Roger Allers and Rob Minkoff, 1994) and the gargoyles in *The Hunchback of Notre Dame* (Gary Trousdale and Kirk Wise, 1996), as well as in Disneyesque productions from other studios, such as the dragons Devon and Cornwall in the Warner Bros. film *Quest for Camelot* (Frederik Du Chau, 1998). As Michael Barrier notes, these sidekick characters are rendered in more exaggerated cartoonal animation than the era's typically realistically drawn protagonists, and this graphic looseness is mirrored in their intertextual awareness.[21] Musical numbers, most commonly those of the sidekicks, also often play host to adult-oriented references alongside a cavalcade of other stylistic deviations; Chris Pallant explains that these sequences "typically provide an opportunity for the otherwise restricted animators to embrace their creative impulses, though this artistic freedom is usually framed in such a way as to legitimize any departure from the established story world."[22] This is certainly true in *Quest for Camelot* and *The Hunchback of Notre Dame*, where the sidekicks' respective musical numbers take place against a series of minimalist, featureless backdrops, rather than in the scene's ostensible setting. This has the effect of presenting the musical performance as semidiegetic, either expressionistic or entirely imagined, so that when, say, characters impersonate Jason Voohrees (*Quest for Camelot*) or Liberace (*The Hunchback of Notre Dame*), it remains incongruous for the informed without jarring the innocent.

Looking at the way in which the Genie and his unique intertextual qualities are introduced to the audience, as well as at the formal qualities of the gags themselves, further reveals how segmentation facilitates double coding while retaining narrative and tonal continuity. It bears noting that Genie doesn't make his entrance for thirty-five minutes, more than a third of the way into the film, by which point its realist designs and logical principles are fully established. Also, a factor for more experienced filmgoers is Disney's more-or-less consistent adherence to these same logical principles in its animated features over the preceding six decades. Having become virtually synonymous with both children's film and cinematic animation, Disney itself (as well as the first half-hour of *Aladdin* specifically) provides a fixed point against which the Genie can orient himself, setting the stage for his aggressive incongruities. These incongruities present themselves thick and fast upon his debut. In his introductory scene, a roughly five-minute sequence, Genie transforms himself into sixteen different forms, among other displays of his plasmatic physicality such as changing size or duplicating himself. Of these sixteen forms, six are nonhumanoid (e.g., a dog, a firework, a fruit machine); four are generic human characters (e.g., a Scotsman, a boxing coach, a waiter), and six are based on celebrities: Arnold Schwarzenegger, Ed Sullivan, Groucho Marx, Cab Calloway, William F. Buckley Jr., and Peter Lorre. Schwarzenegger, arguably the most famous and certainly the most contemporary—therefore the most recognizable—is the first of these, following the Scotsman and his dog. By starting with such an obvious caricature of such a famous man, Williams and Goldberg prime the audience for the rapid-fire parade of likenesses to come. This rapidity is key: in one twenty-second line of dialogue—"What would you wish of me? The ever-impressive, the long-contained, often imitated but never duplicated Genie of the Lamp! Right here, direct from the lamp . . . "—Genie transforms or otherwise contorts himself five times, synchronized to his speech. He becomes Schwarzenegger ("impressive"), trapped in a box ("contained"), a ventriloquist ("imitated"), an army of duplicates ("duplicated"), and, finally, Sullivan ("direct from the lamp"). Within minutes of his introduction, then, Genie is established as incongruous in relation to both *Aladdin*'s diegesis and Disney's body of work by virtue of his plasmatic physicality and his cultural awareness and potentially adult-oriented frames of reference.

We've seen that Genie's transformations are not all explicitly intertextual; nor are they aimed exclusively at an adult audience. Besides the generic characters he inhabits, he draws on children's texts, specifically other Disney films, transforming, for example, into the title character from *Pinocchio* (Ben Sharpsteen and Hamilton Luske, 1941) and briefly conjuring Sebastian from *The Little Mermaid* (Ron Clements and John Musker, 1989). However, the execution and form of the transformations that *are* both adult-oriented and explicitly intertextual differs markedly from those that are neither. As a waiter, a Scotsman, a boxing coach, or any other generic figure, Genie retains his default facial structure, sporting only a different outfit and, occasionally, facial hair (Figure 5.1). Meanwhile, unsurprisingly, the Disney characters are directly transposed; Genie's head transforms completely into that of Pinocchio or of *Aladdin*'s own Jafar, leaving no residual traces of Genie himself. The celebrity impersonations have their own set of requirements: they must be instantly recognizable to the informed viewer but retain continuity with Genie's default features for the benefit of the uninformed. To achieve this balance, Goldberg drew on the work of Al Hirschfeld, revered caricaturist at the *New York Times*, whose style the animator described as "a pinnacle of boiling a subject down to its essence, so that you get a clear, defined statement of a personality."[23] For the celebrity impersonations, Goldberg morphs, to varying degrees, the shape and features of the Genie's face in a way not deemed necessary for the generic figures, mapping a Hirschfeldian distillation of the subjects' essential qualities on to Genie's head but

FIGURE 5.1. *Aladdin*'s Genie morphs into a generic Scotsman, retaining his essential facial features (1992, Disney). Frame-grab.

FIGURE 5.2. Genie mimics Jack Nicholson, involving a much more detailed facial transformation (1992, Disney). Frame-grab.

retaining certain trademarks, such as his blue skin. The hybridized celebrity faces are noticeably more detailed than the genie's default face and, for that matter, the faces of most of the film's other characters (Figure 5.2). This level of detail grants them a specificity that marks them as incongruous within the broader canon of Genie's transformations, let alone within the film as whole, even when the viewer is without knowledge of their referent.

This pronounced specificity separates these sites of reference them from the embedded allusions in *The Baby Boss* and *Madagascar*. While in those examples the references were specific enough to register with an informed audience, they also fit neatly within the context in which they were presented. Here, however, the use of Hirschfeldian carica-ture in the celebrity transformations, which frames them as logically irreconcilable with the film's established diegesis and serving no readily apparent function within the narra-tive, renders them what Mikhail Iampolski would term "anomalies," seemingly foreign lexical elements that "impel us toward an intertextual reading":

> Every "normative" narrative text possesses a certain internal logic. This logic motivates the presence of the various fragments of which the text is made. If a frag-ment cannot find a weighty enough motivation for its existence from the logic of the text, it becomes an anomaly, forcing the reader to seek its motivation in some other logic or explanatory cause outside the text. The search is then conducted in the realm of intertextuality.[24]

This is essentially the difference between Genie's impersonations of Jack Nicholson and of Jafar. Jafar is an established component of the film's world and, as such, doesn't read as anomalous; whereas Nicholson, up to the point that Genie assumes his form, is alien to it. This is what separates *Aladdin*'s deployment of adult-oriented intertextu-ality with that of *The Boss Baby* and *Madagascar*. The *Glengarry Glen Ross* and *American Beauty* references in those films don't introduce new, anomalous elements; they simply rearrange the language of their story worlds—verbally, in the case of "cookies are for closers"; visually, in the case of Alex's imaginary steaks—into something recognizable to informed audiences. Through the force of its specificity, the Nicholson reference in *Aladdin* demands to be read as intertextual—or else as nonsense—in a way that these other examples don't. It's a bolder gambit, which risks alienating the uninformed audi-ence, yet it is one facilitated by the segmentation of these hyperspecific references within the figure of the Genie, a character who is inherently nonsensical.

Wells asserts that the cartoonal context of these allusions was a crucial factor in their reception. "It little mattered," he writes, "that children would not understand the pop-ular culture references in the Genie's performance in *Aladdin*, as the film was clearly borrowing Warneresque tropes as one of the conditions of its approach."[25] As noted, many Disney sidekicks in the 1990s embody these "Warneresque" cartoonal qualities to some degree, and many of their musical numbers provide a semidiegetic space in which to exercise these qualities with impunity. Genie is only the conduit for the most explicit and densely packed collection of adult intertextual references because his very nature as an atemporal, physically plasmatic character makes him naturally suited to exhibiting cartoonal traits. He openly defies logic, and as such he teaches his audience not to seek logic in his actions, in his transformations. This is in keeping with Suzanne Buchan's description of the viewer's developing relationship with the world of an animated film;

the spectator, she writes, must "actively engage in developing new hypotheses that relate [their own experience of the world] to developing comprehension of and engagement with the animated 'world.' "[26] Faced with a reality whose rules diverge from those of our own, we as audience members interpret the film's "cues" in order to develop a hypothesis of how this other reality operates. *Aladdin* and Genie actively and consistently work to acclimatize the audience to the character's cartoonal qualities in order to enable this. Genie's atemporality and metamorphic abilities are established by having him warp and stretch his form, remove his head from his body, and appear as a kilted Scotsman before taking on his first celebrity role. The audience can hypothesize *Aladdin*'s story world as one in which a character like Genie, who is not only aware of contemporary artefacts but can make them manifest, can and does exist. An audience, particularly a young one, may not recognize every caricature that the Genie transforms into, but after "living" with him for even a brief moment they should recognize that he transforms, that the cartoon logic of illogic applies in this situation. By segmenting adult-oriented cultural references within comic cartoonal characters like the Genie, or in semidiegetic, expressionist musical sequences, a film doesn't negate the process of rationalizing an anomaly through an appeal to intertextuality, but for the uninformed it can neutralize the imperative.

Normalizing Chaos

The development of hypotheses on the part of the audience to facilitate an understanding of a world whose rules seem different to our own is also crucial to the third strategy for integrating adult-oriented intertextual references into children's films. I term this strategy *normalization*. Instead of integrating the references in the text, or segmenting them in certain characters and scenes that follow cartoon logic, normalization extends this cartoon logic, allowing it to permeate the film's entire diegesis. The *Shrek* movies, *Shark Tale* (Vicky Jenson, Bibo Bergeron, and Rob Letterman, 2004), and the *Lego Movie* franchise (2014–2019) all jettison realist principles to some extent, taking the postmodern cartoonal qualities of *Aladdin*'s Genie and framing them not as incursions into an otherwise rational story world, but as inherent constituents of that world's internal logic. These films normalize semiotic chaos on a grand scale. Any explicit, obtrusive intertextual reference, whether to specifically adult-oriented hypotexts or otherwise, is simply one node in a broader canvas of anarchic comic beats, anachronisms, and non sequiturs.

Shrek and its sequels, for example, take place in a generic Medieval European fairytale setting—innately intertextual, in that it incorporates characters and settings from a large number of fairy tales, but also rife with anachronism, including versions of contemporary brands, locations, music, and TV shows. A variety of adult-oriented intertexts are mentioned or shown to exist in the films' world, either as themselves or adapted to suit the pseudo-medieval context. *COPS* becomes *KNIGHTS*, for instance, and *Lethal Weapon* becomes *Lethal Arrow*. Similarly, *Shark Tale* is set in an undersea city inhabited by fish, featuring "fishified" versions of real-life brands and cultural texts while also drawing heavily on tropes and iconography from hip-hop culture and gangster movies, in particular *Goodfellas* (Martin Scorsese, 1990), *The Godfather* (Francis Ford Coppola, 1972), and *The Untouchables* (Brian De Palma, 1987). The *Lego franchise's* settings are a literal "*brick*-olage," pieced together from Lego sets past and present, as well as several that have never existed, effectively combining a wide range of pop-culture worlds into one. This has included characters and objects from such adult-oriented texts as *The Matrix* (the Wachowskis, 1999), *Beetlejuice* (Tim Burton, 1988), *The Terminator* (James Cameron, 1984), and *Die Hard* (John McTiernan, 1988) and real-world figures, such as Supreme Court Justice Ruth Bader Ginsburg, with whom few children can be expected to be familiar. Yet all of these films are so dense with intertextual gags that the adult-oriented examples given here are in the minority; they appear alongside other reference points that children are much more likely to recognize—for example, *Shrek's* fairy-tale creatures, *Shark Tale's* fishified versions of all-ages brands like Coca-Cola, and the *Lego* franchise's use of the family-friendly characters of Superman and the *Star Wars* cast. This, combined with other devices like anachronism and metareferences (which signal the inherent illogic of these story worlds), contributes to fostering a very particular hypothesis in both the adult and child audience concerning the workings of these films' settings: that they are in and of themselves wholly irrational. As with segmentation, this hypothesis facilitates references to adult-oriented texts without compromising continuity for the uninformed because the importance of continuity itself is de-emphasized, allowing these jokes to remain explicit without the double coding present in the embedded examples.

This effect is a variation on the concept of the "comic climate" proposed by Gerald Mast, "the notion that an artist builds signs into a work to let us know that he considers it a comedy and wants it to be taken as such." These signs "let us know the action is taking place in a comic world," thus allowing, and encouraging, laughter, particularly at situations that could be taken seriously if presented as such.[27] Mast gives examples of such signs, one of which involves foregrounding the artificiality of the diegesis: "Any hint of artistic self-consciousness—that the filmmaker knows he is making a film—can wrench us out of the illusion of the film and let us know that the action is not to be taken seriously."[28] Drawing on Elder Olson's definition of comedy as "the imitation of a worthless action,"[29] Mast claims that this kind of self-consciousness "reminds the audience it is watching something artificial, 'worthless.'"[30] This, then, suggests an inverse correlation between the extent to which a film highlights its status as fiction and the extent to which it is taken seriously. The films mentioned above, and others that engage in normalization, all foreground their artificiality by including intertextual references and other cartoonal elements that contradict the notion that there is a discrete, internally logical story world. As such, their diegeses read as "worthless," neutralizing our need to rationalize the kind of logical anomalies identified by Iampolski. Of course, relative to live-action cinema, many animated films highlight their artificiality in the sense that their characters and worlds are manifestly manufactured, with no indexical link to reality. This goes some way toward explaining why adult-oriented intertextual gags are much more common in animation than live-action. As Brown writes, "Foregrounding intertextuality has…served an important role in Hollywood animation retaining its narrative distinctiveness from non-animated family films, where postmodern narrative strategies have never been as pronounced."[31] Indeed, of the live-action children's films that do incorporate the kinds of overt references to adult-oriented intertexts discussed in this chapter, many are adaptations of animated TV series, such as the *Scooby-Doo* (2002–2004), *Alvin and the Chipmunks* (2007–2015), and *Smurfs* (2011–2013) franchises, transposing the comic climate of the original and often making heavy use of computer-animation themselves. In essence, the more overtly artificial the film's world is, the less seriously it begs to be taken, and the easier it is to foreground explicit references to adult-oriented texts without concern about disrupting the narrative and tonal continuity.

This natural disparity between live-action and animation in terms of the latter's obvious artificiality relative to the former is foregrounded in *Space Jam* (Joe Pytka, 1996), which is an exemplary model of the normalization strategy in both the explicitness of its adult-oriented references and the artificiality of its diegesis. In fact, the contrast between the live-action human world and the animated land of the Looney Tunes is one of the film's key comic dichotomies; the staid live-action world serves as a straight man of sorts to the cartoonal antics of Bugs Bunny and company, a yardstick for "reality" against which to measure their incongruities. The film centres on retired basketball star Michael Jordan, who is spirited away by the Looney Tunes to compete in a high-stakes game against the evil, alien Monstars. The crux of both Jordan's and the Toon Squad's arc during the game is learning how to harness their innate cartoonal abilities to gain advantage, with the Tunes resorting to ever more chaotic tactics as the game goes on, and Jordan scoring the crucial final points by contorting his body like a Tex Avery character. The chaos and illogic of the goings on in Looney Tunes Land are emphasized by their constant juxtaposition with scenes set in the live-action "real" world, which, though not devoid of humour, take on a more prosaic, sometimes even sombre tone. We see earnest flashbacks in which a young Jordan practices basketball with his now-deceased father, for example, or scenes of the athlete questioning his momentous decision to retire and pursue baseball. The contrast is heightened because these scenes adhere to Jordan's real-life biography; the athlete's career arc as chronicled in the film did indeed play out in reality, albeit without the participation of the Looney Tunes.

I focus on *Space Jam* and the steps it takes to emphasize the anarchic climate of its animated sequences because the film contains an exceptionally direct and explicit reference to an overtly adult-oriented text, and therefore perfectly illustrates the extent to which normalization can be used to integrate these kinds of gags into children's films. The moment comes in the second half of the climactic basketball game. Having suffered a resounding defeat in the first half at the hands of the superpowered Monstars, the Looney Tunes bounce back after a halftime pep talk from Jordan and Bugs. What follows is a rapid-fire montage sequence in which the Tunes leave behind the strictures of traditional basketball and take on the alien adversaries in their trademark chaotic cartoon style. Sylvester the Cat removes one Monstar's shorts with a fishing rod; Daffy Duck unleashes a raging bull on another; Pepé Le Pew gasses his opponents with his infamous stench, and so on. At one point, in a classic Looney Tunes manoeuvre, Wile E. Coyote rigs the basket with dynamite, which explodes and blasts the attacking Monstar. In revenge, the alien grabs Wile E. by the throat but is stopped short when a hail of bullets, fired from offscreen, shatter his teeth. The question of the bullets' source is quickly answered in a cut to Yosemite Sam and Elmer Fudd holding smoking pistols (Figure 5.3). The pair wear matching suits, and Elmer sports an earring. As any informed viewer will recognize, they are meant to resemble Jules and Vincent, the hitman protagonists of Quentin Tarantino's R-rated gangster movie *Pulp Fiction* (1994), a smash hit released two years before *Space Jam*. The connection is cemented with the inclusion of the surf rock classic "Misirlou," *Pulp Fiction*'s iconic opening title music, which interrupts *Space Jam*'s original score. The shot of Sam and Elmer is followed by an abrupt cut to a slow-motion shot of Jordan dribbling the ball, with the film's original score returning to interrupt "Misirlou" mid-bar, as the montage of the Looney Tunes's antics continues apace. Overall, the entire allusion lasts less than four seconds, a small component of a larger sequence characterized by fast-moving, gleeful anarchy.

The humour at play throughout the montage is frequently crude and cartoonishly violent, but none of the gags read as exclusively "adult" in the same way the *Pulp Fiction* reference does. Tarantino's film was rated R by the Motion Picture Association of America for "strong graphic violence and drug use, pervasive strong language and some sexuality."[32] For informed adults, it's the ideal subject matter for a joke centred on the incongruity of invoking a supposedly inappropriate adult-oriented text in a children's film. Although it's not impossible for young children to see the movie, or at least to become aware of its iconography through osmosis, their engagement with it is highly

FIGURE 5.3. Elmer Fudd and Yosemite Sam briefly impersonate *Pulp Fiction*'s protagonists in a shot from *Space Jam* (1996, Warner Bros.). Frame-grab.

discouraged and therefore unlikely. With that said, the way this gag is deployed and executed is remarkable in both its specificity and its bold, obtrusive placement in the film. In this sense, it is a perfect example of Iampolski's notion of a textual anomaly whose presence can only be rationalized by an appeal to intertextuality. And yet, by virtue of its contextualization in the chaotic, cartoonal world of the Looney Tunes and, in particular, its positioning within the montage, its anomalous qualities are obscured. After all, it is not unusual for the Looney Tunes to dress in costume or behave out of character for the sake of a quick gag, a proclivity that is well-established in *Space Jam* itself and in the long tradition of cartoons that preceded it. Elsewhere in this montage alone, Bugs dresses as a mailman to highjack the ball, while Tweety unexpectedly breaks into a sequence of impressive martial arts moves. Additionally, though the *Pulp Fiction* joke might be said to come out of nowhere, it is not a complete non sequitur; in the *Looney Tunes* canon, Sam and Elmer are well-known for using firearms in their never-ending pursuit of Bugs, which was doubtless a factor in the decision to have these particular characters perform this gag. Most importantly, the animated world of *Space Jam* has, by this point, been established as a place where *anything can happen*, to the extent that the film's narrative and emotional climax centres on Jordan flying through the air while stretching his arm half the length of the basketball court. The montage in which the *Pulp Fiction* gag appears has the narrative purpose of precipitating this climax by highlighting the absurd capabilities of the Looney Tunes at the peak of their chaotic power. The brief, four-second shot of Elmer and Sam dressed as Vincent and Jules is subsumed in this chaos, an anomaly in a sea of anomalies.

Further, the heightened tonal qualities of the shot—arising, in part, from the very un–Looney Tunes–like outfits, props, and music—work to ensure that even an audience unfamiliar with *Pulp Fiction*, such as a child audience, understands the comic incongruity at play. Michael Dunne, asking how "references might communicate with an audience probably unfamiliar with their original sources," suggests that "one way...is simply through tone."[33] Referring to the "Dudley Do-Right" segments of *The Rocky and Bullwinkle Show* (1959–1964), which parody silent-film melodramas, he explains that "outdatedness is emphasized...so the conventions of silent-screen serials can be ironically italicized even for viewers who have never personally seen one of these serials."[34] The notion that the connotations of intertextual references can be interpreted by uninformed audiences on a purely tonal level is invaluable here, because it allows for the possibility that, even without recognizing *Pulp Fiction* specifically—without realizing that one is seeing an allusion to a graphically violent, sexual, and profane movie inserted into what is ostensibly a children's film—one can still perceive an incongruity in this sequence. Instead of being rooted in the juxtaposition of adult media and children's media, the incongruity is rooted in the shift in tone between the cartoonish slapstick violence occurring in the surrounding montage and the more serious violence suggested by Sam's and Elmer's decidedly realistic-looking handguns looming large in the frame. It is visible in the transition from the bouncing kineticism of the basketball game to the cold, rigid expressions and stances of the characters as they stare down their victim, and the shift from a Carl Stalling–esque cartoon score to the sinister surf guitar of "Misirlou."

The uninformed audience may not experience the same joke as those who get the reference, but they experience an analogous joke that plays on similar incongruities. This can be seen in other films employing normalization as well. *Shrek 2*'s *Knights* sequence, with its shaky "camera" movements, deliberately blurry footage, and macho voice-over narrator, jars with the tone one expects in a fairy tale, recognizable regardless of one's familiarity with the TV show *Cops*. Meanwhile, one doesn't necessarily need to know who Ruth Bader Ginsburg was to recognize the tonal incongruity of her brief appearance in *The Lego Movie 2*, dressed in judicial attire and introduced by her full name, couched between such cartoonish characters as "Chocolate Bar," "Banana," and the Tin Man from *The Wizard of Oz* (Victor Fleming, 1939). In these films, then, the intrinsic illogic of the diegesis facilitates explicit adult-oriented intertextual references by normalizing anomaly to account for their specificity, while the gags' tonal contrasts are often able to convey the spirit of their humour for the uninformed.

As with the films that employ segmentation, those that apply the normalizing strategy to intertextual adult humour boldly foreground their allusions in an unambiguous appeal to knowledge ostensibly unavailable to their child audience. Along with embedding, all three of these strategies work to ensure that such knowledge isn't assumed or demanded of the viewer. These techniques don't allow uninformed children to access, as Rose terms it, "the space between" childhood and adulthood, which manifests as the knowledge gap; instead they obscure its existence. Although each strategy operates in unique ways, tailored to the tonal, narrative, and aesthetic qualities of the film in question, they ultimately serve the same purpose. Just as the use of adult-oriented intertextual jokes—a form of humour that has been a staple of Western children's cinema since the 1990s—is designed to both play on the arbitrary distinction between childhood and adulthood and simultaneously reinforce it through constructions of childhood innocence, these strategies seek to *preserve* this innocence. Modulating and recontextualizing the anomalous qualities of intertextual references insulates the child audience from their "inappropriate" connotations until such time as they encounter the intertexts themselves. Therefore, understanding and dissecting the ways in which children's films present their adult-oriented intertextual jokes is vital to the full comprehension of their comic ecosystem and its modes of address.

Notes

1. Paul Wells, *Understanding Animation* (London: Routledge, 1998), p. 140.
2. Julian Cornell, "No Place like Home: Circumscribing Fantasy in Children's Film," in Karin Beeler and Stan Beeler (eds.), *Children's Film in the Digital Age: Essays on Audience, Adaptation and Consumer Culture* (Jefferson, NC: McFarland, 2014), pp. 9–27, at 18.
3. Noel Brown, "*Toy Story* and the Hollywood Family Film," in Susan Smith, Noel Brown, and Sam Summers (eds.), *"Toy Story": How Pixar Reinvented the Animated Feature* (London: Bloomsbury, 2018), pp. 21–38, at 28.
4. Brown, "*Toy Story* and the Hollywood Family Film," pp. 28–29.

5. Stan Beeler, "Songs for the Older Set: Music and Multiple Demographics in *Shrek*, *Madagascar*, and *Happy Feet*," in Beeler and Beeler, *Children's Film in the Digital Age*, 28–36, at 34.

6. Beeler, "Songs for the Older Set," p. 32.

7. John Morreall, *Taking Laughter Seriously* (New York: State University of New York Press, 1983).

8. Jerry Palmer, *Taking Humour Seriously* (London: Routledge, 1994), 94.

9. Gérard Genette, *Palimpsests: Literature in the Second Degree* (Lincoln: University of Nebraska Press), p. 23 (emphasis added).

10. Andrew Stott, *Comedy* (London: Routledge, 2005), p. 137.

11. Stott, *Comedy*, 137.

12. Jacqueline Rose, *The Case of Peter Pan, or the Impossibility of Children's Literature* (Philadelphia: University of Pennsylvania Press, 1984), pp. 1–2.

13. Cornell, "No Place like Home," p. 18.

14. Ibid.

15. Brown, "*Toy Story* and the Hollywood Family Film," p. 27.

16. Ibid.

17. Paul Wells, *Animation and America* (Edinburgh: Edinburgh University Press, 2002), pp. 109–110.

18. Wells, *Animation and America*, p. 110.

19. Cornell, "No Place like Home", p. 18.

20. Wells, *Understanding Animation*, p. 186.

21. Michael Barrier, *Hollywood Cartoons: American Animation in Its Golden Age* (Oxford: Oxford University Press, 1999), p. 571.

22. Chris Pallant, "Developments in Peplum Filmmaking," in Michael G. Cornelius (ed.), *Of Muscles and Men* (Jefferson, NC: McFarland, 2011), pp. 175–186, at 176.

23. Charles Solomon, "*Aladdin*'s Inspiration? They Rubbed Hirschfeld," *Los Angeles Times*, November 8, 1992. https://www.latimes.com/archives/la-xpm-1992-11-08-ca-5-story.html. [accessed June 12, 2020.

24. Mikhail Iampolski, *The Memory of Tiresias: Intertextuality and Film* (Berkeley: University of California Press, 1998), p. 30.

25. Wells, *Animation and America*, p. 110.

26. Suzanne Buchan, "The Animated Spectator: Watching the Quay Brothers' 'Worlds,'" in *Animated Worlds*, ed. Suzanne Buchan (Eastleigh, UK: John Libbey, 2006), pp. 15–38, at 25.

27. Gerald Mast, *The Comic Mind: Comedy and the Movies* (Chicago: University of Chicago Press, 1979), p. 9.

28. Mast, *Comic Mind*, p. 10.

29. Elder Olson, *The Theory of Comedy* (Bloomington: Indiana University Press, 1968), p. 46.

30. Mast, *Comic Mind*, pp. 10–11.

31. Brown, "*Toy Story* and the Hollywood Family Film," p. 29.

32. Kenneth Turan, "*Fiction*: Quentin Tarantino's Gangster Rap," *Los Angeles Times*, October 14, 1994, https://www.latimes.com/archives/la-xpm-1994-10-14-ca-50020-story.html. [accessed June 12, 2020]

33. Michael Dunne, *Intertextual Encounters in American Fiction, Film, and Popular Culture* (Bowling Green, KY: Bowling Green State University Press, 2001), p. 156.

34. Dunne, *Intertextual Encounters*, p. 156.

BIBLIOGRAPHY

Beeler, Karin, and Stan Beeler, eds. *Children's Film in the Digital Age: Essays on Audience, Adaptation and Consumer Culture*. Jefferson, NC: McFarland, 2014.

Brown, Noel. *Contemporary Hollywood Animation: Style, Storytelling, Culture and Ideology since the 1990s*. Edinburgh: Edinburgh University Press, 2021.

Dunne, Michael. *Intertextual Encounters in American Fiction, Film, and Popular Culture*. Bowling Green, KY: Bowling Green State University Press, 2001.

Palmer, Jerry. *Taking Humour Seriously*. London: Routledge, 1994.

Rose, Jacqueline. *The Case of Peter Pan, or the Impossibility of Children's Literature*. Philadelphia: University of Pennsylvania Press, 1984.

Smith, Susan, Noel Brown, and Sam Summers, eds. *Toy Story: How Pixar Reinvented the Animated Feature*. London: Bloomsbury, 2018.

Summers, Sam. *DreamWorks Animation: Intertextuality and Aesthetics in "Shrek" and Beyond*. London: Palgrave Macmillan, 2020.

Wells, Paul. *Animation and America*. Edinburgh: Edinburgh University Press, 2002.

CHAPTER 6

CHILDREN'S FILM AND THE PROBLEMATIC "HAPPY ENDING"

NOEL BROWN

IN the popular consciousness, children's films and happy endings are regarded as virtually synonymous. Though far from unique to children's film, there is perhaps no other tradition of cinema—not even the musical or the romantic comedy—where the narrative centrality of the happy ending is so firmly established, and where its occasional absence is more keenly observed.[1] However, the concept has proven to be problematic in the study of children's film in two distinct ways. First, it has been a stick to beat the genre with for reasons of supposed clichéd predictability, simplemindedness, and sentimental denial of reality. Second, it is far from easy to pin down what it actually means. Indeed, in theory and in practice, the happy ending has remained largely ignored by scholars. This neglect may reflect a general reticence to examine the narrational patterns of children film, or else an understandable degree of caution when discussing such an elusive and controversial aspect of the genre.

There may well be a vague, but lingering, suspicion that attempts to define the *happy ending* are futile, since the term appears to convey emotional affect rather than specific structures of storytelling. However, distinctions must be drawn between the formal elements that invite a happy ending (i.e., those encoded in the film via the orchestration of narrational and representational strategies) and their impact on audiences (i.e., what spectators derive from the film), even if there is a strong causal relationship between them. As James MacDowell notes, the happy ending is a "platonic ideal," like genre itself: there is no single happy ending; nor can we assume that all spectators will respond to an ending in the same way.[2] Instead, the task of the critic is to analyse the textual strategies that aim to arouse a pleasurable emotional state. Although it is clearly beyond the gift of any work of fiction to *make* people feel a particular way, it is nonetheless often true, as Carl Plantinga usefully observes, that "a film's *intended* affective focus can be reasonably well determined."[3]

There is some degree of consensus regarding the prerequisites for a happy ending. MacDowell claims that it requires that the film's characters, audiences, or both, are left "happy," whereas screenwriting guru Robert McKee describes "all emotions…[being] satisfied."[4] Relatedly, Susanne Nobles (via Natalie Babbitt) claims that "hope" is an essential component.[5] In all these cases, the link between the outcome for the fictional protagonists and the emotions of the spectators is emphasized. Yet even in endings where the outcome for the characters appears to be wholly positive, it is worth noting Celestino Deleyto's claim that "ambiguity and variety are relatively frequent" in happy endings, and may even be "part of the convention itself."[6] That is to say, even the most apparently straightforward happy endings have the potential to be ambiguous; equally, the spectator may perceive ambiguity without conscious "subversion" on the part of the filmmaker. Building on these ideas, this chapter explores some of the most common narrative patterns and emotional ambiguities associated with the happy ending in children's cinema.

NOTES ON NARRATION IN THE CHILDREN'S FILM

A large proportion of children's films are retellings of fairy tales, folk tales, and stories from other mythological structures that have their roots in Western traditions of narrative drama and comedy. As N. J. Lowe observes, "classical plotting" strongly emphasizes "unit and closure to the narrative structure, with particular importance attached to a firm and satisfying ending."[7] Story, according to Aristotle, "should stand as an organic whole, a single self-contained causal chain—closed at beginning and end, and bound together internally by links of probable and necessary consequence."[8] By the third century, what Lowe calls the "classical plot paradigm" had been refined and adapted into "the three narrative forms in which it was passed on to the Renaissance, and which remain the basis for subsequent developments: epic poetry, tragic and comic drama, and the novel or short story."[9] Lowe sees this view of narrative as a "closed system" as a "natural" way of viewing the world based on our own experiences and worldview, since "it presses into service a cognitive mechanism we use instinctively from infancy onwards in structuring our experience of the real world. We may believe that our view of the outer universe is fully open and unrestricted, but the very way we process experience guarantees that it is not."[10]

Nevertheless, most children's texts didn't have happy endings (as pertaining to the ultimate happiness of the central child figure) until the nineteenth century.[11] Hitherto, as Walter Pape argues, childhood was viewed as a "hazard" to be negotiated, not—as with the Romantics—an arcadian realm to be celebrated and preserved.[12] As such, earlier children's texts were often cautionary tales in which the fictional child's misfortune or death was intended to avert real-life tragedies.[13] As Jack Zipes points out, the literary fairy tale for children—one of the main precursors of modern children's fiction and film—did not exist until the 1700s, when it became an instrument for introducing "morals to children that emphasized the enforcement of a patriarchal code of *civilité*," primarily to children of the French upper classes.[14] It was the increasingly sentimentalized Romantic German fairy tale (*Märchen*), now most associated with the Brothers Grimm, that popularized the happy ending, inaugurating what Pape calls "the beginning of the modern culture of childhood."[15]

The children's literary convention of the happy ending was firmly in place by the time cinema came into being at the very end of the nineteenth century. Many early children's films adopted and codified it. As Zipes notes of Georges Méliès's adaptation of *Little Red Riding Hood* (1901), the director "went to great lengths to transform Perrault's text into a comic adventure with a happy ending."[16] Furthermore, Méliès made it plain that commercial considerations, based on the perceived undesirable effects of an unhappy ending on a paying public, were the major factor in this transformation:

> The public will very much accept viewing how the poor grandmother is eaten, because this episode is treated in a comic fashion. But to view the wolf eating Little Red Riding Hood (a sympathetic character, spoiled but charming child) would certainly be a disagreeable spectacle, even odious that would badly terminate a play destined to entertain more than anything else. Moreover, this ending would not have any dash to it and would leave a troublesome impression on the spectators.... [M]y only goal was to create an amusing and presentable spectacle for all audiences.[17]

It may be significant that Méliès speaks of addressing "all audiences," not just children. This was a period in which motion picture spectators were viewed, on the whole, as homogenous, impressionable, and uneducated. In his memoirs, British film pioneer Cecil Hepworth recalled, "It was said at one time, and it is still largely true, that cinema audiences were of an average mental age of eleven to thirteen years."[18] The key point, though, is that the convention of the happy ending was present in early films for "family audiences" in both the United States and United Kingdom, such as those starring Mary Pickford, Alma Taylor, and Jackie Coogan. Its institutionalization reflected popular aesthetic preferences (usually underpinned by commercial pragmatism) and moral considerations, such as the perceived need to "protect" children from premature exposure to overly traumatic or pessimistic realities.

A primary function of the happy ending is that of imposing order on the text and, by extension, on the extra-diegetic universe. A sense of "wholeness" is a basic pleasure of many works of fiction. Even when divested of their emotive resonances, children's films might prompt pleasurable feelings at a higher cognitive level: the beauty of form, the appreciation of order and precision. Novelist Iris Murdoch spoke of her difficulty resisting the redemptive "consolations" of what she called "crystalline form," while Colin MacCabe notes that the restored equilibrium of story resolution in classical cinema engenders "the effect of harmony—almost in the musical sense."[19] There would appear to be a significant correlation—in art as in life—between *order* and *happiness*.

Few children's films end messily or chaotically, and while the idea of pleasurable dis-order in the "real" world may not seem far-fetched, it is not how fictional narratives, with their almost clockwork "tock-tick" structures (as Frank Kermode has it), operate.[20] Perhaps the only exception is that of anarchic comedy, a mode in which the kind of comic destructiveness that, say, Tom and Jerry wreak on each other is purposely *amoral*: it is joyous because it bears little resemblance to the "real world," and because it is free from consequence.

This sense of order, then, is not just structural and aesthetic; it is also moral. An early screenplay manual (Frederick Palmer's *Palmer Plan Handbook: Photoplay Writing, Simplified and Explained*, published in 1921) claims that the happy ending is "nothing more or less than the balancing of justice, wherein retribution overtakes the guilty, and virtue and innocence are rewarded."[21] As David Bordwell points out, this is essentially a shorthand exposition of the seventeenth-century philosophy of "poetic justice," and it is one that recurs with particular force throughout the larger histories of children's litera-ture and film.[22] An especially writerly passage in William Goldman's *The Princess Bride* explicitly conflates happy endings and moral justice: "One thing you know when you're ten is that no matter what, there's gonna be a happy ending... in the long run justice is going to win out."[23] This moralistic interpretation of the "happy ending" is founded on ideological reassurance: good things happen to those that deserve them, while those who commit unworthy acts will be punished accordingly. It is the satisfaction of cosmic balance restored and reaffirmed, the imposition of a "natural" and agreeable moral order on a capricious, chaotic universe. As we have seen, the pronounced importance of moral justice in children's fiction serves a didactic function, attempting to inculcate in children the values and behavioural codes that (adult) society regards as central to well-ordered civilization. Since the alternative invites nihilism, there are good reasons why individual children and adults alike would choose (or desire) to believe in moral justice.

A sizeable body of research in the field of child psychology supports the view that chil-dren desire and expect moral justice to be served, both in the "real world" and in fiction. Paul E. Jose and William F. Brewer's study of children aged six to ten found that "readers will prefer stories structured so that good characters obtain positive outcomes and bad characters obtain negative outcomes"; Susan R. Goldman and Connie K. Varnhagen also found, among children of a similar age, an expectation for "heroes and positively described characters to meet their goals but villains and negatively described characters to fail."[24] These expectations reflect the successful instillation of what Melvin Lerner terms the "just world hypothesis," which begins to form early in the developmental pro-cess when "children learn to expect that their misbehavior will be punished and good behavior rewarded."[25] Eventually, this belief becomes "generalized," so that it pertains to everyone the child knows, including characters in stories."[26] This evidence accords with the view that moral satisfaction is an important component in happy endings.

For these reasons, it is in the nature of children's films that "happy endings" appear not just natural and organic ("motivated," to use David Bordwell's term), but a narrative inevitability, in the sense that they are anticipated by audiences and prefigured by the events of the film. Frank Kermode memorably suggested that fictional endings exert a "gravitational pull" on readers.[27] Two of the dominant metanarratives of children's film—the quest story ("the hero's journey") and the coming-of-age story—imply a destination that must be reached in order to resolve the narrative satisfactorily: the "teleological rhetoric" that Franco Moretti identifies as central to the classical Bildungsroman, where "the meaning of events lies in their finality."[28] Certainly, the appearance of "gravitational pull" might be engendered by genre conventions that, as Richard Neupert points out, "serve to limit possible conclusions."[29] Endings lead spectators towards a preferred reading, narrowing the range of alternative interpretations. But it bears repeating that this prefiguring is not just structural; it is bound up in aspects of mise-en-scène and cinematography (lighting, colour, shot choices, scenery, costume), music, and performance. Thierry Kuntzel argues convincingly that opening scenes often contain visual and auditory "clues" that establish tone, mood, and structural patterns, so that the entire narrative may be hinted at (or condensed) at the very outset.[30] It is worth pointing out that films' generic identities are often established through profilmic discourses such as paratextual materials (e.g., trailers, ads, reviews) and shared understanding of institutional contexts and genre conventions more broadly. Audiences, then, bring a host of preconceptions to a film before the opening credits roll—expectations regarding genre, performance, and how a film will make them "feel."

So, it is not true to suggest that children's films *only* attain meaning in their final scene. It is the work of the film to position the ending as an organic and even inevitable consequence of what has gone before. This is why "unmotivated" happy endings in films in which a pessimistic conclusion appears to be the natural outcome—for example, *Suspicion* (Alfred Hitchcock, 1941)—are so remarked upon, and also why it is so unusual to find unexpectedly downbeat endings (like the dysphoric "twists" at the end of many horror films) in children's cinema. Nonetheless, Neupert is correct in his observation that endings are scanned by spectators for their "anchoring proof and condensed summary" of the film's narrational and representational codes.[31] Endings confirm, deliver, and validate the profilmic and intrafilmic expectations outlined above. Representational elements, such as performance and musical closure, work in tandem with narrational codes to orchestrate a sense of narrative closure—a semantic counterpoint to the syntactic mechanisms of classical story construction.

Discussion of such narrational and representational strategies can easily give rise to a sense of rigid formula. This is probably one of the reasons film endings have received such scant attention: critics naturally gravitate toward art that seems innovative, if not radical. Happy endings, as MacDowell points out, are often perceived as a "bad object."[32] In particular, films with an "unmotivated happy ending," in Bordwell's terms, exhibit ideological as well as aesthetic conservatism, surrendering to "the demands of social institutions (censorship, studios) which claim to act as delegates of audience desires."[33] Worse, such endings are often seen as pandering to the base inclinations of a naive or self-delusionary audience. Kermode suggested as much when he observed that "simple fictions are the opium of the people," while scriptwriting "guru" Robert McKee bluntly asserts that "happy endings always make more money than tragic endings because life turns many people into emotional cowards who cannot face tragedy in life or fiction."[34]

This reading of happy endings as little more than cynical, commercially motivated chicanery may account for the fact that some scholars have equated the convention primarily with mainstream Hollywood cinema.[35]

There is some truth to such claims, but they grossly oversimplify the situation. Moreover, dismissing the happy ending on such grounds (shaky as they are) is extremely unhelpful, because it validates the critical neglect of a convention that is of fundamental importance to the genre. The danger becomes one of overemphasizing counter-examples that appeal to the scholar's own sensibilities, either because they align with a particular set of aesthetic preferences or because they reaffirm a specific (usually oppositional) worldview. In the process, what David Bordwell, Janet Staiger, and Kristin Thompson describe as the "quietly conformist film"—one that is somehow "typical" or "conventional"—can easily fall by the wayside.[36] Of course, the careful critic must also avoid marginalizing genuinely innovative films and consider the likelihood that the "quiet conformist" is actually more complex and subversive than it first appears.

While this chapter is not primarily concerned with questions of value, at this point the seemingly pervasive association between happy endings and disposability must be tackled. Part of this pattern of disparagement surely stems from the sense that happy endings, as Kermode puts it, "obscure our sense of reality... [and] represent some kind of surrender or false consolation."[37] Even more pertinent is Perry Nodelman's observation that they render children's books fundamentally dishonest, a claim that is all the more striking given that Nodelman regards happy endings as "the main import" of children's fiction. Indeed, according to Nodelman, happy endings make the text a "utopian fantasy."[38] The apparent implication is that of "childishness" in its most pejorative guises: unsophisticated, simpleminded, cosseted, illusory. Of course, it is not uncharacteristic of older children and teenagers to repudiate optimism and embrace a more cynical worldview predicated on seeing things "as they really are." Still, to say that a film (or any other work) has a happy ending is really to say very little about its value. For all this talk of clichéd or "unmotivated" endings, the intellectual and emotional appeal of many children's films may rest on what J. R. R. Tolkien called "the sudden joyous turn," which he saw as essential to "all complete fairy-stories."[39] Tolkien called this *eucatastrophe*—literally "good catastrophe," the binary opposite of tragedy, and "the true form of fairy-tale."[40] In his estimation, the resonances of the "happy ending" go far beyond mere emotional "uplift" and attain a transcendent *joy*—an "echo of evangelium in the real world" (he views the biblical narrative, and particularly the story of Christ, as the quintessential *eucatastrophe*, the joyful overcoming of tragedy).[41]

Theological considerations aside, it is surely true that the poignancy of the "joyous turn" at the end of, say, *The Railway Children* (Lionel Jeffries, 1970)—a film that fully indulges the *possibility* of tragedy—is magnified by the knowledge (among adults, in particular) that not all endings, in fiction or in reality, can be so happy. In the film, the patriarch of an Edwardian English family is arrested on false charges of selling state secrets to a foreign power, driving his wife and three children into penury and forcing them to move to a rural village adjacent to a railway station. In the memorable and powerfully affecting closing scenes, Father (Iain Cuthbertson) emerges from a cloud of steam on the station platform and is met by his eldest daughter, Bobbie (Jenny Agutter). The euphoria of their reconciliation, as she runs toward him and they embrace (a moment preserved via a freeze-frame), is heightened by the film's earlier hints of disquiet: in the trauma of Father's disappearance, which the children experience via distantly observed, unfathomably half-heard conversations; in the untold but presumably horrendous ordeal Father undergoes as a suspected national traitor; in the exile and separation from his family suffered by a pre-communist Russian dissident; and in Mother's (Dinah Sheridan) barely glimpsed grief.

In such circumstances, a happy ending is not a denial of reality. Instead, it could simply acknowledge that there is a place—and perhaps even a ritualistic need—for utopianism, as for drama and tragedy. We may ponder the significance of the line C. S. Lewis (like Tolkien, a staunch Christian) gives to Puddleglum in *The Silver Chair* about the "play-world which licks your real world hollow" to the relation between the utopianism of children's film and the banalities of quotidian life.[42] None of this is intended as a blanket defence of "bad" children's films, many of which do indeed utilize uplifting endings in a commercially motivated attempt to manipulate the audience's emotions. But the same is true of the narrative strategies employed in many genres, including melodrama, suspense, and horror films (which evoke pleasurable feelings of dysphoria for similarly mercenary ends). It is reductive to attribute happy endings to mere naked commercialism or facile optimism, and even worse to dismiss the convention purely on that basis. This takes us back to MacDowell's and Deleyto's points about the diversity of the happy ending and its built-in ambiguities. Just as we take for granted that the pessimistic endings of, say, *Hamlet* and *The Conversation* (Francis Ford Coppola, 1974) are of a very different order from one another, so we must acknowledge that not all happy endings in children's films are made equal.

CHILDREN'S FILM AND THE UTOPIAN DRIVE

At this point, I would like to turn my attention to perhaps the most famous kind of ending in children's film, which is characterized by a utopian drive somewhat akin to Tolkien's "glimpse of evangelium." The utopianism that Richard Dyer regards as integral to the musical (a mode with close "family resemblances" to mainstream children's film) is a useful point of comparison here. In this form, utopianism is not the precise social structure that Thomas More envisaged, but rather, as Dyer famously observed, a projection of "what utopia would feel like rather than how it would be organized."[43] The appeal of this vision rests on its ability to "offer the image of 'something better' to escape into, or something we want deeply that our day-to-day lives don't provide."[44] Dyer's five markers of utopianism include: (a) community (togetherness, sense of belonging, network of phatic relationships); (b) energy (capacity to act vigorously; human power, activity, potential); (c) abundance (conquest of scarcity; having enough to spare without a sense of the poverty of others; enjoyment of sensuous material reality); (d) transparency (a quality of the relationship between represented characters, such as true love, or between performer and audience); and (e) intensity (experiencing of emotion directly, fully, unambiguously, "authentically," without holding back).[45]

Music, of course, gives expression to feelings of these kinds, being "a tonal analogue of emotive life."[46] Given the particular prominence of musical structures in children's film, it follows that a high proportion of quintessentially utopian endings are predicated on the intersection of satisfactory narrative closure and fulsome bodily representations of emotion through song and dance. These representations give free rein to the expression of characters' inner feeling in a way that dialogue can only hint at, and they also elicit these emotions in a more powerful way because their pleasures are partly physiological. Endings of this kind are too numerous to detail, but a select list might include most of the Disney animated musicals from *Snow White and the Seven Dwarfs* (David Hand et al., 1937) to *Frozen* (Chris Buck and Jennifer Lee, 2013), *Mary Poppins* (Robert Stevenson, 1964), *Oliver!* (Carol Reed, 1968), *Annie* (John Huston, 1982), and many Bollywood family films made in the so-called masala style.[47]

Yet the utopian drive is visible in many non-musical children's films. In story terms, it commonly takes one of several recurrent forms, including celebrations of friendship (particularly between children and animals or groups of children), representations of unfettered play, reaffirmations of community, restorations of family, and heterosexual union. Utopian endings are most prevalent in mainstream commercial cinemas such as Hollywood and Bollywood, where the populist aesthetic lends itself both to narrational closure and to pleasurable expressions of feeling. But they are also evident in a good many international films which may not be musicals but which nonetheless embody some combination of Dyer's categories of utopian feeling. For our purposes, the most pertinent of Dyer's categories are "community," "transparency" and "intensity." When operating in synchronicity, they present the sign of perfect relationships between individuals and groups of people: relationships marked by absolute truth and sincerity and underpinned by unalloyed joy. A very select (and generically diverse) list of international films with endings that conform to these patterns of emotion includes the German *Emil and the Detectives* (Gerhard Lamprecht, 1931), the Russian *Cinderella* (Nadezhda Kosheverova and Mikhail Shapiro, 1947), the British *Yellow Submarine* (George Dunning, 1968), the Indian *Goopy Gyne Bagha Byne* (Satyajit Ray, 1969), the Japanese *My Neighbour Totoro* (Hayao Miyazaki, 1988), and the French-German-Italian *Asterix and Obelix vs. Caesar* (Claude Zidi, 1999).

Here, I turn to *The Wizard of Oz* (Victor Fleming, 1939) as a case study of how the utopian drive may function in mainstream children's film. First, it should be emphasized that the film's ending is pre-empted by textual strategies that have been laid out beforehand. Furthermore, although I will confine the following discussion to the film's narrative and representational strategies, it is worth remembering that audiences bring awareness of genre conventions to every spectatorial experience. Famously, the film opens in sepia, and its initial scenes evoke the disenchantment of the child protagonist, Dorothy Gale (Judy Garland), with her dull life on her aunt and uncle's farm in rural Kansas. Around five minutes into the film, Dorothy wistfully sings the Harold Arlen and Yip Harburg ballad, "Over the Rainbow," a song that expresses her fantasy of escape from her arid, colourless life. Approximately sixteen minutes into the film, a tornado strikes the farm, and Dorothy is transported "over the rainbow" to the Technicolored fantasy land of Oz. While she explores the magical landscape, the first few bars of "Over the Rainbow" repeat, reinforcing her sense of release from constraint. However, in a dramatic reversal, Dorothy is cursed by the Wicked Witch of the West (Margaret Hamilton), and much of the remainder of the film concerns her attempts to return home. This necessitates a trip to the Emerald City to seek the assistance of the eponymous Wizard (Frank Morgan) and culminates in her capture by the Witch and the latter's eventual death at the hands of Dorothy and her allies, the Scarecrow (Ray Bolger), the Tin Man (Jack Haley), and the Cowardly Lion (Bert Lahr)—all magical versions of friendly farmhands back in Kansas. Order restored to Oz, Dorothy transports herself back to the farm by tapping together her pair of ruby slippers and repeating the incantation, "There's no place like home."

Dorothy's return home is established as a structural imperative almost from the moment she arrives in Oz, and the representational elements of music and performance—which capture the idiom of the children's fairy tale—promise a satisfactory resolution. In the final scene, Dorothy awakens to her quiet, rural life in Kansas, lying in bed surrounded by her friends and family and overcome with happiness (Figure 6.1). *Eucatastrophe* is strongly marked in the film's final act, which teases the possibility of a

FIGURE 6.1. "There's no place like home." The utopian ending of *The Wizard of Oz* (1939, MGM). Frame-grab.

much less optimistic conclusion through disturbing elements like the demonic flying monkeys and the scene in which the Wicked Witch sets the Scarecrow on fire. The emotional uplift associated with this homecoming is interspersed with—and heightened by—relief that a tragic or unpleasant ending has been averted. The film signals its optimism in other ways. It deals with clear moral binaries, positing a straightforward battle between Dorothy and her friends (good) and the Wicked Witch and her followers (evil). The defeat of the Wicked Witch represents the restoration of order and the commencement of benign rule by her benevolent sister, Glinda (Billie Burke). Dorothy's longed-for return to Kansas provides narrative closure and sees her restored to a comfortable and loving domestic setting. Auntie Em (Clara Blandick) and Uncle Henry (Charley Grapewin) are embodiments of kindly familial solicitude, and all of her beloved friends from Oz—the Wizard, Scarecrow, Tin Man, and Cowardly Lion—are present in their "human" forms. The apparent implication that the Oz adventure was "only" a dream rationalizes it as a child's fantasy and eliminates the potentially disquieting possibility that it was a real-life adventure.

The musical reprise of the instrumental version of "Over the Rainbow" in this sequence confirms that Dorothy has reconciled herself to the pleasures of the quotidian. This is underlined in the film's final lines of dialogue before the music swells to a final crescendo and the title card definitively announces, "The End": "Anyway, Toto, we're home. And this is my room. And you're all here. And I'm not going to leave here ever, ever again. And…Oh, Auntie Em, there's no place like home!" MacDowell argues that the impression of "promised continuation" is fundamental to the happy ending, and this is no doubt true of many other genres (such as the romantic comedy). However, many children's film endings of this type instead privilege a sense of timeliness, an enchanted stability—*happily ever after*—that no imagined future activity (e.g., ageing, conflict, sickness, ennui, death) can besmirch.[48] More fundamentally, we are led to imagine that there is nothing *after* the happy ending: utopian feeling is beyond such worldly concerns. The diegetic world is preserved in amber at its brightest and most seductive. That utopian endings of this kind are not subject to logic or reason, or real-world practical constraints, is not necessarily a narrative defect. In fact, it is often intrinsic to the emotional and affective pleasures (and the social reassurances) they offer.

Broadly speaking, the utopian drive is stronger in film than it is in literature. This is partly to do with cinema's formal specificity. As Plantinga points out, film presents a "packaged experience" of affective and emotional cues, and its audio-visual channels allow these to be presented more emphatically than in written forms.[49] To take just one example, both of the sound-era Hollywood adaptations of *A Little Princess* (1905)— Fox's *The Little Princess* (Walter Lang, 1939) and Warner Bros.' *A Little Princess* (Alfonso Cuarón, 1995)—transform Frances Hodgson Burnett's ending into something positively utopian. The book already has what could reasonably be called a happy ending: after she discovers that she is a wealthy heiress, the orphaned child, Sara Crewe, is delivered from the misery of her life at a strict boarding school in London, and she and her friend Becky, a downtrodden scullery maid, are taken in by her father's old friend, Carrisford.

However, the films resurrect the deceased father (lost in the Boer War early in the novel) and conclude with scenes of emotional reconciliation between Sara and her amnesiac father, who suddenly and joyfully regains his memory when they meet again. This example points to the intensification of feeling that is characteristic of many children's films, and underlines the sense that, though cinema is not necessarily a more optimistic medium than literature, it is a more emotional one.

THE ROLE OF THE SPECTATOR

However, it is not quite sufficient to describe a film—even at the most uplifting end of the spectrum—as utopian and leave it at that. Utopia, as presented in children's films, is not so much a defined structure (much less a tangible time and place) than a set of emotional prompts. Even when seemingly divorced from its cultural specificities, it is always a social construct; it follows that "utopia" is relative and subjective. More precisely, the emotive potential of any given film rests partly on recognition and approval of the *kind* of utopia it presents, which itself depends on individual and social contexts such as race, class, gender, race and ethnicity, religion, culture, national identity, political affiliation, and historical period—the internalized, largely unarticulated situatedness that Pierre Bourdieu called "habitus." Dyer's follow-up piece to his ground-breaking "Entertainment and Utopia" article, entitled "The Colour of Entertainment," expounds on how racial identity has been "consummately processed" by the Hollywood musical.[50] In another consideration of race and gender in the musical, Susan Smith argues that the genre "is unable to imagine its fantasies of escape in ways that do not end up reproducing—or at least being severely compromised by—existing social structures."[51] It is as well to remember that whatever ends up on screen is always product of labour, both physical and emotional. As Dyer points out, for all the finished product's apparent sincerity, "making that jolly tale of the road to happiness, *The Wizard of Oz*, sounds like it was misery from end to end" for many of the cast and crew.[52]

In earlier generations, children's films rarely made much of an effort to reconcile their visions of utopia with contentious worldly realities. Disney, as Jack Zipes tellingly observes, has always sought to "establish ownership of utopia."[53] Hollywood family entertainment often papers over ideological cracks by ignoring, occluding, or actively suppressing social and political fractures that, if given full expression, would annihilate the utopian illusion.[54] This usually goes unnoticed, not just because of the apparent ideological naturalness of what is shown, but also because the mechanisms of pleasure are designed to subsume thought and dissent to unalloyed feeling. As Plantinga points out:

> Movies are less like blank slates than they are like an immersion into a virtual environment in which responses are largely manipulated by strong sensual cues. Resistance is hardly futile, but resistance isn't what draws audience to the experience in the first place, and resistance takes a lot of effort.[55]

Research into children's engagement with visual media suggests that appreciation of happy endings is considerably higher among children than adults, and one study found that 90 percent of second graders and 91 percent of fifth graders prefer "no obstacle" to "obstacle" endings simply because they "like happy endings."[56] It is not clear whether these are aesthetic preferences or a moral ones based on inculcated "just world" ideologies (as Lerner postulated), but it seems fair to presume that the ability, as well as the desire, to read happy endings against the grain increases throughout the maturation process.

As I have suggested, *The Wizard of Oz* appears to be a quintessential happy ending featuring classical elements of narrative closure, ideological reassurance, and emotional uplift. Yet I am far from convinced that it is the most pleasurable of endings for modern audiences. The meanings people attach to endings are not universal; nor are they stable or immutable. As a child, I could never quite comprehend Dorothy's eagerness to return to the life on the Kansas farm that she despises. Even now, I find that there is something staid and unconvincing in her apparently blissful reintegration into the domestic confines of the farm. This sense is exacerbated considerably by the apparent foreclosure of fantasy and rationalization of Oz as a dream. This may have suited the ideological mood of 1930s America, with its "return to the soil" ideology and its valorisation of home, community, and tradition in the wake of the Great Depression, but its apparent disavowal of the oneiric fantasy now appears bathetic and unnecessarily buzz-killing. Indeed, many later children's fantasies that feature excursions into alternative worlds—such as *Time Bandits* (Terry Gilliam, 1981), *Labyrinth* (Jim Henson, 1986), *Coraline* (Henry Selick, 2009), and, perhaps most significantly, Baum's sequels to his original novel—preserve the diegetic truth of the fantasy, and even allow its partial assimilation into the "real" world. In the books, Dorothy eventually settles in Oz and gets married there.

The significance of *The Wizard of Oz*'s foreclosure of fantasy and reconciliation to the quotidian pleasures of "normal life" is that it represents emphatically "adult" conceptions of desirable maturation. It seems to insist that the Freudian pleasure principle is repudiated and that the child voluntarily adopts the routines and the responsibilities of adulthood: orderliness, work, marriage, parenthood, and so on. The same dispiriting attitude suffuses the coda to Lewis Carroll's *Alice's Adventures in Wonderland* (1865), in which the fiercely independent, anarchic Alice is reconstituted as an adult (in her older sister's dream) as an embodiment of contented Victorian domesticity:

> She pictured to herself how this same little sister of hers would, in the after-time, be herself a grown woman; and how she would keep, through all her riper years, the simple and loving heart of her childhood; and how she would gather about her other little children, and make *their* eyes bright and eager with many a strange tale, perhaps even with the dream of Wonderland of long-ago; and how she would feel with all their simple sorrows, and find a pleasure in all their simple joys, remembering her own child-life, and the happy summer days.[57]

As John Batchelor remarks, "If this paragraph were out of context one would assume that its author had not read the events of Wonderland (let alone written them)."[58] Such a vision of adulthood is one most children today—and probably most adults too—would find unappealingly conformist. But notwithstanding current ideologies, endings of this type remain emblematic of a paternalistic tradition in children's fiction—one that seeks to appease bourgeois adult conceptions of childhood and maturation. From this perspective, we might even reinterpret Carroll's coda as an "unmotivated sad ending" (to misquote Bordwell). Happy endings are often inherently unstable, particularly at the ideological level.

Some endings, no doubt, are more stable than others. Affective and emotional responses may be less bound to sociocultural norms because they often require less cognitive processing. Stan Laurel and Oliver Hardy's films, for instance, are predicated on an essentially childlike anarchism, and thereby largely transcend differences in age and background. The Oscar-winning French short *The Red Balloon* (Albert Lamorisse, 1956) is another such example because of the simplicity of its metonymic narrative and complete lack of dialogue. It centres on a lonely Parisian boy who makes friends with an anthropomorphized, perfectly spherical red balloon, which is mercilessly hunted and eventually destroyed by a gang of rival children. After the desolation of the sequence in which the balloon is pelted by stones, falls to the ground, and slowly deflates, the ending perfectly captures Tolkien's concept of *eucatastrophe*: thousands of balloons of different colours from all over the city descend on the boy and lift him up on a magical flight over the metropolis. We may surmise that most contemporary spectators would respond to this joyous, celebratory final scene in ways not dissimilar to 1950s audiences.

We are likely to see greater variance in responses to texts that uphold a particular worldview, because their ideological assumptions, no matter how naturalized they are made to appear, are much more historically and culturally specific. An extreme example is the fluctuating reputation of Disney's notorious 1940s musical *Song of the South* (Wilfred Jackson, 1946), which in recent years has become something of an embarrassment to the company owing to persistent accusations of racism and been suppressed (it has not received a DVD or Blu-ray home video release, and is omitted from the list of films included on the video-on-demand platform, Disney+). More broadly, "classical" works such as *Alice's Adventures in Wonderland* and *Pinocchio* are recognizably products of a far more didactic period of children's fiction and film. Their preoccupation with the child's learning of honesty, decorum, and responsibility reflects (adult) social requirements for an ordered civilization. We may recall Aristotle's and Freud's arguments in favour of an enforced rejection of childish irresponsibility with the onset of mature adulthood (ironically, Pinocchio only becomes a "real boy" after he eschews childish make-believe), and the fact that the modern literary fairy tale originated as part of a French bourgeois programme of instilling the sociobehavioural codes of upper-class adult society. Homilies of this kind are not presented as explicit moral impositions, especially when adapted into children's films. Rather, they masquerade as emotional truths.

Yet many endings offer sufficient scope to adduce some level of ambiguity or ambivalence. Even films that obey "the unspoken laws" of the genre and supply the appearance of absolute utopian closure do not foreclose the possibility that audiences will add their own "dimension[s] of irony to the affirmations of image [and] music," or even reject them altogether.[59] In cases where *only* affirmative feelings would appear to be cued, avenues of resistance are still possible. Hypothetically, the ending of *The Wizard of Oz* could prompt any number of responses. Young children might feel deflated because the adventure has ended; cynics might object to the excessive whimsy and sentiment; pragmatists might enquire, "what happens *after* the happily ever after?"; realists might wonder at the practicalities of Dorothy's intention never to leave home again or imagine that her boredom with her stultifying home life will soon return; people whose identity or way of life is not represented by the film may feel alienated; and misanthropes (or satirists) might wish to squash the ingratiatingly precocious child's head into a bloody pulp.

AMBIGUITIES AND COUNTER-TRENDS

It should be evident by now that even the most apparently "closed" endings can contain ambiguities (conscious or otherwise) and avail counter-interpretations. This does not negate the idea that the happy ending is a central feature of children's cinema, but it does qualify it. This section explores the ways that some films further problematize the convention, either through deliberate generic subversion (as in several Hollywood films) or, in a few cases, by advancing different models of children's film.

First, we need to consider the place of eucatastrophe within the broader context of the happy ending. Major family-oriented blockbusters like *Return of the Jedi* (Richard Marquand, 1983) and *Harry Potter and the Deathly Hallows—Part II* (David Yates, 2011) deal with disturbing or traumatic issues but ultimately emphasize eucatastrophe in their redemptive final scenes. Indeed, the presence of unpleasant elements ultimately heightens the pleasurable feelings associated with their eucatastrophic endings. Tolkien's claim that the possibility of "sorrow and failure" is "necessary to the joy of deliverance" is substantiated by research on emotional responses to film.[60] Hoffner and Cantor point out that "outcome uncertainty" is "necessary for the experience of suspense" because

> individuals cannot or do not perceive differences in the physiological arousal produced by different sources. Consequently, arousal from suspenseful scenes should carry over and intensify the viewer's positive response to a subsequent happy ending, thus producing a rewarding, enjoyable emotional experience. Conversely, if the resolution is unhappy and produces sadness or disappointment, residual arousal from suspense should intensify viewers' dysphoria.[61]

Among participants aged three to eleven in Hoffner and Cantor's study, "physiological arousal, facial expressions of both fearfulness and positive affect, and liking for the program increased as the degree of suspense increased."[62] As we know, horror films are often materially unpleasant, yet still induce feelings of pleasure.

For these reasons, popular understandings of what constitutes "happy" and "unhappy" endings might not accord with what audiences actually experience while watching them. A blandly perfunctory happy ending that resolves the narrative, upholds the ideological consensus, and ends satisfactorily for its protagonists may be a far less pleasurable experience for the spectator than a thrilling, visceral horror film with a pessimistic final act. Clearly, *perceptions* of happy endings rest as much on the ideological assumptions of society-at-large—involving questions of propriety, moral acceptability, and consensus—as on the presumed responses of the audience. Even if we suppose that few commercial films, ultimately, would try to make spectators feel "bad," structured optimism remains an especially central element in the children's film because of the moral, didactic, and ritualistic functions that underpin the genre.

Yet there are numerous examples of ambivalent or pessimistic children's films that subvert, resist, or otherwise opt out of this convention. They tend to fall into one of two categories: those that do not end satisfactorily for their main character(s), and, relatedly, those that perceive something fundamentally wrong with the world at large. These ambiguities in their various inflections could well be the basis of a much longer discussion than space allows here, but I would like to spend some time considering the particular taboo surrounding representations of death. First, it is necessary to point out that, however upsetting films that portray death may be, they often have a valedictory quality. The death of the child's beloved animal companion is often framed as a formative experience in the lives of young people, one that promotes learning and the ability to cope with adversity. In Disney's *Old Yeller* (Robert Stevenson, 1957), the boy's anguished but resolute decision to shoot his faithful pet Labrador, which has gone rabid, proves his mettle as the kind of rugged individualist valorised in North American culture. (Arguably, this is the male-gendered equivalent of the inauguration of female domesticity in other Hollywood family films of the period, such as *Meet Me in St. Louis* [Vincente Minnelli, 1944] and *On Moonlight Bay* [Roy Del Ruth, 1951].)

Often, moments of surmountable trauma are introduced in the narrative to instantiate the metanarrative of the child's coming of age. In two of the most famous Chinese children's propaganda films, *Chicken Feather Letter* (Shi Hui, 1954) and *Sparkling Red Star* (Li Jun and Li Ang, 1974), the boy protagonists endure tremendous personal loss before ultimately playing major roles in the Chinese army's military campaign during the Second Sino-Japanese War. In some ways, these coming-of-age endings represent the children's film at its most conservative and didactic; they celebrate the culmination of the socialization process, the end of the foolishness of childhood, and the onset of responsible, self-reliant adulthood. Although some children's films are concerned with preserving the timelessness of childhood, often as part of a womb-like, arcadian fantasy of presexual, presocial freedom closed off from adult considerations, others frame narrative events as rites of passage that prepare the child for an idealized, ideologically acceptable version of adulthood. Children's films in the second category are suffused with complex, valedictory endings of this type.

A much more radical critique of modernity emerges in a parallel tradition in non-Hollywood animal-centred films, such as the British *Ring of Bright Water* (Jack Couffer, 1969), *The Belstone Fox* (James Hill, 1973), and *Tarka the Otter* (David Cobham, 1978), and the Australian *Storm Boy* (Henri Safran, 1976). In these films, the death of the animal symbolizes a much broader loss of innocence and puts little in its place. While rejecting the overt pastoralism of the Romantics, these productions nonetheless perceive a savage truthfulness in the natural world (Tennyson's "nature red in tooth and claw") that humankind fails to measure up to. This disavowal of modernity gains additional force in *Ring of Bright Water* and *Tarka the Otter* because there is no central child figure to serve as a symbol of optimism after the senseless, violent deaths of the films' animal protagonists. Worse still, in the more adult-oriented *Kes* (Ken Loach, 1968), the cruel killing of the child protagonist's pet kestrel by his own brother leaves him bereft and hollowed out, apparently marking the death of his hope for a better future.

Few films for children are quite so nihilistic. The endings of *Storm Boy* and the celebrated British animated short, *The Snowman* (Diane Jackson, 1982), contain sequences where the child stands over the remains of his dead companion in inarticulate, almost uncomprehending grief. The visceral impact of these scenes embodies an implicit belief that cosseting children ultimately harms them more than exposing them to death, violence, and other quotidian realities in the mediated, relatively "safe" space of children's fiction. Raymond Briggs, British author of *The Snowman*, gave voice to this conviction in a typically unsentimental admission: "I don't believe in happy endings. Children have got to face death sooner or later. Granny and grandpa die, dogs die, cats die . . . all die like flies. So there's no point avoiding it."[63] However, there are ambivalent, if not redemptive, aspects to both scenes. In *The Snowman*, we are liable to come away with feelings of sadness at the apparent death of the snowman and empathize with the boy protagonist, who stares, voiceless and unmoving, at the melted remains of his friend in the morning sun (Figure 6.2). But these feelings may be leavened by other emotions: aesthetic pleasure at

FIGURE 6.2. The child's inarticulate grief in the final shot of *The Snowman* (1982, TVC). Frame-grab.

the beauty of the animation and the gorgeous wistfulness of the song (Howard Blake's ballad "Walking in the Air"); feelings aroused by our own memories of people we have loved and lost; and perhaps, for adults, realisation that such moments of learning can prepare young people for the physical, moral, and behavioural demands of adulthood.

In *Storm Boy* the dreadful stillness of the scene in which the boy (Greg Rowe) discovers that the wild pelican with whom he has made friends, Mr. Percival, has been shot is partly but not wholly redeemed by a short coda. The boy's aboriginal friend, Fingerbone (David Gulpilil), takes him to a freshly hatched chick on a pelican nesting spot. The implication of rebirth and renewal is reinforced when Fingerbone says, "Perhaps [it is] Mr. Percival starting all over again. Bird like him never die." The closing shots—a flock of pelicans taking off and flying in close formation intercut with the boy and his friend smiling, and finally a shot of a bird on the wing—convey a more optimistic faith in nature's plenitude and represent its indefatigably life-affirming aspects (freedom, openness, interconnectedness) when separated from humanity's predilection for destruction. There are other ambiguities in this final scene: Fingerbone's closing dialogue hints at reincarnation, and the pelicans taking off and the subsequent shot of a single pelican in flight might suggest Mr. Percival's spiritual ascension (suggestively, the initially plangent piano score becomes warmer at this point). Such endings are not simply "unhappy." Rather, degrees of complexity and ambiguity are deliberately worked into the films' narrative and representational strategies.

It is one thing for beloved friends to die—or even parents or guardians, as in *A Dog of Flanders* (James B. Clark, 1959), *Stepmom* (Chris Columbus, 1998), *A Monster Calls* (J. A. Bayona, 2016), and *Kubo and the Two Strings* (Travis Knight, 2016). It is quite another for child protagonists themselves to die. Showing the on-screen death of children remains taboo, but it also radically alters the potentiality of the happy ending in another way, by precluding the possibility of the child's continued maturation and their more symbolic role of offering hope for a more enlightened future. Only a very small proportion of films for children take this route, such as the Hollywood productions *My Girl* (Howard Zieff, 1991) and *The Book of Henry* (Colin Trevorrow, 2017) and the Kenyan film *Supa Modo* (Likarion Wainaina, 2018). Ultimately, though, these can still be read as hopeful (if hardly "happy") narratives whose endings uphold several of the core features of children's film, including the coming-of-age of the dead boy's best friend (*My Girl*), the reaffirmation of family unity (*The Book of Henry*), and celebrations of friendship and community (*Supa Modo*).

Supa Modo, in particular, develops a strong focus on local community and collective responsibility. The film centres on Jo (Stycie Waweru), a girl with a terminal illness living in the village of Maweni, who channels her energies into creating stories featuring her superhero alter ego, Supa Modo. During Jo's final weeks, the local council discusses the possibility of reallocating funds initially earmarked for her medical treatment to the production of a community-made film starring Jo as Supa Modo. Despite objections to the plan, one of the villagers justifies it, reminding the others, "That child is ours. Even if we aren't her mother." Dozens of community members then come together to make Jo's movie. After she dies midway through production, her place in the film is taken by a group of her friends, each one announcing, "I am Supa Modo," an expression of kinship that suggests that her best qualities are inherited by other children in the community. Subsequent scenes focus on her positive legacy: the entire village watches the completed movie; the vibrant posters she drew are distributed to children at the local hospital; and finally, a shot of Jo's mother returning to her daughter's favourite spot overlooking a valley, smiling, is immediately followed by a final shot of the girl in the same location, dressed as Supa Modo, also smiling and then lifting off the ground, as if to begin her flight (in a surely unconscious parallel to the final scene in *Storm Boy*).

Any discussion of the possibilities and the constraints of children's cinema must take account of social and industrial contexts. Conventions in any genre—let alone one so shaped by the perceived moral needs of the spectator—are formed not just through repetition and consensus, but also through institutional parameters. The sense that the happy ending is partly a function of the institutionalization of children's film (generic, industrial) is supported by the fact that most of the relatively few films that do feature "sad" or deeply ambivalent endings are made outside well-established film industries or national traditions of children's film. In 1970s Britain and Australia, or in present-day Kenya, the relative absence of institutional frameworks to enforce perceived generic conventions may have played a part in enabling films such as *Tarka the Otter*, *Storm Boy*, and *Supa Modo* to be made. To a lesser degree, this is also true of Japanese anime, where expectations of a happy ending are much lower than in Western children's film. Disney's dub of the Oscar-winning Studio Ghibli anime *Spirited Away* (Hayao Miyazaki, 2001) replaces the ambiguous silence of the original ending (in which the child and her parents return home from the "other world") with two additional lines of dialogue in which the mother asks the girl whether she is looking forward to her new school and is told, "I think I can handle it." This line is much more in keeping with the tendency in Western children's film to articulate, unambiguously, the suggestions of growth and maturation that are only latent in the film's original release.

Genre conventions are more imagined than real. Allegedly, the producer of *Time Bandits* objected to the comic extermination of the child protagonist's deeply unsympathetic parents at the end of the film on the grounds that it would "alienate the audience."[64] Although this instance of comic anarchy disturbed the conservative sensibilities of some adult gatekeepers, test screenings subsequently revealed that this ending was, in fact, extremely popular with children.[65] For similarly paternalistic reasons, *My Girl* was released with a PG-13 rating in the United States, but was reclassified with a more child-friendly PG rating after the producers protested.[66] Narrative patterns are shaped not only by narrative conventions or ideologies, but also by industry norms and prejudices.

Tellingly, perhaps, the Laika animated feature, *Kubo and the Two Strings*—one of the few commercial Hollywood films that consciously challenges the convention of the happy ending—exhibits a high degree of self-consciousness. In the final scene, having begun to come to terms with the murder of his parents earlier in the narrative, Kubo, the film's adolescent hero, addresses their ghostly apparitions: "This was a happy story. But it could still be a whole lot happier... I still need you. So I can say this has been a happy story, or I could feel it—we could all feel it. Then we could end this story together." These lines of dialogue also serve as a rationalization of a deeply ambivalent ending, one that is likely to invoke pensiveness and introspection rather than the more standard, packaged emotional experience of the Hollywood family film. Of course, creative decisions of this kind also entail a certain degree of risk. *Kubo and the Two Strings* was a critical success but underperformed at the box office, particularly compared to contemporaneous Hollywood features with more conventionally uplifting endings, such as *Frozen* and *Moana* (Ron Clements and John Musker, 2016).

It scarcely needs pointing out that, beyond the seemingly unalloyed joy of the utopian climax, the boundaries of the happy ending are somewhat unclear. As we have seen, Babbitt and Nobles have "hope" as their baseline prerequisite.[67] Whereas utopian endings visualize (and attempt to elicit) a sense of unity, "hopeful" endings merely defer it to a probable or possible future beyond the confines of the narrative. This more liberal definition risks stretching the accepted meaning of "happy ending" almost to breaking point, but context is crucial. The slight ray of hope in the final scene of *The Painted Bird* (Václav Marhoul, 2019), perhaps the most unremittingly bleak child-centred film ever committed to celluloid, hardly "redeems" it (in the sense of restoring moral justice and emotional equilibrium). The most it does is leaven the sense of dysphoria that builds gradually and remorselessly over the course of the film, which chronicles the many forms of abuse inflicted upon a Jewish boy during the Second World War. This film is an extreme example, not least because, like other famously pessimistic child-centred films, such as *Bicycle Thieves* (Vittorio De Sica, 1948), *Kes*, and *The Boy in the Striped Pyjamas* (Mark Herman, 2008), it is intended primarily for adults. However, ambivalent endings of this kind may be entirely in keeping with children's films that challenge one or more genre conventions: neither *Kubo and the Two Strings* nor *My Life as a Courgette* (Claude Barras, 2016) end entirely happily for their protagonists, and the tone of their final scenes is decidedly bittersweet. Films like these can be seen in the context of a wider trend in contemporary children's and family film in which a more complex array of emotional responses may be prompted and boundaries of acceptability are challenged, and issues that would once have been considered off-limits are handled with more directness.[68] In such cases, ambiguous endings may stem from ambivalent narratives (particularly in the social realist mode) in ways that appear entirely "motivated."

The happy ending resides at the intersection between narrative, ideology, and emotion. Although it has long since passed into idiomatic cliché—and while its imprecision certainly requires layers of nuance—the happy ending does encapsulate a truism of children's film: it is primarily emotion, not a sense of logic or structure, that most children's films aim to evoke in their final moments. Of course, emotional uplift is also aroused by complex interrelations of logic and feeling: the cognitively developed emotions brought about by the narrative construction of utopian feeling; the blissful emergence from the struggles of the preceding story (eucatastrophe); the almost mathematical neatness of the plot resolution and foreclosure of ambiguity ("crystalline form"). Although happy endings extend carefully orchestrated "invitation[s] to feel" to audiences, they are also deeply subjective, and responses to them are liable to depend on all kinds of individual and cultural variables.[69] Yet for all that, there is something prototypical about the happy ending. Although it descends from much older story structures, it remains an assuredly transcultural convention in contemporary children's cinema. What many of the best-remembered endings in children's films leave us with—and what the term so evocatively captures—are the powerful carriers of feeling.

NOTES

1. Noel Brown, *The Children's Film: Genre, Nation and Narrative* (New York: Columbia University Press, 2017), p. 15.
2. James MacDowell, *Happy Endings in Hollywood Cinema: Cliché, Convention and the Final Couple* (Edinburgh: Edinburgh University Press, 2013), p. 8.
3. Qtd. in MacDowell, *Happy Endings in Hollywood Cinema*, pp. 13–14.
4. Ibid., p. 26; Robert McKee, *Story* (New York: Harper Collins, 2010), p. 47.
5. Susanne Nobles, "'Why Don't We Ever Read Anything Happy?' YA Literature and the Optimistic Ending," *ALAN Review* 26:1 (1998), n.p.
6. Qtd. in MacDowell, *Happy Endings in Hollywood Cinema*, 192.
7. N. J. Lowe, *The Classical Plot and the Invention of Western Narrative* (Cambridge, UK: Cambridge University Press, 2000), p. x.
8. Lowe, *Classical Plot*, p. 62.
9. Ibid., pp. x–xi.
10. Ibid., p. 29.
11. Walter Pape, "Happy Endings in a World of Misery: A Literary Convention between Social Constraints and Utopia in Children's and Adult Literature," *Poetics Today* 13:1 (1992), pp. 179–196.
12. Pape, "Happy Endings in a World of Misery," 183.
13. Ibid., 184–185.
14. Jack Zipes, "The Origins of the Literary Fairy Tale for Children or, How Script Was Used to Tame the Beast in Us," in Gillian Avery and Julia Briggs (eds.), *Children and Their Books: A Celebration of the Work of Iona and Peter Opie* (Oxford: Clarendon Press, 1989), pp. 119–134, at 124.
15. Pape, "Happy Endings in a World of Misery," pp. 189, 190.
16. Jack Zipes, *The Enchanted Screen: The Unknown History of Fairy-Tale Films* (New York: Routledge, 2011), p. 136.
17. Zipes, *Enchanted Screen*, 136.
18. Cecil M. Hepworth, *Came the Dawn: Memories of a Film Pioneer* (London: Phoenix House, 1951), p. 95.
19. Iris Murdoch, qtd. in Frank Kermode, *The Sense of an Ending: Studies in the Theory of Fiction* (Oxford: Oxford University Press, 2000), p. 130; Colin MacCabe, qtd. in Richard Neupert, *The End: Narration and Closure in the Cinema* (Detroit, MI: Wayne State University Press, 1995), p. 71.
20. Kermode, *Sense of an Ending*, 45–46.
21. Qtd. in David Bordwell, "Happily Ever After: Part Two," *Velvet Light Trap* 19 (1982), pp. 2–7, at 6–7..
22. Bordwell, "Happily Ever After," 6–7.
23. William Goldman, *The Princess Bride* (1973; repr. Boston: Houghton Mifflin Harcourt, 2013), 237.

24. Paul E. Jose and William F. Brewer, "The Development of Story Liking: Character Identification, Suspense, and Outcome Resolution" (Technical Report No. 291, University of Illinois at Urbana-Champaign, October 1983), pp. 2–28, at 5; Susan R. Goldman and Connie K. Varnhagen, "Comprehension of Stories with No-Obstacle and Obstacle Endings," *Child Development* 54 (1983), pp. 980–992, at 990.

25. Jose and Brewer, "Development of Story Liking," p. 5.

26. Ibid., 5.

27. Kermode, *Sense of an Ending*, 150.

28. Franco Moretti, *The Way of the World: The Bildungsroman in European Culture* (London: Verso, 2000), p. 7.

29. Neupert, *The End*, p. 38.

30. Thierry Kuntzel, "The Film Work," *Enclitic* 2:1 (1978), pp. 38–61; Kuntzel, "The Film Work, 2," *Camera Obscura* 5 (1980), pp. 7–68.

31. Neupert, *The End*, 32.

32. MacDowell, *Happy Endings in Hollywood Cinema*, 6–7.

33. Bordwell, "Happily Ever After: Part Two," 7.

34. Kermode, *Sense of an Ending*, 179; Michael Margolis, "Interview with Robert McKee: The Storytelling Movie Master," getstoried.com, https://www.getstoried.com/interview-with-robert-mckee-the-storytelling-movie-master/ [accessed July 7, 2020].

35. Iris Shepard and Ian Wojcik-Andrews, "Conclusion: Criticism and Multicultural Children's Films," in Alexander N. Howe and Wynn Yarbrough (eds.), *Kidding Around: The Child in Film and Media* (New York: Bloomsbury, 2014), pp. 223–231, esp. 227, 228–229.

36. David Bordwell, Janet Staiger, and Kristin Thompson, *The Classical Hollywood Cinema: Film Style and Mode of Production to 1960* (London: Routledge, 1985), 10.

37. Kermode, *Sense of an Ending*, 124.

38. Perry Nodelman, *The Hidden Adult: Defining Children's Literature* (Baltimore, MD: Johns Hopkins University Press, 2008), pp. 216–217.

39. J. R. R. Tolkien, "On Fairy Stories" (1947), pp. 1–27, at 22–23. https://excellence-in-literature.com/on-fairy-stories-by-tolkien/ [accessed March 31, 2020].

40. Tolkien, "On Fairy Stories".

41. Ibid.

42. C. S. Lewis, *The Silver Chair* (London: Macmillan, 1955), 155.

43. Richard Dyer, "Entertainment and Utopia," in *Only Entertainment*, 2nd ed. (New York: Routledge, 2002), 19–35, at 20.

44. Dyer, "Entertainment and Utopia," p. 20.

45. Ibid., pp. 22–23.

46. Ibid., p. 21.

47. For more on Indian children's films, see Noel Brown, "A Brief History of Indian Children's Cinema," in Noel Brown and Bruce Babington (eds.), *Family Films in Global Cinema: The World beyond Disney* (London: I.B. Tauris, 2015), pp. 186–204.

48. MacDowell, *Happy Endings in Hollywood Cinema*, p. 35.

49. Carl Plantinga, *Moving Viewers: American Film and the Spectator's Experience* (Berkeley: University of California Press, 2009), p. 6.

50. Richard Dyer, "The Colour of Entertainment," in Dyer, *Only Entertainment*, pp. 36–45, at 45.

51. Susan Smith, *The Musical: Race, Gender and Performance* (London: Wallflower, 2005), p. 13.

52. Dyer, "Colour of Entertainment," p. 36.

53. Zipes, *Enchanted Screen*, p. 23.

54. See, particularly, Noel Brown, "Ways of Being: Identity and Hollywood Animation," in *Contemporary Hollywood Animation: Style, Storytelling, Culture and Ideology since the 1990s* (Edinburgh: Edinburgh University Press, 2021), chap. 4.

55. Plantinga, *Moving Viewers*, p. 14.

56. Goldman and Varnhagen, "Comprehension of Stories," p. 991.

57. Lewis Carroll, *Alice's Adventures in Wonderland* (Chicago: VolumeOne, 1998), 192.

58. John Batchelor, "Dodgson, Carroll, and the Emancipation of Alice," in Gillian Avery and Julia Briggs (eds.), *Children and Their Books: A Celebration of the Work of Iona and Peter Opie* (Oxford: Clarendon Press, 1989), pp. 181–199, at 188.

59. Bruce Babington and Peter William Evans, *Blue Skies and Silver Linings: Aspects of the Hollywood Musical* (Manchester, UK: Manchester University Press), p. 159.

60. Tolkien, "On Fairy Stories," pp. 22–23.

61. Cynthia Hoffner and Joanne Cantor, "Factors Affecting Children's Enjoyment of a Frightening Film Sequence," *Communication Monographs* 58:1 (1991), pp. 41–62, at 42.

62. Ibid., pp. 42–43.

63. Benjamin Secher, "Raymond Briggs: 'I Don't Believe in Happy Endings,'" *The Telegraph*, December 24, 2007, p. 24.

64. Robert Sellers, *Very Naughty Boys: The Amazing True Story of HandMade Films* (London: Metro, 2003), n.p.

65. Sellers, *Very Naughty Boys*, n.p.

66. *Variety*, September 23, 1991, n.p.

67. Becky Parry, in this volume, makes a similar point about the necessity of "hope."

68. See Noel Brown, "Change and Continuity in Contemporary Children's Cinema," in Casie Hermansson and Janet Zepernick (eds.), *The Palgrave Handbook of Children's Film and Television* (Cham, Switzerland: Palgrave Macmillan, 2019), pp. 225–244.

69. Greg M. Smith, *Film Structure and the Emotion System* (Cambridge, UK: Cambridge University Press, 2003), p. 12.

Bibliography

Bordwell, David. "Happily Ever After: Part Two," *Velvet Light Trap* 19 (1982), pp. 2–7.

Brown, Noel. *The Children's Film: Genre, Nation and Narrative*. New York: Columbia University Press, 2017.

Dyer, Richard. "Entertainment and Utopia." In *Only Entertainment*. 2nd ed. New York: Routledge, 2002, pp. 19–35.

Kermode, Frank. *The Sense of an Ending: Studies in the Theory of Fiction*. Oxford: Oxford University Press, 2000.

MacDowell, James. *Happy Endings in Hollywood Cinema: Cliché, Convention and the Final Couple*. Edinburgh: Edinburgh University Press, 2013.

Neupert, Richard. *The End: Narration and Closure in the Cinema*. Detroit, MI: Wayne State University Press, 1995.

PART II

CHILDREN, CHILDHOOD, AND GROWING UP

CHAPTER 7

···

THE COP AND THE KID
IN 1930S AMERICAN FILM

···

PAMELA ROBERTSON WOJCIK

NOWADAYS in America, any discussion of cops and kids tends to detail shootings of children and teens by police, in some cases kids as young as six years old.[1] At best, in accounts of these shootings the cops are seen as poorly trained, unable to distinguish between child and adult, or between threats (e.g., guns) and innocence (e.g., phones or toys). At worst, they seem like trigger-happy racists, too quick to demonize Black kids, especially (though White kids have also been shot). In these instances, kids are seen as innocent victims—in large part, because nothing they could have done could possibly have justified that response. Rather than safeguards of our children's lives, police are often seen as the danger children face in city streets.

This image of cops and kids goes against such reassuring images as Norman Rockwell's famous 1958 painting for a *Saturday Evening Post* cover *The Runaway*, which shows a benevolent policeman sitting on a stool at a diner counter next to a young male runaway, presumably treating the child to a meal or a snack before taking him home. As Joseph Scales suggests, "In the painting, Rockwell portrayed an idyllic version of small-town America. In his sweet, safe universe, no child is ever in danger and no task is more pressing for an officer of the law than to spend a morning with a young runaway." Describing the police officer as "fatherly," Scales views the scene as one of "comfort and safety."[2]

Of course, Rockwell's image was always already more fantasy than reality, the "Platonic ideal of a diner" that placed both cop and kid on pedestals.[3] It is not surprising, then, that expressions of cynicism about America's police and their relation to children, especially Black children, would use Rockwell's image to register a different perception. For example, in 2014, following the shooting of Michael Brown, an unarmed African American teenager, by a White policeman in Ferguson, Missouri, Anthony Freda created a parodic version of *The Runaway*. In Freda's version, digitally superimposed over Rockwell's, the policeman wears a riot helmet and bulletproof vest, and there is an assault weapon by his feet. Next to him is a frightened-looking Black boy. In response to the same event, *Mad Magazine* created a very similar image, titled "The Militarization of Officer Joe," that showed a cop in full riot gear leaning down toward a Black kid whose face registers absolute distress.[4] These images suggest that, as Max Kutner argued, "half a century later, America is a long way off from the quintessential Americana associated with Rockwell's work."[5]

I start with these images and ideas of cops and kids as a way of thinking through very different ways in which cops and kids have been represented. In particular, I am interested in Hollywood films from the 1930s, when cops and kids routinely shared the frame. Of course, kids and cops will interact differently in different historical moments and national contexts, particularly in relation to police brutality toward Black youth, as we can see in African American films such as *Boyz n the Hood* (John Singleton, 1991), or the "Red, White and Blue" episode of Steve McQueen's *Small Axe* (2020) anthology series about Black British life. The kids I will be looking at are all White, as Hollywood representations of Black kids and cops do not become prominent until later, under very different circumstances. Here, I am interested in the way these early images counter both Rockwell's idyllic portrait and our contemporary view.

This chapter examines some of the numerous moments in 1930s Hollywood films when kids encounter the police, particularly beat cops. In films starring the Dead End Kids, Shirley Temple, Jane Withers, Jackie Cooper, and other child actors, kids freely wander urban streets, have encounters with adults, and run into the police. Rather than treat the children as innocents who need protection from the streets, these films view them as miscreants and troublemakers—their presence on city streets taken for granted, but not welcome. These narratives trouble traditional notions of childhood by representing children as tough, street-smart, experienced, and not tethered to family or institutional life. At the same time, they offer a different view of police, showing them as neither wholly benevolent nor as threats, but as largely ineffectual figures. Crucially, they show cops and kids as adjacent figures in the public sphere, mutually aware of each other and in frequent contact.

THE CHILD-CENTRED FILM AS EXPERIENTIAL MODERNISM

To interrogate the meaning of the cop in 1930s Hollywood films, it is necessary to consider the ideological work that child-centred films of the period do. The Great Depression was the era of the child-centred film. Shirley Temple, Jackie Cooper, Freddie Bartholomew, Dickie Moore, Virginia Weidler, Deanna Durbin, Judy Garland, Mickey Rooney, Jane Withers, and the ensemble actors of the Jones Family, the Dead End Kids, and the Our Gang films series dominated the screen. Beyond these stars, the comics and radio showcased the kids of "Little Orphan Annie" and "Gasoline Alley." The presence of child stars and child-centred texts was not entirely new. Nineteenth-century theatregoers witnessed the ascent of the child star Elsie Leslie, who at age seven played Little Lord Fauntleroy; and the silent-film era featured the adult actresses Mary Pickford and Lillian Gish in numerous childlike roles, as well as the child star Jackie Coogan, Chaplin's sidekick in *The Kid* (Charlie Chaplin, 1921). However, the proliferation and dominance of child stars and child images during the Depression was extraordinary, and those child stars often featured in urban narratives of neglect and poverty.

Some have argued that the rise of children in Hollywood film was a response to the Motion Picture Production Code's clamping down on violence and sexuality in films.[6] Certainly, child-centred films circulate in a context of concern about media influence. However, to posit that child-centred films in the 1930s were presented as a better influence on children ignores the role they already played in silent cinema and does not explain the children's appeal to audiences or the complexity of their representations. Child-centred films were not marketed as children's films: in the 1930s, no ratings system existed. Children watched a wide range of films, including gangster pictures, romances, melodramas, and screwball comedies as well as, potentially, child-child-centred films.[7] More likely to be targeted to children were serials, westerns, and adventure stories. Surprisingly, perhaps, Universal horror films of the 1930s were especially appealing to children.[8] Accordingly, child-focused films should be considered adult or family fare: their target audience and fan base seem to have been adults as much as children. Indeed, Noel Brown argues that, while child-star films were successful, there is no evidence that juvenile audiences were the dominant spectators. Thus, the images of childhood neglect must appeal to adult fantasies and fears of childhood as much, if not more, than provide sources of identification for children.

Some critics have argued that Hollywood child films were not just a strategic sop to censors, but provided a "palliative" counter to the miseries of the Great Depression.[9] If, however, these films provided an escape, they did so in complicated ways. In part, these Hollywood child films function much like the musicals and other forms Richard Dyer analyses in the chapter "Entertainment and Utopia" in his *Only Entertainment*. Dyer takes the usual dismissal of entertainment as "escape" and "wish-fulfilment" seriously to suggest that entertainment responds to real needs in society, by offering forms of non-specific utopianism, or "what utopia would feel like rather than how it would be organized."[10] He argues that, to make spectators feel better, entertainment doesn't just offer us visions of a better world (pretty people, nice cars, lavish sets); it also, and more importantly, provides the illusion that it solves problems. However, entertainment delimits the needs and desires of society even as it addresses them: it only offers solutions to some needs and problems, which enables us to ignore others. The problems it offers to solve are, in Dyer's account, the generic problems of people in capitalist societies rather than more specific ones. They work at the level of affect. So, exhaustion related to the condition of living and working under capitalism is resolved filmically through scenes that convey energy (tap dancing, for example). Scenes of abundance (expensive sets, images of wealth, and lots of extras) counter a sense of scarcity. Emotional intensity (conveyed, for example, in torch songs) counters feelings of dreariness; images of community offset feelings of alienation; and transparency (characters speaking or singing their feelings directly) neutralizes the effects of being manipulated and lied to. Like the "solutions" of capitalism—buying more products—these texts create the problems internally and re-solve them within the film, deflecting the real concerns that might have brought you to the movie theatre seeking escape in the first place, providing only a false and temporary respite.

In child films of the 1930s, the feelings of utopia are produced, for example, through energetic musical performances in the case of Shirley Temple and Jane Withers; heart-felt expressions of sentiment in the case of Temple, Withers, and Jackie Cooper; scenes of community in Our Gang and the Dead End Kids; intensity in moments of crisis, a child's tears; and so on. Abundance figures occasionally, such as when the urban child encounters wealth. Still, these films do not completely direct attention away from real-world concerns. Instead of deflecting or ignoring the traumatic effects of the Depression in a purely escapist mode, images of childhood in the 1930s acknowledge and work through many of the anxieties of the Depression. However, in line with Dyer's argu-ment, direct topical references to the Depression or the New Deal are rare (Temple's film *Just Around the Corner* [Irving Cummings, 1938], is an exception that will engage the New Deal directly). Instead, the social issues and the status of children are refracted into longer-term, lingering issues of modernity accentuated by the Depression, including ur-banization, industrialization, overcrowding, massification, immigration, and changing social mores and family structures.

Instead of reading these films as a direct response to the strictures of the Production Code or assuming that the images of childhood innocence they present will cheer audiences, we need to think of the "palliative" effects of child-centred films and their relation to the Depression in more complex terms. The rise of the child in American film needs to be placed in the context of a number of intersecting trends and issues in American culture that galvanize images of childhood neglect for adult audiences. The Depression engendered many contradictory discourses around children. In the 1930s, the displacement of children from the home, loss of parents, and loss of income created a sense of crisis around childhood, with fears about child homelessness, runaways, tru-ancy, and risk, all potentially leading to child endangerment and the loss of innocence.[11] Parental abandonment and desertions also raised questions about the value of the child and family, as more and more children were placed in custody or left to fend for them-selves.[12] At the same time, as Viviana Zelizer explains, from the late nineteenth century through the 1930s, perceptions of childhood shifted from the view that children are ec-onomically worthwhile participants in public and family life to the opinion that they are economically "worthless," but emotionally "priceless."[13] However, the transition was uneven: nineteenth-century working-class children were still expected to contribute wages and household assistance to the family even as the middle-class began viewing children differently; and the Depression restored the need for "useful" children across a wide range of families.

Images of youth thus worked to reassert the pricelessness and innocence of childhood at a time when the status of the child—his or her worth, and his or her innocence—were up for grabs. Most viewers and commentators today nostalgically assume that the child-star era was an age of innocence. However, in Depression-era texts children are very often orphaned, displaced, or homeless; they are shown being trapped in poverty or falling out of the middle or upper classes into poverty; often, they are workers or petty criminals, subject to the economy, not outside it. Films focused on children in this period situate the child in an urban milieu structured by economic status and, often, outside traditional family structures. Many of the texts from this period assert innocence, if at all, only in the face of the child's experience and knowingness. The urban child unnerves precisely because, in the context of a culture of "pricelessness," she registers as out of place, too adult, not innocent. There is sweetness and sentiment in these films, to be sure, and moral virtue, but never a lack of knowledge or complete insulation from harsh realities.

Because they raise the spectre of so many issues associated with urbanization and modernity, child films of the 1930s can be read in terms of what Miriam Hansen has termed "vernacular modernism."[14] As opposed to modernist aesthetics, the concept of vernacular modernism will "encompass cultural practices that both articulated and mediated the experience of modernity."[15] In her figuration, classical Hollywood cinema can be "imagined as a cultural practice on a par with the experience of modernity, as an industry-produced, mass-based, vernacular modernism."[16] Rather than merely reflect modernity, vernacular modernism must, in some way, reflect *upon* modernity. Hansen writes: "The question was, and continues to be, how particular film practices can be productively understood as *responding to*—and making sensually graspable our responses—to the set of technological, economic, social and perceptual transformations associated with the term modernity."[17] This reflexivity differs from the self-reflexive style often associated with modernism, and indeed, vernacular modernism encompasses "plenty of films that transmute conflicts and contradictions arising from modernity into conventional narrative and compositional forms."[18] Vernacular modernism thus differs from what Liesl Olsen has identified as the modernist penchant for representing and describing the ordinary, insofar as Olsen's argument still balances the ordinary as *subject* against modernism as *style*.[19]

In the late nineteenth and early twentieth centuries, the image of the child focalized anxieties over increased urbanization, and the growing squalor of industrialized cities, including overpopulation, tenements, and slums. The urban child in cinema, then, could function as a palimpsest showing the effects of modernity. In particular, 1930s child-focused films depict what David Pike, in his consideration of subterranean spaces in nineteenth-century literature, has characterized as "a burgeoning modernity perceived personally—through the lived space of the child—rather than solely as representation, as modernism."[20]

In the first half of the twentieth century, the presence of children on city streets was so common as to be viewed as something of a nuisance by city planners and pedestrians. The question was not whether children existed in the city, but whether they should be allowed to play on the streets and sidewalks or be relegated to playgrounds and parks, both for their own safety and as a way to regulate their actions. The urban child was viewed as potentially "both at risk in [the] public sphere, and as a cause of trouble in public space," both subject to social forces and available to contact and encounter the world of adults and the public.[21] In Depression-era films, the contradictions of modernity are played out through the figure of the child, by balancing, on the one hand, a kind of social miserabilism, or woeful sociological gaze, and, on the other, a sense of mobility, spatial freedom, and play. But by showing kids as subject to economic and social forces and as figures of neglect, these texts also show kids as independent, resourceful, and playful—able to navigate urban life with amazing pluck and skill.

The 1930s Hollywood representations of urban childhoods can be taken as producing an abiding imaginary of the urban child. These representations both reflect and produce the urban and the child as intertwined ideas and ideals. They present a philosophy of, or a reflection on both urbanism and the child. Looking to these representations, we can think about the values ascribed to urban childhood. In particular, I am interested here in considering kids as members of the public; how the representation of kids in urban space counters notions of childhood innocence, at least insofar as innocence is understood as a lack of knowledge; and how the street-smart kid can be seen as navigating not only urban space but also encounters with adults and strangers. The interaction between cops and kids, in particular, enacts a form of vernacular modernism that negotiates anxieties about increased urbanization, public life, and immigration.

CHAPLIN'S *THE KID* AS PROTOTYPE

Although my primary focus is on the 1930s, it is useful to consider the silent film *The Kid* as establishing a template for thinking about the cop and the kid together. In a seemingly throwaway scene, we see a very young boy (Jackie Coogan) sitting on the kerb, cleaning his nails, while a cop stands behind him. The child gets up to walk into his house, passing the cop and barely marking his existence, as the cop observes, but does not interact with the child. This serves to establish the urban space, the child's place within it, and the presence of police. Cop and kid exist in proximate space, barely acknowledging each other. Later in the film, the cop and the kid will come into contact. First, the child will commit a crime. The child throws a rock to break a window, whereupon his adoptive father, Chaplin's Tramp, arrives, seemingly by chance, with a repair kit to fix the window for a fee. As the kid runs to a new corner and pulls his arm back, getting ready to throw another rock, his arm touches a policeman who has walked up behind him. The kid points across the street to distract the policeman, and then runs away while the cop is looking in the other direction. Though the kid reacts to the cop's presence nervously, aware of his crime and of the threat the cop poses to his family's criminal con, the cop appears cheerfully oblivious, unsurprised by the child's presence on the city street and untroubled by his behaviour (Figure 7.1). Eventually, the cop becomes aware of the crime. As the cop chases Chaplin's Tramp away, we see the child again. As the Tramp and the kid run away from the policeman, we see the Tramp kick the kid away, not to protect

FIGURE 7.1. The kid (Jackie Coogan) nervously reacts to the cop's presence in *The Kid* (1921, First National). Frame-grab.

him from the cop, but to distance himself, literally, from the crime; and we see the cop as rather hapless, unable to fully figure out the crime or to apprehend the criminals.

By the end of *The Kid*, the cop will again be seen as a benevolent figure. First, when the police discover that the kid is not the Tramp's legal son, they take the kid/Coogan away. Then, at the police station, they reunite him with his biological mother, who had abandoned him. Finally, when a policeman finds the Tramp lying despondent in the street, devastated by the loss of the child, the cop picks him up and takes him to the mother's house, where he is reunited with the boy and welcomed into the mother's home. Notably, the cop's actions here seem to be dictated by the mother, and are not the result of police work per se.

The Kid encompasses a few tropes that will recur across films of the 1930s. First, the adjacency of child and cop: both are taken-for-granted figures in the urban landscape. Second, the child as street-smart and knowing, a potential or real menace on the street. Third, the cop's relative inadequacy in handling the kid, his role as inept and ineffectual comic foil to the child, which allows the kid to routinely outsmart and outrun him. And finally, the policeman is revealed to be more benign than menacing. These tropes, in varying combination, will structure the depiction of the police in most of the Depression-era child-centred films.

The Cop as Signifier of the Urban

Cops are a taken-for-granted part of the mise-en-scène in the Dead End Kid films. The Dead End Kids are an ensemble of actors who gained stardom on the stage in Sidney Kingsley's sensational play *Dead End* (1935), starred in numerous films in the 1930s, and then became the Little Tough Guys, the teenage East Side Kids, or the grown Bowery Boys in films that continued through the 1950s. In the 1930s, the Dead End Kids are White, ethnic, lower-class boys living on the Lower East Side or in other ghettos.[22] The Dead End Kids will add an African American character as the series continues (largely for comedic effect), but they initially exist in a White world populated by Greek, Italian, Irish, and Jewish immigrant working-class families. Most often, in the Dead End Kid films, women are relegated to maternal or sisterly roles, though one girl teams with the boys in *Angels Wash Their Faces* (Ray Enright, 1939). Parents are absent and neglectful. For most of the boys, parents are off-screen—a mother yelling for her son to come home, or a boy casually describing his father drunkenly beating the boy's mother (in the film *Dead End*). Generally, the main boy protagonist lives only with his older sister, who cares for him and tries to protect him from street life. Other siblings are absent and never mentioned. The boys are generally associated with low-level criminality. The films usually involve run-ins with the police and other institutions of government, including school and the mayor's office. Those institutions are imagined to be corrupt. The boys sometimes triumph over some form of corruption or evil, but are not reformed or significantly altered in their manners, behaviours, or attitudes. The films are comedic overall but allow some romance—usually for a Kid's sister—and some melodramatic moments. Crucially, the Dead End Kids operate as a gang. As a gang, they antagonize neighbours, shopkeepers, and other kids. Occasionally, the boys remind each other of how to behave, and they adhere to a strictly coded law of the streets that demands loyalty to the group—and no squealing.

In Dead End Kid films, policemen are often used as a kind of shorthand to establish the urban setting. In the opening of the Dead End Kids film *Crime School* (Lewis Seiler, 1938), for example, the opening shot shows a depopulated image of the New York skyline, signalling the larger view of the city, its most perfect image. But a speedy horizontal wipe to the right quickly removes that image and replaces it with one of the Lower East Side. This shot contrasts the more abstract image of New York with an image of the local, marked as lower class. We see crowded streets and laundry hanging out windows, street vendors, cars, and pushcarts side by side, and children playing everywhere—on the sidewalk, in the street, and on fire escapes. And incidentally, in the lower right corner of the frame, we see a policeman hop into his car.

In another Dead Ends Kids film, *Dead End* (William Wyler, 1937), a cop similarly serves as an anchor signifying the urban setting (Figure 7.2). The film's opening moves from a larger view of the city to one of a specific neighbourhood. A title explains the process of gentrification and the curious juxtaposition of high-rise luxury and tenements.

FIGURE 7.2. The policeman (Robert Homans) serves to establish the urban mise-en-scène in *Dead End* (1937, United Artists). Frame-grab.

Behind it, we see the skyline. The camera crane then lowers vertically, from the lofty height of the skyscrapers down into the tenement district, "as if to mimic the perspective of the rich tenants who gaze down into the ghetto from the safe vantage point of their opulent apartments."[23] The image darkens as the camera descends, and then the camera pans left through the tenement blocks. It is the early in the morning, and the streets are largely empty. A visual shorthand establishes the neighbourhood as poor: laundry hanging to dry, tenants sleeping on fire escapes, and garbage cans. A beat cop (Robert Homans) walks past a milkman, and we follow the cop's progress down the street until he passes a doorman scrubbing the front of an oddly incongruent luxury high-rise and then pokes a man sleeping on a bench and forces him to move.

In these two films, the policeman functions like the laundry hanging outside, the bum sleeping on the bench, and the milkman, as a representative urban feature, part of the everyday. In particular, the cop's presence is tied to the street. Siegfried Kracauer, whose work emphasizes cinema's role in both reflecting and revealing reality, argues that films "evoke a reality more inclusive than the one they actually picture" and describes this reality as the "flow of life," which he regards as open-ended.[24] The flow of life can be seen, Kracauer argues, in representations of the quotidian, everyday life, which nonetheless reveal aspects of reality that we would not see without cinema. The quotidian and cinema's revealing function are equated, in Kracauer's writings, with the street: "The street in the extended sense of the word is not only the arena of fleeting impressions and chance encounters but a place where the flow of life is bound to assert itself."[25]

Not only the policeman but also the child is associated with the street in this period. Noting the importance of the street for the urban child, sociologist Allen Hoben observed that "the street become(s) an extension of the home. It is alike the parlour and the playground of the poor."[26] For geographer Hugh Matthews, the street is "a space that is deeply invested with cultural values that forms part of the spatiality of *growing up*."[27] While reformers long tried to dislodge kids from the city streets, kids in the early twentieth century often opted for the unstructured life on the streets over the more structured play spaces in playgrounds and parks. Because cops and kids function are both everyday signifiers and inhabitants of the urban street, they are often adjacent.

THE KID AS TROUBLEMAKER

In the 1930s, the Dead End Kids typify the child miscreant. *Crime School* shows the kids as troublemakers and situates them within disciplinary institutions. In the film, one of the Kids, Frankie Warren (Billy Halop) is always getting into trouble. Frankie's older sister Sue (Gale Page) moves him to what she thinks is a stable neighbourhood that will keep him from crime. However, there, he meets up with other kids who are involved in criminal activity. The local cop on the beat has his eye on the kids, but he is ineffectual in preventing crime. They steal a variety of items in the neighbourhood and bring them to "Junkie" (Frank Otto), a fence and junk shop owner, to get some petty cash. One night, Junkie only offers them a small payout for a large haul. Spike (Leo Gorcey), the most violent of the kids, hits Junkie over the head and knocks him out. The six boys are rounded up and brought to juvenile court. They refuse to "rat out" one of their own, so Judge Clinton (Charles Trowbridge) sentences them all to do time at Gatesville Reformatory. Much of the narrative centres on the efforts of Deputy Commissioner Mark Braden (Humphrey Bogart) to simultaneously clean up the reform school and date Frankie's sister. The film shows kids, cops, and the judicial system as mutually aware of each other, and kids not only being criminal but also having oppositional familiarity with legal systems.

In *Dead End*, the kids are similarly portrayed as menacing. They hang out at the end of the street, the eponymous "dead end," where the tenement district and the East River abut the back entrance to a new high-rise building, the East River Terrace Apartments. Due to a problem with the elevator, the residents of the high-rise must use the back entrance, and thus they are exposed to the slum boys who use the dock as a hangout and swimming hole. The Dead End Kids intimidate the wealthy high-rise residents and antagonize the doorman. In particular, they berate and eventually attack the child whom Jeffrey Turner, borrowing from Leslie Fiedler, characterizes as the "Good Good Boy," the effete, sheltered, and wealthy Philip (Charles Peck).[28] When the boy's beating is discovered, one of the kids, Tommy (Billy Halop), knifes Philip's father after he has threatened to have Tommy arrested. Tommy gets away and hides from the police. Later, the police catch another slum boy, Spit (Leo Gorcey), who squeals on Tommy. Tommy attacks Spit and attempts to cut him with the "mark of the squealer," but his sister Drina intervenes and convinces him to surrender to police. The film end as Tommy is taken away to jail.

Rather than functioning as outliers, the representation of the Dead End Kids resonated well with other child-centred films at the time, and with analyses of urban boys by activists and social scientists that circulated from the late nineteenth century forward, none of which viewed boys as innocent and all of which considered urban boys to be a social problem, if not a menace.[29] Depictions of the urban boy as social and knowing, if not corrupt, often conflict with notions of childhood innocence. As Kathryn Bond Stockton argues, "Experience is still hard to square with innocence, making depictions of streetwise children, who are often neither White nor middle class, hard to square with 'children.'"[30] The urban ideal works to situate the child within an experiential model of modernity that moves him way from an ideal of purity or unworldliness.

THE COP AS COMEDIC FOIL

Crime School and *Dead End* are topical and address the plight of urban youth via a progressive emphasis on social justice, thus their depiction of children's relation to police emphasizes the more sobering effects of the kids' criminal activities. Most other 1930s films downplay the kids' menace and underscore their sense of fun, spatial mobility, and autonomy. These films treat the relation between kids and cops comedically, and the cop is seen as largely ineffectual.

In the Dead End Kids film *Angels with Dirty Faces* (Michael Curtiz, 1938), the kids are still somewhat hardened delinquents, and the hapless cop's abilities are no match for their verve, but the interaction is still played comedically. One scene shows Bim (Leo Gorcey), Swing (Bobby Jordan), and Patsy (Gabe Dell) walking through a crowded Lower East Side neighbourhood. In the space of a single block, they swipe a flask off one pushcart and a tomato off another, then swap packs of stolen cigarettes. Brushing past one portly man, Bim says, "Outta the way Blubberhead, the famine is on." When a policeman (Robert Homans) passes them, they first pretend to be very respectful, bowing and scraping as they say, "How do you do?" Then, Swing bets Patsy, "A nickel you don't conk him." Patsy pulls the stolen tomato out of his shirt and, without looking back, throws it over his head toward the policeman, where it grazes his head before falling to the ground. Crosscutting shows the cop scratching his head, baffled, then walking away from, not toward the boys. The boys then casually commandeer a baby carriage with a baby in it, shove the carriage back down the sidewalk when its parents complain, mocking the father's ethnic accent as they do so, and then join the rest of their gang on a stoop before they attempt to spontaneously and opportunistically rob Rocky Sullivan (James Cagney).

The Busby Berkeley musical number "Pettin' in the Park" in *Gold Diggers of 1933* (Mervyn LeRoy, 1933) contains one of the more cartoonish versions of the trope of the ineffectual cop. In it, Little Person Billy Barty portrays the child who menaces the cops. At first, Barty sits in a baby carriage, dressed in a baby bonnet and frilly dress. A large group of cops, about a dozen, laugh at Ruby Keeler's nervous rube as she navigates the park, and Barty sends a spitball directly on to one cop's neck. As the cops turn to catch Barty, he jumps out of the carriage and roller-skates away. The cops pursue him on skates until Barty points up at the sky (Figure 7.3), and when the cops look up, slides under their legs as they skate over him. Barty's mischievous behaviour will continue later in the musical number as he pulls up the curtain hiding women as they change clothes and then provides Dick Powell with a can opener when he confronts Ruby Keeler's unyielding metal costume.

Even Shirley Temple has comedic encounters with the cops. In *Dimples* (William A. Seiter, 1936), Temple plays a street performer whose grandfather is a thief. When Temple and the rest of her singing group—a mixed-race group of boys—perform at a party at a rich woman's house, her grandfather, unbeknownst to her, sneaks in upstairs to rob the

FIGURE 7.3. Billy Barty, on roller skates and dressed as a baby, taunts policemen in the number "Pettin' in the Park" from *Gold Diggers of 1933* (1933, Warner Bros.). Frame-grab.

guests. When the cops are called, Temple and the other kids scramble away. But Temple is caught. Two Irish cops bring her in to the house and tell the woman, Mrs Drew (Helen Westley) that "this one was stuck in the balustrade." Mrs Drew looks at tiny Temple next to the two tall policeman and snidely says to them, "I trust you were not injured in the struggle," before sending the "gallant" officers upstairs to investigate the real crime.

Perhaps the most consistent comedic interactions between cops and kids occur in the films of the child star Jane Withers. Now remembered mostly, if at all, as "Josephine the Plumber" in commercials for Comet Cleanser throughout the 1960s and 1970s, Withers was an extremely successful child star, appearing in over forty films between 1932 and her initial retirement in 1947 and among the top-ten box office stars of 1937 and 1938. Withers can be seen as what Sally Mitchell, riffing on the New Woman, characterizes as a "new girl"—a figure defined by independence and freedom—who produces a version of the urban as a space of contact and encounter. Withers was characterized the "Yin to Shirley Temple's Yang," as "a tomboy rascal"[31], and "America's favorite problem child": "wild-eyed, mischievous, uncontrollable...the noisy, brawling youngster actually making a mess of the living room before departing, strictly against orders, for some neighborhood gangland Mayhem."[32] Zierold describes her as more ferocious and tomboyish than Temple, her characters often in trouble or "fixes," and prone to brawls.[33] Tough, but essentially good, Withers played lower-class characters willing to stand up for themselves and for others.

In Withers's films, as in others, children are seen as a potential menace, and police as ineffectual. *Pepper* (James Tinling, 1936), for example, opens with an unsuccessful plea by the police for children to behave. We see the Commissioner of Police at a microphone making a radio broadcast:

> And so I appeal to the young people of our great city for a safe and sane Fourth of July. Enjoy yourselves my little friends, but do not forget the rights of others. Remember that good citizenship pays and that you, our youth and greatest pride, have the solemn responsibility to maintain good order.

A dissolve begins a montage sequence in which we see numerous explosions, gushing open fire hydrants, people calling the police to complain of broken windows, and kids, who are shown to be creating the mayhem. At the end of it, we meet Withers's character Pepper, who appears with a gaggle of kids who have been running around the city together. The terms are set: kids are seen as dangerous and in need of control and cops are seen as helpless against them.

Across Withers's films, she interacts with policemen, always outsmarting them. In *Ginger* (Lewis Seiler, 1935), for example, we see her uncle picked up by the police, as Ginger (Withers) and two male friends look on. Ginger throws a rock through a butcher's window to distract the cop. Then, as he walks back toward the window and the butcher shouts, complaining, Ginger yells, "Hey Joe," from across the street, successfully luring the cop away in a chase. She and her friends run down city sidewalks with the policeman in pursuit, while her uncle calmly walks away. Ginger slides down a coal chute in the sidewalk and the cop leaps over it, still running. In *This Is the Life* (Marshall Neilan, 1935), similarly, she outsmarts cops looking for an escaped convict. In this case, she helps a stranger who has just minutes before broken into her room. As the convicts attempts to escape down the fire escape, the cops see him. He runs back into the dressing room where Geraldine (Withers) had met him. She hides him in her closet, then, when the police come to her room, she sends them outside, telling them he ran that way.

In *Little Miss Nobody* (John G. Blystone, 1936), Withers is an orphan named Judy at the Sunshine Home for Children. Having gotten into trouble too many times, Judy is being sent to reform school. When the bus she is on stops for a break, Judy tricks the woman who is escorting her and runs away. On a busy city sidewalk, she tries to blend into the crowd by walking along with a family. However, when the four kids in the family notice her, they tell her, "You got the wrong family." Suddenly realizing that the family is African American, Judy apologizes and darts into the street. She is run over by a bicycle deliveryman. When a kindly Irishman (Stanley Blystone) offers assistance and asks Judy where she is going, she says she is visiting an uncle, then improvises further, giving a name and address she reads off a pet store advertisement. The Irishman shows her his badge, revealing himself to be a plainclothes policeman, and takes her to the pet shop. There, Judy pretends to know the owner and the Irishman falls for her performance. Taking sympathy on the girl, the man, John Russell (Harry Carey), himself on the run from the law, takes her in and they live together as uncle and niece.

THE COP AS BENEVOLENT

Certainly, the cop is also seen as a benevolent figure occasionally, though still largely in-effectual. The Monogram Pictures film *Boy of the Streets* (William Nigh, 1937), starring Jackie Cooper, features a caring and compassionate Irish policeman, Officer Rourke (Robert Emmett O'Connor), who tries to keep Cooper's character Chuck Brennan on the straight and narrow. The film posits that the urban boy is a product of his environment. We see a tug of war between good and bad influences on the boy, all localized within the neighbourhood. The opening scenes—similar to the opening of *Pepper*—show kids engaged in creating Halloween mayhem. As we see Chuck and his gang of male friends plan and execute numerous pranks—calling in false burglaries and murders to the police, for example—we see Rourke and another Irish cop, Gratton (Jack Cheatham), observing the bedlam and treating the boys' pranks as largely amusing. Rourke tells Gratton that the boys have a hard time and points to the "rat traps" they live in as causal. Later, after arresting the boys and then sending them home without charging them with anything, Rourke says that the boys are not bad; they only try to be tough because they have grown up in bad circumstances.

In *Boy of the Streets*, Chuck worships his father, whom he believes to be an important man. He discovers that his father is not the high-minded civic leader he has imagined but, instead, an unemployed "stooge." However, before discovering his father's lowly position, Chuck views Rourke in largely friendly terms, and we view Rourke as largely benign. For example, when a girl in Chuck's tenement is left alone, likely orphaned, her mother having been sent to the hospital, Rourke and Chuck join forces to deceive the child-welfare services, who want to remove her to foster care, by pretending that the girl is Chuck's sister. Once Chuck's illusions about his father have been shattered, however, Chuck is lured into crime by local hotshot gangster Blackie Davis (Matty Fain). Rourke is no match for the criminal influence in Chuck's life; he disappears from the narrative and is unable to keep Chuck away from Blackie. When Davis shoots Officer Rourke, Chuck turns against Davis and gets shot himself trying to protect him. Ultimately, though, rather than Rourke effecting any real change in Chuck's life, we see that Chuck's only option to escape the influence of Davis and rise to a better position than his father, and his only means out of the neighbourhood, is to join the Navy.

The Cop as Immigrant

It is no accident that Officer Rourke in *Boy of the Streets* is Irish. His strong accent marks him as a recent immigrant, even though the narrative asserts that he grew up in the same neighbourhood as Chuck. Rourke is hardly unique. In virtually every 1930s film, to the degree that we can know a cop's ethnic heritage, he is usually marked as Irish through his accent and name. The cops in Temple's film *Dimples* and Withers's film *Little Miss Nobody*, for example, are explicitly Irish. In *Boy of the Streets*, not only Rourke but also Officer Gratton and the desk sergeant at the jail are also Irish.

The Irish cop is a frequent stereotype from the early twentieth century forward, and a figure who marks the complex process of assimilation for the Irish in America. Famously, following mass Irish immigration in the mid-nineteenth century, the Irish in America shifted from being denigrated as dirty, drunk, criminals to being success-fully assimilated, largely through their affiliation with civil service. As Thaddeus Russell argues, "In 1840 at the beginning of the great wave of Irish immigration, there was only a handful of Irish police officers on the force," but "by the end of the year, Irish made up more than one quarter of the police, and by the end of the century more than half the city's police" were Irish Americans, and the "Irish were disproportionally represented among prosecutors, judges, and prison guards," as well.[34] In what came to be a cycle of favours and influence, as the Irish moved into municipal politics, and were elected mayors in Boston, New York, and Chicago, they relied on the Irish vote; and these mayors and police chiefs filled newly created jobs with Irishmen.

Any film with Irish cops might trigger associations with immigration, but Jane Withers's film *Paddy O'Day* (Lewis Seiler, 1936) makes immigration and assimilation its central concern. Withers plays Paddy, an Irish girl who travels to America from Ireland to join her mother, who has been working as a maid. But her mother dies before Paddy arrives, and so she is detained at Ellis Island. The immigration officers she meets are both kind Irishman, who tell her that her mother is "sick." Anxious to see her, Paddy escapes via a dairy truck, taking the dog she has smuggled from Ireland with her. She hops out of the truck on a busy city street and sits on the kerb, within sight of the Empire State building. A series of dissolves show her wandering the streets, interwoven with shots of trains, skyscrapers, and crowds. When she encounters a group of boys playing on a sidewalk, they treat her as an unwanted alien. They mock her outfit—a rather old-fashioned skirt and heavy tights—and once they hear her accent they call her "a Greenhorn fresh from Ireland." After one of the boys squirts her face with a trick novelty ring, Paddy pummels him. A motorcycle cop (Charles Anthony Hughes) arrives. In a heavy Irish accent, he asks "Whaddya doin'?" The boys all run away. When the cop hears Paddy's accent, he immediately takes her side, then asks, "Tell me, darling, what are you doin' in this neighborhood?" Paddy, unaware that her mother is dead, says she is going to see her mom. The cop says he can't take her all the way to Long Island because he has to get home for his dinner, but a cut shows Paddy and her dog riding on the motorcycle. Sometime later, the cop pulls over a motorist and forces him to take Paddy the rest of the way.

Paddy O'Day is a melting-pot narrative that hinges on the idea of immigrants helping each other. Paddy befriends a Russian family on-board the ocean liner that brings her to New York. They plan to eat Irish stew and borscht together when they arrive. When Paddy goes to the house where her mother worked as a servant, she meets an eccentric rich man, nephew to two prudish aunts. Before meeting Paddy, the nephew, Roy Ford (Pinky Tomlin), spends all his time alone studying his taxidermy birds. After Paddy arrives—hiding from the aunts in Roy's study —she introduces him to her Russian friends. Taken with Tamara Petrovich (Rita Hayworth, billed as Rita Cansino), Roy begins frequenting her uncle's nightclub, Café Padushka. His introduction to lower-class ethnic life is authenticating and rejuvenating. By the time his aunts return home from a trip, Roy is drinking vodka and smoking; has replaced his dead birds with live ones; has become an investor in the club; and is writing songs for a revue. The aunts try to have Paddy and Tamara deported, as Paddy is in the country illegally and Tamara is hiding her. However, the Irish immigration officer from Ellis Island, Tom McGuire (Francis Ford), comes to the rescue and suggests that Paddy could be adopted. Ultimately, Roy and Tamara marry, with the promise that they will adopt Paddy, thus forming a blended WASP American-Russian-Irish family.

Conclusion

Across these films, we see cops and kids as adjacent participants in public life, with the police largely benign figures and children as powerful and mobile. Equally, kids are seen as able to both trust and manipulate adults, to manage encounters with hapless cops and both decent and criminal adults. Clearly, much has changed between then and now. Police, once part of the mise-en-scène of everyday life, have—like many of us—become sealed away in cars, walled off from the people of the community. Kids, too, have been walled off—islanded in child-sanctioned spaces, driven from place to place, and removed from the possibility of encounters with adults apart from family or approved caregivers. In our effort to protect our children from so-called stranger danger, we have removed them from the most vital components of urban life: contact and encounter. In making all contact strange, we have made all contact dangerous.

Our collective nostalgia tells us that children were more innocent in the early twentieth century than they are now; but representations of them tell a different story. These films tell us that kids were once perceived as knowing; available to encounter, streetwise; as inhabitants of the streets; and as influential. I am not suggesting that we can or should nostalgically return to an era of beat cops and affable urchins, or abandon our children and give up efforts to protect them. But we need to reconsider what we are protecting them from, and how. We need to ask: What would it look like to imagine an urban child who is mobile and free and able to encounter police and other adults without always imagining that child as already a potential victim?

Notes

Portions of this chapter appear in Pamela Robertson Wojcik, *Fantasies of Neglect: Imagining the Urban Child in American Film and Fiction* (New Brunswick, NJ: Rutgers University Press, 2016), esp. 35–51, 91–96.

1. For example, Jeremey Mardis, age six, was killed by police in Louisiana in 2015; Tamir Rice, twelve, was killed by police in Ohio in 2014; Cameron Tilman, fourteen, was killed by police in Louisiana, 2014; Tyree King, thirteen, was killed by police in Ohio in 2016; Jesse James Romero, fourteen, was killed by police in Louisiana in 2015; Ciera Myer, twelve, was killed by police in Pennsylvania in 2015.

2. Joseph Scales, "Protect and Serve: Discover the Symbolism in Norman Rockwell's Famous Painting 'The Runaway'," *Saturday Evening Post*, June 24, 2014, https://www.saturdayeven ingpost.com/2014/06/the-rockwell-files-protect-and-serve/ [accessed May 20, 2019].

3. Scales, "Protect and Serve."

4. "If Norman Rockwell Depicted Today's America: 'The Militarization of Officer Joe'," *MAD Magazine*, August 21, 2014, https://www.madmagazine.com/blog/2014/08/21/if-norman-rockwell-depicted-todays-america-the-militarization-of-officer-joe> [accessed May 20, 2019].

5. Max Kutner, "Rethinking Rockwell in the Age of Ferguson," Smithsonian.com, August 24, 2014, https://www.smithsonianmag.com/arts-culture/rethinking-rockwell-time-fergu son-180952485/ [accessed 20 May 2019].

6. Jane Hampton, "Robbing the Cradle for Stars," *Photoplay*, November 1934, pp. 34–35, 98.

7. Noel Brown, "'A New Movie-Going Public': 1930s Hollywood and the Emergence of the 'Family' Film," *Historical Journal of Film, Radio and Television* 33:1 (2013), pp. 1–23, at 2.

8. Brown, "New Movie-Going Public," p. 15.

9. Ibid., 17; Charles Eckert, "Shirley Temple and the House of Rockefeller," *Jump Cut* 2 (1974), pp. 1, 17–20.

10. Richard Dyer, "Entertainment and Utopia," in *Only Entertainment* (New York: Routledge, 1992), pp. 19–35, at 20.

11. Steven Mintz, *Huck's Raft: A History of American Childhood* (Cambridge, MA: Belknap Press of Harvard University Press, 2004), 235–248.

12. Mintz, *Huck's Raft*, p. 237.

13. Viviana A. Zelizer, *Pricing the Priceless Child: The Changing Social Value of Children* (Princeton, NJ: Princeton University Press, 1985).

14. Miriam Bratu Hansen, "Tracking Cinema on a Global Scale," in Mark Wollaeger and Matt Eatough (eds.), *The Oxford Handbook of Global Modernisms* (New York: Oxford University Press, 2012), 601–626. For more on vernacular modernism in relation to children in cinema, see Pamela Robertson Wojcik, "Vernacular Modernism as Child's Play," *New German Critique, No.* 122 41:2 (Summer 2014), pp. 87–99.

15. Miriam Bratu Hansen, "The Mass Production of the Senses: Classical Cinema as Vernacular Modernism," in Christine Gledhill and Linda Williams (eds), *Reinventing Film Studies* (New York: Oxford University Press, 2000), pp, 332–350.

16. Hansen, "Mass Production of the Senses," p. 337.

17. Hansen, "Tracking Cinema on a Global Scale," p. 608.

18. Ibid., p. 613.

19. Liesl Olsen, *Modernism and the Ordinary* (New York: Oxford University Press, 2009).

20. David L. Pike, "Buried Pleasure: Doctor Dolittle, Walter Benjamin, and the Nineteenth-Century Child," *Modernism/Modernity* 17:4 (2010), pp. 857–875, at 872.

21. Gill Valentine, *Public Space and the Culture of Childhood* (Burlington, VT: Ashgate, 2004), p. 1.

22. For the sake of simplicity, I will call their territory the Lower East Side. The Kids' particular neighbourhood is never named. *Dead End* situates the kids at Sutton Place and East 53 Street, but the particularities of this address—its juxtaposition of rich and poor—are not typical of the cycle. The Kids could be in East Harlem, another White ethnic ghetto. However, as they later become the East Side Kids and Bowery Boys, and since the Bowery was initially part of what was then referred to as the Lower East Side, assuming the Lower East Side seems apt. In at least one film after *Dead End*, they live near what is labelled Dock Street, so proximity to the East River can be assumed. Gorcey speaks in a Brooklyn accent, which further confuses the setting.

23. Amanda Ann Klein, *American Film Cycles: Reframing Genres, Screening Social Problems, and Defining Subcultures* (Austin: University of Texas Press, 2011), p. 64.

24. Siegfried Kracauer, *Theory of Film* (Princeton, NJ: Princeton University Press, 1997), p.71.

25. Kracauer, *Theory of Film*, p. 72.

26. Allen Hoben, "The City Street," in Sophonisba Breckinridge (ed.), *The Child in the City: A Series of Papers Presented at the Conferences Held during the Chicago Child Welfare Exhibit* (Chicago: Department of Social Investigation, Chicago School of Civics and Philanthropy, 1912), 451–460, at 451.

27. Hugh Matthews, "The Street as Liminal Space: The Barbed Spaces of Childhood," in Pia Christensen and Margaret O'Brien (eds), *Children in the City: Home, Neighborhood and Community* (New York: Routledge Falmer, 2003), pp. 101–117, at 103.

28. Jeffrey Turner, "On Boyhood and Public Swimming: Sidney Kingsley's *Dead End* and Representations of Underclass Street Kids in American Cultural Production," in Caroline F. Levander and Carol J. Singley (eds), *The American Child: A Cultural Studies Reader* (Piscataway, NJ: Rutgers University Press, 2003), 208–225, at 218.

29. For more on this, see Wojcik, *Fantasies of Neglect*, esp. pp. 54–61.

30. Kathryn Bond Stockton, *The Queer Child, or Growing Sideways in the Twentieth Century* (Durham, NC: Duke University Press, 2009), p. 32.

31. "All Dolled Up! Childhood Star Jane Withers Tours the Nation With Her Dolls... One Last Time," *PR Newswire*, June 9, 2004, http://bi.galegroup.com.proxy.library.nd.edu/essentials/article/GALE|A117931997/0925daad6657bd3f85c1423e980c94e4?u=nd_ref [accessed 2 January 2021]; Norman J. Zierold, *The Child Stars* (New York: Coward-McCann, 1965), 97, 98–99.

32. Norman J. Zierold, *The Child Stars* (New York: Coward-McCann. 1965), 97, 98–99.

33. Zierold, *Child Stars*, pp. 100–101.

34. Thaddeus Russell, *A Renegade History of the United States* (New York: Free Press, 2010), p. 151.

BIBLIOGRAPHY

Brown, Noel. "'A New Movie-Going Public': 1930s Hollywood and the Emergence of the 'Family' Film." *Historical Journal of Film, Radio, and Television* 33:1 (2013), pp. 1–23.

Christensen, Pia, and Margaret O'Brien, eds. *Children in the City: Home, Neighborhood and Community*. New York: Routledge Falmer, 2003.

Dyer, Richard. "Entertainment and Utopia." In *Only Entertainment*. New York: Routledge, 1992), pp. 19–35.

Hansen, Miriam Bratu. "Tracking Cinema on a Global Scale." In Mark Wollaeger and Matt Eatough (eds.) *The Oxford Handbook of Global Modernisms*. New York: Oxford University Press, 2012, pp. 601–626.

Hansen, Miriam Bratu. "The Mass Production of the Senses: Classical Cinema as Vernacular Modernism." In Christine Gledhill and Linda Williams (eds.), *Reinventing Film Studies*. New York: Oxford University Press, 2000, pp. 332–350. Originally published in Modernism/Modernity 6:2 (1999), pp. 59–77.

Holloway, Sarah L., and Gill Valentine, eds. *Children's Geographies: Playing, Living, Learning*. New York: Routledge, 2000.

Klein, Amanda Ann. *American Film Cycles: Reframing Genres, Screening Social Problems, and Defining Subcultures*. Austin: University of Texas Press, 2011.

Mintz, Steven. *Huck's Raft: A History of American Childhood*. Cambridge, MA: Belknap Press of Harvard University Press, 2004.

Valentine, Gill. *Public Space and the Culture of Childhood*. Burlington, VT: Ashgate, 2004.

Wojcik, Pamela Robertson. *Fantasies of Neglect: Imagining the Urban Child in American Film and Fiction*. New Brunswick, NJ: Rutgers University Press, 2016.

Wojcik, Pamela Robertson. "Vernacular Modernism as Child's Play." *New German Critique 122* 41:2 (Summer 2014), pp. 87–99.

Zelizer, Viviana A. *Pricing the Priceless Child: The Changing Social Value of Children*. Princeton, NJ: Princeton University Press, 1985.

....

CHAPTER 8

HISTORY, *FORBIDDEN GAMES*, CHILDREN'S PLAY, AND TRAUMA THEORY

....

IAN WOJCIK-ANDREWS

THE much-debated categories of children's film and young adult film consistently intersect with twentieth-century history; the theme of war; the trope of children's play; and the unpredictable, lasting effects of trauma. Some critical studies discuss history, war, and film or film and play, but analyses in which history, war, and play overlap with trauma theory are a neglected area of study within children's cinema. This lack of scholarly attention to how movies starring children interconnect with trauma studies is unsurprising. First, the subject is complicated because it involves multiple areas of overlapping enquiry, such as film studies and trauma studies, but also issues of memory and representation. Second, recent developments in trauma theory by such critics as Cathy Caruth have made us aware that a person's or nation's emotional turmoil is not resolved in a single therapeutic, recuperative act (a film, a work of art, a discussion): a war film featuring a child protagonist doesn't resolve an audience's anguish over the actual death of children in the specific war the movie addresses.[1] According to Caruth, it is more likely that the repetition of certain tropes associated with childhood innocence and loss that are constantly invoked in war films generally points to an unresolved, underlying, and, historically and culturally speaking, ongoing trauma that produces "trauma cultures" or "wound cultures."[2] In this regard, the individual and the collective find themselves in a traumatizing loop as the event from the past is brought into the present, which, in turn, recreates the original crisis the film is supposed to resolve.

This latter point—the paradox of a film recreating the original trauma or crisis it was designed to resolve—is perhaps connected to how children's film is defined. This subject of definition is explored implicitly throughout the chapter and specifically in the conclusion, where Bazin's response to *Forbidden Games* (*Jeux interdits*, René Clément, 1952) as a children's film only raises more questions about what children's film is than provides definite answers. In the absence of an original, clearly identifiable moment when the first children's film was born, the idea that film is a medium through which audiences young and old grapple with catastrophic events remains relevant, especially in discussions of movies such as *Forbidden Games*, which defies easy classification by critics as either a children's film or an adult film.

World War II, specifically the years 1943 to 1944 during Germany's occupation of France, is the setting of Louis Malle's autobiographical film *Au Revoir Les Enfants* (1987), which focuses on the close friendship between Julien Quentin and Jean Bonnet, the latter a Jewish boy whose real name is Jean Kipplestein and who is granted secret asylum by the school priest, Pierre Jean, to escape the prying eyes of the German soldiers. Mark Herman's controversial adaptation of John Boyne's 2006 novel *The Boy in the Striped Pyjamas* (2008) is set near what Bruno, one of the film's two child protagonists, thinks is a local farm but turns out to be a Nazi concentration camp in German-occupied Poland overseen by his newly promoted commandant father. In defiance of his parents, Bruno befriends Shmuel, a Jewish boy whose striped pyjamas mark him as an inmate of the camp, with tragic consequences: the friendship sends them both to the gas chambers. The global impact of World War II, the sheer overwhelming physical carnage and traumatic scarring of adults and children alike that remains to this day, has meant that even emerging film industries, such as that of South Korea, fight to establish themselves in part through war movies focused on the plight of young people. Twenty-first-century films, such as *The Never-Ending Story* (Heedeok Ahn, 2014), as well as a number of Young Adult novels, such as Sook Nyul Choi's *Year of Impossible Goodbyes* (1993), harrowingly dramatize the sexual enslavement of South Korean comfort girls during Japan's occupation of Korea in the 1930s and 1940s.

More recently, US military involvement in the Middle East during the 1990s—which consisted largely of the Gulf War, or Persian Gulf War, code-named Operation Desert Storm—has had lasting geopolitical and human consequences well into the twenty-first century. This decades-long conflict is the broad historical context for Bahman Ghbodi's *Turtles Can Fly* (2004) and Siddik Barmak's *Osama* (2004). Both movies, and especially *Turtles Can Fly*, show distraught child protagonists who have been physically and emotionally brutalized by war. Featuring Avaz Latif as Agrin, a young girl who carries on her back the child born as a result of her gang rape by soldiers, *Turtles Can Fly* humanizes the real-life tragedies behind what was often dubbed a "video-game war" by setting itself in a Kurdish refugee camp on the Iraq-Turkey border, the kind of camp still very much in existence to this day on the southern borders of the United States, where caged Mexican children separated from their parents await either political asylum or deportation. Siddik Barmak's *Osama*, set in a Taliban-occupied Afghanistan village, concerns a preteen girl named Osama (Marina Golbahari) whose mother and grandmother cut her long hair hoping that her boyish appearance with short hair will help her survive the Taliban's cruelty toward women and girls. Sadly, the disguise fails, Osama is sold into marriage, and in the closing scenes, we see her being taken to the aged Mullah's compound, a child prisoner sold into sexual slavery.

Paradoxically, one common feature among these often difficult-to-watch films set in a wide variety of historical periods and war zones is children's play. Three points are worth making here. The first is that play generally allows directors to make obvious (but important) points about, for example, the inhumanity of war, the accompanying loss of life, and its lasting effect on children. In "Impact of War on Children and Imperative to End War," Joanna Santa Barbara notes that children suffer "differently than adults" during war[3] and that a child's whole "life trajectory" is likely to be adversely affected. From *Empire of the Sun* (Steven Spielberg, 1987) to *Grave of the Fireflies* (Isao Takahata, 1988) to *Osama*, audiences are made to see and feel the long- and short-term consequences of war on children. George Eisen, in his book *Children and Play in the Holocaust: Games among the Shadows*, points out that the relationship between war and children's play, whether in reality (as in the Holocaust) or in books or in films such as *The Boy in the Striped Pyjamas* suggests a "perplexing contradiction" about whether "mass murder and play [can] exist side by side.[4] Genocide and children playing are at such opposite ends of the spectrum that they are almost incomprehensible when linked together. Third, linking war and children playing at the very least debunks the conventional, idealized notion that "children's play" is nothing other than childish, innocent fun. It most definitely is not, as Dutch historian and cultural theorist Johan Huizinga wrote in the 1930s, just the "direct opposite of seriousness."[5]

Eisen's "perplexing contradiction" raises the fourth question about spectatorship and trauma. In "The Children Are Watching Us," Bert Cardullo writes that, as a result of questions of censorship after the 1979 Islamic revolution, Iranian directors, much like Italian neorealist directors in the 1940s, became adept at "cloaking grown-up themes in the metaphorical raiment of children's stories."[6] Perhaps one barely disguised grown-up theme that runs through most of the aforementioned movies, and is thus at the heart of the "perplexing contradiction" of which Eisen speaks, is the adult spectator's compulsion to make and watch movies featuring children playing amid the rubble of war. This raises questions not just about how films use children's stories to reflect grown-up themes, as Cardullo suggests or indeed, about whether the searing portrayals of those themes might traumatize young viewers (though both questions are important). The question, from an adult's point of view, is whether the compulsion to produce and then watch films featuring war and children playing is akin to Chronos devouring his children to prevent their succession to the throne, a conscious or unconscious way of controlling otherwise repressed traumas born in childhood. The tendency of adults to create the trope of children playing as war rages around them, and to consume such tropes through the medium of children's films or, at least, films featuring child protagonists, bespeaks the experiences of grown-ups more than the innocence of the young people—a "perplexing contradiction," indeed.

HISTORY

The historical background for Réne Clément's *Forbidden Games* is France's long and complex political and military relationship to Germany. Specifically, the movie

draws on a seminal historical moment in that relationship, the exodus of French citizens in the wake of the French military's failure to prevent Germany's occupation
of Paris in and around the summer of 1940. Much of *Forbidden Games* concerns
itself with the taboo games played by the orphaned, five-year-old Paulette (Brigitte
Fossey) and her eleven-year-old friend, Michel Dollé (Georges Poujouly) in their
makeshift cemetery. Nonetheless, war, the exodus, and the traumatic aftershocks felt
in family conflicts constantly return in scenes in *Forbidden Games*. For example,
Monsieur Gouard's (André Wasley) proud, nostalgic recollections of the fighting in
World War I ("In 1918 we didn't need to run") are contrasted with the recent return
of his son Francis (Amédée), who we learn deserted his post on the front lines as the
German forces advanced toward Paris: "I can't marry France," the son replies to his
father's accusations. And there is the dreaded, fearful sound of daytime and night-
time air raids that appear throughout the film as ever-present, constant reminders
of the war and its dangers. In one scene, Paulette and Michel are stealing crosses at
night. As they hurry back to the cemetery with their ill-gotten gains, the bombing
starts again, and the children sing to themselves to calm their fears. It would be understandable if French citizens wanted to bury the memories of these events and
the difficult, existentialist, nationalist-inflected questions they pose: Would I die
from the bombing? Did the French military fail because French refugees were clog-
ging up the roads and slowing down the transportation of military supplies to the
front lines? Were French citizens and officials who collaborated with the German
occupying forces engaged in treason or resistance? What effect would the Vichy government have on France's standing in the world, asks Simon Hall in *The World in
Revolt*, especially because after "the Allied defeat of the Axis powers, France sought
to maintain its Empire…the world's second largest…against a rising tide of anti-colonial nationalism."[7] Thus, in 1952, *Forbidden Games* played an important role for
French audiences because it used the trope of children playing amid the rubble of
war to provide what Hanna Diamond calls one of the first "retrospective views of the
exodus in the early post-war years."[8] In other words, *Forbidden Games* takes a long,
hard look back at a pivotal moment in French history, and does so through the lens
of child's play.

Hanna Diamond has examined the evacuation of Paris and the exodus of refugees
from the city to the countryside. Drawing on a range of archival materials, including
both the diaries, letters, and photographs of ordinary citizens and of famous feminist existentialist writers, such as Simone de Beauvoir, Diamond reports that there
were close to four million civilians from a range of social classes, moving en masse
but in a mostly orderly fashion, who fled the impending German occupation of Paris
and headed south into rural France with whatever possessions they could gather and
carry. They transported their possessions using farmyard carts, bicycles, prams, and
horses; in short, "vehicles of all kinds."[9] Wealthier people used cars; poorer people
walked. Issues of social class aside, these different modes of transport were crammed
with pots, pans, mattresses, pets, and, of course, people, mostly women, children.
and the elderly: surviving photographs and diary entries clearly show grandparents

being carried in prams. Diamond notes that for many refugees, including evacuees from Belgian, Holland, and Luxembourg, which had already fallen to the advancing German troops, the exodus south sometimes felt like an extended, albeit forced, camping trip during which shared concerns, warm summer weather, beautiful scenery, and kids playing made the journey tolerable.[10] But other refugees expressed grave concerns that the homes they had left would be pillaged, their limited supplies would soon run out, or they would be killed on the road by the indiscriminate bombing of the German planes. According to reports retrieved during and immediately after the exodus, still others recognized the irony—that by fleeing the capital in farmyard carts and horses they were symbolically returning to the Middle Ages or, at the very least, to the "peasant origins" recent generations of Parisian had only just left behind in search of a more modern life in the industrial north, the very place they were now evacuating.[11]

Much of this history, especially the specific details of the exodus (including the deaths of adults by bullets fired from airplanes and the orphaning of children) finds its way into the opening scenes of *Forbidden Games*, no doubt shocking contemporary (grown-up) audiences into remembering the events of June 1940, the month in which the film is set. Clément's opening scenes show harried refugees on an open road trying to avoid being shot by roaming German airplanes. As bullets strafe the road, killing refugees who were too slow to hide, a close-up of a woman's screaming face reveals the pain, anguish, and fear many of the refugees no doubt felt and now remembered. When the bombing temporarily stops, the refugees collect their belongings, stumble back to the road, and move on. Unfortunately, the car Paulette's parents are driving stalls. Terrified that they will get shot by the German planes that are once again lining up to attack, the refugees push the car off the road and down the embankment to clear a path. Paulette and her parents retrieve their belongings from the car including their dog Jock, climb back on to the road, and rejoin a group of refugees who are now scrambling toward the bridge. Jock breaks free from Paulette's grip, runs across the bridge, and is frantically chased by Paulette, who is just as frantically chased by her terrified parents. Just as they are all reunited at the far end of the bridge, the parents fling themselves to the ground to protect Paulette, and they are shot in the back by the German planes, the bullets whizzing past Paulette but piercing the bodies of her parents and Jock. Eventually, shell-shocked and realising that her parents are dead, Paulette clutches the body of her dog and wanders off into the French countryside, traumatized by the loss of her family. Refugees who had survived the "terror of the air raids" climb out of the ditch, emerge from behind the trees that lined the road and from any other place of safety they had found to hide, and continue their journey across the bridge deep into rural France.[12] A perfect example of art imitating life, these opening scenes would have taken French audiences of the 1950s back generally to World War II. More specifically, they would have taken them back to the disasters of June 1940, and more specifically still, to the exodus into the French countryside of Parisian refugees. No doubt the film would have awoken mixed emotions in which sadness for those who died is tempered with joy for the children who survived.

PLAY

In the 1930s and 1940s, the decades leading directly up to the production and release of *Forbidden Games*, several important theorists of the day found themselves grappling with the question: What is play? The work of two critics in particular—the Dutch cultural theorist Johan Huizinga and the Soviet psychologist Lev Vygotsky—directly bear on *Forbidden Games*. Huizinga, writing in the 1930s, defined *play* as a "voluntary activity" not "bound up with notions of obligations and duty."[13] Play is absorbing but relatively innocent, the "direct opposite of serious."[14] Play begins but then ends at a certain moment. Although games are is often repeated—"repetition is one of the most essential qualities of play"—they remain time-bound but also spatially bound: a game exists within a "playground," a "forbidden spot," where special rules apply that lend to play a profound sense of order as well as secrecy.[15] What might to an outsider seem simple and innocent—a view of play that aligns itself with an appropriately conventional view of childhood—is, in fact, highly structured and meaningful to the participants. Echoing Walter Benjamin's observations about children's play as messianic, Huizinga notes that the features of a forbidden spot are not dissimilar to the "primary characteristics of a sacred act."[16] For Huizinga, the difference between a time-and-rule-bound secret space marked for children's play and a space designated for a sacred purpose is minimal, and "leads us deep into the problem of the nature and origin of religious concepts."[17] Writing roughly contemporaneously with Huizinga, Lev Vygotsky, a Russian theorist, argued that play is important from a social and cultural perspective. He rejects the idea that children's play as only innocent and '...as only innocent and "fun", a key term for Vygotsky—one that has had lasting implications for theorists of play and child development specialists—is the "zone of proximal development."[18] This term refers to an increase in the skills a young person might acquire with the help of a more knowledgeable person. Huizinga's work is more relevant for the purposes of this chapter; but it is important to note the irony in the film that it is eleven-year-old Michel who is the more informed, older person who mentors the five-year-old Paulette, teaching her not just about prayers and when to say them, which the village pastor is unable to do, but about life and death through the games they play.

Huizinga's observation that play takes place in a forbidden, secret spot where rules and order apply is central to an understanding of the importance of children's play in *Forbidden Games*. The morning following her first night at the Dollé farm, Paulette finds an old, abandoned mill, whose only inhabitant is an ancient barn owl, which Michel declares is a hundred years old. Because the derelict mill is not used, its place on the farm fulfils an important function in relation to the children's forbidden games. An abandoned building is a perfect secret space for Paulette and Michel, who, without interference or pressure from unsuspecting adults, can now voluntarily construct what Michel calls a "little cemetery" with makeshift graves for all the animals they hope to accumulate and bury. Given the age of the children, the games must contain rules, such as using an appropriate cross for the size of the animal. Thus, the neglected building is a place of supreme importance, for it is where the forbidden games—but also the choices and deceptions underlying them—are housed.

Huizinga notes that play has an element of repetition. Over the course of the movie, the abandoned, derelict mill, and the manger-type room where they create their cemetery, is the hidden spot, set apart from the main family cottage, to which they constantly return, day and night, with the increasingly attractive crosses they steal to repeat the same burial process. Eventually, too, the mill is where the forbidden games come to end. In the beginning, the abandoned mill is Eden-like in its setting and atmosphere, a quasi-sacred spot where the children can play their forbidden games. However, by the end, the derelict mill, the place where their "first disobedience" (*Paradise Lost*) takes place, becomes a site of cruel physical punishment, emotional betrayal, and revelation. Monsieur Dollé beats Michel to get the truth about their games, as Paulette screams at Michel to reveal the whereabouts of the graves and the crosses. Ultimately, Monsieur Dollé, despite his promise, and despite Michel's pleading, hands the orphaned Paulette over to the police and thus to the Red Cross Centre. Devastated by his father's lies, and torn over the loss of his five-year-old partner in crime, Michel destroys the cemetery and the graves. The mill is now not only the place where the games end, but also a site of lies and deceit, disloyalty, and revenge.

The mill is also important because it is the embodiment of Vygotsky's idea of the zone of proximal development, and a common trope in child-oriented films, where Michel teaches Paulette about a number of religious issues. At first, we see Paulette in the abandoned mill with a farmyard tool, attempting to dig a shallow grave for her dog. Michel interrupts her and proceeds to dig a deeper grave while explaining to Paulette, in response to her questions about her dead parents, that they are in "a hole" so that they "can be together and stay dry." This explanation seems to satisfy Paulette, at which point what was simply a naive attempt by Paulette to bury her dog becomes a game in which their cemetery of appropriately sized graves entombs moles, lizards, hedgehogs, rattlesnakes, lions, and tigers. Their verbal game of embellishment and exaggeration ends only when they suddenly realise that the next big thing to bury after the animals would be "parents." At this point, Michel, always the mentor, explains to Paulette what a cemetery is—"where they put the dead to be together"—and that they will "put up crosses." Shocked that Paulette does not know what a cross is, Michel, amused but exasperated, asks, "What did your parents teach you?" The irony of the question would not have escaped the attention of the French audiences of the 1950s. By the end of the scene, the children have found a secret place for their games that is consistent with Huizinga's theories of play and culture and Vygotsky's notion of the zone of proximal development and its relation to play.

Traditionally, critics have been shocked by the forbidden games played by Paulette and Michel. Yet during the 1950s, writers and directors of children's literature and film commonly fused the trope of children playing against the backdrop of war with the archetype of the secret space to examine children's play, especially the kind that emerges in the absence of adults. An especially famous example, and one that's relevant here, is

William Golding's *Lord of the Flies* (1954), though it should be added that other famous children's books, such as *The Lion, the Witch and the Wardrobe* (1950) and *The Witch of Blackbird Pond* (1958), also utilize a secret space to explore the intersections of children playing within the context of the brutality of war.[19] *Forbidden Games* is set in the French countryside in June 1940 as millions of refugees were fleeing the German occupation of Paris. The backdrop of *Lord of the Flies* is a fictional atomic war in the 1950s; the novel is set on a lush, uninhabited island in the South Pacific where a group of stranded English schoolboy evacuees must learn to fend for themselves as they await rescue by the authorities. In both films, children are separated from their parents (and adults generally) as a result of war and transplanted to what seems an Edenic secret space, where innocent, childlike, uninhibited play at first prevails. As these stories develop, the children's games become either increasingly violent (*Lord of the Flies*) or macabre, sacrilegious, and deadly (*Forbidden Games*).

I would argue that, for writers such as Golding and directors such as Clément, the trope of children playing as a function of war and in the absence of adult supervision was convenient for exploring the prevailing philosophy of the 1950s: existentialism. (Obviously, this is not the place for a full assessment of existentialist thinking, notwithstanding its increasing cultural presence today vis-à-vis popular music, gun violence, climate change, immigration, and White supremacy uprisings in the United States). In the 1950s Jean-Paul Sartre, Simone de Beauvoir, Albert Camus, and others coined several key phrases and terms that became part of the existentialist lexicon, such as "existence precedes essence," "alienation," "freedom," and "choice," and are relevant to *Forbidden Games* and children's play.[20]

A central phrase for existentialists is Sartre's "existence precedes essence."[21] In contrast to the long-held belief that human beings are defined by an essential quality—an essence, a transcendent self—that makes them, fundamentally, who they are—existentialists argued that who we are resides first and foremost in the independent, responsible, conscious choices we make and act upon. It's those choices and thus how we live that define our existence, not an "essence." Two more terms from the existentialist lexicon are also relevant here: "authentic" and "bad faith." A fully realised life is an authentic life: to live otherwise is to live what Sartre called an "inauthentic life," a life of "bad faith." Of course, the question of how an authentic or inauthentic life is determined (and by whom) lies at the heart of existentialism, especially when one considers the notions of freedom, meaning, and happiness and their opposites: enslavement, meaninglessness, and despair. Logically, an authentic life is one in which we make choices that maximize freedom: being free gives our lives true meaning, and thus a sense of happiness. However, existentialists argue, in the final instance, people shy away from real freedom—think of the fictional discussion between the Grand Inquisitor and Jesus in Dostoyevsky's *The Brothers Karamazov* (1880)—and instead, adopt and hide within conventions and roles that appear to signify real freedom, meaning, and happiness, but in fact perpetuate a life of bad faith that results from a succession of false choices.

The existentialist notion that existence precedes essence relates to *Forbidden Games*. At the beginning of *Forbidden Games*, Michel and Paulette are presented clearly as children, albeit for different reasons, and thus marked as containing an essence by which they are defined. Adult spectators feel sympathy, especially, for Paulette, in part because she lost her family, but in part because she is perceived *as a child*, and the loss ironically reinforces the idea that she is innocent and helpless, and that childhood more generally is a state of being marked by similar qualities. This sense that she is "merely" a child—a spoiled Parisian child used to certain luxuries—is the reason Monsieur Dollé allows her into the family: she can be a companion for and looked after by Michel, their youngest child, so the adults can continue their work of maintaining the farm, adult farm-work here standing in direct contrast to the kind of children's barnyard play one finds, for example, in E. B. White's *Charlotte's Web* (1952).

But as the relationship between Michel and Paulette develops, they begin to define themselves less in terms of essence—less in terms of the way they are perceived as children—and more in terms of the choices they make about play, choices that seem profoundly adult and shocking precisely because they challenge the way a child and play are typically perceived. Through their play, and the ethical and moral choices that frame the games they play, Michel and Paulette begin to challenge and defy the essentialist assumptions underlying the category "child," as they have been labelled by Monsieur and Madame Dollé. They define themselves in terms of "existence"—that is, the physical and thoughtful actions of planning, strategizing, hiding, stealing, digging, burying, and so forth. Paulette and Michel do not suddenly cease to be children: they don't turn into demonic child monsters (a not unrelated genre, historically speaking). And though the initial framing of *Forbidden Games* during the opening credits is a children's picture book—suggesting to audiences that they watch the movie through a fairy-tale lens, as in Clément's *Beauty and the Beast* (*La belle et la bête*, 1946)—the very serious point of *Forbidden Games* is an examination of human nature and what it means to be a real human child affected by a real war. The children deconstruct the way they are perceived not by *not* playing—a negation of the negation—but, once they are unsupervised and can conduct their games in secret, by making choices that are not typically associated with children, especially in the 1950s. They themselves, as children, put away childish things (Corinthians).

Unsurprisingly, given the global effects of World War II (perhaps most famously summed up by the phrase "God is dead"), other key existentialist terms in the immediate postwar period were "alienation" and "crisis," both of which also connect to *Forbidden Games* and children's play. In existentialist philosophy, broadly speaking, to be alienated means to be separated from yourself, isolated from someone else, and estranged from God. As Mehdi Hojjat puts it: "In existential writing, the concept of alienation is used primarily to refer to a kind of psychological and spiritual malaise which is pervasive in modern society though it is not specific to it."[22] *Forbidden Games* is a story about alienation, especially as it applies to Paulette. In the beginning, Paulette is clearly alienated both from herself and from someone else because of the death of her parents and dog. And as the web of lies and dishonesties that surround her games with Michel take her further from any kind of divine, revelatory truth, she is, arguably, alienated from God. Her meeting with the village pastor is significant, for the result of the discussion is an acknowledgement of her lack of religious understanding. The theme of alienation is reiterated in the movie's final scene at the Red Cross shelter. Paulette wanders into a crowd of adults because she hears a disembodied voice calling, "Michel." Mistakenly looking for someone who she thinks is her friend, she drifts away into a crowd of teeming adults, an exile, alienated in her own country.

In his short essay on *Forbidden Games*, Andre Bazin notes that the children occupy a place in the narrative that is essentially "identical to the one adult characters might have occupied."[23] The most obvious example of this revolves around the adult and child graveyards, where the human and animal burials take place. The village pastor oversees the official graveyard adjacent to the church. Paulette and Michel build their own cemetery, which contains graves adorned by matching crosses the children have spent much time and energy stealing (Figure 8.1).

Although the children's cemetery is hidden inside a deserted mill far away from adults' prying eyes while the adult cemetery is outside the church for all to see, what happens to both cemeteries is the same. In a sequence to which many critics have objected because of its mockery of the French peasantry, the warring Dollé and Gouard families desecrate the church cemetery by fighting and, ultimately, falling into the freshly dug grave meant for Georges, Michel's older brother, who had died as a result of being struck by a horse and cart. The Paulette and Michel's cemetery, which, ironically, is a place of wonder, pride, and enchantment for them both—a place to play—is destroyed by Michel, who had told his father where it was on the promise that he would not hand Paulette over

FIGURE 8.1. The cemetery in which Paulette and Michel bury the dead animals they find (*Forbidden Games*, 1952, Rialto Pictures). Frame-grab.

to the police, only to find that his father lied and, in fact, had every intention of letting the police take Paulette away to the Red Cross centre. In both instances, death begets death or, at least, destruction. Of course, the two scenarios have their differences: the desecration of the official graveyard by the two patriarchs is presented comically, while the destruction of the unofficial graveyard by Michel is deadly serious. However, the differences are clearly designed so that audiences see the adult games and behaviour mimicked in the games of the children.

With regard to play, the film seems to acknowledge what, in *The Ambiguity of Play*, Brian Sutton-Smith calls "the play of the gods."[24] Drawing on the work of Wendy Doniger O'Flaherty, Don Handelman, and Erik Erikson—critics whose backgrounds are in the disciplines of cosmology, mythology, dreams, and play theory (as well as other areas, of course)—Sutton-Smith suggests that human beings across history, time, and cultures are captives of the "play of fortune and luck...God's favor...[or] the play of the last chance."[25] For these and other critics, Sutton-Smith argues, one way children's play might be defined is as the "illusion of mastery over life's circumstances."[26] In some obvious sense, Paulette and Michel respond to the circumstances in which they find themselves by creating a physical and emotional place where they can create their own games and accompanying rules. Regardless of how macabre the games might seem to an adult outsider—the outsiders being either the adults in the film or the adults watching the film—they serve a specific function for Paulette and Michel. For Paulette, whose parents were killed because they ran across the bridge to protect her, the games provide a momentary sense of physical and emotional control over a life that seems very much out of control (or, in existentialist terms, meaningless). For Michel, the games provide a means by which he develops what he hopes will be a lasting relationship with Paulette, a point not lost on Madame Dollé.

However, in other ways, the film reveals that the control and mastery Paulette and Michel innocently think they have is illusory: much of what happens in *Forbidden Games*, as in life, is determined by either luck or fate—the play of the gods. Characters make deliberate choices, but these are just as likely to reap unintended consequences. Many of the refugees are fated to die, as they are all easy targets for roaming airplanes. It is luck that Paulette survives the bullets that whistle past her and murder her family. At the beginning of the film, the injury George, Michel's older brother, receives from a spooked horse may seem completely accidental and unforeseen, yet was highly likely given the fleeing refugees' confusion and terror caused by the planes. The long, simmering conflict between Monsieur Dollé and Monsieur Gouard, which finally erupts in the graveyard scene when Michel hints to his father that Monsieur Gouard probably stole all the crosses from the hearse, unintentionally reveals the identity of the real thieves: Paulette and Michel, the two children perpetuating the lie. Thus, in attempting to control the narrative, to maintain the deception sometimes playfully sometimes seriously, the truth about the lie is revealed. Michel and Paulette's thinking that through play they will be able to control their short- and long-term futures—she will overcome her parent's death; he will develop a relationship with Paulette—is seen as illusory. This doesn't diminish the role of play. Rather, it reinforces the notion of humans as the playthings of the gods.

TRAUMA

Critics typically see *Forbidden Games* through a World War II lens and the aesthetics of Italian neorealism. Bosley Crowther, writing in 1952, argued that for French audiences, *Forbidden Games* does for World War II what *The Grand Illusion* (*Le Grande Illusion*, Jean Renoir, 1937) did for World War I.[27] Contemporary critics such as Peter Mathews see Italian neorealism and French postwar films like *Forbidden Games* as expressions of European and American film industries grappling with what Anne Marie Kelley calls the "psychic scar [that] was left on the world" after World War II.[28] *Forbidden Games* occupies a central place in the history of children's cinema and film (however those terms are defined), not just because of its relation to history, war, and children's play but because of how all three intersect with the lasting effects of trauma.

Cathy Caruth argues that trauma is not just a "simple and healable event" located in a "violent or original" moment in an individual, character, or nation's past.[29] For Caruth, trauma is ongoing, the aftershocks erupting and continuing long after the initial experience. In a text, a character might reveal their trauma in obvious ways—anguished looks or cries of pain—but also in less obvious ways. Caruth suggests that trauma is revealed through an "itinerary of insistently recurring words or figures" that at first seem unconnected to the initial event but that eventually, over time (time in real life or time in a fictional life) reveal the extent of the trauma.[30] She cites examples such as "departure, falling, burning, or awakening," words that seem innocent enough at first but in repetition, in their constant occurrence, in fact "bear witness to some forgotten wound."[31] In short, the repetition of these words and phrases might suggest an event healed through language—a talking cure—but for Caruth, they more likely highlight the degree to which the original conflict, and its violence, remains unresolved even as it cries out for resolution through language.

We might think of *Forbidden Games*, children's play, and trauma, this way. Critics typically focus on the play of the children that occurs as a result of the death of Paulette's parents. The forbidden games Michel and Paulette play involve stealing crosses for the graves in their makeshift cemetery, and one might argue that each grave dug goes toward resolving the initial crisis of her parent's death and that, therefore, the games do indeed function therapeutically (Figure 8.2).

Caruth's point, however, is that a traumatic event is not simply healable through one act. Quite the opposite, in fact: the unresolved nature of the trauma is revealed through the repetition of words and phrases and actions. Furthermore, Caruth points out, "What returns to haunt the victim is not only the reality of the event but the reality of the way its violence has not been fully known."[32] Thus, we would argue that, for Paulette at least, the trauma of seeing her dead parents (she does not witness the actual moment of their deaths) is not resolved through the various burials; rather, each burial re-enacts the way the violence of the trauma is not yet fully known or realised. The trauma of parental loss is not resolved through the actions of choosing a new grave, excavating it, burying an

FIGURE 8.2. Paulette and Michel stealing fourteen crosses in the middle of the night (*Forbidden Games*, 1952, Rialto Pictures). Frame-grab.

animal, and stealing the right size cross to mark the grave. Rather, the sequence awakens the violence of the unresolved trauma even as the trauma is thought to be laid to rest through the repeated sequence of actions. In a sense, the trauma of play becomes the play of trauma.

A key term for Caruth is the idea of "double telling," whereby a trauma narrative reflects an "encounter with death [and] the ongoing experience of having survived it."[33] In part, the lasting success of *Forbidden Games* (and similar films) lies in this realm. The movie's narrative enacts a double telling. Overall, from the beginning to the end there are characters who die as a result of the war, and those who live. It's about the death of loved ones, but also the ongoing life of the survivors, Michel and Paulette, because of the games they play.

From *Empire of the Sun* to *Forbidden Games*, films about children playing during war are made by adults, and perhaps one grown-up theme cloaked in the archetypal raiment of the child is that of adult trauma. As discussed, *Forbidden Games* is set within a particular historical context, that of World War II. The fictional world of the film—the setting for and the drama of the forbidden games the children play—is framed by the historical narrative. For example, in an early scene of *Forbidden Games*, Monsieur Dollé is reading a newspaper whose headlines and stories confirm the date and events of June 1940. Other scenes in the film allude to actual, historically verifiable events: the exodus itself, the death of numerous refugees, the orphanage, and so forth. In this context, the historical narrative informs audiences, positions them as spectators to bear witness to the reality of what happened. However, Caruth's argument is that trauma reveals itself through the repetition of insistently recurring words and phrases that point to the violence of the trauma yet to be known. The repetition of historical scenes in *Forbidden Games* are the insistently recurring words and phrases—individual mise-en-scènes, if you like—that appear to bring to the adult audiences' attention a sense of history. But the historical allusions, skilfully woven into the fabric of the film, also point to the trauma that has yet to be realised and thus resolved. In other words, the movie's historical narrative doesn't resolve the trauma, but is complicit in its cover-up. History functions here as sleight-of-hand, distraction, illusion. It is the archetype of the children playing in an abandoned mill that begins the process of excavating the buried wounds. Through play, the trauma buried by historical reference is reawakened and brought to the surface.

Conclusion

What is a children's film? The significance and influence of *Forbidden Games* was such that Andre Bazin and other important French film critics felt compelled to discuss the film in terms of adaptation and definition. In his 1952 essay of the same name, Bazin compares *Forbidden Games* to other roughly contemporaneous children's film adaptations, including *Road to Life* (Nikolai Ekk, 1931), *Emil and the Detectives* (Gerhard Lamprecht, 1931), and *Hue and Cry* (Charles Crichton, 1947). In doing so, Bazin finds these other films wanting. As adaptations, Bazin argues, they are fundamentally closer to fairy tales and sacred parables than to realist novels, and thus tend to idealize and romanticize the child characters by projecting onto them conventional tropes of innocence, including the mistaken belief that the association between fairy tales and children mandates a happy ending. For Bazin, these and similar children's films pale in comparison to the "originality" and "uniqueness" of *Forbidden Games*, which "refuses to play along" with the conventional wisdom regarding the innocence of childhood, most obviously because of the presence of "necromantic fantasies and…obsessive death rituals in [the] animal cemetery they create," but also through the absence of a happy ending.[34] Monsieur Dollé does not regret beating Michel and forcing him to reveal the whereabouts of the crosses. Paulette and Michel are not reunited. Quite the opposite: Michel destroys the cemetery and Paulette gets lost in the crowd. In other words, for Bazin, *Forbidden Games* is the "first example of its kind on the screen…to tell the truth" about the realities of some children's lives, that there is no place like home at the end of the rainbow.[35]

Half a century later, in 2015, Anat Pick's "Reflexive Realism in René Clément's *Forbidden Games*," which focuses on the film's symbolic use of animals (especially Paulette's dead dog, Jock), makes a similar point about definition, that *Forbidden Games* is neither "a children's film, a war film, or an animal film," and that though the movie figures the death of Paulette's pet dog as the death of innocence, "Childhood…is not simply a victim of war, as would be the case in the conventional war and children's film."[36] In short, critics then and now see *Forbidden Games* as raising lasting, perplexing, and contradictory questions about definition as a function of how stories focused on children are adapted from their adult source material. As in numerous other war films featuring children, its central protagonists are children, a central trope is that of children's play, and the closing scenes of Paulette frightened and alone clearly allude to questions of trauma. Yet, just as canonical children's texts such as *Alice's Adventures in Wonderland* (1865) escape easy classification as children's literature, *Forbidden Games*, despite, or because of, its emphasis on history, war, play, and trauma, refuses to be marked simply as a children's film. Enigmatic then and now, *Forbidden Games* occupies a singular place in children's film history.

NOTES

1. See Cathy Caruth, *Unclaimed Experience: Trauma, Narrative, and History* (Baltimore, MD: Johns Hopkins University Press, 1996).
2. The terms derive from E. Ann Kaplan, *Trauma Culture: The Politics of Terror and Loss in Media and Literature* (New Brunswick, NJ: Rutgers University Press, 2005); and Mark Seltzer, *Serial Killers: Death and Life in America's Wound Culture* (London: Routledge, 1998).
3. Joanna Santa Barbara, "Impact of War on Children and Imperative to End War," *Croatian Medical Journal* 47:6 (2006), pp. 891–894.
4. George Eisen, *Children and Play in the Holocaust: Games among the Shadows* (Amherst: University of Massachusetts Press, 1988), 5.
5. Johan Huizinga, *Homo Ludens: A Study of Play-Element in Culture* (New York: Roy Publishers, 1950), p. 4.
6. Bert Cardullo, "The Children Are Watching Us," *Hudson Review* 54:2 (2001), pp. 295–304, at 298.
7. Simon Hall, *1956: The World in Revolt* (New York: Pegasus, 2015), 31.
8. Hanna Diamond, *Fleeing Hitler: France 1940* (Oxford: Oxford University Press, 2007), p. 213.
9. Diamond, *Fleeing Hitler.*, p., 1.
10. Ibid., p. 2.
11. Ibid., p. 3.
12. Ibid., p. 27.
13. Huizinga, *Homo Ludens*, pp. 7, 8.
14. Ibid., p. 5.
15. Ibid., p. 10.
16. Ibid., p. 19.
17. Ibid., pp. 20, 25.
18. Saul Mcleod, "Vygotsky," *Simply Psychology*, 2020, https://www.simplypsychology.org/vygotsky.html [accessed, November 23, 2021].
19. See also Innocent Sinners (Philip Leacock, 1958).
20. For a concise discussion of main existentialist ideas, see Gordon Marino, *The Existentialist's Survival Guide: How to Live Authentically in an Inauthentic Age* (New York: HarperCollins, 2018), pp. 36–56.
21. Marino, *Existentialist's Survival Guide.*

22. Mehdi Hojjat and Esmaeel Daronkolace, "A Survey of Man's Alienation in a Modern World: Existential Reading of Sam Shepard's *Buried Child* and *True West*," *International Journal of Humanities and Social Sciences* 2:7 (April 2012), pp. 202–209, at 202.

23. Andre Bazin, "*Forbidden Games*," in Bert Cardullo (ed.), *Bazin at Work: Major Essays and Reviews from the Forties and Fifties*, trans. Alain Peitte and Bert Cardullo (New York: Routledge, 1997), pp. 129–135 at 134.

24. Brian Sutton-Smith, *The Ambiguity of Play* (Cambridge, MA: Harvard University Press, 1997), p. 53.

25. Sutton-Smith, *Ambiguity of Play*, 53.

26. Ibid., p. 54.

27. Bosley Crowther, "*Forbidden Games*, the Winning French Film at Venice Fete, Opens at Little Carnegie," *New York Times*, December 9, 1952, https://www.nytimes.com/1952/12/09/archives/the-screen-in-review-forbidden-games-the-winning-french-film-at.html [accessed November 23, 2021].

28. Peter Matthews, "*Forbidden Games*," *Classic Art Films* (blog), August 6, 2015, www.classicartfilms.com/forbidden-games-1952 [accessed December 2, 2019]; Anne Marie Kelley, "Hit Me with Your Best Shot: *Forbidden Games*," *We Recycle Movies*, March 20, 2013, https://werecyclemovies.wordpress.com [accessed December 2, 2019].

29. Caruth, *Unclaimed Experience*, pp. 3–4.

30. Ibid., p. 5.

31. Ibid., 5, 7.

32. Ibid., p. 6.

33. Ibid., pp. 8, 7.

34. Bazin, "*Forbidden Games*," 133, 135; Diamond, *Fleeing Hitler*, p. 213.

35. Bazin, "*Forbidden Games*," p. 135.

36. Anat Pick, "Reflexive Realism in René Clément's *Forbidden Games*," *Yale French Studies* 12 (2015), pp. 205–220, at 218, 220.

BIBLIOGRAPHY

Bazin, Andre. "*Forbidden Games*." In Bert Cardullo (ed.), *Bazin at Work: Major Essays and Reviews from the Forties and Fifties*, trans. Alain Peitte and Bert Cardullo. New York: Routledge, 1997, pp. 129–135.

Cardullo, Bert. "The Children Are Watching Us." *Hudson Review* 54:2 (2001), pp. 295–304.

Caruth, Cathy. *Unclaimed Experience: Trauma, Narrative, and History*. Baltimore, MD: Johns Hopkins University Press, 1996.

Diamond, Hanna. *Fleeing Hitler: France 1940*. Oxford: Oxford University Press, 2007.

Eisen, George. *Children and Play in the Holocaust: Games among the Shadows*. Amherst: University of Massachusetts Press, 1988.

Hall, Simon. *1956: The World in Revolt*. New York: Pegasus Books, 2015.

Huizinga, Johan. *Homo Ludens: A Study of Play-Element in Culture*. New York: Roy Publishers, 1950.

Marino, Gordon. *The Existentialist's Survival Guide*. New York: HarperCollins, 2018.

Sutton-Smith, Brian. *The Ambiguity of Play*. Cambridge, MA: Harvard University Press, 1997.

CHAPTER 9

CHANGING CONCEPTIONS OF CHILDHOOD IN THE WORK OF THE CHILDREN'S FILM FOUNDATION

ROBERT SHAIL

THE Children's Film Foundation (CFF) was a unique British organization. From its creation in 1951 until its demise as a production company in the early 1980s, the CFF produced sixty-minute feature films, slapstick comedy shorts, cliffhanger serials, and assorted educational items for screening across a network of Saturday film clubs throughout the United Kingdom, and beyond; this work was aimed exclusively at children. Generations of British youngsters were introduced to filmgoing through the foundation's work and kept the habit into adulthood. In their final years, they became the Children's Film and Television Foundation (CFTF), and their productions were also seen on the small screen. After the 1980s, when their state funding was cut, they moved from filmmaking into script development, and then finally found an advisory role as they struggled to secure further funding. More recently, they have changed name again and are now a campaigning organization called the Children's Media Foundation (CMF), which champions young media users in the United Kingdom.

Apart from making a huge impact on the cultural and social lives of children in Britain, the foundation was an experiment that sought to demonstrate the power of film to positively influence the citizens of tomorrow. Inherent in this approach was both a belief in the ability of cinema to influence audiences and a commitment to a set of civic values deemed to be largely self-evident. Consequently, its films frequently reflect or respond to dominant cultural conceptions regarding the nature of childhood at any given time.[1] In the 1960s and again in the 1980s, the foundation revised its underpinning value system in response to changing attitudes in the United Kingdom, perceiving a more liberal shift in attitudes to race, gender, and class with which it needed to keep pace. This chapter considers the CFF's intentions toward its audience through an examination of its changing output and through primary research into the responses of its audience so as to both gauge its influence and understand how its value system shaped the work it produced.

THE CHILDREN'S FILM FOUNDATION: AN OVERVIEW

To understand how the Children's Film Foundation developed its ethos, it is useful to trace the growth of children's filmgoing in Britain prior to its appearance in the early 1950s. In this, we will see how pressure grew on the film industry to regulate the way it catered to a young audience, providing a context for the creation of the CFF. According to Terry Staples, the first screenings specifically for children, which can be traced back at least to 1900, were "straightforwardly commercial and exploitative."[2] Children's screenings proliferated as cinema managers realised they were a way to make use of an auditorium in time slots that were otherwise going to be empty: Saturday mornings. The formal organization of regular screenings for children, rather than ad hoc arrangements, is usually credited to the Granada chain and began in 1927.

An aspect of these screenings, crucial for the creation of the CFF, was the lack of care taken by some cinema managers over both the content and, on occasions, the organization of the screenings. The latter led to a series of dreadful accidents—including the worst-ever cinema disaster involving children, which took place on December 31, 1929, at the Glen Cinema, in Paisley, Scotland, when seventy-five children died in the panic that followed a fire. As the 1930s progressed, and such incidents ceased, these anxieties focused on concerns over content. Staples charts the furore over what was screened to children from 1909 to the early 1940s. This concern was initially channelled via local authorities who could refuse to grant licences based on issues of programme content. An attempt by the industry to challenge this was defeated in the High Court, opening the floodgates to individuals and pressure groups besieging local licensing authorities with complaints over the screening of material they saw as inappropriate.[3] Many of these organizations had a religious agenda and were focused on what they saw as the damaging effects of cinema on the behaviour of children. They were particularly alarmed by what they saw as the increasing lack of respect shown by youngsters for traditional values and those in authority.

A series of public inquiries followed the High Court's ruling and continued throughout the interwar period. The results were inconclusive but, as Staples shows, critics of children's screenings could select from different reports the elements that seemed to support their case.[4] By the late 1930s, producers had started to respond to the climate of criticism by making films aimed exclusively at children. Ironically, the most influential model in the United Kingdom actually came from the United States, in the form of the Mickey Mouse Club. A number of British cinema chains began to follow their format, including the ABC cinema chain, which developed the ABC Minors in 1937. The success of the ABC Minors led to imitations from other chains, such as Gaumont. However, the development of an organized system of children's screenings in the 1930s did little to stop the flow of criticism or the plethora of public inquiries, which continued well into the 1940s. Typical of the criticism was an article in *The Times* in 1946 by the sociologist J. P. Mayer, who suggested not enough films were being made with an audience of children in mind.[5] Further regionally based reports followed, along with more letters to *The Times*, and a conference organized by the British Film Institute. The debate eventually reached the House of Commons in the winter of 1946.

The industry was keen to forestall legislation and therefore finally took its own steps to respond to the public criticism. Key to this response was J. Arthur Rank, head of the Rank Organization, who, by the early war period, had acquired ownership of both the Granada and Odeon chains. A devout Methodist and former Methodist Sunday School teacher, Rank took an interest in the potential for the clubs to serve as a moral beacon. As Geoffrey Macnab puts it, Rank was keen "to inculcate youth with 'good Christian values.'"[6] One of Rank's companies, Gaumont-British Instructional (GBI), was tasked with producing a ten-minute film for children extolling the importance of honesty. The film, titled *Tom's Ride* (Darrell Catling, 1944), was released to the clubs and laid the foundation for what became the CFF. Rank deemed the film a success, and in 1947 appointed Mary Field to head a new Children's Film Department (CFD) at GBI, later renamed Children's Entertainment Films (CEF). Field had trained as a teacher but, in the early 1920s, worked in the film industry as an adviser to GBI and was then appointed as their Education Manager. Her background couldn't have been more appropriate, particularly in terms of her commitment to the educational value of films. A crucial step in the creation of the CFF was the publication, on May 5, 1950, of Wheare's Departmental Committee Report on children and cinema. It came to the broad conclusion that Saturday cinema clubs for children were a good thing. More importantly, they held up the CEF as an exemplar of good practice.

Mary Field had already made her own, rather idiosyncratic attempt to make the case for public sector investment by doing an experimental survey. She was keen to show that children's films made by the CEF had more impact than ones produced commercially. In 1948, she tried to obtain evidence by taking still photographs during a live screening with the aid of a flash, which didn't go down well with the young audience. In 1951, she did a similar experiment, this time using an infrared camera. Many of her findings, such as the need to avoid child audiences receiving unexpected frights and the importance of encouraging their positive identification with characters, became guidelines for the subsequent CFF output.

At this point, Rank was suffering serious financial problems. Needing to make cutbacks, the Rank Organization GBI tried to shift responsibility for taking-up the recommendations of the Wheare Report to the wider industry. The four major trade associations agreed to step in to create a new production body to be called the Children's Film Foundation. Funding was to come from the British Film Production Board, which would put part of the revenue from the Eady Levy—a small tax on cinema admissions—towards the CFF. The foundation was to be non-profit-making, with any income generated put back into the production pot. The official launch of the CFF was announced on July 4, 1951. The management board was chaired by Rank himself, with Mary Field as CEO. They announced the production of three feature films, along with two projects that were still in the script stage. The foundation divided cinemas into four groupings: Odeon, Gaumont, ABC, and independents. By 1952, the foundation had begun to release its first productions to these cinema chains: two feature films, four shorts, and travelogues, and published the first editions of *Our Magazine*. Field described these first films as "exploratory," and suggested that the CFF would be keeping a close eye on children's responses.[7] On October 20, 1952, an audience of three hundred school children were invited to a test screening at the Haymarket cinema in London; the results were positive. Further support came when the president of the British Board of Film Classification (BBFC) then gave his approval to the moral content of the CFF films.[8]

The CFF settled into a typical production rate of five or six films per year. The intention was that a complete programme running ninety minutes would be available to each Saturday cinema club. Its output during this period shows the strong influence of Mary Field. A gang of assorted kids, typically ranging in age from four to fourteen, uncover the plans of a criminal gang. Unable to go to the police (for some reason provided by the script), they have to catch the villains themselves. Alternatively, they find themselves in a competition, sporting or otherwise, with a rival gang whose underhand methods our heroes challenge, eventually winning by fair means. Boys usually take the lead, and girls have a supporting role. Bravery, resourcefulness, loyalty, and honesty are prized, whereas the villains are the cheats and bullies. Britain is a White country; its children are polite and smartly dressed, and show due deference to adults, particularly teachers and policemen. The accents are middle class, even when the settings aren't (Mary Field was keen on overdubbing dialogue and preferred to use trained acting-school graduates). Not everyone was enthusiastic about these tendencies. One reviewer bemoaned the fact that the children in *The Secret Cave* "are so excessively well-behaved and nicely spoken that they suggest Kensington Gardens and governesses instead of a Wessex village."[9] During the next six years of production, the CFF released twenty-eight titles. Of these, ten were adventure serials. Field put much of her energy into the cliffhanger serials that characterize the output during these years. The style was set by the first release, *Five on a Treasure Island* (Gerald Landau, 1957), which was adapted from one of Enid Blyton's popular Famous Five novels.

In 1960, the foundation published a comprehensive report assessing its first ten years of operation.[10] It set out three aims: to provide "healthy recreation" for children, to set high standards of taste and behaviour, and to employ the highest technical qualities. It made a promise that there would be "no sensationalism or unhealthy excitement or vulgarity." The language was redolent of Mary Field's ethos in the 1950s. However, the mid-1960s saw the foundation undergoing a significant change of direction. In 1964, the *Journal of the Society of Film and Television Arts* published a special issue on children's films, which included essays by Field and Henry Geddes; Geddes had already made several films for the CFF and was to take over as CEO that year. Most of Field's article is spent looking back at the achievements of the CEF. Geddes' piece looks to the future. He puts some distance between himself and the posture of the earlier foundation: these are "healthy" films for youngsters, certainly, but the principal job of the CFF is to provide regular entertainment for children. He limits the potential for "moral" influence to examples such as *Valley of the Kings* (Frederick Goode, 1964), which, he argues, encouraged children to take an interest in archaeology.[11]

There seems to have been a feeling among the members of the foundation's board that, in the age of Beatlemania and youth culture, the CFF's audience was changing. In 1964, it commissioned a survey of the foundation's activities, for which 1,500 interviews with audience members were carried out across forty-two cinemas. The results were published as *Progress Report: The CFF in the Sixties*. Among the findings was that the average age of club members was now only 8.8 years, which indicated a downward trend. The board was concerned that the foundation was losing half its potential audience and felt that it had to address their needs. In a turn that would probably have dismayed Mary Field, it was suggested that the high moral tone of the CFF's films should be softened. A programme of "new look" films was already underway, an indication of the CFF's awareness that a change was needed. These included *Go Kart Go* (Jan Darnley-Smith, 1963), *Seventy Deadly Pills* (Pat Jackson, 1963), and *Daylight Robbery* (Michael Truman, 1964). Another area covered by the survey was audience preferences, and the finding suggested that there was a gender divide. These findings were taken to validate the bias that the foundation took as self-evident. Henry Geddes responded to the report by issuing a new set of guidelines for filmmakers: he told them that children wanted stories with lots of action and excitement and a strong sense of right and wrong. The films should encourage children to be "fair, tolerant and responsible but without preaching." The changing mood is indicated by a specific reference to racial tolerance. However, the spirit of Mary Field hovers in the suggestion that the films will help children to "become responsible adults."[12]

The 1970s mark the CFF's last golden era of production before its fortunes began to decline. The films of this period provide a record of changing styles, habits, and environments. The children here are informal in comparison with their predecessors. They address adults with a degree of sardonic irreverence rather than the formal politeness of old; outside the classroom, there is little use of the term "sir" to address adult males. Most adults are less formal too, including the schoolteachers, who often have a careworn air about them but remain kindly and well-intentioned. The villains are a good deal more realistic and menacing. The influence of popular crime shows from television like *The Sweeney* (1975–1978) is evident. Britain is a more racially diverse place, and gender differences are less pronounced, though the narratives are still dominated by male characters and interests. Class barriers have broken down somewhat, and there is greater emphasis on working-class characters, as opposed to the middle-class characters of the past. The cultural revolution of the 1960s was largely ignored in terms of direct content in the stories told by the CFF, but its consequences are there to be seen.

By the late 1970s, the context was changing again. A report in *Screen International* in 1978 showed a dramatic drop in the number of cinemas that were running clubs; the total was down to just 350, less than half the number at the start of the decade.[13] Saturday-morning children's television was undoubtedly a major factor. On October 2, 1976, the BBC launched *Multi-Coloured Swap*, hosted by Noel Edmonds, which replicated many features the Saturday clubs. It ran for the better part of three hours, taking up the whole morning. The programme was immediately popular and established a Saturday-morning viewing trend. Nearly three years later, in May 1979, a Conservative government was elected. Later that year, the Cinematograph Films Council (CFC), which advised the Board of Trade on film policy, recommended reducing the Eady Levy payments to the Foundation by half. The Levy funding had already begun dwindling as UK cinema audience levels fell. But the most important factor, providing fuel for those in government and the industry who favoured the closure of the CFF, was the decline of the Saturday clubs. By the autumn of 1981, both EMI and Rank had discontinued their Saturday clubs, leaving only the independents, which now numbered about a hundred and generated roughly ten thousand admissions per week. The reduced funding allowed the foundation to make just one film for release in each of the following three years, totalling a mere ten films in 5 years.

But just as the foundation was on the brink of closure, J. Arthur Rank threw them a lifeline. In 1982, a new deal was announced, just as their Eady Levy grant was completely cut. In exchange for the foundation releasing films from their back catalogue to screening on television, Rank would fund the CFF for three years, with three new feature films to be made each year. These films might have a limited cinema run, but they would also be broadcast on television. Rank's thinking seems to have been that this three-year period would allow the foundation to establish itself as a provider of children's drama for television, perhaps on a semicommercial basis. This might have a longer-term future. By 1983 the new arrangement was in place, and the foundation had changed its name to Children's Film and Television Foundation. Among the CFTF's output were two of the most impressive films in the foundation's history: John Krish's *Out of the Darkness* (1985) and *Terry on the Fence* (1985), which were as morally challenging as they were toughly realistic.

Early in 1986, however, Rank made clear their intention not to renew their funding; they had financial challenges of their own and could no longer provide a safety net for the CFTF. Any hope of renewed funding from the Eady Levy died when the Conservative government closed the company down in 1985, and it soon became apparent that the domestic television broadcasters were not interested in extending their foundation contracts. By the close of 1986, the CFF had effectively come to the end of its 35-year existence as a producer of children's films.

THE CFF'S IDEOLOGICAL FRAMEWORK
IN PRACTICE

The "improving" ideology of the CFF is particularly apparent in the films it produced in the 1950s under the supervision of Mary Field. Her values, reflective of her middle-class upbringing between the wars, were assumed to represent a national consensus regarding what constituted a "good" childhood, this, in turn, building a solid foundation for a productive adult life as a British citizen. A close reading of two films from the fifties indicates the nature of these assumptions and their ideological boundaries, as well as Field's conviction that these values could be constructively communicated via cinema.

Johnny on the Run (Lewis Gilbert, 1953) was one of the most ambitious of the CFF's early features, with a seriousness of intent that helped establish its reputation. It showed a willingness to engage with topical subjects that was not always followed up in the company's later 1950s output, but which they did return to in the 1970s and 1980s. Here the topic is the treatment of refugees made homeless in the aftermath of World War II, in particular, the plight of orphaned children. Johnny, or rather Janek (Eugeniusz Chyiek), is a boy from Poland whom we first meet when he is being fostered by a less than welcoming family in Edinburgh. The foster mother, Mrs MacGregor (Mona Washbourne), is more interested in the money she gets from the state for his upkeep than his welfare, and her eldest son resents this "cuckoo in the nest." After being neglected at home and bullied by children in the streets, Johnny runs away in an effort to get back to Poland. On his journey, he falls into the hands of two inept housebreakers, played by Sydney Tafler and Michael Balfour (typical comic villains in the mode preferred by the CFF), but finally gets away from them and makes his way to a village in the Scottish countryside made up entirely of children who have been orphaned by the war. (Remarkably, this place actually existed in Renfrewshire, Scotland, where 640 orphaned children lived together in their own community under adult supervision.) Johnny is finally happy. But his new home is almost lost to him when the crooks turn up looking for their lost booty, and then Mrs MacGregor arrives on a similar mission.

The film benefits from location shooting in an atmospheric Edinburgh and the Scottish countryside. The children's performances are naturalistic and supported by experienced adult performers. The director was the young Lewis Gilbert, who would go on to a distinguished career that included directing three James Bond films. Gilbert brings style and pace to the film, which marks it out from the conservative approach to camera work and editing usually evident in the foundation's 1950s films. The film's real core strength, however, is in combining an exciting narrative with a message about understanding between nations in the postwar era of reconstruction. The depiction of the village, with its idyllic setting, where the children are involved in tending animals and where they operate a system of democracy in which they elect their own president, offers a vision of postwar progress and consensus. Pat Latham's script even manages a gentle commentary on social inequality when Johnny finds that the cost of a ticket to Poland is the impossible sum of £17, while the parents of a rich child are seen buying him a radio for the same amount. The film is at pains to smooth out the challenges of the period, which prove solvable through cooperation and generosity. The vision is a benevolent one.

Five on a Treasure Island is a more standard CFF product of the period and reveals the inherent conservatism of Field's vision. This eight-part serial is based on the first of Enid Blyton's popular Famous Five books. Originally published in 1942, it was followed by more than twenty volumes detailing the adventures of siblings Julian, Ann, and Dick; their cousin George (Georgina, but known as "George," as she is a tomboy)—played by Richard Palmer, Gillian Harrison, John Bailey and Rel Grainer, respectively—and George's dog, Timmy. The serial was scripted by Michael Barnes; Frank Wells was in charge of the production and provided the initial treatment. The project was considered important enough for Rank themselves to produce; it was directed by the experienced editor Gerald Landau, in his only credit as director. The CFF format for adventure serials had been established, first in 1955, with *Raiders of the River*, followed a year later by *Five Clues to Fortune* (Joe Mendoza, 1956); both films were produced by Merton Park, but it was the popularity of *Five on a Treasure Island* that established the importance of the formula, which the CFF exploited for the next fifteen years. It was followed by *The Carringford School Mystery* (William Hammond, 1958), *Mystery in the Mine* (James Hill, 1959), and, eventually, by a direct sequel, *Five Have a Mystery to Solve* (Ernest Morris, 1964). The narrative *Five on a Treasure Island* unfolds over eight episodes of roughly fifteen minutes, each with a cliffhanger ending. Each new episode opens with a recap, featuring brief clips from previous episodes.

The story finds the Five on summer holiday with George's parents on the south coast of England. George's father owns an island on which there is a ruined castle. Nearby is a shipwreck that contains clues to a treasure. While diving at the wreck The children find a box containing a map that leads them to a network of underground tunnels on the island and eventually to a horde of gold bars. Two crooked antique dealers are on the trail of the treasure, and the plot develops through a series of reversals as first the children and then the villains find themselves locked-up on the island. Help arrives from the mainland, and the crooks are caught. The story is episodic but each instalment has its own chase sequence before climaxing in the expected cliffhanger. Pleasure is afforded by an idealized image of childhood summers, albeit privileged ones—there is plenty of time for picnics. The children are loyal, have happy relationships with the adults (other than the villains), and triumph through tenacity and courage. Blyton has been criticized by some contemporary commentators for her alleged sexism, class consciousness, and xenophobia. There is little evidence of the latter in the film, but there is material that falls into the first two categories. Despite his financial problems, Uncle Quentin lives in a mansion. He and the other characters have middle-class accents; there are many exclamations of "gosh" and "old chap." Both girls are involved in the action, but George's tomboy status is confirmed by her hair being short. She also has the indignity of being told, as an intended complement, that she couldn't have done better if she had been a boy. If these attitudes seem chauvinist and snobby, the CFF was reflecting values still held by parts of British society at this time. In this respect, *Five on a Treasure Island* is indicative of a backward-looking conservatism that dominated the company's conception of childhood in the 1950s.

Adapting to Changing Conceptions
of Childhood

The degree to which ideological constructions of childhood are related to their wider context of production is evident in the changing ethos of the foundation over the next three decades, as it recalibrated its sense of what a productive childhood was. *Cup Fever* (1965) provides telling evidence of how the CFF struggled with developments in its young audience during the 1960s. Here, the young players of Barton United in Manchester are playing in their local cup competition when their hopes of success are sabotaged by the underhand machinations of a corrupt local councillor (David Lodge). What follows is a typical CFF adventure in which the humble Barton United players use their ingenuity to find new training facilities before appearing in the cup final. The sort of class undercurrents evident in *Go Kart Go* emerge again and reflect the changing social landscape in Britain. The Barton players have homemade shirts, a shed for a changing room, and practice in the street. Despite this, they never resort to the dishonest tactics used by their wealthier opponents and triumph in the end. As always in the foundation's films, it's not just winning that matters but how you achieve it. The film has a sense of realism, enhanced by location shooting, from the opening shot of a muddy football field fronting a block of flats. Further evidence of change at the foundation is provided by the appearance of a Black character and that there are Mancunian accents among the familiar London and Home Counties ones. But if the realism is indicative of the foundation's revised style in the 1960s, its attitudes to gender haven't shifted. This is a boys' film; girls are reduced to the secondary role of washing the club's shirts and heating water for their showers. The nadir comes when the girls are not allowed to join the visit to Old Trafford and volunteer instead to spend their time sewing new shirts for the boys.

The values of the Mary Field era cast a long shadow, as evidenced by director John Krish's account of working for the CFF in the late 1950s. Complaining that child actors were from middle-class backgrounds, even when the setting and subject were working class, he said: "Mary Field insisted on this. In my opinion, there was a case for renaming them as the "Middle Class Children's Film Foundation" at that time... I have to say that I felt her view of childhood was out of touch with most children's lives and out of date, even in the 1950s."[14]

By the final years of production, the CFTF had shifted ground considerably, particularly in relation to class. One of the most mature films in the foundation's history, *Terry on the Fence*, is evidence of this. Bearing more than a passing resemblance to the BBC's ground-breaking children's television series *Grange Hill* (1978–2008), it presents a world of moral ambiguities with a toughness that goes further than any previous production. The film begins with one of the foundation's favourite themes, the runaway. Terry (Jack McNicholl) has a row at home with his mother and when she slaps him he runs off. Wandering around, he accidently comes across a gang of tough kids led by the menacing Les (Neville Watson). They force Terry to lead them to his school and show them where to find a cupboard full of radios. When the radios go missing, suspicion falls on Terry, but he won't give up the identity of Les, having witnessed at firsthand the brutal treatment he receives from his own mother. In the end, justice is done, and Terry is acquitted, but he is also able to speak on behalf of Les, for whom he feels considerable sympathy.

Terry on the Fence has a grittiness that is exceptional for the foundation. For the first time a film children are heard swearing, albeit using mild terms like "bloody." Les has a knife that he uses to break into the school, and there is an underlying threat in the first scenes between Terry and the gang. There is even the acknowledgement of the racial tensions in a Britain being hit by race riots when a Black boy and White boy in Les's gang exchange insults. The film's depiction of violence led to the first conflict between the foundation and the British Board of Film Classification (BBFC) as a result of which the use of a knife by Les to threaten Terry was removed, although the depiction of his scar (including an eye-watering moment when he scratches it to show Terry he is serious) was left in. In addition, *Terry on the Fence* follows the example of other late CFTF films like *Friend or Foe* (John Krish, 1982) in presenting its young audience with moral challenges far from the certainties of its earlier work. Les is initially a frightening figure, but when we learn about his life we see him differently. Unlike the foundation's early films, there is nothing reassuring here; moral decisions can be hard.

The film's writer, Bernard Ashley, confirms that such attempts to reflect the reality of children's lives—which he witnessed as a teacher—could still pose difficulties in the 1980s: "I remember that the BBFC objected to a scene in which Terry is threatened with a knife; so, bizarrely, this was altered to have Terry threatened with being imprisoned and left to starve! The BBFC would not grant a U certificate with the knife in the film."[15] In its attempts to conceptualize the morality of childhood, the CFF found itself needing to adjust to a shifting value system and a developing context. The Britain of the 1980s was a different from the Britain of the 1950s, and in the foundation's attempts to adjust to changing audience expectations was an implicit admission that it was now more likely to reflect a wider moral agenda than to set the agenda itself.

INVESTIGATING THE FOUNDATION'S AUDIENCE

By the late 1950s, the network of Saturday morning children's film clubs had settled into a pattern. Generations of children became familiar with the foundation's logo: a shot of Trafalgar Square with the pigeons rising into the air while the bells of St. Martin's sound in the background. A typical Saturday morning programme was divided in two sections with an intermission. During the first half there was a series of short items, including cartoons, two-reel comedies, educational shorts, and an episode from a serial. The second half was a feature film. The intermission might simply act as a break, but it could be an opportunity to supplement the programme with competitions, birthday announcements, and the like. The first half of the programme included contributions from the CFF, but much non-foundation material was also used. This ranged from silent comedy shorts to various serials in the western and science fiction genres. The majority of these were American, as were the cartoons. However, the feature used in the second half was usually a CFF production. These were deliberately made to run for sixty minutes so as to provide a balanced programme. The CFF's records suggest that during their peak period of operation, from the mid-1950s to the mid-1970s, there were around eight hundred cinemas taking part (about half the United Kingdom total), with weekly attendance between 320,000 and 500,000, probably averaging about 400,000; total annual admissions were around twenty million. These were communal gatherings that allowed children to escape from the home and the influence of parents into a place that was still safe, as well as being cheap to access, but where they could socialize with friends, exercise their imaginations, and indulge in a degree of mild misbehaviour without fear of the consequences. What may have confused, and disappointed, Mary Field is that the educational influence of the films seems to have been negligible. More fascinating is the degree to which the screening provided evidence of the general dissatisfaction of children with their daily round and their desire to find two hours in the week when they could shake this off.

In writing my own book-length study of the CFF, I undertook to investigate the nature of the impact the screenings had on their audience. This is particularly relevant considering the Foundation's avowed aims, which went beyond simply providing entertainment. The CFF meant to shape the British citizen of tomorrow, not just into a cinema-goer but into a conscientious and moral citizen who would know right from wrong, who would be willing to stand up to the bullies, and who had a developed sense of fair play. These concerns seem relevant today at a time when the allegedly pernicious effect of the media on children is still the subject of tabloid debate. The view of the CFF was the opposite, seeing the potential for a constructive influence in the lives of future adults.

My three surveys were carried out during 2013 and 2014. The first made use of work colleagues by surveying staff and students from the University of Wales, Trinity St. David at its campuses in Lampeter, Carmarthen, and Swansea. I received close to a hundred responses. I used a questionnaire as a starting point for conversation or correspondence. The questions covered basic quantitative information and asked about their memories of both the films and the events themselves. The second survey used the letters page of two major newspapers in Wales to seek respondents. The final survey used the letters page of the *Bristol Post* newspaper and its website to the same purpose. These efforts only produced a total of about twenty responses, although some were highly detailed. I will not make claims for the empirical robustness of the survey, but it did succeed in producing a slew of personal memories. I believe that they do provide an insight into the experience of being an audience member at the Saturday clubs and of the lasting impression they left. In addition, I attempted to contact individuals who had experiences from the other side of the screen, those who actually helped to run the Saturday clubs. I was able to track down a few, who had vivid recollections of organizing the children's film clubs.

If the testimonies contradict the assumptions the foundation made about the susceptibility of their audience, they do confirm the power of public cinema events for children in providing a social activity of significance to the development of that audience. One theme that emerged from the respondents was that their experiences were affected by their location, particularly if it was rural because it meant they might attend a screening at a tiny local cinema or in a neighbouring village or have to make a journey to the nearest town. Some walked considerable distances or cycled; others took public transport: "It was a bit of an adventure as we lived in a village about 5 or 6 miles from Huddersfield. It was the first thing my brother and I did on our own after initially travelling into town by bus with our mother, who would go shopping."[16] The trip was often made in the company of friends or siblings; it was rare to attend with your parents. If it was an older brother or sister, they were expected to keep younger siblings in order. Being in charge of younger children could be a chore but often brought rewards in terms of a valued sense of responsibility. Rivalry between school groups was common, usually manifested in good-humoured taunts. The clubs could be the venue for burgeoning romance, usually of the most innocent kind, as one man recalled: "We were too busy swapping seats until I took Elaine, a girl in my class, and we sat next to each other in the balcony, quietly... well, I was only eight!"[17]

In relation to the specific programmes seen, many recalled what they described as B movies, along with serials and cartoons. Both the B features and the serials were dominated by the cowboy film and science fiction adventures. Comedy was also at the fore with the shorts by Laurel and Hardy, Charlie Chaplin, Harold Lloyd, and Abbott and Costello. The films made by the CFF don't seem to have had the impact they would have wanted. Some respondents were less than enthusiastic about the CFF's output, and one described them as "complete rubbish compared to the cartoons and US action stuff." Another said, "They were very middle class in their values and the kind of performers they used. They seemed to have the same locations each week, usually London or some country house, and the same plots where the kids discover a gang of smugglers, a runaway or treasure."[18] Some respondents who attended in the 1970s and 1980s noted the shift into more serious subject matter with approval. A number could recall having seen them but only vaguely. Some of the young stars made an impact with recollections of seeing Dennis Waterman (*Go Kart Go*), as did the established character actors like Bernard Cribbins and Roy Kinnear, who were popular. Celebrity cameos such as Roger Daltrey of The Who (*Pop Pirates*) also made an impact. Even if the CFF itself wasn't always directly identified, a description of the content of the films recalled can identify their origin: "I remember weekly serialized children's dramas. These conjure up images of lank-haired kids in snorkel parkas, Raleigh Chopper bikes, and petty criminals operating from a disused gasworks."[19]

The impression left seems to differ depending on the period in which individuals attended, so that the image of country houses, hidden treasure, and children with cut-glass accents dominates in the 1950s, while flares, tank-tops and council estates are the prevalent memory image from the 1970s. The CFF's Famous Five films seem to have had a particular impact with a number of people specifically associating them with the foundation, especially if attending in the early 1960s. The sixty-minute features were remembered by many as a key part of the programme, if not always in any detail. The formulaic aspect of the foundation's output may have been a factor here. Specific titles that were recalled with affection included *The Glitterball*. The effect of the CFF films could be positive:

> A lot of the CFF films have stayed with me. There was *The Johnstown Monster* where the kids create a fake creature for the tourists in Ireland and *Supersonic Saucer* which was a sort of precursor to *E. T.* with a friendly alien. I remember *Our Magazine* which showed children with exotic lifestyles like gypsies or kids who lived on long boats. I also remember watching *Treasure at the Mill* without any sound. Their films were hit and miss. They had interesting casts with good young actors and some famous faces. They were good fun, distinctively British and not too long, but they were so kid centred. I didn't identify with films that were about groups of kids.

The latter comment contradicts one of the foundation's principles, namely that children prefer to watch other children on screen.

If the foundation's films struggled to make the intended impact, the Saturday morning screenings themselves offered much in terms of social engagement. Things could get lively indeed. One interviewee remembered the Odeon in Bolton: "It was a bit of a free for all at times with the local town lads ruling it over everybody else who'd rolled in from the moors; lots of free-flying toffees and crisps. I remember at least one pitched battle. Loads of fun!."[20] Similar stories abound, such as one from someone in Southsea: "The events were very well attended and utterly chaotic. It was anarchy that subsided to some degree when the cartoons and films started but mostly there were kids running up and down the aisles, climbing over the seats, arguing, bickering, fighting, screaming, laughing and throwing things."[21] A favourite spot from which to start a sweet bombardment was the balcony, from where items could be rained down on the unfortunates below. One interviewee shamefacedly confessed to capturing two birds, smuggling them into the cinema, and then releasing them. Attendance doesn't appear to have been adversely affected by the riotous behaviour; quite the opposite, as most respondents described packed auditoriums and queuing around the block to get in. For those who were members of the official clubs organized by the ABC chain or Rank, a regular feature was the sing-along where the audience was encouraged to take part by following lyrics printed on the screen, with the additional aid of a "bouncing ball" to help them keep up; the ball would move from one word to the next in time with the melody. Both the Odeon clubs and the ABC Minors had their own club songs and many interviewees could still recite the words or sing them. After so many years the memory of the songs and the massed ranks of children booming them out remained vividly joyful.

Overwhelmingly, respondents pointed to the social aspect of attending the Saturday morning screenings as being their most important feature. This tended to significantly overshadow the impact of the films being screened: "It was just such a pleasure to be with hundreds of other kids without our mums. It was a social highlight."[22] A key part of this was to be outside of parental control, where comparative freedom allowed boundaries to be tested: "Saturday morning pictures were a parent free zone. Happy carefree days of children growing up and learning about the world."[23] Such experiences played their part in the process of growing-up and becoming independent: "I remember feeling very grown up because I was out without my parents. I always felt safe; there was never any trouble, just lots of enthusiasm and laughing."[24] If the moral tone of the films frequently went unheeded, it was at least recognized. This was especially true for the audience of the immediate post-war period: "We imbibed the sense of adventure, the battle between right and wrong, adversity overcome and virtue rewarded. Perhaps being the generation just after World War Two made us identify with the fight for things that were right."[25] If things were more unruly for later audiences, with less respect for the status quo, there was still a recognition of the moral distinctions drawn in the CFF films: "It was always noisy, especially when the baddy did something horrible. Children are so judgemental, right and wrong are black and white, no grey!"[26]

James Taylor-Godard's love affair with the foundation began at a young age and took him on a journey from being just a member of the audience to a role behind the screen as an organizer, and then into his professional career working in cinema exhibition:

> Many of the features were mediocre. Some could hold the attention but the audience was often tired by the time the main feature came on. Good features that I remember included *The Boy Who Turned Yellow*, *The Glitterball*, *Raising the Roof*— which was set in a cinema with one gang of 'good' kids and one gang of 'bad' kids involved in a competition organized by the cinema about who had the most unusual pets – and *Break Out*. This one had strong content; the Foundation sometimes depicted villains sympathetically or as anti-heroes in the later films. The later films, from the end of the 1970s, were increasingly serious. *Terry on the Fence* was in the catalogue but I don't remember it being released to us. I suspect this was because its content was considered too dark. Some of the films became quite adult in their content, such as *Hide and Seek* which was about a boy running away from home to find his estranged father, who turns out to be uninterested in him as he is a criminal planning a robbery. *Haunters of the Deep* and *The Man from Nowhere* were genuinely scary and intense, or even disturbingly ambiguous. They sometimes had ghostly figures but these were dealt with seriously, whereas in the past films with ghosts were usually comic. The attraction of the Foundation films was that they seemed to make these fantasies real. It was like seeing your own day-dreams of adventure come alive. As a kid I wanted to be in the films, to do what the characters in the stories did.

If the foundation's role as educator is difficult to support in these testimonies, there is evidence of their reflecting prevailing social attitudes and marking how those changed. Ironically, their later films which incorporated greater moral ambiguity appear to have had more impact than the certainties they portrayed in the 1950s.

Concluding Thoughts

A number of patterns emerge from the responses to the survey. In terms of gender, the audience appears to have been evenly divided between girls and boys. Girls were frequently irritated by what they saw as the male bias of the programmes. Two age groups attended, those between six and 10 years of age and those from 11 to 14. At 14, attendance peters out as the children identify the activity as something intended for younger kids. A major factor in the decline in attendance from the late 1960s onwards was the competing attraction from television, with many respondents recalling the arrival at home of their first television set. The decision by the BBC and then ITV to expand their Saturday morning provision also had an impact. In the 1950s and 1960s there is a strong sense that the Saturday clubs filled a gap in the entertainment available to children.

The clubs were hugely popular, with few negative comments recorded. The films themselves played their part, with a strong reaction to the simplicity of the narratives and the clear outcomes presented. The excitement of fast-paced action and the humour of slapstick comedy were appreciated. However, the foundation was probably wrong to believe that the films screened could shape the moral outlook of their young audience; their interaction with their peers seems to have had more impact on their attitudes. However, the films did help to establish an awareness of the values deemed significant by adult society and therefore formed part of a wider ethical framework. The CFF feature films had a mixed response; many preferred the Hollywood films on offer. The higher production values and professionalism were differences often noted. The early CFF films were criticized for their middle-class bias and formal acting, but the later films were appreciated for their increasingly gritty realism and social relevance. The opportunity to see a film on the big screen in which the characters and setting were close to your own experiences was important. A love of cinema more generally has certainly been one of the legacies of the clubs.

Overshadowing the films themselves was the attraction of the clubs as a social event. Even if the details of the films have faded from memories, the actual experience of being in the auditorium remains vivid. The pleasure of being out of the home, away from parents, and having a safe place to go to with friends was of enormous importance. A key factor in this social activity was the chance to gently misbehave, within boundaries. The opportunity to be noisy, to move about freely, throw things (relatively harmlessly), and push against the rules or mock authority figures were all appealing and seemingly beneficial. While recognizing that the films often decried badly behaved children, the kids themselves actually enjoyed a degree of bad behaviour and adjudged it to be morally insignificant. A healthy disregard for unnecessary rules was combined with an awareness of where the line should be drawn. Real harm or aggression was totally absent. The opportunity to be away from parental control was significant; for many, this helped build a taste for independence and developed self-confidence. Far from undermining relationships with their parents, it seems to have strengthened them, as many remembered thinking that it was good for their parents to have time without them. Ultimately, these social aspects of the screenings seem to have had a stronger influence on behaviour and identity than the "improving" content of the CFF's films. Clearly, an agenda to shape children morally through film is one that seems unlikely to succeed. The lastingly successful CFF films were those that, like *Terry on the Fence*, encouraged children to question and think critically about the world around them.

Notes

1. See Allison James, Chris Jenks, and Alan Prost, *Theorizing Childhood* (Cambridge, UK: Polity Press, 1998); and Allison James and Alan Prost, *Constructing and Reconstructing Childhood* (New York: Routledge, 2014), for an outline of theoretical approaches to the cultural construction of childhood.
2. Terry Staples, *All Pals Together: The Story of Children's Cinema* (Edinburgh: Edinburgh University Press, 1997), 2.
3. Staples, *All Pals Together*, 9.
4. Ibid., 38–39.
5. J. P. Mayer, "Films for Children," *The Times* (London), January 5, 1946. See also Mayer's *The Sociology of Film* (London: Faber and Faber, 1946).
6. Geoffrey Macnab, *J. Arthur Rank and the British Film Industry* (London and New York: Routledge, 1994), 149.
7. Mary Field interview, *Today's Cinema*, August 19, 1952, 3.
8. Sidney Harris, "The Child and the Cinema," *Film Teacher*, Summer 1952, p. 3.
9. "Saturday Morning Matinee," *Look and Listen: Modern Technologies in Education and Training* 8:1 (January 1954), p. 6.
10. Children's Film Foundation, *Report on the Work Done by the Children's Film Foundation, 1951–1960* (London: CFF, 1960).
11. Henry Geddes, *Progress Report: The CFF in the Sixties* (London: CFF, 1964), pp. 23–25.
12. Geddes, *Progress Report*, pp. 23–25.
13. Quentin Falk, "The Case for a Top UK Export," *Screen International* 132 (April 1, 1978), p. p. 1.
14. Robert Shail, *The Children's Film Foundation: History and Legacy* (London: Palgrave/BFI, 2016), pp. 100–101.
15. Shail, *Children's Film Foundation*, p. 99.
16. Ibid., p. 119.
17. Ibid., p. 121.
18. Ibid., p. 125.
19. Ibid., p. 126.
20. Ibid., p. 127.
21. Ibid.
22. Ibid., p. 133.
23. Ibid., p. 134.
24. Ibid.
25. Ibid.
26. Ibid.

Bibliography

Agajanian, Rowana. "'Just for Kids?': Saturday Morning Cinema and Britain's Children's Film Foundation in the 1960s." *Historical Journal of Film, Radio and Television* 18:3 (1998), pp. 395–409.

Children's Film Foundation. *Report on the Work Done by the Children's Film Foundation, 1951–1960.* London: CFF, 1960.

Brown, Noel. *British Children's Cinema: From The Thief of Bagdad to Wallace and Gromit.* London: I.B. Tauris, 2016.

Geddes, Henry. *Progress Report: The CFF in the Sixties.* London: Children's Film Foundation, 1964.

Macnab, Geoffrey. *J. Arthur Rank and the British Film Industry.* London: Routledge, 1994.

Shail, Robert. *The Children's Film Foundation: History and Legacy.* London: Palgrave Macmillan/BFI Publishing, 2016.

Staples, Terry. *All Pals Together: The Story of Children's Cinema.* Edinburgh: Edinburgh University Press, 1997.

CHAPTER 10

MIGRANT CHILDREN AND THE "SPACE BETWEEN" IN THE FILMS OF ANGELOPOULOS

STEPHANIE HEMELRYK DONALD

CHILDHOOD is a category of difference within sameness, a form of being that is intrinsic to all human life, and yet which, simultaneously, is unavailable to adult humans. In the context of global migrations, childhood occupies an even more ethereal space of belonging and exclusion. This chapter advances earlier work on Angelopoulos,[1] and follows the example of many other scholars working on the great auteur.[2] His death in 2011 notwithstanding, Angelopoulos's work still resonates with ongoing twenty-first-century historical conditions; and it is that resonance I wish to explore here, particularly in relation to his achievements in representing the experience of migration and childhood. The child migrant's journey through actual and imaginary borders—of innocence and knowledge, security and alienation—epitomizes the transience of childhood itself, within which there must always be accumulation of understanding and preparation for survival among adults. I argue that through Angelopoulos's use of what French cinematography terms *l'intervalle*, or "space between," he visualizes both the negative impact of migration on the collective (generally, the family) and, simultaneously, the ways in which children attempt to reformulate mores of belonging to contingent units of identity and emotional comfort. I do not claim that the filmmaker was making (or, indeed, should have been making) a scientific argument about the damage of the dislocations of intimacy. I do, however, suggest that looking at his work with current and recent tragedies in mind allows insight into how children may act on their own behalf, and how filmmakers might imagine their contributions against the odds they face.

Exilic

The work of a great European filmmaker, Angelopoulos's oeuvre is known to cinephiles and world cinema experts for its grasp of Greek history, profound connections with southeast European (and, specifically, Balkan) trauma, and immense contributions to late modernist style onscreen. His sensitivity to the presence of childhood in adults nearing the end of life should also be acknowledged as a gift to cinema. The children in Angelopoulos' films are always both young and eternal, incandescent, and spectral. I would go so far as to suggest that those dislocations between child and death prompt forms of auto-morality and progress of the human spirit. Although these films are not explicitly made for children, they treat the child protagonist with absolute respect, such that, were children to watch them, they would feel present in the film's haptic and emotional address.

Eternity and a Day (*Mia Aioniotita Kai Mia Mera*, 1998) and *The Weeping Meadow* (*To Livadi pou Dakrizei*, 2004) share the focus of this discussion. Both films concern children in conditions of migration and arrival, and both consider how their core relationships are sundered or forged in the processes and contingencies attached to such turmoil. Visually and in terms of narrative affect, the films deploy the *l'intervalle* (literally, "the space between") between protagonists, between stages of life, and between states of perception. They achieve this through cinematography and shot design, as well as through narrative direction and emphases. *L'intervalle* is a French concept that speaks across the form and poesis of cinema and that Alain Bergala has both described in film analysis and used as a core principle of poetic narrative in his work with young people.[3] This notion of "cinematic space" is that which holds the revelatory capacity to show human motivations, experience and, especially, to both acknowledge and explore social and emotional relationships that are antagonistic or surprising.

Eternity and a Day meditates on an ageing man's preparation for death. The meditation engages ideas of exile, language, and love, and it does so in no small measure by presenting the immanence and luminosity of childhood and revealing how its special and uncompromising energy and desire for human connection compels us to be more, better, or different in the world. Alexandre (Bruno Ganz), a poet, is the adult protagonist. He is ill with cancer and preparing to leave his house by the sea and go to hospital, and he does not expect to recover. He drives around the wet streets of Thessaloniki, saying goodbye to his family, his dog, and his memories. He meets a child (Achilleus Skevis), who is washing car windshields with a group of other boys, Albanian refugees or trafficked labour, or both. The remainder of the film develops the man and the child's friendship as Alexandre discovers that this small Albanian boy's demands on his time, care, and attention awaken in him the capacity to complete a sequence of responsibility and reciprocity with another being, from first sight to meaningful farewell, something that he has failed to do even with close relatives—his unresolved relationships with his mother, wife, and daughter are presented in the storyline and in flashback. The Albanian boy is, of course, especially vulnerable. It is the late 1990s, a period of intense Albanian migration to Greece after the fall of the Communism in 1992 and a time when migrant children were especially at risk of exploitation. The boy needs to be saved from the police; from deportation back to Albania, where he has no family; from child traffickers, and from utter loneliness after the drowning death of his great friend and fellow child migrant, Selim (uncredited). In these respects, his situation is far more perilous than that of Alexandre, who is facing death but has his work, his memories, and his privileged life behind him. Despite these inequities, the boy serves as a generous teacher and guide for the older man, thus problematizing the concept of vulnerability and highlighting the agency of the refugee child.

The first indication of the boy's moral power is his incandescent smile at his first meeting with Alexandre, a smile that lights up the screen. "Light up the screen" is a casual phrase, but it refers a theoretical conception of the phenomenology of film. Saige Walton, in her excellent book on flesh and the baroque in film, quotes Sobchack's "cinesthetic subject" as always returning to childhood "the open sensual condition of the child at birth." Walton recognizes that the "inter-sensory-perception" of childhood and the "sensuous density" of cinema make natural companions.[4] That insight allows us to better understand the luminosity of the migrant child's eruption into *Eternity and a Day*.

The boy steps out of a car, turns to Alexandre, and smiles. It is an ordinary but also exceptional human gesture. His smile is toothy and disarming. It alters the mood from ordinary kindness to the possibility of intangible gifts, and invokes an involuntary, smaller smile from the depressed older man. The film has already introduced us to childhood. In the film's opening sequence, a boy wakes up in a very beautiful house—the same house the older man will leave a few scenes later. He gets out of bed, slips past his parents, and runs down to the beach to play with his friend. The boy, of course, is the young Alexandre. The interval in space, time, and fortune between the privileged boys in the graceful house next to the water and the Albanian boy running through a city street decades later, a boy, we later see, who lives with other young refugees in a deserted factory, is bridged by the man's sudden impulse to help to the child and broached by the child's open smile.

The boy's grace continues as he pays Alexandre the respect of attention as their friendship matures, listening carefully to the older man's stories of exile and return. Alexandre is working on the unfinished final work of another poet, Dionysius Solomos (b. 1798–d. 1857, played in the film by Fabrizio Bentivoglio). Thus, Alexandre's last work is entangled with another's, and we realise, neither will be completed. Alexandre tells the boy that Solomos had collected and paid for words of his native tongue when he returned from exile to his mother's island. For Solomos, the words create a currency of reciprocation with a homeland, his mother, and her people. Alexandre deals in words but is less skilled at making those words forge a contact with his place in the world of others. By contrast, the boy plays within the logic of the poet's story by collecting words and selling them to his new friend. This transaction imbues the story with immediacy and mimetic urgency.

His witty riposte fuels the fire of language that Alexandre so desperately needs to understand the end of his own life and to articulate his own regrets.

The traffic in words is a preoccupation of Alexandre and a revelation in the playful response of the boy, and it occurs across several sequences. The most extraordinary exchange comes in a long scene set at the harbour's edge. It is constructed thus: first, man and boy emerge from a dispersed crowd walking by the harbour. The tiny boy (his small size accentuated by his proximity to the bulky adult) looks up at the man with concern. The man bends over in pain as they sit on a bench facing out to the sea. The boy says, "I see you're smiling, but you're sad. [*stands, smiles*]. Shall I get you some words? They may even be expensive! [*laughs, walks to the water's edge*]." The boy walks away and stands between two small groups of men. (Is he listening to their conversation, collecting a word? Or is he looking out to sea, at the ships and boats moored on the far edge of the bay, remembering a word that has shaped his childhood so far?) He turns and walks back toward the camera, and towards Alexandre, his pace somewhere between a stride and run, indicating his untapped potential, his youthful energy, his boundlessness. He returns with a word that articulates the condition he shares with the dying writer: "Xenitis." It translates as "exilic," "an exile," "a stranger everywhere." As Alexandre bends in agony at his failing body, the boy stands next to him, close enough, but also respectfully distant. He inhabits and exudes the exilic, at once absolutely hopeful and absolutely forlorn, boundless but also constrained by his childish size and the pressure of belonging to a place that has insufficient imagination to accept him. It is the role of the emigrant, described by Vilèm Flusser, who must "attempt to experience, identify, and assess [their expulsion] as a sort of stimulus. If they succeed in this, their unsettledness will be transformed into resolve."[5] At the end of the sequence, there is a disturbance

FIGURE 10.1. Man and boy. *Eternity and a Day* (1998, Paradis Films). Frame-grab.

down by the water. The boy's friend, Selim, has drowned; we surmise later that it was at the hands of child traffickers. Strangers carry Selim along the harbour walk, his tiny body sodden and limp.

The sequence is defined first by Angelopoulos' trademark long take, whereby the protagonists' movements toward and away from the camera define our attention even as the peripheral groups of bystanders remind us of a larger world of inference and connection. This is not quite the pan of his earlier work, whereby space, history, and the group are mutually engaged in action or intent at the invitation of the camera; as Julian Murphet notes, "The pan gathers anonymised, distributed agents into a circle, a knot, of political or ethical energy."[6] The long take described by Murphet might be co-interpreted as a collaboration with the affordance of the space between, *l'intervalle*, to open and close, creating a visual mnemonic of Flusser's paradox—expulsion as re-solve. The camera draws on the momentary poesis of these two humans—one old and one young—to draw them close onscreen, yet their game of words requires that they will walk from and into the group (not quite a crowd) in order to play. The man remains stationary on the bench and the boy walks away, but never beyond the *fort da* of connection and return. In a narrative about adults, this would be the string of desire, but here it is the thread of reciprocity that maintains the connection and the emotional density of *l'intervalle*. In the sequence, the crowd has a role, too, in this revelation. They are small in number and casual in character, rather than large and energized around any obvious political intent, really just individuals-become-social taking the air. Yet somehow, the boy takes from this group the word for *exile*. And yet, too, from these people comes a tragic collective purpose when they retrieve the dead child from the water and carry him away from the sea and to the city morgue. The space between and among them now refers back to the boy as they retrieve his friend. Thus is presented the essential relationship between immediacy and potentiality, life, death, childhood, adult anxiety, and poetry. The long take, combined with the deployment of *l'intervalle*, suggests that time is present, unstoppable, and mutual; that this man and this boy, this sequence of events, this discovery of words, and these actual and intimated deaths are precious to the protagonists, but nevertheless sutured into a much larger human narrative. If there were only one scene in the film, and it was this one, we would still understand the narrative punctum.

WATER

The Weeping Meadow is also fascinated by the longue durée of exile, here envisaged through a mythological epic situated across watery, "weeping" borders: rivers, floods, and the ocean. Eleni (Alexandra Aidini), sequentially and cumulatively an orphan, a refugee, and a political prisoner, carries the film. Panayiota Mini summarizes Eleni's mythological role as sister (Antigone) and grieving mother of tragically fratricidal twins,[7] as much as her heroic, part-Greek twentieth-century history, which takes her from refugee in the exodus from Odessa (1919–1923)[8] to DAG (Democratic Army of Greece, Δημοκρατικός Στρατός Ελλάδας, "ΔΣΕ") sympathizer and prisoner of conscience in the Civil War (1946–1949).[9]

The materiality of the film is drenched in the accumulated sorrow across the span of this woman's life. Again, the film starts with a small child, here the young Eleni, arriving from Odessa with her adoptive parents and brother. Eleni, we are told in voiceover, was found in Odessa, a child weeping over the dead bodies of her parents, and was subsequently taken with other refugees to Greece after the Turkish (Muslim)-Greek (Pontic-Orthodox) population swap in 1923. Alexis, her adoptive brother (Nikos Poursanidis), and Spyros (Vasilis Kolovos), her adoptive father, both fall in love with her as she grows up. Her twin children (Alexis is the father, but the two are too young to marry) are born in secret and given up for adoption. The family—Eleni, Alexis, and the boys—is reunited for a few years, but separated again when Alexis migrates to America, and Eleni is subsequently imprisoned for assisting DAG fighters and fugitives during the Occupation. Alexis is killed fighting in the Japanese war as an American GI, a war in which he had enlisted only to gain right-of-entry visas for his family. Eleni's losses are complete when the twins die fighting on opposing sides in the civil war. As Mini describes the end of the film, "Eleni's posture and cry over her son's corpse echo a mother's universal grief for her dead child, as represented in ancient theatre."[10]

The life of Eleni as a series of parallels with the wider experience of Greek refugees and exiles, of historical and political alignments in the first half of the twentieth century, and of the disappearances and bereavements of Greek mythology are only too clear. I argue that so, too, are contemporary issues of border crossing, rights of abode, and the risks associated with migration. Eleni may be understood as everyone's child, everyone's mother, and every woman in a conflict zone, even though she is also clearly embedded in a specific and contingent temporality. She suffers what Greece and Greeks have suffered in a fractured nation-space with uncertain borders, but she also suffers the kinds of losses that anyone in war, particularly civil war, might endure. Her sorrow washes across the membrane of the film. In *The Weeping Meadow*, the protagonist is not so much luminous as she is porous, and it is that sensorial conceit and load that transports Eleni's story across the "membrane" of historical space and into a European present of mobility and mass dispossession. As Marks argues, "For intercultural artists it is most valuable to think of the skin of the film not as a screen, but as a membrane that brings its audience into contact with the material forms of memory."[11] In another, even more pertinent, articulation of skin and porosity, film theorist and German studies scholar Andrew Webber comments (in response to Alexander Kluge's thoughts on human skin and film),

> To inhabit time as your "own" is also to fulfil it in a subjective sense. But this, in turn, implies openness, responsiveness, to connection with the time of the other: the time of the subject and that of the other come into a form of reciprocity in order to maintain an ethically proper relation. According to this model, film and human skin, respectively, have a temporality—a life-time—that is their own, but that can also allow appropriate accommodation, or mutuality, between them.[12]

How does Angelopoulos create a film and a protagonist of such temporal porosity? In part, he does so through a literal response to material dissolution, in water. Eleni weeps in many sequences of the film. When we first hear her story, she is a refugee child weeping for her dead parents. Then she weeps for her lost twins and, later, for her lost husband, and then again for her children. The relation of refugees to water-as-border defines both films. The Albanian boy is exiled from everyone he has known before by a tall fence enshrouded in mist, and he is separated from his friend Selim by the ravages of sea water even as he discovers and sells the word "exile." The baby Eleni is named aloud over a watery reflection of the exiled Odessa Greeks as they wait for entry into Greek territory. They are standing on one side of a flooded plain; settlers are listening to their story on the other shore.

In the parallel structure of the film's final sequence, Eleni sits in a collapsed house on a flooded river, weeping. Weeping, that extraordinary wetness of being, the collapse of flesh into water, the admission humans make to the fluidity of their composition when there is nothing left to say, takes her back into the river, sinking into grief with her dead son. As Sohi and Khojastehpour have noticed, one of the few close-ups in the film, from a filmmaker known to avoid close-ups, is this final image of Eleni, weeping for her son (Figure 10.2).[13] The shot is indeed a close-up, but it is not an extreme close-up that probes her face for emotional clues to character. Rather, Angelopoulos "gathers" Eleni into the "molar trajectory" of bereavement, and postconflict despair.[14] We see only her head and shoulders, in profiled against the water, as her body lurches, and her head is thrown back in grief; the camera continues past her, pans upward, and rests on the waves of the unaccountable river. The grammatical sense of the film's narrative peaks and the visual grammar of its theme of migration and loss operate in such observations of *l'intervalle*

FIGURE 10.2. Eleni's grief. *The Weeping Meadow*. (2004, Theo Angelopoulos Films). Frame-grab.

as a key symbolic choreographic gesture. It is not Eleni's grief we should remember, but the precise distance between, and relationality of, the expression of that grief and the waters of Europe.

EUROPE NOW

> As European cinemas have collapsed, Angelopoulos has continued to cultivate a national identity that is neither isolating nor insulating. Angelopoulos persists in the view that Greek national culture can be a lens though which to observe all human concerns, much as Joyce used Irish culture.[15]

Dan Georgakas's observation, made after the Balkan wars of the 1990s but before the 2011 debacle in Syria (ongoing, at the time of writing), is prescient. In the films of Angelopoulos, one sees at work not just a cultural sensibility that speaks to European malaise and nostalgia, but also a vision that captures the crises of the present day, most particularly the plight of refugees, the agony of aging in exile, and a profound recognition that we are failing our children even as we call them into emotional service to remediate that failure. I don't have an answer to the proposition that European cinema has collapsed; I am not sure what that might mean. It is possibly fair to say that European cinema is not offering or achieving a complete global language through which to share the true traumas of today's world—from climate change to the continuing violence against women and children to the re-invention of cultural borders and the exclusion of refugees. But the understanding that Angelopoulos was an artist whose work resists final categorization as the world unfolds beyond his own historical references is well taken. It is also notable that, in Frederic Jameson's essay a quarter of a century later, the differences between Joyce and Angelopoulos are also noted (re: *The Travelling Players*) when he argues that the use of paratactic historical episodes "do not at all suggest some eternal return, some Viconian or Joycean cycle of history, but rather simply ask us to review the events. To gather them together in one unique memory....They construct a past."[16] This paratactical narrative is an outcome of *l'intervalle*. Stories and protagonists occupy the conditions of humankind and of history, and as such there will necessarily be passages of juncture and recognition between one sequence of separations and losses and another, taking place somewhere else and as the result of a different war.

The Weeping Meadow and *Eternity and a Day* observe the endlessly replicated tragedies of two generations of migrants, the Pontic Greeks displaced from the East, and the Albanians displaced by economic collapse.[17] In *The Weeping Meadow*, angry and judgemental villagers ("those peasants from the East," as Eleni's foster aunt describes them) take vengeance on the young couple returning with their illegitimate children to the house after the funeral of their father, Spyros. The villagers have strung up a flock of sheep, a living part of Eleni and Alexis's inheritance, on the tree outside the family home. They hang like pathetic festive baubles, blood dripping to the ground below. The following day floods arrive. The sheep carcasses now float in the water as the boats of escaping villagers nudge through them. I found myself comparing that image in a temporal parataxis to the efforts of filmmakers in the past few years to draw our visceral attention to the five thousand souls who drowned in the Mediterranean Sea in 2016, and the thousands more who had drowned in the years before that. In Marc Wilkins's short film, *Bon Voyage* (2016), a Swiss couple sailing their luxury yacht to Egypt encounters a boat crammed with refugees. Afraid of being overwhelmed by the numbers of people they see jumping into the water, they sail away, calling out that they will seek assistance. Overnight, the refugees' boat founders, and in the morning the hapless holiday couple sail through a sea of drowned people; men, women, and children become corpses bobbing against the yacht's hull. They find a small group of survivors and bring them on board, but these, too, they deceive, and eventually deliver to the Libyan coastguard, whence they will returned to Libyan camps to be beaten, enslaved, or imprisoned.[18] The European couple's betrayal is lodged in their incapacity to understand the difference between blind adherence to the idea of law as the ultimate arbiter, which they interpret as meaning they should deliver the refugees back to the nearest shore, and the underpinning reciprocity of the international law of the sea—which they have already broken by sailing away from those in trouble but which they nonetheless cite to themselves as a reason to call the coastguard. Wilkins's story of this individual failure of responsibility ends with the one child survivor coming out of a hiding place (where her mother had stowed her in the few frantic moments available to save someone, if not herself). Her parents lost, the girl stands, enraged, at the cabin hatch. Her stare at the Swiss couple is an unabashed denunciation of failed reciprocity between nations and peoples. We might recall, in contrast, the brilliant smile delivered to Alexandre in recognition of his first, dying, step towards mature kindness.

Daphne Matziaraki's documentary, *4.1 Miles* (Greece, 2016), offers a more positive account of humanity.[19] Matziaraki follows the work of a coastguard captain and his crew from the island of Lesbos, who respond tirelessly to emergency calls and sightings of refugee boats in trouble. The short film explores a man who finds himself at a juncture of history and responds with his humanity, taking risks, being a leader to his crew, plucking people from the water, administering first aid, taking them to shore, and refusing to give up on anyone, dead or alive. His only fear is that "someone has been left behind." His absolute and practical commitment to the international law of the sea, the utter porosity of legal mutual responsibility, is a timely and potent recuperation of hope.

It seems, at the time of writing, that Angelopoulos's contribution to "human concerns" (as Georgakas has it) deepens as time passes.[20] The films do not only teach us about Greece's civil scars and wounds, or about the trembling borders of Asia Minor in the twentieth century, or even about the intense poeticism and gestural strength of Greek storytelling and theatre. His films also instruct us on how we think about our predicament, our shared "human concerns," now. Paula Rabinowitz's description of Walter Benjamin's (and Paul Klee's) "angel of history," "whose face turns towards the past as she is blown towards the wreckage of the future," aims at the relationship between historical memory and the work of the documentarist.[21] And the angel's turning head is surely echoed both in the ethical searching of the Greek lifeguard, and the profoundly unethical departure of the fictional Swiss sailors (fictional, but, of course, performative metaphors for most of Europe). Benjamin's vivid and confused angel shows us so clearly what this might feel like, both being in exile and observing the family receding in our wake.

Ghosts

Storytellers who use ghosts, spectres, and visual and aural interventions to reveal the degree to which we walk in company with the figures of our past are crucial to an era, ours, when lies have accrued such threatening substance. There is a sequence in *Eternity and a Day* when, like words purchased for a poet's unfinished masterpiece, diegetic sound is both of the present and past such that the flesh of the film is pregnant with ghosts of its own devising. The older Alexandre hears singing on the quay, and the sky turns to the blue of a holiday in 1967. The slippage continues to the dénouement of the film; his long-dead wife dances with him on the beach where he played as a boy, and then she laughs, walks backward, and leaves him finally alone. The final shot zooms backwards slowly and slightly, echoing front on her stage-left departure moments earlier. Alexandre's face and three-quarters of his body remain in medium shot with the grey sea behind him. He stands, still asking questions of the past, caught between an eternity of memories, and his imminent disappearance into black. I am precisely not suggesting that Angelopoulos's films are "about" a present moment of which he could not have been fully aware at the time of the films' making, but rather about the subjects he explicitly espouses and represents. Nonetheless, given his capacity to recognize that memory and being are saturated with the past to the extent that one hears in different registers and sees in different colours the closer one comes to death, I do suggest that the imagery, pathos, and human reciprocity that Angelopoulos creates in his work afford us a lens through which to bear a kind of witness to the persistence of present human suffering in our midst and on our doorstep. The present cannot tell us how to view the past, but the membranes of film can afford a distanciation and a lens through which to engage with the overwhelming propinquity of the present. This, too, speaks to the capacity of childhood to inhabit a present that is saturated with itself, rather than with a prospective and retrospective desire.

Referring, then, to the question of whether the works of Angelopoulos might also address children themselves, my glib or, rather, my pragmatic answer would be that it depends on the child. When designing a Virtual Reality version of the migrant journey to Europe, advisers who had made similar journeys as child refugees themselves commented on the dreamlike quality of the experience, on the size and intractability of the adult form, and on the realisation that no one treated you like a child when you were deemed illegal or a supplicant. No one, for instance, crouched down to your level to ask a question. Their comments recall Chiko Kinoshita's assessment of

Mizoguchi's use of space within the frame, *l'intervalle*, to explore power relations between protagonists as a process of internal montage. The movement between poles of the axis of the shot combines with the relative scale of figures in the image, to denote power as a class relation within the shot.[22] I note that Angelopoulos also understands that childhood innocence is lost once that childhood is mobile and bordering, and that children must literally "look up" to adults.[23] That is why the reciprocity when the boy smiles at Alexandre on the boy's plane of sight is so revelatory, and might indeed be of interest to a child spectator. Both Angelopoulos and Wilkins position a child's judgement, whether a smile of grace, or a stare of denunciation, in the centre of the frame and at the heart of the film's meaning. Addressing the question more practically, the status of a film—for children or about children—also depends on whether a child spectator is required to watch the whole film or only the sections when a child is present on screen. In my general observations over many decades, young audiences respond with intellectual and emotional acuity to stories and protagonists where a child's agency is the subject of the scene, sequence, or entire film. It doesn't really pertain whether that film is "meant" for them or not. I have not screened either of the films under discussion here to young audiences. I have however, screened many clips from art cinema to younger viewers, eight to sixteen years in age, in China, Australia, and the United Kingdom. Without exception, the responses have been sensitive to the perception of the child on the screen. The adult characters, meanwhile, blur, or are stock figures—good, bad, nice, nasty—in their subsequent accounts of the action.[24]

In claiming that the films made a few years before we guessed how bad things would get this century, having already been so terrible in the last, I follow up on Jameson's point that Angelopoulos' later films—Jameson refers to *Voyage to Cythera* (*Taxidi sta Kythira*, 1984)—carried "a spatiality which would not have been fully perceptible to anyone before the 1980s and the final triumph of the transnationals."[25] The "transnationals" may refer to the filmmakers and filmgoers who moved past national and Hollywood cinema towards the transnational moment that characterized film analysis in the 1990s.[26] Helpfully, Higbee and Lim have, more recently, revisited the concept and argued for the blurring of identity borders both internal to the nation and across postnational and postcolonial spaces of identity and belonging.[27] Perhaps today, we have taken up their advice and think more along the lines of transculturality, regional cinemas, world cinema (the multi-sited, polycentric cinema described by Lúcia Nagib),[28] as well as the functional, globally distributed national film industries producing narratives and compromises to underscore the politics of soft power they are funded to support.

Jameson's reference to the transnationals' "triumph" is insightful—he acknowledges the extended cinematic imaginary of late twentieth-century culture, where the many border crossings of the century's fraught history come into view as a summation of three generations of exile, and he infers the psychosocial, intergenerational borders of contemporary transnational visualization and experience. It is not just that Angelopoulos pays attention to people returning home or that he understands how profoundly they will find it altered; it is that the multiple returns and exiles of individuals, families, communities, and peoples result in the decentring of home itself. It is a world in which exile is the only certainty. There is just so much water. So many walks to and along the beach, the seafront, the headlands. Ships come in carrying an old man (*Voyage to Cythera*) and leave carrying a young musician who will end up on the battlefields of Japan (*The Weeping Meadow*) or a tiny boy (*Eternity and a Day*) off to make his fortune. When the sea is out of sight, the rivers rise and fall; the rain comes down in sheets. New boats veer into view, with new generations of exiles on board. A century of displacement, expulsion, and return renders place itself uncertain, and space stretches to encompass time past, time lost, and time regained. Space stretching to embrace time has always been a tactic in Angelopoulos's films, because he has always made room for migrants.

Jameson continues in a semicritical mode, insofar as he regrets the individual protagonist at the centre of later films. Notwithstanding his later rethinking of this so-called humanist turn,[29] I would hold him to that description on the "individual protagonist" and suggest that he somewhat misreads the status of these men and women and their actor-interpreters. I argue that the performances, especially of Ganz and Aidini, do not "substitute an old-fashioned individual pathos" within the films.[30] Rather, they subsume cumulative human experience in unknowable but emotionally demanding personae who present pathos and despair onscreen, but who neither siphon performance into small bottles of individual realism nor let it flood out as an amorphous, free-for-all humanism. Instead, they present time in perpetuity, with the caveat that this is not a presentist cinema in the philosophical sense of the hierarchy of the present in the revisioning of the past.[31] Rather, the past is constantly intervening as spatial and spectral incursions,[32] and the future is visible through the lens of the protagonists' horizontal scans of their time on earth.

As brought to us through Angelopoulos's filmmaking, these performances present age, despair, and exile, but keep childhood in sight. Whether heard in the massive cry of the grieving mother or caught in the downwards look of the bereaved lover who is bereft of a future and knows it (I am thinking of Bruno Ganz's penultimate decisive look downward in *The Dust of Time* [2008] before he climbs the steps on the barge in preparation for suicide), or ineffable hope relayed in the smiles between a young child and an older man, we are *not* perhaps observing *all* human concerns, but we are privy to the presentation of sublime moments of the human condition, always subject to specific and grounded crises—impending death, an inescapable understanding of one's own exile, a recognition of another human actor in suffering and thankfulness.

Psychopathology indicates an incapacity to distinguish the past from the present. Sufferers may endure nightmares, or they may find themselves acting out certain passages of their pasts or reincarnating through their own bodies the results of their previous actions upon other people's. Nagib's essay on *The Act of Killing* (Joshua Oppenheimer, 2012) beautifully explores this in the context of that singular documentary, wherein a serial murderer produces a presentist, somatic response—choking and coughing—to his own re-enactment of a mode of killing, garrotting, he has inflicted on hundreds of victims.[33]

Angelopoulos' protagonists are also affected with presentism, although never as gar-ishly repulsive as the murderers in *The Act of Killing*.[34] Angelopoulos' child migrants (and indeed returning adults—as if children embarking on a new world on the way to death) are, however, not only engaged with the past but relive it over the course of the film, criss-crossing a membrane between pathological naivety and mature self-know-ledge. *Voyage to Cythera*'s Spyros, perhaps the most revenant in the films, is not naive. He begins his traffic of the film disembarking from the ship and uttering the words "It's me." He knows who "me" is, and what "me" means as a historical returnee. Subsequently, he resists the way things have become; he dances belatedly for his fallen comrades; and he finally crosses the border to a different consciousness, again on water. He is a spectre in his own return, although his haunting is not so much pathological as a choice to re-main as "me," an exile, and as such, true to a version of time that others can no longer countenance.

The relation between and across the child refugees of Angelopoulos and more recent and pointed takes on refugeeism in Europe is a cinematic phenomenon of reciprocity and recognition. It indicates current situations that produce mutual cross-border responsibilities towards the causes, outcomes, and probable impacts of how we act on our own and others' behalf. The relation is materialized in the membrane between cin-ematic knowing, political responsibility, and audience empathy. It operates across tem-poral and spatial borders: it fords streams, bridges rivers, and ploughs through oceans. It rings in the opening sequence of *The Weeping Meadow*: a voice calling across a river and asking people for their stories, just as refugees today are asked, over and over again, for a story. A man, a woman, and two children—the three-year-old girl reaching out to grasp the hand of the older boy—have, of course, barely begun their story. The older boy will live with the girl, love her, escape with her, and finally die for her in a foreign battle. The little girl will grow alongside him, will carry their children, defend their political homeland, and weep for him and their children when they fall in battle. All this tragedy is before them when they arrive at the water's edge. This reminds us that, though asking for a story and offering sanctuary is the beginning of reciprocity, it does not stem the tides and floods of history. The refugees cross the flood, but their exile continues. Stories do not stop at the border.

Nowness

I conclude, though, with some thoughts on how the images that stick from the films, the *nowness* of their address, achieve that intense meaning, that immanence. To do so I re-turn to the idea of *l'intervalle*. Daniel Colucciello Butler argues that Theodor Adorno's philosophical method, and subsequently Steve Reich's music (in particular, the piece "Different Trains" [1988]), might help us understand how immanence is paratactically created—how it is "mobile"—"a consistent disequilibrium," "a force-field and all things at once." His explication of Reich's music, where melodies follow the tonal patterns of voices (alongside and in contrapuntal play with other materially produced sounds and soundscapes), is that *mimicry*, however exact and confounding, "does not preclude our continuing awareness of the distinction between the sound of the voices and the sound of the strings." "The piece thus provides a differential immanence of sound, where sound is too immanent to be divided up and yet too differential to escape the sense of disequilibrium."[35] Butler reminds us that Reich's objective is to address "the imma-nence of these trains'—the train which Reich catches as a child travelling between his parents" separate houses in New York and Los Angeles, and the trains carrying other, less geographically fortunate Jews of that period to their deaths.[36] The music creates immanence through its chiasmic deployment of difference, and Reich's motivation, or possibly intimation, is served.

This explanation—and the use of Reich as an example—though it does not specif-ically address either cinema or Angelopoulos, nevertheless elucidates for me the filmmaker's methods of using the on-screen space between protagonists in weaving history, memory, and growing old into and through historical events, agonies of exile, child life, and overpowering grief. When Alexandre takes the boy to the Albanian frontier (Figure 10.3), they see bodies hanging off the other side of the border fence. The bodies are at once Christlike, sheeplike, spectral, and threatening. They look as though they are dead. But when the pair turn and run away from a border official, the hanging bodies just climb down, the show over. The exact spatial relation between the travellers and those hanging on the fence is ruptured. The suspension of the latter is no longer meaningful. But why not? Are they ghosts of those who never made it over the border alive when it was their turn to run, and as such, are they visible only to fellow refugees? Are they a kind of morbid scarecrow *chora*, warning the boy not to return,

FIGURE 10.3. Approaching the border. *Eternity and a Day* (1998, Paradis Films). Frame-grab.

captives and soothsayers in the paratactic space of no-man's land? Do they constitute the "interstitiality" of Angelopoulos' visual thought (interstitiality being the crack where thought is produced)?[37] And indeed, to return to the question of a child spectatorship, is this an indication of childhood perceptions of external reality as a circus, wherein the acrobats and clowns penetrate the consciousness of childhoods as manifestations of primal fear? And, while this is not a discussion of the address of a grinning clown or swooping trapeze artist, what childhood entertainment is not premised on the terrifying uncertainty of a world run by unreliable adults, whether or not that child is also a refugee?

The paratactic approach to the internal indexicality in Angelopoulos's cinema (and, of course, prompted by the idea of the crack) made me think again of Doris Salcedo's 2007 installation *Shibboleth*, promptly nicknamed the Crack, in the Tate Modern's Turbine Hall.[38] Salcedo's intention was to recognize the cracks, the shibboleths in and between European societies and populations, between those who belong and those who do not, between those who know all the words and those who must purchase them one by one or, worse, who are silenced by the very sound of their own voices. The Crack was just that, a long crack of varying widths stretching the length of the Turbine's concrete floor. The most emblematic image from the installation was of visiting children jumping from one side of the crack to the other and laughing, blissfully and naively broaching the border with their bodies and their voices.[39] Angelopoulos's method is on a continuum with those of Reich and Salcedo (and vice versa). By leaving cracks in time and in space he allows other stories to come through the work and into the frame. For an auteur with so much control over the detail and choreography of his

FIGURE 10.4. Approaching the border, Odessa refugees. *The Weeping Meadow* (2004, Theo Angelopoulos Films). Frame-grab.

narratives, he is also utterly, profoundly generous with the opening of time to history, and to childhood.

Notes

1. *Child life* is a coined term associated with Agamben's ideas on *bare life*. However, while *bare life* indicates the least of living, the reduction of the human spirit, and the destruction of sociality and hope, *child life* refers to "the transient and crucial being-in-the-world that is childhood, an ontology that grounds us all." Stephanie Hemelryk Donald, *There's No Place like Home: The Child Migrant in World Cinema* (London: I.B. Tauris, 2018), p. x.

2. Panayiota Mini, "The Historical Panorama in Post-1974 Greek Cinema: *The Travelling Players, Stone Years, Crystal Nights, The Weeping Meadow*," *Journal of Greek Media and Culture* 2:2 (2016), pp. 133–153; Julian Murphet, "The Cinematography of the Group: Angelopoulos and the Collective Subject of Cinema," in Angelos Koutsourakis and Mark Steven (eds.), *The Cinema of Theo Angelopoulos* (Edinburgh: Edinburgh University Press, 2015), pp. 159–174; Les Roberts, "Non-places in the Mist: Mapping the Spatial Turn in Theo Angelopoulos' Peripatetic Modernism," in Wendy Everett and Axel Goodbody (eds.), *Revisiting Space: Space and Place in European Cinema* (Oxford: Peter Lang, 2005), pp. 325–344.

3. Alain Bergala, "De *l'intervalle* chez Mizoguchi," *Cinémathèque* 14 (1998), pp. 28–43.

4. Saige Walton, *Cinema's Baroque Flesh: Film, Phenomenology and the Art of Entanglement* (Amsterdam: Amsterdam University Press, 2016), p. 98.

5. Vilèm Flusser, *The Freedom of the Migrant Objections to Nationalism* (Urbana: University of Illinois Press, 2003), p. 26.

6. Murphet, "Cinematography of the Group," pp. 162–166.

7. Mini, "Historical Panorama," pp. 146–147.

8. Emilia Salvanou, "From Imperial Dreams to the Refugee Problem: Population Movements during Greece's Decade of War 1912–22," in Peter Gatrell and Liubov Zhvanko (eds.), *Europe on the Move: Refugees in the Era of the Great War* (Manchester: Manchester University Press, 2017), pp. 284–303, at 294–298.

9. Alan James, "The Civil War in Greece (1947–1954)," in *Peacekeeping in International Politics: Studies in International Security*, ed. (London: Palgrave Macmillan, 1990); Nikos Marantzidis, "The Greek Civil War (1944–1949) and the International Communist System," *Journal of Cold War Studies* 15 (2013), pp. 25–54.

10. Mini, "Historical Panorama," p. 147.

11. Laura U. Marks, *The Skin of the Film: Intercultural Cinema, Embodiment, and the Senses* (Durham, NC: Duke University Press, 2000), p. 243.

12. Andrew Webber, "The Seen and the Un-seen: Digital Life-Time in Christian Petzold's *Etwas Besseres als den Tod* (2011)," *Oxford German Studies* 46 (2017), pp. 345–459.

13. Behzad Ghaderi Sohi and Adineh Khojastehpour, "Beginning in the End: Poetry of Greek Tragedy in Theo Angelopoulos's *Ulysses' Gaze* and *The Weeping Meadow*," *Literature/Film Quarterly* 38:1 (2010), pp. 59–72, at 68.

14. Murphet, "Cinematography of the Group," p. 164.

15. Dan Georgakas, "Angelopoulos, Greek History and *The Travelling Players*," in Andrew Horton (ed.), *The Last Modernist: The Films of Angelopoulos* (Trowbridge: Flicks Books, 1997), pp. 27–42, at 40.

16. Frederic Jameson, "Angelopoulos and Collective Narrative," in Angelos Koutsourakis and Mark Steven (eds.), *The Cinema of Theo Angelopoulos*(Edinburgh: Edinburgh University Press, 2015), pp. 99–113 at 109.

17. See Martin Baldwin-Edwards, "Albanian Emigration and the Greek Labour Market: Economic Symbiosis and Social Ambiguity," *South East Europe Review* 7:1 (2004), pp. 51–65. There is a general overview in a section on Albanian migration to Greece in Martin Baldwin-Edwards and Katarina Apostolatou, "Greece," in Heinz Fassmann, Ursula Reeger, and Wiebke Sievers (eds.), *Statistics and Reality: Concepts and Measurements of Migration in Europe* (Amsterdam: Amsterdam University Press, 2009), 233–267, at 235–233.

18. The deals struck between Italy (with the support of the EU) and Libya are now well documented. See the account as of August 11, 2019, at "Libya," "About us," the UN Refugee Council (UNHCR) UK website, figures updated October 23, 2017, https://www.unhcr.org/uk/libya.html. Jeff Crisp, who has been unremitting in casting a light on the conditions experienced by returned migrants, provides a more critical perspective. See "Leaving Libya by Boat: What Happens after Interception?" (*blog*), Refugees Study Centre website, University of Oxford, April 5, 2018, https://www.rsc.ox.ac.uk/news/leaving-libya-by-boat-what-happens-after-interception-jeff-crisp [accessed September 20, 2019].

19. Available for Freeview through *New York Times* online, archive, https://www.nytimes.com/video/opinion/100000004674545/41-miles.html [accessed October 18, 2019].

20. Georgakas, "Angelopoulos, Greek History and *The Travelling Players*," p. 40.

21. Paula Rabinowitz, "Wreckage upon Wreckage: History, Documentary and the Ruins of Memory," *History and Theory* 32:2 (1993), pp. 119–137.

22. Chika Kinoshita, "Choreography of Desire: Analysing Kinuyo Tanaka's Acting in Mizoguchi's Films," *Screening the Past*, 2001, n.p., http://www.screeningthepast.com/2014/12/choreography-of-desire-analysing-kinuyo-tanakas-acting-in-mizoguchis-films/accessed [accessed October 11, 2019].

23. The observations about dreams were made in consultations in 2019. Currently, I do not have permission to publish the names associated with the consultation. For more discussion of the inappropriate language of innocence, see Stephanie Hemelryk Donald, "Landscape in the Mist: Thinking beyond the Perimeter Fence," in Angelos Koutsourakis and Mark Steven (eds.), *The Cinema of Theo Angelopoulos* (Edinburgh: Edinburgh University Press, 2015), pp. 206–218.

24. Stephanie Hemelryk Donald, "Follow the Yellow Brick Road: The *Passeur*, the Gatekeeper, and the Young Migrant Film-maker," *Film Education Journal* 2:1 (2019), pp. 48–61.

25. Frederic Jameson, "The Past as History, the Future as Form," in Andrew Horton (ed.), *The Last Modernist: The Films of Angelopoulos* (Trowbridge, UK: Flicks Books, 1997), pp. 78–95, at 78.

26. Sheldon Hsiao-Peng Lu (ed.), *Transnational Chinese Cinemas: Identity, Nationhood, Gender* (Honolulu: University of Hawai'i Press, 1997).

27. Will Higbee and Song Hui Lim, "Concepts of Transnational Cinema: Towards a Critical Transnationalism in Film Studies," *Transnational Cinemas* 7 (2010), p. 21.

28. Lúcia Nagib, *World Cinema and the Ethics of Realism* (New York: Bloomsbury, 2011).

29. Jameson, "Angelopoulos and Collective Narrative."

30. Jameson, "Past as History, the Future as Form," note 25.

31. Eleftheria Thanouli, *History and Film: A Tale of Two Disciplines* (New York: Bloomsbury, 2018).

32. Webber, "Seen and the Un-seen."

33. Lúcia Nagib, "Non-cinema, or the Location of Politics in Film," *Film-Philosophy* 20:1 (2016), pp. 131–148.

34. Oppenheimer codirected the film with Christine Cynn and an anonymous Indonesian.
35. Daniel Colucciello Butler, *Deleuze and the Naming of God: Post-Secularism and the Future of Immanence* (Edinburgh: Edinburgh University Press, 2014), p. 193.
36. Butler, *Deleuze and the Naming of God*, 193.
37. Ibid.
38. Doris Salcedo, *Shibboleth* (2007). Details of the installation at the Tate Modern are available at the Khan Academy website, see "Doris Salcedo, Shibboleth," n.d., https://www.khanacademy.org/humanities/ap-art-history/global-contemporary/a/doris-salcedo-shibboleth [accessed October 22, 2019].
39. Mention of the entanglement between the Crack/Shiboleth and the visiting public is canvassed in relation to refugee studies in the following (downloadable) publication: Dionysios Gouvias, Chryssanthi Petropoulou, and Charalampos Tsavdaroglou, *Contested Borderscapes. Transnational Geographies vis-à-vis Fortress Europe*, Cultural Commons.com, http://aoratespoleis.wordpress.com [accessed October 22, 2019].

BIBLIOGRAPHY

Bayraktar, Nilgun. *Mobility and Migration in Film and Moving Image Art: Cinema Beyond Europe*. New York: Routledge, 2015.

Berghahn, Daniela. *Far Flung Families in Film: The Diasporic Family in Contemporary European Cinema*. Edinburgh: Edinburgh University Press, 2013.

Berghahn, Daniela, and Claudia Sternberg, eds. *European Cinema in Motion: Migrant and Diasporic Film in Contemporary Europe*. New York: Palgrave Macmillan, 2010.

Donald, Stephanie Hemelryk, Emma Wilson, and Sarah Wright, eds. *Childhood and Nation in Contemporary World Cinema: Borders and Encounters*. London: Bloomsbury, 2017.

Donald, Stephanie Hemelryk. *There's No Place like Home: The Migrant Child in World Cinema*. London: I.B. Tauris, 2018.

Horton, Andrew. *The Films of Theo Angelopoulos: A Cinema of Contemplation*. Princeton, NJ: Princeton University Press, 1997.

Iordanova, Dina, David Martin Jones, and Belén Vidal. *Cinema at the Periphery*. Detroit, MI: Wayne State University Press, 2010.

Karalis, Vrasidas. *A History of Greek Cinema*. London: Continuum, 2012.

Karalis, Vrasidas. *Realism in Greek Cinema: From the Post-War Period to the Present*. London: I.B. Tauris, 2017.

Koutsourakis, Angelos, and Mark Steven, eds. *The Cinema of Theo Angelopoulos*. Edinburgh: University of Edinburgh Press, 2015.

Lebeau, Vicky. *Childhood and Cinema*. London: Reaktion Books, 2008.

Loshitzky, Yosefa. *Screening Strangers: Migration and Diaspora in Contemporary European Cinema*. Bloomington: Indiana University Press, 2010.

Nagib, Lúcia. *World Cinema and the Ethics of Realism*. New York: Bloomsbury, 2011.

Rollet, Sylvie. *Voyage à Cythère: La poétique de la mémoire d'Angelopoulos*. Paris: L'Harmattan, 2003.

Williams, James. *Space and Being in Contemporary World Cinema*. Manchester, UK: Manchester University Press, 2013.

Wilson, Emma. *Cinema's Missing Children*. London: Wallflower Press, 2003.

Wright, Sarah. *The Child in Spanish Cinema*. Manchester, UK: Manchester University Press, 2013.

CHAPTER 11

IRANIAN CINEMA AND A WORLD THROUGH THE EYES OF A CHILD

JOHN STEPHENS

ONE of the finest—and also most unique—bodies of film for or about children was produced in Iran in the years following the Islamic Revolution of 1979. There had been an emerging children's cinema in the 1970s, mainly produced and funded by the Centre for the Intellectual Development of Children and Adolescents (colloquially referred to as "Kanoun"), which was founded in 1969 with the primary objective to produce pedagogical films and documentaries. One of Iran's greatest filmmakers, Abbas Kiarostami, began his career with Kanoun, where he made nine short educational films between 1970 and 1982. These are mostly didactic works, but only in the sense that they explore such themes as the contrasting effects of cooperation and conflict or the difference between order and disorder and thereby promote prosocial behaviours. Kiarostami, who had not previously made any films, later came to consider that these early works were inartistic, but they demonstrate how he was developing strategies and techniques that persist in his later works. His first film, *Bread and Alley* (1970), is a nine-minute study of how a small boy, returning home after going out to buy bread, works out how to pass a seemingly unfriendly dog in a narrow alley. A lack of connection between the world of adults and the world of children is often conveyed in later Iranian films, and already, here, various passersby remain oblivious to the boy's plight. He finally decides to brave the dog by bribing it with a piece of bread, and the dog promptly becomes his friend. The film closes with the dog cornering the next child to walk along the alley carrying food. Will this child also realise that the dog is hungry and will respond to kindness?

Marked by documentary realism and a minimalist approach, and a pace that quickens and slows not by action but by the contrasting lengths of takes, *Bread and Alley* is a remarkable first film. Meaning in film is often suggested by means of metonymy to the extent that film tends toward metonymy to a much greater degree than toward metaphor.[1] The visual element of film is essentially metonymic; that is, what viewers see is part of a larger whole; images signify literally but also have symbolic, and hence thematic, meaning. Kiarostami expressed this principle through the four main components of the film: the boy, the dog, the narrow alley, and the bread (an oblong sheet of Persian flat-bread the boy carries tucked under an arm). The story is simple: the boy fears the dog but must pass it in the narrow alley in order to deliver the bread and complete his errand. The figurative potential of the narrative is realised in two ways.

First, the story is a version of a familiar script, best known as an international folktale type in which a traveller encounters a stranger on the road who tests the protagonist's capacity for altruism.[2] If he or she proves worthy, the stranger will offer some kind of assistance. As Shanti Fader summarizes it, "The hero or heroine…must show compassion to everyone and everything he or she encounters, or there is no chance of living happily ever after."[3] The required gesture often entails offering food to the stranger, so when the boy thinks to offer the dog a piece of the bread, he is allowed to pass, and the dog accompanies him to the gate of his house. Second, visual images function metonymically especially when they are placed in juxtaposition. Figure 11.1 shows the moment after the boy has thrown some bread to the dog. In this carefully designed frame, the centrally placed camera creates a vector that links dog (stranger), boy (protagonist), bread (item of exchange), and the end of the alley (destination), bringing the four

FIGURE 11.1. *Bread and Alley*, visual image as metonymy (1970, Kanun Parvaresh Fekri). Frame-grab.

symbolic components of the film into meaningful relationship. The dog has turned aside to eat, and the chiaroscuro effect produced by a hand-held camera, natural film lighting, and the confined setting brings the cavity the boy has torn at the edge of the bread into sharp relief against the dark shadow at the centre of the frame. The boy's crouching posture and placement in the scene render him smaller than the dog but also indicate that he has adopted a non-threatening stance. Not only has the conflict been resolved by the literal and symbolic sharing of bread, so that the boy is free to pass, but these metonymic juxtapositions convey a moral (not moralistic) perception about human engagement with the everyday world built on a valorising of openness and consideration for others.

The thematic effect is underpinned by a dual perspective that is characteristic of Iranian children's films. Visual perspective alternates between a point of view that observes the child and, from around three minutes into the film, the point of view of the child as he stands at the intersection of two alleys and gazes along each in turn. He watches a man with three donkeys go to the end of the wider alley and turn out of sight, and then he watches a cyclist go along the narrower alley past the dog. It is often observed that Iranian films are shot from a child character's perspective, but it is more accurate to say that a child's point of view is constituted diegetically as a cognitive stance from which the world can be viewed.

Hamid Reza Sadr suggests that after the early 1980s, presentation of the diegesis from a child perspective indicates "a new generation confronting a new world," although the cinema of the 1970s had already developed this strategy.[4] When a film industry re-emerged after the Islamic Revolution, new filmmaking regulations were in place. For adult films, these regulations concerned the erasure of Western influence, especially in expressions of romantic or sexual love; the banning of singing and dancing; and the imposition of dress codes for women. *Bread and Alley* contains some elements that would not have been permissible in the next decade. For example, when the boy arrives home, the door is opened by a woman who is wearing Western clothes, including a skirt that falls above the knee, and a flower in her hair rather than *hejab*.[5] More centrally, the role of the dog would be unlikely, since the presence of dogs on the streets, or even being transported in a car, has been forbidden. Western scholars often assume that directors were drawn to children's films because they were less closely regulated, but major filmmakers of the mid-1980s had been at work during the 1970s. Directors of the three greatest films of the 1980s—*The Runner* (Amir Naderi, 1985); *Bashu, the Little Stranger* (Bahram Beizai, 1985); and *Where Is the Friend's Home?* (Abbas Kiarostami, 1987), all made for Kanoun—had made excellent films in the previous decade, Beyzai with *Journey* (1972), Naderi with *Harmonica* (1974), and Kiarostami with his several films. A more significant aspect of the post-Revolution period is that with adult films pegged back to be a mediated reflection of (Islamic) social reality, directors saw children's film as an opportunity to explore some of the artistic possibilities of cinema. It is no accident that *The Runner, Bashu, the Little* Stranger, and *Where Is the Friend's Home?* are widely regarded as three of the greatest films in Iranian cinema history. They were also perhaps the first post-Revolution Iranian films to attract notice outside Iran.

These three films are in a realist mode, which is often, but not essentially, attributed to the influence of Italian neorealist cinema. Their realism is characterized by such production features as location shooting; non-professional actors; poor and working-class protagonists; a blurred boundary between fiction and documentary-style realism; non-linear narration; slow-paced action; pace varied by alternating between long takes and short takes; and the extensive use of ambient sound instead of non-diegetic sound, especially music, to supply contextual atmosphere, in contrast to typical Hollywood films. Realist techniques impart a sense of immediacy to events and actions, which in turn reinforces the ethical perspective of each film. Set in the period following the Revolution and during the Iran-Iraq war, the three films share a social ecology. Each protagonist is a young boy, and only *Bashu* has a significant female presence. The core of social ecology is the concept of flourishing, the well-being of people in their interactions within the surrounding world—that is, interactions with habitation and social, institutional, and cultural contexts—and the bearings such interactions have on notions of wholeness, humanness, naturalness, and place in the larger order of things.[6]

How can children flourish in a hostile environment? Amino (Majid Niroumand), the protagonist of *The Runner*, is an orphan or abandoned child who lives in a wrecked, beached ship that is adjacent to an oil field, an industrial wasteland, and a small airfield. A recurrent image is the flaring as gas from oil drilling is burned off, a fiery image used as a backdrop in scenes shot from a distance with a shallow depth of field. The effect is simultaneously to embed characters in the industrial scene and exclude them from it. Similarly, Amino has a passion for aeroplanes and rejoices when he sees them take off and land, which seems to be metonymic of a desire for a better life. Amino fends for himself: in the course of the film, he is shown scavenging for recyclables in a garbage dump, collecting bottles washed up near the shore, selling iced water, and shining shoes, but none of these is without the risk of violence or exploitation, especially by adults. Amino's community consists of a rabble of boys whose main pleasure is to run races during which they trip and push each other. Amino strives to excel in this group, but he eventually discovers that to change his life he must become literate and finds a school that will accept him. He then wins the film's last race. Just as literacy presages a way out of a seemingly inescapable environment, the film suggests, children may be the forebears of enlightenment at this moment of Iranian history.

A similar suggestion emerges from *Bashu, the Little Stranger* (Bahram Beyzai), a story about the impact of war and the constitution of minorities. While the film positions its audience to reflect upon the intersections of inequality which constitute minoritized subjectivities, it is particularly optimistic about the possibilities of change. Having witnessed the deaths of his parents and sister when their village in Khuzestan Province was bombed, Bashu (Adnan Afravian) hides in the back of a passing truck that takes him to Gilan Province in the north of Iran. People here speak Gilaki, a Caspian language Bashu (an Arabic speaker) does not understand and eventually begins to learn. Given shelter by Naii (Susan Taslimi), a young mother who is working a farm while her husband is away seeking work, Bashu becomes a great asset and is eventually adopted by her (and her husband on his return). The film is thematically very complex in depicting Bashu's struggles to deal with post-traumatic stress and the racism and xeno-phobia of the Gilaki villagers, while Naii strives to affirm female independence against the views of her neighbours. A consequence of the film's thematic complexity is that viewers will stress diverse aspects of the film. Bashu is a minoritized child, and although representations of minoritized children normally deal with them as individuals, the subject will usually be metonymic, so that an individual's situation is integrated with perceptions of institutional marginalization. The displaced and ethnically othered child is thus the focus for problematizing Persian ethnocentrism and the myth that Iran is linguistically, racially, and culturally unified. Rather, as Nasrin Rahimieh observes, the film shows that "cultural and linguistic diversity rather than uniformity are character-istic of the space represented as Iran."[7] The efficacy of this perspective, along with the film's challenge to Iranian gender politics, is evident in the film's reception: the Iranian authorities initially withheld screening permission and cancelled Beyzai's licence to make films.

The approach to the themes of *Bashu* is thus intersectional and highlights how categories of difference such as gender, national origin, race, class, and age can overlap and interact. From this perspective, then, it is important to emphasize that identity categories and the means we use to analyse them are not separable; but as an intersecting bundle, they produce systemic social inequalities which in turn mutually produce minorities. Bashu is defined by his dark skin colour (Naii initially tries to wash it off), his lack of family, his "foreign" origin, his homelessness, and his limited access to the regionally dominant language. Change operates at the intersection of these minority categories as a bottom-up cooperation whereby minoritized subjects are integrated into a wider community.

Bashu's integration is completed when Naii's husband returns, apparently from Khuzestan. The only work he could find was with the military, and he has lost his right arm as a result. As he approaches his home through the rice fields, he has a chance en-counter with Bashu, and though neither knows who the other is, the ground is laid for final acceptance. When shortly afterwards another boy tells Bashu that Naii's hus-band has returned, he hurries to the house, where Naii and her husband are engaged in a fierce argument about him. Bashu threatens to attack the husband, who suddenly declares that he is Bashu's father. Bashu offers to shake his hand, but the man indicates that he has no hand to shake. Bashu embraces him as a fellow victim of war. This scene can be interpreted in multiple ways—an attempt to reassert male control in a domain so far governed by Naii; a partial resolution of Bashu's war trauma in his recognition of a fellow victim; or, considering the husband's loss of his right arm, an implicit sugges-tion that patriarchal power has been weakened and a more equal family unit might now emerge. However it is interpreted—and the second interpretation does not preclude the third—there is an affirmation that Bashu has crossed the xenophobic boundary and will now take his place as the family's missing right arm.

That an altruistic child can be a model for adults, if they will only see, is exemplified in *Where Is the Friend's Home?* (Abbas Kiarostami, 1987). Nevertheless, this is not a di-dactic film, but a major example of the fusion of children's film and artistic cinema.

When Ahmad (Babek Ahmedpour) discovers that he has inadvertently picked up the workbook of his desk-mate Mohammad Reza (Ahmed Ahmedpour), he realizes he has caused a crisis. During class that day their bullying teacher had told Mohammad Reza that if he failed to submit his homework in his workbook he would be expelled. Ahmed knows that Mohammad Reza lives in a neighbouring village, possibly Poshteh, and sets out from Koker to deliver the book.

A striking aspect of *Where Is the Friend's Home?* is its richness in metonymic significance, and especially its capacity to express multiple possibilities. The homework book Ahmad is striving to deliver is such a metonymy. It has a literal presence and function in the narrative, but also various figurative possibilities. A book is a common metonymy for knowledge or learning, which the boys desire but is suddenly in jeopardy. The context also shapes significance, and the *homework* book can also represent the power adults wield over children, the use of education as a means of oppression, and so on. At one point an adult takes the book from Ahmad and tears out a page for his own use, despite Ahmad's protests, which expresses a careless disregard for children's agency and their learning. The action harks back to the moment near the beginning of the film when the teacher tears up Mohammad Reza's homework because he has done it on loose sheets, not in the book.

The effectiveness of metonymy is both that it carries its extra weight of significance lightly and imparts deeper and more complex meanings to "ordinary," literal objects. It may also emerge from a juxtaposition of shots or sequences. An example occurs during the first nine minutes of the film, which are mostly taken up with the teacher berating Mohammad Reza for not writing his homework in his book. The classroom sequence ends with a long take (37 seconds) in which the teacher lectures on discipline, a theme running throughout the segment and a recurrent motif in the film. The action then cuts to the children running outside to play, and soon Mohammad Reza falls and hurts himself. Then follows another long take (36 seconds) in which Ahmad looks after his friend, which signifies empathy and responsibility. The film is thus structured so that the two long takes are a contrasting pair, each metonymic of how humans relate to one another, and then suggesting a further metonymy, a need for social change towards a more caring and less authoritarian society. A dismissive attitude toward children permeates the film, as when people in Poshteh give useless or unhelpful answers to Ahmad's questions. Finally, unable to find Mohammad Reza's house, Ahmad returns home feeling depressed, but after his parents have gone to bed he finds the solution: he completes not only his own homework but also his friend's, and the following morning the teacher commends Mohammad Reza's excellent work.

Commenting on the observation that his films provide closure that leaves characters with something less tangible but more significant than was expected, Kiarostami remarked, "In *Where Is the Friend's Home?* the child who is looking for his friend didn't find the house, but instead he earned his friendship."[8] Like metonymy, this use of material metaphor (a search) to instantiate an abstract theme creates complex meaning. It is well-known that both the title and theme of the film draw on "Address," a modern Sufi poem by Sohrab Sepehri, which begins, "Where is the friend's house? in the morning twilight the rider asked."[9] Atefeh Akbari Shahmirzadi argues that although the first line of the poem indicates that the horseman is searching for a particular friend, anyone to whom the question is posed knows who is being referred to. Kiarostami has inverted this assumption, however, in that no one knows Mohammad Reza. Nevertheless, Kiarostami does concur that "the path to meeting the friend is more important than the friend itself," because it transforms the seeker.[10] The sacred, therefore, does not inhere in the supernatural but in everyday life.

Lost and Found: The Emergence of Girls in the 1990s

An important shift in the 1990s was the release of films with girls as protagonists or second leads. The most famous of these in the West is Jafar Panahi's feature film debut, *The White Balloon* (1995), which won the Caméra d'Or at the 1995 Cannes Film Festival. Shortly afterwards, in 1997, Hadani Ditmars offered a caveat—not specifically aimed at *The White Balloon*—that there is "a vast distance between what the Iranian public likes to watch and what European art festivals screen," and she further commented that the most popular film in Tehran's cinemas in 1996 was "a melodramatic remake of *The Parent Trap* called *Strange Sisters*."[11] Better known as *Long Lost Sisters* (Kiumars Pourahmad, 1995), this film is the fifteenth live-action film adaptation of Erich Kästner's 1949 German novel *Das doppelte Lottchen*. *Long Lost Sisters* is an excellent example of how an adaptation reflects the morality and aesthetic of the milieu in which it is produced. Ali Dadras (2005) argues that it is rare for an Iranian film to succeed so well in appealing to the tastes of both adults and children.[12] Its success may be due to the central "lost and found" theme, which pervaded children's cinema in the 1990s. In this film, the two sisters have been lost to each other, each has been lost by one parent, and the parents have lost love and happiness. Ditmars referred to *Long Lost Sisters* as a remake of the Disney film *The Parent Trap* (David Swift, 1960), although the film itself acknowledges Kästner's novel as its source. Certain cinematic moments, such as the shot-reverse-shot sequence in which the two girls, responding intuitively to the sense of a dissociated self, sneak glances at one another following their first encounter, are clearly derived from *The Parent Trap* (see Figure 11.2) but the girls' plan to fake their own disappearance may show the influence of the second German remake, *Charlie & Louise* (Joseph Vilsmaier, 1994). However, it would have been culturally impossible to reproduce many elements of either the Disney plot and its social landscape or the actual flight of the two girls in *Charlie & Louise*. Amid the plethora of adaptations, it is thus more appropriate to regard *Long Lost Sisters* as a version of a *separated twins script* that has supplanted a specific pretext.

Throughout the world, in mythology and folktale, the *separated twins script* resonates with audiences, both because it has a history in international mythology and folktale,

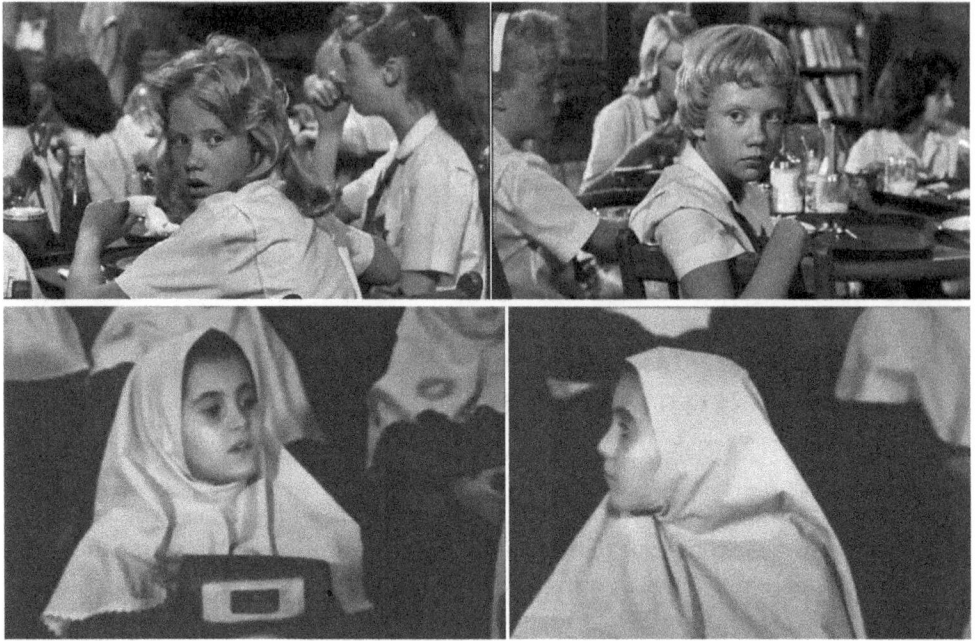

FIGURE 11.2. Images of the dissociated self: (*top*) *The Parent Trap* (1960, Disney), with Hayley Mills playing both twins; (*bottom*) *Long Lost Sisters* (1995, Sureh Cinema Development Organization), played by identical twins Elaheh and Elham Allahyari. Frame-grab.

in which twins symbolize duality of the self, and because it has a strong affective appeal in beliefs about the special bond between twins and in real-life stories about separated twins. This appeal is particularly acute in the image of a self that has become estranged from its twinned other because of the breakdown of the family. Around the mid-1990s, the divorce rate in Iran, particularly in the middle-class suburbs of Tehran, was beginning to rise sharply, and both the film and its enthusiastic box-office reception may be seen to reflect this social climate. In contrast to the physical distance and sociological differences between the parents that constitute barriers in *The Parent Trap*, in *Long Lost Sisters* the father (Khosro Shakibai) and mother (Afsaneh Bayegan) are creative people, she a designer of wedding dresses, and he a composer of children's songs. They do not live at a great distance from each other, and near the end of the film the mother discloses that she has secretly observed her lost daughter, Narges (Elham Allahyari), for years. Another major difference lies in the circumstances in which the girls meet: not at a summer camp, but at an interschool festival, where choirs of girls sing religious songs composed by Narges's father. The first, sung during the film's titles, begins, "Your name is the best beginning, without your name I would begin no deed," which alludes to the sentence which begins almost all chapters of the Qur'an. Thus, where in a mythic perspective the girls' chance meeting might signify a destiny sparked by unconscious memory and desire, here, the framing imbues it with a religious worldview. The parents might therefore be seen to be in breach of the social order and to need to embrace the children's view of how to live. The girls "trap" their parents, with the aid of their maternal grand-mother, instantiating the lost-and-found motif by going missing and thus prompting the parents to roam the city together in search of them. When the parents realise that they have been tricked, they give up the search and have dinner together, a resonant symbol, as they begin to find each other instead. The resolution of the actual and sym-bolic estrangement is reached at the grandmother's house: she dresses the girls in iden-tical clothes, and their oneness is confirmed when neither parent can tell them apart. The twins thus not only reunite themselves but reforge the family unit as their parents become reconciled.

Having found what they did not know had been lost, Narges and Nasrin perform their desire to live as sisters through their devious and often naive struggle to surmount the limited agency endemic to female childhood. The theme of limited agency is found in other films employing the motif of things lost and found, such as Majid Majidi's religious-themed *Children of Heaven* (1997) and *The Colour of Paradise* (1999), but it is most eloquently represented in *The White Balloon*. On the eve of Nowruz, the Iranian New Year festival, a seven-year-old girl, Razieh (Aida Mohammadkhani), sees beau-tiful goldfish while in the bazaar with her mother, and wants to buy one for the festival. At Nowruz, goldfish symbolize new life and new beginnings, so Razieh stresses the plumpness of her desired fish in contrast to the skinny fish in the pond of their com-munal courtyard. After persistent nagging, and with the help of her older brother, Ali (Mohsen Kalifi), Razieh prevails. Her mother (Fereshteh Sadr Orfani) gives her the last five hundred toman note in her purse and orders Razieh to return four hundred toman as change. On her way to buy the fish, Razieh loses the money twice, first when it is taken (then returned) by a pair of charlatan street performers and second, when she drops it, and it falls through a grating.

The story unfolds as a lost-and-found folktale script in which the protagonist loses something of value, only to have it returned through the intervention of one or more helpers. A Nowruz story must have a positive outcome. Sanaz Hamoonpou has demonstrated that a still older script underlies the Nowruz festival: Nowruz coincides precisely with the vernal equinox, so that what has been lost and found is Spring itself, embodied in the victory of Spring over the Demon of Winter. What was originally a Zoroastrian religious belief has become a formative script in folklore and persisted de-spite the Arab Islamic invasion of 633–651 CE and the Islamic Revolution of 1979.[13] It first appears in children's picture books in Manouchehr Neyestani's *Here Comes Flower, Here Comes Spring*.[14] Hamoonpou's observation that Nowruz ceremonies have always begun with perplexity, disorder, and agitation because the disruption of order is one of their basic characteristics can also serve as an apt comment on why things keep going awry in *The White Balloon*.

The film's lost-and-found theme is established implicitly in the opening three minutes, which consist of two long takes. The first (2:05 minutes) introduces the setting and characters using the long-take technique of following a character with a tracking shot until another character or moving object crosses the path, and the camera then tracks the newcomer. Several characters who appear later in minor roles are here introduced as figures in the scene. At the seventy-second point of the opening shot, the camera picks up an anxious middle-aged woman, who is clearly searching for someone, and follows her. She pauses to seek information from a teenage Afghan balloon seller, whom the camera had briefly lingered on earlier, and then walks off in the direction he indicates. She eventually finds a little girl, her daughter, Razieh, and proceeds to take her home, thus completing the opening lost-and-found narrative.

Razieh's subsequent attempts to find and then recover the money she has lost occupy the last hour of the film. The story of this small-scale film is of little consequence, but the lost-and-found structure is used to convey a young child's perspective of adult authority. Razieh lacks the agency to achieve her goals unaided, and must instead depend on her cuteness, tears, and persistent nagging to elicit help, although in the end it is her brother and the Afghan balloon seller who save the day. As Amir Ali Nojoumian observes of Iranian films more generally, "Adults are either over-protective of children because they see them as weak, incapable and in need of discipline, or indifferent toward and neglectful of the young people's desires and needs."[15] *The White Balloon* visually reinforces the child-adult dis-connection by subtle camera placement: while scenes are not obviously shot from a low angle, which might suggest a child's view of the world, much of the film is shot from a position slightly below the central horizontal axis, which means that the adults are literally always looking down at Razieh. This strategy is very apparent in the scene in the tailor's shop adjacent to the closed-up shop where Razieh has lost her money. She has been left here by a kindly elderly woman who has helped her locate the money, but who reprimands her for going where a girl should not go and ultimately fails to follow through with her help. The tailor is a bully who is indifferent to Razieh's problem and more interested in squabbling with a dissatisfied customer. The three characters are presented from different camera heights: first, a head and shoulders shot of Razieh's profile fills the screen but shows her looking up; second, a head and shoulders image of the tailor is shot from below the centre point; third, the unhappy customer is shot from above the centre point and from farther away to underline that he occupies a powerless position similar to that of a child. The scene is presented from Razieh's perspective and hints at a political implication in this depiction of authoritarian power. The placing of an adult in the powerless position of a child is a way of engaging with everyday life in an authoritarian society, where anyone can feel as helpless as a child.

FILMS ABOUT CHILDREN

Western viewers may doubt that *The Runner, Bashu,* or *Where Is the Friend's Home?* are films for children rather than about them, but the Kanoun signature on the title screen of each indicates that a child audience is intended. Other films, however, are more overtly about children. Two examples are Samira Makhmalbaf's *The Apple* (1997) and Marziyeh Meshkini's *The Day I Became a Woman,* part 1 "Hava" (2000). *The Apple* is the more widely known, in part because Samira Makhmalbaf was only seventeen when she made it and international festival audiences were intrigued by the idea of a teenage girl making a film about women in Iran. The film itself earned praise because of its eloquent pervasive symbolism, and because it metacinematically features characters who play themselves in a blend of reality and fiction and, thus, like many Iranian films, foregrounds the porous boundary between fiction and reality. An elderly man, sixty-five-year-old Ghorbanali Naderi, and his blind wife have imprisoned their twelve-year-old twin daughters, Zahra and Massoumeh, for their whole lives. The girls have never left the house; have impaired speech development (although they have a capacity for speech); are emaciated and walk in an awkward way, presumably because of persistent malnutrition and severe vitamin D deficiency; and lack social skills. After neighbouring families submit a petition to the Welfare Department requesting intervention, a social worker, Azizeh Mohamadi (played by herself), takes the girls away and engages in a prolonged tussle with the parents over their well-being.

The blending of fact and fiction is an intriguing aspect of the film. It is not a documentary, since the characters are either re-enacting things they had previously done or performing a new scene set up by the film's director. And even though the whole film was shot in only eleven days, it does not consist of first takes, and so scenes that seem spontaneous were shot several times from different angles. The powerful scene in which Mrs Mohamadi locks Ghorbanali behind the barred gate that had imprisoned his daughters and then gives him a hacksaw and an order to saw his way out (destroying the gate) is a Makhmalbaf invention, not a re-enactment. It makes the father complicit in the liberation of the girls, albeit unwillingly, and is a component of his ambivalent representation. He is not depicted as a monster but as an incompetent parent wedded to an archaic gender ideology. Nevertheless, his repeated complaint that he has been dishonoured by the neighbours' intervention and the newspaper reports about his treatment of the girls consistently misses the point that he is a perpetrator, not a victim, and has damaged his children. In the last scene in which he appears with the girls, they are going off together to the marketplace, which they had never done before, foreshadowing some kind of happier future. A documentary, in contrast, would have added a coda or an epilogue explaining that the girls were soon after permanently removed from their parents and placed in foster care.

The shifting line between fact and fiction is also evident in the underlying *social isolation script*, which can be found both in actual cases and works of fiction, and which facilitates judgments about some elements of this particular case. For example, Mrs Mohamadi's solution of setting the girls loose in the street is naive and dangerous, as they know nothing about traffic, money, or how to interact with other children; they are fortunate to encounter two tolerant younger girls who befriend them. This script normally entails a period of education before the socially isolated child can act independently. The incorrect newspaper report that the girls had been kept chained is derived from the script as realised in the story of Kasper Hauser, for example. *The Apple* can thus be compared with such films as *The Enigma of Kaspar Hauser* (Werner Herzog, 1974) or *Nell* (Michael Apted, 1994).[16]

The social isolation script is a variant of the *feral child script* that appears in films such as François Truffaut's *L'enfant sauvage* (1970). Both *Kaspar Hauser*, based on an actual case, and *Nell*, which is entirely fictional, follow a script about a young person who has lived with little or no human contact and is suddenly brought into society. The script usually consists of a representation of the physical, linguistic, and social state of the principal subject, an account of a companion or captor (if included), and a history of the attempts to impart cultural knowledge and speech capacity to the subject. Because the time frame of *The Apple* involves only a few days, the script is truncated so that the acquisition of improved speech or social behaviour is telescoped into brief episodes, and an indeterminate period during which the girls are held at an orphanage is an unrepresented back story. A common element in examples of both the *social isolation* and *feral child* scripts is an affirmation that essential humanity can survive physical and emotional abuse but needs to be nurtured by intersubjective relationships that offer positive role models and affirmative pathways for growth. An image of essential humanity is shown in the film's starkly beautiful and overtly symbolic opening frames. Against the background of a roughly rendered wall, a thin arm reaches out and attempts to pour water from a cup onto a meagre plant growing in a pot, but most of the water falls outside. On the one hand, the gesture discloses a possible awareness that something cannot flourish unless it is nurtured; on the other hand, it soon becomes obvious that the girls themselves are in need of physical and cognitive nurturance.

Ghorbanali Naderi's solipsistic, benighted dictum that girls are like flowers—who will wilt if they go outside and are seen or touched by men or boys, bringing dishonour upon their fathers, finds comparable expression in Marziyeh Meshkini's *The Day I Became a Woman*. This portmanteau film, set on Kish Island in the south of Iran, consists of three short films about girls and women at separate life stages. Since my concern at this point is with films about children, I will focus on the first film, "Hava" (Eve), which tells of the attempts by Hava (Fatemeh Cherag Akhar) to hold on to childhood after she is told on her ninth birthday that she is now a woman.[17]

Most of the film's images represent the proximal processes of family and peer relationships and interactions with the immediate physical environment, which together are deployed as a critique of the process whereby patriarchal norms and values are inculcated within the family. In Muslim regions, veiling and sex segregation, legitimated by appeal to the Qur'an and other sacred writings, are part of the gender system.[18] The film's characters belong to the Arab ethnic minority in the south of Iran and are therefore presumably Sunni Muslims, whose women are reputed to be more restricted than in the Shia majority. This ethnic marking is indicated by the wearing of a *battoulah*, a face mask traditionally worn by Muslim Arab women in Persian Gulf states and in southern Iran, though now less commonly among younger urban women. Hava's grandmother (Ameneh Passand) is never seen without a *battoulah*, whereas her mother (Shahr Banou Sisizadeh) and other younger women don it only when they leave the house. The *battoulah* signifies that the grandmother has internalized the gender system she recites when instructing Hava: "Hide your hair, don't sin; don't talk to boys; God will be angry." Hava receives permission to have one last hour of play with her best friend, a boy. She is given a stick, which, when placed upright in the ground, will tell the time as the sun moves overhead and the shadow shortens. The shrinking shadow acts as a measure of her anxiety about her disappearing childhood and symbolizes her diminishing freedom. Going to the beach to wait for her friend, she encounters two boys who are building a raft; in need of a sail, they persuade her to give them her headscarf in exchange for a toy fish. This sequence is not subtle: the exchange of objects symbolizes Hava's desire for a persisting childhood in contrast to the agency that is available to the boys and their freedom to explore the world.

The film closes with a montage of three brief scenes. First, Hava's mother comes to fetch her, covers her with a chador, and leads her away in a final demonstration of women's role as the key agents of the socialization of children.[19] Hava's last words, and the final, poignant words of the film, are "Goodbye Hassan. The shadow has gone now." The second image, intercut with the first, shows Hassan gazing in mute grief through a barred window as the cherished companion he will never see again walks away. The image encapsulates the trauma of this painful separation. Finally, the film ends as the raft builders launch their craft into the sea and float away from the shore. The closing frame, a close-up of the raft's sail (that is, Hava's scarf) fluttering in the breeze, images the freedom denied to Hava and encapsulates gender inequality. The unsuccessful quest for agency becomes a theme in YA films at the very end of the 1990s, notably in *The Girl in the Sneakers* (Rasul Sadr Ameli, 1999) and subsequent films.

FEMALE AGENCY IN YOUNG ADULT FILMS IN THE TWENTY-FIRST CENTURY

The emergence of interrogative YA films in Iran coincides with what Shahram Khosravi defines as "the battle over the right to identity."[20] This battle is between the theocratic state's attempt to determine a hegemonic identity for young people and young people's resistance to a subject position imposed on them from above. Because Iran lacks the debate platforms afforded by traditional political parties, cinema often provides social and political commentary, within the constraints of a strict censorship regime.[21] In the late 1990s, some degree of social liberalization seemed possible following the election of the reformist President Mohammad Khatami in 1997 and the student uprising in Tehran in July 1999, and Iranian cinema began exploring youth issues in the context of generational conflict. Themes such as youth culture, love, teenage anxieties, and the repressive impact of the strict patriarchal family and family values entered the politics of representation. However, although Khatami lacked the power to bring about change, his support among young people led a conservative judiciary to reassert the criminalization and violent repression of a large part of youth culture. The nature and consequences of the repression of pop music, for example, are played out in Bahman Ghobadi's fiction-documentary *No One Knows about Persian Cats* (2009), a film which continues to be banned in Iran. The film's title alludes to laws that forbid walking dogs in public or transporting dogs (or cats) in cars. The law is not simply an example of the criminalization of selected aspects of culture but a response to a perceived Westernization of culture. Hence, any increase in pet ownership attracts a more active application of the law. Dogs are considered "unclean," and thus occupy a place in culture comparable to that of the illegal "Western-influenced" pop music.

Filmed illegally over seventeen days, *No One Knows about Persian Cats* depicts the semi-fictional attempt by two pop musicians to form a band and travel to London to participate in a music festival. Having previously been beaten and imprisoned for putting on a concert, Ashkan (Ashkan Kooshanejad) and Negar (Negar Shaghaghi) must obtain passports and visas through the black market. In search of band members, their main contact, Nader (Hamed Behdad), takes them to various locations where music is surreptitiously performed or rehearsed. The narrative is fragmented, as scenes are connected mainly by the presence of the main characters, but this structure also enables symbolic vignettes. The most poignant of these is a scene in which police stop Ashkan and Negar's car and take Negar's little dog from her, presumably to be killed. The scene is a *mise-en-abyme* of the film's larger *repression* script in that it both enacts the extreme social and political limitation on agency and foreshadows the death of the music. At the close of the film, a concert to host the duo's final performance before leaving Iran is raided by the police. Ashkan tries to escape but falls from a high window and is critically injured; shortly afterward, Negar stands on a rooftop and, recalling her experiences of the repression script—her loss of Ashkan, of her dog, and of her music—throws herself off the roof.[22]

Persian Cats is one of the darkest instantiations of the repression script in Iranian YA films. As Negar Shaghaghi subsequently writes,

> For girls interested in rock music there were even more restrictions. The idea of a female musician was unthinkable. In the male-oriented society of Iran, a woman is protected by her male relatives, first her father and brother and later her husband.... Women are seen as vulnerable members of society, as well as representing the moral values of the family. So images of women with distinctive looks and movements not considered "suitable" for a young lady do not fit well.[23]

Development toward maturity in young adults in Western fiction and film generally adheres to a script which concludes with agentic subjectivity by affirming social awareness, empathy with others, and an adequately developed Theory of Mind (the ability to predict other people's motivations and actions). In Iranian YA film, the underlying narrative arc is a version of the repression script whereby the struggle for agency remains subordinated to the family and the social mores the protagonists strive to resist. In contrast to the pattern of struggle and gain typical of Western YA narratives, these films are more apt to consist of a sequence of failures or defeats. The female protagonists are positioned as searchers who do not find what they seek. Their emotional states and mental conditions are expressed through a sustained feminine point-of-view expressed via the simple dual-perspective technique discussed above, wherein the camera position shifts between a representation of the character and the character's subjective perspective on what she observes. The audience can then draw upon basic Theory of Mind knowledge to attribute thoughts and feelings to the character that are not overtly articulated within the film's diegesis.

These structures are readily apparent in *At Five in the Afternoon* (Samira Makhmalbaf, 2003), a tragedy set in Afghanistan just after the fall of the Taliban. The title of the film reproduces the first line of Federico García Lorca's poem about violent death, "Lament for Ignacio Sanchez Mejias," and the opening lines are whispered on the soundtrack as two women appear, leading a horse and walking toward the camera in a stony desert. The film ends with the same scene, now showing the women walking away from the camera as Lorca's "Lament" is again whispered on the soundtrack. These women are Noghreh (Agheleh Rezaie) and her sister-in-law Leylomah (Marzieh Amiri). The framing by repetition, a common technique, suggests that the cycle of deprivation and death is inescapable. While the film has positive elements—women have greater freedom, can attend school, and can aspire to careers—Noghreh's desire for education and her dream of becoming Afghanistan's first female president prove to be delusional, rendered impossible by the ongoing search for water, food, and shelter and her limited ability to disobey her traditionalist, fundamentalist father. Thus, the strength and optimism with which Noghreh approaches life is offset by a sequence of failures that are epitomized in the deaths of Leylomah's husband and her starving baby and in the father's fatal decision to take his daughters away from the godlessness of NATO-occupied Kabul and into the desert in search of an imagined Islamic utopia.

The effectiveness of shifting point-of-view between directorial representation and the character's subjective perspective is evident in many moments in the film. A particularly expressive example is when Noghreh searches a war-ravaged palace trying to find water to fill her water jars. Striding through the deserted passages in her secret (non-hejab) white court shoes, she can hear water dripping but cannot find it. It is up to viewers to determine what this unseeable water is a metonym for, but possibilities are the source of life, the fecundity and wealth that have been lost from this site and, most importantly, Noghreh's own future. When she looks through a window at the ruined wing of the palace across the courtyard (see Figure 11.3), she sees the surreal image of her father leading his horse along a third-floor walkway. This interchange of subjective seeing and the objects seen is a powerful means to attribute a mental state to the character.

One of the first Iranian YA films to challenge traditional family and social structure was Rasoul Sadr Ameli's *The Girl in the Sneakers* (1999), which concerns the attempt of a 15-year-old girl, Tadai (Pegah Ahangarani), to run away from home in search of Aideen (Majid Hajizadeh), who she imagines herself in love with. As Amir Ali Nojoumian has proposed, it is one of the first Iranian YA films to reflect the vicissitudes of adolescent love in conflict with an insensitive adult society.[24] The opening scene, in which the couple walk together in a park during only their third meeting, emphasizes their naivety: as they imagine a future together, Tadai walks in a childlike way on the edge of the curb while Aideen fantasizes a life based on a literal reading of Carlos Castaneda's

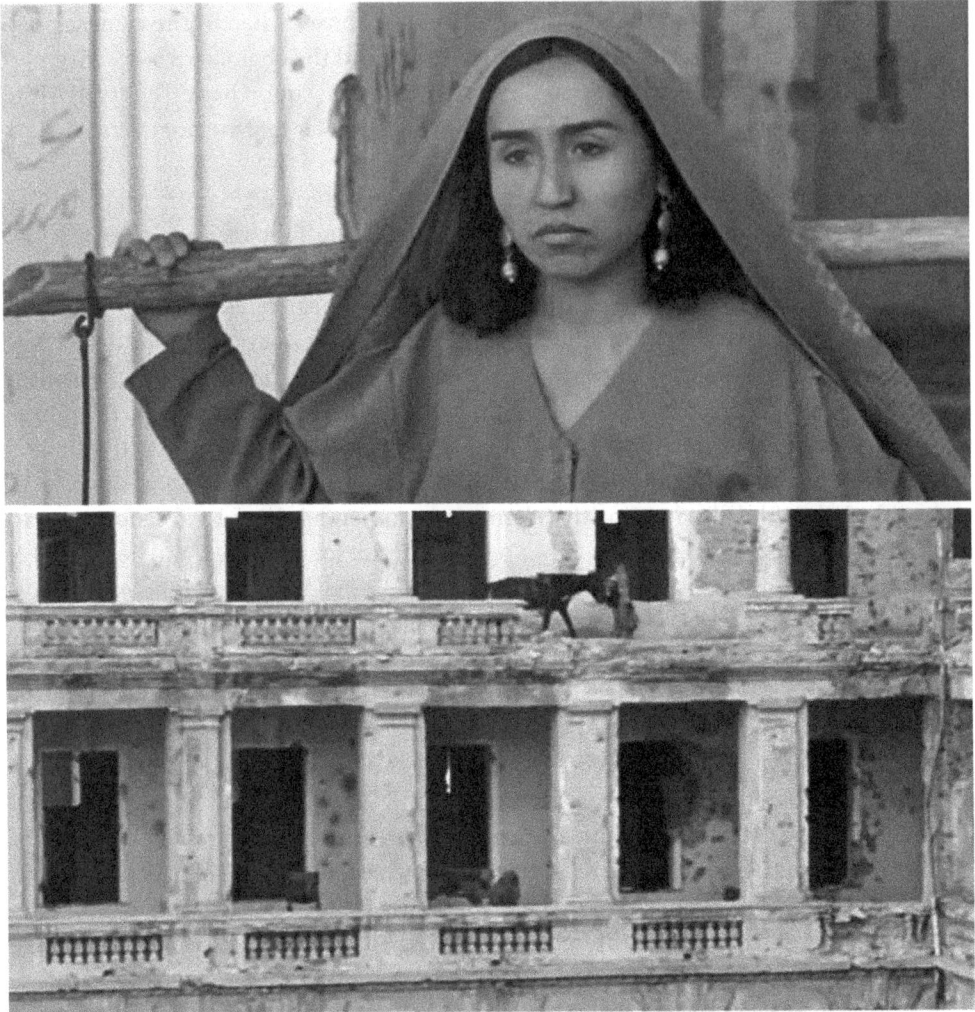

FIGURE 11.3. *At Five in the Afternoon.* Noghreh pauses in her search for water to gaze at the opposite wing of the destroyed palace (2003, Bac Films). Frame-grab.

The Teachings of Don Juan. Their behaviour marks how unprepared they are for adult experiences and the rude shock that comes when they are arrested by the moral police and charged with sexual misconduct. Released after a humiliating virginity check and ordered never to contact Aideen again, Tadai decides to run away and spends a day and night wandering through Tehran's seedier districts. Only her sequestered innocence and the intervention of a self-interested gypsy woman protect her from male predation and return her to her home, with no more agency than before despite her romantic disappointment.

Other significant films based on the *repression* script are "Ahoo" (part 2 of *The Day I Became a Woman*) and the satirical comedy *Offside* (Jafar Panahi, 2006). Of these films,

Offside has received the most attention outside Iran. Neither film had a local release. The plot concerns several young women who disguise themselves as men so they can watch an international soccer match but are apprehended and held in a pen, where they wait to be punished for their "cultural crime." Under absurd codes of care and protection women are forbidden in sports stadiums because players wear shorts and spectators use language unsuitable for female ears. The young soldiers assigned to guard them have little enthusiasm for the task and less knowledge of the game than most of the girls. On the way to delivering the girls to the police station that evening, the soldiers' van is brought to a halt by the multitude of people celebrating Iran's victory in the match; the jubilant crowd pulls the soldiers from the van, and the girls seize the opportunity to melt into the throng. As Adrian Danks observes, *Offside* rigorously investigates the effect on a small group of young females of a simple but somewhat ill-defined regulation that excludes women from a particular social-cultural activity. It explores the absurdity of the situation and in so doing, casts light on other social restrictions within Iranian society.[25]

A regulation that excludes women constitutes an acute constraint on female agency, based on the (male) belief that women are innately inferior and cannot make moral judgments, a belief that impacts upon all aspects of women's lives, large and small. Set within the Muslim community of Kish, "Ahoo" is a surreal tale in which the eponymous protagonist, in defiance of the gender ideology of the men of her tribe, participates in a bicycle race with a group of other chador-clad young women. Although it is not illegal for a woman to ride a bicycle in Iran, it is considered immodest, and a female cyclist is vulnerable to physical attack by moral vigilantes. Ahoo is exposed to a series of four interventions by men (they on horseback, she on her bicycle) during her determined attempt to complete the race. Iran's Civil Code (Article 1105) defines the husband as the head of the family and thus his wife must obey his orders: a wife's disobedience can be used to justify domestic violence and can constitute legal grounds for divorce, but in modern Iran divorce can only be pursued through the court.[26] When her husband threatens divorce, Ahoo exercises her agency, replying, "So, divorce me," and her husband fetches an imam who, following tribal practice, declares the couple divorced. Ahoo's father and tribal leaders (riding half-naked in a further signifier of tribal primitiveness) next attempt to assert male authority, and finally, her two brothers block the path and take away her bicycle. As the final confrontation unfolds, the camera assumes the vantage point of Ahoo's main rival in the race, and then zooms out until the arguing group becomes tiny figures in the far distance. What happens to Ahoo then or later remains unknown, which suggests that the possibility of female agency is still unknown.

Unlike these other films, *Red Nail Polish* (Seyyed-Jamal Seyyed-Hatami, 2016) was released in Iranian cinemas. This female coming-of-age film, which is intended for a primarily young adult and female audience, is a variant of an *overcoming* script rather than the *repression* script.[27] At the opening of the film, the protagonist, sixteen-year-old Akram (Pardis Ahmadieh), is presented as a schoolgirl interested in all things feminine, experimenting with nail polish and hair styles and speculating about marriage, but soon has to endure a sustained series of disasters. Her drug-addict father, Arsalan (Behnam

Tashakkor), dies in an accident; the landlord asks the family to leave the house, as the rent has not been paid for two months and Arsalan had borrowed a large sum of money from him; Akram tries to raise money by hawking the wooden toys Arsalan had been making when he died, but then is arrested because Arsalan had concealed his drugs inside the toys. When Akram is in detention her mother has an abortion, suffers a mental breakdown, and disappears, and Akram's small brother and sister are taken into care. The film was presumably acceptable to the Iranian censors because it implicitly affirms the traditional family in contrast to this dysfunctional family that has been destroyed by the moral failure of drug addiction. Further, the second half of the film places Iranian society in a positive light through the account of Akram's ultimately successful negotiations with firm, but caring and reasonable, social and legal agencies to win the right to act as parent for her brother and sister.

Akram's coming of age is expressed not only narratively, through her growing strength and persistence, but also symbolically. At the close of the film, the elements of the "girly" discourse with which the film began have been transformed by Akram's creative observation of a wedding procession, which makes striking use of the dual-perspective camera shift technique. It is not articulated as such in the moment, but here, Akram's perception also shifts—from a girl's to a woman's. On her return home, she takes apart some of the wooden figures made by her father and reassembles them as brides. She paints their mouths with her nail polish, cuts up her mother's wedding dress to make gowns and head scarves for them, and trims a few centimetres of her own hair to make hair for the dolls. As she makes her first sale in a busy shopping area, a doppelgänger, wearing the same school uniform Akram was wearing in the opening scene and embodying Akram's girlhood, mounts the footpath and walks away down the street until the scene cuts to black. Like the other YA films, the ending is open, but now it is also reassuring, offering hope that Akram will find creative and mature solutions to the difficulties before her.

Some of the films discussed here have not been released in Iran; others, such as Beizai's *Bashu*, remained in censorship limbo for years. These circumstances make it difficult to discern directions and traditions in Iranian children's films. Western perspectives are apt to ground a sense of continuity in "art cinema," for which Iran is famous, but this thinking is, to some extent, a misrepresentation. Films such as *Long Lost Sisters* and *Red Nail Polish*, which are more obliquely interrogative and more overtly conformist, may be more indicative of the mainstream. However, it is often difficult to locate copies of mainstream films, especially with subtitles, so an idea of what constitutes the core of films for children and young adults may remain elusive.

Notes

1. V. V. Ivanov, "The Categories and Functions of Film Language," trans. Roberta Reeder, *Film Criticism* 11:1–2 (1986), pp. 173–189, at 177; Sung-Ae Lee, Fengxia Tan, and John Stephens, "Film Adaptation, Global Film Techniques and Cross-Cultural Viewing," *International Research in Children's Literature* 10:1 (2017), pp. 1–19, at 3.

2. A *script* is a familiar narrative sequence that consists of essential and optional components and is instantiated by invoking one or more of the essential components. A script in this sense is different from a film script since scripts apply in everyday life as well as in folktales and creative narratives of all genres. See John Stephens and Sung-Ae Lee, "Transcultural Adaptation of Feature Films: South Korea's *My Sassy Girl* and its Remakes," *Adaptation* 11:1 (2018), pp 75–95, at 77.

3. Shanti Fader, "Compassion," in Josepha Sherman (ed.), *Storytelling: An Encyclopedia of Mythology and Folklore* (London: Routledge, 2015), p. 97.

4. Hamid Reza Sadr, "Children in Contemporary Iranian Cinema: When We Were Children," in Richard Tapper (ed.), *The New Iranian Cinema: Politics, Representation, and Identity* (London: I.B. Tauris, 2002), pp. 227–237, at 230.

5. In Iranian usage, *hejab* refers to Islamic clothing in general, not just the veil.

6. See John Stephens, "Cognitive Maps and Social Ecology in Young Adult Fiction," *International Research in Children's Literature* 8:2 (2015), pp. 142–155, at 143 .

7. Nasrin Rahimieh, "Framing Iran: A Contrapuntal Analysis of Two Cinematic Representations of Postrevolutionary Iran," *Edebiyât* 9:2 (1998), pp. 249–275, at 269.

8. In *Cahiers du cinema*, cited in Jerry White, "Children, Narrative and Third Cinema in Iran and Syria," *Canadian Journal of Film Studies* 11:1 (2002), pp. 78–97, at 83.

9. The pre-titles dedicate the film to Sepehri. See the extended discussion and review of literature in Atefeh Akbari Shahmirzadi, "'Where Is the Friend's Home?': New World Landscapes in Sohrab Sepehri's Poetic Geography," *Cambridge Journal of Postcolonial Literary Inquiry* 6:3 (2019), pp. 322–327. See also Khatereh Sheibani, "Kiarostami and the Aesthetics of Modern Persian Poetry," *Iranian Studies* 39:4 (2006), pp. 509–537.

10. Shahmirzadi, "Where is the Friend's Home?," p. 323.

11. Hadani Ditmars, "Talking Too Much with Men," *Sight and Sound* 7:4 (1997), pp. 10–12, at 12.

12. Cited in Amir Ali Nojoumian, "Constructing Childhood in Modern Iranian Children's Cinema: A Cultural History," in Casie Hermansson and Janet Zepernick (eds.), *The Palgrave Handbook of Children's Film and Television* (Cham, Switzerland: Palgrave Macmillan, 2019), pp. 279–294, at 292.

13. Sanaz Hamoonpou, "Rapithwin, the Demon of winter and Baba Barfi: An Archetypal Battle of Survival and Transformation in Iranian Children's Literature of the Twentieth Century," *Persian Literary Studies Journal* 6:10 (2017), pp. 37–38.

14. Manouchehr Neyestani, *Gol oumad, Bahar oumad* [Here comes flower, here comes spring], illustrated by Parviz Kalantari (Tehran: Centre for the Intellectual Development of Children and Adolescents, 1971).

15. Nojoumian, "Constructing Childhood," p. 280.

16. Bert Cardullo, "Mirror Images, or Children of Paradise," *Hudson Review* 52:4 (2000), pp. 649–656, at 650.

17. Under Iranian Shi'a law still in force in Iran in 2000, a girl reached puberty (and hence marriageable age) at nine lunar years (eight years and nine months). The minimum age of marriage for girls was raised to thirteen in 2002, although hard-line clerics objected that the change contravened Islamic law. See Mohammad Hossein Nayyeri, "Gender Inequality and Discrimination: The Case of Iranian Women," Iran Human Rights Documentation Center, website, March 5, 2013, sec. 2.1.1. "Minimum Age for Marriage," http://www.iranh rdc.org/english/publications/legal-commentary/1000000261-gender-inequality-and-dis crimination-the-case-of-iranian-women.html [accessed April 8, 2020].

18. Farhad Kazemi, "Gender, Islam, and Politics," *Social Research* 67:2 (2000), pp. 453–474, at 454.

19. Kazemi, "Gender, Islam, and Politics," p. 458.

20. Shahram Khosravi, *Young and Defiant in Tehran* (Philadelphia: University of Pennsylvania Press, 2008), p. 1.

21. Noushabeh Amiri, *Bulletin of the 10th Festival of Films from Iran*, October 24, 1999, cited in Khosravi, *Young and Defiant in Tehran*, p. 130.

22. The "real" Negar and Ashkan did manage to leave Iran, attend the Cannes Film Festival, where *Persian Cats* won the Un Certain Regard Special Jury Prize in 2009, and promote the film and their music in London. In 2009, after the arrest of Bahman Ghobadi and the apparent judicial murder of the band's drummer, Ali Ghomashchi, after he had returned separately to Iran, Negar and Ashkan sought and received political asylum in the UK.

23. Negar Shaghaghi, "Sounds of Silence," *Index on Censorship* 39:3 (2010), pp. 51–58, at 54.

24. Nojoumian, "Constructing Childhood," p. 292.

25. Adrian Danks, "The Rules of the Game: Jafar Panahi's *Offside*," *Australian Centre for the Moving Image*, March 23, 2020. https://www.acmi.net.au/ideas/read/rules-game-jafar-panahis-offside [accessed April 8, 2020].

26. Nayyeri, "Gender Inequality and Discrimination," sec. 2.2 "Divorce."

27. "Our film is mostly for girls and in general it's about women and their relationship with the society and their families." Seyyed-Hatami, in a brief interview with iFilm, https://en.ifilmtv.com/News/Content/268/iFilm-exclusive-on-Red-Nail-Polish [accessed April 11, 2020].

BIBLIOGRAPHY

Brown, Noel, and Bruce Babington. "Introduction: Children's Films and Family Films." In Noel Brown and Bruce Babington (eds.), *Family Films in Global Cinema: The World Beyond Disney*. London: I.B. Tauris, 2015, pp. 1–16.

Dabashi, Hamid. *Close Up: Iranian Cinema, Past, Present and Future*. London: Verso, 2001.

Dabashi, Hamid. *Masters and Masterpieces of Iranian Cinema*. Washington, DC: Mage, 2007.

Dabashi, Hamid. "Dvandeh/The Runner." In Gönül Dönmez-Colin (ed.), *The Cinema of North Africa and the Middle East* (London: Wallflower Press, 2007), pp. 81–88.

Dempsey, Anna M. "Telling the Girl's Side of the Story: Heterotopic Spaces of Femininity in Iranian Film." *Comparative Studies of South Asia, Africa, and the Middle East* 32:2 (2012), pp. 374–390.

Gengye, Szolt. "Subjects and Objects of the Embodied Gaze: Abbas Kiarostami and the Real of the Individual Perspective." *Acta Universitatis Sapientiae: Film and Media Studies* 13:1 (2016), pp. 127–141.

Khosravi, Shahram. *Young and Defiant in Tehran*. Philadelphia: University of Pennsylvania Press, 2008.

Langford, Michelle. *Allegory in Iranian Cinema: The Aesthetics of Poetry and Resistance*. London: Bloomsbury, 2019.

Moore, Lindsey C. "Women in a Widening Frame: (Cross-)Cultural Projection, Spectatorship, and Iranian Cinema." *Camera Obscura: Feminism, Culture, and Media Studies* 20:2 (2005), pp. 1–33.

Naficy, Hamid. "Iranian Cinema under the Islamic Republic." *American Anthropologist*, new series, 97:3 (1995), pp. 548–558.

Naficy, Hamid. *A Social History of Iranian Cinema*. Vol. 4. Durham, NC: Duke University Press, 2012.

Nojoumian, Amir Ali. "Constructing Childhood in Modern Iranian Children's Cinema: A Cultural History." In Casie Hermansson and Janet Zepernick (eds.), *The Palgrave Handbook of Children's Film and Television*. Cham, Switzerland: Palgrave Macmillan, 2019, pp. 279–294.

Sadr, Hamid Reza. "Children in Contemporary Iranian Cinema: When We Were Children." In Richard Tapper (ed.), *The New Iranian Cinema: Politics, Representation, and Identity*. London: I.B. Tauris, 2002, pp. 227–237.

Sprio, Margherita. "Filmic Performance: Authenticity and *The Apple*." *Wide Screen* 1:1 (2009), pp. 1–9.

White, Jerry. "Children, Narrative and Third Cinema in Iran and Syria." *Canadian Journal of Film Studies* 11:1 (2002), pp. 78–97.

Zeydabadi-Nejad, Saeed. *The Politics of Iranian Cinema: Film and Society in the Islamic Republic*. New York: Routledge, 2010.

CHAPTER 12

THE AMERICAN TWEEN AND CONTEMPORARY HOLLYWOOD CINEMA

TIMOTHY SHARY

We're not kids, we're tweens!
—Max (Jacob Tremblay) in *Good Boys* (Gene Stupnitsky, 2019)

IN *Love Finds Andy Hardy* (David Snell, 1938), the fourth film of what became an enormously popular series about a teenage boy and his coming of age in a Middle American town, the eponymous hero juggles the affections of different girls. One of them, played by rising star Judy Garland, is a twelve-year-old named Betsy, who gets along well with Andy (Mickey Rooney) but is ostensibly too young to date him—after all, he's old enough to drive and take high school girls to dances. Alone and agitated about her age, she breaks into song:

> I'm past the stage of doll and carriage
> I'm not the age to think of marriage
> I'm too old for toys and I'm too young for boys
> I'm just an in-between...
> I'll be so glad when I have grown some
> All by myself, I get so lonesome
> And I hope and pray for the day
> When I'll be sweet sixteen
> Then I won't have to be an in-between.

And this is the essence of torment for a population that is stuck in the middle of growth between childhood and adulthood: the tween. Adults comprise the majority of the population and by far the greatest number of protagonists in movies, while young children and teenagers have for generations enjoyed widespread media visibility despite their minority status. Yet this has not always been the case for that vital age population that is "in-between" and seeking identity and distinction. This chapter traces the emergence of a youth cohort on the edge of adolescence, from its genesis in the early twentieth century to its thriving notoriety today. It argues that tween culture has been acculturated by, and is now often symbiotic with, North American movies. The evolution of particular themes common to tween movies, and the generic patterns that have emerged from the industry's exploitation of those themes, further indicates that these films have cohered into a crucial commentary on American cultural concerns about children ageing out of their supposedly innocent impulses into the responsible realm of adulthood. At the dynamic intersection of those two phases in life is the tween, surrounded by ambiguity and arising as a character, a market, and an attitude.

IDENTIFYING THE TWEEN

The state of being "in-between" the recognized status of different social groups is indeed tormenting. The detachment, alienation, and lack of solid identification that arise from such cultural "liminal" conditions has been studied in the fields of anthropology, sociology, and psychology.[1] Those who are not wholly within certain groups—in terms of race, gender, sexuality, religion, health, and so on—often feel diffidence for and encounter scrutiny by the more assured members of groups who are verifiably included, and this is most quantifiably the case with groups determined by age.

Starting at birth, children are identified by age markers, first by weeks and months. Many parents continue to express their children's ages in months for some time after the first year, if only because an eighteen-month-old has distinct developmental differences from a twelve-month-old, even if both are technically one-year-olds. The demarcation of months tends to fade after the first few years; by the age of three or four years—when American children begin preschool—even the former designations of "infant" and "toddler" tend to give way to "child." After children start grade school, they are often identified by their class level: kindergartener, first grader, second grader, and so on.

This continues until about the age of eleven, when a sensitive ambiguity sets in, for both children themselves and the educational institutions that label them. In most American school districts, the first years of compulsory education (known as "grade" or "elementary" school) are divided from the later years (known as "high" or "secondary" school) by a two- or three-year period called "middle school" (previously referred to as "junior high school"). The middle-school grades tend to be the sixth or seventh through the eighth, and the age of middle-school students is typically eleven to thirteen. There is no national age standard for middle school, though most American school districts have one. Starting middle school clearly signals to those students that they are no longer children, but not yet the young adults that populate the higher-level schools they have yet to enter.

Before the twentieth century, most American schools educated children only until the early teen years, since few children went on to high school.[2] With increasing indus-trialization and urbanization after 1900, however, communities found incentives to ed-ucate children in specialized skills to prepare them to enter the workforce during their teenage years, and they began using public funds to build more secondary schools as they passed more compulsory schooling laws to occupy the minds and time of youth. By no coincidence, the emergence of movies and movie theatres by 1910 was also viewed by moral guardians as a contributing factor to juvenile delinquency.[3]

The reasons American middle schools were established are less evident. According to Douglas MacIver and colleagues, the creation of a school level between elementary and secondary levels in the early twentieth century gave "young adolescents a curric-ulum that was more substantial and more differentiated than that offered in elementary schools," and the new buildings also addressed "common practical problems such as the overcrowding of K–8 elementary schools and high rates of students leaving school after grade eight."[4] In some areas, the "junior high school" became a way to "entice greater numbers of non-college-bound youths to stay in school at least through grade nine by offering them commercial, domestic, and vocational curricula," and thus by the 1940s, the majority of adolescents were attending such schools.[5]

However, after World War II, resistance arose to mixing older and younger teens within schools, and educators began questioning the specialization of topics now being used in junior high curricula. Educators saw a better option in a middle-school design that would prepare students academically for high school but still maintain a transi-tional population between primary and secondary schooling. By the 1970s, an increasing number of school districts had established middle schools for grades 6 to 8 (ages 11–13) and high schools for grades 9 to 12 (ages 14–17). By the 1980s, most communities had middle schools, and research organizations (such as the Carnegie Corporation and the Kellogg Foundation) had affirmed the need to educate early adolescents separately from younger and older age groups based on their developmental idiosyncrasies.[6]

The concerns about adolescent development that arose in American education in the early twentieth century had originated in the field of psychology, which, after the pub-lication of G. Stanley Hall's foundational work *Adolescence* in 1904, began suggesting a behavioural and cognitive division of older and younger children.[7] Society became acculturated to the idea of a vital time in the "turn" from childhood to adulthood, characterized physically by the onset of secondary sexual characteristics (elevated amounts of sex hormones in children leading to bodily changes) and manifested psy-chologically in curiosity about sexual activity, questions about self-identity, and conflicts with social expectations. Children at this stage inevitably experienced a wide, sometimes dramatic, range of emotions: in addition to wondering about their changing bodies, they become less satisfied with previously pat answers to questions about repro-duction, sexuality, and life itself. Under the Victorian-era repression of the late 1800s, adults had abhorred such unrest in children; yet with the Industrial Revolution flour-ishing in the early 1900s, more children were becoming centralized in American cities, and thus forming a youth culture with some levels of internal influence, from illicit neighborhood gangs to sanctioned groups aimed at channelling wayward impulses. Accordingly, the Boy Scouts of America was created in 1910, and the Girl Scouts followed in 1912.

Beyond schooling and psychology, American culture slowly recognized the emergent youth population as a force of its own. Paid child labour (unlike chores imposed at home and work on farms) increased in the early 1900s. Industrialization led to children being paid for factory work and selling items on the streets (particularly newspapers), though their parents tended to take in their income.[8] These jobs, as well as the increased mobility of children, who could use public transportation to get around the city, meant that urban youth were taking on even more activities outside the home and adult control, and so schooling was a logical solution to regain some of that control. After World War I and the relatively prosperous 1920s, more schools were built across the expanding suburban landscape of America, and with more single-family houses populating those suburbs, children began enjoying the new freedom of individual bedrooms to be used as personal spaces. Popular culture also engaged children with comic strips in newspapers (which would evolve into a comic book industry starting in the late 1930s), while the relatively new medium of radio produced shows often based on child characters in those comics, such as *Little Orphan Annie* (1930) and *Jack Armstrong, the All-American Boy* (1933).

Though its etymology is somewhat ambiguous, the term *teen-ager* emerged around 1922, having evolved from the prevailing term *teener* to describe youth, which had been in use since the 1890s. Despite Betsy's labelling of herself as an "in-between" in the *Andy Hardy* film from 1938, the term *tween-ager* did not come into use until the 1940s, and the label *tween* to mean a "child nearing puberty" did not come into common use until after 1988.[9] Regardless of the semantics, by the end of the 1930s American culture was recognizing these "older children" as a distinct presence, as was evident when Hollywood started making movies that were clearly *about* teenagers, and thus cultivating a youth audience. As adolescents developed an "elevated" status from children, they gained unprecedented standing in society, By 1935 the American Youth Congress had been formed, and presented its *Declaration of the Rights of American Youth* to the United States Congress the following year.[10] This new standing would be yet another reason for teenagers' wanting to establish their own hierarchy, not unlike the one the school system promoted, so that they would be viewed as more mature and sophisticated than younger children. Those who temporarily languished between the poles of younger and older childhood would become the frustrated, displaced, and disempowered tween population.

THE TWEEN ON-SCREEN

When movie theatres came to America in the early twentieth century, the fledgling film industry tended to traffic in general fare that could be enjoyed by a wide range of age groups; these primarily took the form of adventures that were suitable for a family audience. Such stories were largely drawn from popular literature—historical accounts, travelogues, romances, westerns, and some science fiction—almost all of which focused on adult characters. With the rise of the studio system in the 1920s, filmmakers and theatres began seeking more sophisticated approaches to reach certain audiences, catering stories to racial, ethnic, and religious groups, for instance, and by the 1930s, Hollywood had clearly established ongoing genres to entertain the expanding range of audience interests. Movies that explored more mature content were, however, effectively banned after the enforcement of the Production Code in 1934 (which eliminated most topics related to sex and immorality that had been seeping into films by the early Depression years), and thereafter few movies were made that would have necessarily excluded young audiences—although certain subjects may have been less appealing to them.

Notwithstanding the growing divide between preadolescent "kids" and identifiable "teenagers" in popular culture after the 1930s, Hollywood was understandably reluctant to embrace the abstruse—not to mention narrow and financially precarious—tween population. After all, this is a group that resists its own marginalized status in society and likely cringes at the very notion of being represented in the first place. While there was *some* money to be made in producing films about youth that went beyond the anodyne fare of many family films, the industry may not have seen the sense in making movies that older children would resist and younger children might find too complicated, leaving adults potentially uninterested altogether. Noel Brown has commented on this dilemma as it relates to movies made for tween audiences in the 2010s, and his explanation also applies to the tween films of much of the twentieth century: "The relative inaccessibility of the enormously lucrative teen market, the perceived unprofitability of the narrowly conceived 'child audience,' and the desire to appeal to parents accompanying children to the cinema all necessitate, in mainstream popular cinema, a multi-layered mode of address calculated to secure a broad, trans-demographic clientele."[11] Deviating from that necessity to make films that portray and please tweens would be a risky proposition.

Constrained by the moral boundaries of the Production Code, the studios certainly knew they needed a safe address for audiences. They soon found salvation in the promotion of child stars, who could appeal to young and old; these included Jackie Cooper, Jane Withers, Freddie Bartholomew, and Judy Garland. In fact, two highly successful child actors remained the top box-office draws for seven years after the Code went into effect: Shirley Temple, from 1935 to 1938, and Mickey Rooney, from 1939 to 1941. During her heyday, Temple played preteen characters (from about the ages of 6 to 9), and Rooney, though he had some preteen roles, did not become as hugely popular until his later teen years, primarily through his Andy Hardy movies. Thus Temple played distinctly childish roles, and Rooney was an "older" young adult (i.e., could drive, date, and had some autonomy in his social decisions). Tellingly, neither actor represented the tween population, and the movie industry continued to largely dismiss that transitional age group.

Perhaps the leading explanation for Hollywood's previous avoidance of adolescent depictions is the awkward subject of sexuality. While sex was not addressed for older teens in movies until the 1950s, keeping an emphasis on "pre-sexual" children like Temple's characters meant the subject could be avoided altogether, and with older teens like Andy Hardy, knowledge of sexual development could be assumed.[12] Tween characters might have had reasonable questions about their changing bodies and thoughts, and their curiosity about sex may have needed to be addressed. But Hollywood in the early twentieth century was quite invested in maintaining repressed moral codes for a neutral audience.

These conditions began to change after World War II, and especially in the 1950s, when Hollywood saw movie audiences declining because of the popularity of television, and the nation saw its youth population growing thanks to the postwar baby boom. The studios slowly saw the logic of making films for a youth audience that might actually exclude their parents, as Thomas Doherty surmised in his analysis of the rock-and-roll movies of the mid-1950s.[13] Again, these films tended to focus on older teenagers in high school or college, and the tween population was generally dismissed (Figure 12.1).

FIGURE 12.1. Hollywood was less receptive to Shirley Temple as a tween, seen here with Nella Walker in *Kathleen* (1941, MGM), though as a younger child she had been the most popular movie star of the 1930s. The industry did not fully embrace tween characters for many more years. Frame-grab.

Yet a significant development in the representation of tween characters had begun in the 1940s, when Hollywood slowly started to recognize the dramatic value of later childhood.[14] Temple moved into tween roles herself in *Young People* (Allan Dwan, 1940) and *Kathleen* (Harold S. Bucquet, 1941), and by 1942 was playing a more mature teen role in *Miss Annie Rooney* (Edwin L. Marin, 1942), a film that was brazenly promoted as delivering her first screen kiss.[15] The war years (1941–1945) were, of course, taken up with stories of combat and crime, but immediately thereafter the industry found success in a string of films about tween characters played by previously unknown performers: Peggy Ann Garner in *A Tree Grows in Brooklyn* (Elia Kazan, 1945), Claude Jarman Jr. in *The Yearling* (Clarence Brown, 1946), and Lanny Rees in *Home in Oklahoma* (William Witney, 1946). These stories were all set in earlier eras, which not only evoked nostalgia but avoided confrontations with concerns about contemporary adolescence. Alas, this acceptable use of tweens did not persist into the 1950s, and more sensational stories about older teens garnered far more attention. There were significant tween characters in films like *The Member of the Wedding* (Fred Zinnemann, 1952) and *The Space Children* (Jack Arnold, 1958), but they were few and far between, and the industry continued to sideline this age group for the next two decades, sporadically producing minor hits like *The Parent Trap* (David Swift, 1961) and *The Fool Killer* (Servando González, 1965).

As movie attendance continued to decline into the 1970s, the industry had experienced an unexpected revival by the end of decade, with blockbusters such as *Jaws* (Steven Spielberg, 1975), *Star Wars* (George Lucas, 1977), and *Superman* (Richard Donner, 1978), all of which generated sequels. These films did not feature tweens or even teens (except for *Star Wars*'s Luke Skywalker), but they certainly appealed to those age groups, as well as to adults, and perhaps most crucially, they were "certified" to be appropriate for youth in the ratings system that had emerged at the end of the 1960s. The implementation of the Motion Picture Association of America's rating system in 1968 did away with the vague Production Code approval, which had theoretically made all films acceptable for children. In its place, the rating system gave the industry a standard for designating films that might require "parental guidance" for children (the PG rating) and could restrict children from seeing films without an adult guardian (the R rating). The rating system meant that even the gory violence of *Jaws* was ruled permissible for young viewers since it was rated PG. As the ratings system evolved throughout the 1970s, the G rating (generally acceptable without reservation) began to disappear, if only because the industry and the ratings administration understood that more mature topics were finding their way into almost all Hollywood features.

But by the early 1980s, the studios began chafing against the limits of the PG rating as they began promoting movies with more violence. The MPAA then introduced the PG-13 rating in 1984, which explicitly told the tween audience that "some material may be inappropriate" for them. The crucial difference between PG-13 and R ratings was that only the R rating empowered theatres to actually turn away children who were not accompanied by a parent or an adult guardian. The PG-13 rating allowed children to attend these movies without adult supervision; and in terms of the evolving home-video market at the time, it expanded the range of titles that parents might feel safe allowing their children to watch alone. Not coincidentally, the first PG-13-rated film was *Red Dawn* (John Milius, 1984), about teenagers, which followed by a few months the film that had ostensibly provoked the MPAA to reconsider the R-rated boundaries of violence, *Indiana Jones and the Temple of Doom* (Steven Spielberg, 1984). For the rest of the decade and into the 1990s, almost every major American blockbuster was a PG-13 film, many of them quite inviting to young audiences.

The distinctions wrought by the ratings system—whereby films *about* tweens could be made that were not intended *for* tweens—had also betrayed a crucial shift in the representation of children and the address of the child audience. Although a few films about "evil children" had gained notoriety before the 1970s (notably, *The Bad Seed* [Mervyn LeRoy, 1956] and *The Children's Hour* [William Wyler, 1961]) and were likely viewed by parents as inappropriate for their children to see, movies the Hollywood studios made about youth were generally deemed suitable for a young audience. Yet the ratings system clearly codified films intended for adults that would be explicitly restricted for child audiences, spawning stories about tweens in R-rated films like *Taxi Driver* (Martin Scorsese, 1976) and *Pretty Baby* (Louis Malle, 1978). Thereafter, any academic study of films about children needed to be conscious of this discrepancy, because movie studios could then make movies about youth that were outside the bounds of permissible childhood viewing.[16]

As Hollywood gradually saw the bigger profits to be made from more spectacular (and juvenile) fare during the rise of 1970s blockbusters, the studios also slowly gained evidence of the lucrative market for tween characters, and began featuring them in family-friendly stories like *The Black Stallion* (Carroll Ballard, 1979) and *E.T. The Extra-Terrestrial* (Steven Spielberg, 1982).[17] The tween film nonetheless remained in a larval stage for another decade as Hollywood's interest in older teen characters, who could carry more mature stories about sex and violence, revived, and even emergent tween classics like *The Goonies* (Richard Donner, 1985) and *Stand By Me* (Rob Reiner, 1986) featured older teens in supporting roles to avoid the appearance of being mere "children's films" that might otherwise have limited appeal.

STUDYING THE TWEEN

In pioneering works, David Considine (1985) and Thomas Doherty (1988, revised 2002) considered the stakes of representation for adolescent characters in films going back to the 1930s, and further studies by Lewis (1992), Shary (2002, revised 2014), Tropiano (2006), Driscoll (2011), and Smith (2017) illuminated the complexity of teenage roles and the impact of their messages.[18] Yet again, the emphasis has mostly been on "older youth"—the prevailing scholarship, and the industry itself, has apparently found more interest in the population of youth that has achieved high school status. To be sure, by the later teens, youth have begun to form more complex social and sexual relationships, are more active consumers, and are closer to becoming the adults who are employed by studios (and schools), all reasons for the industry to pay more attention to them than their younger counterparts.

Many of these studies into adolescence do consider films about younger teens (typically characters down to age 12), yet otherwise the realm of "children's cinema" has been relegated to prepubescent youth. About that realm of "younger youth" many cogent studies have been written, such as ones by Jackson (1986), Sinyard (1992), Wojcik-Andrews (2000), Lury (2010), and Brown (2017), but none of them take up the distinct tween population that began emerging in American movies in the 1980s.[19] Instead, in recent years there has been more work on tween culture in the social sciences, such as that of Natalie Coulter (2014), who argues that the tween identity emerged as a market demographic in the 1980s; Ingvild Kvale Sørenssen (2015), whose analysis of Disney yields persuasive classifications of tweens; and Fiona MacDonald (2016), who takes on the influence of media for tween girls.[20]

I still contend that youth *before* the later teens are worthy of serious consideration, even if films about them are not as numerous and they may appear less interesting to some academics. After all, in addition to the moral standard they set for an industry pursuing the prized PG-13 demographic, tweens offer dramatic appeal because of the liminal state they navigate en route to adulthood, because almost all children by the time of their "double-digit years" have become cognizant enough to seek autonomy in their self-identification, and more crucially for the movie industry, they have begun to voice their preferences for entertainment options.

THE EMBRYONIC TWEENS

This chapter can only cover a fraction of the tween movies that have emerged since tweens were first named as such in the 1980s. Rather than aim for a complete history, then, I outline the relevant trends and key texts that have emerged. As mentioned, there is some academic rationale for distinguishing between films made *for* youth and films made *about* youth, though I remain concerned with the broader representation of tween characters, regardless of the intended audience. Given the expanding number and visibility of tween movies since the turn of the current century, I focus on the past two decades.

In the 1980s, as the advent of home-video systems slowly made the secondary market for the "kid vid" truly expansive, the number of tween characters in Hollywood productions noticeably increased.[21] Tween stories in previous decades had developed consistent plot themes in these films—family reunification, romantic curiosities, and influential friendships—with the occasional foray into paranormal exploration. These themes would continue to signify a curious moment of transition for youth as they graduate from childish stories about cute animals and cheerful adventures to mature topics they will encounter in adulthood, while still retaining connections to fundamental elements of psychological development, such as self-identity, sexual interest, socialization, and confrontations with the mysterious forces of grown-up life. Indeed, tween films offered nourishing narratives of empowerment and growth for children in their liminal stage, and at least two dozen examples made their way to American theatres in the 1980s. By the 1990s, more than twice that number appeared, which was enough for certain subcategories of tween storylines to arise, similar to those in teen films going back to the 1950s.[22]

Family reunification plots were, in many ways, emblematic of postwar trauma, and they had become increasingly common by the 1960s. The children in these films were occasionally affected by their parents' efforts to get on with their lives after the death of a spouse (*The Courtship of Eddie's Father* [Vincente Minnelli, 1963]; *With Six You Get Eggroll* [Howard Morris, 1968]; *Yours, Mine, and Ours* [Melville Shavelson, 1968]); and before long, the increasing divorce rate provoked the studios to consider the impact of this trend on youth (*Kramer vs. Kramer* [Robert Benton, 1979]; *Rich Kids* [Robert M. Young 1979]; *Firstborn* [Michael Apted, 1984]; *Irreconcilable Differences* [Charles Shyer, 1984]). Thus, we see a longing for family harmony after disruption in many of these tween characters, providing the drama in *Murphy's Romance* (Martin Ritt, 1985), *Empire of the Sun* (Steven Spielberg, 1987), *This Boy's Life* (Michael Caton-Jones, 1993), and *Tumbleweeds* (Gavin O'Connor, 1999). In the 1990s, the commonness of family tensions allowed some films to treat the subject with a degree of levity, for example, in *All I Want For Christmas* (Robert Lieberman, 1991), *Getting Even with Dad* (Howard Deutch, 1994), *Unstrung Heroes* (Diane Keaton, 1995), and the popular remake of *The Parent Trap* (Nancy Meyers, 1998). In the more extreme cases, tweens who cannot reconcile the family dissolution seek parental surrogates in, say, a foster father (*Free Willy* [Simon Wincer, 1993]), a lawyer (*The Client* [Joel Schumacher, 1994]), or an aging circus performer (*The First of May* [Paul Sirmons, 1999]).

Portraying romantic interests among tweens may seem premature, but many prepubescent children begin to have such longings from an early age. Films made before the 1990s had generally avoided any kind of sexual element (except in those rare instances where adults induced a tween's sexual experience, as in *Taxi Driver, Pretty Baby, Forty Deuce* [Paul Morrissey, 1982], and *Big* [Penny Marshall, 1988]).[23] But in the 1990s, tween characters began asking more mature questions about sex, and occasionally experiencing first kisses, as in *My Girl* (Howard Zieff, 1991), *The Sandlot* (David Mickey Evans, 1993), *The Baby-Sitters Club* (Melanie Mayron, 1995), *Casper* (Brad Silberling, 1995), *Now and Then* (Lesli Linka Glatter, 1995), *Welcome to the Dollhouse* (Todd Solondz, 1995), and *Jungle 2 Jungle* (John Pasquin, 1997). Some features began broaching decidedly mature issues for tween characters, such as same-sex attraction (*This Boy's Life*), prostitution (*Milk Money* [Richard Benjamin, 1994]), threatened rape (*Welcome to the Dollhouse*), and childbirth (*Manny & Lo* [Lisa Krueger, 1996]). Otherwise, these tween characters, as with tweens in real life, were unfamiliar with sustained romantic relationships, even as some odd couples formed, usually under dramatic rather than casual conditions, such as after death in *Casper*, while coping with disease in *The Baby-Sitters Club*, or through trauma in *Pups* (Ash Baron-Cohen, 1999).

Another aspect of adolescent development tweens experience is the increasing importance of friendships, which begins to displace the prominence of family contact

FIGURE 12.2. *The Goonies* (1985, Warner Bros.) indicated the burgeoning presence of tweens in American culture and in Hollywood movies. *Left to right*: Corey Feldman, Ke Huy Quan, Martha Plimpton, Kerri Green. Frame-Grab.

(particularly parental). As youth seek independence from their parents—despite their ongoing reliance on the security of the family unit—they turn to peers in an effort to socialize beyond the home, usually in school. While the occasional film tested the nature of tween alliances, usually through rivalries (*Troop Beverly Hills* [Jeff Kanew, 1989], *Lord of the Flies* [Harry Hook, 1990], *The Sandlot*, and *Little Men* [Rodney Gibbons, 1998]), the greater emphasis in tween films remained on the vital synergy that friends bring to each other, which was celebrated in *The Goonies* (Figure 12.2), *Stand by Me*, *Big*, *The People under the Stairs* (Wes Craven, 1991), *Richie Rich* (Donald Petrie, 1994), *The Cure* (Peter Horton, 1995), *Tom and Huck* (Peter Hewitt, 1995), and *The Mighty* (Peter Chelsom, 1998).

We begin to see the fourth notable theme of tween films in the 1980s, one that will have even prominence in the next century—that is, encounters with the paranormal. Youth have an inherent fascination with the bizarre and macabre, and Hollywood knew from the ongoing success of horror and sci-fi franchises going back to the 1970s that young audiences were eager for sensational subjects. Films with more- graphic horror—with psychopathic killers and copious gore—were directed to older teens, particularly those that could breach the films' R ratings, although some tween characters had roles in these films, beginning with *The Exorcist* (William Friedkin, 1973) and *Damien: Omen II* (Don Taylor, 1978), and continuing in *The Pit* (Lew Lehman, 1981) and *Children of the Corn* (Fritz Kiersch, 1984). The *Corn* films were heavily sequelized, with the release of three more instalments in the 1990s; two other R-rated horror films about tweens appeared in that decade as well: *The People under the Stairs* and *The Good Son* (Joseph Rubin, 1993). Stories of the paranormal for tween audiences focused on more benign phenomena, such as creepy mysteries (*The Goonies, The Gate* [Tibor Takács, 1987]), space aliens (*E.T., Flight of the Navigator* [Randal Kleiser, 1986]), and body-swapping (*Big, Vice Versa* [Brian Gilbert, 1988]). In the 1990s, there were curiously few examples of these, as industry interest shifted to tweens (and older teens) in stories about animals, which followed the success of *Free Willy* in 1993, after which came a remake of *Lassie* (Daniel Petrie, 1994), as well as *Fly Away Home* (Carroll Ballard, 1996), *Air Bud* (Charles Martin Smith, 1997), and *Wild America* (William Dear, 1997).

These predominant topics for tweens would persist into the new century, although the industry did occasionally offer variations on these themes and traversed generic interests, as in the spy adventure *Cloak & Dagger* (Richard Franklin, 1983); the political commentary of *Amazing Grace and Chuck* (Mike Newell, 1987); the historical drama of *Convicts* (Peter Masterson, 1991); and the odd trio of films about tweens who get involved with pro baseball in *Rookie of the Year* (Daniel Stern, 1993), *Angels in the Outfield* (William Dear, 1994), and *Little Big League* (Andrew Scheinman, 1994). By the end of the century, not only had the tween audience emerged as a profitable market for Hollywood studios, but tween movies had taken on a complexity and consistency that ensured their characters and stories had enough recognizable qualities to endure.

TWENTY-FIRST-CENTURY TWEENS

With the tween market now clearly established, the 2000s continued the expansion in the number and topics of tween movies being made. Most of these were still directed to the tween audience itself, and their stories featured tween characters in PG- and PG-13-rated movies based on the four themes that had emerged in the 1990s, yielding enough examples to reveal further industry patterns.

Stories about family reunification have actually declined in the past two decades in comparison to the attention divorce and family upheaval received throughout the 1980s and 1990s (at least, in realistic films; fantasies are different, as I detail below). Increasingly, tweens were directed to learn coping skills with single parents, predominantly single mothers struggling to overcome strife without their children's missing fathers. This was on prominent display in *Double Parked* (Stephen Kinsella, 2000), *12 and Holding* (Michael Cuesta, 2005), *Dear Lemon Lima* (Suzu Yoonessi, 2009), *Janie Jones* (David M. Rosenthal, 2010), *St. Vincent* (Theodore Melfi, 2014), *So B. It* (Stephen Gyllenhaal, 2016), *Mid90s* (Jonah Hill, 2018), and *Coffee & Kareem* (Michael Dowse, 2020). The protagonists in all these films have some level of respect for their mothers' efforts, though the plots are often driven by some challenge posed by the tween child. A paradigm (if notorious) case would be *Pay It Forward* (Mimi Leder, 2000), in which a most insightful boy tries matchmaking to encourage his mother to cope with her alcoholism, trying to set her up romantically with his influential schoolteacher. The true depth of the adults' pain is beyond the tween's understanding, yet, as in many of these stories, the tween protagonist is the catalyst for greater change.

The estranged fathers are notably missing from these films. When dads are present, they tend to be depicted as protective patriarchs to tweens, maintaining—in the following films—some semblance of the family coherence the single mothers are unable to sustain: *Domestic Disturbance* (Harold Becker, 2001), *Zathura: A Space Adventure* (Jon Favreau, 2005), *Kick-Ass* (Matthew Vaughn, 2010), and *Eighth Grade* (Bo Burnham, 2018). Other kinds of patriarchal figures nurture tweens from broken families as well, such as coaches (*Rebound* [Steve Carr, 2005], *The Longshots* [Fred Durst, 2008], *The Karate Kid* [Harald Zwart, 2010]); teachers (*Pay It Forward, Akeelah and the Bee* [Doug Atchison, 2006], *That's What I Am* [Michael Pavone, 2011], *Queen of Katwe* [Mira Nair, 2016]); and, in a more recent mode, potential foster fathers to orphans (*Let Me In* [Matt Reeves, 2010], *Hugo* [Martin Scorsese, 2011], *Moonrise Kingdom* [Wes Anderson, 2012], *The Retrieval* [Chris Eska, 2013], *Annie* [Will Gluck, 2014], and *Lamb* [Ross Partridge, 2015]). The tween characters almost always learn that fathers (and father figures) know best, as in the haunting *Leave No Trace* (Debra Granik, 2018), in which a traumatized veteran has fled from the pressures of civilized life to forage in the wilderness with his tween daughter. After they are given the option of a more typical life but later move off the grid again, the girl makes the difficult decision to stay with a commune and let her father continue on his own.

Many films since the 1950s have tried to show the troubles of youth lurking behind the happy facades of American households (*Rebel Without a Cause* [Nicholas Ray, 1955], *The Graduate* [Mike Nichols, 1967], *Ordinary People* [Robert Redford, 1980], and *Happiness* [Todd Solondz, 1998]); and in twenty-first-century movies, tween families remain rather tense, even when conditions seem favourable and both parents are present. Curiously, tweens whose parents remain together often face difficulties despite the appearance of family coherence. The title character in *Max Keeble's Big Move* (Tim Hill, 2001) is having enough trouble adjusting to middle school when he learns that his parents are suddenly moving the family far away. In *Off the Map* (Campbell Scott, 2003), a home-schooled girl watches her family endure a financial crisis that sinks her father into a deep depression. Another girl, in *Bee Season* (Scott McGehee, 2005), finds herself stuck in a family crisis as her parents try to cope with religious doubt and past trauma while she works to become a champion speller. The heroine in *The Greening of Whitney Brown* (Peter Skillman Odiorne, 2011) is distraught by her parents' sudden lack of wealth and loss of social status. And everything goes terribly wrong for the family in *Hereditary* (Ari Aster, 2018): still trying to cope with the death of a grandparent, the surviving parents are gravely traumatized by the brutal death of their tween daughter.

Even in deliberately light-hearted fare, the nuclear family is somehow imbalanced, such as in the three *Diary of a Wimpy Kid* films (2010–2012), where resentment arises from the large age differences between three siblings. The animated celebration of a tween girl's emotional growth, *Inside Out* (Pete Docter, 2015), features two loving parents struggling with relocation and its impact on their only child. Another tween girl endures the disruption of relocation in *Permanent* (Colette Burson, 2017), while her parents face financial troubles and adulterous temptations. And we might expect that the title character in *Alexander and the Terrible, Horrible, No Good, Very Bad Day* (Miguel Arteta, 2014) will undergo a trying time given the title, but actually, his entire family is in turmoil. His dad is unemployed, his mom has major burdens at work, and his three siblings have their own crises, all of which is aggravated by Alexander's wish that the rest of his family join in the anguish of his bad day. Tweens thus continue to be given clear messages about family life: its normal state is one of turbulence, and parents are unreliable (if often sympathetic) leaders. In keeping with the increased drive toward independence that teens enact during puberty, movies steer tweens toward friends for more reliable relationships, so that the peer group becomes a more profound influence on their identity and activities, and the depreciation of family becomes an inevitability.

Romantic and sexual themes for tweens have not markedly increased in prominence in the past two decades, despite the suspicion that children have been gaining more access to sexual content through the Internet. Most tween forays into romance remained rather tame, with filmmakers taking up the subject only sporadically. (The persistent popularity of the Olsen twins, Mary-Kate and Ashley, in the early 2000s was an exception: they began a six-year franchise of cloying travelogues across different international cities with *Passport to Paris* [Alan Metter, 1999], and each film predictably featured a pair of cute boys to woo the girls.) Understandably, the most common scenario explored first love among tweens, which could result in unrequited torment (*George Washington* [David Gordon Green, 2000]; *Children on Their Birthdays* [Mark Medoff, 2002]; *Dear Lemon Lima*; *Diary of a Wimpy Kid: Rodrick Rules* [David Bowers, 2012]; *Eighth Grade*), or unfulfilled curiosity (*The Lizzie McGuire Movie* [Jim Fall, 2003]; *Little Manhattan* [Mark Levin, 2005]; *Flipped* [Rob Reiner, 2010]; *Standing Up* [D. J. Caruso, 2013]; *Jessica Darling's It List* [Ali Scher, 2016]). After all, characters who are too young to marry even with parental consent are poor candidates to depict as living "happily ever after" in a romantic relationship.

Yet the past decade began offering some tweens a certain level of promise in their initial amorous pursuits, even when their situations are compromised, such as the growing affection between a boy and his vampire girlfriend in *Let Me In*. Although he must necessarily confront the latent evil the girl represents, the vampire ultimately saves his life and he ascends to the role of her protector. The preternaturally dedicated tween couple in *Moonrise Kingdom* realise that their guardians would not understand the intensity of their affection for each other, so they run away to create an idyllic retreat for their romance. Their juvenile paradise is soon enough shattered by the demands of grownups, yet their peers rally to reunite the pair, then preside over a pretend wedding before the couple cooperates with the adult authorities. The quiet heroine of *Eighth Grade* has a painful crush on a hip boy, only to discover his selfish banality, and then cautiously turns her attention a boy who, like her, is an awkward outsider and likely a more promising romantic option, or, at least, a better friend. And the proudly bawdy *Good Boys* (Gene Stupnitsky, 2019) parades its three title tweens through a rigorous crash course on acceptable sexual behaviour, with a refreshingly responsible message about informed

FIGURE 12.3. Tween depictions took a radical leap with *Good Boys* (2019, Universal), which features the title characters navigating carnal questions within a preadolescent domain of misinformation leavened with profanity. *Left to right*: Keith L. Williams, Jacob Tremblay, Brady Noon. Frame-grab.

consent, culminating in an ultimately tenuous first foray into romantic conquest (Figure 12.3).

Given the nascent nature of adolescent romance, in movies and in real life tweens continue to rely on their friendships to provide social order and verify many aspects of status, such as popularity, loyalty, and congeniality. Most friend groups in tween movies are sincere and supportive, resisting the petty competitiveness and suspicion that can fester within groups of teenage friends. Most tween films eschew dyadic friendships, where two friends support each other (as in the *Diary of a Wimpy Kid* franchise), in favor of trios and small groups who gather around a protagonist who leads the story, as in *George Washington*, *Catch That Kid* (Bart Freundlich, 2004), *Hoot* (Will Shriner, 2006), *Super 8* (J. J. Abrams, 2011), *Earth to Echo* (Dave Green, 2014), *It* (Andy Muschetti, 2017), and *Mid90s*. Quite often, a mission is set in motion—to solve a mystery, right a wrong, or confront adult authority, or all of the above—and the narrative follows the characters accordingly. Such is the case in *Dear Lemon Lima*, where a Yup'ik girl struggles to adjust to her exclusive Alaskan school and enlists her "athletically impaired" friends to compete against more skilled students in a field-day contest. Not only do her friends eventually win, but they also legitimize their outsider status against the prevailing social order and rigid school administrators.

Gender plays an increasingly important role in adolescent relationships over time, although among tween friends, girls often have closer bonds than boys, who are not only later bloomers in bodily development, but who tend to assume the socialized rites of male bonding later than girls embrace group allegiances. The same Hollywood sexism that decrees most movies will be about male characters persists in tween stories, yet in recent years some films have integrated a lone girl into the boys' friend groups (in *Super 8*, *Earth to Echo*, *Time Toys* [Mark Rosman, 2016], and *It*). Alas, films devoted to groups of tween girlfriends are relatively few, such as *Sleepover* (Joe Nussbaum, 2004), *Summer Eleven* (Joseph Kell, 2010), and *The Fits* (Anna Rose Holmer, 2015).

Going beyond the typical experiences with family, friends, and crushes, some tween films continue to delve into the unrealistic yet fascinating world of the paranormal, and after the British *Harry Potter* films (2001–2011) began their ten-year run celebrating sorcery, Hollywood may justifiably have been expected to deliver more such fare for tweens. However, the *Potter* effect primarily showed itself in tales about older teens dabbling in supernatural sensations (*Final Destination*, 2000–2011; *Spider-Man*, 2002–2007; *Twilight*, 2008–2012); tweens were less often exposed to the potential dangers of inexplicable phenomena.

The initial *Spy Kids* trilogy (2001–2003) became increasingly occupied with the spectacular imagery of its tween fantasy yet did not entertain the level of cosmic depth that *Zathura* did in 2005, as signalled in its subtitle: *A Space Adventure*. Three siblings are playing with an old board game and discover that it turns their home into a spaceship, which carries them away on a mission to bring peace to their broken family. This kind of appeal to family reunification would permeate other sensational stories of tweens who find self-esteem and belonging in ersatz family units: the overweight tween in *Zoom* (Peter Hewitt, 2006), who gains respect among a group of dubious superheroes; the clairvoyant tween in *Push* (Paul McGuigan, 2009), who recruits a father figure to help her find her missing mother; the tween pals in *Super 8*, who evade the troubles of their beleaguered parents by bonding over the search for a space alien; the tween trio of *Earth to Echo*, who forestall their families' threatened evictions by discovering a space alien; the tweens in *It*, who confront the traumas of their past that persist in their parents as they search for missing children. If more realistic films about tweens seem largely to have resolved the former concerns about damaged families, the fantasy realm is still rife with worries about abusive, absent, and ambivalent parents whose children turn to alternate realities in an effort to find stability.

Conclusion

Hollywood has embraced tweens as characters to consider and a market to exploit. In identifying and depicting this particularly narrow age group, the movie industry betrays its efforts to profit from a specific audience formation, yet films about tweens also confirm the complex and unique nature of adolescence itself, even though some are clearly not made for tween audiences. As psychologists have long demonstrated, childhood is the most formative time in just about everyone's life, and all the learning and growth we endure in those years is profound. Most "children" in movies are assigned stated ages, if only because each childhood developmental stage can be so distinctly different, and the characters between the ages of eleven and thirteen who populate the tween film are arguably the most distinctive of all.

FILMOGRAPHY: TWEEN FILMS, 2000–2020

The age of the protagonist is next to the title when known. For mixed-age groups, no age is given.

2000:
Double Parked (13)
George Washington
Our Lips Are Sealed
Pay It Forward (11)

2001:
Domestic Disturbance (12)
Lloyd
Max Keeble's Big Move (12)
Spy Kids

2002:
Children on Their Birthdays (13)
Spy Kids 2: Island of Lost Dreams

2003:
The Lizzie McGuire Movie
Off the Map (11)
Spy Kids 3-D: Game Over

2004:
Catch That Kid (12)
Clipping Adam
Sleepover
13 Going on 30 (13)

2005:
Bee Season (11)
Little Manhattan
Rebound
12 and Holding (12)
Zathura: A Space Adventure

2006:
   Akeelah and the Bee (11)
   Half Nelson (13)
   Hoot
   A Very Serious Person (13)
   Wild Tigers I Have Known (13)
   Zoom
2007:
   The Girl Next Door
   Hounddog (12)
2008:
   Harold (13)
   The Longshots (12)
   Spy School (12)
2009:
   Alabama Moon
   Dear Lemon Lima (13)
   Sam Steele and the Jr. Detective Agency (13)
   Push (13)
2010:
   Diary of a Wimpy Kid (11)
   Flipped
   Janie Jones (13)
   The Karate Kid (12)
   Kick-Ass (11)
   Let Me In (12)
   Standing Ovation
   Summer Eleven
2011:
   A Bag of Hammers (12)
   Diary of a Wimpy Kid: Rodrick Rules (12)
   The Greening of Whitney Brown
   Hick (13)
   Hugo (12)
   The Sitter
   Super 8
   That's What I Am (12)
   Spy Kids: All the Time in the World in 4D
2012:
   Diary of a Wimpy Kid: Dog Days (12)
   Moonrise Kingdom (12)

2013:

 The Retrieval (13)
 Stand Clear of the Closing Doors (13)
 Standing Up (12)

2014:

 Alexander and the Terrible, Horrible, No Good, Very Bad Day
 Annie (11)
 Boyhood
 Earth to Echo
 Like Sunday, Like Rain (12)
 Sex Ed
 St. Vincent (12)

2015:

 The Fits
 The Great Gilly Hopkins (12)
 Inside Out (11)
 Jack of the Red Hearts (11)
 Lamb
 Pan (12)
 Sex, Death, and Bowling (11)

2016:

 Better Watch Out
 Cents
 Jessica Darling's It List
 Little Men (13)
 Middle School: The Worst Years of My Life
 Queen of Katwe
 So B. It (12)
 Time Toys

2017:

 Diary of a Wimpy Kid: The Long Haul (12)
 It
 Jurassic School
 Permanent (13)
 Wonderstruck (12)

2018:

 Eighth Grade (13)
 Family (11)
 Hereditary (13)
 Leave No Trace (13)
 Mid90s (13)

2019:

Brightburn (12)

Doctor Sleep

The Goldfinch (13)

Good Boys

Honey Boy (12)

Little (13)

The Lodge

Mysti

2020:

Coffee & Kareem (12)

Magic Camp

Magic Max

Timmy Failure: Mistakes Were Made (11)

We Can Be Heroes

NOTES

1. Within anthropology, Victor Turner is most often credited with popularizing the concept of "liminality" as a state of ambiguity and instability for individuals enduring a transition in status between social groups or between rites of passage. His oft-noted study *The Forest of Symbols: Aspects of Ndembu Ritual* (Ithaca, NY: Cornell University Press, 1967) borrowed from the foundational work of Arnold van Gennep, specifically *Les Rites de Passage*, 2nd ed. (1909; repr. Chicago: University of Chicago Press, 2019), which advanced the now familiar concept of "rites of passage" encountered during the growth process. Tensions of liminality, although not named as such, were examined in some of the psychoanalytic work by Freud and Jung in the early twentieth century, and in his studies Jung applied the concept to his theories about the individuation process. See *Psychological Types*, ed. Sir Herbert Read, vol. 6 of *C. G. Jung: The Collected Works* (1921; New York: Routledge, 2014).

2. "In 1910 just 9 percent of American youths earned a high school diploma, but by 1935 40 percent did." Claudia Goldin and Lawrence Katz, "Human Capital and Social Capital: The Rise of Secondary Schooling in America, 1910 to 1940," *Journal of Interdisciplinary History* 29 (Spring 1999), pp. 683–723, at 684–685.

3. Social reformer Jane Addams famously lamented the impact of movie houses on children in "The House of Dreams," a chapter in her 1909 book *The Spirit of Youth and the City Streets*. The chapter was reprinted in Gerald Mast (ed.), *The Movies in Our Midst: Documents in the Cultural History of Film in America* (Chicago: University of Chicago Press, 1982), pp. 72–78.

4. Douglas J. MacIver, et al., "High-Quality Learning Opportunities in High Poverty Middle Schools: Moving from Rhetoric to Reality," in Thomas S. Dickinson (ed.), *Reinventing the Middle School* (New York: Routledge Falmer, 2001), pp. 155–175, at 156.

5. MacIver et al., "High-Quality Learning Opportunities," p. 157.

6. Joyce L. Epstein and Douglas J. MacIver, *Education in the Middle Grades: National Practices and Trends* (Columbus, OH: National Middle School Association, 1990), p. 5.

7. G. Stanley Hall, *Adolescence: Its Psychology, and Its Relations to Physiology, Anthropology, Sociology, Sex, Crime, Religion, and Education* (New York: D. Appleton & Company, 1904).

8. Lucy Rollin, *Twentieth-Century Teen Culture by the Decades: A Reference Guide* (Westport, CT: Greenwood Press, 1999), pp. 8–12.

9. Douglas Harper, *Online Etymology Dictionary*, https://www.etymonline.com/ [accessed August 18, 2019].

10. Steven Mintz, *Huck's Raft: A History of American Childhood* (Cambridge, MA: Belknap Press at Harvard University Press, 2004), pp. 245–247. The American Youth Congress, like other socialist efforts of the New Deal era, became suspect during the World War II years and was dissolved.

11. Noel Brown, *The Children's Film: Genre, Nation and Narrative* (New York: Columbia University Press, 2017), p. 20.

12. Temple's first roles were in the notorious *Baby Berlesks* series of short films, made in 1932 and 1933, which featured preschoolers in parodies of adult dramas. Temple's first speaking role, in *War Babies* (Charles Lamont, 1932), at the age of four, was as a vamp drawing the attention of male suitors, and in six subsequent appearances she also played decidedly sexualized roles. Presumably, this level of carnal content in films about children was permissible owing to the incongruity of the actors' ages. For Temple's transition to teen roles, see Ilana Nash, *American Sweethearts: Teenage Girls in Twentieth-Century Popular Culture* (Bloomington: Indiana University Press, 2006), pp. 163–165.

13. Thomas Doherty, *Teenagers and Teenpics: The Juvenilization of American Movies in the 1950s* (Philadelphia: Temple University Press, 2002), pp. 57–79.

14. Because young characters' ages are sometimes ambiguous, identifying tween roles can be difficult across movie history, especially before World War II. In more recent decades, characters' ages often are clearly noted, and I have focused on such examples in this study. Of course, an argument can be made that the "maturity" of youth has changed over generations, so that numerical ages are less important than developmental stages; yet trying to codify such stages using psychological markers may yield specious results, particularly when considering fictional characters.

15. While *Miss Annie Rooney* exploited the supposed novelty of Temple's first screen kiss, in reality, she'd had her first screen kiss many years earlier, in *War Babies*. The sleazy moment is made more depraved by the fact that four-year-old Temple furtively kisses one boy while she is in the arms of another.

16. I make this case at length in my entry "Children's Films," in Barry Keith Grant (ed.), *The Schirmer Encyclopedia of Film* (Detroit, MI: Schirmer Reference, 2007), pp. 117–120. Other studies of children in cinema would offer similar qualifications.

17. While this study primarily focuses on protagonists aged eleven to thirteen, there are many notable films that generally qualify as tween depictions even though the characters may be slightly older or younger, such as the Elliott (Henry Thomas) character in *E.T.*, who is ten.

18. David M. Considine, *The Cinema of Adolescence* (Jefferson, NC: McFarland, 1985); Thomas Doherty, *Teenagers and Teenpics*; Jon Lewis, *The Road to Romance and Ruin: Teen Films and Youth Culture* (New York: Routledge, 1992); Timothy Shary, *Generation Multiplex: The Image of Youth in Contemporary American Cinema* (Austin: University of Texas Press, 2014); Stephen Tropiano, *Rebels and Chicks: A History of the Hollywood Teen Movie* (New York: Back Stage Books, 2006); Catherine Driscoll, *Teen Film: A Critical Introduction*

(New York: Berg, 2011); and Frances Smith, *Rethinking the Hollywood Teen Movie: Gender, Genre and Identity* (Edinburgh: Edinburgh University Press, 2017).

19. Kathy Merlock Jackson, *Images of Children in American Film: A Sociocultural Analysis* (Metuchen, NJ: Scarecrow Press, 1986); Neil Sinyard, *Children in the Movies* (London: B. T. Batsford, 1992); Ian Wojcik-Andrews, *Children's Films: History, Ideology, Pedagogy, Theory* (New York: Garland, 2000); Karen Lury, *The Child in Film: Tears, Fears, and Fairytales* (London: I.B. Tauris, 2010).

20. Natalie Coulter, *Tweening the Girl: The Crystallization of the Tween Market* (New York: Peter Lang, 2014); Ingvild Kvale Sørenssen, "The Social Construction of Everyday Concepts: Constructing the 'Tween,'" *Barn* 33:2 (2015), pp. 81–90; Fiona MacDonald, *Childhood and Tween Girl Culture: Family, Media and Locality* (London: Palgrave Macmillan, 2016).

21. The home-video market that emerged in the 1980s led some studios to make movies for release directly on video, particularly for the children's market. Some of those films no doubt appealed to tweens, but here I am studying primarily theatrically released features.

22. In my original assessment of American teen films of the 1980s, I identified five subgenres—school, delinquency, horror, science, and romance; yet by the 1990s it was clear that the "science subgenre" had faded, and by the 2000s "horror" had become more supernatural than scary. See Shary, *Generation Multiplex*, pp. 8–9.

23. The sordid *Forty Deuce* oddly revolves around a twelve-year-old boy who dies from a drug overdose in the opening scene.

BIBLIOGRAPHY

Addams, Jane. "'The House of Dreams,' from *The Spirit of Youth and the City Streets*. 1909. Reprinted in Gerald Mast (ed.). *The Movies in Our Midst: Documents in the Cultural History of Film in America*. Chicago: University of Chicago Press, 1982, pp. 72–78.

Brown, Noel. *The Children's Film: Genre, Nation and Narrative*. New York: Columbia University Press, 2017.

Considine, David M. *The Cinema of Adolescence*. Jefferson, NC: McFarland, 1985.

Coulter, Natalie. *Tweening the Girl: The Crystallization of the Tween Market*. New York: Peter Lang, 2014.

Doherty, Thomas. *Teenagers and Teenpics: The Juvenilization of American Movies in the 1950s*. Philadelphia: Temple University Press, 2002.

Driscoll, Catherine. *Teen Film: A Critical Introduction*. New York: Berg, 2011.

Epstein, Joyce L., and Douglas J. MacIver. *Education in the Middle Grades: National Practices and Trends*. Columbus, OH: National Middle School Association, 1990.

Goldin, Claudia, and Lawrence Katz. "Human Capital and Social Capital: The Rise of Secondary Schooling in America, 1910 to 1940." *Journal of Interdisciplinary History* 29 (Spring 1999), pp. 683–723.

Hall, G. Stanley. *Adolescence: Its Psychology, and Its Relations to Physiology, Anthropology, Sociology, Sex, Crime, Religion, and Education*. New York: D. Appleton & Company, 1904.

Harper, Douglas. *Online Etymology Dictionary*. https://www.etymonline.com/.

Jackson, Kathy Merlock. *Images of Children in American Film: A Sociocultural Analysis*. Metuchen, NJ: Scarecrow Press, 1986.

Jung, C. G. *Psychological Types*. Vol. 6 of *C. G. Jung: The Collected Works*. Edited by Sir Herbert Read. New York: Routledge, 2014.

Lewis, Jon. *The Road to Romance and Ruin: Teen Films and Youth Culture*. New York: Routledge, 1992.

Lury, Karen. *The Child in Film: Tears, Fears, and Fairytales*. London: I.B. Tauris, 2010.

MacDonald, Fiona. *Childhood and Tween Girl Culture: Family, Media and Locality*. London: Palgrave Macmillan, 2016.

MacIver, Douglas J., Estelle Young, Robert Balfanz, Alta Shaw, Maria Garriott, and Amy Cohen. "High-Quality Learning Opportunities in High Poverty Middle Schools: Moving from Rhetoric to Reality," in Thomas S. Dickinson (ed.), *Reinventing the Middle School*. New York: Routledge Falmer, 2001.

Mintz, Steven. *Huck's Raft: A History of American Childhood*. Cambridge, MA: Belknap Press at Harvard University Press, 2004.

Nash, Ilana. *American Sweethearts: Teenage Girls in Twentieth-Century Popular Culture*. Bloomington: Indiana University Press, 2006.

Rollin, Lucy. *Twentieth-Century Teen Culture by the Decades: A Reference Guide*. Westport, CT: Greenwood Press, 1999.

Shary, Timothy. *Generation Multiplex: The Image of Youth in Contemporary American Cinema*. Austin: University of Texas Press, 2014.

Sinyard, Neil. *Children in the Movies*. London: B. T. Batsford, 1992.

Smith, Frances. *Rethinking the Hollywood Teen Movie: Gender, Genre and Identity*. Edinburgh: Edinburgh University Press, 2017.

Sørenssen, Ingvild Kvale. "The Social Construction of Everyday Concepts: Constructing the 'Tween.'" *Barn* 33:2 (2015), pp. 81–90.

Tropiano, Stephen. *Rebels and Chicks: A History of the Hollywood Teen Movie*. New York: Back Stage Books, 2006.

Turner, Victor. *The Forest of Symbols: Aspects of Ndembu Ritual*. Ithaca, NY: Cornell University Press, 1967.

van Gennep, Arnold. *The Rites of Passage*. 2nd ed. Chicago: University of Chicago Press, 2019.

Wojcik-Andrews, Ian. *Children's Films: History, Ideology, Pedagogy, Theory*. New York: Garland, 2000.

CHAPTER 13

....

GROWING UP ON
SCANDINAVIAN SCREENS

....

ANDERS LYSNE

REPRESENTATIONS of youth have been present in Scandinavian film cultures since the advent of post–World War II cinema. Starting with the juvenile-delinquency films that accompanied the rise of teenage culture in the 1950s and backed by an internationally unique tradition of favouring and stimulating the production of films made for and about children and young people through public funding, the region's filmmakers have sought to explore every aspect of the pain and pleasure of growing up in Scandinavia. But despite the fact that the region's unique tradition of producing youth films is frequently mentioned in the ever-increasing body of scholarly work on Scandinavian cinema, studies on films for and about young people are conspicuously absent from otherwise authoritative accounts that have sought to explore Scandinavia's film and media cultures, such as *Transnational Cinema in a Global North* (2005), *Crime and Fantasy in Scandinavia* (2008), *Nordic Genre Film* (2015), *A Companion to Nordic Cinema* (2016), and *Nordic Film Cultures and Cinemas of Elsewhere* (2019).[1] In comparison, international interest in youth films within the academy is growing rapidly. A decade ago, most studies of youth film would usually begin by pointing to the lack of studies, but a substantial body of scholarly work now offers an impressive range of sociological, aesthetic, and industrial perspectives on the youth film. However, as illustrated by the recent works *The Aesthetic Pleasures of Girl Teen Film* (2017) and *Rethinking the Hollywood Teen Movie* (2017), the omnipresence of Hollywood films in global cinema has meant that scholarly interest has continued the predominant tradition of focusing on the US teen films.[2]

The lack of attention to youth films in Nordic film studies may be attributed to the particular slipperiness of the youth film genre label in Scandinavian cinema. Unlike the Hollywood tradition of the teen movie—that is, movies catering specifically to the teenage demographic—Scandinavian youth films have traditionally addressed audiences of a much wider age range than that of the young people represented onscreen. Originating in the film historical tradition of realism and the social-problem films of the 1940s, their inclination towards stylistic and thematic seriousness has often blurred the generic boundaries between youth film and adult drama, making youth films primarily films *about* youth rather than films made specifically *for* a youth audience. These blurred boundaries may also be related to Scandinavian cinema's status as "minor," characterized by small consumer markets, language barriers, and a dearth of avenues of international distribution beyond the festival circuit.[3] All this makes it difficult to sustain a film production targeted solely to a narrow youth audience. Another complicating factor is the recurrent confusion about the boundaries between youth film and children's film, which may appear equally ambiguous. Predating the youth film genre by less than a decade, the children's film emerged in Scandinavia in the 1940s, but it has largely been characterized by a similar cross-generational address, one that insists on taking children and childhood seriously in content as well as form. From the 2000s onward, following a greater market orientation in film policies and production climate, the fluid boundaries between the two genres of youth film and children's film have been further effaced by the development of tween-targeting films that infuse a recognizable Scandinavian childhood with family-friendly comedy, romance, and occasional musical numbers. Broadly viewed, youth films may be distinguished from these and other varieties of the children's film by their inclusion of age-inappropriate adult elements, such as a sustained pessimistic tone, frightening mood, or verbal representation of explicit violence and sexuality. Across the region, the presence of these elements in youth-oriented films has grown steadily over the last decades. This development is also reflected in the films' suitability ratings, which predominantly classify them as unsuitable for audiences under the age of eleven or twelve (depending on national classification standards). Finally, the question of definition is further complicated by the more theoretical question of who the term "youth" in youth film actually refers to (a question also frequently asked in children's film studies, and no less difficult to answer there).[4] Generally, but by no means exclusively, "youth" is taken to designate either (a) an intended audience (films *for* youth); (b) a textual feature, such as central characters or key thematic concern (films *about* youth); or (c) an empirical audience (films *watched by* youth).[5] Even though scholars and critics alike tend to conflate these dimensions, films about young people are not necessarily made to be consumed by young people, and vice versa.[6] Nor is either necessarily a film that young people will watch.

Despite these persisting difficulties, however, categorization is necessary to make sense of the continued development and appeal of the youth film in Scandinavian cinema. This chapter will apply a textual perspective to the question of definition, using the label *youth film* to refer to films that share a thematic focus on the issues of adolescence. *Adolescence*, as Timothy Shary has noted, is an ambiguous term in that it does not refer solely to biological age; instead, it emphasizes the psychological and social process of leaving childhood and entering adulthood.[7] Recognizing that a definitional focus on the transitional phase of adolescence inevitably points to the porous boundaries both downward towards childhood and upward towards adult life, this thematic delineation delimits a category broad enough to contain films addressing youth issues that may, or may not, target a youth audience but excludes films that merely feature young people or are watched by young people that do not thematically engage with the issues of youth. Adopting a regional perspective to explore the historical development of the youth film in Danish, Norwegian, and Swedish cinema, the chapter will identify four major strands in the historical development of the youth film across Scandinavia: (a) the juvenile-delinquency film; (b) the coming-of-age film; (c) the medium-concept youth film; and, finally, (d) the generic turn in the postmillennial era. With a dual focus on textual features and contextual factors, the chapter argues that the Scandinavian youth film has evolved from being primarily films *about* youth to, increasingly, being films *for* youth, all the while retaining an inherent ambiguity informed by a continuous negotiation of pedagogic, aesthetic, and commercial objectives.

THE JUVENILE-DELINQUENCY FILM

Young people featured prominently in Scandinavian cinema of the postwar period. In Denmark, the critically acclaimed realist dramas *Ditte, Child of Man* (Bjarne Henning-Jensen, 1946) and *Jenny and the Soldier* (Johan Jacobsen Jr., 1947) sensitively depicted struggling young characters on the brink of adulthood, but ultimately, the age of the characters functioned less as a thematic concern of its own than as a way of adding to their vulnerability to increase audience empathy. Similarly, the popular farce series *Father of Four* (1953–1961) and the extremely successful adaptations of author Morten Korch's rural melodramas, most notably, *The Red Horses* (Jon Iversen and Alice O'Fredricks, 1950, Denmark), employed young central characters as representations of the reconcilement of tradition and modernity.[8] In Norway, young people featured in two popular romantic dramas by director Edith Carlmar, *Better Than Their Reputation* (1955) and *The Wayward Girl* (1959). The latter (Figure 13.1) starred Liv Ullman in the titular role as the reckless young woman Gerd, whose well-behaved boyfriend, Anders (Atle Merton), takes her to a deserted cabin in the idyllic Norwegian woods to escape the perilous city; but urban temptations catch up with them when the young drifter and petty criminal Bendik (Rolf Søder) shows up and seduces Gerd. But the film ends squarely on a reconciliatory note as the parents of the stray lovers show up, the police arrive to arrest Bendik, and Anders forgives Gerd and promises to look after her. As film historian Gunnar Iversen has pointed out, the film's distinct openness about sexuality and its positive linking of nature and nudity had much in common with the contemporary Swedish films *One Summer of Happiness* (Arne Mattsson, 1951) and Ingmar Bergman's *Summer with Monika* (1953),[9] stories of impermanent summer romances between young lovers set in the lush Swedish archipelago. Their liberal attitude towards sexuality and explicit depictions of nudity made them international sensations, but their metaphorical connection between the seemingly unavoidable stagnation of adult life and the seasonal change from warm summer breeze to cold autumn chill gestured towards an art cinema tradition and the targeting of a broader audience, beyond the youth they depicted.[10]

FIGURE 13.1. Liv Ullmann and Atle Merton in *The Wayward Girl* (1959, Carlmar Films). Frame-grab.

However, just as in the United States, it was the image of juvenile-delinquency that marked the emergence of youth film as its own genre in Scandinavian cinema. The thematic coupling of youth and danger intensified in the mid-1950s, but had already begun in the 1930s. Uneasiness over the effect of mass culture on young people had ignited panic in the media and moral campaigns against "trashy literature"[11] and, later, in the post-war years, against comics.[12] The rise of youth culture in the 1950s signalled a shift in intensity in which young people no longer were merely the target group for certain kinds of media content associated with mass culture but had become an integral part of the content itself. Across types of media, the image of youth embodied a period-specific ambiguity of fascination and fear, perhaps nowhere more evident than in cinema. Thus, during the 1950s, and coinciding with a similar pervasive trend in the United States and Great Britain, Scandinavian countries (Denmark and Sweden especially) produced an array of films about young people gone morally astray.[13] Aesthetically, the films were social melodramas. Often conjoining a documentary-style realism with affectively charged pathos and moralism, and borrowing heavily from the iconography of the Hollywood juvenile-delinquency films, they also brought fame to local actors such as Ib Mossin in Denmark and Tage Severin in Sweden, both of whom became national teenage idols, combining the brooding images of James Dean and Marlon Brando with Scandinavian lustiness.

The opening sequence of *Dangerous Youth* (Lau Lauritzen Jr., 1953, Denmark) is a particularly lucid example of how, in the films, "elements of culture, sexuality, social problems and Americanization [are] convened as a clearly metaphorical and symbolic expression of modernity."[14] Beginning with a close-up of legs clad in jeans and sneakers dancing the jitterbug and the sound of an up-tempo ragtime-infused piano, the film's title—written across the screen in huge letters—immediately signals a characteristic double bind of warning and titillation. Abruptly, we cut to the image of three young men throwing a rock through the window of a jeweller's shop and hurrying in to rob the place before escaping in a big American car. A frantic car chase ensues as the police pursue the young men through the busy streets of Copenhagen before the film cuts away to a newspaper stand and a headline announcing a continued rise in youth crime that is worrying authorities. *Dangerous Youth* was a national sensation on its release and is widely perceived to have inaugurated the youth film genre in Denmark. Its main protagonist is Egon (Ib Mossin), a decent young man who has moved to the big city to live with his relatives and become an engineering apprentice. He meets the sensible Ruth (Anni Stangerup), and they fall in love. But unfortunately, Egon is also susceptible to the lure of danger. He becomes involved with a gang of petty criminals, and when they assault a drunk man to steal his money, the police catch them and Egon ends up in juvenile detention. Following his release, and hardened by his rejection by Ruth and his family, he decides to plan another break-in. But when his new girlfriend tips off the police, Egon is caught again, and this time, he is sentenced to real jail. Characteristically, the film does not depict Egon as villainous, suggesting instead through different stylistic strategies that his actions are the result of his feeling let down by the people around him. This expression of the film's attitude is perhaps most evident during Egon's final break-in attempt, when the musical score shifts from a short, staccato motif that underlines the suspense into a slower, more sorrowful, melodic mode that suggests a tragic perspective on the story.[15] As such, the film embodies a well-meaning, but unequivocal, paternalistic attitude that seems as clearly aimed at an audience of concerned adults as the jeans and jitterbugging of the opening sequence targeted their rebellious teenagers.

This distinct adult perspective permeated every aspect of the youth films, from their tone to their titles. In *Sin Alley* (Palle Kjærulff-Schmidt, 1957, Denmark), youth unemployment leads the young male protagonist into prostitution; and *The Young Have No Time* (Johannes Allen, 1956, Denmark) centres on rebellion among upper-class youth. The similarly titled *Youths in Danger* (Per G. Holmgren, 1946, Sweden) is equally archetypical. Released a year before the infamous Gögatan riot, in which thousands of young people clashed violently with the police in the south of Stockholm, *Youths in Danger* was one of the first films in Sweden to depict a new kind of rebellious distrust of adult society. A young man from a troubled family background, Wille (Kenne Fant), and a gang of his friends stand trial for car theft. Wille walks away with a milder punishment than the others. A sympathetic social worker (Gunnar Sjöberg) offers to help him find a new home and a job, and Wille is finally able to articulate his feelings for his girlfriend (Nita Värhammar). However, the momentary bliss is interrupted when the criminal gang leader (Sven-Eric Gamble), known as "The Scar," shows up, convinced that Wille ratted him out and seeking revenge. Thematically, *Youths in Danger* establishes a clear structural contrast between the destructive forces of the old criminal milieu that Wille is struggling to escape, and the edifying presence of the social worker, his girlfriend, and the cheerfully wholesome members of the local youth club, who all come to Wille's rescue in the end. As an early entry into the genre, the film's depiction of juvenile delinquency ends on an optimistic note. Like most of its successors, *Youths in Danger* depicts "the youth problem," a common term employed by the media at the time, as the result of weak and problematic family relations. With absent or nonresilient parent figures, the films seemed to stress, inherently vulnerable youth all too easily fall prey to criminal temptations, while the narrative structure repeatedly highlights well-meaning authority figures, like the social worker in *Youths in Dangers*, who can surely get the young, lost, mostly male protagonists back on track.

Unlike in Denmark, where films having an educational purpose could benefit financially because they were exempt from so-called entertainment tax, the Swedish juvenile-delinquency films seemed more clearly aimed at a youthful audience because they "portended the animosity towards adults in youth culture which would dominate the entire entertainment market during 1960s."[16] According to film historian Leif Furhammer, "The subcultural function of the films was emphasised by their low prestige value with the established cultural opinion, represented for instance by film censorship and film criticism. They were seen as catering to the lower instincts of the audience."[17] As the commercial value of the films increased, they grew more fatalistic in tone. In *Fartfeber* (Egil Holmsen, 1953, Sweden) and *The Vicious Breed* (Arne Ragneborn, 1954, Sweden), sensational scenes of sex and violence connected to media debates about drugs, prostitution, and vandalism were prominent, while the positive authority figures from earlier films like *Youth in Dangers* had vanished from the narrative.

The Coming-of-Age Film

Historically, the wave of juvenile-delinquency films was short-lived, and by the beginning of the 1960s, it had largely disappeared, giving way to films depicting youth in a decidedly more sympathetic tone. The coming-of-age film emerged as broad narrative category in Scandinavian cinema throughout the 1970s and early 1980s. It quickly established itself as a perennial favourite with audiences and critics, and drew international attention through "a popular and ever-present selection at film festivals and in art film theatres."[18] Delineating a thematically diverse group of realist dramas, the coming-of-age film shares with the literary tradition of the Bildungsroman a narrative focus on identity formation and the maturation of a young protagonist on the cusp of adulthood.[19] In a proliferation of films, including *A Swedish Love Story* (Roy Andersson, 1970, Sweden), *The Summer I Turned 15* (Knut Andersen, 1976, Norway), *The Tree of Knowledge* (Nils Malmros, 1981, Denmark), and *My Life as a Dog* (Lasse Hallström, 1985, Sweden), filmmakers explored themes of first love, sexuality, loneliness, bullying, mental health, and death, while straddling aesthetic registers ranging from social realism to nostalgia and "feel good." Unlike the juvenile-delinquency films of the 1950s and early 1960s, where youth itself had been a problem that needed solving, these films instead emphasized the problems faced by youth, and shifted the narrative focus to the intimate spheres of family, friendship, and love, and thus they signalled a significant shift in perspective from the overt parental didacticism of the juvenile-delinquency films to an inherently sympathetic perspective on adolescent life.

Reflecting a cultural climate permeated by solidarity with—even idealization of—children and young people,[20] these films often depicted their young protagonists as involved onlookers of sorts, simultaneously "wanderers and voyeurs"[21] in a fractured adult society, detachment from which became the most viable solution for successful maturation. Released in 1970, Swedish filmmaker Roy Andersson's debut feature film, *A Swedish Love Story*, serves as an early paradigmatic example. Aesthetically anchored in a social realist tradition but notably breaking with the emphasis on structural injustice that was predominant in Swedish films at the time, the poetic and political focus of Andersson's film was the micro-sociology of everyday life. Taking inspiration from the art-cinema realism of the Czech New Wave, the films of Miloš Forman especially,[22] *A Swedish Love Story* self-reflexively opens with the image of a theatre curtain rising and continues to unfold in long, episodic stretches, thus anticipating the signature tableaux aesthetic of the director's later films, but in a notably more accessible narrative form. Thematically, the film contrasts the lyrically heightened emotional drama of a budding love affair between fifteen-year-old Pär (Rolf Sohlman) and fourteen-year-old Annika (Ann-Sofie Kylin) with a scathing critique of their petite bourgeoisie families. While Pär's parents seem slightly more balanced, seemingly content with the life their small garage business affords them, Annika's family represents an adult generation tormented by emptiness and failure. Her father, John (Bertil Norström), is a refrigerator salesman whose stagnated career prompts him regularly to spit venom at Annika's mother, Elsa (Margreth Weivers), a woman thoroughly disillusioned by her status as a traditional housewife, while her neurotic sister Eva (Anita Lindblom), who has given up on her dreams of becoming a flight attendant, attempts to numb her feelings of existential misfortune by engaging in destructive love affairs. In comparison, the film presents Annika and Pär as fragile creatures, still in a state of unspoiled innocence, gently staging the awkwardness and sensitivity of their incipient romance through furtive looks, delicate gestures, and frequent narrative stretches of silent dialogue.

Invoking Andersson's trademark tonal combination of grotesque comedy and tragic humanity, the film distils its politics most sharply in the closing sequence. Dressed in bibs and clown hats, the two families have come together for a traditional crayfish feast at a country estate. When John attempts to make "a speech to humanity" nobody seems to care, and he proceeds to wander drunkenly into the woods, talking to himself and occasionally laughing hysterically. Later, when the rest of the company decides to go for a spot of night fishing, they discover his hat floating in the lake, and panic ensues. As the camera alternates between close-ups and panning long shots, the family members, now acutely sober, scamper around the foggy woods desperately calling out his name. But John soon reappears and, without uttering a word, blends in with the others as if nothing has happened. As they make their way back to the house in the early morning light, the film cuts to Pär and Annika tumbling playfully around in the woods, blissfully unaware of all the commotion. As they stop and puzzlingly observe the cheerless cohort of adults, the film frames them in a frontal close-up looking straight into the camera as if to suggest the complicity of the audience (Figure 13.2). It is an arresting image, one that embodies the film's empathic gaze on the younger generation as equally vulnerable and reassuring, even if the director's caustic critique of the parents' generation solidifies the narrative perspective as inherently adult.

Two factors contributed substantially to the rise of the coming-of-age film. First, the introduction of television in the mid-1950s and early 1960s took a major toll on film industries across the Nordic region. As financial success based on domestic returns became increasingly impossible, governments introduced various forms of state support to secure the survival of national film production and ensure cultural diversity, notably, by creating film institutes and film schools in Sweden and Denmark in the early to mid-1960s. Second, and inherently intertwined with the first, the expansive rise of television led to a change in cultural attitudes towards cinema. Television rapidly became the preferred source of popular entertainment, a shift that coincided with the international rise of art cinema and the auteur concept, in which film was increasingly viewed as an art form having intrinsic value and an important cultural expression of national identity in a broader sense, in addition to its function as popular entertainment.[23] Consequently, by establishing forms of public funding based on artistic and cultural criteria, government film policies functioned to steer parts of film production towards what was regarded as more "valuable" cinematic forms, notably art cinema.[24] Although genre films, especially comedies, largely dominated domestic production and box offices across the region,

FIGURE 13.2. Ann-Sofie Kylin and Rolf Solman in *A Swedish Love Story* (1970, Europa Film). Frame-grab.

art cinema (primarily from Denmark and Sweden) became the main cinematic export, spearheaded by auteurs like Ingmar Bergman and Carl Th. Dreyer.

The coming-of-age film both benefitted from and contributed to the notion that art and auteur cinema was the gold standard of Scandinavian cinema, which came to characterize filmmakers' discourse, popular criticism, and institutional function from the 1960s to the late 1980s.[25] Adding to this was the fact that many directors of coming-of-age films explored issues of growing up in several films, which meant that the films could then be exported as auteur cinema to film festivals and art-house cinemas abroad, leading to a slew of prestigious awards and nominations.[26] But the success of the coming-of-age film may equally be attributed to formal issues. Mostly eschewing the distinct reliance on the self-reflexivity and ambiguity associated with art cinema,[27] these films generally favoured a "realist" approach that retained an accessible and emotionally engaging narrative form, but simultaneously employed certain art film conventions such as episodic narratives, open endings, and complex characters.[28] In this way, coming-of-age films often shared the seriousness and cultural prestige commonly associated with the art film, which, in turn, helped them secure favourable critical reception and guaranteed their presence on the international film festival circuit, all while also appealing to wider audiences.

Curiously, despite a relative surge in youth film studies since the turn of the millennium, very little scholarly work has been done on the coming-of-age narrative as a cinematic form.[29] Highlighting New Zealand cinema in the first book-length study of the coming-of-age film, Alistair Fox identifies four distinctive characteristics of these films, which may be applicable to similar "small nation cinemas" like those of Scandinavia.[30] The first is a predominant dialogue with the nation's literature, which points to the fact that most coming-of-age films have been adaptations of well-known literary sources. Second is the idea of the coming-of-age film as personal cinema in the sense that most of the films, albeit to varying degrees, are autobiographical, with connections to the childhood of either the director or the source author, which lends them an added aura of auteur cinema. Third is that they are frequently staged in rural settings, which—among other things—tend to serve as a metaphor for emotional experience. And finally, the films generally share a thematic preoccupation with "the vulnerability of children to the unresolved issues of parents; to dysfunction within families; and to the effects of more general environmental factors such as oppressive social codes and cultural value systems, socio-economic deprivation, marginalization, and cultural dispossession."[31]

Even if Fox's book does not aim to flesh out a more general theory, his study does situate the coming-of-age film as "an international phenomenon generally, especially with the regard to the important place it occupies in virtually all cinemas."[32] Adding to the analytical framework established by Fox's characteristics is Swedish film scholar Birgitta Steene's short but frequently cited article on what she terms "the adult children's film": films about childhood, but intended for an adult audience.[33] Steene surveyed a number of Scandinavian films from the 1970s and 1980s featuring children on the verge of puberty, and identified four recurring thematic motifs that often seem to blend into one another: (a) the child discovers sexuality; (b) the child is confronted with a Christian moral code; (c) the child experiences death or evil; and (d) the child is bullied, misunderstood or separated from friends or family. Together, Steene argues, these conventions seem to delineate a group of films about children and young people, but predominantly address an adult audience.

A closer look at three influential examples—*Pelle the Conqueror* (Bille August, 1987, Denmark), *The Other Side of Sunday* (Berit Nesheim, 1996, Norway), and *Evil* (Mikael Häfström, 2003, Sweden)—will illustrate how a combination of Fox's and Steene's approaches may illuminate the form and function of the coming-of-age film in Scandinavian cinema.[34] Representing three decades of cinema, these three films all achieved both national and regional critical and commercial success, earned international accolades, and were widely distributed on the film festival and art-house cinema circuit. *The Other Side of Sunday* and *Evil* both received Academy Award nominations for Best Foreign Language Film, in 1997 and 2004 respectively. *Pelle the Conqueror*, a Danish-Swedish coproduction, won the Palm D'Or in 1988 and a Golden Globe and an Academy Award for Best Foreign Language Film in 1989, and, in effect, significantly contributed to the internationalization of Danish cinema that began in the late 1980s. In addition, all three films were adaptations of critically acclaimed and widely read literary works. *Pelle the Conqueror* was adapted from the first of a four-volume historical novel of the same name. Written by Danish author Martin Andersen Nexø and published in 1906, the book marries the maturation plot of the Bildungsroman with a story of the rise the labour movement set in the late nineteenth century. *The Other Side of Sunday* and *Evil* are both based on autobiographical novels about, respectively, the post-war youth of Norwegian author Reidun Nortvedt and of Swedish author Jan Guillou. As such, the film versions exemplify Fox's notion of the coming-of-age film as personal cinema, in that they connect the audience with the formative experiences that led the authors to write the novels in first place, and simultaneously spark self-reflection among audience members themselves.

Further, *Pelle the Conqueror* and *The Other Side of Sunday* both make significant use of nature as a metaphor to represent subjective and affective dimensions of growing up. In *Pelle the Conqueror*, the final shot shows the titular protagonist (Pelle Hvenegaard) leaving behind his loving but docile father (Max von Sydow) and their life of near slavery as he runs along a snowy beach towards an open future and thus completes the film's bittersweet maturation plot. Concluding on a similar note of disruption as a signal of personal growth, *The Other Side of Sunday* ends with the fourteen-year-old protagonist, Maria (Marie Theisen), finally standing up to her pietistic father (Bjørn Sundquist), the local priest, when she suddenly gets up and walks out of his church in the middle of Sunday communion. The film's closing shot shows her in slow motion, strolling along a sunny forest road, smiling defiantly, to the sound of "You're Nobody 'Till Somebody Loves You," by the Mills Brothers, suggestively equating the idyllic Norwegian countryside with the equally open future ahead of her. In *Evil*, the Swedish boarding school at which the main character arrives at the beginning of film is also located in the lush countryside, but this one soon proves to be anything but idyllic. The film's plot revolves around fifteen-year-old Erik (Andreas Wilson), who lives in Stockholm with his docile mother (Marie Richardson) and sadistic stepfather (Johan Rabaeus), who regularly beats him. When Erik is expelled from school for fighting, he is sent to a reform school, where the teachers encourage the older students to systematically bully the younger students as a means of maintaining discipline. Aesthetically, *Evil* favours suspense and exterior action over interior drama and emotional conflict; the film maintains an external focalization and a sober audiovisual style, restricting the audience's access to the subjectivity of its tormented protagonist. However, despite its social realist probing of the structural dynamics of institutionalized violence, the film remains anchored in the coming-of-age narrative, depicting the protagonist's eventual ability to overcome the systemic violence as the result of an identity-formation process that involved his separation from friends and family, the discovery of sexuality, and, of course, the experience of evil.

Beyond the fundamental recognition that growing up is a universal formative experience and a basic point of identification for cross-generational audiences, an important aspect of the films' popularity may also be attributed to their ability to connect the past and the present through the combination of recognizable historical settings and open-ended narratives. Thus, when the young protagonists in *Pelle the Conqueror* and *The Other Side of Sunday* set out towards their open futures at the end of each film, they leave behind the historical past and approaching the future of the contemporary moment inhabited by the audience. Most commonly, the films render this suggestive link between past and present in a poetic mode. However, this link may also function as a social critique by breaking the fourth wall, as in *A Swedish Love Story*, where the final shot of Pär and Annika gazing puzzlingly into the camera seems to reflexively confront the adult spectator with the image of the miserable adult world as represented on screen. Similarly, in in the final moment of *Evil*, the protagonist turns his back, quite literally, on his childhood of institutionalized violence, as the camera frames him bicycling towards the future in a frontal medium shot, seemingly steering straight towards the audience with a confrontational look in his eyes.

Unlike the juvenile-delinquency film—which emerged as a subgenre of the social melodrama—the coming-of-age film is a broader narrative category, which necessarily raises the question of categorization. Some scholars have argued that "coming-of-age" should be considered a narrative motif that encompasses a range of films focused on adolescent characters cutting across genres, styles, and specific target-audience groups.[35] Others agree that "coming-of-age" delineates a specific category of films and is a genre of its own, different from the youth films that target younger audiences.[36] The form and function of the films highlighted here make a strong case for the latter. Even if they marked a significant shift from youth as a social problem to "social values and practices as a problem for youth," their narrative perspective, broad realist dramatic form, frequent literary connections, and historical settings all suggest appeal to a wider age group than the young people they depict, and mark them as films *about* young people rather than *for* young people.[37]

Since the 1990s, a shift towards greater market orientation across the Scandinavian region has seen an increased commercial focus on teenage and young adult demographics and stimulated the production of youth films made specifically for youth. Still, the coming-of-age film has maintained a prominent position in postmillennial film production in all Scandinavian countries, with notable examples including *King of Devil's Island* (Marius Holst, 2010, Norway), *Behind Blue Skies* (Hannes Holm, 2010, Sweden), *The Orheim Company* (Arild Andresen, 2012, Norway), *Speed Walking* (Niels Arden Oplev, 2014, Denmark), and *The Day Will Come* (Jesper W. Nielsen, 2016, Denmark), which have all achieved success with indigenous critics and audiences and are popular offerings in international film festivals.

THE MEDIUM-CONCEPT YOUTH FILM

Films made specifically for a children's audience had been prevalent since the mid-1940s; early examples included *Ten Boys and One Girl* (Alexy Zaitow, 1944, Norway), *The Children* (Rolf Husberg, 1945, Sweden), and *Those Blasted Kids* (Astrid and Bjarne Henning-Jensen, 1947, Denmark). However, youth films—understood as films made specifically for an adolescent audience—did not come about until the mid-1970s. Institutionally, the tradition originated in Denmark with the Danish government's decision in 1976 to appoint a part-time film consultant to promote the production of films for children and young people.[38] The effect was immediate, and over the next five years, twelve films went into production. When the national film policy was revised in 1982, the government made the decision, unprecedented internationally, to allocate 25 per cent of all public funding to films for children and young people, and to appoint a full-time children's and youth film consultant with authority over distributing the funds. Thus, from the mid-1970s to the late 1980s youth film became an international brand for Danish cinema, a development frequently highlighted in film historical surveys.[39] Although the films made during this period benefitted from the success of the earlier adult-oriented coming-of-age films and shared with them the popular art cinema form and emphasis on psychological realism, they also differed in a number of ways. First, their narrative focus was less on maturation catalysed by cross-generational conflict; instead, they homed in on the youth peer group to explore the formative potential of themes such themes as first love and unlikely friendship, as we see distilled in the titles of *Wanna See My Beautiful Navel?* (Søren Kragh-Jacobsen, 1978, Denmark) and *Me and Charly* (Morten Arnfred, 1978, Denmark), two of the most successful films of the period, as well as in the coming-out drama *Friends Forever* (Stefan Henzelman, 1987, Denmark). Second, because there was greater emphasis on placing young people in their own social spaces, youth in these films often removed themselves from adult society, and excursions, holiday trips, or summer camps were frequent settings. Third, the films used music in new ways. Popular music had, of course, played an important role in the juvenile-delinquency films, establishing the youth-culture setting, and thereby solidifying their appeal to a youthful audience. However, in films like *Wanna See My Beautiful Navel?* and *Me and Charly*, the contemporary pop songs did not just function as diegetic music, playing in the background at discos or bars. Instead, the music was often composed especially for the films and functioned both to cue moods and as a poetic narrative voice highlighting the films' solidarity with their young protagonists.[40]

Initially, films for young people were primarily a Danish phenomenon, and the film cultural debates in Norway and Sweden were primarily preoccupied with children's film. The Swedish government, in particular, managed to vitalize its children's film culture by trying out new modes of exhibition and providing financial support, resulting in aesthetically experimental and genre-bending children's films such as *Elvis! Elvis!* (Kay Pollack, 1976) and *The Brothers Lionheart* (Olle Hellbom, 1978). But in the late 1980s things began to change in Norway and Sweden as well. In Norway, the government and the organization that represented municipal cinemas, Film & Kino, jointly hired a film consultant to promote the production of children's and youth films, though without the same financial mandate as in Denmark, and by increasing the so-called "ticket subsidy," a box-office bonus based on a film's commercial success, from 55 per cent to 100 per cent of box-office gross for films made for younger audiences. The incentives proved successful—half of the films produced in Norway in the first half of the 1990s were children's or youth films.[41] In 1990, *The Death at Oslo C* (Eva Isaksen) represented a new and different kind of youth film. Based on a popular novel about the friendship between two teenagers, Pelle (Håvard Bakke) and Proffen (Tommy Karlsen), the plot centres on their quest to find Pelle's girlfriend Lena (Helle Beck Figenschow), a drug addict who has suddenly gone missing. Mixing an indigenous tradition of children's detective stories with elements from the coming-of-age film and the action and crime films that dominated Norwegian film at the end of 1980s, which is often referred to as the "the helicopter period,"[42] the film was an enormous success and was followed by two sequels. In Sweden, there was a similar development between the late 1980s and the early 1990s. In his study of Swedish film genres between 1985 and 2000, film scholar Anders Marklund points to the film *Black Lucia* (Rumle Hammerich, 1992) as marking the advent of a different, notably darker kind of youth film.[43] *Black Lucia* is a psychological thriller about a young high school girl (Tova Magnusson) who develops a sexual obsession with her teacher (Figge Norling), who may or may not be guilty of the murder of one of her female classmates. The film traded on the contemporary popularity of the erotic thriller, transporting the genre's stylized tropes to a recognizable Swedish high school setting.

Despite national differences, the 1980s and 1990s saw Scandinavian youth films develop from simply being films about young people that addressed a wider audience to adopting increasingly youth-oriented strategies of address. The context was the rise of state support of filmmaking across the region that, according to media scholars Ib Bondebjerg and Eva Novrup Redvall, was based on the perception that "a unique [film] culture exists, which respects and provides children and young people with a broader freedom of expression," which promoted variety in terms of styles and themes.[44] However, two broader tendencies can also be identified. The first is a preoccupation with depicting the conditions of modern, and increasingly multicultural, urban life, evident in such films as *The Searchers* (Peter Cartriers and Daniell Fridell, 1993, Sweden), *Nightbuss 807* (David Flamholic, 1997, Sweden), and *Schpaa* (Erik Poppe, 1998, Norway), all of which feature young people in suburban ghettos or on the streets of big cities dealing with drugs, racism, violence, and conflicts among gang members. The second is the production of films that are closer to the-coming-of-age film in having a narrative focus on identity formation and the emotional dimensions of youth more than on than exterior action. These films also differ from the former in their foregrounding of female subjectivity. An example is the Danish film *Ballerup Boulevard* (Linda Wendel, 1986), The creative result of a call from the Danish Film Institute to increase the number of "girl films" in the youth film output,[45] *Ballerup Boulevard* revolves around fourteen-year-old Pinky (Stine Bierlich), who dreams of starting a band with her two friends but becomes socially isolated when her mother (Helle Hertz) is sent to prison for tax fraud she has committed in an attempt to save the family business. Thematically, the film's social realism is seen in the conflict between the individual and the social structure. This combines with a contemporary pop sensibility that strengthens the film's youthful address, incorporating pop songs into the story through Pinky's musical aspirations and giving the film's episodic narrative structure continuity. Concluding with a long take in which Pinky, wearing a puffy pink skirt, gazes out her bedroom window, lost in thought, as the film's catchy title song is turned up on the soundtrack, the film illustrates an awareness of the youth audience even as it seeks to be recognizable and relevant to a broader audience. The films are indicative of what we might term the "medium-concept youth film." As defined by film scholar Andrew Nestingen, who takes his inspiration from Justin Wyatt's seminal book on "high concept" moviemaking from 1994,[46] *medium-concept* filmmaking can be understood as "filmmaking that involves the adaptation of genre models and art-film aesthetics; an engagement with political debates, lending the films cultural significance; and that integrates with these elements a marketing strategy designed to reach a specific audience."[47] For Nestingen, a medium-concept film is one that mixes the dramaturgical structures and continuity style of the genre film with the excess that is characteristic of the art film. The medium-concept film gained prominence in Scandinavian film production in the mid-1990s when national film institutes went from being aesthetic gatekeepers to being cultural-economic gatekeepers by altering decision-making schemes to stimulate greater market orientation and diversification in the types of films produced.[48] The ambiguity inherent in Nestingen's concept was condensed in premillennial youth films. On the one hand, these films were emblematic of a cultural political engagement, offering a quality alternative to the dominant Hollywood tradition, anchored in local language and culture. As such, they pointed to the seriousness and cultural cachet associated with the realist and art cinema tradition.[49] But at the same time, the period's intensified attempts to appeal to younger audiences affected the films in a way that gestures to the very same US film and media culture that they were situated in opposition to in film policy and institutional discourse.

The most prominent medium-concept youth film was also the most successful one, critically and commercially. Sweden's *Show Me Love* was the debut feature film of director Lukas Moodysson. Released in 1998, the film was celebrated by critics as a milestone in Swedish cinema. More than 900,000 Swedes flocked to see it in cinemas, cementing its status as an instant classic (Figure 13.3).[50] The story of friendship, love,

FIGURE 13.3. Alexandra Dahlström and Rebecka Liljeberg in *Show Me Love* (1998, Memfis Film). Frame-grab.

and desire between two teenage girls growing up in a conformist, oppressive small-town community in Sweden represented a breakthrough for youth cinema in a number of ways. It signalled a shift from the narrative focus on young male protagonists, the rough urban lifestyle, and gang crime that was predominant in Swedish representations of youth in the 1990s. It also announced the beginning of what film scholar Tommy Gustafsson has referred to as "youthful youth films": films made for younger audiences by younger directors.[51] The overwhelming success of *Show Me Love* was unprecedented, nationally as well as regionally. By combining contemporary social realist concerns with issues of social class, bullying, teen suicide, and homosexuality, a visual style linking it to the contemporary Danish Dogme 95 movement, a fundamentally uplifting story of self-realisation and first love, and a character gallery and dramaturgical structure akin to contemporary US teen movies, it crystalized the ambiguity inherent in Nestingen's notion of the medium-concept film.

THE YOUTH GENRE FILM

In the new millennium, youth film continues to be both enhanced and challenged by the increased market orientation at the institutional, production, and aesthetic levels across the Scandinavian countries, a shift that began in the late 1980s. This means that the so-called consultant schemes—in which support for film projects is based on aesthetic and cultural criteria—are now supplemented by schemes in which support for films is based on commercial criteria.[52] The most important result has been a stronger orientation towards commercial genre cinema. This has occurred partly because youth films are being influenced by a wider palette of genres, and partly because of the development of new generic formulae in the youth cinema firmament. For instance, a string of commercially successful films was released in the mid to late 2000s that could be considered Scandinavian iterations of the US high school comedy.

The films *The Ketchup Effect* (Teresa Fabik, 2004, Sweden), *Just Bea* (Petter Næss, 2004, Norway), *Bitter Sweetheart* (Hella Joof, 2007, Sweden), *Triple Dare* (Christina Rosendahl, 2007, Denmark), and *Turn Me On, Dammit!* (Jannicke Systad Jacobsen, 2011, Norway) all centre on what Frances Smith has argued is "the primary determiner of what constitutes a Hollywood teen movie," namely, "the sexual coming-of-age narrative."[53] Combining recognizable contemporary Scandinavian settings with an expressive audiovisual style and narrative conventions lifted from the romantic comedy genre, these films draw inspiration from a certain strand of "clever," female-driven US high-school comedies, represented by *Mean Girls* (Mark Waters, 2004), *Juno* (Jason Reitman, 2007), and *Easy A* (Will Gluck, 2010), and exhibit a number of parallel characteristics. This is particularly evident in the representation of the female protagonist as self-reliant, active, and competent; whereas the male characters generally come across as more reactive and less assertive. Similarly, the films often feature school settings (even if the characters are rarely seen in class or studying); a gallery of stock characters, including the jock, the nerd, and the rebel; and a clearly defined narrative goal, most commonly the loss of virginity. Third, the influence of the Hollywood teen film is evident in the films' marketing, which gestures towards the "high concept," with slogans like "Love is hell" (*Tommy's Inferno*) and "The first time sucks" (*Just Bea*) and movie posters that highlight the film's highly recognizable teen archetypes. However, the most striking influence may be in tone—the films have generally traded in the seriousness associated with the realist and art cinema tradition for "the light comedy, feel good and only slightly embarrassing modality" that has characterized the affective appeal of most mainstream US teen films since 1960s, according to media scholar Anne Jerslev.[54] In *The Ketchup Effect*, a ketchup bottle thus becomes a recurring visual metaphor for masturbation; and the female protagonist in *Just Bea* is persuaded by her girlfriends to try out different positions of the Kama Sutra in a fully-packed study hall, while they go searching for literary inspiration for her first sexual experience.

Just Bea revolves around the titular character's quest to overcome sexual inexperience. Bea (Kaia Foss) is sixteen and writes for the high school paper, but she is also the only one of her friends who hasn't had sex. When she falls in love with the most popular guy in school, Daniel (Espen Klouman Høiner), her friends convince her that "the first time always sucks" and that she should lose her virginity to someone else before she has sex with Daniel. So, Bea experiences a realistically rendered, awkward sexual initiation with her oblivious guinea pig, the shy and slightly older agronomy student Anders (Kim S. Falck-Jørgensen). When she finally has sex with Daniel, he turns out to be selfish and narcissistic. In the end, Bea realizes that she wants Anders, and in the final scene she assertively seduces him, and they have passionate sex in an airport toilet before she leaves for Canada to pursue her writing ambitions, completing her maturation arc. The narrative is developed around these three sexual interludes. This strategy of structuring the film around three scenes of intercourse as three major turning points in Bea's sexual coming-of-age contributes to the film's tightly woven dramaturgy. More importantly, it also allows the film to highlight its frank depiction of sexuality, which, together with the characters' direct language, makes it recognizable and offers its target audience points of identification, and this differentiates it from the more sanitized versions of high school sex that characterize the film's Hollywood role models.

Another notable characteristic of these films, and of the postmillennial youth film in general, is the marginalization of the parent figure. Whereas cross-generational conflict has always been a central narrative component of youth film, postmillennial youth films chiefly happen in the sphere of the peer group, relegating adults to the periphery or making them mere caricatures who provide comic relief.[55] Nevertheless, through strategies in characterization and narrative structure, the films arguably retain an adult perspective. In *Turn Me On, Dammit!*—a quirky, highly successful comedy based on Olaug Nilssen's best-selling novel, whose deadpan humour is closer to *Juno* than *Mean Girls*—fifteen-year-old Alma (Helene Bergsholm) tries to overcome the boredom of growing up in a tiny Norwegian town by creating her own excitement, which primarily consists of nonstop sexual fantasies and relentless masturbation. When her classmate Artur (Matias Myren), the object of many of her fantasies, joins her outside at a party at the local youth club and unexpectedly flashes her, Alma is excited and runs to tell her friends. But they don't believe her, and when Artur denies it, Alma quickly becomes a pariah and a laughing stock. Refusing to be oppressed, Alma defiantly engages in rebellious behaviour such as smoking weed in public and continues her habit of calling her favourite phone-sex hotline. However, the film eventually has her run away to Oslo, where she realizes that there is a bigger, more accepting world outside her tiny hometown, and when she returns, more mature and self-assertive, Artur publicly admits his lie and they finally reunite.

The endings of both *Just Bea* and *Turn Me On, Dammit!* (Figure 13.4) also show how the romantic storylines of these films, like their US counterparts, generally follow a narrow, heteronormative trajectory. With just a few exceptions, the success of *Show Me Love*, with its tender, complex exploration of coming out, did not lead to an increase in LGBTQ+ characters or storylines in subsequent youth films; sex and love largely remain a heterosexual privilege.[56] As such, the gender and sexuality politics of these films are emblematic of how the youth film has retained a general ambiguity throughout its different iterations in Scandinavian film history. Even as both films seemingly promote a sex-positive message, taking seriously their protagonists doubts as well as desires, their narrative representation and structure equate sex with romantic heterosexual love. Thus, the final passionate sex scene in the airport toilet between Bea and Anders in *Just Bea* makes for an unequivocally empowering happy ending, but the film's equally unequivocal message is that sexual fulfilment only happens when you're with someone you are truly in love with. Similarly, *Turn Me On, Dammit!* may put fantasy and reality on equal footing by blurring the boundaries of internal and external focalization in rendering Alma's sexual fantasies (ranging from public masturbation to lesbian lovemaking),

FIGURE 13.4. Helene Bergsholm and Matias Myren in *Turn Me On, Dammit!* (2011, Motlys). Frame-grab.

but the film's wistfully comedic, sweetly ironic tone not only wisely prevents it from being exploitative, but also safely tempers the transgression and makes us believe in its girl-gets-boy ending.

Notes

1. Andrew Nestingen and Trevor G. Elkington (eds.), *Transnational Cinema in a Global North: Nordic Cinema in Transition* (Detroit, MI: Wayne State University Press, 2005); Andrew Nestingen, *Crime and Fantasy in Scandinavia: Fiction, Film, and Social Change* (Seattle and Copenhagen: University of Washington Press and Museum Tusculanum Press, 2008); Tommy Gustafsson and Pietari Kääpä (eds.), *Nordic Genre Film: Small Nation Film Cultures in the Global Marketplace* (Edinburgh: Edinburgh University Press, 2015); Mette Hjort and Ursula Lindqvist (eds.), *A Companion to Nordic Cinema* (Chichester, UK: Wiley Blackwell, 2016); and Anna Westerstahl Stenport and Arne Lunde (eds.), *Nordic Film Cultures and Cinemas of Elsewhere* (Edinburgh: Edinburg University Press, 2019).

2. Samantha Colling, *The Aesthetic Pleasures of Girl Teen Film* (New York: Bloomsbury, 2017); Frances Smith, *Rethinking the Hollywood Teen Movie: Gender, Genre and Identity* (Edinburgh: Edinburgh University Press, 2017).

3. Mette Hjort, *Small Nation, Global Cinema* (Minneapolis: University of Minnesota Press, 2005), pp. ix–x.

4. Noel Brown, *The Children's Film: Genre, Nation and Narrative* (New York: Columbia University Press, 2017), pp. 2–19.

5. Kirsten Drotner, "Filmkultur i børnehøjde: Danske Børne- og ungdomsfilm," in Ib bondebjerg, Jesper Andersen, and Peter Schepelern (eds.), *Dansk Film 1972–97* (Copenhagen: Munksgaard-Rosinante, 1997), pp. 134–165.

6. Steve Neale, *Genre and Hollywood* (London: Routledge, 2000), p. 119.

7. Timothy Shary, *Generation Multiplex: The Image of Youth in American Cinema since 1980* (Austin: University of Texas Press, 2014), p. 20.

8. Ib Bondebjerg, *Filmen og det moderne. Filmgenrer og filmkultur i Danmark 1940–1972* (Copenhagen: Gyldendal, 2005), p. 330.

9. Gunnar Iversen, *Norsk filmhistorie: Spillefilmen 1911–2011* (Oslo: Universitetsforlaget, 2011), p. 168.

10. Leif Furhammer, *Filmen i Sverige: En historia i tio kapitel* (Stockholm: Wiken, 1991), p. 226.

11. Bondebjerg, *Filmen og det moderne*, p. 330.

12. Henrik G. Bastiansen and Hans Fredrik Dahl, *Norsk Mediehistorie* (Oslo: Universitetsforlaget, 2003).

13. On the US, see Timothy Shary, *Teen Movies: American Youth on Screen* (New York: Columbia University Press, 2005); and Thomas Doherty, *Teenagers and Teenpics: The Juvenilization of American Movies in the 1950s*, 2nd ed. (Philadelphia: Temple University Press, 2002). On Britain, see John Hill, *Sex, Class and Realism: British Cinema 1956–1963* (London: British Film Institute, 1986).

14. Bondebjerg, *Filmen og det moderne*, p. 330.

15. Birger Langkjær, *Realismen i dansk film* (Frederiksberg: Samfundslitteratur, 2012), p. 179.

16. Bengtsson, Bengt. "The Youth Problem Film in the Post-War Years," in Mariah Larsson and Anders Marklund (eds.), *Swedish Film: An Introduction and Reader* (Lund: Nordic Academic Press, 2010), pp. 147–164, at 147.

17. Furhammer quoted in Bengtsson, *Youth Problem Film*, p. 148.

18. Trevor G. Elkington, "Costumes, Adolescence, and Dogma: Nordic Film and American Distribution," in Nestingen and Elkington, *Transnational Cinema in a Global North: Nordic Cinema in Transition*, pp. 31–54, at 39 (p. 39).

19. Philippa Zielfa Maslin has elaborated thoroughly on the relation between the Bildungsroman and the coming-of-age film in "'Contemporary British Coming-of-Age Films (1979 to the Present)" (unpublished PhD diss., University of London, 2018).

20. Drotner, *Filmkultur i børnehøjde*, pp. 134–165.

21. Birgitta Steene, "Barnvoksenfilmen—en ny genre?" *Z filmtidsskrift* 4 (1992), pp. 31–37.

22. Anne-Helene Sommarström and Clas Österholm, "En kärlekshistoria," Svenska Filminstitutet, February 2014, https://www.filminstitutet.se/contentassets/100707d4c b7b4a28868f68d150e42163/enkarlekshistoria.pdf [accessed August 14, 2019].

23. Hjort and Lindqvist, *Companion to Nordic Cinema*.

24. Gustafsson and Kääpä, *Nordic Genre Film*, p. 4.

25. Nestingen, *Crime and Fantasy in Scandinavia*, p. 109.

26. Notable examples include Swedish director Kay Pollack, who directed Elvis! Elvis! (1976), Children's Island (1980), and Love Me! (1986). In addition to *Pelle the Conqueror*, Danish director Bille August explored childhood and adolescence in Zappa (1983), Twist and Shout (1984), and Buster's World (1984), originally a hugely popular drama series for the national public broadcaster DR. In Norway, director Berit Nesheim made Frida (1991) and Beyond the Sky (1993), the former also a beloved drama series for the national public broadcaster NRK, before going on to direct *The Other Side of Sunday*.

27. David Bordwell, "The Art Cinema as a Mode of Film Practice," *Film Criticism* 4:1 (1979), pp. 56–64.

28. See Birger Langkjær, "Realism as a Third Film Practice," *MedieKultur* 51 (2011), pp. 40–54, for a discussion of realism as a third film practice between genre and art films in Scandinavian cinema.

29. See Maslin, "Contemporary British Coming-of-Age Films," pp. 45–69, for a survey of the scholarship on the coming-of-age film.

30. The term "small nation cinema" is lifted from Mette Hjort and Duncan Petrie, *The Cinema of Small Nations* (Edinburgh: Edinburgh University Press, 2007).

31. Alistair Fox, *Coming-of-Age Cinema in New Zealand* (Edinburgh: Edinburgh University Press, 2017), p. 24.

32. Fox, *Coming-of-Age Cinema in New Zealand*, p. 4.

33. Birgitta Steene, *Barnvoksenfilmen*.

34. The three films were all critical and commercial successes nationally and across the Scandinavian region, and received wide international distribution through the film festival and art-house cinema circuit. The most successful of the three, *Pelle the Conqueror*, won the Palm D'Or in 1988, a Golden Globe, and an Academy Award for Best Foreign Language Film (1989), and *The Other Side of Sunday* and *Evil* were both nominated for the latter in 1997 and 2004, respectively.

35. Catherine Driscoll, *Teen Film: A Critical Introduction* (New York: Bloomsbury, 2011); Maslin, *Contemporary British Coming-of-Age Films*.

36. Steene, *Barnvoksenfilmen*; and Fox, *Coming-of-Age Cinema in New Zealand*.

37. Fox, *Coming-of-Age Cinema in New Zealand*, p. 4.

38. Ida Zeruneith (ed.), *Wide-Eyed: Films for Children and Young People in the Nordic Countries 1977–1993* (Copenhagen: Tiderne skifter, 1995).

39. Peter Cowie, *Scandinavian Cinema* (London: Tantivy Press, 1992); Tytti Soila, Astrid Söderbergh Widding, and Gunner Iversen, *Nordic National Cinemas* (London: Routledge, 1998); Anne Jerslev, "Youth Films: Challenging Genre, Performing Audiences," in Kirsten Drotner and Sonia Livingstone (eds.), *International Handbook of Children, Media and Culture* (London: SAGE, 2008), pp. 183–195, at 185.

40. Langkjær, *Realismen i dansk film*, p. 296.

41. Gunnar Iversen and Ove Solum, *Den norske filmbølgen: Fra Orions belte til Max Manus* (Oslo: Universitetsforlaget, 2010).

42. Gunner Iversen, "Learning from Genre: Genre Cycles in Modern Norwegian Cinema," in Nestingen and Elkington, *Transnational Cinema in a Global North: Nordic Cinema in Transition*, pp. 261–278, at 266.

43. Anders Marklund, *Upplevelser av svensk film: En kartläggning av genrer innom svensk film under åren 1985–2000* (Lund: Lunds Universitet, Litteraturvetenskapliga Institutionen, 2004).

44. Ib Bondebjerg and Eva Novrup Redvall, *A Small Region in Global World: Patterns in Scandinavian Film and TV Culture* (CeMES Working Paper No. 1 Center for Modern European Studies, University of Copenhagen, 2011), p. 94.

45. Zeruneith, *Wide-Eyed*.

46. Justin Wyatt, *High Concept: Movies and Marketing in Hollywood* (Austin: University of Texas Press, 1994).

47. Nestingen, *Crime and Fantasy in Scandinavia*, p. 53.

48. Ibid., p. 67.

49. Bondebjerg and Redvall, *Small Region*.

50. Anna Westerståhl Steport, *Lukas Moodysson's Show Me Love* (Seattle and Copenhagen: University of Washington Press and Museum Tusculanum Press, 2012), p. 3.

51. Tommy Gustafsson, "Ett steg på vägen mot en ny jämlikhet? Könsrelationer och stereotypier i ung svensk ungdomsfilm på 2000-talet," in Erik Hedling and Ann-Kristin Wallengren (eds.), *Solskenslandet: Svensk film på 2000-talet* (Stockholm: Atlantis, 2006), pp. 171–193.

52. Bondebjerg and Redvall, Small Region.
53. Smith, *Rethinking the Hollywood Teen Movie*, p. 18.
54. Jerslev, "Youth Films: Challenging Genre, Performing Audiences," p. 185.
55. Jo Sondre Moseng, "Himmel og Helvete: Ungdom i norsk film 1969–2010" (unpublished PhD diss., Norwegian University of Science and Technology, 2011).
56. Exceptions are discussed in Anders Lysne, "Straight Eye for the Queer Guy: Gay Youth in Contemporary Scandinavian Film," in Christopher Pullen (ed.), *Queer Youth and Media Cultures* (New York: Palgrave MacMillan, 2014), pp. 211–223; and Meryl Shriver-Rice, *Inclusion in New Danish Cinema: Sexuality and Transnational Belonging* (Bristol, UK: Intellect, 2015).

BIBLIOGRAPHY

Bengtsson, Bengt. *Ungdom i fara: Ungdomsproblemen i svensk spelfilm 1942–62*. Stockholm: Stockholms Universitet, 1998.

Bengtsson, Bengt. "The Youth Problem Film in the Post-War Years." In Mariah Larsson and Anders Marklund (eds.), *Swedish Film: An Introduction and Reader*. Lund: Nordic Academic Press, 2010, pp. 147–164.

Bondebjerg, Ib, and Eva N. Redvall. *A Small Region in Global World: Patterns in Scandinavian Film and TV Culture*. CeMES Working Paper No. 1, 2011. Center for Modern European Studies, University of Copenhagen.

Christensen, Christa Lykke. "Making a Life of Your Own: Danish Children's and Youth Film in the 1970s and the 1980s." In Claire Thomson, Pei-Sze Chow, and Isak Thorsen (eds.), *A History of Danish Cinema*. Edinburgh: Edinburgh University Press, 2021, pp. 128–139.

Cowie, Peter. *Cool and Crazy: Modern Norwegian Cinema 1990–2005*. Oslo: Norwegian Film Institute, 2005.

Cowie, Peter. *Straight from the Heart: Modern Norwegian Cinema 1971–1999*. Oslo: Norwegian Film Institute, 1999.

Jerslev, Anne. "Youth Films: Challenging Genre, Performing Audiences." In Kirsten Drotner and Sonia Livingstone (eds.), *International Handbook of Children, Media and Culture*. London: SAGE, 2008, pp. 183–195.

Langkjær, Birger. "Realism as a Third Film Practice." *MedieKultur* 51 (2011), pp. 40–54.

Lysne, Anders. "Straight Eye for the Queer Guy: Gay Youth in Contemporary Scandinavian Film." In Christopher Pullen (ed.). *Queer Youth and Media Cultures*. New York: Palgrave MacMillan, 2014, pp. 211–223.

Lysne, Anders. "On Becoming and Belonging: The Coming of Age Film in Nordic Cinema." In Jakob Lothe and Bente Larsen (eds.), *Perspectives on the Nordic*. Oslo: Novus Press, 2016, 127–142.

Marklund, Anders. *Upplevelser av svensk film: En kartläggning av genrer innom svensk film under åren 1985–2000*. Lund: Lunds Universitet, Litteraturvetenskapliga Institutionen, 2004.

Moseng, Jo Sondre. "Himmel og Helvete: Ungdom i norsk film 1969-2010." Unpublished PhD diss., Norwegian University of Science and Technology, 2011.

Mulari, Heta. "New Feminisms, Gender Equality and Neoliberalism in Swedish Girl Films 1995–2006." Unpublished PhD diss., University of Turku, 2015.

Steene, Birgitta. "Barnvoksenfilmen—en ny genre?" *Z filmtidsskrift* 4 (1992), pp. 31–37.

Stenport, Anna W. *Lukas Moodysson's Show Me Love*. Seattle and Copenhagen: University of Washington Press and Museum Tusculanum Press, 2012.

Troelsen, Anders. "Ungdom, utilpassethed og utopi: Om ungdomsfilm efter 2. Verdenskrig." In Anders Troelsen (ed.). *Levende billeder af Danmark*. Copenhagen: Medusa, 1980, pp. 121–234.

Zeruneith, Ida, ed. *Wide-Eyed: Films for Children and Young People in the Nordic Countries 1977–1993*. Copenhagen: Tiderne skifter, 1995.

PART III

CHILDREN'S FILM AND PERFORMANCE

CHAPTER 14

ALMA TAYLOR, MARY PICKFORD, AND GIRLHOOD IN EARLY BRITISH AND HOLLYWOOD CINEMA

MATTHEW SMITH

AT the turn of the twentieth century, the girl-child in cinema became central to understanding, reflecting on, and rationalizing the changes taking place in both Britain and America. In this period, the girl on-screen works in the interstices between a Victorian past and an approaching modernity, between traditions of family and patriarchy, and an increasingly independent and self-actualized female body politic. As Kristen Hatch suggests, the figure of the girl helped to assure uncertain nations that, just as the mutable adolescent matures and grows into the stable adult, so, too, the nation will survive its own growing pains.[1] Christine Gledhill suggests that the girl's liminal cultural status allowed and perhaps still allows her to function productively in moments of social change:

> If psychologically the "threshold" implies a state of transition, the Girl is its archetypal representative: her culturally assigned femininity open to empathic feelings; her youth to mutability; her body and psychology to physical and emotional change; her cultural position veering between the care free irresponsibility of childhood and the idealism of the young adult.[2]

In literature and film, the boy is often understood to enjoy an ascent toward adulthood through the structure of the Bildungsroman, a narrative form that describes the individual's formative years and spiritual edification and achievement of a socially defined manhood.[3] Although this reading problematically obscures the multitudinous complexity of boyhood, it offers a productive contrast to the growth of the girl who, by virtue of her liminality, frequently oscillates between subject positions, performative, mutable, nebulous, and fraught with danger.

As two pre-eminent stars of early cinema, the American Mary Pickford and the British Alma Taylor provide a site from which to explore the discursive history of the girl-child on screen and the changing role of the woman in Britain and the United States. What makes Pickford and Taylor such potent resources is the incredible popularity they both enjoyed in the 1910s, a period of rapid maturation for the cinema and of social change in both Britain and America. With their unconstrained bodily performance and predilection for slapstick, Pickford's and Taylor's films were intended for, and appealed to, cross-demographic "family" audiences. At this point, there was little distinction between "children's films" and "adult films." As Rachel Low has suggested, children had yet to be defined as a discrete consumer group, and they flocked to see the crime stories, westerns, and melodramas already being shown.[4] Yet Pickford's and Taylor's work also appealed to an audience fascinated by the emergence of the adolescent girl, and both stars provided a social model for young females and, as Diane Anselmo argues in her study of fan letters, promotional materials, and poems from the period, an escapist vision of emerging adolescence that appealed to liminal girls moving toward adulthood.[5]

Pickford and Taylor also allow us to examine the efficacy of the figure in reconciling competing discourses of tradition and modernity, and female emancipation in a moment of historic social change. When assessing these figures, academic analysis has often focused on the way in which Mary Pickford, in particular, represents a *child-woman*, a figure ambiguously inscribed with characteristics of both the adult woman and the child. For Gaylyn Studler, this inscription allows Pickford to function in the interstices of a range of often competing discourses.[6] Studler suggests that Pickford absorbs and reflects a variety of desires and emotional needs and argues that the physical and emotional qualities of stars like Pickford and Taylor, combined with girls' capacity to embody competing ideologies, underpin their popularity and reflect the Victorian anxiety toward new womanhood and the adolescent girl. With specific reference to Pickford, Studler argues:

> On one hand, male fantasies were easily attached to her. She represented a dangerously attractive female whose masquerade of childishness appealed to adult men raised in the late Victorian period. Those men might find her enticing innocence a comforting alternative to the models of feminine sexual subjectivity offered by the flapper and the new woman. On the other hand Pickford's child woman heroines also could serve an identificatory function for women and girls who might read her as a comforting "asexual" figure of freedom whose youth released her from the demands—including the sexual demands—of adult femininity.[7]

Studler's reading is compelling. It highlights a capacity to embody competing ideologies and describes the important cultural function the on- and off-screen personae of Pickford (and, I would argue, Taylor) fulfilled in a moment of social rupture. It also highlights the accessible and acceptable sexuality of these girls, as is evident in the prurient responses in contemporary criticism to their "little bodies" on the screen. I suggest that their performance as tomboys serves a similar function, absorbing, reflecting, and reframing a range of desires, needs, and discourses through a figure culturally associated with maturation and growth. Consequently, this chapter argues that the figure of the tomboy is another important representational apparatus through which early twentieth-century cinema works to ameliorate the fears around the changing position of the girl. Centrally, the ascription of immaturity and adolescent growth associated with the tomboy allows Pickford and Taylor to behave in ways that would otherwise not be appropriate for girls and women and, at the same time, to provide an acceptable social model of transitory girlhood.[8] The anarchic characters Pickford and Taylor inhabit function as a cultural escape valve, as the comic absurdity of their performance relies on the incongruity between their actions and the innocence of childhood and traditional womanhood.

I do not wish to suggest that cinema in this period embodies an entirely conservative attitude toward gender. Janet Staiger, Richard deCordova, and Jon Burrows have all argued that cinema encouraged and participated in several progressive debates about the figure of the new woman being produced by cultural upheavals in British and American society.[9] However, in the persistence of the tomboy figure on-screen in this moment, it is possible to understand the work of Taylor and Pickford as embodying a preoccupation with the uncertain state of girlhood. Through the tomboy figure, multilayered expressions of femininity, independence, childhood, and sexuality emerge that help to control and obfuscate societal unease around the changing place of women and girls by offering a controlled expression of female independence that is associated with an acceptable period of self-discovery. In the films of Pickford and Taylor, the tomboyish instincts of these young girls provide a familiar vision of nonconformist gender identification that, ultimately, reassuringly reforms into compliant modes of femininity, the tomboyism on display becoming a culturally acceptable expression of female subjectivity.[10]

This chapter discusses the consistency with which Pickford's and Taylor's work uses the tomboy figure as a productive model for negotiating a complex terrain of changing values in the early twentieth century in Britain and the United States. It begins by establishing the historical moment in which Pickford, Taylor, and the cinema emerge, and then discusses how fears of modernization and nostalgia for Victorian tradition organized themselves around the girl. I suggest that the critically flexible figure of the tomboy, in the late nineteenth and early twentieth centuries, comes to describe emergent fears of new womanhood, and that, in the films of Pickford and Taylor, a vision of acceptable gender transgression is figured through their performance as tomboys. Underpinning this is the rigorous, extratextual construction of both stars as girlish, dainty, sweet, small, and naive. Finally, through close textual analysis of *Fanchon the Cricket* (James Kirkwood Sr., 1915), *Poor Little Peppina* (Sidney Olcott, 1916) and the *Tilly the Tomboy* series (Cecil Hepworth, 1910–1915), the chapter shows how these tomboyish tendencies are resolved narratively by a return to the patriarchal norm, heteronormative marriage, or, alternatively, the termination of tomboyish behaviour and the return to a performative girlhood.

In *Fanchon the Cricket* and *Poor Little Peppina*, Pickford plays a dynamic and active girl who displays clearly masculine or tomboyish qualities but maintains a clear association with the natural, the pure, and the feminine.[11] In *Fanchon the Cricket*, she is physical, single-minded, and assertive but displays a clear vulnerability and actively pursues heterosexual love; in *Poor Little Peppina*, Pickford's character dresses as a boy to escape the overtures of an unwanted suitor and facilitate a transatlantic journey to Europe. She then eschews this overt performance of maleness to return to a position of dependent femininity and a fulfilling marriage. Both films balance masculine performance with the reiteration of or return to the feminine, a thematic characteristic underpinned by the mobile tomboy figure. Similarly, Alma Taylor, as Tilly in the *Tilly the Tomboy* series, represents a self-contained and controllable expression of suffragist anger. The series represents the transgressions of its tomboy characters in a formally consistent way that resolves in Tilly's ultimate return to a traditional vision of girlhood. In the case of both Taylor and Pickford, the tomboyish performance is underpinned by the carefully constructed star personae of both actresses and the textual return to clearly defined gender norms. While the child-woman figure as described by Studler navigates a variety of sexual desires and emotional needs in a period of cultural change, the tomboy perhaps offers a comforting vision of transitional girlhood that provides a bridge between a Victorian past and an oncoming modernity.

Dangerous New Womanhood and the Tomboy

Mary Pickford (1892–1979) and Alma Taylor (1895–1974) were born in the same decade as the cinema itself and rose to stardom in a period of cultural obsession with girlhood. The Victorian period saw the roles of men and women become more clearly defined than ever before, as the female who stayed at home and the male who went to work described new spheres of domestic and public space. Underpinning this ideology were developing social scientific and physical anthropological theories of the innate characteristics of femininity and masculinity, which argued that disparities in physical ability, intelligence, and temperament were physically and anthropologically demonstrable.[12] Charles Darwin's theories of evolution encouraged the emergence of the pseudo-scientific discipline of social Darwinism, which suggested that social groups and peoples are subject to the same laws of evolution as plants and animals. As Cynthia Eagle Russett describes, Charles Darwin, in the *Descent of Man* (1871), tentatively argued that characteristic differences of temperament that are observable in the animal world would likely extend to human beings. Despite these clearly insubstantial foundations, retrograde readings of women as biologically and mentally inferior and the subsequent uncertainty around their capacity to function in the public sphere resulted in the emergence of the "angel of the house" (a figure defined and glorified by Coventry Patmore in his poem of the same name, published between 1854 and 1862). With the emergence of the suffragists' movement and the National Union of Women's Suffrage Societies in 1897, along with health and educational reform, the role of the woman began to change in the later part of the nineteenth century and the early part of the twentieth century. As Kristen Hatch has argued, "During this period, a new generation of women—more diverse and more radical than the feminists of previous generations—began to rally for women's suffrage and sexual freedoms, rejecting the ideal of the 'angel in the house' that defined middle-class femininity in terms of sexual purity and self-sacrifice."[13]

The suffrage movement also coincided with the emergence and early development of film, and suffragists became expert at ensuring that newsreel cameras were not only present at the major moments of movement's history but also offered the best vantage points from which they could film those moments. For instance, the newsreel *Suffragette Pageant* (1911) captures an estimated 66,000 suffragists taking part in a procession through London, where the newsreel cameras were situated to capture the magnitude and scale of the event. *Suffragettes Again* (1913) shows the aftermath of a fire set at a Plymouth timber yard by suffragists in retaliation for the arrest of Emily Pankhurst. Finally, *Palace Pandemonium* (1914) shows Pankhurst once again arrested, this time outside the gates of Buckingham Palace.[14] With the emergence of social Darwinism, sexology, and phrenology and the radical new womanhood embodied by the suffragist movement, attacks by the social and scientific community on the New Woman and her adolescent precursor, the tomboy, became common.

Emerging in its recognizable contemporary form in the mid-nineteenth century,[15] the tomboy, as Judith Halberstam suggests,

> tends to be associated with a "natural" desire for the greater freedoms and mobilities enjoyed by boys. Very often, it is read as a sign of independence and self-motivation, and tomboyism may even be encouraged to the extent that it remains comfortably linked to a stable sense of a girl identity.[16]

As Halberstam suggests, and notwithstanding these potential liberatory qualities, tomboyism was not seen as a suitable lifelong identity. Michelle Ann Abate suggests, in the late nineteenth and early twentieth centuries the phenomenon of tomboy taming emerges, and young girls are now expected to slough off their tomboy traits when they reach a specific stage of life, usually adolescence or the onset of puberty.[17] Similarly, in the early part of the twentieth century, and in a specifically US context, a mediated vision of tomboy behaviour emerged in the figure of the "American girl," who, as Renée M. Sentilles suggests, supposedly differed significantly from the tomboy in that she did not resist conventionality or maturity and was not a misfit.[18] The American girl featured in series of books for girls and in print culture and helped to normalize the idea of the active girl. Fair-skinned, wholesome, and frequently placed outside in the sunshine, the American girl's stubborn resentment against growing up and the tomboy's innate individualism represented a shift toward a more positive stance that celebrated youth rather than disparaged maturity.[19]

Notwithstanding the American girl's eventual ubiquity, the figure of the tomboy, an incalcitrant outsider, endured on both sides of the Atlantic. If physical girlhood as a preparatory stage for marriage and motherhood signified health and potentially high reproductive potential, this desirable coding rarely extended to the tomboy. For young girls, tomboyism was a breeding ground for the mannish[20] and, perhaps—as Judith Halberstam suggests—read as an antecedent to lesbianism.[21] The tomboyish vision of girlhood Taylor and Pickford offered arguably embodied many of these concerns. These capable, independent, energetic, and boisterous visions of the girl-child existed outside the domestic space, outside the mediating influence of female peers, and they frequently proved themselves physically and emotionally superior to their male counterparts. However, this gender nonconformity was textually resolved in a heteronormative marriage or a return to girlhood and existed in contrast to an extratextual construction of Pickford's and Taylor's respective star personae, which privileged their innocence, sweetness, naivety, feminine charm, and, ultimately, their girlhood.

CONSTRUCTIONS OF STARDOM: GIRLHOOD AND PERFORMANCE

Jonathan Burrows argues that Taylor's and Pickford's star personae are constructed differently and with sensitivity to the specificities of national reception. Burrows suggests that the extratextual construction of Alma Taylor's stardom, though indebted to the North American model, is distinct in its attitude toward performance, class, and personality. For Burrows, the American star model offered a microcosm of democracy in which any individual could become a star; it privileged consumerist ideals and embraced the cult of personality that surrounded new stardom. The British model, as defined by Cecil Hepworth and inflected, typically, by class politics, drew its stars from the middle classes, painted Taylor as an active non-consumer, and sought to foreground the dramatic qualifications of its associated stars by connecting their screen performance with the supposedly more technically demanding and transformative art of stage performance.[22]

Fusing these visions of stardom is the consistent focus in trade magazines, reviews, and critical comment, on both sides of the Atlantic, on the innocence and naivety of Pickford and Taylor, their "girlishness," and their bodies. For example, critics described Pickford in her performances on-screen as "never sweeter,"[23] "dainty and spontaneously playful,"[24] as a "little queen of the screen,"[25] and a "winsome little star,"[26] and one suggested that "every scene is made more appealing by the beauty and grace of this beloved little film-star."[27] Similarly, Chrissie White, Alma Taylor's co-star in the *Tilly the Tomboy* films, was described by one critic as "quite a little feast in herself,"[28] and the *American Bioscope* magazine described White and Taylor as "delightful young persons [who] are so refreshingly young, and real, and full of life."[29] Series producer and

creator Cecil Hepworth suggested that "the great aim and object of these Tilly girls…
was to paint the town extremely red" and that the "great charm of these delightful
little comedies" was the "joyfully disarming way in which they thoroughly did it." For
Hepworth, the series embodied the recipe for successful child story pictures in that it
represented the mischievousness of youth but without any of the sting.[30] Commentators
delighted in the physicality of the actors and the abandon with which they performed,
as well as echoing Romantic notions of the child as synonymous with the natural world.
In the descriptions of Chrissie White as a "little feast," the Tilly girls as refreshingly
young and real, and Pickford as dainty, beautiful, and little, a voyeuristic investment
in the girl-child that privileges the spectacle of the body and her appealing *girlishness* is
clear. Jon Burrows offers another example of the centrality of innocence and naivety in
the extratextual construction of Alma Taylor, noting that, in 1915, when she was twenty,
Taylor's life story was serialized in ten weekly instalments by the Scottish women's magazine *Home Weekly*. Divulged in these articles were tales of her childhood and an examination of authentic life experiences (working on a barge and travelling on a steam
train) that, supposedly, informed her later on-screen work. Similarly, stories circulated
about Taylor being filmed, without her knowledge, as a child as emblematic proof of
the unique sincerity and intuitive spontaneity with which she was educated in the art of
film acting.[31]

The centrality of the girl to discourses of social control, equality, and political reform
becomes central to the figure's emergence in the early part of the twentieth century as a
cultural icon, and to the emergence of both Taylor and Pickford as stars. As Christine
Gledhill argues in her discussion of Pickford's stardom (in a reading one can extend to
include Alma Taylor), Pickford's career did not last beyond the 1920s, as her stardom
was rooted in the 1910s and 1920s transatlantic investment, in the girl-child.[32] Similarly,
Diane Anselmo suggests that, in this period, the girl remained an enigmatic figure in
spite of the rapid technological, scientific, and psychoanalytical advancements of the
period. In remaining unknowable, Anselmo argues, this adolescent girl, caught between
childhood and womanhood, carried a thrill for early twentieth-century audiences,[33]
found a representational home in the elliptical and spectral medium of cinema, and, in
her liminality, helped assuage fears of new womanhood:

> On one hand, the drummed-up emphasis on the redeeming powers of girlhood's elu-
> siveness and transformability warded off anxieties about the galloping industrializa-
> tion, modernization, and weaponization of modern civilizations. On the other hand,
> the figure of the coy and hapless adolescent girl preserved a nostalgic idealization of
> subservient and domestic femininity, which a new generation of independent, edu-
> cated, and freethinking young women had, by the mid-1910s, begun to challenge.[34]

The dual notions of a coy adolescent girl and the nostalgic idealization of subservient
femininity are seemingly central to the construction of both Taylor's and Pickford's
star personae. Pickford's success was predicated on her appearances between 1917 and
1920 in a series of adaptations of classic children's novels, including *Poor Little Rich Girl*

(Maurice Tourneur, 1917) and *Rebecca of Sunnybrook Farm* (Marshall Neilan, 1917), in which she portrayed strong-willed, independent girls contending with cruel relatives. However, her films before this describe a far more eclectic on-screen career. As John Tibbetts notes, Pickford had previously appeared as

> a deposed Bosnian queen in *Such a Little Queen* (1914), the mother of an illegiti-mate child in *Hearts Adrift* (1914). The rebellious wife in *Behind the Scenes* (1914), an Alaskan Inuit in *Little Pal* (1915), the cross-dressing spy in *Nell Gwynn* (1915), a factory worker who protested sweatshop labor in *The Eternal Grind* (1916) and the suicidal mothers in *Hearts Adrift* (1914) and *Madame Butterfly* (1915).[35]

The overlooked diversity of Pickford's oeuvre; the rigorous extratextual construc-tion of "little" Mary Pickford and Alma Taylor as sincere, natural, and refreshing; and the orthodoxy within contemporary criticism that privileged smallness, sweetness, and beauty suggests a deep cultural investment in the figure of the girl. As Tibbetts argues, Pickford's little-girl roles indisputably established her as the highest-paid, most recognized, most idolized, and most powerful female star in the entertainment busi-ness,"[36] while Taylor reached her critical and commercial peak in 1915, after producing all eighteen films in the Tilly series. This period also coincides with what Michelle Ann Abate has identified as the zenith of the tomboy in American literary fiction, a mo-ment that saw the appearance of classic tomboy novels including Louisa May Alcott's *Little Women* (1867), Sarah Orne Jewett's *A Country Doctor* (1884), and Kate Douglas Wiggin's *Rebecca of Sunnybrook Farm* (1903).[37] British literature also saw the arrival of the tomboy in this period; Peggy Vaughan in Angela Brazil's *Terrible Tomboy* (1904) was popular on both sides of the Atlantic, and she imitated the wild and active antics of her North American counterparts. These transatlantic tomboys are the literary forerunners of Pickford and Taylor, and their prevalence and popularity perhaps suggest that cer-tain attitudes and anxieties around femininity and girlhood were, to an extent, inter-changeable and intercontinental. The following analysis of *Fanchon the Cricket*, *Poor Little Peppina*, and *Tilly the Tomboy* articulates both the prevalence of these themes in the films of two hugely popular early films stars, and also illuminates the way the visions of tomboyism on display describe a broader cultural desire to soothe fears around tran-sitory girlhood and the new woman.

TOMBOYISM: *FANCHON THE CRICKET* AND *POOR LITTLE PEPPINA*

Fanchon the Cricket, based on *La Petite Fedette* (1848) by George Sand,[38] tells the story of Fanchon (Mary Pickford), a girl who lives with her grandmother (Gertrude Norman) in a small cabin in the French woods.[39] Fanchon is ostracized by the children who live in the nearby village. Her unkempt appearance is a source of ridicule; and her grandmother's inequitable reputation as a witch, a source of fear. Fanchon watches the interactions of the village children from afar until a prank she plays during a May Day picnic catches the attention of Landry (Jack Standing), the son of a rich merchant and the group's most popular male. After Fanchon saves Landry's brother, Didier (Richard Lee), from the attentions of a local bully and subsequently saves Landry himself from drowning, the pair fall in love. Unhappily, Landry is set to marry the pompous and priggish Madelon (Lottie Pickford) at the behest of his controlling father. Landry resolves to ignore his father's wishes and to marry Fanchon instead, but Fanchon refuses to wed Landry until she has his family's approval. At the end of the film, Fanchon's grandmother dies and Landry falls ill with a fever. Landry's father visits Fanchon in the woods and gives his blessing to her relationship with his son in the hopes that it will help cure his illness. Fanchon visits Landry, who makes a miraculous recovery.

Fanchon the Cricket is organized dramatically around moments that suggest the potential benefits of gender nonconformity as a catalyst for Fanchon's ultimate acceptance into Victorian society. For example, Fanchon's defeat of Didier's bully offers a progressive and aggressive vision of femininity figured through Fanchon's tomboy behaviour, introduces Fanchon to Landry's family, and sets in motion a series of events that culminate in a heteronormative courtship. This sequence begins with Fanchon observing Didier and his bully from a nearby gate as they begin to struggle. Fanchon remonstrates with the bully, who threatens to punch her, raising his fist in anger. Unperturbed, Fanchon approaches him, and the two begin to wrestle. They fight, but Fanchon wrestles the boy to the ground and punches him in the stomach. She even kicks him on the backside when he attempts to stand up, underscoring her total victory. As the bully escapes with his friends, Fanchon reprimands Didier for not protecting himself and tells him to stop crying, because he is "not the one who got hurt." Juxtaposing this image of female toughness and physical aptitude is the scene that introduces Madelon. Madelon is depicted as priggish, prim, and difficult, a cold and unappealingly proper vision of Victorian womanhood.[40] In contrast to Fanchon, she is passive, compliant, and unassertive; associated with the domestic space rather than the natural world; and reminiscent of Patmore's "angel of the house." Whereas Fanchon rolls down hills, climbs trees, fights off bullies, and plays in fields, the cosseted Madelon retreats from the natural world. For example, Landry and Madelon stand beside a small river, which Madelon refuses to cross unless Landry agrees to carry her. Witnessing this, Fanchon mocks Madelon's stuffiness by stamping through the water with exaggerated, prim femininity, pinching her ripped skirt and lifting it demurely as she strides through the river.

Masculine performance and the rejection of conventional womanhood are carefully counterbalanced in the film with Fanchon's clearly articulated desire to develop her feminine qualities and to affiliate herself with the village children, and, centrally, Landry. As the village children celebrate the festival of St. Audoche, Fanchon watches them forlornly, and embarrassed by her clothes, feels unable to attend. Her grandmother finds her lying alone in the grass and asks what is wrong; Fanchon tells her, "I can never go where the other girls go. I never have anything to wear." The grandmother escorts Fanchon home and reveals a chest filled with clothes. An intertitle in the form of a note reveals that the clothes were bequeathed to Fanchon by her mother on her death. Dressed in her new clothes, Fanchon is now empowered to attend the festival with the other children. Articulating a newfound femininity, Fanchon moves from obscurity to significance; despite the continued ridicule of the village children, she catches Landry's attention, and their courtship begins. Fanchon's masculine performance, then, is admissible as part of a stated desire to participate in traditional gender roles and as an aspect of her transition toward adulthood and proper femininity. Another intertitle tells us that Fanchon craves "what she has never received ... Affection." This further legitimizes Fanchon's pursual of Landry and her transition from the tomboyish to the feminine and suggests that these tomboyish tendencies may be the result of her upbringing and being raised outside a traditional family unit.

With this in mind, it is possible to contrast Fanchon's free-spirited and tomboyish girlhood with another, apparently less appealing vision of femininity embodied by the spinster figure of Fanchon's grandmother. If Madelon represents a subtle critique of an already outdated model of Victorian femininity, and Fanchon, in the amalgamation of tomboyish freedom and paradigmatic femininity, a mitigated new womanhood, then Fanchon's grandmother represents a third feminine form. She is elderly, unattractive, and unmarried and symbolizes an admonition to her granddaughter about the importance of requited heterosexual romance and the danger of persistent gender nonconformity. Rather than being an example of the possibilities of nonconformism, Fanchon's grandmother, in her loneliness and isolation, is emblematic of the importance of gender norms. The film's climax reveals that Landry's father had discouraged his brother from having a relationship with Fanchon's grandmother in their youth. When confronted with this information, Fanchon's grandmother says, "Many years ago you prevented me from marrying your brother; but if these children love each other, you shall not ruin their lives as you did mine." Here, unfulfilled romantic love is directly responsible for the grandmother's "ruined life."

The film's coda is instructive in outlining Fanchon's development from rambunctious tomboy to refined woman, the replacement of physicality and wildness with demure sweetness, and the maintenance of the comforting aspects of traditional Victorian womanhood in the face of the new woman.[41] After Fanchon has awoken Landry from his fever-induced sleep, the screen fades to black before opening on a field of wheat gently blowing in the wind. Fanchon, initially hidden by the wheat, stands with her arms outstretched. Moving through the field, the now expensively dressed Fanchon approaches the foreground of the frame; addressing the camera directly, she smiles, turns, and skips away through the field as the camera fades to black. Fanchon is no longer the brazen, bullish, and outspoken tomboy, but has been tamed by romantic love; her naturalism and spontaneity are now ordered and controlled. As Kristen Hatch suggests, characters like Fanchon signify American modernity by updating a stock figure in sentimental fiction and proving that the nation can still hold traditional values; the figure of the tamed tomboy thus becomes a conduit for this relationship between the old and new.[42]

Poor Little Peppina

Poor Little Peppina is the first seven-reel film of Mary Pickford's career, making it her longest up until this point. The film tells the story of the Torrens family, wealthy Americans living in Italy with their baby daughter, Lois. Soldo (Antonio Maiori), a mafia chief masquerading as a butler in the Torrens' employ, "drinks too freely" of the family's wine and is caught by fellow employee Pietro (Ernest Torti). Fired, the furious Soldo kills Pietro; however, the police apprehend Soldo and imprison him. Liberated by his Mafia counterparts one month later, Soldo conspires to kidnap the Torrens' daughter. Having taken the child, Soldo leaves her with his poor Italian relatives before escaping to New York. Several years pass and the girl, now age fifteen and known as Peppina (Mary Pickford) works in the fields with her adoptive family. An American heiress known as the Duchess has taken an interest in Peppina during this time, teaching her to read and to speak English. Peppina becomes engaged against her will to the family's employer, Bernardo, who offers a substantial dowry for her hand in marriage. Escaping on the eve of their wedding, Peppina—with the help of her stepbrother, Beppo (Jack Pickford)—disguises herself as a boy to avoid detection. Peppina decides to escape to New York and seeks assistance from the Duchess. She is given an amount of money and the address of the Duchess's brother, whom she is told to visit on her arrival.

Peppina stows away on a ship bound for America and while searching the upper-class cabins for food meets Hugh Carroll (Eugene O'Brien), a sympathetic New York district attorney travelling home from Italy. Taking pity on the "boy," Carroll provides him with food and assures his safe passage by finding him a space in steerage. The ship arrives in America and the boy pays the unscrupulous ship's stoker to allow him entry into the country. Seeing the money, the Stoker agrees to help the boy, and takes him to an East Side bar now owned by Soldo. Soldo, the Stoker, and their accomplice take the boy's money and force him to work at the bar. Wearying of the men's cruelty, Peppina escapes to become a messenger boy. Fate intervenes and leads Peppina, still masquerading as a boy, to the shop where a little while before she had innocently paid for a hat with a counterfeit bill. Arrested, Peppina reveals her identity, and Soldo and his accomplices have to go before the district attorney, who happens to be Hugh. Recognizing the boy, now revealed to be Peppina, Hugh ensures that the criminals are brought to justice and Peppina is reunited with her family. We learn that Hugh is, in fact, the Duchess's brother and the address given to Peppina by the Duchess was Hugh's. The film concludes three years later with Hugh and Peppina married and living in wealth and prosperity.

The film rehearses many themes familiar to Pickford's work (and, as I will show, to the Tilly series). Transitional girlhood features centrally, as do themes of liminality, bodily change, masquerade, and surveillance. Familiarly, the film climaxes with a return to the ideological security of heterosexual romance, and the material security offered by a wealthy and successful man. As Tibbetts observes, Mary Pickford portrayed boys in a number of her roles, including *The Poor Little Rich Girl* and *Little Lord Fauntleroy* (Alfred E. Green, 1921), and cross-dressing scenes abound in the actor's work.

Tibbetts highlights a sequence from *Poor Little Rich Girl* in which Pickford's character, Gwendolyn, is dressed as a boy by her father as a punishment. Regarding herself in the mirror, Gwendolyn finds the image reflected back to be pleasing, and especially enjoys the luxury of trouser pockets.[43] But if *Poor Little Rich Girl* nods toward the freedoms of boyhood, *Poor Little Peppina* offers a sustained articulation of the different forms of mobility available to the boy, and its title points ironically and literally to the potentially impoverished social and economic status of the girl.

Significantly, the film opens with a sequence that describes Lois's privileged and loving upbringing. An "iris in" transition opens on the Torrens family. Three-year-old Lois stands on a park bench, as her mother and father fuss over her, the proceeding intertitle has described the Torrens as a wealthy American family living in Italy. The sequence is reminiscent of Louis Lumière's *Repas de bébé* (1895) in its brief picture of a bourgeois family and apparently naturalistic depiction of the world, and is uncannily familiar in its representation of the family and the centralization of the child.[44] It also, perhaps unconsciously, consolidates the vision of Victorian life that is represented through the Torrens family, by situating its opening sequence within the context of early actuality footage. In locating Lois within the context of the Victorian family structure, both formally and narratively, the child's transition from Lois to Peppina to boy and then back to a remade Victorian woman who combines aspects of Lois and Peppina is more striking. Moreover, it expresses the transition from Victorian girlhood to the rural, agricultural, and physical girlhood of Peppina and the return to the patriarchal family unit represented by Lois/Peppina's marriage to Hugh.

The cultural anxiety that surrounded girlhood, the girl, sexuality, new womanhood, and bodily performance is expressed in *Poor Little Peppina* through acts of surveillance and the protagonist's desire to avoid examination. Having resolved to run away, Peppina and Beppo escape into woods near the family home and begin working to disguise Peppina as a boy, cutting her hair and dressing her in Beppo's old suit. Contemporary commentators felt that Pickford lost none of her appeal with the loss of her curls, one critic noting, "Miss Pickford in boy's clothes with short hair is altogether adorable, but she is that in her peasant clothes and later in the frock of a young woman of fashion."[45] However, the symbolic act of hair cutting is meaningful, and stripping Pickford of her famous blonde ringlets foregrounds the liminality of her own girlhood and the lack of individuality associated with girlhood culturally, and points toward Pickford's later attempts to shed her "Little Mary" image (which were thwarted by a cinemagoing public desperate to consume the stable and familiar vision of girlhood Pickford embodied).[46] Later in her career, Pickford was all too aware that, as far as her fans were concerned, the screen's epitome of the "growing girl" must never herself grow old.[47]

Yet despite Pickford's extratextual fixity and eternal youth, transition and movement are central to the plot of *Poor Little Peppina*. Underpinning the journey between subject positions are the literal act of travel between Italy and the United States and the recognition of Peppina as a boy during the liminal phase of transatlantic travel. The passage between the United States and Europe introduces Peppina to her future husband, Hugh, who reads Peppina as a boy, determines to help the child, and even photographs Peppina on the ship's deck. In her performance of boyhood and interaction with her prospective lover, Pickford in *Poor Little Peppina* offers the clearest articulation of Studler's characterization of Pickford as both asexually appealing to Victorian girls, who read Pickford as liberated from the demands of adult femininity and sexuality, and her appeal to Victorian men as enticingly innocent. In her performance of boyhood, Pickford elides the threatening sexual agency of modern womanhood and proves liminal enough to negotiate a wide range of sexual desires and identifications.[48] Moreover, the knowledge that Pickford is really "Mary" masquerading as a girl who is masquerading as a boy evades the potentially homoerotic implications of Hugh's subsequent attraction and marriage to Peppina.

Counterbalancing the subversive and potentially homoerotic male masquerade is the ultimate resolve into a familiar model of heterosexual romance and the return to the normative patriarchal family structure. Three years pass between Hugh's rescue of Peppina and her reunion with her parents. Hugh asks Lois's father for her hand in marriage, and he consents on the condition that Hugh and Lois "always make a home near us." Hugh agrees and rushes to find Lois. We are reintroduced to Lois/Peppina, now age twenty-one, as she descends the stairs in the family's large Victorian home. The girl has grown, assuredly into the model of Victorian femininity; her long ringlets have returned, and she is once again dressed, as in the climactic scene of *Fanchon the Cricket*, expensively in an ornate white dress. Here, as in much of Pickford's body of work, the potentially problematic adolescence of the girl is navigated via the freeing performance of masculinity, this time overtly in Peppina's performance of boyhood, but frequently through the appropriation of tomboyish qualities. Ultimately, in its familiar climax the film offers a reassuringly conventional resolution.

Tilly the Tomboy

As the preceding analysis suggests, Mary Pickford's characters frequently participate in an overt gender play that assuages ideas of problematic new womanhood by positioning tomboyish behaviour as an aspect of adolescent growth. These narratives indicate that everything will be fine with the preservation of the patriarchal structure. A similar exchange takes place in the *Tilly the Tomboy* movies. Beginning in 1910, the same year as the United States' first large-scale suffrage parade and the Black Friday march that protested the failure of the conciliation bill, the Tilly series obfuscates the political and cultural discomfort caused by the actions of the suffragists by concealing acts of female self-actualization beneath the familiar facade of tomboyish performance.[49] Tilly and Sally assume the cultural codes of girlishness and childishness in order to precipitate their tomboyish behaviours, before reverting to a masquerade of femininity. The narrative structure encapsulates the liminality of girlhood described earlier by Gledhill, Hatch, and Studler, and creates a diegetic space in which moments of transgression are bookended by the return to a proper vision of femininity, even if this femininity is performative and self-conscious.

Tilly the Tomboy Visits the Poor (Lewin Fitzhamon, 1910), the first film in the series, begins in what becomes conventional Tilly fashion, with the foregrounding of a deliberate femininity. Tilly and Sally's father explains to them that they are to visit Mrs Smith, an elderly woman who has fallen ill. Tilly and Sally stand demurely as their father speaks, performing their child status in self-conscious gestures and poses. The camera frames the trio in a medium long-shot and holds it as the girls clasp their hands together innocently and bow their heads in deference to their father. He exits, and the camera remains focused on the now unobserved sisters, watching as the facade quickly fades and they begin playfully pushing each other. As Tilly and Sally make their way to Mrs Smith's home, framed from behind, again in medium long-shot, they continue to mock their girlish status through exaggerated performance. They move with a knowing balletic grace, daintily holding hands and performing a semi-curtsey before entering the house.[50] However, their behaviour quickly turns again. Once inside Mrs Smith's home, they begin to torment her. Framed in a three-shot, Tilly and Sally spin Mrs Smith's sick bed in circles, pull books from the shelves, and eventually jump furiously up and down on the old woman's bed, as she lies helpless. The long-shot helps to create a stage on which Tilly and Sally may perform and increases the theatricality of their actions, exaggerating the performance of their mischievous tomboyism.

The public performance of girlhood combined with Tilly and Sally's private anarchy is important and reflects a distorted version of what Mary Ann Doane and Joan Riviere have both referred to as the masquerade of femininity.[51] Unlike the suffragists, Tilly and Sally make sure that their actions go largely unnoticed; when confronted by authority figures they play to notions of girlish innocence and femininity, which allows them freedom of movement and ensures that their actions go unpunished. Tilly, Sally, and Pickford wear femininity like a mask that can be removed.[52] For example, as the action moves from Mrs Smith's bedroom to the street, the girls begin to torment a number of working men. They tie a rope around the end of a ladder, which they then use to knock down a man carrying a stack of baskets, and steal a laundry van, throwing the contents on the street as they drive away. Locating the camera behind the action and observing the girls as they drive away from their pursuers helps to highlight their destructive tendencies.

In the sequence, the camera in its medium long-shot position observes the dirty laundry being thrown from the van by a laughing Sally. The van's owner and a number of other interested adults chase the girls, attempting to collect and occasionally tripping over the discarded washing. Tilly and Sally's rampage ends as they ransack a bakery, pushing the bakers into a vat of flour. Importantly, all of these acts underpin the girls' anonymity and mobility. None of their victims actually sees who has perpetrated the crimes against them, and instead they simply follow the trail of the destruction the girls leave behind. However, Tilly and Sally are always too fast and too adept at navigating their surroundings. The film's payoff comes as the girls re-enter Mrs Smith's home with the angry mob in hot pursuit. They once again begin to perform their innocence, carefully tending to Mrs Smith. The baying mob enters to witness the scene: Tilly reading to Mrs Smith and Sally feeding her soup. On witnessing the girls' charity, the confused mob withdraws, apologizing for their incursion. Tilly and Sally's mobility throughout this escapade is in stark contrast to their immobile, subservient, and deferential performance of feminine childhood when they are observed by figures of authority.

Tilly's Party (Lewin Fitzhamon, 1911) offers further evidence of the ways in which Tilly and Sally perform femininity and girlishness in order to engage in an unabashed performance of tomboyism. Tilly and Sally sit bored on the periphery of a party given by their father. Two midshipmen enter the frame on bikes and immediately approach the girls; they talk to them briefly before Tilly and Sally's father interrupts, eager to speak to the returning seaman. While the rest of the party is distracted, Tilly and Sally grab the unguarded bikes, and under the guise of wheeling them from the room, forcefully ram them into the party guests, who stand talking in a group. The cluster of guests tumbles over in a mix of limbs and spinning wheels, while the girls look on, stifling laughter and proclaiming their innocence. They once again clasp their hands apologetically and effect their familiar look of contrition. Their father is unmoved and evicts the girls from the party, sending them instead to their music lesson. During the sequence, the camera once again foregrounds ideas of seeing and not seeing. The wide framing allows the viewer to note the lack of attention given to Tilly and Sally, the group of adults talking excitedly with their backs turned while the girls plot behind them, and the ability of the two girls to navigate the confined space without being observed by or disturbing, until they choose to, the adults.

After their father leaves the scene, the two midshipmen return to talk to Tilly and Sally. The girls see this as their opportunity for some fun and hatch a plan to have their suitors climb up into their bedroom through the window. Their plan in place, the girls leave the scene, escorted to their room by a typically matronly housekeeper. In their bedroom, Tilly and Sally proceed to lock the housekeeper in a cupboard and, moving to the window, haul up the waiting midshipmen. Now that the girls are free from adult supervision, pandemonium ensues. The girls sabotage the party food, wreck their father's home, and generally create complete and unbridled mayhem. They escape the house with the assistance of the midshipmen and their bikes, their father and his furious guests in hot pursuit. The chase sequence is formally similar to the one in *Tilly the Tomboy Visits the Poor*, and again contrasts the speed of movement enjoyed by Tilly and Sally with the relative slowness of the adults. Tilly, Sally, and the midshipmen race toward the camera before moving out of the frame. The action remains framed in the same manner as we wait for the chasing pack of adults to catch up, a sequence that articulates the literal gap between the two parties. In the next moment, Tilly and Sally traverse a wooden gate and make their way into a field, Tilly breaking the fourth wall and acknowledging the camera (and, by extension, the viewer) with a wave, as the audience becomes complicit in their escape. As they again leave the frame, their father arrives, stumbling over the gate and failing to keep pace with the girls.

Tilly and Sally race to the home of their piano teacher, barge inside, and seat themselves at the piano. Their lesson begins just moments before the chasing pack enters the room. The girls again feign outrage at the unwelcome interruption, innocently turning to their instructor and asking him to expel the trespassers. He obliges, sending a barrage of abuse toward the girls' father and the party guests. The text again employs the visual motif of Tilly and Sally sitting innocently while their adult pursuers leer at them over the piano. This moment of visual parity bookends the film, but it also visually articulates the way power and agency has oscillated throughout the course of the narrative. What becomes clear from these readings is that the *Tilly the Tomboy* series offers a more ambivalent solution to the issue of emergent new womanhood than we see in the films of Mary Pickford. Instead of an absolute return to a patriarchal norm, the films present an oscillatory vision of girlhood, boyhood, and womanhood that has the Tilly girls use their femininity as a mask that allows them to hide their tomboyish behaviour and the destruction it brings. This reiteration of girlhood echoes what Cecil Hepworth earlier described as mischief without the sting: the cathartic performance of tomboyish behaviour that resolves in a return to girlhood and offers a vision of acceptable transgression in a moment of suffragist revolution.[53]

Conclusion: Transatlantic Tomboyism

This chapter has not attempted to read back or historicize Pickford and Taylor or to map contemporary concerns of gender representation onto these figures. Instead, it suggests that anxieties around female sexuality, adolescents, and independence find a representational outlet in the newly developed medium of cinema in the early part of the twentieth century through the figure of the tomboy. On-screen, Pickford and Taylor can be read as culturally acceptable articulations of a defiant girlhood. Off screen, their careful extratextual construction as innocent, naive, spontaneous, and *small* counterbalances this portrayal and underpins their popularity with an uncertain Victorian audience and allows a range of competing ideological discourses to exist through these figures simultaneously. In the expressive possibilities of the two figures, drawn large by the cinema screen, we are able to investigate the way girlhood and the masquerade of femininity and masculinity come to articulate a range of transatlantic fears about the changing position of the woman and the girl, and underline the mutability and liminality of the girl-child on screen. As Vicky Lebeau suggests, these figures raise questions about what constitutes womanhood, girlhood, femininity, and masculinity and describe cinema's long history of investing in the child—both as an image and idea—as a figure of instability and indeterminacy.[54]

Cinema continues to ask these questions and frequently frames them around the girl-child. *Tomboy* (Céline Sciamma, 2011), *We Are the Best!* (Lukas Moodysson, 2014), and *The Fits* (Anna Rose Holmer, 2015) explore the place of unorthodox girlhood in contemporary culture and further illuminate the continued uncertainty around the figure of the girl. As this chapter has worked to show, Taylor and Pickford provide the prototypical cinematic example of this tendency and evidence of the way in which the cinema screen frequently deploys the figure of the child in order to explore and explain attitudes toward gender, nationhood, history, and identity. Facilitating these representational approaches is the medium of early silent cinema itself, which tended toward an anarchistic and slapstick visual approach that sought to engage a mixed-age and predominantly working-class audience. Schematic plotting and the absence of diegetic sound—combined with the necessarily excessive physicality of early film performers—all underscored ideologies of mobility, performativity, and self-expression, while also heightening the juxtaposition between the modes of being outlined previously: tomboy, girl, boy, woman, adult, and child. As such, early cinema became the ideal vehicle through which to explore and express these states, providing an accessible and recognizably rendered vision of transitional childhood. These women, playing girls, playing boys, ameliorated transatlantic fears about the position of the girl and changing notions of female adolescents.

Notes

1. Kristen Hatch, "'America's Sweethearts': Mary Pickford, Shirley Temple and the 'Decline of Sentiment,'" in *Shirley Temple and the Performance of Girlhood* (New Brunswick, NJ: Rutgers University Press, 2015), p. 32.
2. Christine Gledhill, "Mary Pickford: Icon of Stardom," in Jennifer M. Bean (ed.), *Flickers of Desire: Movie Stars in the 1910s* (New Brunswick, NJ: Rutgers University Press, 2011), pp. 43–68, at 53.
3. Examples abound and include *David Copperfield* (Charles Dickens, 1850), *Kim* (Rudyard Kipling, 1901), and latterly the Harry Potter series (J. K. Rowling, 1997–2007).
4. Taylor was voted the most popular British screen star of 1915, beating Charlie Chaplin, who came in second. See Jonathan Burrows, "'Our English Mary Pickford': Alma Taylor and Ambivalent British Stardom in the 1910s," in Bruce Babington (ed.), *British Stars and Stardom: From Alma Taylor to Sean Connery* (Manchester, UK: Manchester University Press, 2001), pp. 29–41, at 30; Rachael Low, *The History of the British Film 1906–1914* (1950; repr. London: Routledge, 1997), pp. 32–33.
5. Diane W. Anselmo, "Betwixt and between, Forever Sixteen: American Silent Cinema and the Emergence of Female Adolescents," *Screen* 58:3 (2017), pp. 251–284.
6. Gaylyn Studler, "Oh, 'Doll Divine': Mary Pickford, Masquerade, and the Paedophilic Gaze," in Jenifer M. Bean and Diane Negra (eds.), *A Feminist Reader in Early Cinema* (Durham, NC: Duke University Press, 2002), pp. 349–373.
7. Studler, "Oh, 'Doll Divine,'" p. 367.
8. Sally Mitchell, *The New Girl* (New York: Columbia University Press, 1996).
9. See Jon Burrows, *Legitimate Cinema: Theatre Stars in Silent British Film, 1908–1918* (Exeter, UK: University of Exeter Press, 2003); Richard deCordova, *Picture Personalities: The Emergence of the Star System in America* (Urbana: University of Illinois Press, 2001); and Janet Staiger, *Bad Women: Regulating Sexuality in Early American Cinema* (Minneapolis: University of Minnesota Press, 1995).
10. Michelle Ann Abate, *Tomboys: A Literary and Cultural History* (Philadelphia: Temple University Press, 2008); Judith Halberstam, *Female Masculinity* (Durham, NC: Duke University Press, 1998), pp. 7–9. Abate argues that the tomboy figure appears in antebellum children's literature and persists via various expressions and in a number of forms throughout the nineteenth, twentieth, and twenty-first centuries.

11. *Little Pal* and *Rags* (James Kirkwood, 1915), and *The Foundling* (John B. O'Brien and Allan Dwan, 1915) are just three further examples of this tendency.

12. Cynthia Eagle Russett, *Sexual Science: The Victorian Construction of Womanhood* (Cambridge, MA: Harvard University Press, 1991), p. 3.

13. Hatch, "America's Sweethearts," p. 37.

14. All of these films are available at the BFI Player website http://player.bfi.org.uk/ and help to form part of the *Make More Noise: Suffragettes in Silent Film 1899–1917* (2015) collection.

15. Michelle Ann Abate suggests the figure of the tomboy has a complex discursive history and argues that the term "tomboy" emerges in Britain as early as the sixteenth century. *Tomboys: A Literary and Cultural History*, p. 15.

16. Halberstam, *Female Masculinity*, pp. 5–7.

17. Abate, *Tomboys: A Literary and Cultural History*, p. 19.

18. Renée M. Sentilles, *American Tomboys, 1850–1915* (Amherst: University of Massachusetts Press, 2018), p. 148.

19. Sentilles, *American Tomboys*, p. 149.

20. Abate, *Tomboys: A Literary and Cultural History*, pp. 50–53.

21. Halberstam, *Female Masculinity*, p. 6.

22. Burrows, "Our English Mary Pickford."

23. *Moving Picture World*, May 22, 1915.

24. *New York Times*, Mary Pickford in Boy's Masquerade; Movie Favorite a Kidnapped Foundling in *"Poor Little Peppina"*. Amusing but Improbable Long Arm of Coincidence is Wrenched Badly, But Spectators Like it. February 21, 1916.

25. *Variety*, October 15, 1915.

26. "Rags", *Moving Picture World*, August 14, 1915.

27. Grace Kingsley, *At the Stage Door, Los Angeles Times*, January 3, 1915.

28. Geoffrey Macnab, *Searching for Stars: Stardom and Screen Acting in British Cinema* (London: Continuum, 2000).

29. Macnab, *Searching for Stars*, p. 13.

30. Cecil Hepworth, *Came The Dawn: Memories of a Film Pioneer* (London: Phoenix House, 1951).

31. Burrows, "Our English Mary Pickford," pp. 30–33.

32. Gledhill, "Mary Pickford: Icon of Stardom," p. 52.

33. Anselmo, "Betwixt and Between," pp. 276.

34. Ibid., p. 256.

35. John C. Tibbetts, "Mary Pickford and the American Growing Girl," *Journal of Popular Film and Television* 29:2 (2010), pp. 50–62.

36. Tibbetts, "Mary Pickford and the American Growing Girl," p. 51.

37. Abate, *Tomboys: A Literary and Cultural History*, p. 15. Notably, Pickford would star in the film version of *Rebecca of Sunnybrook farm* in 1917.

38. George Sand was born Amantine Lucile Aurore Dupin and was a notable example of a nineteenth-century European woman who chose to wear men's clothing and appropriate a conventionally male name. The non-traditional gender expression of the author reflects in the character of Fanchon as performed by Pickford.

39. In the novel, the three central protagonists are fourteen-years-old; however, in the silent film no age is specified.

40. Madelon is played by Pickford's younger sister, Lottie, and the bully is played by Pickford's brother, Jack.

41. Studler, "Oh, 'Doll Divine,'" p. 357.
42. Hatch, "America's Sweethearts," p. 31.
43. Tibbetts, "Mary Pickford and the American Growing Girl," p. 58.
44. Vicky Lebeau, *Childhood and Cinema* (London: Reaktion Books, 2008), pp. 23–25.
45. ""Mary Pickford in Boy's Masquerade; Movie Favorite a Kidnapped Foundling in 'Poor Little Peppina,'" *New York Times*, February 21 1916.
46. In her autobiography, Pickford recalls being mistaken by members of the public for her child characters "now and again," and notes, "I had allowed myself to be hypnotized by the public into remaining a little girl." Mary Pickford, *Sunshine, and Shadow* (New York: Doubleday, 1955), pp. 250–253.
47. Tibbetts, "Mary Pickford and the American Growing Girl," p. 59.
48. Studler, "Oh, 'Doll Divine,'" p. 368.
49. The Conciliation bill sought to extend the rights of British women by ensuring a limited number of women had the right to vote according to their property holdings and marital status.
50. This is similar to the masquerade of femininity that Pickford participates in during *Fanchon the Cricket.*
51. See Mary Ann Doane, "Film and the Masquerade: Theorising the Female Spectator," *Screen* 23:3–4 (1982), pp. 74–88; and Joan Riviere, "Womanliness as Masquerade," in Hendrik M. Ruitenbeek (ed.), *Psychoanalysis and Female Sexuality* (New Haven, CT: College and University Press, 1966) pp. 303–313.
52. Doane, "Film and the Masquerade," p. 81.
53. Devious and mischievous children were a mainstay of early silent cinema; in fact, *Our New Errand Boy* (James Williamson, 1905) pre-dates the Tilly series by five years and depicts a comparable paragon of rascality behaving in a similarly impish way to Tilly and Sally. On a broader level, it is also possible to compare Tilly and Sally with the anarchic, individualistic, and picaresque adventures of Huckleberry Finn. This suggests a further transnational element to representations of childhood in this period.
54. Lebeau, *Childhood and Cinema*, p. 94.

BIBLIOGRAPHY

Bean, Jennifer M. *Flickers of Desire: Movie Stars of the 1910s*. New Brunswick, NJ: Rutgers University Press, 2011.
Brown, Geoff, and Laurence Kardish. *Michael Balcon: The Pursuit of British Cinema*. New York: Museum of Modern Art, 1984.
Brown, Noel, and Bruce Babington, eds. *Family Films in Global Cinema: The World beyond Disney*. London: I.B. Tauris, 2015.
Cunningham, Hugh. *Children and Childhood in Western Society since 1500*. New York: Longman, 1995.
Donald, Stephanie, Emma Wilson, and Sarah Wright, eds. *Childhood and Nation in Contemporary World Cinema: Borders and Encounters*. London: Bloomsbury Academic, 2017.
Gledhill, Christine. *Reframing British Cinema, 1918–1928: Between Restraint and Passion*. London: British Film Institute, 2003.
Gledhill, Christine. *Gender Meets Genre in Postwar Cinema*. Urbana: University of Illinois Press, 2012.

Halberstam, Judith. *Female Masculinity*. Durham, NC: Duke University Press, 1998.

Halsey, A., ed. *British Social Trends since 1900: A Guide to the Changing Social Structure of Britain*. 2nd ed. Basingstoke, UK: Macmillan Press, 1988.

Harris, Anita. *All about the Girl: Culture, Power, and Identity*. New York: Routledge, 2004.

Higson, Andrew. *Dissolving Views: Key Writings on British Cinema*. London: Bloomsbury, 2016.

Kearney, Mary Celeste, ed. *Mediated Girlhoods: New Explorations of Girls' Media Culture*. Oxford, UK: Peter Lang, 2011.

Lebeau, Vicky. *Childhood and Cinema*. London: Reaktion Books, 2008.

Olson, Debbie, and Andrew Scahill, eds. *Lost and Othered Children in Contemporary Cinema*. Lanham, MD: Lexington Books, 2014.

Studler, Gaylyn. *Precocious Charms: Stars Performing Girlhood in Classical Hollywood Cinema*. Berkeley: University of California Press, 2013.

Wojcik-Andrews, Ian. *Children's Films: History, Ideology, Pedagogy, Theory*. New York: Garland, 2000.

....

CHAPTER 15

CRAFT AND PLAY IN LOTTE REINIGER'S FAIRY-TALE FILMS

....

CAROLINE RUDDELL

DESPITE the fact that Lotte Reiniger's films are animated and often based on fairy tales, they are usually not, perhaps surprisingly, associated explicitly with children. This chapter seeks to interrogate the relationship, or lack of one, between Reiniger and children's culture in a number of key areas. First, because Reiniger is perhaps best known for her animated films based on fairy tales, the chapter will position her alongside, or within, a long-held societal and cultural association between fairy tales and children. Second, even though animation is wide-ranging and multifaceted, it is often, like fairy tale, aligned with children's culture. As Amy Ratelle notes, "On a broad scale, animation has been historically devalued and dismissed as 'kids' stuff."[1] Third, the trade press often portrayed Reiniger herself as a childlike figure, as well as—ironically and paradoxically—a maternal presence. As I have argued elsewhere, in a book chapter co-authored with Katharina Boeckenhoff, much of the writing about Reiniger (in the trade press and in scholarly works) "suggest[s] she has magicked these films out of nowhere,...links her with children's culture; and finally...characteris[es]...her as maternal and unthreatening."[2]

I seek to move beyond these arguments to consider Reiniger and children's films in relation to notions of craft and play. As such, the chapter is organized into three sections exploring respectively animation, fairy tale, and play. The concept of craft provides the overall framework to the discussion. What sets Reiniger's work apart from most other animation associated with children (such as the many examples of computer-animated television) is her method—silhouette animation; her characters are silhouetted paper cut-outs, a form of stop-motion animation. This method is time-consuming and distinctly "crafty." Ewan Kirkland, in writing about the TV series, *Charlie and Lola* (2005–2008), aligns paper cut-out animation with children's culture, and argues that the collage aesthetic, even when achieved through computer-generated animation, "faithfully reproduces the design of the book series on which the [*Charlie and Lola*] franchise is based, while more broadly exploiting animation's proximities to sequential art, picture books and other visual culture aimed at children."[3] Craft and play, then, are self-evidently also associated with children's culture in some cases, and will provide a lens through which to examine the relationship between Reiniger's films and/as children's culture.

REINIGER AND METHOD: SILHOUETTE CUT-OUT ANIMATION AND CHILDREN'S CULTURE

Ratelle argues that the eighteenth century saw a sea change in terms of publishing for children, who for the first time were being valued as a separate audience from adults.[4] Indeed, published books of fairy tales would have been part of this movement, which saw that the "emergence of children's literature as a vehicle for cultural values tied household economic advancement to Locke's ideals of social advancement through education."[5] In an increasingly commercial context, then, education combines with economic progress in a potentially "win-win" situation. As Ratelle goes on to argue, children's media at large, including animation, can be seen as an extension of this eighteenth-century move toward children's literature as a "delicate balance between education and entertainment."[6] It is interesting to place Reiniger within such debates and contexts. Famously difficult to contextualize,[7] Reiniger clearly does not fit into animation that is mass produced for a young audience, and she is hard to contextualize in many other ways as well (such as in relation to the Weimar Republic, German expressionism, and the like).[8]

For the purposes of this chapter, it is important to acknowledge that Reiniger's method of production does align her with children's culture, but also *doesn't*, and this is because of the technique she uses. Silhouette cut-outs made by hand can never be produced on a mass scale because of the time needed to create them; hence the two techniques used to create animation in the mainstream studio settings have been, traditionally, cel animation, later followed by computer-generated imagery and digital processes. Reiniger's animation method, then, warrants further interrogation because it cannot, in most ways, be situated alongside mass-produced children's culture (which, as Ratelle, drawing on Paul Wells, notes, is problematically derided for being "loud, often obnoxious, poorly written and frivolous").[9] Although there are many deeply problematic implications in critiques that have called Reiniger's work "frivolous," she certainly does not fit the other descriptions; she creates work that is often described as "pretty" (equally problematic), never "loud" or "obnoxious."[10] Instead, her work is meticulous and cannot be replicated in a large-scale industrial setting.

As several scholars have noted, "children's films" cannot be defined solely through textual strategies.[11] Noel Brown argues that to understand children's films, it is also important to consider contexts and paratexts, and suggests that there are at least five contextual processes that allow for defining children's films.[12] These are (a) the ways films are marketed and the distribution materials/strategies used; (b) censorship and suitability ratings; (c) critical reception; (d) merchandising; and (e) exhibition strategies, which might, for example, include children's matinees. These five processes all feed into how we might understand, or be encouraged to receive, a film as a children's film. Brown also suggests that these categorizations are just as relevant to television, noting that television shows aimed at a younger audience are shown in the child-friendly mornings or afternoons, rather than at supposedly "adult-only" times.[13] For Brown, the generic identity of the children's film "is not just a matter of what appears on screen. It is subject to broader, largely uncoordinated processes of negotiation" between bodies such as review boards, producers, audiences, and critics, as well as merchandisers and exhibitors.[14]

This is important to acknowledge, because one of the reasons it is hard to locate Reiniger in discussions of "children's film/culture" is that those contexts, paratexts, and processes of negotiation don't necessarily apply. For example, Reiniger's films were not accompanied by the large-studio practice of merchandising. It may also be the case that those wider contexts or paratexts are less accessible to us now. In the case of *Die Abenteuer des Prinzen Achmed*, archival research on its critical reception in the trade press (one of Brown's processes that does relate to Reiniger's output) when the film was first released in Germany suggests it was not necessarily received as a children's film; the initial screenings seemed to have been attended by a more adult "arts" crowd, of which Reiniger was very much a part.[15] In the twenty-first century, our lack of knowledge about how children did or do relate to Reiniger's films is compounded by the fact that most people who engage with them in a contemporary context are adults, cineastes, or scholars, as I will explore. The films are arguably even more distant from children now than when they were produced.

It is also worth noting that, according to Michael Cowan, silhouette methods had long been associated with portraiture, before photography became ubiquitous.[16] He argues that "the era of photography did not so much suppress the silhouette as it marginalized it, forcing it to migrate into less 'serious' domains, particularly that of children's illustration."[17] That is, the silhouette method migrated from the "serious" work of capturing likeness in portraiture to the much "less serious" world of children's culture, notably fairy tale. Such associations, which predate any later links with fairy tale, demonstrate the precariousness of such interconnections; associations are led by industrial and commercial practices rather than by intrinsic qualities that automatically entwine with certain demographics. The silhouette method and increasing links with children's culture and fairy tale can be considered a precursor to animation's becoming associated at large with children with the advent of mass media and, in particular, television.

It is possible to chart the process by which animation became associated with children's culture in the United States through developments in the moving-image industries, both cinema and television. Undeniably, Disney targeted a child or family audience, but some of the animation in the United States provided more adult content; Felix the Cat, for example, engaged in all sorts of "adult" behaviours, such as drinking and going to clubs.[18] With the legal action that resulted in the removal of exhibi-tion chains to the industry's oligopoly and the dismantling of the vertically integrated system, practices such as block booking (which had been integral to the survival of the animated short) began to wane.[19] Television became a lucrative medium, and children were clearly the target audience for much of the animation it produced, historically and now. This can be linked to Brown's argument about the wider context of the different processes that position children's media—with the development of mass media, across film and television, lucrative markets reveal themselves in the children's demographic. This is related not just to the films and television shows, but also to practices like mer-chandising.[20] Of course, we cannot contextualize Reiniger in such ways. Although her works were shown on television and—in the case of *Aladdin and the Magic Lamp* (1954) and *The Magic Horse* (1954)—sometimes commissioned for US television, she has never been associated with mass-produced children's television programming. Her commissioned television work also includes advertisements, which Tashi Petter refers to as "useful" films,[21] suggesting that they were made with commercial interests in mind. Her more personal projects were produced outside the mainstream studio context, which is not uncommon among animators, who very often work across different sectors and industry contexts. How, then, is Lotte Reiniger aligned with children's culture in terms of her animation method, if indeed she is at all?

Much of the academic literature on animation that explores its association with children focuses on television, and understandably so, given the amount of animated children's television on offer, and though Reiniger's work was shown on television, as noted, it is never considered in the field of television studies. Brown provides a useful critical framework for children's cinema to provide a broad definition of children's films and their modes of address. Noting that there are always exceptions to the rule, he argues that the children's film generally avoids "unsuitable" topics, such as sex or drug abuse; features a sympathetic protagonist; has an easy-to-follow narrative; and has clear moral binaries, where good always wins out in the end.[22] Ultimately, he says, children's films uphold social norms.[23] Given that many of Reiniger's films are fairy tales, many of Brown's arguments apply, because most fairy tales famously aim to condition chil-dren into understanding their place in the social world. Brown also makes the point that children's films often aim to appeal to as wide an audience as possible; this could also be said of Reiniger's work, given that fairy tales have wide appeal[24]

Rachel Moseley also provides some useful frameworks based on her work on stop-motion animation of the 1960s and 1970s, in which she looks at production companies such as Smallfilms (a small British animation studio). Moseley argues that the anima-tion studies literature has largely ignored stop-motion that does not meet these criteria: "[there is] an address to an adult audience; the perception that it is 'international,' avant-garde or, at least, art; [and it is distributed] as film."[25] She makes the point that compared to animated children's television generally, stop-motion of the kind she interrogates is doubly ignored, neglected in both television studies and animation studies. For Moseley, then, animation made for children has not been considered "important" enough to merit scholarly attention. Noting that stop-motion animation for children is associated with the terms "lightness," the "playful," and the perhaps even more loaded term "whimsy,"[26] Moseley suggests that these connotations are "indicative of the lack of attention paid to children's television in general histories of television and perhaps also of the perception of this particular form of pre-school television as simple and self-apparent in its meaning and address."[27]

Once again, it is difficult to place Reiniger alongside Moseley's examples of stop-motion animation because, as noted, her work does not fit neatly alongside standard preschool children's programming. It is also worth noting that her works are referred to as "films." Perhaps more poignantly, it is also the case that her work is far closer to what Moseley loosely describes as "art" than are such stop-motion examples as *The Clangers* television series (1969–1974; 2015–). Thus, Moseley's assertion that the kinds of stop-motion that have attracted critical attention are "'international,' avant-garde, or, at least, art" applies to Reiniger in multiple ways. The concept of what constitutes "art" is a thorny issue, but in fact her work is often shown in museums, as in the permanent exhibition in Tübingen.[28] It is also the case, and again, I have argued this elsewhere, that although we can't really categorize her work distinctly as avant-garde, there are elements of 1920s avant-garde animation in *Die Abenteuer des Prinzen Achmed* (see Bettina Kümmerling-Meibauer, this volume, for more discussion), which is often, somewhat problematically, attributed to some of her collaborators.[29] As a German national and someone who produced animation in multiple locales throughout her career (notably, across Europe), she is also "international" in terms of Moseley's categorizations. Once again, we can see that Reiniger is difficult to categorize; in this instance, she falls between an "artistic," innovative use of stop-motion methods and popular narrative storytelling. She also cannot be contextualized in the ways that both television studies and animation studies have tended to categorize and discuss either children's programming or stop-motion methods.

If it is difficult to contextualize Reiniger in relation to these histories of stop-motion animation and children's culture, it is important to consider why and how her work skirts around the edges of children's culture. Here, we can turn to the notion of play, which has been undertheorized in animation studies (though Chris Pallant provides very useful thoughts on the notion of play in relation to video games, which, of course, as he points out, are examples of animation). Identifying the similarities between play in a playground, where children move within a particular bounded space (e.g., a fenced-off section of the playground), and animated play, which moves within the boundary of the frame, Pallant writes that this

> highlights an important tension between the potential freedoms afforded by play/animation and the regulation imposed by the playground/frame (perhaps a narrative framework, or principles of verisimilitude, or the physical limits of space itself if projection mapping is the type of animation employed).[30]

I turn to aesthetics in more detail below, but first it is important to consider the thematic use of play in Reiniger's work, which would broadly come under Pallant's "narrative framework."

The notion of play is captured thematically in *The Grasshopper and the Ant* (1954), which opens with a butterfly, followed by a dragonfly, and then more butterflies, flitting among flowers at the peak of summer. This idyllic scene is set to music, played by Grasshopper, and the impression is that the insects are dancing to the tune: the butterflies fly in synchronized patterns, and then the frogs on lily pads start to dance to the music too. Woodland creatures join in, and then everyone is dancing to Grasshopper's tune (Figure 15.1). The joyful scene is interrupted by the severely cut (with scissors, not editing) Ant, who ignores the festivities in favour of collecting food for the winter. What then plays out is pertinent for a number of reasons. Firstly, the film plays as a moral tale for children, as is common in the fairy tale narrative. Grasshopper plays his fiddle all summer, and come winter nearly dies because he has not collected any food. Ant, in her cosy home full of food, turns Grasshopper away when he asks for help, thinking him foolish for not preparing for winter properly. When Ant is lonely and seeking company, Grasshopper, now recovered thanks to the kindness of the woodland animals, invites her in and plays the fiddle for her.

The moral of the story, then, is that we need to balance work and play: too much play and we will not thrive, too much work and we will become detached and isolated. A further moral of the story is to be kind to others, which is demonstrated by a number of the woodland creatures, including Grasshopper, who overlooks Ant's former unkindness

FIGURE 15.1. Woodland creatures dance joyfully to the grasshopper's tune in *The Grasshopper and the Ant* (1954, Primrose Productions). Frame-grab.

and welcomes her in. Reiniger's version differs in its tone and message (as well as style) from the 1930s Disney adaptation, *The Grasshopper and the Ants* (Wilfred Jackson, 1934). Disney's grasshopper, also does not prepare for the winter; instead, he happily plays his fiddle while an army of ants work hard gathering food. But in the Disney version, when the grasshopper needs food and shelter, the ants take pity on him and feed him. The grasshopper is ashamed and learns the lesson that hard work is required in order to thrive, and although he plays music for the ants, the film very much comes down on the side of the ants' industriousness (possibly reflecting its 1930s New Deal Depression-era social context) rather than the grasshopper's self-indulgent play.

Reiniger's adaptation of *The Grasshopper and the Ant* is also interesting because it demonstrates her love of music (the movement in her animation often likened to dancing and ballet). In archives, it is possible to find some of her preproduction drawings that render her characters "in motion," as if they are dancing. The marks on the pages form circular movements with notes making them appear like choreographed movements, which indeed they are. The notion of play is also thematized in this film, and indeed, we can consider play to be fundamental to the moral storytelling that is common to the fairy tale; it is often the case in fairy tales that "straying from the path," in whatever form that may take, is akin to allowing too much play and pleasure into one's life. To further explore the association (or lack thereof) between Reiniger's work and children's culture, it is necessary to further explore the notion of fairy tale.

Fairy-Tale Films

As noted earlier, Reiniger's work is often associated with the fairy tale, due, in large part, to the fact that her feature-length film, *Die Abenteuer des Prinzen Achmed*, is based on the Middle Eastern tale *The Thousand and One Nights*, or *Arabian Nights*, and that she is also well known for her short fairy tale films, most of which were produced in the mid-1950s (with some exceptions) and released on DVD by the British Film Institute in 2009. It is well documented that fairy tales have long been associated with children's culture. As Andrew Teverson points out with respect to the fairy tale as an emerging literary genre, they were often "used in the moral education and 'socialisation' of children."[31] And while it would be straightforward to analyse Reiniger's fairy-tale films in light of their moral instruction (as I have done in the *Grasshopper and Ant* example), it is potentially more useful here to consider her fairy-tale films from a different angle, and one that is entirely to do with the fact that they are animated. Here we turn to the concept of *metamorphosis* because it is fundamental both to animation and to fairy tales. Lucy Fraser's extended study of the fairy tale and pleasure argues that transformation is key to understanding fairy tale in multifaceted ways:

Transformation is the magic that is built into the fairy tale, which is also known as the "wonder tale." Magic regularly manifests itself in events of metamorphosis, impossible changes in form, as when a fantastical creature such as a mermaid gains human legs or morphs into an air spirit. Transformation also structures the fairy tale genre, in which the fairy tale morphs constantly into new shapes but remains somehow recognizable.[32]

For Fraser, metamorphosis is crucial to understanding the fairy tale (and its pleasures) because fairy tales morph across time and borders, and also, as a matter of convention, feature characters and objects that magically and marvellously change form through the genre or mode's "tendency to replicate and mutate."[33] Writing about *Prinzen Achmed*, Rachel Palfreyman argues that it

> does not set out to overturn the patriarchal premises of the traditional fairy tale. Not part of the feminist or Marxist revision of the genre, it is a tale in which a handsome prince goes off on an amazing odyssey, spies upon a fairy princess skinny-dipping in an exotic lake, and the tale ends with not one, but two princesses rescued into marriage.[34]

Palfreyman's article outlines some key ideas about Reiniger's output and reception, full discussion of which is beyond the scope of this chapter. But it is worth noting that, though it is clear that Reiniger does not subvert the patriarchal ideology of so many fairy tales, Palfreyman acknowledges that she does have much to offer feminists, largely in what she calls a "celebration of transformation and metamorphosis."[35] This raises two important questions: first, because metamorphosis is considered key to an under-standing of animation, what is the relationship between fairy tale, metamorphosis, and animation?[36] Second, what does this relationship contribute to our understanding of the interplay of Reiniger's films and play?

In discussing the ability of animation to engage space differently from live-ac-tion, because we can see "in between" the frames, Aylish Wood argues, "The sus-tained metamorphoses of resolving transitions, the dimensional play, and space which defies abstraction variously reveal the versatility of animation to depict spaces where possibilities have not yet fully subsided."[37] This opening up of spaces of possibility could equally be applied to the narrative spaces of fairy tales, where, because of their fantastical nature, the possibilities also "have not yet fully subsided." In *The Golden Goose* (1944), for example, the young hero of the story, Dummling, meets an old man in the forest with magical abilities. Because Dummling is kind to the old man and offers him bread and water (unlike his older brothers who selfishly refuse him), the old man bestows on him several gifts, perceiving that he has a "good heart." First, he will turn the water into wine; second, he will turn the bread into a roast chicken; lastly, he tells the young man that if he cuts down an old tree in the forest, he will find a great gift at the root. Then the jug begins to wobble and shake and is transformed into a bottle of wine. The bread walks, flips over, and becomes a roast chicken.

The sequence shows how metamorphosis works in terms of the production method, the animation, and the space that fairy tale gives to the transformation of objects and things. The animation—specifically the use of the paper cut-outs—allows for metamorphosis in exactly the way that Wood describes: we can see in-between the frames. It is also the case that the slightly "jerky" movement of the stop-motion allows us to perceive how each frame morphs into the next. When Dummling cuts down the tree, a number of magical rings begin emanating from the tree, and then a golden goose rises from the roots, in that familiar stop-motion movement that lacks the fluidity of other techniques. This lack of fluidity allows us to see the transition from frame to frame, and this metamorphosis is doubled by the magical appearance of the goose with golden feathers.

Similarly, in *Aladdin and the Magic Lamp* (1954), when Aladdin rubs the lamp, we see a bright circle of light appear as the genie emerges from the lamp. The use of the magical light here and in *The Golden Goose* acts as a signpost telling the audience that a magical transformation is about to take place. The genie is rendered in what looks like paint instead of as a paper cut-out, and he gradually fills the space by bubbling and smudging into the form of the genie. Because of the different method (paint as opposed to paper) there is a distinct contrast in the scene between the genie and Aladdin: the genie has no solid edges and is constantly shifting and morphing, while the paper cut-out Aladdin retains his hard edges. The genie is also pale against the black silhouette of Aladdin. The sequence highlights Wood's argument that metamorphosis acts in a variety of ways depending on the method of animation used, and in this instance the metamorphosis is doubled by the magical transformation of empty space into the genie. In this sense, these films fit Wood's "view of space as not easily defined, and which may even remain obscure."[38]

This doubled use of metamorphosis—made possible by the combination of animation and fairy-tale conventions—begs the question of what this contributes to an understanding of how her films sit alongside both children's culture and the concept of play (play not necessarily being simplistically aligned with children's culture, but also applicable to adults). Palfreyman's assertion that Reiniger's "fairy tale narratives combine to develop a conceptual engagement with life and death, subject and shadow, flatness and depth, shifting shapes and metamorphosing bodies" potentially allows for thinking of Reiniger's films as containing more adult themes.[39] Yet this would be to oversimplify the distinction between what appeals to adults and what appeals to children. The argument that aligns animation with children's culture does not allow for the fact that there is much crossover in what appeals to children and what appeals to adults, and this is particularly evident in Reiniger's output. As Kirkland argues, "Pleasure in magic, or its representation on the screen, is not exclusive to child audiences."[40] Metamorphosizing bodies and transformative objects appeal to a wide range of audiences, albeit possibly in different ways.

Ewan Kirkland has suggested that "children and the child-like have historically functioned as a means whereby adults negotiate discomforting aspects of modern life, culture and art in the age of mechanical reproduction."[41] The enduring appeal of magic is showcased in Reiniger's films in relation to transformation (which is replicated in children's imaginative play), and if we take Kirkland's point, is likely to appeal to both children and adults. Magical transformation is also reminiscent of the idea that objects might have power, being what Jane Bennett describes as "stuff that commands attention as vital and alive in its own right, as an existant in excess of its reference to human flaws or projects."[42] Magical transformation in the examples discussed here evokes both the childlike and play and the idea that things might possess "thing power: the curious ability of inanimate things to animate, to act, to produce effects dramatic and subtle."[43] Bennett's discussion of "thing power" is useful in that it allows for seeing the doubling effect of metamorphoses, where the animation of some "thing" is happening at the level of Reiniger and her paper and card, and where, at the thematic and narrative level, inanimate objects possess the power to "produce effects."

Play and Craft

Reiniger used scissors to make her cut-outs or silhouettes, which, if we follow Kirkland's argument, is associated with craft activities that are popular with children. Craft-based activities are a major component of toys and activities marketed to children. What's more, the very concept of craft, or aesthetics that prioritize a "handmade" look, often informs and underpins animation regardless of how it was produced, whether with scissors and paper, digitally, or otherwise.

I have noted throughout this chapter that there is no easy way to situate Reiniger in traditional contexts of what is perceived as children's culture, even though much of her work is both fairy tale and animation. Kirkland points out that "notwithstanding the demonstrable popularity of animation with adults, the form has persistent associations with child audiences."[44] What complicates an association between Reiniger's work and children's culture are the many ways she cannot be contextualized, as pointed out by Palfreyman in 2011. Although she uses popular narrative storytelling in the form of fairy tales, we can also detect avant-garde elements in her work. It is also important to acknowledge that in order to see Reiniger's work in a public space, it usually means encountering her films in a museum or at a film screening, neither of which is necessarily at a children's venue. For example, in the event run by *Fantasy/Animation* in October 2019 where *Die Abenteuer des Prinzen Achmed* was screened for a paying audience at the Cinema Museum in London, the late-evening timeslot, Q&A, and venue all suggest a more grown-up audience.[45] Palfreyman notes that Reiniger's work is shown in a variety of festival contexts and at special screenings targeting both adult and child audiences.[46] Given Reiniger's likely multifaceted appeal, then, it is useful to consider the content of her films in relation to a further consideration of play, notably in terms of aesthetics; regardless of the actual demographic that might find pleasure in her films, the concept of play allows for further interrogating her films in terms of both the method of production and thematic content.

Kirkland argues that the (imaginary) figure of the child, and childhood, embodies a number of ambiguities as well as problematic notions of nostalgia:

The imaginary figure of the child comes to embody many contradictions, anxieties and hopes of the very era which brought it into being. The child functions to articulate adult dislocation from modernity, and anxiety about the speed of social, cultural and technological change.[47]

Kirkland is discussing the fictional child depicted in television or film, as in *Charlie and Lola*, to name one. However, his arguments also apply to the concept of play in interesting ways. Indulging in play (and for adults play is seen as an indulgence) can allow that "dislocation from modernity" and distance from the kinds of anxieties that Kirkland notes. The concept of the child or childhood is a complex but useful framework for considering how Reiniger's films intersect with play and, by extension, craft. If Reiniger's films offer viewers some form of escapism, it may be in those fairy tales that revert to stories long known, told and retold throughout generations; but it may also have to do with their crafted nature. As many have noted, watching/seeing/viewing crafted items invokes a haptic quality, encouraging us to imagine what it would feel like to craft those things ourselves. In museums showing Reiniger's work, it is not uncommon to find a space where visitors can make their own silhouette cut-outs, as is in the permanent collection of her work at Tübingen museum. This is another example of her appeal to both children and adults.

The "perceived lack" of realism in stop-motion movement, according to Moseley, needs to be reframed "in favour of an 'aesthetics of child's play,' through which we understand the slight hesitancy and unevenness of the movement created as commensurate and 'realistic' with the movement of the small object in the hand of the child at play."[48] It is interesting to map such an "aesthetics of child's play" on to Reiniger's work. To do that, it is necessary to think of the stop-motion object (whatever it might be) as a toy. This is easier to do with 3-D animated objects than with those like Reiniger's that are flat and 2-D. It is quite straightforward, for example, to think of Bagpuss or the knitted Clangers as objects that could easily translate from stop-motion animated movement to being played with in a child's hand. This is less easy to do Reiniger's flat, 2-D silhouettes, in part, because of their fragility, which one senses when watching the films. Michael Cowan terms her work "ornamental," and her use of paper and card objects are less easy to imagine as playthings than something closer to a soft toy, such as the Clangers.[49] What the paper does insinuate are craft-making and scissor play. An example is Reiniger's 1922 adaptation of *Cinderella*.

The film's title page, framed within a clearly scissor-cut border, introduces the story of Cinderella and explains that the tale will be "told by a pair of scissors on a screen." Scissors then appear, moving, apparently, with a life of their own, and are followed by a pair of hands (presumably Reiniger's), which proceed to cut a figure out of paper or card at a higher frame rate that speeds up the process. The introduction thus supports Moseley's assertions: instead of imagining the stop-motion animated puppet or object in the hand of the child, we might imagine the scissors in our own hands, attempting to cut-out these figures as Reiniger does. The film also self-consciously references its crafted method of production, as the subtitles frequently state "snip!" before revealing narrative development. Reiniger's work foregrounds a crafted aesthetic, made explicit through the very material of the films themselves.

Here we can return to Moseley's "aesthetics of child's play," which, for Moseley, encapsulates both the specifics of the movement of stop-motion animation, but also how this movement could translate into the movement of the toy as played with by a child. The delicacy of the paper lends it a "weightlessness," according to Cowan, who cites Reiniger on the matter: "The puppets lay flat on the surface. They are missing that centre of gravity which gives the marionette such a charming unreality...But in exchange, they are masters of this surface, and there is no limit to their delicate mobility."[50] For Cowan, this weightlessness is explained by a lack of gravity and "laws of mechanics," which are a direct result of two-dimensional space where all figures appear flat.[51] For Reiniger, the material of paper allows for a "delicate mobility." The weightlessness associated with the flat 2-D paper images is emphasized in sequences where characters or animals fly through the air. A good example is the magical horse in *Die Abenteuer des Prinzen Achmed*, who takes to the skies with Achmed on his back, and Achmed is for some time unable to work out how to make the horse descend. The figure on the horse soaring through the sky embodies the lack of gravity associated with the flat 2-D paper or card images. Similarly, in *Aladdin and the Magic Lamp*, the genie's magic lifts Aladdin out of the cave as if he were as light as a feather.

It is possible to consider Reiniger as falling between camps in relation to this "aesthetics of child's play": on the one hand, her use of stop-motion fulfils Moseley's conceptualization, creating that jerky movement lacking in fluidity. On the other hand, that movement is not quite so straightforward with Reiniger's use of paper and card. Lacking 3-D "substance," it is less easy to imagine them as toys being played with. It is much easier to think of them on a flat surface being crafted.

Conclusion

It is possible to see Reiniger's fairy-tale films as part of the tradition of silhouette cutouts that were increasingly aligned with children's culture. As Cowan argues:

> If the silhouette appeared as such an appropriate genre for these illustrated children's stories, this was precisely on account of its newfound status as a medium opposed to the documentary medium of photography: that of a "naïve" art whose flatness holds the illusionism of three-dimensional representation at bay.[52]

Despite the silhouette's long association with portraiture, its perceived "naivety" and flatness positions it as a useful medium for children's storytelling, and, as Cowan rightly asserts, this is the result of industrial and contextual shifts in production rather than any intrinsic quality to the silhouette form. For Reiniger, though, her work is not usually explicitly discussed in relation to children's culture, and this is due to the fact that very often she falls between several camps; the works I have considered here are based on popular narrative storytelling in the form of fairy tale, and she uses animated methods, both long associated with children's culture. Yet she is an international artist; her work is distributed as film. Her use of animation is stop-motion rather than the more usual forms of mass-produced children's culture, and she cannot be contextualized in the traditional ways that both animation studies and television studies have placed stop-motion. Play informs her work both thematically and aesthetically. Play in relation to fairy-tale moral narratives feature in her work, but we can also turn to Moseley's "aesthetics of child's play," which allows us to see that though Reiniger's work does indeed embody that jerky stop-motion movement, it is less easy to translate this into imagining her silhouette cut-outs as toys in a child's hand. As ever, Reiniger cannot be easily categorized or contextualized.

Finally, it is also worth noting that this chapter continues to problematize notions of what constitutes children's culture and how these conceptions are realised. As Kirkland notes:

> Certain narrative aspects undoubtably recur throughout histories of children's media, such as fairy stories, talking animals and alternative worlds. Animation also seems to be fairly consistently associated with children, evident in film, television and digital media. But to connect these recurring qualities with some innate aspect of children's, in contrast to adults', pleasures disregards the extent to which those tastes have been shaped by adult-informed institutions.[53]

Reiniger reminds us quite clearly that there is no easy way to distinguish between what might appeal to children and what adults find pleasure in; the metamorphoses and transformations so prominent in her fairy tale works dissolve such boundaries.

NOTES

1. Amy Ratelle, "Animation and/as Children's Entertainment," in Nichola Dobson, Annabelle Honess Roe, Amy Ratelle, and Caroline Ruddell (eds.), *The Animation Studies Reader* (London: Bloomsbury, 2019), pp. 191–202, at 191.
2. Katharina Boeckenhoff and Caroline Ruddell, "Lotte Reiniger: The Crafty Animator and Cultural Value," in Caroline Ruddell and Paul Ward (eds.), *The Crafty Animator: Handmade, Craft-Based Animation and Cultural Value* (Cham, Switzerland: Palgrave Macmillan, 2019), pp. 75–98, at 92–93.
3. Ewan Kirkland, "Handmade Aesthetics in Animation for Adults and Children," in Ruddell and Ward, *The Crafty Animator*, pp. 127–156, at 133.
4. Ratelle, "Animation and/as Children's Entertainment," pp. 192–193.
5. Ibid., p. 193.
6. Ibid.
7. See Caroline Ruddell, "Contextualising Lotte Reiniger's Fantasy Fairy Tales," in Christopher Holliday and Alexander Sergeant (eds.), *Fantasy/Animation: Connections between Media, Mediums and Genres* (London: Routledge, 2018), pp. 109–125. See also Rachel Palfreyman, "Life and Death in the Shadows: Lotte Reiniger's *Die Abenteuer des Prinzen Achmed*," *German Life and Letters* 64:1 (January 2011), pp. 6–18.

Ratelle, "Animation and/as Children's Entertainment," p. 191.

8. See Palfreyman, "Life and Death in the Shadows."
9. Ratelle, "Animation and/as Children's Entertainment," p. 191.
10. Boeckenhoff and Ruddell, "Lotte Reiniger."
11. See, for instance, Ewan Kirkland, *Children's Media and Modernity: Film, Television and Digital Games* (Bern: Peter Lang, 2017); and Noel Brown, *The Children's Film: Genre, Nation, and Narrative* (New York: Columbia University Press, 2017).
12. Brown, *Children's Film*, p. 5.
13. Ibid., p. 10.
14. Ibid.
15. Boeckenhoff and Ruddell, "Lotte Reiniger."
16. Michael Cowan, "The Ambivalence of Ornament: Silhouette Advertisements in Print and Film in Early Twentieth-Century Germany," *Art History* 36:4 (2013), pp. 784–809.
17. Cowan, "Ambivalence of Ornament," pp. 793–794.
18. Ratelle, "Animation and/as Children's Entertainment," p. 193.
19. Jason Mittell, "The Great Saturday Morning Exile: Scheduling Cartoons on Television's Periphery in the 1960s," in Cecile Stabile and M. Harrison (eds.), *Prime Time Animation: Television Animation and American Culture* (New York: Routledge, 2003), pp. 33–54.
20. Brown, *Children's Film*.
21. Tashi Petter, "Sponsored Silhouettes: Lotte Reiniger's 'Useful' Films in Britain," in Malcolm Cook and Kirsten Moana Thompson (eds.), *Animation and Advertising* (Cham: Switzerland: Palgrave Macmillan, 2019), pp. 73–88.
22. Brown, *Children's Film*, pp. 11–15.
23. Ibid., p. 19.
24. Ibid., pp. 20–24.
25. Rachel Moseley, *Hand-Made Television: Stop-Frame Animation for Children in Britain, 1961–74* (Basingstoke, UK: Palgrave Macmillan, 2016), p. 13.
26. Moseley, *Hand-Made Television*, p. 4.
27. Ibid., p. 9.
28. Boeckenhoff and Ruddell, "Lotte Reiniger."
29. Ruddell, "Contextualising Lotte Reiniger's Fantasy Fairy Tales."
30. Chris Pallant, "Video Games and Animation," in Nichola Dobson, Annabelle Honess Roe, Amy Ratelle, and Caroline Ruddell (eds), *The Animation Studies Reader* (London: Bloomsbury, 2019), pp. 203–214, at 205.
31. Andrew Teverson, *Fairy Tale: The New Critical Idiom* (London: Routledge, 2013), p. 59.
32. Lucy Fraser, *The Pleasures of Metamorphosis: Japanese and English Fairy-Tale Transformations of The Little Mermaid* (Detroit, MI: Wayne State University Press, 2017), p. 4.
33. Fraser, *Pleasures of Metamorphosis*, p. 4.
34. Palfreyman, "Life and Death in the Shadows," p. 10.
35. Ibid., p. 15.
36. See Aylish Wood, "Re-Animating Space," *animation: an interdisciplinary journal* 1:2 (2006), pp. 133–152, at 150.
37. Wood, "Re-Animating Space," p. 150.
38. Ibid., p. 147.
39. Palfreyman, "Life and Death in the Shadows," p. 18.
40. Kirkland, *Children's Media and Modernity*, p. 20.

41. Ewan Kirkland, "Handmade Aesthetics in Animation for Adults and Children," in Ruddell and Ward, *The Crafty Animator*, 127–156, at 131.
42. Jane Bennett, "The Force of Things: Steps towards an Ecology of Matter," *Political Theory* 32:3 (June 2004), pp. 347–372, at 360.
43. Bennett, "Force of Things," p. 351.
44. Kirkland, "Handmade Aesthetics in Animation," p. 129.
45. See *Fantasy/Animation* at http://www.fantasy-animation.org, run by Christopher Holliday and Alexander Sergeant.
46. Palfreyman, "Life and Death in the Shadows," p. 7.
47. Kirkland, *Children's Media and Modernity*.
48. Moseley, *Hand-Made Television*, p. 14.
49. Cowan, "Ambivalence of Ornament."
50. Lotte Reiniger, cited in Cowan, "Ambivalence of Ornament," p. 790.
51. Ibid.
52. Ibid., p. 796.
53. Kirkland, *Children's Media and Modernity*, p. 21.

BIBLIOGRAPHY

Boeckenhoff, Katharina, and Caroline Ruddell. "Lotte Reiniger: The Crafty Animator and Cultural Value." In Caroline Ruddell and Paul Ward (eds.), *The Crafty Animator: Handmade, Craft-Based Animation and Cultural Value*. Cham, Switzerland: Palgrave Macmillan, 2019, pp. 75–98.

Brown, Noel. *The Children's Film: Genre, Nation and Narrative*. New York: Columbia University Press, 2017.

Cowan, Michael. "The Ambivalence of Ornament: Silhouette Advertisements in Print and Film in Early Twentieth-Century Germany." *Art History* 36:4 (2013), pp. 784–809.

Kirkland, Ewan. "Handmade Aesthetics in Animation for Adults and Children." In Caroline Ruddell and Paul Ward (eds.), *The Crafty Animator: Handmade, Craft-Based Animation and Cultural Value*. Cham: Switzerland: Palgrave Macmillan, 2019, pp. 127–156.

Kirkland, Ewan. *Children's Media and Modernity: Film, Television and Digital Games*. Bern: Peter Lang, 2017.

Moseley, Rachel. *Hand-Made Television: Stop-Frame Animation for Children in Britain, 1961–74*. Hampshire: Palgrave Macmillan, 2016.

Palfreyman, Rachel. "Life and Death in the Shadows: Lotte Reiniger's *Die Abenteuer des Prinzen Achmed*." *German Life and Letters* 64:1 (January 2011), pp. 6–18.

Petter, Tashi. "Sponsored Silhouettes: Lotte Reiniger's 'Useful' Films in Britain." In Malcolm Cook and Kirsten Moana Thompson (eds.), *Animation and Advertising*. Cham: Switzerland: Palgrave Macmillan, 2019, pp. 73–88.

Ratelle, Amy. "Animation and/as Children's Entertainment." In Nichola Dobson, Annabelle Honess Roe, Amy Ratelle, and Caroline Ruddell (eds.), *The Animation Studies Reader*. London: Bloomsbury, 2019, pp. 191–202.

Ruddell, Caroline. "Contextualising Lotte Reiniger's Fantasy Fairy Tales." In Christopher Holliday and Alexander Sergeant (eds.), *Fantasy/Animation: Connections between Media, Mediums and Genres*. London: Routledge, 2018, pp. 109–125.

Andrew Teverson. *Fairy Tale: The New Critical Idiom* (London: Routledge, 2013.

CHAPTER 16

....

DISNEY'S MUSICAL
LANDSCAPES

....

DANIEL BATCHELDER

THE animated world is one of boundless possibilities. Characters, objects, and scenery alike may be effortlessly bestowed with the gift of vibrant life. Gravity may serve as a mere suggestion rather than a law, as may all other properties of a world that is limited only by its creators' imaginations. More often than not, music saturates the animated world, functioning as a cog that is seamlessly, often inseparably integrated into the colourful on-screen action. Yet because of animation music's deep entrenchment into the very fabric of its visual surroundings, scholarly approaches and the attendant vocabulary used to analyse music in live-action films frequently fall short of doing justice to its unique positioning.[1]

This chapter traces the early development of music-image relationships in the animated films of the Walt Disney Studio. Disney was not the first studio to incorporate sound into animated productions, but it was arguably the first to perfect the technological logistics of sound synchronization in animated film. Yet as Disney refined these practical exigencies, its early short films increasingly mobilized music to create innovative diegetic spaces, thereby exploring the aesthetic potential of music in animation. I argue that Disney's earliest sound films present a utopic, idealized vision of the world that blurs the boundaries between images and sounds. As the studio moved from cartoon shorts to animated features, it progressively pursued this style of synaesthetic presentation, providing prewar audiences with immersive escapist spaces. By the time of its nearly disastrous collapse into bankruptcy in 1942, Disney had established itself as the world's premiere animation studio. It had also made tremendous strides in forming and exploring a new mode of dramatic presentation: the animated musical.

It is somewhat anachronistic to label the films under investigation in this study—namely, the cartoon shorts and animated features that collectively constitute Disney's so-called "Golden Age," which lasted from *Steamboat Willie* (Ub Iwerks, 1928) through *Bambi* (David Hand et al., 1942)—as "children's films."[2] Disney's feature films, especially, have historically drawn viewers from across age demographics.[3] More specifically,

Depression- and prewar-era animated shorts and features provided audiences of all ages an escapist respite from the harsh realities of life, a fact vividly demonstrated by the climax of Preston Sturges's *Sullivan's Travels* (1941).[4] Yet the enduring appeal of these films to young viewers cannot be denied. Thus, though this chapter does not address children or the broader strokes of children's film per se, the attractiveness of Disney's fantastical musical landscapes to young eyes and ears remains pertinent throughout.

MICKEY MOUSING IN THEORY

To a student of film music, the notion of audiovisual alignment in Disney animation will inevitably conjure up the term *mickey mousing*. Because definitions vary somewhat in scope from source to source, I will immediately cast a wide net by describing mickey mousing as *discrete instances of precise synchronization between diegetic action and a nondiegetic musical sound source*. I shall also refer to isolated instances of audiovisual synchronization as "hits" in accordance with traditional film music parlance. Mickey mousing thus may consist of a single hit—for example, a single staccato chord that accompanies an on-screen smack across the face—or a series of hits, as in a descending scale that mirrors the footsteps of a character walking down a flight of stairs. Deliberately open-ended and unstable, these designations acknowledge the ultimately subjective limits of what can constitute "synchronicity," a "diegesis," and even what counts as "music." The following phenomenologically informed reading, however, embraces such ambiguity because it allows us to explore these limits with abandon.

In discussions of live-action film music, scholars frequently cast mickey mousing in derogatory terms, perceiving the effect as superfluous, cheapening, or just plain silly. "Apart from its essential redundancy," writes Mervyn Cooke, "catching the action at every available opportunity presents a serious impediment to continuity."[5] The term seems to have been coined as a slur of sorts, reportedly first used by David O. Selznick to describe the "hyperexplicit, moment-by-moment musical illustration" that was a key feature of Max Steiner's scores.[6] Steiner's overreliance on the technique came to be considered in his lifetime an affected tic, and Hollywood composers quickly agreed that mickey mousing in live-action film was undesirable for dramatic moments, except to achieve specific, often comedic, effects.[7]

Whence this anxiety over precise audiovisual synchronization? Kathryn Kalinak's insightful commentary on the supposed value of the technique merits quoting at length:

> To the modern listener, mickey mousing may seem excessively obvious and even distracting, but ironically it was a practice founded in the very principle of inaudibility. The vocal track in classical cinema anchors diegetic sound to the image by synchronizing it, masking the actual source of sonic production, the speakers, and fostering the illusion that the diegesis itself produces the sound. Mickey mousing duplicates these conventions in terms of nondiegetic sound. Precisely synchronizing

diegetic action to its musical accompaniment masks the actual source of sonic production, the offscreen orchestra, and renders the emanation of music natural and
consequently inaudible. Musical accompaniment was thus positioned to effect perception, especially on the semiconscious level, without disrupting narrative credibility. Mickey mousing, like other elements of the classic score, was harnessed to the
narrative, catching an action to solidify its importance.[8]

Kalinak suggests that mickey mousing's tight alignment of score and film allowed the
audiences of early talkies to cross the tacitly understood phenomenal barrier between
the two, situating the orchestral hits as organic extensions of the on-screen action. Yet
in the context of classical Hollywood film-scoring style, a sonic gesture that falls outside
the underlying score's musical continuity can be jarring. Ironically, overly precise synchronization in this context *reveals* the artificiality of the nondiegetic sound source (that
is, the orchestra) rather than masking it.

This perceived violation relates to a deeper anxiety about the expected place of music
in a filmic space. "The classical narrative sound film," Claudia Gorbman posits, "has
been constituted in such a way that the spectator does not normally (consciously) hear
the film score."[9] In the traditional Hollywood film, music comments continuously on
the diegetic events, most commonly amplifying dramatic shifts by contributing affectively appropriate soundscapes, but moviegoers typically expect the score to play
a submissive, ancillary role to the visuals and dialogue. Mickey mousing thus allows
nondiegetic music to undesirably permeate the film's diegesis, thus ruining the illusion
of reality being presented on-screen.

Furthermore, apprehension regarding mickey mousing in classical cinema may be
linked to ambivalence as to whether tightly synchronized sounds are proper music.
Broadly speaking, a recognition of musicality—that is, determining what does and
does not "count" as music—relies in part on the audience's ability to perceive the apparent source of a sound as a familiar musical instrument with the attendant qualities
of timbre, pitch, articulation, duration, and so on. Although some instances of mickey
mousing meet these criteria, in a filmic context, the resulting sounds do not appear to
be motivated by the rhetoric of phrasing, tonality, meter, or any of the other compositional parameters that typically inform music. The musical logic of mickey mousing instead finds explicit motivation from *visual* stimuli, even though the audience knows that
the performing musicians do not exist in the on-screen diegesis. In this sense, mickey
mousing overlaps with, but is nonetheless distinct from, sound effects. To this end,
mickey moused sound effectively occupies a nebulous space between music and noise,
and the resulting cognitive dissonance similarly destroys the live-action film's diegetic
illusion.

Viewers thus perceive mickey mousing as a violation of cinematic reality on at least
two fronts. The technique both calls attention to its nondiegetic sound source and is
motivated by non-musical impetuses, thereby losing its sense of identity as "proper"
music. But what of an animated film, whose entire on-screen universe is fabricated from
pen and ink and contains no possibility of organically occurring sound?

MICKEY MOUSING IN PRACTICE

Disney's *Steamboat Willie* was not, as some sources indicate, the first sound cartoon.[10] It was, however, the first animated work to feature a fully integrated and fully synchronized soundtrack, complete with continuous music, sound effects, and a sort of mumbled, not-quite-intelligible dialogue. To ensure proper synchronization, Walt Disney, director Ubbe "Ub" Iwerks, and Wilfred Jackson, an animator with some musical training, developed a system that allowed the advance planning of visual and sonic events with a high degree of precision. Once *Steamboat Willie*'s creators had agreed on the film's gag-based storyline and corresponding sounds, Jackson used a metronome to convert the film's frame rate, soon to be standardized at twenty-four frames per second, into a steady musical pulse. The team then mapped the score, a medley of popular tunes, on to what is known as a bar sheet, or lead sheet, a chart that "paired each measure of [Jackson's loosely notated] music with a description of the corresponding screen action."[11] This side-by-side graphic representation helped to align visible and musical gestures, but Disney and Jackson also worked closely to ensure extreme precision by preparing exposure sheets—"frame-by-frame instructions for the cameraman"—that indicated exactly where moments of audiovisual alignment would occur and synchronized each musical beat within 1/24 of a second accuracy.[12] After the studio shot the film, a small orchestra followed superimposed animated footage of a bouncing ball to record the score at a predetermined tempo directly on to the film using Patrick Powers's Cinephone sound-on-film system. The resulting cartoon was something of a marvel—a flashy, noisy testament to human and technological ingenuity. "By using the bar sheet," historian Michael Barrier summarizes, "Disney had made possible an airtight fit between music and animation."[13]

Because of this precise pre-planning of music and images, *Steamboat Willie* presents an animated world in which *everything*—from the characters and props to scenery that bounces and sways—moves in time to a constant stream of steadily paced music. In the film's opening scene, for instance, an establishing shot of the steamboat against laterally panning background footage reveals a waving flag, a spinning paddlewheel, and two large smokestacks that alternatively compress and expand as they emit rings of smoke (Figure 16.1). Iwerks animated each of these moving parts in small, repeating cycles of varying duration. Each cycle in turn directly aligns with even subdivisions of the cheery rendition of Bert and Frank Leighton's song, "Steamboat Bill," played by the small ensemble recorded on the soundtrack. A rasping sound accompanies the jolly smokestacks, audibly punctuating the orchestra's tempo with a steady quarter note pulse. Sheer technical necessity inextricably links the physical and musical gestures, and all the sounds fit squarely within the omnipresent music's fixed pulse.

These tight connections between score and image have not escaped scholarly attention. *Steamboat Willie*, writes Daniel Goldmark, "overflows with synchronized movements, both obvious and subtle...the animation is not just supported by the music,

FIGURE 16.1. The opening shot of *Steamboat Willie* (Disney, 1928). Frame-grab.

then, but is entirely interdependent with the soundtrack."[14] A constant barrage of clever synch points obstinately insists upon the close alignment of the sonic and the visual gestures, each one "catching an action to solidify its importance," as Kalinak notes.[15] Yet the film seamlessly weaves these relentless audiovisual hits into the fabric of constant music governed by a prevailing pulse. The short also gives what would normally be thought of as unmusical sound effects, such as the rasping smokestacks, an unusually high level of musicality, which owes to their precise location within the score's pulse. Moreover, every visible gesture appears to be motivated by an audible rhythmic impetus.

The Disney studio's approach to audiovisual synchronization in *Steamboat Willie* draws a clear and immediate distinction with the problematic experience of mickey mousing described above. The classic Hollywood model of live-action film scoring typically condemned music to a subservient, supplemental role in a film; now Disney's organization of all sounds according to a prevailing pulse effectively flaunts animation's artificiality by collapsing this hierarchy of perception.[16] The relentless visible affirmations of what would normally be considered background music close the phenomenological distance between sound and image, thereby making mickey mousing's off-screen sonic reinforcements of individual on-screen gestures part of a dance-like continuum rather than jarring exceptions.

The medium of animation itself also informed the aesthetic ramifications of Disney's bar sheet system. Cartoons created long before—and, for that matter, long after—*Steamboat Willie* often exploited their flexible diegeses for comic effect, as witnessed in the oft-used sight gag wherein a character reaches his or her hand *just* off-screen to produce an unexpected object. In *Steamboat Willie*, the persistent, symbiotic affirmation of sonic and visible gestures similarly flaunts the cartoon's impossible audiovisual space, affording sounds both with and without an apparent visual source a phenomenological equivalence that markedly breaks with classical Hollywood sound-design traditions. So, while Kalinak asserts that mickey mousing in live-action film transfers the "illusion that the diegesis itself produces the sound" onto nondiegetic sound, animation's ability to complicate the boundaries between these two categories essentially flattens the distinctions between diegetic and nondiegetic sound that have been hotly debated in film music studies for decades.[17]

As such, while it is possible to refer meaningfully to cartoon sounds, images, characters, and so on, belonging or not belonging to a diegesis—which Gorbman usefully describes as "the narratively implied spatiotemporal world of the actions and characters"—the limits of diegetic space in animation extend far beyond those in a live-action film.[18] More to the point, these early sound cartoons demonstrate the possibility of music being simultaneously diegetic and nondiegetic. Because of their continuous, mickey moused reinforcement by visual cues, sound shorts like *Steamboat Willie* effectively locate their scores within what Robynn Stilwell terms the "fantastical gap," the ambiguous perceptual space that film music occupies when it procedurally transmogrifies between clearly set diegetic/nondiegetic poles.[19] Far more conspicuous than mere underscoring, yet often lacking the logical justification typically afforded to on-screen musicking, Disney's early scores exist in a liminal space between the diegetic and the nondiegetic, foreground and background.

Furthermore, the close, constant connection between music, sound, and movement in these early shorts also works to neutralize mickey mousing's abovementioned crisis of musicality. A bizarre but pertinent example: in an early *Steamboat Willie* scene, antagonist Peg-Leg Pete bites into a piece of chewing tobacco. As he shakes his head to tear the chaw loose, a percussive rattling effect confined within exactly three beats of the backing orchestral scoring sounds. Pete chews audibly eight times, and each chomp falls precisely on a half-beat. He looks to the left and to the right (one beat each) to see if anyone is watching before parting his lips (one beat) as his front teeth split apart (one beat) and he spits through the gap. A slide whistle mimics the spit's downward trajectory (one and one-half beats) before Pete's teeth clack shut (one-half beat). As Pete repeats the process, wind blows his second putrid tobacco wad backwards, where it hits a bell behind his head. The resulting clang marks a major cadential point in the music that has been accompanying the scene all along. The film's constant audible and visual reinforcement of this steady pulse provides a sort of justification for the placement of sound effects—both those supplied by traditional musical instruments (e.g., the slide whistle and bell) and by non-traditional instruments (e.g., the rattling and chewing sounds)—thereby blurring distinctions between music, sound, and noise.

The unique sound-image paradigm that resulted from what was initially a pragmatic solution to a practical problem also provided Disney with new ways to pursue the comedy that audiences expected from pre-feature animated shorts. At a memorable point in *Steamboat Willie*, a goat eats a copy of the sheet music for "Turkey in the Straw." Mickey then turns the goat into a phonograph, its tail serving as a crank, and the song emanates from the creature's mouth. The mischievous mouse proceeds to play along with the tune, using a number of on-board objects and creatures as instruments: pots and pans, a cat, a duck, suckling pigs, and a cow's teeth. Here, the animated medium's ability to transform and redirect sounding bodies allows typically non-musical objects, like a cow's teeth, to serve double duty as a musical instrument—that is, a xylophone. What's more, this connection constructs a sort of timbral analogy between the perceived actions required to carry out the displayed gesture (hitting a cow's hard teeth with mallets) and the physicality required to produce the attendant sound (light, terse, percussive strokes of the xylophone keys). Such audiovisual puns, extremely common in Disney's shorts, flagrantly permit the invisible recorded orchestra on the soundtrack to assert its presence in the cartoonal diegesis. In a verbal pun, Jeff Smith explains, "two frames of reference are connected by a principle of aural similarity,"; however, in *Steamboat Willie*, these audiovisual puns communicate humour by comically riffing on the audience's bisociative perception of sound and image as a synchronized whole.[20] Clearly, this novel approach to film scoring allowed Disney's early cartoons to explore equally novel dramatic possibilities: new ways of telling a story, of allowing characters to interact with one another in space and time, and of making audiences laugh.

Utopic Spaces

Following the popular success of *Steamboat Willie* and the reliability of the bar sheet system, the Disney studio continued to make synchronized sound cartoons starring Mickey Mouse. These early shorts contain little to no plot per se; rather, they unfold as a series of slapstick gags and on-screen performances of everything from burlesque stripteases to Rachmaninoff preludes. The studio's reliance on exposure sheets meant that music was a necessary component of the planning process: Disney's gag meetings took place in a so-called music room that came equipped with a piano, demonstrating the close early collaboration between the studio's animators and composers.[21]

In 1929, the year after *Steamboat Willie* was released, Disney and Iwerks joined forces with the composer Carl Stalling to develop a second series of cartoon shorts that ran parallel to the Mickeys. Beginning with *The Skeleton Dance*, the *Silly Symphony* series represented an even more concentrated exploration of the expressive and comedic potential of synchronizing animation to continuous music.[22] In these balletic shorts, musical rhetoric motivates actions all the more directly: not only with pulse as in the Mickeys, but also with meter, form, melodic contour, and the like. Individual choreographic actions in *The Skeleton Dance*, for instance, tend to take shape in even four- and eight-bar phrase lengths—all of which, of course, match the music perfectly. At one point, a chorus line of four dancing skeletons performs an eight-bar vaudevillian dance routine heading to the right of the screen before repeating the same routine to the left. The combined result is a complete visualization of the antecedent and consequent phrases of the sixteen-bar periodic musical structure that accompanies them. Here, even more so than in *Steamboat Willie*, music structures the limitless possibilities of the animated world. "The early Silly Symphonies [1929–1939] and Mickey Mouse cartoons," writes Lea Jacobs in her thorough study of mickey mousing in Disney's early animation, "should be considered synchronization experiments. They explore and showcase the possibilities the technology opened up through their precise and inventive matches of sound and image."[23]

Although these cartoons often contain embedded performance spaces, the registral shifts required to enter into these spaces are so slight as to be negligible. Due to their organization of on-screen events based on the repetitive and predictable structures of musical rhetoric, the constant potential for musicking essentially renders the entirety of each film as a performance of sorts. In these shorts, claims Michel Chion, "we see a cartoon creature sing and make music with anything, hitting this or blowing on that. The whole world becomes a wind, string, or percussion instrument creating a jazzy music that sets everyone and everything to dancing."[24] What results can be described as an idealized space in which harmonious sound replaces disruptive noises, and all the action is informed by music's apparently logical structures of tonality, even tempi, phraseology, and the like.

The fantastical, hypermusical spaces in Disney's early sound cartoons are evidence of Richard Dyer's famous assertion that entertainment provides audiences with escapist projections of utopianism. Products of mass entertainment, he maintains, provide images of abundance, energy, and community that serve to counteract the real-world issues of scarcity, exhaustion, and isolation. Dyer especially sees this tendency in classic Hollywood musicals that "try to dissolve the distinction between narrative and numbers, thus implying that the world of the narrative is also (already) utopian."[25] This description easily applies to Disney's early shorts, wherein the constant musical affirmation of physical gestures significantly softens the boundaries between plot and performance in an absorbing synthesis. In these films, cause-and-effect linearity is to an extent usurped by continuous cycles of musical and gestural repetition with variation. As such, they provide ideal escapist fodder in no small part because they present viewers with a pleasing phenomenological alternative to the real-world experience of existing in linear time. Given their insistent location of music and movement within a whimsically unpredictable perceptual space, Disney's first sound cartoons represented an incredibly fertile mode of fantastical entertainment.

The phenomenon of interpreting of Disney's early cartoons as utopic spaces is not new. At the time of his death, influential director and film theorist Sergei Eisenstein left behind unpublished notes praising the studio's shorts. To Eisenstein, "the epos of Disney is 'Paradise Regained.' Precisely paradise. Unreachable on Earth. Created only by a drawing...Disney...is a complete return to a world of complete freedom...freed from the necessity of another primal extinction."[26] "Disney's films," he continues, "are a revolt against partitioning and legislating, against spiritual stagnation and greyness. But the revolt is lyrical. The revolt is a daydream."[27] For the Soviet director, Disney's early cartoons, with their freewheeling transformations of the recognizable world, served as appealing projections of a primordial, and therefore liberated, society.

In her path-breaking analysis in *The Oxford Handbook of the American Film Musical*, Susan Smith builds upon Eisenstein's vivid celebration to articulate the unique expressive properties of the music in Disney animation:

> [Eisenstein's] claims that Disney's cartoons convey a sense of 'Paradise Regained' gestures toward the animated film's capacity to offer a more satisfying sense of what that utopia would look like, not just feel like (as Dyer famously contended). The idea that an animistic impulse underpins the creative process of animation also seems absolutely crucial in understanding the special kind of utopian sensibility associated with [the animated musical].[28]

For Smith, the tendency in animation (especially early Disney animation) to generate a diegetic world that is apparently organically infused with music allows the animated film musical to stand as a distinct mode of creative expression.

Yet while the present analysis of sound cartoons as hypermusical utopias has, to this point, fallen neatly in line with Eisenstein's and especially Smith's readings, these latter two studies do not take into account the seismic aesthetic shifts that occurred during the first decade and a half of the Disney studio's history. As the 1930s progressed, the fantastical, plasmatic metamorphoses that Eisenstein had celebrated became increasingly unrepresentative of Disney's output. Over the course of the studio's Golden Age—a period of massive growth culminating in the production of five feature-length films between 1937 and 1942—Disney fixed its sights on a set of increasingly ambitious artistic and dramatic objectives. Coupled with an influx of new talent being added to the studio's personnel list, these ambitions reworked and diversified the way Disney approached the union of music and animated images.

New Developments

The Disney studio's success with integrated sound meant that, by the early 1930s, audiences expected all American cartoons to use sound to enhance the "trick" of animation.[29] By 1934, New York's Fleischer and Hollywood's MGM and Warner Bros. studios had all adopted the format of musical slapstick gags interspersed with phenomenal performances in their *Happy Harmonies* (1934–1938), *Betty Boop* (1930–1939), *Merrie*

Melodies (1931–1969), and *Looney Tunes* (1930–1969) series (note the derivative variations on the *Silly Symphonies* moniker). Disney had to discover new ways to delineate
its films from those of competing studios. One response to this dilemma came from
Disney's continued dedication to technological advancements. *Flowers and Trees* (Burt
Gillett, 1932), for instance, was the first-ever film produced in three-color Technicolor,
and by 1936, the studio had developed and patented the multiplane camera, which made
it possible to create an animated illusion of three-dimensional depth of field.[30]

Another response came in the form of a general change of focus in the studio's humour strategies. Instead of relying on animation's customary body morphing,
perspective-bending feats, Disney's shorts increasingly emphasized personality and
narrative. The studio imbued their anthropomorphic stars with appealing character
traits, and, as animation scholar Paul Wells puts it, Disney's cartoons began "deriving...
humour from the recognition of comic aspects within the human character."[31] Pluto,
Donald Duck, Goofy, and others became regulars in the Mickeys, balancing out the title
character's rather bland personality. These mechanical and stylistic changes were not
mere novelties; rather, they were signs of a fundamental shift in Disney's approach to the
medium of animation. No longer satisfied with frivolous, diverting cartoon shorts, the
studio embarked on a well-documented process of telling compelling stories with convincing, even life-like, characters.

Disney's animators began attending compulsory life-drawing classes at the nearby
Chouinard Art Institute, where they were under the supervision of instructor Donald
Graham. In a famous and often-cited 1935 memo to the artist, Walt Disney articulated
his views on the complex interactions between animation and reality:

> The first duty of the cartoon is not to picture or duplicate real action or things as they
> actually happen—but to give a caricature of life and action—to picture on the screen
> things that have run thru [*sic*] the imagination of the audience [or] to bring to life dream
> fantasies and imaginative fancies that we have all thought of during our lives... The
> point must be made clear to the men that our study of the actual is not so that we may
> be able to accomplish the actual, but so that we may have a basis upon which to go into
> the fantastic, the unreal, the imaginative—and yet to let it have a foundation of fact, in
> order that it may more richly possess sincerity and contact with the public.
>
> I definitely feel that we cannot do the fantastic things, based on the real, unless we
> first know the real.[32]

In Wells's view, this trend heralded a transition towards what would soon become the
studio's prevailing aesthetic sensibility. "With each technical development... Disney
moved farther from the plasmatic flexibility of many of the early *Silly Symphonies* and
coerced the animated form into a neo-realist practice."[33] Deftly avoiding the pitfalls of
ascribing the possibility of realism to animation, Wells appropriates Jean Baudrillard
and Umberto Eco to locate a quality of hyperrealism in "the kind of animation which
aspires to the creation of a realistic image system which echoes the 'realism' of live-action film."[34] Given the cartoon's obviously painted appearance and inclusion of magical

or otherwise impossible events, few would have mistaken even the studio's most life-like films for live-action photography. Yet throughout the 1930s, Disney productions increasingly avoided the loony, illogical free-for-all that defined other studios' cartoons and instead pursued a brand of fantasy that relied ever more heavily on generous doses of plausibility. Disney's Depression-era adjustments—the infusion of markedly human personalities, the addition of colour, the simulation of depth, and the convincing alignment of sound and animated image—may thus be understood as steps away from cartoonish zaniness and towards a prioritization of verisimilitude.

MUSICAL LANDSCAPES

Throughout the 1930s the exposure sheet system continued to be refined, allowing animators to mobilize gestures and sound effects increasingly independently from obvious subdivisions of the score's pulse. As Jacobs explains:

> Most of [Disney's] cartoons of the 1930s and later continued to 'match' music and movement in some way, even as other considerations such as conforming movement to the laws of physics and the creation of more rounded and palpable figures also became important to animators. That is, the filmmakers at Disney did not simply abandon musical rhythm as an organizing principle as they experimented with more complex and realistic movement but, rather, developed more subtle and varied methods for synchronizing the music and image tracks.[35]

In other words, the studio did not discard continuous mickey mousing, and in fact it became an ever-more sophisticated expressive tool. Yet Disney increasingly treated the device as a discrete dramatic mode rather than a consistent and necessary approach. The moments in Disney's later shorts and eventual feature films that rely on a paradigm of constant audiovisual synchronization largely align with the moments in which these films deviate the most from a sense of carefully constructed verisimilitude and lapse into a more fantastical and temporally non-linear form of storytelling.

While the Mickeys of the 1930s increasingly resembled live-action musical comedies by separating performance and plot, the *Silly Symphonies* largely continued to revel in the choreographic possibilities of constant audiovisual synchronization. The series generally retained its reliance on musical structures as governing principles, with through-scored and even through-sung features that remain determinedly performative from beginning to end. Yet even as they maintained the tight connections between audible and visual signs that audiences had come to expect from cartoon shorts, the *Silly Symphonies* gradually moved away from the cartoon-as-series-of-loosely-connected-gags model and began demonstrating greater dramatic cohesion by introducing simple plots and non-recurring characters. To be sure, MGM's *Happy Harmonies* and Warner Bros.' *Merrie Melodies* also tended to feature through-composed scores and basic plotlines featuring frequent musical performances. Yet both these series, with their satirical and mildly bawdy humour and regular inclusion of current popular songs, represented a rather coarser and more urban-centric approach to cartoon comedy than was found in the refined and often pastoral *Silly Symphonies*.[36] Although the animated movements in the *Silly Symphonies* films still tend to be strictly aligned to a prevailing musical pulse, these synchronicities appear more balletic than ever, and much of the later *Silly Symphonies*'s pleasure lies in the appreciation of choreographed gestures in service of a story told through music and dance.

The creative manpower the studio invested in the *Silly Symphonies* therefore yielded an unparalleled exploration of the expressive potential of mickey mousing. Studio composer Leigh Harline was particularly celebrated, as Barrier puts it, for his "ability to work on two levels, picking up details of the action while maintaining longer musical lines, [which] made for a richer score and a more cohesive film."[37] In Harline's first assignment, the through-sung biblical parable *Father Noah's Ark* (Wilfred Jackson, 1933),

> both music and action are divided into miniature movements, or acts; each of those units advances the story, but there is also an abundance of elaborate synchronization within each one. In the first few minutes of the cartoon, for example, Noah's family and the animals carry out the construction of the ark to a theme adapted from the first of Beethoven's contredanses.[38]

Even this relatively early project demonstrates far more nuanced and sophisticated connections between sound and image than were found in the studio's previous experiments. Following several short gag scenes of Noah's family assembling their menagerie and stockpiling the ark—all in perfect step to the orchestral scoring, of course—the inevitable rain begins to fall from the heavens. Here, Harline's score, mirroring the characters' panicked rush to the ark, shifts from its earlier F major joviality (which transposes its Beethovenian source up a perfect fourth) to a new *minore* section in the parallel minor characterized by four-bar melodic figures that feature a terse, repeating sixteenth-sixteenth-eighth eighth-eighth pattern (a retrograde of the rhythm that opens the B section of Beethoven's contredanse).[39] As pairs of giraffes, elephants, alligators, and other animals scurry along, animated walk cycles of varying duration observe the different sizes of the animals' gaits: lion footsteps occur on quarter note beats; bears' paws hit the ground on eighth notes; and a pair of frogs hops in two-beat cycles and lands on the off-beats in a sort of visualized syncopation. Although the score's prevailing pulse still utopically motivates these movements, such subtleties draw the viewer's attention away somewhat from the behind-the-scenes practical process of the short's creation, erasing the animator's metaphorical fingerprints to reveal a relatively more lifelike representation of animal movement.

The creative possibilities for both large- and small-scale audiovisual synchronicities reached an apex in Harline's score for *The Old Mill* (Wilfred Jackson, 1937). After the credits have rolled over a robust G major introduction, an opening iris reveals bucolic scenes of woodland flora and fauna going about their hyperrealist daily lives as Harline introduces a pastoral melodic theme that begins in a 2/2 G major and then modulates, nineteen measures later, to a 6/8 A major as violas take over the lush melody (Figure 16.2).[40] This shift marks a seamless change from the film's opening multiplane camera pan into an intimate scene of two birds sharing a worm. The grand A theme covers four such episodes in total: the opening shot, the birds, a transitional sequence that depicts the business of sleeping bats in the mill's rafters (complete with mickey moused celesta hits as the nocturnal creatures open their eyes) and a concluding shot of closing water lilies accompanied by a cadential return of the primary musical theme.

What follows this shot, though, is decidedly different. In total silence, a frog emerges from a lake onto a lily pad and croaks tentatively, with a croaking sound effect that perfectly aligns with a four-note ascending scalar gesture played by a solo bassoon. This process repeats until a second frog "responds" both with a croak and with a new complementary melodic fragment that extends the initial four-note figure to six notes. The two frogs then croak in dialogue as the bassoon repeats its six-note gesture, until a third frog surprises its companions—and the audience—with its own call that simultaneously adds an additional two notes to the accompanying melody. After a final grand pause, the three frogs croak madly to one another as the score sounds the now-completed eight-note theme. Harline gives this theme variety by adding flutes and a gossamer filigree of celesta that represent chirping crickets and hovering

FIGURE 16.2. Hyperrealism in *The Old Mill* (Disney, 1937). Frame-grab.

fireflies.[41] Once again, the composer uses mimetic mickey mousing to achieve cohesive musical rhetoric.

A wordless women's chorus simulating a howling wind halts the comic proceedings and introduces the next section: a violent storm that threatens to destroy the mill and the animals that reside therein. In this thematically unstable portion of the score, fragmented melodic material jerks wildly through changing keys, meters, and shifts in orchestration. Yet these seemingly unpredictable vicissitudes are not random: many of them directly align with the dramatic action presented on-screen. Rapid *staccatissimo* xylophone and string hits provide the sound of the huge rain drops that rhythmically pelt the mill's roof, while terrifying cymbal crashes give voice to a loose shutter that violently bangs against its encasement in the wind. More broadly, the quick shifts in melodic material mirror, and are mirrored by, fast cuts between shots of the storm and shots of the havoc it threatens to wreak. These destabilizing manoeuvres independently work to build tension, and their tight alignment heightens the dramatic effect. When the storm finally passes, a series of chromatic gestures transition Harline's score back to its opening theme, as peace is restored at the mill.[42]

Although the foregoing description may appear pedantic, it illustrates the extreme care with which the Disney studio crafted immersive diegetic spaces governed by music. Small-scale audiovisual hits still occur in *The Old Mill*, but the music and action also cohere on a larger scale. The cartoon's meagre plot delineates significant events with clearly noticeable thematic shifts in the score, giving the short a prevailing dramatic structure that sets the scene, establishes an expository state of affairs, deviates from this status quo (first with a shift in tone, and then with the threat of chaos), and then returns to the sense of normalcy constructed in the exposition.

Returning now to our initial description of mickey mousing—instances in which diegetic action is synchronized with a nondiegetic musical sound source—we see that Disney's shorts elaborated this relatively simple and initially practical technique into a tool that carried enormous expressive and dramatic potential. Unlike the rupture of cinematic illusion caused by mickey mousing in live-action films, the through-scored comedy in the *Silly Symphony* series in fact allowed the constant close communication between on- and off-screen elements to enhance, in ever more sophisticated ways, the appearance of a consistent diegesis. Music in these cartoons takes on a semantic value that is instantaneously decoded, and thus enforced, by visual gags. Whereas the omnipresence of music in Disney's early sound shorts had the effect of flattening or erasing the distinctions between images and sound, the studio's later shorts demonstrated a sensitive collaboration between audible and visual impulses, resulting in a discursive paradigm in which music and images playfully interact with and react to one another with far greater dimension and agency than before. Given these constant and multivalent symbiotic affirmations of music and gesture, *Silly Symphonies* like *The Old Mill* still present spectators with the sights and sounds of a fantastical, utopic space in which all occurrences motivate and are motivated by coherent, euphonious music. In fact, one could argue that the marked verisimilitude of this short, with its hyperrealist depictions of animal appearance and behaviour, constitutes a *more* utopic space than Disney's earlier through-scored films: in this world, close audiovisual synchronization translates even relatively lifelike events into music in real time.

FEATURE ATTRACTIONS

From a strictly aesthetic viewpoint, it is unsurprising that Disney became the first major animation studio to venture into feature film productions. The vocabulary of comedic narratives it had developed in the *Mickey Mouse* shorts gave audiences the cartoonish antics they expected, while the *Silly Symphonies* explored artistic and dramatic procedures that added personal and critical interest to what would have otherwise been, in a theatrical feature, an exhausting ninety-minute series of gags. More specifically, the now-familiar sights and sounds of an entire diegetic world that seems to operate according to a music-driven unity became, for the studio, a natural point of entry into audience expectations of Hollywood musical comedies.[43]

The studio's balletic visualizations of musical rhetoric were clear predecessors to *Fantasia* (Ben Sharpsteen et al., 1940), whose mostly plotless segments read like extended *Sillies*, animated to complement extant symphonic literature.[44] Yet the influence of the studio's expressive, dramatic approaches to audiovisual synchronization are also woven into the studio's plotted features. As the Disney studio ventured into the production of feature-length animated films, it continued to deploy these utopic musical landscapes—only now it did so more strategically, as a tool to enhance the drama of much longer narratives. In her discussion of Disney's Golden Age features, Smith describes the new expressive possibilities that the medium of animation offered to the form of the film musical, offering that "Disney animated films...often contain songs that, while absolutely essential to the emotional fabric of their narrative worlds, wouldn't necessarily be considered musical numbers in the conventional sense."[45] I submit that this diegetic fluidity was, in large part, made possible by the studio's sophisticated approach to sound-image unification.

The opening twenty-five minutes of the studio's first feature, *Snow White and the Seven Dwarfs* (David Hand et al., 1937; music by Frank E. Churchill, Leigh Harline, and Paul J. Smith), favour rhyme, music, and song over straightforward dialogue and sound effects, privileging aestheticized modes of expression over directness.[46] Here, Disney mobilizes the heightened expressive potential of constant music that it had been exploring in its shorts, and it conspicuously frontloads this approach as if to declare a statement of purpose. At times, *Snow White* seems to insist on the novel possibilities of its artificial diegetic space, working against the studio's aspirations towards verisimilitude. About ten minutes into the film, after a terrifying flight through the forest, Snow White collapses, sobbing, in a clearing.[47] As the sun comes up, woodland animals begin to approach her at different paces that do not have any discernible rhythmic relationship to the score. The startled princess lets out an exclamation, and the animals scatter into hiding as the pace of the music suddenly quickens. The simulated camera cuts now fall on every downbeat, and the score begins to mickey mouse certain gestures as the animals pop their heads out of their hiding spots.[48] Snow White begins speaking to the animals, out of time with the score at first, but then in an increasingly recitational manner that slips into rhymed verse in a kind of spoken recitative. Spoken verse turns into coloratura vocalise as Snow White imitates a bird's song, and then finally begins to sing conventionally, as the musical number "With a Smile and a Song" begins in earnest.[49] This extremely gradual and subtle transition from mood-appropriate underscoring to full-fledged musical number demonstrates the Disney studio's continued reliance on audiovisual synchronization to delineate performance spaces. Just as mickey mousing violates the boundary between diegetic and nondiegetic music in a live-action film, so, too, does it blur the lines between "song" and "not-song" in these animated films.

Moreover, by allowing a character to engage in song, Disney explicitly mobilizes the animated medium's ability to transform and redirect sound through artificial sources. In the hyperrealist and hypermusical diegesis of *Snow White*'s opening scenes, the chirping of a forest bird provides a rhythmically and tonally conventional counter-melody to the singing of a human character, simultaneously recognizing and modifying real-world distinctions between seemingly random, natural birdsong and deliberately crafted human song (Figure 16.3). Singing allows Snow White to channel the music that appears

FIGURE 16.3. Snow White communes with nature through song (*Snow White and the Seven Dwarfs*, 1937). Frame-grab.

to govern everything around her, erasing the distinctions between her body and every other form in the surrounding diegesis. This exploitation of ontological equivalency helps to contextualize Snow White's predilection for communicating with the flocks of nonverbal forest creatures that constantly surround her, especially as she uses song to command the animals in "Whistle While You Work."

The use of music to construct utopic spaces the films of Disney's Golden Age reached a climax in *Bambi*, the film that also represents the height of the studio's hyperrealist aesthetic priorities. If several scenes in *Snow White* made ample use of the expressive potential of closely linked music and images, *Bambi* maintains this approach through the entirety of its ninety-minute running time. Frank Churchill and Ed Plumb's lush score provide even the slightest gestures with audible confirmations. The title character's first awkward steps, his comical attempts to ice-skate, the stags' leaping off a rock—all of these actions find relentless musical affirmations. As before, this approach to scoring allows music to participate in on-screen actions in a way that does not seem awkward or forced but, rather, creates an aestheticized space that sublimates all sonic and visual elements into a co-operative symbiotic totality.

As a musical, however, *Bambi* holds an extraordinarily unique profile. Although the film contains four distinct musical numbers, none of them are performed by on-screen characters. Instead, an unseen off-screen chorus delivers each song. While these voices obliquely comment upon the on-screen actions, there remains a clear phenomenological distance between the chorus and the visible characters. The song "Little April Shower," for instance, accompanies images of woodland creatures scurrying to avoid rainfall. Yet though the animals' footsteps fall in perfect subdivisions of the song's pulse, their mouths remain shut, denying viewers an apparent source of the audible voices. "The non-diegetic song that we hear on the soundtrack," writes Smith, "is thus not constructed as the *source* [original emphasis] of the music as such but instead as a reflection of a natural musicality that…is already inherent within the narrative and superior to its own."[50] If the songs in *Snow White* seemed to flow from the core of the musical diegesis via the singing characters, then *Bambi*'s delocalized songs appear to well up directly from the film's diegesis. And because *Bambi*'s hyperrealist forest setting demonstrates an inextricable connection to music, the songs that spontaneously arise from the film's continuous underscoring seem to represent the voice of nature itself.

This striking effect is compounded when one considers the other roles that the off-screen chorus plays in this film. Looking for Romance (I Bring You a Song) that accompanies Bambi and Faline's courtship, two solo voices suggest the interior monologues of the on-screen characters. The remainder of the chorus wordlessly adds "ooh" and "ah" syllables, accompanying the soloists but simultaneously serving another function indicated by the on-screen action. If the constant audiovisual alignment in earlier Disney films permitted a facile negotiation between speech and song, here the device also works to collapse the distance between music and sound. In the conductor's score to this section, the wordless chorus carries a marking that reads "ZEPHYR EFFECT," and indeed, this instruction corresponds to a shot of a breeze blowing through tall grass.[51] Such instances render the notion of music in *Bambi* as functioning as the voice of nature quite literally.

What's more, throughout the film Larry Morey's lyrics consistently work towards this conflation of music and nature. "Little April Shower" likens the sound of rain to "a tune," and both "Gay Little Spring Song" and "Looking for Romance" use the idea of song as a metaphor for love and sex. Finally, the Oscar-nominated "Love Is a Song" is a virtuosic juggling of references to music, life, and love, encapsulating and bookending all of the film's major themes:

> Love is a song that never ends
> Life may be swift and fleeting
> Hope may die yet love's beautiful music
> Comes each day like the dawn
> Love is a song that never ends
> One simple theme repeating
> Like the voice of a heavenly choir
> Love's sweet music flows on.

This relentless insistence on situating music as a part of nature carries broad dramatic implications. By weaving music into the fabric of a cohesive film world, *Bambi* places music on the same plane of reality as the characters and landscape that seem to be innately attuned to its sounds. The version of nature presented in this film effaces the boundaries that separate sound, image, and movement, resulting in a diegesis in which aesthetic concerns become synonymous with life itself. In this utopic space, the entire hermetically sealed universe can communicate through the legible and structurally predictable form of a popular song, with its familiar patterns of formal repetition and harmonic fulfilment. In drawing its audience's attention towards this engrossing alternate reality, Disney simultaneously draws the focus away from the materiality of the film. Though viewers may be aware that every colour, every gesture, and every sound represents the over-determined result of painstaking labour on behalf of the studio, *Bambi* counteracts this recognition by creating the absorptive illusion of an apparently organic universe ruled by art and aesthetics.[52]

The initial critical reception of *Bambi* provides a fitting close to this study. The film, which had been in delayed production for years, fell victim to poor timing when it was released mere months after the Japanese bombing of Pearl Harbor, the event that incited the United States to end its lengthy policy of isolation and enter into World War II. Critics reacted negatively to the sealed-off forest community depicted in *Bambi*, and several denounced the vilification of Man, the film's unseen but powerfully destructive antagonist.[53]

Yet as we have seen, *Bambi*'s strong escapist tendencies owed in no small part to the Disney studio's unique use of music. The studio's initially practical approach to sound-image synchronization had yielded a novel mode of entertainment, in which sonic and visual gestures seemed to link in a symbiotic relationship. The resulting films presented audiences with imaginative and absorptive diegetic worlds governed by the received logic of musical rhetoric. As Disney pursued increasingly ambitious projects, these fantastical audiovisual creations became powerful dramatic tools, giving voice to characters and even entire settings through the vivid register of song. Though in many ways this practice aligned Disney's Golden Age films with the escapist tendencies of their contemporary Hollywood productions, these utopic musical landscapes also stand as clear markers of a studio discovering the unique expressive potential of the animated musical.

Postscript: Musical Landscapes after the Golden Age

It is generally unwise to ignore the Disney studio's long and often thorny history by considering all of its films along a single set of critical or aesthetic guidelines. Still, though an investigation of how Disney's musical practices shifted in the decades since *Steamboat Willie* and *Snow White* lies far outside the scope of this chapter, it is possible to gesture towards the influence of the musical landscape paradigm Disney developed during its Golden Age on the studio's later productions. We have already witnessed, for instance, how Snow White's songs channel the innate musicality of her world, thereby allowing the character to manipulate her natural surroundings. The subtly magical event of a human character—almost always a female—communicating with animals or otherwise controlling nature in the space of a song has become one of the most persistent, and most parodied, tropes of "the Disney musical," writ large.[54] Human-animal duets became mainstays of Disney films in the post-war period: in *Cinderella* (Clyde Geronimi et al., 1950), the eponymous heroine sings with birds and mice; in *Sleeping Beauty* (Clyde Geronimi et al., 1959), she sings with forest creatures, trading coloratura vocalises with a songbird as Snow White did; and in both the animated and live-action portions of *Mary Poppins* (Robert Stevenson, 1964), she sings and whistles with birds.[55] The Disney self-parody *Enchanted* (Kevin Lima, 2007) lambasts this broad convention when princess Giselle summons pigeons, rats, and cockroaches to tidy a modern-day New York City apartment. In each of these instances, the girl-singing-with-nature device serves, in part, as evidence of the character's essential goodness: she is so pure and gentle that even animals know to trust her implicitly. Yet this device also suggests a supernatural connection with, and agency over, the natural world—which, in these filmic spaces, maintains intimate connections with music.

Although the device of humans directly engaging animals in song dwindled after Walt Disney's death, the studio maintained and even amplified the musical landscapes in later features, presenting *Bambi*-like symbiotic relationships between music and nature. Much of *Pocahontas* (Eric Goldberg and Mike Gabriel, 1995) powerfully recalls Eisenstein's writings on Disney as the film deploys music and images to evoke a Native American version of animism. Like *Bambi*'s "Love Is a Song," the climactic "Colours of the Wind" conflates music, images, and nature, urging the listener to synaesthetically "sing with all the voices of the mountains" and to "paint with all the colours of the wind." In *Tangled*

(Nathan Greno and Byron Howard, 2010), Rapunzel activates her magical hair through song, whereas the title character of *Moana* (Ron Clements and John Musker, 2016) sings to tame an angry volcano god. In *Frozen* (Chris Buck and Jennifer Lee, 2013), Elsa fabricates an ice palace and creates the anthropomorphic snowman Olaf, while she sings "Let It Go"—a song that, notably, contains the lines "I am one with the wind and sky" and "my power flurries through the air into the ground"—and in *Frozen II* (Chris Buck and Jennifer Lee, 2019), a disembodied voice causes Elsa to awaken elemental spirits.

Of course, these later examples are several steps and nearly a century removed from the pragmatic bar sheet system the studio devised for *Steamboat Willie*'s novel synchronization of sound and image. Yet the frequency with which Disney has returned to a magical, musical version of nature suggests that its Golden Age technical developments have had tremendous influence on the development of the studio's fundamental aesthetic principles. Now a firmly established form, the animated musical remains a formidable escapist tool, providing viewers of all ages with the stylized images and sounds of a world better than our own.

Notes

1. See Daniel Goldmark, *Tunes for 'Toons: Music and the Hollywood Cartoon* (Berkeley: University of California Press, 2007), p. 4.
2. Steven Watts, *The Magic Kingdom: Walt Disney and the American Way of Life* (Columbia: University of Missouri Press, 1997), p. 61.
3. For a particularly astute study of the effects of Disney media on children, see Nicholas Sammond, *Babes in Tomorrowland: Walt Disney and the Making of the American Child, 1930–1960* (Durham, NC: Duke University Press, 2006).
4. Donald Crafton, *Shadow of a Mouse: Performance, Belief, and World-Making in Animation* (Berkeley: University of California Press, 2013), pp. 242–246.
5. Mervyn Cooke, *A History of Film Music* (Cambridge, UK: Cambridge University Press, 2008), p. 86.
6. Claudia Gorbman, *Unheard Melodies: Narrative Film Music* (Bloomington: Indiana University Press, 1987), p. 88.
7. Cooke, *History of Film Music*, p. 86.
8. Kathryn Kalinak, *Settling the Score: Music and the Classical Hollywood Film* (Madison: University of Wisconsin Press, 1992), p. 86.
9. Gorbman, *Unheard Melodies*, p. 31.
10. Robert C. Sickels, "Steamboat Willie and the Seven Dwarves: The Disney Blueprint for Sound and Music in Animated Films," in Graeme Harper, Ruth Doughty, and Jochen Eisentraut (eds.), *Sound and Music in Film and Visual Media: An Overview* (New York: Continuum, 2009), pp. 602–611, at 602. For an accurate history of the first sound cartoons, see Daniel Goldmark, "Before *Willie*: Reconsidering Music and the Animated Cartoon of the 1920s," in Daniel Goldmark, Lawrence Kramer, and Richard Leppert (eds.), *Beyond the Soundtrack: Representing Music in Cinema* (Berkeley: University of California Press, 2007), pp. 225–245.
11. Michael Barrier, *Hollywood Cartoons: American Animation in Its Golden Age* (New York: Oxford University Press, 1999), p. 51.

12. Barrier, *Hollywood Cartoons*, p. 51.

13. Barrier, *Hollywood Cartoons*, p. 54. For detailed descriptions of this process, see Barrier, *Hollywood Cartoons*, pp. 48–57; Sickels, "Steamboat Willie and the Seven Dwarves," pp. 604–605; Thomas F. Cohen, "The Click Track: The Business of Time, Metronomes, Movie Scores and Mickey Mousing," in Harper, Doughty, and Eisentraut, *Sound and Music in Film*, pp. 105–106.

14. Daniel Goldmark, "Drawing a New Narrative for Cartoon Music" in David Neumeyer (ed.), *The Oxford Handbook of Film Music Studies* (New York: Oxford University Press, 2013), pp. 229–244, at 231. See also Susan Smith, "The Animated Film Musical," in Raymond Knapp, Mitchell Morris, and Stacy Wolf (eds.), *The Oxford Handbook of the American Musical* (New York: Oxford University Press, 2011), pp. 167–178, at 169.

15. Kalinak, *Settling the Score*, p. 86.

16. See Robynn Stilwell, "The Fantastical Gap between Diegetic and Nondiegetic," in Goldmark, Kramer, and Leppert, *Beyond the Soundtrack*, pp. 184–220, at 188–189.

17. Ibid.; Annahid Kassabian, "The End of Diegesis as We Know It?," in John Richardson, Claudia Gorbman, and Carol Vernallis (eds.), *The Oxford Handbook of New Audiovisual Aesthetics* (New York: Oxford University Press, 2013), pp. 89–106; David Neumeyer, "Source Music, Background Music, Fantasy and Reality in Early Sound Film," *College Music Symposium* 37 (1997), pp. 13–20; Jeff Smith, "Bridging the Gap: Reconsidering the Border between Diegetic and Nondiegetic Music," *Music and the Moving Image* 2:1 (2009), pp. 1–25; Ben Winters, "The Non-Diegetic Fallacy: Film, Music, and Narrative," *Music & Letters* 91:2 (2010), pp. 224–244; and Daniel Yacavone, "Spaces, Gaps, and Levels: From the Diegetic to the Aesthetic in Film Theory," *Music, Sound, and the Moving Image* 6:1 (2012), pp. 21–37.

18. Gorbman, *Unheard Melodies*, p. 21.

19. Stilwell, "Fantastical Gap," p. 187.

20. Jeff Smith, "Popular Songs and Comic Allusion in Contemporary Cinema," in Pamela Robertson Wojcik and Arthur Knight (eds.), *Soundtrack Available: Essays on Film and Popular Music* (Durham, NC: Duke University Press, 2001), pp. 407–432, at 416.

21. Barrier, *Hollywood Cartoons*, p. 60; Frank Thomas and Ollie Johnston, *The Illusion of Life: Disney Animation* (New York: Disney Editions, 1981), p. 80.

22. Mike Barrier, "An Interview with Carl Stalling," in Daniel Goldmark and Yuval Taylor (eds.), *The Cartoon Music Book* (Chicago: A Cappella Books, 2002), pp. 38–41.

23. Lea Jacobs, *Film Rhythm after Sound* (Berkeley: University of California Press, 2015), p. 65.

24. Michel Chion, *Film: A Sound Art*, trans. Claudia Gorbman (New York: Columbia University Press, 2009), p. 39.

25. Richard Dyer, *Only Entertainment*, 2nd ed. (New York: Routledge, 2002), p. 28.

26. Sergei Eisenstein in Jay Leyda (ed.), *Eisenstein On Disney*, trans. Alan Upchurch (Calcutta: Seagull Books, 1986), p. 3.

27. Ibid., p. 4.

28. Smith, "Animated Film Musical," p. 172.

29. Norman M. Klein, *7 Minutes: The Life and Death of the American Animated Cartoon* (New York: Verso, 1993), p. 18.

30. Barrier, *Hollywood Cartoons*, pp. 80, 249.

31. Paul Wells, *Understanding Animation* (London: Routledge, 1998), p. 129.

32. "Walt Disney Productions Inter-Office Communication to Don Graham from Walt Disney dated 23 December 1935," pp. 3–4. Reproduced on Michael Sporn Animation (*blog*), http://www.michaelspornanimation.com/splog/?p=618 [accessed April 29, 2020].

33. Wells, *Understanding Animation*, p. 23.
34. Ibid., p. 25.
35. Jacobs, *Film Rhythm after Sound*, p. 72.
36. Goldmark, *Tunes for 'Toons*, p. 17. The inclusion of popular songs is particularly prevalent in the cartoons produced by Warner Bros., whose pre-feature shorts were contractually obliged to plug tunes produced by the many Tin Pan Alley publishing houses that the studio owned.
37. Barrier, *Hollywood Cartoons*, p. 101.
38. Ibid., p. 101. The score also liberally quotes the spiritual "Who Built the Ark?"
39. This assumes a 4/4 time signature, at a tempo of approximately quarter note = 145 BPM.
40. Leigh Harline, *The Old Mill*, box 19, piece 3, pp. 1–3, University of Cincinnati Archives and Rare Books Library.
41. Harline, *Old Mill*, pp. 4–11.
42. Ibid., pp. 22–31.
43. See Rick Altman, *The American Film Musical* (Bloomington: Indiana University Press, 1987), pp. 90–128.
44. Indeed, the entire film grew around the *Sorcerer's Apprentice* sequence, which was originally conceived as a Silly Symphony. See Barrier, *Hollywood Cartoons*, pp. 242–244.
45. Smith, "Animated Film Musical," p. 168.
46. An extended version of the discussion of this film appears in Daniel Batchelder, "*Snow White* and the Seventh Art: Cultural Politics of the Animated Musical," *American Music* 39:2 (Summer 2021): 138–153.
47. Frank Churchill, Larry Morey, Leigh Harline, and Paul J. Smith, *Walt Disney's "Snow White and the Seven Dwarfs" Master Score* (Milwaukee: Hal Leonard Corporation, 2015), p. 30.
48. Churchill et al., *Walt Disney's "Snow White"*, p. 32.
49. Ibid., pp. 32–33.
50. Smith, "Animated Film Musical," pp. 168–169.
51. Frank Churchill and Ed Plumb, *Bambi* score (1942), Library of Congress item 168, Sequence 11.0, p. 2.
52. See Smith, "Animated Film Musical," p. 172.
53. David Whitley, *The Idea of Nature in Disney Animation* (Aldershot, UK: Ashgate, 2008), p. 74; Barrier, *Hollywood Cartoons*, p. 368.
54. See Ryan Bunch, "Soaring into Song: Youth and Yearning in the Animated Musicals of the Disney Renaissance," *American Music* 39:2 (Summer 2021): 182–195.
55. *The Jungle Book* (Wolfgang Reitherman, 1967) reverses this paradigm as various jungle animals, and eventually a human, attempt to influence Mowgli through song.

BIBLIOGRAPHY

Barrier, Michael. *Hollywood Cartoons: American Animation in Its Golden Age*. New York: Oxford University Press, 1999.

Batchelder, Daniel, ed. *American Music* 39, No. 2 (Summer 2021). "Special Issue on Music and Sound in Disney Media."

Crafton, Donald. *Shadow of a Mouse: Performance, Belief, and World-Making in Animation*. Berkeley: University of California Press, 2013.

Dyer, Richard. *Only Entertainment*. 2nd ed. New York: Routledge, 2002.

Eisenstein, Sergei. *Eisenstein on Disney*. Edited by Jay Leyda. Translated by Alan Upchurch. Calcutta: Seagull Books, 1986.

Goldmark, Daniel. "Before *Willie*: Reconsidering Music and the Animated Cartoon of the 1920s." In Lawrence Kramer and Richard Leppert (eds.), *Beyond the Soundtrack: Representing Music in Cinema*. Berkeley: University of California Press, 2007, pp. 225–245.

Goldmark, Daniel. *Tunes for 'Toons: Music and the Hollywood Cartoon*. Berkeley: University of California Press, 2007.

Goldmark, Daniel. and Yuval Taylor, eds. *The Cartoon Music Book*. Chicago: A Capella, 2002.

Gorbman, Claudia. *Unheard Melodies: Narrative Film Music*. Bloomington: Indiana University Press, 1987.

Jacobs, Lea. *Film Rhythm after Sound*. Berkeley: University of California Press, 2015.

Kalinak, Kathryn. *Settling the Score: Music and the Classical Hollywood Film*. Madison: University of Wisconsin Press, 1992.

Rodosthenous, George, ed. *The Disney Musical on Stage and Screen: Critical Approaches from "Snow White" to "Frozen."* London: Bloomsbury, 2017.

Smith, Susan. "The Animated Film Musical." In Raymond Knapp, Mitchell Morris, and Stacy Wolf (eds.), *The Oxford Handbook of the American Musical*. New York: Oxford University Press, 2011, pp. 167–178.

Stilwell, Robynn. "The Fantastical Gap Between Diegetic and Nondiegetic." In Daniel Goldmark, Lawrence Kramer, and Richard Leppert (eds.), *Beyond the Soundtrack: Representing Music in Cinema*. Berkeley: University of California Press, 2007, pp. 184–204.

Thomas, Frank, and Ollie Johnston. *The Illusion of Life: Disney Animation*. New York: Disney Editions, 1981.

Watts, Steven. *The Magic Kingdom: Walt Disney and the American Way of Life*. Columbia: University of Missouri Press, 1997.

Wells, Paul. *Animation and America*. New Brunswick, NJ: Rutgers University Press, 2002.

Wells, Paul. *Understanding Animation*. Abingdon: Routledge, 1998.

Whitley, David. *The Idea of Nature in Disney Animation*. Aldershot, UK: Ashgate, 2008.

CHAPTER 17

HAYLEY MILLS AND THE DISNEYFICATION OF CHILDHOOD

DAVID BUCKINGHAM

In the early 1960s, Hayley Mills was the most popular child star in the Western world. Though she is most remembered for her performances in six Disney movies, she also played leading roles in several British-made film dramas of the time. In this chapter, I will focus on Mills's first two British films and first two Disney releases, made during the same period. As I will show, these films raise several broader questions about the phenomenon of child stardom, and about the representation of childhood—and specifically of *girlhood*—during this period of impending social and cultural change.

THE MAKING OF A CHILD STAR

Hayley Mills was born in London on April 18, 1946. Her father was the prominent film actor Sir John Mills, and her mother was the writer Mary Hayley Bell. Hayley later appeared in several films alongside her father and in two written by her mother: *Whistle Down the Wind* (Bryan Forbes, 1961) and *Sky West and Crooked* (John Mills, 1965). She made her screen debut as a baby in her father's film *So Well Remembered* (Edward Dmytryk, 1947)—although some accounts suggest that her parents were not necessarily keen for her to pursue an acting career.

Mills was brought up on her parents' four-hundred-acre dairy farm in Sussex, though she attended a private boarding school for most of her childhood. One day, the director J. Lee Thompson was visiting her father to discuss his role as a police superintendent in Thompson's forthcoming thriller *Tiger Bay* (1959). The director noticed twelve-year-old Hayley playing in the garden, apparently spoofing television commercials. He was so impressed by her that he immediately decided to change the lead role in the film—that of a child who witnesses a murder—from a boy to girl: he apparently cast Hayley without a screen test. Released in 1959, the film was a great critical success. Hayley Mills won the British Academy Award (BAFTA) for Most Promising Newcomer to Film and an award at the Berlin Film Festival.

After *Tiger Bay*, Hayley went back to school. However, the film eventually brought her to the attention of Walt Disney. On a trip to London, Disney's wife, Lillian, saw the film more or less accidentally, while seeking shelter from the rain. Disney asked the film's distributor, Rank, to send him a print, but they refused. His wife was so insistent that Disney finally came over to London, where he met Hayley and her parents in the swanky Dorchester Hotel. At the time, Disney had been casting for his forthcoming film *Pollyanna* and had already tested 350 girls for the title role, without success; apparently, he was at the point of dropping the project. Shortly after meeting Mills, he signed her to a five-year contract, again without a screen test.

Pollyanna, released in 1960, was something of a sensation, not least because of Disney Studios' energetic pre-publicity. Amid a high-profile cast, Mills won very positive reviews, and was awarded a special miniature Juvenile Academy Award. It seems that her parents didn't tell her about this, however, and she wasn't there to collect it, having once again gone back to her strict boarding school. The award was presented by the leading child star of a previous generation, Shirley Temple, and collected on Hayley's behalf by a fellow Disney child actor, Annette Funicello.

Despite the critical acclaim, *Pollyanna* was not a major box-office success. Apparently Disney put the blame for this on the title, which he believed was a turn-off for male cinemagoers. However, Mills's second Disney film, the comedy *The Parent Trap* (David Swift, 1961), in which she played identical twin sisters, was far more popular: it has made more than $25 million at the box office to date, and spawned several sequels. Mills's performance of the song "Let's Get Together," written by Robert and Richard Sherman, was a top-ten chart hit and led to an album.

Walt Disney took a close personal interest in Mills's career and became friendly with her family: she later described how she was "looked after . . . like a cherished daughter" at Disney.[1] Yet Hayley Mills was also a leading earner for the studio. During this period, she regularly appeared on lists of the most popular female screen actors on both sides of the Atlantic. In 1961, she was the most popular star overall at the US box office. Mills was on the receiving end of a tidal wave of fan adoration: she reportedly received between 6,000 and 7,000 letters and gifts every week. Evidence from her recent public appearances, and from extensive video tributes and comments on YouTube, suggests that this fandom continues today—albeit, of course, with a strong element of nostalgia.

After *The Parent Trap*, Mills continued to appear in Disney films, but she also had a parallel career in British films, often made with her parents. A year after *Pollyanna*, she played the lead role in a version of her mother's novel *Whistle Down the Wind*. In 1964, she co-starred with her father in the melodrama *The Chalk Garden* (dir. Ronald Neame) and then did so again in the comic adventure *The Truth about Spring* (Richard Thorpe, 1965), made for Universal Studios. Towards the end of this period, Mills was beginning to transition out of her role as a child star—which was effectively put to an end when she appeared in a modest but much-discussed nude scene in the British comedy *The Family Way* (John and Roy Boulting, 1966), at the age of twenty.

Understanding Child Stardom

Of course, there is a long history of child stardom that can be traced back to well before the advent of cinema. But the Hollywood lineage extends from Mary Pickford, in the 1910s and 1920s, through Shirley Temple and Mickey Rooney and on to more contemporary examples such as Macaulay Culkin, Drew Barrymore, and Miley Cyrus. Inevitably, there are significant differences among these stars, not least in terms of how successfully they make the transition from child to adult roles. Yet broadly speaking, child stars function in two principal ways: as *commodities* and as *representations*.[2]

Like other stars, child stars have an economic function for the film industry. They operate as "unique selling points" for films, enabling producers to draw attention to their products in a crowded and competitive marketplace, and thereby create a degree of predictability in an uncertain business. Stars are bankable, in a way that relatively few directors or screenwriters are, though the economic and legal position of child stars as paid employees has often proven complex.[3] Meanwhile, stardom can also prove difficult for the industry to handle, not least because stars live off-screen lives that can sometimes conflict with the roles they play on-screen. Considerable work goes into managing public perceptions of these off-screen lives, on the part of publicists, agents, and studio executives.

Meanwhile, child stars also function as representations of childhood itself. They perform particular versions of childhood, and thereby embody assumptions about what children (and, by extension, adults) are, or ought to be. These actors are children, but they are also *playing the role* of children: childhood is, at least partly, a kind of masquerade. Again, there is a good deal of diversity here, but it is hard to ignore the dominant tendency to idealize and sentimentalize childhood. This is certainly apparent in a good deal of Hollywood cinema, but it has a longer history in the Romantic view of childhood, expressed, for example, in nineteenth-century literature and painting (Wordsworth, Dickens, and the pre-Raphaelites). The child here is often seen as "cute" or a "loveable moppet"—as a beautiful, pure, free spirit, an object of unquestioning adult wonder and joy.

In her book *Precocious Charms*, Gaylyn Studlar has explored these representations of childhood in the films of six leading Hollywood child stars, including Pickford and Temple, as well as actors, such as Deanna Durbin and Jennifer Jones, who are less well remembered today.[4] In performing childhood, she argues, these child stars also mark out the boundaries, and the relationships, between childhood and adulthood. Indeed, the child is often seen to have something to teach adults: childhood is a repository of fundamental human values, such as honesty, loyalty, and affection, with which adults sometimes seem to have lost touch. The child is innocent in these films and yet somehow intuitively knows and speaks the truth—even if that truth is something that adults seek to deny. The child is often a peacemaker or a healer, with the power to make adults better people. Like some kind of sticky emotional glue, the child has a unique ability to reunite or reassemble the family and, in some cases, the wider community as well. One especially striking aspect here is the preponderance of sick and orphaned children in these films. These vulnerable children typically evoke or reawaken feelings of pity and affection among the adult characters and a hidden wish to care for and protect. This is especially notable among potential father figures, who thereby become more human and domesticated and can be integrated back into the family.

The majority of child stars are female, and the girl star also embodies particular ways of being feminine and therefore mediates assumptions about what females are or ought to be. This can obviously take the stereotypical form of prettiness and passivity, but girl stars are also often represented as independent and physically assertive. From Pickford and Temple on through, they often play the role of the tomboy or the hoyden, who is feisty and rebellious. This is a child who is determined to be free of adult constraints and to resist adult authority, and she often takes on conventionally masculine characteristics in doing so. Even so, this is frequently a temporary starting position: these girls generally learn a more traditional form of femininity, though they may use it to further their own interests.

In such narratives, the spectre of sexuality is often lurking, albeit generally off-screen. Freud notwithstanding, children are traditionally considered to be presexual, or asexual: it is assumed that children know nothing about adult sexuality, let alone experience sexual feelings of their own. However, numerous commentators have argued that the child star can become an *object* of sexual desire. Some have suggested that these films invoke a "paedophilic gaze" that is equivalent to the "male gaze" of mainstream Hollywood cinema. The most infamous instance of this was seen in the novelist Graham Greene's reviews of Shirley Temple in 1936 and 1937, which commented on the star's "voluptuous" appeal, her "dubious coquetry," and her "dimpled depravity"—reviews for which he was successfully sued by Temple's studio, Twentieth Century-Fox.[5] There is no doubt that some adult men may find such images of girlish innocence erotic; and images of cute girls may be more palatable and comforting in this respect than images of sexual adult women. However, as Studlar points out, the fans of Temple and other girl stars were by no means only adult men, and even for them, the appeal may have been more about a search for a lost childhood than anything overtly sexual. The role of the adult male (re)discovering a fatherly desire to protect the child may hold a genuine appeal both to male and female viewers.

Nevertheless—and especially in the case of female stars—the issue of sexuality is frequently a key point of tension, not least in making the transition from child star to adult actor. The industry's publicity machine may have to work overtime to reassert conservative notions of childhood and femininity that the stars themselves urgently wish to jettison, and resort to extreme tactics in seeking to do so (Miley Cyrus is a recent case in point). As we'll see, these characteristics are apparent in several ways in the case of Hayley Mills. However, Mills was not just a Hollywood star. She was also an actor in

British films—films whose style and approach reflected a very different context of production, and whose representations of childhood (and girlhood) were rather different from those in her American movies. I begin by looking at two of these films before contrasting them with Disney's vision of childhood.

Tiger Bay

Released in 1959, Hayley Mills's first film still seems remarkably fresh and contemporary. Directed by J. Lee Thompson, who went on to direct several notable (and less notable) Hollywood action movies, *Tiger Bay* co-starred the German actor Horst Buchholz in his first English-language film, along with Hayley's father John Mills. As I have noted, it was Thompson's meeting with Hayley that prompted him to change the central character from a boy (as in the original short story, "Rodolphe et le Revolver," by Noel Calef) to a girl. Apparently, he was impressed by what he saw as her natural talent and her "wonderful big eyes"—eyes that play a crucial role in the film.

Briefly, the story concerns a young girl named Gillie Evans, who witnesses a murder. Looking through the letterbox of a flat in her apartment block, she sees a Polish sailor, Bronislaw Kochinsky (Horst Buchholz), shoot his lover in a fit of jealousy. Kochinsky hides the gun, but Gillie retrieves it. Kochinsky then tracks her down to the church, where she has been singing in the choir. At first, she threatens him with the gun, but they go on to form a friendship. The police are on Kochinsky's trail, but the two manage to escape capture. Gillie is eventually apprehended, but she denies all knowledge of Kochinsky, and helps to implicate another man. Kochinsky tries to abscond on a ship bound for Caracas. However, in the final scenes, the police catch up with him. Gillie falls off the ship, and Kochinsky rescues her, but the police pull him from the water and arrest him.

Tiger Bay is essentially a fast-paced suspense thriller: several scenes are very tightly choreographed and edited, and the chase sequences build to an effective climax. However, there are also elements of social realism, especially in the matter-of-fact portrayal of the shabby, multicultural Cardiff neighbourhood where the film is set. Despite the casting of John Mills in the role of the police superintendent, it is striking how the point of identification throughout the film remains with the child and her association with the wrongdoer rather than with the authorities. The murder is a crime of passion. As Steve Chibnall argues, "Criminality stems from weakness and the inability to deal with the emotions created by interpersonal relationships"—a repeated theme in Thompson's other early films.[6] Kochinsky fails to heed the warning given to him by an Indian doctor early in the film: "Don't let your emotions rule your life." For much of the film, he is panicking, out of his depth, which is why he has to rely on the child to help him.

Mills's performance is a long way from the cute "moppets" played by the likes of Shirley Temple. Her acting is quite naturalistic, with the occasional fleeting facial tics and ungainly expressions that became a kind of trademark of her style. Her character is feisty, sometimes insolent, and very defiant towards authority. As is often the case in films featuring child stars, she is without parents. She has moved to Cardiff from London, and is living with her aunt, who struggles to control her. From the very start, she is depicted as a liar: she swindles her aunt, keeping the change from her shopping trip to buy a toy, and she immediately lies to the police about what she witnessed. Later, she falsely identifies the murderer in an police line-up, and she continues to insist until the very end—despite great pressure from the police—that she knows nothing about Kochinsky. However, this is not inveterate lying: it is motivated initially by her desire to keep the gun, and then by her loyalty to Kochinsky. Both Gillie and Kochinsky are outsiders: Kochinsky dreams of marriage, but he is constantly drawn by his love of the sea, and Gillie is parentless, a Londoner in an alien city and country, who struggles to find a way into the street games of her peers. Both are looking for belonging, yet also for escape.

One recurring issue in the films I'll be discussing is children's agency—that is, their ability to drive and influence events. A key aspect of agency has to do with *knowledge*. This is partly a matter of how the film manipulates the viewer's access to information, as well as that of the various characters, through narrative; but in this case it is also to do with the different kinds and levels of knowledge possessed by the children and the adults. In the early part of the film, Gillie has most of the knowledge, which the viewer shares: she knows where the gun is and conceals it; she knows that the gun is not loaded, though Kochinsky does not know this when she aims it at him; and she constantly conceals key facts about the murder from the police. At the same time, the viewer knows it is unlikely that Kochinsky will take her with him, despite her wishes; and we see several threats to her safety that she does not see herself (notably, in a scene on a ferry when a gate swings open and Kochinsky rescues her).

Tiger Bay also comments more directly on assumptions about childhood, most notably, in the scene where Gillie takes the gun to church and conceals it under her surplice. She then proceeds to sing in a very pure and "angelic" way; yet she also swaps a bullet from the gun for some chocolate with one of the choir boys, and they clinch the deal while singing in time to the psalm. As we see in her interrogations at the hands of the police, it seems that Gillie is very skilful in turning on the persona of the innocent, wide-eyed child when the context suits her.

Another key issue here is gender. Thompson's use of a girl rather than a boy in the leading role may have been somewhat fortuitous, but it opens up some interesting questions. Gillie is a tomboy; she has a short pudding-basin haircut and is dressed in trousers and a dark t-shirt throughout the film. When we first see her, she is framed behind railings, looking on at a group of (mainly) boys playing a game of cowboys and Indians or gangsters in the street. The boys refuse to allow her to take part on the grounds that she doesn't have a toy gun and tell her to go back to London. When Gillie fights back, the boys tell her that their game is not for "ladies," and she retorts "I'm not a lady." Gillie's desire for a gun, and her eventual acquisition of a *real* gun, is her initial motivation to lie. Some critics have read this in tiresomely Freudian terms: Gillie is suffering from penis envy, and the gun is (needless to say) a phallic symbol. According to Melanie Williams, the film's title is a reference to vagina dentata.[7]

Freudian symbol-hunting aside, Williams is correct to suggest that *Tiger Bay* offers a vision of girlhood, not only on the cusp of adolescence, but also on the cusp of the social revolutions of the 1960s. In one scene, Kochinsky invites Gillie to look forward to the romantic relationships that lie ahead for her as a woman—although from his rather embittered perspective, this is a matter of her having "all the power in the world, for good or bad, just with your little finger, a few words, to make [men] happy or unhappy." If Kochinsky's lover Anya (Yvonne Mitchell) clearly represents this femme fatale version of female power, the other women in the film (such as Gillie's aunt) are less than powerful; yet, as Williams argues, Gillie herself anticipates the more liberated young women of 1960s cinema.

At the same time, it's possible to see the relationship between Gillie and Kochinsky as a kind of romance. (Mills later reported that she fell "instantly in love" with the handsome Buchholz.) In one scene, they are onlookers at a West Indian wedding celebration, and the two of them are scattered with confetti; and the closing shots, in which they embrace after he has rescued her from the sea, are accompanied by a rather insistent swell of romantic strings. However, it is Kochinsky's desire to *protect* Gillie that pulls us to his side—for example, in the scene on the ferry and when he rescues her from the sea instead of choosing to stay on the ship and save himself (even the police superintendent is bound to admit that he has shown himself to be "a brave man"). When the two of them briefly escape to the countryside before Kochinsky can catch his ship, we see him acting out playful stories for her, more like a young father than a lover. In this scene, as in the wedding scene and elsewhere, there are constant reminders of Kochinsky's passionate love for the woman he has killed. By contrast, the bond between him and Gillie is one of loyalty and friendship between outsiders: it is affectionate, but there is no implication of sexual attraction.

Whistle Down the Wind

This bond formed between the child and the criminal recurs, in a rather different way, in *Whistle Down the Wind*. Released in 1961, it was produced by Allied Film Makers, a small independent company that made a total of six films between 1959 and 1964 (including, most famously, the gay drama *Victim* [Basil Dearden, 1961]).[8] Two members of the company were mainly involved: Richard Attenborough as producer, and Bryan Forbes in his debut as a director. The script, based on a novel by Hayley Mills's mother Mary Hayley Bell, was written by Keith Waterhouse and Willis Hall, who went on to become leading television writers.

The film focuses on three children living on a Lancashire farm who discover a fugitive hiding in their barn. When they stumble upon him, he exclaims, "Jesus Christ!" in shock. Heavily influenced by stories they have heard told at Sunday School, and by the Salvation Army, the children believe that he is Jesus come again. We learn fairly soon that the fugitive is wanted for murder, although the children remain unaware of this. Initially confused by their willingness to protect him from discovery, he makes no attempt to correct their mistake. Most of the children in the nearby village eventually learn that "Jesus" is living in the barn, but it is only when the news finally reaches an adult, the children's father, that police are called in to apprehend him. The criminal surrenders and is taken away, watched by a large audience of local children.

Here again, the issue of children's agency and knowledge is a key theme. Mills's character, Kathy, is the oldest of the children, and for much of the film she has knowledge that she deliberately conceals from the adults (and some of the other children). And yet, on another level, she suffers from a kind of blind faith, or ignorance: the adult viewer obviously knows that the fugitive, Blakey (Alan Bates), is not Jesus, whereas Kathy herself does not acknowledge this until the very end. Initially, Blakey does not understand why the children are protecting him and only gradually realizes the reason. Meanwhile, the viewer sees information (for example, on newspaper billboards) about the hunt for Blakey that the children do not see. These differences in knowledge—between the child characters, their parents, Blakey, and the viewer—are manipulated throughout, for various reasons: to create tension, to encourage or undermine the viewer's identification, and at times for comic or ironic effect. It isn't without significance that the game the children play at a birthday party towards the end of the film is one of Blind Man's Buff (Figure 17.1).

FIGURE 17.1. Kathy (Hayley Mills) and Blakey (Alan Bates) in *Whistle Down the Wind* (1961, Allied Film Makers). Frame-grab.

It is only in the final scenes that these disparities in knowledge are resolved. The adults (and the police) find Blakey, and Kathy appears to learn what the adults know. Nevertheless, the ending is somewhat ambiguous. Rather than explicit dialogue, a series of extended close-ups on Kathy seem to imply that she is finally registering the truth about Blakey's criminal identity. However, when a couple of much younger children approach her and ask to see Jesus, she replies that they have missed him this time; but she reassures them that he will be coming again another day. The significance of this is open to debate: it is possible to infer that Kathy continues in a state of blind faith, although it seems more likely that she has made the transition to adult knowledge, and simply wishes to protect the younger children from disillusionment—rather as though she might not want to tell them the truth about Santa Claus.

Indeed, it could be argued that the film as a whole takes a rather ambiguous stance on these questions of knowledge and faith. As Sandy Brewer has noted, the story of Jesus was central to British children's primary-school education in the 1950s.[9] At the start of the film, we see the Salvation Army proselytizing in the streets of the village, and we also see the children at their religious Sunday school—though in both cases, their questions about whether Jesus will come again receive unclear and unsatisfactory answers. The posters outside the church and the comments of the local vicar suggest that organized religion is in decline. Later, the children approach the vicar, trying to get some definitive judgement about the rebirth and return of Jesus, but he appears preoccupied with thefts of metal guttering and lead from his church. As they leave him, the youngest child, Charles, says, "He doesn't know, does he?" Indeed, it is Charles who acts as a kind of disbelieving truth-teller throughout the film: he seems to lose his faith when he finds that "Jesus" hasn't protected his pet kitten, and he later asserts, "It isn't Jesus, it's just a feller."

Yet at the same time, the film is overflowing with religious symbolism—to an extent that some contemporary critics found contrived. "Jesus" appears in a stable, and the children of the village bring him offerings (including a plastic "Arabian charm bracelet" from a children's magazine); and at the very end of the film, he holds out his arms in a crucifixion pose as he surrenders to the police. The children (his "disciples," as they are called in the final credits) have to "sin" (to steal and lie) to help him; and in one scene, an older bully forces a younger child to deny three times that he knows Jesus, while a train whistle blows (or a cock crows). A version of "We Three Kings" plays on several occasions when we see the three children approaching or disappearing into the distance. All of this could be read as ironic, or at least playful; but in combination with the other elements I have discussed, it contributes to a wider sense that the boundaries between knowledge and ignorance (or blind faith) are perhaps not entirely clear-cut.

From the outset, the film portrays the children's world as largely separate from that of adults. In the opening scene, the three children, unseen, follow a farmworker as he goes to drown some unwanted kittens. They promptly rescue them and hide them in the barn. Here, as in their later attempts to conceal Blakey, they effectively evade adult control and surveillance, often through outright lying and deceit—and despite the adults' repeated attempts to boss them about. As Kathy says, the return of "Jesus" has to be kept hidden: "It's got to be a secret society from the grown-ups." As Noel Brown points out, the film represents adulthood—for example, in the characters of the children's father and their aunt—as "overburdened with worldly vices: pragmatism, cynicism, brutality, lack of imagination and connection with nature."[10] To some extent, the children are free to come and go as they please, although Kathy (aged about twelve) is delegated to take charge of the younger ones. The film offers a vision of rural childhood, but it is by no means a pastoral idyll of the kind presented in Mills's Disney films: the landscape is rugged, the weather is unforgiving, and farming is clearly very hard work.

On the one hand, this view of the child's world might be seen to reflect the "lost freedom" of 1950s childhoods,[11] although it also generates some concerns about the children's safety—as when their father, having heard that Blakey is on the run, warns them about the danger of talking to strangers or the "funny people [who are] about these days." Significantly, the children's mother is missing from the story, and (as in *Tiger Bay*) a rather reluctant aunt has taken her place. Their father is generally somewhat distant— "I don't know what they're up to half the time," he admits. These absences might be seen to reflect the concerns about the need for emotional attachment within the family that were strongly emphasized in child development theories at the time (for example, in the work of psychologists John Bowlby and Donald Winnicott).[12] Kathy is, on one level, an active agent with a certain degree of power and authority—and as Brown suggests, this may anticipate the countercultural movements that emerged later in the decade.[13] Nevertheless, she is also rather lost and bewildered, and by the end of the film, she appears to have crossed over into a state of adult disillusionment.

Debating "Disneyfication"

It was on the strength of her performance in *Tiger Bay* that Hayley Mills was awarded her contract with Disney—although it is hard to think of many films featuring children at this time that were *less* like those Disney was producing. Before moving on to look at Mills's Disney features, it is important to consider Disney's significance in relation to ideas about childhood, and to unpack the idea of "Disneyfication."

In the three decades before the 1960s, Disney's rise had largely been due to its intensive targeting of the children's market—although Disney himself always insisted that his films were intended as "family entertainment," which would draw in parents as well (and hence prove even more lucrative). From *Steamboat Willie* (Ub Iwerks, 1928) and the early Mickey Mouse cartoons right through to its contemporary productions, such as the *Toy Story* (1995–) films, *Cars* (John Lasseter, 2006), and the various "Disney Princesses," Disney has become almost synonymous with a particular, dominant definition of American childhood. Even today, Disney films tell both parents and children powerful stories about both childhood and the transition to adulthood.

In his book *Babes in Tomorrowland*, Nicholas Sammond describes how claims about the harmful effects of media on children gained traction in the early 1930s, especially after the coming of sound.[14] Although this led to greater censorship (in the form of the

Hays Code), it also implicitly raised the question of how movies might be *beneficial* for children—how they might help children grow up to be good citizens, and not simply mislead them into bad ways. This effectively created a market opportunity: it enabled Disney to present itself as a company whose accumulation of commercial profit could be compatible with "doing good" for children. By carefully cultivating its wholesome brand identity—and constructing Walt himself as an avuncular but efficient self-made man—the company was able to embed its enormous range of media products and merchandise into the everyday family lives of most Americans.

Sammond shows how ideas about child-rearing had changed from the highly regulated behaviourist approach of the 1920s and 1930s, based on ideas of "scientific management" that were being applied in industry, to the moderately permissive approach that arose in the 1950s, most often identified with Dr Benjamin Spock. As Sammond argues, these changing ideas were tied up with anxieties about the United States' national identity and its position in the world, initially around the Depression and the New Deal and, subsequently, during the Cold War. Media consumption was a particular concern—especially considering the way cinema brought different racial groups and social classes together. According to Sammond, Disney's approach involved the imposition of White, middle-class norms of behaviour; and even as it cautiously embraced the more permissive ideas of the 1950s, it also urged the child to conform to narrowly stereotypical but apparently innate gender roles, not only in its cartoons, but also in its nature documentaries.

Sammond's account goes beyond the familiar arguments about ideological manipulation that are often laid at Disney's door. He points out that these arguments about child-rearing, which were widely circulated in women's magazines and other popular advice literature for parents, effectively created a climate in which Disney could thrive. Disney, he argues, was not an all-powerful agent of thought control, imposing a kind of false consciousness on its audiences: rather, it was meeting (and also helping to shape and define) an already perceived need.

However, the view that Disney films were a means of brainwashing is the one that prevails in much of the critical commentary. Despite Walt Disney's status as a kind of American icon, there is a long history of condemning Disney's output, which gathered force in the 1960s. In 1965, the critic Frances Clarke Sayers published a classic essay in a children's literature journal, in which she claimed that Disney productions—its animated cartoons in particular—were vulgar, sentimental, and clichéd.[15] Disney's versions of classic fairy tales, she argued, were crude and simplistic, ironing out moral complexities in favour of a one-dimensional image of "sweetness and light." Three years later, Richard Schickel went further: "Disney's machine," he argued, "was designed to shatter the two most valuable things about childhood—its secrets and its silences—thus forcing everyone to share the same formative daydreams."[16] Disney was a force for ideological conformity, driven by rampant commercialism.

For more recent critics, of whom there have been many, Disney is also a purveyor of sexism, racism, classism, imperialism, and a whole legion of other obnoxious prejudices.[17] The charge of Disneyfication, in this account, is partly about a kind of simplification or sanitization: moral tension and complexity are ironed out in favour of simplistic, dumbed-down tales of good and evil. It is also about sentimentality: genuine and profound emotions are replaced with superficial mawkishness and mush. The criticism implies a rejection of Disney's commercialism—and, in particular, the transformation of "classic" or sacred children's texts into profitable commodities. Yet it is also, finally, a political charge: Walt Disney himself is presented (admittedly, with some good evidence) as a reactionary, even a kind of crypto-fascist, as well as a peddler of xenophobic prejudice.

While these critical views of Disney were not widely shared in the early 1960s, some of the films of that time—including the ones I consider next—would certainly have provided Disney's detractors with valuable ammunition. On the other hand, we might also expect to see (as we arguably do in *Tiger Bay* and in *Whistle Down the Wind*) at least some intimations of the changes in the position of children and young people and of women that began to gather momentum as the decade progressed. Gender was one significant aspect in this respect. As Sammond explains, Disney's live-action films at the time were largely targeted at boys: his hiring of Mills represented something of a departure—*Pollyanna* was his first live-action feature with a central girl character.[18]

Pollyanna

Sandwiched rather incongruously between the two British films I have discussed was Mills's first Disney feature, *Pollyanna*, released in 1960. Unlike both *Tiger Bay* and *Whistle Down the Wind*, which are, arguably, films for adults, *Pollyanna* is clearly a children's film, or at least one intended as "family entertainment": there is hardly anything in this film that would not be understood by most children of cinemagoing age. The director, David Swift, had previously worked on Disney's animation and TV productions, and this was his first feature film; it enjoyed a relatively high budget of over $1 million. Walt Disney took a close personal interest in the project, and reportedly often wept while viewing the daily rushes; he refused Swift's requests to cut the running time, which is just over two hours.

The film is set in the small town of Harrington in the early 1900s: the set resembles "Main Street USA" at Disneyland. Pollyanna, a twelve-year-old orphan, arrives to live with her wealthy and domineering Aunt Polly (Jane Wyman), who effectively runs the town. Pollyanna is a cheerful, talkative, and optimistic child. She tells the inhabitants of the town about the "glad game" her father had taught her: you should always find something to be glad about, she says, no matter how bad things may seem. As she settles in, Pollyanna gradually transforms the entire community, including the hypochondriac Mrs Snow (Agnes Moorhead), the grumpy recluse Mr. Pendergast (Adolphe Menjou), and the hellfire-and-brimstone preacher Reverend Ford (Karl Malden)—and, ultimately, even her Aunt Polly. When most of the townspeople want a run-down orphanage rebuilt, Aunt Polly opposes the idea, but they defy her by planning a bazaar to raise funds. Pollyanna subtly persuades Reverend Ford to support the idea, and this proves decisive: the bazaar is a great success. Although Aunt Polly refuses to allow Pollyanna to attend, her playmate Jimmy Bean (Kevin Corcoran) helps her to escape from the house by climbing down a tree outside her bedroom window. However, when she returns, she slips and falls from the tree and is badly injured. Her legs paralysed, Pollyanna becomes severely depressed, jeopardizing her chance of recovery: it seems that the "glad game" can no longer do the trick. However, when the townspeople learn about the accident, they arrive en masse at Aunt Polly's house with gifts and good wishes. The film ends with Pollyanna leaving Harrington for an operation in Baltimore, which is hoped to secure her recovery (Figure 17.2).

If ever a film was open to the charge of Disneyfication, it would be *Pollyanna*—although in this respect I reserve a special place in my heart for *Summer Magic* (James Neilson, 1963), which followed it a couple of years later. However, it should be noted that both films have their origins in a long tradition of "sentimental fiction," particularly aimed at girls and women.[19] While this tradition arguably extends back to the early days of the novel (for example, Samuel Richardson's *Pamela* [1740]), it continued in the nineteenth and twentieth centuries in the enormously popular *Little Women* (1868), *What Katy Did* (1872), *Anne of Green Gables* (1908), and *The Secret Garden* (1911), and their numerous adaptations for film and television.

FIGURE 17.2. Pollyanna (Hayley Mills) as a force of transformative sunniness and optimism (*Pollyanna*, 1960, Disney). Frame-grab.

The original source for *Pollyanna* was a novel by Eleanor Porter, published in 1913. The book sold more than a million copies, and was first adapted for film in 1919, significantly featuring an earlier child star, Mary Pickford. The success of Porter's novel generated a sequel, *Pollyanna Grows Up* (1915), and a series of at least fourteen subsequent Pollyanna books by other writers (collectively known as the "Glad Books").[20] The book was adapted again for television by the BBC in the 1970s, and by the UK commercial network Carlton in 2003. More implausibly, it also generated a fifty-one-episode *anime* series on Japanese TV, and two Disney musicals with largely African American casts in the late 1980s and early 1990s.

The central theme of these "sentimental novels" is children's agency. The child is seen to have the power to transform everybody around her—not only her extended family (as in *Summer Magic*), but also the wider community, as in *Pollyanna*. One of the closing shots of the film shows the citizens attaching a new sign to the train station as Pollyanna leaves for Baltimore: no longer called just "Harrington," in reference to the control exercised by Aunt Polly's family, it has also become "the Glad Town." As Judy Rosenbaum puts it, Pollyanna is a kind of "junior fairy godmother": she changes negatives into positives, encouraging all she meets to look on the brighter side of life and thereby transform themselves.[21] She unfreezes those who are emotionally frozen or blocked, and humanizes those who are repressed and miserable, enabling them to fulfil the desires they cannot admit even to themselves. By the end of the film, a whole set of new partnerships is formed, both romantic (Aunt Polly and the doctor) and familial (Jimmy Bean is adopted by Mr. Prendergast, and Aunt Polly finally accepts Pollyanna as her daughter).

At the same time, Pollyanna helps to precipitate a kind of democratic revolution that empowers the citizens of the town and challenges the quasi-aristocratic position of her aunt. In the early scenes, we see the townspeople's resentment of Aunt Polly's charity, as well as their failure to fully stand up to her wealth and power. The bazaar represents self-help, as opposed to charity; yet here too, the people need Pollyanna to set them free. In particular, she enables the priest to liberate himself from Aunt Polly's control, which has extended to defining the tone and content of his sermons: it is Pollyanna's claim that "nobody can buy a church" and then her mention of the "glad texts" in the Bible that most incite him to change. Although Aunt Polly takes on an almost villainous air, especially when she refuses to allow Pollyanna to attend the bazaar, she, too, is eventually transformed by the power of Pollyanna's love: in the closing scenes, she becomes both a wife and a mother. This all happens at some personal cost to Pollyanna—in that she becomes an invalid—but the ending suggests that this will only be temporary. While the film's politics are far from radical, they do reflect a kind of democratic populism that is very prevalent in Disney (and, indeed, in mainstream Hollywood more broadly).

Pollyanna arrives in a world where adult authority is not to be questioned. In the opening scenes, she is persistently bossed about and told off for showing curiosity about her new environment. Yet as we have seen in other child-centred films, Pollyanna uses her growing knowledge, gained though eavesdropping and observing adults, to manipulate them. She may lie or deceive, but she does so for good reasons, and she has an ability to speak truths (for example, by drawing attention to her aunt's considerable wealth) that adults may wish to efface or conceal.

Pollyanna is significantly more "girlish" than the characters in Mills's British films, although she retains elements of the tomboy persona. She seems uncomfortable with her Aunt's attempts to make her more "ladylike," and prefers to run around with Jimmy Bean, getting her new dresses dirty in the process. As in her British films, Mills's performance conveys a degree of unpolished spontaneity—she screws up her face into ungainly expressions—although in this context, the act seems somewhat contrived and cute.

Of course, there is a good deal of sentimentality in *Pollyanna*—although (as Rosenbaum implies) it is debatable whether this is any more apparent than it was in the original novel, or even in the broader tradition of fiction from which it comes. The ending brings together all the characters, playing on all the heartstrings at once; and it is certainly difficult (perhaps particularly for a British viewer) to stomach the sight of Hayley Mills at the bazaar, wrapped in the American flag singing "America the Beautiful." Between the release of Porter's original novel and Disney's version almost fifty years later, the word "Pollyanna" had come to represent a kind of saccharine sentimentality—which, once Pollyanna is paralysed, devolves into mawkishness. Although the film makes some changes from the original novel—playing up Aunt Polly's power in the town and playing down Pollyanna's talkativeness—it doesn't by any means escape this charge; although, again, Mills's subsequent Disney film *Summer Magic* probably wins that award.

The Parent Trap

Released in 1961, *The Parent Trap* was Mills's second Disney film. Like *Pollyanna*, it was written for the screen and directed by David Swift, and based on a novel—in this case, *Das Doppelte Lottchen* (*Lotte and Lisa*, 1949) by the popular German children's author Erich Kästner. The film was a great success at the box office, generating almost ten times the revenue of *Pollyanna*.

The story begins when two very similar-looking girls, Susan and Sharon, meet at summer camp: both are played by Hayley Mills, using stand-ins and a variety of split-screen and matte effects. Unaware that they are, in fact, identical twins, the girls initially become rivals, pulling pranks on each other. Eventually, they figure out that they are sisters who were separated shortly after birth when their parents (Mitch and Maggie) divorced. They decide to switch places, each eager to meet the parent she has never known, and when camp ends, they return to each other's homes in Boston and California, respectively. They also hatch a plan to get their parents back together, suspecting that they still love each other despite their mutual hostility. However, they discover that Mitch (Brian Keith) is shortly due to be remarried to a gold-digging younger girlfriend named Vicky (Joanna Barnes). To stop this from happening, Susan and Sharon decide to reveal their true identities, and the whole family reassembles in

California. Through a variety of means, and with their mother's help, the girls con-
spire to sabotage Mitch's marriage plans. Just in time, they succeed: Mitch and Maggie
(Maureen O'Hara) rekindle their romance. The film ends with their wedding, and the
girls are maids of honour.

The Parent Trap might be described as a romantic comedy, although it is one in which
children occupy the central roles. As in a conventional romcom, the inevitable romantic
conclusion is deferred through a variety of obstacles, and the couple realise their true
feelings for each other only at the very last minute. The girls eventually get in league
with their mother, but it is they who engineer the eventual reunion and, hence, the
reassembling of the family. As in the other films I have discussed, the twins possess a
considerable degree of agency: they often know more than the adults, extracting information from them that they can later use, and they deceive and manipulate them for
their own purposes. In doing so, they often choose to play the role of the angelic, innocent child, even if the viewer knows better (Figure 17.3). Once again, the child (or children plural, in this case) plays the role of the healer who magically rights the wrongs that
have been caused by the mistakes or delusions of the adults. While some of the adults
in *The Parent Trap* can be trusted—the wise, benevolent grandfather; the honest family
servant—others (such as those who run the summer camp) are seen as merely inept figures of fun.

Nevertheless, there are limits to this fantasy of child empowerment. The children do
play mischievous pranks on Mitch's villainous girlfriend Vicky, but they hardly ever
challenge their parents' authority: only at one point, when they resist their parents'

FIGURE 17.3. The twin girls representing a form of Disneyfied youthful rebellion in *The Parent
Trap* (1961, Disney). Frame-grab.

attempts to make Sharon return home, do they do so directly. Their rebellion may be effective, but they are essentially harmless and childlike, and they serve as a primary source of the film's rather basic slapstick comedy.

Furthermore, the children's agency is entirely directed towards the reconstitution of the traditional nuclear family. Steven Watts describes *The Parent Trap* as "Disney's ultimate expression of domestic ideology"; yet this is an ideology that appears to be implicitly under threat.[22] At several points, the girls refer to the breakdown of the modern family and its consequences for their friends. Thus, Susan remarks, "It's scary how nobody stays together any more. Pretty soon there's going to be more divorces than marriages." Both girls resist one potential solution to their problem, that their parents could share them: the "six month split," they argue, would leave them feeling like a "yo-yo" or a "bathroom towel."

While this might be seen to reflect the social changes of the time, rates of divorce in the United States actually fell during the 1950s and did not start to rise significantly until the 1970s. Yet for Disney in 1961, it appears that the nuclear family is in need of support. The embroidery sampler bearing the legend "Bless Our Broken Home," which appears in the animated credits at the start of the film, is replaced at the end by one that says "Bless Our Happy Home": "broken" families, it seems, cannot be happy ones. And in case we missed it, the message is also reinforced by the song "Let's Get Together" that the girls perform for their parents, whose melody recurs in later scenes.

The unspoken problem here, of course, is sex. It seems that Mitch has been sexually manipulated by his much younger girlfriend, whose motives are primarily financial (and who is supported in this by a scheming future mother-in-law). Although Mitch is conventionally masculine (and is described as such), this is not to say that Maggie is passively feminine: she repeatedly stands her ground against Mitch and, at one point, even hits him in the eye. However, her determination primarily arises from her desire to win back her man. With the girls' help, she takes the lead in trying to rekindle their relationship. Following the not-so-subtle hints of her father, Maggie gets a new hairstyle and wears more sexually alluring clothes ("using her femininity," as Mills's character in *Summer Magic* is taught to do); and when the children are out of the picture, she engineers an embrace with Mitch while she cooks a meal for them. What Maggie and Mitch are missing, it appears, is not so much sex as romance, and the girls work hard to evoke their memories of the early days of their relationship, for example, by restaging the scene of their first date.

Significantly, however, Mitch seems just as interested in Maggie's abilities in the kitchen. He looks back wistfully to the domestic realities of femininity "behind the scenes"—the wet stockings drying in the bathroom, his razor that is blunt because she used it to shave her legs. He even fondly recalls looking after the girls as babies, feeding them and changing their diapers. Even "masculine" men need romance, but it would seem that they also crave a degree of domesticity. Women are by no means entirely passive here, and men are not merely hunters and warriors. Even so, the gender roles remain highly conventional: if women perform their domestic and romantic roles adequately, it seems, men can be drawn back into the traditional family.

The girls implicitly understand some of this, but as children they remain outside it. In one scene, Sharon tells her father that "when a girl gets to a certain age, she misses her mother." Mitch takes this as a cue for the "father-daughter talk" about sex, and clumsily makes a start. However, it isn't clear to either of them what they are actually talking about, and in any case, Sharon claims, "I've known about all that for simply years." Later, Sharon torments her father's girlfriend by referring to the large number of other women he is seeing, and Vicky warns her not to "play with the big girls." Yet for the moment, even at the age of thirteen, the girls remain children, whose knowledge of the adult world needs to be strictly limited.

COMING OF AGE

As I have noted, one of the key difficulties faced by child stars (and perhaps especially by girls) is how they will revise their image as they grow up, and how successfully they can make the transition to adult roles. Some effectively continue as children: Mary Pickford, for example, was still playing "little Mary" when she was well into her twenties. Others—perhaps those who were more implicitly or explicitly sexual in the first place—seem to make the transition more smoothly: Elizabeth Taylor or Jodie Foster, for example. Many appear to crash and burn in their private lives, attracting a great deal of voyeuristic publicity in the process: examples here might include Drew Barrymore or Macaulay Culkin (or, indeed, Michael Jackson). Yet others simply withdraw from the public gaze, or find alternative adult roles, such as Deanna Durbin or Shirley Temple.

In Mills's case, it seems that this was not an easy transition to make. She felt increasingly constrained by the image Disney constructed for her, both on screen and off—although to be fair, Disney's publicity machine worked hard to dispel the rather old-fashioned image that *Pollyanna* had created, and present her as an active "modern" girl.[23] The difficulty of this transition was also apparent in some of the films from the final stages of Mills's career as a child star, such as the British-made melodrama *The Chalk Garden* (Ronald Neame, 1964) and her last Disney film, the comedy *That Darn Cat!* (Robert Stevenson, 1964). In different ways, both films illustrate some of the difficulties of a child star "coming of age"—particularly in the mid-1960s. As Mills later acknowledged in discussing *The Chalk Garden*, "That was a difficult time for me ... I was moving out of childhood and developing into another kind of actress, because I was developing into a woman. It was new territory, and I wasn't sure of myself." If she appears uncomfortable and implausible as a troubled adolescent in this film, her role in *That Darn Cat!* seems bland and lacking in individuality. Sexuality might serve as one obvious marker of a transition to adulthood. Yet while sex is certainly referred to in *The Chalk Garden*—albeit primarily as a means for Mills's character to outrage the adults—in *That Darn Cat!* it seems to be largely repressed.

At the same time, both films also seem to reflect difficulties in making the transition from the 1950s to the 1960s. *The Chalk Garden* makes implicit reference to the "youth revolution" of the 1960s; however, Mills's character is mostly confined to the claustrophobic atmosphere of the house and family. There are no other young people in the film, and no evidence of anything remotely approaching "youth culture." Likewise, the young people of *That Darn Cat!*—like much else in the film—seem to have walked straight out of the 1950s: they are bland, suburban, and entirely wholesome. In different ways, the style of these films also seems to look backwards—to 1950s melodrama and to comedy capers of an earlier age, respectively. Ultimately, both seem distinctly old-fashioned for their time: unable to take account of emerging changes in the social position of young people more broadly, and of young women in particular.

If Mills found the inevitable end of her career as a child star to be uncomfortable, the contrast between her experiences in low-budget British films and with Disney Studios must have made things even more difficult. *Tiger Bay* and *Whistle Down the Wind* offer very different representations of childhood from the Disney version—and very different opportunities for Mills as an actor. Of course, the production context of Disney Studios was (and still is) very different from that of independently produced British cinema, in all sorts of obvious ways. Yet in the two British films discussed here, there is an element of genuine spontaneity in her performances, and perhaps also a sense that different, more powerful, roles for children and young people (and specifically for young women) were beginning to emerge in the wider society.

It was this spontaneity that Disney clearly noticed, and yet in taking it and using it, he transformed it into something merely cute. Mills later credited her time at Disney for giving her the opportunity to "learn her craft." But in fact it was a particular kind of craft she was learning—and one that did not easily transfer to more mature adult roles. In her Disney films, it is as though Mills is self-consciously *acting the part* of a child and doing so in quite narrowly defined terms. When she could no longer do this, there was really nowhere for her to go. In this sense, Hayley Mills herself was "Disneyfied," in a way that did not ultimately serve her very well.

Notes

1. This chapter is part of a larger online project, *Growing Up Modern: Childhood, Youth and Popular Culture since 1945*. More information about it and illustrated versions of all the chapters (including a much longer version of this chapter) can be found on my website, David Buckingham, https://davidbuckingham.net/growing-up-modern/. Surprisingly, there is no biography (official or unofficial) of Mills, and very little in the way of memoir or autobiography. I have gleaned information from various popular magazine stories available online, and from a variety of more-and-less reputable sources, including the Internet Movie Database, Wikipedia, and Reel Classics, as well as various TV and radio interviews to be found on YouTube. I have also drawn on Brian McFarlane's interview with Mills in An Autobiography of British Cinema, and on a revealing British TV interview, conducted in 1967, available online from the British Film Institute, https://player.bfi.org.uk/free/film/watch-hayley-mills-1967-online.

Interview with Mills, in Brian McFarlane, *An Autobiography of British Cinema* (London: Methuen, 1997).

2. See Richard Dyer, *Stars* (London: British Film Institute, 1997).

3. Viviana Zelizer, *Pricing the Priceless Child* (Princeton, NJ: Princeton University Press, 1994).

4. Gaylyn Studlar, *Precocious Charms: Stars Performing Girlhood in Classical Hollywood Cinema* (Berkeley: University of California Press, 2013).

5. For a discussion, see Kristen Hatch, "Discipline and Pleasure: Shirley Temple and the Spectacle of Child Loving," *Camera Obscura* 27:1 (2012), pp. 127–155.

6. Steve Chibnall, *J. Lee Thompson* (Manchester, UK: Manchester University Press, 2000), pp. 234–249.

7. Melanie Williams, "'I'm Not a Lady!'": *Tiger Bay* (1959) and Transitional Girlhood in British Cinema on the Cusp of the 1960s," *Screen* 46:3 (2005), pp. 361–372.

8. See Sally Dux, "Allied Film Makers: Crime, Comedy and Social Concern," *Journal of British Cinema and Television* 9:2 (2012), pp. 198–213.

9. Sandy Brewer, "'Who Do You Say I Am?': Jesus, Gender and the (Working-Class) Family Romance," in Sally R. Munt (ed.), *Cultural Studies and the Working Class* (London: Bloomsbury, 2000), pp. 167–179.

10. Noel Brown, *British Children's Cinema: From The Thief of Bagdad to Wallace and Gromit* (London: I.B. Tauris, 2016), p. 133.

11. See Matthew Thomson, *Lost Freedom: The Landscape of the Child and the British Post-War Settlement* (Oxford: Oxford University Press, 2013).

12. See Denise Riley, *War in the Nursery: Theories of the Child and Mother* (London: Virago, 1983).

13. Brown, *British Children's Cinema*, pp. 133–136.

14. Nicholas Sammond, *Babes in Tomorrowland: Walt Disney and the Making of the American Child* (Durham, NC: Duke University Press, 2005).

15. Francis Clarke Sayers, "Disney Accused: Interview with Charles M. Weisenberg," *Horn Book Magazine* 41 (1965), pp. 602–611.

16. Richard Schickel, *The Disney Version: The Life, Times, Art, and Commerce of Walt Disney*, 3rd ed. (Chicago: Ivan R. Dee, 1997).

17. See David Buckingham, "Dissin' Disney: Critical Perspectives on Children's Media Culture," *Media, Culture and Society* 19 (1997), pp. 285–293.

18. Sammond, *Babes in Tomorrowland*, chap. 5.

19. Susan Larkin, "The Sentimental Novel: Community, Power and Femininity," in Kathy Merlock Jackson and Mark I. West (eds.), *Walt Disney, from Reader to Storyteller* (Jefferson, NC: McFarland, 2015), pp. 127–138.

20. William McReynolds, "Disney Plays 'The Glad Game,'" *Journal of Popular Culture* 7:4 (1974), pp. 787–796.

21. Judy Rosenbaum, "Adapting *Pollyanna* for the Space Age," in Jackson and West, *Walt Disney, from Reader to Storyteller*, pp. 115–126, esp. 119–122. Similarly, John F. Kasson argues that Temple's smile is a kind of "emotional labour" that promised to heal the emotional crisis of the Great Depression. John F. Kasson, "Shirley Temple's Paradoxical Smile," *American Art* 25:3 (2011), pp. 16–19.

22. Steven Watts, *The Magic Kingdom: Walt Disney and the American Way of Life* (Columbia: University of Missouri Press, 1997), p. 333.

23. Watts, *Magic Kingdom*, p. 333.

BIBLIOGRAPHY

Brown, Noel. *British Children's Cinema: From The Thief of Bagdad to Wallace and Gromit.* London: I.B. Tauris, 2016.

Buckingham, David. "Dissin' Disney: Critical Perspectives on Children's Media Culture." *Media, Culture and Society* 19 (1997), pp. 285–293.

Dyer, Richard. *Stars.* London: British Film Institute, 1997.

Jackson, Kathy Merlock, and Mark I. West, eds. *Walt Disney, from Reader to Storyteller.* Jefferson, NC: McFarland, 2015.

Sammond, Nicholas. *Babes in Tomorrowland: Walt Disney and the Making of the American Child.* Durham, NC: Duke University Press, 2005.

Sayers, Francis Clarke. "Disney Accused: Interview with Charles M. Weisenberg." *Horn Book Magazine* 41 (1965), pp. 602–611.

Schickel, Richard. *The Disney Version: The Life, Times, Art, and Commerce of Walt Disney.* 3rd ed. Chicago: Ivan R. Dee, 1997.

Studlar, Gaylyn. *Precocious Charms: Stars Performing Girlhood in Classical Hollywood Cinema.* Berkeley: University of California Press, 2013.

Watts, Stephen. *The Magic Kingdom: Walt Disney and the American Way of Life.* Columbia: University of Missouri Press, 1997.

Williams, Melanie. "'I'm Not a Lady!'": *Tiger Bay* (1959) and Transitional Girlhood in British Cinema on the Cusp of the 1960s." *Screen* 46:3 (2005), pp. 361–372.

CHAPTER 18

DANNY KAYE AS CHILDREN'S FILM STAR

BRUCE BABINGTON

DANNY Kaye is indelibly associated with children, partly because of his off-screen role as the first Goodwill Ambassador for UNICEF (United Nations International Children's Emergency Fund), partly because his screen and vocal performances are so child-friendly, and partly because of the benign light that *Hans Christian Andersen* (Charles Vidor, 1952; prod. Samuel Goldwyn) sheds backwards and forwards over his career and has led to a virtual conflation in many minds of the actor-comedian and the film's biographically simplified Andersen. It might therefore seem surprising that he almost never plays a literal parent in his films. Perhaps the explanation is that parenthood, with its narrower interest, is felt to constrain wider empathies with all children. *Merry Andrew* (Michael Kidd, 1958) does end with Kaye's antic schoolteacher, Andrew Larrabee, with his new Italian circus family, very briefly singing a song about having a future "fat bambino" with Selena (Pier Angeli); however, *The Five Pennies* (Melville Shavelson, 1959) is the only film in which Kaye plays a biological parent (omitting the minor case of Mr. Darling in a TV production of *Peter Pan* [Dwight Hemion, 1976]), and much of the film's narrative is focused on "Red" Loring's relationship with his daughter. More than this, children belonging to anyone are conspicuously absent from most of his films. Where they *are* very much present, in *Hans Christian Andersen*, above all, and in *Merry Andrew*, Kaye appears as a benign avuncular figure to other people's children, gifting them games, imagination, songs, self-confidence, and precious life advice.

Few major comedians interact happily with children on-screen, more often ignoring their existence, as with Harry Langdon and Mae West, or even being hostile to them, as with W. C. Fields. Mostly, this is because the comedian's persona almost always contains a pronounced element of the child, cutting out empathy for smaller competing narcissists. Kaye was exceptional in swerving so strongly from this pattern: not only was he often childlike himself, as are so many comedians, but he tenderly related to children in his on- and off-screen performances. This chapter's focus on Danny Kaye as the paradigmatic children's star of his time has an implicitly larger reach: most of the writing on comic stars and their films, though it pays lip service to their appeal to the juvenile segment of the dual child-adult audience, in practice bypasses any attempt to analyse the child audience's response, preferring the less difficult terrain of the adult audience's reaction. Thus, the particulars of Kaye's persona and performances and their attractions for children addressed here point to more general issues attached to family films and their dual audience's responses.

Traits of Kaye as performer that were especially appealing to children are his candid, fresh-faced looks—that "nice face" that both Miss Shanley (Virginia Mayo) and a policeman remark on in *Wonder Man* (H. Bruce Humberstone, 1945); his gentleness; his ability to speak in broad funny voices and accents (aspects of the mimicry Freud saw as "the child's best art and the driving motive of most of his games");[1] his penchant for nonsense; his trademark scatting; occasional eruptions into non-lexical noises; and his ultra-rapid delivery of infernally tongue-twisting lyrics, working the cusp between sense and nonsense. Further, there is the "ugly duckling" transformational nature of his characters' narrative trajectories; the moral simplicities of the plots he inhabits, which feature lots of chases in their finales; his doing what Freud also famously observed children love—letting himself as an adult "down to their level";[2] his empathy with animals; the saving grace for a child of the lack of intense romantic interactions in his plots; and the occasional resemblance of his manic moments to childish tantrums. There is also what Peter Ustinov called "a fundamental helplessness,"[3] with which the child may be thought to identify, analogous to his or her own situation, and which occasions much comedy based on his incorrigible accident proneness.

Kaye's significant, though rare, on-screen interaction with children comes in three films: *Merry Andrew*, *The Five Pennies*, and, most famously, *Hans Christian Andersen*. *Hans Christian Andersen* will be addressed at length in this chapter's second part. In *Merry Andrew*, though Kaye's Andrew Larrabee eventually swaps teaching classics for the circus, he is a schoolteacher for much of the narrative, though of a very different sort from his enemy the Gradgrindish pedant in *Hans Christian Andersen*. Kaye has three numbers in *Merry Andrew* in which he (a) instructs his pupils in mildly anarchic liberty in a paean to Pan ("The creature bacchanalian / No good Episcopalian / Believes in"), (b) turns geometry into play on the croquet lawn, and (c) gives, with Selena, the boys' dormitory a more sober lesson in deferred gratification ("You can't always have what you want / I'm sorry to say that it's so"), quasi-anarchic release balanced by realism. However, *The Five Pennies*, a biopic of the jazz musician Red Loring deploying familiar musical biopic thematics—the clash of career and family, achievement blighted by tragedy, retirement, and comeback—gives narrative centrality to the protagonist's relationship with his daughter (Susan Gordon and Tuesday Weld at different ages). Red retires out of guilt over her catching polio when he was touring; she finally pushes him to do a comeback concert, during which she is able to abandon her crutches and dance with him. Four of the film's numbers are sung to or with his daughter. With his wife and the band, he sings "Lullaby in Ragtime" to the baby; he sings "The Five Pennies" and "The Music Goes Round and Round" to his daughter (Susan Gordon) in the winningly casual, teacherly mode that is so pronounced in *Hans Christian Andersen*. And finally, he performs in a trio with his daughter and Louis Armstrong in which she holds her own against the other two.

On very rare occasions, Kaye appears as a literal rather than a metaphorical child. In *Knock on Wood* (Melvin Frank and Norman Panama, 1954) Jerry/Kaye's adult self regresses to childhood under hypnosis and starts speaking in the immature voice that is heard in some of Kaye's later children's sound recordings. Then young Jerry, played by a child actor, watches as his father (in an oedipal trope, played by Kaye himself) performs on stage, and then precipitates a marital quarrel that reveals the infantile sources of both Jerry's fear of marriage and his love of the theatre. Jerry's ventriloquist's doll, Clarence, his miniature double, functions as his disruptive infantile self. In *On the Riviera* (Walter Lang, 1951), the most wholly adult of his comedies, Kaye performs "Popo the Puppet", not as a child but as a child's toy, speaking immaturely: "I went to the zoo with my mummy and saw all the animals, didn't I," he says, then mispronounces the names of animals and plants, for example, "ephelant." In other films, the child, though absent, is invoked. In *The Secret Life of Walter Mitty*, for example, when Mitty daydreams being an RAF fighter pilot hero, the party piece he performs for his fellow officers is a child-audience-directed impersonation of an ancient Germanic music professor lecturing on the instruments of the orchestra, which in terms of realistic motivation is hardly plausible, since the military audience would surely have wanted more adult—in both senses of the term—or more sentimental mess room entertainment. In *On the Riviera*, which is not just the most adult, but also the most sexually suggestive of his films, the number "Popo the Puppet," in which Kaye is attached to strings like a marionette and sings and dances as if being operated by a puppeteer seems equally odd considering the film's sophistication, but here again, it emphasizes the comedian's recurrent child motif that turns up even in one of his least child-oriented roles.

Although the presence of children in a children's film provides the child audience with obvious points of identification, it is in no way necessary because comedians will endear themselves to the child audience by acting childishly or in other ways that children find appealing, even in wholly adult-populated narrative environments. Most of Kaye's comedy inhabits this terrain. The opening of *The Inspector General* (Henry Koster, 1949), illustrates this clearly. Here, Kaye, in the role of the illiterate peasant Georgi, is first shown aiding his unscrupulous boss Yakov (Walter Slezak) in a scam selling villagers a cure-all elixir that is actually furniture polish. Georgi's introduction is, of course, that of the much-anticipated comedian star behind the character, who (like Abbot and Costello, Laurel and Hardy, Martin and Lewis, and the Three Stooges) was certainly known to 1940s and 1950s children far more than any non-comedian stars. Georgi first appears as an apparently bodiless head, in a warm-up for the hard sell, after which, supposedly recovered from total paralysis, he begins energetically touting the elixir. In his sales spiel, he recounts the many childhood diseases he had and doctors he consulted before finding this cure. When he sees that one of his victims of his scam is a frail old woman, his conscience rebels; he confesses the fraud to her but is overheard by the now-angry customers; the confidence men are forced to flee, running for their lives.

Three factors regulate the comedic flow in *The Inspector General*. The first is *velocity*, the comedian's and the sequence's constant prestissimo (the musical terminology, apt because of the structural role music plays throughout is a reminder, if we needed it, that Kaye's comedies are musicals). The confluence of the comedian's linguistic and bodily velocities (he is reintroduced bursting feet first through a screen), moving fast and talking and singing even faster, is self-referentially articulated when, frenetically rhyming the names of the diseases (laryngitis, pharyngitis, appendicitis, and so on) the elixir supposedly cures, he collapses into a spectator, gasping, "Have you ever been short of breath?" There is no division of child and adult audience here, since admiration for the super-rapid tempi crosses any potential barrier. The second is Kaye's trademark swerving mid-action from topic to topic, character to character, mode to mode, register to register, with extreme agility (most famously on view in the Hollywood movie parody in *Up in Arms* [Elliott Nugent, 1944]). The technique elicits admiration across age brackets (although, on occasion, some of the allusions may escape children). The third is Kaye's ability to address both his child and adult audiences equally, and often simultaneously. One instance is the micro-segment at the beginning of *The Inspector General* of Georgi's recital of medical conditions ("Do you get colds or prickly heat?") with its four "hiccups," where the word, on each occasion, is bracketed, decelerated, separated from the verbal flow, and expanded into four increasingly distorted variations that resist conventional description. This sequence, without doubt, is equally open to child and adult audiences; after all, everyone is familiar with hiccups and their disruptive somatic effects.

Similarly, other comic moments—often beginning at a simple, child-directed level—attain adult admiration through their expertise. For instance, there is Kaye's explosive tantrum, directed at the old man with the ear trumpet after Kaye has asked him, "Are you bothered by quiet?" and gets no reply. Georgi's gentle repetition of "quiet," fails again to get a reply, which provokes a prolonged manic bellowing of the word, with stamping feet, flailing arms, and extreme bodily contortions. When Georgi has finished, the unfazed elder remarks admiringly about Georgi's "nice" dancing, which pushes adult memory back to an image of Kaye and Dinah Shore jiving in *Up in Arms* several years earlier. But the moment, we may speculate, still works for children, who do not have that memory but can still revel in the incongruity of Kaye's frenetic actions. The musical allusions in Georgi's *sprechgesang* presume adult knowledge that only a minority of children might have shared: "Hungarian Rhapsody Number 2," the 1908 pop standard revived by Betty Grable in *Coney Island* (Walter Lang, 1943). Yet the classical music's infectious rhythms and the lilt of the pop song easily cross differences of age and knowledge.

There are no such barriers to be negotiated in the parts of the aforementioned scene in *The Inspector General* in which the comedy is concentrated in close-ups on the star's facial gestures. In the sequence's first segment, Kaye's supposedly severed head responds, sometimes comically ineptly, to his boss's commentary, and the simplest child-oriented comedy here involves the most basic parts of the comic's most fundamental physical repertoire: risible eye movements, an independently moving ear; happy and sad gurnings; comic distress when he is forced to drink the elixir, his unwilling mouth forced open by

Yakov, who pulls Georgi's ear like a lever. In the fourth segment, a more complex comedy of facial movements forms around Georgi's account of his childhood diseases, following the pattern "When I was one" (*facial twitch symptomatic of the disease*), "When I was two" (*different facial move symptomatic of another disease*), and so on, up to "When I was eight," each age accompanied by a different facial symptom. These micro-diagnostics peak at "When I was four" and "When I was nine," where, instead of a single twitch, there are retrospective successive flurries of the previous symptoms, three at "four," but as many as six at "nine," constituting a minute tour de force of non-tendentious comedy.

As noted, velocity, much emphasized in *The Inspector General*, is a major feature of Kaye's comic performances, but not of his role in *Hans Christian Anderson*, which utilizes a different, quieter set of his skills (something C. A. Lejeune, in her contemporary review of the film, remarked upon).[4] As a harbinger of that performance, the sequence's final segment (when, overcome with guilt at cheating the old woman, Georgi confesses the fraud to her) is important. The comedy here of the old woman's unexpected resistance to his virtuously trying to take away her bottle of elixir and in Kaye's classic double-take when he realises that his confession has been overheard emphasize beneath the trickster's pranks, the character's and comedian's niceness, his good-heartedness, are always present in the films, but are overtly emphasized here, as they will be in *Hans Christian Andersen*.

Steve Seidman's influential definition of "comedian comedy" (i.e., centred on comedians, like Kaye, whose film personae are derived from other branches of entertainment—in Kaye's case, stand-up comedy, revue, cabaret, radio, and the Broadway stage—and take precedence over the usual modes of characterization by foregrounding the comedian's persona over that of the narrative character), lists various generic motifs widely shared among comedian-comics. The most important of these are "childishness," "animalism," "identity confusion," "dual or multiple roles," "the threat of madness," "the mirror motif," uninhibited "erotic impulses" (but at the same time, "displacement" of them), and "sexual confusion."[5] All these attributes feature more or less with Kaye, all modulated comically. The destabilizations of the double, devoid of the uncanny, tend much less to fear than to fun (think of the comedy generated by Kaye's doubling roles in *Wonder Man* and *On the Double* [Melville Shavelson, 1961], as well as *On the Riviera*). Threats of madness benignly contained have their comic parallel in comedians' extremes of linguistic and behavioural disorder (with Kaye, flights of semi-manic explosiveness are found, especially in the early films). Two more of Seidman's categories, the topoi of animality and of sex and gender ("uninhibited erotic impulses, but at the same time displacement of them, and sexual confusion") are attached to Kaye in characteristic ways examined below in the context of his child audience's pleasure.

Animals/Animality. The primary quality that comics respond to with animals is ferality, which is associated positively with unrepressed, unsocialized energy. Kaye certainly often fits this schema: witness his associations with Daffy Duck in the Looney Tunes cartoon *Book Revue* (Bob Clampett, 1946) and Bugs Bunny in Merrie Melodies' *Hot Cross Bunny* (Robert McKimson, 1948); both cartoons are testament to Kaye's cross-generational stardom at the time and to children's enjoyment of the wilder characteristics, the mild anarchism, of his early films. In *Up in Arms*, when Mary (Constance Dowling) is in danger of being discovered on board the ship, Kaye/Danny Weems distracts the searchers by crouching on all fours and imitating a barking dog; when he is apprehended, he blows a raspberry in his interrogator's face and scoots off, barking again. In *Wonder Man*, when Edwin telephones Miss Shanley (Virginia Mayo), a dog barks when she asks where he is working at midnight (which the plot requires him to keep from her) and his reply, improvised from the dog's barking, is that he's in a pet shop. When the dog inconveniently won't bark again, Kaye launches into an imitation of a whole menagerie—chickens, dogs, cats, owls, and even a talking parrot. Such recurring moments clearly have child appeal, but what is unusual (though hardly unique) in emphasis and extent with Kaye is his empathetic relationship with animals; he treats them as fellow beings to befriend and converse with, reminding us of Freud's insight that "children show no trace of the arrogance which urges civilized men to draw a hard-and-fast line between their own nature and that of all other animals. Children have no scruples over allowing animals to rank as their full equals."[6] In a publicity still for *Merry Andrew*, the female star, Pier Angeli, is on Kaye's right, and the chimpanzee he befriends, Angelina, is on his left. Pier Angeli is not touching him, but Angelina is resting her head on his shoulder. It is a comically hyperbolic statement of Kaye's characters' relation to the animal world, often at a tangent from comedian comics' usually more feral one, as when Angelina is drenched by rain, and Andrew, worried that she will catch a cold, caringly puts his jacket around her.

Examples of Kaye's characters' attachment to animals abound—for instance, his relationship with his milk-cart horse, Agnes, in *The Kid from Brooklyn*; Andrew's replying "how do you do?" to a workhorse's whinnying in *Merry Andrew*; or Mitty opening his office window to feed the pigeons with a "good morning everybody." And then there is Georgi, starving in *The Inspector General*, politely asking a horse for some of his oats. Later, when Georgi asks some soldiers if he can share the scraps they're giving to their dog, they make him beg for them, doglike, and then force him to race the dog for a chunk of meat; but when the dog wins, Kaye courteously lets him have it, telling him, "You won it fair and square." Or Hans, hitting the road for Copenhagen in *Hans Christian Andersen* and stopping to fix his shoes and talk to a large dog, telling him, "You're lucky you don't have to wear shoes," and musing on the expression "a dog's life." Though instances of feral comedy may outnumber the gentler kind, the latter are particularly characteristic, with only Mitty's understandable dislike of his fiancée's unlovable lapdog an exception. With Kaye's characters it's not just the trait of liking animals but something deeper, that sense of a childlike equality with them Freud remarked on in *Totem and Taboo*.

Masculinity. Serious writing on sex and gender motifs that has attached to Kaye has moved away from rather crude, unevidenced attempts to "out" him to a more useful emphasis on performative ambiguities along a spectrum of masculinities.[7] Such analyses implicitly laud the actor-comedian's skills as an impersonator across that spectrum, from the woman-hating "Antoine of Paris" in *Walter Mitty* to the promiscuously heterosexual Henri Duran in *On the Riviera* to, most virtuosically, the dazzling switching between the ineffectual Hubert and his mesmerized transformation into the parodically macho swordsman-seducer Giacomo in the hypnosis scenes in *The Court Jester*. *Wonder Man* and *On the Double* are built around doublings that split Kaye into a nervously deficient and a comically macho male, with *On the Riviera* a similar but more nuanced version. In these films, Seidman's uninhibited "erotic impulses" are placed with the hyper-macho figure, and the "displacement of them" with his antithesis, while the "sexual confusion" is found in the extremes of masculinity within the doubles, and in the traces of androgyny many have seen in Kaye.

Whatever these types may signify to adult audiences, the question we are considering here is their meanings for Kaye's child viewers. We might speculate that there were four: (a) underlying everything else, delight in caricatures of types of masculinity known to children, but largely innocent of adult socio-sexual interpretations; (b) laughter at the passive Kaye characters' naivete and spasms of anxiety, but at the same time identification with those traits as they have been experienced by a child; (c) laughter at the typical Kaye character's diffidence around women but, simultaneously, a more complex identification in which the child sees in that relationship him- or herself figured in relation to the mother; (d) and lastly, the non-macho elements in the Kaye persona (celebrated most unambiguously in *The Court Jester*, where Jean [Glynis Johns] falls in love with him when he is singing a lullaby to the baby) may be thought to appeal to children by virtue of a softened masculinity lightened of aggressive (or even frightening) characteristics, or, at least, suggesting, as with the other doubles, a middle way between extremes of masculinity, with more emphasis on the softened ones.[8] Whatever credence we give to such speculations, it is important to stress that they only have meaning in the context of the comic delight created by the performer.

HANS CHRISTIAN ANDERSEN

I'm Hans Christian Andersen, Andersen that's me.
—sung by Danny Kaye in the film

Kaye's appointment in 1954 as the United Nations International Children's Fund's Goodwill Ambassador for Children was a case of life imitating art, for it was doubtless the recurrent images of Kaye as Andersen singing Frank Loesser's musical versions of the famous tales, either surrounded by spellbound children or in single encounters with lonely, vulnerable small individuals, that led Maurice Pate, who had been the executive director of UNICEF since 1947, to offer Kaye the post, which he filled until his death in 1987. Those who are curious could look at the beginning of *Assignment Children* (1954)—the documentary short film advertising Kaye's new off-screen role—to see him recounting a meeting with Pate, Madame Pandit (India's ambassador to the United States), and Dag Hammarskjold that initiated the project. Kaye's commitment to this much-publicized role, whatever it may have contributed to his already stellar reputation, was wholehearted, as shown in his trip to India, where he visits a Malaria Institute, a DDT plant, and encourages villagers to give children an anti-tuberculosis vaccine; takes in a polio ward in Japan; and, of course, entertains non-English-speaking child audiences with non-linguistic antics and interacts with the cutest individual children.

Hans Christian Anderson gathered together many previous workings of the child motif in Kaye's earlier comedies, and in doing so, underwritten by his later UNICEF activities, became remembered as a paradigm of the child-oriented family film, despite the various conflicting ambiguities traced below. As Kaye's film box office success dimmed in the late 1950s and early 1960s, the recording career he'd had in the 1940s revived, largely because of the lasting resonance of his performances of the Frank Loesser songs in the film. Because Kaye's vocal numbers are important moments in nearly all his films, it is useful to begin with an overview of that career with an emphasis on the songs most appealing to children. In "Dinah" (1942), he used his crazed Russian character, mild surrealism, and hectic scatting to grotesquely distort the popular sentimental song ("Deena is there anyone feena, in the state of Caroleena?"), ending with nearly a half minute of accelerated scatting.

Nearly all the songs Kaye recorded with the Andrews Sisters between 1947 and 1949 were also novelty numbers and played on his comedic family film persona, foregrounding comic accents—Scottish in "Amelia Cordelia MacHugh," Latin American in "The Big Brass Band from Brazil," and "Beatin', Bangin', and Scratchin' "—with pronounced onomatapoeic and alliterative effects, such as the "oompah, oompah, cigaloo" in "The Big Brass Band from Brazil" and the "Chinga, ara, sa, sa" of an American military band in the song of the same euphonic name, and lyrics that featured comic rhymes and basic verbal play, for example, the refrain in "Amelia Cordelia MacHugh"—"*MacWho?*" Their cover of the popular "The Woody Woodpecker Song" (1948) combines many of these child-appealing elements with the Woodpecker's manic "oh hohohoho ho" cry and woodpecking sounds made by the orchestra. The most popular of his songs with the Andrews Sisters (briefly third on the Billboard charts in 1947) was "Civilization." The witty lyrics voice the resistance of a native African to missionary propaganda about the benefits of US "civilization"—automobiles, films, false teeth, and so on—culminating in the atom bomb, eliciting the protest, "Bongo, Bongo, Bongo / I don't want to leave the Congo / Oh No! No! No! No! No!" Regardless of which of these allusions younger children might or might not have taken up, they would surely have been delighted by the comic alliteration and assonance of "Bongo Bongo Bongo" and "Bingle Bangle Bungle / I don't wanna leave the jungle / Oh, No! No! No!" (while older children would surely have enjoyed the song's broad ironies).

Cut to two album covers: The cover of *Danny Kaye for Children* (Coral, 1959) is a Norman Rockwell–style painting of a benign Kaye and four excited children, two boys, two girls; it is an updating of images of Kaye/Andersen enchanting children in *Hans Christian Andersen*. The cover of *Mommy Gimme a Drinka Water* (Capitol, 1958) has an elongated Kaye spread out on a wooden chair dressed as a gawky child in long socks, shorts, a child's shirt, and silly hat, with his head and funny facial expression turned to the viewer. Together, the images represent two aspects of Kaye's relationship to children:

first, the empathetic adult charmer-adviser; and second, the adult as child. In films Kaye was usually the child metaphorically rather than literally, but in the songs, he often takes on a child's persona. "All I Want for Christmas Is My Two Front Teeth" (1949, with Patti Andrews) and the songs on *Mommy Gimme a Drinka Water*, such as "I'm Five," act out, for adults as well as children, the traumas and joys of childhood. Kaye's vocal career as he moved into 45s (1949) and LP albums (1948)—with peaks in the late 1940s and the mid- to late 1950s—consisted basically of recording versions of mainstream ballads and soundtracks from the films (especially *Hans Christian Andersen*). Later, many of the earlier albums or new compilations based on older albums were released on CD, cultivating the nostalgia market and demonstrating Kaye's persistence in popular memory.

Though surprisingly large tracts of *Hans Christian Andersen* embrace an adult text about the disillusioning vicissitudes of romantic love, Frank Loesser's charming songs nonetheless encourage children as much as adults to sing along, particularly to songs like "Inchworm," "The King's New Clothes," "The Ugly Duckling," and "Thumbelina"— or, in the less riven parts of the adult sectors of the narrative, the charming "No Two People Have Ever Been So in Love," the affecting "Anywhere I Wander," and the ever-green "Wonderful Copenhagen." During the 1950s, these were complemented by songs more wholly aimed at children, such as "The Little White Duck," "Tubby the Tuba," and "I Tawt I Taw a Puddy Tat," with Kaye playing the role of children's storyteller on albums such as *Grimm's and Hans Christian Andersen's Fairy Tales* (Golden Records, 1953) and *Famous Folk Tales from Around the World Told by Danny Kaye* (Golden Records, 1961). A relaxed, unobtrusive didacticism in "Tubby the Tuba" reassures children that, how-ever overwhelming their disadvantages seem, something fulfilling will happen in their lives (like Tubby's fame-giving Bullfrog Concerto). "The Little White Duck" unobtru-sively gives a lesson in accepting with equanimity the realities of the world's food chain: "Frogs Eat Butterflies, Snakes Eat Frogs, Hogs Eat Snakes, Men Eat Hogs."[9] And even the happy cartoon-reminiscing drama of Tweetypie's fears of being devoured by Sylvester, and Sylvester's frustration at failing to eat him, touches on such realities.

Hans Christian Andersen: Two Narratives

What follows divides this family film into the children's narrative and the adult narrative; the children's narrative centres on Hans and the small children who are his original au-dience, and the adult narrative centres on the melodrama of Hans's doomed passion for the ballerina. The children's narrative welcomes the adult viewer (who, as Bergson and Freud agree, may find nostalgic pleasure in regaining the "lost laughter of childhood")[10] because comic elements that are pleasing to the child are often also pleasing to adults, awakening in them pleasurable pre-adult feelings and nostalgia. The relation of children to the adult narrative is more problematic and will not be centrally addressed here.

Paradoxically, Kaye's performance in the children's narrative of *Hans Christian Andersen* is in many ways unlike those in his earlier comedies. Elements in his earlier films marked particularly attractive to children, such as those anarchic flights and spasms that first brought him to fame, the slapstick elements of his style, the tongue-twisting lyrics, exist here only in an occasional, diminished form. For instance, when Hans puts down the schoolmaster with his fantastical invention of numbers getting married and having children, or his performance for Peter of the courtship of the table and chair. Other elements of his persona are emphasized instead: his gentleness, the daydreaminess of a kind of Nordic Walter Mitty, his combination of jauntiness and vulnerability, his sensitivity, the quickness and inventiveness evident in all his roles, his grace of movement (here subdued), all overlaid by the candidness, kindliness, and perspicacity that the performer exudes.

Four Songs

The defining moments of the children's text are Kaye's performances of four charming Frank Loesser songs. Complexly relational and intimate, the three songs addressed to

FIGURE 18.1. Hans and the Ballerina in the adult melodrama text in *Hans Christian Andersen* (1952, RKO). Frame-grab.

individual children (the inchworm counts as a surrogate child) are the antithesis of the brilliant numbers written for Kaye by Sylvia Fane, where the solo performer displays applause-demanding virtuosity and often adopts outlandish comic personae. Indeed, thinking of children's rapt attention when Kaye is doing one of his UNICEF gigs, one might feel that a major marker of the seemingly unmediated transparency of Kaye's performance is the convincing response he draws out of the children in Hans's scenes, most memorably, from Peter J. Votrian as the "Ugly Duckling" and, to a lesser degree, Beverly Washburn, the little girl in "Thumbelina." Both were accomplished child actors, but we also see such responses from the many uncredited nonprofessional children in the group scenes.

Evident across the songs are various of Kaye's performance characteristics in this film: (a) his spellbinding but uncoercive presence (he often asks the children for permission—"Do you want me to tell a story? Should I go on?") is the opposite of authoritarian, as are his relaxed, informal gestures and postures, mostly sitting, or crouching near the inchworm on the marigold; (b) his ability to convey sympathetic immersion in the children's worlds; and (c) without breaking that bond, to convey Hans's own self-conscious reactions to his dramatizations, and, in the case of "Thumbelina," to divide, or rather, expand, attention to four characters (the girl he's addressing, himself, Thumbelina, and her playmate); and (d) his gentle tactility, particularly with the thumb puppets in "Thumbelina," the sick boy in "The Ugly Duckling," and even when he lovingly caresses the marigold in "Inchworm" (it should be emphasized that audiences in 1952, that different and, in some ways, less sexually fraught era, would have found nothing untoward in Hans's tactility with the "Ugly Duckling"). The intimacy of these songs yields maximum gain from minimal staging, most notably evident in the metamorphosis of Kaye's thumbs into Thumbelina and her playmate. Though gentle empathy is dominant, the songs and Kaye's light baritone voice vary in their registers: the juvenile naughtiness of the finale of "The King's New Clothes"; the demotic of "The Ugly Duckling" ("Pwak, get outta town"); the bounciness of "Thumbelina"; and the meditational quiet of "Inchworm."

"The King's New Clothes"

After opening with a view of Andersen's home village of Odense, the film moves on to indelible images that resonate in the memory as its defining moments: Andersen/Kaye surrounded by children excitedly responding to his preamble and song, with a kite—symbol of the aspiring imagination—high in the sky but prevented from disappearing by the textbooks anchoring it to the ground. This trope suggests a melding of imagination and facts rather than their complete opposition, an early hint that the numbers may be less simple than expected. The group sweetness is not completely unalloyed: the little girl arriving late kisses Hans, and though she is courteously thanked, she is also tenderly reprimanded and told not to be late again; the scene suggests a discipline that Hans's enemies—the burgomasters and schoolteacher—fail to understand; a second complicating hint. A third follows quickly with the curious business of the Queen of China doll, which Hans transforms into a King simply by adding a moustache.

The doll sequence contains several ambiguities; there are adult-oriented sexual overtones in Hans's comment that one would be surprised how many kings are just queens with moustaches, but this is also readable as asserting the equality of boys and girls (though with an innuendo of juvenile investigation of sexual difference when altering the doll's sex, he admonishes, "No peeking!"). It also leads to a minor crisis when a stubbornly obstreperous little boy refuses Hans's invitation to imagination by insisting that the transformed queen with a moustache is not a king. Hans's reaction to this challenge to his storyteller's authority is a little put down of the small sceptic; but then, in an implicit reversal, his song treats the difficult child's argumentativeness as a positive, his refusal to accept unquestioningly the storyteller's claim linking him with the child in the story, whose unprejudiced eye sees through the conforming adults' misperceptions. The rollicking song that develops from a straightforward, attenuated version of the tale "The Emperor's New Clothes" has characteristics not present in the other three numbers—occasionally rowdy join-ins from the children, and an ingenuity of lyrics marginally closer to Kaye's trademark patter songs, with the wit of the repeated "altogether" (for example, "The suit of clothes is altogether...the most remarkable suit of clothes that I have ever seen") culminating in the juvenile naughtiness of "The King is in the Altogether, the Altogether, the Altogether / He's altogether as naked as the day that he was born." Unlike the other songs that offer healing (curing Thumbelina's and the Ugly Duckling's loneliness, hopefully opening the inchworm/schoolchild's eyes a little wider), "The King's New Clothes" celebrates the deconstructive insight of the child, the bolshy little boy of the beginning, down-to-earth rather than imaginatively floating, like the kite which functions as a symbol of the untrammelled imagination here and in the closing repeat scene. Here it's the villains of the story, the confidence men promising the King wonderful magic clothes who represent the imagination, but put to ill uses, as distinct from the imaginative talents with which Hans dramatizes the story.

"Thumbelina"

The three later songs have in common that Hans performs them not to the happy group, but to individuals (the inchworm is a caterpillar, but as already said, it is also a surrogate schoolchild) who are unhappy in some way. They also show Hans, despite his own problems, reaching out in empathy to others with his art, a lesson for older as well as younger watchers. In "Inchworm," despite Hans's victimization by the authorities, he still empathizes with the inchworm. In "Thumbelina," even from jail he sympathizes with the little girl watching him. In "The Ugly Duckling," though distressed by Doro's (Zizi Jeanmaire) departure, he still responds to the shaven-headed little victim of an undefined illness. Whereas the plight of the "Ugly Duckling" is written all over him, that of the seemingly outgoing young girl in "Thumbelina" is masked by her prettiness and her confident replies to Hans—"Are you all alone in there?" "Are you scared?" Responsive viewers might sense that Hans understands her questions to be self-directed, confessing her loneliness, which—as with the more obviously traumatized "Ugly Duckling"— contrasts with the utopically happy children in the group scenes.

Although the miniature proscenium-stage (the barred window ledge) spectacle Hans fashions for the girl invokes literal anatomical smallness ("though you're no bigger than my thumb," "tiny little thing"), the girl—as distinct from Thumbelina, to whom the words are directed—is actually far from dwarfish. The references to her smallness are therefore neither literal nor the song's dominant subject, but instead seem to represent childhood *feelings* of smallness and of being lost in the big world. Hans's diagnosis leads him—after courteously asking permission—to perform for her, which he does with his usual unassuming didacticism. Rather than follow the original literary tale of the minuscule Thumbelina's adventures (near-forced marriages to the mole and toad, escape with the swallow, eventual marriage to the tiny prince, and so on), this performance of the song is built around an endearing miniature puppet drama that is largely on the theme of loneliness; Hans first transmogrifies his thumb into Thumbelina, a playmate for the lonely girl, and then, after discovering that the Thumbelina he has brought to life also suffers from loneliness, imprints her face on his other thumb, to make a playmate for the little puppet (Figure 18.2).

The resulting sequence involving Kaye/Hans, the little girl, and Thumbelina and her new playmate is played out in multiple interactions, so that Hans, in addressing the girl,

FIGURE 18.2. Hans with Thumbelina and her friend in a moment from the children's text in *Hans Christian Andersen* (1952, RKO). Frame-grab.

also intimately addresses Thumbelina, the playmate he has devised for her, and himself, performing a micro-version of other virtuoso comic interactions with multiple people all demanding his attention that are one of his comic trademarks. Such performances require quicksilver changes and adaptations, as when he finds himself a fugitive in the large-scale, rambunctious Italian opera and Russian ballet sequences in *Wonder Man* and *Knock on Wood*. The "digital" ballet he invents for the girl is a dexterous tour de force, perhaps comparable (if at a lesser level of invention and mastery) only to Chaplin's forked bread rolls metamorphosed into dancing shoes in *The Gold Rush* (Charles Chaplin, 1925). Hans's fingers delicately coax Thumbelina's miniature head into lifting and falling in answer to his questions, and then bring the companion thumb to life in a dance duet with Thumbelina, which concludes with a lesson for the child that "when your heart is full of love, you're nine foot tall," lifting Thumbelina high into the air along with the words. At the finish, the little girl looks experimentally at her own thumb (as she has done earlier in the performance), underlining that the gist of the number is less about her literal size than a lesson for the lonely child in self-creating her own resources.

"The Ugly Duckling"

In the moments prefacing the song, darker sides of childhood (scapegoating, victimizing, oppressive peer pressure) are embodied by the sad-faced little boy standing apart—expelled from the storytelling circle by his peers, persecuted for his odd looks, then pushed aside by them in their rush back to school—his hat knocked off, clutching his strangely bald head. Just before Hans notices the boy, a sombre city official has directed silent hostility towards the storyteller, recalling the disapproving Odense of- ficialdom. Hans, having sent his audience off to school, notices the vulnerable child, and asks, "What's the matter? Are you unhappy? Would you like me to tell you a special story?" The boy, clutching his shaven head, eventually nods in cautious assent, edging closer as Hans beckons to him, but also half retreating as he does, the first of a series of delicate shifts of position and emotion that eventually bring him closer to Hans. Kaye's sidelong glance, followed by the camera, makes the audience aware that the steps he is sitting on look on to a lake. The sight of two impeccable swans gives him an idea for a song, and he starts singing, "There once was an ugly duckling with feathers all stubby and brown"; the lyrics move from a dramatization of difference leading to rejection, with repetitions of the demotic, anachronistic "Tsk, Get outta town," to the final meta- morphosis into a desired and accepted adulthood: "All through the winter in his lonely clump of weed / Till a flock of swans spied him there and very soon agreed / You're a very fine swan indeed." As in the other numbers, Kaye's is a more than a straightforward singing performance; rather, it is one of constant, empathetic rapport with the child— at one point he pauses to ask, "Would you like me to tell you the rest of the story?"— drawing the boy more and more into the song.

Interestingly, this is the only number in which there is physical contact between Kaye and a child (apart from the girl who embraces him, not vice versa, in the preamble to "The King's New Clothes" and again at the film's end). Touch has been discreetly re- served for this most difficult encounter. The increasing physical closeness of singer and child leads to Hans's playful gestures, as when, for example, at the line "with [swan's] head so noble and high," he lifts the boy's head as gently he had Thumbelina's, pinches his nose softly, holds his hand, swipes him gently with his index finger, pokes him playfully in the stomach, and then answers the question, "Say, who's an ugly duckling?" with "Not I."

Unexpectedly, though, because the boy's gradually mollifying trauma is so deeply engrained, there is a partial break in confidence at the number's end, when Hans says of the children who have been persecuting him, "So it shouldn't make any difference if they won't play with you," and the boy contradicts him, "But it does, I want to play with them, but they make fun of me, just because I was sick and the doctor shaved my head." Hans replies encouragingly, "But look what happened to the ugly duckling." Touching the boy's arm and putting his hat back on his head, Hans adds, "One day soon you'll look in the mirror, much sooner than you think, and your hair will be grown out and you'll be just like the ugly duckling. You'll be better than any of them, I promise." Doubtful, the boy asks, "Are you sure, Hans?" "Very sure," he answers, nodding firmly and sending the boy off to school. Here, the nearby presence of the hostile official is re-established, and Hans looks up at him nervously, expecting a negative judgement (has his song promised the child too much?). But the official nods and smiles his approval. He departs. Hans relaxes thankfully as the scene returns to a bustling ordinariness as a woman collects her husband's shoes. The sequence, and the song, is a happy ending to the initial drama of alienation, but it differs from the others in its hesitating moments of precariously resolved doubt.

"Inchworm" and Cultural Memory

In a well-remembered sequence, Hans and his young apprentice, Peter, are walking home after the authorities have broken up Hans's storytelling session with the schoolchildren, Peter draws Hans's attention to an inchworm, "the first one of the year," crawling slowly along a marigold. (The tiny larvae of the geometer moth are called "inchworms" because of their odd inching movement.) Hans crouches beside Peter, looks intently at it, and then sings to the tiny creature, which is unseen by the audience:

> Inchworm, inchworm
> Measuring the marigolds
> You and your arithmetic
> You'll probably go far
> Inchworm, inchworm
> Seems to me you'd stop and see
> How beautiful they are.

Not based on an Andersen story, the song is Loesser's and the film's invention, though it is in the spirit of Andersen's other anthropomorphic creatures and animated objects. Like its subject, the song is extremely short, less than a minute, though there are nearly two minutes of contextualizing build-up as the pair pass the school and the children's rote chanting of the times tables floats out from the building ("Two and two are four / Four and four are eight / Eight and eight are sixteen / Sixteen and sixteen are thirty-two") and continues as a counterpoint to Kaye's address to the inchworm. The antipathy between the rigid schoolmaster's and the storyteller's philosophies is accentuated when the schoolmaster, seeing a child waving at Hans, slams the door. Before beginning to sing, Hans looks intently at the marigold and the inchworm and then in the direction of the children's chanting, shaking his head slightly, suggesting scepticism about the value of the lesson if it is not accompanied by other perspectives. This gesture is repeated when he finishes his song with a fleeting look of sadness for children trapped in a delimiting view of the world. Yet for all that it is a rote lesson, Kaye's enactment of Loesser's lyrics and melody is too subtle to create a simple binary opposition (i.e., arithmetic bad, imagination good), for the children's counterpoint is no harsh drone but is, rather, ethereal and beautiful, something not to be denied, but placed within wider values. Kaye sings to the tiny unseen creature with the particular ability he has as an actor to produce the effect of transparent intimacy and sympathy with children and animals; he does not mock the inchworm's dogged measuring, so that when he sings "you'll probably go far," it is without satiric inflection, only the suggestion of things missed out on in pursuing stolid progress alone. A considerably older Kaye (now sixty-eight) performs a charming repeat of the song on *The Muppet Show* (season 3, episode 16, 1979), extending his empathy to the Muppets as he sings to them and conducts them, and encourages the inchworm, here a small green puppet, to crawl onto his hand ("Get your head up and look around").

David Bowie's 2003 statement that Kaye's performance of Loesser's song was a big influence on "Ashes to Ashes" (1980) and, indeed, on many of his songs, created some stir. While asserting the connection's deep-rootedness, Bowie recognized that it might seem hermetic:

> I loved it as a kid and it stayed with me forever. I keep going back to it. You wouldn't believe the amount of my songs that have sort of spun off from that one song. Not that you'd really recognize it. Something like "Ashes to Ashes" wouldn't have happened if it hadn't been for "Inchworm."[11]

Bowie also noted the "child's nursery rhyme element" and "something so sad and mournful and poignant about it."[12] Though there are many cover recordings of the song (by Bowie himself, Cleo Laine, Doris Day, Anne Murray, Paul McCartney, and others), it is clearly the original Kaye version in its audiovisual form that affected Bowie. The same is true of the Hollywood film star Jake Gyllenhaal, who listed "Inchworm" as one of five pieces to be played when he was guest DJ on the radio station KCRW (Santa Monica), saying "Danny Kaye was and is still a huge influence on me as an actor and a performer. I just watched him so much when I was a kid and he had this love of entertaining, I think I heard also about him this real love for children and caring for them and you can tell that it [*sic*] in this song."[13] The alto saxophonist, David Sanford, has also talked about *Hans Christian Andersen*'s impact on him, mentioning "Inchworm," "Thumbelina," "Wonderful Copenhagen," and "Anywhere I Wander."[14] It is this last song that Sanford singled out most: "That particular song was so moving to me, because it just had such a bittersweet yet hopeful quality to it" (though he added, " 'Inchworm' was a great song").[15] Responding to the interviewer's comment, "What a beautiful movie... I'm afraid that *Hans Christian Andersen* has fallen out of the culture," Sanford replied, "I'm so emotionally attached to it that I can't really evaluate it with anything close to objectivity."[16] I can't resist adding to these responses by musicians and actors those of two colleagues, both distinguished professors of English Literature, who still know all the songs by heart; one of them even gifted me his own cover of "Inchworm" over beers in a Newcastle pub.

For me and, I suspect, many who saw the film in early life, such moments fill the memory. But perhaps the film's most perceptive critic when it was released, C. A. Lejeune, took a different view. Celebrating its pleasures—"such a charming entertainment, full of happiness and pathos,"— she declared, "Samuel Goldwyn's film, it must be plainly understood, is not primarily a children's entertainment.... Its niceties, which include a good deal of brilliant ballet from Roland Petit and his prima ballerina, Renée Jeanmaire, are addressed to adults and adolescents rather than to the junior spectator."[17] Perhaps aware that she had gone too far in demoting its child-friendly attractions, she restored the balance a little, adding, "I should hesitate to say that children won't love it."[18] It is, however, true that much of the later narrative is adult and adolescent oriented. Apart from Lejeune's sensitivity to Kaye's nuanced performance ("I had not imagined that it was in his power to play a part so gently, to resist every temptation to exaggerate voice or gesture"), her review, nicely titled "Dan's Andersen," is also notable for cutting through high critical embarrassment at the film's flagrant infidelity to biographical facts, writing, "It would also be misleading to suggest that the biographical background of this picture is anything more solid than the take-off needed for a flight of fancy." In this, she, of course, alludes to the film's notorious epigraph: "Once upon a time there lived in Denmark a great storyteller named Hans Christian Andersen. This is not the story of his life, but a fairy tale about the great spinner of fairy tales."

Lejeune most certainly underestimates the film's juvenile audience appeal, but the adult orientation of the ballet scenes and the surrounding melodrama is undeniable. Indeed, in several countries, Hans's obsession with Doro took titular pre-eminence— for example, *Hans Christian Andersen et la Danseuse* in France and Belgium; *Hans Christian Andersen und die Tänzerin* in West Germany and Austria. Large tracts of the second half of the film are devoted to Andersen's doomed love for Doro, a relationship quite unlike any found in the conventional family film romance plot ending with conjoined parents-to-be such as a child might tolerate while also being comforted by its familial conclusion or having stably married parents throughout. Instead, its hero is a naive, tortured, solipsistic lover pursuing the unreachable, a ballet dancer who recalls Andersen's real-world obsession with the soprano Jenny Lind and other unsuccessful objects of desire of both sexes. One can see in Hans elements of Kaye's persona that, in other circumstances, would be at home in a children's narrative (the incorrigible fantasist, the comically anxious, the accident-prone naïf) darkened here to melodramatic inflections.

HART TROUBLES: MOSS HART'S NARRATIVE

After many versions of the script had been rejected by Samuel Goldwyn (whose long-standing pet project it was),[19] the legendary Broadway figure Moss Hart was brought in to write the screenplay. It may seem that Hart was a strange choice for the job, but he had distinguished stage and film credits. He had written (with Kurt Weill and Ira Gershwin)— the most intellectual of Broadway musicals, *Lady in the Dark* (1941), in which Kaye had a part that helped launch his film career—and the screenplays of *Gentleman's Agreement* (Elia Kazan, 1947) and *A Star is Born* (George Cukor, 1954), a musical with tragic strains. Hart's credentials suggest that the narrative of *Hans Christian Andersen* should not be simplistically scorned by critics, as it often has been over the years on account of its supposed cloying sentimentality. Instead of complaining at what is missing (for example, Andersen's actual biographical circumstances, his literary apprenticeship, work in other genres, his shambling unattractiveness and narcissism, and his dislike of being classed as a children's writer), critics might pay attention to what actually *is* there, which shows Andersen as a subject with multiple resonances for Hart. Both, for instance, wrote extraordinary but unreliably self-mythicizing autobiographies, Hart's *First Act* (1959), Andersen's *The Fairy Tale of My Life* (1847); both had poverty-stricken childhoods; both were bisexual; both suffered from depression; both escaped their constricted childhoods and entered glamorous art worlds. "I have a pet theory of my own, probably invalid, that the theatre is an inevitable refuge of the unhappy child,"[20] wrote Hart, and the concentration on the theatre in the second half of *Hans Christian Andersen* references not only Hart's milieu but also Andersen's early theatre connections. Within its limitations and paradoxical freedoms, the film's faux naive account of Andersen's life is altogether less simple than it may appear.

Troubled in later life, Hart was said to have been analysed twice daily.[21] We also know of his sessions with two New York psychoanalysts Gregory Zilboorg and Lawrence S. Kubie, the latter of whom apparently aimed to counter the homosexual element in his bisexuality.[22] Considering this and the celebrated psychoanalytic thematics of *Lady in the Dark*, we should hardly be surprised to find the celluloid Andersen's trajectory shadowed by such concerns and the oneiric sequences of the film's second half. When the naively enraptured Hans is called upon to make new shoes for Doro, he takes her denunciation of the angry ballet master as "that unkind man" literally. Later, his young apprentice, Peter, after observing the married pair's verbal and physical violence to each other, comprehends their sadomasochistic erotic bond that Hans is blind to. In one of several daydream sequences, Hans fantasizes rescuing Doro as she submissively dances to her husband's sadistically beating stick. Moving through an expressionist Caligarian mise-en-scène in which he imagines Doro calling for help, he crashes through a door hyper-masculinely. Fighting acrobatically like Stewart Granger in a period action-romance (*Scaramouche* [George Sidney, 1952] and *The Prisoner of Zenda* [Richard Thorpe, 1952] were released in the same year), Hans wrestles the ballet master to the ground; but, with him at his mercy, contemptuously only breaks his phallic stick and turns as victor to face Doro rushing towards him, only for the illusion to break before she reaches him.

Hans's love dream continues in another oneiric sequence where they marry and sing the charming honeymooners' duet "No Two People (Have Ever Been So in Love)"—recapitulating the marriage fantasy in *Up in Arms*, Kaye's first feature, and ending equally unhappily (though in the earlier film another bride repairs the loss). The relationship between Hans and Peter also founders when Peter tries to convince Hans of his misunderstanding of Doro's relationship with her husband. Though their relationship is chastely presented, we might feel that beyond Peter's ironic role as father figure to the older Hans, there are intimations of unconsummated homosexual desire, at least on the part of Hans. Hans's second gift to Doro, the "Little Mermaid" ballet, is another story of failed impossible desire, with parallels between the female victim of unrequited love and Hans himself. Also, notably, Hart's ballet narrative avoids the optimistic relief of the original tale's path to human life and immortality for the mermaid, ending on the contrary in her return to death and materialist dissolution in the sea, and the Prince's inability to stop her.

CHILD, ADULT, CHILD-ADULT

The dichotomy outlined here between the child-oriented narrative with its master images of Andersen storytelling to children and the adult melodrama of obsessive love, with a third strand, connected to the first, of Andersen's rise to initial literary success, is, of course, too absolute for a narrative that moves between all three. (For instance, the oneiric sequence "No two people have ever been so in love" has a mise-en-scène and music of child-entrancing prettiness.) Further, it might be argued that the child-adult narrative division can be suggestively recast into two different sorts of child-centred narratives (literal for children, metaphorical for adults), one typical of the "children's film" and one of the "child film" (i.e., films such as *The Fallen Idol* [Carol Reed, 1948] and *The Exorcist* [William Friedkin, 1973] in which the central protagonist is a child, but the audience is definitely adult).[23] So, while in the child-oriented narrative Hans is a benign surrogate parent, the adult narrative transmutes him from parent to child, a trajectory with marked oedipal characteristics: the man-child anxious to please the impossible object of desire mother with gifts, his love for her blocked by a stern powerful father figure, her husband, the ballet master, who exerts dominance over Doro both in the boudoir and on stage.

Hans's incorrigible childlikeness is emphasized by his misreading of Doro's and her husband's sadomasochistic games—making him like a child misinterpreting the primal scene as the couple locked in combat, the father beating the mother (the psychoanalytic allusions are unavoidable, given Moss Hart's great investment in psychoanalysis in his life as well as art). Hans's immaturity in the world of adult passions contrasts with the maturity of his apprentice, the adolescent Peter's understanding of the passions misinterpreted by the older Hans. Cruel though the comedy is, both Doro and her husband find the innocent Hans amusing, condescendingly laughing at him (though with a certain guilt on her part) as adults laugh at the antics of a child imitating something beyond his understanding or physical capacity. In a visual trope, subtle but powerful, the characteristic pose in which the Ugly Duckling stands before Hans during their encounter, hands in front of body clasping his cap, is transferred to Hans in various moments of the melodrama plot, most strikingly where he carries the differently-coloured ballet shoes made for Doro in front of him like a posy, echoing the unhappy child's posture. And when he insists on delivering the shoes to Doro just before the performance, the husband/father figure treats him like a naughty child, locking him away in a scenery storage room as if he were being sent up to bed in disgrace. All these intimations are augmented by that slightly asexual aspect Kaye as actor often projects in amorous situations, so that his passion for Doro never seems very physical at all.

The third narrative strand is Andersen's rise from his supposed beginnings as a cobbler in provincial Odense to a printed metropolitan author. Its defining moment takes place in the newspaper office where the editor, the Ugly Duckling's father, rewards Hans by printing his story, thus establishing him as the published literary figure of Andersen's jaunty song of biographical triumph, "I'm Hans Christian Andersen, Andersen that's me" (underwritten when he sees his theatrical billboard listing as the author of the book of the "Little Mermaid" ballet). A last variation on the child/adult dichotomy/relationship is played out ambivalently in Hans's end-of-narrative return from Copenhagen to Odense, which seems to prioritize a simple orality (child) over written literature (adult) as we see in the film's final scene, a near repetition of its opening with Hans singing favourite stories in a "greatest hits" sort of sequence to the children.

However, it is not quite identical. Whereas in the opening scene the only adults are the hostile schoolteacher and burgomasters interrupting Hans's stories, here at the end as the view widens adults are revealed, including even the schoolteacher (requesting a favourite song), standing behind the children, thus imaging the duality of Andersen's stories and the film's double child/adult audience. Earlier as Hans and Peter walk back to Odense, Hans says that he will give up telling stories, which Peter contradicts with, "You'll tell stories, you'll even write stories" and, with a homage to Loesser's songs, "you'll even sing stories." This convolution of the apparently simple return to orality is further complicated, even denied, by the images of printed texts of some of the most famous stories—*The Steadfast Tin Soldier* (1838), *The Little Mermaid* (1837), *Thumbelina* (1835), *The Red Shoes* (1845)—superimposed on their journeying in a partial binding of the twin children's and adults' texts that jostle for predominance in this rewarding film.

Notes

1. Sigmund Freud, *Jokes and Their Relation to the Unconscious*, Pelican Freud Library 6 (Harmondsworth, UK: Penguin Books, 1992), p. 291.
2. Freud, *Jokes*, p. 292.

3. *Danny Kaye: Nobody's Fool*, South Bank Show, dir. Ken Howard, ITV: 1994.

4. C. A. Lejeune, "Dan's Andersen," *Observer*, December 21, 1952, p. 6.

5. Steve Seidman, *Comedian Comedy: A Tradition in Hollywood Film* (Ann Arbor, MI: UMI Research Press, 1981), pp. 78–121.

6. Sigmund Freud, *Totem and Taboo*, Pelican Freud Library 13 (Harmondsworth, UK: Penguin Books, 1985), pp. 126–127.

7. Especially Martha Bayless, "Danny Kaye and the Fairy Tale of Queerness in 'The Court Jester,'" in Kathleen Coyne Kelly and Tison Pugh (eds.), *Queer Movie Medievalisms* (Farnham, UK: Ashgate, 2009), pp. 185–200.

8. Bayless, "Danny Kaye and the Fairy Tale of Queerness."

9. Wallace Stevens, *Collected Poems of Wallace Stevens* (London: Faber & Faber, 1955), p. 78.

10. Freud, *Jokes*, p. 289.

11. Qtd. in "Danny Kaye 'Inchworm' and 'Ashes' Correlation," David Bowie Wonderworld forum, https://www.tapatalk.com/groups/bowiewonderworld/danny-kaye-inchworm-and-ashes-correlation-t77533.html [accessed May 20, 2020].

12. Ibid.

13. "Jake Gyllenhaal," Guest DJ Project, KCRW, December 2, 2009, https://www.kcrw.com/music/shows/guest-dj-project/jake-gyllenhaal [accessed May 20, 2020].

14. Mike Ragogna, "Jazzin' Around: Conversations with David Sanborn, Lee Ritenour and Kurt Elling," HuffPost, October 5, 2012, https://www.huffpost.com/entry/jazzin-around-conversatio_b_1941485 [accessed May 20, 2020].

15. Ragogna, "Jazzin' Around."

16. Ibid.

17. Lejeune, "Dan's Andersen."

18. Ibid.

19. David Koenig, *King of Jesters* (Irvine, CA: Bonaventure Press, 2012), pp. 141–151 has useful information about Goldwyn's project and the many scripts before Hart took over.

20. Frank Rich, "The Greatest Showbiz Book Ever Written," *New York*, March 7, 2014. nymag.com/news/frank-rich/act-one-moss-hart-2014-3/ [accessed May 21, 2020].

21. Malcolm Goldstein, "Moss Hart Stars in Act Two: A Charmed and Troubled Life," *Observer* (New York), March 7, 2014. <https://observer/2001/04/moss-hart-stars-in-act-two-a-charmed-and-troubled-life/> [accessed June 1, 2020].

22. Rich, "Greatest Showbiz Book Ever Written"; Bruce Kirle, *Unfinished Show Business: Broadway Musicals as Works in Process* (Carbondale: Southern Illinois University Press, 2005), p. 189.

23. As defined in Noel Brown and Bruce Babington, "Introduction: Children's Films and Family Films," in Noel Brown and Bruce Babington (eds.), *Family Films in Global Cinema: The World beyond Disney* (London: I.B. Tauris, 2015), pp. 1–16, at 13–14.

BIBLIOGRAPHY

American Film Institute. "Hans Christian Andersen." AFI Catalog online. https://catalog.afi.com/Catalog/moviedetails/50501 [accessed May 31, 2020].

Andersen, Hans Christian. *The Fairytale of My Life: An Autobiography*. 1947. Lanham, MD: Cooper Square Press, 2000.

Gottfried, Martin. *Nobody's Fool: The Lives of Danny Kaye*. New York: Simon and Schuster, 1994.

Hart, Moss. *First Act: An Autobiography*. New York: Random House, 2002.

Koenig, David. *King of Jesters*. Irvine, CA: Bonaventure Press, 2012.

Lejeune, C. A. "Dan's Andersen." *Observer*, December 21, 1952, p. 6.

Seidman, Steven. *Comedian Comedy: A Tradition in Hollywood Film*. Ann Arbor, MI: UMI Research Press, 1981.

Tynan, Kenneth. *He That Plays the King*. London: Longman Green and Co., 1950.

Wullschlager, Jackie. *Hans Christian Andersen: The Life of a Storyteller*. Chicago: University of Chicago Press, 2002.

CHAPTER 19

REAL ANIMALS AND THE PROBLEM OF ANTHROPOMORPHISM IN CHILDREN'S FILM

CLAUDIA ALONSO-RECARTE
AND IGNACIO RAMOS-GAY

THIS chapter addresses the significance of the use of real animals in Western children's and family films, at both a narrative and an industrial level. As narrativized and highly mediated bodies that are anthropomorphized through genre conventions, animals signify modern visual culture's strained semiotics between the authentic and the artificial, even as they are integrated within shared assumptions about childhood affective development. By unearthing how the children's film, as a genre, prescribes and conditions representations of animals, and by examining the multiple ways in which anthropomorphism colonizes their subjectivity, this chapter approaches the consequential ethical implications that struggle to accommodate genre expectations while appeasing public concern for animal welfare.

APPROACHING GENRE, DECIPHERING ANIMALITY

In recent years, a number of scholars have undertaken the task of analysing animals in film. Notably, Derek Bousé's *Wildlife Films* (2000), Gregg Mitman's *Reel Nature* (1999), David Ingram's *Green Screen* (2000), Akira Mizuta Lippit's *Electric Animal* (2000), and Jonathan Burt's *Animals in Film* (2002) have all tried to articulate how animality is made sense of through the types of narratives and technologies afforded by film.

The attempt at reconciliation between the technological and the natural, they argue, has paved the way for the formulation of a series of filmic conventions, discourses, and strategies (most notably that of anthropomorphism) that have systematized and standardized the modes of animal representation in different filmic genres. Welling defines the anthropomorphizing of animals as "the one-way projection of uniquely human emotions and characteristics onto non-human beings conceived of as radically 'other.'"[1] Thus, for example, a diachronic study of the underlying narratives of wildlife documentaries will reveal how the artifice of editing and scripting of animals' lives has fomented specific social and political ideologies and, ultimately, delivered a distorted version of animality that, though inauthentic, does satisfy audiences' sense of order through established structures. Horror cinema, to consider another example, in its most monstrous manifestation, often resorts to a blurring of the boundaries between the animal and the human in such a way that the anthropomorphic endeavour enlivens animals that exist "beyond the ethical, as do other characters in horror cinema, such as zombies, monsters and psychopathic killers."[2]

Children's film presents challenges of its own that reach far into the nature of anthropomorphism. Amy Ratelle's *Animality and Children's Literature and Film* (2015) exemplifies how criticism of children's literature and of modern philosophical thought inform the medium of cinema. Indeed, an adequate analysis of animality in children's film certainly demands a close inspection of the previous ideology and aesthetic practice that made anthropomorphism the signature rhetorical device applied to animals; but we must also move the discussion towards consideration of how the very instability of the concept of animality intersects with and tests the limits of children's film as a genre in order to appreciate the extent to which animals are supplied as constructs in our crafting of childhood culture.

In *The Children's Film: Genre, Nation and Narrative* (2017), Noel Brown describes the features and structures that allow spectators to recognize patterns and classify productions as children's films. After examining several variables, including audience profiles, ratings, possible censorship, publicity and merchandizing, and narrative strategies and appropriateness (all of which are dependent on the cultural ideology at hand), he concludes that, though hard to categorically define, children's films tend to adhere to five broad principles: (a) "the reaffirmation of family, kinship and community"; (b) "the foregrounding of child, adolescent and teenage figures and their experiences," including those of "symbolic children" that may come in the shape of "lovable animals"; (c) "the exclusion and/or eventual defeat of disruptive social elements"; (d) "the minimization of 'adult' representational elements"; and (e) the resorting to "endings [that] are predominantly upbeat, emotionally uplifting, morally unambiguous and supportive of the social status quo."[3]

The films that will be examined in this essay adhere to the abovementioned features, although some productions may prove more defiant than others. Because the family film genre is also reliant on such characteristics, we shall equally consider these types of productions. Moreover, given that family films are commercially designed to attract parents, guardians, or other family members as much as children,[4] the subject of real animals has particular interest precisely because adults and children relate very differently to them: children are encouraged to empathize with animals, whereas being adult involves the "realistic" acceptance of animal exploitation within an established social order. Current understandings in developmental psychology endorse the stimulation of children's affectivity through animal representations and human-animal relationships. Children's clothing, accessories, books, and toys constitute systematic reproducers of an animal imagery whose object is to elicit a social response from the infant and child, such as empathy, stewardship, caretaking, and other interspecies emotional displays deemed as positive by the culture at hand.[5] When watching a children's film with real animals, many adult viewers will probably deliberate about the moral inconsistencies between the on-screen representation of animality and how capitalist structures of consumption actually harvest animal products and byproducts. As Ratelle contends, "The civilizing process that children go through has been mediated by the animal body. Children are asked both implicitly and explicitly to identify with animals, but then to position themselves as distinctly human through the mode of their interactions with both lived animals and those depicted in literature and film."[6] Outgrowing empathy for animals, in other words, is symptomatic of a graduation into normative adulthood. As an act of affirmation of one's ontological status as human (versus animal), the transition involves a gradual revelation of the extent to which anthropocentrism is institutionalized on different levels.

Brown also emphasizes that "recurrent features in the children's film…are prescribed by what (adult) society believes children *ought to see*."[7] When it comes to real animals, not only does this signify that children are shielded from the actual material interests behind their objectification; it also raises the question of what *seeing an animal* actually implies within today's postmodern and posthuman cultural context. John Berger's oft-cited *Why Look at Animals?*, written in 1977, defines modern capitalism as the ideology that truly fractures the mediation between man and animal. Modernity, in Berger's view, is characterized by the disappearance of the animal, by its commodification in a visual culture where the reproduction of the animal replaces and extinguishes the subject's original animality (a thesis later elaborated on by Lippit). Berger specifically evokes the visual semiotics of zoos to prove his point. It is in the zoo, parents believe, that children can be conveniently and safely exposed to the originals of the animal reproductions they have learned to empathize with (through toys, books, illustrations, films, and other media). Yet as caged animals are ruthlessly abandoned to the monotony of their own apathy and inaction, the tension between the real and the duplicated version of the animal becomes clear:

> The animals seldom live up to the adults' memories, whilst to the children they appear, for the most part, unexpectedly lethargic and dull. (As frequent as the calls of animals in a zoo are the cries of children demanding: Where is he? Why doesn't he move? Is he dead?) And so, one might summarize the felt, but not necessarily expressed, question of most visitors as: Why are these animals less than I believed?[8]

Similarly, Randy Malamud writes:

> Animals in visual culture are often disguised in some way—costumed, or masked, or distorted, or disfigured. Mockery of animals is another harbinger of disguise, as is decontextualization. These are all disguises because they prevent us from seeing the authentic animal beneath the cultural flippery. Animals are disguised because the authentic animal would be too depressing, or too scary, or too boring, for the viewer to endure.[9]

In the context of children's film, the replacement of the authentic animal with the artificial or attenuated animal is a well-established gesture. What children *ought to see* is not just a matter of censoring or dulcifying the more disagreeable facts that come with life in the wilderness (the graphic bloodshed of predatory hunting, sexual encounters, social behaviours that range from masturbation to the killing or maiming of one's offspring, "cruel" neglect of the weaker members of the social group, etc.) or in spaces designed for exploitation (factory farms, fur farms, zoos and aquaria, laboratories, etc.). What children *ought to see* is, for the most part, also a greatly distorted animal whose subjectivity is violated both through the manipulation of its immediate environment and through a misrepresentation of its communicative skills as a social being. In children's films, it is indeed how animals interact among themselves and with human beings (particularly children or youths) that is at the heart of anthropomorphism.

Anthropomorphism, as a form of thinking with and through the animal, is not exclusive to popular culture of course. As Daston and Mitman remind us, animals "evoke an immediate, almost irresistible pulse of empathy: humans past and present, hither and yon, think they know how animals think, and they habitually use animals to help them do their own thinking about themselves."[10] Yet, they point out, it is a cognitive process that excites suspicion in the fields within which it is invoked, including philosophy and psychology or the more scientifically harnessed domains such as biology, ethology, or genetics. The stigma anthropomorphism cannot seem to escape is its association with a sentimental, social, and emotional capacity that is traditionally denied to animal subjectivity. Practices or arguments perceived as anthropomorphic are often regarded as unpolished and immature (i.e., childish). And yet, in the twenty-first century, the ethological study of several species has revealed critical evidence supporting the theory that consciousness of the self is not exclusive to the human condition, thus challenging civilization's long-standing assumptions about animal ways of thinking. From Alexandra Horowitz's bestselling *Inside of a Dog* (2010) and renowned animal behaviourist Marc Bekoff's *Canine Confidential* (2018) to Brakes and Simmond's compilation of studies on cetacean culture and communication,[11] and from multiple studies in primatology extending from the work of Dian Fossey and Jane Goodall to that of Frans DeWaal, to Jonathan Balcombe's study of the more ambiguous fish species,[12] to name just a few examples, it is gradually becoming more evident that not only are animal minds extremely complex, but their social and communication skills, although unique, can in some ways be said to resemble our own. If, as Thomas Nagel (1974) once argued, it is ultimately impossible for us to know what it is like for a bat to be a bat, and the best we can do is know what it would be like for a human to be a bat,[13] then we could argue that our best shot in approaching animal subjectivity is through its symptomatic resemblance to human consciousness. Given that, according to this theory, our assimilation of species otherness can only truly be fathomed through emotions and cognitive processes that we are able to experience, the metaphorization of animal subjectivity does prove useful to advance scientific thought. Applied to the entertainment industry, however, it seems the aim is not so much to decipher animality as it is to use such likeness to reassert genre expectations on human character types.

Anthropomorphism in children's and family films requires, for the most part, idiosyncratic and recognizable forms of animal characterization that enhance and reaffirm the genre's general features. However, how the variables are handled within the patterns may determine whether a film is deemed to be representative of one genre or another. If we consider, for instance, films that revolve around the child-animal bond—a prominent theme in children's films, such as *The Black Stallion* (Carroll Ballard, 1979), *The Horse Whisperer* (Robert Redford, 1998), the Hungarian production *White God* (Kornél Mundruczó, 2014), or the more recent *Alpha* (Albert Hughes, 2018)—we would still hesitate to regard them as representative of the genre, even if they share some of its attributes. Admittedly, this may have to do with their inclusion of adult-oriented themes (adulterous desires in *The Horse Whisperer*), the depiction of a sordid and disturbing urban setting (*White God*) or the use of overtly experimental cinematographic techniques (*The Black Stallion*; *Alpha*). Yet part of it also has to do with the limitations on the type of anthropomorphism that is typical in children's films: physiognomy is not altered (and even if computer-generated imagery is occasionally employed, as in *Alpha*, the aim is to emulate the authentic facial features of the animal, not to evoke human gestures); the animals do not employ human language; and their intuitive responses to the emotionally troubled child are, for the most part, consistent with their species-specific behaviour.

The verisimilitude of actual animal behaviours, of conduct that portrays animal subjectivity without succumbing to anthropomorphic excess, pulls away from artifice towards realism. And so, when that "contract" between the representation and the attempt at realism is compromised, the films shift towards the conventions of other established genres. The second part of *The Black Stallion*, for instance, seems inclined to accommodate the conventions of children's films when it comes to both plot and symbolism. This was not lost on Roger Ebert, who wrote, "We've seen the second half before—the story of the kid, the horse, the veteran trainer, and the big race. But the first hour of this movie belongs among the great filmgoing experiences. It is described as an epic, and earns this description."[14] And *White God* takes a drastic turn into full-fledged horror and vengeance when the protagonist dog, who is abandoned by the father of his child-owner, retaliates against humans by leading a pack of vicious canines through the city. The anthropomorphic displays on which genre rests are carefully calculated by production teams in accordance with marketing strategies targeted to specific audiences. Let us now examine how anthropomorphism is systematized in children's and family films through patterns and motifs that safeguard the genre.

RECURRENT PATTERNS AND SYMBOLS: FROM DISNIFICATION TO PET CULTURE

Steve Baker has famously addressed how animal representation and affectivity become inextricably linked through what he terms "disnification"—that is, the process whereby the animal is belittled through the dynamics of visual culture in a way that accommodates our desires and expectations surrounding animality. "The animal is the sign of all that is taken not-very-seriously in contemporary culture; the sign of that which doesn't really matter," he writes. He goes on to add that "the basic procedure of disnification is to render [the animal] stupid by rendering it visual."[15] Doubly implicating Disney's "processing" of animal natures and the semiotics of signification, Baker describes a cultural colonization of the animal through the visual. "The animal is only ever knowable in mediated forms," he claims,

> To see animals at all is to see them *as* something—as something that we have made meaningful, even if that something is only the display of our own investment in the idea of an authentic nature, a natural order of things, for which the animal is the ideal icon under the order of disnification.[16]

Within filmic discourses, disnification may be easily accomplished through animation, animatronics, and computer-generated imagery (CGI); but representations of real animals also come into play, especially in children's film. Animal subjectivity tends to be reduced to psychological processes children can identify with, and it is normally exercised in contexts they can relate to (usually the family or a family-like community, presented at a temporary moment of crisis, which the animal helps them overcome). It is the animal's capacity to restore order that ultimately amounts to a disnification process. To give just a few examples, we might consider how in *Old Yeller* (Robert Stevenson, 1957), the dog integrates himself within the domestic sphere by adjusting to the Coates's frontier family values; how in *Benji* (Joe Camp, 1974) the stray dog figures out that two children are being held hostage and finds a way to lead the investigators to the kidnappers; how in *The Journey of Natty Gann* (Jeremy Kagan, 1985), the wolf wisely steps in as the surrogate protector of a teenage girl until she is reunited with her father; or how in *Free Willy* (Simon Wincer, 1993), the captive orca identifies the troubled foster child's pain as his own.

One might be tempted to argue that the animals in these films are not being rendered stupid as much as upgraded to the category of humanoids that can not only solve crimes but, more importantly, also repair the emotional damage caused by the hardships of an unstable family environment that no therapist could possibly have remedied. Little explanation is ever given for the animals' restorative powers, thus projecting the idea that the child-animal bond cannot be violated by the rational and operates instead in the domain of the telepathic. A somewhat recurrent visual motif that sublimates this type of interspecies connection is that of the child/youth's hand reaching out to kindly touch their kindred animal, either for the first time or as a first gesture in a new relationship based on caretaking, love, and respect. This gesture, which has been produced in poignant emotional scenes in films such as *Free Willy* (Figure 19.1), *The Black Stallion*, and *White Fang* (Randal Kleiser, 1991), recalls and reinvents Michelangelo's classic image of the hands of God and Adam in the Sistine Chapel, which symbolizes the moment in which the Creator makes his human creation in own image. What the transposition of this mythical motif into children's films suggests is that the animal is "reborn" into a new communal existence. The child's hand makes that particular specimen unique, and this great creation consists in the individualization of that one animal, who is now an ambassador of something beyond its species. Through the child, the animal transcends his/her own nature to emerge as a "chosen" figure inhabiting the in-betweenness of species.

And yet, this type of anthropomorphism that bends animal subjectivity to the needs of the child "stupidifies" the animal, insofar as it annuls its species-specific consciousness, turning it instead into a character that befits the developmental patterns of childhood and adolescence. Often, the annulment or objectification (or both) of animal subjectivity is assisted by the evocation and re-enactment of an ancient story or myth. These myths not only help to contextualize or justify that telepathic connection; they also answer to Hollywood's penchant for romanticizing the wilderness through the incorporation of traditional (usually Native American) narratives, a pattern that David Ingram has traced in productions that have marketed themselves as environmentalist films.[17] The conservationist agenda in the United States began to gain more prominence in the media with the advent of television, and drew on romanticized equivalences between purity and what is conceived as primitivist, finding in native cultures the trademark of authenticity.

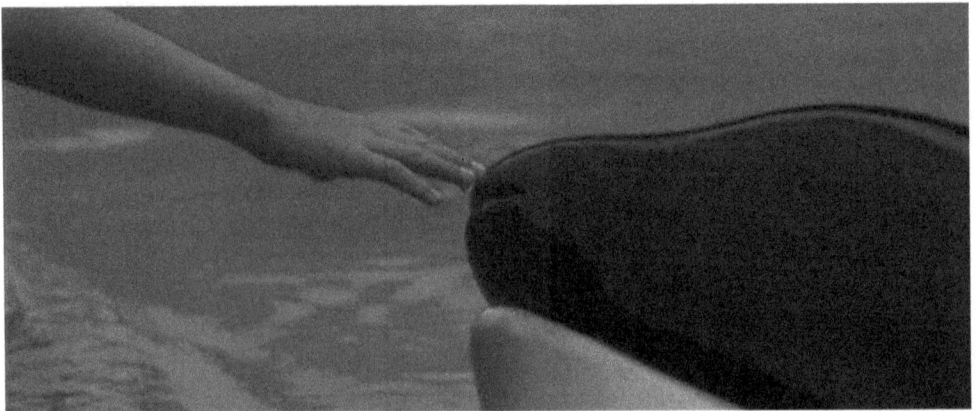

FIGURE 19.1. In *Free Willy* (1993, Warner Bros.), Jesse, the child, reaches out to touch Willy, the whale, in a moving scene that symbolizes interspecies communion and represents the individualization of the animal. Frame-grab.

This process of green-washing scripts certainly became very notable in 1980s and 1990s children's and family films, and myths (often accompanied by totemic figures cherished by the child) became fairly common featured in the storylines. With unapologetic cultural appropriation, Caucasian children were often portrayed as the natural conveyors of native oral traditions, suggesting that they were able to transcend not only species boundaries, but also ethnic ones. In *The Golden Seal* (Frank Zuniga, 1983), it is a ten-year-old white boy who, attuned to the mysticism of an elderly Inuit and his foundational myth, struggles to save a seal and her pup from the greedy hands not only of his father and another white hunter, but also another Inuit. In *Free Willy*, Jesse, a foster child, ritualizes an ancient Haida myth he learns from Randolph, the Native American keeper of the aquarium, who also gifts him with a small wooden figure of an orca. Jesse and Randolph's simultaneous prayer in Haida, it is suggested, is the chant that gives Willy the faith and power to successfully jump over the wall, beyond which there is freedom. Similarly, in *Dolphin Tale* (Charles Martin Smith, 2011), the fictionalized true story of Winter the dolphin, whose amputated tail is replaced with a prosthetic one, we find a white boy named Sawyer, whose efforts to save his cetacean friend lead to a ritualistic reconstruction of an old Chumash legend. According to the story, dolphins were originally Chumash children who fell from a rainbow. Not only is Sawyer aligned with the dolphin totem through a small figurine he was gifted with, but the imagery of the legend is also re-enacted towards the end, when several children jump into the water to swim with Winter.

Gregg Mitman describes how wildlife films and documentaries have, throughout the history of film and television, been progressively inclined to commodify animals into ideologies of domesticity and American family values.[18] Placing particular emphasis on nature documentaries such as Disney's *True-Life Adventures* series (1948–1960) and the television programme *Zoo Parade* (1950–1957), he unearths the artifice of anthropomorphism that accommodates middle-class domestic morality. Part of the distortion, he argues throughout, involved representing wild animals as domestic pets of sorts, thus emphasizing the central role that household companions have in consolidating normative family ethics, conduct, and spaces. This allocation of animality within the specifics of modern Western domestic culture finds its origin in the Victorian gentility and ideology that made its way across the Atlantic.[19] The Victorian and Edwardian eras are crucial periods in the proliferation of a type of children's literature that advocated against animal cruelty. As industrialization gradually pushed animals to the outskirts of cities and concealed exploitative practices from the public eye, scenes of deliberate cruelty to animals aroused public indignation within cities. Anna Sewell's literary classic *Black Beauty* (1877) is a testament to the violence inflicted on horses within class-based urban structures (the book was most recently faithfully adapted into a children's film in 1994, under the direction of Caroline Thompson). In nineteenth-century Britain (and then in the United States), laws and policies regulating the visibility of animal cruelty in different industries (sports and entertainment, the food industry, as transport, and in scientific experiments) began to shape contemporary animal welfare culture. Coupled with a growing middle-class consciousness that was determined by a highly gendered division of spaces (the public domain being masculine and reserved for males, whereas the domestic sphere was feminine and relegated to women and children), modern pet culture emerged as an acceptable practice of animal stewardship within the household. Being in contact with a pet, integrating it within the family setting and providing it with a singular status in the domestic social order certainly enhanced the educational value of animals for children, as kindness and humaneness were instilled as virtues to be exercised by the young. The animal-child link was further strengthened by the recognition that "pets were transformed, like children, into beings that had sentimental rather than economic value."[20] This emotional connection to an animal was thought to reflect and be manifest in family dynamics and patterns, and so pet-keeping "provided an opportunity for children to reproduce and internalize familial affection, acting toward pets as their own parents did toward them."[21]

Children's films have consistently explored processes of maturation and moral cleansing associated with pet-keeping. These often culminate in the resolution of the main conflict: the family crisis. In *The Journey of Natty Gann*, a wolf takes on the role of both pet and paternal figure as he accompanies a young girl across America in search of her father. In *Free Willy*, the liberation of the orca (who, by virtue of the interspecies emotional bonding, had acquired the social status of a pet) is paired with Jesse's acceptance of his foster family. *Homeward Bound: The Incredible Journey* (Duwayne Dunham, 1993) remakes Fletcher Marker's 1963 original with an added subplot about the children's acceptance of their stepfather, which is linked to the moment when the pets return home. In another Disney family film, *Iron Will* (Charles Haid, 1994), the lead dog of a dogsled team helps a young man come to terms with the death of his loving father; and in Alan Shapiro's 1996 version of *Flipper*, the dolphin (who, incidentally, seems more inclined to live in close contact with the human population, as if he were a pet, than to roam free in the ocean) emerges as an unexpected sidekick that helps a disenchanted teenager cope with his parents' divorce.

This ritualized step into the child's coming of age frequently involves the assertion of normative gender roles. Beyond the child's integration within a gendered and sexualized social structure in which he or she will face new kinds of challenges, what the transition often indicates is an anthropocentric assimilation of the ultimate human superiority over animals: thus, becoming a man or a woman frequently involves the shedding of an idyllic, infant stage when animals were prioritized and the centre of affection. Having mastered the moral requirements of responsible pet-keeping, the child is ready to safely move on to conventional human relationships. One of the most famous examples of this is, of course, *Old Yeller*. Set on a Texas farm after the Civil War, the film revolves around Travis, a boy who is left to protect his mother and younger brother while the father is away on a cattle drive, and his relationship with a dog he calls Old Yeller. Travis's love for the loyal canine is crushed by the inevitable violence and harshness of the "real" adult world after he has to shoot a rabid Yeller at the end of the film (Figure 19.2). Travis's paternalistic understanding that it is he who must be the dog's executioner reasserts the assimilation of his manhood within the frontier ethic, precipitating the loss of innocence.

FIGURE 19.2. A grieving Travis prepares to shoot his beloved dog in *Old Yeller* (1957, Disney), a moment that represents the character's coming of age into normative, masculine adulthood. Frame-grab.

Sometimes, child and animal come of age together. In these cases, the child's undertaking of paternal or maternal responsibilities that climax with the animal's independence proves to be the necessary step into gendered young adulthood. *Fly Away Home* (Carroll Ballard, 1996) fictionalizes the story behind a visionary project in the late 1980s and early 1990s that aimed to lead migrating geese in flight by use of an ultra-light aircraft. A young girl named Amy has lost her mother and now must live with her estranged father. The father-daughter bond develops as Amy's maternal instincts are imprinted onto a group of goslings that she must later push into adulthood by leading the flock in the air.

In yet another film that simultaneously depicts the coming-of-age and aging of different animal species, *Charlotte's Web* (Gary Winick, 2006), normative femininity is also asserted by and through the child figure. It is significant to note here that the child, Fern, transitions from mother figure (to her pig, Wilbur) to blossoming young girl, while the teleology of other characters leads to quite a different destiny: Wilbur's coming-of-age will bring about his slaughter, and Charlotte, the spider, learns to accept her fate: she will die once she has laid her eggs. At the beginning of the film, Fern's mother is concerned about her daughter's excessive fondness for animal company. She consults a doctor whose diagnosis is clear: "There is a name for her condition," he explains. "It's called childhood phase. And sadly, it's something she'll grow out of." Fern's transition out of this phase is shown by her interest in a boy (which also troubles her mother), and the film leaves little room to develop a gendered identity beyond that of being a mother figure or an object of interest to the male gaze.

Becoming gendered into normative roles is also a developmental feature in *The Journey of Natty Gann*. Natty, a tomboyish teenager, experiences her first kiss during her quest to find her father but also an attempted sexual assault. Significantly, it is a wolf that saves her from the molester (Figure 19.3), in the same way Natty herself had helped rescue the animal from being forced into dogfighting. Beyond the unexpected inclusion of scenes and references to dogfighting and sexual assault in a Disney family film, what the narrative suggests is that Natty is growing into a sexualized female figure, whose virtue must be protected by the father she longs to reunite with—or by his proxy, the wolf. The wolf in *Natty Gann* reverts back to his wildness just before Natty finds her father, leaving her to complete the last part of her quest on her own. The act of being freed can itself be regarded as a coming-of-age moment of the wild animal, whose temporary uniqueness as a pet of sorts will dissolve in the more impersonal biodiversity of the wilderness. In this way, the film also reaffirms anthropocentric values that claim the separation of nature and culture to be the "natural" order of things. As with the separation of gendered spheres in the Victorian era, wild animals and children are allocated in spaces that are meaningful because they oppose one another (nature versus culture, and the wilderness versus the domestic sphere), or so the moral of the films suggests. The temporary crisis makes the pet-like interaction between the wolf and Natty acceptable, even necessary; but once it is overcome, each must return to their proper place, both spatially and socially. *Free Willy*, *Cheetah* (Jeff Blyth, 1989), and *Mr. Popper's Penguins* (Mark Waters, 2011) are also examples of this pattern, although it should also be noted that sometimes the animal chooses *not* to revert, opting instead to reaffirm his or her domestic status, as with the wolf in Disney's adaptation of *White Fang*.

Sometimes the animal has to "prove himself," both emotionally and spatially, to acquire pet status. Dogs are often the species of choice for this task. In one of the first Rin Tin Tin movies, *Where the North Begins* (Chester M. Franklin, 1923), the loyal German

FIGURE 19.3. As if sensing danger, the wolf remains vigilant behind the rear window, just moments before breaking through the glass to rescue Natty from her molester (*The Journey of Natty Gann*, 1985, Disney). Frame-grab.

Shepherd is only truly integrated within the domestic setting after it is revealed that he risked his life to protect the family baby. In *Lassie Come Home* (Fred M. Wilcox, 1943), the Carracloughs agree to hide Lassie from her new legal owners when they realise the trials she must have gone through trying to return to them and to their young boy, Joe. In *Old Yeller*, Travis gradually takes in the dog as he overcomes the expectations associated with the ideals of family loyalty. Similarly, in *Benji*, the single father only accepts Benji as a pet after he saves his children from the kidnappers, despite his initial aversion to his being a street mutt. And in *Babe* (Chris Noonan, 1995), the pig is symbolically transformed from edible body to pet when the farmer invites him to enter the house.[22] The invitation comes because Babe has shown his abilities as a sheepdog, suggesting that his transcendence into canineness must be rewarded with domesticity.

This is just a shortlist of the many films that have adapted the conventions of the highly popular nineteenth-century dog melodramas for the screen. Such theatrical productions represented the culmination of the use of on-stage canines, which had gradually shed their original value during the Renaissance as mere props or embellishments to become heroic figures within the Victorian imagination.[23] In the early 1800s, plays like *The Caravan; or the Driver and His Dog* and *The Dog of Montargis* were popular with audiences, as eager crowds packed theatres to see heroic dogs saving the day in the highly sentimentalized productions. Their impressive stunts included jumping into water to save a supposedly drowning child—a feat that was repeated in the family film *Beethoven* (Brian Levant, 1992)—or sniffing out and subduing the villain before the innocent eyes of the community. These canine melodramas resonated deeply with the domestic ethos of Victorian culture and found themselves eventually re-enacted in children's films.[24]

As evinced by the limited range of animals that are disnified through children's film and made to excel in their role as pets, there are some species that are more common to the genre than others. In his negative review of *The Golden Seal* in 1983, Roger Ebert suggested that the film's inadequate choice of animal species and anthropomorphic excesses were mostly to blame for its overall lack of quality, and he predicted that in no time the upcoming Disney production *Never Cry Wolf* (Carroll Ballard, 1983) would overshadow the movie and its seal:

> Seals are cute. But they are not charismatic animals....If we could only see them doing what seals do, that would perhaps be interesting. Instead, we are given anthropomorphic seals who can apparently listen to young boys, understand what is told to them, and respond....Wolves: Now there's an animal with charisma.[25]

The film had actually used sea lions (not seals), which would, in time, be used in other children's films—most prominently in *Andre* (George Miller, 1994). But Ebert was on to something with his notion of animal charisma. In the second half of the twentieth century, environmentalists began to highlight the natural charisma of wild animals, termed "charismatic megafauna," to attract public attention to environmental issues. These "flagship species" emerged as chosen, symbolic figures that strengthened the pragmatics of discourses of threatened extinctions even as they served, in visual culture, as objects of human affection.[26] Usually mammals, their attractiveness lies in their "cuteness," their furriness, and cuddliness, although the majestic beauty of birds of prey, cetaceans, and large reptiles and fish has also successfully seduced the public.

Whether for conservationist or marketing purposes, charismatic megafauna direct public attention to *what ought to be seen* and *how it ought to be seen*, thus again compromising the nonhuman animal other's authenticity, and deliver instead a distorted type of animality that satisfies affective needs and expectations of humans. As noted, children's film has both taken advantage of and promoted these species' charisma, often by exacerbating anthropomorphic qualities and editing or censoring certain behaviours. Mitman dedicates a chapter of his book to the study of how the dolphin overcame its stigmatization as vermin prone to graphic sexual activity to become a television and Hollywood sensation.[27] Birds aren't furry, but they can capture audiences' attention, especially when anthropomorphism is shown through group behaviour and is combined with CGI, such as in *Mr. Popper's Penguins*. The disnification and charismatization of real animals in children's film is enhanced by their neoteny. As Baker argues, the preservation of youthful physical attributes (namely, the roundness of a healthy physique versus the sharpness of the bony frame of the aging body) excites more favourable responses to the visual imagery of the animal.[28] To emphasize animals' neotenous continuity into their adult forms, it is not unusual in children's films to introduce them in their infant stage, whether as a puppy (such as in *Son of Lassie* [S. Sylvan Simon, 1945], *White Fang*, or *Beethoven*, among others), as a piglet (*Charlotte's Web*), a cub (*Cheetah*; *Alaska* [Fraser C. Heston, 1996]), a foal (*Black Beauty*), or as goslings (*Fly Away Home*). Shabby or "funny-looking" specimens may have supporting roles in these films, but the lead animal's charisma is ensured through the visual exhibition of its impressive neoteny.

Children's Films and Animal Ethics

As animals are anthropomorphized, the restrictions or recommendations regarding what ought to be shown condition the imagery. Certain taboos are more prominent than others: zoophilia, for instance, is a far less common theme or motif in mainstream cinema than other forms of animal cruelty. Yet even the simulation of animal cruelty is dependent on the genre of the film in question, which determines what imagery is acceptable and unacceptable.[29] In this sense, children's and family films are deserving of further study on how they manage, script-wise, to deal with moral inconsistencies when it comes to non-human otherness. For one thing, although the brutality of factory farming and slaughtering are the underlying reason pigs like Wilbur or Babe, in quasi-existentialist desperation, seek to save themselves, neither film seems all that invested in promoting vegetarian or vegan practices. In fact, certain images in the films border on the aesthetics of horror and post-humanist science fiction. Consider the opening sequence of *Charlotte's Web* (Figure 19.4), when Fern saves Wilbur from being killed

FIGURE 19.4. After rescuing the pig runt from a sure, violent death, Fern embraces it, indicating both her acceptance of her mother role towards the animal and a shift from the film's sobering and disturbing opening scene to the family-related themes that are more typical of children's films (*Charlotte's Web*, 2006, Paramount). Frame-grab.

with an axe by her father, or of *Babe*, when several piglets, torn from their mother, must suckle machines to get their milk. But such nuances do not so much question the totality of the system of exploitation as address the experience of a single, special pig. Aimed at mainstream family audiences, the films are protective of normative childhood development, which involves the regular consumption of meat. Paradoxically, films with a more overt vegan agenda, such as Netflix's *Okja* (Joon-ho Bong, 2017), which also resorts to the pig-pork motif through a CGI upgraded hog species, also fail to completely reject anthropomorphism. Renouncing (or at least limiting) anthropomorphism would give the narrative an opportunity to build a case for a species, not because of its empathetic capacities or because of its potential to become a pet, but because it is an end unto itself, a moral being worthy of consideration. Like *White God*, *Okja* hardly qualifies as a children's film despite its reliance on the child-animal combination—and yet it misses the chance to de-anthropomorphize the animal; instead, the film continues to rely on ethical standards that measure animal worth according to subjective likeness to humans.

The social normativity of consuming meat, however, is exceptionally problematic when contrasted with other forms of animal exploitation that are denounced in children's films. True to the original Victorian ethos, animal suffering and pain are considered crueller when the object of torment is a pet or an animal in a "relatable" family structure that echoes the meaningfulness of domesticity. Thus, Cruella de Vil's villainy in Disney's *101 Dalmatians* movies is grounded not so much on the consumption of fur, but on the breaking of the cultural taboo that separates dogs from other animals used for clothing. Or, in the case of *Old Yeller*, Travis proves his moral worth when he refrains from shooting a doe and her fawn but has no problem killing a lone buck, thus integrating supposed ethics of hunting within an ethos of domesticity, deviating from which would be perceived as degenerate.

In children's films, moral deviancy is also often embodied by agents of corporate capitalism that seek profit through the exploitation of a wild animal, such as in *Cheetah* or *Free Willy*, or of an ecosystem. Their acts result in threats to the local biodiversity, as for example in *Hoot* (Will Shriner, 2006). Paradoxically, such greed is sometimes ascribed to characters who are meant to support animal welfare practices. In *Mr. Popper's Penguins*, the film's moral ambivalence towards zoos is accentuated by making the zoo-keeper (who had initially appeared genuinely interested in the penguins' well-being) the profit-seeking villain. In *Beethoven*, as if revitalizing Victorian anti-vivisectionist imagery, it is the family's vet who is fixated on using their dog as an experimental subject. A likely reason behind these initiatives may be found in the very nature of melodrama, which traditionally revolves around a threat to the domestic by an evil incarnate who, more often than not, turns out to be a trustworthy friend or authority figure. Melodrama achieves closure and the restoration of order with the exposure and defeat of the rather flat, one-dimensional villain, who is fixated on his one purpose involving the animal and whose lies and distortions have contaminated the domestic setting.

But the fictionalization of animals and animality in the children's and family film genre also affects the supra-structures of filmmaking. It goes hand in hand with the commodification of animals as "actors" or "performers" in a multi-billion dollar industry. Indeed, audiences have become more sceptical of the behind-the-scenes treatment of animals as studies on animal cognition and animal rights and welfare regulations have begun to occupy more of the discursive and legal public space. Hence, beyond Baker and Malamud's position that anthropomorphism, distortion, and disnification compromise animals' integrity, the monitoring of the production process is also integral to an understanding of how animality and film come together as an apparatus.

Because how animals are narrativized in film is inseparable from how they are narrativized as actors, genre continues to be essential in the determination of ethical standards, though of course, beyond any genuine interest in animal welfare, the commercial value and publicity of the film are really at stake.[30] The public is particularly vigilant when it comes to whether children's and family films practice what they preach precisely because of the genres' strong dependency on melodramatic conventions and on the accentuation of morality. Knowing a film has the certified approval of competent authorities eases audiences into a viewership comfort zone that yields to cinema's suspension of disbelief. In the United States, representatives of the American Humane Association (AHA) have been monitoring the welfare of film animals since the public outcry against the killing of a horse in *Jesse James* (1939), which led to an agreement between the AHA and the Hays Office (and later also with the Screen Actors Guild). In Britain, the Cinematograph Films (Animals) Act, first developed as a bill in 1937, also marked the beginning of supervision of both the treatment of animals and the depiction of animal cruelty on screen.[31] The evolution of these policies and practices not only shows the extent to which leading film companies in the West acknowledge that animal welfare is a public concern, which, if not guaranteed, can seriously damage the marketing of a film, but also the extent to which modern culture has gradually integrated animal ethics discourses within the semiotics of the mediatized animal.

Since, as we argued in the section titled "Approaching Genre, Deciphering Animality" in this chapter, modernity is defined by the disappearance of animals and their incorporation within mediatized visual constructions that reaffirm cultural expectations about animality, it follows that the intimacy between viewers and nature developed through cinematography is an affective contract built on artificiality. The tensions between the desire for authenticity and the inevitable artifice of the rendering of animality in visual culture lead the marketing and merchandizing of film production to manufacture discourses to appease viewers who are concerned about the welfare of animals. Originally, animal stars were packaged for consumption as performers whose past was stylized in human-interest stories.[32] In time, the more melodramatic events of their biographies (for instance, having been a rescue animal in the case of the Metro-Goldwyn-Mayer lion, Fearless Fagan, in the 1950s) were marketed as further reassurance of their present well-being. Film companies today often make behind-the-scenes footage of animals on the set available to the public (often including it in DVD extras) as a strategic move to persuade viewers that the animals are not being treated as expendable commodities. Because of the unique moral position of children's and family films, public judgment about the consistency of treatment in the on-screen and behind-the-scenes domains is an issue that the genre has to cope with. "Making-of" shorts inform viewers that Old Yeller, for instance, was played by a rescue mutt named Spike; that the owls and other wildlife specimens featured in *Hoot* were properly taken care of through both humane and scientific practice that adjusted training methods to their natural species behaviour; that Winter, the maimed dolphin who played herself in *Dolphin Tale*, was completely undisturbed by the filming process; or that all the pigs in *Charlotte's Web* were given proper homes and would be monitored for the rest of their lives by Animals Australia to ensure they were properly taken care of (even though, as mentioned earlier, the film itself is not completely conducive to vegan ethics).

This transparency may be driven by marketing concerns, but their educational value in promoting animal welfare initiatives should not be underestimated. These efforts are laudable and to be encouraged, especially when the film promotes environmentalist principles as in the case of *Hoot*. Ethical breaches have not gone unnoticed by viewers, who have on occasion made a public cause out of them. Most famously, the campaign to free Keiko, the charismatic orca in *Free Willy*, received widespread media coverage that did not miss the opportunity to point out the moral incoherence of using a captive whale to create an anti-captivity-themed children's film. Ratelle observes that the textual subplot about whale and dolphin shows in aquaria, "perhaps unintentionally, encourages the film's viewers to sense their own complicity in the consumption of the species as entertainment."[33] This invitation to reflect on the ethics of spectatorship must have contributed to the support for Keiko's release. Yet the idealized back-to-the-wilderness ending celebrated in the movie was far from consummated in real life: after twenty years in captivity and numerous health and behavioural problems resulting from living isolated in a tank, Keiko only managed to survive four years in the wild, during which time he struggled to adapt socially to other whales and to the new environment.

Children's films that do not live up to animal welfare standards are often blacklisted in online forums. Reports of alleged animal cruelty in 1980s children's films such as *The NeverEnding Story* (Wolfgang Petersen, 1984) and the popular Japanese movie *The Adventures of Milo and Otis* (Masanori Hata, 1986) have lived on in Internet rumourology. More recent productions where evidence of animal suffering has been more carefully recorded have precipitated many viewers' distrust of the supervision carried out by the AHA. The investigation into the circumstances surrounding the deaths of two horses during the filming of *Flicka* (Michael Mayer, 2006) yielded disparate findings: the Department of Los Angeles Animal Services declared the deaths to have been preventable, while the AHA absolved the production company of all responsibility.[34] Especially alarming was leaked footage of how a scene in the family film *A Dog's Purpose* (Lasse Hallström, 2017) was shot. The footage showed what appeared to be a distressed German Shepherd on the verge of drowning. Despite the production team's high-gear efforts to do damage-control during the promotion of the film, the box office and the reputations of Amblin Entertainment and the AHA Film and Television Unit severely suffered. Active campaigning on the part of animal rights organizations such as People for the Ethical Treatment of Animals argued that the presence of an AHA representative was no guarantee of the animals' well-being and proclaimed that its undercover footage offered true transparency (versus the artificial discourses of making-of and behind-the-scenes documentaries) through which to judge the entertainment industry's ethical standards and practices. As an instrument of intervention and "call-out culture," the Internet is the most powerful tool through which to denounce malpractice by animal trainers and handlers. By "guilting" potential viewers into boycotting children's and family films, organized or individual animal welfarists and rightists are not just asking consumers of visual culture to position themselves on the "right" side of entertainment history; they are aiming at a generational moral renovation through which children will be educated in the practice of animal ethics, one that aspires to become truly standardized and naturalized.

CONCLUSION: WELCOMING ARTIFICE

This chapter has addressed the ways through which real animals are integrated within the genre of children's and family films, which are themselves products of our own cultural constructions of the concept of "childhood." We have attempted to describe how these somewhat elusive filmic genres have been instrumental to the progressive disappearance of animals in modernity. The paradox lies in the fact that even though real animal bodies are systematically allocated on the screen, their compartmentalization within a rhetoric of anthropomorphism (effected through recognizable patterns, symbols and motifs that commodify animality within an ethos of domesticity) has extinguished the possibility of authenticity. Such are the instincts of visual culture: within the semiotics of representation, the animal has little chance of retaining any trace of its authentic animality. Against the limits of our human ability to know what "being an animal" is and means, children's films offer themselves as decisive tools for exploring what to make of the animal through the child and what to make of the child through the animal. And because the genre must live up to its distinctive prescriptiveness of educational values, how animals *ought to* be reflected involves issues pertaining to animal welfare both on the screen and throughout the filmmaking process.

A final word should be said, nonetheless, about the current substitution of real animals for technological surrogates that range from animatronics to CGI. In recent years we have seen an increase in the use of such devices for the complementary representation of the animal body. This shift has affected other cinematographic genres, including horror, fantasy, and science fiction. Children's films have exhausted many of the possibilities such resources afford: special effects have been used for mouth replacement to disnify the animal as a verbal creature, and animatronics, puppetry, and CGI have artificially reproduced entire specimens to overcome the actual physical limitations of the original animal body. A quick diachronic overview of Hollywood productions that have resorted to some or a combination of such methods reveals the extent of technological advancement since the 1990s: the *Babe* (1995–1998), *Dr. Dolittle* (1998–2009), *Free Willy* (1993–2010), and *Cats and Dogs* (2001–2010) franchises; *Marmaduke* (Tom Dey, 2010), *Charlotte's Web*, and *Mr. Popper's Penguins*, to name but a handful of popular children's films, attest to the increasing presence of artificial animal bodies, to the point that the real bodies (especially those of wild animals) have become practically extinguished as an on-screen presence, as shown for example in *The Jungle Book* (Jon Favreau, 2016), *The Greatest Showman* (Michael Gracey, 2017), *Peter Rabbit* (Will Gluck, 2018), *Dumbo* (Tim Burton, 2019), *The Lion King* (Jon Favreau, 2019), and the Swedish film *Monky* (Maria Blom, 2017). Undoubtedly, CGI and animation are a much-welcomed alternative that helps to eradicate long-standing practices of abuse and neglect in the training of animals for the entertainment industry. The public's increasing awareness of animals as sentient and cognitively complex beings has increased demand for cruelty-free and animal welfare-oriented forms of filmmaking, although one must remain wary about the behind-the-scenes use of animals in the animation process.[35]

As the literature concerning this phenomenon struggles to catch up with the post-humanist momentum causing the human, the animal, and the machine to blend into one another, an interesting question to raise is how this will affect children's perceptions of animality in the future. The real animal body, as argued throughout this chapter, was always to be distorted through children's films that package animality as an artifice. What CGI and other alternative technologies suggest is that artifice no longer even pretends to be authentic but, rather, delights in its own unnaturalness. In a world of Photoshop and social networks, in which representation of the self proves to be an improvement over the original, the deictic preference for the artificial signifier is symptomatic of an exacerbated assimilation of the illusory. It seems that the animal, at least as far as children's films go, is destined to reassert its subjection to anthropomorphism, sinking further into the elusive and unknowable. And yet the real, cryptographic flesh of the wild species will welcome this surrogate, for it just might mean that they will then be left to inhabit that place where their instincts have always led them: away from the eyesight of man, into the land of the unseen.

Notes

1. Bart H. Welling, "On the 'Inexplicable Magic of Cinema'": Critical Anthopomorphism, Emotion, and the Wildness of Wildlife Films," in Alexa Weik von Mossner (ed.), *Moving Environments: Affect, Emotion, Ecology, and Film* (Waterloo, CAN: Wilfrid Laurier University Press, 2014), pp. 81–101, at 81.

2. Katarina Gregersdotter, Nicklas Hållén, and Johan Höglund, introduction to Katarina Gregersdotter, Nicklas Hållén, and Johan Höglund (eds.), *Animal Horror Cinema: Genre, History and Criticism* (Basingstoke, UK: Palgrave Macmillan, 2015), pp. 1–18, at 7.

3. Noel Brown, *The Children's Film: Genre, Nation and Narrative* (London: Columbia University Press, 2017), pp. 13–15.

4. Brown, *Children's Film*, p. 3. See also Noel Brown and Bruce Babington, "Introduction: Children's Films and Family Films," in Noel Brown and Bruce Babington (eds.), *Family Films in Global Cinema: The World beyond Disney* (London: I.B. Tauris, 2015), pp. 1–16, at 2.

5. See Boris Mayer Levinson, *Pets and Human Development* (Springfield, IL: Charles C. Thomas, 1972); Gail F. Melson, *Why the Wild Things Are: Animals in the Lives of Children* (Cambridge, MA: Harvard University Press, 2001); and Matthew Cole and Kate Stewart, *Our Children and Other Animals. The Cultural Construction of Human-Animal Relations in Childhood* (Farnham, UK: Ashgate, 2014).

6. Amy Ratelle, *Animality and Children's Literature and Film* (Basingstoke, UK: Palgrave Macmillan, 2015), p. 10.

7. Brown, *Children's Film*, p. 15.

8. John Berger, *Why Look at Animals?* (1977; repr. London: Penguin, 2009), p. 33.

9. Randy Malamud, *An Introduction to Animals and Visual Culture* (Basingstoke, UK: Palgrave Macmillan, 2012), p. 72.

10. Lorraine Daston and Gregg Mitman, introduction to Lorraine Daston and Gregg Mitman (eds.), *Thinking with Animals: New Perspectives on Anthropomorphism* (New York: Columbia University Press, 2005), pp. 1–14, at 1–2.

11. Philippa Brakes and Mark Peter Simmonds (eds.), *Whales and Dolphins: Cognition, Culture, Conservation and Human Perceptions* (Abingdon, UK: Earthscan, 2011).

12. Jonathan Balcombe, *What a Fish Knows: The Inner Lives of Our Underwater Cousins* (New York: Farrar, Straus and Giroux, 2016).

13. Thomas Nagel, "What Is It like to Be a Bat?," *Philosophical Review* 83:4 (October 1974), pp. 435–450.

14. Roger Ebert, "*The Black Stallion*," rogerebert.com, October 17, 1979. https://www.rogereb ert.com/reviews/the-black-stallion-1979 [accessed February 2 2019].

15. Steve Baker, *Picturing the Beast: Animals, Identity, and Representation* (1993; repr. Urbana: University of Illinois Press, 2001), p. 174.

16. Baker, *Picturing the Beast*, p. 180.

17. David Ingram, *Green Screen: Environmentalism and Hollywood Cinema* (2000; repr. Exeter, UK: University of Exeter Press,2010).

18. Gregg Mitman, *Reel Nature: America's Romance with Wildlife on Film* (1999; repr. Seattle: University of Washington Press, 2009).

19. See Katherine C. Grier, *Pets in America: A History* (Chapel Hill: University of North Carolina Press, 2006).

20. Susan J. Pearson, *The Rights of the Defenseless: Protecting Animals and Children in Gilded Age America* (Chicago: University of Chicago Press, 2011), p. 32.

21. Pearson, *Rights of the Defenseless*, p. 33.

22. Ratelle, *Animality and Children's Literature and Film*, p. 86.

23. See Michael Dobson, "Renaissance Dogs: The Transformation of the Onstage Canine, 1550–1850," *Performance Research* 5:2 (2000), pp. 116–124.

24. See Claudia Alonso-Recarte, "Canine Actors and Melodramatic Effects: *The Dog of Montargis* Arrives on the English Stage," *Cahiers Victoriens et Édouardiens* 86 (Autumn 2017), pp. 1–19; and Philip Howell, *At Home and Astray: The Domestic Dog in Victorian Britain* (Charlottesville: University of Virginia Press, 2015), pp. 41–45.

25. Roger Ebert, "*The Golden Seal*," rogerebert.com, October 12, 1983. https://www.rogerebert. com/reviews/the-golden-seal-1983 [accessed February 15, 2019].

26. See Nigel Leader-Williams and Holly T. Dublin, "Charismatic Megafauna as 'Flagship Species,'" in Abigail Entwistle and Nigel Dunstone (eds.), *Priorities for the Conservation of Mammalian Diversity: Has the Panda Had Its Day?* (Cambridge, MA: Cambridge University Press, 2000), pp. 53–81.

27. Mitman, *Reel Nature*, pp. 157–179.

28. Baker, *Picturing the Beast*, pp. 181–184.

29. See Jonathan Burt, *Animals in Film* (London: Reaktion Books, 2002), p. 141.

30. See Abigail Perdue and Randall Lockwood, *Animal Cruelty and Freedom of Speech: When Worlds Collide* (West Lafayette, IN: Purdue University Press, 2014), p. 19.

31. Burt, *Animals in Film*, pp. 85–163.

32. See Claire Molloy, *Popular Media and Animals* (Basingstoke, UK: Palgrave Macmillan, 2011), pp. 40–63.

33. Ratelle, *Animality and Children's Literature and Film*, p. 132.

34. Edward A. Boks, Letter from the Los Angeles Department of Animal Services to the American Humane & TV Unit, Animal Advocates website, October 17, 2006, http://www. animaladvocates.us/Flicka_Incident.pdf [accessed February 25, 2019].

35. See Malamud, *Introduction to Animals and Visual Culture*, p. 82.

BIBLIOGRAPHY

Baker, Steve. *Picturing the Beast: Animals, Identity, and Representation*. 1993. Urbana: University of Illinois Press, 2001.

Berger, John. *Why Look at Animals?* 1977. London: Penguin, 2009.

Bousé, Derek. *Wildlife Films*. Philadelphia: University of Pennsylvania Press, 2000.

Brooks, Peter. *The Melodramatic Imagination: Balzac, Henry James, Melodrama, and the Mode of Excess*.1976. New Haven, CT: Yale University Press, 1995.

Brown, Noel. *The Children's Film: Genre, Nation and Narrative*. London: Columbia University Press, 2017.

Brown, Noel, and Bruce Babington. "Introduction: Children's Films and Family Films." In Noel Brown and Bruce Babington (eds.), *Family Films in Global Cinema: The World Beyond Disney*. London: I.B. Tauris, 2015, pp. 1–16.

Burt, Jonathan. *Animals in Film*. London: Reaktion Books, 2002.

Cole, Matthew, and Kate Stewart. *Our Children and Other Animals: The Cultural Construction of Human-Animal Relations in Childhood*. Farnham, UK: Ashgate, 2014.

Daston, Lorraine, and Gregg Mitman. Introduction to Lorraine Daston and Gregg Mitman (eds.), *Thinking with Animals: New Perspectives on Anthropomorphism*. New York: Columbia University Press, 2005, pp. 1–14.

Grier, Katherine C. *Pets in America: A History*. Chapel Hill: University of North Carolina Press, 2006.

Howell, Philip. *At Home and Astray: The Domestic Dog in Victorian Britain*. Charlottesville: University of Virginia Press, 2015.

Ingram, David. *Green Screen: Environmentalism and Hollywood Cinema*. Exeter, UK: University of Exeter Press, 2010.

Levinson, Boris Mayer. *Pets and Human Development*. Springfield, IL: Charles C. Thomas, 1972.

Lippit, Akira Mizuta. *Electric Animal: Towards a Rhetoric of Wildlife*. Minneapolis: University of Minnesota Press, 2000.

Malamud, Randy. *An Introduction to Animals and Visual Culture*. Basingstoke, UK: Palgrave Macmillan, 2012.

Melson, Gail F. *Why the Wild Things Are: Animals in the Lives of Children*. Cambridge, MA: Harvard University Press, 2001.

Mitman, Gregg. *Reel Nature: America's Romance with Wildlife on Film*. 1999. Seattle: University of Washington Press, 2009.

Molloy, Claire. *Popular Media and Animals*. Basingstoke, UK: Palgrave Macmillan, 2011.

Pearson, Susan J. *The Rights of the Defenseless: Protecting Animals and Children in Gilded Age America*. Chicago: University of Chicago Press, 2011.

Ratelle, Amy. *Animality and Children's Literature and Film*. Basingstoke, UK: Palgrave Macmillan, 2015.

Turner, James. *Reckoning with the Beast: Animals, Pain and Humanity in the Victorian Mind*. Baltimore, MD: Johns Hopkins University Press, 1980.

Welling, Bart H. "On the 'Inexplicable Magic of Cinema': Critical Anthropomorphism, Emotion, and the Wildness of Wildlife Films." In Alexa Weik von Mossner (ed.), *Moving Environments: Affect, Emotion, Ecology, and Film*. Waterloo, CAN: Wilfrid Laurier University Press, 2014, pp. 81–101.

PART IV

CHILDREN'S CINEMA, SOCIETY, AND NATIONAL IDENTITY

CHAPTER 20

NATION, IDENTITY, AND THE LARRIKIN STREAK IN AUSTRALIAN CHILDREN'S CINEMA

ADRIAN SCHOBER

THIS short account of Australian children's cinema takes as its starting point a certain anti-authoritarian streak in the national character that has helped define Australia's identity: the *larrikin streak*. According to Professor E. Morris's *Dictionary of Austral English* (1898), the word *larrikin* has "various shades of meaning between a playful youngster and a blackguardly rough. Little street-boys are often, in a kindly way, called *little larrikins*."[1] Its etymology is much debated, but its earliest recorded use in an article in the Melbourne *Herald* in 1870 was in reference to loutish behaviour. As Melissa Bellanta chronicles in *Larrikins: A History*, this was when the term was inextricably linked to the gangs or "pushes" in the inner-city suburbs of Brisbane, Melbourne, and Sydney in the late nineteenth and early twentieth centuries: "By the 1880s, it was caught up in a moral panic about out-of-control adolescents," which became the "scourge of urban colonial society."[2] Amid reports of violence on the streets, this culminated in the so-called Mount Rennie Outrage of 1886, involving the horrific gang rape of a sixteen-year-old girl by larrikins of Sydney's "Waterloo Push." *Larrikinism* became associated with not only violence but drinking, gambling, and other vices.

By the turn of the new century the larrikin began to acquire a more positive connotation. In the First World War, Australian soldiers, or "diggers," of the Australian and New Zealand Army Corps (ANZAC) embraced *larrikin* not as a term of notoriety but as a badge of honour. This was personified in ANZAC serviceman David Barker's iconic image of the "larrikin-like digger," reproduced in the 1916 trench publication *The ANZAC Book*.[3] Defiance was said to be exhibited in the refusal of soldiers to salute their

British superiors. Enshrined in Australia's mythology about itself, this reappropriated larrikin came to be seen as

> almost archly self-conscious, too smart for his own good, witty rather than humorous, exceeding limits, bending rules and sailing close to the wind, avoiding rather than evading responsibility, playing up to an audience, mocking pomposity and smugness, taking the piss out of people, cutting down tall poppies, born on a Wednesday, looking both ways for a Sunday, larger than life, sceptical, iconoclastic, egalitarian yet suffering fools badly, insouciant and, above all, defiant.[4]

As this new concept of Australian identity was gaining a foothold, it found expression in the new art form that was fascinating to the nation: the cinema. The history of the Australian film industry has been characterized by film historian Graham Shirley as going "through a perpetual replay of rise and fall": "These cycles usually started with the discovery that Australia could and should be making features, moved into a period of public welcome for the reappearance of a national film identity, then went into decline as that identity failed to develop or was simply taken for granted."[5] An early landmark of the silent era was Charles Tait's *The Story of the Kelly Gang* (1906), about Australia's most famous bushranger Ned Kelly (1854–1880) and his band of outlaws. Kelly has been immortalized as the larrikin anti-hero, the symbol of resistance to established authority.[6] However, it was Raymond Longford's box-office smash, *The Sentimental Bloke* (1919), based on C. J. Dennis's bestselling book of verse *Songs of a Sentimental Bloke* (1915), that did much to advance the "institution" of larrikinism as a sign of Australianness. In Shirley and Brian Adams's précis, it is the "story of a city barrowman [the Bloke from the slums, played by Arthur Tauchert] redeemed from his larrikin ways by the love of a good woman—but always on the brink of being lured back by his mates into another bout of heavy drinking and a flutter of two-up."[7] In adapting Dennis, Longford shifted the backdrop from the Little Lonsdale Street push in central Melbourne to the Sydney dockside suburb of Woolloomooloo, which had formed part of the "larrikin belt" of the city.[8] The "robust larrikin" of this film ushered in a new male stereotype that was consolidated in Longford's sequel *Ginger Mick* (1920) and spinoff *The Dinkum Bloke* (1923), the films of New Zealand-born comic Pat Hanna (as the "Digger") and popular actor Chips Rafferty.[9] And as we shall see, the historic silent influenced the expression of larrikinism in Australia's early children's cinema.

At the same time, this cinema represents a continuation of a loose larrikin tradition in children's literature found in Ethel Turner's *The Little Larrikin* (1896), Dorothy Wall's Blinky Bill books about an anthropomorphic koala, Fred Davison's *Duck Williams and His Cobbers* (1939), the post-war "Smiley" books of Moore Raymond, and Ray Harris's *The Adventures of Turkey, Boy of the Australian Plains* (1952).[10] Turner may have conceived the titular hero of *The Little Larrikin* as the antithesis to the saintly Cedric Errol of Frances Hodgson Burnett's *Little Lord Fauntleroy* (1886).[11] In it, six-year-old Lol Carruthers becomes the leader of a small-boy push in urban Sydney. Turner also describes some unruly children in *Seven Little Australians* (1894). Before beginning her story proper, Turner offers "a word of warning" to readers:

> If you imagine you are going to read of model children, with perhaps a naughtily inclined one to point a moral, you had better lay down the book immediately and betake yourself to *Sandford and Merton* [by Thomas Day], or similar standard juvenile works. Not one of the seven is really good, for the excellent reason that Australian children never are.
>
> In England, and America, and Africa, and Asia, the little folks may be paragons of virtue, I know little about them.
>
> But in Australia a model child is—I say it not without thankfulness—an unknown quantity.
>
> It may be that the miasmas of naughtiness develop best in the sunny brilliancy of our atmosphere. It may be the land and the people are young-hearted together, and the children's spirits not crushed and saddened by the shadow of long years' sorrowful history.
>
> There is a lurking sparkle of joyousness and rebellion and mischief in nature here, and therefore in children.
>
> Often the light grows dull and the bright colouring fades to neutral tints in the dust and the heat of the day. But when it survives play-days and school-days, circumstances alone determine whether the electric sparkle shall go to play will-o'-the-wisp with the larrikin type, or warm the breasts of the spirited, single-hearted, loyal ones who can alone can 'advance Australia.'[12]

Thus, in subverting romantic models of childhood, the larrikin child may be seen as Australia's counterpart to Tom Sawyer or Huckleberry Finn, paralleling the "free, adventurous, and subversive spirit of a Twainian 'rough-and-tumble' boyhood, connected with nature."[13] On a finer point, we may see the larrikin child—like its opposite number in Twain—as the site of tensions between Romantic and Puritan/Evangelical models of childhood, as encapsulated in Leslie Fielder's description of the Good Bad Boy: "The Good Boy does what his mother must pretend to the rest of the world (even to herself) that she wants him to do: obey, conform; the Good Bad Boy does what she *really* wants him to do: deceive, break her heart a little, so that she can forgive him, smother him to the embrace that seals him back into her world forever."[14] Maurice Saxby agrees: though Turner's children in *The Little Larrikin* and *Seven Little Australians* or Wall's Blinky Bill "may subvert the image of childhood innocence, and although they may be mischievous, even naughty, they are not bad. They are not louts. From the literature itself it can be argued that the larrikins are distinct from the louts or hoodlums."[15] In other words, the larrikin child is likeable; the lout is not.

In the crossover from literature to film it can usefully be argued that much Australian children's cinema is, at its root, a larrikin cinema. As a body of work, it is not as rich or voluminous as, say, British children's cinema.[16] But the "larrikin streak" is an aspect that sets Australian cinema apart from other indigenous cinemas. In analysing this streak across a range of films from the silent to post-war eras to the Australian film revival of the 1970s and 1980s, this chapter argues that larrikinism—and a larrikin childhood in particular—speaks directly to questions of history, nation, and identity. This throws into sharp relief so-called aspects of the Australian character, or *mystique*—what historian Russel Ward famously termed the Australian Legend.[17] Combining film history with textual analysis and an analysis of critical and commercial reception, this chapter seeks to chart a course for the larrikin children's film in Australia.

THE KID STAKES AND THOSE TERRIBLE TWINS

Following in the larrikin tradition of children's literature, two of Australia's most be-loved comic-strip creations dating from the early 1920s, Fatty Finn and Ginger Meggs, have perhaps best cemented the idea of a larrikin childhood in the public imagination.[18] They inhabit the same time-capsule world of billy-carts, slingshots, marbles, smoke bombs; gangs, fistfights, and blood oaths; mates, bullies, and sweethearts; and colourful street vernacular like "bonzer," "beaut," and "mutt." "In his tilts with authority and in acting out his most characteristic roles (battler, con man, mischief maker)," the char-acter of Ginger Meggs, created by Jimmy Bancks for the Sydney *Sunday Sun*, was "fun-damentally a larrikin—sturdily optimistic, self-confident, quick thinking, independent, spirited."[19] Hubert "Fatty" Finn was created by Syd Nicholls for the Sydney *Sunday News* to rival Ginger in prankish behaviour. Both are good bad boys in the Australian tradi-tion and direct descendants of the Sentimental Bloke.[20] It's fitting that Australia's first children's films from the silent period drew on these creations.

In the same manner that C. J. Dennis appears writing at his desk at the beginning of Longford's *The Sentimental Bloke*, Nicholls has a self-referential cameo at the beginning of *The Kid Stakes* (1927). Here, the flesh-and-blood Fatty confers with his creator at the drawing board (Figure 20.1). Actor Tal Ordell, who had starred in films for Longford, directed his one and only feature, which displays the influence of American cinematic forms, the *Our Gang* series (1922–1944), Charlie Chaplin's *The Kid* (1921), and, in the highly celebrated goat race at the end of the film, Fred Niblo's *Ben Hur* (1925).[21] However, the single greatest influence on the film is *The Sentimental Bloke*, and it's significant that Ordell recruited Longford's regular cinematographer, Arthur Higgins, on the film. From its predecessor, *The Kid Stakes* lifts the realistic Woolloomooloo setting as well as larrikin sentiments. As Shirley and Adams note, the "assumptions about slum larrikins are basically the same, although conveyed with sharper slapstick that derives from gang-ster rivalry in miniature."[22] Indeed, in its representation of gang life, these elements of loutishness remain. Like Lol in *The Little Larrikin*, Fatty Finn (as played by the director's son, Robin "Pop" Ordell) is the leader of the gang, with his "trusted lieutenant" Tiny King (Charles Roberts) and others in tow. Bruiser Murphy (Frank Boyd) is the leader of a rival gang. He browbeats Fatty into entering his goat Hector in a billycart race against his own champion goat, Stonker. Shirley and Adams also note that "Fatty is tougher,

FIGURE 20.1. Fatty Finn (Robin "Pop" Ordell) confers with his creator, Syd Nicholls, at the drawing board in *The Kid Stakes* (1927, Ordell-Coyle Productions). Frame-grab.

sometimes surlier, than his cartoon counterpart; Bruiser, his adversary, is every inch the hood of the future. Bruiser and his toughs look less comfortably brought up, are worse dressed and more disposed to larrikinism [of the loutish kind]."[23] What's more, Bruiser smokes!

Both sides require unswerving conformity to the codes and initiations of gang life, which underlines the importance of that traditionally male Australian institution: mateship. Thus "sissyboy" Master Algie Snoops (David Lidstone), who strays from the affluent Potts Point into the gangland slums, must prove his mettle with his fists first (at Fatty's taunts) before he can join the gang. And Bruiser's plot to sabotage the race by having a traitor in Fatty's ranks let Hector loose for "a glassy and six stinkies" (i.e., marbles) is an affront to the code of loyalty embodied in mateship. Later, Fatty has his gang sign a blood oath "not to be traitors to each other" and to save Hector from impoundment in a mansion (and almost certain destruction because the goat has gorged himself on the rare plants of its owner's garden) so that he can compete in "the kid stakes." The climactic goat race crystallizes the association of gambling with sport and competition that is seen to figure so large in the Australian character. As Fatty and Bruiser face off with their goats, Ordell deploys cross-cutting and emphatic intertitles to convey energy and excitement. Hector wins by a short beard!

When *The Kid Stakes* had its premiere on June 9, 1927, critics reviewed it principally as a children's film, while recognizing its appeal to grown-ups. Many singled out the naturalistic performances of the children and the goat race at the end of the film (filmed over the border in Queensland because goat racing was illegal in New South

Wales at the time). *The Brisbane Courier* thought it a "rollicking comedy of boyhood adventures."[24] Implicit in *The Adelaide Saturday Journal*'s review was an appreciation of the larrikin elements: "Not only the young ones in the audience, but the old ones, too, can enter with zest into the harum-scarum pranks, the boyish schemes, and, last but not least, the exciting goat race."[25] Despite the positive reviews, the £4,000 production returned only a small profit on its initial release, whereupon it was edited into comedy shorts.[26] To commemorate the rediscovery of the long-thought-lost film in the 1950s, painstakingly reconstructed for a special screening, the tabloid *Pix* observed that it was an important historical document of the age—that is, the larrikin age: "*The Kid Stakes* brings back the Sydney of the 1920s, the ragged urchins of Woolloomooloo, the brawling, free-fisted waterfront characters, the old streets and shops long since changed."[27]

The surviving fragment of *Those Terrible Twins* (1925) predates *The Kid Stakes*. Not a great deal is known about the circumstances of its production. It was directed by the Papuan adventurer J. E. Ward, whose previous credits were jungle monologues.[28] Shot on location in Sydney's backstreets, the silent dramatizes the knockabout antics of "partners in crime" Ginger Meggs and Bluey (Ray Griffen and Billy Canstell). One episode has the boys laying a smoke bomb on Ginger's unsuspecting sister Susan (Kitty Willoby) and her gentlemen caller. Fleeing the scene of the crime, the boys bowl over their father, who has a pratfall and in Calvinist/Puritan fashion, punishes them with a few licks of the strap ("Whack! Whack!"). Later, on a tram, the boys cause a gentleman's newspaper to catch fire, sparking an altercation with another man. They also cause mayhem (a series of slapstick incidents) at a local gym. Because they are good bad boys, we're encouraged to laugh at their antics; they are not actually wicked, as we see later when they help rescue Susan, who has been kidnapped by jewel thieves. Susan's new beau, Graham Trent (actor unknown), a well-known cricketer, also comes to the rescue, leading to some protracted fisticuffs. At the end, Trent and Susan are married. The boys complain about having to dress up for the occasion, which is suggestive of the straitjacketing of a larrikin childhood. "Struthe, Ginge," says Bluey in the Australian vernacular, "I feel more like I'm goin' to a funeral than a weddin'," while Ginger wishes he were "dead."

Those Terrible Twins was shown in a private screening on May 12, 1925, before its premiere at the Haymarket Theatre in Sydney on July 25, 1925. The *Sydney Morning Herald* opined that it was "plainly modelled on the pictures that come pouring into our midst from America," and noted that in its efforts to patch together miscellaneous elements—pie-slinging episodes, bathing beauties, crooks—the film leaves "the story rambling and incoherent. It is, in fact, but a series of incidents."[29] It is a film that plays fast and loose with its sources; it is not considered part of the Ginger Meggs canon (for the record, Ginge did not have a twin). Fascinatingly, it may be that the film is not a Ginger Meggs movie at all, but was based on a different property: the Terrible Twins, created by the now-forgotten comic-strip artist, Cyril Samuels.[30] The naming of Ginger and Bluey may have occurred after the fact to enhance the film's box-office appeal. If so, the ploy failed. The film sank into obscurity in the annals of Australian silent cinema, and we had to wait more than fifty years for the release of a bona fide Ginger Meggs feature.

SMILEY AND SMILEY GETS A GUN

Both *The Kid Stakes* and *Those Terrible Twins* were made during a peak in Australian film production that lasted until the coming of sound. With the Great Depression taking hold during the 1930s, few films—let alone children's or family films—were being produced. Most notable is Ken G. Hall's *Orphan of the Wilderness* (1936), which revolves around an orphaned kangaroo named Chut who is trained to box in a travelling circus. Although the film was not specifically targeted at children, Chut was extremely popular with them, which led to product tie-ins (Chut dolls), "personal appearances," and the se- rialization of the story in children's magazines—pre-empting by decades the eponymous marsupial of the Australian children's television series *Skippy the Bush Kangaroo* (1968– 1970), which became a global phenomenon.[31] In contrast, Arthur Collins's lacklustre adaptation of Ethel Turner's novel *Seven Little Australians* (1939) met with an equally lacklustre reception. The Second World War put a virtual halt on film production, which continued well into the post-war years. However, several British productions, including Ralph Smart's *Bush Christmas* (1947) from Children's Entertainment Films (founded by the British mogul J. Arthur Rank), were made on Australian soil and featured regional themes and characters. In the mid-1950s, American studios such as Columbia Pictures and Twentieth Century Fox also invested in films made (and set) in Australia. *Smiley* (1956) and *Smiley Gets a Gun* (1958) were both produced and directed by Englishman Anthony Kimmins and released by Twentieth Century Fox.

It may seem odd to lump films with multinational origins into this discussion of Australian children's cinema, but, as Bruce Molloy notes, *Smiley* "has an authentic Australian feel."[32] Indeed, it could be argued that it often takes a foreign director to bring out the Australianness in filmic depictions—witness Englishman Nicolas Roeg's *Walkabout* (1971) or Canadian Tod Kotcheff's *Wake in Fright* (1971).[33] *Smiley* was a long time in development—Alexander Korda of London Films purchased the rights to Australian journalist-turned-fiction writer Moore Raymond's popular novel right after it was published in 1945. Book reviewers drew parallels between the characters Smiley Greevins and his mate Blue (renamed Joey in the film) and Huck Finn and Tom Sawyer.[34] Smiley was the subject of two other books: *Smiley Gets a Gun* (1947) and *Smiley Roams the Road* (1959). The film transposed the subversive spirit of larrikinism from the city to the country, and, Saxby writes, the "characters, the attitudes and predicaments in *Smiley* are as recognizable and as Australian as Ginger Meggs," adding, "Smiley him- self…is part of the Australian legend, the hero, the little Digger, the larrikin with a heart of gold."[35] Colin Petersen was chosen to play Smiley after a nationwide search, which provided some valuable pre-publicity for the upcoming film. Bruce Archer was selected to play Joey. Raymond wrote the screenplay with Kimmins.

Set in the fictional township of Murrumbilla, in western Queensland, during an in- determinate period of the first half of the twentieth century, *Smiley* has the titular pro- tagonist set on buying a Raleigh bicycle he has seen in a mail-order catalogue. As well as selling crayfish to the townsfolk, Smiley does various odd jobs for his parents and the well-meaning Sergeant Flaxman (Chips Rafferty) to meet his "four quid" target. First though, he must work off the cost of the repairs for buckling the wheel of Sarge's bicycle. He is also put to work as a bellringer ("One penny per tintinnabulum") by the Reverend Lambeth (Ralph Richardson), then as a rouseabout (sheep shearing hand) where he is joined by his faithful companion Joey. He is even retained by the town publican, Mr. Rankin (John McCallum), unwittingly, as a courier to deliver opium to the Aboriginal settlement on the fringes of town, under the ruse of a secret service operation (shades here of Kipling's *Great Game*). But each time Smiley is about to reach his goal, his imprudent conduct costs him his hard-earned savings, and he must start the process all over again. To be fair, it's not always the little scamp's fault (feeling down on his luck, Smiley briefly contemplates suicide with Joey!).

Smiley has been read, validly, as a valorisation of the Protestant work ethic, reflecting both egalitarian principles (through hard work one can enjoy the spoils of growth) and Australian Prime Minister Robert Menzies's post-war economic and masculine ideals of upward middle-class mobility.[36] Chelsea Barnett notes that the film was promoted as "'the story of a lovable Australian boy who proves himself a man!,' reflecting the connection made between specific ideas of Australian masculinity as they operated in the fifties, and the process of childhood development, of a boy 'becoming' a man."[37] But any discussion of *Smiley*'s representation of masculinity and "coming of age" is necessarily incomplete unless we read it as a narrative of the process of taming one's larrikin impulses, which largely stand in the way of Smiley's development.

When Smiley's washerwoman mother (Margaret Christensen) upbraids her son for suspected mischief, she tells him, "You're getting more like your old man every day. He doesn't care if I have to do the washing for half this town, as long as when he gets back droving he's got all his money to spend on booze!" Failing the masculine-breadwinner ideal, Pa Greevins's (Reg Lye) semi-nomadic existence as a drover conforms to Russel Ward's infamous characterization of the "typical Australian" who "swears hard and consistently, gambles heavily and often, and drinks deeply on occasion."[38] He is a warning of what Smiley might become if he doesn't curb his larrikin impulses soon. Like father, like son, Smiley squanders part of the money he has earned as a hand at the shearing station in an illicit game of two-up (lured by the prospect that "if you don't speculate, you don't accumulate"). A game with a long tradition in Australia, two-up was a favourite among diggers during the First World War, despite—and because of—anti-gaming laws dating back to the late 1800s. Later, when Pa returns from his droving, he good-naturedly donates to his son's bicycle fund. But it's as if his period of abstinence produces an insatiable desire for drink and gambling that must be fulfilled to brutal excess. Why Smiley prays to save up for his bicycle *before* his father gets home only becomes apparent when his father plunders his son's savings to play two-up and loses. This is the ultimate betrayal of childhood. So distraught is Smiley that he accidentally knocks his father unconscious with a cricket bat. Thinking he has killed him, he flees, implying that the son must "slay" the father to carve out his own identity.

Australian critic Paul Byrnes writes that the "film is partly about the fight for Smiley's soul. Will he succumb to the dark side, represented by his father the drunk and Rankin the drug runner, or will he become more responsible and upright, working hard for his money and saving to buy material rewards for his honest labour—in this case, a bicycle?"[39] Byrnes astutely frames this struggle in terms of Australian historiography and the much-written-about "conflict between the English and Irish influences—order or rebellion, sobriety or drunkenness. *Smiley* is primarily a moral lesson in favour of temperance, rectitude and religious principles, situating itself firmly on the British side."[40] (Author Raymond, it is worth noting, was of Irish and Scottish extraction). Concomitantly, we may construct the film's moral dilemma in terms of the so-called wowser-larrikin nexus: the wowser, or "puritan," whose moral conservatism has its roots in Catholic and Protestant religion, and the more defiant and "godless" larrikin. Ward notes how Anglican clergyman as chaplains became particularly identified with the "government machinery of repression" among the convicts in penal Australia.[41] In the development of an Australian ethos, Ward finds that Irish convicts and working-class immigrants brought with them a distinctly anti-British attitude, which became associated with "troublesomeness," a sense of rebellion.[42] With excessive drinking seen as a stereotypical Irish trait, it's not surprising that early larrikinism was closely linked to the Irish-Australian character.[43]

Knowing that Smiley lacks a strong father figure, Sarge takes a special interest in the boy, helping to keep him on the straight and narrow. But it's Smiley's refined schoolteacher, Miss Workman (Jocelyn Hernfield), and upstanding schoolmaster Mr. Stevens ("Bud" Tingwell), who embody English middle-class restraint. They privately chuckle at his insubordination in the classroom, but outwardly enforce the rules and discipline they believe are necessary to his development. Smiley also receives moral guidance from the Reverend Lambeth, who, the novel intimates, belongs to the Bush Brotherhood, a special Anglican order of travelling parsons that ministered to remote areas of Australia.[44] It is he who baptizes Smiley in the opening sequence, and it's plain that he has had an influence on the boy's moral development; before donating to the bicycle fund, he has Smiley recite his catechism. Given his practical-cum-muscular Christianity, the Reverend also gives his nod of approval to "rough justice in the Old Testament fashion" when Smiley tells him that he "stoushed" (socked) a schoolmate for tale-telling (the schoolmaster's toffee-nosed son Fred [Gavin Davies], who had earlier belittled Smiley's poverty). It's noteworthy that this brand of justice is compatible with larrikinism of the loutish kind—even the Reverend is not above stoushing the shady Rankin when he tries to make a hasty escape from the town. So much for turning the other cheek.

By the same token, a certain larrikin spirit can be morally improving. Ma Greevins uncharacteristically praises her son to the visiting Sergeant for his cheerful persistence and resilience in the face of adversity: "I'll say this about him, it doesn't matter how many times he takes a knock, he'll always get up again and have another go." Of course, the well-worn egalitarian Australian notion of a "fair go," and willingness to "have a go," needs to be weighed against the film's frank depiction of the vices associated with working-class masculinity.

A key scene in which Smiley sings for money at the local pub illustrates the ambivalent nature of the nexus between working-class masculinity, "Australianness," and nationhood. It's significant that Smiley's choice of song is the bush ballad "Waltzing Matilda," with lyrics by Australia's premier poet, Banjo Paterson (Figure 20.2). Carrying an anti-authoritarian theme, the ballad about a sheep-stealing swagman has been read as Paterson's response to the Australian shearers' strike of 1894.[45] Before "Advance Australia Fair" replaced "God Save the Queen" as the official national anthem in 1984, Clement Semmler could argue that the song is the nearest thing Australians "have to a national anthem, and in the minds of many Australians, it is automatically that. It is learned at school and sung with pleasure, and becomes the one song that adults sing, as a group, naturally and unselfconsciously."[46] What's more, "the elements of 'fair go,' of the little man against the big man, of anti-authority, of bravado, and of the setting of the outback give the song that added appeal to the average Australian conscious of his colonial beginnings."[47] Earlier, we spy Smiley in a tree playing at Captain Cook "discovering

FIGURE 20.2. The irrepressible Smiley (Colin Petersen) sings Australia's de facto national anthem "Waltzing Matilda" in *Smiley* (1956, London Film Productions). Frame-grab.

Australia"—a fallacious view of history that was taught to generations of Australian school children. As an Australian-born son of the British Empire, Smiley is the focal point for nationalistic fervour, symbolic of the young nation (which only federated in 1901) asserting its place in the larger world, and the men in the pub join in a hearty rendition of Australia's de facto anthem—until the Sergeant walks in. Whereas Rankin and Miss Workman see no harm in Smiley's sing-along, Sarge knows better: "As his schoolteacher, I'd have thought you'd know better than to let him mix with a mob of boozers like this [sic]." He knows all too well that this sort of company can only steer the boy into a life of drunkenness and waste.

The oft-dismissed sequel, *Smiley Gets a Gun*, more clearly articulates the larrikin-taming theme. In the opening, Smiley (now played by Keith Calvert, chosen after a nationwide search for a replacement after Colin Peterson moved to England to star in films) is caught by the Sergeant firing his catapult at chickens outside the Murrumbilla police station. After cataloguing Smiley's transgressions in the town, he tells him, "If you don't reform soon, you're gonna drive me and everybody else in Murrumbilla crackers!" When Sarge reprimands Smiley for being in possession of a dangerous weapon, Smiley asks whether he'd had a catapult when he was a boy. "No, I didn't," Sarge lectures the youth, "I wasn't a young larrikin like you. I was responsible. I was allowed to have a .22 rifle. In fact, this one [*taking it off the wall*]." The rifle becomes the coveted prize in a bargain between the lawman and the "lawless" boy. It is based on a reinforcement-punishment system, one that turns Smiley into a poster boy for Skinnerian conditioning. For every responsible act, the Sergeant explains, he will give him one more "nick" (i.e., notch) with an axe in the tree, but for every irresponsible act, he will wipe out one or more of the nicks he has earned. Eight nicks and the gun is his. Sarge will even throw in twenty rounds of ammunition free. As in *Smiley*, achieving his heart's desire is not without its setbacks.

Despite a few lapses of judgement, the little larrikin this time round is more sinned against than sinning. One may apprehend a subtext about *listening* to the child. On one occasion, Sarge fingers Smiley for starting a bushfire on the outskirts of the town. When he finds out that Smiley was only "protecting his cobber"—Joey, the real fire-starter—he reinstates the nicks and awards him two extra for good conduct. In the valorising of mateship, "honour among thieves" trumps tale-telling every time. Most serious of all, Smiley is accused by Murrumbilla's oldest inhabitant, the eccentric Granny McKinley (Sybil Thorndike), of stealing her hidden box of gold sovereigns when she was called away to officiate at the opening of the town's newly struck bore. He is almost sent to trial before the real culprit (a peripatetic writer) is found. At the end, Granny gets her gold back and Smiley gets his gun. As Smiley undergoes his changing fortunes, he becomes the subject of a "sporting proposition," the menfolk betting on whether he will be able to earn his eight nicks or not. Smiley's Pa has reformed since the events of the first film, having swapped a life of droving for blacksmithing, but he still falls woefully short of the father ideal. He actually bets *against* his son winning with bore worker Mr. Stiffy (Grant Taylor). What's more, Pa attempts to derail his son's progress by having him recite the vulgar poem, "The Dog's Meeting," at a public performance.

Released in the United Kingdom on June 28, 1956, and in Australia on October 18, 1956, *Smiley* was a great critical and popular success. *The Australian Women's Weekly*, awarded the film two stars out of three (above average) and received it warmly: "A wonderful film for children, *Smiley* brings smiles of warm indulgence to grown-up lips as well."[48] The *Monthly Film Bulletin* wrote that "*Smiley* is, perhaps, the most refreshing film with an Australian background since *Bush Christmas*, with which it can be compared in many ways."[49] However, *Smiley Gets a Gun* did not match the success of the original. For presenting a much more sanitized portrayal of childhood, family, and town life, the *Monthly Film Bulletin* dismissed it as a children's film with nothing to offer adults: "This story is written and told entirely in juvenile terms, and is acceptable only on that level…Children of twelve or under will enjoy it."[50] Ignoring the reviewer's obvious prejudices, one might nonetheless argue that the sequel watered down the larrikin elements of the first film. Because of its lacklustre box-office performance, a proposed third film was cancelled.

LET THE BALLOON GO AND THE AUSTRALIAN FILM REVIVAL

The 1950s and 1960s in Australia have been described as "cinematically barren."[51] Yet the first stirrings of the Australian film revival in the early 1960s included a handful of films made for children. Tim Burstall, a key figure in the revival, began his career directing the children's shorts *The Prize* (1960; winner of the Bronze Medal at the 1960 Venice Film Festival) and *Nullarbor Hideout* (1965), as well as the 1963 children's television series *Sebastian the Fox*. In 1962, only one feature film was produced in Australia, and it was a children's film: *They Found a Cave*, directed by Andrew Steane. It was followed by the children's musical-comedy, *Funny Things Happen Down Under* (Joe McCormick, 1965), starring ingénue Olivia Newton-John, and *The Intruders* (Lee Robinson, 1969), a spin-off of the hit television series *Skippy*. None of these films were commercially successful, though. Responding to the note of despair regarding an indigenous film industry, the Vincent Report of 1963 made recommendations aimed at stimulating the film industry—including tax concessions for investors and producers—that were ignored. But as Australian film critic Brian McFarlane points out, the report "played its role in fostering the growing determination of Australian filmmakers and their supporters that there should once again be an active film industry in this country."[52]

It has been acknowledged that 1969 was a watershed year in the Australian film revival. In December, the "larrikin" prime minister, John Gorton of the conservative Liberal Party, announced that he would be adopting unreservedly the recommendations of the Interim Report of the Australian Council for the Arts. This included establishing a national film and television school, an Australian film and television development corporation, and an experimental film and television fund.[53] However, it was the 1972 election of the more "cultured" Labour prime minister Gough Whitlam that saw funding of a national film industry reach its apotheosis. The immediate result of this government intervention: "ocker" films that celebrated (or satirised, depending on one's point of view) an uncultivated, "uncouth" Australian masculinity with its attendant vices and obsessions, which often went hand in hand with sex comedies. Writing in 1974, film producer and social commentator Phillip Adams situated the ocker films *Stork* (Tim Burstall, 1971), *The Adventures of Barry McKenzie* (Bruce Beresford, 1972), and *Petersen* (Tim Burstall, 1974) within a "larrikin tradition" dating back to Longford's *The Sentimental Bloke*, the "Dad and Dave" series, and films of George Wallace. These films represented a variant of larrikinism, and Adams saw them as a necessary part of the revival: "For Australia will always need to make its larrikin films for the simple reason that there are a vast number of larrikins at all levels of our population."[54]

The 1970s and 1980s also saw the release of a number of films for the children's and family market, including *Strange Holiday* and *Little Jungle Boy* (both 1970, Mende Brown), *Marco Polo Junior versus the Red Dragon* (Eric Porter, 1972), *Avengers of the Reef* (Chris McCullugh, 1973), *Ride a Wild Pony* (Don Chaffey, 1975; a fine Disney production made on Australian soil), *Storm Boy* (Henri Safran, 1976; remade 2019), *Barney* (David Waddington, 1976), *Let the Balloon Go* (Oliver Howes, 1976), *Dot and the Kangaroo* (Yoram Gross, 1977), *Blue Fin* (Carl Schultz, 1978), *Fatty Finn* (Maurice Murphy, 1980), and *Ginger Meggs* (Jonathan Dawson, 1982). Films like *Ride a Wild Pony*, *Let the Balloon Go*, *Fatty Finn* and *Ginger Meggs* work within the tried-and-true larrikin tradition. *Storm Boy* was an unqualified success, both critically and commercially. It also sold well overseas. However, the failure of so many Australian children's films at the time can not only be put down to audience indifference for home-grown product but to unfair exhibition practices: *Marco Polo*, Australia's first animated feature, *Dot and the Kangaroo*, and *Let the Balloon Go* were only shown at matinees. As film historian Eric Reade vented in 1979: "This relegation to matinees is really infuriating to those people who wish to see Australian-made films accepted in their own country. This will neither help nor encourage production of Australian features for children."[55]

Let the Balloon Go was publicly funded by Film Australia for the Australian Film Commission, established by the Whitlam Government in 1975. It was adapted from the 1968 book of the same name by Australian children's author Ivan Southall, who, as a "British subject", won the prestigious Carnegie Medal for 1971. Critic David Stratton, noting the problematic nature of family films in the Australian market, writes, "The film experienced tremendous difficulties in finding distribution, and its release was considerably delayed. When it eventually emerged, it caused hardly a ripple."[56] It had its premiere in Los Angeles on December 8, 1976, and picked up a couple of American awards for outstanding children's film, but critical reception was mixed. In its homeland, the *Australian Women's Weekly* was pleasantly surprised: "The makers [of the film] have avoided most of the obvious tear-jerking situations and rarely get carried away with sentiment. The result is a fine film that most people should enjoy watching even though it's aimed at children."[57] But the Sydney *Sunday Telegraph* couldn't "work up any positive enthusiasm" for the movie despite its best intentions.[58] The film's star Robert Bettles was familiar to audiences as the "wild colonial boy" of *Ride a Wild Pony* and the terminally ill son in the Australian drama *The Fourth Wish* (Don Chaffey, 1976), and his performance as the physically disabled boy was widely praised. Outside Australia, the *Variety* reviewer felt there wasn't much Bettles could do "to overcome inept direction, which makes him bad-tempered and willful, rather than a sympathetic striver after independence, trying and succeeding in overcoming his handicap."[59] Lacking cultural context, this reviewer failed to grasp the unsentimental larrikin implications in his coming of age: exceeding limits, bending rules. Interestingly, the larrikin intersection is missing from the book.

In stamping the source material with the requisite Australianness, the unassuming children's film transposes the contemporary (i.e., late 1960s) setting of the novel outside Melbourne to the historical setting of "Munaroo, 1917" in rural New South Wales (actually the town of Carcoar, southwest of Bathurst). From the outset, John Clement Sumner, who wears callipers on his legs because of his polio affliction and suffers from epilepsy, is presented as a "wannabe larrikin." The film begins with the local children gate-crashing a military exercise involving the local fire service, under acting fire chief Gifford (Bruce Spence) and Constable Baird (John Ewart), which has them "at war" with the neighbouring town of Wyalong. When they are discussing tactics, it is John who suggests pelting the "enemy" with flour bombs at Bennett's Bridge. But on the way to the bridge, he is waylaid by his mother (Janet Kingsbury), who wants to take him home. He manages to slip away to watch the exercise from afar; his expression of longing as he witnesses this carnival of misrule speaks volumes. John is confined to bed for the rest of the day, "not as a punishment," his mother reminds him, but as a precaution against overexerting himself. The next day at church John has a seizure, and that evening he's visited by a doctor who proposes an innovative surgery. Adamant that "they're not going to cut me up," John has a nightmare in which he breaks free from the operating table as he is pursued by a team of masked surgeons with their instruments of torture. This transforms into a light-at-the-end-of-the-tunnel fantasy in which he triumphantly competes in a hurdle race, as school mates cheer him on.

When John rides with his mother in a horse-drawn cart, he witnesses his hell-raising mates throwing stones on the tinned roof of the house of Major "Tiddly" Fairleigh (Kenneth Goodlet), who comes out brandishing his sabre. John joins in the chorus of name-calling, "Tiddly Fairleigh, Tiddly Fairleigh" until his mother reprimands him. When John asks why he can't call the Major names (reasoning that "everyone else does"), she counters: "It doesn't matter what everybody else does, we don't say things like that about people who are...different, do we?" Given the "cripple" insults John has to endure, she has a point. Yet this sort of unruly behaviour can be understood as a larrikin rite of passage. Like Granny McKinley in *Smiley Gets a Gun*, the Major is an eccentric, for every small town must have one. What's more, the character provides the link between larrikin and soldier.

John has a Mitty-like moment when he imagines his able-bodied self in a mounted infantry charge across the desert. His self-aggrandizing nationalistic fantasy following the Sinai-Palestine campaign of the First World War is triggered by the sight of a procession of enlistees from the neighbouring town—specifically, a man with an "arabesque" head-band. Director Howes uses superimposition and trickery to convey a sense of the grandeur and scale of the event, as bayonet-wielding soldiers on horseback advance across the undulating desert riven by explosions. The fantasy ends with victor John holding the Australian flag. *Variety* identified 1917 and the war as "a difficult period for today's kids to relate to since war then was an honorable enterprise, and jingoism rife. This factor may pose problems in acceptance of film by audiences outside [its] country of origin."[60] The charge notably evokes the Australian Light Horse Brigade's part in the Battle of Beersheba, on October 31, 1917, which led to the liberation of Jerusalem. This battle is also depicted in George Lambert's 1920 painting "*The Charge of The Australian Light Horse at Beersheba, 1917*," Charles Chauvel's propaganda war film *Forty Thousand Horseman* (1940), and *The Lighthorsemen* (Simon Wincer, 1987). In Australian culture, it has been dwarfed by the much-mythologized story of ANZAC sacrifice in the 1916 Gallipoli campaign, seen as a defining moment in the country's sense of national self-awareness and identity, giving rise to the Anzac Legend.[61] The larrikin is also seen to have come of age at Gallipoli. Why, then, does the film evoke Beersheba and not Gallipoli or, for that matter, the battlefields of France, where John's brothers are fighting? Is it because Beersheba, as an unequivocal victory and not failure, fits in better with the film's narrative of *uplift*?

Further fuelling John's heroic wish fulfilment fantasy is his visit to the Major's house. Wearing full military regalia, the Major talks proudly of fighting dervishes in the Anglo-Sudan War of 1881—1899. Says the impressionable boy, "I would have liked to have been there, sir." "You could have been there, boy," replies the Major. "You can do anything you want, provided you put your mind to it and don't let the enemy get in the way. Never surrender, boy, never surrender." We are meant to unproblematically accept this fervent belief in empire, in war as a great adventure, as a metaphor for the battlefield of life. The film thus conflates larrikinism with a certain courage and spirit underwritten by the "romance of war." But having the town eccentric, a living relic of a bygone age, convey these sentiments is problematic. It may well be that *Let the Balloon Go* is subtly undercutting the pro-war sentiment.

As John is about to leave, the Major offers him a final word of advice that spells out the film's message: "And a balloon is not a balloon until you cut the string and let it go" (or, as the Australian daybill shouted, "A boy's first step toward manhood—like the balloon—he wants to be free!"). The transparent symbolism is foreshadowed in images of an air balloon being readied for flight. When he's left alone in the house by his mother for the first time, John does something that no one in the town thinks he can do: climb a tree (Figure 20.3). From the top, he watches the air balloon go rogue. As in Albert Lamorisse's famous French short *The Red Balloon* (1956), the balloon functions "as a psychological mirror of the child protagonist."[62] But John's "rogue" act of independence is spoiled when the townspeople rally around him. Gifford and Baird comically stage a rescue; it hasn't occurred to them that the boy doesn't need rescuing. John sustains minor injuries when he falls from the tree. But as far as he is concerned, it has been worth it. For the mother can begin to process her son's need for independence and finally "let go." Against her first instincts, she lets him ride on the fire engine with the other kids. Abandoning

FIGURE 20.3. John Sumner (the talented Robert Bettles) climbs to freedom in *Let the Balloon Go* (1976, Film Australia). Frame-grab.

the truck, they run across the field to chase the balloon as it struggles to get airborne. At long last, John can partake in the larrikin life of the town.

Fatty Finn and *Ginger Meggs*

Released close together, *Fatty Finn* and *Ginger Meggs* help bring this discussion of the larrikin streak in Australian children's cinema full circle. Both comic-strip adaptations recall Mark Twain's hopes in the preface of *The Adventures of Tom Sawyer* (1876):

> Although my book [and here we may substitute "film"] is intended mainly for the entertainment of boys and girls, I hope it will not be shunned by men and women on that account, for part of my plan has been to try to pleasantly remind adults of what they once were themselves, and of how they felt and thought and talked, and what queer enterprises they sometimes engaged in.[63]

Writer-producer Michael Latimer cannily reflected on the different directions a film about Ginger Meggs could take: "For whom were we making the film? Bancks *aficionados*? Australian kids? A worldwide 'family' market?...In the end our intuition prevailed, fortunately in total agreement. We would try to relate *Ginger Meggs* to a 1980s audience anywhere: we would make a commercial family film with modern music."[64] This would be no mean feat after the release of a new type of "children's film" that became a Hollywood game-changer: George Lucas's *Star Wars* (1977). Although they are intended mainly for children, *Ginger Meggs* and *Fatty Finn* make appeals to an adult nostalgia that is restitutionist in its implications; neither is particularly distinguished.

Publicly funded by the Children's Film Corporation and the Australian Film Commission, *Fatty Finn* is in certain respects a remake of *The Kid Stakes*. Set in the Sydney suburb of Woolloomooloo in 1930, the film reworks key scenes—like the cricket match, the sacred blood oath, the goat-cart race—of its predecessor, but with less flair and self-assurance. The film *Fatty Finn* most resembles is *Smiley*. The episodic plot deals with Fatty's (Ben Oxenbould) attempts to acquire 17 shillings and 6 pence to buy a crystal set to listen to batsman great Don Bradman from Australia "spifflicate" Britain in the First Test. There are only thirteen days before the match will be broadcast, and Fatty has to "use his enterprise"—as the pawnbroker puts it—to acquire the money in time. Fatty is, of course, thwarted by Bruiser (Greg Kelly) at every turn, which leads to a series of revenge-driven escapades between their respective gangs. The wastrel Mr. Finn (played by Australian television personality Bert Newton) is a more charming version of Smiley's Pa. In one scene, Fatty catches him raiding his money box, so that he can buy Mrs Finn (Noni Hazelhurst) a clothes mangle for Mother's Day. On a budget of AU$350,000, the film grossed a decent AU$1,064,000 at the domestic box office against fierce competition from *The Empire Strikes Back* (Irvin Kershner, 1980) and *Superman II* (Richard Lester, 1980). Geoff Mayer of the Australian journal *Cinema Papers* praised the film for its unique Australian sense of humour (one that is indubitably larrikin): "For the film is crude, irreverent, direct and egalitarian in its determination to prick any sign of pretentiousness and pomposity."[65]

Yet there doesn't seem to have been much faith in the project. First-time director Maurice Murphy seemed surprised that both children and adults patronized the film.[66] And scriptwriter Bob Ellis was unhappy with the end result, blaming it on meddling; in the "realisation on screen [it] doesn't come half way up to Disney, and is arguably garish, unfunny and miscalculated."[67] While praising the film's energy and visual style, he called the performances—except Newton's—"dreadful."[68] Revisiting the film today, one feels inclined to agree.

Even more thinly plotted than *Fatty Finn*, *Ginger Meggs* has all the familiar ingredients in a film about the street larrikin with the heart of gold: Ginger (Paul Daniel) getting up to mischief, getting even with enemies Eddie Coogan (Daniel Cumerford) and Tiger Kelly (Drew Forsythe), clashing with his parents (a hammy performance by comedian Garry McDonald as the at-the-end-of-his-tether dad), brawling in the schoolyard, running away, and so on. Like *Fatty Finn*, the film forgoes much of the street realism for a colourful comic-strip aesthetic. It is marred by an anachronistic rock-music score, which jars against the period setting (circa late 1940s). Despite the high hopes for the film, it grossed a meagre A$990,000 at the domestic box office on a budget of A$1.3 million. Its director, Jonathan Dawson, would never make another feature film. Released so soon after *Fatty Finn*, it may have suffered from over-familiarity. For Australian reviewer Derham Groves, writing for *Variety*, it was "an engagingly unpretentious, gentle film targeted primarily at the age 5–13 brigade."[69] But the *Sydney Morning Herald* believed it had missed its target audience: "Whatever dear old Ginger Meggs may mean to his remaining fans—and they must be getting on a bit—he's come up looking just a bit out of date for 1982…I suspect it's more likely to appeal to nostalgic adults than to fun-seeking youngsters."[70] Mayer, who gave the thumbs up to *Fatty Finn*, resorted to special pleading in his review. He sensed the film had "'softened' the character of Ginger," most notably its larrikin aspect.[71] Judging by the box-office receipts, one wonders whether the character's quaint larrikinism was able to speak to a younger generation being weaned on the special-effects-laden films of the "Lucas-Spielberg industry." It would seem that the window of opportunity for making such nostalgic children's fare had passed.

CONCLUSION

A unique larrikin sensibility or streak has been a feature of Australia's children's cinema for most of its history, and is part of a broader larrikin tradition in its literature and culture. As couched in terms of children and childhood out of bounds, it's a streak that reflects and refracts facets of the Australian character: its class consciousness, resistance to authority, egalitarian and mateship qualities, heightened sense of militarism and nationalism, and vices and obsessions. Since the 1980s, the two animated features made about Dorothy Wall's larrikin koala, *Blinky Bill: The Mischievous Koala* (Yoram Gross, 1992), and *Blinky Bill: The Movie* (Deane Taylor, 2015), have flaunted a token Australianness, while the animated *The Magic Pudding* (Karl Zwicky, 2000) bothered critics and fans alike for its departures from Norman Lindsay's classic children's novel, sacrificing much of the idiosyncratic (that is to say, larrikin) language and humour. The underperformance of *The Magic Pudding* (earning just over AU$1 million on an AU$10 million budget) and others is, of course, symptomatic of the underperformance of Australian films more generally in a context where Australians seem to have little interest in paying to watch local films.[72]

Australia's most successful larrikin export remains Paul Hogan's "crocodile hunter" Mick Dundee from the highly successful *Crocodile Dundee* (1986, 1988, 2001) series; and Hogan/Dundee's real-life successor, Steve Irwin, scored a moderate hit with the family film *Crocodile Hunter: Collision Course* (John Stainton, 2002). The late Irwin's puckish larrikin persona was well-received overseas, but some Australians were not so comfortable with the perpetuation of the stereotype.[73] Perhaps tellingly, fewer children's or family films today evince the larrikin streak. In the pursuit of the world family market, investors, producers, and directors seem less willing to embrace this aspect of the Australian character—the surprise family hit *Red Dog* (Kriv Stenders, 2011), about a "four-legged larrikin," did not travel well overseas. There are also signs that the larrikin no longer has cultural currency in a multicultural and diverse Australia, where nation and identity are much more contested. As Jessica Milner Davis and Lindsay Foyle lament: "The Australian self-image that applied for most of last century seems now to be passing. This is a shame. Australians simultaneously loved the larrikin and were embarrassed by it, but now the cringe is proving stronger than the affection."[74] Whether this signals the end for a larrikin children's cinema in Australia remains to be seen.

Notes

1. Edward E. Morris, *A Dictionary of Austral English* (1898: Project Gutenberg, 2009), s.v., "larrikin." http://gutenberg.net.au/ebooks09/0900231h.html [accessed January 8, 2019].

2. Melissa Bellanta, *Larrikins: A History* (St. Lucia: University of Queensland Press, 2012), p. xiv.

3. Bellanta, *Larrikins*, p. xv. See C. E. W. Bean (ed.), *The ANZAC Book*, 3rd ed. (Sydney: University of New South Wales Press/Australian War Memorial, 2010), p. 35.

4. Clem Gorman, "Round Up the Usual Suspects!," in Clem Gorman (ed.), *The Larrikin Streak* (Chippendale: Pan Macmillan Australia, 1990), pp. ix–xiii, at x.

5. Graham Shirley, "Australian Cinema: 1896 to the Renaissance," in Scott Murray (ed.), *Australian Cinema* (St. Leonard's: Allen & Unwin and the /Australian Film Commission, 1994), pp. 5–44, at 5.

6. See, in particular, Graham Jones, *Ned Kelly: The Larrikin Years: the Rise and Fall of the Prince of Larrikins* (Wangaratta, VIC: Charquin Hill, 1990).

7. Graham Shirley and Brian Adams, *Australian Cinema: The First Eighty Years*, rev. ed. (Sydney: Currency Press, 1989), pp. 53–54.

8. Bellanta, *Larrikins*, p. 9.

9. Andrew Pike, "Chapter 2: The Life and Times of *The Sentimental Bloke*," in *Raymond Longford's The Sentimental Bloke* (Canberra: National Film and Sound Archive, 2009), pp. 37–62, at 53–54, 58. Accompanying booklet to *The Sentimental Bloke: the Restored Version*, directed by Raymond Longford (1919; Canberra: NFSA/Madman Entertainment, 2009), DVD.

10. Stella Lees and Pam Macintyre, *The Oxford Companion to Australian Children's Literature* (Melbourne: Oxford University Press, 1993), p. 64.

11. Brenda Niall, *Seven Little Billabongs: The World of Ethel Turner and Mary Grant Bruce* (Ringwood, AUS: Penguin, 1982), p. 99.

12. Ethel Turner, *Seven Little Australians* (Camberwell, VIC: Puffin, 2003), pp. 1–2.

13. Adrian Schober, "Renegotiating Romanticism and the All-American Boy Child: Alfred Hitchcock's *The Trouble with Harry*," in Debbie Olson (ed.), *Children in the Films of Alfred Hitchcock* (New York: Palgrave Macmillan, 2014), pp. 127–159, at 144.

14. Leslie Fiedler, "The Eye of Innocence," in Henry Anatole Grunwald (ed.), *Salinger: A Critical and Personal Portrait* (New York: Harper & Row, 1962), pp. 218–245, at 224–225.

15. Maurice Saxby, *Images of Australia: A History of Australian Children's Literature 1941–1970* (Lindfield, NSW: Scholastic Press, 2002), p. 450.

16. See Noel Brown, *British Children's Cinema: From The Thief of Bagdad to Wallace and Gromit* (London: I.B. Tauris, 2016).

17. Russel Ward, *The Australian Legend* (1958; repr. Melbourne: Oxford University Press, 1970).

18. Lees and Macintyre, *Oxford Companion to Australian Children's Literature*, pp. 162, 183; Saxby, *Images of Australia*, pp. 451–452.

19. Barry Andrews, "Ginger Meggs: His Story," in *Nellie Melba, Ginger Meggs and Friends* (Malmsbury, VIC: Kibble Books, 1982), pp. 211–229, at 221.

20. Not only was Nicholls influenced by Dennis's *The Sentimental Bloke*, but he also produced the titles for the Longford adaptation.

21. Adrian Danks, "*The Kid Stakes*," *Metro Magazine: Media & Education Magazine* 118 (1999), p. 79.

22. Shirley and Adams, *Australian Cinema*, pp. 86–87.

23. Ibid., p. 86.

24. "Wintergarden Theatre," *Brisbane Courier*, June 9, 1927, p. 22.

25. George Galway, "Fatty Fin [*sic*] as a Screen Hero: 'The Kid Stakes,' a Success at Haymarket," *Adelaide Saturday Journal*, July 2, 1927, p. 20. Reprint of a review in the *Sunday Evening News*.

26. Andrew Pike and Ross Cooper, *Australian Film 1900–1977: A Guide to Feature Film Production* (Melbourne: Oxford University Press/Australian Film Institute, 1980), p. 178.

27. "Old Sydney Lives Again," *Pix*, October 30, 1954, p. 42.

28. Pike and Cooper, *Australian Film*, p. 165.

29. Anon., *Sydney Morning Herald*, May 13, 1925, p. 10.

30. See Camille Scaysbrook, "The Mystery of 'Those Terrible Twins' (1925), Part 1-6", "Brooksie's Silent Film Collection," 2009–2017, https://brooksiescollection.tumblr.com/tagged/ttt/chrono [accessed November 13, 2017].

31. Pike and Cooper, *Australian Film*, p. 231.

32. Bruce Molloy, "*Smiley*," in Brian McFarlane, Geoff Mayer, and Ina Bertrand (eds.), *The Oxford Companion to Australian Film* (Oxford: Oxford University Press, 1999), pp. 457–458, at 457.

33. As Scott Murray argues, the films by Roeg and Kotcheff are "classic examples of how foreign eyes can see and understand local issues with a clarity often unimagined at home." In *Wake in Fright*, this includes the dark side to drinking, gambling, and mateship. Scott Murray, "Australian Cinema in the 1970s and 1980s," in Scott Murray (ed.), *Australian Cinema* (St. Leonards: Allen & Unwin and the Australian Film Commission, 1994), pp. 71–148, at 72.

34. "Sylvan," review of *Smiley*, *The Argus*, January 15, 1946, p. 16.

35. Saxby, *Images of Australia*, p. 457.

36. Emma Hamilton, "Smiley," in James E Bennett and Rebecca Beirne (eds.), *Making Film and Television Histories: Australia and New Zealand* (London: I.B. Tauris, 2012), pp. 153–157, at 154–155; Chelsea Barnett, "'Working Hard and Saving Up': Australian Masculinity and Meanings of Work and Class in *Smiley* (1956)," *Lilith: A Feminist History Journal* 21 (2015), pp. 97–105.

37. Chelsea Barnett, *Reel Men: Australian Masculinity in the Movies, 1949–1962* (Carlton, VIC: Melbourne University Press, 2019), p. 75.

38. Ward, *Australian Legend*, p. 2.

39. Paul Byrnes, "*Smiley* (1956)" [curator's notes], Australian Screen/National Film and Sound Archive (NFSA). https://aso.gov.au/titles/features/smiley/notes [accessed February 17, 2019].

40. Byrnes, "*Smiley*."

41. Ward, *Australian Legend*, p. 90.

42. Ibid., pp. 52–53.

43. Bellanta, *Larrikins*, pp. 25–26.

44. Moore Raymond, *Smiley* (London: Sylvan Press, 1945), pp. 22–23.

45. See Matthew Richardson, *Once a Jolly Swagman: The Ballad of Waltzing Matilda* (Melbourne: Melbourne University Press, 2006), pp. 93–94.

46. Clement Semmler, *The Banjo of the Bush: The Work, Life and Times of A. B. Paterson* (Melbourne: Lansdowne, 1975), p. 101.

47. Semmler, *Banjo of the Bush*, 101.

48. "Talking of Films," *Australian Women's Weekly*, December 19, 1956, p. 73.

49. B. H. T, review of *Smiley, Monthly Film Bulletin* 23 (August 1956), p. 100.

50. Anon., review of *Smiley Gets a Gun, Monthly Film Bulletin* 25 (June 1958), p. 78.

51. Murray, "Australian Cinema in the 1970s and 1980s," p. 71.

52. Brian McFarlane, *Australian Cinema 1970–1985* (Richmond, VIC: William Heinemann, 1987), p. 20.

53. "1969: Interim Report of the Film Committee, Australian Council of the Arts," in Albert Moran and Tom O'Regan (eds.), *The Australian Film Reader* (Sydney: Currency Press, 1985), pp. 171–174, at 172.

54. Phillip Adams, "There'll Always Be Celluloid Larrikins," *Sydney Morning Herald*, November 16, 1974, p. 9.

55. Eric Reade, *History and Heartburn: The Saga of Australian Film 1896–1978* (Sydney: Harper & Row, 1979), p. 268.

56. David Stratton, *The Last New Wave* (London: Angus & Robertson, 1980), p. 272.

57. Harriet Veitch, review of *Let the Balloon Go, Australian Women's Weekly*, December 15, 1976, p. 111.

58. Review of *Let the Balloon Go, Sunday Telegraph*, January 2, 1977, p. 74.

59. "Miha," aka M. Harris, review of *Let the Balloon Go, Variety*, May 5, 1976, p. 19.

60. "Miha," *Let the Balloon Go* review, p. 19.

61. John Robertson, *Anzac and Empire: The Tragedy and Glory of Gallipoli* (Port Melbourne: Hamlyn Australia, 1990), pp. 259–267.

62. Noel Brown, *The Children's Film: Genre, Nation and Narrative* (New York: Columbia University Press, 2017), p. 81.

63. Mark Twain, preface to *The Adventures of Tom Sawyer* (New York: Penguin, 1986), n.p. (Original work published in 1876).

64. Michael Latimer, "Finding Ginger Meggs," in John Hogan (ed.), *The Golden Years of Ginger Meggs* (Sydney: Pan Books, 1982), pp. 10–14, at 10–11.

65. Geoff Mayer, review of *Fatty Finn, Cinema Papers* 31 (March–April 1981), p. 66.

66. Dave Sargent, "Maurice Murphy [interview]," *Cinema Papers* 35 (Nov.–Dec. 1981), p. 444.

67. Richard Brennan, "Bob Ellis [interview]," *Cinema Papers* 29 (Oct.–Nov. 1980), p. 386.

68. Brennan, "Bob Ellis," p. 386.

69. "Dogo," aka Derham Groves, review of *Ginger Meggs, Variety*, December 29, 1982, p. 16.

70. "Ginger, How You've Aged!," *Sydney Morning Herald*, December 19, 1982, p. 86.

71. Geoff Mayer, review of *Ginger Meggs, Cinema Papers* 42 (March–April 1983), p. 65.

72. See Jordi McKenzie and David Walls, "Australian Films at the Box Office: Performance, Distribution and Subsidies," *Journal of Cultural Economics*, 37:2 (2013), pp. 247–269.

73. Janaki Kremmer, "'Croc Hunter' Painted Controversial Picture of Aussies," *Christian Science Monitor*, September 5, 2006. https://www.csmonitor.com/2006/0905/p12s01-woap.html [accessed August 1, 2019]. Interestingly, Irwin's voicing of an albatross in the broadest of Australian accents in the US-Australia animated co-production *Happy Feet* (George Miller, 2006) was cut from the film.

74. Jessica Milner Davis and Lindsay Foyle, "The Satirist, the Larrikin and the Politician: An Australian Perspective on Satire and Politics," in Jessica Milner Davis (ed.), *Satire and Politics: The Interplay of Heritage and Politics* (Cham, Switzerland: Palgrave Macmillan, 2017), pp. 1–36, at 26.

BIBLIOGRAPHY

Bellanta, Melissa. *Larrikins: A History*. St. Lucia: University of Queensland Press, 2012.

Gordon, Clem, ed. *The Larrikin Streak*. Chippendale: Pan Macmillan Australia, 1990.

McFarlane, Brian. *Australian Cinema 1970–1985*. Richmond: William Heinemann Australia, 1987.

McFarlane, Brian, Geoff Mayer, and Ina Bertrand, eds. *The Oxford Companion to Australian Film*. Oxford: Oxford University Press, 1999.

Murray, Scott, ed. *Australian Cinema*. St Leonard's: Allen & Unwin and the Australian Film Commission, 1994.

Oz Movies. Various film entries, 2018. https://www.ozmovies.com.au/ [accessed August 10, 2019.]

Pike, Andrew, and Ross Cooper. *Australian Film 1900–1977: A Guide to Feature Film Production*. Melbourne: Oxford University Press and the Australian Film Institute, 1980.

Reade, Eric. *History and Heartburn: The Saga of Australian Film 1896–1978*. Sydney: Harper & Row, 1979.

Saxby, Maurice. *Images of Australia: A History of Australian Children's Literature 1941–1970*. Lindfield: Scholastic Press, 2002.

Shirley, Graham and Brian Adams. *Australian Cinema: The First Eighty Years*. Rev. ed. Sydney: Currency Press, 1989.

Southall, Ivan. *Let the Balloon Go*. Harmondsworth, Middlesex: Puffin Books, 1981. (Originally published 1968).

Ward, Russel. *The Australian Legend*. Melbourne: Oxford University Press, 1970.

CHAPTER 21

NATIONALISM IN SWEDISH CHILDREN'S FILM AND THE CASE OF ASTRID LINDGREN

ANDERS WILHELM ÅBERG

THERE is a widespread conception that children's films were always there, right from the advent of narrative cinema. This is Ian Wojcik-Andrews's stance in his influential account of the history of children's film, *Children's Films: History, Ideology, Pedagogy, Theory* (2000).[1] From this perspective, one might want to argue that, for example, the Lumière brothers' comic short *L'Arroseur Arrosé* (*The Sprinkler Sprinkled*, 1895) is the original "rascal film." The rascal film has indeed, over time, become one of the major subgenres of children's film, featuring mischievous young protagonists getting the better of adult antagonists. A different, though related, line of reasoning is that classic children's literature was adapted very early in the history of cinema, with films such as Cecil M. Hepworth's version of *Alice in Wonderland* (1903) and Georges Méliès's *Le petit chaperon rouge* (*Red Riding Hood*, 1901). The argument is that the intermedial connection to stories that have come to be associated with children would make their adaptations children's films. Whether these are valid claims largely depends, of course, on how the term "children's film" is defined. I would suggest that an institutional definition of children's film paves the way for a clear account of the gradual appearance of a peculiar type of film for children. Hence I propose "children's films" are

> *films produced for, marketed to, and exhibited for a child audience (and sometimes accompanying adults) that are considered by experts (i.e., directors, scriptwriters, and others related to the film industry, film critics, teachers, other guardians of children, and the like) to be especially suited for and aimed at such an audience.*

Children's films defined this way began to be produced in Sweden in the 1940s. This happened after decades of discussion and debates about children and the cinema, especially about the risks the new medium posed for children.[2] Since the early years of the twentieth century and the establishment of film theatres in Swedish cities, children have constituted a considerable proportion of the audience, as reported, for example, in contemporary newspapers.[3] After the regulation of film exhibition in 1911, some films were prohibited for children under the age of fifteen; all other films were therefore deemed appropriate for—or, rather, not obviously harmful to—younger children.[4] Admittedly, a few films were produced in the early 1920s that are, by any standard, rascal films. However, I see those films as precursors, with all-age appeal in marketing and critical reception.[5] If anything, they seem to have been deemed *unsuitable* for children.[6] It was not until in the late 1930s and early 1940s that a discourse on children's film appeared in Sweden that is still recognizable as such. That is, a discourse in which the conception of a certain type of film produced for children interacts with the production decisions in the film industry and the film and media policies of civil society (i.e., women's clubs and other associations), and after some delay, the government. By the 1940s, films for children became subject to national film policy, and there was a political ambition formed to support the production of children's film in various ways. This can be seen in several official reports of the Swedish government instigated in the 1940s and published in the late 1940s or early 1950s, above all, "Ungdomen och nöjeslivet" (Youth and entertainment) and "Barn och film" (Children and film). It is clear that the discourse on children's film at this point is part of a wider national discourse—that is to say, a discourse about Sweden and Swedishness, national identity and distinctiveness, and national ambitions and hopes for the future. Two quotations that are quite typical of children's film discourse of the period illustrate this state of affairs. They both treat children's film as a phenomenon of national significance, which, by definition, makes it an important societal issue. Sweden's leading film critic, Robin Hood (a nom de plume for Bengt Idestam-Almquist), went straight to the core of this new focus on children's film:

> Slowly but steadily, a new attitude towards children has presented itself. . . . It starts to dawn on people that the children are the nation's most important asset, the children, they are us, the continuation of us, and those plants needs to be cared for. . . . What do we do for children in terms of film? One can safely answer: nothing.[7]

"Barn och film," one of the reports within the framework of the big inquiry on film begun in 1949, was the first official report in Sweden dedicated exclusively to the issue of children's film. It examined children's film-going habits and the characteristics of a "good" children's film, and considered questions of how to support and encourage their production. The nation-building functions of children's films are stressed:

> In light of what was stated earlier about children's film-habits, the committee finds it important that society enables a continued production of good *Swedish* [italics in original] children's films. Because film for large numbers of children and youth is the main mediator of impressions outside of the home and school, it must be a societal interest that children get those impressions also in Swedish design, in films mirroring a Swedish environment, Swedish living and Swedish culture.[8]

In this chapter, I will trace the development of Swedish children's film from the focal point of the national discourse. I will argue that children's films, especially those with significant audience appeal, tend to be a part of the national discourse and tend to promote ideas about Sweden and Swedishness, as well as elicit pleasurable feelings associated with the Swedish nation and people. To structure the analysis, I concentrate on several films, and one TV series, adapted from the literary work of Astrid Lindgren, although other examples will also be discussed.

CHILDREN'S FILM AS NATIONAL EDUCATION

The 1930s and 1940s are considered the formative years in the creation and growth of the so-called Swedish Model for a modern welfare society, leading to a period of unprecedented modernization and prosperity in the decades after the Second World War. In popular political discourse (not to say propaganda), the image of this society is that of the Swedish nation as a home for the people, or in Swedish: *Folkhem*. In modern Swedish history, the period between, roughly, the early 1930s to the early 1980s is often referred to as the *Folkhem* era. The early decades of this era, in particular, were characterized by an ambition to educate the citizens. These didactic impulses drew partly from conservative paternalism, but also from the more progressive mission of nineteenth-century popular (or social) movements such as the temperance movement, the revival movement, and the labour movement. The work to reform and modernize society in the early welfare state demanded enlightenment and a fostering of modern citizenship.

There were great hopes during this time that the modern film medium could be used as a channel of communication in this context, despite a generally pessimistic view of the quality and effects of the actual output in terms of feature films in commercial theatres. However, it has been noted that contemporary film, in various ways, mirrored and problematized important social and political issues, and that it frequently used an educational (some would say merely tendentious or propagandist) mode of address. Swedish film historian Per Olov Qvist has shown that Swedish feature films produced in the 1930s propagated national consensus among social classes—that is, the working class, upper class, and upper-middle class.[9] This was in line with the official political stance and rhetoric of the governing Social Democratic Party. The films also celebrate the social virtues of self-discipline, courtesy, honesty, a keen sense of justice, naturalness, hard work, sense of duty, helpfulness, loyalty, optimism, moderation, modesty, and common sense. As Swedish film historian Michael Tapper has noted, these virtues are universal, but the films made then clearly depict them as specifically Swedish, and the marks of decent Swedishness.[10] In contrast, characters who display the opposite demeanour are often portrayed as suspiciously foreign. In this way, popular culture incorporates, processes, and disseminates self-images and ideals that are framed as national.

After film became a popular-entertainment medium in the beginning of the twentieth century, the issue of children and film was initially treated mostly as a social problem. Simultaneously, there were hopes about the didactic potential of film in schools. Children's film as a genre appears at the intersection of these fears and hopes. The formation of a discourse and of practice of production and support for children's film takes place as a result of political debate and societal intervention. This means that children's film can be seen as a result of social reform within the framework of the Swedish welfare state, much as with, for example, kindergartens. During the 1940s, a small number of films were finally produced that corresponded to the hopes for a type of film suited to the needs of children as outlined in the various government reports mentioned above and in the previous debates. The authors of "Ungdomen och nöjeslivet" (Youth and entertainment) made a brief note of this trend, citing *Det var en gång* (*Once Upon a Time*, Arne Bornebusch, 1945) and *Barnen från Frostmofjället* (*The Children*, Rolf Husberg, 1945), two of about ten productions released during the 1940s that could be considered children's films.[11]

Per Olov Qvist has further demonstrated that the Swedish feature films of the 1930s use a number of "ethnic strategies."[12] Concretely, this means that their recurring themes and motifs are embedded in a national context. Values that can be conceived as "Swedish"—and are indeed marked as such in the films—are thus repetitively reinforced, while potential threats to the constructed community around those same values are demonized and marked as alien. The children's films of the 1940s are constructed in the same way.

With a caveat about a few precursory rascal films in mind, it seems reasonable to regard the 1944 film *Rännstensungar* (*Guttersnipes*, Ragnar Frisk) as Sweden's first children's film. It has come to be considered as a classic, and it has been remade several times. The 1944 film exemplifies the kind of ethnic strategizing described by Qvist. It tells the story of a collective of children living in a run-down apartment building in a poor area in the centre of a city. The protagonist is an orphaned girl, Ninni (Birgitta Hoppeler), who is confined to a wheelchair. The landlord is the unkind capitalist, Mr. Högstrand (Bertil Brusewitz). Ninni is cared for by the penniless artist, Fahlén (Adolf Jahr) and the social worker Miss Sanner (Britta Brunius). After a series of highly melodramatic complications involving Fahlén being enticed to falsify art by a crooked art dealer and unfairly accused of stealing money that was actually stolen by two sketchy street musicians, the film ends on a positive note: Fahlén finds success as an artist and decides to marry Miss Sanner, and the couple will adopt Ninni; Fahlén and Högstrand reconcile; and Ninni is cured and learns how to walk. This new sense of community is celebrated with an outing in the countryside, where the guttersnipes of the title are playing in the pastoral landscape, far from the cramped and unhealthy environment of the city. At this very spot, Fahlén and Högstrand decide to build a holiday camp for poor children.

The film reiterates one of the major themes of 1930s cinema: the peaceful reconciliation of social classes within a framework of national community. It also has what Qvist calls an emancipatory theme that stresses the possibility of upward social mobility, which is characteristic of a good society (the *Folkhem*). Furthermore, the film ethnifies the construction of community among the social classes by contrasting this with the ethnic outsiders in the story. With a keen sense of symbolic and narrative economy, the Swedish proletarian-cum-upper-class centre (the Fahlén–Högstrand union) in the end of the film is defined by mutual antagonism with a Jewish art dealer (Josef Norman; upper class, non-Swedish) and the street musicians (Erik Ahlfors and Gösta Tönne), coded as "pikies" (proletarian, non-Swedish). Swedes should stand united and counteract the potentially disruptive force of class antagonism. Then "we" can move towards a better, more equal modern society, where children can flourish. Figuring out that this is the "message" of the film does not require a lot of interpretive ingenuity. It is quite clear and unambiguous, which brings us back to the didactic theme. There is a lesson to be learned here, and the address to a child audience may be the reason this lesson is so pedagogically and unequivocally designed. The film is *obviously* about the value of class reconciliation, and it *obviously* relates to the kind of thinking voiced by Robin Hood in his call for a better film for children: the children are our (the nation's) future. This makes it a perfect example of the trend of civic education in the *Folkhem*-era popular culture.

Finally, the film uses a trope that is one of the most characteristic ways to signal (or evoke) Swedishness in twentieth-century art, including film. The last scene of the film is a celebration of community in a serene, pastoral setting. The landscape is replete with symbolic significance. First, it can be attributed to *romantic agrarianism*, a body of ideas popularized in Sweden, and in other countries in Europe, in the second half of the nineteenth century, that feeds into the national Romantic movement in Sweden around the turn of the twentieth century. In agrarianism, perhaps most famously conceptualized by Ferdinand Tönnies, the ills of modernity and various forms of social anomie are associated with life in the big cities.[13] By contrast, an aboriginal sense of community—or *Gemeinschaft*—is thought to characterize the traditional ways of life developed in the countryside, incused by the agrarian landscape and wild nature. This chimes well with the film's narrative, where, in the final scene, the misery and contentions of city life are transformed to paradisiac and utopian unity. Secondly, and in line with the former, there is a tenacious conception that the cornerstone of Swedishness is worship of (Swedish) nature and the (Swedish) landscape. This theme was heavily emphasized in the national discourse and in the arts, especially painting and literature, around the turn of the twentieth century. For example, Gustaf Sundbärg, a statistician who was responsible for the official investigation of Swedish emigration carried out between 1907 and 1913, is best remembered today for his highly influential treatise on the characteristics of the Swedish people, *Det svenska folklynnet* (*The Temperament of the Swedish People*), where he writes:

> The most profound tenet of the temperament of the Swedish people, and that which largely explains the nature of our people in all, is *a strong love of nature* (italics in original). It is this warm devotion that has created our great natural scientists, our inventors, and our explorers; it has also bestowed us with our lyrical poets, our

beautiful folk songs, and classical Swedish singing, yes, it has given Swedish *fantasy* itself its peculiar flight.[14]

Hence, the final scene of *Rännstensungar* joins in a tradition in Swedish art of charging natural settings with national pathos. It depicts and elicits feelings towards (to use a term coined by ethnologist Orvar Löfgren) "a patriotic nature."[15] In the next section, we will see how this device will be a recurring feature of Swedish children's films, not least in the works belonging to the Lindgren tradition in Swedish literature and film.

SWEDEN AS IDYLL: THE START OF THE LINDGREN TRADITION

Astrid Lindgren (1907–2002) was one of comparatively few Swedish authors to achieve worldwide fame in the twentieth century. This puts her in a small and exclusive group of people who are objects of national pride, simply because they draw the eyes of the world to our small country, and their achievements are recognized internationally (other examples include the film director Ingmar Bergman and the tennis player Björn Borg). It is well documented that Lindgren is considered a "national icon" in Sweden. This is not exclusively because of her international fame; it also owes to specific values attributed to her public persona and her literary work. These are the values participants in a study by the literary scholar Helene Ehriander considered to typify (positive) Swedish values, such as common sense, the ability to "be oneself" despite fame and fortune, and a penchant for fairness.[16]

Lindgren made her debut as an author of literature for children and youth in 1944, and she followed up her first book, *Britt-Marie lättar sitt hjärta* (*Britt-Marie speaks from her heart*, 1944) with her breakthrough work *Pippi Långstrump* (*Pippi Longstocking*) in 1945. She became a presence in film when one of her novels, *Mästerdetektiven Blomkvist* (*Bill Bergson, master detective*, 1946), was adapted for the big screen under the title *The Master Detective Bill Bergson* (*Mästerdetektiven Blomkvist*, Rolf Husberg, 1947). This release marked the beginning of what it seems reasonable to call the Lindgren tradition in Swedish children's film. During the long 1950s (1945–1965), thirteen of about thirty children's films produced in total were based on works by Lindgren, along with a hugely popular original TV series. Lindgren's stories continue to be adapted for the screen. From 1955, Lindgren acted as scriptwriter in many of the productions, and worked intimately with directors such as Olle Hellbom. No reliable box-office data from the 1940s and 1950s are available to researchers, but by all accounts, the Lindgren films were successful and had great impact. This is especially true from the mid-1950s, when the popular child star Eskil Dalenius played different characters (though all, confusingly, named Rasmus) in several films and in radio dramatizations. Both Bill Bergson and Pippi Longstocking became phenomena with a wider—and, in Pippi's case, controversial—cultural meaning. Pippi was debated as a (bad) role model for children, and "Bergsonery" was the popular term for the activities of vigilant children, especially with a keen eye to possible spies in the somewhat paranoid Cold War atmosphere of the 1950s.[17] It is significant of Lindgren's position within children's film at the time that the Social Democratic youth organization Unga örnar (the Young Eagles), together with Kooperativa förbundet (The National Cooperative Association) and Arbetarnas bildningsförbund (the Workers Education Institute), implemented an extensive campaign called the Bullerby (Noisy Village) action. It was a nationwide attempt to engage children aged six to twelve in educational play in the youth clubs, stimulated by screenings of one, or possibly both, of Olle Hellboms Noisy Village adaptations *Alla vi barn i Bullerbyn* (*The Children of Bullerby Village*, 1960) and *Bara roligt i Bullerbyn* (*Only Fun in Bullerby Village*, 1961).[18]

Furthermore, beginning in the 1960s, Lindgren's stories were circulated in many media: books, films, radio dramatizations, stage plays, and on television.[19] There are other examples of artists using such multimodal distribution in this period, of course. In Lindgren's case, however, the business model has been developed and refined over the decades, and it has come to include multiple forms of merchandize and tie-ins (toys, clothes, and the like) as well as international syndication of her characters (Pippi especially), a theme park—Astrid Lindgrens Värld (Astrid Lindgren's World)—in the author's birthplace, Vimmerby, as well as other forms of cultural tourism in the Småland region.

A very noticeable aspect of the children's films of the 1950s and early 1960 is their pastoral and idyllic character. The children's film historian Margareta Norlin claims that the image of contemporary Sweden in these films is, in a sense, whitewashed and rid of all possible controversy. The bigger cities vanish from the screen, and most children's films are set in rural environments or small towns with white picket fences. Norlin states, "It is obvious that there is no interest to depict a society characterized by the special political interest of different groups. Society is depicted as a unity—the *Folkhem*."[20] Film scholar Malena Janson has attributed this development to Lindgren's breakthrough and speaks of a "Bullerby discourse" in Swedish children's film, with reference to the books and films about the children of Noisy Village, which is a fairly literal translation of the meaning of the name of the imaginary geographical location Bullerbyn.[21] This discourse has, according to Janson, continued as a dominant idyllic current in Swedish children's film.

The political scientist Patrik Hall has specialized in the origins and historical development of nationalism in Sweden. He describes a distinct shift in the middle of the twentieth century. By that point, nationalism had become "institutionalized," and was primarily manifested as "banal nationalism" of the kind Michael Billig has analysed. Hall stresses that World War II marked a divide over how conceptions of nationality were publicly expressed: "In Sweden institutionalized nationalism has [since the war] been particularly subdued, in comparison to the extreme nationalism dominating Swedish culture in the pre-war period."[22] One of the many paradoxes of the post-war era is that modern Swedishness is typically characterized by a lack of openly expressed patriotism. The historian Martin Wiklund has described this as "a form of nationalism that is difficult to detect, with a very subdued expression, which identified Swedishness with democracy, neutrality, and internationalism, and in time with the welfare society."[23] Hence it was "typically Swedish" to abstain from patriotic excesses, which were now regarded as irrational and outdated.

Seacrow Island occupies a central place in Swedish culture. First, it is shorthand for a collection of works consisting of TV productions, films, and books. Second for generations of Swedes, it has come to connote the ideal summer paradise in the Stockholm archipelago. The TV series *Vi på Saltkråkan* (*The Children of Seacrow Island*, Olle Hellbom) consists of thirteen parts, each about thirty minutes long. It first aired from January to April 1964, and it was immensely popular. The first feature film about Seacrow Island was shot in the spring of 1964. It was called *Tjorven, Båtsman och Moses* (*The Little Girl, the Dog, and the Seal*, Olle Hellbom), and it premiered in October 1964. The same autumn, a novel was published, a part-novelization of the TV series. During the 1960s, three additional feature films about Seacrow Island were produced, along with a feature film edited from the original TV series. The films were among the highest-grossing of the decade, which is unusual for children's films. The four features were, in turn, edited into a second TV series in 1977. The original series has been re-run more than fifteen times on national television and is now available on the streaming site of the national broadcasting company.

The TV series and films tell the story of the Melkersson family and their summers on Seacrow Island, focusing on the everyday adventures of the Melkersson children and their island peers. It is set in a pastoral tradition, and Mr. Melkersson's (Torsten Lilliecrona) (he is a widower) concluding words in the series can be read as Astrid Lindgren's intended moral of the story, and, indeed, of the fictional world of Seacrow Island:

> Yes, it's a dream alright. I get to keep it all. My children get to keep their summer dream, and live their summer life, the sweet, secret, and wild. The life that Man can experience only when he is a child, and forgets when he grows up and no longer has the same right to paradise.[24]

Lindgren's books often depict small town idylls, such as Lillköping (Smallville), and pastoral environments, such as Seacrow Island or Noisy Village. In this, she seems clearly inspired by 1920s Swedish literature, particularly the novels of Hjalmar Bergman and the poetry of Birger Sjöberg. The literary scholar, Martin Kylhammar, has analysed what he terms "pastoral patterns of composition" in this literary tradition, and it is easy to see that Lindgren uses these patterns in her work.[25] The visual aesthetics of the TV series and films add powerfully to this pastoral effect. In terms coined by the film scholar Martin Lefebvre, they "turn setting into landscape." This means that the spectator is invited to enjoy the landscape as an attraction in its own right, apart from the narrative function of the setting.[26] The landscape imagery is derived from national romantic painting from the latter part of the nineteenth century and around the turn of the twentieth century. This kind of imagery is highly mediated in a multitude of ways; it is found on postcards, in schoolbook illustrations , in Swedish Tourist Society pamphlets, and so on. In a sense, it has been generalized; it has become a visual style with national connotations, apart from the painters who created it. It is, however, possible to identify specific paintings that are models for some of the compositions in the TV series and films in the work of artists such as Axel Sjöberg, Prince Eugen, Bruno Liljefors, and Carl Larsson. Hence, the landscape of Seacrow Island obviously becomes a version of the "patriotic landscape." The represented surroundings of the island connote certain values and historical conceptions, making it the epitome of Swedishness, in much the same way a representation of Monument Valley in a John Ford western connotes "the spirit of the frontier" or "manifest destiny."

This is a historical development that has taken place over time. It is possible to illustrate how it works by briefly tracing the reception history of the Seacrow Island cycle. The first phase, during the 1960s, treats the cycle as a new and contemporary phenomenon. The bulk of published material consists of reports from the productions of the films, interviews with the budding child stars, and the like. But there are also a number of reviews of the films, in particular. (TV series were not seriously reviewed in Swedish newspapers at this time.) The references to Sweden and Swedishness are legion, but general; there are positive references to the films' depictions of "a Swedish vacation paradise" or of the eldest daughter in the Melkersson family, Malin, as a veritable "propaganda for Sweden."[27] In the changing political and cultural landscape of the 1970s, the cycle is viewed as old-fashioned and perhaps out of touch with contemporary Sweden. On the occasion of the premiere of the second TV series, the columnist Britt-Marie Svedberg wrote, ironically, in the leading Swedish newspaper *Dagens Nyheter*:

> No, "Seacrow Island" could never have been produced as children's television today. It doesn't depict social problems in suburban areas. It has nothing to say about how the closing of factories affect local communities, nor about the conflicts of children with divorced parents. Not even a single brushy protest singer interrupts the action. "Secrow Island" is just fun.[28]

The second phase of reception, during the 1970s, marks the low point for any kind of overt patriotism in political and public discourse in Sweden. The decade is characterized by institutionalized nationalism in its most subdued form. There are few newspaper articles about the Seacrow Island cycle, and those that do exist make no clear references to a national discourse This is unusual, because writing on children's film tends to do precisely that, both in earlier and later decades.

The third phase is initiated during the 1980s, and continues into the 1990s and 2000s, with re-runs being shown in more frequent intervals. When *Vi på Saltkråkan* was re-run in 1991, Swedish national television issued a press release describing series as a beloved classic: "Astrid Lindgren's and Olle Hellbom's tale of summer vacation that was recorded on the islet Seacrow Island by Norröra outside Blidö in the Stockholm archipelago has become the most Swedish thing we have."[29] The newspapers took the bait, and this evaluation of the series was repeated in several of the articles written with regard to the re-runs in 1991, and again in 1993.[30] The metamorphosis of the Seacrow Island cycle is now complete: it has transformed from a nice piece of family entertainment focusing on children to an important part of the Swedish cultural heritage.

During this phase, articles about the Seacrow Island cycle tend to focus on Swedishness and nostalgia. A representative example illustrates the role of the Seacrow Island cycle in the culture at large. In 1991, journalist Lena Valtonen wrote about the dual form of nostalgic pleasure that *Vi på Saltkråkan* elicits. She starts with the assumption that most people in their thirties—as she was at the time—would have seen the series before, probably for the first time, when they were children themselves. This is in all likelihood an understatement: given the frequency of the reruns, it is probable that large portions of the population of all ages shared memories of watching the series. Valtonen describes her own memories of watching the series as a child in 1964. The neighbours gathered in the home "of the family that had managed to purchase the first TV-set in the neighbourhood."[31] It was a ritual of community, where lemonade and buns were served to nearly thirty people, Valtonen remembers. Layered over these childhood memories of watching the series are the memories of the series itself: "Vi på Saltkråkan gave us the image of the ultimate summers paradise. An idyllical image, of course. And absolutely irresistible!"[32] She ends by pointing out that a lot has changed on the island Norröra, where the series was shot: "But in Vi på Saltkråkan, everything stays the same. Pristine. That is nice to know for all nostalgic people, who can now return to paradise, and bring a new generation of children along for the ride."[33]

Valtonen's amalgamation of these idylls—real childhood memories of watching the series and the childhood represented in *Vi på Saltkråkan*—illustrates how the idyllic landscape in *Vi på Saltkråkan* has become part of the collective memory of the space of childhood for generations of Swedes. This process, and Valtonen's eloquent rendition of it, coincides with a veritable cult of nostalgia in Sweden that by that time had become a crucial factor for the production and reception of children's film.

NOSTALGIA FOR THE *FOLKHEM*: LINDGREN REVISITED IN THE 1980S AND 1990S

There is wide agreement that the *Folkhem* era is a relic of the past, though there is some disagreement about when it ended. By the 1980s, a sense of social change seems to have set off nostalgic impulses, especially for the aesthetics and culture of the 1940s and 1950s. This was, by and large, an international phenomenon that had started in the 1970s, but in Sweden it specifically evoked nostalgia for the *Folkhem* era. The memory of the *Folkhem* era has become even more significant since the 1980s. The period is often referred to in art, scholarly debate, journalism, and political discourse and has in the process (except, perhaps, in scholarly discourse) become mythified. For example, the Swedish nationalist and populist party, Sverigedemokraterna (the Swedish Democrats), tends to project Sweden in the *Folkhem* era as an ideal, indeed, a national paradise, before "the fall" brought on by globalization, immigration, and multiculturalism.[34]

In her overview of Swedish film history in *Nordic National Cinemas*, the film scholar Tytti Soila makes note of the increasing interest in children's culture in Sweden starting in the mid-1970s and onward. There is, in a sense, a new wave of children's film—as well as of films about childhood produced for adult or all-age audiences—in the 1970s that included several aesthetically and morally challenging films depicting the contemporary lives of children. From the beginning of the 1980s and into the 1990s, however, children's films tended to look back nostalgically at history. Solia makes the productive observation that films in this nostalgic mode could be considered a type of heritage cinema for children, looking back at the *Folkhem* era:

> The extraordinary thing was that the metaphor of the folkhem could not be discarded, but was rather projected into the past. Both the childhood films and the Lindgren films create the concept of a utopian past and is a Swedish version of heritage cinema whose occurrence became a pan-European phenomenon in the 1980s.[35]

Lindgren continued to be a presence in Swedish children's film in the 1970s, with three films about Pippi Longstocking, three about Emil, and adaptations of the books about Karlsson on the roof, the brothers Lionheart and Madicken (also known as Mischievous Meg, or Mardie). Still, it is possible to speak about a revival of her work in children's film in the 1980s and 1990s. The period saw a number of franchises and remakes based on Lindgren's books, both in films distributed in cinemas and in serialized form on television. This body of work includes another film about Madicken and the remake *Rasmus på luffen* (*Rasmus and the Tramp*, Olle Hellbom, 1981) and Bill Bergson films and two films about the Children of Noisy Village. The books about Lotta on Troublemaker Street were adapted for the first time in two films, as was *Ronja Rövardotter* (*Ronia— The Robber's Daughter*, Tage Danielsson, 1981), which was a huge hit. *Seacrow Island* was released in a stage version produced for television in 1995. Furthermore, two short stories became films for younger children—*Peter och Petra* (*Peter and Petra*, Agneta Elers-Jarleman, 1989) and *Nils Karlsson Pyssling* (*Simon Small*, Staffan Götestam, 1990)—and Pippi Longstocking was launched as an international animated franchise. In addition, a number of short films based on Lindgren's work were produced for television.

As observed by Soila, Norlin, and others, these Lindgren films had a nostalgic quality, and they were released in a cinematic context where many other films for children were also set in the past or, even when set in the present, had a retro quality. This is true, for example, of the top-grossing children's/family film of the period, *Sunes sommar* (*Sune's Summer*, Stephan Apelgren, 1993), where a family abstains (out of necessity) from going on a vacation abroad, and instead revives the somewhat old-fashioned vacation habit of travelling in the Swedish countryside with a caravan. Nor was the trend for nostalgia seen only in children's films. On the contrary, children's films are part of a wider nostalgic current running through various aspects of culture, such as interior design, fashion, and architecture, as well as, as mentioned, political discourse. Among the most successful films for adult audiences were the *Sällskapsresan* (*Package Tour*) franchise (1980–1999; an additional prequel was released in 2011), directed by and starring Lasse

Åberg, and the melodrama *Änglagård* (*House of Angels*, Colin Nutley, 1992). Though set in the present, these films are saturated with a powerful nostalgic sentiment and, in the case of *Änglagård*, romantic agrarianism. So, in a sense, the nature of children's films of the period can be understood as a product of adaptation to marketplace trends, especially compared to some of the commercially less appealing and more experimental children's films of the 1970s.

In the mid-1980s, the high-profile director Lasse Hallström was entrusted with the project of adapting Lindgren's stories about the children of Noisy Village, which resulted in the feature films *Alla vi barn i Bullerbyn* (*The Children of Noisy Village*, 1986) and *Mer om oss barn i Bullerbyn* (*More about the Children of Noisy Village*, 1987). These films can also be considered remakes of Olle Hellbom's adaptations from the early 1960s. The production company, Svensk Filmindustri, wrote in an application for financial support from Svenska filminstitutet (the Swedish Film Institute) that an important reason to make the films was that the Hellbom adaptations were out of circulation. They now exist, it was argued,

> only in our memory, but that is of no avail for today's kids. For them, the Swedish countryside (a long time ago) with cows and pigs, pranks in the hayloft, looking for the Neck [Näcken, the water spirit] late at night, crayfishing, lambkins, going to a Christmas party by sleigh etcetera, has become almost exotic. That is why we want to tell the story about the six children of Noisy Village in the three Noisy Village farms. That is why we want to make a film about the Noisy Village.[36]

The letter is indicative of didactic ambitions in the field of popular ethnography and cultural history. At the very least, it shows that the officials at Svensk Filmindustri imagined that this would be a successful argumentative strategy at this point in time.

This didactic agenda clearly suffuses the finished films. It is fairly prominent in the literary original as well. Like the books, the films are episodic, which enhances the impression of a cavalcade of customs and traditions. The episodes can be grouped in two types. One group portrays the traditional celebrations of religious or secular feasts, such as Easter, Walpurgis night, Pentecost, Midsummer festival, Christmas, and the New Year. The other is more generally focused on lifestyle: going to school, children's labour (running errands, helping with haymaking and harvest, crayfishing), and leisure activities (bathing, fishing, excursions, treasure quests, and so on). Considering also that the iconography of the films is an extremely clear case of cinematic national romanticism—including virtual re-enactments of famous paintings such as Ernst Josephson's *Näcken* (*The Neck*) of 1882 (several versions of this painting exit)—it is reasonable to associate the film with the general enthusiasm for putatively aboriginal aspects of historical mores and popular culture that are characteristic of the national romantic era. The Swedish ethnologist Artur Hazelius and his grand projects come to mind: the Nordic Museum and the open-air ethnographic museum Skansen in Stockholm, founded in 1873 and 1891, respectively. The films work in the same mode as Skansen, which is famous for its re-enactments of aspects of traditional culture (weddings, dances, harvests, etc.) in an "authentic" setting composed of historical buildings collected throughout the country and reconstructed in Stockholm. The films are actually a form of late-twentieth-century open-air museum for children, which seems to be what the producers intended. The Skansen museum itself was an expression of nationalist sentiments around the turn of the twentieth century. The films' affinity with this kind of nationalist ethnography, as well as the painterly iconography, made it quite obvious to some contemporary critics that the films had revamped this kind of nationalism.[37]

Dramaturgically, the two films follow a pastoral pattern of composition by making Noisy Village a secluded idyll, far from the dangers of modern life, which are only present in the form of recounted stories from the newspapers, as a form of contrast. The village is presented as the emblematic "small world," a closely knit community of family, friends, and neighbours. With the possible exception of the mean shoemaker—ironically named Snäll (Kind)—and his scary dog, this small world contains nothing threatening and hardly any conflict. The films also express a pastoral ideal characteristic of a *Geminschaft*: life is ideally led in a small community, governed by the shifting of the seasons: sow, grow, harvest, repeat. The narrator, one of the children named Lisa, expresses a childishly utopian hope that the three girls and the three boys of Noisy Village will marry each other, and never have to leave the village. Harmless as this may seem, the ideology of blood-and-earth looms beneath the surface of this celebration of home and family.

The attractive tableaux from Noisy Village are derived from the visual aesthetics and popular motifs of the painter Carl Larsson. One of Larsson's projects was the decoration and artistic documentation of his home, Lilla Hyttnäs. Like his contemporary, Ellen Key, he was inspired by the arts and crafts movement. Key and Larsson were the most famous proponents of an ideology of the good home as the foundation of a new, better, and more enlightened society in the early twentieth century. Historian Yvonne Hirdman has emphasized Key's importance in the rhetoric of "the good home" that the leader of the Social Democrats, Per-Albin Hansson, embraced when he launched the powerful political metaphor of Sweden as a *good home for the people*, a *folkhem*, in a speech in 1928.[38] *Alla vi barn i Bullerbyn* and *Mer om oss barn i Bullerbyn* are both set in 1928–1929, and they seem designed to recall the very model—the ideal—that modern Swedish society aimed to realise in the *Folkhem* era. Metonymically, Noisy Village *is* Sweden.

The two films discussed are not isolated cases, though they are extreme in their intertextual borrowings from early twentieth-century art. On the contrary, the pastoral mode characterizes many children's films of the period. If nationalism and issues of nation seem to be expressed or addressed in an indirect, albeit indisputable, way in the Noisy Village films, there are other films where this is less subtle. To give but one example outside the Lindgren oeuvre, the Hallström film, *Mitt liv som hund* (*My Life as a Dog*, 1985), tells the story about the boy Ingemar, who must relocate from the city to a small village when his mother dies. At the end of the film, Ingemar has settled in the village and is now truly part of the community. The final scene takes place on the night the Swedish boxer, Ingmar Johansson (and Ingemar's namesake), became the heavyweight champion of the world, in June 1959. In a montage sequence, we watch the people in the village listening to the radio broadcast. Ingemar and his friend Saga fall asleep and miss the end of the fight. When the commentator announces Johansson's victory, people rush into the street in the middle of the bright Nordic night, or open their windows, and the last line of dialogue is an orgiastic shout: "Heja Sverige!" (Go Sweden!).[39]

The historical children's films of the period make past social and physical landscapes the setting of, for a lack of a better concept, "the good life." It is a life characterized by security, confidence, mutual care, warmth, and community. These words may appear trite, but the films invite the spectator to experience their content emotionally. Feelings of these kinds are then associated with issues of nation in varying ways. There is a continuum, where one extreme is patriotic outbursts, as in *Mitt liv som hund*, and the other is the depiction of a strikingly monocultural society. Sweden before the increase in immigration in the 1980s and 1990s appears as ethnically uniform in comparison to the society where the films were distributed, and is, in this regard, "more Swedish." This impression is enhanced by the occasional appearance of ethnic outsiders, whose must either leave (as in *Lotta 2—Lotta flyttar hemifrån*, Johanna Hald, 1993), or are generously invited into the Swedish community (as in *Mitt liv som hund*).

The films of the period contribute to a nationalization of feelings. They reference to historical memories that most of the intended audience does not share personally. Still, they invite audience members to invest feelings in those memories. Thus, the films work as emotion-saturated history textbooks, creating and disseminating collective memories in a certain national context. The recurring motif of community can thus both be understood and felt as a symbol of national community.

Conclusion: From Nation-Building to Longing

In the Swedish political debate after the turn of the millennium, ethnicity has become a charged and controversial issue. Central to this is the question of Swedish ethnicity. Should Swedes be regarded as one ethnic group among others in a multicultural society? The populist and nationalist party, Sverigedemokraterna, has made gains among the electorate in recent elections, achieving a 17.5 percent share of the vote in the election for the Swedish parliament in 2018, making it Sweden's third largest political party. Sverigedemokraterna has appropriated the term "ethnic Swedes," by implication distinguishing "real Swedes" from others. This kind of political rhetoric is divisive. Still, from an anthropological perspective, Swedes do seem to be an ethnic group, recognized as such by, for example, members of other ethnic groups living in close contact with Swedes in Sweden, which is pretty much the scholarly definition of an ethnic group.[40] The controversy concerns, of course, the political intentions and consequences of pitting groups of Swedish citizens against each other.

However, operating with the concept of (Swedish) ethnicity, it is possible to make the crucial observation that Swedish feature films for children have been unrealistically mono-ethnic in terms of representation. Over the course of more than sixty years from 1944 to 2006, only a handful—literally no more than five or six, even allowing for oversight—of the child protagonists or leading roles in children's film played by children have been marked as other than Swedish (or in some cases, unspecified "Nordic"). In 2006, an effort was made to change this state of affairs with the film *Förortsungar* (*Kidz in da Hood*, Ylva Gustavsson and Catti Edfeldt). It is a remake of *Rännstensungar*, which is significant. It tells the same story—the protagonist is an orphaned refugee girl (Beylula Kidane Adgoy) who is cared for by a musician (Gustaf Skarsgård)—but is set in a contemporary high-rise suburb of Stockholm, and overlays the story about antagonism between social classes with the issue of ethnic diversity, specifically the division between ethnic Swedes and other ethnicities (immigrants and refugees living in the suburbs). It is fair to say that the film is going for the same kind of emotionally satisfying reconciliation as its predecessor, and it is a transparent call for unity and understanding of the plight of refugees. However, the ending is bleak compared to the earlier film, leaving the gap, so to speak, between the Swedish majority and the immigrants and refugees open; in the final scene, a new family of "illegal" refugees comes to the neighbourhood and the cycle begins again.

To sum up: the early Swedish children's films of the 1940s had a nation-building function. They mirror as well as disseminate ideals of citizenship and Swedishness and equate the two. This does not distinguish children's film from other types of film; on the contrary, films for adult audiences function in the same way. However, the didactic stance of the children's films may make their effort to transmit nationally coded social virtues even more overt. These virtues develop in a society where various tensions need to be alleviated. The goals the films strive for, such as class reconciliation and unity in *Rännstensungar*, are attained within a context of nationally coded community. Throughout the 1950s and 1960s, this community is increasingly depicted as an idyll, especially in the imaginary places like Seacrow Island and Noisy Village created by Astrid Lindgren. These have come to be read as miniature versions of Sweden that already had nostalgic appeal when they first appeared on the screen. After a break in the 1970s, when the discourse about children's films relinquished issues of nation and Swedishness, a powerful wave of nostalgia reasserted itself in the 1980s and 1990s. The work of Astrid Lindgren, in particular, came to the fore as a source for adaptations, but her works are part of a pervasive retrospective trend.

This coincides with, and fuels, nostalgic sentiments for the *Folkhem* era in Swedish culture and society-at-large. One of the most visible, and novel, political expressions of this nostalgia is the emergence of populist, nationalist, and (at least to some extent) overtly xenophobic political parties in the mainstream, first the short-lived Ny demokrati (New Democracy, 1991–2000), and now Sverigedemokraterna (1988–), whose support has grown steadily. Infamously, Sverigedemokraterna's leaders have referred to the fictional world of Astrid Lindgren in their political rhetoric.[41] While this is, in a sense, disingenuous—it has annoyed members of the Lindgren family, and other critics, who protested that Lindgren would not sympathize—it does point to the fact that Sverigedemokraterna is sensitive to the national significance of Lindgren's work, not least in its filmed form, in Swedish culture at large. In contemporary society, it has become quite common to speak about "the new Sweden"—that is, a country that has gone through changes due to increased immigration. In "the new Sweden," ethnic diversity has become a key factor in social stratification, and one of the hot political topics (specifically, racism, discrimination, dealing with the needs of refugees, ghetto-ization, and so on). *Förortsungar* tries to address these complexities by depicting the suburb as a place where a new sense of community can grow. Interestingly, the remaking of *Rännstensungar* is, in itself, an attempt to mobilize nostalgia, to solicit the powerful sense of national community of the *Folkhem*-classic in a new political and cultural context.

NOTES

1. Ian Wojcik-Andrews, *Children's Films: History, Ideology, Pedagogy, Theory* (New York: Garland, 2000), pp. 53–57.
2. Cf. Tommy Gustafsson, "Film, censur och videovåld under 1900-talet," in Tommy Gustafsson and Klara Arnberg (eds.), *Moralpanik och lågkultur: Genus- och mediehistoriska analyser 1900–2012* (Stockholm: Bokförlaget Atlas, 2013), pp. 41–93.
3. Torgny Wallbeck-Hallgren (Waldeck), "Den fattiges teater," *Svenska Dagbladet*, March 1,1905.
4. Gustaf Berg, *Barn och biograf: En orientering med hänsyn till censuruppgift och gällande förordning* (Stockholm: Filmbladet, 1916), p. 20.
5. For an alternative view, see Margareta Rönnberg, *Vänstervridna? Pedagogiska? Av högre kvalitet? 70-talets barnteveprogram och barnfilmer kontra dagens* (Visby: Filmförlaget, 2012), pp. 125–127.
6. Tommy Gustafsson, *En fiende till civilisationen: Manlighet, genusrelationer, sexualitet och rasstereotyper i svensk filmkultur under 1920-talet* (Lund: Sekel Bokförlag), p. 75.
7. Bengt Idestam Almquist (Robin Hood), "Barnen och filmen," *Stockholmstidningen*, March 18, 1945.
8. *Barn och film*, Statens offentliga utredningar (1952), pp. 51, 37.
9. Per Olov Qvist, *Folkhemmets bilder: Modernisering, motstånd och mentalitet i den svenska 30-talsfilmen* (Lund: Arkiv förlag), pp. 369–426.
10. Michael Tapper, *Snuten i skymningslandet: Svenska polisberättelser i roman och på film 1965–2010* (Lund: Nordic Academic Press, 2011), pp. 81–82.
11. *Ungdomen och nöjeslivet*, Statens offentliga utredningar (1945), pp. 22, 271.
12. Qvist, *Folkhemmets*, pp. 286–293.
13. Cf. Ferdinand Tönnies, *Community and Civil Society* (Cambridge, UK: Cambridge University Press, 2001), pp. 22–92.
14. Gustaf Sundbärg, *Det svenska folklynnet: Aforismer*, 7th ed. (Stockholm: P. A. Norstedt & söners förlag, 1911), p. 4.
15. Orvar Löfgren, "Nationella arenor," in Billy Ehn, Jonas Frykman, and Orvar Löfgren (eds.), *Försvenskningen av Sverige: Det nationellas förvandlingar* (Stockholm: Natur och kultur, 1993), pp. 21–117, at 25.

16. Helene Ehriander, "Astrid Lindgren—den motvilliga celebriteten," *Humanetten* 39 (2017), pp. 10–14.

17. Marie Cronqvist, *Mannen i mitten: Ett spiondrama i kallakrigskultur* (Stockholm: Carlssons, 2004), pp. 201–205.

18. "Vår verksamhet 1963. Unga Örnars Skånedistrikt," p. 6, and "Vår verksamhet 1964: Unga örnars Skånedistrikt," p. 5.

19. Cf. Mats Rohdin, "Att sprida stoffet för alla vindar: Astrid Lindgren, filmen och mediernas mångfald," *Biblis* 59 (2012), pp. 27–41.

20. Margareta Norlin, "Blomkvisteri, idyller och Arne Sucksdorff," in *Svensk filmografi* 5 (Stockholm: Svenska Filminstitutet, 1983), pp. 643–648, at 645.

21. Malena Janson, *Bio för barnens bästa? Svensk barnfilm som fostran och fritidsnöje under 60 år* (Stockholm: Acta Universitatis Stockholmiensis, 2007), pp. 83–92.

22. Patrik Hall, *Den svenskaste historien: Nationalism i Sverige under sex sekler* (Stockholm: Carlsson, 2000), p. 282.

23. Martin Wiklund, *I det modernas landskap: Historisk orientering och kritiska berättelser om det moderna Sverige mellan 1960 och 1990* (Stockholm/Stehag: Symposion, 2006), p. 118.

24. Quoted from the DVD-release of the TV series, my translation.

25. Martin Kylhammar, *Maskin och idyll: Teknik och pastorala ideal hos Strindberg och Heidenstam* (Malmö: Liber förlag, 1985), pp. 14–15.

26. Martin Lefebvre, "Between Setting and Landscape in the Cinema," in Martin Lefebvre (ed.), *Landscape and Film* (New York: Routledge, 2006), pp. 19–59.

27. Cf. I. Å. [real name not known)], "I sommarparadiset," *Upsala Nya Tidning*, December 20, 1965; and Jolanta (Margareta Sjögren), "Välsignat naturliga människor," *Svenska Dagbladet*, December 12,1965.

28. Britt-Marie Svedberg, "'Roliga Saltkråkan' vore ogörbar idag," *Dagens Nyheter*, October 31, 1977.

29. Press release (copy) from Sveriges Television (1991), "Vi på Saltkråkan," VIPÅSALT.134 ÅW.

30. Cf. "An en gång 'Vi på Saltkråkan—något av det svenskaste vi har," *Arbetet*, October 23, 1993.

31. Leena Valtonen, "Bullfest för Tjorven & Co," *Röster i Radio-TV* 33 (1991), pp. 8–9, at 8.

32. Valtonen, "Bullfest för Tjorven & Co," p. 8.

33. Ibid., p. 9.

34. For example, in the party's manifesto for the election of 2006. It is no longer available at Sverigedemokraternas official homepage but can be accessed here: https://toreboda.sd.se/valmanifest_2019/ [accessed June 9, 2019].

35. Tytti Soila, "Sweden," in Tytti Soila, Astrid Söderbergh Widding, and Gunnar Iversen (eds.), *Nordic National Cinemas* (London: Routledge, 1998), pp. 142–232, at 231.

36. Quoted in Petter Karlsson and Johan Erséus, *Från snickerboa till Villa Villekulla: Astrid Lindgrens filmvärld* (Stockholm: Forum, 2004), p. 25.

37. Cf. Per Olov Qvist, "Ormens väg genom Bullerbyn," *Filmhäftet* 57 (1987), pp. 55–60.

38. Yvonne Hirdman, *Att lägga livet till rätta—studier i svensk folkhemspolitik* (1989; Stockholm: Carlssons, 2000), p. 89.

39. Quoted from the soundtrack.

40. Thomas Hylland Eriksen, *Ethnicity and Nationalism: Anthropological Perspectives* (1994; repr. New York: Pluto Press, 2010), pp. 15–20.

41. Björn Söder, then party secretary, in a speech at Sverigedemokraternas convention in 2009, http://www.sverigedemokraterna.net/nyhet.php?action=fullnews&id=1194 [accessed November 4, 2009]. The transcription of the speech has been removed from this site.

BIBLIOGRAPHY

Åberg, Anders. "Seacrow Island: Mediating Arcadian Space in the Folkhem Era and Beyond." In Erik Hedling, Olof Hedling, and Mats Jönsson (eds.), *Regional Aesthetis: Locating Swedish Media*. Stockholm: National Library of Sweden, 2010, pp. 125–140.

Åberg, Anders. "Conceptions of Nation and Ethnicity in Swedish Children's Films: The Case of Kidz in da Hood (Förortsungar, 2006)." *Journal of Educational Media, Memory and Society* 2:5 (2013), pp. 92–107.

Gustafsson, Tommy. *Masculinity in the Golden Age of Swedish Cinema: A Cultural Analysis of 1920s Film* (Jefferson, NC: McFarland, 2015.

Holmlund, Christine. "Pippi and Her Pals." *Cinema Journal* 42 (Winter 2003), pp. 3–24.

Janson, Malena. *Bio för barnens bästa? Svensk barnfilm som fostran och fritidsnöje under 60 år*. Stockholm: Acta Universitatis Stockholmiensis, 2007.

Kümmerling-Meibauer, Bettina, and Astrid Surmatz, eds. *Beyond Pippi Longstocking: Intermedial and International Aspects of Astrid Lindgren's Works*. New York: Routledge, 2011.

Lindgren, Anne-Li. "Att utbilda barn till ett nationellt medborgarskap: folkhemmet och föreställningar om 'vi' och 'de andra.'" *Historisk tidskrift* 122 (2002), pp. 29–53.

Marklund, Anders. *Upplevelser av svensk film: En kartläggning av genrer inom svensk film under åren 1985–2000*. Lund: Critica Litterarum Lundensis, 2004.

Metzdorf, Ragna. *Stilwandel des Kinderfilms: 1960er bis 1980er Jahre*. Frankfurt: Peter Lang, 2011.

Rönnberg, Margareta. *Vänstervridna? Pedagogiska? Av högre kvalitet? 70-talets barnteveprogram och barnfilmer kontra dagens*. Visby: Filmförlaget, 2012.

Rydin, Ingegerd. *Barnens röster: Program för barn i Sveriges radio och television 1925–1999*. Stockholm: Stiftelsen etermedierna i Sverige, 2000.

CHAPTER 22

UNREALITY, FANTASY, AND THE ANTI-FASCIST POLITICS OF THE CHILDREN'S FILMS OF SATYAJIT RAY

KOEL BANERJEE

FAERIE, the magical domain of the fairy story, is a realm as treacherous as it is fantastic. J. R. R. Tolkien, a seasoned traveller in this land, warned his readers of its dangers in no uncertain terms: "Faerie is a perilous land, and in it are pitfalls for the unwary and dungeons for the overbold."[1] It holds many wonders for all those who wander there, but it gives little away in the way of information. And though it has perils in store for the bold, it threatens to close its doors forever on the curious who ask too many questions. Although Tolkien does not squarely equate the fairy story with children's literature, he concedes that children, perhaps more than adults, are capable of a literary belief whose rigour far surpasses the "willing suspension of disbelief" required by most literary works. For Tolkien, the author of a fairy story creates a secondary world, a world where the fantastic is not just the only truth but, for that very reason, remains not fantastic at all, but is commonplace, the very law of the land. The inability to marshal belief calls not only for the banishment of the reader from this secondary world, but also signals the limitations of its magic and, alongside it, the failure of the literary work and its creator.

In a similar vein, Ursula K. Le Guin warns about the dangers of superimposing the travails of Poughkeepsie on Elfland, reminding her readers that one cannot make oneself at home in Elfland.[2] Comparing fantasy literature to a dream rather than a reverie, she comments on its relationship to reality:

> It is a different approach to reality, an alternative technique for apprehending and coping with existence. It is not antirational but pararational; not realistic, but surrealistic, superrealistic, a heightening of reality.... Fantasy is nearer to poetry, to mysticism, and to insanity than naturalistic fiction is.[3]

Fantasy, then, does not cancel reality; instead, it augments it. As is the case with Tolkien's Faerie, the fantastic is the quotidian in Le Guin's Elfland, for dragons outnumber bears in this realm. Elfland, she adds, provides "no comfortable matrix of the commonplace to substitute for the imagination, to provide readymade emotional response, and to disguise flaws and failures of creation."[4] Just as the curious can be banished from Faerie simply for asking too many questions, the writer, too, can lose sight of Elfland. Le Guin ends on another note of caution: "Elfland is not Poughkeepsie; the voice of the transistor is not heard in that land."[5]

This chapter examines *Hirak Rajar Deshe* (*Kingdom of Diamonds, 1980*), the second film in Satyajit Ray's Goopy Gyne Bagha Byne series (1969–1990), as an allegory of India during the Emergency, a period of curtailment of civil liberties imposed by the Indira Gandhi government in India between 1975 and 1977. The first film of the series, *Goopy Gyne Bagha Byne* (Satyajit Ray, 1969), which chronicles the adventures of the titular protagonists, belongs to genre of the fairy story. *Hirak Rajar Deshe*, however, deviates from the conventional fairy story, as it spells out its political referents more directly than did its predecessor. Instead of a fairy tale, a staple genre of children's film and literature, *Hirak Rajar Deshe* offers a cautionary note to authoritarian regimes; and to its intended audience (i.e., children) it offers hope as it reminds them that even fearsome dictators will ultimately fall. Ray, often criticized for his reluctance to take a political stand in his films, even during the political turmoil of the 1960s, uses the fantasy genre to launch a scathing attack on the fascist tendencies of the government during the Emergency. The chapter maps how the fantasy form—which releases Ray from the demands of naturalism in his earlier films—not only invites an allegorical reading, but in being structured as an allegory, also transcends its own time and becomes an allegory for fascist politics, including those of our present moment.

FROM FAIRY STORY TO ALLEGORY

True to Le Guin's demands of all fantastic art, the first instalment of the Goopy Bagha series, *Goopy Gyne Bagha Byne*, adapted from Ray's grandfather Upendrakishore Ray Chowdhury's short story, is set in a land where the voice of the transistor has never been heard. Instead, in a mythical village called Amloki, the day breaks on Gopinath Gyne (Tapen Chatterjee), or Goopy, practicing his vocal lessons. Goopy wants to be a singer, and a classical singer at that, but he shows no discernible evidence of talent. But if aspiring to be a classical singer is a lofty and futile task for Goopy, the village grocer's son, he continues to practice, much to the amusement of the local upper-caste men who egg him on to sing for the king. Although it is mythical, Amloki is not magical, for it, too, is subject to the conventions of the world outside its diegesis. The audience knows, for instance, that Goopy will fail as a musician not only because of his dearth of talent, but also because the aspiration to be a classical musician is laughable for a poor, low-caste villager like him. The fairy story thus acknowledges the laws of everyday life to which it stands in opposition. The king, upon being rudely awakened by Goopy's enthusiastic but off-key music, banishes him from the village. Lost in a forest, a scared Goopy finds Bagha Byne (Rabi Ghosh), another aspiring musician who, similarly, has been exiled from his village, Haritoki.

Happy to forge new friendships at the end of what has been a taxing day, Goopy and Bagha sing to their hearts' content as they pass the night in the forest. Unbeknownst to them, the forest is enchanted—Bhooter Raja, the King of Ghosts, dwells there. Their music pleases the King of Ghosts, and they are granted three wishes. It is this moment of benediction that frees the protagonists from the laws that govern everyday life. Goopy and Bagha receive magic slippers that can take them anywhere they want, they can conjure up any food they desire by clapping their hands, and can mesmerize any audience with their music. Being thus blessed, Goopy and Bagha go on to do many fantastic things. They lift the curse of muteness from the inhabitants of the kingdom of Shundi, and even manage to stop a disastrous war about to be waged on Shundi by the evil minister of Halla, a rival kingdom. And finally, in true fairy story fashion, after saving the kingdoms of Halla and Shundi, the heroes marry their princesses. At the end of the film, we leave Goopy and Bagha to what we safely assume to be their happy ever-afters.

Hirak Rajar Deshe, the sequel to this fantastic tale, begins where the fairy tale of Goopy and Bagha ends. In the opening scene, Goopy and Bagha, dressed in regal clothes, sing about their good fortune now that they are royalty (Figure 22.1). Addressing the camera,

FIGURE 22.1. Goopy and Bagha sing about their princely lives in *Hirak Rajar Deshe* (1980, Government of West Bengal). Frame-grab.

Goopy and Bagha sing about how their lives have changed since the audience last saw them. They now live a life of comfort, blessed with wealth, children, and the promise of a kingdom. The song, intercut with the opening credits, recaps the events of the previous film, and telescopes the decade that has passed. Although this song highlighting the happy state of affairs is, in many ways, an ode to the "happily ever after" life of the fairy tale, this joyous feeling is fleeting, for it is soon followed by Goopy and Bagha's unrest as they long for more adventures. Their magic slippers, a gift from the King of Ghosts, which could transport them anywhere, have not been used in a long time and are now gathering dust. The transitory nature of the happily ever after of the fairy tale is underscored by frequent cuts to an hourglass that hangs in the room where Goopy and Bagha lounge. The happy ending of the fairy tale works precisely because time does not impede it. Here, with the hourglass and the gathering of dust on a prized possession, time works its way into the narrative. With time and its ravages finding their way into the film's opening sequence, the possibility of yet another fairy tale is foreclosed at the very onset. Unlike the protagonists of fairy tales, Goopy and Bagha feel the passing of time. Their father-in-law, the kind-hearted king of Shundi, realizes that Goopy and Bagha want to travel and sends them to the Kingdom of Diamonds, Hirak, as his representatives at the kingdom's anniversary celebrations.

In *Goopy Gyne Bagha Byne*, the almost-imminent war between Halla and Shundi is prevented by the songs of its two protagonists. However, Hirak proves to be a bigger challenge for these seasoned troubadours. Hirak, the kingdom of diamond mines, is ruled by a greedy, despotic king (Utpal Dutt), who exploits his subjects by increasing taxes, overworking the diamond miners, and suppressing dissent with an iron fist. His ministers are puppets who do not dare question the tyrant's dictates. The king, emboldened by his riches and unchallenged in his authority, has invited kings from all over to join the kingdom's anniversary celebrations, which will culminate with the unveiling of the king's statue and formally mark the beginning of *Hirakabda*, "the era of Hirak" (Figure 22.2). To finance this rather expensive endeavour, he had levied high taxes on his subjects, and forced his taxpayers—the poor citizens of Hirak—into makeshift camps so that the royal guests would not see the persistence of poverty despite the kingdom's prosperity.

Although the king is reluctant to forgive taxes or spend state wealth on the welfare of his subjects, he has invested a lot of money on a laboratory for a scientist who has promised to create technology that will help him manage his kingdom. After six months of toiling away in his *jantar mantar* (laboratory), the scientist has invented a machine that will brainwash dissenters. Those who dare to question the king are put into a chamber of the *jantar mantar*, and are, literally, brainwashed with the release of a lever in the complex machine. Appropriately, the chamber of horrors is shaped like a scary giant with a mechanical tongue that replaces dissent with couplets carefully crafted by the king's court poet. The tyranny of the king is translated into the tyranny of rhyme. The court poet has composed different rhymes for different complaints. For example, the peasant who pleads to the king to reduce his taxes is now brainwashed to repeat (and *believe*): "Baki rakha khajna, mote bhalo kaaj na" (Keeping taxes pending is not a good thing

FIGURE 22.2. The King of Hirak doles out diamonds to his sycophants in *Hirak Rajar Deshe* (1980, Government of West Bengal). Frame-grab.

/ Even you do not eat food, you must make your taxes good). Similarly, the diamond miner who complains about his poor working conditions is brainwashed into thinking (and saying out loud) that "Anahaare nahi khed, beshi khele baare medh" (there is no harm in starvation; food only makes one fat"). Rhyme thus reproduces sameness while gesturing towards difference.

Talking in rhyming couplets is nothing new in the world of Goopy and Bagha. In *Goopy Gyne Bagha Byne*, the King of Ghosts speaks in rhyme when he grants Goopy and Bagha the three wishes. Rhyme is an exception to the prosaic nature of everyday speech. The use of musical verse in the sequence featuring the King of Ghosts is set up as an aural foil to the everyday (or life as Goopy and Bagha have known it thus far). Commenting on Ray's adaptation of the sequence, Mihir Bhattacharya observes:

> Upendra Kishore's king of the ghosts is a genial soul, fond of music (with plenty of loud noises, as in the original performance of the duo) and of simple people, and he himself speaks in the rustic accents of the labouring poor. Ray stylizes his speech into a performance in musical verse, with a brilliant recourse to electronic distortion (he recorded his own voice and speeded it up), and the distancing itself sets up the trans-actional model for the commerce between the two worlds. The ghostly apparatus is

the other of mundane authority, with powers to override the latter's dictates, though arbitrary in its appearance and incomprehensible in its practice. As a machinery for reparative justice, it does not insist on retribution, though many other folkloric agencies do, and its endowment of the duo is contingent on the latter's initiative, motivation and enterprise for the direction the gifts will take. One of its principal narrative roles is in the direction of providing the initial impetus and the permanent means for a regime of pleasure.[6]

Not only does the sequence stand out because of the use of musical verse, it is also a visual contrast to the rest of the film. Ray, noted for his careful deployment of a naturalist cinematic style, uses an unusual technique for this supernatural sequence.[7] Although the King of Ghosts speaks in verse, he also speaks in the accents of the ordinary village folk. And despite the rhyming, his language is modelled on the "language of men." The King of Ghosts, unlike spectral characters found in most ghost stories, does not induce fear. Unlike the kings of Amloki and Haritoki, he is benevolent and rewards the aspiring musicians for their (as yet non-existent) talents.

Although the use of rhyme in the first film is liberating in that it frees Goopy and Bagha from their mundane existence, it is equally important that it marks the moment of benediction that frees them from the need to work. As Bhattacharya notes:

> What matters to the liberated heroes is that they do not have to work for the things which they desire. Food, in the experience of the likes of Bagha and Goopy, has to be produced with enormous, complicated and exhausting labour, performed largely under duress, and consumed mostly by those who are born to enjoy the fruits of others' labour.... This is the everyday world from which the duo wished to escape into music.... The most characteristic utopia for the labouring poor in such a society would invariably be marked by the absence of labour, and its obverse, the access to plenitude.[8]

In contrast to the use of verse in the first film, rhyme serves a different function in the sequel. Although the King of Ghosts speaks in rhymed couplets, he speaks in the language of labouring men, and with a marked rustic accent. The king of Hirak and his sycophantic courtiers, on the other hand, speak in a more crafted verse. And the court poet's rhyme, unlike that deployed by the King of Ghosts, does not free people from their misery. Rather, it chains them to their state of privation and wipes away all traces of dissent. The tyranny of the king translates into the tyranny of rhyme when the over-taxed farmer and the over-worked miner, after being brainwashed by the new machine, say, "Jai jodi jak pran, Hirak er raja bhogoban" (Whether we flourish or perish, the king of Hirak is god). Thus rhyme becomes oppressive, forcing people into submission and subjugation by erasing all opposition.

There is, however, one person in Hirak who does not speak in verse. The dialogue of Udayan Pandit (Soumitra Chattterjee), the schoolteacher, is written in prose. When he is introduced, Udayan is teaching his pupils the *Hitopadesha* (*Beneficial Advice*). The choice of text is not insignificant. *Hitopadesha*, a Sanskrit text from the twelfth century, consists of fables featuring both animals and humans. Udayan is narrating the story of Sanjeevaka, the ox, who became friends with Pingalaka, the lion, and two foxes, Damanaka and Karataka. Udayan draws his own conclusion from the beast fable. He tells his pupils that no force in nature is more calamitous than the wrath of the king. If the despotic king's subjects have to die, they are better off doing so while defying the king's demands. And, as if to prove his point about royal tyranny, the king's education minister and the court poet arrive at the school with a small army. They inform Udayan and his students that their school has now been closed. The court poet reads the king's decree to Udayan and his students. The king has proclaimed: "lekhapora kore je, anahaare more she" (one who studies too much, dies of starvation), that "janar kono shesh nai, jaaanar chesta britha tai" (there is no end to knowledge, it is futile to learn), and that "bidyalaabhe lokshen, nai artho, nai maan" (learning is wasteful, it confers neither riches nor garners respect). After forcing Udayan and his pupils to repeat the king's devious verses, the minister leaves Udayan to the task of closing down the school.

The intertextual reference to the beast fable of *Hitopadesha* marks the moment when *Hirak Rajar Deshe* folds the allegory proper into its allegorical schema. Fredric Jameson has pointed out that the disappearance of personification indicates not only the transition from the classical or traditional allegory (to which *Hitopadesha* belongs) to the modern allegory, but also signals the emergence of modernity:

> …modern allegory involves a kinship between processes, unlike the personifications of classical or traditional allegory: it is the inter-echoing of narratives with one another, in their differentiation and reidentification, rather than the play with fixed substances and entities identified as so many traits or passions, for example, incarnated in individual figures all the way to the caricatural or the stereotypical. We will find ourselves reverting again and again to this insight: that it is the disappearance of personification that signals the emergence of modernity.[9]

The traditional allegory employs personification and relies heavily on fixed tropes and stereotypes, while the modern allegory is polysemous. The use of the beast fable (i.e., the traditional allegory) in *Hirak Rajar Deshe*, however, unites the two phases of the allegory—the classical and the modern. The classical or traditional allegory invoked here in the form of a lesson (both as principle and classroom instruction) invites the audience to view the film as an allegory. In other words, the traditional allegory opens the film to be viewed or read allegorically. The fragment of the beast fable referenced in the film serves as a metacommentary on two levels. First, the didactic track buttresses the film's plot about the evil machinations of a despotic king. Second, the moral tract of the beast fable helps Ray make a political point that transcends the film's narrative. The use of the beast fable, then, not only serves to unite the traditional allegory with the modern allegory; it opens up the film to multiple diegesis, one that ties the fictional Hirak to the very real India under the leadership of the-then Indian Prime Minister, Indira Gandhi. In this manner, the beast fable helps Ray bypass, what some of his contemporary critics have claimed is his hesitation to make political statements.[10] For Ray's intended audience (primarily children), the placement of the traditional allegory or the beast fable—a familiar form in children's literature and cinema—alerts them to an underlying subtext. Thus, for children, it is the provisional moral lesson about tyranny that provides the framework for interpretation even if they are unable to connect it to actual political events.

ALLEGORIZING THE EMERGENCY

Almost a decade before filming *Hirak Rajar Deshe*, Ray had come under severe criticism from his peers for not responding to the political unrest that marked the late 1960s and the 1970s in India, particularly in West Bengal. When Ray returned to Calcutta after filming the first instalment of the Goopy Bagha series, Calcutta was in a state of unrest and political turmoil. In 1967, the Congress-led government of West Bengal lost the election to the United Front, a coalition government formed by the Communist Party of India–Marxist (hereafter, CPI-M) and the Bangla Congress. In 1969, under the leadership of Charu Majumadar, the radical wing of the CPI-M split from the party to form the Communist Party of India–Marxist Leninist (CPI-ML).[11] The CPI–ML demanded that its activists assassinate not only class enemies as a part of their warfare against landlords, but also university teachers, police officers, and politicians. The movement had started in Naxalbari (earning the CPI-ML members the moniker "Naxalites"), but by the early-1970s it had gathered momentum in Calcutta. The West Bengal state government imprisoned several Naxalite leaders. In acting against the Naxalites, the police committed several civil and human rights violations, including detention, torture, and staged shoot-outs. The political unrest was exacerbated by a worsening food crisis, an economic recession, the Bangladesh Liberation War, and a mass migration of refugees from Bangladesh. In 1972, the Congress came back to power in the state and the new chief minister, Siddhartha Shankar Ray, targeted both the CPI-M and the CPI-ML activists, along with trade unionists, peasant organizers, and students. When Ray returned to the city to shoot his Calcutta trilogy, many of his critics charged that he—unlike his contemporary, Mrinal Sen—was not making a political statement through his films. Although Ray abandoned his classical naturalism in his Calcutta trilogy, *Pratidwandi* (*The Adversary*, 1970), *Seemabaddha* (*The Company Limited*, 1971), and *Jana Aranya* (*The Middleman*, 1975), his new style was regarded by many as mere "gimmick."[12]

If the political unrest in Bengal motivated Ray to adopt a new cinematic idiom in his Calcutta trilogy, the policies adopted by Indira Gandhi's union government potentiate the narrative and motivate the allegorical structure of *Hirak Rajar Deshe*. On June 26, 1975, Gandhi declared a state of emergency (hereafter, the Emergency) throughout the country. Commenting on the rationale behind the Emergency, political theorist Sudipta Kaviraj observes:

> Imposition of the Emergency from the government side was done on the excuse that two things were getting out of hand and the Central government required

exceptional powers to deal with them. The first of course was a threat to the unity and integrity of the country, dubiously equated with the ruling party's dominance. A second and perhaps more popular rationalisation of the Emergency was that it was meant also to negotiate the inflationary situation—an immensely popular slogan, understandably, for the middle and the lower classes.[13]

The Emergency was a period of unprecedented draconian measures that essentially curtailed democratic processes, including suspending elections, mass imprisonment of dissenters, censorship of the press, and curtailment of civil liberties. Exhibiting a blatant disregard for human rights, Indira Gandhi's son, Sanjay Gandhi, spearheaded a mass-sterilization campaign, one that targeted the lower classes, particularly the religious minorities.[14]

While the poor were the most affected by policies implemented during the Emergency, it also made the political elite powerless. As Kaviraj notes,

> the well-known unconstitutional uses of power and irrational excesses of the family planning and beautification drives...naturally fell most heavily on the poorest. It also carried to its extreme the internal reallocation of power within the Congress elite, leading to the gradual decline of the group of more professional advisers around Indira Gandhi.[15]

The after-effect of the curtailment of the freedom of the press, the stifling of political opposition, and the erosion of the independence of the judiciary, continued to be felt even after the Emergency was withdrawn on March 21, 1977. In many ways, as this chapter will discuss in the section, "A Cautionary Tale for the Present", it created a precedent for authoritarianism in India.

By the time President Fakhruddin Ali declared the Emergency, Ray's politics had already been under intense scrutiny. Many felt that Ray simply was not saying enough. When the Emergency was imposed, Ray did not issue a political statement condemning the government actions. Ray was filming the final instalment of his Calcutta trilogy, *Jana Aranya*, in 1975. Although it is arguably one of the darkest satires on the social milieu in Bengal at the time, targeting the failing education system and the severe unemployment crisis, the film does not directly address the policies of the central government. Instead, the crisis of democracy is, quite literally, in the background of the film. In *Jana Aranya* there is a sinister caricature of Indira Gandhi drawn on a wall. Ray, a skilled painter, drew the graffiti himself. While graffiti in the background in a tracking shot is not the strongest political protest, it made Ray's sentiment about the new measures amply clear. In a later interview, Ray further clarified his stance:

> Obviously in a situation like that (i.e. the Emergency) an artist can hope to do things at a very great risk, and I thought that instead of direct attack I should indicate by some means that I was not in favour of the Emergency and I was not going to help them in any way.[16]

If *Jana Aranya* provided a glimpse of a sinister Indira Gandhi, *Hirak Rajar Deshe* completes the story. It recreates the Emergency in the imaginary kingdom of Hirak. The seemingly unlikely genre of the children's film becomes, in this rendition, the mode of Ray's most direct political critique.

The similarities between Hirak and India during the Emergency are clearly spelled out in the film. Early in the film, as Hirak prepares for its big celebration, the poor of Hirak are forced into colourful, makeshift tents that are meant to hide every sign of squalor for the viewing pleasure of the king's royal guests. Indira Gandhi and her son, Sanjay, launched a demolition drive, one supposedly motivated by a desire to beautify the Indian capital city, Delhi. This move, aimed at removing the slums and temporary low-income housing from the city, was met with resistance by the urban poor who would otherwise be denied their right to the city and be pushed to the city's margins. In April 1976, the residents of Turkman Gate protested the government's attempts to bull-doze their dwellings. The police, backed by the union government, shot the protestors, who were also run over by the government's bulldozers.[17] Ironically, Indira Gandhi's campaign slogan in the 1971 election bid had been *garibi hatao* (remove poverty). The populist slogan won her the popular mandate, but it was more jingoistic than effective. Meant to woo the urban and rural poor, the slogan found success on the electoral plat-form, but the programmes that it spearheaded were poorly managed. By the time the Indira Gandhi–led government declared the state of internal emergency in 1975, its stance on poverty seemed to have undergone a radical shift. Far from the rallying cry "remove poverty," the government now aimed solely at removing the poor from their city. Demolishing the temporary dwellings of the urban poor was an integral part of the beautification drive of the government, which increasingly positioned itself as anti-poor rather than anti-poverty. Ray captures this impulse behind the city beautification drives, when the poor of Hirak are forced into beautiful tents that hide them from view. The incarceration of the poor is further highlighted when the camera focuses on a bird cage abandoned outside the makeshift encampment as the king's soldiers force the poor into the tent. The bright colours of the tent are a stark contrast to the bleakness that they hide from view. Aesthetics, like rhyme, becomes a source of tyranny.

The Emergency, Kaviraj notes, "represented...a massive decline of ideology."[18] Commenting on its long-lasting political consequences, he observes that by weakening the political opposition and by reallocating power within the political elite that supported the move, the government ensured that there were no challenges to the anti-poor policies it implemented:

> Under normal conditions of democracy, political initiatives, when they show un-popular or dysfunctional consequences, make for their own abandonment. In an authoritarian regime such dysfunctionalities could continue unchecked; for it is in-conceivable that any political regime would have continued with the excesses of the sterilisation drive or could have been so uniformed or insensitive towards popular opinion. Authoritarianism made the government behave more ignorantly.[19]

Similarly, the king of Hirak surrounds himself with a coterie of sycophantic ministers who neither have the power nor the desire to oppose the king. The ministers fear the king and are desperate to please him. They help the king to crush any sign of dissent from his over-taxed and underpaid subjects.

The king's monopoly over the diamond mines further weakens the possibility of opposition. Not satisfied with controlling the mines, the king seeks to augment his treasury by imposing even more taxes on the farmers and reducing the miners' wages. The period of the Emergency, similarly, saw the government further weaken working-class movements. Although the era immediately preceding the Emergency had been one of economic stagnation and a decline in wages, particularly for the rural and urban poor, the Emergency resulted in the alignment of politics and capital in unprecedented ways.[20] In its quick turn from populism to authoritarianism, the government declared a moratorium on strikes, supported wage-freezes, and, even as the country faced a job crisis, supported lay-offs by multinational companies. The Indira Gandhi government did not merely squash its political opposition, but also enfeebled and disciplined labour.[21] In many ways, this move, coupled with drastic cuts in social welfare programmes, set a precedent for the implementation of anti-working-class neoliberal fiscal reforms a decade later.

As the government reduced spending on education, health and nutrition programmes, and urban development, it also spearheaded mass sterilisation campaigns aimed at controlling population growth. In this new Malthusian consensus, family and children's welfare came to be equated with forced sterilisation. This was the authoritarian government's biggest move to contain the working class, and it had a long-term impact on the union government's family planning policies. In Ray's allegory, the king's secret weapon against his own subjects is *mogoj dholai* (brainwashing). Hirak, created in the image of India during the Emergency and similarly tyrannized by its ruler, is a kingdom that exacerbates poverty by denying the workers a basic living wage and overtaxing them. However, the king of Hirak does not sterilize his subjects. He does not stand in the way of reproduction of his reserve army of labour. He does something more heinous—he brainwashes them.

Ray's Hirak, in this manner, comes to represent the India during the period of the Emergency. For a director who had, at least thus far, resisted making overt political statements, *Hirak Rajar Deshe* is uncannily political. Here, uncanny or *Unheimliche*, as Freud points out, is at once familiar and unfamiliar, symbolizing being at home and feeling unhomely.[22] The form of the children's film allows Ray to recreate the tyrannical regime of the Emergency which, in this retelling, is both distanced by the careful deployment of the fantastic elements and rendered closer by the film's allegorical subtext. Ray, flouting Le Guin's advice to the practitioners of the fantasy form, does not merely transport the troubles of Poughkeepsie to Elfland; he recreates Poughkeepsie itself. However, as Tolkien points out, fantasy and reality are not antithetical:

> Probably every writer making a secondary world, a fantasy, every sub-creator, wishes in some measure to be a real maker, or hopes that he is drawing on reality: hopes that the peculiar quality of this secondary world (if not all the details) are derived from Reality, or are flowing into it . . . The peculiar quality of the "joy" in successful Fantasy can thus be explained as a sudden glimpse of the underlying reality or truth.[23]

Fantasy, then, sources its subject from the real and offers a horizon of possibility, an alternative, or a way out of the troubles of the real world. This approach is not escapist, but marks the utopic vision associated with the most revolutionary literary and cinematic creations. The children's film offers Ray not only the chance to critique the ways of tyrants, but more significantly, it allows him, via the resolution, to show a way out. The fantastic world of Hirak, created in the image of India under Indira Gandhi's authoritarian regime in the mid-1970s, is almost the same but not quite. In this interplay of sameness and difference, Ray offers not only a scathing indictment of despotic rulers but—true to the form of the children's film—also adds the hopeful message that even the most feared of tyrants ultimately fall. Ray does not deploy the fantasy film to escape the grim political reality of his time. By making what Raymond Williams calls "hope possible, rather than despair convincing," Ray's film takes a truly radical stance.[24]

While the fantasy genre allows Ray to make his most radical political film during an era that was marked by censorship aimed at silencing dissent and criticism of the government's actions, the film also uses songs to further highlight its social commentary. The songs play an important function in the first instalment of the adventures of Goopy Bagha, and the second instalment is no exception. In the first film, the heroes stop the evil minister of Halla from waging a war on Shundi as they arrest the march of his army with their song (and by making all kinds of food magically drop, like manna from heaven). Ray's use of songs in his children's film serves a dual purpose. They play a vital narrative function: in *Goopy Gyne Bagha Byne*, for instance, the song *Ore Baba Dekho Cheye* marks the film's denouement. The song also offers a larger socio-political metacommentary, as it spells out the evils of warfare and the persistence of hunger and poverty as India recovers from a war with China.

The songs in *Hirak Rajar Deshe* serve similar social and narrative functions. The song, *Kotoi rango dekhi duniyai* ("I see so much absurdity in this world"), sung by a folk singer of Hirak, comments on the inequities of the world where the good of heart are forced to live in dire circumstances, while the evil one perches himself on the throne. The song highlights the plight of the farmers and miners of Hirak. The film song, functioning as a metacommentary, serves a tutelary function that is in line with the genre of children's fiction, both literary and cinematic, as it elucidates for its young spectators the exploitation of labour. The use of the folk song, which serves a pedagogic task, aligns the film with Jawaharlal Nehru's vision for the children's film in India, a genre that he believed was, thus far, uncharted by the Indian film industry. Nehru believed that the children's film should educate the nation's children as it entertained them. However, for the children's film to be a powerful developmental tool, producers had to figure out a way to avoid the temptation to sermonize because that would run the risk of alienating its intended audience.[25] Ray uses the film song to achieve this balance; it teaches its viewers about the conditions of the working class without being pedantic. The use of the folk song is significant, because it uses the words, rhymes, and rhythms of the very people who are oppressed by the king's tyrannical regime. In this manner, it paves the way for Ray's more direct use of the beast fable and its associated moral lesson in a later scene.

If *Kotoi rango dekhi duniyai* links the diegetic world of Hirak and its extra-diegetic referent of contemporary India via the precarity of labour in both, then the song *Nohi Jantra* (I am not a machine) directly addresses the tyrants in both worlds. When the king and his ministers attempt to brainwash Udayan and his pupils, the only people in the kingdom who dare to question the king, the machine seems to malfunction. Instead of the rhyme the court poet had composed for Udayan and his pupils, Goopy and Bagha emerge from the shadows, proclaiming the end of the evil machinery. The build-up to the song is ominous and features close-ups of the machine, especially its demonic eye, its cavernous mouth, along with other equipment in the laboratory, including a skeleton. The dimly lit room, saturated with red overtones, amplifies the menacing atmosphere (Figure 23.3). Goopy, emerging from the shadows, walks up to the king and his ministers who, because of the music's magical quality, are unable to move. To this captive audience, Goopy proclaims that he is aware of the king's evil ways. Goopy looks the king in the eye and declares him to be greedy, corrupt, and cruel, and says that he has brought only misery and misfortune to his poor subjects. The king, Goopy continues, in a reckless bid to save his throne, has oppressed those who dare to defy him. Goopy and Bagha, though now royals themselves, are not dressed in their finery but in ordinary clothes; they are the Goopy and Bagha from the previous film. In their attire and

FIGURE 22.3. The brainwashing machine in *Hirak Rajar Deshe* (1980, Government of West Bengal). Frame-grab.

their diction, Goopy and Bagha stand in for the common folk the king ceaselessly and mercilessly seeks to oppress. In this final stand-off, it is the will of the people that ultimately puts an end to their own subjugation. The film culminates with the king, having been brainwashed by his own machine, gleefully joining the crowd as they take down his statue, marking an end to the despotic regime.

A Cautionary Tale for the Present

Hirak Rajar Deshe, as I have argued, is an allegorical take on the Emergency and its various injustices; however, its structure opens up its critique to almost any other era of similar draconian measures. The film ceases to be a mere critique of its own times and serves as a primer on authoritarian regimes, including those that mark our present moment. For instance, the film, transcending its own temporal and political referents, offers an allegorical account of the current rise of Hindu hyper-nationalism in India. The brainwashing, in the current scenario, is not mass sterilisation, but the processes by which authoritarianism garners popular and electoral consent. Scholars of South Asia have speculated about the form that a Hindu nationalist fascism will take and debated its sociopolitical consequences since the demolition of the sixteenth-century Babri Masjid in 1992. Yet such fascism ceased to be only another object of academic enquiry and became a lived reality for many, particularly the poor and religious minorities, after the election of the Narendra Modi–led National Democratic Alliance (hereafter, NDA) in 2014.[26] The populist NDA election campaign promised to accelerate economic growth, extend the seemingly successful but contested "Gujarat Model" to the rest of India, and end political corruption. The unprecedented success of the NDA, particularly the Bhartiya Janata Party (BJP), and the successful makeover of Modi's image from that of his former role as the Chief Minister whose term in office witnessed the 2002 Gujarat riots to that of an economic visionary not only demonstrates how deeply the logic of neoliberalism has penetrated civil society, but also highlights the connections between the market and fascist forces. The country has witnessed a sharp increase in attacks on religious minorities and Dalits, as well as on political and social activists, while the government maintains a stoic silence.

Majoritarian fascism, in this instance, manufactures mass consent because it creates a populist narrative of national prestige and economic growth. And at the same time, it draws on the myth of majoritarian persecution to justify violence against minorities. It must be noted that the Hindu right-wing does not frame its agenda solely on religious grounds, but also speaks the language of the market—that is, development. Development has ceased to refer solely to the economy and now includes aspects of life (e.g., religion) that, hitherto, were considered to be outside the economic domain. What grants the current regime's hyper-nationalist programme its popularity is the promise it makes to the underclass—that is, people without any stake in the sphere of production—of inclusion in the economic sphere. In a world of rapidly dwindling state welfare, religious identity remains the issue of last resort for the government to convince the growing underclass that they have some stake in the political sphere. Identity, in times of unprecedented economic polarization, reasserts its primacy through violence and through repeated recourse to the politics of blood and belonging. If the king of Hirak decimated political opposition by brainwashing them and Indira Gandhi achieved the same results through mass sterilisation and internment of political opponents, then the current regime obliterates opposition by invoking arcane colonial laws of sedition and making religion the cornerstone of national identity. The latter is, perhaps for the same reason, more alarming, as it refashions fascism and authoritarianism as desirable polities.

That the allegorical referents of *Hirak Rajar Deshe* shift from its own times to another moment, one similarly marked by the appeal of authoritarianism and the threat of fascism, is not merely a result of allegorical interpretation. Rather, it pertains to the very nature of the allegory. Drawing on Northrop Frye's investigation of allegory, Craig Owens points out that the polyphony of the palimpsest serves as the paradigm for all allegories. And, Owens continues, "Conceived in this way, allegory becomes the model of all commentary, all critique, insofar as these are involved in rewriting a primary text in terms of its figural meaning."[27] Allegory is not an act of interpretation or hermeneutics, but a structural element of the work itself. Approached in this manner, *Hirak Rajar Deshe* does not limit itself to its own immediate political context because the allegorical element is not a cosmetic frill or an added aspect of interpretation, it is the structuring principle of the text. It is an allegory of authoritarian regimes, wherever they might be located, temporally or spatially. And like all classic allegories, this one, too, has a moral to impart to its intended audience. Even if the opening sequence of *Hirak Rajar Deshe* disavowed the happy ever after of the fairy story, the film echoes Brecht as it reminds its viewers that there will be singing, even in dark times.

NOTES

1. J. R. R. Tolkien, "On Fairy-Stories," in *The Tolkien Reader* (New York: Ballantine Books, 1966), p. 33.
2. Ursula K. Le Guin, "Elfland and Poughkeepsie," in David Sandner (ed.), *Fantastic Literature: A Critical Reader* (Westport, CT: Praeger, 2004), pp. 144–155, at 145.
3. Le Guin, "Elfland and Poughkeepsie,"' p. 145.
4. Ibid., p. 154.
5. Ibid., p. 145.
6. Mihir Bhattacharya, "Conditions of Visibility: People's Imagination and Goopy Gyne Bagha Byne," *Journal of the Moving Image* 2 (2001), pp. 77–105. https://jmionline.org/article/conditions_of_visibility_peoples_imagination_and_goopy_gyne_bagha_byne [accessed December 11, 2019].
7. For a detailed discussion on the realist aesthetics of Ray, see Ravi Vasudevan, "Nationhood, Authenticity and Realism in Indian Cinema: The Double Take of Modernism in the Work of Satyajit Ray," *Journal of the Moving Image* 2 (2001), pp. 52–76. Also see Keya Ganguly, *Cinema, Emergence, and the Films of Satyajit Ray* (Berkeley: University of California Press, 2010).

8. Bhattacharya, "Conditions of Visibility."

9. Fredric Jameson, *Allegory and Ideology* (London: Verso, 2019), p. 48.

10. See Chidananda Dasgupta, *The Cinema of Satyajit Ray* (New Delhi: Vikas, 1980).

11. For a detailed discussion of the Naxalite movement, see Kheya Bag, "Red Bengal's Rise and Fall," *New Left Review* 70 (2011), pp. 69–98.

12. Dasgupta, *Cinema of Satyajit Ray*, p. 50.

13. Sudipta Kaviraj, "Indira Gandhi and Indian Politics,'" *Economic and Political Weekly* 21:38–39 (1986), pp. 1697–1708, at 1704

14. Kaviraj notes that the effect of the Emergency was felt in multiple spheres, including politics and media: "With public discussions suspended, some of the worst features of our ancient culture began to assert themselves—openly dynastic suggestions, gratuitous abasement of political leaders, medieval sycophancy. "Relocation" of poor people for reasons of offending middle or ruling class aesthetics, use of massive force in sterilisation campaigns all showed the state was becoming used to conditions of unaccountability and the usual insensibility of third world authoritarianisms. Obviously, this pursuit of sterility and beauty created intense opposition to itself, and it made an equally violent retribution to itself inevitable. As resistance to its policies grew, it was beset with inefficiencies of authoritarianism. First was the paradox of censorship. By destroying press freedom, the government simultaneously destroyed the credibility of its own – the only available – media." Kaviraj, "Indira Gandhi and Indian Politics," p. 1705.

15. Ibid., p. 1704.

16. Andrew Robinson, *Satyajit Ray: The Inner Eye; the Biography of a Master Filmmaker* (London: I.B. Tauris, 2004), p. 207.

17. For an overview of the measures taken by the government during the Emergency, see "The Shah Commission Final Report: General Observations," *Indian Journal of Public Administration* 36:3 (July 1990), pp. 695–701.

18. Kaviraj, "Indira Gandhi and Indian Politics," p. 1699.

19. Ibid., p. 1704.

20. Andre Gunder Frank, "Emergence of Permanent Emergency in India,'" *Economic and Political Weekly* 12:11 (1977), pp. 463–475.

21. Frank, "Emergence of Permanent Emergency in India," pp. 463–475.

22. See Sigmund Freud, "The 'Uncanny,'" in *Standard Edition of the Complete Psychological Works of Sigmund Freud*, vol. 17 (London: Hogarth Press, 1955), pp. 219–220.

23. Tolkien, "On Fairy-Stories," pp. 87–88.

24. Raymond Williams, *Resources of Hope: Culture, Democracy, Socialism* (London: Verso, 1989), p. 118.

25. For a discussion of the Nehruvian vision of the children's film in India and an overview of the genre in Indian cinema, see Noel Brown, "A Brief History of Indian Children's Cinema," in Noel Brown and Bruce Babington (eds.), *Family Films in Global Cinema: The World beyond Disney* (London: I.B. Tauris, 2015), pp. 186–204.

26. See Aijaz Ahmad, *Lineages of the Present: Ideology and Politics in Contemporary South Asia* (London: Verso, 2000); and Aijaz Ahmad, *On Communalism and Globalization: Offensives of the Far Right* (New Delhi: Three Essays Collective, 2007).

27. Craig Owens, "The Allegorical Impulse: Toward a Theory of Postmodernism," *October* 12 (1980), pp. 67–86, at 69.

BIBLIOGRAPHY

"The Shah Commission Final Report: General Observations." *Indian Journal of Public Administration* 36:3 (July 1990), pp. 695–701.

Ahmad, Aijaz. *Lineages of the Present: Ideology and Politics in Contemporary South Asia*. London: Verso, 2000.

Ahmad, Aijaz. *On Communalism and Globalization: Offensives of the Far* Right. New Delhi: Three Essays Collective, 2007.

Bag, Kheya. "Red Bengal's Rise and Fall." *New Left Review* 70 (2011), pp. 69–98.

Bhattacharya, Mihir. "Conditions of Visibility: People's Imagination and Goopy Gyne Bagha Byne." *Journal of the Moving Image* 2 (2001), pp. 77–105.

Brown, Noel. "A Brief History of Indian Children's Cinema." In Noel Brown and Bruce Babington (eds.), *Family Films in Global Cinema: The World Beyond Disney*. London: I.B. Tauris, 2015, pp. 186–204.

Dasgupta, Chidananda. *The Cinema of Satyajit Ray*. New Delhi: Vikas, 1980.

Frank, Andre Gunder. "Emergence of Permanent Emergency in India." *Economic and Political Weekly* 12:11 (1977), pp. 463–475.

Ganguly, Keya. *Cinema, Emergence, and the Films of Satyajit Ray*. Berkeley: University of California Press, 2010.

Jameson, Fredric. *Allegory and Ideology*. London: Verso, 2019.

Kaviraj, Sudipta. "Indira Gandhi and Indian Politics." *Economic and Political Weekly*, 21:38–39 (1986), pp. 1697–1708.

Le Guin, Ursula K. "Elfland and Poughkeepsie." In David Sandner (ed.), *Fantastic Literature: A Critical Reader*. Westport, CT: Praeger, 2004, pp. 144–155.

Robinson, Andrew. *Satyajit Ray: The Inner Eye; the Biography of a Master Film-maker*. London: I.B. Tauris, 2004.

Tolkien, J. R. R. "On Fairy-Stories." In *The Tolkien Reader*. New York: Ballantine Books, 1966, pp. 33–90.

Vasudevan, Ravi. "Nationhood, Authenticity and Realism in Indian Cinema: The Double Take of Modernism in the Work of Satyajit Ray." *Journal of the Moving Image* 2 (2001), pp. 52–76.

Williams, Raymond. *Resources of Hope: Culture, Democracy, Socialism*. London: Verso, 1989.

CHAPTER 23

GENDER, IDEOLOGY, AND NATIONALISM IN CHINESE CHILDREN'S CINEMA

YUHAN HUANG

No one can be a child forever, but childhood often remains in one's memory for a lifetime. Remembrance and the imagination of childhood not only reflect hopes and regrets that are deeply ingrained in individual experience but also contribute to a collective consciousness concerning the past and future of society. Chinese intellectuals started to pay attention to children and childhood early in China's history and placed tremendous importance on education and moral enculturation following the Confucianist tradition. The shift from viewing children mainly as subordinates in kinship to viewing them as "the symbol of hope for the future" took place in the early twentieth century, when under the Western influence, elite intellectuals sought to modernize Chinese culture and began advocating for concepts of individualism, humanity, and the nation, as well as for scientific methods and democratic values.[1] The reconceptualization of childhood did not happen in isolation but was imbricated with the transformation of women's status and rights, social reform, and revolution. It was also when the local film industry sprouted in China, and films representing the lives and fates of children constituted an essential body of work that traced the trajectory of the Chinese discourse on nation, history, and gender in which the frameworks of kinship and nation alternate and amalgamate.

Films about children and for children are not clearly differentiated in China, and they have been enjoyed by both young and adult audiences. This was the case in Republican China (1911–1949) and the Maoist era under the People's Republic of China (henceforth PRC, 1949–). In fact, the first commercially successful locally produced feature film in China, *An Orphan Rescues His Grandpa* (Zhang Shichuan, 1923), tells the story of a boy raised by a widowed mother. The film heralded a series of child characters in an orphaned or half-orphaned state, giving rise to a popular archetype in Chinese cinema. *The Winter of Three Hairs* (Zhao Ming and Yan Gong, 1949) provides a perfect example of this trend and is one of the most famous children's films in China, which also signalled a transition to new images of children as heroic soldiers and workers in China's socialist era. In Maoist China films featuring children enjoyed as much support as those on other topics. One of the best-known socialist films, *Sparkling Red Star* (Li Jun and Li Ang, 1974), is about a boy war hero. Produced during the Cultural Revolution (1966–1976), the film was a key cultural project supported by the state (and supervised by the wife of Mao Zedong), making it a fine specimen of Chinese socialist culture. Besides live-action films, animation also contributed to some of the most memorable films in Chinese children's cinema. Animation artists, working in specialized studios and having marginal status in the film industry, enjoyed comparatively less political control. *The Heroic Sisters of the Steppe* (Qian Yunda and Tang Cheng, 1965), an animated film based on real events, was one of the best-known children's film at the time and continued to be viewed after the socialist era had ended. It contributes to the representation of a socialist girlhood, and the intersection of ethnicity, gender, and nationalism reveals a nuanced political articulation.

Although educators have made efforts to draw the line and identify films suitable to show young audiences at school screenings, there is still no state-imposed age-sensitive rating system for cinema in mainland China. Teachers and parents are responsible for selecting the contents for children to watch. Children's cinema specifically created for children's education and entertainment did not develop as a separate industry until the 1980s when Yu Lan, a prominent actress, founded the first specialized studio for children's film production in Beijing. The Economic Reform and Opening-Up policies China implemented in the following decades took away much of the state support for the Chinese film industry, which gradually shifted to a commercial model that resorts to the market to support the making and distribution of films. In this process, children's film studios, along with animation film studios, suffered from a drain of resources and talent. At the same time, renewed attention to childhood became noticeable in films targeting adult audiences, some of which appealed to young audiences as well. *Thatched Memories* (Xu Geng, 1998) and *11 Flowers* (Wang Xiaoshuai, 2011) explored the lives of children in Maoist China, providing an important lens on China's recent past as seen by its anti-hero characters to reflect on the social reality in present-day China.

This chapter examines the representation of gender and nation in Chinese children's film, and defines *children's film* loosely as films for children or that centre on children's experience. By tracing how cinematic images of children have changed throughout mainland China's film history, the chapter analyses the construction and deconstruction of notable archetypes of children characters in their political and historical context, showing how discourses of nationalism and socialism are established in children's cinema in China. Although the chapter proposes three archetypes of child characters—the orphaned child, the young hero and heroine, and the anti-hero—it does not aim to chart them as isolated cultural products of a given historical period. Instead, this research highlights continuities, departures, and returns to dominant motifs and ideas about children and childhood as filmmakers actively envision the past and future of the children's world. Furthermore, by examining the intersection with issues of gender,

ethnicity, and social class in these cinematic archetypes, the research reveals a complicated process of cultural imagination of children and childhood.

A CHILDHOOD IN HARDSHIP:
ORPHAN AS ARCHETYPE

The Winter of Three Hairs (1949) was the first film to premiere in the PRC. It was based
on one of China's most popular children's stories, which is still being adapted today. The
story follows a child's sorrowful experience of being orphaned in the Sino-Japanese War
in WWII and left to live on the street. The film represents the culmination and epitome
of the orphan characters developed in early Chinese films. The first half of the twentieth century in China was a time of immense social instability amid political conflict,
war, and foreign invasion, which gave rise to a nationalistic sentiment and calls for
unity and social reform. Issues of children's and women's welfare were at the forefront
of discussions on the urgent need to advance national power and political development.
The theme of children in hardship, particularly orphans or half-orphaned children, was
prevalent in family-ethics films, which often evoked much audience sympathy and,
when the youngsters in the films rose above their adversities, projected a sense of communal hope for a brighter future.

The cinematic image of children overcoming hardship had started with *An Orphan
Rescues His Grandpa*, one of the earliest Chinese feature-length films. The full film no
longer exists, but related records document its importance in Chinese film history. It
features a fortuitous story in which a widow, expelled from the family estate, raises her
child alone. The boy, born after his father's death and unknown to the paternal family,
saves a rich man from an ill-conceived scheme and later finds himself to be the man's
long-lost grandson. Their eventual reunion validates a social order that aligns with
Chinese values of familial and communal lineage, and during this time of social upheaval, the film provides a locus of cathartic relief, celebrating a satisfying ending that
was not always actualized in real life. With its happy plot twist and moral message
reaffirming family ethics, the film resonated with local Chinese audiences; it was the first
local Chinese film to achieve major commercial and critical success, and it helped define
the genres and themes of early Chinese cinema.[2] Zhen Zhang observes the emergence of
a genre of family-ethics melodrama films after the success of *An Orphan*, geared towards
communal sentiment, kinship, and market demands.[3] The trend to combine social advocation with more pragmatic concerns approximates what the film pioneer Zheng
Zhengqiu called "commercialism with a dose of conscience."[4]

Although the 1923 film was not intended as a children's film, it unequivocally focused
on a young character and centred on children's issues at the time. Considering its influence on future films in China, including films for children, it is understandable that
film scholar and historian Zhang Zhilu calls it China's first children's film.[5] In 1925 alone,

four of the eight full-length films produced in China featured orphans or half-orphans as their protagonists; and among the twenty-one full-length live-action children's films produced before the founding of the PRC in 1949 (as listed in Zhang's history), sixteen involved orphans or half-orphans. The preoccupation with orphans and neglected children in early Chinese cinema manifests a shared sense of mission among the Chinese elites who were living at a time of fast-paced modernization and Westernization amid political unrest and natural disasters. Chinese reformers in the twentieth century often took addressing children's problems as vital to national survival. Lu Xun, one of the most influential intellectuals in twentieth-century China, made an appeal to "save the children" in his famous short story "A Madman's Diary" (1918), which is a gruesome modernist tale portraying China as a society with thoroughly corrupt, cannibalistic adults, whose only hope for the future rested on children.[6] Lu Xun was not alone in regarding children as the source and agent of national renewal. Chinese filmmakers echoed this view but conveyed it in a manner that catered to a plebeian taste, accommodating both the pedagogical mission and the market demand for pleasurable film experiences.

It is worth noting that family-ethics films often develop intricate plots that interweave children's hardship and women's issues in family and society. Many films about orphans or half-orphans also feature single mothers. Compared to films that were dedicated to promoting "New Women," family-ethics melodramas centred on children's issues often present a more conservative view of women's obligations within the family. A comparison between the films *New Women* (Cai Chusheng, 1935) and *The Singing Girl Saves Her Mother* (Zhang Shichuan, 1938) is an excellent example of the difference in gender perspective between films about women's liberation and those about family-ethics film centred on children's welfare, even though both themes were central to the discourse of national modernization in China during the early twentieth century. *New Women* is about the difficulties faced by a single mother who is trying to live in society independently. The protagonist, Wei Ming, is an educated woman who decides to marry a man against her family's will but is deserted by her husband shortly after the marriage. With a young daughter and no means of support, Ming goes to work in Shanghai, where she rejects a rich man's sexual advances and gets into a series of troubles. Ming loses her job and, in dire poverty, watches helplessly as her child dies from a fever, and she commits suicide afterward. The film ends with Ming calling out, "I want to live."[7] The film's tragic ending makes a sharp social criticism. *New Women* calls attention to the exploitation of women as sexual objects and profoundly sympathizes with the female predicament in a patriarchal society. *The Singing Girl Saves Her Mother*, though it shares a similar plot, sends a very different message through its happy ending. The film involves a high-born man and a low-born woman who are secretly betrothed, against the wishes of the man's parents. When his parents find out about the relationship, they separate the couple and drive the woman away. She later gives birth to a daughter and raises her alone. The story ends in a happy reunion when the daughter finds her father and reunites her parents, saving her mother from being incarcerated by mistake. Although *Singing Girl* is sympathetic to the woman's misfortune, it allows her little agency and sees her child as the

solution to her social predicament, in an ending that reaffirms existing order of the patriarchal family.

Although both girls and boys featured as protagonists in orphan-themed films,
male characters became more prominent in the late 1930s and 1940s, when the leftist
filmmakers and artists started to frame orphans in the light of war, revolution, and
social-class division, presenting children as both the victims of social unrest and potential contributors to a proletariat revolution. The film *A Lamb Astray* (1936), directed by
the prominent pro-communist filmmaker Cai Chusheng, provides an early example of
the orphan-proletariat child. The film tells the story of an orphan boy who, after being
adopted by a wealthy man, feels rejected in the upper-class social circle and returns to
his cohort of homeless children. Unlike earlier films about orphans that advocated for
family-ethics, Cai's film emphasizes the division between children from different social classes, drawing attention to systemic social inequality in the distribution of wealth
and resources. There is no happy ending to cater to the commercial marketplace; the
film's ending is open. *A Lamb Astray* was the inspiration for the 1949 film *The Winter of
Three Hairs*.

Sanmao, or Three Hairs, is one of the most, if not *the* most, memorable and successful
characters in Chinese children's stories. Sanmao means "three-hairs" in Chinese, a reference to his iconic three strands of hair. Sanmao is mostly known as an orphan; however,
the characterization has undergone notable changes since the character first appeared in
a serialized comic strip by cartoonist Zhang Leping (1910–1992) in 1935. At first, Sanmao
was a boy in a happy middle-class family, whose mischievous but lovable personality put
him and his family in many humorous situations. The delightful comic serial enjoyed
instant popularity with both children and adults, but its publication was interrupted in
1937 when Japan's attack on China signalled the approach of a full-scale war. During
wartime, Zhang participated in artistic and political activism against the Japanese invasion, working on the Sanmao comics only sporadically. When the war ended in 1945,
the cartoonist depicted Sanmao as a homeless orphan in two new serials, expressing an
unmistakable political undertone that had not been there before the war. Sanmao's personality also changed; he now showed great compassion for the poor, and his mischievousness turned into a quick-wittedness in his dealings with the police and bullies.

The reinvention of Sanmao's most likely grew out of the cartoonist's experiences
moving around the country to engage in resistance art and interactions with those who
were suffering most because of the war. Among Zhang's wartime cartoons, "Sanmao's
Broadsword" depicts Sanmao trying to enlist in the army; though he is underage, he
proves himself by cutting down two trees with a borrowed broadsword.[8] In her examination of Chinese wartime resistance art, Laura Pozzi cites "Sanmao's Broadsword" as
an example of representations of children as fighters and activists. She points out that
the cartoon is not literally an encouragement for underage children to join the army; instead, it elevates children as role models for both children and adults by suggesting that
"with enough willpower, even children could overcome the Japanese."[9] The image of
Sanmao taking up arms anticipated other changes that would take place in Zhang's post-
war cartoons and how the orphan motif would evolve in children's cinema. The shift in

Zhang Leping's artistic preoccupations was characteristic of made artists in China in the late 1930s and early 1940s. Many artists had taken part in the national resistance, and their wartime activism gave rise to voluntary politicization and allegiance to nationalism. It also contributed to the solidarity of a circle of leftist writers, filmmakers, and artists who made social inequalities their central concerns. As Zhang re-invented the image of Sanmao after the war, he continued his exploration of children's lives in China in *Sanmao Joins the Army* (1946) and *The Wanderings of Sanmao* (1947); the latter placed a new focusing on social class divisions. The story, from which the film is adapted, recounts Sanmao's unfortunate experiences after being orphaned in the war. He seeks help from the orphanage and welfare office, but both turn him away, and he is forced to live in the streets, hungry and cold.

When the Shanghai-based, left-leaning Kunlun Film Company brought Sanmao to the screen, his characterization underwent another round of changes. The comic books convey his strong sense of sympathy for the poor, but they do not portray the young Sanmao as a revolutionary agent with class conscious and a political agenda. The film made the orphan more revolutionary. A significant change concerns the adoption story. In the comic, a kind-hearted working-class family takes Sanmao in but later has to give him up after a fire destroys everything they own. In the film, Sanmao is instead adopted by a wealthy but childless family. He feels rejected by the members of family's social circle and becomes intolerant of upper-class formalities and hypocrisy. Sanmao secretly invites his street friends to the house for a feast. When the family finds out, they call the police. Defending his friends, Sanmao renounces his adoptive family and goes back to live on the streets. Borrowing from *A Lamb Astray*, the film presents Sanmao's adoption as a clash of social classes. The boy's act of rebellion insinuates a class consciousness that marks his sense of belonging to the proletariat. By taking food from the rich and giving it to the poor, Sanmao completes a quasi-revolutionary act of wealth redistribution. And finally, when Sanmao voluntarily leaves his adoptive family for a life on the streets, he shows the defiance and self-sacrifice that often characterize revolutionary heroes.

The different versions of the ending in the story of Sanmao's life on the streets shed light on how political ideology shapes the representation of children. As discussed, in the difference between family-ethics films and left-leaning films about women's liberation, a happy ending or a tragic ending can radically transform a film's meaning. The comic serial, published in 1947, presents a bleak future for Sanmao. In the comic's last panel he is being driven away from a Children's Day celebration. Realising that only rich kids are allowed to take part, Sanmao leaves the scene in disappointment.[10] On the other hand, the film adaption offers a bright prospect for Sanmao. It is said that, initially, a dark ending had been planned.[11] And Sanmao's return to street life after leaving his adoptive family is a vision consistent with the film's fierce criticism of social inequalities and the lack of social welfare for children. However, the film's final cut adds an additional scene in which he joyously joins a city parade as the Communist Party enters Shanghai. The PRC was founded just before the film's premiere, and it is likely that the filmmakers felt a need to depict the new social reality in a favourable light. The changed ending also anticipates further transformations of the Sanmao cartoon character, who becomes a happy boy living in this new society; from then on, the comic series made little reference to his orphanhood. As the first film to be premiered under the PRC, and one of the most popular Chinese children's films ever, *The Winter of Three Hairs* occupies a unique place in Chinese film history. The film was the product of deliberate efforts by the left-leaning filmmakers, writers, and artists to represent China's social reality through children's stories. In the national narrative, Sanmao epitomizes the orphan as a victim of social unrest and an agent of social change. In addition, the happy twist at the end of the film signals a transition that anticipates the construction of communist little heroes and heroines in the Chinese children's cinema.

FASHIONING OF THE IDEAL CHILD: NATIONAL HEROES AND HEROINES

The founding of the PRC brought significant changes to the film industry. The Chinese Communist Party saw films as a powerful tool to cultivate mass culture and transmit political messages about socialist construction. New regulations were implemented, and political campaigns were launched to transform the industry. Privately owned film studios were gradually taken over and consolidated as state-run studios, where most of the existing corps of filmmakers and technicians continued to work.[12] Children's films were part of a national project, produced and distributed by the state-owned studios, with financial support from the state. In his historiography, Zhang Zhilu observes three new motifs in Chinese children's cinema in the decades following the founding of the PRC: (a) the good behaviour and deeds of children; (b) the lives of children in a new society transitioning to socialism; and (c) little war heroes.[13] The first two themes focus on the everyday lives of children at school and at home and are often set in the present under the PRC government. These films highlight communal life and provide role models for children; for example, in *Flowers of the Motherland* (Yan Gong, 1955), a group of fifth-grade students help a careless, indolent boy and a self-centred, unfriendly girl change their behaviour and develop warm friendships. The film exemplifies a recurring theme of personal transformation and identification with the values of collectivism. The film has no villains, and the community cherishes its children as the "flowers of the motherland" of the title. In sharp contrast to a peaceful and protected childhood under the PRC, historical films provided vivid depictions of children's struggles and misfortunes during wartime and social instability. The deliberate contrast between childhood in the past and in the present pays explicit tribute to the founding of the PRC, and the reimagination of wartime childhood contributes to a national narrative that seeks to restructure the Communist party's political history. Wartime stories also provide an outlet for cinematic excitement and action. Equally didactic in their central messages about socialism and collectivism, the war films' plots feature more conflict and physical action that would stimulate the audience than the films set in the peaceful contemporary time of the 1950s and the early 1960s. Although they only accounted for one-fifth of the total production of films for children, the films about little war heroes and heroines were among the most popular and best-remembered children's films from socialist China, and they are often remembered with nostalgic sentiment today.

Sparkling Red Star is one of the most frequently discussed works of Chinese socialist cinema, and its young protagonist serves as an ideal model of the Communist child hero. The film is set in central China in the 1930s and features a boy named Pan Dongzi from a revolutionary family. His father, a soldier in the Red Army of the Chinese Communist Party, leaves home to continue the revolution when the Red Army relocates its base camp. Dongzi's mother is also a loyal supporter of the Communist Party. She stays behind with the boy and takes the lead in the local resistance. In a battle against the local landlord, she sacrifices herself to save others. Having witnessed his parents' devotion to the Communist cause, Dongzi is eager to do his part for the revolution. He becomes an apprentice to seasoned revolutionaries and makes significant contributions to the local guerrilla war effort. Dongzi also revenges his mother's death in a battle against the landlord. At the end of the film, he joins the Red Army, becoming worthy of the red star that symbolizes the revolutionary army and the Communist Party.

The film is a curious reimagining of the Chinese revolutionary history in a Bildungsroman story, turning the image of a child who is a victim of war and also an active agent who fights the war into one heroic figure. The film starts with an adult narrator speaking over the image of a young boy in the woods:

> Everyone has a childhood. My childhood started in the bitterness of class oppression, and I spent it in the fire of class struggle. It was about forty years ago. I was only seven in the turbulent year of 1931. People said that the Communist Party's Red Army led by Chairman Mao had arrived at nearby mountains, and was about to come to our region.[14]

The opening narration situates the audience in China's recent wartime history, giving a very specific point of reference in time and location, thus explicitly paying homage to Mao Zedong. By narrating the story as an adult who has survived the war and contributed to the founding of the nation, the child character gains legitimacy as a role model. The story does not establish Dongzi as the perfect child at the beginning of the film. He is a playful boy who feels a strong attachment to his parents. But as Dongzi experiences various challenges in life—bidding goodbye to his father, being driven away from home, losing his mother, and facing dangerous enemies—the audience grows sympathetic to him. Although he shows moments of vulnerability, he is never presented as a passive victim of events; he never cries on-screen and always tries to fight back. Gradually, one's sympathy for the boy turns into feelings of amazement and awe. When Dongzi finally avenges his mother's death, vows his allegiance to the Communist Party, and reunites with his father, he has completed the trial, metamorphosing from an ordinary child protected by the adults into a legendary Communist hero.

Dongzi's story maintains an underlying continuity to the orphan motif prevalent in earlier films about children's lives in wartime China. However, it brings a significant shift by transforming the basis of the family from kinship to a shared revolutionary allegiance. Although Dongzi's parents provide support for much of the film, he is mentored and guided by his senior communist comrades. In addition, his beloved parents' absence and sacrifice have further motivated him to commit to the revolutionary cause. In this way, communist camaraderie replaces family kinship, and the nation becomes the symbolic home for the orphaned child. The film presents the orphan turned child-hero as a voluntary and active agent in the society he lives in, but it no longer challenges the social reality in which the film has been produced and viewed. The sense of agency derives from a historical imagination, a performance of the past. By identifying with Dongzi and his longing to have a home, the audience goes into "imaginative ideological labour" of political nation-building and connects the orphaned children with a community of motherland.[15] Thus, the film represents a paradigm shift from a leftist narrative that challenges the social status quo to a national narrative disguised in historical imagination that confirms the dominant ideology.

Films similar to *Sparkling Red Star* mostly feature boys as the protagonists; girls seldom appear as war heroes, and if they do, they show up as supporting members in a group of children. However, heroic girlhood was not absent in Chinese socialist discourse. The legendary story of Longmei and Yurong is a fascinating case in which issues of nationalism, ethnicity, and gender are intertwined in the ideological dynamics of making socialist girl heroines. The story is based on an actual event that took place in Inner Mongolia in February 1964—two sisters, aged eleven and nine, encountered a snowstorm when they were taking care of a flock of sheep entrusted to them by their father, who had gone out to help his neighbours. The sheep, frightened by the gusty wind, scattered and ran farther into the pastoral. To protect the sheep, which were the local commune's collective property, the two sisters followed them and were forced to stay out in freezing cold weather for a day and a night. At last, they reached a railway station more than thirty-five kilometres away, saved by a local railway worker. Both girls had frostbite, and the younger sister, Yurong, having lost one boot in the storm, suffered a severe injury in one foot and later became crippled. They protected the commune's 380 sheep, with only two dying in the blizzard. The local government, hearing about the incident, praised the two girls' heroic deeds and publicized it as exemplary behaviour nourished by communist thoughts. The news spread rapidly through the country, and the two girls became well-known socialist heroes. The Shanghai Animation Studio's animated film *The Heroic Sisters of the Steppe* (1965) was based on their story. It became an instant classic in children's cinema and continued to be aired and viewed until the 1990s.[16]

The stories of socialist heroes always claim to be based on real events, but the construction of the heroic discourse has been subject to much scrutiny. A study of the film by Uradyn E. Bulag revealed historical inaccuracies and the deliberate fabrication of ethnic harmony in the telling of the story. The discrepancy concerned the ethnic identity of the person who saved the two sisters at the end of their arduous journey. Both the news reports and the film adaptation presented the saviour as Han Chinese, the ethnic majority in mainland China. The news reports contrived a story in which both a Han Chinese railway signal operator and a Mongolian pastoral lord discovered the girls. Although the railway worker managed to save the injured children, the pastoral lord took advantage of the opportunity to steal sheep. The film version did not have the sheep-stealing subplot but, it presented the head of the local commune, a Han Chinese communist, as the leader of the rescue team. Bulag's research, which included evidence from news archive from the 1990s and interviews with people who had been involved in the incident, shows that the girls' real saviour of the girls was a Mongolian man called Haschuluu, who was serving a sentence of labour and under surveillance in the area where the girls lost the sheep.[17] Bulag suggests that it was a deliberate falsification, but not by the Han Chinese leaders at the top of the bureaucracy. It was "a political strategy of Mongols" to claim allegiance to Han communists' central government and "to present themselves as posing no threat."[18] The truth of this political myth is still largely unknown today.

The politics of ethnicity embedded in this story is closely related to the politics of gender. In depicting two Mongolian girls espousing communist ideals, falling into danger, and then being saved by a Han Chinese, the story feminizes ethnic minorities to make their heroes appear less threatening to the Han government. It is not to say that the two girls, Longmei and Yurong, have less agency than their male counterparts, such as Dongzi in the film *Sparkling Red Star*. Like Dongzi, who has been guided and mentored by senior communist comrades who serve as parental figures, the two girls are under a similar power structure between a communist father and the child, in their case interwoven with the ethnic power relation. The gender dynamic is particularly prominent in the film adaptation, which visualizes the life and deeds of the two girl heroines.

The Heroic Sisters of the Steppe focuses mostly on the two sisters' heroic deeds and their subsequent rescue, fully exploiting the visual form to enhance the psychological impact of the story. The film opens with an idyllic scene of life on the plateau, where the sheep are grazing on the hill. As the camera pans to modern settlements and zooms in on one particular household, the film introduces the girls' family. The film depicts the family's room décor in detail—the portrait of Mao Zedong, various awards—to show the revolutionary background. It is the only time in the film that the girls' mother appears, working in the yard and checking on two toddler boys in the room through the window. The two protagonists enter into the scene with hoes in their hands, and then their father—who needs help to run the commune—entrusts them to care for the flock of sheep. The sisters take the herd to a hill covered with lush grass. While the sheep eat, they sit down to read a book about Lei Feng, a Han communist exemplar of noble character and altruistic personality. The reference to Lei Feng serves as a prelude to the sisters' heroic endeavour and sets up a political context as a source of the heroines' inspiration and strength.

When the snowstorm hits, the two girls demonstrate deep sisterly love, mighty physical strength, and devoted perseverance to accomplish the work their father has entrusted them with. Having a hard time to keep the sheep in a flock, Longmei tells

Yurong to go back and ask the adults for help. Yurong, concerned about the safety of her older sister and the sheep, will not go back alone. Thus both girls stay with the herd, despite the severe weather. There is a spectacular scene of the two girls lifting ewes and rams out of the snow, becoming protectors of animals larger and heavier than themselves. The scene reverses the typical depiction of children as helpless stray lambs, such as in *The Lamb Astray*. The girls show a resolute determination to help themselves in dangerous situations. When Yurong falls into a crack in the snowy field, she does not wait helplessly to be rescued. She carves into the icy ridge and climbs out. To contemporary audiences, these depictions may seem extreme or incomprehensible because they seem to encourage children to put themselves in hazardous situations for reasons of ideological necessity. However, viewed in the context of the socialist era, when there was a growing representation of women as equally capable of doing work traditionally done by men, the story of Longmei and Yurong sent a positive message to girls about women's liberation and advancement in the society.

Just as the national discourse reimagines the parent-child connection as a nation-child relationship in children's war films, it plays a similar role in the story of two heroic sisters, replacing kinship with communist camaraderie and equating familial affection with communal solidarity. In all the representations of Longmei and Yurong's story, the girls' biological parents play a minuscule role. As noted, their mother appears only once in the film version, and their father is mostly a vehicle for introducing and conveying the film's communist ideals. When Yurong falls in the deep snow and crawls towards the sheep, she cries out, "Father says that the herd is our commune's lifeline. I cannot leave the herd."[19] The line indicates that the father-daughter affection does not rest on their mutual caring for each other, but on the mutual obligation to defend communal benefit and property. The film thus creates a symbolic father-daughter relationship that overrides biological kinship. In the political sense, the girls are children of the local commune that sent out a rescue team, of which their biological father is a member. In the spiritual sense, the two girls are successors to socialist exemplars like Lei Feng, heirs of the communist ideal embodied in the image of Mao Zedong. This father-daughter relationship is echoed in children's films in the post-Maoist era, but as one would expect, radically challenged and restructured.

THE ANTI-HERO AND THE RISE OF THE CHILDHOOD FILM IN POST-MAO CHINA

The passing away of Mao Zedong in autumn 1976 brought an end to the decade-long Cultural Revolution, closing a communist era that prioritized political movements and ideological allegiance above everything else. The following decades witnessed a series of political and economic reforms that brought tremendous social and cultural change to the lives of the Chinese people. The 1980s in China—often referred to as the

New Era—celebrated Western modernist thought and aesthetics and introduced state-sanctioned modernization and China's integration into the capitalist world market. The modernist advocation of individualism and freedom was seen as enlightenment against communist collectivism and Maoism. Along with other arts, the film industry invested in comparatively more diverse and explorative endeavours than in the previous decades. Humanism became a central theme in mainstream films, and intellectuals returned as legitimate characters, a shift from the dominance of characters of workers, farmers, and soldiers on the socialist screen. Representations of female characters framed the pursuit of feminine beauty as part of an overarching theme of individual freedom and pursuit of happiness. As in the early twentieth century, when women and children were first put on the agenda of national modernization, issues of femininity and education in the 1980s are subsumed in a new enlightenment discourse.

The soul-searching of a wilful, independent-thinking girl was a popular trope in films for children and young adults during the 1980s, including *The Girl in Red* (Lu Xiaoya, 1985), *The Missing Girl-Student* (Shi Shujun, 1986), and *A Time of Dreams* (Lin Hongtong and Ge Xiaoying, 1988). These films touch upon social issues related to gender and class inequalities, children's welfare when parents divorced, individual freedom under a collectivist education system, while at the same time emphasizing themes of beauty, love, and individual happiness. *The Girl in Red* best encapsulates this archetype; it features a middle-school girl, An Ran, who gets in trouble for wearing a fashionable bright-red shirt. She further alienates herself from her classmates by openly confronting their teacher for a mistake in her lecture, an act of defiance against the commonly accepted value of respecting one's seniors in China. Although Ran is an outstanding student, her classmates and teacher think she is too aloof and lacks humility. She is confused by their rejection and worries that she will lose an award given to the best students. Ran's older sister tries to help by bribing the teacher with hard-to-come-by film tickets, and the teacher gives Ran the award discreetly. After thoughtful reflection and internal struggle, Ran abjures her award in an act of protest, establishing herself as an anti-hero against the heroic paradigms of revolutionary discourse, choosing independent thinking over the recognition from the community, individualism over collectivist conformity. Compared to children's films from the Maoist era, *The Girl in Red* represents a diametrically different relationship between the child and the community. Instead of fitting in, the protagonist wants to stand out and act on her own accord. The colour red also gains a new meaning. In revolutionary discourse, red is a symbol of communism and the spirit of self-sacrifice, as in the film *Red Sparkling Star*. But in this post-Mao film, Ran's red shirt represents her spirited, self-willed defiance and the pursuit of beauty, associating femininity with personal freedom and happiness.

Although the film markedly diverges from the socialist representation of the relationship between children and the community, the gender framework in which it constructs girlhood and womanhood is unchanged from previous decades. The representation of girlhood and womanhood is always subsumed into a "grander" discourse of national survival, revival, and enlightenment. In *The Girl in Red*, parents play important roles, and they represent different views on life when they offer suggestions to the girl. Both parents are intellectuals and have suffered from political antagonism during the previous decade, but their conclusions about how their daughter should see the community turn out to be quite different. Her mother criticizes Ran's acts of self-alienation and encourages her to hold back her strong personal opinions to earn the student award, which will help her college application in the future. Ran emphatically disagrees and becomes estranged from her mother, at times betraying a contempt for the mother's pragmatism. Ran's father, an unrecognized painter, represents an enlightened figure of idealism. He defends Ran's individualism, saying that "only a poor artist wears other's eyeglasses."[20] Ran, aligned with the idealistic vision, shows a clear affinity with her father. The father-daughter relationship here, though restoring the sense of kinship erased in revolutionary discourses, still bears the imprint of the symbolic structure of nation-building, this time in the name of modernist enlightenment.

The era of modernist enlightenment was short-lived and ended when the government clamped down on appeals for political freedom at the Tiananmen Square Protests in 1989; China remained politically communist, even as economically, it further entered the global capitalist system and consumer culture. In analysing the complexities and paradox of capitalism in a socialist country, scholars who study contemporary Chinese culture and society commonly describe PRC in the 1990s and afterward as "postsocialist."[21] The word indicates an entanglement of a rapidly globalizing consumer culture with historical roots in socialism. The 1990s saw a massive wave of marketization in China, and it was also around this time that the Chinese film industry went through a process of reform, allowing private companies to produce art and commercial films in China, though ideological censorship is still in place. A group of young filmmakers who started as underground artists now can produce films for a more general audience. Often referred to as the "sixth generation," these filmmakers have a more individualistic approach to cinema, differentiating themselves from their predecessors who often reflect on Chinese society and its past by taking a panoramic view of history.[22] Notably, childhood emerged as a significant theme even though the films are not intended for children. Autobiographic accounts of childhood and youth have produced some of the most memorable postsocialist representations of Maoist China, such as *The Blue Kite* (Tian Zhuangzhuang, 1993), *Little Red Flowers* (Zhang Yuan, 2006), and *11 Flowers*. These are best described as "childhood films."[23] Still, the line between childhood film and children's film is quite ambiguous; some of these films not only feature child characters as the protagonists but also appeal to a young audience because they retell the experience of growing up in the Maoist era, such as *Thatched Memories*. These films often feature protagonists, mostly males, who are not so glorious and suffer from self-doubt, inaction, and a sense of loss. They are China's beat generation. Many of the stories include autobiographic references to the director's personal experience.

Among these childhood films, Wang Xiaoshuai's *11 Flowers* provides a telling case to analyse the politics of memory and gender. The plot of *11 Flowers* follows the unveiling of a violent incident to an eleven-year-old boy during the Cultural Revolution. The story starts when a castrated corpse is found in the village where the boy, Wang Han, lives. The boy later has a brief encounter with the fugitive murderer and learns that the man had committed the crime to avenge the rape of his sister. Eventually, the fugitive will be caught and sentenced to death; however, the encounter makes a deep impression on the boy, who starts to understand the complexities of justice and that things are not as simple as black and white. He gradually develops feelings of compassion for the murderer's family and a secret affection for Juehong, the rape victim, which leads to his sexual awakening. The film, focusing on the boy's perception of the series of events, is a Bildungsroman story of personal awakening. The sense of awakening is both political and sexual. Set at the time of the Cultural Revolution, when the political orthodoxy championed an absolute vision of morality and associated sexual desire with degradation, the film intersects with a postsocialist discourse that seeks to redefine China's socialist past, associating the boy's personal awakening with a political revisioning of the Maoist China. When asked why he made the film, Wang Xiaoshuai emphasized a shared sense of awakening felt by his generation:

> The film is not about a moment of a particular person at 11-years-old. It is about a generation born in the mid-60s and reached their teens at the end of the Cultural Revolution. There is a sense of shock and alarm, suddenly awoke from simple-mindedness. It is as if we came to an abrupt halt when charging forward with Mao's Red Book held up high in our hands.[24]

Wang Xiaoshuai uses the story to convey a collective awakening as China transitions into a postsocialist society. His vision of the past is markedly different from the optimistic view that saturated films in the 1980s. He evokes a strong sense of shock and bewilderment commonly expressed in other postsocialist childhood films. These films highlight a sense of urgency about developing a historical articulation derived from self-conscious reflection and a redemptive relationship to the past; in Walter Benjamin's words, "to seize hold of a memory as it flashes up at a moment of danger."[25] The lens of childhood plays a vital role in these films for several reasons. First, the sense of betrayal and disillusionment the six-generation directors want to express about contemporary China is deeply rooted in their childhood experience. Mostly born in the 1960s, this generation of filmmakers spent their formative years in the political fever of Maoist China. They were witnesses to a bygone era before they could understand it. Filmmaking is thus the perfect medium for re-enacting and reflecting on such an experience. Secondly, having a young protagonist allows the filmmakers to present events during the Cultural Revolution from an unknowing, unjudgmental viewpoint that can help circumvent the political censorship in the film industry. Thirdly, by incorporating personal memories of Maoist China, the sixth-generation filmmakers have constructed a distinctly different narrative from existing discourse developed in the 1980s, giving them a unique voice and registering their presence in retelling China's recent history.

In discussing postsocialist cinema, cultural critic Jinhua Dai makes an important observation on the gender dynamic in a "process of man regaining power."[26] Although girl protagonists enjoyed brief popularity in children's films of the 1980s within a framework that of highlighting modernist enlightenment and the return of intellectuals, the postsocialist childhood films see a return to male protagonists as the agent and narrator. *11 Flowers* is distinctive in this respect. Whereas the boy in the film experiences an awakening in observing the unfolding of events in the film, the girl Juehong is depicted as a passive victim. In fact, Juehong's story is featured in another film directed by Wang Xiaoshuai, *Shanghai Dream* (2005). Even when the girl is the protagonist and focal point of the film, she has little agency, and few options to get out of her predicament. Her victimhood and acceptance of what has happened to her are apparent. This phenomenon exemplifies the problem with predominantly male filmmakers representing the history and reality of Chinese society from their personal perspective.

CONCLUSION

Although there are different opinions on how children's film should be defined, scholars generally agree on the importance of a contextual approach to examining cinematic works for and about children because children's cinema provides "a metacommentary on film and society,"[27] and offers "insights regarding social, cultural, and ideological meanings."[28] It is also very relevant to constructing national identity, "both as propaganda and as resistance."[29] A contextual approach is essential to studying Chinese children's cinema, which possesses no film rating system based on age appropriateness and for most of its history has had few studios dedicated to the production of children's films. This chapter has examined some of the canonical works in Chinese children's film, some of which are specifically intended for a young audience, while others have been enjoyed by both children and adults. The study does not claim to be an exhaustive review; however, the emphasis has been on films that participate in a continuous construction of children's images on the screen and in society. By observing thematic and narrative connections between films from different periods, the current study identifies three cultural archetypes that recur in films with numerous variations: the orphan, the revolutionary child-hero, and the anti-hero. These archetypes should not be treated as rigid categories. Instead, they are many intersections that show how one archetype gradually transitions to the next, such as the orphan-turned-proletariat in *The Winter of Three Hairs*. Furthermore, the gendering of the image of children is an under-discussed topic in the scholarship on Chinese children's cinema. This chapter has examined how girl protagonists fall in and out of favour in films for and about children in China, showing an underlying power relationship that always subsumes women's liberation and advancement into the national discourse of survival and enlightenment, the symbolic father-daughter relationship being the backbone of this gender structure. Despite the limited narrative space and opportunity given to female characters, Chinese children's cinema has produced some extremely memorable stories about strong and independent girls, such as the little heroic sisters on the Mongolian steppe. In describing children's cinema as a genre for everyone, not just the young audience, Noel Brown rightly points out that "children's films are objects of pleasure, fascination, and nostalgia."[30] This is certainly the case with Chinese children's cinema, and many of the films discussed in this chapter are fondly remembered and re-watched regardless of their strong political association.

NOTES

1. Mary Ann Farquhar, *Children's Literature in China: From Lu Xun to Mao Zedong* (New York: Routledge, 2015), p. 1.
2. Early Chinese filmmaking was mostly independent and underfunded, relying heavily on foreign expertise. Production companies rose and fell quickly, many having made only one picture. The phenomenal success of *Orphan Rescues Grandfather* was therefore an important milestone and engendered great financial support for Zhang Shichuan and Zheng Zhengqiu, the co-founders of Mingxing (Star Motion Picture Company), the most influential Chinese film studio in the 1920s. See Yingjin Zhang, *Chinese National Cinema* (New York: Routledge, 2004), pp. 13–27.
3. Zhen Zhang, "Transplanting Melodrama: Observations on the Emergence of Early Chinese Narrative Film," in Yingjin Zhang (ed.), *A Companion to Chinese Cinema* (Chichester, UK: John Wiley & Sons, 2012), pp. 30–39.
4. Zhang, *Chinese National Cinema*, p. 19.
5. Zhang Zhilu, *Zhongguo shaonian ertong dianying shilun* [A history of Chinese youth and children's cinema] (Beijing: Zhongguo dianying chubanshe, 2005), p. 9.
6. Lu Xun, "A Madman's Diary," in Joseph Lau and Howard Goldblatt (eds.), *The Columbia Anthology of Modern Chinese Literature*, 2nd ed., trans. Yang Xianyi and Gladys Yang (1918; repr. New York: Columbia University Press, 2007), p. 16.
7. *Xin nüxing* [New woman], dir. Cai Chusheng (1935), DVD, East Asian Library and Learning Resources Center's Project, Minneapolis, 2008.
8. Zhang Leping, "Sanmao de dadao" [Sanmao's broad sword], Sanmao Comics website, http://www.sanmao.com.cn/father/artwork/comic/sanmao/15zhanluan/01.htm. [accessed June 15, 2020].
9. Laura Pozzi, "'Chinese Children Rise Up!': Representations of Children in the Work of the Cartoon Propaganda Corps during the Second Sino-Japanese War," *Cross-Currents: East Asian History and Culture Review* 4:1 (2015), pp. 333–363, at 347.
10. Zhang Leping, *Sanmao liulangji quanji* [The wanderings of Sanmao] (1947; Shanghai: Shanghai kexue jishu wenxian chubanshe, 2010), p. 261.
11. Lanjun Xu, "The Child and the Future of China in the Legend of Sanmao," in David Der-wei Wang (ed.), *A New Literary History of Modern China* (Cambridge, MA: Harvard University Press, 2017), pp. 406–414, at 412.
12. For a detailed discussion of the nationalization of the film industry under the PRC, see Zhuoyi Wang, *Revolutionary Cycles in Chinese Cinema: 1951–1979* (New York: Palgrave Macmillan, 2014), pp. 25–43.
13. Zhang, *Zhongguo shaonian ertong dianying shilun*, pp. 30–31.
14. *Shanshan de hongxing* [Sparkling red star], dir. Li Ang and Li Jun, Bayi dianying zhipian chang, Beijing, 1974, 1905 (website), n.d, https://www.1905.com/vod/play/86069. shtml?__hz=6e0721b2c6977135 [accessed June 15, 2020].
15. Geoff Eley and Ronald Grigor Suny, introduction to *Becoming National: A Reader* (Oxford: Oxford University Press, 1996), pp. 3–37, at 8.

16. Animated films produced by Shanghai Animation Film Studio (SAFS), including *The Heroic Sisters on the Steppe*, enjoyed monopoly status on the Chinese screen until the late 1980s. As China entered the global economy, SAFS's status declined. Foreign animation and joint productions saturated the Chinese market, a great variety of new works with fast-changing themes and styles were produced. Animated films from SAFS before the 1990s felt outdated but nostalgic. For discussions of the Chinese animation industry, see Daisy Yan Du, *Animated Encounters: Transnational Movements of Chinese Animation, 1940s–1970s* (Honolulu: University of Hawai'i Press, 2019), pp. 181–186; and Sean Macdonald, *Animation in China* (Abingdon, UK: Routledge, 2017), pp. 174–206.

17. Uradyn E. Bulag, "Models and Moralities: The Parable of the Two 'Heroic Little Sisters of the Grassland,'" *China Journal* 42 (1999), pp. 21–41, at 34–35.

18. Bulag, "Models and Moralities," p. 29.

19. *Caoyuan yingxiong xiao zimei* [The heroic sisters of the Steppe] (1965), dir. Qian Yunda and Tang Chengm, DVD, Shanghai dianying yinxiang chubanshe, Shanghaim, 1997.

20. *Hongyi shaonü* [Girl in red], dir. Lu Xiaoya (1985), DVD. Emei dianying zhipianchang yinxiang chubanshe, Chengdu, 2005).

21. Xudong Zhang, "Epilogue: Postmodernism and Postsocialist Society – Historicizing the Past," in Arif Dirlik and Xudong Zhang (eds.), *Postmodernism and China* (Durham, NC: Duke University Press, 2000), pp. 399–442, at 401.

22. The development of Chinese cinema was mainly a process of apprenticeship before the 1980s. Therefore studies and critique of Chinese cinema often draw on age cohorts to identify common patterns and stylistic choices in each generation of directors. The sixth generation includes directors Jia Zhangke and Wang Xiaoshuai. For a discussion on generational divisions of Chinese filmmakers, see Harry H. Kuoshu, *Celluloid China: Cinematic Encounters with Culture and Society* (Carbondale: Southern Illinois University Press, 2002), pp. 1–20.

23. Noel Brown, *The Children's Film: Genre, Nation and Narrative* (New York: Columbia University Press, 2017), p. 12.

24. Wang Xiaoshuai, "Wang Xiaoshuai caifang quanji [Collected interviews of Wang Xiaoshuai]," LeTV, http://www.le.com/ptv/vplay/1597894.html#vid=1597894 [accessed June 15, 2020],

25. Walter Benjamin, "Theses on the Philosophy of History," in Hannah Arendt (ed.), *Illuminations: Essays and Reflections*, trans. Harry Zohn (New York: Schocken Books, 1969), p. 255.

26. Dai Jinhua, *Xingbie zhongguo* [Gendering China] (Taipei: Maitian chubanshe, 2006), p. 83.

27. Ian Wojcik-Andrews, *Children's Films: History, Ideology, Pedagogy, Theory* (London: Garland, 2000), p. 20.

28. Brown, *Children's Film*, p. 12.

29. Stephanie Hemelryk Donald, Emma Wilson, and Sarah Wright, introduction to Donald, Wilson, and Wright (eds.), *Childhood and Nation in Contemporary World Cinema: Borders and Encounters* (New York: Bloomsbury Academic, 2017), pp. 1–14, at 3.

30. Brown, *Children's Film*, p. 10.

BIBLIOGRAPHY

Brown, Noel. *The Children's Film: Genre, Nation and Narrative*. New York: Columbia University Press, 2017.

Bulag, Uradyn E. "Models and Moralities: The Parable of the Two "Heroic Little Sisters of the Grassland." *China Journal* 42 (1999), pp. 21–41.

Dai, Jinhua. *Xingbie zhongguo* [Gendering China]. Taipei: Maitian chubanshe, 2006.

Donald, Stephanie Hemelryk, Emma Wilson, and Sarah Wright, eds. *Childhood and Nation in Contemporary World Cinema: Borders and Encounters.* New York: Bloomsbury Academic, 2017.

Du, Daisy Yan. *Animated Encounters: Transnational Movements of Chinese Animation, 1940s–1970s.* Honolulu: University of Hawai'i Press, 2019.

Eley, Geoff, and Ronald Grigor Suny. "Introduction: From the Moment of Social History to the Work of Cultural Representation." In Geoff Eley and Ronald Grigor Suny (eds.), *Becoming National: A Reader.* Oxford: Oxford University Press, 1996, pp. 3–37.

Farquhar, Mary Ann. *Children's Literature in China: From Lu Xun to Mao Zedong.* New York: Routledge, 2015.

Kuoshu, Harry H. *Celluloid China: Cinematic Encounters with Culture and Society.* Carbondale: Southern Illinois University Press, 2002.

Macdonald, Sean. *Animation in China.* Abingdon, UK: Routledge, 2017.

Pozzi, Laura. "'Chinese Children Rise Up!': Representations of Children in the Work of the Cartoon Propaganda Corps during the Second Sino-Japanese War." *Cross-Currents: East Asian History and Culture Review* 4:1 (2015), pp. 333–363.

Wang, Zhuoyi. *Revolutionary Cycles in Chinese Cinema: 1951–1979.* New York: Palgrave Macmillan, 2014.

Wojcik-Andrews, Ian. *Children's Films: History, Ideology, Pedagogy, Theory.* New York: Garland, 2000.

Xu, Lanjun. "The Child and the Future of China in the Legend of Sanmao." In David Der-wei Wang (ed.), *A New Literary History of Modern China.* Cambridge, MA: Harvard University Press, 2017, pp. 406–414.

Zhang, Xudong. "Epilogue: Postmodernism and Postsocialist Society; Historicizing the Past." In Arif Dirlik and Xudong Zhang (eds.), *Postmodernism and China.* Durham, NC: Duke University Press, 2000, pp. 399–442.

Zhang, Yingjin. *Chinese National Cinema.* New York: Routledge, 2004.

Zhang, Zhen. "Transplanting Melodrama: Observations on the Emergence of Early Chinese Narrative Film." In Yingjin Zhang (ed.), *A Companion to Chinese Cinema.* Chichester, UK: John Wiley & Sons, 2012, pp. 25–41.

Zhang Zhilu. *Zhongguo shaonian ertong dianying shilun* [A history of Chinese youth and children's cinema]. Beijing: Zhongguo dianying chubanshe, 2005.

CHAPTER 24

ETHNIC AND RACIAL DIFFERENCE IN THE HUNGARIAN ANIMATED FEATURES *MACSKAFOGÓ/ CAT CITY* (1986) AND *MACSKAFOGÓ 2/CAT CITY 2* (2007)

GÁBOR GERGELY

THE 1986 animated feature *Macskafogó/Cat City* (József Nepp and Béla Ternovszky, 1986) is a common reference point for a whole generation of Hungarians now in their thirties and forties.[1] It tapped into new cultural trends, playfully engaging with new technology, as well as long-established tropes of Hungarian adventure stories stretching back to Jenő Rejtő's (aka P. Howard) mock-colonial yarns (e.g., *A tizennégy karátos autó/The Fourteen Carat Convertible*, 1940). The film came out as the ruling party, Magyar Szocialista Munkáspárt (MSzMP), was beginning to make cautious overtures to emerging organized opposition groups. As the USSR, under Mikhail Gorbachev, adopted glasnost and perestroika as its official objectives, the central committee of the MSzMP in Hungary gradually opened up the public sphere to a plurality of voices. This was most clearly apprehended in the cultural sphere. The musical *István a király/King Stephen* (by youth culture icons Levente Szörényi and János Bródy) premiered in 1983. It featured the punk singer Feró Nagy and a host of other singers and performers who, periodically, had been banned or blacklisted in the past. For the first time in the state socialist era, Hollywood films were shown in Hungarian cinemas as part of their first global run, starting with *Star Wars* (George Lucas, 1977), released in Hungary in 1979, just two years after its US premiere. It was followed in 1981 by *Alien* (Ridley Scott, 1979).

E.T. The Extra-Terrestrial (Steven Spielberg, 1982) and *The Empire Strikes Back* (Irvin Kershner, 1980) were released in 1983, and *Return of the Jedi* (Richard Marquand, 1983) and *Raiders of the Lost Ark* (Spielberg, 1981) came out in 1984. A new commercial radio station, Danubius, was established in 1986. In the same year, Queen gave an arena concert at Népstadion, and a memorandum of understanding was signed to set up the first MacDonald's outlet near Budapest's premier shopping street, Váci utca.

As Zoltán Varga notes in his overview of Hungarian animation, *Cat City* draws on a range of cultural tropes that were commonly associated with Western popular culture in the late Cold War period and anticipates the generic hybridity, intertextuality, and postmodern bricolage that characterize twenty-first-century animated features.[2] Varga argues that the film combines elements of the war film, the espionage thriller, the adventure film, the musical, horror, and science fiction.[3] The film thus bears evidence of the increasing permeability of the Iron Curtain and the gradual opening up of the Hungarian cultural scene to hitherto-suppressed trends. Although set apart by its generic hybridity and bewilderingly rich intertextuality, the film is also firmly rooted in a domestic tradition of arch satire masquerading as children's entertainment.[4] It fits into its creators' body of work with equal ease: writer József Nepp made his name with the macabre animated short *Öt perc gyilkosság* (*Five Minutes of Murder*; József Nepp, 1966) and teamed up with director Béla Ternovszky to make the animated science-fiction sitcom *Mézga Aladár különös kalandjai* (*The Curious Adventures of Aladár Mézga*; József Nepp and Béla Ternovszky, 1972), to become Hungarian animation's leading creative duo. Their films were characterized by a playful excess of cultural references, bleak humour, and inventive use of language. The film fits into the Hungarian tradition of animation which, in turn, sits comfortably in a broader Central European regional tradition drawing on folk and fairy tales as well as a transnational exchange of personnel, practices, and resources in the state socialist era. Indeed, Ternovszky's previous project was the successful Hungarian-West German co-production *Meister Eder und sein Pumuckl* (*Master Eder and His Pumuckl*; 1982).

As Gabriella Székely proudly notes in her otherwise negative review of the film, the Hungarian animation studio Pannónia, where *Cat City* was made, was an established production centre with a good international reputation for doing high quality work at low cost.[5] René Laloux and Moebius, among many others, made films there (e.g., *Les Maîtres du temps* [*Time Masters*], René Laloux, 1982). Indeed, one of Székely's issues with *Cat City* is that it does not live up to her expectations of the studio's technical brilliance. Animation being a reasonably cheap (if painstakingly produced) form of entertainment, Pannónia was a key source of children's programming in communist Hungary, and a prolific exporter to Warsaw Pact countries.[6] By Hungarian standards, the film was widely distributed to export markets: it was shown at the Los Angeles International Animation Celebration in 1987, and was released in Bulgaria, Czechoslovakia and the USSR in 1989, and in the Netherlands in 1991.

This chapter focuses on *Cat City* as an exemplary text in the Nepp-Ternovszky oeuvre and in the canon of Hungarian popular culture during the state socialist period. As such, it reveals dominant attitudes to race, gender, sex, and state power in entertainment

aimed predominantly at a youth audience. Notwithstanding the film's enduring popularity and status as a cult favourite, it has received very little critical attention, and, to my
knowledge, this chapter is the first extended treatment of *Cat City* and its sequel. I will
argue that the films construct a binary opposition between the desirable mouse society
and the hateful cat order. In imagining competing social arrangements as irreconcilable racial difference, the films give evidence of deeply ingrained racist and anti-Semitic
reflexes in the Hungarian popular discourse of the 1980s, and in the 2000s.

It is worth pausing to note here that popular discourse during state socialism is always inflected by the state's intrusion into all aspects of life. Popular discourse is policed,
constrained, prompted, and supervised by the state. By necessity, therefore, popular discourse reflects the official line mandated by the state and, by and large, toed by society,
but it is also a reflection of popular views, which may be in tension with or fit comfortably into the general line. The chapter, then, analyses the crude national and racial
stereotypes on show as the film and its sequel paint the nightmare vision of *nemzethalál*,
"death of the nation," a recurring theme in Hungarian nationalist thinking. It contends
that the films are not exceptional. Rather, they are typical expressions of Hungarian
ideas of nationhood that were central to the Horthy era's nationalist policies and later
adapted in the state socialist era, and thus remained in currency. Under the nationalistic and étatist governments of Viktor Orbán, their Horthy-era meanings have been
recovered and fully embraced once more.

Bahun argues that the status of animation was somewhat ambiguous in state socialist
Central and Eastern Europe: it was simultaneously singled out for generous state support and remained relatively free of the type of stifling control the state exercised in other
areas of cultural production.[7] Although (as Varga's book on Hungarian animation's rich
variety shows) there is plenty of evidence that animators were able to pursue their own
interests in their work, I think it is worth remembering Miklós Haraszti's caustic *The
Velvet Prison*, which insists that participation in any state-sustained creative industry as
an artist is a crucial accommodation with the regime, which benefits from the creative
work.[8] Indeed, *Cat City* writer Nepp acknowledged in a 2009 interview that self-censorship had made more active censorship redundant. "We knew what was taboo, it never
occurred to us to cross the line, we wanted to live," he told his interviewer.[9] For this
reason, this chapter does not seek to position *Cat City* as oppositional, but neither does
it argue that it is a straightforward reflection of state socialist Hungary's official ideological positions. Rather, it suggests that as an animated film produced in the context of a
privileged segment of state socialist Hungary's creative industries, it gives expression to
widely shared attitudes, among which discourses of race, gender, sex, and nation preferred by the state sit alongside, in tension or tandem with, popular discourses of race,
gender, sex, and state power.

It is worth noting here that while censorship in pluralistic societies ostensibly aims
to protect society from exposure to material that may pose a threat to individual and
collective morality and thereby ensure that popular entertainment remains "wholesome,"[10] censorship under repressive regimes has tended to focus on policing ideological content.[11] *Cat City* is a good example: as I will note later on, the film's ideological

positions on capitalism, state power, and an ideal society are compliant with state socialist tenets, while the film's references to sex, highly eroticized rendering of female characters, and frequent instances of callous violence sit oddly with *Cat City*'s children's film status. Nonetheless it was marketed, consumed, and is remembered as a film aimed at a child audience. Indeed, the sequel is available on the video streaming site *Mese Online/Tales Online* (meseonline.hu) as a children's film, even though its primary audience includes—or, perhaps more appropriately, consists of—the now middle-aged fans of the original.

While *Cat City* was an enormous and enduring hit with its target audience, it was less well received by critics. The 1986 review in the leading Hungarian film magazine *Filmvilág* was remarkably negative. In just three short paragraphs, Gabriella Székely savages the film for its many references to Hollywood films; the co-production arrangements, which stretch the film into a cross-border zone of liminality (an East-West co-production; a Warsaw Block film made with German *deutschmarks* and US dollars); and its failure to satirize Western tropes, which she argues the film simply adopts rather than critiques.[12] Székely suggests that the film is ideologically unsound and sees its playful intertextuality as elitism, demonstrating the filmmakers' failure to draw inspiration from the lived reality of their audience, and their privileged access to certain texts, such as the latest outing of "agent 07[*sic*]."[13] Still, the review concedes that the films cited did run in Hungarian cinemas (the then most recent Bond film, Roger Moore's *A View to a Kill* [John Glen, 1985], was released in Hungary in 1985), which suggests an attempt to frame the film as distant from its audience and therefore not reflecting current popular cultural trends. In truth, the film was evidence of increasingly easy access to culture produced outside the state socialist era's command economy. What the critic saw as primitive mishmash is clearly identifiable as postmodern intertextuality, which can be linked, in turn, to the decline of the institutional background and infrastructure of the film sector in late-communist Hungary.

CAT CITY: RACIAL CONFLICT AS ALLEGORY OF IDEOLOGICAL OPPOSITION

Cat City tells the story of a peaceful, orderly mouse society under existential threat by an international gang of sadistic cats. On the verge of final destruction, the mice gamble all their available resources on one last roll of a dice: a mysterious machine, designed by an absent-minded professor, Fusimishi (István Szatmári), in Pokyo. The machine, the "cat catcher," which gives the film its Hungarian title, promises to reverse the fortunes of the mice and eliminate the feline threat for good. The secret agent, Grabowski (László Sinkó), is brought out of retirement for one last mission: to deliver the blueprints for the machine to the underground production facility from which the mice plan to launch their counteroffensive.

An initial sequence shows the daily outrages the cats visit upon the innocent mice: mouse casualties are in double digits as a converted tank hoovers up gold from a bank vault; an elderly mouse couple endure a devastating home invasion as a brutal cat ransacks their tastefully furnished home; a mouse-driven car is totalled by a cat-chauffeured American town car; and a young newspaper-mouse is forced at gunpoint to eat the full print run of the daily he is selling. The film immediately establishes a set of key differences between the cats and mice beyond their respective perpetrator-victim status. Many of the cats are dressed in sharp suits familiar from Hollywood gangster films. Fedoras, sunglasses, and Tommy guns complete their looks. Others are dressed in military gear: the cigar-chomping cat who leads the assault on the bank wears a bomber jacket, army-issue lace-up boots, and a tank-commander's helmet. The film's emblematic villain, Mr. Fritz Teufel (Miklós Benedek)—whose surname is the German for "devil"—wears a smartly cut, slim-fit double-breasted suit in gunmetal grey. The chunk missing from his ear, his eye-patch, and his bionic hand indicate practical experience of strong-arm tactics. While the cats are imagined as more-or-less individualistic but highly disciplined members of a hierarchical organization united by shared bloodlust, age, and class, the members of mouse society are imagined as ordinary, but varied citizens of a coherent but accommodating community. Thus, we see foot soldier, specialist, and manager cats, their status clearly indicated by the tools of their trade: guns, lab-coats, high-tech gear, and executive suites. By comparison, the mice we see range in age from the young child to the wizened old man, in social class from the harbour urchin through bank manager to the top brass, in ethnic or racial identity from white (signalled as unmarked) to Black (indicated via crude markers of race).

The relative homogeneity of the cats compared to the variety of the mice is worth closer attention. The narrow set of characteristics shared by all the cats mark them out as representatives of that which falls outside the norm. The norm, as a consequence, is what the cat perfidy and cruelty threaten. Given that the norm, or the desirable, is defined as that which is not feline, the norm is an accommodating category, which includes all that is mouse. Indeed, mouse society is characterized by a degree of heterogeneity, albeit illusory. The mice are imagined as ethnically mixed: markers of mouseness are shaded by markers of racial difference. Thus the hero Grabowski, and members of Intermouse (the provisional global mouse government) are coded as white. They have white or blond hair, and Anglo-American names (e.g., Nick Grabowski, John Edlington, Bob Poljakov, Lusta, and Lazy Dick) and are dressed in suits and ties (except for Grabowski, who matches high-waist light blue slacks with trainers and a blue-and-red T-shirt with a large gold G logo). The vampire bats who rescue the crash-landed Lazy Dick (István Mikó), sent to Pokyo the long way to draw attention away from Grabowski, are drawn with a dark complexion, thick stubble and thicker lips. They wear ponchos and sombreros and speak a Spanish-accented Hungarian peppered with stereotypical Mexicanisms (Figure 24.1). They are sentimental, music-loving, trigger-happy bloodsuckers. Their appetite is not only nourishment oriented but also libidinous, and in fact, the only act of bloodsucking we see involves a highly sexualized female cat as its victim. Other racial stereotypes include the street urchin in the harbour, who is drawn

FIGURE 24.1. Fat, stubbly, dark-skinned Mexican vampire bat Maxipocak (Gyula Bodrogi) tells Intermouse sergeant Lazy Dick (István Mikó) that his fate is sealed. A reprieve swiftly follows Lazy Dick's final sorrowful trumpet solo, invoking racist stereotypes of Latin passion and sentimentality, *Macskafogó/Cat City* (1986, International Publishing House IPH Kft). Frame-grab.

with a dark complexion and thick lips to suggest Blackness, and the professor and his assistant in Pokyo, who are drawn as powerfully condensed orientalist caricatures. Thus, Professor Fusimishi has a long, sparse beard and wears a lab coat over a pair of striped morning trousers, which allude to the Japanese emperor's habit of wearing a morning suit on formal occasions. His assistant Chino San (Vera Pap) wears a kimono and is stereotypically diffident (Figure 24.2). Overall, then, the mouse community is accommodating, and appears universal. By contrast, cat society is dispersed, relatively homogenous, and not associated with a specific geographical location but with the spaces of business, technology, and luxury entertainment.

Cat City may look to the West for its references, but its representation of mouse society seems to reflect a well-learned lesson about power behind the Iron Curtain. The film's opening montage of anti-mouse violence is followed by a meeting of the chief representatives of mouse society. We see a senior mouse official enter the top secret Intermouse headquarters. He has to undergo a biometric identification procedure, including tail verification and a full-body X-ray. The highest decision-making organ of the mouse establishment, hidden beyond impenetrable security arrangements (which are nonetheless breached by the all-pervading surveillance technology of the cats), is a

FIGURE 24.2. *Cat City* hero Grabovski (László Sinkó) rescues absentminded Professor Fusimishi (István Szántó) and his assistant, the demure, kimono-clad Chino San (Vera Pap) in *Macskafogó/ Cat City* (1986, International Publishing House IPH Kft). Japaneseness and Asianness are marked through clothing and orientalist tropes of diffidence and physical frailty. Frame-grab.

committee of secret policemen. The reference may be to Bond turning up in M's office to take his orders, but though we are rarely in doubt that Bond's orders, relayed by M, come from the Prime Minister, here the orders come from a moustachioed and benevolent old chairman of the committee: Bob Poljakov (Ferenc Kállai). Benevolent he may seem, but the chairman of the central committee of the secret police is the highest authority in mouse society. There is no parliament, no council, no government, just a kindly old man at a round table of secret policemen. (And they are *all* men.) The filmmakers may have sought to lampoon the West, but they ended up revealing a truth about where power resides at home: in a small committee of men, one of whom is more equal than the others.

If mouse society's police state is the desirable norm, cat society's capitalist power structure, propped up by all-pervasive surveillance technology and the military para-phernalia of Prohibition-era American gangsters, represents the repudiated and ideo-logically corrupt social arrangements associated in official state socialist discourse with the imperialist West (Figure 24.3). The cats are led by a crime syndicate chaired by Mr. Giovanni Gatto (János Körmendi), a purring, indolent white cat surrounded by a host of hostesses and personal assistants. His second-in-command, Teufel, spends most

FIGURE 24.3. Sadistic villain Fritz Teufel (Miklós Benedek) spies on the all-male central committee of the mouse secret police chaired by Bob Poljakov (Ferenc Kállai in *Macskafogó/Cat City* (1986, International Publishing House IPH Kft). Frame-grab.

of his screen time sadistically tormenting his own personal assistant, Safranek (Péter Haumann). In between meting out brutal off-screen corporal punishment for his many missteps, Teufel lectures Safranek on management principles. With Safranek's hand heavily bandaged, bearing evidence of a high price paid for a costly mistake, Teufel purrs, "You don't like me, do you, Safranek?" Safranek's stuttered reply is, "I love you, sir." Teufel approves: "Good. Staff should love their manager. This is the founding principle of the corporation." Teufel dismisses Safranek, and then dials Gatto to give a progress report on efforts to seize the cat-catcher blueprints, only to find himself on the receiving end of the same treatment: he is threatened and humiliated by his boss. Teufel rings off and collapses into his executive office chair. We then cut to Safranek's home—an American-style detached suburban house complete with porch and integrated garage—where he, in turn, sends his daughter to bed without dinner for her persistent refusal to terminate her friendship with a mouse. Although the film is grim in its assessment of the living conditions of the mice, it does not blame them for their misfortune. By contrast, the cats' permanent state of terror and victimization is rooted in their character—it is of their own making.

In addition to the stereotyped representation detailed above, the film features a number of racist jokes. One such joke is a seeming critique of racist attitudes, which puts the racist comment in the mouth of the villain. I argue, however, that given the film's enthusiastic embracement of a racial logic that underpins the narrative, the examples of racism found in the film are not anti-racist in their effect. I turn to the scene where, in response to the mice's plan to recover the blueprints for Professor Fusimishi's anti-cat device, Teufel summons Schwartz (Gyula Buss) to recommend mice who are willing to carry out covert operations for the cats. A cross between a talent agent and a pimp for assassins, a fat black cat dressed in a crumpled suit turns up. In contrast to the representation of other ethnic characters in the film, he is not marked with crude signs of race. His name is Schwartz. Although *Schwartz* means "black" in German, this is not a reference to Blackness. In the films' system of representation, Blackness is indicated through external racial markers, or corporeal inscriptions of race such as thick lips or dark skin. Although Schwartz has luxurious black fur, his muzzle is white, and his lips are pencil thin. The name Schwartz, then, must be a label of Jewishness. As he himself insists when Teufel persists in calling him plain Schwartz, he is *von* Schwartz. It is his name, and the implicit aspiration to a nobility that is denied by those around him, as well as his job, his malice, and manner of obsequious dissimulation that fully unmask him as the cunning, ambitious, boastful Jew of anti-Semitic propaganda. With contempt tinged with approval, Mr. Teufel tells him, "Schwartz, you are an extortionist." Schwartz replies with a familiarity that few risk in Teufel's presence: "Thanks for the compliment, old boy, but you are the true master." The implication is that they are cut of the same cloth. Mr. Teufel pays him and remarks, "I'll never deal with Blacks again." The tasteless double joke is that Teufel's seeming anti-Black racism is, in truth, anti-Semitic. Given the film's attribution to the cats of stereotypical characteristics associated with the figure of the Jew in anti-Semitic propaganda, the joke has a third layer: Teufel, a driver of hard bargains, a creep, and a cat who lives off the sweat of others, is a Jew-hating Jew.

It is worth pausing here to discuss the assassins on Schwartz's books: they are a gang of four rats, newly minted contract killers, having recently retired from the ballet. Schwartz presents a promotional tape to Mr. Teufel, whose disbelieving reaction to the extended musical number that acts as the gang's calling card is the exclamation, "What is this rubbish?…These are rats!" Schwartz retorts, "You're not a racist, Mr. Teufel, are you? And what if they are rats? What difference does it make?" The four make chaotic and ineffective assassins, but they are dogged in their pursuit of Grabowski, and are the only characters in the film that are neither cat nor mouse. Their loyalties and actions may be said to be rooted in race, inasmuch as *rat* is a byword for duplicity in Hungarian, as in English. Their position in an unpredictable zone of liminality is underscored by their shifting proportions: in one scene they are small enough to squeeze into Grabowski's Volkswagen Beetle; in another, the glass bottle thrown from the window of a cat-piloted biplane by Buddy (András Kern), the rat gang's leader, is big enough for Grabowski to slip into and use as a life raft after he is shipwrecked in the middle of the ocean. The rats' shifting proportions serve as a visual reminder of their duplicitous nature and their uncertain position in the film's racial hierarchy. If cats are evil, and the mice upstanding by nature, the rats' nature is to be cynical and amoral.

In a comic fight between the hapless Billy (Gyula Szombathy) and Buddy, the former calls the gang's leader a *macskabérenc*, a twist on the racist slur *zsidóbérenc* (a hireling in the pay of a Jew or the Jews). *Macska* being the Hungarian for cat, *macskabérenc* means a hireling working for the cats. The slur applied to those in their pay reveals how the filmmakers imagine the cats: as an international Jewish conspiracy.

The film's racism and anti-Semitism are not limited to stereotyped representation or use of language. It is not all so oblique. From the outset, the film fits into a broader anti-Semitic discourse underpinned by the notion of *nemzethalál*, or death of the nation, invoked repeatedly in Hungarian nationalist discourse. *Cat City* opens with a pastiche of the famous *Star Wars* crawl. As in the original it parodies, the *Cat City* crawl sketches the vision of the final destruction of a beleaguered community:

> The bloodthirsty cats organized into perfectly-equipped and highly disciplined mul-tinational gangs crudely trampling over law and order and breaching the historical conventions existing between cats and mice have sought to bring about the final de-struction of mouse society. But the mice, on the very brink of complete annihilation when the most learned mouse leaders began to contemplate the idea of planetary exodus, unexpectedly found a new ray of hope ...

This introduction, which eerily echoes the justifications of Hungary's anti-Jewish meas-ures in the 1930s,[14] resurrects the idea of an indigenous population threatened with ex-pulsion from its rightful place by a multinational criminal business organization. Not insignificantly, the film's establishing shot is of a neon-lit metropolis nestled at the feet of the easily recognized triple-peak of Budapest's Hármashatárhegy. The opening crawl's vision of mouse society on the brink of final destruction echoes the Hungarian anti-Semites' claim to the role of defenceless victim in their fatalist fantasies of a nation in the throes of death, and the concomitant grotesque misrepresentation of the true power re-lations between the dominant majority and the gradually excluded and disenfranchised Jewish minority blamed for all social, economic, and political crises and misfortunes in the interwar period. The film's plot can be seen as the last efforts of a homogenous race to stave off complete physical and economic destruction at the hands of a nationless but racially homogenous and parasitic group.

I contend that the film uses anti-Semitic stereotypes to invest its villains with cer-tain characteristics: avarice, cruelty, a tendency to exploit others, a thirst for power, and a conspiracy to subvert the established order. The scene with Mr. Teufel and (von) Schwartz illustrates how, though inferiority is constructed in the film through racial markers, Jewishness is constructed through behaviour and an attitude to power. Just as Schwartz bows and scrapes to Teufel, so Teufel bows and scrapes to his own boss. Thus, in the film's internal logic, Jewishness is a set of racially determined behaviours (we see these traits only among the cats) that can exist alongside other external racial markers, such as a swarthy complexion or thick lips. The cats are thus overinvested with markers of difference. In this system of representation, corporeal inscriptions of Blackness and Asianness are used to illustrate power. Blackness stands for a lack of intellectual or political power or both, and Asianness indicates a lack of economic or physical power (or both). Jewishness, however, is revealed in behaviour, in the need for economic, political, and cultural power, and is fixed as catness by the discourse of zoological race in the films. Thus, the idea of irreconcilable racial difference between Jew and non-Jew can be apprehended in the representation of the world as split into cats and mice, where ideas of persecution and victimhood are made manifest in raced embodiment.

CAT CITY 2: RACIAL CONFLICT, BUT NOT AN ALLEGORY

Twenty years after the original film, a sequel, *Cat City 2: Cat of Satan* (Béla Ternovszky, 2007), was released. It had been hotly anticipated, given *Cat City*'s cult status, which was strongest among those who were, by the middle of the 2000s, beginning to ascend to positions of significant cultural, economic, and political influence. It is something of a commonplace to state that the political landscape had changed dramatically over a time span of two decades, but it is worth noting just how far things had come compared to 1986. In just three short years from the film's release, Hungarian state socialism deflated like a balloon. Poland's trade union Solidarity had loosened the USSR's grip on the region, and the Hungarian foreign minister, Gyula Horn, took wire cutters to the Iron Curtain in June 1989. On October 23 of that year, the anniversary of the 1956 uprising, speaker of the Hungarian parliament, Mátyás Szűrös, declared the Hungarian Republic (as opposed to the People's Republic) and became its provisional president, with general elections called for spring 1990. When *Cat City 2* came out, four free elections later, Hungary—as a member of NATO (since 1999) and the European Union (since 2004)—was a fairly typical emerging economy in post-communist Central and Eastern Europe: accumulating public debt, putting off essential reforms, and marked by deep political divisions after decades of forcibly imposed unity. As in other countries of the region, a rapidly growing economy papered over various cracks. The infamous 2006 Balatonőszöd speech to the parliamentary MSzP party of the then newly re-elected socialist prime minister, Ferenc Gyurcsány, proved a significant flashpoint. A leaked recording of the speech, which was intended to be a sobering assessment of the reality of the country's economic situation and a rallying call for action to set the tone for the government cycle ahead, prompted riots in Budapest and has kept the socialist party—successor to the one-party system's MSzMP—out of power ever since.

With the film industry infrastructure dismantled or sold off in the early 1990s, domestic commercial film production stalled in the post-communist period.[15] The old state-owned production facility, which had originally been set up by Alexander Korda in the 1910s, was asset stripped and, by November 1994, employed just seven hundred people, down from 2,452 in 1984, and a further 428 jobs were earmarked for redundancy.[16] Alongside a continued, but declining, output of art films financed from a

Treasury-backed film fund, commercial production ground to a halt, and in 1994 not a single film was completed at Mafilm.[17] Pannónia was not spared, either. Taxpayer subsidies were discontinued,[18] and the once internationally renowned studio was asset stripped. Its old stable of filmmakers dispersed and now mostly operated freelance.[19] That a feature-length animated film was completed at all, therefore, is in itself remarkable, a testament to the enduring appeal of the original, and a perceived demand to revisit a film that had provided a foundational experience for many.[20] The sequel, for which writer Nepp and director Ternovszky teamed up once more, was not well received. Indeed, József Nepp told an interviewer in 2009 that because of the excessive interference by the producers, he had asked his script credit to be changed to "based on a script by."[21] His bitterness about the sequel, however, did not sour his relationship with Ternovszky, nor his affection for the world of *Cat City*: at the time of the interview, the pair were trying to raise funds for a prequel titled *Fight of the Vampires* (Szóró 2009). Nothing came of the project.

Cat City 2 tells the story of a primitive cat tribe in Africa that has continued to terrorize the indigenous mouse population, unaware of the mouse victory throughout the known world. The cats stumble across the truth, and summon Moloch (Gábor Reviczky), a daemon from hell, to help free their brothers, who are now kept docile with the aid of a device built into the ribbons their mice masters compel them to wear. Mouse society is ill-prepared for a cat uprising. Poljakov is in a retirement home, and Grabowski is busy with his successful spinach-canning factory. Of the original film's mouse leadership, only Edlington remains active, but he has grown complacent in his high-tech command centre. Moloch leads the insurgent cats across the electrified fence that keeps the jungle space isolated from mouse-controlled territories. Moloch defeats the mouse army, but the cat catcher is redeployed, and it pacifies all but a small number of cats, who surrender to Grabowski. In their generosity of spirit, the mice offer the cats a treaty declaring a ninety-nine-year truce, and both parties are allowed to retain all the assets they have accumulated to date. The cheesy song over the end credits, however, warns of pointy claws hidden in velvet paws, suggesting that the feline threat is biologically determined, inherent in cat embodiment, and cannot be eliminated without eliminating the cats themselves.

Just as in *Cat City*, the sequel imagines a heterogeneous and universal mouse society that accommodates a range of ethnic, racial, sexual, and class identities. More directly linked to the P. Howard novels (which also informed the original), *Cat City 2* opens with a jungle sequence: Henry Morton Stanley (Péter Rudolf) slashes through lianas and animal tails indiscriminately as he searches for Livingstone in the jungle. Although his disregard for the jungle and its inhabitants might seem to give the film an anti-colonial critical edge, any notion that we may be watching a film opposed to imperialism is immediately dispelled by the sight of Stanley's companions: "native" mice, drawn with the thick lips and dark skin we saw examples of in the original. Here, the racism is clearer, louder, and cruder: the Black mice are inferior in every way to the white mice. They are dumb, feeble (even as they are used purely for labour), ugly, and the butt of jokes. They endure servitude because they lack the courage, strength, and initiative to resist the cats who rule over them. In the original, even captured mice showed bravado in the face of cat oppression, whereas now, the Black mice of the sequel are expressions of a perceived racial hierarchy. The vampire bats are back, too, and also rendered in racist manner. We see Lazy Dick (István Mikó), sitting forlornly on the stoop of his ramshackle hut as an unseen woman nags him ceaselessly. A message in a bottle washes up at his feet: he is recalled to duty to help the mice fight off Moloch and the insurgent cats. Lazy Dick dashes off, and his wife flaps into the open: she is a thickset, pockmarked, ugly woman. Nominally Latin American, she could equally easily be read as Gypsy. Her ugliness is in her nagging, rooted in her femininity, and linked to her prolificacy, which is racially determined. There is no semblance of a critique of the orientalism that underpins capitalist exploitation (which could be perceived with a heavy dose of the benefit of the doubt in the original), and there is no affection for the character (something that is in ample evidence in the first film). The character (credited only as Dick's wife and voiced by Kati Lázár, doyenne of shrew roles) is no more than a racist caricature whose only purpose is to score cheap and cruel laughs at the expense of women of colour.

The cats, once more, are a relatively homogeneous community united by cruelty, venality, and bloodlust; but the cats of *Cat City 2* are more varied in appearance than the cats in the first film. The influence of the P. Howard novels, set in the demimondes of ports operated by European colonial powers (Singapore, Hong Kong, Oran, etc.), can easily be apprehended in the indiscriminate intermingling of the traditional garb of disparate peoples. Thus, the cats' costumes and corporeal inscriptions of racial difference condense a set of markers of colonial otherness. The leader of the cat tribe wears a kepi and military medals on his chest; another wears a Bedouin headscarf and flowing white robes; and a third sports a stack of metal rings on his neck. The colonizer's disregard for the subaltern's identity and sensibilities is made manifest in the representation of the cats. Although P. Howard's authorial position is complicated by his own precarious position as a Jew under Hungarian anti-Semitic legislation (Acts 15 of 1938 and 4 of 1939) and his satirical, irreverent colonial adventure stories can be said to reproduce the orientalism of the works they parody, *Cat City 2* was not made by an oppressed and penniless sufferer of racist state violence, but by a long-established and highly regarded creative duo able to command significant resources.[22] The representational regime of *Cat City 2* is not part of a grimly comic fantasy; it is the outcome of a position of power.

In their book on racial stereotyping in animated films, King and colleagues note that, by 1995, Disney "rejects ugly images of indigenous women [that were] still acceptable" when *Peter Pan* (Clyde Geronimi et al., 1953) was made,[23] arguing that

> in many respects "difference" has changed, or, better said, the manners in which individuals and institutions describe it, interpret it, and account for it have changed: appeals to biology have given way to culture and society; overt expressions of racism and (hetero)sexism have become taboo, replaced by covert and coded formulations.[24]

By comparison, notions of difference had not significantly changed, at least as apprehended in Hungarian popular culture, suggesting that Hungarians were still comfortable with that sort of imagery in 2007. Indeed, racism is not cited as the reason for the film's poor critical reception and box office.

In a film teeming with crude racist stereotypes and lacking the satirical bite of a dystopic vision, which did inflect the original, we see the cats subjugated and brainwashed, expropriated and disenfranchised, under total control and surveillance. They are menial labourers, assigned tasks requiring no intellectual prowess. If they take momentary breaks from work, to light a cheap cigar, for instance, they receive a painful electric shock to punish them for their idleness. The film serves up the chilling vision of a Nazi utopia: a vanquished racial foe kept in subjugation for the service of the more deserving race. The tiny tribe of primitive African cats who learn of the global rule of the master race turn to their deity, not in the heavens, or in nature, but in the depths of hell. They summon Moloch. To link this to anti-Semitism we may turn to any of the vast wealth of scholarship on anti-Jewish prejudice. For instance, Cohn's *Warrant for Genocide* notes: "In the Middle Ages Jews had been seen as agents of Satan ... it is one of the achievements of the modern anti-Semitic movement that in the late nineteenth century it was able to revive this archaic superstition."[25] The summoning spell itself ramps up the anti-Semitism: the incantation is in legalese; it is a literal contract between a people and their deity. It can be seen quite clearly that in envisioning the daemon-assisted rise of a justly oppressed race, *Cat City 2* taps into a long-running discourse of anti-Semitism and echoes the neo-Nazi trope of a job half done.

The cats and Moloch set off to break the shackles, the ribbons that bind their race. They breach the steel mesh fence (reinforced with barbed wire) that marks the boundary of the land beyond which the cats are slaves and the mice masters. They succeed in liberating some cats—chiefly the main characters of the original—and destroy much of the military capabilities of the mice. But their cause is not a just one. The cat-catcher puts an end to the reign of terror of Satan's left-hand, and the cats, defeated once more, must bow to the rightful victors, the mice. In their generosity, the mice offer the cats a settlement that leaves them with their free will and any property that they may hold. But this must be none, since they had been expropriated, disenfranchised, and enslaved for two decades. Therefore, the treaty sanctifies the seizure of cat assets that must have taken place at the end of the first film, since in the sequel, we see the mice in exclusive ownership of all wealth. And still, the film ends with the reference to sharp claws in velvet paws, a not-too-subtle reminder of the racially determined untrustworthiness of cats in their dealings with members of a race that they regard as prey.

It is worth considering this dénouement in light of the following, taken from a speech by the interwar anti-Semitic agitator László Budaváry at the national conference of the Association of Awakening Hungarians:

> We, Hungarians, have given you rights, you had a period of grace, too, some fifty years, during which you could have shown that you are fit to exercise your rights,

or not. You convinced us of the contrary, you convinced us that you have grossly abused the confidence placed in you by the nation, and therefore the sovereign nation, which granted you these rights, has the power to withdraw them, to the extent that the nation sees fit. We are happy to settle for a less than total withdrawal of your rights, and it is up to you, Jews, to convince us not to go all the way.[26]

Read against the opening crawl of the original *Cat City*, the similarities are too close for comfort: "the cats…crudely trampling over law and order and breaching the historical conventions existing between cats and mice have sought to bring about the final destruction of mouse society."

Cat City and its poor sequel both tap into the discourse of the treacherous racial enemy of the homogenous and victimized nation. Both imagine this racial enemy as having reneged on past agreements and overthrown conventions. Both films suggest that special measures are necessary to limit this racial enemy. They imply that imposing restrictions on the freedom of self-disposition of a multinational yet racially homogenous group that is working in concert to leech off the nation's wealth is a fair response to the threat it poses. It would be going too far to attribute anti-Semitic or racist intent to the filmmakers, but the reading rehearsed in this chapter indicates the troubling persistence of anti-Semitic and racist stereotype in Hungarian popular discourse, and suggests that, if anything, things have gotten worse over the past three decades.

Notes

1. See Dávid M. Kovács, "Megérdemelte a Macskafogó a ráncfelvarrást," *Index*, September 14, 2018.
2. Zoltán Varga, *A magyar animációs film: Intézmény- és formatörténeti közelítések* (Budapest: Apertúra, 2017), pp. 185–190.
3. Varga, *A magyar animációs film*, pp. 185–186.
4. See also the epic poem *Lúdas Matyi/Matt the Goose Boy*, by Mihály Fazekas (1815–1817); the novel *A beszélő köntös/The Talking Robe*, by Kálmán Mikszáth (1889); or, indeed, the Hungarian-born John Halas's adaptation of George Orwell's Animal Farm (co-directed with Joy Batchelor, 1954).
5. Gabriella Székely, "Macskafogó," *Filmvilág*, November 1986, p. 54.
6. Sanja Bahun, "The Human and the Possible: Animation in Central and Eastern Europe," in Sanja Bahun and John Haynes (eds.), *Cinema, State Socialism and Society in the Soviet Union and Eastern Europe, 1917–1989* (London: Routledge, 2014), pp. 186–208, at 190.
7. Bahun, "The Human and the Possible," p. 190.
8. Miklós Haraszti, *The Velvet Prison* (London: I.B. Tauris, 1988).
9. Ildikó Szóró, "Remekművek megrendelésre: Interjú Nepp Józseffel, a magyar rajzfilmgyártás egyik doyenjével," *Hetek*, July 10, 2009.
10. Annette Kuhn, *Cinema, Censorship and Sexuality, 1909–1925* (1988; repr. London: Routledge, 2016), p. 22.

11. See, for instance, the 1928 censorship handbook: János Bingert, *A mozgófényképüzemek és filmügyek rendészete* (Budapest: Magyar Mozi és Film, 1928). See also András Gervai, *Állami álomgyár* (Budapest: L'Harmattan, 2017), pp. 19–25.

12. Székely, "Macskafogó."

13. Ibid.

14. See Budaváry, cited in János Gyurgyák, *Ezzé lett magyar hazátok: A magyar nemzeteszme és nacionalizmus története* (Budapest: Osiris, 2007), p. 243.

15. Gervai, *Állami álomgyár*, pp. 236–263.

16. Ibid., p. 260.

17. Ibid., p. 262.

18. Varga, *A magyar animációs film*, pp. 78–79.

19. Ibid., p. 83.

20. The other animated features of the decade were the art films *A szalmabábuk lázadása/Revolt of the Straw Men* (György Palásthy, 2001) and *Ének a csodaszarvasról/Song of the Miracle Stag* (Marcell Jankovics, 2001); the "hood" comedy *Nyócker/The District* (Áron Gauder, 2004); the first fully computer-generated Hungarian animated feature, *Egon & Dönci* (Ádám Magyar, 2007); and *Kis Vuk/A Fox's Tale* (György Gát and János Uzsák, 2008).

21. Szóró, "Remekművek megrendelésre."

22. Edward Saïd, *Orientalism* (New York: Pantheon, 1978).

23. C. Richard King, Carmen R. Lugo-Lugo, and Mary K. Bloodsworth-Lugo, *Animating Difference: Race, Gender and Sexuality in Contemporary Films for Children* (Plymouth, UK: Rowman and Littlefield, 2011), p. 16.

24. King et al., *Animating Difference*, p. 16.

25. Norman Cohn, *Warrant for Genocide: The Myth of the Jewish World Conspiracy and the Protocols of the Elders of Zion* (London: Serif, 1996), p. 46.

26. János Gyurgyák, *Ezzé lett magyar hazátok: A magyar nemzeteszme és nacionalizmus története* (Budapest: Osiris, 2007), p. 243; my translation.

BIBLIOGRAPHY

Bahun, Sanja. "The Human and the Possible: Animation in Central and Eastern Europe." In Sanja Bahun and John Haynes (eds.), *Cinema, State Socialism and Society in the Soviet Union and Eastern Europe, 1917–1989*. London: Routledge, 2014, pp. 186–208.

Balogh, Gyöngyi, Vera Gyürey, and Pál Honffy. *A magyar játékfilm a kezdetektől 1990-ig*. Budapest: Műszaki Könyvkiadó, 2004.

Bingert, János. *A mozgófényképüzemek és filmügyek rendészete*. Budapest: Magyar Mozi és Film, 1928.

Cohn, Norman. *Warrant for Genocide: The Myth of the Jewish World Conspiracy and the Protocols of the Elders of Zion*. London: Serif, 1996.

Gervai, András. *Állami álomgyár*. Budapest: L'Harmattan, 2017.

Gyurgyák, János. *Ezzé lett magyar hazátok: A magyar nemzeteszme és nacionalizmus története*. Budapest: Osiris, 2007.

Haraszti, Miklós. *The Velvet Prison*. London: I.B. Tauris, 1988.

King, C. Richard, Carmen R. Lugo-Lugo, and Mary K. Bloodsworth-Lugo. *Animating Difference: Race, Gender and Sexuality in Contemporary Films for Children*. Plymouth, UK: Rowman and Littlefield, 2011.

Kuhn, Annette. *Cinema, Censorship and Sexuality, 1909–1925*. 1988. London: Routledge, 2016.

Saïd, Edward. *Orientalism*. New York: Pantheon, 1978.

Varga, Zoltán. *A magyar animációs film: intézmény- és formatörténeti közelítések*. Budapest: Apertúra, 2017.

....

CHAPTER 25

NEGOTIATING EAST AND WEST WHEN REPRESENTING CHILDHOOD IN MIYAZAKI'S *SPIRITED AWAY*

....

KATHERINE WHITEHURST

IN this chapter, I consider how the figure of the child gives us insight into the construction of the Japanese nation and culture in *Spirited Away* (Hayao Miyazaki, 2001).[1] Building on Susan Napier's 2006 article, "Matter Out of Place: Carnival, Containment and Cultural Recovery in Miyazaki's *Spirited Away*," I explore how the intersection between Eastern and Western ideologies in *Spirited Away* sees the child navigate varied cultural expectations to seek a resolution and become the embodiment of potentially utopic social change in an imagined Japan.[2] In her consideration of Japanese society, Napier asserts that "Japaneseness" is embodied in the tension between Japanese cultural identity and otherness. This division, she suggests, might be understood through the ideas of *kokusaika* (internationalization) and *furusato* (native place or old hometown).[3] Napier concludes that the negotiation of these two ideas informs the ambiguity of Japanese national identity and draws into question the viability of Japaneseness, particularly because the quintessential Japanese traits of "purity, self-sacrifice, endurance and team spirit" appear to be threatened by the homogenization seemingly promised by globalization.[4] In Napier's usage, *furusato* becomes associated with traditional Japanese values, and *kokusaika* with ideas of globalization. From this perspective, Miyazaki's exploration of cultural identity and cultural collapse in the film highlights, for Napier, "certain problematic issues, including toxicity between generations, environmental pollution and the waning of traditional mores and customs that are central to modern Japanese society."[5]

Building on Napier's consideration of *kokusaika* and *furusato*, this chapter more narrowly considers how *kokusaika*, with its associations with Western individualism and *furusato*, with its associations with Eastern collectivism, are negotiated and intertwined in Miyazaki's depiction of an imagined Japanese national identity. Thus, while Napier suggests that "the film may be viewed as an ambitious attempt at the rehabilitation of certain aspects of an idealized traditional Japan,"[6] I believe that by revisiting the ideas of *kokusaika* and individualism and *furusato* and collectivism in relation to the child, the film can be seen to highlight communal dissolution with the incorporation of neoliberalism in the modern Japanese state. Further, when read through the child, I argue that *Spirited Away* does not create a singularly nostalgic longing for past traditions but offers a utopic avenue to reimagine the nation.

In exploring the figure of the child within *Spirited Away*, I will not specifically consider the figure of the *Shōjo* (young girl).[7] Napier offers a fruitful reading of the *Shōjo* in *Spirited Away*, and the *Shōjo* has been extensively considered in relation to Miyazaki's other films and anime more broadly.[8] Instead, this chapter explores how a broader understanding of the institutionalization of childhood and of the child in Japan can provide insights into the imagined Japanese society depicted in *Spirited Away*. In detailing how the child becomes entwined in the construction and perception of the nation, I illustrate how the child on screen functions as a symbolic figure whose negotiation of national and cultural expectations reveals the structure of the nation, and the path to reimagine the potential of the state. As Stephanie Hemelryk Donald, Emma Wilson, and Sarah Wright assert in their consideration of the child on screen,

> Allegorically, the child can feel pressure from the past (even when that past is imaginary), and yet be called upon to also represent hopes for the future. This makes the child a powerful symbol for nations coming to terms with shifting political or social changes, both as a mode of representation to themselves and as a projection to the wider world.[9]

In exploring this symbolic potential of the child, I illustrate how the child in *Spirited Away* serves as a site to question past ideals of the nation, to resist neoliberal greed, and to project a hopeful future that sees Japan re-craft the interplay between Japanese collectivist values and Western individualism. To do this, I first outline how, historically, the child became entwined with the state. This historical account will frame my reading of the function of the child within *Spirited Away*.

JAPAN AND THE CHILD: THE ROLE OF THE CHILD IN NATION-BUILDING

In Japan, during the Edo period (1600–1868), the child was a part of family strategies, and contributed to household management and economic activities.[10] As Walthall asserts, "Children came to be seen as treasures to be carefully raised and educated."[11] This increased value of the child in Japanese society can be seen in the social marking of a child's development in ceremonies conducted by families, including naming ceremonies, *Kamioki* ceremonies,[12] as well as other formal changes in hair and clothing that were used to indicate a child's movement towards and into adulthood.[13] However, despite this attention and care for the child, the category of childhood during the Edo period was flexible and often determined by cultural expectations rather than a biological age.[14] As such, while the child came into increased focus during this time, it was only when children's lives were more uniformly shaped by education policies—and Japan developed further ties with the West—that modern Japan began to apply clear definitions for the state of childhood.[15]

The history of the child and the institutionalization of childhood in Japan are intertwined with the changing landscape of education in Japan. While popular schooling existed between the seventeenth and eighteenth centuries,[16] it was largely confined to wealthy commoners or the upper class.[17] Although, initially, there were restricted opportunities for education, like Europe and America, which in the seventeenth and eighteenth centuries saw the expansion of widespread education as a means to address moral ills within the community,[18] in the first half of the nineteenth century Japanese society was "inspired by the desire to regenerate their communities amidst what they perceived to be a widespread moral and economic crisis."[19] Japan's focus on education and, by extension, the development of a modern understanding of the child, mirrors the West, though as Platt notes, with a slight delay.[20] Despite these similarities, as this early educational reform and Japan's changing perception of the child occurred prior to "Japan's encounter with Western imperialism,"[21] and thus before the West demanded that Japan end its isolation, Japan was not imitating the West.[22]

Considering the relationship between the state, education, and childhood, Platt, Uno, and Stearns all assert that the rising threat of imperialism from the West led to "fundamental changes in the relationship of schooling and childhood in modern Japan."[23] In addition to "recogniz[ing] the importance of adopting Western military technology" to secure national independence,[24] a small portion of the leadership in Japan felt that Western power resided in their ability to mobilize its people.[25] As Platt notes, when the Japanese leadership set out to harness the power of their human resources, "they set about creating institutions to accomplish this goal,...[recognizing in particular the] importance of the school."[26] Japan's remodelling of its schools sees the child repositioned as a tool and resource for the nation, particularly for the government's goal of sustained independence.

The Japanese elite began to explore the educational practices that they perceived as the root of Western strength. As Pratt and Stearns both note, a team of government officials were sent to the West to report on the benefits and limitations of Western education. Japan saw the value of reflecting the West's focus on science and innovation rather than tradition, which led to a reform of their Confucian-principled education.[27] In addition to their interest in the materials taught by the West, some intellectuals in Japan felt that the education system should reflect the Western Enlightenment movement. These intellectuals felt that education should be used as a means to liberate citizens to "unlock...the potential of the individual and [to] cultivat[e] his or her independence."[28] Although the Meiji government sympathized with ideas of social enlightenment, ultimately these perspectives were not meaningfully reflected in its policies in the nine-teenth century.[29] This is not to suggest that the Meiji government completely dismissed the ideas of individualism that were at the heart of the social enlightenment movement. Instead, the government felt that individual success was only valuable if used in support of the nation and government.[30]

The state's desire to mobilize its youthful citizens through education still found reso-nance with traditional Japanese values. As Stern notes,

> Conservative counterattack against too much Western influence crystalised in a pronouncement by the Emperor in 1879. An ensuring Memorandum for teachers insisted that "loyalty to the Imperial House, love of country, filial piety toward parents, respect to superiors, faith to friends…constitute the great path of human morality."[31]

This "moralistic" framing of education saw individualistic (read: Western) ideologies set at odds with a conservative Japanese ideal. The importance of collectivism in Japanese education, though framed as a moral response, largely reflects the priorities of a vertical collectivist society, with its emphasis on hierarchies and the submission to authorities. Educating the child was seen as a way to ensure the continuance of this vertical collec-tivist system and, by extension, the Japanese nation. The Emperor's Memorandum, and its promotion of collectivist values, reflected the government's goals for a vertical col-lectivist society and highlighted Japan's mixed response to Western education and indi-vidualism. Thus, though Japan drew on some components of the West, at this time (the mid-nineteenth century) "almost no one advocated [for] complete Westernization."[32]

A central aspect of Japan's early resistance to the Western model is its balance between collectivism and individualism. Japan is often separated from the West based on its col-lectivistic nature.[33] However, as Toshie Imaga notes, "It is important to recognize that individualism and collectivism are not always the opposite, and both may coexist within a given culture."[34] This is certainly the case in the West more broadly, as well as in Japan. In the nineteenth century, Western education systems encouraged national loyalty whilst praising and encouraging individual success and achievement in the classroom, while in Japan, collective and group success was rewarded and encouraged, with indi-vidual success largely valued when in pursuit of the common good.[35] What we can see in both these models is a negotiation of collectivist and individualist models, with the West leaning more closely towards individualism with some collectivist aspects, and Japan towards collectivism with some individualist aspects. What is important to note is that while Japan did not completely accept a Western model as it was deemed too individu-alistic for the purposes of the Japanese state, Western values surrounding individualism were not completely rejected. Rather, individualism was incorporated within a broader umbrella of collectivism.

With the child caught at the centre of these changes, their identities and roles within society saw them negotiate traditional Japanese perspectives with Western ideological influences and pressures. This balance between collectivism and individualism within the education system has shifted over the years in response to Japan's relationship to the West, and has constantly placed different demands and expectations on to its young citizens. As Stearns notes, during the American occupation (1945–1952), nationalism was played down and individualism was encouraged.[36] Similarly, in the 1980s the government encouraged a movement from uniformity to diversity of expression to position Japanese youths as future competitors on the global market.[37] While we might read this as Japan's movement towards a Western, individualist frame, at the same time, as Stearns notes, there has been resistance from nationalists within Japan.[38] For example, in the 1980s nationalists argued against the government's push towards diversity of expression by asserting that Japanese children were already out-performing their global competitors in academic competitions, and that it was the rest of the world (i.e., the West) that needed to catch up to Japan.[39] This tension within the Japanese education system demonstrates how the balance between collectivism and individualism is in flux within Japan.

The child continues to be put at the epicentre of these debates, forced to negotiate a system that sees the value of individual development and innovation commonly associated with individualism, take shape within an education system which is historically structured and informed by a collectivist identity. The child must learn to negotiate Eastern and Western values through its negotiation of individualism and collectivism. We can see this interplay within the Japanese education system play out in the lives of contemporary Japanese youths. In Sugimura and Mizokami's discussion of contemporary Japanese youths, they suggest that individualism and collectivism underpin Japanese adolescents' identities and that Japanese adolescents "value 'individualistic collectivism,' enjoying individuality within a collectivistic society."[40] Although Sugimura and Mizokami are discussing adolescence, this negotiation of individualism and collectivism is reflected in the education that has informed these adolescents' early years. It is perhaps unsurprising that these youths' identities are intertwined with a negotiation of individualism and collectivism that has long been at the heart of the nation and central to the formation of the education systems that have sought to define their roles as Japanese citizens.

THE CHILD, THE NATION,
AND SPIRITED AWAY

In *Spirited Away*, the main protagonist, the child Chihiro, must navigate social systems that vary in their engagement with collectivism and individualism. Through this engagement the film highlights some of the limitations and possibilities afforded by these varying social systems. The film challenges, problematizes, and reimagines the interplay between collectivism and individualism within the broader social context of the film's primary location, the bathhouse, and the Japanese society Chihiro has come from. The chapter considers how the child is shaped by these social systems and how the child can stand as a figure of hope for the reform of these systems in the face of neoliberalism. While Chihiro's narrative is not set in a formal educational institution (like the Japanese children who had to learn to navigate individualism and collectivism within the education system), Chihiro must similarly learn to navigate the interplay between these isms as she learns about her role/place within the bathhouse. Further, as this film is, at least in part, a coming-of-age narrative, at the heart of the film is a story about emotional growth and education. As my analysis will demonstrate, Chihiro's successful navigation of the social world of the bathhouse creates a narrative of hope and reform for the future.

The Japanese social system—and, more specifically, the institute of the family at the start of the film—is marked by a lack of care between members, a strong sense of individualism and an obsession with material consumption that seems to override the importance of relationships. This Japan is far from the collectivist ideal normally associated with the country, and which we saw historically promoted within the Japanese education system. At the outset of the film, Chihiro, unlike many other Miyazaki's young protagonists, is depicted as whiny, materialistic, and self-centred. Moping about having to move, Chihiro is initially non-responsive to her parents' attempts to engage her, and refuses to be coaxed into any level of excitement about her new town or school. Instead, she becomes upset about the death of her flowers which she was given as a farewell gift. Her concern over the flowers seems, at least in part, to be rooted in their material value. This material importance becomes clear through Chihiro's complaint about having received her first bouquet of flowers when she was moving. Though she is reminded that she was given a rose for her birthday, her dismissal of the flower, remarking, "One rose isn't a bouquet", sees the value of the rose diminished due to the limited quantity of flowers given in comparison to a bouquet. This dismissal suggests that the sentiment behind the giving is not as important as the material value of what has been given. Similarly, rather than remarking on how sad it is to leave her friends, her claim that it is sad that she has only received a bouquet upon her departure again suggests that the material item has been elevated above the relationships they represent. Finally, in not noticing that she has in fact dropped the card that has accompanied her flowers, she puts less value in the symbolic gesture of care and friendship that the card, alongside the flowers, represents.

This suggests that Chihiro is, at least to some degree, a materialistic child, and it highlights her individualism. Her lack of expressed care for the friends she is leaving behind shows her fixated on her own wants and needs. Similarly, her sullenness suggests that she can't look beyond herself to consider the challenge this move poses to her parents. Within this opening scene, her mother expresses a concern about the isolation of the new residence, and seeks to remind Chihiro that this day is a big one for all of the family. In highlighting the challenges the family, and she in particular, might be facing as a result of this move, she draws attention to how Chihiro's self-pity and inward-looking behaviour has blinded her to the needs and concerns of her parents. Chihiro's individualism reflects early concerns in Japan about the impact individualism would have on the formation and stabilization of a collective, with the family standing in for the collective in this instance. Her indifference to her family's needs, concerns, and desires also puts her at odds with traditional Japanese values of filial piety towards parental figures, and sees her embody the breach from Japanese morality that was feared would occur through Western influences.

Chihiro is not alone in her individualism and materialism. As Napier notes, "Not only are the parents shown as dependent on credit cards and imported cars, they are also completely insensitive to their daughter."[41] Her mother and father are both depicted as strongly individualistic and focused on ownership, consumer power, and consumption. This focus sees them repeatedly drawn away from the relationships that surround them and distracts them from the mutual care they might otherwise provide. For example, rather than speaking to Chihiro about why she is sad, her mother instead remarks on her own concerns about the nearness of the shops in which she might buy material goods. Similarly, when Chihiro becomes concerned that they may have become lost en route to the new house, her father fails to respond to her concerns, instead asserting, "We're fine, we've got four-wheel drive." Not only does this reply not answer Chihiro's question about being lost, but it suggests that the ownership of the car justifies his dismissal of both his daughter's and later his wife's concerns.

Materialism and individualism are depicted as centrally entwined in the characters' relationship to the world around them and are framed as the central factors in their isolation from one another. One example of this is when the family seeks to cross a stone river to visit what they think is a theme park that went bust in the 1990s. The father is depicted reaching back to help his wife across the stone river. However, catching the smell of food, his attention is redirected to the food they might buy and eat. Allowing his arm to go limp, he no longer seeks to provide support for his wife, and she is depicted stumbling forwards into him. Similarly smelling the same food, Chihiro's mother makes no effort to help her, and instead instructs her to hurry up. Chihiro, shown struggling over the rocks on her hands and feet, is left by her mother and father to cross the stone river on her own, despite her calls for them to wait. In this moment we see a chain of disconnection, as the care that might be offered amongst the family members are abandoned in the pursuit of consumption and individual pleasure.

Napier suggests that "from the opening shots of Chihiro's sullen family in the Audi, Miyazaki is clearly setting up a contrast between a materialistic and de-territorialized modern Japan and a more authentic indigenous Japan and doing so in a far more critical style than anything in his previous work."[42] Rather than concluding that this negative portrayal is a depiction of modern Japan as Miyazaki interprets it, I would suggest, instead, that the parents' individualism and consumptive practices provide a means to interrogate the relationship between individualism, consumerism, and neoliberalism. Whether the parents' sudden drive for immediate consumption is a reflection of the lives they already live or is influenced by their arrival in the theme park with its connections to the 1990s bust (i.e., the neoliberal consumerism associated with this period) is not clear. What the spectator is positioned to see is how an imbalance between collectivism and individualism in a neoliberal society leads to the decay of the family unit.

This collapse of the family unit, brought about by a fixation with consumption and individual desire, comes to the forefront as Chihiro is left to wander the empty theme park on her own while her parents distractedly eat large quantities of food without restraint or regulation. Chihiro is depicted at the corner of a long and empty street (Figure 25.1). This image not only highlights how the child becomes isolated within her family, but the film links this empty space to a broader, shared culture that is seemingly empty of substance.

The architecture of the theme park, which Miyazaki has described as pseudo-Western, is modelled on houses and shops from the Meiji and Taishō periods, periods that were influenced by Japan's relationship with the West. While one might read this Western reference as an insinuation that the greed and consumption that has isolated the family is a result of Western influences. As Yoshioka notes,

> By "pseudo-Western" Miyazaki means a style that mixes Western and traditional Japanese features.... One of the reasons Miyazaki gives for adopting this style is to emphasize the rich diversity that makes up traditional Japanese culture.... Miyazaki sees the Japanese pseudo-Western styles as itself "traditional" since it is a bricolage of the newest bits and pieces added to a dynamically evolving Japanese culture.[43]

As a facade of Japanese history that was recreated and rooted in a period (the 1990s) marked by materialistic mass consumption, the theme park's representation of Japanese culture is seemingly hollowed out by the capitalistic manipulation of heritage for consumer purposes. In this way, instead of depicting a society that has lost its way through Westernization, this scene suggests that the rich diversity found in Japanese culture is

FIGURE 25.1. Chihiro is depicted in isolation and surrounded by a facade of Japanese history that has been created for consumer purposes in *Spirited Away* (2001, Studio Ghibli). Frame-grab.

lost through the privileging of neoliberal consumerist values, and an over-emphasis on individualism within this system.

Though Chihiro starts off in an environment heavily weighted towards individualism and neoliberalism, as she leaves the theme park and becomes situated in the bathhouse, she must learn to navigate a collectivist system that is tinged with elements of individualism. The bathhouse is most obviously situated as a vertical collective. Vertical Collectivism emphasises hierarchies where people must "submit to authorities or large group to the point of self-sacrifice".[44] Individual desires are contained within this vertical collectivism as Yubaba, the witch who runs the bathhouse, controls the flow of goods and services, designates roles and positions within the bathhouse, enforces staff subservience through their labour, claims their name and thus symbolically their identities, and uses her power threateningly. This vertical collectivism broadly reflects the conservative elements of the early Japanese education system and moral values, and the Meiji government's efforts to mobilize its citizens in support of the nation. While one might be tempted to read this vertical collectivism as reflective of a traditional Japan, as detailed in the above consideration of Japanese education policies, this conservative promotion of vertical collectivism was as much shaped by a fear and response to the West. As such, these values do not simply reflect Japanese values, but a Japanese negotiation of *furusato* and *kokusaika*.

The negotiation of Japan and the West is hinted at in the bathhouse through the use of dialogue and costume. Two clear examples of Western influence can be seen shortly after Chihiro arrives at the bathhouse. Sent by Haku (Yubaba's apprentice) to Kamaji (who runs the bathhouse's boilers) to request work, Chihiro is unsuccessful in obtaining work from him. However, he puts her in the care of Lin, a bathhouse attendant, instructing Lin to bring Chihiro to Yubaba so that she can request employment. After Chihiro thanks Kamaji for this help, he replies to her in English, stating "good luck". Kamaji's use of English suggests that the bathhouse is not isolated within a purely Japanese past, but is linked to the Western world.[45] Similarly, when first introduced to Yubaba, despite her role as the ruler of a Japanese bathhouse, she wears a nineteenth century Western-styled dress. These Western references suggest that the bathhouse is not a purely Japanese space, but rather reflects the diversity found in Japanese culture. As such, while Napier suggests that the bathhouse is "dangerously vulnerable to cultural pollution from various forms of otherness",[46] I would argue that it is not cultural pollution that threatens the bathhouse, but, as I will demonstrate, neoliberalism that threatens the collective strength of the bathhouse, and by extension the nation.

Despite the dominance of the vertical collectivist system within the bathhouse, the bathhouse is not devoid of individualism. Individualism takes shape in two forms within the bathhouse. One form of individualism is informed by self-reliance, initiative, and self-realisation which benefit the group. The other form of individualism is informed by anarchy, greed, and social atomisation that make it vulnerable. In terms of strengthening the collective, Chihiro is taught the value of individualism when it works in support of the collective. This lesson reflects the values taught to children in Japan following the educational reforms of the Meiji government. For example, when set the task to care for what is mistakenly believed to be a stink god, Chihiro is shown determinately trying to clean the creature, and seeking to find her own solutions to do so, namely by refilling the tub with the herbal soak. In so doing, she discovers a "thorn" in his side. The presence of this "thorn" signals to Yubaba that this is not a stink god. With Lin's help, and subsequently help from the rest of the bathhouse attendants, Chihiro removes a bicycle and other garbage from the god, revealing a river god beneath. The River god rewards Chihiro individually, through the gifting of a magic dumpling, and the bathhouse through the payment of gold. Chihiro's individual success for the collective is reaffirmed and celebrated by Yubaba when she hugs Chihiro, observes that Chihiro has made them a fortune and that others could learn from her, and that sake is on the house. In this moment, Yubaba reaffirms Chihiro's individual value/contribution, recognizes her as a part of the bathhouse rather than an outsider, and gains her favour with the rest of the attendance through the shared reward of sake. While the stink god scene is often read as a critique of environmental and/or spiritual pollution,[47] this scene also gives insight into how individualism is partnered with vertical collectivism in the bathhouse, with Chihiro's initiative seeing her gain confidence, find her place within the bathhouse and sees the collective strengthened, primarily in economic terms.

The bathhouse also contains scenes where individualism undermines the order and power structure of the vertical collective. For example, at the start of the film, Lin is bribed by Kamaji with a roast newt to go against Yubaba's will in aiding Chihiro to get a job. Lin's desire for the newt outweighs her concern about Yubaba's wishes and the potential punishment she might receive if she gets caught. Lin's individual desires and greed pose a threat to the structure and power Yubaba seeks to enforce. While these small acts of individualism don't ultimately disrupt the vertical collectivist structure, under a neoliberal influence, these desires become catastrophic for the community.

Neoliberalism is embodied within the bathhouse in the character No Face. Scholars have read No Face allegorically as "a scathing indictment of the ethos of 'consumerism,'"[48] as a figure representing "a lonely young Japanese person who does not know how to make friends,"[49] or as both the "emptiness and desire…[of] the contemporary soul…[and the] grotesque body…of repressed Japanese tradition."[50] Building on Alistair Swale's and Tai Wei Lim's assertions, I contend that No Face is a figure of neoliberal economics.

When we are introduced to No Face, the unlimited production, innovation, and capitalism promised by neoliberalism through deregulation takes utopic form. This becomes clear when No Face helps Chihiro navigate around the bathhouse's power structure, which is inhibiting her from completing her job to the best of her ability. Sent by Lin to the foreman to request a token for an herbal soak for the large tub, Chihiro is denied the token and instructed to clean the tub by hand. No Face, appearing behind the foreman, turns invisible before selecting a token and giving it to Chihiro. After Chihiro has successfully filled the tub, No Face joins her in the tub room and offers her multiple tokens, for which she has no immediate use. She turns down his offer, and he disappears, leaving the tokens behind. Shortly after this exchange, Chihiro finds herself in need of the additional tokens to clean the river god. When Yubaba questions how she has come into possession of these tokens, the spectator is reminded of how No Face has enabled Chihiro to bypass the regulations that would otherwise have inhibited her from completing her job and helping the river god. In this way, Chihiro's engagement with No Face initially represents the promise of neoliberalism through de-regulation.

However, as No Face interacts with the other bathhouse attendants, his propensity for deregulated greed and consumption becomes destructive to the vertical collective. His influence becomes clear after the bathhouse attendants rush to collect the gold the river god has left behind. Yubaba insists that the gold belongs to the bathhouse, rather than to individual bathhouse attendants. When they are told that they must hand over the gold, the attendants begin to complain. No Face briefly comes into view behind the characters during this scene. Whether No Face's presence influences the characters' greed in this moment is not entirely clear. However, as No Face is shown briefly looking down at his hand, the one he later uses to produce gold to give to the attendants, the desire and greed the attendants show in this moment becomes the avenue for the deregulation that No Face subsequently explores and exploits.

Like the individualist world that Chihiro comes from, the vertical collectivist society of the bathhouse, and the relationships fostered within this environment, are similarly threatened by neoliberalism. Just as Chihiro finds acceptance and belonging within the bathhouse, the emergence of No Face sees her similarly abandoned and isolated within her community. Waking from a nightmare, Chihiro, for the first time since arriving at the bathhouse, finds herself alone. All the other attendants who share a room with Chihiro, including her friend Lin, have left her upstairs while they go in pursuit of No Face's gold. This gold, given to the individual rather than the bathhouse in exchange for food, drink, and attention, frames the attendants' material pursuit as driven by individual desires and greed.

As No Face's consumptive practices and the bathhouse attendants' financial gain is unregulated, this exchange can be read as a neoliberal economic relationship. This exchange is largely framed as exploitative, not only in terms of how the bathhouse attendants are exploiting the bathhouse by keeping the money for themselves, but also in their treatment of other staff, such as Kamaji, who, woken to work outside his normal hours, is described by Lin as in a "foul mood." Because Kamaji works in the boiler room and thus does not have access to No Face, it is unlikely that he is receiving additional payment for this labour. As the rules and order of the bathhouse become deregulated, the economic balance and the consumptive practices within the bathhouse become lawless, exploitative, highly individualistic, and centred on greed.

When Yubaba first learns about No Face, she asserts that the bathhouse attendants' greed has attracted No Face to the bathhouse. This suggests that the attendants are desiring subjects despite, or more likely as a result of, their position within a vertical collective. In fact, one might argue that the greed the bathhouse attendants display stems from the desire for escape and freedom that the bathhouse's vertical collective inspires. Prior to No Face's admittance into the bathhouse, characters such as Lin and Haku express a desire to escape the bathhouse and Yubaba's control. As this desire later fuels the greed characters display when seeking gold from No Face, the repressive nature of the vertical collective seemingly creates the initial space for greed to be developed.

The bathhouse is, of course, a business centrally concerned with capital. Despite the collectivist structure, its collectivism is predicated on making money rather than promoting the relationships within the collective. For this reason, the vertical collectivist structure, like the individualist world Chihiro comes from, is easily undermined and corrupted, as the pursuit of capital falls under the influence of neoliberalism.

With the bathhouse attendants distracted by neoliberal greed, Chihiro repeatedly finds herself alone. This is first represented, as indicated above, through her waking up without the company and care of Lin and the other attendants. However, she is also made to deal, in isolation, with the monster No Face has become. Where she was aided by and part of a team when she was seeking to help the river god, despite his repulsive smell, when she faces No Face she is shoved into a room while other attendants and Yubaba wait outside. When the foreman asks Yubaba if Chihiro is safe alone in the room with No Face, Yubaba asks if he would like to take her place, which evidently, he does not. The child is no longer supported by her community and is left to face this challenging and dangerous situation alone. This suggests that, as neoliberalism is introduced within a vertical collective, the communal support that would otherwise occur when facing group challenges is eradicated, while the expectations of one's submission to those in power or a large group are maintained. This creates a deeply fractured, repressive, and destructive community.

In addition to the neglected and/or exploited relationships brought about by this neoliberal greed, the bathhouse and, as a result, the attendants, experience a financial loss from taking part in neoliberal activities. Mirroring the financial crash in the 1990s brought about by poor lending practices and bad debt, the bubble created through No Face's consumption bursts when, shortly after his departure, the gold he provided degrades into sand. The expense of his consumption and the staff's labour result in financial loss for the bathhouse and the community as a whole. Thus, neoliberalism is revealed as socially and financially destructive when incorporated within a vertical collective.

When Chihiro leads No Face from the bathhouse, she concludes that he does not belong there, and that he becomes ill, or rather corrupted, in the bathhouse. When asked by Lin where No Face should be taken, Chihiro indicates that she is not sure. To Chihiro's knowledge, there exist two worlds, her world and that of the bathhouse. Her assertion that she is not sure where No Face should go suggests that his unregulated behaviour is a threat in either of these social structures.

In fact, the corruption of the bathhouse reflects the corruption found in Chihiro's own world. The selfishness of her parents, their consumptive habits, emotional disconnection, and reference to the economic crash in the 1990s that led Japan into a recession, all mirror the destructive force of No Face within the bathhouse. In recognizing neoliberalism as problematic for the bathhouse's vertical collectivism, and having this problematic relationship mirror the interplay between neoliberalism and individualism in

Chihiro's own world, the film asks us to reconsider how collectivism, individualism, and neoliberal values can be rebalanced within an imagined Japan.

As Chihiro's goals and desires are not materialistic (instead, she wishes to be reunited with her family and to save Haku), No Face's neoliberal excess has nothing to offer her. As Chihiro tells No Face, "You can't help me with what I want." This suggests that neoliberal excess cannot foster community and personal relationships. In privileging the value of personal relationships, Chihiro's engagement with the collectivist system of the bathhouse is horizontal in nature. Horizontal collectivism occurs when "equality and harmony is emphasized and people engage in mutual sharing and caring."[51] Of course, this horizontal engagement is not innate to Chihiro's character. At the start of the film, she is a materialistic, selfish, and individualistic child. Her lack of care for others suggests that prior to arriving at the bathhouse she did not engage in the mutual sharing and caring found within horizontal collectivism.

Instead, she learns these skills in the bathhouse, where (under the surface of vertical collectivism) there exists an undercurrent of horizontal collectivism. For example, though in public Lin and Haku are initially dismissive of Chihiro and treat her as an inferior within a vertical collectivist system, in private, they draw attention to the performative nature of their dismissive attitude and reaffirm their caring positions. Thus, while Lin publicly complains when Chihiro is assigned to be her assistant, in private she draws attention to the performative nature of her complaints by enthusiastically congratulating Chihiro on securing work and by helping Chihiro settle in. Lin and Haku care for Chihiro by finding and helping to secure her work in the bathhouse, bringing her food to help her recover during stressful times, and by supporting her endeavour to save her parents. Lin and Haku are not alone in this generosity. Kamaji cares for Chihiro by helping her to obtain work, by covering her in a blanket when she has fallen asleep below him, and by providing her with train tickets when she wishes to seek out Zeniba (Yubaba's twin sister) to save Haku. As Chihiro flourishes under this encouragement and support, her relationship to both individualism and collectivism shifts, moving from the dominance of individualism and vertical collectivism, towards the caring and supportive structure of horizontal collectivism.

Relationships rooted in caring help Chihiro to navigate the world of the bathhouse and enable her to maintain her identity within the vertical collective. For example, shortly after signing a contract with Yubaba in which Chihiro trades her name, and by extension her identity, in exchange for work, Haku takes Chihiro to see her parents, who have been transformed into pigs. Upset about her parents' transformation, Chihiro experiences two acts of kindness, one new and one renewed, that help to restore her sense of self. The first act of kindness and caring comes from Haku, who returns Chihiro's clothing from her world to her. Her clothes serve as a reminder of where Chihiro has come from and are items she will need to eventually return to her world. In returning the clothes, Chihiro discovers within them the card that had originally accompanied her flowers. Here, the material value of the flowers is usurped by the symbolic value of the farewell card, with her friend's farewell note reminding Chihiro of her own name and identity. Her friend's original act of caring is renewed because now Chihiro knows and appreciates the value of the sentiment the card expresses (of knowing and caring for Chihiro). It is through these relationships that Chihiro maintains her sense of self and individualism in the repressive structure of Yubaba's bathhouse.

Although the importance of horizontal collectivism to Chihiro's development is apparent in Yubaba's vertical collective, it is an undercurrent rather than the dominant structure within the bathhouse. In contrast, in Zeniba's home, horizontal collectivism and individualism are privileged. This is demonstrated in three ways: firstly, upon the arrival of Chihiro, No Face, Bôh (Yubaba's baby, who has been transformed into a mouse), and Yubaba's bird, Zeniba seeks to care for them, providing them with tea, cakes, biscuits, and rest. Unlike the initially threatening space of the bathhouse, Zeniba's home is a place of care. Secondly, her differing approach is seen through her description of her relationship to Yubaba. She asserts: "My sister and I are two halves of one whole, but we really don't get along." If we read this whole as collectivism more broadly, Yubaba and Zeniba can be seen to represent two different aspects of collectivism, vertical and horizontal, with the power and repressive potential of Yubaba's vertical collectivism seemingly at odds with the equality and care found in Zeniba's horizontal collectivism.

Finally, Zeniba is aligned with horizontal collectivism through her engagement with the principles of equality, mutual sharing, and caring. This is seen in Zeniba's crafting of a hairband that she says will protect Chihiro. When making this hairband she works with and alongside No Face, Bôh, and Yubaba's bird to spin and knit the hairband. She is depicted kindly teaching and praising the work of Chihiro's friends, who have willingly taken up the labour. Their shared labour reinforces a horizontal collectivist value of equality. Further, as this hairband is intended to protect Chihiro, the labour behind this effort is also driven by care.

Zeniba reinforces the power of horizontal collectivism by asserting that magic alone could not do what they have collectively accomplished when creating the hairband. In suggesting that their shared labour and care is more powerful than magic, Zeniba undermines the seemingly all-powerful strength of Yubaba—who rules through the use of magic alone—and by extension, the hierarchal power found in the vertical structure of Yubaba's bathhouse. Zeniba's assertion thus suggests that the power of the vertical structure is inferior to a horizontal collectivist structure. As Chihiro already embodies the values found within a horizontal collective prior to arriving at Zeniba's home, Zeniba's assertion serves to reaffirm Chihiro's wisdom and strength, while also pointing towards her future potential. Reflecting Donald, Wilson, and Wright's consideration of the child on screen,[52] Chihiro's social alignment and future potential sees her function as a symbolic tool representing the potential for social change and the hope for the future.

The end product of No Face, Bôh, Yubaba's bird, and Zeniba's work is a very small hairband. Unlike the gift of the rose that Chihiro dismissed at the start of the film due to its limited material value, she now remarks on the hairband's value by commenting on its beauty and by thanking them for making it for her. Her acceptance of the hairband highlights her growth and development as a character as she is distinguished from the materialistic and selfish child she was at the start of the film. Yet, despite this movement away from materialistic greed, Chihiro is not expected to abandon her individualism.

Individualism is equally incorporated within the horizontal collectivism found in Zeniba's home. Unlike the bathhouse, Zeniba lives in a thatched cottage. This architecture makes a clear reference to Western culture and, by extension, the individualism associated with this culture. Paired with this architecture, Zeniba seems to live in isolation.

In considering the markers of an individualist society, Ogihara asserts that Household size is another behavioural indicator of individualism. [...] [I]n individualistic societies, family relationships are more likely to be freer and looser, leading people to live separately and independently of other family members.[53] Zeniba's isolation within her home (she appears to be the only occupant) and from her sister further links her—and thus the social system in which Chihiro is immersed by staying with Zeniba—to individualism. This link to individualism is seen in her conversations with Chihiro. After asking for Zeniba's help, Zeniba tells her that while she would like to help Chihiro, she cannot. She then informs Chihiro that Chihiro will have to save her parents and Haku on her own. This emphasis on Chihiro's own agency sees a privileging of individual action, and repositions it as important to Chihiro's own development and success. Rather than framing individualism as something to avoid, the film firmly roots individualism and individual action as central to the success and resolution Chihiro seeks.

Consequently, Zeniba promotes a horizontal collectivism that incorporates individual initiative and action. As Chihiro actively responds to and reflects the care provided through this system, with Chihiro saving both Haku and her parents, this combination of collectivism and individualism fosters growth and stability. In some ways, the film's pairing of individualism and collectivism reflects the values of the Meiji government, particularly its belief that individual success was of value when in support of the collective. However, as the Meiji government's incorporation of individualism within a collectivist frame largely saw individualism as ideally working in support of the nation and government, individualism was imagined and contained within a vertical collectivist structure. In contrast, the film depicts individualism within a horizontal structure, as Chihiro's individual actions provide care for community members, namely her parents, Haku, No Face, and the bathhouse attendants more broadly. The use of individualism to pursue the values of horizontal collectivism both harkens back to Japan's past (namely the confinement of individualism within collectivism), without directly reflecting or idealizing a past rhetoric that confines individualism within vertical collectivism.

The horizontal collectivism and individualism embodied by Zeniba and Chihiro is presented as the means to control and regulate No Face and, by extension, neoliberalism. This becomes apparent in Chihiro's resistance to No Face's offers in the bathhouse, as detailed previously, in her regulation of No Face's behaviour and in Chihiro's ability to find No Face a home. Travelling to Zeniba's home, Chihiro tells No Face that he can come with her as long as he behaves. No Face's accompaniment of Chihiro as she leaves the bathhouse is symbolic of her liberation from the rules and regulations of the bathhouse. However, as she has moved beyond the confines of the bathhouse to save Haku and protect the bathhouse, this de-regulation does not derive from a place of greed but a place of respect and care. It is notable that, on this journey, No Face once again becomes unthreatening and is seemingly controlled by the purpose and drive of Chihiro's goal. Chihiro's engagement with the values found in horizontal collectivism consequently control and regulate the neoliberalism No Face embodies.

When Chihiro and her companions (No Face, Bôh, and Yubaba's bird) enter Zeniba's home, No Face remains placid. Even when provided with food and drink, No Face's consumption remains confined as he eats slowly with a fork and does not request further food. Zeniba also includes No Face and the others in the production of the hairband. Yet again, instead of engaging in excess, No Face does not seek to create more hairbands than required. As he becomes neither monstrous in his consumption or his production, the excess and greed associated with neoliberalism is controlled, while the deregulation, creativity and utopic production promised by neoliberalism is mobilized for the care of others. It is notable that, as Chihiro prepares to return to the bathhouse and subsequently her home, No Face does not accompany her. Instead, Zeniba asks him to stay and be her helper, and No Face agrees. Consequently, the question of where No Face belongs is resolved as he is seemingly managed within the horizontal structure of Zeniba's home and the individualism it incorporates.

The film ends with Chihiro wearing the hairband created for her in the spirit of horizontal collectivism and individualism. As No Face participated in the creation of this hairband, it is also associated with his neoliberal nature. Chihiro's wearing of the hairband suggests that she carries with her the knowledge of an alternative way to live in a neoliberal society. The ending of *Spirited Away* is in some ways ambiguous. It ends much as it began with Chihiro clutching to her mother as they go back through the tunnel that had brought them to the spirit world. Although Chihiro's regression casts doubt over whether she remembers her time in the spirit world, as Zeniba told her during their visit, "Nothing that happens is ever forgotten, even if you can't remember it." Zeniba's words haunt this scene and suggest that the values Chihiro has learned will not be forgotten. This notion is reaffirmed as the film draws the spectator's attention to the hairband as a bright light emanates from it in a close up shot of Chihiro (Figure 25.2).

In drawing attention to the hairband the audience is reminded not only of her journey and education, but the values that are embodied by the hairband. As the carrier of this hairband, Chihiro becomes the hope for the future of Japanese society, with the negotiated values of horizontal collectivism and individualism that are represented by the hairband serving as the means to combat the destabilizing elements of neoliberalism.

This same reading cannot be applied to the dubbed English-language version of the film released by Disney. In the Hollywood version of this film, the ending is less ambiguous. As Adachi notes, "The English translation of *Spirited Away* has 16 lines in total that are added as voice-overs,"[54] five of which are added in the final scene. In an exchange with her parents in the final scene, both parents try to comfort Chihiro about starting at a new school. Their remarks are met with an upbeat reply from Chihiro that "[she] thinks [she] can handle it". In concluding the film with a resolution centrally focused on Chihiro's coming to terms with the family's move, the broader social and national discourse found in the Japanese version is replaced with a more traditional (Western)

FIGURE 25.2. Attention is brought to Chirhiro's hairband, as its glow reminds the spectator of the journey she has undergone, *Spirited Away* (2001, Studio Ghibli). Frame-grab.

coming-of-age ending, rooted in narratives of personal growth and development of the kind that typically underpin Hollywood family films. Further, Chihiro's newfound confidence in her own abilities align her with the ideologies of exceptionalism and individualism that are commonly found and celebrated in Disney films. She is presented as uniquely capable of handling her family's move and of rescuing Haku and her parents.

Finally, where Zeniba asserts in the Japanese version of the film that "nothing that happens is ever forgotten", in the Disney version Zeniba alternatively states "once you've met someone you never really forget them." In rooting remembrance in a person rather than in a happening, the film closes down the possibility that Chihiro will remember an alternative way to live in society and instead suggests that she won't really forget Haku. This puts emphasis on individual and personal (romantic) relationships rather than her place and role in broader society. As the dialogue in the Hollywood version spends more time emphasizing the love between Chihiro and Haku, the potential for her to remember the love between herself and Haku is given a higher priority. The differences between the two versions reveal their variant ideological framings, with each version of the film speaking to different national ideologies and perspectives.

Throughout the Japanese version of this film, Chihiro must navigate the different expectations set for her within social systems that incorporate various elements of individualism and collectivism. Chihiro's journey reflects the journey of many Japanese youths who have had to negotiate an education system that, at different periods, has valued different aspects of individualism and collectivism. In reflecting the early debates around education and the values and systems that will help to create a strong and stable Japan, *Spirited Away* highlights the strengths and limitations of these systems as they become intertwined with neoliberalism. The film suggests that the high level of individualism often associated with the West and the vertical collectivism that is clearly present throughout Japan's history are both susceptible to the greed and social abuse often caused as a result of neoliberal excess and deregulation. Rather than seeking to eradicate neoliberalism, the film—through the child's journey—suggests that society can make use of neoliberalism by containing it within a system that balances horizontal collectivism with individualism. As Chihiro's accomplishments highlights the success of this balance between neoliberalism, individualism, and horizontal collectivism, the child embodies how this social structure might take physical manifestation within society more broadly.

In understanding the deep ties between Japan and the West, and the way this relationship has shaped the history of the child in Japan, it becomes clear that the historical periods to which the film refers reflect the interplay between East and West that has long been at the heart of Japanese society. The Japanese version of *Spirited Away* reflects this long-standing relationship in its depiction of both "modern" and "historic" Japan. The film's negotiation of Western individualism and Eastern collectivism does not put these two systems at odds with each other. Instead it explores how the various manifestations of the interplay between these systems can leave society vulnerable to or protect citizens from the exploitative aspects of neoliberalism. Further, as the child, historically, has played a significant role in the shaping of the Japanese nation, the use of the child in the resolution of the problems caused by neoliberalism suggests that the child's success is the success of the nation. Rather than simply presenting a coming-of-age narrative, in the Japanese version, the conclusion is less about the future potential of Chihiro as it is about the future potential of her society as it evolves in a neoliberal world.

Notes

1. This article is based on a subtitled version of the Japanese film. I have indicated in text when I refer or compare the Japanese version of the film to Disney's version of the film.
2. Susan Napier, "Matter out of Place: Carnival, Containment, and Cultural Recovery in Miyazaki's 'Spirited Away,'" *Journal of Japanese Studies* 32:2 (2006), pp. 287–310, at 287.
3. Napier, "Matter out of Place.", pp. 287–288.
4. Ibid., p. 289.
5. Ibid., p. 291.
6. Ibid.
7. The *Shōjo* is an iconic figure in Japanese popular culture. The *Shōjo* is a depiction of the feminine rooted in liminality. Neither a child nor an adult, this figure is a representation of girlhood rooted in cute culture. The figure is often linked to purity, female beauty, and traditional femininity. See Napier, "Matter out of Place," and Saito, "Magic, Shōjo, and Metmorphosis," for further discussion.
8. See Napier, "Matter out of Place"; Susan Napier, *Anime from Akira to Princess Mononoke: Experiencing Contemporary Japanese Animation* (New York: Palgrave, 2001); Kukhee Choo, "Girls Return Home: Portrayal of Femininity in Popular Japanese Girls' Manga and Anime Texts during the 1990s in Hana Yori Dango and Fruits Basket," *Women: A Cultural*

Review 19:3 (2008), pp. 275–296; Kumiko Saito, "Magic, 'Shōjo,' and Metamorphosis: Magical Girl Anime and the Challenges of Changing Gender Identities in Japanese Society," *Journal of Asian Studies* 73:1 (2014), pp. 143–164; Mark W. MacWilliams, ed., *Japanese Visual Culture: Explorations in the World of Manga and Anime* (Armonk: M.E. Sharpe, 2008); and Frenchy Lunning, "Under the Ruffles: Shōjo and the Morphology of Power," *Mechademia* 6:1 (2011), pp. 3–19.

9. Stephanie Hemelryk Donald, Emma Wilson, and Sarah Wright (eds.), *Childhood and Nation in Contemporary World Cinema: Borders and Encounters* (New York: Bloomsbury, 2017), p. 2.

10. Luke S. Roberts, "Growing Up Manly: Male Samurai Childhood in Late Edo-Era Tosa," in Sabine Frühstück and Anne Walthall (eds.), *Child's Play: Multi-sensory Histories of Children and Childhood in Japan* (Oakland: University of California Press, 2017), pp. 41–59, at 42.

11. Anne Walthall, "For the Love of Children: Practice, Affect, and Subjectivities in Hirata Atsutane's Household," in Frühstück and Walthall, *Child's Play*, pp. 60–80, at 60–61.

12. A Kamioki ceremony marked the infant's becoming a toddler. According to Roberts, it took place around the age of three, and saw sons and daughters grow out their shaved hair. See Roberts, "Growing Up Manly."

13. Roberts, "Growing Up Manly," pp. 43–44.

14. Or Porath, "Nasty Boys or Obedient Children? Childhood and Relative Autonomy in Medieval Japanese Monasteries," in Frühstück and Walthall, *Child's Play*, pp. 17–40, at 17.

15. Peter N. Stearns, *Childhood in World History* (New York: Routledge, 2006), p. 77.

16. Kathleen Uno, "Civil Society, State, and Institutions for Young Children in Modern Japan: The Initial Years," *History of Education Quarterly* 49:2 (2009), pp. 170–181, at 173.

17. Brian Platt, "Japanese Childhood, Modern Childhood: The Nation-State, the School, and 19th-Century Globalization," *Journal of Social History* 38:4 (2005), pp. 965–985 (p. 976).

18. Colin Heywood, *A History of Childhood: Children and Childhood in the West from Medieval to Modern Times* (Cambridge, UK: Polity Press, 2017), pp. 21–22.

19. Platt, "Japanese Childhood," p. 967.

20. Ibid., p. 966.

21. Ibid.

22. Stearns, *Childhood*, p. 73.

23. Platt, "Japanese Childhood," p. 970.

24. Ibid., p. 971.

25. Ibid.; Stearns, *Childhood*, p. 73.

26. Platt, "Japanese Childhood," p. 965.

27. Stearns, *Childhood*, p. 74.

28. Platt, "Japanese Childhood," p. 973.

29. Ibid.

30. Ibid.

31. Stearns, *Childhood*, p. 76.

32. Ibid., p. 74.

33. Toshie Imada, "Cultural Narratives of Individualism and Collectivism: A Content Analysis of Textbook Stories in the United States and Japan," *Journal of Cross-Cultural Psychology* 43:4 (2012), pp. 576–591, at 577; also see David Matsumoto, Tsutomu Kudoh, and Sachiko Takeuci, "Changing Patterns of Individualism and Collectivism in the United States and Japan," *Culture and Psychology* 2:1 (1998), pp. 77–107.

34. Imada, "Cultural Narratives," p. 577.
35. Stearns, *Childhood*, p. 76.
36. Ibid., p. 80.
37. Ibid.
38. Ibid.
39. Ibid., p. 81.
40. Kazumi Sugimura and Shinichi Mizokami, "Personal Identity in Japan," *New Directions for Child and Adolescent Development* 138 (2012), pp. 123–143, at 124.
41. Napier, "Matter out of Place," p. 299.
42. Ibid.
43. Shiro Yoshioka, "Heart of Japaneseness: History and Nostalgia in Hayao Miyazaki's *Spirited Away*," in MacWilliams, *Japanese Visual Culture* (Armonk: Routledge, 2014), pp. 268–285, at 260.
44. Imada, "Cultural Narratives," p. 579.
45. This intersection between East and West is lost in the English dubbed version of *Spirited Away*, as the characters only speak in English.
46. Napier, "Matter out of Place," p. 293.
47. See Napier, "Matter out of Place"; Tai Wei Lim, "*Spirited Away*: Conceptualizing a Film-Based Case Study through Comparative Narratives of Japanese Ecological and Environmental Discourses," *Animation* 8:2 (2019), pp. 149–162; andJames W. Boyd and Tetsuya Nishimura, "Shinto Perspectives in Miyazaki's Anime Film 'Spirited Away,'" *Journal of Religion and Film* 8:2 (2004), pp. 1–14.
48. Alistair Swale, "Miyazaki Hayao and the Aesthetics of Imagination: Nostalgia and Memory in *Spirited Away*," *Asian Studies Review* 39:3 (2015), pp. 413–429, at 426; also see Lim, "Spirited Away"; andHiroshi Yamanaka, "The Utopian 'Power to Live': The Significance of the Miyazaki Phenomenon," in MacWilliams, *Japanese Visual Culture*, pp. 249–267.
49. Noriko T. Reider, "Spirited Away: Film of the Fantastic and Evolving Japanese Folk Symbols," *Film Criticism* 29:3 (2005), pp. 4–27, at 19.
50. Napier, "Matter out of Place," p. 304.
51. Imada, "Cultural Narratives," p. 579.
52. Donald, Wilson, and Wright, *Childhood and Nation*, p. 2.
53. Yuji Ogihara, "Temporal Changes in Individualism and Their Ramification in Japan: Rising Individualism and Conflicts with Persisting Collectivism," *Frontiers in Psychology* 8:695 (2017), pp. 1–12, at 3.
54. See Reito Adachi, "Dubbing of Silences in Hayao Miyazaki's *Spirited Away*: A Comparison of Japanese and English Language Versions," *Perspectives: Studies in Translatology* 24:1 (2019), pp. 142–156, at 149.

BIBLIOGRAPHY

Donald, Stephanie Hemelryk, Emma Wilson, and Sarah Wright, eds. *Childhood and Nation in Contemporary World Cinema: Borders and Encounters*. New York: Bloomsbury, 2017.

Imada, Toshie. "Cultural Narratives of Individualism and Collectivism: A Content Analysis of Textbook Stories in the United States and Japan." *Journal of Cross-Cultural Psychology* 43:4 (2012), pp. 576–951.

Napier, Susan. "Matter out of Place: Carnival, Containment, and Cultural Recovery in Miyazaki's 'Spirited Away.'" *Journal of Japanese Studies* 32:2 (2006), pp. 287–310.

Platt, Brian. "Japanese Childhood, Modern Childhood: The Nation-State, the School, and 19th-Century Globalization." *Journal of Social History* 38:4 (2005), pp. 965–985.

Stearns, Peter N. *Childhood in World History*. New York: Routledge, 2006.

Yoshioka, Shiro. "Heart of Japaneseness: History and Nostalgia in Hayao Miyazaki's Spirited Away." In Mark W. MacWilliams (ed.), *Japanese Visual Culture* (London: Routledge, 2014, pp. 268–285.

CHAPTER 26

COMING-OF-AGE IN SOUTH KOREAN CINEMA

SUNG-AE LEE

COMING-OF-AGE stories in South Korean (henceforth Korean) media are part of a vast network of interrelated generic forms aimed at a wide audience. This audience crosses over from teenagers (or "young adults") to "emerging adults"—defined by Jeffrey Jensen Arnett as "the age period from the late teens through the mid-to-late 20s (roughly ages 18–25)"—and also to adult.[1] The stories appear not only in films but also as comic books (both printed *manhwa* and online productions known as *webtoons*) and television dramas. There is also considerable adaptation from one genre to another, especially from *manhwa/webtoon* to drama. Comic formats appear serialized as, in most cases, short, weekly or semi-weekly chapters and may run for two or more years. The long time span and the looseness of structure mean that adaptations may be created before the comic has reached its conclusion. The most common drama format, 16 one-hour episodes, is better suited to adapt the loose narrative form of the comic than is film, but films do often adapt comics. Thus, *Student A* (Lee Gyeong-Sup, 2018) synthesizes in one hour and 54 minutes a webtoon of 125 chapters posted between February 2015 and June 2017.[2] To accomplish such an adaptation, a film will eliminate sub-plots and side stories and reduce the material to a familiar coming-of-age narrative script.[3]

An informative example of the coming-of-age script is the drama miniseries *Ma Boy* (Lee Jeong-Min, 2012). Set in a creative-arts high school, this romantic comedy deals with a cast of characters who are 17–18 years old, and appeals to a broad teen audience: the leading female role of 17-year-old Jang Geu-Rim is played (very impressively) by Kim So-Hyeon—an already experienced actress who was only 13 at the time, so that her youth added to her appeal across a range of teen viewers. Having recovered from a year in hospital, Geu-Rim seeks to shed her past suffering and make a fresh start at a new school, where she encounters both celebrities and bullies (including cyberbullies) and falls in love with her roommate Hyeon-U (Kim Seong-Ung), a cross-dressing boy. She and Hyeon-U have become a couple by the close of the series, so Geu-Rim completes a coming-of-age journey from insecurity to social and personal well-being. The series includes a lot of silliness and humour, some bizarre characters of both sexes, jokes about the Korean pop-music industry, and satire of the paparazzi who spin stories about young celebrities. The repetition in very popular dramas of a script which includes such a range of motifs provides both a solid foundation for films and an audience well educated in the patterns and functions of this script.

The coming-of-age story in film takes various forms, but at the most general level follows one of two variant scripts. Each, in turn, is differentially instantiated according to whether the protagonist is male or female. The films under discussion in this chapter mostly address a crossover audience (young adult, emerging adult, and adult), although some—such as *Burning* (Lee Chang-Dong, 2018) and *Plum Blossom* (Gwak Ji-Gyun, 2000)—are primarily adult oriented, while others—*No Breathing* (Jo Yong-Seon, 2014), *Student A* (Lee Gyeong-Sup, 2018), *Fashion King* (O Gi-Hwan, 2014), and *Fantasy of the Girls* (An Jeong-Min, 2018), for example—are more obviously directed toward an early teen to young adult audience. As in the West, where crossover young adult film franchises, whether fantasy such as *The Hunger Games* (2012–2020) or romance such as *To All the Boys I've Loved Before* (2018–2021), have flourished, appealing both to teen and emerging adult audiences, South Korean coming-of-age films attract a wide demographic. Following the principle that pre-adult audiences have a strong interest in the challenges that concern and confront characters at their next life stage, we can assume that a film set in a senior high school will attract attention from students in middle school. The same principle applies to "emerging adult" characters who attend university or are striving to establish themselves in the workforce. Thus, the huge success of the coming-of-age film *My Sassy Girl* (Gwak Jae-Yong, 2001) can, in part, be attributed to its appeal to a diverse audience, even though the characters' university attendance is largely a background marker of their immaturity.

FOUNDATIONAL NARRATIVE SCRIPTS: THE WELL-BEING SCRIPT

The first of the two narrative scripts follows a Bildungsroman pattern familiar in Young Adult films and novels created for Western audiences, but with some variation in the weighting of the components; in films with female protagonists, for example, there is stronger critique of social and gender hierarchies. The protagonist is a young person who is, in some way, a social outsider but is often also marked by a particular talent (most often creative or sporting); they may be displaced from their usual home to a contrasting location (either from country to city, or city to country), where they experience a different kind of learning; they are increasingly alienated from their family; the individual has a conflictual relationship with the institutions that construct their subjectivity (family and other relatives, school, local authorities);[4] they experience unsatisfactory or unrequited feelings of affection, which may be superseded by a requited relationship; the protagonist finds at least one other person who provides unconditional support as they turn experience into understanding and begin to grow to maturity; formal education may contribute to growth, but the main shaper of character is the education that comes from life experience; at the close the protagonist has resolved their conflicts, experienced personal fulfilment and a change of social state, and is (re-)incorporated into their social community.

While no film is likely to realise every element of this narrative script, the concurrence of a majority of its components indicates a generic relationship among films that may differ in many other ways. Franco Moretti makes the important point that this narrative script has a "teleological rhetoric," in that the meaning of events lies in their conclusion; that is, "events acquire meaning when they lead to one ending, and one only."[5] Whereas Moretti further argues that this structure in European Bildungsroman is usually normative and socially conservative, Korean films pay close attention to social practices and pressures which generate high levels of anxiety among young people, so that a positive ending may incorporate persisting resistance to social norms. I will refer to this script as the well-being script.

In contrast, the second principal narrative script is what I identify as the "dysphoria script." I have adopted this term from Nancy K. Miller, who, writing of eighteenth-century European fiction with female protagonists, distinguishes between the "euphoric" plot, which leads to social integration, and the "dysphoric" plot, which leads to alienation and exclusion.[6] *Euphoria* is not an appropriate descriptor for the well-being script in Korean cinema, however, and especially for films with female protagonists, as it would substitute happiness for the modicum of well-being the protagonist attains in many films. Thus, positive relations with others, harmony with social ecology, a sense of meaning and purpose in life, self-acceptance, and self-determination, for example, constitute well-being rather than euphoria.[7] Such elements of well-being apply precisely to the ending of *Yong Sun* (Shin Jun, 2016), for example, in which an unruly schoolgirl, bristling with resentment against parents, teachers, and peers, is extricated from the folly of an affair with an athletics coach, reconciles with her father and stepmother, decides not to leave the district, and devotes her attention to athletics rather than romance. With a new sense of purpose and self-determination, she has found well-being.

Well-being seems more elusive in the critically acclaimed film *Take Care of My Cat* (2001), by female director Jeong Jae-Eun, which offers a rare image of the lives of young South Korean women following graduation from a vocational high school. Five school friends gradually drift apart because of their different circumstances (and hence different capabilities) to deal with the vulnerability and marginalization they endure as young women with limited social and economic resources. The delineation of the five characters constitutes a configuration metonymic of the place of young women in the Korean masculinist, neo-Confucian hierarchy, and so coming-of-age within the well-being script would necessitate redefining it according to the narrow conception of that hierarchy. Yu Tae-Hui (Bae Du-Na), who strives to preserve the group's friendship, comes from a well-off, middle-class family but has worked for a year in the family business without remuneration. Korea's patriarchal son-preference denies her opportunities for self-determination. Ambitious Shin Hae-Ju (Lee Yo-Won) is the only one of the five with a regular job, as an office girl in a brokerage company. Her role is to send faxes, make photocopies, and fetch coffee. She is bullied by the male staff and it is made clear to her that her employment will never change unless she completes a degree. By the end of the film she has become the most abjected of the five, lonely, and devoid of hope. Twins Lee Bi-Ryu (Lee Eun-Shil) and Lee On-Jo (Lee Eun-Ju) live together and earn money by making and selling jewellery on the street; their role in the film is small and lies outside the coming-of-age narrative.

Finally, Seo Ji-Yeong (Ok Ji-Yeong) is the most disadvantaged of the group: she dreams of working in textile design but is an orphan living in a shanty with her elderly grandparents. As she is still a minor, the Korean employment system denies her a regular job because she has no parent to stand as guarantor. When, 25 minutes before the end of the film, the roof of the shanty collapses, killing her grandparents, she is left homeless and destitute, and, quite unjustly, ends up in a Juvenile Detention facility. The roof collapse is a turning point in the narrative trajectory, since up until then viewers can only predict a dysphoric outcome. When Ji-Yeong is to be released, Tae-Hui calculates how much her father should have paid her and steals it from his hoard. She then meets Ji-Yeong outside the facility and announces that they will travel abroad together and begin new lives, and the film closes as a plane departs from Incheon Airport. The story of a coming-of-age film is often open-ended in this way, while at the same time the film has reached thematic closure through its representation of what has been overcome and by leaving viewers with sense that well-being is possible for some of the characters, especially altruistic Tae-Hui, though not for all of them. Tae-Hui's farewell message to her family (see Figure 26.1) encapsulates the barriers that confront the Korean female

FIGURE 26.1. Tae-Hui's farewell message to her family in *Take Care of My Cat* (2001, CJ Entertainment). Frame-grab.

protagonist of a coming-of-age film. She has taken the patriarchal family photograph and excised her own image, thus defining her place in the family, both past and future.

WELL-BEING SCRIPTS AND MALE PROTAGONISTS

Well-being scripts with male protagonists are apt to adopt a more comedic mode, no doubt because they are underpinned by the possibilities of male privilege. *Twenty* (Lee Byeong-Heon, 2015) relates the adventures of three boys between graduating school and beginning compulsory military service as they contend with unrealised dreams, financial uncertainties, and societal expectations. Such challenges generate more comedy than maturation, however, and what the three have learned by the end of the film is that if they take the wrong path they can turn back and try another. In a clever parody of the LIFE IS A JOURNEY conceptual metaphor, which underlies many coming-of-age stories, at the close of the film the boys have set out to spend a week walking across the country to the military camp.[8] As they walk along the road, they share a sense of camaraderie and well-being and bicker about girlfriends, which takes the narrative back to the squabble over a girl which originally brought them together. They have not yet grown up.

Coming-of-age narratives with a more euphoric outcome generally pivot on personal accomplishment in a creative or sporting field; examples include *Student A*, *No Breathing* (Jo Yong-Seon, 2013), and *Fashion King* (O Gi-Hwan, 2014). The most conventional of this group is *No Breathing*, which tells the story of two boys who are striving to represent their country in an international swimming competition. As rivalry gradually develops into bromance, and each comes to terms with the legacy of his father, they come to realise that enjoying the process matters more than the end goal. The film emphasizes this point by concluding as the two enter the pool area together to compete for Olympic gold—it is of no consequence which, if either, wins the race.

The deferral of the outcome is also a strategy employed at the close of *Fashion King*, an adaptation of a popular web comic of the same name. This film also has a predictable plot, but it is distinguished by its often bizarre fashions and the exaggerated over-acting as a reflection of comic book action. U Gi-Myeong (Ju Won) is a homely wuss who frequently transfers schools to escape the constant bullying he suffers. At his new school he is smitten with the prettiest girl in the school and decides to gain her attention by transforming himself by means of fashionable clothing. His desire is misplaced and the truly lovable girl, of course, turns out to be his next-door neighbour. In his quest for style he meets a "fairy godfather" in the fashionista Kim Nam-Jeong (Kim Seong-O), who introduces him to *ganji* ("dopeness" in English), a concept which blends aura, coolness, charisma, and unique taste, style, and sense of fashion. In a simple sense, *ganji* means that someone has acute fashion sense and puts things together well. As a street style it is associated with famous brands, but in his own workshop Nam-Jeong produces imitations of these brands and asserts that *ganji* is more than a superficial appearance. Further, it is the only weapon lower economic groups have against the strong. The cultivation of *ganji* is thus the key to the film's coming-of-age narrative and Gi-Myeong's aspiration inevitably puts him in competition and conflict with Kim Won-Ho (An Jae-Hyeon), the school's current fashion king. The film climaxes in a fashion contest between them, but Gi-Myeong is attacked by Won-Ho's bully boy on his way to the venue and left injured with his outfit destroyed. While Won-Ho parades on the runway in a carefully constructed and crafted outfit, Nam-Jeong dresses Gi-Myeong in bits and pieces of clothing and accessories he borrows from their friends, but his improvisation demonstrates the art of putting things together well. As Gi-Myeong, battered and bleeding, takes his turn on the runway, to tumultuous applause, he reflects on the moment in voice-over, interspersed with the compere's announcements. The film concludes with a euphoric assertion of self-acceptance and self-determination:

> Gi-Myeong: I'm not wuss Gi-Myeong anymore…
> (*Compere: The Fashion King is…*)
>   I am U Gi-Myeong.

Again, it is irrelevant who the winner of the competition is since Gi-Myeong has demonstrated the superior force of his *ganji*.

Comparable with *Fashion King* in such aspects as self-conscious overacting and some amusing shifts between live-action and animation, and between realism and fantasy, the romantic comedy *Fantasy of the Girls* (literal title: *Girls' World*, 2018) is a rare example in film of a comedic well-being script with female protagonists. Writer/director An Jeong-Min has a strong grasp on the coming-of-age genre which enables him to use a predictable plot to develop quirky, amusing characters as the basis for humour. Most of the adult characters, for example, are melodramatically comic, as is common in films for pre-adult viewers. Set in a girls' school, *Fantasy of the Girls* revolves around a girl crush developed by mid-teen Seon-Hwa (No Jeong-Ui) when she accidentally acquires the role of Juliet in the school production of *Romeo and Juliet*. The part of Romeo is played by Ha-Nam (Gwon Na-Ra), a beautiful older girl who is the crush object of almost every girl in the school. Ha-Nam is also a lesbian (she rides a motor scooter and usually walks with her hands in her pockets and is thus attributed with "masculine" traits) and is receptive of the affection shown by Seon-Hwa as the play brings them together. While production of the play is not the major focus of the action, *Romeo and Juliet* is an astute choice because of its climax in a double suicide in response to thwarted love. The film thus plays with the possibility that Seon-Hwa, naïve and inexperienced, may stumble into a dysphoria script because of her crush and the resentment it attracts from Su-Yeon (Jo Su-Hyang), producer of the play, who also loves Ha-Nam. A production of a Shakespearean tragedy also proves to be a useful source of comedy as it enables emotional girls intrigued by the idea of romantic love to be depicted dramatically over-acting in auditions and rehearsal in their attempts to perform emotions beyond their comprehension. The film thus opens with Seon-Hwa helping her best friend Ji-Eun (Kim Ye-Na) to prepare to audition for the role of Juliet, but Ji-Eun is awkward and graceless and overacts terribly, so that viewer response mixes amusement and embarrassment on her behalf. Seon-Hwa is in part sustained by her fantasy life in which she is an astronaut, and even shouts, "To the Universe!" when there is a gap in conversation, asserting that this takes her into the fourth dimension.

Seon-Hwa ends the relationship with Ha-Nam when she discovers that Ha-Nam and Su-Yeon have a mutual past, and drops out of the play before the opening night performance, passing the role to Su-Yeon. Later that night Ha-Nam visits Seon-Hwa and gives her a jar of sweets, telling her that if she eats one each day her sorrow will be gone with the last sweet. The film closes with a montage sequence that shows Seon-Hwa happily immersed in girlhood activities, and then a final space travel fantasy in which she removes her spacesuit, eats the last sweet, and gazes at a rainbow in a night sky above a waterfall. Within the film's symbolism, the rainbow denotes that all characters have found happiness, but the natural landscape also instantiates the conceptual metaphor COMING-OF-AGE IS A PLANT THAT BLOSSOMS, which I discuss further below.

THE DYSPHORIA SCRIPT

The dysphoria script includes much the same components as the well-being script, but is driven by an alternative teleological rhetoric which leads to an outcome negative for the main character(s). The components take relentlessly negative form, so that alienation from family, conflict with social institutions, emotional isolation, and lack of any support preclude any possibility of social reincorporation. At the close of the film the protagonist has been denied the change of social state necessary for positive coming-of-age and is thus left in a liminal, abject situation or commits suicide. The contrapuntal inter-relation of the two scripts is explored in *Plum Blossom*, in which male friends Ja-Hyo (Kim Rae-Won) and Su-In (Kim Jeong-Hyeon) follow different trajectories by the close of the film, in that Su-In commits suicide by jumping from a cliff into a river and Ja-Hyo commits himself to an intersubjective love relationship. Other films may follow one trajectory and then quite suddenly reverse direction. *Student A* opens with an image of a schoolgirl falling to her death from the roof of a school building; viewers will assume that she is a "suicide jumper," and therefore the film will lay out the chain of events that led to this moment. Suicide has been the most common cause of death among young South Koreans for many years, and the suicide of schoolgirls by roof jumping or autodefenestration is a trope established and sustained by the *Whispering Corridors* film series (1998–2009), notably in *Whispering Corridors* (Park Gi-Hyeong, 1998), *Memento Mori* (Kim Tae-Yong and Min Gyu-Dong, 1999), *Voice* (Choe Ik-Hwan, 2005), and *Blood Pledge* (Lee Jong-Yong, 2009). Viewers who draw the obvious conclusion that the opening image of *Student A* foreshadows its close thus do so with the knowledge that suicide jumping is a common cinematic trope. Of the dysphoric coming-of-age films mentioned in this chapter, the suicide jumping of a schoolgirl appears in *Plum Blossom*, *Han Gong-Ju* (Lee Su-Jin, 2013), and *After My Death* (Kim Eui-Seok, 2018). The ending of *Student A* mocks this expectation, however, and discloses that the girl Jang Mi-Rae (Kim Hwan-Hui) accidentally fell and landed unhurt in a tree, wins approval through her achievement in creative writing, and develops firm friendships with a group of her peers. She has become firmly situated within the well-being script.

An even more abrupt substitution in which dysphoria is replaced by well-being occurs within the frame of *The Harmonium in My Memory* (Lee Yeong-Jae, 1999). The film opens with a 45-second segment during the title sequence in which a woman, viewed in part and from behind, searches in a cabinet for an LP record of the early 1960s Connie Francis compilation *My Greatest Songs* and puts it on a turntable. The record is to play a significant function in the film, but at the outset viewers are not informed of the purpose of this scene. The body of the film ends with the female protagonist, Hong-Yeon (Jeon Do-Yeon), disconsolately watching the departure of Su-Ha (Lee Byeong-Heon), the object of her unrequited love. Inside the moving car, Su-Ha unwraps a farewell present she has sent to him, a copy of *My Greatest Songs* to replace his broken copy, and he seems to realise his mistake. The camera then lingers on Hong-Yeon at middle distance, where she stands beside the *jangseungs*, carved wooden figures that mark and guard the village boundary. Hong-Yeon is thus left standing in a liminal place, at a moment of loss, but also of possibility. By indicating her position at a physical boundary, the *jangseungs* visually reinforce that she inhabits a particular position within the conceptual metaphor COMING-OF-AGE IS A JOURNEY. This (temporary) ending is an appropriate outcome for a dysphoria script, but the scene now dissolves into the frame: with her back still to the camera, the woman sits in the same room and the same time as in the opening frame and looks at the record cover (see Figure 26.2). There are three out-of-focus photographs in the room. The woman turns in response to the doorbell, and we see it is Hong-Yeon. As the credits roll, each of the photographs is displayed: Hong-Yeon and Su-Ha's wedding; a photo with their first child; and a photo with four children. The framing indicates that Hong-Yeon selects this record because she is reminiscing about her journey from dysphoria to well-being.

FIGURE 26.2.   *Left*: Hong-Yeon in liminal space. *Right*: Onset of closing frame, *The Harmonium in My Memory* (1999, Art Hill). Frame-grab.

Conceptual Metaphors and
Coming-of-Age

The growth of Hong-Yeon and Su-Ha's family indicates that they have flourished in a manner socially valued in 1960s Korea (and East Asia more generally). The transition from Hong-Yeon standing at a boundary while watching a departure to the images of the flourishing life she and Su-Ha lead brings together the two conceptual metaphors on which the concept of coming-of-age is grounded: COMING OF AGE IS A JOURNEY and COMING OF AGE IS A PLANT THAT BLOSSOMS. These metaphors are sub-sets of the more general conceptual metaphors LIFE IS A JOURNEY and THE HUMAN LIFE CYCLE IS THE LIFE CYCLE OF A PLANT. A conceptual metaphor is a system of correspondences between a concrete domain of experience (the "source domain") and an abstract domain (the "target domain"). In the conceptual metaphor LIFE IS A JOURNEY, one of the most frequently evoked metaphors, the source domain, journey, is much more concrete than the target domain, life. In everyday use, the metaphor allows us to "map" stages of life as stages of a more concrete journey—departures, encounters, delays, detours, arrivals, and so on. The retrospective view from the frame of *The Harmonium in My Memory* thus redefines Su-Ha's departure from Sanri as a detour. The formulation (in English) of "coming-of-age," which has been directly adopted as a critical concept into Korean, has already built in a journey aspect in the continuous participle *coming*, which describes a process of motion toward some point.

There is an overlap with the plant metaphor, however, as when we speak of "plants coming into bloom." In Western discourse, human growth and maturation have long been metaphorized as vegetative growth,[9] but critical analysis of coming-of-age narratives has predominantly identified them as mapped onto the journey.[10] Roberta Trites lists several other metaphors of growth, such as filling a container or shaping the self like a sculpture, but the metaphor of particular interest for this study is "cultivating life as if it were a plant."[11] This metaphor is particularly prevalent in East Asia, especially in countries such as Korea and Japan, which have been deeply influenced by Chinese philosophy. Sarah Allan contrasts Western discourses—which distinguish plants from animals—and the Chinese conceptual scheme, in which "plants and animals are classified together in a single category,"[12] which pivots on plant growth and regeneration: "the principles of plant growth are [thus] extended from plants to an understanding of all living things, including humans. Thus, people are not 'reasoning animals' but living things which have a certain potential for growth when they are nurtured properly."[13] Because natural phenomena were a basis for conceptual metaphors, they remain inherent in vocabulary and concepts. This inherency probably explains why coming-of-age films in East Asia make more use than Western films of an embodied COMING -OF-AGE IS A PLANT THAT BLOSSOMS metaphor. Since the principles of plant growth are extended to other living things, animals may also function as the source domain of the metaphor. A larger study may show that of the two metaphorical source domains in East

Asian coming-of-age films the plants metaphor predominates in a film's visual elements and the journey metaphor in more verbal elements.

COMING-OF-AGE IS A PLANT THAT BLOSSOMS AND THE WELL-BEING SCRIPT: IM SUN-RYE'S *LITTLE FOREST* (2018)

COMING-OF-AGE IS A PLANT THAT BLOSSOMS is a metaphor well suited to films that instantiate the well-being script. In Korean cinema, an explicit embodiment of the metaphor as the core of the film is *Little Forest* (2018). This film is an adaptation of the Japanese *Little Forest* chain—a manga (2004) by Igarashi Daisuke and a two-part film (2014 and 2015) directed by Mori Junichi—and the Japanese source has probably contributed to the use of the conceptual metaphor. However, the Japanese works are best known for scenes that depict cooking and eating (the manga includes a recipe with each episode), whereas the Korean is more concerned to develop the coming-of-age element and the plant metaphor and so develops a grounding ecotopic discourse that goes beyond the information that the protagonist cooks what is available to be harvested at particular times of the year. The film deals with a crucial 18 months in the life of Hye-Won (Kim Tae-Ri), a young woman who has returned to her childhood home in a rural Korean village after failing to successfully combine study and part-time work in Seoul. Earlier, her widowed mother (Mun So-Ri) had abruptly left their home after Hye-Won's Entrance Examinations, declaring that it was now her time to experience things she had never attempted because she was so young when she married. What these things are is not disclosed to the audience, nor to Hye-Won, as the mother only appears in the film within Hye-Won's memories.

Hye-Won's attempt to come to terms with her mother's departure is one part of a set of themes imbricated throughout the film. There are a few ancillary characters, but only four main characters and two storylines subsumed into a social ecological narrative. These storylines are (a) the relationship between Hye-Won and her mother, which gives the coming-of-age theme an eco-feminist slant; and (b) an inexplicit and inarticulate love triangle involving Hye-Won and her friends Jae-Ha (Ryu Jun-Yeol) and Eun-Suk (Jin Gi-Ju), who had all been at school together. Human interactions are central to the narrative, but the two story strands in which Hye-Won is involved are not central to what the film is about, but rather feed into the representation of a life unfolding according to the rhythms of the ecosystem and the celebration of a harmonic balance among human subjects and between human subjects and natural environment. Time of year, for example, is felt corporeally as Hye-Won ingests produce she has earlier preserved: "Glazed chestnuts tasting this good means it is deep into autumn"; "If dried persimmons taste this good it means it is deep into winter." The *what* and *how* of representation in the film, including the metaphorical implications of these examples, thus, on the one hand, offers a critical perspective on the grounding concept and, on the other, tunes in to what was trending term in South Korea, *sohwakhaeng*, "a small but certain happiness," which, more simply, is a sense of well-being. A good example occurs late in the film when Hye-Won returns after a second attempt to live in Seoul, harvests two onions she had planted the previous autumn, hollows, stuffs, and cooks them, and is interrupted by the return of her beloved dog Ogu, delivered by Jae-Ha, who has been caring for him during her absence. Hye-Won had returned to Seoul in her quest to find meaning in her life, but with the coming of spring the film presents a montage which contrasts high-rise buildings and the haecceity of frogs and bees in the country, and these juxtapositions constitute an affective tipping point which prompts Hye-Won to return to her rural home. The day after her return she repairs the roof of the house, an action which symbolizes permanence. Throughout, narrative is secondary to such schematic image schemas and conceptual metaphors, which encapsulate how this film integrates Hye-Won's coming-of-age with the development of a "small but certain happiness."

The metaphor COMING-OF-AGE IS A PLANT THAT BLOSSOMS also lies within an ecological perspective that explores the interdependencies of place and the social and cultural networks that shape the cognitive development of a person. *Little Forest* seeks to persuade its audience to desire a positive interaction with the physical environment in three main ways: through representations of animals and plants whose haecceity glows on the screen, whether it is a snail, a daisy, or a frog; through the simple but aesthetically pleasing cooking segments, which begin by depicting the gathering or harvesting of the ingredients and culminate in the pleasures of presentation and eating; and by its representation of the symbiosis between human habitation and seasonal cycles as embodied metonymically in seasonal foods. The well-being of people depends upon their interactions with the world they live in: that is, interactions with habitation (environment) and social, institutional, and cultural contexts, and the bearings such interactions have on notions of wholeness, naturalness, and a sense of belonging. The desirable outcome is a kind of contentment more than some notion of happiness. The film encapsulates this sense in Jae-Ha's idea of himself as a farmer and the equanimity he shows after his rice field and apple orchard have been devastated by a typhoon: he can still identify a "sufficient" level of well-being in his life—a principle that Hye-Won fails to grasp until the end of the film and thus after her second attempt to live in Seoul.

As the "stuffed onions" sequence illustrates, *Little Forest* communicates more by image than story, and its numerous micronarratives are characteristically incomplete. The closing frames of the film, indeed, offer a visual and narrative gap: Hye-Won arrives home on her bicycle to find the door open and the curtains parted and smiles with pleasure within a freeze-frame and fade to black. Viewers may think or hope that her mother has finally returned but can never know. However, this ending seems to invite viewers to connect the most specific and most general components of the cognitive map that informs the narrative: that is, the proximal processes of family relationships and the overarching temporal frame of departures and arrivals that can be seen as analogous to the seasonal cycle—winter-spring-summer-autumn-winter-spring—which the film follows. This framework that spans the proximal and distal and is the context for the development of subjectivity encapsulates Hye-Won's coming-of-age story. Most of the film's images represent the proximal processes of family and peer relationships and interactions with the immediate physical environment in its changing climatic phases and the frequent juxtaposition of gathering what grows without planting and the intensive labour of planting and weeding. Intermediate domains encapsulate the interdependencies of place and the social and cultural networks that shape the cognitive development of a person.[14] Thus, individual development expresses the need for Hye-Won to acquire more interactive communication skills and to be agentic and productive rather than just busy. A further domain evokes more distant environmental contexts—that is, the representation of rural life and frequent contrasts with urban life.

The film's title is a simple metaphor for ecotopia, as articulated late in the film when Hye-Won reflects on her mother's interaction with place: "For mother, nature, cooking and her love for me have been her little forest. I should find my own little forest too."[15] Life in the village is simple, with some overtones of an ecological utopia, but it is also neither primitive nor indolent. There is no conscious aspiration to an ideal of living close to nature, but it is realised in daily practice and is the essence of Hye-Won's coming of age.

DYSPHORIA SCRIPTS AND SOCIAL CRITIQUE

There may be many ways for people to find their own little forest, but when the metaphor COMING-OF-AGE IS A PLANT THAT BLOSSOMS appears in films grounded in the dysphoria script its function seems to be to express a missed possibility or to indicate the depth of a character's abjection. In *Nunbal* (*A Stray Goat*, Jo Jae-Min, 2016) Ye-Ju (Ji U), a high school student, has been ostracized because she lives in a motherless family and her father has been suspected of a serious crime. She has done nothing wrong and is a very likeable girl but is subjected to both physical and emotional bullying. Unexpectedly, she finds a friend in newcomer Min-Shik (Jin Yeong), and they become a couple. One day in the forest they rescue a small, stray goat which has fallen into a pit, and Ye-Ju adopts and nurtures it. Her nurturing is the "plant" metaphor, since her display of care and affection expresses what she does not receive in her own life. However, her exclusion and persecution by other students and the powers of patriarchal Christianity are unrelenting, and when she is raped by the original owner of the goat and abandoned by Min-Shik in an act of cowardice, she disappears and viewers must assume she has committed suicide. The film closes with an image of Min-Shik, belatedly repentant but deeply mired in abjection, lying in a muddy field and weeping, as snow begins to fall. In this example, the negative effect of the "plant" metaphor intensifies the film's bleakness.[16]

Like *Nunbal*, films based on the dysphoria script usually contain some elements of social critique. In several interviews, Lee Chang-Dong, director and co-writer of *Burning*

(2018), has explicitly commented on this aspect of his film. In an interview with Patrick Frater for *Variety*, for example, he stated:

> For a long time, I've wanted to tell a story about young people, and in particular, the young people of this generation. . . . The rage of young people is a particularly pressing problem. The millennials living in Korea today will be the first generation that are worse off than their parents' generation. They feel that the future will not change significantly. Not able to find the object to direct their rage at, they feel a sense of debilitation. This film is about young people who feel impotent, with rage bottled up inside them.[17]

In such a context, the prospect of social integration as an outcome of the coming-of-age seems very unlikely. The film's strategy for creating viewer uncertainty is to present the mise-en-scène from the perspective and feelings of Jong-Su (Yu A-In), one of the three principal characters, but also to represent that perspective as unreliable. Jong-Su grew up on a farm in Paju, a village close to the boundary between North and South Korea and which is depicted as lacking sophistication. He completed a college degree and aspires to be a writer but has not yet written anything. He has been unable to find an appropriate job since graduation and lives a life of precarity doing part-time work. At the opening of the film he encounters Hae-Mi (Jeon Jong-Seo), who also comes from Paju and lives a similar precarious life, and who invites him for a drink. While in the bar she demonstrates her skill as a mime, which she is studying as a hobby, and asks Jong-Su to feed her cat while she is away on a trip to Africa. They return to her small apartment, where they have sex. Jong-Su returns to Paju to look after his father's farm while his father is in prison and drives back and forth to feed the cat. On her return from Africa Hae-Mi is accompanied by Ben (Steven Yeon), a wealthy young man who drives a Porsche and has a luxury apartment in Gangnam. The introduction of this third character is a basis for social critique in themes of privilege and the ever-widening economic gap between the plutocracy and ordinary people.

A central aspect of the film's mystery is recurrent hesitation over whether an event depicted should be accepted as having happened within a realist narrative. Because Jong-Su is an aspiring writer, there is a lingering suspicion that he may have created much, if not all, of the story. An audience is thus drawn into a process of dual interpretation and either chooses between understanding events as realism or fantasy or performing a kind of double reading. Lee Chang-Dong alludes to this latter possibility in an interview with *Hollywood Reporter*, when, with reference to the film's final scene in which Jong-Su stabs Ben to death and burns his body in the Porsche, Lee remarks, "that may or may not have been a part of reality" but it is part of the wider strategy to induce the audience "to follow Jong-Su's narrative and put themselves in his perspective and feel his confusion and emotions, but at the same time distance themselves and look at him critically."[18] Coming-of-age narratives undergirded by the dysphoria script often favour open or ambiguous endings, and *Burning* is no exception.

Two metaphors near the beginning of the film point to the interpretive duality. First, when Hae-Mi mimes peeling a tangerine her explanation of viewer's role has a metacinematic *mise-en-abyme* effect: don't imagine that the tangerine is there, but forget that it *isn't* there. When soon after she takes Jong-Su to her room and explains that the cat is hiding, he asks if it isn't an imaginary cat and if, when he comes to feed it, he should forget that it isn't there. Subsequently, he never sees the cat in her room but does find traces of its existence in its litter tray. When just past the midpoint of the film Hae-Mi disappears, the same conundrum emerges: does she still exist, or did she ever exist? Viewers are invited to ponder the ontological status of represented events when, late in the film, Jong-Su is shown sitting in what was Hae-Mi's room typing and it may thus be concluded that he has used his own room as a setting for part of the story he is creating. The dual reading involved in this ambiguity generates an unusual perspective on the coming-of-age narrative: on the one hand, it depicts a realistic dysphoric narrative in which a young man, seething with class resentment, is out of his depth socially and emotionally and is driven to murder an upper-class psychopath he suspects of killing the woman he himself desires; on the other hand, it explores the creative process of a budding writer who uses the world around him, a created persona for himself, and his favourite authors (Faulkner, Scott Fitzgerald) to engage critically with social issues that trouble his world. The ambiguity perhaps also helps audiences to comprehend the narrative's crucial metaphor, the greenhouse.

Because they are a site in which plants are grown and nurtured by the production of a special climate, greenhouses have the potential to express the metaphor COMING-OF-AGE IS A PLANT THAT BLOSSOMS. A more obvious example appears twenty minutes into *Plum Blossom*, when Ha-Ra (Yun Ji-Hye), a single-minded young woman, takes Ja-Hyo to a greenhouse (used for growing flowers) where she seduces him. The setting seems idyllic but fails to express the "plant that blossoms" metaphor because Ja-Hyo's masculinist mindset, grounded in a neo-Confucian ideology of male dominance, is repelled by the experience. As he later explains to his friend Su-In, he thinks girls should be repressed and sensitive rather than sexually aggressive. A central part of his coming-of-age is to learn to embrace the "new breed of girl" who expresses her desires and hence a new version of the "blossoming" metaphor. Although the episode conforms to Jerome Buckley's "ordeal by love" as an early stage of the (male) Bildungsroman, the film itself seems confused about this girl.[19] She is depicted as mentally unbalanced by her obsessive desire and Ja-Hyo's subsequent rejection of it, and the episode is closed when she jumps to her death from the school roof and thus joins the long list of girls in film who are pushed to suicide by inimical social ideology and its practice.

Hae-Mi is another girl who enacts her desires. When she initiates love-making with Jong-Su, she is clearly in control and experienced, managing her own blossoming. The greenhouse is introduced in *Burning* near the middle of the film when Hae-Mi and Ben unexpectedly visit the farm one evening. This is also the last time Jong-Su sees Hae-Mi, and in terms of the realist story it may have been one of the last days of her life. On this evening, Ben tells Jong-Su about his hobby of burning down derelict greenhouses, sites of ugliness in the countryside. As his disquisition unfolds it is a psychopath's manifesto:

there is no right or wrong; he does not judge but is as impartial as natural forces; when he has done his work, it is as if the object never existed. He further explains that he has found his next target, the best ever, one that is "very, very near" Jong-Su. Whether or not the character in this role did burn farm buildings is the central mystery of the film's main pre-text, Haruki Murakami's story "Barn Burning." Lee Chang-Dong reports that his co-writer, O Jeong-Mi, saw it as a metaphor that discloses that the character is a se-rial killer of young women, and *Burning* incorporates hints that Ben is such a killer—for example, on a visit to Ben's apartment after Hae-Mi vanishes, Jong-Su finds her wrist-watch in a drawer containing various female trinkets, and a cat Ben has acquired is pos-sibly Hae-Mi's cat. A re-viewing of the farmhouse conversation suggests in retrospect that Ben is talking about Hae-Mi. Jong-Su subsequently sets up a meeting with Ben in a farm area on the outskirts of the city. The murder of Ben is the culmination of a mon-tage sequence consisting of four vignettes linked by the presence or absence of Hae-Mi. Cinematically, the sequence has a high level of realism, not least because it consists of a series of long takes: it runs for 11 minutes and 16 seconds, with only nine shots.[20] On the other hand, the presumed reality of events is called into question. In vignette one, the first shot shows Jong-Su lying on his/Hae-Mi's bed with Hae-Mi cuddling him from behind and giving him a handjob. The second shot, a 20-second static take, shows him lying in the same position, but now alone, so the previous shot was a dream or a fan-tasy. The next vignette, already mentioned, shows him in what was previously estab-lished as Hae-Mi's room. The bed, the bedside lamp, and the cupboard are the same, but there is no sign of Hae-Mi's clutter or of women's clothing. Viewers might assume that he imagined those, and the crucial positioning of this scene, as he pauses, thinks for a mo-ment, then resumes typing, suggests that the surrounding vignettes are his creation. The third vignette begins with Ben in his bathroom putting in his contact lenses and then, in a second shot, he applies make-up to Hae-Mi's face. The film has not previously shown either character when Jong-Su is not present, so this sudden change of perspective places the scene within Jong-Su's novel. Perhaps Ben is preparing Hae-Mi for her death.

The final vignette, which begins with a very long shot of six minutes and eight seconds, depicts the murder of Ben. Ben arrives first at the meeting place and greets Jong-Su with a few words that taunt him with a collage summary of the plot:

> Hey, Jong-Su! I see there are a lot of greenhouses here. [*Sniggers*]. Where's Hae-Mi? You asked me to join you and Hae-Mi. Isn't she with you?

Ben's conjunction of Hae-Mi's absence and greenhouses works to confirm both that the burning greenhouses are a metaphor for serial killings and that Hae-Mi was the most recent victim. Jong-Su says nothing but repeatedly stabs Ben in the stomach. That Jong-Su strips naked and throws his clothes into the Porsche with Ben's body is the culmina-tion of the film's ambiguity. The action is a practical destruction of evidence, but also stresses the contrast between the bare life of everyday Koreans and the absurd wealth of the over-privileged who consume but produce nothing. Finally, it has a novelistic touch in the parallel between the burning Porsche and a burning greenhouse, and in the implication that to destroy a greenhouse is to erase the metaphor COMING-OF-AGE IS A PLANT THAT BLOSSOMS. Hae-Mi is represented with an optimistic disposition and a hunger for meaning, but, in the reading of the film's action as realistic, she dies in her mid-twenties. As he leaves the murder scene, Jong-Su is represented as utterly abject in his nakedness and horror at what he has done. In a reading of the action and characters as products of Jong-Su's imagination, the dysphoria script expresses deep criticism of a social malaise that precludes coming-of-age as well-being. A third parallel reading of the ending, also as literal realism and social dysphoria, is to argue that Hae-Mi has chosen to disappear because of the credit card debt that plagues young Koreans and Ben dies because of Jong-Su's jealousy and resentment. Nevertheless, all reading options are variants of the dysphoria script.

OPEN AND AMBIGUOUS ENDINGS IN THE DYSPHORIA SCRIPT

The ambiguity of the ending of *Burning* is unusually complex, even though, as I observed above, open or ambiguous endings are a feature of films based on the dysphoria script. Coming-of-age is a process, not an ending, so of the films discussed here only *The Harmonium in My Memory* seems to have reached a point of stasis. In contrast, the closure of one part of life and the beginning of a new phase, as in *Take Care of My Cat*, is an expected outcome. The disjunction between open-ended story and thematic closure exemplified by this film is broadly typical of dysphoric films, but arguably takes a different form depending on the gender of the protagonist. The dysphoria script with a female protagonist is apt to represent girls as depressive and sensitive to peer behaviour and prone to consider suicide as a solution to life's challenges. This schema appears infrequently amongst male protagonists, who are more likely to be victims of disadvantageous social practices as in *Set Me Free* (Kim Tae-Yong, 2014) and *One Way Trip* (Choe Jeong-Yeol, 2016). Many of the young characters in dysphoria script films are depicted as already disadvantaged: they inhabit a lower socio-economic stratum, are orphans, come from broken families, or have neglectful or overbearing parents.

Set Me Free focuses on a duplicitous protagonist, Yeong-Jae (Choe U-Sik), who was abandoned by his irresponsible father and has grown up in a group home run by the Catholic Church. Now about to turn 17, when he must leave the home and return to his hated father, Yeong-Jae pretends to have a religious vocation and strives to qualify for admission to a seminary. When he fails, he is sent to live at an institution in the country. As a coming-of-age story, the outcome is bleak, since Yeong-Jae is unlikely to blossom in his future life. The film has resolved thematically, however, in the painful imbrication of natural moral justice and South Korea's dystopian social practices. *One Way Trip* is an even darker narrative. Four young men go off to spend time together before one of their number Sang-U (Su Ho) leaves for military training, but their trip and their lives go awry when they witness a man beating his wife and attempt to intervene. However, they knock the man unconscious, the wife phones her lover, who has the husband killed, and the wife lies to the police, placing the blame on the boys. During a police pursuit, Sang-U (Su Ho) is struck by a car and critically injured. When she is located, the woman is found to be a high-profile television anchor and does not want her unsavoury private life disclosed, so her station's CEO contacts senior police and asks for the case to be dealt with quietly and expeditiously. Two elements that militate against the friends are the capacity of the rich and powerful to use money and influence to circumvent law and the corruption of the police force, many of whose members are willing to solve cases in favour of people with power and do not bother investigating if a suspect is young and from a powerless family. The three remaining friends are imprisoned and, in this mire of corruption, take the immoral decision to blame Sang-U for the "murder." Once they are sentenced to fines and released, nothing further is told about them. Sang-U dies soon after, and only one of his friends attends the funeral. In contrast to the open-endedness of the story, thematic closure is strong in its portrayal of appalling failure in public and private morality.

FEMALE-CENTRED DYSPHORIC NARRATIVES

Comparable failures of morality in female-centred dysphoric coming-of-age narratives are products of how the behaviour of girls is constructed and policed to a great extent by the internalization and reproduction of social ideology by girls themselves, and this also explains why teenagers commit suicide and resort to violence. When Yeong-Hui (Jeon Yeo-Bin), the protagonist of *After My Death*, is suspected of complicity in the death of another student, Gyeong-Min (Jeon So-Ni), she is ostracized and physically assaulted by her class peers, but their attitude is summed up in the question, "Is it true that you put bad ideas into other people's minds?" In other words, her crime is being different and thinking differently. Eventually, her father's indifference to her and the bullying by the girls and by Gyeong-Min's mother, whose fierce campaign against Yeong-Hui is intended to mask her own contribution to her daughter's suicide, drive Yeong-Hui to attempt suicide herself.

The attempted regulation of girlhood is encapsulated in a suicidal girl schema constructed early (around 13 minutes) in the film when the school principal is leading the staff in a discussion to find an "acceptable explanation" for the suicide of 11th grade student, Gyeong-Min. An "acceptable" explanation is one that exonerates the school, a purpose which only emphasizes the gap between male authority and female teens. The suicidal girl is schematized as extremely clever, so communicates poorly with her peers; she is mentally unstable, depressive, with a dark side; she compounds her mental darkness by listening to dark music (in Gyeong-Min's case, 1990s Northern European music), which proves she was influenced by undesirable foreign cultures. One of her class peers confirms that she didn't listen to K-pop, which suggests she was alienated and probably insane. Underpinning this schema, once again, is a normative masculinist perspective on the position and behaviour of women in society. Why Gyeong-Min jumped off a bridge into a river is still unclear at the close of the film, but it is strongly implied that a significant catalyst is an unhappy home life attributable to the values of a money-hungry society. The ambiguity of Gyeong-Min's suicide comments forcefully on the concerns of schools and parents to save face ahead of any concern for the well-being of young people.

This neglect of the well-being of the young is eloquently expressed in *Han Gong-Ju*. Dysphoria script narratives characteristically employ multiple flashbacks, usually to furnish explanatory context, but this film only releases this information as it begins to be known by characters within the film. Gong-Ju (Cheon U-Hui) is a transfer student about whom nothing is known. She is reticent and does not attempt to make friends. Over time, however, she learns to swim, and when some of the prominent girls overhear her singing they invite her to join their a capella group. In short, she is beginning to blossom. However, when one of the group posts a clip of her performing online, it all begins to unravel. Gong-Ju and her friend were victims of a vicious gang rape and she has been relocated not so much for her own benefit but for the benefit of her former school. Her mother refuses to know her, and her drunken father is only interested in gaining money from the families of the perpetrators (South Korea's unjust legal system is again pertinent, since the wealthy can buy acquittal for a crime if the victim will sign a request for the charge to be dismissed). Her father visits and tricks her into signing a dismissal document for one of the perpetrators, and with her location disclosed online the classroom is suddenly invaded by all the families, demanding signatures. Distraught, she packs her suitcase and leaves. Next morning, she jumps from a bridge leaving the suitcase at the point from which she jumps (see Figure 26.3), in accordance with a filmic convention whereby a suicide jumper leaves objects behind (for example, in *After My Death* Gyeong-Min leaves her backpack and shoes on the bridge). Viewers don't see Gong-Ju jump (although a careful inspection of the preceding, long-distance shot of the bridge shows her standing outside the rail), so the sudden appearance of the abandoned suitcase prompts viewers to infer suicide. But then, in an astonishingly humorous switch, the camera shows a vertical down-shot of the river, and Gong-Ju breaks the surface and begins to swim with the current. A voice-over conversation explains the switch to a quest for well-being:

Eun-Hui (friend): Why do you swim so hard?
Gong-Ju: In case I want to start over. Because my mind could change.

The conversation brings viewers within the cognitive frame of Gong-Ju's memory and imagination, as the soundtrack proceeds to introduce the imagined voices of a crowd chanting her name to urge her on, as in a race, which then mingles with the film's a capella theme and ends in a victory cheer as Gong-Ju swims out of the bottom of the screen into her future. Perhaps. Some viewers infer that the dysphoria script is played out to its conclusion, and she drowns, but inferences based on narrative gaps can be inconclusive, and I argue that the film is an example of script switching at the close.

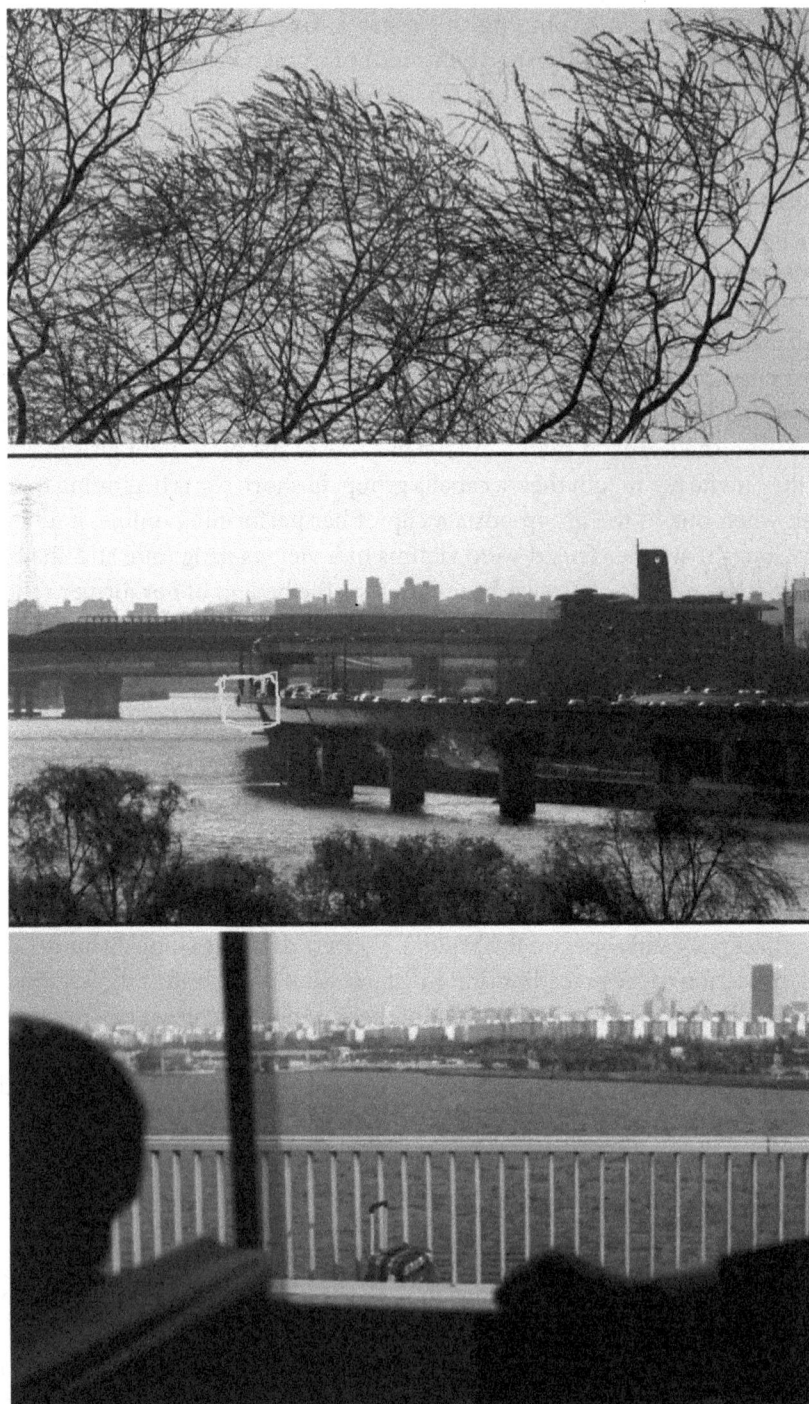

FIGURE 26.3. Montage sequence from *Han Gong-Ju*: Rhetoric of the ending (2013, Vill Lee Film). Frame-grab.

In conjunction, the conversation and the visual image evoke the potent symbolism of rivers, especially symbolism of change and of death and rebirth, and underlying these symbols in turn are the metaphors, COMING-OF-AGE IS A JOURNEY and COMING-OF-AGE IS A PLANT THAT BLOSSOMS. The latter is reinforced by an image of trees in bud interpolated as the first image in a montage consisting of the trees, an extreme long-distance shot of the place from which Gong-Ju jumps (highlighted in Figure 26.3), and the image of her suitcase (Figure 26.3). The suitcase thus develops a double meaning: first, it tells the world that Gong-Ju has died; and second, it signifies that she has transitioned to a new life and left her past behind her. It thus becomes as potent an image as the defaced photograph in *Take Care of My Cat*. Once more, Gong-Ju's story after this point is not told but the last message she received on her mobile was an invitation from a recording company to come in for an interview, which suggests a new pathway might open. Nevertheless, her decision, as she fell to the water, to start over—find meaning, purpose, and self-determination in living—already provides a satisfying closure.

CONCLUSION

A distinctive contribution Korean coming-of-age films have made to the genre is to the rhetoric of the ending in films with female protagonists. When the parents of Gong-Ju's rapists invade her classroom and physically attack her, aiming to compel her to sign forms that would exonerate their sons and release them from imprisonment, one of them laments, "Today is my son's birthday. I couldn't even cook for him." The utterance encapsulates the mentality that makes it so difficult for girls to achieve well-being. Recurrent motifs in Korean cinema are the excessive value placed on sons and the assumption long embedded in Confucianist ideology that young women have neither rights nor subjective agency, an assumption internalized by many women themselves. The victims of sexual violence may thus be blamed and persecuted, as in Gong-Ju's case.[21] Young women who seek agency, and push against the limits and constraints imposed by society, become targets for victimization and may not survive. Why is Hae-Mi the most exhilarating target serial killer Ben (*Burning*) has ever encountered? Presumably because she ignores social constraints more than most young women and so must be suppressed.

Most of the female-centred films discussed in this chapter have plots with a dysphoric trajectory that is diverted into a well-being script at a very late point of the narrative. A film plot requires drama and conflict, needless to say, but the lateness of the shift from one script to the other suggests that within Korea's hierarchical and masculinist ideology such outcomes are unlikely, a deus ex machina twist. That this structure still appears in a film as recent as *Student A*, released in 2018, indicates that filmmakers are not optimistic that Korean society is likely to change in the foreseeable future and they must keep pushing against its conservatism. After the classroom invasion dislocates Gong-Ju's precarious blossoming her situation becomes an exposition of a dysphoric society: the school Principal indicates that she will be expelled; the local police chief, who is in collusion with the perpetrators, advises Mrs Jo (Lee Yeong-Ran), with whom she is staying, to send her away and insinuates that she is the perpetrator, not the victim; Gong-Ju phones her father, who tells her to come home, but she realizes that he intends to betray her again; she phones the teacher who arranged her transfer, but he fobs her off; she phones her friend, Eun-Hui (Jeong In-Seon), but she is too appalled to pick up. In this hopeless situation, Gong-Ju grasps the agency she has striven for since she began to learn to swim and reverses the direction of the film in its final minute.

Comedic films such as *King of Fashion* or *Twenty* presuppose mishaps and reversals, but the effect of the final reversal in *King of Fashion* is very different from that in *Han Gong-Ju*. *King of Fashion* conforms to a common comedic pattern within which the protagonist's journey is from misfortune or abjection to triumphant well-being. Viewers have no doubt this outcome will prevail over the protagonist's ups and downs, whereas the precariousness of Gong-Ju's daily composure is foregrounded by flashbacks which gradually disclose the violence and abuse which shape her present, with the result that suicide is a predictable outcome. Temporal disruption by means of flashbacks is widely employed in coming-of-age films, and especially those grounded in a dysphoria script. Flashbacks contribute to the teleological rhetoric that, according to Moretti, makes a predetermined ending inevitable. An important strategy of coming-of-age films, then, is to identify that rhetoric and overthrow it with a counter-rhetoric that refuses the anticipated close. This strategy is one of the most important contributions Korean coming-of-age films have made to the genre.

NOTES

1. Jeffrey Jensen Arnett, "Emerging Adulthood: What Is It, and What Is It Good For?," *Child Development Perspectives* 1:2 (2007), p. 68.
2. Personal names appear in the normal Korean order—that is, family name followed by given name. Romanization of Korean follows Revised Romanization, except when a different system has been employed in quoted published work.
3. The sense of *script* I am using here has been adopted from everyday cognition into (for example) cognitive narratology. Individuals normally hold in memory specific, detailed knowledge of standard actions or situations, such as dining in a restaurant; similarly, as a narrative form, a script enables us to formulate inferences about the direction of a recognizable sequence of events on the basis of some core components, although such a script is a skeletal structure whose narrative realisation is flexible and its components are multifarious.
4. Roberta Trites, *Literary Conceptualizations of Growth: Metaphors and Cognition in Adolescent Literature* (Amsterdam: John Benjamins Publishing Company, 2014), p. 20.
5. Franco Moretti, "The Bildungsroman as Symbolic Form," in *The Way of the World: The Bildungsroman in European Culture* (London: Verso, 1987), p. 82.
6. Nancy K. Miller, *The Heroine's Text: Readings in the French and English Novel 1722–1782* (New York: Columbia University Press, 1980).

7. See further the discussion of well-being in Sung-Ae Lee and John Stephens, "From Anxiety to Well-Being: Openings and Endings of Children's Films from Japan and South Korea," in Casie Hermansson and Janet Zepernick (eds.), *The Palgrave Handbook of Children's Film and Television* (Cham, Switzerland: Palgrave Macmillan, 2019), pp. 170–171.

8. I follow the normal practice of identifying conceptual metaphors by placing them in small capitals.

9. Trites, *Literary Concepts of Growth*, pp. 3–4.

10. Ibid., pp. 21–25.

11. Ibid., p. 28.

12. Sarah Allan, *The Way of Water and Sprouts of Virtue* (Albany: State University of New York Press, 1997), p. 95.

13. Ibid., pp. 95–96.

14. For the relationship of cognitive maps and social ecology in Young Adult texts, see John Stephens, "Cognitive Maps and Social Ecology in Young Adult Fiction," *International Research in Children's Literature* 8:2 (2015), pp. 142–155.

15. The term ecotopia, referring to the notion of an ecological utopia, entered "green" discourses from Ernest Callenbach's 1975 novel, *Ecotopia: The Notebooks and Reports of William Weston* (New York: Bantam Books, 1977). Callenbach's utopian vision sought to combine environmental concepts with clean high technology.

16. For an extended analysis of *Nunbal* see Sung-Ae Lee, "SOCIETY IS A FAMILY: Social Exclusion and Social Dystopia in South Korean Films," in Bernard Wilson and Sharmani Patricia Gabriel (eds.), *Asian Children's Literature and Film in a Global Age: Local, National, and Transnational Trajectories* (Shanghai: Palgrave Macmillan, 2020).

17. Patrick Frater, "'Burning' Director Lee Chang-dong: Still Angry After All These Years," *Variety*, 3 December 2018, https://variety.com/2018/film/asia/lee-chang-dong-burning-cannes-1202812485/ [accessed 9 January 2020].

18. Patrick Brzeski, "HKIFF Interview: South Korea's Lee Chang-dong on the Many Mysteries of 'Burning,'" *The Hollywood Reporter*, 10 December 2018, https://www.hollywoodrepor ter.com/movies/movie-news/oscars-interview-lee-chang-dong-burning-1167869/ [accessed 9 January 2020].

19. Jerome Hamilton Buckley, *Season of Youth: The Bildungsroman from Dickens to Golding* (Cambridge, MA: Harvard University Press, 1974), p. 18.

20. See the discussion of the length of takes in East Asian film in Sung-Ae Lee, Fengxia Tan, and John Stephens, "Film Adaptation, Global Film Techniques and Cross-Cultural Viewing," *International Research in Children's Literature* 10:1 (2017), p. 18.

21. Young-Hee Shim, "Feminism and the Discourse of Sexuality in Korea: Continuities and Changes," *Human Studies* 24:1 (2001), p. 146.

BIBLIOGRAPHY

Abel, Elizabeth, Marianne Hirsch, and Elizabeth Langland. *The Voyage In: Fictions of Female Development*. Hanover, NH: University Press of New England, 1983.

Allan, Sarah. *The Way of Water and Sprouts of Virtue*. Albany: State University of New York Press, 1997.

Arnett, Jeffrey Jensen. "Emerging Adulthood: What Is It, and What Is It Good For?" *Child Development Perspectives* 1:2 (2007), pp. 68–73.

Buckley, Jerome Hamilton. *Season of Youth: The Bildungsroman from Dickens to Golding.* Cambridge, MA: Harvard University Press, 1974.

Lee, Sung-Ae. "'How Can I Be the Protagonist of My Own Life?': Intimation of Hope for Teen Subjectivities in Korean Fiction and Film." In John Stephens (ed.), *Subjectivity in Asian Children's Literature and Film: Global Theories and Implications.* New York: Routledge, 2012, pp. 95–114.

Miller, Nancy K. *The Heroine's Text: Readings in the French and English Novel 1722–1782.* New York: Columbia University Press, 1980.

Moretti, Franco. "The Bildungsroman as Symbolic Form." In *The Way of the World: The Bildungsroman in European Culture.* London: Verso, 1987.

Stephens, John. "Cognitive Maps and Social Ecology in Young Adult Fiction." *International Research in Children's Literature* 8:2 (2015), pp. 142–155.

Trites, Roberta. *Literary Conceptualizations of Growth: Metaphors and Cognition in Adolescent Literature.* Amsterdam: John Benjamins Publishing Company, 2014.

PART V

HOLLYWOOD AND FAMILY AUDIENCES

....

CHAPTER 27

THE WALT DISNEY COMPANY, FAMILY ENTERTAINMENT, AND HOLLYWOOD'S GLOBAL HITS

....

PETER KRÄMER

THE Walt Disney Company released *Star Wars: The Force Awakens* (J. J. Abrams, 2015) three years after it had taken over Lucasfilm Ltd., ten years after the last film in the series made by George Lucas (*Star Wars: Episode III—Revenge of the Sith* [2005]) had been released, and thirty-eight years after the original release of *Star Wars* in 1977 had helped to change Hollywood. Conceived, marketed, and widely understood as a film in the Disney tradition—a modern fairy-tale "aimed at kids—the kid in everybody"—*Star Wars* came out after a decade (1967–1976) in which Hollywood had largely turned away from family entertainment. By contrast, since 1977 the major studios have been most successful, both in the United States and in the rest of the world, with films addressed to an all-inclusive mass audience (including children and their parents as well as teenagers and young adults), mostly in the science fiction and fantasy genres.[1] Many of the biggest hit movies since 1977 tell, just as *Star Wars* did, stories about large-scale, even all-encompassing threats and destruction.[2] Also like *Star Wars*, these films often focus on families or family-like groups, especially on the often traumatic relationship between children and their parents or parental substitutes.[3]

Star Wars played a central role in reorienting the output of the major Hollywood studios and the viewing patterns of cinema audiences around the world; however, it did not do so on its own. Several big-budget science fiction films, notably Steven Spielberg's *Close Encounters of the Third Kind* (1977) and the DC comic book adaptation *Superman* (Richard Donner, 1978), both of which had already been in production by the time *Star Wars* was released, also helped to set the stage for future developments, and two films George Lucas produced in the wake of *Star Wars* consolidated the overall trend. Indeed, a list of the top-grossing films in cinemas around the world for the five-year period from

1977 to 1981 has *Star Wars* (later retitled *Star Wars: Episode IV—A New Hope*) at number one; its first sequel *Star Wars: Episode V—The Empire Strikes Back* (Irvin Kershner, 1980) at number two; the fantastic (in places decidedly supernatural, even religious) adventure *Raiders of the Lost Ark* (Steven Spielberg, 1981), a Lucas-Spielberg collaboration, at number three; *Close Encounters* at number five; *Superman* at number six; and the space-themed James Bond movie *Moonraker* (Lewis Gilbert, 1979) at number eight (as a rule, I look at the top ten, but the Box Office Mojo list I am using here does not include films below number eight).[4]

A comparison with the ten biggest hits in global cinemas for the five-year period from 2012 to 2016 reveals striking continuities, which is quite surprising considering that the (home-based and portable) media technologies competing with cinema-going have changed so much in the meantime, as have global cinema markets (most notably through the explosive growth of box office revenues in China). The chart for 2012–2016 looks eerily similar to that of 1977–1981, insofar as it includes a *Star Wars* film at number one (*Star Wars: The Force Awakens*); *Jurassic World* (Colin Trevorrow, 2015)—a sequel to Steven Spielberg's near-future science fiction film *Jurassic Park* (1993)—at number two; and four superhero movies (based on Marvel rather than DC comics): *The Avengers* (Joss Whedon, 2012, at number three), *Avengers: Age of Ultron* (Joss Whedon, 2015, at number five), *Iron Man 3* (Shane Black, 2013, at number seven); and *Captain America: Civil War* (Joe Russo, 2016, at number nine).

Unlike the list for the years from 1977 to 1981, the 2012–2016 top ten also include two animated features: the fairy-tale adaptation *Frozen* (Chris Buck and Jennifer Lee, 2013, at number six) and the *Despicable Me* prequel *Minions* (Pierre Coffin and Kyle Balda, 2015, at number eight). And unlike the earlier chart, these top ten are dominated by Disney, which produced *Frozen* and, through its fairly recent takeovers of Lucasfilm and Marvel Entertainment (acquired in 2009, although Marvel films up to and including 2011 were distributed by Paramount), is also responsible for five more films. From having no film among the ten top-grossing films for 1977–1981, Disney thus moved to have six films in the top ten for the years 2012–2016.

As of April 2020, Disney accounted for seven of the top ten films released since 2017, including the top five. The seven films are three more Marvel movies (two of them—*Avengers: Infinity War* [Anthony and Joe Russo, 2018] and *Avengers: Endgame* [Anthony and Joe Russo, 2019]—dealing with a genuinely universal threat, with half of all life in the universe being wiped out and a totally clean sweep being attempted as well), another *Star Wars* film and two "live-action" remakes (which in fact consist largely of computer-generated imagery) of 1990s animated features: *The Lion King* (Jon Favreau, 2019) and *Beauty and the Beast* (Bill Condon, 2017). The seventh title is *Incredibles 2* (Brad Bird, 2018) by Pixar Animation Studios which Disney had acquired in 2006 (though it had already owned all of Pixar's features from 1995 onwards).

As if this was not sufficient proof of Disney's dominance of global cinema, in March 2019 the company completed its takeover of 21st Century Fox, which means that it now controls all aspects of the *Star Wars* franchise and also owns the rights to James Cameron's *Avatar* (2009), arguably still by far the highest-grossing theatrical release of all time (if it were possible to adjust box-office revenues to changes in ticket prices around the world, *Avatar* would leave the official number one, *Avengers: Endgame*, far behind). Cameron has been working on four *Avatar* sequels, the first of which is scheduled to be released in 2022.[5]

The first section of this chapter examines how Disney achieved its current dominance; the second section shows that Disney paved the way for *Star Wars* and helped to reshape the operations of the other major studios as well. My analysis focuses on Hollywood's biggest global hits, highlighting their appeal to an all-inclusive mass audience and the internationalism of their stories, characters, and themes, with a special emphasis on the centrality both of parent-child relationships and of global threats and devastation.[6]

DISNEY'S HITS AND COMPANY HISTORY

For the Walt Disney Company today, its corporate history, which goes back all the way to 1923 (when it was called the Disney Brothers Cartoon Studio), is more alive and more relevant than for almost all other entertainment companies, because, highly unusually, Disney's intellectual property from many decades ago is still of enormous value.[7] This concerns not just the name and likeness of Mickey Mouse, which the company has used since 1928, making numerous films and licensing a myriad of products as well as featuring Mickey in all kinds of live performance, but also the first five animated feature films it produced between 1937 and 1942. With the exception of *Snow White and the Seven Dwarfs* (David Hand et al., 1937), these were not major hits during their original theatrical release, but Disney re-released them into cinemas on a regular basis for decades, and also had enormous success with their video releases, so that today they are among the biggest movie hits of all time. It is important to note that, from the outset, Disney's animated features were by no means targeted exclusively, or even predominantly, at young children.[8] They were also meant to appeal to the parents who would accompany their children to the cinema, and to the cinema-going public more generally. Through their many re-releases across the decades, these films could specifically build on the nostalgic feelings of adult audiences who had first seen them during their childhood.

While Box Office Mojo's all-time chart of all movies that have grossed in excess of $200 million in cinemas around the world (789 titles as of September 30, 2019) is probably not very reliable for the decades before the 1970s (due to insufficient data on foreign grosses), it is interesting to note that three of the four films released before 1972 included on this list are Disney animated features. *Bambi* (David Hand et al., 1942) is only beaten by *Gone with the Wind* (Victor Fleming, 1939, with numerous re-releases thereafter); the other two are *One Hundred and One Dalmatians* (Clyde Geronimi et al., 1961) and *The Jungle Book* (Wolfgang Reitherman et al., 1967).

Much more reliable and informative than Box Office Mojo is an all-time US box office chart that is adjusted for ticket-price inflation and includes revenues from all re-releases (it lists 300 titles).[9] Although this chart cannot tell us about the foreign earnings of Hollywood films, it is quite likely that many, if not most, of the films that did particularly well in the United States were also export hits.[10] The top-grossing films from 1937 to 1941 are, in this order: *Gone with the Wind*, *Snow White and the Seven Dwarfs* and two more Disney films, *Fantasia* (James Algar et al., 1941) and *Pinocchio* (Ben Sharpsteen et al., 1940). The only Disney animated feature made in this five-year period missing from the list is *Dumbo* (Ben Sharpsteen et al., 1941). *Bambi* is the top-grossing film from 1942 to 1946. To put the success of these films in perspective, in the all-time adjusted US chart the top-grossing films of the last twenty years—*Star Wars: The Force Awakens*, *Avatar*, and *Avengers: Endgame*—are all ranked below *Snow White*, and just ahead of *Fantasia*.

Another measure of success are rankings in the all-time sales charts for VHS tapes, DVDs, and Blu-ray discs. I have only found US charts, but once again, as a rule of thumb, we can assume that films that sell particularly well in the United States also do so in the rest of the world. Videotape was the dominant medium for movie rentals and sell-through from the late 1970s to the early 2000s, when it was overtaken by DVD; Blu-ray discs have been selling in significant numbers since 2006, but these numbers are far lower than for DVDs.[11] In recent years, both DVD and Blu-ray sales have collapsed (and video has disappeared altogether), so that it is unlikely that the recently compiled all-time charts will see much change at the top from now on.[12]

As with the adjusted box office chart, *Dumbo* is missing from the all-time US sales chart for VHS tapes (listing the top twenty-five titles), but the other Disney titles from 1937 to 1942 did extremely well on their video release in the late 1980s and 1990s, outperforming the vast majority of recent movies (and all other movies released theatrically before 1982, except for two more Disney animated features: *Cinderella* [Clyde Geronimi et al., 1950] and *One Hundred and One Dalmatians*). *Snow White and the Seven Dwarfs* (first released on video in 1994) comes in at number two, beaten only by Disney's *The Lion King* (Roger Allers and Rob Minkoff, 1994; on video in 1995); *Fantasia* (on video in 1991) follows at number seventeen, *Pinocchio* (on video in 1993) at number eighteen and *Bambi* (on video in 1989) at number twenty-one.

Although these earliest Disney animated features did not sell quite so well on DVD and Blu-ray discs, an all-time Blu-ray sales chart (listing the top ten titles) has *Snow White* (first released on Blu-ray in 2009) at number ten, and a consolidated all-time sales chart for all formats (listing the twenty top titles) has it at number three, beaten only by *The Lion King* and Pixar's *Finding Nemo* (Andrew Stanton, 2003). Apart from *Snow White*, there is no film on the Blu-ray chart released theatrically before the 2000s, and on the all-formats chart only *Snow White* and two other Disney animations (once again, *Cinderella* and *One Hundred and One Dalmatians*) were released before the 1990s.

Unlike other film companies, Disney has thus been able to keep re-releasing its oldest features for many decades, in theatres and on VHS, DVD, and Blu-ray, each time with considerable if not outstanding success. As clichéd as it may sound, it does seem to be the case that these animated features do not age like other movies; they are timeless. This is one of the main reasons for the company's financial success. However, an even more important reason has been the success of its theme parks, the first of which, Disneyland, opened in 1955 in California, while the second, Walt Disney World, opened in 1971 in Florida. By the mid-1970s, these two theme parks generated the majority of Disney's revenues and profits, and they continued to do so until the mid-1990s, when, in the wake of Disney's takeover of Capital Cities/ABC in 1995, television became the company's main source of revenues and profits.[13]

The theme parks were intimately connected with Disney's classic shorts and features, bringing many of their characters (among them Mickey Mouse) and settings (among them Sleeping Beauty's castle) to life, and thus drawing on their popularity. While the theme parks owed a lot of their success to Disney movies, the steady income generated by Disneyland (and later Walt Disney World) allowed the company to sustain, and eventually enlarge, its film operations. These operations had already changed in the 1940s, when, having complemented the company's initial output of animated short films and its licensing of all kinds of merchandise with the release of animated features from 1937 to 1942, the company branched out into live-action films, initially focusing on documentaries and live-action/animation hybrid features, and then also including live-action features, starting with *Treasure Island* (Byron Haskin, 1950). After eight years during which Disney's feature-length animations were all anthologies of short films, in 1950 the company also started releasing "proper" animated features again. In 1954, the company produced its first television show (*Disneyland*), among other things to advertise its soon-to-be-opened first theme park and its new movie releases. And in 1953, Disney set up its own distribution network in the United States, Buena Vista Distribution, adding an international distribution arm in 1961. In the 1950s and 1960s, Buena Vista released, on average, five films a year.

Continuing with the breakdown of the inflation-adjusted all-time US chart into five-year periods allows us to track the huge box office success of Disney films of the 1950s and 1960s, in the case of animated features mostly achieved through regular re-releases. *Cinderella*, which marked Disney's return to animated features in 1950, is the top-grossing film from the years 1947–1951. *Lady and the Tramp* (Clyde Geronimi et al., 1955) is the fifth highest-grossing film from the years 1952–1956, and *Peter Pan* (Clyde Geronimi et al., 1953) is at number eight. *One Hundred and One Dalmatians* is the top grosser from 1957 to 1961; *Sleeping Beauty* (Clyde Geronimi et al., 1959) is at number three, and the live-action adventure *Swiss Family Robinson* (Ken Annakin, 1960) is at number six. *Mary Poppins* (Robert Stevenson, 1964), another live-action film (which includes some animation), is at number three for 1962–1966. *The Jungle Book* is the second highest-grossing film from 1967–1971, and the live-action *The Love Bug* (Robert Stevenson, 1969) is just outside the top ten at number eleven.

Again, there is more to the success of these films than these box office rankings. *Cinderella* was also very successful on VHS, DVD, and Blu-ray (at number ten on both the all-time VHS and all-formats charts). *One Hundred and One Dalmatians* is at number twelve on the all-time VHS sales chart for the United States, and at number 18 on the sales chart combining all formats. *The Jungle Book* is the thirty-fifth best-selling DVD of all time in the United States; no other title released theatrically before 1989 is among the forty-two films listed in this chart.

None of the films that Disney released between *The Love Bug* in 1969 and the late 1980s could match the huge commercial success of the titles discussed above, but Disney had successful theatrical re-releases of its classic animated features both in the United States and abroad during this period. The company also released these films on video (making them available for only a limited period of time before withdrawing them again, awaiting another re-release). Disney and Jane Fonda, with her immensely popular exercise videos, dominated annual video sell-through charts in the United States from the mid-1980s onwards. Indeed, the sell-through market (as distinguished from the sale of videos to rental shops), which by the early 1990s had become Hollywood's single most important source of income, was in many ways created and sustained by the success of Disney's (and Fonda's) releases.[14]

During the 1980s, Disney branched out from its exclusive focus on family entertainment, first by setting up the more adult-oriented Touchstone Pictures, whose first release was *Splash* (Ron Howard, 1984), an updated and mildly risqué live-action version of the "Little Mermaid" fairy-tale. Later Disney added Hollywood Pictures (set up in 1984, but its first film, the horror comedy *Arachnophobia* [Frank Marshall, 1990], was released only several years later), and it acquired the "indie" studio Miramax in 1993. The takeover of Capital Cities/ABC then added more and soon-to-be dominant (in terms of revenues and profits) products and services, which did not fall under the Disney brand (one of Disney's most important assets, for example, is the sports cable network ESPN).[15] In the new millennium Disney refocused its film operations once again on family entertainment, not least through the acquisitions of Pixar, Marvel, and Lucasfilm. One of the main reasons for this was the extraordinary success of a new batch of Disney movies from the late 1980s onwards; all but one were family films.

The ten top-grossing films around the world from 1987 to 1991 included the Touchstone release *Pretty Woman* (Garry Marshall, 1990, at number five)—a romantic comedy which presents itself as a modern fairy-tale but features a prostitute—the animated *Beauty and the Beast* (Gary Trousdale and Kirk Wise, 1991, at number nine), and the live-action/animation hybrid *Who Framed Roger Rabbit* (Robert Zemeckis, 1988, at number ten). While the animated *The Little Mermaid* (Ron Clements and John Musker, 1989) came in only at number twenty-six, it is at number twenty-five on the list of the all-time best-selling videos in the United States (with *Beauty and the Beast* at number five), at number twenty-two on the list of the all-time bestselling DVDs, and at number nine on the list of the all-time best-selling films across all formats (*Beauty and the Beast* is number four, the same rank it has on the all-time Blu-ray sales chart for the United States).

From this point onwards, Disney was once again producing outstanding hits on a regular basis, placing at least two films among the ten global top grossers for each of the following five-year periods (if we include all the Pixar films, and all the Marvel films on this list, and the *Star Wars* movies Disney released after the Lucasfilm takeover): two in 1992–1996, three in 1997–2001, two in 2002–2006, four in 2007–2011 and, as already mentioned, six in 2012–2016. It is also important to note that, as a consequence of its takeover of Lucasfilm and Fox, Disney now (co-)owns *Home Alone* (Chris Columbus,

1990), the number one film of 1987–1991; *Independence Day* (Roland Emmerich, 1996), *Mrs Doubtfire* (Chris Columbus, 1993), and *True Lies* (James Cameron, 1994), respectively numbers three, seven, and ten for 1992–1996; *Titanic* (James Cameron, 1997) and *Star Wars: Episode I—The Phantom Menace* (George Lucas, 1999), the two top films for 1997–2001; *Star Wars: Episode III—Revenge of the Sith* (George Lucas, 2005), the number eight for 2002–2006; and *Avatar*, the number one for 2007–2011 (as well as, for example, the Indiana Jones films, which did particularly well in the 1980s).

Several of these huge box office hits from the last three decades—as well as other Disney releases—were also placed highly in the all-time video, DVD, Blu-ray and all-formats sales charts for the United States, with, for example, *Frozen* at number one on the Blu-ray chart, *Finding Nemo* at number one on the DVD chart, and *The Lion King* at number one on the VHS and all-formats charts. Indeed, all these charts are dominated by Disney releases, making up six of the top ten on the Blu-ray chart, five of the top ten on the DVD chart, and seven of the top ten both on the VHS chart and the chart for all formats. If we add older films that Disney has acquired through its recent takeovers, the numbers are seven, six, nine, and nine.

The global reach and future potential of many of the features Disney has released up to now is further demonstrated by the company's increasing output of remakes and sequels, including live-action remakes of, as well as live-action sequels to, animated features;[16] by the (in some cases hugely) successful launch of stage musicals based on both animated and live-action features, which run for years in theatres all around the world;[17] and by the expansion of rides or themed areas based on certain film franchises, such as *Star Wars* and *Avatar*, in Disney's parks (in addition to California and Florida, these can now be found in Tokyo, Paris, Hong Kong, and Shanghai). Disney's features are also the main attraction of the company's new streaming service Disney+, launched in November 2019. Furthermore, these features drive the sale of all kinds of merchandise, ranging from picture books and toys to clothes and collectibles. In other words, Disney's global hits are everywhere. And, as we will see next, the rest of Hollywood has done much in recent decades to emulate the Walt Disney Company.

DISNEY AND HOLLYWOOD'S GLOBAL HITS

Like Disney, today's other major Hollywood studios—Paramount (now part of National Amusements/Viacom), Warner Bros. (AT&T), Universal (Comcast), Sony Pictures Entertainment (formerly Columbia), as well as Disney's recent acquisition Fox—can trace their corporate histories back to the early decades of the twentieth century. These studios (and other majors that have since disappeared [RKO] or been reduced to a much diminished status [Loew's/MGM, United Artists]), quite unlike Disney, organized the production of large numbers of feature films (most of them eventually settling on one film a week) across the 1910s and 1920s.[18] In addition to their production plants in and around Los Angeles and their international distribution networks, several of the majors also owned large movie theatre chains in the United States and, to a lesser extent, abroad, mostly in Canada and Europe.

From early on, the major Hollywood studios tried out various forms of self-regulation (of potentially problematic content), culminating in the Motion Picture Producers and Distributors of America (later Motion Picture Association of America) Production Code, which operated from 1930 onwards, so as to reduce the interference of official censorship (which in the United States existed at the municipal and state levels but not at the federal level) and to make sure that, in principle, each film was suitable (but not necessarily attractive) for all age groups.[19] The film industries of many, possibly most, other countries were subjected to more extensive official censorship and also early on introduced age ratings, which excluded young children and, in many cases, most teenagers from screenings of particular films.[20] Through their contacts with censorship boards and other organizations around the world, the Production Code Administration tried to ensure that Hollywood exports would encounter minimal controversy and censorship abroad, especially in Europe, the most important export market.

From the outset, American feature-film producers invested a lot of money in films set in Europe (as well as other foreign parts) and/or featuring European characters in stories that were often based on well-known European source material, such as fairytales, novels, and plays.[21] Both published studio ledgers and studies of box office charts in various European countries indicate that these European-themed films tended to be Hollywood's biggest export hits.[22] Many of them also were big hits in the United States. From the 1910s to the late 1940s, however, American-themed films were more successful at the top of the US charts than the European-themed productions, as exemplified most clearly by the extraordinary success of two Civil War epics, *The Birth of a Nation* (D. W. Griffith, 1915) and *Gone with the Wind*.[23]

This situation changed in the late 1940s when, as the result of an anti-trust case, the major studios had to divest themselves of their domestic theatre chains and also confront rapidly declining ticket sales in the United States (while the European market was growing), to which they responded with a reduction in, and a reorientation of, their output.[24] These and other developments (such as changes in public opinion and audience preferences) led to the increased production of European-themed films. Quite surprisingly, from the late 1940s to the mid-1960s, such films (especially historical epics, international adventures, and musicals) dominated the US box office charts. The thirteen biggest non-Disney hits of this period were mostly set outside the United States: the historical epics *The Robe* (Henry Koster, 1953), *The Ten Commandments* (Cecil B. DeMille, 1956), *The Bridge on the River Kwai* (David Lean, 1957), *Ben-Hur* (William Wyler, 1959), *Cleopatra* (Joseph L. Mankiewicz, 1963), and *Doctor Zhivago* (David Lean, 1965); the international adventures *Around the World in Eighty Days* (Michael Anderson, 1956), *Goldfinger* (Guy Hamilton, 1964), and *Thunderball* (Terence Young, 1965)—at a stretch one might also include *The Greatest Show on Earth* (Cecil B. DeMille, 1952) in this category because of its itinerant, international cast, though all the action takes place in the United States; and the musicals *West Side Story* (Robert Wise and Jerome Robbins, 1961), an updated and Americanized version of *Romeo and Juliet, My Fair Lady* (George

Cukor, 1964), and *The Sound of Music* (Robert Wise, 1965).[25] These films also did well abroad, especially in Europe.[26]

Upon its initial release in 1937, Disney's *Snow White and the Seven Dwarfs* immediately became the highest grossing European-themed film of all time in the United States (according to not-inflation-adjusted figures, but the film would probably maintain the top position, without its re-releases, even in an adjusted chart).[27] As discussed in the previous section ("Disney's Hits and Company History"), through regular re-releases, many of Disney's subsequent pre-1970 animated features (and several live-action films), almost all European-themed, also became massive hits in the United States—and, following the general patterns identified here, presumably in export markets as well, especially in Europe (still Hollywood's largest export market but increasingly challenged by Latin America and Asia).

Like most of Hollywood's other top hits before the late 1960s, Disney's biggest hits from *Snow White* to *The Jungle Book* and *The Love Bug* tended to be set not only abroad, but also in the past (*The Love Bug* being one of the rare exceptions), and like a good proportion of these other top hits, most of them were musicals.[28] They frequently revolved around familial or family-like relationships, especially between young children or teenagers and their parents (or stepparents or other parental substitutes) and all kinds of associated emotional trauma, themes surprisingly absent from, or only marginally present in, most of Hollywood's biggest non-Disney hits during this period. Disney hits from the late 1930s to the 1960s (and beyond) featured incomplete and dysfunctional families; orphans and children left to their own devices and exposed to mortal danger; cruel, even murderous maternal characters; and, famously, a child having to deal with the death of his mother (in *Bambi*).

Also unlike other top hits before the late 1960s, Disney's best box office performers emphasized fantastic elements, such as magic, talking animals, a sentient car, and so on. When supernatural elements appeared in Hollywood's biggest non-Disney hits, it was mostly in the context of biblical epics, and thus they were associated with religious faith rather than fantasy. Furthermore, Disney produced a series of substantial science fiction hits dealing with the impact of advanced technology both in the future and in the past, starting with *20,000 Leagues under the Sea* (Richard Fleischer, 1954) and including, for example, *The Absent-Minded Professor* (Robert Stevenson, 1961). In fact, these Disney movies were, together with James Bond movies featuring futuristic technologies, the highest-grossing films in the United States that could be classified as science fiction before the release of *2001: A Space Odyssey* (Stanley Kubrick, 1968) and *Planet of the Apes* (Franklin J. Schaffner, 1968).[29]

Some of Disney's most successful science fiction films and animated features echo a key theme among the top hits produced by the other major studios, namely, the threat and/or enactment of large-scale destruction in many historical epics and international adventures, caused by, for example, armed conflict, divine intervention or a supervillain. The echoes of the theme of large-scale destruction in Disney hits include the devastating fire (caused by human intrusion into the forest) in *Bambi* and the advanced military technologies (including a nuclear bomb) deployed by Captain Nemo in *20,000 Leagues under the Sea.* Through their emphasis on fantasy or science fiction and on parent-child relationships (with the possibility of throwing a global threat into the mix), Disney films thus prepared the ground for *Star Wars.*

The company also exerted an enormous influence on the way in which the other studios conducted their business. When compared to the rest of Hollywood, from the mid-1950s to the 1970s Disney stood out because it was consistently and highly profitable with its focus first on one, then two theme parks, on a small number of features (few of which required huge budgets), television programmes, and all kinds of merchandise. All the company's offerings were addressed to family audiences and many of them referenced each other, thus potentially generating additional business for each other (a process later to be called synergy).[30]

By contrast, the other studios focused on a larger number of often extremely expensive movies, which were rarely related to the other products and services the studios offered (for example, television programmes) or the other businesses of their parent companies (which were often in completely unrelated industries). Being largely dependent on the income their films generated in movie theatres, first and foremost in the United States, the other studios were particularly strongly affected by the dramatic decline in ticket sales in the United States from the late 1940s onwards, reaching a historical low point in 1971 (it appears that, by and large, export markets had been shrinking since the late 1950s, but it is unclear when they bottomed out).[31]

The historical low point in the United States had a lot to do with what was in effect a suspension of the Production Code in 1966 (it was replaced by a rating system based on age appropriateness in 1968). This led to the production of a series of high-profile and often extremely successful taboo-breaking films that alienated large audience segments from the cinema-going experience and left a preponderance of young, educated urbanites in the cinema audience.[32] With a shrinking market and an increasing number of big-budget flops, several of the major studios took huge losses in the years around 1970.

In this situation, the Disney company provided a model for the reorientation of the American film industry. Some filmmakers, notably Lucas and Spielberg (who cited Disney movies among their inspirations for *Star Wars* and *Close Encounters*; indeed, both films, as well as later Lucas/Spielberg releases, were widely understood by the press as Disneyesque),[33] and some studio executives saw the possibilities for making movies for an all-encompassing family audience once again, and also for synergy.[34] Warner Bros. used its ownership of DC as the basis for the big-budget *Superman* movie, and Paramount converted fan favourite *Star Trek* (1966–1969), a TV show produced by its television subsidiary, into the equally big-budget *Star Trek: The Motion Picture* (Robert Wise, 1979), its "G"-rating (standing for "General audiences. All ages admitted") being by that time closely associated with children's films. The licensing of all kinds of merchandise (especially items for children) for these and other productions of the late 1970s and beyond also became ever more important.

In the 1980s, *synergy* became a buzz word, leading to the reorganization of existing conglomerates, several of which came to focus on media and entertainment instead of operating across diverse industries, and the formation of new media conglomerates.[35] The idea was that the entertainment products and services offered by these conglomerates would promote each other—but, unlike in the case of Disney, there is serious doubt about whether this strategy was, in fact, successful.[36] There is little doubt, however, that the types of Hollywood movies that were the most successful changed dramatically. Having been pushed aside by the taboo-breaking hits of the late 1960s, family entertainment returned to the top of the charts a decade later.

The ten top hits in the United States for 1967–1971 included the erotic comedy-drama *The Graduate* (Mike Nichols, 1967, at number one) and the graphic war and hospital movie *M*A*S*H* (Robert Altman, 1970, number six). The biggest US hits for 1972–1976 included *Jaws* (Steven Spielberg, 1975, number one), which featured nudity, mutilated bodies, and graphic depictions of shark attacks; *The Exorcist* (William Friedkin, 1973, number two), in places a highly sexualized horror film featuring obscene, sacrilegious talk and images of a grossly disfigured child's body; and the extremely violent gangster movie *The Godfather* (Francis Ford Coppola, 1972, number four). These three films also were Hollywood's biggest global hits during this period.

Between 1967 and 1976, historical films continued to be prominent on the US charts (and probably also abroad)—for example, *The Jungle Book*, *The Sting* (George Roy Hill, 1973), and *The Godfather*. Unlike historical films made in the preceding two decades, these top hits were mostly set in the United States rather than abroad, and in the recent rather than the distant past, and they had largely lost their epic dimension; that is, they did not deal with events and developments that had changed the course of history. Both international adventure movies and musicals had a much reduced presence on the US charts during this decade (although the former, especially the James Bond movies, appear to have performed much better abroad).[37]

Newly prominent hit patterns in the decade 1967–1976 concerned, as we have seen, films breaking long-standing taboos to do with sex, violence, race, and religion, and also films—usually labelled *disaster movies*—about threats to large numbers of people and large-scale death and destruction caused by a combination of human error, technological failure, and natural catastrophe (thus putting a different spin on the threatening developments and destructive events so often central to historical epics and international adventures).[38] These films, which, compared to Hollywood's taboo-breakers, were often perceived as a return to old-fashioned family entertainment, included *Airport* (George Seaton, 1970, number five in the US top ten for 1967–1971); *The Towering Inferno* (John Guillermin, 1974, number seven for 1972–1976); and *The Poseidon Adventure* (Ronald Neame, 1972, number ten for 1972–1976; *Earthquake* [Mark Robson, 1974] was just below the top ten).

Importantly, since the mid-1960s the relationship between parents and children, long a staple of Disney's output, had also emerged as a key theme in many non-Disney hits—notably in *The Sound of Music* (1965, the top hit in the United States for 1962–1966) and *The Exorcist*, but also, with regard to (young) adult characters and their parents, in *The Graduate*, *Love Story* (Arthur Hiller, 1970, at number four in the United States for 1967–1971), and *The Godfather*.

One way to understand the huge impact of *Star Wars* and *Close Encounters of the Third Kind* had in 1977 around the world is to see them as films that avoided the taboo subject matter and narrow focus on the United States that was characteristic of so many hits between 1967 and 1976, and managed to combine most of the other hit patterns of the preceding decades—that is, epics, international adventures, Disney fantasy films, and disaster movies with a particular emphasis on the parent-child relationship and a sense of global threat. In doing so, these two films were able to connect with key cinema experiences of the different generations of people who were going to the movies at the time (whereby younger people had often become familiar with older hits through theatrical re-releases and television broadcasts).

Star Wars is a fairy-tale (beginning with "A long time ago…") featuring magic-like spirituality ("the Force") and talking machines. It tells a story that is not set in the United States and does not feature American characters (although the actors are mostly Americans) about an orphan who loses the people who raised him, as well as his recently acquired mentor. It is a historical and futuristic epic about the fate of whole civilizations (all about to be absorbed into an Evil Empire); an interstellar (not merely international) adventure, ranging across a whole galaxy; and a film that both threatens and enacts ultimate disaster (the Death Star's explosion of Alderaan, an almost successful attack on the rebel moon). It was also designed and marketed to appeal to all age groups, and commentators at the time acknowledged that it had, in fact, managed to assemble an all-inclusive mass audience.[39]

Similarly, *Close Encounters of the Third Kind* is an epic movie and international adventure (key scenes are set outside the United States, and a globe-trotting Frenchman is a central character) about contact with an extra-terrestrial civilization. The film revolves around two families who are being torn apart (in one a single mother is violently separated from her son; in the other a father pushes away his wife and children), with musical (and, in some versions of the film, dialogue) references to Disney's *Pinocchio* and a quotation from the biblical epic *The Ten Commandments*, which is shown on television in an early scene and suggests a religious interpretation of the story of *Close Encounters* (about a man called to climb up a mountain, where he encounters heavenly beings). There is a sense of threat—after all, the aliens have vastly superior technology and abduct children, military pilots, and others, and a secretive international organization keeps the world's population from learning about all this—but the emphasis is on the possibility of what we might call transcendence, or perhaps redemption, offered by contact between humanity and extra-terrestrials. Like *Star Wars*, *Close Encounters*, despite its many disturbing thematic and formal elements, was widely understood as entertainment for the whole family.[40]

Since 1977, most of Hollywood's biggest global hits have, in different ways, been inspired by the synthesis of preceding hit patterns achieved by *Star Wars* and *Close Encounters*.[41] Some hits focus only on a subset of the elements making up this synthesis; others replicate it in full.[42] The latter include the *Star Wars* sequels and prequels. As already noted, most of these films were top-ten global hits for the five-year periods in which they were released.

The *Harry Potter* movies (2001–2011) also stay close to the *Star Wars* model (or perhaps, it is better to say that they stay close to the source novels, which are, to a considerable degree, modelled on *Star Wars*). They feature another young orphan who belatedly learns about the fate of his parents, from whom he has inherited the potential to master a mysterious force (here called *magic*), and another villain who is building an evil empire, initially only in the United Kingdom but surely intended to be expanded later, thus constituting a threat to the global political order and changing the overall course of history. The films centrally revolve around the relationship between young children (later, teenagers) and their parents and parental mentors, and they are neither set in the United States nor have American protagonists. Much the same can be said about the *Lord of the Rings* movies (2001–2003), with the important exception that the four hobbits at the centre of the story are in some respects childlike, but they are not children, and their parents do not play an important role in the story, although parental mentors do. Unlike the *Harry Potter* films, the *Lord of the Rings* movies range across different lands. Based on best-selling books for children and teenagers, these two film series made up half of the global top ten for the years 2002–2006, and three of the top ten for 2007–2011.

Arguably, many of the adaptations of superhero comic books also stay close to the *Star Wars* model, starting with *Superman*. Based on a comic strip that most people would first have come across as children, the film focuses on a child losing his parents, finding loving foster parents (and also encountering a ghostly projection of his dead father), and travelling across the galaxy and then all around Earth. It depicts global destruction (of Superman's home planet) and a large-scale disaster in California, involves supernatural abilities, and allegorizes religious tales by sending a young male to Earth, where he will do great things for humankind. The protagonist is an immigrant to the planet rather than a native-born American. *Avengers: Infinity War* and *Avengers: Endgame* contain variants of most of these elements, taking, as already noted, the epic scope of the story and the global threat it revolves around to the furthest extremes and also the internationalism—or rather, *interstellarism* (if this word existed)—of the settings and cast, with parent-child relationships quite central as well, especially those of the antagonist and his (adult) daughters. These and other superhero movies occupy one place each in the global top tens for 1977–1981, 1987–1991, 2002–2006, and 2007–2011, and four places in the global top ten for 2012–2016, and they are shaping up to dominate the global top ten for 2017–2021.

While the *Star Wars* and *Lord of the Rings* films are set in an imaginary past, and the *Harry Potter* and superhero films in a kind of alternative present, there are also a number of science fiction films set in the (near) future in the global top ten for the various five-year periods. Films like *Terminator 2: Judgment Day* (James Cameron, 1991, number three for 1987–1991), *Independence Day* (number three for 1992–1996), *Men in Black* (Barry Sonnenfeld, 1997, number five for 1997–2001), *Armageddon* (Michael Bay, 1998, number six for 1997–2001), *The Matrix* (Lana and Lilly Wachowski, 1999, number nine for 1997–2001), *Avatar* (number one for 2007–2011) and *Transformers: Dark of the Moon* (Michael Bay, 2011, number three for 2007–2011) deal with, actual or possible, turning points in human history, including the very end of that history. They not only emphasize the threat of large-scale destruction but also enact it on-screen, and they engage in different ways with biblical ideas about the apocalypse (as indicated already by the titles of *Terminator 2: Judgment Day* and *Armageddon*). These films may focus on American characters and settings, but they also include scenes set in other countries, in space, or in a future in which the United States is long gone. Several, especially *Terminator 2*, focus on the relationship between parents and their (in some cases adult) children. Similarly, the near-future science fiction films *Jurassic Park* (number two for 1992–1996), *The Lost World: Jurassic Park* (Steven Spielberg, 1997, number four for 1997–2001), and *Jurassic World* (number two for 2012–2016) centre on the threat and reality of large-scale destruction and the relationship between adults and children, and though they mostly feature American characters, they largely take place in exotic locations.

In addition, the top hits since 1977 include a series of historical films, among them *Raiders of the Lost Ark* (number three for 1977–1981), *Indiana Jones and the Temple of Doom* (Steven Spielberg, 1984, number six for 1982–1986), *Indiana Jones and the Last Crusade* (Steven Spielberg, 1989, number four for 1987–1991), *Dances with Wolves* (Kevin Costner, 1990, number six for 1987–1991), *Robin Hood: Prince of Thieves* (Kevin Reynolds, 1991, number eight for 1987–1991), and *Titanic* (number one for 1997–2001). Most of these films also have an epic scope and deal with (the threat of) large-scale destruction. Thus, the first and third *Indiana Jones* films concern the rise of the Nazis and their attempt to utilize divine power to achieve their evil purposes; *Dances with Wolves* traces the ongoing destruction of Native American societies; *Robin Hood* features a kingdom in disarray; and, somewhat allegorically, the sinking of the Titanic represents the final disintegration of Victorian culture. Apart from *Dances with Wolves*, none of these films is primarily set in the United States (and even *Dances with Wolves* is set on land that in the film's time frame has only just begun the process of being integrated into the United States), and the first three could be described as international adventures. Several of them deal centrally with the relationship between parents and their (young) adult children, and, to a greater or lesser degree, they can all be regarded as family entertainment.

This last point certainly applies to almost all the films in the final two groups that I want to discuss—namely, ghost stories and fairy-tales. The former include *Ghost* (Jerry Zucker, 1990, number two for 1987–1991), *The Sixth Sense* (M. Night Shyamalan, 1999, number three for 1997–2001), and the three *Pirates of the Caribbean* movies, which are placed at number two for 2002–2006 and at numbers five and seven for 2007–2011. The fairy-tales include *Beauty and the Beast* (number nine for 1987–1991), *Aladdin* (Ron Clements and John Musker, number five for 1992–1996), and *Frozen* (number six for 2012–2016) and the parodic *Shrek 2* (Andrew Adamson, 2004, number five for 2002–2006), as well as *Alice in Wonderland* (Tim Burton, 2010, number six for 2007–2011), which is not based on an actual fairy-tale but has most of the characteristics of such tales. It is unclear how exactly to categorize the following four animated hits: *Toy Story 2* (John Lasseter, 1999, number seven for 1997–2001), *Finding Nemo* (number three for 2002–2006), *Toy Story 3* (Lee Unkrich, 2010, number four for 2007–2011), and *Minions* (number eight for 2012–2016). They are not, strictly speaking, fairy-tales, but they do feature quasi-magical elements: toys that are alive, talking fish, and the eponymous fan-tastic creatures in *Minions*.

Of the films mentioned in the preceding paragraph, most are addressed to an all-in-clusive family audience, and many explore, at least in parts, the experiences of children and child-like characters and their relationship to parents or parental figures. The ma-jority are set outside the United States and have no American characters. All of them are characterized by drastic departures from everyday reality that we may label fantastic, su-pernatural, or, indeed, religious. The religious dimension is fairly explicit in *Ghost* and *The Sixth Sense*, which both feature souls who linger in this world after their deaths, be-fore they can finally move on, and in the first and the third *Indiana Jones* movies, which emphasize the reality of divine power (through the ark of the covenant and the holy grail).

I want to end this overview of global movie hits since 1977 by taking a closer look at *The Lion King* (number one for 1992–1996), which is the cornerstone of one of Hollywood's most successful franchises. Even without taking merchandise sales, television income, and many other revenue streams into account, the numbers are truly impressive:

- Global box office revenues for the 1994 and 2019 films: $0.97 billion and $1.64 bil-lion, respectively (the former figure would be much higher if one were to adjust it for inflation);[43]
- US VHS and DVD sales revenue for the 1994 film: $0.52 billion and $0.22 billion, respectively, plus $0.30 billion in VHS sales revenue for the straight-to-video se-quel *The Lion King II: Simba's Pride* (Darrell Rooney, 1998) (again, these figures would be higher if they were adjusted for inflation; the film is likely to have earned a similar amount on VHS and DVD abroad);[44]
- Revenues for the stage version of the 1994 film, which was launched in 1997 in the United States and has since been presented all around the world: $8 billion (as of 2017).[45]

Not coincidentally, *The Lion King* comes very close to the synthesis of preceding hit patterns achieved by the *Star Wars* saga (of which here I mainly invoke Episodes IV–VI). In the film's truly epic narrative, much of the animal kingdom is under threat because of the rise of an evil king; indeed, after his ascendance, the kingdom comes close to total ruin, shown in scenes of horrendous devastation. A young male lion (Simba), who has lost his father—a powerful leader who makes ghostly appearances after his death, of-fering spiritual guidance—is at the heart of the story. This young male goes on a journey across different lands, but in the end, must return home because only he can defeat the evil king and restore the kingdom. Needless to say, neither the setting nor the characters are American (in the dubbed versions shown in the non-English-speaking world, the voice actors are not American either).

The element that sets *The Lion King* apart from the original *Star Wars* trilogy is that Simba witnesses his father's death and is made to feel responsible for it (whereas in *Return of the Jedi* [Richard Marquand, 1983], Luke refuses to kill his father and, in fact, redeems him by rousing him to turn against the Evil Emperor).[46] In this respect, *The*

Lion King reaches back to a foundational moment in Disney storytelling—namely, the death of Bambi's mother. This reminds us that, though *Star Wars* has provided the model for most of Hollywood's biggest global hits since the late 1970s, among the preceding hit patterns *Star Wars* synthesized so well Disney's animated features stand out. When it comes to exploring the traumas associated with the relationship between children and parents, Disney has always tended to go much further than *Star Wars* or Hollywood's other big global hits.

Conclusion

Starting with the release of its first animated feature in 1937, the Walt Disney Company produced a series of extraordinarily successful, and impactful, movies until 1969. The majority were (musical) adaptations of fairy-tales or of more or less fairy-tale-like children's books. From the late 1940s to the mid-1960s, the largest group among the biggest hits for the other Hollywood studios in the United States and, it seems, abroad were historical epics (including biblical tales), followed by international adventures and musicals. Like most of Disney's biggest hits, these films were mostly set in the past and outside the United States (in Europe, especially), and they had few American protagonists. They were designed to be suitable for and, ideally, to appeal to people of all ages, both in the United States and abroad (again, especially in Europe). Indeed, we might want to call all of them "family films."

As Noel Brown has argued, "family film" is a complex category, and applying it in any particular case may require, in addition to an analysis of the film itself, extensive research into contextual factors (to do, among other things, with the marketing and critical reception of a film).[47] A movie may fit the category "family film" when it is presented in some contexts, but not in others (I have argued that *2001: A Space Odyssey* functioned, for most people, as a family film during its original US theatrical release but has rarely been regarded as such in other contexts).[48] To clarify the status of Hollywood's biggest hits from the 1930s to the 1960s as "family films" would therefore necessitate research into where, when, and how these hits were presented to which audiences, obviously a mammoth task that goes far beyond the possibilities of a chapter such as this one.

The same applies to Hollywood's global hits since the 1970s. Although some can easily be ruled out (it is, for example, very hard to imagine circumstances under which people would regard *The Exorcist* as a film for the whole family), and others just as easily ruled in (under what circumstances would a Disney animated feature *not* be regarded as a family film?), there are many films that may function as family entertainment in some contexts and not in others. Based on previous research but also, admittedly, on anecdotal evidence and hunches, in this chapter I have suggested that the vast majority of Hollywood's biggest global hits since the late 1970s are, in effect, family films; that is, they function as family entertainment for most people in most circumstances. I have also suggested that the enormous commercial success and impact of *Star Wars* had a lot to do with the fact that it had synthesized most of the key hit patterns of the past to do with epics (in the case of *Star Wars*, futuristic as well as historical), including biblical epics (belief in "the Force" in *Star Wars* taking the place of Judeo-Christian faith); international (now interstellar) adventures; and Disney fairy-tales ("A long time ago" instead of "Once upon a time," and magic being replaced by "the Force").

Like many epics and international adventures, as well as the 1970s cycle of disaster movies, *Star Wars* revolved around the threat of large-scale destruction and the actual, spectacular display of such destruction (here taken to the extreme of an exploding planet, this display of power being in the service of subjecting all the known universe to the rule of an Evil Emperor). Like many Disney fairy-tales, *Star Wars* was also centrally concerned with the difficult, even traumatic relationship between a young person and parents as well as parental substitutes. And, like the vast majority of both Disney hits and the biggest hits from other Hollywood studios between the late 1940s and the mid-1960s, *Star Wars* was neither set in the United States nor featured American characters.

Finally, I have tried to show that most of Hollywood's biggest global hits since 1977 have, more or less directly and more or less strongly, been influenced by *Star Wars* and, therefore, through the mediation of this film, have in many ways continued the hit patterns of the more distant past. However, the orientation in most of these films has been more global than it was in the pre-1970s hits. For instance, the non-American settings are no longer primarily European, but might be anywhere on Earth or, indeed, elsewhere in this or an alternative universe. The Bible and Judeo-Christian faith are also less important, while other forms of spirituality play a larger role. Last but not least, the threats to people's freedom, happiness, and lives that many of the stories revolve around relate to much larger groups than ever before, in some cases to all humans (as well as non-human animals) on Earth, or even all life in the universe. Thus, with its biggest hits, Hollywood is telling truly global stories for a global audience. At the same time many of these stories also concern the most intimate human relationship, the one that is the foundation for everything else: that between children and their parents.

Notes

1. This chapter is a summation of research I have conducted over the last three decades. To avoid listing countless primary and secondary sources in the endnotes, I draw on several of my previous publications. With regard to the topics covered in the first few sentences, see Peter Krämer, "'It's Aimed at Kids—the Kid in everybody': George Lucas, *Star Wars* and Children's Entertainment," in Yvonne Tasker (ed.), *Action and Adventure Cinema* (London: Routledge, 2004), pp. 358–370, on the making, marketing and reception of *Star Wars*. On changing hit patterns in the United States between the late 1940s and the early 1980s, see Peter Krämer, *The New Hollywood: From Bonnie and Clyde to Star Wars* (London: Wallflower, 2005). On global hit patterns since the late 1970s, see Peter Krämer, "Hollywood and Its Global Audiences: A Comparative Study of the Biggest Box Office Hits in the United States and Outside the United States since the 1970s," in Richard Maltby, Daniel Biltereyst, and Philippe Meers (eds.), *Explorations in New Cinema History: Approaches and Case*

Studies (Oxford: Wiley-Blackwell, 2011), pp. 171–184. Also see Noel Brown, *The Hollywood Family Film: A History, from Shirley Temple to Harry Potter* (London: I.B. Tauris, 2012), on the various definitions and the changing status of family entertainment, and James Russell and Jim Whalley, *Hollywood and the Baby Boom* (New York: Bloomsbury Academic, 2018), on changing hit patterns in the United States from the 1950s to the present.

2. Peter Krämer, "Welterfolg und Apokalypse: Überlegungen zur Transnationalität des zeitgenössischen Hollywood," in Ricarda Strobel and Andreas Jahn-Sudmann (eds.), *Film transnational und transkulturell: Europäische und amerikanische Perspektiven* (Paderborn: Wilhelm Fink Verlag, 2009), pp. 171–184.

3. Peter Krämer, "Would You Take Your Child to See This Film? The Cultural and Social Work of the Family-Adventure Movie," in Steve Neale and Murray Smith (eds.), *Contemporary Hollywood Cinema* (London: Routledge, 1998), pp. 294–311.

4. Based, as are all subsequent five-year global charts, on Box Office Mojo, "All-Time Box Office: World-Wide," https://www.boxofficemojo.com/alltime/world/?pagenum=1&p=.htm [accessed September 30, 2019]. One of the reasons for looking at five-year periods is that global box office revenues are not comparable over longer periods of time due to ticket price inflation, fluctuating exchange rates and changes in the overall size of the global cinema market. Within each five-year period, the influence of these factors on the ranking of films can be expected to be minimal. Five-year breakdowns also are a good way to track historical changes and continuities.

5. Sarah Whitten, "*Avatar* Sequels Are a Huge Risk for Disney, But You Can't Doubt James Cameron," CNBC.com, July 26, 2019, https://www.cnbc.com/2019/07/26/james-camerons-avatar-sequels-are-a-huge-risk-for-disney.html [accessed September 30, 2019].

6. For a discussion of the reasons for studying hit movies, see, for example, Peter Krämer, "Big Pictures: Studying Contemporary Hollywood Cinema through Its Greatest Hits," in Jacqueline Furby and Karen Randell (eds.), *Screen Methods: Comparative Readings in Film Studies* (London: Wallflower, 2005), pp. 124–132; see also Krämer, *New Hollywood*, pp. 6–37.

7. For a succinct history of the Disney company, see Janet Wasko, *Understanding Disney: The Manufacture of Fantasy* (Cambridge, UK: Polity, 2001), pp. 6–69.

8. See, for example, the discussion of *Snow White*, *Pinocchio* (1940), and *Fantasia* (1940) in Leonard Maltin, *The Disney Films*, 3rd ed. (New York: Hyperion, 1995), pp. 25–45.

9. Box Office Mojo, "Domestic Grosses Adjusted for Ticket Price Inflation," https://www.boxofficemojo.com/alltime/adjusted.htm [accessed October 22, 2019].

10. In a previous study, I have shown that there is considerable overlap between Hollywood's biggest domestic and export hits from the 1970s to the early 2000s. One key difference is the greater success of non-American-themed films outside the US. As most of Disney's biggest hits in the US are neither set in the US, nor do they feature American characters, they are quite likely to have replicated their domestic success abroad. See Krämer, "Hollywood and Its Global Audiences," pp. 171–184.

11. Paul McDonald, *Video and DVD Industries* (London: British Film Institute, 2007).

12. Samuel Axon, "DVD and Blu-ray Sales Nearly Halved over Five Years, MPAA Report Says," ArsTechnica.com, April 12, 2019, https://arstechnica.com/gadgets/2019/04/dvd-and-blu-ray-sales-nearly-halved-over-five-years-mpaa-report-says/ [accessed 30 September 2019]. The all-time VHS, DVD, Blu-ray and all-formats sales charts for the US that I am going to use are from Wikipedia, "List of Best-Selling Films in the United States," https://en.wikipedia.org/wiki/List_of_best-selling_films_in_the_United_States [accessed 30 September 2019].

13. This paragraph and the one that follows are partly based on Peter Krämer, "Disney and Family Entertainment," in Michael Hammond and Linda Ruth Williams (eds.), *Contemporary American Cinema* (Maidenhead: Open University Press, 2006), pp. 265–266.

14. Peter Krämer, "Disney, George Lucas und Pixar: Animation und die US-amerikanische Filmindustrie seit den 1970er Jahren," *Film-Konzepte* 33 (February 2014), pp. 6–21.

15. For a detailed breakdown of Disney's divisions, see the company's annual financial reports; the one for 2018 can be found at https://www.thewaltdisneycompany.com/wp-content/uploads/2019/01/2018-Annual-Report.pdf. For an international study of perceptions of the Disney brand, see Janet Wasko, Mark Phillips and Eileen R. Meehan (eds.), *Dazzled by Disney? The Global Disney Audiences Project* (Leicester, UK: Leicester University Press, 2001).

16. Wikipedia, "List of Disney Live-Action Adaptations and Remakes of Disney Animated Films," https://en.wikipedia.org/wiki/List_of_·Disney_live-action_remakes_of_animated_films [accessed September 30, 2019].

17. Wikipedia, "Disney Theatrical Productions," https://en.wikipedia.org/wiki/Disney_Theatrical_Productions [accessed September 30, 2019].

18. For an overview of the development of the major Hollywood studios, see Douglas Gomery, *The Hollywood Studio System: A History* (London: BFI Publishing, 2005).

19. This paragraph is based on Ruth Vasey, *The World According to Hollywood, 1918–1939* (Exeter, UK: University of Exeter Press, 1997).

20. See Daniel Biltereyst and Roel Vande Winkel (eds.), *Silencing Cinema: Film Censorship Around the World* (New York: Palgrave Macmillan, 2013).

21. Sheldon Hall and Steve Neale, *Epics, Spectacles, and Blockbusters: A Hollywood History* (Detroit, MI: Wayne State University Press, 2010).

22. Joseph Garncarz, *Wechselnde Vorlieben: Über die Filmpräferenzen der Europäer 1896–1939* (Frankfurt: Stroemfeld, 2015), pp. 127–134, 203–251. Information on the biggest export hits of several Hollywood studios in selected years before the 1970s can be found in their internal ledgers which were published as microfiche supplements to the following essays: H. Mark Glancy, "MGM Film Grosses, 1924–1948: The Eddie Mannix Ledger," *Historical Journal of Film, Radio and Television* 12:2 (June 1992), pp. 127–143; Richard B. Jewell, "RKO Film Grosses, 1929–1951: The C. J. Tevlin Ledger," *Historical Journal of Film, Radio & Television* 14:1 (March 1994), pp. 37–50; and H. Mark Glancy, "Warner Bros. Film Grosses, 1921–51: The William Schaefer Ledger," *Historical Journal of Film, Radio and Television* 15:1 (March 1995), pp. 55–74.

23. Joel W. Finler, *The Hollywood Story* (London: Octopus, 1988), pp. 276–277.

24. This paragraph is largely based on Peter Krämer, "'Faith in Relations between People': Audrey Hepburn, *Roman Holiday* and European Integration," in Diana Holmes and Alison Smith (eds.), *100 Years of European Cinema: Entertainment or Ideology?* (Manchester, UK: Manchester University Press, 2000), pp. 195–206; and Peter Krämer, "Stanley Kubrick and the Internationalisation of Postwar Hollywood," *New Review of Film and Television Studies* 15:2 (June 2017), pp. 250–269.

25. Krämer, *New Hollywood*, pp. 19–27, 111–115.

26. See, for example, Joseph Garncarz, *Hollywood in Deutschland: Zur Internationalisierung der Kinokultur 1925–1990* (Frankfurt: Stroemfeld, 2013), pp. 91–97; 185–200.

27. Finler, *Hollywood Story*, p. 276.

28. Krämer, *New Hollywood*, pp. 19–27, 111–115.

29. Peter Krämer, *2001: A Space Odyssey* (London: BFI Publishing, 2010), pp. 31, 37–38, 90–95.

30. This paragraph and the next two are largely based on Krämer, "Disney and Family Entertainment," pp. 265–269.

31. For changing cinema attendance levels in Europe, see Ginette Vincendeau (ed.), *Encyclopedia of European Cinema* (London: BFI Publishing, 1995), pp. 466–467.

32. Krämer, *New Hollywood*, pp. 47–63.

33. Peter Krämer, "'The Best Disney Film Disney Never Made': Children's Films and the Family Audience in American Cinema since the 1960s," in Steve Neale (ed.), *Genre and Contemporary Hollywood* (London: BFI Publishing, 2002), pp. 185–200, at 187, 190. Also see Krämer, "It's Aimed at Kids—the Kid in Everybody," pp. 358–370; and Peter Krämer, "Spiritual Science Fiction for the Whole Family: Spielberg, *Close Encounters of the Third Kind* and 1970s Hollywood," in David Roche (ed.), *Steven Spielberg, Hollywood Wunderkind and Humanist* (Montpellier: Press universitaires de la Méditerranée, 2018), pp. 35–49.

34. Krämer, "Disney and Family Entertainment," pp. 269–276.

35. Thomas Schatz, "The Return of the Hollywood Studio System," in Erik Barnouw (ed.), *Conglomerates and the Media* (New York: New Press, 1997), pp. 73–106.

36. Jonathan A. Knee, Bruce C. Greenwald, and Ava Seave, *The Curse of the Media Mogul: What's Wrong with the World's Leading Media Companies* (New York: Portfolio, 2009).

37. See, for example, the West German charts in Garncarz, *Hollywood in Germany*, pp. 193–196.

38. Krämer, *New Hollywood*, pp. 63–65.

39. Krämer, "It's Aimed at Kids," pp. 358–370.

40. Krämer, "Spiritual Science Fiction for the Whole Family," pp. 35–39.

41. The absence of an explicit and forceful threat to large groups of people, and of the enactment of large-scale destruction, makes *Close Encounters* a less influential model for future global hits. However, the film's emphasis on transcendence and redemption, in the absence of global threats, is also arguably a key element of, for example, *E.T. The Extra-Terrestrial* (1982, the number one global hit for 1982–1986), *Ghost* (1990, number two for 1987–1991), *Forrest Gump* (1994, number four for 1992–1996), *The Sixth Sense* (1999, number three for 1997–2001) and *Finding Nemo* (number three for 2002–2006). Four of these five films—as well as, for example, *Home Alone* (number one for 1987–1991)—also centre, just like *Close Encounters*, on the relationship between young children (or childlike characters) and their parents.

42. Cp. Krämer, "Would You Take Your Child to See This Film?," pp. 294–311; "Disney and Family Entertainment," pp. 275–276; "Disney, George Lucas und Pixar," pp. 6–21; and "Big Pictures," pp. 124–32.

43. Box Office Mojo, "All-Time Box Office: World-Wide," https://www.boxofficemojo.com/alltime/world/?pagenum=1&p=.htm [accessed October 22, 2019].

44. Wikipedia, "List of Best-Selling Films in the United States," https://en.wikipedia.org/wiki/List_of_best-selling_films_in_the_United_States [accessed October 22, 2019].

45. Wikipedia, "*The Lion King* (musical)," https://en.wikipedia.org/wiki/The_Lion_King_(musical) [accessed October 22, 2019].

46. In fact, *The Lion King* goes as far as suggesting that, on some level, Simba did indeed wish his father to die; after all, he sings "I Just Can't Wait to Be King," thus expressing a desire that can only be fulfilled if the old king dies. On this and other intriguing aspects of this film, see Peter Krämer, "Entering the Magic Kingdom: The Walt Disney Company,

The Lion King and the Limitations of Criticism," *Film Studies* 2 (Spring 2000), pp. 44–50. Interestingly, the *Star Wars* prequels revolve around Anakin Skywalker's separation from his mother and his mourning of her death, and also around his responsibility for the death of his wife. And in the recent sequels, the antagonist Kylo Ren kills his father.

47. Brown, *Hollywood Family Film*, pp. 6–8.
48. Peter Krämer, "'A Film Specially Suitable for Children': The Marketing and Reception of *2001: A Space Odyssey* (1968)," in Noel Brown and Bruce Babington (eds.), *Family Films in Global Cinema: The World beyond Disney* (London: I.B. Tauris, 2015), pp. 37–52.

BIBLIOGRAPHY

Brown, Noel. *The Hollywood Family Film: A History, from Shirley Temple to Harry Potter.* London: I.B. Tauris, 2012.

Garncarz, Joseph. *Hollywood in Deutschland: Zur Internationalisierung der Kinokultur 1925–1990.* Frankfurt: Stroemfeld, 2013.

Garncarz, Joseph. *Wechselnde Vorlieben: Über die Filmpräferenzen der Europäer1896–1939.* Frankfurt: Stroemfeld, 2015.

Hall, Sheldon, and Steve Neale. *Epics, Spectacles, and Blockbusters: A Hollywood History.* Detroit, MI: Wayne State University Press, 2010.

Krämer, Peter. "'The Best Disney Film Disney Never Made': Children's Films and the Family Audience in American Cinema since the 1960s." In Steve Neale (ed.), *Genre and Contemporary Hollywood.* London: BFI Publishing, 2002, pp. 185–200.

Krämer, Peter. "Big Pictures: Studying Contemporary Hollywood Cinema through Its Greatest Hits." In Jacqueline Furby and Karen Randell (eds.), *Screen Methods: Comparative Readings in Film Studies.* London: Wallflower, 2005, pp. 124–132.

Krämer, Peter. "Disney and Family Entertainment." In Michael Hammond and Linda Ruth Williams (eds.), *Contemporary American Cinema.* Maidenhead: Open University Press, 2006, pp. 265–279.

Krämer, Peter. "Disney, George Lucas und Pixar: Animation und die US-amerikanische Filmindustrie seit den 1970er Jahren." *Film-Konzepte* 33 (February 2014), pp. 6–21.

Krämer, Peter. "'A Film Specially Suitable for Children': The Marketing and Reception of *2001: A Space Odyssey* (1968)." In Noel Brown and Bruce Babington (eds.), *Family Films in Global Cinema: The World beyond Disney.* London: I.B. Tauris, 2015, pp. 37–52.

Krämer, Peter. "Hollywood and Its Global Audiences: A Comparative Study of the Biggest Box Office Hits in the United States and Outside the United States since the 1970s." In Richard Maltby, Daniel Biltereyst, and Philippe Meers (eds.), *Explorations in New Cinema History: Approaches and Case Studies.* Oxford: Wiley-Blackwell, 2011, pp. 171–184.

Krämer, Peter. "'It's Aimed at Kids—the Kid in Everybody': George Lucas, Star Wars and Children's Entertainment." In Yvonne Tasker (ed.), *Action and Adventure Cinema.* London: Routledge, 2004, pp. 358–370.

Krämer, Peter. *The New Hollywood: From Bonnie and Clyde to Star Wars.* London: Wallflower, 2005.

Krämer, Peter. "Welterfolg und Apokalypse: Überlegungen zur Transnationalität des zeitgenössischen Hollywood." In Ricarda Strobel and Andreas Jahn-Sudmann (eds.), *Film transnational und transkulturell: Europäische und amerikanische Perspektiven.* Paderborn: Wilhelm Fink Verlag, 2009, pp. 171–184.

Krämer, Peter. "Would You Take Your Child to See This Film? The Cultural and Social Work of the Family-Adventure Movie." In Steve Neale and Murray Smith (eds.), *Contemporary Hollywood Cinema*. London: Routledge, 1998, pp. 294–311.

Russell, James, and Jim Whalley. *Hollywood and the Baby Boom*. New York: Bloomsbury Academic, 2018.

Wasko, Janet. *Understanding Disney: The Manufacture of Fantasy*. Cambridge, UK: Polity, 2001.

Wasko, Janet, Mark Phillips, and Eileen R. Meehan, eds. *Dazzled by Disney? The Global Disney Audiences Project*. Leicester, UK: Leicester University Press, 2001.

CHAPTER 28

....

READING *JASON AND THE ARGONAUTS AS A CHILDREN'S FILM*

....

SUSAN SMITH

GUIDED by a figurehead made in the form of Hera (Honor Blackman), queen of the gods and wife of Zeus (Niall MacGinnis), the Argo ship has just landed with its crew on the Isle of Bronze in *Jason and the Argonauts* (Don Chaffey, 1963). Warned by Jason (Todd Armstrong, dubbed by Tim Turner), in line with Hera's decree, against taking anything from the island except food and water, Hylas (John Cairney) and Hercules (Nigel Green) chase after a herd of goats only to find themselves suddenly in a clearing, ring-fenced by statues. In the foreground is the imposing bronze figure of Talos, standing crouched, sword in right hand, on a plinth. Set apart from the shore where the boat and its crew have just landed, the openness combined with isolation of this location—accentuated by the now more prominent sounds of the wind and birds—imparts the sense of it as a theatrical arena of a private kind, one in which a compelling psychological fantasy is about to be played out.

The impact of our initial sighting of the formidable-looking Talos (captured by a dramatic side-long view of him alone, followed by a frontal shot that has him still in the foreground but now encompasses the other statues behind him) is heightened by the reintroduction of Bernard Herrmann's score at this exact moment, its bold, brass-laden tones aptly heralding the giant man of bronze's first appearance. Overawed by what they see, Hylas and Hercules stand looking up at the statue, at which point Hylas wonders aloud whether Talos is "one of the Titans." "He might be—he's big enough," muses Hercules. "Didn't Jason say something about Talos?" continues Hylas, before starting off towards the statue, followed by Hercules. After more shots of Talos, Hylas exclaims: "This must be where Hephaestus moulded the statues of the gods!" "Yes," replies Hercules in a hushed, reverent tone as he gazes around, "and set them up for all the world to see." As Hylas and Hercules get closer to Talos, their tiny, ant-like figures contrast with the imposing size of this and the other statues. Following a shot of first Hylas on his own, and then of both men looking up at Talos, interspersed with an even closer shot of the man of bronze (his rusted surface now all the more prominent), the camera slowly tracks down the statue's body before coming to rest on his name on the plinth beneath, located just above a door. "Hercules…?" says Hylas, inviting his friend to join him, which the older man duly does, and both walk towards this entrance.

Once they open the door (accompanied by a loud creaking sound), a pulsating harp-based cue (reminiscent of Herrmann's score for *Vertigo* [Alfred Hitchcock, 1958]) strikes up evoking the mysterious nature of the two men's discovery as a detached interior shot shows them crossing the threshold. "It's a treasure chamber!" declares Hercules. "The treasure chamber of the gods," exclaims Hylas, and then both men hurry towards a pile of riches heaped inside a chest in foreground of the frame. Having cried out in excitement on finding and holding up a pearl, Hylas chides Hercules for mistaking a brooch pin for a javelin. Then, as rusty metallic sounds begin to intrude ominously on the soundtrack, Hercules maintains, "Well, whatever it is, it'll make a useful weapon! Let's get back to the ship." Hylas cautions Hercules to put the brooch pin back on account of what Jason said, but the older man persists: "Well, it won't be missed. Anyway, if the gods leave all this lying around unguarded, they obviously don't want it." "Come on!" he urges his younger friend, just as the door clangs shut. Their initial attempts to open the door prove futile, until Hercules braces himself and musters all his strength to force it ajar, allowing both men to escape. On scurrying outside, a high-level view shows them looking around trying to figure out why the door mysteriously closed. Cut to another high-level view, this time solely of Hercules as he speculates: "It must have been the wind." At this, the camera adopts an over-the-shoulder position from behind Hercules as he continues to look around, only to be jolted back to looking at Talos, just as the statue, with a terrible grating, creaking sound, turns its head slowly and menacingly towards Green/Hercules (Figure 28.1).

So begins arguably one of most memorable sequences in stop-motion special effects history where Talos, now stirred to life, proceeds to wreak havoc on the Argonauts and their ship, only to eventually be destroyed by Jason. Heeding advice from Hera (in the fourth and penultimate instance of help allowed by Zeus), the hero "looks to [Talos's] ankles" and, opening the plug he spies there, releases the mythical bronze statue's *ichor* (life blood), causing the now stricken statue to clutch at his throat, scream in apparent agony, crack, and fall to the ground (Figure 28.2). This event, in turn, brings about Hylas's death, when the young man runs back in a fatal attempt to retrieve the brooch pin or "weapon" taken by Hercules from the deities' chamber, and is crushed by the collapsing Talos. Ray Harryhausen,[1] a pioneer of stop-motion special effects and the creative force behind this and other fantasy episodes in *Jason and the Argonauts*, is also credited as an associate producer of this movie directed by Don Chaffey,[2] whose contribution has been overshadowed by Harryhausen's growing reputation as the main auteur of films featuring his work.[3] The sequence involving Talos is the first of several in this version of *Jason and the Argonauts* that were created using Dynamation, a process developed by Harryhausen that used split screens and rear projection to integrate the models seamlessly into the live-action footage.[4] Approximately eight feet tall in the original legend,

FIGURE 28.1. Talos awakens. *Jason and the Argonauts* (1963, Charles H. Schneer Productions). Frame-grab.

FIGURE 28.2. The death of Talos. *Jason and the Argonauts* (1963, Charles H. Schneer Productions). Frame-grab.

Talos is transformed by Harryhausen into a giant hundred-feet monster who terrorizes the crew both on shore and, once, in their boat, although the animatronics model itself was only twelve inches high.[5] Departing from the Apollonius of Rhodes story, the episode involving Talos in the 1963 movie version is the first of several Jason experiences on his hero's quest to find the Golden Fleece in which creatures from Greek mythology intervene to obstruct his progress.[6] The other main Harryhausen fantasy sequences that follow include those involving the Harpies, who are called on by Zeus to torment the blind man Phineas (Patrick Troughton); the "Clashing Rocks" where demigod Triton (Bill Gudgeon) rises up out of the water to hold back the cliffs and help the Argo ship pass through on its way to the land of Colchis;[7] the seven-headed Hydra that guards the Golden Fleece and fights Jason to prevent its theft; and, finally, the warrior skeletons whose famous uprising and battle with Jason and two of the Argonauts is considered by many to be the crowning example of Harryhausen's stop-motion special effects work.

With the Talos sequence in mind as emblematic of the fantasy stop-motion sequences overall, this chapter aims to offer an individual contemplation of what it is about the movie's textual properties that make it capable of exerting such childlike fascination and appeal (this isn't to say, of course, that the film doesn't exert a hold over an adult viewer, though it's possible that any such appeal will have its roots in childhood). We'll begin by considering Talos's awakening in terms of its censoring purpose. Before doing so, though, it's worth noting that while this entire episode (culminating in Talos's death) can be read partly in terms of its moral function, the film as a whole is characterized by a muted didacticism alongside a spirit of defiance evocative of the 1960s that is prevalent throughout the story. Compared to movies typically produced during the so-called classical era of cinema, *Jason and the Argonauts* was released in 1963, early in what has been termed as the post-classical era of moviemaking when censorship and other restrictions began to relax. The fact that Jason's quest, culminating in his theft of the Golden Fleece, is treated by the film without any sense of censure seems indicative of this loosening of moral resolve. As Paul Wells points out, the film never questions the "morality" of Jason's quest, taking it as a given that the protagonist is justified in his actions.[8] For Noel Brown, too, the film's "plotline offers little more than basic heroic motivation; the substance of the movie experience lies within the various dangers Jason and his crew encounter during their voyage."[9] The emphasis on spectacle (exemplified in Harryhausen's exciting fantasy sequences) and a less obvious form of didacticism arguably makes the film a precursor to the Spielberg/Lucas style of blockbuster family-adventure film. As such, *Jason and the Argonauts* might be seen to capture a transitional moment in Hollywood's children's film: on the one hand, hearkening back to a more overtly didactic form of cinema and, on the other, pointing forward to a less discernibly moralistic mode.

On the face of it, of course, *Jason and the Argonauts* doesn't appear to be a children's film due to its lack of actual child characters. The only exceptions occur near the beginning when Jason and his youngest sister, Philomena, are briefly and anonymously shown as infants being rescued or carried into the temple of Hera for protection (respectively) during Pelias's murderous attack on their father Aristo, then King of Thessaly. When recounting the defining principles of the children's film, Noel Brown cites the presence of child characters as one of the main qualifying criteria. He goes on to acknowledge, however, that "the on-screen presence of children is not a pre-requisite for classification as a children's film," with "many productions" instead featuring "what might be called 'symbolic children,'" a "highly mutable" category consisting of "non-child figures in which 'childlike' attributes...are invested."[10] That *Jason and the Argonauts* features adult characters as "symbolic children" who are controlled and guided on their quest (emblematic of the child's journey towards adulthood) by the gods (figuratively, their "parents") is visualized early on in the sequence, when Jason is transported to Mount Olympus and miniaturized to the size of the pieces on a map-like chessboard, becoming only inches tall in front of Zeus, Hera, and the other divinities. In a reversal of what happens in *The Wizard of Oz* (Victor Fleming, 1939), where Dorothy Gale (Judy Garland), in a literal rendering of the "adult-like" responsibility now placed on her shoulders, has to grow up on reaching Munchkin city, emerging from her aunt and uncle's house in the land of Oz a seemingly (she doesn't physically increase in height) much taller person (relative to the diminutive inhabitants she encounters there), Jason gets smaller when he is brought face-to-face with the much larger (and hence symbolically more parental, in terms of stature) gods.

The fact that the film is a fantasy/adventure fable taken from classical mythology is often cited as further proof of its credentials as a children's film. This chapter looks beyond platitudes about the timeless appeal to children of the creatures and adventures from classical mythology, and argues instead that there is more to understanding what might make this cinematic retelling of the Jason and the Argonauts legend so compelling to a younger viewer. It won't try to explain the film's interest for a young audience through empirical research, however, given the challenges of attempting to reconstruct the responses of audiences who may have been children in 1963 but are now adults. Instead, it takes the film's special attraction for children after 1963 as a given, enlisting by way of support the tributes that abound online and elsewhere highlighting the impact of Harryhausen's work on people growing up[11] (whether this will remain the case and, if so, to what degree are interesting questions but lie beyond the scope of this chapter), not to mention the lasting impression it made on this author as a child.[12] It's worth recalling, too, how many notable special-effects creators, directors, and other filmmaking personnel have said that watching Harryhausen's special effects in childhood was a major formative influence on their creative development.[13] Harryhausen himself often said that his own career had been inspired by seeing *King Kong* (Merian C. Cooper and Ernest B. Schoedsack, 1933) for the first time as a young adolescent, attributing its lasting power to Willis O'Brien's transformation of an inches-high model of Kong into a giant ape.[14] Given Harryhausen's frequent testimony that his childhood experience of watching King Kong had ignited his life-long passion for stop-motion animation, and taking into account the seminal influence and impact that ordinary cinema-goers and film industry professionals ascribe to Harryhausen's work when they were growing up, it seems reasonable to suggest that *Jason and the Argonauts* is a film whose stop-motion fantasy animation, along with its enduring legacy, was forged in the crucible of childhood.

Recalling the moment in the film when Talos comes alive, it's easy to see how a standard reading might dwell on the moral function, whose repressive, censoring power is realised with such unsettling force that it may well leave a lasting impression on a youthful imagination. In exploring the childhood allure of this sequence (and, by extension, the film as a whole), we shall begin, therefore, by thinking about its more conventional role before considering what it is, exactly, that might make Talos's awakening, pursuit of the argonauts, and subsequent death resonate more subversively from a childhood perspective. From there, we shall move on consider a much overlooked and often dismissed aspect of the film: its narrative. Contrary to what others have maintained,[15] this chapter argues that *Jason and the Argonauts*'s narrative may also be central to understanding the movie's resonance for a child, although the contradictions inherent therein (more on this later) may make it more responsive to the confusions and dilemmas of childhood than capable of advancing a coherent moral standpoint.[16]

FINDING DIDACTICISM IN THE
TALOS EPISODE

Triggered directly by Hercules's disobedience in stealing the brooch pin from the treasure chamber, the man of bronze's coming alive and destructive pursuit of the film's mythical strong man and his friend Hylas (not to mention the entire crew of the ship, eventually) invites the reading that this is a punishment of these two characters. As the episode's "symbolic children" because of their errant behaviour, Hercules and Hylas are implicitly admonished for going against "parental" rule (represented by Hera's order—conveyed via Jason—not to take anything except food or water from the island). It's a punishment that results in the death not only of Talos but also of Hylas himself, whose tragic end is a direct result of his attempt to retrieve the brooch pin Hercules had wrongfully taken from the treasure chamber. reconstrued in this movie's retelling of the legend,[17] Hylas's untimely demise (and Hercules's guilt-ridden refusal to accept his young friend's death) bears out that "it is a firm structural principle of the [children's film] genre that individuals and/or groups that violate accepted codes of society will eventually get their comeuppance."[18] As such, the Talos episode can be understood to conform fairly conservatively, on this level, to notions of what a children's film is meant to do.

That it is Hercules, not Hylas, who takes the brooch pin and survives, might seem to contradict this kind of reading and meting out of moral justice, especially given the older man's implied status as a kind of symbolic father figure for his young friend, his "son." In engineering the narrative so that Hercules survives, the film broadly follows Apollonius's original story.[19] But Hercules's responsibility for the theft is never in doubt; it is clear from the moment the awakening Talos first directs his accusatory gaze towards him[20] to the moment the older man admits his guilt just before leaving the ship for the final time in search of his friend: "Why kill a boy for my grave fault?" a penitent Nigel

Green/Hercules asks Jason. Because of the camera set-up when Talos turns his head, it seems, disconcertingly, that he is looking straight at us, the viewers, too, creating a frisson of danger that may carry a heightened charge for a young member of the audience. Notwithstanding this, the fact that it's Hylas who warns Hercules not to take anything from the treasure chamber might still make the young man's death seem like an excessive punishment, especially given the minor nature of the two men's misdeed. That it is Hylas (the "son") who suffers the ultimate punishment for the wrongdoing of Hercules (the "father") might also fuel a child's a sense of the injustice of taking the blame for the sins of a "parent." Indeed, if Hylas ultimately has to shoulder the blame, it further strengthens the logic of the older man's guilty admission of culpability afterwards.

Hercules's theft of an item from the treasure chamber also anticipates Jason's theft of the Golden Fleece. As such, it could be argued that the film enacts a *twofold* psychological displacement as it switches from Jason to Hercules and then to Hylas, the character most representative of the child, who is left to assume responsibility and make the ultimate sacrifice. It might, therefore, make more sense to think of Hylas's death as a substitute for the moral judgement that isn't enforced on Jason within the narrative proper, even though he has plundered another country to get the Golden Fleece. The skeleton sequence is quite explicitly construed as an act of vengeance by an angry King Aeetes (Jack Gwillim), the ruler of the kingdom of Colchis, on Jason and his crew for the theft. Yet even here, Armstrong's Jason manages to escape (even if his two argonauts and fellow fighters don't) and as I argued earlier, there's no suggestion that the film itself condones Aeetes's retributive deed, presenting the king instead as merely another potentially deadly (and not altogether likeable) antagonist. Perhaps, then, it's during fantasy sequences like the Talos episode that moral judgement is dispensed indirectly and in an overdetermined fashion, so that Hercules's and Hylas's removal of nothing more than a brooch pin anticipates and stands in for Jason's more serious theft of the Golden Fleece near the end of the film. Indeed, if Hercules functions in the narrative as a kind of foil for Jason's taking of the fleece, then Talos's pointed targeting of the older man during this first fantasy episode makes sense both psychologically and ideologically, linking the story's arch strongman to Jason (perpetrator of the narrative's ultimate larceny) and acknowledging Hercules (not Hylas) as originator of this episode's more minor wrongdoing.

SUBVERSIVE CHILDHOOD FANTASIES AWAKENED BY TALOS

Having considered the Talos episode from a psychoanalytical perspective that bears out *Jason and the Argonauts*'s conventional ideological workings as a children's film, it is important to recognize that this sequence can also be experienced in a radically different and potentially more subversive way. The moment where the man of bronze comes alive arguably takes us to the heart of this movie's childlike allure, and to grasp the full significance of this we need to contemplate its animistic powers. Slowly turning his head with a creaking sound evocative of an indefinably long period of time spent rusting motionless on his plinth, Talos's transition from inanimate statue to sentient being invested with movement and life encapsulates something quintessential about the nature of animation itself, especially the impulse known as *animism* (concerning an ability to breathe life into the inanimate) that scholars claim is fundamental to the form.[21] The grating sounds that herald Talos's shift from inert to moving statue are especially crucial in alluding to his inanimate origins even at the very point where he awakens, creating a sense of ambiguity regarding whether he is animate or inanimate that for Freud (drawing on Jentsch and writing more broadly) is a condition for generating feelings of the uncanny.[22]

As Harryhausen's own comments make clear, he was all too conscious of the irony of having to exaggerate Talos's mechanical rustiness—an unusual practice, given how the famed stop-motion animator was typically more preoccupied with trying to make his creatures' movements seem as fluid as possible.[23] Harryhausen was right, though, to exaggerate Talos's rusty condition, since it's precisely this quality that amplifies the sense that the bronze statue is coming to life, drawing attention to the animistic process by which the weathered figure is brought into being and stressing the difficulty of Talos's discovery of movement after such a long period of immobility. But if Talos's awakening encapsulates something fundamental about the animistic impulses inherent in Harryhausen's stop-motion special-effects work in general, then it acquires a particular imaginative significance when it comes to reading *Jason and the Argonauts* as a children's film.

Perhaps part of the childlike appeal of the Talos episode stems from its ability to encapsulate something about the young viewer's fascination with inanimate objects of play and a desire to invest them with life. If so, then the sequence can be understood to enact a fantasy of attaining a god-like power over such playthings, which may, in turn, help to explain the attractiveness of animation (stop-motion animation, in particular) as a form capable of fulfilling such a desire. That the bronze statue of Talos (like the Harpies, Hydra, and skeletons that follow) is an animatronics model brought to life through Harryhausen's stop-motion special effects is suggestive of this, making the moment where he awakens and turns his head archetypally suggestive of a child's wish-fulfilment fantasy. Moments such as this when creatures like Talos are stirred into being and run amok realise this fantasy in a manner that's simultaneously thrilling (it's as if the child's plaything acquires not just the breath of life but an omnipotent power that previously could only be imagined) and terrifying (the object's power is such that it outstrips the child's control, evoking feelings of vulnerability and helplessness instead).

If one accepts this kind of reading, then a young viewer is no longer merely the transgressor and the victim in a drama where Talos functions as the implied avenger, an agent of (parental) retribution doling out punishment to Hercules and Hylas, the sequence's "symbolic children." Rather, in this cinematic dream-turned-nightmare, the child is able to indulge in a fantasy of power that positions Talos as the symbolic toy, model, or other plaything who is now magically invested with the breath of life and transformed into a living, moving being, whose subversive energies may be at once both deeply pleasurable and unsettling, which ultimately requires their containment and the killing off of the monster. Such a childlike investment in a more subversive side to Talos may be accentuated by the statue's much-noted sympathetic qualities, especially during his final death throes, the compelling nature of which enables him to become more than a repressive agent of parental punishment and an even stronger figure of identification for a young, viewing other.[24] The man of bronze's awkward, stiff movements potentially heighten his pathos-inducing qualities, evocative as these are of a growing child's feelings of bodily discomfort and physical gaucheness. This dramatic inversion of Talos's role (whereby the statue transforms from agent of parental oppression, on one reading, into a subversive identification figure for the child, on the other) is reflected in the gods' position. No longer are they merely representatives of an intrusive form of parental authority; on this reading their control over humans (especially evident in the game of chess Zeus and Hera play using pieces symbolizing their counterparts on earth) now invites comparison with the child's manipulation of the inanimate plaything.[25] Indeed, given that the gods' control over humans has sometimes been compared (in documentaries and elsewhere) to Harryhausen's power, as stop-motion animator, over his models-turned-mythical creatures, this recognition that the film's attractiveness to a juvenile spectator may reside in the child's own animistic impulses and fantasies with regard to the inert object of play implicitly associates the creativity of stop-motion animation itself with a childlike sensibility.[26]

So far, we've explored two diametrically opposed ways of interpreting Talos's role, so much so that the episode involving him appears highly ambivalent when *Jason and the Argonauts* is considered as a children's film. Such is the deep-rooted uncertainty underpinning this episode that it becomes impossible to determine whether the giant man of bronze performs a punitive or an empowering function from the perspective of childhood (not to mention his "uncanny" blurring of inanimate and animate states) and thus can be read as offering either a child's nightmarish playing out of parental control or a fantasy of gaining release from that. Rather than this profound sense of tension or contradiction at the heart of *Jason and the Argonauts* being a fatal flaw, however, it may be the very thing that makes the film resonate so strongly for a young audience, enabling it to speak to some of the inconsistencies and incongruities of childhood. By way of illustrating this sense of ambivalence in the film, we've focused on the episode involving Talos as a major example of the film's fantasy special-effects sequences. But, as we're about to see, though Harryhausen's memorable stop-motion feats usually attract the most attention, *Jason and the Argonauts*'s much-overlooked narrative world is also important in articulating the child's sense of confusion about authority and the desire to rebel.

THE IMPORTANCE OF NARRATIVE IN
JASON AND THE ARGONAUTS

Of particular significance here is the way certain characters are wont to question, with growing explicitness and indignation, the degree of power the gods (again, readable as symbolic parents) exert over humans, creating a sense of resentment and hostility towards their divine "superiors" that is specific to this movie adaptation. Initially, the narrative presents this power as contradictory and confusing for those humans on the receiving end, but increasingly, it shows key personages openly defying the gods' authority over them, and eventually countenancing the possibility of rebellion. The ambiguous degree of power the gods exert over humans is established from the outset via Pelias (Douglas Wilmer), Jason's arch-enemy. In the first scene, Pelias is told by a priest (Michael Gwynn), who reads Pelias's future in the ashes, that he will conquer the kingdom of Thessaly that night and kill its King (Aristo) "because Zeus commands it." But no sooner has Pelias laid his sword on the fire in thanks to the gods, professing, "If I am protected by Zeus, I will have no need of this," than he is cautioned by the same priest: "Pelias. It is also foretold, that although you will win the throne of Aristo, you will, when Zeus ordains, lose it to one of Aristo's children." Frustrated by this prophecy, which denies him control over his destiny, a determined Pelias tries to thwart this fate by killing Aristo's children. Pelias sets off into battle, and the next scene shows him entering the temple of Hera, where an adult Briseis (Davina Taylor), one of Aristo's children, kneels in prayer before the statue of the goddess, having brought her infant sister (Philomena) with her. Pelias asks Briseis to confirm who she is, but is silenced by Hera (who emerges—her identity unbeknownst to him—in shadowy, human form from a corner of the temple). Having been told by Hera that Briseis called upon the goddess, who heard her prayer, Pelias kills the young woman by plunging his sword into her, asking that prayers be said for him, too, as he does so. In an exchange worth quoting in full, Pelias then tries to absolve himself of responsibility for what he has just done by construing his murder of Briseis as an act of divine ordination, only to be challenged by Hera:

PELIAS: It is the will of Zeus.
HERA: It is not the will of Zeus. It is your will. Zeus has given you a kingdom. The rest will be your own doing. The gods abandon you, Pelias. A one-sandaled man shall come and no gods shall protect you from him.
PELIAS: A one-sandaled man?
HERA: The child who has escaped you: Jason.
PELIAS: Then why was I not told the whole prophecy? Why did Zeus drive me to kill this girl when the only one I needed to kill was Jason?
HERA: Zeus cannot drive men to do what you have done. Men drive themselves to do such things that the gods may know them and that men may understand themselves. The killing of Jason will do you no good. Kill Jason and you kill yourself.

Pelias's villainy in this opening part of the film establishes him as Jason's main human adversary (and vice versa), and Hera's prophecy is fulfilled when Wilmer's character (who is now King of Thessaly) is later saved from drowning by the one-sandaled hero (Jason having grown into a young man). But, as the above exchange between Pelias and Hera indicates, it is through this arch-enemy of Jason that the film arguably first gives vent to the child's confusion about authority and sense of injustice: "Why wasn't I told the whole prophecy?" Pelias demands in obvious frustration upon discovering that his murder of Briseis has been pointless (Figure 28.3). Hera's reply is typically ambiguous: to begin with, she tells Pelias that he cannot deflect responsibility for what he has just done onto the gods and presents his action here as akin to a test that reveals his true nature to himself and the deities. But then she denies him all possible control over his destiny by telling him that if he kills Jason, it will be a self-destructive act that will result in his own death.

Through this kind of contradictory commentary, Hera at once condemns Pelias as being guilty of murder (and hence capable of agency) yet also construes him as a passive servant of an ordained fate, unable to change a destiny decreed by the gods. As such, Pelias has the potential to become an implied figure of identification for a child who, like him, may feel the weight of expectation from parents and society to develop a sense of accountability for their actions, yet at the same time is liable to feel controlled by that same authority. Given that Pelias initiates a questioning of the gods that culminates in Jason's explicit voicing of rebellion against them during the 'Clashing Rocks' episode, it is possible to read these two characters as psychological twins despite their ostensible

FIGURE 28.3. "Why wasn't I told the whole prophecy?" Pelias asks Hera. *Jason and the Argonauts* (1963, Charles H. Schneer Productions). Frame-grab.

enmity, Pelias representing a more transgressive side of the hero. Jason's affinity with Pelias is, in fact, gestured at long before the Clashing Rocks sequence where he can be heard admitting to Hermes (Michael Gwynne) that he doesn't believe in the gods, just moments before being transported to Mount Olympus. The psychic kinship, or inter-dependency, of the two men is also hinted at in Hera's advice to Pelias not to destroy Jason—a point the perfidious King of Thessaly revisits later when explaining his actions to his son Acastus (Gary Raymond): "Kill Jason and you kill yourself."

In an attempt to buy time and exert at least a limited degree of control over his fate, Pelias advises Jason to undertake his quest to find the Golden Fleece before returning to claim the throne of Thessaly (thereby overthrowing Pelias himself as the incumbent king). Once Jason's long odyssey begins, Pelias recedes from the film and is represented instead by his treacherous son, Acastus (who becomes a prominent member of Jason's crew and eventually betrays him to King Aeetes). Pelias's role as a mouthpiece for questioning the authority of the gods (and, by implication, for expressing the child's resentment of parental control) is performed by the blind Phineas during the episode (immediately after the one involving Talos) detailing the unsighted character's perse-cution by and eventual liberation from the Harpies. That the Harpies deprive Phineas of his food seems telling in this context, evoking as it does, a traditional punishment (or threat of punishment) of the misbehaving child by the parent ("to bed without supper!"). Pelias's previous sense of injustice is in turn couched more explicitly by Phineas. Moments before Jason arrives with his crew, and following the latest attack by the Harpies, the blind man questions why Zeus would punish him daily despite the fact he didn't sin every day. Then, upon meeting Jason, Phineas explains that Zeus blinded him and ordered the Harpies to torment him as a penalty for misusing his powers of prophecy. Having made clear that "the gods have ordered [him] to tell [Jason] what-ever [he wants] to know," Phineas nevertheless proceeds to claim, resentfully: "But the gods have gone too far with me. They can punish a man so much, and then one day he abandons them. He says, 'Alright, Zeus. Throw a thunderbolt. Let the earth swallow me. I defy you!'" There is a clap of thunder (timed to suggest an angry retort by Zeus), and Phineas, refusing to be cowed, looks up at the skies and shouts, "You growl away all you like, Zeus. I mean what I say!" He then offers to help Jason, but only if he is freed from "these tormenting Harpies" in return. Warned by Acastus not to interfere, Jason none-theless agrees (itself a mutinous gesture) to Phineas's condition (prompting another thunderclap), and the next sequence shows the argonauts capturing and encaging the Harpies and treating Phineas to a feast he can now enjoy in peace.[27]

This voicing of rebellion by Phineas is echoed by Jason during the Clashing Rocks se-quence that follows. Having announced his decision to go through the Clashing Rocks, despite just witnessing another ship's doomed attempt to do likewise (from the other end), and no longer able to call on Hera's help, Jason first observes sarcastically (by way of criticism) to Acastus, "The gods want their entertainment." Following a transi-tion to Mount Olympus, Zeus, watching the hero's dilemma via the pool, observes tes-tily: "Jason goes too far," only for Hera (asserting her loyalty to Jason and the human world) to retort: "Because he speaks the truth when the gods themselves go too far?" On returning to the Clashing Rocks, which start up once more as the Argo ship begins to travel through the narrow causeway, Argos (Laurence Naismith) tells Jason to turn back ("We're trapped," he warns him). There is another switch to Mount Olympus, where Hera, now seated opposite Zeus at their large chess-like table (which also has a map detailing Jason's voyage), comments (on hearing her husband echo Argos's final word), "It seems so. You've left me only one move." Moving a piece resembling Triton next to a ship symbolizing the Argo, she proceeds to make a gesture of help (despite having exhausted the number of times she can assist Jason) that openly undermines Zeus's authority. A cut to a shot showing Jason grasping the amulet of Triton (given to him by Phineas) around his neck (Figure 28.4) heightens his subversive kinship with Hera (not to mention with Jason and the blind man), and this link between Jason and the Queen of the gods is strengthened even more by his rebellious action of then throwing the amulet into the water. Just before he does so, a more dutiful Argos urges, "Pray to the gods, Jason," only for Armstrong's character to reply angrily, "The gods of Greece are cruel. In time, all men shall learn to do without them!"

Jason's ireful response is thus construed by Naismith's character as an outright rejection of the gods' help. But the force of his rebuttal is undercut by the film's continued insistence on Hera's protective concern for her human charge, her act of divine intervention in this case seeming to prompt Triton (Bill Gudgeon) to appear at the very place where the amulet thrown by Jason disappears. Rising out of the water, this demigod (son of Poseidon) holds back the cliffs long enough to enable the ship to pass through before then sinking back into the deep whence he came. On watching Jason and his crew overcome

FIGURE 28.4. Jason clutches the amulet before throwing it into the water during the Clashing Rocks sequence. *Jason and the Argonauts* (1963, Charles H. Schneer Productions). Frame-grab.

the Clashing Rocks, Zeus and Hera have an exchange that is directly relevant to the focus of this chapter (and that develops the idea of Hera's kinship with the human world):

HERA: Jason dared to speak of the end of the gods…and yet you let him live.
ZEUS: If I were to punish every blasphemy I'd soon lose all loyalty and respect.
HERA: You are the god of many men. Yet when those men no longer believe in you then you'll return to nothing.
ZEUS: You understand that, and yet you remain with me.
HERA: You think it weak of me, my lord?
ZEUS: Not weak. Almost human.

That the film countenances an eventual end to the gods' rule over humans suggests a more sombre side to its envisioning of the Jason legend. In terms of the child viewer, this contemplation of a time when the gods will no longer hold sway over humans (a form of manipulation that is presented rather like a game, as suggested by the recurring motif of chess played by Zeus and Hera) gestures towards the child's growing up and newfound independence and self-determination from one or both parents. One could go further and construe the film's entire odyssey as a kind of rite of passage or coming of age for Jason (another feature of the children's film cited by Brown).[28] Hence, Jason begins his journey to find the Golden Fleece under the maternal protection of the goddess Hera, only to discover his romantic desire for Medea (Nancy Kovack, dubbed by Eva Haddon) by the end. If one pursues this kind of psychological reading, the sequence depicting the Clashing Rocks can be read as symbolic of the traumatic moment of birth itself, the rocks themselves—as they close in on their victims—serving as a metaphor for the infant's tumultuous movement through the constricting birth canal. Hence, the Argo ship and crew battle through the narrowing passageway created by the rocks on either side only to be saved by Triton. The role performed by this male demigod (especially in using his strength to help the argonauts through the Clashing Rocks) could be read as emblematic of the crew's destiny (he helps them out of the narrow causeway, representative of the pangs of labour, and towards patriarchy). To read Triton in this way is complicated by his gender ambiguity, however: he is a merman, after all, and invoked not by Zeus but by the maternal goddess Hera. If the Oedipal trajectory for the male infant traditionally involves the latter's movement away from the mother and towards the father, moreover, then Hera nevertheless remains an appropriately distant yet still concerned presence, watching from afar at Mount Olympus and manipulating her game of "chess" with Zeus to help Jason even when, technically, she is no longer allowed to.

If Triton's rescue of the Argo seems to be initiated in part by Hera's "maternal" intervention, then this demigod's emergence is also triggered, as argued earlier, by Jason's rebellious act of throwing the amulet (which is fashioned in the image of Triton) into the sea. Such ambiguity regarding who initiates Triton's appearance (is it Jason, Phineas, Hera, or a combination of all three?) maintains a sense of the film's ambivalence regarding whether humans are controlled by the gods or in charge of their own destiny. As such, the movie continues to articulate tensions in the child's experience by enacting a struggle for control over her or his sense of destiny and identity. The main ambiguity surrounding whether humans are regulated by the gods or in charge of their own lot is embodied, perhaps above all, in Phineas's gift to Jason of the amulet, an object that in many ways signifies rebellion. It is given to the film's protagonist by the blind man (who is no longer willing to accept the daily torment inflicted by Zeus) as a good luck charm in repayment for being freed from the Harpies (Jason's capturing of these creatures is itself, as suggested earlier, an overruling of Zeus's command). Mirroring the blind man's rebelliousness, Jason, in turn, throws the amulet into the water during the Clashing Rocks' sequence at the very point when he, too, is at his most defiant. But Phineas's gesture is also prompted by his discovery that Jason and the argonauts no longer have the gods' protection, and so can be regarded not just as an alternative, autonomous good luck charm that suggests the ability of humans to survive independently from the gods but as a small, compensatory token intended to stand in for the help the deities might otherwise have offered to enable the ship to pass through the Clashing Rocks.

That Hera nevertheless still helps Jason by moving a chess piece resembling the amulet effectively overwrites the need for Phineas's gift, which, in the process, loses its more defiant, independent human force by becoming symbolic of her divine benevolence. But such a link between Hera and Phineas also implies the goddess's affinity with the blind man's spirit of rebellion against the accepted "higher" order. It's worth remembering, too, that in helping Jason by invoking Triton, Hera is defying her husband Zeus's decree that she can only help her human charge five times (a gesture redolent of the film's 1960s' context and the "battle of the sexes" tensions inherent in her marriage). As Zeus intimates, Hera's dialogue during this sequence also suggests her instinctive sympathy for human feelings of sedition and, in countenancing the end of the gods, Hera is, of course, throwing into question her own future power. This is partly averted by her implied rescue of Jason during the Clashing Rocks sequence, although, ironically, it is this act of mercy by Hera that results in his first encounter with Medea, a survivor of the other ship (travelling from Colchis), which sank trying to pass through the vexatious causeway before the Argo. Jason's romantic involvement with Kovack's character signals the waning of Hera's power over him, both as goddess and implied maternal figure. Embodied most of all in the Honor Blackman character's jealous response to Jason's otherwise typical romantic coupling with Medea at the end of the film, Hera's reaction on seeing them kiss (as she steals another glimpse of Jason via the pool, only to be taken aback by what she sees) makes explicit an Oedipal tension inherent in her protective feelings for him throughout.

But if Hera's reaction to Jason and Medea's kiss suggests this goddess's fading influence over her human charge, Zeus allows the couple's romantic clinch because he has further plans for the story's hero and hence will remain a controlling influence over him: "For the moment, let them enjoy a calm sea, a fresh breeze and each other. The girl is pretty and…I was always sentimental. But for Jason, there are other adventures. I have not yet finished with Jason. Let us continue the game—another day" he says to Hera. Hence, he couches the human couple's romance as a mere temporary interlude or hiatus for Jason and, in doing so, rejects Hera's challenge to his authority through her suggestion (accompanied by her contention she is "a worthy opponent") that "the game is over." If one considers *Jason and the Argonauts* through the lens of a children's film, then Zeus's final comments mean that it ends somewhat bleakly with the suggestion that the hero's independence is still not wholly possible and that "parental" control (or some other form of manipulation or authority) will extend beyond the point of narrative closure, continuing to forestall Jason's quest for self-determination, even in adulthood. One might argue that the film's ending is thus laced with a sense of realism in the implication that the journey into adulthood is ongoing rather than finite and that the conventional romantic clinch (as a typical mark of the "happy ending") is thereby qualified (perhaps thought necessary given the film's tacit status as a children's film). It's a chastening moment, nonetheless, that qualifies the sense of success underpinning Jason's fulfilment of his quest, implying that there are certain limits on his passage towards independence and selfhood and raising questions regarding what a child viewer may in practice learn from a film of this kind.

The ending of *Jason and the Argonauts* can be contrasted with that of a more contemporary children's film, Pixar's *Toy Story 4* (Josh Cooley, 2019). In contrast to the temporary reprieve the earlier film grants Jason, *Toy Story 4*, it could be claimed, follows through on its preoccupation with Woody's narrative journey towards self-determination. Hence, the cowboy doll first selflessly gives up his voice box (and hence his usefulness as a child's plaything) to the female doll Gabby Gabby (Christina Hendricks). Then he renounces his very role as a child's toy (formerly crucial—so he thought—to his identity) and finally says a fond goodbye to his toy friends (previously so central to the franchise yet more marginalized in this film), including his close buddy Buzz Lightyear (Tim Allen), before setting off (freely, in a more modern-day, implied romantic alliance) with an already emancipated Bo-Peep (Annie Potts) at the end. Challenging the previous aims and raison d'être of the *Toy Story* franchise (in ways that risk alienating the latter's devoted legions of fans), the fourth film's closing sequence subversively plays on the idea that Woody is no longer "lost," overturning the notion that once a toy doesn't have a child owner it becomes a "lost toy." It may be unfair to judge a film released in 1963 alongside such a recent work. Bearing in mind, too, the claim made in 1992 by Tom Hanks (who would, of course, become the voice of Woody in the *Toy Story* films) that *Jason and the Argonauts* is "the greatest film ever made,"[29] one is reminded of the shifting nature of cinematic canons, even movies iconoclastically seized upon as such by audiences, suggesting that any such claims perhaps need to be understood as relative to which audiences view what films and when. Perhaps it would be fairer to evaluate *Jason and the Argonauts*'s significance as a children's film not so much according to its ending but in terms of "the amount of dust the story raises along the road" (a phrase Laura Mulvey invoked to explain the strength of the melodrama form and its appeal for 1950s' female audiences).[30] That dust, this chapter has argued, must be understood in relation both to the memorable fantasy sequences *and* the narrative of this cinematic retelling of the Jason and the Argonauts myth. In the first case, plenty of "dust" is certainly stirred up by Talos and the other mythical creatures with the help of a form of stop-motion animation that has no equivalent in the computer-generated

Toy Story franchise, even if the latter deals with the idea of inanimate figures coming to life as well. Yet, as this chapter has explored, the narrative of this 1963 film also contains elements that are imaginatively expressive of seditious uprising and rebellion, not just censoring and punishment. Both strands (the fantasy sequences and the narrative) are significant, therefore, and may go some way towards explaining the de facto spell the film has long cast over children.

Notes

1. For an overview of the work of Ray Harryhausen (including an interview with him), see Paul Wells, *Animation: Genre and Authorship* (London: Wallflower Press, 2002), pp. 90–101.
2. Don Chaffey was a British film and television director whose other notable films include One Million Years B.C. (1966, also with Harryhausen); *Greyfriars Bobby: The True Story of a Dog* (1961); *The Three Lives of Thomasina* (1963); *Pete's Dragon* (1977); and *The Magic of Lassie* (1978). Chaffey often made movies aimed at children, and some of the most successful outside his collaboration with Harryhausen were either child-centred (*The Three Lives of Thomasina*, for example, which starred a young Susan Hampshire) or their content makes them eligible to be considered children's films. To what extent Chaffey was able to bring this authorial interest to bear on *Jason and the Argonauts* isn't clear in light of accounts that have appeared elsewhere that Harryhausen's involvement in the filmmaking extended beyond the stop-motion animation process itself to taking part, for example, in meetings with the producer and writer (see the interview with Harryhausen in Wells, *Animation: Genre and Authorship*, p. 93).
3. For a discussion of the issues and debates surrounding Harryhausen's auteur status, see Wells, *Animation: Genre and Authorship*, pp. 90–101.
4. As Nigel Andrews points out, "Harryhausen invented and patented with [film producer Charles] Schneer the screen process Dynamation (also known as SuperDynamation), a method of matting together foreground and background footage so that effects appear seamless." Nigel Andrews, "Ray Harryhausen, Film Animator," *Financial Times*, 2013, https://www.ft.com/content/bef678e2-b988-11e2-9a9f-00144feabdc0 [accessed July 1, 2019]. For a more detailed overview of the Dynamation process, see Lee Krystek, "Harryhausen's Dynamation," Museum of Unnatural Mystery website, 1999, http://www.unmuseum.org/dyna.htm [accessed July 1, 2019].
5. According to Greek legend, not only was Talos much shorter, but the way he posed a threat was by heating himself in a fire and then embracing his victims. It was Harryhausen who decided to turn Talos into a giant bronze statue, which at one point straddles the harbour like the ancient Colossus of Rhodes. See Ray Harryhausen and Tony Dalton, *Ray Harryhausen: An Animated Life* (London: Aurum Press, 2003), pp. 156–159. For an edited extract, see also Ray Harryhausen, "Model Heroes," *The Guardian*, 2003, https://www.theguardian.com/books/2003/dec/20/featuresreviews.guardianreview16 [accessed July 1, 2019].
6. In Apollonius of Rhodes's famous epic poem *Jason and the Argonauts*, from the third century BC (the earliest full written source), Talos appears late in Argo's return voyage after the Golden Fleece has been obtained. Apollonius of Rhodes, *Jason and the Argonauts*, trans. Aaron Poochigian (New York: Penguin Books, 2014). Repositioning this episode so that it's the first fantasy sequence to occur on the outward part of Jason's odyssey gives it dramatic prominence.

7. The moment when Triton (demigod and son of Poseidon) appears out of the water isn't animated (and hence doesn't employ Dynamation). Instead of using an animatronics model, Triton was performed by actor Bill Gudgeon, and the sequence was filmed in a water tank in Shepperton Studios, England, using miniature cliffs and ships. For more on the creation of the Clashing Rocks, see Harryhausen and Dalton, *Harryhausen: An Animated Life*, pp. 162–163. Harryhausen also discusses making this episode in his interview with director John Landis. See John Landis and Ray Harryhausen, *Jason and the Argonauts: An Interview with Ray Harryhausen* (Columbia TriStar Home Video, 1995).

8. Wells, *Animation: Genre and Authorship*, p. 53.

9. Noel Brown, *The Hollywood Family Film: A History, from Shirley Temple to Harry Potter* (London: I.B. Tauris, 2012), p. 134.

10. Noel Brown, *The Children's Film: Genre, Nation and Narrative* (New York: Columbia University Press, 2017), p. 13.

11. For just one example of such tributes, see the user postings on the IMDb website, https://www.imdb.com/title/tt0057197/reviews?ref_=tt_urv [accessed July 1, 2019].

12. For another female child's account of the impact of the moment when Talos first moves, see Aurora Bugallo, "When Talos Turned His Head, Ray Harryhausen Made My Childhood," *getTV*, July 7, 2016, https://www.get.tv/gettv-blog/when-talos-turned-his-head-ray-harryhausen-made-my-childhood [accessed July 1, 2019].

13. For further details of high-profile figures who have acknowledged the seminal influence on their careers of Harryhausen's fantasy creations and sequences, see the special features on the DVD and Blu-ray transfers of *Jason and the Argonauts*, including The Harryhausen Chronicles (Richard Schickel, 1998) documentary. See also Ray Harryhausen: Special Effects Titan (Penso, 2011) and Episode 22 of the Ray Harryhausen podcast, "Interview with Mark Gatiss," http://www.harryhausen100.com/podcasts/ [accessed July 1, 2019].

14. Ray Harryhausen's account of watching *King Kong* for the first time as a child has been widely quoted, but he discusses it first-hand in *The Harryhausen Chronicles* and *Ray Harryhausen: Special Effects Titan* documentaries.

15. In this regard, I disagree with Alex Sergeant's contention that *Jason and the Argonauts* "[isn't] that interested in narrative." See https://www.fantasy-animation.org/all-episodes/episode-3-jason-and-the-argonauts-don-chaffey-1963[accessed July 4, 2019]. Noel Brown similarly claims that "in Harryhausen films, the narrative exists only to frame the special-effects sequences that lay at the heart of their appeal"; Brown, *Hollywood Family Film*, p. 134.

16. Lacking a strong moral scheme, the film instead concludes quickly after the skeleton battle, "the viewer [being] merely left to assume that Jason returns home and comfortably reclaims his throne." Brown, *Hollywood Family Film*, p. 134.

17. In Apollonius's poem, Hylas still disappears, but instead of being crushed to death by a falling Talos, he is abducted by a nymph while fetching water from her spring. Apollonius, *Jason and the Argonauts*, pp. 47–48, 52.

18. Brown, *Children's Film*, p. 14.

19. In Apollonius's poem, Hercules plays no part in Hylas's disappearance, although, as in the film, he leaves the argonauts' voyage at this point to go in search of Hylas (Apollonius, *Jason and the Argonauts*, 49). In the two-part television miniseries (Nick Willing, 2000), Hercules (Brian Thompson) remains part of the quest until the argonauts reach Colchis and seek the golden fleece. Once under attack, he sacrifices himself heroically defending them.

20. In the cut to a wider shot that follows both men are standing in the frame, but the fact that this iconic moment when Talos comes alive is first registered via an over-the-shoulder shot from Hercules's vantage point makes clear its particular relevance to Green's character.

21. On animism and its relevance to animation, see Paul Wells, *Understanding Animation* (London: Routledge, 1998), p. 10.

22. See Sigmund Freud, *The Uncanny*, trans. D. McLintock (1919; London: Penguin Books, 2003), p. 124. In interviews, Harryhausen was wont to maintain that stop-motion animation is especially well-suited to capturing a sense of fantasy or the dream world. In *The Harryhausen Chronicles*, for example, he claims: "Fantasy is essentially a dream world, an imaginative world, and I don't think you want it quite real. You want an interpretation. And stop motion to me gives that added value of a dream world that you can't catch if you try to make it too real. And that's the essence of fantasy—transforming reality into the imagination." Harryhausen thus marks out stop motion as distinct from other types of animation by virtue of its heightened capacity to create an "interpretation" of the real world, thereby "transforming reality into the imagination," all of which seems suggestive of the "uncanny" nature of Talos's awakening. On the growing scholarly interest in the relationship between fantasy and animation, see Christopher Holliday and Alex Sergeant's edited collection *Fantasy/Animation: Connections between Media, Mediums and Genres* (London: Routledge, 2018), along with their Fantasy/Animation Research Network website. See "Episode 3: Jason and the Argonauts (Don Chaffey, 1963)," podcast, *Fantasy/Animation.org*, https://www.fantasy-animation.org/all-episodes/2018/8/30/episode-3-jason-and-the-argonauts-don-chaffey-1963?rq=jason%20and%20the%20argonauts [accessed July 1, 2019].

23. See, for example, Harryhausen, "Model Heroes."

24. Talos's capacity to elicit a potentially subversive pathos invites comparison with Robin Wood's notion of the "sympathetic monster" in the American horror film (for Wood, it makes this figure more than simply an embodiment of evil and thus complicates our attitude towards "normality"). See Robin Wood, "The American Nightmare: Horror in the 70s," in *Hollywood from Vietnam to Reagan...and Beyond* (New York: Columbia University Press, 2003), pp. 63–84.

25. In Clash of the Titans (1981, Desmond Davis), Harryhausen's last film, the chess-like board game is replaced by "a miniature arena with tiny statues as the niche pieces"; Harryhausen and Dalton, Ray Harryhausen: An Animated *Life*, p. 155.

26. This analogy between gods and stop-motion animator is briefly broached in *The Harryhausen Chronicles* documentary and the fantasy-animation.org podcast on the film. It can also be applied to *Clash of the Titans*, where Zeus and the other gods are again shown, now more explicitly, frequently manipulating models or figurines of the characters they control.

27. This rebellious gesture is absent from Apollonius's story. There, Zetes, one of the winged twin sons (part of Jason's crew), instead seeks assurance that by helping Phineus (note the spelling variation) by driving off the Harpies they "shall not incur the gods" disfavor." Apollonius, *Jason and the Argonauts*, p. 62.

28. Brown, *Children's Film*, p. 16.

29. At the 64th Academy Awards ceremony in March 1992, Tom Hanks paid the following, frequently quoted, tribute to Ray Harryhausen, who was about to receive the Gordon E. Sawyer Award for technological achievement from his friend, the author, screenwriter, and colleague Ray Bradbury: "Some people say *Casablanca* or *Citizen Kane*...I say *Jason*

and the Argonauts is the greatest film ever made." A clip showing Hanks's tribute is available on the Ray and Diana Harryhausen Foundation Facebook page, https://www.faceb ook.com/RayHarryhausen/posts/some-people-say-casablanca-or-citizen-kane-i-say- jason-and-the-argonauts-is-the-/1276202372513598/ [accessed July 1, 2019].

30. Laura Mulvey, "Notes on Sirk and Melodrama," *Movie* 25 (Winter 1977/78), pp. 53–57.

BIBLIOGRAPHY

Brown, Noel. *The Children's Film: Genre, Nation and Narrative.* New York: Columbia University Press, 2017.

Brown, Noel. *The Hollywood Family Film: A History, from Shirley Temple to Harry Potter.* London: I.B. Tauris, 2012.

Fowkes, Katharine A. *The Fantasy Film.* Oxford: Wiley-Backwell, 2010.

Freud, Sigmund. *The Uncanny.* 1919. Translated by David McLintock. London: Penguin Books, 2003.

The Harryhausen Chronicles. Dir. Richard Schickel, 1998. Re-released on the Blu-ray transfer of *Jason and the Argonauts.* Sony Pictures, 2010.

Ray Harryhausen: Special Effects Titan. Dir. Gilles Penso. Frenetic Arts in conjunction with the Ray and Diana Harryhausen Foundation, 2011.

Harryhausen, Ray, and Tony Dalton. *The Art of Ray Harryhausen.* London: Aurum Press, 2005.

Harryhausen, Ray, and Tony Dalton. *A Century of Model Animation: From Melies to Aardman.* London: Aurum Press, 2008.

Harryhausen, Ray, and Tony Dalton. *Ray Harryhausen: An Animated Life.* London: Aurum Press, 2003.

Harryhausen, Ray, and Tony Dalton. *Ray Harryhausen's Fantasy Scrapbook: Models, Artwork and Memories from 65 Years of Filmmaking.* London: Aurum Press, 2011.

Holliday, Christopher, and Alexander Sergeant. *Fantasy/Animation: Connections between Media, Mediums and Genres.* London: Routledge, 2018.

Holliday, Christopher, and Alexander Sergeant. "Episode 3: Jason and the Argonauts (Don Chaffey, 1963)." Podcast. *Fantasy/Animation.org,* n.d. https://www.fantasy-animation.org/ podcasts/2018/8/30/episode-3-jason-and-the-argonauts-don-chaffey-1963 [accessed July 4, 2019].

Wells, Paul. *Animation: Genre and Authorship.* London: Wallflower Press, 2002.

....

CHAPTER 29

HOLLYWOOD AND THE BABY BOOM AUDIENCE IN THE 1950S AND 1960S

....

JAMES RUSSELL

FOR roughly two decades between the mid-1940s and mid-1960s, North American society was reshaped by a relatively unprecedented surge in birth rates. This phenomenon is commonly agreed to have begun in 1946, "reversing a century-and-a-half long decline in fertility," and to have ended in 1964.[1] Previously, in the mid-1930s, annual birth rates had dipped as low as 2.3 million, but in 1947 alone, 3.8 million babies were born, and the numbers continued to rise.[2] Each year between 1954 and 1963, more than four million babies were born, and the result was a seventy-five-million strong generation: the baby boomers, who at the time collectively ranked as the largest demographic group in the United States by some margin. By 1964, when birth rates began to decline, 40 per cent of the population were aged under twenty.

The earliest baby boomers grew up in a period of notable prosperity, which Landon Jones has described as "a buccaneering orgy of buying and selling that carried all things before it."[3] Consumerist behaviour, and the resources required to support the production and purchase of consumer goods of all kinds, from TVs and fridge freezers to cars and suburban homes, became more firmly entrenched than ever before in American life.[4] Frequently, the young baby boomers were unwitting agents in this consumerist revolution:

> As the kids grew up, so did the markets. Throughout the 1950s the 5–13 age group grew by an additional one million baby boomers every year. The toy industry set records annually after 1940, growing from an $84 million stripling to a $1.5 billion giant. Sales of bicycles doubled, [and] children's toys became a boom market. At its peak, the juvenile market was ringing up a staggering $33 billion annually.[5]

This chapter explores Hollywood's response to the emergence of the baby boom. By the end of the 1950s, the American population incorporated more children than ever before, and the needs of young families, tacitly or directly, drove the growth of American industry. And yet, while American businesses of all kinds expanded sales on the back of the baby boom, Hollywood entered a period of decidedly mixed fortunes. The impact of anti-trust legislation, stock price fluctuation, changes to laws governing the flow of income from overseas markets and, especially, declining domestic theatrical audiences, combined to foster a period of notable uncertainty.

In this context of rapidly growing national prosperity in broad terms, but gradually declining commercial reach in the movie industry, it is worth asking how Hollywood sought to address a newly minted audience of young baby boomers from the early 1950s onwards. How did the industry react to the potential needs of this new audience? What impact did the appearance and rapid proliferation of the baby boomers have on industry structures and on production trends?[6] I seek to answer these questions by looking first Hollywood's understanding of child viewers and at the moviegoing opportunities available for children and families during the period of the baby boom. I then examine, in broad terms, some of the movies that did cater to child audiences, concluding with a look at the fortunes of Walt Disney Productions.[7] The first section, "Hollywood and Child Audiences," is concerned with spaces of movie consumption that were tailored to children, and the second is about the movies that were made for children in the 1950s.

HOLLYWOOD AND CHILD AUDIENCES

Throughout the 1930s and 1940s, the major Hollywood studios made relatively few feature films designed to cater directly to child viewers, preferring instead to focus on "broadly adult-oriented family movies."[8] Feature films aimed at children were certainly successful, as the success of *Snow White* (David Hand et al., 1937) and *The Wizard of Oz* (Victor Fleming, 1939) indicate, but these were outliers—rare features in the major's production schedules. Instead, children's movies were largely the preserve of independent producers and "poverty row" studios such as Monogram and Republic, who produced a range of B-movies and serials about characters such as Tarzan, Flash Gordon, and many others. Where the bigger studios did invest consistently in addressing child viewers was in animation, and most of the majors had established an animation wing that was producing shorts and serials designed to feature on the bill of theatrical entertainments alongside more adult fare. Only Walt Disney, in the 1930s and 1940s an independent producer relying on distributors to release his films, specialized in high-end, feature-length children's films. That said, under the terms of the Production Code which governed movie content, *all* films were meant to be suitable for consumption by child viewers. Noel Brown has observed that at this time, "it was widely accepted that Hollywood was, as its advocates insisted, a family institution. That is to say, it was construed as an amusement fitted to serve all facets of the public, including children."[9] But it is also true that children as a distinct segment of the audience were a relatively low priority for the major studios dominating the industry during the first half of the twentieth century.

This was very much the status quo as Hollywood entered the post-war period, and the baby boom began, but the market conditions that had for decades ensured stability and growth in the movie industry were changing. Most significantly, Americans stopped going to the movies with the frequency and regularity to which the industry had become accustomed. Although no one source has ever provided totally reliable figures, every measure of attendance showed an astonishing decline. According to the US census, weekly attendance dropped from ninety million in 1946 to sixty million in 1950 and to forty million in 1960.[10] Surveys by the US Department of Commerce suggest a more modest spike of 79.4 million weekly ticket sales in 1946, which had dropped to 37.7 million in 1957.[11] The decline didn't stop there. Data gathered by the historian Joel Finler shows that weekly ticket sales dropped below twenty million for the first time in 1964 and bottomed out at sixteen million in 1971.[12]

As early as July 1947, *Variety* reported that "grosses are off about 10% and attendance considerably more when compared to July last year."[13] Noting that employment figures were increasing across the United States, the *Variety* reporter went on to complain, "There doesn't appear to be any real reason for the slump except a general uncertainty about the future which has Johnny Public hanging onto his grouch bag just in case."[14] Studio heads generally agreed that the slump might be arrested by cutting costs and improving picture quality. Hence, Jack Warner's insistence that "this coming year must be the creative year in the motion picture industry. Production must be good, and the public must be convinced that it is good."[15] Only Paramount resident Barney Balaban seemed to recognize that the industry was at the mercy of larger societal forces: "The cost of living kept on rising and there was less money left for pleasure. Some of the easy war cash vanished and a portion of the populations gathered in the big centres for war work purposes dispersed. The increasing numbers and use of new automobiles, the booming of outdoor sports and other forms of recreation made stronger competition for pictures."[16] Balaban's analysis of the forces affecting movie consumption was correct, although, like other studio heads, he suggested that improved movie quality, rather than revised content, would safeguard audiences.

In large part, the unanticipated post-war decline in movie ticket sales is attributable to the changing social and economic circumstances of those young families fuelling the baby boom. When they moved into new suburban tract housing, boomer families were also moving away from the established sites of movie exhibition. As their wealth increased, they would often purchase a television alongside their car and refrigerator, which provided all kinds of free entertainment in the home, a role previously occupied by radio, which had enjoyed a more complementary relationship with the movies.[17] More than five million TV sets were sold every year throughout the 1950s (and annual sales often exceeded seven million), which meant that more than sixty-seven million TVs had been sold by the end of the decade.[18] In 1951, a Warner Bros. poll had found that "television ownership was already responsible for a 3–4% drop in the overall US film audience, with further declines on the way."[19] Audiences had already started to decline before TV ownership became the norm, but purchasing a TV set clearly discouraged people from going to the movies even further.

It is beyond the remit of this piece to explore Hollywood's relationship with television, other than to observe that TV quickly became an important forum for delivering children's entertainment, including Hollywood movies. At the start of the 1950s, the studios resisted licensing television rights to their movies, but by 1958, all the major studios had sold blocks of their pre-1948 movies to television networks across the United States.[20] Movies came to make up the majority of content shown on many TV networks. One of the most influential methods of presenting movies was the show *Million Dollar Movie* (1955–1966), first aired by the independent WOR-TV Channel 9 in New York State in early 1955, and then adopted by other independent local stations across the country. Channel 9 found that it could effectively compete with the larger national networks (and their affiliates) by screening movies every evening over the course of a week. The movie was always a 1930s or 1940s studio picture never before shown on TV (initially drawn from the RKO library), which ran at the same time every night for a week.[21] This meant that children were watching movies during the 1950s, but they were very often older movies released on TV; as a result, the impact of this moviegoing was not commercially visible.

As home viewing increased, Hollywood's most obvious response to the decline in theatrical audiences at the start of the 1950s was to reduce the volume of film productions. In 1948, the major studios released a combined total of 488 movies. In 1952 this number had declined to 253, and by 1963, the number of annual film releases from the major studios was down to 142.[22] The volume of product flowing through movie theatres of all sizes declined, and under the terms of anti-trust rulings, ownership of those theatres was taken over by new national chains. As a result, the industry began to privilege the sort of expensive, spectacular movies that performed well in prestigious first-run theatres, where the majors still accounted for most of their revenue.[23] Meanwhile, the number of regular movie theatres in the United States declined from 16,904 in 1950 to 12,291 in 1960, and worst of all, overall box office receipts fell by over $400 million a year, from $1.3 billion in 1950 to $951 million in 1960.[24]

As theatrical audiences declined, exhibitors spotted a change in their patronage, and tried to make the case for making movies that might draw boomer parents and kids to theatres. In June 1950, *Variety* observed that exhibitors were "almost unanimous" in their desire to see "more family-style entertainment."[25] According to one theatre owner in New Mexico, "The business is here—100,000,000 looking for entertainment. Hollywood should wake up and give it to them. Bring out more comedies and good musicals. Avoid the depressing stuff."[26] Later in the year, these theatre owners seemed to be proven right, when a brief rise in ticket sales was attributed precisely to this "lost" family audience:

> Family-type product has provided the backbone of the improvement in grosses which has been felt by most theatres this summer. It's the kiddies and old folks attracted by these pix that make the difference in grosses, exhibs say. The teen-agers and early 20s group can be counted on pretty much in any case, so the family pix get some of that "lost audience" that has become an industry maxim.[27]

Several polls researching the audience demographics for Hollywood films were carried out in the 1950s, the most thorough coming in 1957. Commissioned by the Motion Picture Association of America. MPAA), the survey divided audiences by age range and assessed frequency of attendance (and a broad range of other issues). It found that 72 per cent of tickets were sold to moviegoers under the age of twenty-nine.[28] These viewers generally went to the movies most frequently and constituted the largest demographic group in the theatre. The survey highlighted the importance of demographic research and encouraged an increased focus on teen audiences, but it also revealed a less remarked-upon fact: children (those aged fourteen or under) attended with greater frequency than almost any other group and made up a massive segment of the audience— 31 per cent of all ticket sales. However, though children were watching more movies than ever in the 1950s, as Edward Jay Epstein has noted, during this period a child rarely paid more than twenty-five cents for admission, and so was not considered a lucrative patron.[29] Children were also less likely to watch movies at first-run theatres or as part of the regular schedule. Instead, children were catered to by weekend matinee screenings and, to some degree, by the relatively new phenomenon of the drive-in theatre.

On Saturday mornings across the United States, junior matinees and junior motion pictures clubs were offered in regional movie theatres. Many were coordinated by regional exhibition chains, for example, the Krazy Kat Club and the Mickey Mouse Club in California, or the Radio Patrol in Chicago.[30] For a few cents' admission, each offered a diverse schedule of entertainment, which usually included a cartoon, a serial, shorts, and a "child-friendly" feature. After 1946, matinees were also supported in part by the Children's Film Library, an MPAA initiative that made "significant family films from all the leading Hollywood studios since the early 1930s available to exhibitors for use in Saturday Matinee shows."[31] The Library's director Marjorie Dawson and her team identified releases it felt would be suitable for children's screenings, and then approached distributors to obtain prints. The films were edited for violence, but, according to Dawson, a key requirement was length: "Children want action and they can't stand a picture that's longer than an hour and a half," she told *Variety*.[32] Dawson also felt that child audiences were reliable in the face of the competition with television; but the screening arrangements secured by the Library generally negated any chance of generating profit. Children participating in its summer screening series, which ran in theatres nationwide, paid $1 for admission to twelve screenings across the summer school vacation.

At its height, over 2,500 theatres used the library, but Noel Brown has argued that "the creation of the Children's Film Library represented a tacit admission on the part of the MPAA that the majority of films were unsuitable for juvenile audiences."[33] Many of the Library's prints were in poor condition, and the MPAA failed to invest in maintaining supply in the mid- to long term. In 1955 *Variety* reported that, even as NATO president Wilbur Snaper was complaining about the "tremendous lack of pictures suitable for children," the Library's inventory had "dwindled to the point where it has become difficult to build programmes."[34]

Drive-in theatres also offered a new opportunity for family viewing. As the number of traditional movie theatres in the United States declined (from 16,904 in

1950 to 12,291 in 1960), the drive-ins proliferated (growing from 2,200 sites to 4,700 over the same period).[35] Drive-ins were successful in the 1950s precisely because they seemed to solve one of the key problems facing the industry—they offered a convenient arena for suburban boomer families (and teens with cars) to watch movies. According to Douglas Gomery:

> Some drive-ins took direct aim at the suburban family with an ever-growing number of young children by tendering free passes to parents of newborns up to three months of age. Many drive-ins passed out free milk. Children age[d] twelve and below nearly always were admitted free…What fantasies it held—for teens desperate for a little privacy or for a family hungry for a cheap night of fun—had little to do with the movie-viewing experience. The lone attraction of the drive-in seemed to be that it was cheap entertainment for baby boom families wanting the occasional night out—two dollars a car for whoever could squeeze in. The slogan for Pacific Theatres' Southern California customers became: "Come as you are in the family car."[36]

In a profile of drive-in operators in 1956, an article in the *Saturday Evening Post* observed:

> In nine out of ten cars you'll see young children asleep on the back seat and on the floor. That's why the ozoners are going over big. The drive-in movie is the answer to the sitter problem and to the downtown parking problem. It's the answer to the young family's night out. It's the neighbourhood theatre of the future.[37]

One Chicago drive-in manager was quoted as claiming, "The drive-in attracts brand new movie patrons: young families with children."[38] However, the major Hollywood studios excluded drive-ins from a position near the top of the system of runs and clearances, which meant that "since drive-in theatres did have problems getting new quality products they opened their arms to B-movies," according to Gary D. Rhodes.[39] As with matinee screenings, this seems to have been because rentals from drive-ins were disproportionately low. To give one example, in June 1954, *Variety* printed a brief story headlined "53 Kids in Bus, $1 admission," which ran:

> Drive-Ins playing up 'family nite' rates of a buck for each carload should take note of what occurred at Ray David's ozoner in Chadron, Neb., recently. After a day of picnicking, the Chadron school superintendent loaded the school bus with Junior class members into the ozoner—53 passengers for $1. However, there was a happy ending: The kids zoomed concession stands sales to a record take.[40]

It may be an apocryphal story (and possibly one that confirmed pre-existing biases) but in this one instance, a large group of children reportedly generated less than a dollar in rentals, and the story captures in microcosm the broader reason why the majority of Hollywood studios often tended not to privilege the needs of child viewers in their production planning: their viewing habits meant that children were not seen as a lucrative, or even commercially viable, audience. Watching TV, at matinees, and at drive-in theatres, children were very much present, but they lacked influence as an audience sector, despite the ever-growing size of the baby boom. So, what films were made for children in the 1950s and 1960s?

THE FILMS

To some degree, then, the major Hollywood studios failed to recognize the potential value of the baby boom audience when the boom was underway, and children's films were a relatively marginal feature of production schedules. Cinema was predominantly constructed as an adult affair, while TV spoke to baby boomers more directly. The boomers have sometimes been characterized as generation defined by their relationship with television. Historian Paul C. Light has claimed, "By the time the average baby boomer had reached age 16, he or she had watched from 12,000 to 15,000 hours of TV."[41] In the words of NBC chief Brandon Tartikoff, "Television itself is a baby boom instrument. The baby boom generation has never known an environment where there wasn't a television."[42] For those boomers who would go on to become filmmakers themselves, TV's influence was particularly significant. For example, Steven Spielberg has said, "I was and still am a TV junkie. I've just grown up with TV, all of us have, and there's a lot of TV in my brain that I wish I could get out of there. You can't help it—once it's in there, it's like a tattoo."[43] By contrast, movies were a less important influence. George Lucas, one of Spielberg's peers and another iconic filmmaker from the baby boom generation has recalled, "Movies had extremely little effect on me when I was growing up. I hardly ever went, and when I did, it was to meet girls. Television had a much larger effect."[44]

But baby boomers did go to the movies, and although Hollywood didn't address them as a vital segment of the audience (as is common today), the industry produced a range of movies which either incorporated an address to children, or which can be understood primarily as children's movies. The most significant development in terms of broadly appealing movies occurred when the major studios each started spending more money on fewer but more spectacular and expensive productions designed to draw family groups back to high-cost auditoriums for a special, one-of-a-kind experience. Early pressure to reduce the number of productions, and privilege "high value" releases, developed in response to changes in booking practices required by the anti-trust laws. Once films were being sold to exhibitors on an individual basis, *Variety* predicted, "only the top product will have the best chance in the coming selective buying market."[45] This resulted in a boom in widescreen spectaculars aimed at the broadest possible audience, including the historical epics *The Ten Commandments* (Cecil B. DeMille, 1956) and *Ben-Hur* (William Wyler, 1959); the musicals *The Sound of Music* (Robert Wise, 1965) and *Doctor Dolittle* (Richard Fleischer, 1967); and prestige literary adaptations such as *Around the World in 80 Days* (Michael Anderson, 1956). Some of these were more obviously targeted to children than others, but almost all were marketed to children.

According to the press kit for William Wyler's *Ben-Hur* (1959):

> Since the opening of *Ben-Hur* special student performances throughout the country have proved a lucrative source of additional revenue. Today, more than ever before, educators, religious leaders and parents are seeking entertainment of a high moral and educational nature for the young people they are guiding. *Ben-Hur* is that kind of entertainment, and for this reason your welcome at various schools and youth organizations will be a hearty one.[46]

The pamphlet went on to suggest various ways that exhibitors might attract the interests of scout groups, girl guides, church youth groups, and schools of all sorts. Similar materials accompanied the release of many roadshow epics. *The Ten Commandments* was promoted with another all-important study guide and a book entitled *The Ten Commandments for Children*.[47] Children were also appealed to with a set of colouring pencils and a book, "manufactured in three denominations—Catholic, Protestant and Jewish."[48] These promotional materials provide some evidence that the grand historical spectacles of the period were considered "children's films" insofar as they were marketed as edifying, potentially educational, viewing experiences.

Epics offered an exceptional alternative to Hollywood's regular content, but many of the established genre releases that hit movie screens in the 1950s seem to have had the same broad appeal for children, just as they had done in the 1930s and 1940s. Effectively, the industry maintained a strategy that had worked well in previous eras, despite the fact that moviegoing habits, and the wider demographic makeup of the country, were changing. Early in 1954, *Variety* suggested that low sales over the Christmas period may have been connected to a paucity of product aimed at children and looked forward to a bumper Easter. "Unlike last Christmas week," ran an editorial published in March 1954, "bookings for the spring holiday season have been carefully selected to supply the small fry market [and] distribs have made available a number of pictures of sufficient entertainment value to encompass the tastes of the whole family."[49] The range of films perceived as child friendly gives some indication of the how Hollywood understood the tastes of child viewers. The sure-fire hits of Easter 1954 included reissues of Disney's *Pinocchio* (Hamilton Luske et al., 1940) and Fox's *Heidi* (Allan Dwan, 1937)—both adaptations of classic children's stories. However, they also included recently produced swashbucklers—notably, MGM's *Ivanhoe* (Richard Thorpe, 1952) and *Knights of the Round Table* (Richard Thorpe, 1953); Fox's *Prince Valiant* (Henry Hathaway, 1954); and Disney-RKO's *Rob Roy, the Highland Rogue* (Harold French, 1953).

These kinds of films—historical adventures filled with action, adapted from myths, legends, and even comic strips—had a clear appeal to children, especially boys. As well as medieval swashbucklers, Hollywood also produced a series of films about pirates, including Disney's adaptation of *Treasure Island* (Byron Haskin, 1950) and Warner Bros.' *The Crimson Pirate* (Robert Siodmak, 1952). The latter was a knockabout parody of the swashbuckler, described by Carl Millikin Jr., Warner's head of research, as "a good natured melodrama—sort of a child's eye burlesque of pirates and their ways."[50] The movie begins with Burt Lancaster's title character admonishing the audience not to take the film too seriously, and then launching into a display of acrobatic swordsmanship. Arthur Pollack wrote in the *LA Daily Compass* that the movie was made up of "all sorts of mad and comical doings, mostly acrobatic, all absurd. Children should be spellbound by it. Nothing makes sense."[51] In the *Hollywood Citizen-Reporter*, Lowell Redelings described it as "an excellent entertainment recommended not only for adults with a sense of humor but for young people and children."[52]

In a similar fashion, mid-budget westerns—which featured heavily in production schedules throughout the period—offered a related form of "boys-own" adventure, even though, again, they are rarely understood as children's films. Some of the most prestigious westerns of the period seemed to focus on the priorities of suburban boomer families, although they often did so with a maudlin air. Perhaps the most famous example is George Stevens's 1953 movie *Shane*, which depicts the relationship between Alan Ladd's titular gunslinger and a young boy who comes to idolize him. In the same year, the John Wayne vehicle *Hondo* (John Farrow, 1953) featured a similar relationship. Both movies share an awareness of the importance of children to the appeal of the western movie and its attendant myths, and both dramatize the relationship between boy viewers and the western heroes they watch at the movies.

Perhaps the most child-friendly western hero of the period was the Lone Ranger, who had first appeared on radio in 1933 and then successfully made the leap to movie serials in 1938, becoming a fixture of the ABC early television schedules in 1949. The Lone Ranger married comic book preoccupations with secret identities and vigilante justice to a frontier setting, and the character was a masked man who, accompanied by his Native American sidekick Tonto, fought villains in the American west. The character had been developed by Detroit-based producer George Trendle, who sold the rights on to Jack Wrather in 1955. Wrather ceased production of the radio serial but produced new episodes of the TV serial for ABC until 1957, and developed a movie based on the character for Warner Bros. in 1956. According to the *New York World Telegram*, "Warner decided to film the veteran program after making movies of *Dragnet* and *Our Miss Brooks*" and *The Lone Ranger* was clearly part of a concerted strategy to build movie hits out of successful TV shows.[53] The movie was little more than an expanded episode of the TV show, and was produced at minimal cost, using the existing production crew and cast. It generated a modest $1.5 million at the box office, representing a strong return for Warner Brothers, but also indicating at the limited commercial capacity of films aimed squarely at the baby boom market.

Beyond westerns, many key comedies of the age can also be understood as retaining a particular appeal for children. The Ma and Pa Kettle series of films were broad comedies about a rural family with fifteen children, who, in the first movie, *Ma and Pa Kettle* (Charles Lamont, 1949) move to a modern suburban home and struggle to cope with proliferation of gadgets it contains. The Kettle movies were one of several long-running comedy series that endured throughout the 1950s, although probably most familiar to early baby boomers were the ones by William "Bud" Abbott and Lou Costello. Abbott and Costello had been a hugely successful comedy duo throughout the 1940s, consistently considered among the most commercially reliable stars from 1940 until the mid-1950s.[54]

Their 1952 release, *Jack and the Beanstalk*, gives some indication of the pair's position as child-friendly performers. Various Warner Brothers' press releases present the movie as part of a concerted effort to speak to younger viewers:

> "Kids are getting too many killings and shootings in their entertainment fare these days," says Costello, "Bud and I plan to give them something exciting and yet not exciting enough to bring on nightmares when they fall asleep." Yes Bud and Lou haven't let their juvenile friends down. They know what it means to have them on their side. For it has been the love and affection they have for children—and that children have for them—that has been the real basis of their unprecedented movie success.[55]

On release, *Variety* suggested that the movie had indeed reached its target audience, with some provisos: "Subject assures hefty response from moppet audiences, but from an adult appreciation standpoint the film probably won't have much appeal."[56] The movie earned $1.6 million in rentals in the United States—a fairly standard return for a low budget, child-friendly movie.

For the majority of Hollywood studios, catering to children and families was a hit-and-miss business. Despite failures such as *Jack and the Beanstalk*, on occasion, children's films could generate significant profits, as was the case with Columbia's *The 7th Voyage of Sinbad* (Nathan H. Juran, 1958), which reportedly cost $650,000 to produce and generated over $3 million in domestic rentals (Figure 29.1). The film was a fantasy adventure built around the special effects of independent producer Ray Harryhausen, whose earlier science fiction and horror films, such as *The Beast from 20,000 Fathoms*

FIGURE 29.1. The huge popularity of Ray Harryhausen's *The 7th Voyage of Sinbad* (1958, Columbia) did not displace Disney's dominance in the family market. Frame-grab.

(Euguene Louire, 1953), arguably held the same kind of implicit appeal to children as the western. *The 7th Voyage of Sinbad* was the first of several films from Harryhausen which combined special effects, fantasy, and myth in a way that influenced a generation of future filmmakers. For this reason, Noel Brown has said that it "can be seen, in retrospect, as the most important family film of the 1950s."[57] Another successful children's film released in 1958 was MGM's *tom thumb*, directed by George Pal. Like Harryhausen's movie, it was a moderate hit, generating $3 million in rentals, and used relatively advanced special effects to tell a classic children's story. However, the solid performance of *tom thumb* and Harryhausen's movies didn't effect a wider change in industry priorities, and by the time they came along in the late 1950s, the market for children's films was largely dominated, and determined, by Walt Disney productions, whose fortunes during the period were very different from those of its competitors.

Disney had made a name for itself in the 1930s and 1940s by producing shorts and animated feature films aimed at children. At the start of the 1950s, Disney represented a reliable brand for children's entertainment, and market conditions in the movie industry were changing in such a way as to facilitate growth in all areas of its operation. The child audience was growing at a dramatic rate; anti-trust laws encouraged new players to enter the distribution market, and the marketing model Disney had developed, which heavily emphasized licensing, was afforded new impetus by the growth in domestic consumerist habits.

Disney then invested in a programme of quality animated features, starting with *Cinderella* (Figure 29.2; Clyde Geronimi et al., 1950). In contrast to the pre-war period, budgets were more tightly controlled, and Walt Disney himself was, by many accounts, less involved than before with the production of these new animated films.[58] Later, Walt Disney told an interviewer that, for him at least, *Cinderella* "was just a picture."[59] However, the film was rapturously received by his contemporaries and film critics. Writing to Walt, the director Michael Curtiz described it as Disney's "masterpiece of all pictures you have done."[60] According to *Variety*:

> *Cinderella* is one of Walt Disney's top achievements as an animated story spinner. He catches the warm and simple charm of the Charles Perrault classic so effectively and with such easy presentation that film truly is a delight, a cinch to please audiences of all ages.[61]

Mandel Herbstman made a similar observation in his review for *Motion Picture Daily*:

> *Cinderella* holds entertainment rewards for audiences of all ages, but there is something about this tale of the pretty little scullery maid who married the Prince Charming that makes ideal screen fare for the youngsters. For *Cinderella* is the symbol of magic fulfilment to every child.[62]

In each case, reviewers made the obvious but undeniable claim that *Cinderella*'s appeal was strongest for child viewers, and the film's astonishing commercial performance

FIGURE 29.2. Disney's *Cinderella* (1950) held the strongest appeal for child audiences, a demographic that other Hollywood studios of the period were failing to exploit. Frame-grab.

provided a clear indication that Disney animation and the child audience were powerful forces that other studios were failing to adequately exploit. Over the course of its run, *Cinderella* generated over $9 million in box-office rentals, making it the highest-grossing film of 1950, and, on re-release, it remained one of the most commercially successful films of the period.[63] *Cinderella* was followed by *Alice in Wonderland* (Clyde Geronimi et al., 1951), *Peter Pan* (Clyde Geronimi et al., 1953), and *Lady and the Tramp* (Clyde Geronimi et al., 1955). In all, between 1946 and 1964, Disney released eleven feature-length animated movies, most of which enjoyed significant commercial success. For instance, *Peter Pan* earned $7 million in rentals, making it the fifth highest-grossing release of 1953, and *Lady and the Tramp* earned $8 million, making it the third highest-grossing movie of 1955.[64]

Disney's cultural reach broadened even further as its post-war offerings for the first time began to include live-action features, initially in the form of short nature documentaries, such as *Seal Island* (James Algar, 1948). In 1950, Disney released its first live-action drama, an adaptation of *Treasure Island* directed by Byron Haskins. The film was a modest hit, earning $3 million in US rentals, but its production had been motivated primarily by operational requirements. Because Disney was unable to release profits from the UK market due to the ongoing post-war trade restrictions, it had instead chosen to re-invest its "frozen" capital in a UK-based film production.

The film's relative commercial success nonetheless encouraged Disney to develop more live-action films in a similar vein, and by 1954, live-action films dominated the company's production schedules. By the early 1960s, Disney was releasing between six and ten live-action films for every animated feature. By 1964 Disney had produced forty-three live-action fiction films and seven feature-length documentaries, along with many short films. The live-action releases were Disney's bread and butter with boomer audiences—generally appealing films that focused on a very broad cross section of child-friendly topics—from prestige movies like *Swiss Family Robinson* (Ken Annakin, 1960) and *Mary Poppins* (Robert Stevenson, 1964) to low-budget boilerplate productions like *The Shaggy Dog* (Charles Barton, 1959) and *Summer Magic* (James Neilson, 1963), starring Disney stalwarts Fred MacMurray and Hayley Mills, respectively.

After 1953, Disney released all of these movies via its newly established distribution wing, Buena Vista Pictures, which freed the company from its reliance on RKO and established Disney as a studio equivalent in terms of operational capacity to any of the other major players in the US film market. Alongside its movies, Disney expansion into TV brought allowed the company to develop an intense relationship with its core audience of baby boomers. The company benefitted immeasurably from a dependable, large, and growing consumer base that was not being exploited by competitors in any serious way. Neal Gabler estimates that as a result, in 1966 alone (the year of Disney's death)

> 240 million people saw a Disney movie, a weekly audience of 100 million watched a Disney television show, 80 million read a Disney book, 50 million listened to Disney records, 80 million bought Disney merchandise, 150 million read a Disney comic strip, 80 million saw a Disney educational film, and nearly 7 million visited Disneyland.[65]

These figures give some sense of Disney's impact on the baby boomers, who would have made up the vast majority of these many millions.

The most remarkable aspect of Disney's commercial expansion in the 1950s is the lack of competition that the studio faced in capitalizing on the baby boom audience. Rather, Disney's success was (and to some extent still is) almost always understood as a direct consequence of Walt Disney's unique character. Bob Thomas writes in *An American Original*, his biography of Disney:

> How could it happen? How could one man produce so much entertainment that enthralled billions of human beings in every part of the world? That is the riddle of Walt Disney's life.[66]

Steven Watts describes Walt Disney as "arguably the most influential American of the twentieth Century," and makes the point that news stories in the 1950s "regularly portrayed Walt Disney as a creative figure whose wondrous powers bordered on the magical."[67] Whether he was celebrated as a visionary or dismissed as a boor, Walt Disney—and, by association, his company—was almost always presented as an

exceptional individual. As a result, Disney's success in the 1950s was invariably understood as the result of Walt's unquantifiable, visionary "genius," not demographic change.

In truth, Disney's success in the 1950s and 1960s was built upon the unceasing expansion of the baby boom audience. The sort of products that Disney specialized in directly
targeted the largest demographic group in the United States (a group that only got larger
as the 1950s rolled on). Consequently, Disney's films, TV shows, theme parks, and other
products engaged a large, ever-growing audience that was largely underserved by all the
other film studios. As Noel Brown has uncovered in his own account of the period, in
1960 *Variety* observed that, apart from Disney, the Hollywood studios had "practically
forfeited the children's market to television."[68] It is no accident that over the 1950s and
1960s, Disney cemented its status as the single most reliable "brand" for family entertainment, and children's films, in the media marketplace.

The value of Disney's commercial appeal was encapsulated by the colossal success
and lasting legacy of the 1964 release, *Mary Poppins*, which starred Julie Andrews as
a magical nanny to two British children at the turn of the century. In its historical setting, literary origins, spectacular song and dance numbers, integration of animation
with live-action, and commercial appeal, the movie not only embodied Disney's address to baby boomers but also brought together many key trends in children's filmmaking of 1950s and 1960s. It was very much in line with the trend for high-budget
spectaculars aimed at family viewers, but it was also, crucially, a Disney release, one
which blended live-action and animation techniques. Despite the historical British
setting, it depicted a suburban family, an overworked father, and children learning
the value of play, magic, and adventure. In many ways, it was the archetypal children's
movie of the baby boom in that it was concerned with themes that spoke directly to
boomers, and it was released into a media environment where these themes were only
infrequently addressed.

CONCLUSION

During the baby boom period, children's films continued to be a marginal feature of
Hollywood's production schedules. Whereas other industries had quickly recognized
the commercial importance of the young family unit, the boomers on their own were
neither old enough nor affluent enough to constitute a viable audience for Hollywood
until at least the end of the 1950s. Consequently, at the very start of the 1950s the baby
boom audience slipped out of Hollywood's field of vision. The industry focused instead
on range of other factors: the impact of anti-trust legislation, calls for a relaxation of
censorship restrictions and a concomitant emphasis on "quality" adult-oriented movies,
growing international markets, and technological changes such as the introduction of
widescreen and widespread adoption of television. Even as they grew older, the potential commercial viability of the child audience remained unclear to most studios, which
continued to release children's movies infrequently.

Disney was a striking exception to this trend, and throughout the 1950s and 1960s, it seized, or perhaps was gifted, almost uncontested access to the largest demographic group in the United States. Baby boomers built the foundation for the company's commercial expansion during this period and, as importantly, . its lasting cultural dominance. For decades to come, Disney would trade on nostalgia for the movies (and theme park rides) it had produced in the 1950s and 1960s.

The children's films that were released during the period were diverse in terms of setting but similar in terms of thematic concerns. Key releases ranged from ancient world epics to medieval swashbucklers and westerns to animated and live-action musicals (frequently with a British or European setting). But except for Disney's releases, the majority of these movies were not directly about children; rather, they focused on action and adventure narratives featuring adults, especially men. A good example is Twentieth Century-Fox's *Prince Valiant*, a comic strip adaptation starring twenty-three-year-old Robert Wagner as a knight facing intrigue and battling enemies in King Arthur's court (Figure 29.3). It failed to recoup its massive $3 million budget following its release in 1954, likely adding to the studio's assumption that children's movies were probably bad business. Yet even though the film starred adults, young Prince Valiant goes on a journey that is not dissimilar to the narrative concerns of a Disney movie: when the movie begins, he is a young, inexperienced squire learning to become a knight under the tutelage of Sterling Hayden's Sir Gawain. The movie ends with Valiant taking his place at the round table, having won the heart of Janet Leigh's Aletta and defeated James Mason's villainous Sir Brack. It is, at its heart, a story focused on education and personal growth from inexperienced youth to mature adult.

Almost all of Disney's child heroes go on similar journeys. In movies from *Cinderella* and *Peter Pan* to *Mary Poppins* and *The Jungle Book* (Wolfgang Reitherman et al., 1967), children navigate a transition from childhood to maturity in fantastical, escapist worlds that to some degree mirror the social environment of the baby boomers. Mowgli, in *The*

FIGURE 29.3. Fox's *Prince Valiant* (1954) typifies the kind of action-adventure swashbuckler about a male protagonist's coming of age that jostled for the attention of the children's audience in the 1950s. Frame-grab.

Jungle Book, is an orphaned Indian boy raised by talking animals during the British Raj, superficially living a life that is quite different from that of the young boomers. But he is also voiced by an American boomer, Bruce Reitherman (the son of the director), and he goes on a journey where he encounters a range of potential parental role models before settling in the man village, enticed to leave the wild jungle by a girl who sings:

> I must go to fetch the water,
> 'Til the day that I'm grown,
> Then I will have a handsome husband,
> And a daughter of my own.

Mowgli's magical journey, like those of many young Disney heroes and heroines, including Prince Valiant, leads inevitably towards the moment when he becomes enculturated into the milieu of the 1950s US nuclear family.

Nicholas Sammond has argued that, in the 1950s at least, child-rearing discourses and Disney's movies both used the figure of the child as "a link between a rapidly modernizing culture and its roots in human prehistory, signifying the grounding of that culture in the natural world."[69] In their stories about children growing up, the Disney movies of this period dramatized the wider fears and hopes for the baby-boom generation: that they would become good citizens and viable contributors to the booming consumerist economy that the baby boom itself had helped to usher in. These narratives continued to circulate in children's films well into the late 1960s, when the wider American movie industry finally recognized the commercial significance of the baby boomers, and of the youth audience more generally. By this point, the baby boomers were entering their late teens en masse, and their tastes appeared to be for more challenging, adult-oriented entertainment.

Notes

1. Herbert S. Klein, *A Population History of the United States* (Cambridge, UK: Cambridge University Press, 2004), p. 174.
2. Klein, *Population History*, p. 175.
3. Landon Jones, "A Booming Baby Explosion," in Stuart A. Kallen, ed.), *The Baby Boom* (San Diego, CA: Greenhaven Press, 2002), pp. 31–41, at 33.
4. Lizabeth Cohen, *A Consumer's Republic: The Politics of Mass Consumption in Post-War America* (New York: Vintage, 2004), p. 3.
5. Jones, "Booming Baby Explosion," pp. 33–34.
6. In seeking to answer these questions, this chapter represents a reworked and much abbreviated account of phenomena also discussed in James Russell and Jim Whalley, *Hollywood and the Baby Boom: A Social History* (New York: Bloomsbury, 2018).
7. Throughout the chapter I will refer to the company as "Disney," and the man as "Walt."
8. Noel Brown, *The Hollywood Family Film: A History, from Shirley Temple to Harry Potter* (London: I.B. Tauris, 2012), p. 57.
9. Brown, *Hollywood Family Film*, p. 17.

10. Data cited in Peter Lev, *Transforming the Screen: The Fifties* (Berkeley: University of California Press, 2003), p. 7.

11. Data cited in Michael Conant, "The Paramount Decrees Reconsidered," in Tino Balio (ed.), *The American Film Industry* (Madison: University of Wisconsin Press, 1985), pp. 537–573; p. 4.

12. Joel W. Finler, *The Hollywood Story* (London: Wallflower, 2003), p. 379.

13. "Record Jobs and BO Boomer," *Variety*, July 16, 1947, p. 1.

14. "Record Jobs," p. 40.

15. "Top Industry Leaders Stress Need for More Creative Films," *Variety*, January 7, 1948, p. 5.

16. "Top Industry Leaders," p. 5.

17. Douglas Gomery, *Shared Pleasures: A History of Movie Presentation in the United States* (Madison: University of Wisconsin, 1992), p. 88.

18. See Tom Genova, *Television History: The First 75 Years*. http://www.tvhistory.tv/Annual_TV_Sales_39-59.JPG [accessed August 19, 2019].

19. Lev, *The Fifties*, p. 9.

20. William Boddy, *Fifties Television: The Industry and Its Critics* (Chicago: University of Illinois Press, 1993), p. 136.

21. Boddy, *Fifties Television*, p. 139.

22. Finler, *Hollywood Story*, pp. 364–365.

23. Sheldon Hall and Steve Neale, *Epics, Spectacles and Blockbusters: A Hollywood History* (Detroit, MI: Wayne State University Press, 2010), pp. 136–140.

24. Lev, *The Fifties*, p. 304.

25. Mike Kaplan, "Exhibs Sour on Formula Pix," *Variety*, June 21, 1950, pp. 9, 18.

26. Kaplan, "Exhibs Sour."

27. Herb Golden, "Family Pix as BO backbone," *Variety*, September 6, 1950, p. 1.

28. Reproduced in Conant, "Impact of the Paramount Decrees," p. 5.

29. Edward Jay Epstein, *The Big Picture: Money and Power in Hollywood* (London: Random House, 2006), p. 13.

30. Gomery, *Shared Pleasures*, p. 138.

31. Brown, *Hollywood Family Film*, p. 88.

32. "Kid Library Wiggle Tests Films," *Variety*, May 19, 1954, p. 17.

33. Brown, *Hollywood Family Film*, p. 89.

34. "Kid Film Library Evaporates," *Variety*, March 16, 1955, p. 7.

35. Lev, *The Fifties*, p. 212.

36. Gomery, *Shared Pleasures*, pp. 92–93.

37. Frank J. Taylor, "Big Boom in Outdoor Movies," *Saturday Evening Post*, September 15, 1956, pp. 31, 100.

38. Taylor, "Big Boom."

39. Gary D. Rhodes, introduction to Gary D. Rhodes (ed.), *Horror at the Drive-In: Essays in Popular Americana* (Jefferson, NC: McFarlane, 2003), pp. 1–14, at 2.

40. "53 Kids in Bus—$1 Admission," *Variety*, June 9, 1954, p. 7.

41. Paul C. Light, *Baby Boomers* (New York: W. W. Norton, 1988), p. 15.

42. Brandon Tartikoff, qtd. in Light, *Baby Boomers*, p. 41.

43. Steven Spielberg, qtd. in Joseph McBride, *Steven Spielberg: A Biography* (London: Faber and Faber, 1998), p. 62.

44. George Lucas, qtd. in John Baxter, *George Lucas: A Biography* (London: HarperCollins, 2000), p. 25.

45. Abel Green, "Pix Production's Dipsy Doodle," *Variety*, February 5, 1947, p. 1.
46. MGM Pictures, *Ben-Hur* press kit, p. 35.
47. Paramount Pictures, *The Ten Commandments* press kit, p. 8.
48. Ibid.
49. "Moppet-Aimed Easter Bookings," *Variety*, March 17, 1954, p. 7.
50. Letter from Carl Millikin Jr., Head of Research at WB, May 12, 1952, Story misc. folder, Crimson Pirate file, Warner Bros Archives, University of Southern California.
51. Arthur Pollock, review of *The Crimson Pirate*, *Daily Compass*, August 28, 1942, Crimson Pirate file, Warner Bros. Archives, University of Southern California.
52. Lowell Redelings, review of The Crimson Pirate, *Hollywood Citizen News*, September 27, 1952, p. 12.
53. Aline Mosby, "Lone Ranger to Cry Hi-Yo on the Silver Screen," *NY World Telegram and Sun*, September 9, 1955, p. 24.
54. Top Ten Moneymakers Poll, reproduced in Lev, *The Fifties*, p. 306.
55. "Undated Press Release," Jack and the Beanstalk file, Warner Bros. Archives, University of Southern California.
56. Review of *Jack and the Beanstalk*, *Variety*, n.d., Jack and the Beanstalk file, Warner Bros. Archives, University of Southern California.
57. Brown, *Hollywood Family Film*, 133.
58. Neal Gabler, *Walt Disney: The Biography* (London: Aurum, 2008), p. xx.
59. Walt Disney, qtd. in Gabler, *Walt Disney*, p. 477.
60. Michael Curtiz, qtd. in Gabler, *Walt Disney*, p. 477.
61. Anon, Review of Cinderella, *Variety*, December 13, 1949, p. 12.
62. Mandel Herbstman, Review of Cinderella, *Motion Picture Daily*, December 13, 1949, p. 10.
63. Figures used here are from Peter Krämer, *The New Hollywood: From Bonnie and Clyde to Star Wars* (London: Wallflower Press, 2005), p. 111. Box office data for Disney releases are complicated by frequent re-releases.
64. Krämer, *New Hollywood*, p. 112.
65. Gabler, *Walt Disney*, p. x.
66. Bob Thomas, *Walt Disney: An American Original* (New York: Disney Editions 1976), p. 3.
67. Stephen Watts, *The Magic Kingdom: Walt Disney and the American Way of Life* (Columbia: University of Missouri Press, 1997), p. 397.
68. "Secret Fear of Family Films," *Variety*, February 24, 1960, qtd. in Brown, *Hollywood Family Film*, p. 110.
69. Nicholas Sammond, *Babes in Tomorrowland: Walt Disney and the Making of the American Child 1930–1960* (Durham, NC: Duke University Press, 2005), p. 374.

BIBLIOGRAPHY

Brown, Noel. *The Children's Film: Genre, Nation, and Narrative*. New York: Columbia University Press, 2017.

Brown, Noel. *The Hollywood Family Film: A History, from Shirley Temple to Harry Potter*. London: I.B. Tauris, 2012.

Lev, Peter. *Transforming the Screen: The Fifties*. Berkeley: University of California Press, 2003.

Leibman, Nina C. *Living Room Lectures: The Fifties Family in Film and TV*. Austin: University of Texas Press, 1995.

Light, Paul C. *Baby Boomers*. New York: W. W. Norton, 1988.

Russell, James, and Jim Whalley. *Hollywood and the Baby Boom: A Social History*. New York: Bloomsbury, 2018.

Sammond, Nicholas. *Babes in Tomorrowland: Walt Disney and the Making of the American Child 1930–1960*. Durham, NC: Duke University Press, 2005.

CHAPTER 30

DON BLUTH AND THE DISNEY RENAISSANCE

PETER C. KUNZE

THE 2009 documentary *Waking Sleeping Beauty* (Don Hahn, 2009) chronicles the so-called Disney Renaissance in animation, a period of revitalization beginning with Roy E. Disney's takeover of the animation division and peaking with a run of films that smashed box-office records for feature animation, including *The Little Mermaid* (Ron Clements and John Musker, 1989), *Beauty and the Beast* (Gary Trousdale and Kirk Wise, 1991), *Aladdin* (Ron Clements and John Musker, 1992), and *The Lion King* (Roger Allers and Ron Minkoff, 1994). *Waking Sleeping Beauty* makes no effort to conceal its self-interest: former president of Walt Disney Feature Animation Peter Schneider and *Beauty and the Beast* producer Don Hahn produced it, and Walt Disney Studios Motion Pictures served as the theatrical distributor. In the story of film and television animation's resurgence since the 1980s, history belongs to the victors: unsurprisingly, Schneider and Hahn focus on Disney animation, even though press coverage during the period also included Hanna-Barbera cartoons, new Bugs Bunny shorts, and Fox's *The Simpsons*.[1] More surprisingly, popular and academic historians of US animation tend to follow Disney's lead, as the attention paid to Disney far outweighs the scholarship of other contemporary animation producers, including Ralph Bakshi, Tom Griffin, and Joe Bacal. The most egregious exclusion was and is Don Bluth, who not only posed a formidable threat to Disney throughout the 1980s, but arguably inspired (at least, in part) the very renaissance that revitalized the struggling company.

Don Bluth has had a long career in animation, first at, then outside of, Walt Disney Productions. He started there in the 1950s but left to complete a mission trip and his education. He returned in the 1970s to work as an apprentice to the senior animators. By the end of the decade, he had emerged as a leading talent among the younger generation, serving as animation director on the ambitious, but ultimately underwhelming *Pete's Dragon* (Don Chaffey, 1977). Growing tensions between the younger animators and both the older animators and the administration led to Bluth's departure with other animators in 1979, and between 1981 and 2000, his production company produced ten animated features, as well as several video games and direct-to-video releases. Despite this productive career, Bluth's role in animation history and the history of film in general continues to be obscured by the influence and ongoing dominance of his former employer. Close attention to his career, however, reveals ebbs and flows in US animation over the past forty years.

It goes without saying that the history of feature animation in Hollywood is largely the history of Walt Disney—but his is not the only story that needs to be told. As Janet Wasko has noted, "Not only does this perpetuate the 'great man' version of history, but this ongoing fascination with Disney and his accomplishments tends to deflect attention away from the corporate nature of his enterprise."[2] Nevertheless, animation historians tend to follow suit, and the academic and trade presses abound with biographies of Walt Disney and histories of Disney animation. Published in 1987, the revised edition of Leonard Maltin's history of American animation affords Bluth a mere three out of 355 pages, in part because it appeared between *An American Tail* (1986) and *The Land Before Time* (1988), which had the highest opening weekend gross ever for an animated feature film at that time.[3] (Disney, of course, receives its own chapter, which is over fifty pages long.) Charles Solomon affords Bluth a similar amount of space in his 1994 revised edition of his animation history, *Enchanted Drawings*, which is about 350 pages long. In 1991, John Cawley published *The Animated Films of Don Bluth*, a trade book sorely in need of updating, and later historians, including Tom Sito and Giannalberto Bendazzi, have been slightly more attentive to Bluth's role. Recently, Chris Pallant suggested that "it was Don Bluth, perhaps more than anyone else, who proved most influential in prompting the Disney Renaissance."[4] Such a claim is strictly based on box-office grosses, and Pallant's focus on Disney feature animation affords him little room to consider Bluth's development and impact, not only on Walt Disney Productions, but on video games and animation more broadly. Similarly, in 2016, Maureen Furniss frames Don Bluth primarily as an unsuccessful competitor for Disney who ultimately faced several stumbling blocks, setbacks, and failures.[5] Although it is difficult to extricate Bluth's career from the fall and resurgence of Disney, he nonetheless deserves greater attention. In this chapter, I turn to interviews, newspaper articles, and trade press coverage to reconstruct Bluth's career from his leaving Walt Disney Productions in 1979 through the release of *An American Tail*. Such analysis of Bluth's career reveals that he, just as much as Roy E. Disney and the team of Eisner-Wells-Katzenberg, was responsible for the renewed interest in animation, and for both reviving the Disney storytelling formula and updating it for the blockbuster era. The critical and commercial failures of his studio have marginalized his position in an industry-wide flourishing in televisual and feature animation, but he remains an important player in this creative boom.

Waking Sleeping Beauty proves an interesting case study in self-mythology for how it both reveals the backbiting and infighting at Walt Disney Studio while simultaneously suggesting each of the warring parties—such as Michael Eisner, Jeffrey Katzenberg, Roy E. Disney, and Peter Schneider—were ultimately working in the best interest of the company and, more importantly (or so we are led to believe), the tradition of Walt Disney entertainment. These men, especially Disney's "idiot nephew," Roy, become the saviours of Disney animation and, by extension, feature-film animation. Of course, as in any Disney film, the story is not without a villain, and in *Waking Sleeping Beauty*, that individual is Don Bluth. Hahn, as narrator, reports:

> [CEO of Walt Disney Productions] Ron Miller knew that Walt's guys were retiring fast. He had to raise a new crop of animators, but he was cautious about it. He'd got burned five years earlier when he entrusted a charismatic animator named Don Bluth to lead the department. But Bluth polarized the animators. Some adored him as the messiah of animation, and others…well, others thought he was just another Walt wannabe.[6]

Don Bluth's defection from Walt Disney Productions and specifically the Animation Division has long been blamed (quite fairly) for the delayed release of *The Fox and the Hound* (Ted Berman, Richard Rich, and Art Stevens, 1981), but *Waking Sleeping Beauty* casts Bluth's departure as an act of treachery, literally deeming it a "betrayal." Hahn later refers to Bluth as "the animator who kicked us when we were down." (Hahn does not mention that he worked with Bluth and fellow animators on the "garage short" *Banjo the Woodpile Cat* [Don Bluth, 1979], a half-hour film they made in their spare time to train themselves as filmmakers and figure out how viable they would be as an independent entity.) Looking back now, of course, Walt Disney Productions and its loyalists see Don Bluth as the defector who nearly brought down the struggling animation division; but this augmented version, unsurprisingly, privileges the storyteller. Yet, as this chapter argues, Bluth's departure ironically—and perhaps inadvertently—accomplished what Walt Disney Productions had brought him on board to do in the first place: save Disney animation.

Don Bluth at Disney, 1971–1979

By the 1970s, Walt Disney Productions was in trouble, and everyone knew it. At the time of his death in 1966, Walt Disney was supervising production of *The Jungle Book* (Wolfgang Reitherman et al., 1967), which went go on to become the second highest-grossing film of the year, behind *The Graduate* (Mike Nichols, 1967). Reitherman was one of Disney's "Nine Old Men," a collective of animators who had worked on every Disney animated feature since *Snow White and the Seven Dwarfs* (David Hand et al., 1937). By the 1970s, they had begun to retire or pass away, leaving no clear successors in place and an uncertain future for Disney animation. Walt's interest in other ventures, the rising cost of animation, and the shifting interests of the movie-going public led to a decrease in feature animation production at Disney throughout the 1960s. The animation studio released only four animated films in the 1970s, and while their grosses were respectable, they were noticeably lower than their predecessors. Disney's reliance on creative properties to motivate interest in its theme parks, by then the most profitable division, exacerbated the studio's creative problems. Concerned for "a continuity of quality Disney animated films for another generation,"[7] Ron Miller, Walt's son-in-law and now a vice president, put Eric Larson, one of the "Nine Old Men," in charge of training a new generation of Disney animators.

Walt Disney Productions reached out to Don Bluth, who, as a young animator, had helped on *Sleeping Beauty* (Clyde Geronimi et al., 1959). After a brief time at Disney, Bluth completed a mission trip in Argentina and started a theatre in Culver City with his brother. He stayed a great fan of Disney, though, and took the opportunity to return in 1971, where he worked on *Robin Hood* (Wolfgang Reitherman, 1973) and *Winnie the Pooh and Tigger Too* (John Lounsbery, 1974). The next major animated feature out of Disney Animation was *The Rescuers* (John Lounsbery, Wolfgang Reitherman, and Art Stevens, 1977), an adaptation of Margery Sharp's popular 1959 children's book featuring the voices of television stars Eva Gabor and Bob Newhart. Many critics saw promise in the film, and it even outperformed *Star Wars* (George Lucas, 1977) in Paris, France, as well as West Germany, where it became the highest-grossing film to date. Unfortunately, it did not revive the critical and artistic reputation of Disney Animation.

Don Bluth emerged as one of the leading talents of the new generation, going on to serve as animation director on *Pete's Dragon*, a mixture of live-action and hand-drawn animation. Released only a few months after *The Rescuers*, *Pete's Dragon* was a modest success on par with *Robin Hood*. Although it was praised for its technological feats, critics blasted its long running time (over two hours), lacklustre musical numbers, and underdeveloped script.[8] Behind the scenes, tension was growing: some of the animators, led by Bluth, felt that story and production values had waned over the past few years, much to the indifference of the executives. The strong storylines and nuanced character development of classics like *Pinocchio* (Norman Ferguson et al., 1940) and *Bambi* (James Algar et al., 1942), Bluth's personal favourite of the Disney canon, had fallen to the wayside in favour of broad characters and episodic narratives. "I always felt the emphasis should be on story first, animation second," Bluth noted.[9] He later reported that the older animators had mostly completed animating *Robin Hood* without even a sense of how it would end. Light entertainment, it would seem, undermined story, a loss that infuriated the younger animator.

Bluth kept busy directing the featurette *The Small One*, which was largely drawn by the trainees (including Gary Goldman, John Musker, and John Pomeroy) and planned for Christmas 1978 release. He had emerged as a leader among the rising generation of animators, and it seemed at Disney and in the press that he was heir apparent to the Nine Old Men. Meanwhile, Eric Larson kept busy developing the younger talent pool, reporting in July 1978 that Disney had found roughly forty-five of the seventy-five animation personnel necessary "to strengthen all the areas."[10] Although Disney had planned *The Black Cauldron*, an ambitious one-film adaptation of two novels in Lloyd Alexander's *The Chronicles of Prydain* (1964–1968) as a showcase for its younger talent and a return to the darker Germanic style of films like *Pinocchio*, production was delayed while Walt Disney Productions moved ahead instead on *The Fox and the Hound*.

News of the growing discontentment behind the scenes at Disney reached executives at Aurora Productions, a new production company established by former Disney executives Richard Irvine and James L. Stewart. They approached Bluth about striking out on his own, an offer the increasingly dissatisfied animator could not turn down. It became clear that the spectre of Walt Disney hung over the studio, especially the Animation Division, and as a result, the studio remained reticent to take the necessary artistic risks, which, ironically, was the opposite of the approach Walt himself embraced. On his forty-second birthday—September 13, 1979—Don Bluth, along with Gary Goldman and John Pomeroy, walked into the office of their boss, Ed Hansen, resigned, and announced their intentions to compete with Disney animation. Eight other animators went with them, and several more followed in the coming weeks.

Of course, this mass departure of rising talent inspired fury throughout the studio, especially because it was in process of trying to revive the lagging animation division. Initially, Ron Miller chastised Bluth for his "lack of loyalty," but diplomatically noted in the *New York Times*, "We develop the finest artists in the field of animation in the world. It's typical of artists to want to spread their wings."[11] Later, he made the uncharacteristic move of calling Bluth a "son of a bitch."[12] Eric Larson was equally critical: "I think young people today [Bluth left when he was forty-two] lack a certain discipline. It's a big problem for them to become a cog in a team effort. But this place is so far ahead of any place else that I welcome competition. It's what we need."[13] Ed Hansen, head of animation, insisted, "We're still smiling"[14]; years later, in 1984, he admitted, "My world collapsed on September 13, 1979."[15] Despite efforts to seem unperturbed and self-congratulatory, executives and animators at Disney were clearly irate and worried, no doubt in part because of their fear for the future of feature animation at in hallowed home.

Bluth himself was critical of where Miller and his fellow executives had steered Walt Disney Productions, but he was also optimistic about both where he and the studio were heading: "There were too many committee decisions. Everything got done by vote. In addition, people can't be left in a room to teach themselves how to become animators. There is a sincere desire on the part of Disney to perpetuate the art of animation, but the studio wasn't *teaching*."[16] Teaching the next generation of animators was not Bluth's only concern; his beloved studio was cutting corners left and right to save money on animation effects, from leaving out smoke and sparkling water to, most famously, the whites of Bernard's eyes in *The Rescuers*. Furthermore, as Bluth later explained, women were often prevented from advancing up the animator ranks in the same manner as their male counterparts,[17] an assessment his colleague Heidi Guedel corroborated in her memoir.[18] Some commentators, including Pamela G. Hollie of the *New York Times*, faulted Disney's commercial focus on theme parks and live-action films as the reason behind the waning quality of Disney animation and, by extension, the departure of the Bluth collective.[19] She claimed their defection would not only delay *The Fox and the Hound*, but "more fundamentally, it has dashed the studio's efforts to rebuild the Disney animation department to its past glory." The shift in focus was somewhat understandable from a business perspective. The theme park provided a steady revenue stream, and the live-action films were relatively inexpensive to produce; feature animation, on the other hand, required up to four years to develop, draw, and film, and there was no promise of financial return. The earlier animated films—often called the "annuities" within the company—proved profitable in re-release on seven-year cycles, so the need for new films from the Animation Division was not as pressing. Finally, with the shift toward niche audiences, especially teenagers, the Hollywood of the 1970s did not have as much need for children's entertainment. In a film landscape dominated by ambitious epics (*The Godfather* [Francis Ford Coppola, 1972], *Jaws* [Steven Spielberg, 1975], *Star Wars*), ribald comedies (*Blazing Saddles* [Mel Brooks, 1974], *The Rocky Horror Picture Show* [Jim Sharman, 1975], *National Lampoon's Animal House* [John Landis, 1978]), and broad action-adventure films (*Dirty Harry* [Don Siegel, 1971], *The Poseidon Adventure* [Ronald Neame, 1972], *Rocky* [John G. Avildsen, 1976]), where was the audience for light-hearted family fare? Most likely at home in front of their televisions. Disney had work to do, and with their heir apparent gone along with a crop of the company's young talent, the drive to succeed seemed more urgent than ever before.

THE EARLY YEARS: *XANADU* (1980) AND *THE SECRET OF NIMH* (1982)

When Don Bluth left Disney in 1979, he felt confident he could deliver his first feature film within the thirty-month time frame (compared to Disney's roughly four-year production cycle) and $7 million budget he had been allotted. The new animation studio, named Don Bluth Productions, also found supplemental work. HBO bought the short film *Banjo the Woodpile Cat* and aired it in February 1980. In June, the company announced it had been hired to animate a two-minute sequence for the film *Xanadu* (Robert Greenwald, 1980). Produced by Lawrence Gordon and Joel Silver and distributed by Universal Pictures, the film included a brief animation sequence as the two lovers, played by Olivia Newton-John and Michael Beck, turn into dancers, then fish, and finally birds. Bluth demonstrates some of his classical Disney values here, including impressive use of colour and light to capture the sparkling couple, fireworks, waterfall, and bubbles. *Xanadu* made an underwhelming $22 million at the box office, losing out in annual gross to, among others, Disney's re-release of *The Lady and the Tramp* (Clyde Geronimi, Wilfred Jackson, and Hamilton Luske, 1955). Yet *Xanadu*'s brief animated interlude testifies to the quality of animation Bluth sought to revive and, in fact, could deliver.

By the time *Xanadu* was released, in August 1980, Bluth and company—roughly forty-three personnel—were hard at work on their first feature film, an adaptation of Robert C. O'Brien's *Mrs Frisby and the Rats of NIMH*, a children's book that had won the prestigious Newbery Medal in 1972. Conflicts with Wham-O, makers of the Frisbee, led to the renaming of protagonist as "Mrs Brisby" and of the film itself as *The Secret of NIMH*. With its use of anthropomorphized mice, the film draws obvious parallels to Mickey Mouse and other Disney creations, including the mice in *Cinderella* (Clyde Geronimi, Wilfred Jackson, and Hamilton Luske, 1950) and, more recently, Bernard and Miss Bianca in *The Rescuers*. Quite obviously, Bluth sought to not only strike out on his own, but to maintain his artistic connection to the Disney tradition.

In the meantime, Disney finally released *The Fox in the Hound* after five years in production. The film grossed $39 million dollars, placing it just behind *Reds* (Warren Beatty, 1981), and far behind Steven Spielberg's *Raiders of the Lost Ark*, which was the top film of the year, with over $200 million in domestic gross alone. The likes of George Lucas and Steven Spielberg had usurped the domain of family entertainment; their spectacles, which were produced on a grand scale and took advantage of the latest innovations in special effects, far outperformed the modest animated fare Disney was producing. As Wayne Warga noted in 1980, "Disney films have fallen victim to the increasing sophistication of audiences of any age. What were once family films are now largely considered made for children. The audience for Disney films is rapidly shrinking."[20] Ron Miller, now the president of Walt Disney Productions, promised that change was coming, though he often admitted that the influence and legacy of his legendary father-in-law loomed over him, causing him to doubt his decisions. Bluth himself had noted the higher-ups, especially Miller, lacked the drive and the backbone to venture into new territory, both thematically and artistically. In truth, the Disney brand, long associated with G-rated entertainment, could only go so far, even as film became increasingly edgier in its representation of sexuality and violence. Miller publicly lamented the state of Disney filmmaking in general:

> They'll have to blindfold and gag me before I'll let them do anything more than a soft P.G....Sure, I'm a hypocrite. I let my children see everything—R's and P.G.'s—the lot. But I have a responsibility to this company. One racy picture could do incredible damage to a name built up over 55 years.[21]

In 1980 Walt Disney Productions recruited twenty-seven-year-old Tom Wilhite to lead creative development and David Ehrman, thirty-one, to serve as executive story editor. The studio had lost its hipness in Hollywood, and Wilhite and Ehrman aimed to recapture it. Wilhite told the *Los Angeles Times* that Disney was open to talk with anyone who was passionate, while Ehrman urged for a broader, more modern, more daring film product at Disney. "We're considered a kid's studio," Ehrman candidly remarked, "and that isn't enough. I want the Disney image to stand for fantasy and adventure, as it always has, but also for some updated drama as well."[22] Among the new projects were a live-action adaptation of S. E. Hinton's Young Adult novel, *Tex* (Tim Hunter, 1982) and the partially computer-animated movie *Tron* (Steven Lisberger, 1982). Both films were rated PG, and the latter became notable, not only for its debt to the increasing influence of video games, but, more importantly, for its bold use of computer graphics.

Ironically, Wilhite's rhetoric at this time aligned with many of Bluth's critiques years earlier, though he, of course, drew no such parallel:

We want to follow the philosophy of Disney himself, who was always interested in progress and change. Perhaps change hasn't occurred as often as it should here, but we feel we're moving in the right direction with the kinds of pictures we have in production now—pictures that are different from what other people are doing and that involve new artists. We're discovering the essence of what made this studio what it is: change, chance, risk-taking, escapes, innovation, upbeat films.[23]

Surely, Don Bluth was chagrined to read about this young executive championing risk-taking and innovation, even at the expense of an overbearing loyalty to tradition. He had lamented Disney's narrow-mindedness during his time there, especially the deference to a misguided notion of what Walt would have done. Bluth was carrying on the Disney tradition of *Bambi*, one that predated his own time at the studio in the 1950s, in his careful attention to renderings of character, backgrounds, and the more volatile elements of landscape, like water and wind. Although Wilhite faulted Bluth for his obsession with early Disney feature animation, the latter attempted to discourage the perception among industry professionals, critics, and audiences that he was simply mimicking his key influence and former boss:

There will be no "second Disney." It's wonderful that his success could occur, and he could show all that animation can be. Unfortunately, his legacy has been left to those who could chop it up and sell it in the meat market. But he didn't tell all the stories. We want to understand how he told stories and then go from here.[24]

Bluth may have been antiquated in his esteem for *Pinocchio* and *Fantasia* (Norm Ferguson, 1940), but it was the necessary catalyst for a new age of American animation.

Don Bluth Productions completed *The Secret of NIMH* on budget, in May 1982, and MGM/Universal Artists released it in July. The press kit proclaims, "The Second Age of Animation is here."[25] Furthermore, the filmmakers prided themselves on their homage to classical animation, in particular their use of numerous costly measures to heighten the film's quality, including multiplane shots, numerous passes of film through the camera (to enhance depth and dimension), close attention to shadows and reflections, the "orchestration of color" (including the use of over 600 colours, 500 of which were created by the studio), and an "uncompromised" plot.[26] Clearly, Don Bluth Productions (in conjunction with MGM/UA) used their press materials to simultaneously damn their former colleagues at Walt Disney Productions; Bluth told *Variety*, "We'll worry them into reformation, with our competition a useful impetus for Disney Studios to make improvements."[27] If the likes of Miller, Hansen, and Larson perceived Bluth as a troublemaker and defector, he obviously positioned himself as the champion, even saviour, of classical American animation. At the same time, Bluth and company intentionally harkened back to an era there where Disney ensured the highest quality and made bold choices to further the art form. If animation were going to captivate audiences, Bluth believed, it would need to return to its classical roots.

The Secret of NIMH situates itself, both narratively and artistically, in the tradition of Disney feature animation. Mrs Brisby is a kindly, soft-spoken heroine, ennobled by the tragic death of her husband (which happened before the film begins). The supporting characters vary from the comical to the villainous, creating the possibility of a range of emotional responses to the film. Characters, highly expressive and meticulously crafted, seem to remain in constant motion against dark, brooding backgrounds that reflect their indebtedness to *Pinocchio* and *Fantasia*. Crafting a fiercely binarized world of light and dark, good and evil, and courage and cowardice, *The Secret of NIMH* aims to provide the entertaining but also morally educational experience of the early Disney films. Yet, as Stefan Kanfer noted in 1997 (just as several critics had in 1982), "Sadly, predictably, the missing ingredient was Walt's story sense and timing."[28]

Aurora Productions and distributor MGM/United Artists rigorously marketed the film across various media platforms and retailers. While feature animation was stagnant at best, Disney's sheer size, fuelled by its expansion into television, theme park entertainment, and merchandise, made it a sizable behemoth to compete with at the box office. "We want to outdo Disney in marketing a G-rated family film," Aurora President Richard Irvine told the *New York Times*. "We needed to be sure enough money was there to compete head-to-head with Disney."[29] In addition to brief stage shows in department stores nationwide featuring actors costumed as the lead characters, *NIMH* merchandise included an ice cream flavour, cups, puzzles, activity books, clothing, toys, and school supplies. Children's book publisher Scholastic published a special edition of O'Brien's original novel with a scene from the film on the cover, while Little Golden Books published Gina Ingoglio's *Mrs Brisby and the Magic Stone* for younger readers. The sheer range of products testifies to the increasing number of corporate partnerships studios pursued in their efforts to fund, brand, and promote their films, especially one as meticulously created as *The Secret of NIMH*.

Critics, however, were not as impressed with *The Secret of NIMH* as its filmmakers obviously were. Sheila Benson, writing for the *New York Times*, commended the technique but felt the story itself fell flat.[30] Nevertheless, she saw promise: "What *NIMH* proves amply is that Bluth's idealistic young company has both technique and heart for the painstaking, expensive work of fully detailed animation."[31] Roger Ebert of the *Chicago Sun-Times* equally tempered his criticism, noting how the characters' body language is itself a commendable feat. Shoddier animation, particularly on the quickly and inexpensively produced programmes shown on Saturday morning television, employed few backgrounds and limited body movement. *NIMH*'s characters are constantly mobile, and therefore, they are quite expressive. Yet, Ebert laments, "It is not quite such a success on the emotional level, however, because it has so many characters and involves them in so many different problems that there's nobody for the kids in the audience to strongly identify with."[32] Vincent Canby of the *New York Times* was no more forgiving, finding the characters well-drawn, yet the story lacking and the characters unworthy of an audience's sympathies. Ultimately, he lays the blame on the weak screenplay by Bluth, Goldman, Pomeroy, and Will Finn—a particularly damning critique, considering how Bluth charged Disney with lacking sufficient attention to plot. Indeed, while the animation delights, the characters rarely resonate in the same way they did in early Disney features.[33]

At the box office, Don Bluth Productions butted heads with an old foe, Walt Disney Studios. Disney personnel were still criticizing the defectors in the popular press nearly two years after Bluth and company had departed. Glen Keane, one of the younger generation of animators, assured Alex Ward of the *New York Times*, "To tell you the truth, it was a relief when they left. The rift developed during the making of *Pete's Dragon* [completed in 1977] and carried over to *The Fox and the Hound*, and it caused a lot of conflicts."[34] A month after Keane's remarks, Don Bluth said in the same newspaper, "The art of animation wasn't growing. The studio was so encrusted with its original and traditional ways."[35] Bluth, again, does not mention specifics regarding these "ways," but this rift allows Disney to discredit Bluth's efforts by portraying him as contentious and derivative, while Bluth himself used the media to cast Disney as outdated and reactionary.

A week after MGM/United Artists released *The Secret of NIMH*, Disney released its own technical marvel, *Tron*. Since both films featured innovative animation, the Rainbow Theater in Tujunga, California, planned to show them both in a double feature. Disney nixed the idea, threatening to pull *Tron* rather than allow the double feature to take place. Dick Cook, general sales manager for Buena Vista Distribution, feared that audiences might confuse *The Secret of NIMH* for a Disney film and preferred instead that *Tron* "be paired with something that was commercially successful."[36] Bluth pointedly responded:

> *NIMH* was never a vendetta or a personal statement against Disney. If anything, I would hope the competition would make them take their jobs more seriously. There is a responsibility for Disney to make the legacy of its animation continue to exist.[37]

Despite claims on both sides that the disagreement was not personally motivated, the invective belies such a suggestion. Universal Artists responded within a week; sales chief Jerry Esbin insisted the films should not be shown together and insisted that *Tron* was not, in fact, animation: "*NIMH* is animated—with live drawings, *Tron* is special effects."[38] Here, one of the first shots is fired in the battle between hand-drawn animation and computer animation as the former underscores the invalidity of the latter. Bluth diplomatically suggested that both be presented together on television; ironically, nearly two decades later, computer animation would effectively render Bluth's loyalty to classical animation obsolete. Yet for its commitment to high production values and strategic response to the state of Disney animation, *The Secret of NIMH* remains a key text in the resurgence of feature animation and is a favourite among animation professionals and fans across of the world.

Audiences at the time, however, agreed with the critics in the popular press, and the film unimpressively grossed less than $15 million domestically. The news must have hit Bluth particularly hard. When he was looking for financing, some potential backers had told him only Walt Disney had ever made a profit doing feature animation.[39] They were right then, and they were still right. Bluth had to look to additional avenues for animation.

SPIELBERG SAVES: *DRAGON'S LAIR* (1983) AND *AN AMERICAN TAIL* (1986)

After *The Secret of NIMH*, Don Bluth became the first animator to play an active role in the increasing popularity of video games. Whereas *Star Wars* had grossed over $300 million since its initial release, *Pac-Man* made over $1 billion in 1981 alone. Indicators pointed to the value of video games as a medium, and Bluth's production company played an integral role in the development of *Dragon's Lair*, an arcade game that used a laser disc to feed information to the machine. Programmed by Advanced Microcomputers Systems and manufactured and distributed by Cinematronics, *Dragon's Lair* featured about twenty-two minutes of animation from Don Bluth, produced at a cost of over $1 million. By February 1984, more than 8,000 machines had sold at a cost of about $4,000 each; Bluth himself estimated a gross revenue of more than $32 million overall.[40] He exalted,

> This market is fantastic for our industry. Games could replace the old theatrical shorts as a training ground for animators and a place where we can experiment.... They can also bring money into the industry, money that can be used to finance projects on a grander scale, like animated features.[41]

Unfortunately, the promise of the video-game industry proved fleeting, and its temporary bust and the underwhelming sales performance of *Space Ace* pushed Bluth out of the market and effectively bankrupted his production company. At one point, the company bank account slipped down to $6,000—half of what it took to run his studio for a week.[42] Video games were not the only problem Don Bluth and his production company faced, however. Soon after the release of *The Secret of NIMH*, they had announced plans for an $11 million film based on a Norwegian fairy tale, *East of the Sun, West of the Moon*. The relative failure of *NIMH* at the box office consequently triggered Aurora's withdrawal from the project.

By the mid-1980s, Disney had become savvier in how it handled animation, both in managing its existing properties and creating new ones—despite the growing concerns about *The Black Cauldron* (Ted Berman, Richard Rich, 1985). After years in development, the film was over budget and underwhelming. Hope was not lost at Disney, as Ron Miller insisted that "Animation is more important to us now that it has been for at least 20 years."[43] Disney began to consider issuing its animated library on to video cassette to tap into the growing home video market, though Miller suggested he would release the "marginal" films rather than the unidentified seventeen he considered untouchable.[44]

By Christmas 1984, Disney had sold over 600,000 units of its Limited Gold Series, which compiled their cartoon shorts.[45] In September that year, Miller was ousted as Disney's CEO (largely because of the controversial handling of an attempted hostile takeover by Saul Steinberg) and replaced by Michael Eisner and Frank Wells. Spurred on by Roy, the studio aimed for a new animated feature every eighteen months, even as budgets for quality animation rose to nearly $8 million per film.

Disney also began to integrate computer animation into their hand-drawn features. In 1982, a team led by John Lasseter (later of Pixar) and Glen Keane used computers to produce a brief scene from Maurice Sendak's classic children's book *Where the Wild Things Are*. Animators employed computer animation technologies in *The Black Cauldron* and *The Great Mouse Detective*, specifically the climactic scene in London's Big Ben. In 1985, Bud Hester of Disney Animation noted,

> This is an art form, like ballet. That's why computers will never replace animators. You can use a computer imager to move an image around a screen, but it doesn't have a life. And that's what an animated character is supposed to have, the extra upturn on a mouth.[46]

Although Hester's comment reveals some scepticism and perhaps even fear about the capabilities of computer animation, his comment also speaks to the limitations of computer animation at the time. John Lasseter even proposed doing *The Brave Little Toaster* (Jerry Rees, 1987) completely on the computer; he was fired soon after the meeting. In particular, animating living beings—humans and animals—proved difficult and yielded artificial-looking results, which one can still see in the baby character in Lasseter's Oscar-winning animated short *Tin Toy* (1988). (Tellingly, both *Tin Toy* and Lasseter's earlier effort *Luxo, Jr.* [1986], bring inanimate objects to life rather than animating living beings.) At best, computer animation was a facilitator, as the technology did not yet allow for a completely computer-animated feature.

During this time, Don Bluth faced more struggles of his own, largely because of the bankruptcy. With his partners, Gary Goldman and John Pomeroy, Bluth joined Morris Sullivan to form Bluth Sullivan Studios, with the latter serving as president. The new company denied employee requests for collective bargaining rights and even "coerced" employees into leaving the union, leading to charges of unfair labour practices.[47] Executives responded by saying the new company was not obliged to honour the old company's contracts, though many saw Bluth Sullivan Studios as simply an extension of the former. Yet the intervention of Steven Spielberg, the same director who was revolutionizing family entertainment and Hollywood spectacle with films like *Close Encounters of the Third Kind* (1977) and *E.T. The Extra-Terrestrial* (1982), breathed new life into the ailing company.

Like Bluth, Spielberg had grown up on Disney animation, yet felt that the heyday of Disney, MGM, and Warner Bros. had long passed. Composer Jerry Goldsmith had turned Spielberg on to *The Secret of NIMH* and Bluth's revival of classical animation, leading Spielberg to talk with Bluth about a possible collaboration. Soon, David

Kirschner came to Kathleen Kennedy at Amblin Entertainment with an idea, and Spielberg took it to Bluth. Negotiations began in December 1984, and by August of the following year, Bluth announced a new film for Spielberg's Amblin, *An American Tail*, another mouse story that boldly took up themes of immigration, identity, and the American Dream. The invaluable opportunity to work with the mastermind behind *Jaws* (1975) and *E.T.*, however, did not protect Bluth Sullivan Studios from continued labour woes. On August 13, 1986, the Motion Picture Screen Cartoonists, a trade union, took out an ad in *Variety* decrying *An American Tail* for using non-union labour and outsourcing to Ireland. Bluth, for his part, complained that the union's call for salary increases, and the dominance of what he called the "Saturday-morning-television school of animation," required him to implement cost-saving measures to remain financially solvent.[48] The Irish government had provided generous subsidies to compel the American animation studio to move from Van Nuys, California, to Dublin, Ireland, with the understanding Bluth and company would train and employ three hundred Irish citizens. In October 1986, Sullivan settled with the union, but Bluth and associates' time in the United States was over for now. In November 1987, Morris F. Sullivan and Don Bluth opened a 42,000 square foot facility in Dublin.

An American Tail clearly demonstrated the imprimatur of its benevolent executive producer, Steven Spielberg. The protagonist, Fievel, was named after Spielberg's own grandfather, a Russian Jew who had also immigrated to United States. Despite Bluth's penchant for the menacing evil of early Disney animation, *An American Tail* is noticeably toned down, in part because Spielberg, now a young father, was, according to Bluth, "very insistent that his son, Max, could watch this without repercussions."[49] Bluth partner John Pomeroy did the bulk of the animation, while Bluth directed the voice talent. The film features the rich, dark tones produced by using the 600-colour palette developed for Bluth's earlier work, and one cannot help but draw comparison yet again to the mettlesome, yet well-meaning mice of *Cinderella* or even the painful devastation of parental separation of *Bambi* (though Bambi's mother dies, whereas Fievel and his family are reunited). Explaining *An American Tail*'s debt to classical animation, Gary Goldman explained:

> Many people—particularly younger people who have not seen the classics—believe that what they see on television will be what they will see in the theaters. We hope to change that perception, not only for now but for future productions in the industry.[50]

Following a lead forged in part by the Lucas-Spielberg spectacles of the 1970s and early 1980s, Bluth and company attempted an to create an animated spectacle that would underscore the essential difference between the theatre-going and home-viewing experiences. As a result, they created what might be considered the first blockbuster animated feature of contemporary Hollywood.

An American Tail consciously revitalizes aspects of a Disney film that had been lacking in animation over the previous two decades. For one, *An American Tail* clearly owes a debt to the musical and early Disney animation, as the mice break out into the joyous "There Are No Cats in America" or, more memorably, Fievel and his sister Tanya's long-distance duet of the Oscar-nominated song, "Somewhere Out There." Although the musical numbers are not as tightly integrated into the plot as in the subsequent Disney animated musicals, the songs are vital contributors to both the narrative development as well as the emotional impact of the film. Furthermore, "Somewhere Out There" is repeated over the end credits, this time covered by pop stars Linda Ronstadt and James Ingram. This use of theme music set the stage for a new era of pop hits coming out of animated feature films. Not only did the song help to promote the film, but it also proved a career highlight for Ronstadt and Ingram, peaking at #2 on the Billboard Top 40 charts.

Furthermore, the film suggests a transition in the use of voice talent. While Walt Disney occasionally used character actors, most of the film's voice talent were unknown so as to preserve the film's verisimilitude. Some famous actors appeared in Disney films in the 1970s, notably Eva Gabor and Bob Newhart in *The Rescuers*, but *An American Tail* actively employs recognizable voice talent for comedic characters in supporting roles. Tiger, the vegetarian cat, is Dom DeLuise doing a Cowardly Lion impression of sorts, and Madeline Kahn channels her turn as Lili von Shtupp in *Blazing Saddles* (Mel Brooks, 1974) for her role as the wealthy German organizer, Gussie Mausheimer. Christopher Plummer is also featured as Henri, a pigeon whose demeanour calls to mind Maurice Chevalier. These actors' performances in part testify to a cross-generational audience: children who will be amused by the exaggerated intonations and accents, and parents who may recognize the allusions to earlier films, as well as the voices of stars who arguably made their names in adult-oriented fare, such as the Mel Brooks movies. Star voices themselves could provide capital for selling the picture, as Disney would learn six years later with Robin Williams as the Genie in *Aladdin*. Even more than Kahn, DeLuise, and Plummer, however, the posters and movie trailers highlighted Steven Spielberg's signature as the producer, even over Don Bluth's animation.

Bluth did find some champions with his latest effort, including Eleanor Ringel of the *Atlanta Journal and Constitution*, who praised the film's artistic superiority to television cartoons: "*An American Tail* celebrates the rich diversity of our melting-pot heritage; it doesn't insult kids (or adults) with fifth-rate Saturday-morning non-animation; and it gives us some wonderfully memorable characters that weren't already sitting on the Toys R Us shelves, waiting for a feature-length plug to stimulate sales."[51] Unfortunately, most critics were no more taken with *An American Tail* than *The Secret of NIMH*. Vincent Canby of the *New York Times* faulted the film's troublesome politics, including its light-hearted representation of a pogrom and its damning conclusion, in which cats are gleefully deported to Hong Kong.[52] The title Charles Solomon's review in the *Los Angeles Times* sarcastically notes that the film "lavishly disappoints," observing that "rarely has so much animated opulence been wasted on such a thin, badly told story."[53] Yet again, Bluth, the great champion of stories rich in emotional complexity that fostered audience identification, was faulted for a feeble screenplay. The fairness of this charge is questionable, as the reunion of Fievel and his parents and the aforementioned duet are highlights of the film. But for all his adorableness, Fievel is ultimately a weak character, drowning in his large clothes and often overshadowed by the more amusing supporting cast. Although critics praised the animation, this was often undercut by the unsatisfying final act, including what some saw as three back-to-back climaxes. Harry McCracken, writing for *Cinefantastique*, chides, "*An American Tail* manages to be a better film than such ramshackle underpinnings suggest largely because of Bluth's insistence on high production values."[54] In the critics' eyes, Bluth's efforts were noble and the artistic results satisfying, yet the foundational elements of his art form—its characters, its plot, its emotional resonance—remained hollow.

Audiences seemed to be warming up to animated features again. Months earlier, in July 1986, Disney had released *The Great Mouse Detective* (Ron Clements et al., 1986), which grossed a staggering $1 million dollars a day in its first five days.[55] Roger Ebert optimistically opined,

> For a long time, I was down on the full-length animated efforts of Disney and others, because they didn't seem to reflect the same sense of magic and wonderment that the original animated classics always had. Who, for example, could ever equate *101 Dalmatians* with *Snow White and the Seven Dwarfs*? But now, maybe thanks to computers, animated movies are beginning to sparkle again.[56]

Disney Animation seemed to be rebounding artistically, though the film ultimately grossed only $25 million. Released in November 1986 by Universal Pictures, though, *An American Tail* blew *The Great Mouse Detective* out of the water, earning an impressive $47 million domestically and another $37 million abroad, easily becoming the highest-grossing family film of the year. Partnerships with Sears and McDonald's drew additional revenue.[57] Spielberg and Bluth announced their next collaboration—a dinosaur film, later titled *The Land Before Time* (Don Bluth, 1988)—but this time another entertainment titan was on board, George Lucas. But Bluth was unhappy with the creative control Spielberg and Lucas had had over his work, and the partnership dissolved after this film. Don Bluth and his independent animation studio had arrived and, with them, a new age for film animation.

The Land Before Time opened higher and ultimately outperformed Disney's *Oliver & Company* (George Scribner, 1988), yet Bluth's remarkable success over his former employer would be short-lived. On November 17, 1989, both studios faced off again with *All Dogs Go to Heaven* (Don Bluth, 1989) and *The Little Mermaid* (John Musker and Ron Clements, 1989). Although both were bested by *Harlem Nights* (Eddie Murphy, 1989), the new comedy starring Eddie Murphy and Richard Pryor , their premieres were still promising. *All Dogs Go to Heaven* opened to $4.7 million in roughly 1600 theatres, and after a slight bump during the Thanksgiving holiday, slowly tapered off over the next five weekends. *The Little Mermaid*, however,, opened in around a thousand theatres but grossed over $6 million. Despite never hitting number one at the box office, it performed solidly through November with spikes around Christmas and Valentine's Day.

Equally important, *The Little Mermaid* toppled *All Dogs Go to Heaven* in the reactions from critics. The reviews of *All Dogs Go to Heaven* were divided, and several critics chided the faulty plotting and modest animation. But most critics celebrated *The Little*

Mermaid as the long-awaited return to form for Disney feature animation. Desmond Ryan of the *Philadelphia Inquirer* noted how *The Little Mermaid*, unlike its immediate predecessors, "looks back to the studio's unrivaled heritage."[58] Roger Ebert, whose top-rated movie-review television show with Gene Siskel was syndicated via Buena Vista, expressed similar enthusiasm in the *Chicago Sun-Times*. Although the popular impression was that feature animation was kids' stuff, Ebert asserted that animated films could have wide appeal as long as the story rose above the typical "dim-witted" fare. "*The Little Mermaid*," Ebert concluded, "has music and laughter and visual delight for everyone."[59] Indeed, the story's romance and the musical numbers cemented its popularity, and the film established the formula the Walt Disney Company would follow for at least the next decade. Despite the impressive box-office performance of his own princess musical, *Anastasia* (Don Bluth, 1997), Bluth would never come close to matching the hundreds of millions of dollars Disney's animated films generated during the next few years or its formidable ability to exploit its creative properties across multiple platforms.[60] Consequently, Bluth's name has largely been marginalized, both commercially and critically, amid the success of the Disney Renaissance films.

CONCLUSION: AN ELEGY

The overlooking of Don Bluth in the history of animation testifies not only to Disney's ability to self-mythologize, but to animation historians' tendency to reinforce that narrative. Even though Disney's meteoric resurgence of via *The Little Mermaid* and its partnership with (and eventual acquisition of) Pixar has allowed the studio to deride Bluth for his perceived betrayal, it seems undeniable that his and his fellow animators' 1979 defection provided the necessary impetus to revitalize the Disney legacy in animated family entertainment. Furthermore, Bluth Studio's partnership with Amblin Entertainment infused a blockbuster mentality into animated features that has resonated in feature animation ever since, from the hit pop music of Elton John in *The Lion King* to the voices of Mike Myers, Eddie Murphy, and Cameron Diaz in *Shrek* (Vicky Jenson and Andrew Adamson, 2001) to the emotional montage sequence at the beginning of *Up* (Pete Docter and Bob Peterson, 2009). Although Bluth did not originate many of these techniques and approaches to filmmaking, his collaboration with Steven Spielberg, and later George Lucas, certainly updated them for a film industry that was increasingly synergistic, transmedial, and globalized. Bluth ultimately fell victim to the digital innovations in his beloved art form, but there is little denying that he remains an integral (albeit underappreciated) instigator, both intentionally and inadvertently, behind some of its greatest modern triumphs. In understanding his contribution, we complicate the historical narrative of Disney's role in contemporary animation and challenge its ability to manipulate and misrepresent the company's role in the film industry and its history.

Notes

1. See Jeffrey A. Trachtenberg, "Playing a Different 'Toon,'" *Millimeter*, January 1985, p. 180; Jack Mathews and John Culhane, "The Old Magic Is Back," *Los Angeles Times*, November 12, 1989, pp. U6–U7, U20; and Charles Solomon, "Toon Town Is Boom Town," *Los Angeles Times*, August 19, 1990, pp. F8–F9, F94.
2. Janet Wasko, *Understanding Disney: The Manufacture of Fantasy* (Malden, MA: Polity, 2001), p. 7.
3. All box office figures are from BoxOfficeMojo.com.
4. Chris Pallant, *Demystifying Disney: A History of Disney Feature Animation* (London: Continuum, 2011), p. 90.
5. Maureen Furniss, *A New History of Animation* (London: Thames & Hudson, 2016), pp. 341–342.
6. Don Hahn, *Waking Sleeping Beauty*, dir. Don Hahn, Walt Disney Studios Home Entertainment, 2010.
7. Ron Miller, qtd. in John Culhane, "The Old Disney Magic," *New York Times*, August 1, 1976, p. 32.
8. Charles Champlin, "Smoke, but No Fire in Dragon," *Los Angeles Times*, December 16, 1977, p. 22.
9. Jay Scott, "Going against the Traditions of Walt Disney," *Globe and Mail*, June 30, 1982, p. 15.
10. Eric Larson, qtd. in Wayne Warga, "Disney's Endangered Species," *Los Angeles Times*, July 2, 1978, p. N25.
11. Ron Miller, qtd. in Aljean Harmetz, "11 Animators Quit Disney, Form Studio," *New York Times*, September 20, 1979, p. C14.
12. Ron Miller, qtd. in "The Rebel Nibbling at Disney's World," *Fortune*, October 4, 1982, p. 68.
13. Eric Larson, qtd. in Harmetz, "11 Animators," p. C14.
14. Ed Hansen, qtd. in Andrew J. Neff, "Two Disney Animators Ankle for Bluth," *Variety*, November 16, 1979, p. 6.
15. Ed Hansen, qtd. in Aljean Harmetz, "Animation Again a Priority at Disney," *New York Times*, August 27 1984, p. C11.
16. Emphasis in original. Don Bluth, qtd. in Harmetz, "11 Animators," p. C14.
17. Harmetz, "Animation Again," p. C11.
18. Heidi Guedel, *Animatrix—a Female Animator: How Laughter Saved My Life* (New York: iUniverse, 2003), pp. 324–325.
19. Pamela G. Hollie, "Animators' Loss Shakes Disney," *New York Times*, October 10, 1979, p. D1.
20. Wayne Warga, "Disney Films: Chasing the Changing Times," *Los Angeles Times*, October 26, 1980, p. O1.
21. Ron Miller, qtd. in Sally Ogle Davis, "Wishing upon a Falling Star at Disney," *New York Times*, November 16, 1980, p. SM36.
22. David Ehrman, qtd. in Warga, "Disney Films," p. O36.
23. Tom Wilhite, qtd. in Charles Solomon, "Will the Real Walt Disney Please Stand Up?," *Film Comment*, July–August 1982, p. 51.
24. Don Bluth, qtd. in Solomon, "Will the Real Walt Disney?," p. 53.
25. *The Secret of NIMH*, press kit, MGM/UA Entertainment, Philadelphia, 1982, p. 1. Archives and Special Collections, Salisbury University, Salisbury, MD.

26. What "uncompromised" meant isn't quite clear. Most likely it refers to a sense that storylines in Disney films at the time had been loose and episodic. Another possibility is that the film does not shy away from, at times, scaring its youngest audience members. (Recent Disney films had fairly innocuous antagonists, though, in fairness, *The Fox and the Hound* features an intense fight sequence.) *The Secret of NIMH* press kit, pp. 2–3.

27. Don Bluth, qtd. in "Bluth Completes Cartoon Feature," *Variety*, May 19 1982, p. 34.

28. Stefan Kanfer, *Serious Business: The Art of Animation in America from Betty Boop to "Toy Story"* (New York: Scribner, 1997), p. 212.

29. Richard Irvine, qtd. in Aljean Harmetz, "Ex-Disney Animators Try to Outdo Their Mentor," *New York Times*, July 14, 1982, p. C17.

30. Sheila Benson, "*NIMH:* A Mixture of Genres," review of *The Secret of NIMH, New York Times*, July 2, 1982, p. H1.

31. Benson, "*NIMH,*" p. H14.

32. Roger Ebert, review of The Secret of NIMH, RogerEbert.com, January 1, 1982.

33. Vincent Canby, "*N.I.M.H.*, Shades of Disney's Golden Era," review of *The Secret of NIMH, New York Times*, July 2, 1982, p. C12.

34. Glen Keane, qtd. in Alex Ward, "New Hands Are Carrying on the Disney Studio's Tradition," *New York Times*, July 5, 1981, p. D13.

35. Don Bluth, qtd. in "Disney Attempts to Reverse Movie Division's Profit Slide," *New York Times*, August 31, 1981, p. D4.

36. Dick Cook, qtd. in Deborah Caulfield, "Disney Vetoes *NIMH* as a Pairing with *Tron,*" *Los Angeles Times*, August 25, 1982, pp. D1, D4.

37. Don Bluth, qtd. in Caulfield, "Disney Vetoes," p. D4.

38. Jerry Esbin, qtd. in Deborah Caulfield, "Warrens Returns to Old Haunts," *Los Angeles Times*, August 28, 1982, p. D7.

39. Don Bluth, qtd. in Gerald Duchovnay, "Don Bluth," in Gerald Duchovnay (ed.), *Film Voices: Interviews from Post Script* (Albany: State University of New Press, 2004), pp. 143–152, 150.

40. David Crook, "Animator Leads with a *Space Ace,*" *Los Angeles Times*, February 21, 1984, p. G9.

41. Don Bluth, qtd. in Charles Solomon, "Fantasy, Technology Meet in *Dragon's Lair,*" *Los Angeles Times*, August 9, 1983, p. G5.

42. Dann Gire, "Bluth on Making *An American Tail* for Steven Spielberg," *Cinefantastique* 17:3–4 (1987), p. 110.

43. Ron Miller, qtd. in Aljean Harmetz, "Animation Again a Priority at Disney," *New York Times*, August 27, 1984, p. C11.

44. Harmetz, "Animation Again," p. C11.

45. Aljean Harmetz, "Video Alter Economics of Movie Animation," *New York Times*, May 1, 1985, p. C19.

46. Bud Hester, qtd. in Trachtenberg, "Playing a Different 'Toon,'" p. 190.

47. David Robb, "Cartoonists File Labor Charge vs. Sullivan Studios," *Variety*, April 4, 1985, pp. 1, 15.

48. Nina Darnton, "Steven Spielberg Ventures into Animation," *New York Times*, November 10, 1986, p. C8.

49. Don Bluth, qtd. in Darnton, "Steven Spielberg," p. C8.

50. Goldman, qtd. in *An American Tail* press kit.

51. Eleanor Ringel, "Beat Path out Door to Better Mouse Tale," *Atlanta Journal and Constitution*, November 21, 1986, p. 1.

52. Vincent Canby, review of *An American Tail*, *New York Times*, November 21, 1986, p. C8.

53. Charles Solomon, "*American Tail* Lavishly Disappoints," *Los Angeles Times*, November 22, 1986, p. H8.

54. Harry McCracken, "Don Bluth Is Good, but He's No Walt Disney," review of *An American Tail*, *Cinefantastique* 17:3–4 (1987), p. 110.

55. Charles Champlin, "*Mouse Detective* Good News for Animation," review of *The Great Mouse Detective*, *Los Angeles Times*, July 12, 1986, p. D1.

56. Roger Ebert, review of *The Great Mouse Detective*, RogerEbert.com, July 2, 1986.

57. Gire, "Bluth on Making," p. 111.

58. Desmond Ryan, "Disney Animators Give Life to *The Little Mermaid*," *Philadelphia Inquirer*, November 17, 1989, p. 3.

59. Roger Ebert, "*The Little Mermaid*," *Chicago Sun-Times*, November 17, 1989. https://www.rogerebert.com/reviews/the-little-mermaid-1989 [accessed July 25, 2020].

60. Of course, it should be noted that *The Rescuers Down Under* (Hendel Butoy and Mike Gabriel, 1990)—neither a musical nor a romance—did not match the success of the other Disney animated films of the period.

BIBLIOGRAPHY

An American Tail. Press kit. Universal Pictures. Universal City, CA. 1986. Archives and Special Collections, Salisbury University, Salisbury, MD.

Bendazzi, Giannalberto. *Cartoons: One Hundred Years of Cinema Animation*. Bloomington: Indiana University Press, 1995.

Duchovnay, Gerald. "Don Bluth." In Gerald Duchovnay (ed.), *Film Voices: Interviews from Post Script*. Albany: State University of New York Press, 2004, pp. 143–152.

Kanfer, Stefan. *Serious Business: The Art of Animation in America from Betty Boop to Toy Story*. New York: Scribner, 1997.

Maltin, Leonard. *Of Mice and Magic: A History of American Animated Cartoons*. Rev. ed.. New York: Plume, 1987.

Pallant, Chris. *Demystifying Disney: A History of Disney Feature Animation*. London: Continuum, 2011.

The Secret of NIMH. Press kit. MGM/UA Entertainment. Philadelphia. 1982. Archives and Special Collections, Salisbury University, Salisbury, MD.

Sito, Tom. *Drawing the Line: The Untold Story of the Animation Unions from Bosko to Bart Simpson*. Lexington: University Press of Kentucky, 2006.

Solomon, Charles. *Enchanted Drawings: The History of Animation*. Rev. ed.. New York: Random House, 1994.

Waking Sleeping Beauty. Dir. Don Hahn. Walt Disney Studios Home Entertainment, 2010.

Wasko, Janet. *Understanding Disney: The Manufacture of Fantasy*. Malden, MA: Polity, 2001.

CHAPTER 31

ON "LOVE EXPERTS," EVIL PRINCES, GULLIBLE PRINCESSES, AND *FROZEN*

AMY M. DAVIS

AT the time of its US release, many reviewers gave *Frozen* (Jennifer Lee and Chris Buck, 2013) a tepid rating at best. Christy Lemire of RogerEbert.com, for instance, described the film's songs as "lively and amusing if not quite instant hits."[1] Meanwhile, Scott Foundas, writing for *Variety*, opined in his opening paragraph that " 'Frozen' should generate considerable box-office heat, if not quite the same level of critical and audience affection that attended the superior 'Tangled' and 'Wreck-It Ralph.' "[2] With hindsight, such descriptions and predictions about *Frozen* are indeed eyebrow-raising; after all, one of those "lively and amusing if not quite instant hit [songs]," "Let It Go," not only reached the top 10 on various charts (going double platinum in the United States) but also won Best Original Song at the 86th Academy Awards in 2014; the soundtrack as a whole reached number one in the Billboard 200 chart for at least thirteen non-consecutive weeks.[3] *Frozen* was the highest-grossing film of 2013, and by the end of 2014 had sold an estimated five billion dollars' worth of merchandizing, a figure that gives some indication that audiences did indeed feel great "affection" for *Frozen*, regardless of its merits in comparison to *Tangled* (Nathan Greno and Byron Howard, 2010) and *Wreck-It Ralph* (Rich Moore, 2012).[4]

Five years later, audiences awaiting the release of *Frozen II* (Jennifer Lee and Chris Buck, 2019) were still excited enough that, in its first twenty-four hours of release, the film's June 2019 trailer was viewed almost ten million times on YouTube alone.[5] In its opening weekend in the United States (November 22–24, 2019), *Frozen II* grossed over $130 million, "becoming the first animated title outside of summer to surpass triple digits in its first weekend. The movie also set a new pinnacle for the Thanksgiving box office, earning $123 million over the five-day holiday frame."[6] By early December, its soundtrack had reached number one on the Billboard 200 chart "with the equivalent of 80,000 album sales in the United States, including 51 million streams and 37,000 copies sold as a complete package."[7] Clearly, these numbers suggest that the Frozen franchise has been enthusiastically embraced by audiences around the world and across multiple demographics in a way that few movies have before, with the strong bonds of sister-hood between its central protagonists, Anna and Elsa of Arendelle, named by fans as one of the most appealing parts. *Frozen's* characters and its positioning of sisterly and familial love as being at least as important as (if not more important than) romantic love have made it seem revolutionary. Certainly, the love the sisters have for each another is central to both films (and, of course, it saves the day), but love—as well as the harm that comes from being bereft of love—is depicted in many forms throughout the films and expressed in many ways by its characters. Its importance is such that it carries over as a major theme in all three (to date) of the first film's sequels: the shorts "Frozen Fever" (Jennifer Lee and Chris Buck, 2015), "Lego/Disney: Frozen Northern Lights" (Steven Spencer, 2016), "Olaf's Frozen Adventure" (Stevie Wermers and Kevin Deters, 2017), "Myth: A Frozen Tale" (Jeff Gipson, 2019), the feature film *Frozen II*, "Once Upon a Snowman" (Dan Abraham and Trent Correy, 2020), and the limited series *Olaf Presents* (Hyrum Osmond, 2021).[8] Love's role throughout the *Frozen* saga, therefore, is the focus of this chapter.

EVIL PRINCES AND GULLIBLE PRINCESSES

Certainly, one of the things that seemed to surprise most of the audience in 2013 was the romantic misdirection that starts the trouble in Arendelle: the arrival of Prince Hans (Santino Fontana) of the Southern Isles, his quickie romance and engagement to Princess Anna (Kristen Bell), and Queen Elsa's (Idina Menzel) refusal to bless their betrothal. Even before we learn later that Hans is using Anna to gain the throne of Arendelle, Anna and Hans's engagement is depicted as mightily naive and stupid. When Elsa hears about it, she is disgusted and angered. When, later, Anna mentions it to Kristoff (Jonathan Groff), whom she has met only a little while before, he is openly shocked and horrified. He is so deeply appalled by the prospect that, shortly afterward, when he and Anna realise that their sleigh is being pursued by wolves, Kristoff initially rejects Anna's help, telling her that he does not trust her judgement, citing her hasty de-cision to marry; indeed, he is so horrified by it that he even mentions it again in *Frozen II* (during one of his series of clumsy, aborted attempts to propose to Anna). Many people saw the narrative's characterization of the speed of Hans and Anna's relationship as rash and imprudent as a comment on the fairy-tale trope of love at first sight, as well as on Disney's inclusion of this trope in many of its fairy-tale adaptations.

Nonetheless, it should be remembered that one of the few firsts that *Frozen* can lay claim to within the Disney canon is that it is the first Disney film in which the (apparent) romantic leads become engaged on the same day they meet. The Prince may serenade Snow White at the beginning of *Snow White and the Seven Dwarfs* (David Hand et al., 1937), but there is no actual betrothal in the film; indeed, months pass between the day they meet and the day the Prince awakens Snow White. Granted, they spend most of that time apart; but even when the Prince rescues her with "Love's First Kiss" and breaks the witch's spell, they only ride away together, presumably to go to one or the other of their kingdoms. Marriage is only implied (or assumed by the audience, who are familiar with the trope), not discussed. Cinderella and Prince Charming *are* quick, but they at least wait a day to become engaged, after the Grand Duke has found Cinderella at her stepmother's house and identified her as the mystery woman who stole Prince Charming's heart. As for Princess Aurora in *Sleeping Beauty* (Clyde Geronimi, 1959), she is betrothed to Prince Phillip as an infant, so their engagement (such as it is) lasts a good 16 years! For Anna and Hans, however, the decision to marry comes only hours after they first meet—Anna is wearing the same dress when Hans proposes that she was wearing when she met him. While, eventually, Kristoff will propose to Anna (and be accepted), this does not happen until near the end of *Frozen II*, some 3 years (we learn that Elsa's coronation took place 3 years prior to the start of *Frozen II*) after they first met, and after they have spent time as a couple and come to know one another. In fact, Kristoff's failed attempts to propose to Anna become a semi-comic subplot of *Frozen II*, helping to impress on its audience that, this time at least, the lead couple's decision to marry will not be a rash move born of infatuation or desperation, but—to borrow a theme from the first film—an act of true love.

Yet in many online and popular discussions of Anna's decision in *Frozen* to accept the hand of a man she has known only for a few hours, almost none acknowledge the reasons why Anna clearly feels so compelled to agree so quickly to marry a stranger. This is despite the fact that the film itself provides numerous clues as to Anna's motivation. The first sign that Anna is very much a bird in a gilded cage is the song and montage "Do You Want to Build a Snow Man." The song begins just after the King (and Queen, one presumes, though we do not hear her speak until *Frozen II*) have shut Elsa away from Anna (supposedly for Anna's protection) and, without understanding why, Anna suddenly—and for the first time—finds herself without a friend to play with. It is also made very clear that Anna absolutely adores her older sister, and finds this abrupt change in their relationship confusing, singing to her sister in the first part of the song, shortly after Elsa is shut away, "We used to be best buddies, and now we're not / I wish you would tell me why!" Over the course of this increasingly emotional song, Anna knocks at Elsa's door, seeking her company. In the first verse, Anna expresses the feeling that "It's like [Elsa has] gone away." Next, she notes:

> I think some company is overdue
> I've started talking to the pictures on the walls!
> It gets a little lonely—all these empty rooms—just watching the hours tick by!

In the song's next section, as Anna passes Elsa's closed door, she pauses briefly as if she would like to knock, but years of rejection have taught her not to bother, and so she moves on to bid her parents good-bye as they prepare for their ill-fated trip. After they are lost at sea, Anna is utterly alone, a solitary, forlorn figure standing next to their memorial stones during the funeral service; the shot transitions to show her alone and grieving in the palace's huge, dim corridors. She approaches Elsa's door, knocks quietly (and with just three ordinary knocks, rather than the jauntier "Tap Tap Ta-Tap Tap" that she uses at the start of the song's earlier verses), and sings:

> Please—I know you're in there.
> People are asking where you've been.
> They say have courage, and I'm trying to—
> I'm right out here for you—
> Just let me in!
> We only have each other—
> It's just you and me—
> What are we gonna do?
> Do you want to build a snowman...?

What we learn from "Do You Want to Build a Snowman," and from the hopes Anna expresses subsequently during one of her "I Want" songs, "The First Time in Forever," is that Anna has spent years essentially on her own. She may live in an opulent palace with servants to wait upon her—and she seems to have a pleasant relationship with the servants—but Anna, clearly an extroverted, affectionate person, has no one with whom she can share her life. Indeed, her song's title implies that she cannot remember the last time that she has shared genuine closeness with another person, suggesting that her status as princess, as well as the fact that the palace's gates have been closed since they were children, has cut her off from forming relationships with any of the people of Arendelle. Certainly, we hear nothing of any friends, nor does Anna seem to have a pet or sidekick. Anna notes that Elsa's Coronation Day and the Coronation Ball—and the fact that people will be joining them in the palace—are the first time she has had the opportunity to meet someone with whom she can share her life. She also expresses her concern that this might be her only opportunity to do so, singing, "I know it all ends tomorrow / So it has to be today!" So, when she is wooed by the charming, handsome, funny Prince Hans—apparently the first person to express friendliness to her on socially-equal terms (since he is, too, is a royal), it appears to her—and to the audience—that her wishes have come true at last, and she seizes the opportunity with both hands before it can slip away.

Her decision to rush into a betrothal may well be highly problematic (particularly to modern Western sensibilities), but one could argue that it is also very pro-active. Essentially, Anna has lost her family and is alone in the world in the sense that her only surviving relative has both metaphorically and (by and large) literally shut her out. She and Elsa may both still live under the same roof, but it is evident that they almost never see each other. This is demonstrated by the scene at the Coronation Ball when Elsa and Anna are announced to the guests, and Anna displays an awkward hesitance at being asked to stand next to Elsa on the dais, then makes small talk with her before her overture—her wishing that they could leave the gates open all the time—is rejected.

Of course, unbeknownst to Anna, Elsa would love to be closer, too, but she is terrified of allowing Anna into her life for fear of harming her further after nearly accidentally freezing Anna's head when they were children. We see Elsa's struggles with isolation and loneliness throughout her childhood during scenes intercut with Anna's singing "Do You Want to Build a Snowman" when, in between each of the song's verses, we see Elsa's struggles to control her powers: her learning from her father (Maurice LaMarche) her mantra "conceal it, don't feel it—don't let it show"; her fear of hurting her parents physically, which makes her push them away as well; her formal (and nervous) good-bye to her parents before their trip; and, lastly, her depression and isolation in a barren room scarred with ice, Elsa holding herself and sobbing with her back to the door, the closest she can get to Anna (who sits against the other side, equally alone). But while the audience may be aware of the true reasons for Elsa's separation from Anna, Anna herself has no idea; indeed, later, in a conversation with Hans, Anna remarks that, "We used to be really close, but then, one day, she just shut me out." So, while Anna's decision to accept Hans's proposal may seem rash (not to mention glaringly poor judgement) to both Elsa and the audience, who know Elsa's reasons for keeping her distance, in Anna's mind, it makes sense. For her, as far as she knows, Hans is her last chance for love, closeness with another, and—through their marriage—a chance to create a new family of her own. She is determined to make the most of this vanishingly rare opportunity, and will not be put off by Elsa's condemnation, particularly given her belief that Elsa only knows how to shut people out, not how to give and receive love.

Of course, the film foreshadows that, contrary to Anna's hopes, Hans will *not* be "The One." The first clue that this is the case comes just seconds before Anna meets Hans. As she sings the final lines of "The First Time in Forever"—"For the first time in forever / Nothing's in my way!"—she bumps into Hans's horse. It may appear to be a goofy, funny "meet cute," but in fact it functions as a clue that, when it comes to finding True Love, it will be Hans who gets in Anna's way for most of the film. The fact of his existence, and his role as Anna's fiancé throughout the entire middle section of the film, keeps her apart (romantically) from Kristoff, the young man with whom she forms a genuine attachment during their quest to find Elsa, and who brings her to the Trolls for help after Elsa has accidentally frozen Anna's heart. Kristoff's knowledge that Anna has a fiancé means that, when he becomes aware of his growing feelings for Anna, he holds back from expressing them. Though the Trolls observe in their song "Fixer-Upper," "Her quote 'engagement' is a flex arrangement / And by the way, I don't see no ring!" and try to marry Anna and Kristoff to one another on the spot, Anna's fainting—whether this is just shock at the Trolls' forwardness or a result of her heart freezing further—puts paid to such ideas. Grand Pabbie's (Ciarán Hinds) declaration that "Only an act of true love can thaw a frozen heart" will give Kristoff the opportunity to bundle Anna up and ride away on Sven the reindeer to get her safely to Hans so that she can be saved by Hans's giving her a true love's kiss. In doing so, Kristoff demonstrates his true love for Anna, as well as creating a scenario for Hans to show that his love for Anna, ultimately, is an opportunistic sham. Granted, Anna's love for Hans is likewise opportunistic—she wants love and intimacy and, as a smart, funny, handsome prince, he'll do the job nicely. But whereas Anna enters their relationship with hope, Hans does so cynically; as he will confess later, he wants a kingdom of his own, and is willing to do away with Elsa and Anna to gain theirs.

Ironically, another possible clue that they are wrong for each other is Hans and Anna's duet "Love Is an Open Door." Unlike the other songs in *Frozen*, "Love Is an Open Door" has a kind of cutsie, pop duet style. Though they say things that, on the surface, sound very playful and romantic, those sentiments are expressed in such a conventional musical form that little genuine emotion comes through. It is as if both characters are acting out a pantomime of love to convince themselves and each other that there is something real between them. Interestingly, during the lines "Say goodbye to the pain of the past / We don't have to feel it anymore," we see the couple dancing at a distance; on the word "pain," the camera actually cuts from watching them dance on the top balcony of a lighthouse to a shot of them in silhouette behind the sails of a ship, again possibly implying that such sentiments are not genuine, but only shadows.

In this section of the film, in fact, it is interesting to observe the number of risky behaviours the couple engage in as they sing of their "love" for one another: in addition to dancing on the lighthouse balcony and one of the booms of a ship's masts, they also leap between balconies, slide in their stocking feet across wooden floors (and nearly fall while doing so), sit on the ridge of part of the palace's roof, leap about on the edge of a bridge, dance among the moving parts of a giant clock, and dance on the edge of a small cliff. It's on the cliff, surrounded by a waterfall, that Hans proposes and Anna accepts; mirroring the beginning of the song, Hans prefaces his proposal with "Can I say something crazy?"; although it comes across initially as sweet and goofy, Anna's reply is itself a foreshadowing of trouble to come: "Can I say something even crazier? Yes!" This indicates that, deep down, Anna recognizes that leaping into an engagement with Hans is not a wise choice. But for Anna, her life has been such a lonely, empty existence, marrying Hans seems like her only means of escape and change. Indeed, the thing that precipitates Anna going off with Hans during the ball is yet another rejection from Elsa, when Anna says she wishes that they could always be sociable and spend time together, and Elsa almost forcefully rejects the notion:

ANNA: This is so nice! I wish it could be like this all the time.
ELSA: Me too. But it can't. [looks away]
ANNA: Well, why not? I mean...
ELSA: [Interrupting angrily, turning her back on Anna] It just can't.
ANNA: [Nods quietly to herself, as if hurt but not terribly surprised] Excuse me
         for a minute.

Anna walks away from the dais and is accidentally knocked into Hans by a careless guest; symbolically, she is pushed into Hans's arms, and he instantly turns on the charm, catching her and pulling her toward him to lead her in a waltz. Yet Hans's obvious sophistication and panache—in a single move, he catches Anna by the hand before she can hit the ground, bows, places his champagne flute on the tray of a passing servant, and pulls her into his arms as romantic music swells—hint that he is a smooth operator, and there is something of a performance about his actions that belies their authenticity. Anna, being very sheltered and naive, has no way of noticing this; more importantly, she has no desire to notice it. This is her "chance to change [her] lonely world—a chance to find true love," and Hans seems like the answer to her prayers.

PRINCE HANS OF THE SOUTHERN ISLES

So yes, there are many clues (if one cares to see them) before the revelation that Hans is a threat who will seek to destroy the sisters and take control of Arendelle. And yet, for all that (ultimately) we are encouraged in *Frozen* to see Hans as a dangerous villain, it is important to note the many links between Anna and Hans. They are both the younger children of royal rulers. They both have difficult relationships with their older siblings that lead them to feel more-or-less alone in the world. Hans and Anna even resemble one another physically to a greater degree than Anna and Elsa. They both wish to im-prove their lives and to make a change…and they both see a marriage as the way to bring about that change.

It is this combination of the ties between Anna and Hans and his cruel, devious plans that positions Hans within the trope of the Demon Lover, and as an expression of Anna's own dark side. According to Wyatt Bonikowski, "The demon lover might be described as the representation of a part of the mind that has been split off and projected outwards, which then returns to pursue the subject with the force of the death drive."[9] Bonikowski links the Demon Lover to Lacan's idea of The Thing, arguing that it is "a development of that aspect of Freud's *Nebenmensch*, the 'neighbour' or 'fellow human being,' which, in the subject's encounter with reality, is split off '*als Ding*,' 'as a Thing'; one aspect of the neighbour is assimilated to consciousness but the Thing cannot be assimilated and remains resistant to representation."[10] In fact, *Nebenmensch* is better understood, not as a "neighbor" or "fellow human being," but as something more akin to Plato's idea of the Split Apart (sometimes termed the "Soul Mate," though without the romantic connotations that idea has acquired).

In this case, Hans serves as Anna's shadow self. Indeed, once could argue that his at-tempt to take the throne of Arendelle by nefarious means foreshadows Anna's even-tual (and more reputable) rise to the throne of Arendelle at the end of *Frozen II* (thus serving as a further link between them). As we see over the course of *Frozen* and *Frozen II*, Anna is the sister who most aligns with patriarchal norms and expectations (whereas Elsa will ultimately align with the feminine and matriarchal). This is stressed through Anna's need for a romantic attachment to a man, as well as (more symbolically) through her rising to occupy her father's throne when Elsa chooses to live among their mother's people. That Hans and Anna are equally drawn to one another is stressed, however, in a moment that *may* be characterized as audience misdirection, but which serves no function of deception within the film itself. After their first meeting, as Anna hurries away to the palace for Elsa's coronation, Hans's horse takes his foot off the boat Hans is standing in and it falls into the water, landing on top of Hans. Hidden from the view of all the other characters—and therefore with no reason to pretend (after all, he is unaware that a non-diegetic audience is watching the story unfold)—Hans watches Anna walk away, and a sweet, goofy expression appears on his face as he sighs; Hans is smitten (Figure 31.1). While much of his subsequent behaviour can be read as an act—after all, other characters are around, and he has his part to play—this moment seems to be for himself alone.

Anna's initial attachment to Hans, as well as his reveal as the film's villain later in the narrative, casts Hans in the unusual role of being both the Prince and the villain of the story. Although, certainly, he is not the only evil princely figure in folklore and fairy tales—indeed, figures such as Bluebeard spring to mind (Marina Warner devotes an entire chapter of *From the Beast to the Blonde* to a discussion of Bluebeard as a Demon Lover)—his appearance in a film, especially a Disney animated feature, is very unusual.[11] There have been earlier male villains, but they have not played any kind of romantic role (genuine or false), even when they have had (or at least pretended) sexual feelings for the heroine. But as Anna's demon lover/shadow self, Hans offers a chance for Anna to emerge as the true heroine of the story, both in the short term (in *Frozen*) and in the long term (in *Frozen II*). Hans is the shadow self that Anna must reject, just as in more traditional fairy-tale narratives, the hero(ine) must reject and defeat the villain to sublimate her better, more heroic self. Anna does this in a number of ways throughout *Frozen*, such as through her quest to save her sister, her willingness to sacrifice herself to save Elsa, and (in a moment that is as funny as it is important to the narrative's symbolism) when she punches Hans in the face and knocks him into the fjord. This rejection of Hans *cannot* be read as a rejection of Patriarchy as a whole. As Anna and Elsa embrace following the

FIGURE 31.1. Hans, hidden under a boat, watches as Anna returns to the palace. *Frozen* (Disney, 2013). Frame-grab.

punch, Anna looks back over her shoulder at Kristoff and smiles warmly. Only a minute later, having given Kristoff a new sled, she kisses him on the cheek, encouraging him to kiss her romantically. Her links to Kristoff remain strong throughout, and by the end of *Frozen II* are made permanent through their decision to marry. But in Hans's role as villain (and initially as Demon Lover), he creates a foil for both Anna and Elsa: he is the entitled side of Patriarchy who will try to take whatever he wants and either kill or condemn whoever tries to stand in his way regardless of the greater claim they may have. That Anna has rejected fully this aspect of Patriarchy is confirmed in *Frozen II* by his failure to return; though he receives a brief mention early in the film and later reappears, in ice form, in Ahtohallan (in a roomful of Elsa's memories; Elsa takes this opportunity to punch him, too), he plays no role whatsoever in the narrative to follow. What is happening here is not necessarily that Hans is fooling us; he does seem to like Anna (indeed, she is hard not to like). The villain is not incapable of love, after all. Rather, what makes the villain wrong, or bad, or a threat, within the fairy tale usually is their inability to value love above desire, and to let go of selfish impulses in favour of helping and caring for others (as a romantic partner, a parent, or as a good citizen of his community).

As Rothman notes in his discussion of Voldemort (a villain who *does* love—not other people—but power, revenge, and himself most of all), "His moral unsightedness resulted in part from a failure to value sexuality, love…and human life in particular—and in part from a failure to engage in moral choice, weighing and if necessary choosing between values."[12] Anna will give all of herself to help others, but Hans is incapable of such sacrifice. Yet that moment when we glimpse what seems to be Hans's genuine affection for Anna may be the moment that allows the narrative to spare his life. Hans is not killed off, after all. Rather, he is thrown into a cell and returned to his twelve older brothers for punishment. In a brief mention in *Frozen II*, we know that his punishment is ongoing. His dreamy gaze from under the boat in *Frozen* is Hans's potential redemption because it indicates that he is not wholly evil. He must be punished, but perhaps will be reformed through his labours. This is different from the fate of the evil King Runeard (Jeremy Sisto)—Anna and Elsa's paternal grandfather—whose selfish desire to capture the lands of the Northuldra people leads to his death and to his soldiers' imprisonment within the Enchanted Forest for 34 years (and 5 months and 22 days). But just as Anna rejects Hans, she also rejects—and she and Elsa work to redress—the sins of the past in order to save the present and protect the future.

THAWING A FROZEN HEART

Toward the end of the film, Hans declares to Anna his intent to allow her to die in an act of passive-aggressive murder/betrayal so that he can seize control of Arendelle; by locking her in a room to die, he almost keeps Anna from the Act of True Love that will save her, Elsa, and Arendelle. But until Hans reveals his scheming to Anna, there are few clues (all easily missed on initial viewing) as to Hans's true nature. He has played his part well, and has Anna, the people of Arendelle, and the visiting dignitaries believing his sincerity as Anna's true love, as a dutiful and altruistic royal (he is even chastised by the Duke of Weselton [Alan Tudyk], the film's red-herring villain, for giving away Arendelle's tradable goods to the suffering people of the kingdom, defending his upholding and interpretation of Anna's orders to protect the kingdom, and even leading a search party to rescue Anna when her riderless horse returns). Later, when he locks Anna in a cold room to die alone and returns to the gathered dignitaries, feigning (as the audience now realizes) his shock and distress that Anna has died (noting that the two had time to say their marriage vows to one another before her death, thereby legitimizing his claim to the throne) before "reluctantly" charging Queen Elsa with treason and sentencing her to death "with a heavy heart," none of the officials question his claim to have married Anna, though there were no witnesses. Likewise, none object to his assumption of the power to charge the queen—the legal and *actual* ruler—with treason, and none insist upon a trial before imposing a sentence on her. In a slightly earlier scene, even Elsa believes Hans's sincerity when he tells her that he is protecting her from the cries for her death from the visiting dignitaries, as well as his worries for the still-missing Anna. In other words, everyone—not just Anna—take Hans at his word, and no one takes any steps to question him, let alone stop him. No one, that is, except for Anna.

Initially, because she falls so quickly and easily for Hans's smooth talk, Anna comes across as gullible. Particularly when she rejects Elsa's condemnation of her decision to marry Hans, Anna seems naive even for someone who has spent most of her life sequestered in a palace.

ELSA: [Disdainfully] You can't marry a man you just met.
ANNA: [Angrily] You *can* if it's true love.
ELSA: [Dismissively] Anna, what do *you* know about true love.
ANNA: More than you! All you know is how to shut people out!

Elsa's reaction to Anna's cutting remark shows that, from Elsa's point of view, it is particularly hurtful, given Elsa's and the audience's (privileged) knowledge. We know that Elsa has kept her distance in order to keep Anna safe—that Elsa loves her sister so dearly that she has sacrificed her happiness for Anna's well-being. Though she must know that Anna does not and cannot know this, to be told that she knows nothing of true love clearly wounds Elsa. We have evidence throughout *Frozen* that Elsa misses her sister deeply, and "Olaf's Frozen Adventure" strengthens this argument when we see that, every Christmas, Elsa has come to look forward with joy to the Olaf-themed cards and gifts that Anna makes for her each year and slips under her door, and that Elsa has kept them and treasures them (Figure 31.2). During "Do You Want to Build a Snowman," we see Elsa's loneliness first-hand. Later, during "Let It Go," we see that Elsa's first conscious use of her powers after fleeing Arendelle is—at long last—to build a snowman: Olaf (Josh Gadd), the character she and Anna had created as children. It is a tangible signal that Elsa's apparent joy in her first flush of freedom is tempered by her love and homesickness for her sister, and her longing for their days of childhood closeness before the accident that led to their separation for Anna's protection.

FIGURE 31.2. Elsa, holding a homemade Olaf doll from Anna, gazes with a bittersweet expression at the door that keeps her necessarily—but sadly—separated from the sister she loves and misses, but for whom she must sacrifice her happiness to keep safe. "Olaf's Frozen Adventure" (Disney, 2018). Frame-grab.

Though this loneliness and love for her sister help to humanize Elsa, ultimately—and particularly within *Frozen II*—Elsa is shown to be a character who is less a fairy-tale princess/queen and more of a figure from mythology. She is linked with the Nokk (the water horse), the Giants, the powers of the Enchanted Forest, and the spirits of Earth, Air, Fire, and Water (indeed, Elsa learns that she is the fifth element, and that she and Anna are meant to serve as a bridge—through their bonds with each other and with their own spheres—between the human and magical worlds). Yet one could argue that it is Elsa's increasing identification with her mother and her mother's people (the Northuldra) that keeps her story rooted in the fairy-tale genre. Sheldon Cashdan claims that "fairy tales are about women and the important role they play in the child's emerging sense of self."[13] Certainly, this becomes a hugely important aspect of Elsa's story in *Frozen II*, an idea that is indicated by the reprising of the song "Vuelie," which begins both films; while the first film has a more masculine version, the second film's reprise is characterized by being an all-female version of the piece's choral element. We learn early in the film that it is a sign that Elsa is worried about something when she wraps herself in her mother's shawl. Indeed, the film begins with us hearing from Iduna (Evan Rachel Wood)—Elsa and Anna's mother—for the very first time. She also sings the first song in *Frozen II*, "All Is Found," which will serve as Elsa's guide when, as adults, she and Anna, Olaf, Kristoff, and Sven go on a quest to learn the source of Elsa's powers. From the beginning, Elsa's greater link to her mother is stressed when Iduna helps little Anna to fall asleep first by stroking her eyes, and then singing "All Is Found" for Elsa alone.

This linking to the Mother—and through the Northuldra people and Iduna's status among them, to the Matriarchal—speaks to a growing desire to reject patriarchal roles and constraints that hold women back, and through that rejection, to find true freedom and fulfilment. As Tanya Krzywinska notes, "[Films about good witches] can be read as articulating desires and conflicts, which cannot easily be separated from a patriarchal context, within contemporary women's lives, and providing a means to symbolize the experience of such contradictions. The seductions of the witch film are indeed bittersweet as they speak of very real conflicts between freedom and constraint."[14] Certainly, this is hinted at even in *Frozen*, before we know anything at all about the silent young queen who dies alongside her husband while away from her daughters. After all, one of the major themes of *Frozen* is the bond of love and sisterhood Elsa and Anna share. Thanks to the well-intentioned but misguided advice given by Grand Pabbie, the leader of the Trolls, and by Elsa's father, Elsa's initial (and, one might argue, forced) alignment with Patriarchy has weakened her and Anna's bond by cutting them off from one another and teaching them to focus more on men. But their triumphing over such toxic masculine characters as Prince Hans and the Duke of Weselton restores and makes permanent their bond—their sisterhood. Certainly, the narratives of all the films in the *Frozen* saga refrain from pitting the sisters against one another. As is typical in films featuring a good witch, Krzywinska notes, "They may occasionally argue with one another, but there is no significant competition set up between the women in [such narratives]."[15] Likewise, though many in Arendelle initially fear Elsa and her powers, the audience knows from early on in *Frozen* that Elsa's powers, though capable of harm, are not at all evil, and that she seeks only to bring joy and happiness to her sister through her use of them. Though she is discussing *Practical Magic* (Griffin Dunne, 1998) here, Krzywinska could easily be describing Elsa: "Witchcraft is rendered Californian-style in terms of healing and protection, and through a very un-postmodern investment in being 'yourself,' which some women regard as empowering."[16] After all, another important theme that runs throughout the saga is of finding and being true to oneself. This idea is at the heart of the song "Let It Go," as well as of "Into the Unknown" and "Show Yourself." Indeed, the reason for the journey in *Frozen II* is the quest to find out the source of Elsa's powers—to learn how and why she is who and what she is.

While Anna aligns with Patriarchy (albeit in what is likely a more enlightened version than that of her father and grandfather) through her marriage with Kristoff and her rise to the throne of Arendelle, Elsa's story arc is one of alignment with the Feminine and Matriarchy. When looked at across the saga as a whole, Elsa's story follows very closely the idea posited by Maureen Murdock (in response to Joseph Campbell's phallocentric "Hero's Journey") as the "Heroine's Journey." As Murdock notes, "This journey is described from . . . the perspective of many of the women . . . who have sought validation from patriarchal systems and found them not only lacking but terribly destructive."[17] Murdock's "Heroine's Journey" entails the following:

- Separation from the Feminine
- Identification with the Masculine and gathering of allies
- Road of trials: meeting ogres and dragons
- Finding the boon of success

- Awakening to feelings of spiritual aridity—death
- Initiation and descent to the Goddess
- Urgent yearning to reconnect with the feminine
- Healing the mother/daughter split
- Healing the wounded masculine
- Integration of masculine and feminine[18]

For Elsa, this journey can be charted as follows:

- Her magic nearly harms Anna permanently, compelling her parents to follow Grand Pabbie's advice to keep Elsa and Anna apart.
- Elsa then follows her father's advice to repress her magic, and also begins her preparations for her eventual role as Queen.
- Elsa undergoes her coronation, which brings external threats (i.e., Prince Hans and the Duke of Weselton); she flees, but ultimately finds that they follow her to arrest or destroy her. She is imprisoned, escapes, and is nearly murdered by Prince Hans.
- Anna saves Elsa; they embrace, and Elsa realizes that love is how she can control her magic. She restores Arendelle, resuming her role as Queen.
- Elsa serves as queen for a time but is not happy. One night, she hears a woman's voice calling out to her from the distance.
- Elsa embarks "Into the Unknown" by going on a quest to discover her magic's source. She separates herself from her companions, journeying beyond the human world into Ahtohallan, where she encounters her mother's spirit and learns of the events that led to her parents' union and her birth. There, she learns that she is the Fifth Element.
- Meanwhile, Anna seeks to find her sister and works to save her; Elsa sings with her mother's spirit in the song "Show Yourself" (which is far more about true self-discovery than "Let It Go") as she seeks answers.
- Elsa and her mother, Iduna, are linked, and Elsa's learning the truth of her grandfather's actions toward the Northuldra causes Elsa to freeze and die.
- Anna realizes her sister has died when Olaf (who was brought to life by Elsa's magic) likewise dies. She mourns deeply but decides to "Do the Next Right Thing." She determines to undo the wrong her grandfather did and finds a way to destroy the dam. This revives Elsa, who comes to save Arendelle from the flood of the burst dam and free the Northuldra people from being trapped in the Enchanted Forest.
- Elsa and Anna hug, bring Olaf back to life, and embrace their new, separate roles as leader of the Northuldra (Elsa) and Queen of Arendelle (Anna), as well as their conjoined role as a bridge between the worlds of Magic and Humanity.

If Elsa performs a limited version of this in *Frozen*, in *Frozen II* her story adheres to Murdock's idea much more closely. We see Elsa's original rejection of the Masculine in *Frozen*; though (as discussed earlier) young Elsa learns initially to identify with the masculine by allowing her father to glove her hands (and thereby repress her magic) and teach her to "conceal it, don't feel it—don't let it show," in a burst of anger and desperation

Elsa lets lose her powers and runs away. At this stage, she fits the idea of the "Angry Girl" as discussed by Kimberley Roberts:

> The angry girl generally…is significant and pleasurable precisely because the expression of anger has hitherto been the unspoken domain of men and boys. The long history of the angry youth in film, canonized by James Dean, has by and large been a male story—one where the individual is valorized and set in conflict with the traditional mores of his parent and the larger society…. [The expectation that girls rebel within a set of carefully contained, specific ways] leaves most teenage girls in a classic double-bind; they believe that their rebellious feelings make them improper as "young women" and, conversely, that their status as young women requires them to leave their rebellious adolescence behind before they have really experienced it.[19]

This particularly comes through in the lyrics of "Let It Go," the smash-hit song of *Frozen* and an anthem to various groups who claimed it as their own "coming out" song. Though the song can have different meanings to those who embrace it, for so many girls and women who love the song, it is likely Elsa's expressions of anger over the control and repression that has been forced upon her for most of her life that most resonates, expressed in the song in such lines as "Don't let them in—don't let them see / Be the good girl you always had to be / Conceal, don't feel—don't let them know / Well now they know!" (said as she whips off her remaining glove and throws it to the wind). It is there, too, when she proclaims, "Turn away and slam the door! / I don't care what they're going to say / Let the storm rage on" and in her declaring, "It's time to see what I can do / To test the limits and break through / No right! No wrong! No rules for me—I'm free!" Elsa is angry, and she revels in being able to express that anger for the first time.

Yet her ability to wield her powers with true control and precision—to decide consciously when and how she will use them—will come only when she recognizes that Love is greater than Anger. Her love for her sister (and the association of the expression of that love through the character of Olaf) is her way into this, but it is a greater form of love—her love and acceptance of herself—that will bring her full control. This aligns with Bowman's argument that,

> based upon Western fairy tales, [such] stories serve as an instruction manual for proper and improper femininity on a surface level. However, when examined from a depth psychology perspective, they articulate the inherent power of the Archetypal Feminine over the psyche, a power which women must learn to navigate within themselves.
>
> The splitting of the Great Mother into the princess and the witch exemplifies the dual nature of the goddess. While clearly preferring the safe, elementary, passive maternal element of the Good Mother, the archetype also offers an explication of the transformative powers of both the Good and Terrible Mother.[20]

It seems that it is her finally expressing years of pent-up anger and frustration that is her most appealing aspect for audiences, if their embracing of "Let It Go" is any indication.

As we learn in *Frozen II*, Elsa's magic comes to her through her mother, as a reward for her mother's act of love and goodness when, as a child, she saves Prince Agnarr's life; Elsa's ultimate transformation into her true, whole self (thereby uniting the Good and the Terrible Mother) comes only at the end of the saga when she embraces this fully and abdicates her throne to live in the Enchanted Forest. This links with Eric Neumann's discussion of the dual nature of the Great Mother and its archetypal links to the witch:

> Because the ecstatic situation of the seeress results from her being overpowered by a spirit that erupts in her, that speaks from her, or rather chants rhythmically from her, she is the center of magic, of magical song, and finally of poetry. She is the source from which Odin received the runes of wisdom; she is the Muse, the source of the words that stream upward from the depths; and she is the inspiring anima of the poets.[21]

As Sheldon Cashdan notes, "Fairy tales [typically] are essentially maternal dramas in which witches, godmothers, and other female figures function as the fantasy derivatives of early childhood."[22]

Yet, though the *Frozen* saga in particular plays with this trope—Elsa is the "witch" in the literal sense, and the sisters' mother, Iduna, is revealed to be the conduit through which Elsa received her powers—ultimately, the narrative's greatest twist is the way that the ties that bind the sisters are what force them apart. Because, as they learn, they are meant to serve as a bridge between worlds, the two must go their separate ways at the end of the film in order to fulfil their true destinies. In other words, the resolution of the narrative—what allows each young woman to be her true self—requires the sisters to inhabit separate worlds (though, happily, they still get to visit from time to time). Elsa, by going to live among the Northuldra in the Enchanted Forest that was their mother's homeland, become permanently a part of the "feminine" realm of magic; Anna, by accepting the role of Queen of Arendelle and marriage with Kristoff, aligns more with the "masculine" realm of her father and grandfather's kingdom. Her little (potentially adult-oriented) quip to the uncharacteristically elegantly dressed Kristoff at the end, that she prefers him in leather, likewise links Anna to power (and pleasure?) and similarly identifies her more with a traditionally masculine approach to overt sexuality. As for Elsa, her entire spiritual journey in *Frozen II* is foreshadowed by Iduna's song "All Is Found"; Queen Iduna (Evan Rachel Wood) sings it for Elsa alone, and looks pointedly at her elder daughter during the line "lay the answers and a path for you," before taking her daughter in her arms affectionately and singing the rest of the song to her:

> Yes, she will sing to those who hear,
> And in her song, all magic flows
> But can you brave what you most fear?
> Can you face what the river knows?
>
> Where the north wind meets the sea,
> There's a mother full of memory
> Come, my darling, homeward bound
> When all is lost, then all is found.

Narratively, the song's function is to provide clues and information that help the sisters on their quest, but its additional function as foreshadowing is stressed by the bridge and final stanza, in the middle of which we get the film's title card, and by the end of which we arrive in the narrative's present, where Elsa, standing on a balcony, first hears the voice calling her. This song, the accompanying visual clues tell us, is the key narrative. But the theme that will enable Elsa to undertake and then complete her stated quest, as well as her greater journey of self-understanding, is Love: her mother's love, but in particular Anna's love, which saves Elsa's life once again, and thereby enables her to complete her journey and her quest.

About Those "Love Experts" . . .

Though the Trolls—and subsequently the other characters—begin to speak of *an* act of true love (which the Trolls posit may mean "a true love's kiss, perhaps"), ultimately, what we see throughout the films are *multiple* acts of True Love. These acts, furthermore, are linked to multiple kinds of love. Elsa's first intentional creation—though we get only the quickest glimpse of it at the time—is Olaf, whom she conjures when she sings the line "Can't hold it back anymore" the first time she sings the chorus to "Let It Go." It turns out that Olaf has enormous significance to the sisters' childhoods; as we learn in the 2018 short "Olaf's Frozen Adventure," Olaf is in fact the centre of the sisters' Christmas traditions, as Anna has made drawings, Christmas cards, and straw dolls of Olaf to give to Elsa every Christmas during their time apart (Figure 31.3). Each time, as we see in

FIGURE 31.3. Anna's Olaf-themed Christmas present to Elsa, which Elsa has saved in a special chest in the attic. "Olaf's Frozen Adventure" (2018, Disney). Frame-grab.

flashback, Anna's offerings of love are delivered under Elsa's door following the leitmotif "Tap Tap Ta-Tap Tap" (as Anna knocks on Elsa's door) that is the start of Anna's song, "Do You Want To Build a Snowman."

Through this, we know that Elsa is performing an act of True Love (however unconsciously) when she first brings Olaf to life because she is thinking foremost of her sister, from whom she has been alienated for most of their lives. It is not her first such act, however; the first is when, as a child, she agrees to hide her powers and keep herself away from Anna so that her beloved sister will be safe. Later, Anna performs her first act of true love when she rushes off to bring Elsa back to Arendelle, alone and at great personal risk. Kristoff performs the next act of True Love. Having come to know Anna over the course of their journey to find Elsa, he has fallen in love with her, and has even come to realise this (at least partially) on a conscious level. Yet when Anna collapses shortly after Grand Pabbie reveals that "Only an act of True Love will thaw a frozen heart," Kristoff, assuming that Hans, Anna's fiancé, is her true love, rushes to return Anna to Arendelle, sacrificing his own love for her. Kristoff, in putting Anna's needs before his own, commits an act of True Love that is linked to romantic love, but a romantic love that is of the purest sort. Yet it is *Frozen*'s final act of True Love—Anna's sacrificing of herself to save Elsa from Hans—that is positioned as *the* Act of True Love in the film, since it is this act which not only saves Elsa's life, but also thaws the ice in Anna's heart and saves her life, too, thereby restoring the sisters to one another. The characters'— and the audience's—realisation that True Love does not have to mean *romantic* love, but simply and purely means *selfless* love—putting others first, no matter what the cost—is very much *Frozen*'s climactic moment.

But this never comes from the Trolls, despite their being described by Kristoff as "Love Experts" when he first tells Anna about them. Interestingly, it is Anna who expresses doubt about their status as experts; when she refers to Kristoff's friends as "Love Experts," you can hear the implied quotation marks in the tone of her voice. This is interesting because it is Anna who will prove to be the true expert on love, both in *Frozen* and in its sequels; while initially she seems to be the most naive because of how she is taken in by Hans, once she sees what he really is, she wastes no time mourning but moves forward decisively. Though initially she runs outside to meet Kristoff, who is running toward her, she changes direction to save her sister from Hans; she sees that Elsa's need is greater and responds accordingly. Even in *Frozen II*, which focuses on Elsa's discovery of the source of her power, we likewise see that it is Anna who is the most selfless and the most capable of being strengthened by love. As in *Frozen*, when she journeys to the North Mountain to bring Elsa back to Arendelle, in *Frozen II* she refuses to stand by when Elsa is in danger (chastising her sister at one point by saying, "You don't want me to follow you into fire? Then don't run into fire"). Later, when Anna realizes that Elsa has died, though she is devastated by her loss, she nonetheless resolves to "do the next right thing" and keep working to save the Northuldra, thereby fulfilling Elsa's promise. Saving the Northuldra will ultimately save Elsa (incidentally, this emphasizes the link between Elsa and the Northuldra), and thereby becomes another great act of True Love that Anna performs.

That Anna is the true expert is hinted at by Kristoff in *Frozen* in his description of the Trolls as he takes Anna to meet them. As he tells her about them, he says, "They can be a little inappropriate. And loud. Very loud. They're also stubborn at times, and a little overbearing." Though the film does not remark upon this, Kristoff's description of the Trolls could be of Anna herself, whose exuberance, occasional awkwardness, and open-heartedness are some of her most charming qualities. While certainly Grand Pabbie is positioned by the narrative as being wise, his wisdom seems more about magic and other elemental subjects. Love, however, is *not* an expertise of the Trolls. After all, they have *no* problem with the idea of Anna and Kristoff marrying immediately, and during their song "A Bit of a Fixer-Upper," they dress Anna and Kristoff for their wedding. Their evaluation of Anna? "Bright eyes, working nose, strong teeth—yes! Yes! She'll do nicely for our Kristoff!" They appraise her much as one might judge a horse; her personality, character, and temperament are apparently not important. While, admittedly, it transpires that Anna and Kristoff *are* in fact a good match, and they do eventually fall in love and decide to be married, there is no indication that the Trolls recognize that true love takes time to grow; it is not evidenced by a "working nose." So, the Trolls are not "Love Experts"; they only seem that way to Kristoff because they were the ones to take him in and become his family when he was a very young child, and his love for them is strong because they were the ones to teach him about love.

That it is Anna who is the true expert is emphasized in *Frozen II* in two early scenes. The first is at the very beginning, when Anna and Elsa are children and are playing "Enchanted Forest." Anna introduces romance into their play narrative, having the prince character proclaim, "Who cares about danger when there's love!," much to young Elsa's disgust. The next scene that links Anna to Love is when the trolls arrive after Arendelle has been evacuated as nature rises up in anger. Though Grand Pabbie chastises Elsa for stirring up angry magical spirits, he calls Anna aside to confide his worries about Elsa and her magic; he is a wise, guardian soul, and he speaks only to Anna as a true equal. It is also Grand Pabbie—in saying, "When one sees no future, all one can do is the next right thing"—who foreshadows Anna's song "The Next Right Thing," as well as her love (for her sister and for the kingdom) being strong enough to help her do what she must. Grand Pabbie may be able to see visions and understand magic, but it is Anna who understands Love, and is its greatest champion.

Do You (Still) Want to Build a Snowman?

One thing that *Frozen*—as both an individual film and as a saga—has been brilliant at doing is tapping into the slowly growing (but, hopefully, growing nonetheless) trend for female-centric narratives seen within the larger film and television industry. Of course, it is worth remembering that Disney's animated features have always been good at this;

of the (at the time of writing) fifty-one single-narrative feature films made by Walt Disney Animation Studios, twenty-seven have a central female character (sometimes she co-stars with a male character, but she is central to the narrative nonetheless). This, as much as anything else, links it to the fairy-tale genre, a group of stories that, on the whole, has tended to have its female-led stories rise to the greatest prominence.

But above this, and beginning with *Frozen*, Disney has consistently begun to show-case stories about heroines where, among other things, a romantic narrative is either sidelined, maligned, or—in the cases of *Moana* (Ron Clements and John Musker, 2016) and *Raya and the Last Dragon* (Don Hall and Carlos López Estrada, 2021)—non-existent. This is a radical choice for stories about women. As Michele Schreiber notes, "Romance itself remains the dominate concern of the contemporary woman in American cine-matic narratives as she negotiates the complicated interplay between and among pri-vate and public, political and personal, and self-identity and group-identity."[23] Indeed, to have a central heroic female character such as Elsa go through the whole of a single film—let alone two feature films and multiple shorts—and *never* associate her with a love-interest of any sort is almost unheard of. It was certainly unusual enough that, in a well-meant response, many fans began to call upon Disney to make Elsa a lesbian and/or queer. Once *Frozen II* was announced in 2016, "Give Elsa a Girlfriend" campaigns be-came so vocal that they generated journalistic coverage. Elle Hunt's May 2016 article for *The Guardian*, "Frozen fans urge Disney to give Elsa a girlfriend in sequel," claims that the hashtag #GiveElsaAGirlfriend was retweeted "more than 1,500 times" in 3 days.[24] The longevity of the popularity of this idea is supported by the publication on February 26, 2018 of a HuffPost article, " 'Frozen' Director Gives Glimmer of Hope Elsa Could Get a Girlfriend."[25] It implies, ultimately, that romance is associated with female characters to such a strong degree that even those who considered themselves to be campaigning for something new and radical were, in fact, arguing for something inherently regres-sive and—ultimately—reactionary. When, at the end of *Frozen II*, Elsa remained single, there were those in the popular press and blogosphere who expressed disappointment that a prominent secondary character from the Northuldra, Honeymaren, who they argued had been positioned in such a way that she easily could have become Elsa's girl-friend, had not been utilized by the story as such. Some have expressed hope that there will be a *Frozen III* in which Elsa will become Disney's first lesbian princess.[26]

The fact remains that, while making Elsa a lesbian and/or queer might be seen as rev-olutionary in some circles, arguably the even more revolutionary move was for her to remain unattached and focused instead on coming to know and accept herself. This, ultimately, is what *Frozen* as a saga has done. For those who need a romantic narrative, this is supplied through Anna and Kristoff. But with Elsa, we get something more: rather than being compelled to project love onto another, Elsa can look within and come to know and love herself. That they have different interests is noted at the beginning of *Frozen II* when we see a young Elsa and Anna playing with snow toys Elsa has made, and the family laughs about how Anna likes to have romantic stories, but Elsa just wants adventures. This is the film letting us know right up front—even before the opening credits—that Elsa will have no time for romance yet again. As we see the narrative unfold, it is obvious that Elsa (and even Anna, who is oblivious to Kristoff's attempts to propose to her until the very end of the film) has more important concerns. Elsa is about to embark on a quest to find out who she is, what she is, what the source of her magic is, and what her true purpose is. And that, the saga makes clear, is more than enough.

This narrative choice becomes clearer when examined from the perspective of depth psychology. As Neumann notes, "When a personality is assailed by the transformative character of the Feminine and comes into conflict with it, this means psychologically that its ego consciousness has already achieved a certain independence.... But when the personality comes into conflict with the transformative character of the Feminine, it would seem—mythologically speaking—as though the Feminine were determined to retain the ego as a mate."[27] In other words, Elsa must first join together the various parts of her personality; she cannot—and does not—look outside herself but rather inside, and thereby unites the two major female archetypes to be found in fairy tales such as those that Disney has typically told. As Bowman puts it,

> This distinction between the Disney princess and her Terrible Mother nemesis is, ultimately, a false dichotomy. Though the films clearly code these two figures as distinct, each character offers personality features present in the Great Mother as a whole: creation and destruction, nurturance and negligence, protection and confinement. Thus, despite the eventual "happy endings" of these films, the princess and villainess figures remain inextricably linked; they are, indeed, defined by one another and thus both create and destroy each other symbolically.[28]

It is as a Great Mother figure that Elsa becomes unique in the canon of Disney princesses. Her learning that she is the Fifth Element, and bringing together Earth, Air, Fire, and Water, position her as a true departure for Disney, and makes her unusual as a female character in cinema as a whole. She is a leader, she is self-sufficient, she is magical and powerful, and she helps to shape the world around her in the most fundamental way, doing so by uniting all aspects of the Great Mother. This is why *Frozen* as a saga is so special, and is why it likely will stand the test of time to become a true Disney classic.

Notes

1. Christy Lemire, "Frozen," RogerEbert.com, November 27, 2013, https://www.rogerebert.com/reviews/frozen-2013 [accessed March 2, 2020].
2. Scott Foundas, "Film Review: 'Frozen,'" *Variety*, November 3, 2013, https://variety.com/2013/film/reviews/frozen-review-1200782020/ [accessed March 2, 2020].
3. Jeff Lundon, "Well into Spring, 'Frozen' Soundtrack Keeps the Charts Cool," NPR.com, May 9, 2014, https://www.npr.org/sections/therecord/2014/05/09/310417407/well-into-spring-frozen-soundtrack-keeps-the-charts-cool?t=1583319166769 [accessed March 5, 2020]. See also Keith Caulfield, "'Frozen' Spends Lucky 13th Week at No. 1, Lindsey Stirling Bows at No. 2," Billboard.com, July 5, 2014, https://www.billboard.com/articles/news/6077608/frozen-spends-lucky-13th-week-at-no-1-lindsey-stirling-bows-at-no-2 [accessed March 5, 2020].

4. Paul Bond, "A Breakdown of 'Star Wars' Mechandise Sales This Year," *Hollywood Reporter*, December 17, 2015, https://www.hollywoodreporter.com/news/a-breakdown-star-wars-merchandise-849861 [accessed March 2, 2020].

5. Viewing numbers checked on YouTube by author, June 12, 2019, 6 p.m. BST, for the Walt Disney Animation Studios YouTube channel: https://www.youtube.com/watch?v=Zi4LMpSDccc.

6. Rebecca Rubin, "'Frozen 2' Is Now the Highest-Grossing Animated Movie Ever," *Variety*, January 5, 2020, https://variety.com/2020/film/box-office/frozen-2-biggest-animated-movie-ever-disney-box-office-1203456758/ [accessed March 2, 2020].

7. Ben Sisario, "'Frozen 2' Soundtrack Debuts at No. 1, without a 'Let It Go' (So Far)," *New York Times*, December 9, 2019, https://www.nytimes.com/2019/12/09/arts/music/frozen-2-billboard-chart.html [accessed March 2, 2020].

8. In summer 2020, a series of Olaf-led shorts were released online; as these shorts in no way contribute to the overarching narrative and themes of the *Frozen* saga and are instead focused on gags that rely on Olaf's bodily plasticity, I have not included them in my discussion (amusing and charming though they are). This is likewise the case with the short Disney+ series *Olaf Presents* (2021), where Olaf re-tells the narratives of Disney animated films, albeit in his own inimitable fashion and mirroring his re-telling of *Frozen*'s narrative to the Northuldra people during *Frozen II*.

9. Wyatt Bonikowski, "'Only One Antagonist': The Demon Lover and the Feminine Experience in the Work of Shirley Jackson," *Gothic Studies* 15:2 (November 2013), pp. 66–88, at 70.

10. Ibid., p. 70.

11. Marina Warner, *From the Beast to the Blonde: On Fairy Tales and Their Tellers* (London: Vintage, 1995), pp. 241–257.

12. Ken Rothman, "Hearts of Darkness: Voldemort and Iago, with a Little Help from Their Friends," in Jamey Heit (ed.), *Vader, Voldemort and Other Villains: Essays on Evil in Popular* Media (London: McFarland, 2011)Kindle eBook, location 3183.

13. Sheldon Cashdan, *The Witch Must Die: The Hidden Meaning of Fairy Tales* (New York: Basic Books, 1999), p. 29.

14. Tanya Krzywinska, *A Skin for Dancing In: Possession, Witchcraft and Voodoo in Film* (Trowbridge, UK: Flick Books, 2000), p. 154.

15. Krzywinska, *Skin for Dancing In*, p. 151.

16. Ibid., p. 150.

17. Maureen Murdock, *The Heroine's Journey: Woman's Quest for Wholeness* (Boston: Shambhala, 1990), p. 4.

18. Murdock, *Heroine's Journey*, p. 5. It should be noted that, in the original, Murdock lists this as a cycle, so that the final stage then leads back to the first.

19. Kimberley Roberts, "Pleasures and Problems of the 'Angry Girl,'" in Frances Gateward and Murray Pomerance (eds.), *Sugar, Spice, and Everything Nice: Cinemas of Girlhood* (Detroit, MI: Wayne State University Press, 2002), pp. 217–233, at 222–223.

20. Sarah Lynn Bowman, "The Dichotomy of the Great Mother Archetype in Disney Heroines and Villainesses," in Jamey Heit (ed.), *Vader, Voldemort and Other Villains: Essays on Evil in Popular Media* (London: McFarland, 2011), Kindle ebook, location 1302.

21. Erich Neumann, *The Great Mother: An Analysis of the Archetype*, trans. Ralph Manheim (Princeton, NJ: Princeton University Press, 2015), Kindle ebook, location 6804.

22. Cashdan, *Witch Must Die*, p. 28.

23. Michele Schreiber, *American Postfeminist Cinema: Women, Romance and Contemporary Culture* (Edinburgh: Edinburgh University Press, 2014), p. 2.

24. Elle Hunt, "Frozen Fans Urge Disney to Give Elsa a Girlfriend in Sequel," *The Guardian*, May 3, 2016. https://www.theguardian.com/film/2016/may/03/frozen-fans-urge-disney-to-give-elsa-girlfriend-lgbt [accessed March 2, 2020].

25. Bill Bradley, "'Frozen' Director Gives Glimmer of Hope Elsa Could Get a Girlfriend," HuffPost, February 26, 2018. https://www.huffingtonpost.co.uk/entry/frozen-director-elsa-girlfriend_n_5a9388c5e4b01e9e56bd1ead?guccounter=1&guce_referrer=aHR0cHM6Ly9jb25zZW50LnlhaG9vLmNvbS8&guce_referrer_sig=AQAAAAet7lE9hKNSIaOo4j4LKFYHhxIEOs5juKMpAf69VCpkgF4oT89pmJdbfauIeojzdLcsU6HoxPoe2vvqGZv-7r4vOpGqStoh2UJ2GdolFm2Kg1iJR3uTGN2l6gASNTKoz9Wr4zD7HZnrXsgoiL36gj6zpbcn3dgtVsoYaoRkJn6V [accessed March 2, 2020].

26. See, for example, Kelsea Stahler, "*Frozen II*'s Director Explains Why Elsa Doesn't Have a Girlfriend—Yet," Refinery29.com, November 26, 2019, https://www.refinery29.com/en-gb/2019/11/8899923/is-honeymaren-elsa-girlfriend-in-frozen-2-interview [accessed July 30 2020]; and Evan Lewis, "Honeymaren Will Reportedly Become Elsa's Girlfriend in Frozen 3," WeGotThisCovered.com, https://wegotthiscovered.com/movies/honeymaren-reportedly-elsas-girlfriend-frozen-3/ [accessed July 30, 2020].

27. Neumann, *Great Mother*.

28. Bowman, "Dichotomy."

Bibliography

Cashdan, Sheldon. *The Witch Must Die: The Hidden Meaning of Fairy Tales*. New York: Basic Books, 1999.

Heit, Jamey, ed. *Vader, Voldemort and Other Villains: Essays on Evil in Popular* Media. London: McFarland, 2011. Kindle eBook.

Krzywinska, Tanya. *A Skin for Dancing In: Possession, Witchcraft and Voodoo in Film*. Trowbridge, UK: Flick Books, 2000.

Murdock, Maureen. *The Heroine's Journey: Woman's Quest for Wholeness*. Boston: Shambhala, 1990.

Neumann, Erich. *The Great Mother: An Analysis of the Archetype*. Translated by Ralph Manheim. Princeton, NJ: Princeton University Press, 2015. Kindle eBook.

CHAPTER 32

HOLLYWOOD, REGULATION, AND THE "DISAPPEARING" CHILDREN'S FILM

FILIPA ANTUNES

Is the Hollywood children's film in crisis? The question is frequently asked in alarmed headlines, often some version of "Is Hollywood ruining children's movies with adult-focused content?"[1] Many in the popular press have already pronounced the genre dead, from *The Atlantic*'s observation that "live-action films for children have largely...been 'decimated'" in Hollywood[2] to *Den of Geek*'s prediction that Disney's decision to aim for a PG-13 for *Mulan* (Niki Caro, 2020) was a "smart move" even if it "will limit the kid/family audience."[3] These sentiments have also become more prevalent in film criticism, where children's titles often become the site for deep ambivalence. *Vanity Fair* critic Richard Lawson, for instance (who, in his own words, has "often complained that live-action children's films have gotten too tame"), felt uneasy about the heavier tone of recent PG-rated children's films, wondering about *Maleficent: Mistress of Evil* (Joachim Rønning, 2019), for example, "Is this the children's movie I've been wanting?"[4]

This chapter explores discourses of crisis surrounding the children's film and argues that worries about the genre are deeply intertwined with concerns over Hollywood's transforming identity. In these crisis debates, the idea of children's film serves as short-hand not for the cultural concepts usually associated with the genre—childhood and family—but for Hollywood's place in America's cultural landscape: a Hollywood without children's film is a diminished, or "disappearing," industry.

The ratings system is often a key tool in this rhetoric of crisis, and expectedly so, as the American ratings system, like film regulation more broadly, is the result of a delicate balance between cultural and industrial expectations. The chapter therefore begins by establishing the link between regulation change and crisis discourses, showing its significance in three key moments: the replacement of the Production Code by the ratings system in 1968, when Hollywood audiences were first segmented according to age; the creation of the PG-13 rating in 1984 and the resulting dissociation between PG films and mainstream appeal; and the contemporary preference for all-ages PG-13 franchises, which is a product of a changed media landscape and new consumer habits. From here the chapter moves to a case study of *The House with a Clock in Its Walls* (Eli Roth, 2018) to explore the nuances of contemporary articulations of crisis discourse.

What's at Stake in the Children's Film?

The children's film has long been defined as a category of diverse texts perceived to have a special link to the idea of childhood and its ongoing cultural construction. The crisis discourses explored in this chapter all seem to point to childhood, too, implying a correlation between Hollywood's "abandonment" of the children's film and a moral failure in the culture to uphold the childhood ideal. But this way of reading the genre, and thus the discourses surrounding it, is incomplete. Although the children's film is dependent on cultural ideals, it is also overtly an industrial product, named after a target demographic and clearly subject to commercial and industrial constraints.

This industrial side is often acknowledged but not valued as a key factor in the meaning of children's film. As we shall see later on, crisis discourses are dominated by concerns that the industry is corrupting the genre, whether through "ratings creep" or a general sense of dismay over the commodification of children's entertainment. In many good academic analyses of the genre, too, the children's film's industrial context is seen to be either detrimental or extraneous to the significance of the text, suggesting that children's film as a category is entirely defined by cultural ideas, usually childhood and pedagogy.[5]

This is not to say that the children's film as an industrial category has been ignored. There are good historical accounts of the children's film industry (particularly focused on Disney and on the British children's film), as well as a pool of research that highlights industrial factors as important points of discussion, particularly by writers interested in the American family film and the intricacies of audience differentiation.[6] Peter Krämer's work on Disney and George Lucas, Noel Brown's history of the Hollywood family film, and Robert C. Allen's work on Hollywood's approach to family audiences in the 1990s are all insightful illustrations of the way children's entertainment navigates its wider industrial context. Yet these studies also tend to use the children's film to demonstrate Hollywood's position as a cultural industry more than they explore the children's film as a category uniquely shaped by its industrial context. Indeed, authors who share this approach are often more interested in the idea of "family entertainment" and all-ages "family" audiences (that is, the mainstream) than the specificities of films narrowly targeted to children and their parents.

Brown's work is particularly interesting here because he separates the children's film and the family film categories but defines both in exactly the same terms: as industrial, cultural, and deeply contextual objects, marked in specific ways by marketing and distribution strategies, ratings, critical reception, merchandizing, and exhibition strategies.[7] The strength of this definition is in the way it positions children's film firmly within an industry and simultaneously underlines that this position can and does shift according to fluctuating cultural attitudes, an approach that significantly opens up the potential of critical readings of the genre.

There is an important implication here, because to read the children's film as a category that exists in relation to the interactions between business and cultural values is to make it closely synonymous with the industry's cultural identity. Indeed, this is what Brown's work on the family film demonstrates: "The 'family film' is Hollywood in its purest, most unadulterated form," because it is not restricted to a set of narratives or aesthetics but changes along with cultural attitudes, such as family values, and with expectations about the universal appeal of Hollywood entertainment.[8] To understand the family film, then, is to understand Hollywood as a cultural industry. Can the same correlation be applied to the narrower category of the children's film?

The current literature on the children's film suggests an immediate obstacle to this hypothesis in its tendency to de-emphasize or compartmentalise the children's film's association with business when discussing it as a category, especially where Hollywood titles are concerned. Drawing on Bazalgette and Staples, Brown proposes that the children's film exists on a spectrum encompassing non-commercial texts (driven by pedagogical and cultural ideals, and often targeted at children primarily) and commercial texts (driven by pleasure and entertainment, targeted at broader all-ages audiences).[9] Hollywood is clearly positioned in the second category, presented not as an image of the whole genre but only of a particular commercial model of children's film. Nevertheless, Brown also notes, it is this specifically commercial face of the genre that has come to broadly define the children's film culturally: even if Hollywood only represents the "children's film as a commercial entity," it "has been the world's most prolific and the most influential producer of children's films [and] the products of a single studio have become virtually synonymous…with the children's film itself."[10]

The paradox here is that Hollywood is representative of "only" the commercial side of children's film (understood as part of the broader commercial model of family entertainment), even as the children's film genre is broadly defined by the parameters set as direct results of Hollywood's industrial concerns. The separation between "commercial" and "non-commercial" examples of children's film does observe a distinction in the contexts and motivations of different texts, but ultimately, this split is not a commentary on the children's film as a generic category but a response to what is perceived to be less than desirable about its articulation—namely, the global dominance of the American industry and business model. In other words, the children's film is not simply understood as a genre, like other film categories; it easily and frequently becomes shorthand for particular values and expectations, used as the expression of a purely cultural ideal.

Crucially, this is also how we talk about Hollywood, which is simultaneously a derided money-spinning industry, a cherished cultural institution, and the most emblematic representative of the Seventh Art's value in everyday culture. The "magic" of film, specifically in its Hollywood facet, has, moreover, been associated with an array of romantic notions and ideals since its very early days (love, family, childhood, the American Dream), a foundation still present in the industry's preference for family entertainment.

It is therefore fitting that the crises of the children's film have been historically aligned to crises in Hollywood's cultural identity. As I will argue, the association of children's film with "pure" culture is used in crisis discourses as a tool to negotiate Hollywood's place in American culture and navigate its changing balance between artistic ideals and business goals.

Film classification is an especially useful tool in this kind of analysis. In studies of the children's film, regulation tends to be primarily addressed as a means of audience identification, as per Brown's definition. But as Krämer's work suggests, there is a strong link between classification models and the visibility of children's film in Hollywood's landscape, a link that he particularly highlights in the years immediately after the end of the Production Code's period of censorship.[11] In my own research I propose that classification is more than an industrial object. Like the children's film, regulation is simultaneously cultural and industrial: it separates film texts based on cultural ideas about childhood and maturity, and it plays a key role in shaping the film industry's output, economic model, and cultural identity. As this chapter will show, regulation is a tangible way to assess what childhood and the children's film are to a given culture, but it is also a measure of how Hollywood itself is culturally understood and of what is considered its appropriate place in popular culture.

The following sections will develop the significance of this connection by exploring three key moments in the history of both Hollywood and the children's film: the end of censorship and the introduction of regulation in the 1970s; the embracing of younger audiences in the all-ages market and subsequent introduction of the PG-13 rating in the 1980s (Figure 32.1); and the market dominance of PG-13 film franchises in the 2010s. I draw on my previous research to summarize the first two moments, and use Scott Mendelson's critical portfolio and a case study to fully explore the contemporary context (Figure 32.1).

FIGURE 32.1. Disney's new brand? Possessed children and other horror tropes in *The Watcher in the Woods* (1980). Frame-grab.

CHILDREN'S FILM AFTER
THE PRODUCTION CODE

Before the introduction of the ratings system in 1968, Hollywood films were censored by the Production Code, a set of rules that ensured all films were, if not children's films per se, at least made under the assumption that there could be children present in the audience. The ratings system did not restrict content in the same way but instead sorted finished productions into four age-based categories, which soon developed broader associations with maturity and genres: broadly speaking, "G" for children, "PG" for an all-ages "everyone," "R" for mature audiences, and "X" for pornography. These categories proved invaluable from an economic perspective because they allowed for much greater diversification in content and tone and, as a result, became instrumental in Hollywood's reinvention as a modern industry, freed from infantilizing censorship. This shift is emblematic of the hard edge of the New Hollywood, where the majority of releases were located in the R and PG categories, rather than the G equivalence suggested by Code restrictions, reframing the film industry as a space for adults.

Naturally, this new Hollywood identity presented an obstacle to the children's film. Disney in particular struggled during this period because its brand had been built during the Code period and was interchangeable with ideas of wholesomeness and traditional family values. Disney films were not strictly children's films but, before the rating system, had existed in an industry that only minimally differentiated children's and all-ages content. After the industry transitioned to a clearly separated market, however, Disney's content did not venture outside the G-rating. Although this was appropriate based on the content of its films, which in the 1970s were indistinguishable in tone from the earlier Code-approved titles, the G label relegated Disney films to a small portion of the market (children and parents) and created unfavourable competition against PG material (constructed as films for everyone).

This PG-rated competition was especially overwhelming because it included the blockbusters *Star Wars* (George Lucas, 1977) and *Superman* (Richard Donner, 1978), which were not only marketed as having broad all-ages appeal, but were, moreover, positioned as better entertainment choices than G-rated films through their use of action and edgier subject matter. *Star Wars*, for example, may always have been envisaged as children's film, but it explicitly embodied a new kind of entertainment, opposed to previous trends in the 1970s and aligned with the tastes and sensibilities of a new Hollywood and a new America.

It quickly became clear—to critics and to Disney's finance division—that maintaining an exclusive association with the G-rating was damaging Disney's reputation. The studio's struggles were not creative, as is commonly theorized; as I have shown elsewhere, Disney's difficulties came out of its attempts to preserve the weight of the Disney brand while navigating Hollywood's new relationship to child and family audiences, who had been the main public under the Code but were now only a niche demographic. Eventually, Disney ventured into the soft PG arena with a bold, though conflicted, decision to embrace the horror genre in the early 1980s. But these films, including the studio's first live-action and animated PG titles, *The Watcher in the Woods* (John Hough, 1980) and *The Black Cauldron* (Ted Berman and Richard Rich, 1985), were met with confusion and proclamations of the studio's death, not because audiences rejected their creative premises but because of the perceived incompatibility between the Disney brand (i.e., children's film) and the PG-rating (i.e., all-ages, not associated with children) (Figure 32.1).[12]

Disney's crisis was thus the result of a transition in regulation connected to a transformation in Hollywood's identity, both of which changed the children's film industrial position. Disney could only overcome the problem when it adapted its business strategy accordingly, primarily through diversifying investments unrelated to the core Disney brand, but also by emphasizing the all-ages appeal of its product as family entertainment rather than children's film.[13]

PG and the Challenge of All-Ages Content

In the early 1980s, the meaning of the PG-rating changed, prompting a new and controversial crisis in children's film. The broad strokes of this story are well-known: in 1984, audiences were shocked that *Gremlins* (Joe Dante, 1984) and *Indiana Jones and the Temple of Doom* (Steven Spielberg, 1984) had been rated PG, prompting the Motion Picture Association of America (MPAA) to add a new rating—PG-13—as a bridge between the PG and R ratings. As with Disney's crisis in the 1970s, this was not a case of creativity gone wrong, or even of bad rating practices, but of a transition in Hollywood's identity.

As film critic Vincent Canby noted in the *New York Times*, the source of the controversy was the increasing ambiguity around the PG rating's relationship to the children's genre: "With the present PG rating, there is no way for parents to know whether or not 'Indiana Jones' would be more or less upsetting to a 6-year-old than, say, 'King Kong' [John Guillermin, 1976], which also received a PG and has nothing remotely as 'strong' as the heart-removal scene."[14] The situation was more problematic still in relation to *Gremlins*, which, for Canby, was less violent but "far more disorienting" because it did not respect the children's film conventions that a PG rating suggested, including a happy ending and a reverence for family values.[15] It's significant that what Canby addressed in this comment was a need for PG to signpost a film's tone as well as its content—in other words, to signal a film's suitability to be watched by children *and* its suitability as a children's film.

This is a different understanding of the PG category than we saw previously with the Disney crisis. Immediately after the rating system replaced the Code, PG was an all-ages rating with no particular association with children, but as we find here, by the early

1980s, the PG category was seen not just as appropriate for all-ages but as an appropriate space for children's entertainment, too. This shift was in no small part a response to the identity cultivated by Hollywood during the 1970s with the aid of the ratings system, when R-rated releases were plentiful and many PG films addressed mature themes and audiences. This status quo only changed after *Star Wars* and subsequent family-friendly blockbusters—which shied away from the G rating for economic reasons—began to widen the scope of the PG category.

The wider scope of the PG rating was at the heart of the problems noted by Canby and which circulated in the crisis discourses of the time. We find an especially clear instance in Alexander Walker's review of *Gremlins* (Figure 32.2), which he deemed "a black adult joke at the expense of innocence" that "lured" children to it with a PG only to "[snatch] the security blanket away from everything that has been held holy in children's movies."[16] Although Walker's comments might remind us of moral panics rhetoric, the critic's point is not about media effects but about a perceived erosion of the place and value of the children's film in a Hollywood focused on attracting broad all-ages audiences, a battle taking place only within the PG category.

To modern eyes it may seem strange to attach concerns over the death of children's film to PG-rated Amblin productions, which are now remembered as childhood classics and symbols of the child-friendly nature of 1980s Hollywood. But we should remember that, at the time of their release (and regardless of ratings controversies), Amblin was seen to be helming a positive modernization of the children's film, bringing it in line with the attitudes of the period in relation to both childhood and the kind of content expected from modern Hollywood. Roger Ebert encapsulated the point in his review

FIGURE 32.2. *Gremlins* subverts children's film expectations in this kitchen scene between mother and "child" (1984, Warner Bros.). Frame-grab.

of *The Goonies* (Richard Donner, 1985): "There used to be children's movies and adult movies. Now Spielberg has found an in-between niche...It's more refreshing than the old Disney technique," by which Ebert meant a tendency to infantilize the audience, as was seen in the times of the Production Code (and continued, by Disney, into the G rating throughout the 1970s and early 1980s).[17]

The introduction of PG-13 thus marks a major cultural and industrial transition, which affected the identities of both Hollywood and the children's film. Since the unrestricted market was now segmented into three categories, all-ages content (PG-13) could be clearly separated from child-oriented films (G and PG), protecting the children's film's cultural associations (childhood, family values, innocence) while also allowing it a more viable commercial position. Furthermore, the genre could now spread over two categories of different intensity, which meant that Hollywood could continue making traditional children's films (Disney-style, animated, rated G), for which there was still a market, along with edgier titles aimed at slightly older children and families (Amblin-style, live-action, rated PG). Not only did this more closely match understandings of the limits of childhood in the 1980s, it also allowed the industry to push its all-ages content further under PG-13 and present the Hollywood film industry as boundary-pushing, culturally relevant, aligned to the dominant attitudes of its time, and not merely to tradition and family values.[18]

THE "PLAGUE" OF PG-13?

The impact of the PG-13 rating on Hollywood cannot be overstated. It has changed the industry and its participation in the broader culture more than any other ratings category, and almost as much as the initial introduction of the ratings system did. The first change to Hollywood's identity happened almost instantly after the creation of the PG-13 rating, when the ratings developed the associations that prevail today: G for young children (a category now almost extinct and reserved largely for animation); PG for wholesome content targeted directly at children and their parents; PG-13 for films aimed at "everyone"; and R for mature content (with NC-17 reserved for a very small portion of the most provocative features).

As had happened in the late 1970s and early 1980s, the industry quickly gravitated toward the all-ages category (now PG-13), hoping to capture adjacent audiences like families and teenagers. Children's film again declined as a result of the PG rating's decreased economic potential, a shift that was particularly noticeable after the 2000s, when America's demographics changed and young families were no longer such a significant part of the market.[19] These factors were further paired with a significant shift in the broader media environment, including the rise of narrowcast television in the 1990s with a variety of child- and family-oriented channels, and, more recently, an explosion of digital content not just tailored to all children but to precise age groups and available on demand. This new status quo affected Hollywood well beyond the range of the children's film. The industry's development of cross-platform franchises and shared universes, and the tendency to produce remakes, sequels, and huge blockbuster franchises are connected to Hollywood's need to compete with other forms of entertainment in today's industrial context.

These transformations in the business model are not just industrial concerns. As I've been demonstrating, industrial change happens in tandem with cultural change: the end of the Production Code was driven by a cultural rejection of censorship; Hollywood's developing identity is led by the culture's developing values (not just around family); and the ratings system itself embodies fluctuating understandings of childhood. Cultural attitudes, Hollywood's identity, and the boundaries of children's entertainment are topics that always merge in discourses of crisis. In the previous sections, I started from cultural views on the children's film's crisis and explained their connections to industrial change; as I move into the contemporary moment, I want to take the opposite approach and show how concerns framed industrially are also attached to cultural ideals, not just in relation to the children's film but to Hollywood's identity more broadly.

To this end, this section examines critic Scott Mendelson's column in *Forbes*, where, over the last two decades, he has addressed the present crisis in children's film. His writing illustrates two key points in my argument: first, ratings and classifications are a vital part of how crisis discourses are articulated; and second, the idea of children's film functions as proxy for an ideal Hollywood identity in these discussions.

For readers unfamiliar with Mendelson, it is important to note that he is the film industry and box office expert for a business-oriented magazine. Mendelson's writing therefore includes film criticism and reviews, but is overall weighted toward analyses of box office numbers, rating decisions, release schedules, and general business strategies. It is relevant, then, that his is one of the most emphatic and consistent voices in the contemporary children's film crisis discourses. Mendelson's comments do not have the backdrop most commonly associated with crisis discourse—namely, concerns over childhood and innocence or commercialism; rather, Mendelson is clear that the "disappearance" of children's films represents a decline not in American culture generally but in Hollywood's business model. See the following passage in a review of *Goosebumps* (Rob Letterman, 2015):

> I talk quite a bit about the death of the out-and-out kid movie. No, I'm not talking about animated features, I'm talking about live-action, G or PG-rated features that are explicitly pitched to a kid-friendly level. [We lost them] in the early 2000's, when the general audience-friendly, PG-13, four-quadrant, global blockbuster fantasy franchise film basically took over the industry…Why bother making a PG-rated film pitched to younger moviegoers when parents are going to just take their kids to *Transformers: Revenge of the Fallen* [Michael Bay, 2009] or *Iron Man 2* [Jon Favreau, 2010]?[20]

Mendelson critiques the hyper-commercialism of contemporary Hollywood here, but his worry here is not for the industry's morals but for the possibility that it will become monotonous and, therefore, insignificant in the broader context of popular culture.

Across his writing, Mendelson frequently lays the blame for this situation at the MPAA's feet, accusing it of increasingly arbitrary practices that have blurred the distinctions between the rating categories. Commenting on the decision to give *Frozen* (Chris Buck and Jennifer Lee, 2013) a PG rating instead of G, Mendelson charted what he believes to be the PG rating's descent into irrelevance:

> We've gone from G-rated films like *Babe* [George Miller, 1995]…that featured… genuinely intense scenes of animal peril and death to *Brave* [Mark Andrews and Brenda Chapman, 2012] getting a PG for a few moments where a big bear roars a couple of times. Once the PG lost its status as box office poison it would seem that the MPAA began tossing it out for pretty much [anything] while the studios make no attempt to fight it. [PG has now become] useless in terms of its stated goal, which is to tell parents [if a given] family film may be a bit much for their youngest kid.[21]

Mendelson's criticisms here—Hollywood's capitalism and the MPAA's arbitrary rating criteria—are two staples of the crisis rhetoric around the children's film. The ratings critique, in particular, is a perennial feature in North American popular and academic debates about children's entertainment, where it is often expressed as a concern over a supposed "ratings creep." As Ron Leone and Nicole Houle have suggested, the ratings-creep theory posits that the MPAA has become increasingly and irresponsibly permissive in the kind of content it allows under the PG-13 and PG ratings. Using content analysis and comparison, the authors argue that many contemporary films rated PG and PG-13 would have received harsher rating in the past, in particular the restricted R rating—the implication being that the ratings no longer serve their purpose of informing audiences about a film's suitability.[22] Mendelson applies a similar logic to his reading of the G and PG ratings: in the past there was a clear distinction between these ratings, but the MPAA today seems to rate all animated films PG regardless of their intensity, diluting the system's usefulness as a result.

Although the ratings-creep argument seems compelling, it cannot sustain rigorous scrutiny. It is founded on an erroneous understanding of ratings as static and clearly defined categories, removed from the culture that creates them, a premise I have already demonstrated to be false. Importantly, the ratings-creep view also suggests that Hollywood is a static industry, or at least one with a static, ahistorical identity, detached from the particulars of US culture and economy.

It is revealing that these imagined ideals of stability—stable childhood, stable Hollywood—are frequently the cornerstone of crisis discourses since these issues are not connected to the form, production, distribution, or reception of the children's film, but only to its cultural ideal. This concern is evident in Mendelson's comments about ratings and the children's film, particularly in the way he conflates two separate views of Hollywood (and the children's film): one as a business grounded in the attitudes and contexts of the time, the other imagined as something pure and pre-cultural.

To address a specific Mendelson example: *Brave*'s PG rating may seem silly next to *Babe*'s G rating, but there are two decades between these ratings decisions and, significantly, between the conditions of production and reception (economic, industrial, and cultural) for each text. As Mendelson himself notes, the PG rating has undergone an important transformation over the last couple of decades, from being given to films perceived as inappropriately intense for animated films in the 1980s ("box office poison") to becoming the standard for these productions in the 2000s and beyond. This transformation did not represent a corruption of the classification system but was the result of a shift in the current understandings of childhood and suitability and in the way Hollywood conceived and marketed its family-oriented product. In other words, the MPAA may have intended PG to mean "parental guidance," but it is understood by audiences and Hollywood producers as a category of "general family entertainment." Similarly, a G rating does not mean "for general audiences," as its official description implies but rather, as audiences, critics, and scholars have noted, "children's film" specifically.

Significantly, this inflexibility is something Mendelson applies exclusively to the children's film. In relation to other Hollywood texts and genres less encumbered by associations with ideals, Mendelson clearly understands ratings as flexible categories defined by changing cultural assumptions and industrial plans. Commenting on the decision to give *RoboCop* (José Padilha, 2014) a PG-13 rating instead of an R, the critic wrote:

> This isn't about whether it deserved a PG-13 rating (it did) or whether that rating affected the film artistically (I'd argue it did), but about how said rating affected the film's box office. [An R rating] would have acted as [a draw] for those adults who wanted a genuinely adult genre entry…If your main competition is a four-quadrant programmer that's doing exceptionally well with younger audiences [*The Lego Movie*, Phil Lord and Chris Miller, 2014; rated PG], including younger boys, your film doesn't benefit by chasing that same demographic while arguably scaring off at least a portion of the older audience by virtue of its rating.[23]

As before, Mendelson is irritated by Hollywood's monotonous preference for PG-13 material, but now the discourse takes on a different tone. The decision to rate *RoboCop* PG-13 or R is understood as part of a strategy of differentiation pursued by the studios, and not dictated by the MPAA's supposed agenda. In other words, when the children's film is not implicated, "ratings creep" and other crisis rhetoric is not invoked. There is something about the children's film that prompts not only a forgetting of shifting cultural contexts (childhood today is not the same as it was in the past) but also of the genre's position in Hollywood (the film industry today is not the same as it was in the past). Sentimentality about childhood may be part of the reason this happens, but I want to suggest that a romanticizing of Hollywood is also at play and that these two factors are deeply intertwined. Note the following passage from another of Mendelson's articles:

> As an adult who doesn't care what a movie is rated, I can say "Do whatever you want to do and let the MPAA judge accordingly." But as a parent, I feel a little silly telling my daughter that she can't see the new *Teenage Mutant Ninja Turtles* [Jonathan

Liebesman, 2014] adventure or wondering whether *Transformers: Dark of the Moon* [Michael Bay, 2011] should have gotten an R.[24]

Though this article is part of Mendelson's portfolio of writings on the PG rating's failures and of the resulting "death" of the children's film, his argument points to an entirely separate problem: it is not that contemporary Hollywood no longer makes children's film (*Teenage Mutant Ninja Turtles* and others could fit that label); rather, it is that films with the potential to be meaningful for child audiences are not getting the PG rating and are not presented as "children's film," or even as "family films," because the studios pursue a PG-13 rating in order to market their productions as films "for all audiences." Concerns over childhood, the children's film, and the stability of the ratings are combined here with a clear concern over the shape of Hollywood itself, revealing the crisis to be not just about a "disappearing" genre or classification but also a "disappearing" industry.

Indeed, the yearning is less for children's film than it is for a version of Hollywood that no longer exists: a Hollywood at the centre of popular culture, serving each segment of the population equally, and not only a profitable, market-researched, imagined "everyone." A Hollywood closer to what it was before PG-13 was introduced and the industry succumbed to what Mendelson calls "the plague of 'All PG-13, all the time.'"[25] The idea of the children's film is absolutely central to this desire because it is the genre most immediately associated with varied audiences and the idea of entertainment for art and other noble purposes beyond simply profit. Moreover, the idea of a diverse market, in which all demographics are more or less equally catered to, evokes past commercial glory, when the theatrical release was an end in itself, and not just a single element in a global multimedia franchise, to a time before streaming and ultra-targeted narrowcasting television.

A "NEW SHOCKING": *THE HOUSE WITH A CLOCK IN ITS WALLS*

The understanding of children's film as a genre in crisis and as shorthand to a crisis in Hollywood is not limited to Scott Mendelson's portfolio; it is an integral part of how contemporary Hollywood children's film is discussed, especially in critical reception. *The House with a Clock in Its Walls* is an ideal case study here. Directed by Eli Roth, who once claimed he would never make a film that wasn't rated R and the first film in a series intended to revive Amblin's 1980s brand of PG-rated children's entertainment, *House with a Clock* immediately prompted discussions of regulation and the children's film: the film's promotion used crisis rhetoric to strategically differentiate *House with a Clock* from other contemporary children's films and attach it to memories of a different Hollywood, whereas the critical reception intertwined crisis discourses with assumptions about Hollywood's proper relationship with child audiences today.

The best place to begin unpacking these discourses is the promotional work done by director Eli Roth, whose presence at the helm of a children's film naturally sparked the public's curiosity and media interest. See this exchange between Roth and a reporter from *Vulture*:

> Q: Amblin is rebooting itself as a company with this movie. Interesting they should choose the hard-R horror guy to do it.
> A: They really wanted to relaunch what Amblin was in the '80s. [W]hen [Spielberg] saw [*House with a Clock*], he said, "Eli, you really did it. You really made a true Amblin movie. It's not mocking or beholden to something before it, yet it feels like it's in the tradition of those. You're really carrying the torch.[26]

House with a Clock was the first of a planned series of new Amblin films that would include remakes and sequels to many of its classic titles, such as *Gremlins* and *The Goonies*. Many commentators had assumed these plans to be a way of riding the current wave of 1980s nostalgia, but note how Roth deflects that association, framing his film not as something from the past but as a firmly contemporary expression of the Amblin sensibility. It's also significant that Roth does not try to divert the interviewer's attention away from his filmmaking history but instead links his reputation as a subversive filmmaker to the Amblin identity of the 1980s. Making a point he often repeated when promoting the film, "The new shocking is doing a PG movie"—to do what Amblin did in the 1980s and so few do in the 2010s.[27]

These are subtle discursive moves, yet they effectively distinguish *House with a Clock* from its competitors by establishing a background of crisis for this release. Roth's message is that Amblin-style children's films have indeed disappeared, and they cannot be replaced by Amblin homage, parody, or nostalgia.[28] This is, of course, savvy marketing, but it worked because it drew on agreed perceptions of the contemporary moment when compared to the 1980s. See this comment in a *Collider* interview (whose sentiments were widely echoed, as I'll show later, in the film's critical reception):

> When I think back to my childhood…The movies that I saw in the theater, when I was 9, 10, 11 and 12, were those scary Amblin movies that were everything to me, like *E.T.* [Steven Spielberg, 1982], *Raiders, Gremlins, Goonies, Poltergeist* [Tobe Hooper, 1982], and even *Ghostbusters* [Ivan Reitman, 1984]. There were other oddball movies, like *Time Bandits* [Terry Gilliam, 1981], where the kid's parents blow up at the end and a guy gets turned into a pig. That was mind-blowing, as a child. I had never seen anything like it. And there were other movies, like *Dragonslayer* [Matthew Robbins, 1981], *The Dark Crystal* [Jim Henson and Frank Oz, 1982] and *Labyrinth* [Jim Henson, 1986], that were much closer to Grimm's Fairy Tales, where characters die.[29]

What Roth recalls here is not Amblin specifically but a much broader idea of what the children's film label entails. He gestures toward this even more clearly in the *Vulture* interview: "I've always wanted to do my version of a kids' movie. And by that I mean a film like *Time Bandits* or *Beetlejuice* [Tim Burton, 1988] or *Gremlins* or *Goonies*. . . . .

There was a danger [in these films] and that's what makes the best children's movies."[30] Though Roth claims this version of children's film as his own, he is in fact describing what the genre was in the 1980s, when the category's boundaries changed explicitly from what they had been under the Production Code, but also when the children's genre had more variety because it spread across different rating categories, including not only G and PG but also the softer side of PG-13 with titles like *The Gate* (Tibor Takács, 1987) or Amblin's own *Arachnophobia* (Frank Marshall, 1990). Indeed, Roth contrasts the films of the 1980s (and his revival of that period in *House with a Clock*) with the attitude of traditional, narrow-range children's film: he wanted to make "a [PG-rated] movie for 9- and 10-year-olds that still has a sense of mischief and danger, that's not about sweetness or some heavy-handed message."[31] The discourse here is thus not only one of crisis but also of criticism, which allows Roth not only to champion a particular view of what the children's film should be but also to present *House with a Clock* as a solution to the present crisis.

As I have suggested, these crisis discourses do not point to a crisis in sentiment but to a struggle with the period's industrial models. As both Roth and Amblin recognize in the creative choices made in *House with a Clock* (more on which later), the problem is not that the children's film ever went away; it is that Hollywood's model—and, indeed, the ratings system itself—changed dramatically since the 1980s, relegating the children's film to an unprofitable niche rating category regardless of its narratives aims or originality.

As with Roth's promotional discourse, most reviews of the film circulate crisis discourses based on a concern over Hollywood's scope and relationship with young audiences. In practical terms, this translated into a tendency to read *House with a Clock* as either too child-oriented (a children's film, out of place in Hollywood) or not child-oriented enough (an all-ages title, out of place in the children's rating category, PG).

FIGURE 32.3. The "family," led here by the "mother," unites against spooky opponents in *The House with a Clock in Its Walls* (2018, DreamWorks). Frame-grab.

Katie Rife's *AV Club* review exemplifies the first position. "The fantasy and horror sections are full of wonder," she allows, "but the screenplay…diverts too often to inert scenes of Lewis' struggles at school, and a subplot about his on-again, off-again friendship with bully Tarby…feels like a distraction from the magical business at hand." Rife's criticism here is not about the narrative's perspective nor about its cohesion. The issues Lewis has at school and with his peers affect a key plot point, but they primarily serve to present him as the story's protagonist and to develop a child's perspective on the story's events. When Rife suggests that these scenes take away from the film's core, she is implying that the film should have focused on the adult characters instead, whose struggles are developed in the main plot and who provide the film with all-ages appeal.

It is no coincidence that this complaint is attached to praise for the film's 1980s-inspired horror sequences, as contemporary retrospectives have stripped these reference points from their context as children's culture, remembering them primarily from adult perspectives.[32] Thus, even as Rife acknowledges *House with a Clock*'s roots in children's culture ("kid-lit horror" and "family-friendly horror" comparable to "the '80s [children's horror] films that inspired it," the children's culture of the critic's own childhood), she nevertheless also describes *House with a Clock* as "a high-end version of one of those direct-to-video kids' movies that play on the Disney channel all throughout October." As the comparison reveals, what makes the film "high end" is not its budget but the assumption that it is something *other* than children's culture: all-ages Hollywood instead of child-oriented Disney.[33] In presenting Lewis as a central focus, then, *House with a Clock*, for Rife, introduced unwelcome confusion about the film's target audience.

The film's approach to its child protagonist was read differently by critics who started from the assumption that *House with a Clock* was a children's film, not an all-ages family release. Emily Yoshida's review in *Vulture*, for example, reaches the opposite conclusion: "The film doesn't trust Lewis's point of view enough; this is a kids' movie that prioritizes the machinations of the adult characters."[34] This view was echoed in *Slant* by Jake Cole, for whom *House with a Clock* has "a maladroit sense of character," particularly in relation to the child protagonist. Cole had some investment in the adult heroes but thought they too were "trample[d] over" in order to highlight the action of the all-ages plot, resulting in a film that "stumbles between awkward, telegraphed jolts and busy, effects-heavy action, completely losing sight of [its] emotional core."[35]

This sense of an emotional core tied to the child character features significantly in most reviews, particularly those that read *House with a Clock* as an underperforming children's film, usually allied with a comment on the film's flaws in either narrative or sentiment. As with Rife's complaints about the distractions of Lewis's child-specific storylines, these were not comments about storytelling but about Hollywood's contemporary relationship with children's film and child audiences. This relationship is particularly highlighted by the critics who most overtly compared *House with a Clock* to the Amblin films of the 1980s, such as Dan Jolin in *Empire* (*House With a Clock* "channels the visual appeal of '80s Amblin adventures while lacking their storytelling appeal")[36] and Robbie Collin in the British *Telegraph*:

The classic Amblin films ran on awe, and framed every magical moment, spooky or otherwise, as formative experiences for their pre-teen heroes. But here, weird happenings are 10 a penny...Too hectic to be scary, and with a plot that's regularly bogged down in optimistic franchise-building spadework, *The House with a Clock in Its Walls* never quite grasps what made its inspirations tick.[37]

As Collin notes, the difference between *House with a Clock* and the children's horror adventures made in the 1980s is that the latter focused on the issues of childhood and early adolescence without shaping them into all-ages franchise material. This observation may underline the difficulty of telling a child-oriented story in today's Hollywood, but it is not, as Collin implies, a problem of sincerity; it stems from a change in Hollywood's role in popular culture: in the 1980s PG (and, by proxy, the children's film) was a profitable category because children and young families were a large portion of America's population, and because that market was not yet overwhelmed by digital and on-demand competitors.[38]

Scott Mendelson's review gestures toward this industrial obstacle more clearly than others, even if the critic himself seems to prefer a different explanation of the film's potential box office failure: *House with a Clock* "is the kind of flick that would be considered a generational classic had it opened in 1984. So the question is whether today's kids, now saturated in unthinkably huge PG-13 fantasy actioners (and copious online entertainment), will appreciate the pint-sized thrills." Notice how Mendelson highlights a change in children's sensibilities (of the growing-too-old-too-quickly variety) as the main culprit in the current children's film crisis, leaving the huge business changes in the background. Elsewhere in his review, however, Mendelson is clearer about the significance of industrial factors in determining the success of films like this one: "The hope [in the film's release strategy] is that [*House with a Clock*] can thrive as a [horror] kid-targeted fantasy alongside the R-rated flicks (*The Nun* [Corin Hardy, 2018], *The Predator* [Shane Black, 2018]), at least until Sony's *Goosebumps 2* [Ari Sandel, 2018] debuts."[39] The problem, as Mendelson implies, is that pushing the boundaries of PG content may have worked for the film's narrative (i.e., a "return" of the children's film), but it is a disadvantage in the industrial terrain, where overt links to children's entertainment are high risk.

In branding terms, *House with a Clock* was equivalent to PG-13 material because it was an edgier horror fantasy directed by a known horror director, so it competed at the box office against R-rated horror and action, a category much more enticing to the profitable teenaged and adult audiences. For similar reasons, the film's window of opportunity would close as soon as *Goosebumps 2* opened because *House with a Clock* would then be competing for a market niche too small to accommodate two simultaneous children's titles. *House with a Clock* would, moreover, be disadvantaged in this competition because *Goosebumps 2* was a much softer PG title, immediately recognizable as suitable for children, and a part of an established multimedia franchise.

It's telling, then, that despite hailing *House with a Clock* as a return to form in the children's genre, Mendelson nonetheless praised the film's all-ages appeal: though it "prioritizes the younger audiences...over their nostalgic parents," *House with a Clock* "expertly blends kid-sized scares with all-ages wonderment," featuring "Jack Black for the kids and Cate Blanchett for the grown-ups" in "a true all-ages movie."[40] This is different view from that expressed by Rife and Collin, but it shares their premise: unlike other contemporary media, such as television and digital platforms, Hollywood cannot easily sustain an association with children's entertainment beyond the all-ages family category.

Indeed, even critics who did not concern themselves with the intricacies of *House with a Clock*'s address to young audiences mostly approached the film as an all-ages release, emphasizing the elements of adult interest in it, such as the practical effects, the Cate Blanchett and Jack Black pairing, and, of course, Eli Roth's move away from R-rated horror. Justin Chang in the *Los Angeles Times* perhaps says it best: *House with a Clock* is a "young-adult fantasy" about "the perils of adolescence," which may "dismember… the [adult] audience's expectations" about Eli Roth's filmmaking but never "violates the codes of a PG rating."[41] In other words, *House with a Clock* is a children's film in the contemporary Hollywood sense: family entertainment, rated PG but with all-ages appeal.

CONCLUSION

This chapter explored the links between discourses around the children's film and those around Hollywood's cultural and industrial identities. It argued that crisis rhetoric related to children's film stems from a struggle to negotiate the genre's (and, by proxy, Hollywood's) shifting position under new cultural and industrial conditions. The goal was to show that analyses of crisis periods are significant in more than one way: they express the cultural meanings of the children's film by highlighting, rather than downplaying, the importance of its industrial position; and they show how these apparently small genre-specific conflicts signal much broader transitions in Hollywood history, adding an additional layer to the children's film's cultural significance.

Crisis discourses feed on the children's film's associations with deeply rooted cultural ideas, such as the "natural" and pre-cultural status of childhood and the need to separate childhood and adulthood by establishing clear limits for children's entertainment. Complaints of cynicism or of inappropriate suitability are thus the bread and butter of crisis discourses, whether these refer to Disney's issues in the 1970s, Amblin's controversies in the 1980s, or the challenges faced by children's film in the 2010s. But, as demonstrated here, crisis rhetoric is more rigorously explained by industrial factors and the cultural impact of different industrial models than by associations with childhood. Debates about the children's film are almost never solely about children and their entertainment; they encompass ideas about the kind of industry and cultural institution Hollywood is or should be.

Indeed, the "disappearance" of the children's film reflects not an objective regression in the genre but a change in Hollywood's relationship with young audiences. During the Production Code, all films had to anticipate the presence of children in the audience, meaning that the difference between a children's film and an all-ages film was quite narrow. After the introduction of the ratings system, children moved gradually to the periphery of Hollywood's concerns, and the children's film became an increasingly niche genre, as it became progressively separated from the main all-ages category (PG and, after the 1980s, PG-13). It should be noted that while this was happening in Hollywood, children's content blossomed in other media, such as television and on digital platforms, which could cultivate niche brands more easily within their industrial models.

Hollywood's identity is one of universality, however—and herein lies the problem. As the current PG-13 debates indicate, the dissatisfaction with the industry's preference for this rating is not that it suggests a Hollywood with broad reach but the opposite: a Hollywood that produces only one thing for one (imagined) demographic. The lack of variety—in genre, budget, tone, and approach—is, in fact, a threat to Hollywood's identity as a universal, culturally-relevant industry. This problem is what the "disappearance" of the children's film represents because this genre is shorthand for niche audiences and for the intrinsic value of film as culture supposedly unencumbered by commercialism. Thus, the bigger question in crisis discourses is not whether the children's film is under threat in Hollywood, but whether a Hollywood without children's film is worth having, or whether this model even constitutes Hollywood at all.

Notes

1. Hollie McKay, "Is Hollywood Ruining Children's Movies with Adult-Focused Content?," *Fox News*, July 15, 2011. https://www.foxnews.com/entertainment/is-hollywood-ruining-childrens-movies-with-adult-focused-content [accessed April 16, 2020].
2. Anya Jaremko-Greenwold, "Why Hollywood Doesn't Tell More Stories for—and about—Girls," *The Atlantic*, June 12, 2016. https://www.theatlantic.com/entertainment/archive/2016/06/why-its-so-hard-to-make-great-films-forand-aboutgirls/486269/ [accessed April 16, 2020].
3. Katiya Burt, "What Mulan's PG-13 Rating Means," *Den of Geek*, February 19, 2020, https://www.denofgeek.com/movies/mulan-pg-13-rating/ [accessed April 16, 2020].
4. Richard Lawson, "Maleficent: Mistress of Evil Is Maybe One of the Most Political Films of the Year," *Vanity Fair*, October 15, 2019. https://www.vanityfair.com/hollywood/2019/10/maleficent-mistress-of-evil-angelina-jolie-review [accessed April 16, 2020].
5. E.g., Ian Wojcik-Andrews, *Children's Films: History, Ideology, Pedagogy, Theory* (New York: Routledge, 2000); Cary Bazalgette and David Buckingham (eds.), *In Front of the Children: Screen Entertainment and Young Audiences* (London: BFI Publishing, 1995).
6. On Disney, see, for example, Chris Pallant, *Demystifying Disney: A History of Disney Feature Animation* (London: Continuum, 2011); Janet Wasko, *Understanding Disney: The Manufacture of Fantasy* (Hoboken: Wiley, 2013). On the British children's film, see Noel Brown, *British Children's Cinema: From The Thief of Bagdad to Wallace and Gromit* (London: I.B. Tauris, 2017); Terry Staples, *All Pals Together: The Story of Children's Cinema* (Edinburgh: Edinburgh University Press, 1996); and Robert Shail, *The Children's Film Foundation: History and Legacy* (London: Palgrave Macmillan, 2016).

7. Noel Brown, *The Hollywood Family Film: A History, from Shirley Temple to Harry Potter* (London: I.B. Tauris, 2012); and Brown, *The Children's Film: Genre, Nation and Narrative* (New York: Columbia University Press, 2017).

8. Brown, *Hollywood Family Film*, p. 18. Brown has argued similar points in "The 'Family' Film, and the Tensions between Popular and Academic Interpretations of the Genre," *Trespassing Journal* 2 (2013), pp. 22–35; and "'Family' Entertainment and Contemporary Hollywood Cinema," *Scope* 25 (2013), pp. 1–22.

9. Brown, *Children's Film*, pp. 19–24.

10. Ibid., p. 35.

11. Peter Krämer, "'It's Aimed at Kids—the Kid in Everybody': George Lucas, *Star Wars* and Children's Entertainment," in Yvonne Tasker (ed.), *Action and Adventure Cinema* (London: Routledge, 2004), pp. 358–370.

12. Filipa Antunes, "'This Could Be Our Exorcist!': Disney, Horror, and the New Rules of Childhood," in *Children Beware! Childhood, Horror and the PG-13 Rating* (Jefferson, NC: McFarland, 2020), pp. 25–43.

13. Antunes, *Children Beware!*, pp. 99–106.

14. Vincent Canby, "Film View; as a Rating, PG Says Less Than Meets the Eye," *New York Times*, June 10, 1984, sec. 2.

15. Canby, "Film View."

16. Antunes, *Children Beware!*

17. Roger Ebert, "The Goonies," RogerEbert.Com. https://www.rogerebert.com/reviews/the-goonies-1985 [accessed April 8, 2020].

18. Filipa Antunes, "Parents Strongly Cautioned: PG-13, a Cultural Turning Point," in *Children Beware!*, pp. 44–64.

19. Filipa Antunes, "Attachment Anxiety: Parenting Culture, Adolescence and the Family Film in the US," *Journal of Children and Media* 11:2 (2017), pp. 214–228.

20. Scott Mendelson, "Review: 'Goosebumps' Is a Scary Good, Kid-Friendly Lovecraftian Horror Comedy," *Forbes*, October 5, 2015, https://www.forbes.com/sites/scottmendelson/2015/10/05/review-goosebumps-is-a-scary-good-kid-friendly-lovecraftian-horror-comedy/ [accessed April 16, 2020].

21. Scott Mendelson, "Disney's 'Frozen' Proves Failure of the PG Rating," *Forbes*, November 26, 2013, https://www.forbes.com/sites/scottmendelson/2013/11/26/disneys-frozen-proves-worthlessness-of-pg-rating/#57c1c1f76d35 [accessed April 16, 2020].

22. Ron Leone and Nicole Houle, "21st Century Ratings Creep: PG-13 and R," *Communication Research Reports* 23:1 (2006), pp. 53–61.

23. Scott Mendelson, "'RoboCop' and the Problem with PG-13," *Forbes*, February 27, 2014, https://www.forbes.com/sites/scottmendelson/2014/02/27/robocop-and-the-problem-with-pg-13/#701ae81c62ba [accessed April 16, 2020].

24. Scott Mendelson, "Why 'Star Wars: The Force Awakens' Should Be Rated PG," *Forbes*, December 1, 2014, https://www.forbes.com/sites/scottmendelson/2014/12/01/why-star-wars-the-force-awakens-should-be-rated-pg/#1ec9e548354c [accessed April 16, 2020].

25. Mendelson, "Why 'Star Wars.'"

26. Chris Lee, "Eli Roth on 'The House with a Clock in Its Walls': 'The New Shocking Is Doing a PG Movie,'" *Vulture*, August 30, 2018, https://www.vulture.com/2018/08/eli-roth-house-with-a-clock-in-its-walls-interview.html [accessed April 16, 2020].

27. Lee, "Eli Roth."

28. For an analysis of the contradictions in contemporary nostalgic texts, see Antunes, *Children Beware!*, pp. 158–161.

29. Christina Radish, "'The House with a Clock in Its Walls': Eli Roth on Creating Gateway Horror for Kids," *Collider*, September 21, 2018, https://collider.com/eli-roth-interview-house-with-a-clock-in-its-walls/ [accessed April 16, 2020].

30. Lee, "Eli Roth".

31. Ibid.

32. Antunes, *Children Beware!*, pp. 158–165.

33. Katie Rife, "Eli Roth, of All Directors, Brings Amblin Magic to the Kid-Lit Horror of 'The House with a Clock in Its Walls,'" *AV Club*, September 19, 2018, https://film.avclub.com/eli-roth-of-all-directors-brings-amblin-magic-to-the-1829180158 [accessed April 16, 2020].

34. Emily Yoshida, "The House with a Clock in Its Walls Never Really Gets Ticking," *Vulture*, September 21, 2018, https://www.vulture.com/2018/09/the-house-with-a-clock-in-its-walls-review.html [accessed April 16, 2020].

35. Jake Cole, "Review: *The House with a Clock in Its Walls*," *Slant*, September 19, 2018, https://www.slantmagazine.com/film/the-house-with-a-clock-in-its-walls/ [accessed April 16, 2020].

36. Dan Jolin, "The House with a Clock in Its Walls Review," *Empire*, September 20, 2018, https://www.empireonline.com/movies/reviews/house-clock-walls-review/ [accessed April 16, 2020].

37. Robbie Collin, "The House with a Clock in Its Walls Review: Frightfully Dull Spielberg-Lite Fantasy," *Telegraph*, September 20, 2018, https://www.telegraph.co.uk/films/0/house-clock-walls-review-frightfully-dull-spielberg-lite-fantasy/ [accessed April 16, 2020].

38. Antunes, "Attachment Anxiety"; *Children Beware!*

39. Scott Mendelson, "Review: 'The House with a Clock in Its Walls' Is a Wonderful Kid-Sized Horror Fantasy," *Forbes*, September 18, 2018, https://www.forbes.com/sites/scottmendelson/2018/09/18/review-house-with-a-clock-in-its-walls-is-a-wonderful-kid-sized-horror-fantasy-eli-roth-cate-blanchett-jack-black/ [accessed April 16, 2020].

40. Mendelson, "Review: 'The House with a Clock in Its Walls.'"

41. Justin Chang, "Review: 'The House with a Clock in Its Walls' Offers Creaky, Freaky Haunted-Mansion Fun," *Los Angeles Times*, September 19, 2018, https://www.latimes.com/entertainment/movies/la-et-mn-the-house-with-a-clock-in-its-walls-review-20180919-story.html [accessed April 20, 2020].

BIBLIOGRAPHY

Allen, Robert C. "Home Alone Together: Hollywood and the 'Family Film.'" In Melvyn Stokes and Richard Maltby (eds.), *Identifying Hollywood's Audiences: Cultural Identity and the Movies*. London: BFI Publishing, 1999, pp. 109–131.

Antunes, Filipa. "Attachment Anxiety: Parenting Culture, Adolescence and the Family Film in the US." *Journal of Children and Media* 11:2 (2017), pp. 214–228.

Antunes, Filipa. *Children Beware! Childhood, Horror and the PG-13 Rating* (Jefferson, NC: McFarland, 2020.

Bazalgette, Cary, and Terry Staples. "Unshrinking the Kids: Children's Cinema and the Family Film." In Cary Bazalgette and David Buckingham (eds.), *In Front of the Children: Screen Entertainment and Young Audiences*. London: BFI Publishing, 1995, pp. 92–108.

Brown, Noel. *The Children's Film: Genre, Nation and Narrative*. New York: Columbia University Press, 2017.

Brown, Noel. "'Family' Entertainment and Contemporary Hollywood Cinema." *Scope* 25 (2013), pp. 1–22.

Brown, Noel. "The 'Family' Film and the Tensions between Popular and Academic Interpretations of the Genre." *Trespassing Journal* 2 (2013), pp. 22–35.

Brown, Noel. *The Hollywood Family Film: A History, from Shirley Temple to Harry Potter.* London: I.B. Tauris, 2012.

Krämer, Peter. "'The Best Disney Film Disney Never Made': Children's Films and the Family Audience in American Cinema since the 1960s." In Steve Neale (ed.), *Genre and Contemporary Hollywood.* London: BFI Publishing, 2002, pp. 185–200.

Krämer, Peter. "Disney and Family Entertainment." In Linda Ruth Williams and Michael Hammond (eds.), *Contemporary American Cinema.* Maidenhead: Open University Press, 2006, pp. 265–271.

Krämer, Peter. "'It's Aimed at Kids—the Kid in Everybody': George Lucas, *Star Wars* and Children's Entertainment." In Yvonne Tasker (ed.), *Action and Adventure Cinema.* London: Routledge, 2004, pp. 358–370.

Krämer, Peter. "'Would You Take Your Child to See This Film?': The Cultural and Social Work of the Family Adventure Movie." In Steve Neale and Murray Smith (eds.), *Contemporary Hollywood Cinema.* London: Routledge, 1998, pp. 294–311.

Leone, Ron, and Nicole Houle. "21st Century Ratings Creep: PG-13 and R." *Communication Research Reports* 23:1 (2006), pp. 53–61.

PART VI

AUDIENCES,
ENGAGEMENT, AND
PARTICIPATORY
CULTURE

CHAPTER 33

....

HOW CHILDREN LEARN
TO "READ" MOVIES

....

CARY BAZALGETTE

IN 1917 the National Council for Public Morals (NCPM), a British lobbying organization concerned primarily with the threat of "racial degeneracy" and the role of "sexual purity" in combating it,[1] published the report of an independent inquiry that it had commissioned on children and the cinema.[2] Given that the cinema-exhibition sector had helped to fund the inquiry, it is not surprising that the report concluded that "the cinema, under wise guidance, may be made a powerful influence for good." However, it immediately follows this cautious acknowledgement with a more trenchant claim: "If neglected, if its abuse is unchecked, its potentialities for evil are manifold."[3] This ostensibly "balanced" judgement betrays underlying prejudices: cinema's "influence for good" depends upon "wise guidance" and is in any case not guaranteed, whereas its "abuse" and potential "evils" are taken for granted.

Over a century later, much research and almost all public debate on children and moving-image media—now broadening to include computer games and social media—still largely operate within the NCPM's binary view. As David Buckingham points out, this fits within a wider and more long-standing construction of childhood—at least in Western societies—as "both a negative and a positive enterprise" that normalizes public discourse about children into similarly binary terms: protecting them from harm and identifying what may do them good.[4] We could term this "the risks and benefits paradigm": it is one that severely limits the scope of inquiry into, among many other things, children's relationships with media that are presumed to present potential risks. The questions generated within this paradigm tend to focus on the effects of such media on children, instead of addressing the specific characteristics of different forms and genres, and the varied range of engagements that children may have with them. Longer-established cultural forms such as books and theatre are not treated so narrowly.

"Movies"

This chapter presents a different way of looking at children's relationships with moving-image media, which sidesteps the risks and benefits agenda by focusing on the distinctive and complex qualities that these media share, whatever platforms or distribution systems they may appear on, and discussing how children learn to understand them. The risks and benefits paradigm is particularly associated with the accelerating development of communication technologies throughout the twentieth century, and, in the twenty-first century, with the digital revolution that has dramatically widened access to all forms of media. It is frequently claimed that these technological developments have "blurred the boundaries" between established cultural forms. While acknowledging that this has been the case to some extent, I argue that moving-image media—film, television, video, and to some extent, games—remain uniquely recognizable. For brevity's sake, I will refer to these media from now on simply as "movies."

Many people assume that movies simply "present" or "capture" reality, which is understandable, given that one of movies' many pleasures is their similarity to real life. Indeed, from its earliest beginnings, the movie industry promoted itself as the most "lifelike" medium. The "founding myth" of movies, based on the behaviour of some viewers' in early screenings, is that viewers automatically believe they are watching "real life," and technological developments since the 1890s have always striven for greater realism.[5] But movies are also a unique and densely multimodal art form. They are full of rhetorical devices that do not reproduce our daily perceptual experiences, such as jump-cuts, parallel montage, shot-reverse shot sequences, non-diegetic sound, and techniques such as animation, computer-generated imagery (CGI) and numerous types of special effect. Every movie-watcher today has learned to interpret the features to which these specialist terms refer and takes them for granted. And the enormous diversity of movies now available on streaming platforms like YouTube continues to establish new tropes and devices, with which users quickly become familiar. But we don't remember our initial efforts to learn movies' rhetorical devices.

Anyone with experience of very young children can infer that they learn something about movies between the ages of 12 and 36 months because babies can't follow an extended movie narrative, but most three-year-olds can. This chapter explains what such learning looks like, describes the contexts in which it is likely to take place, and presents a new theoretical approach to the study of this process. Based on an observational study of dizygotic girl and boy twins between the ages of 17 and 42 months (my own grandchildren) as well as on many other informal observations of children's movie-viewing and listening to comments by parents and teachers, the case for taking such learning seriously is built up and illustrated.

The children watched a wide variety of movies on a random basis: TV series (usually in broadcast video on demand or in DVD collections rather than when broadcast; occasionally feature films, selected by their parents for family viewing sessions, but then sometimes favourite segments would be re-viewed; and selected short films from DVD collections that I owned. The family did not have tablets, so the now-widespread practice of allowing toddlers to view and select movies from YouTube was not part of their viewing practices.[6] After initial offerings by adults, which were usually impulsive and opportunistic, further choices and re-viewings were directed by the children themselves, prompting many arguments over differing preferences. As a result, the progression of their learning about movies was largely self-directed. The following sections describe the phenomena that indicate the nature of this learning process and suggest ways in which we might interpret them.

Focused Attention

Figure 33.1 shows the twins (aged 23 months) watching a short non-mainstream movie for the first time, played from a DVD on a large domestic TV monitor. The film is *Laughing Moon* (Kiyoshi Nishimoto, 2000), a playful Japanese animated movie that shows "tangram" shapes in different configurations e.g., chicken, dog, dinosaur, rock star, each of which is identified by music or sound effects.[7] When the movie started, both children were "caught" in the middle of doing something else: Alfie, in the process of sitting down at the table; Connie, in the middle of trying to open a book (but backwards, and thus impossible to open properly). Once the movie starts, Alfie maintains exactly this position for the whole six minutes, having been startled by a loud sound at the

FIGURE 33.1. Watching *Laughing Moon*. Author's collection.

beginning and then waiting somewhat tensely for other sudden sounds. Connie divides her attention between two different challenges: trying to work out what is going on in the film and trying to work out how to make the book stay open.

The image in Figure 33.1 is a screen grab from a video: one of many that show the intensity with which children of this age can focus their attention on a movie. Both children have one hand placed where it was when their attention was initially seized: Alfie's on the table, Connie's on her belly. Both use the other hand to steady themselves as they watch: at this age, children's centre of gravity is higher than that of an older child or adult and it is harder for them to keep their balance while still being able to move their heads. They are fairly close to the screen, which is just outside the frame in this image. At this distance, they are afforded significant choices about where to look on the 32-inch screen and have to turn their heads to spot objects that appear in different places on the screen or to follow movement. We tend to think of "toddlers" as incessantly active, but here, they hold their bodies almost completely still and gaze open-mouthed at the screen, breathing deeply. At the end of the movie, they instantly ask for "more"—that is, to watch it again.

Unfortunately, on this occasion it wasn't possible to immediately show them the movie again. Their second viewing was a month later, the day after their second birthday, and in my house rather than in theirs, where the first viewing occurred (see Figure 33.2). This time, the movie is not being sprung on them as a surprise, so they know what is coming and have selected places from which to watch it: this time, farther away from the screen. Again, their responses differed. Connie has gained a favoured viewing position

FIGURE 33.2. Second *Laughing Moon* viewing. Author's collection.

in the armchair, but instead of relaxing into the chair she holds her head forward, jaw jutting. Alfie is still anxious about the loud noises and stands to watch, leaning against the sofa. Both watch intently and a bit anxiously for the first couple of minutes of the movie. Watching it with them, and concerned about what they will make of it, I keep uttering almost involuntary noises e.g., "ooh" and "uh-oh" in response to the sudden sounds and changes of image. Both jump at loud noises such as rock music, which at first seems almost unmotivated.

But within a minute, both children have figured out the movie's project. It's a guessing game. The tangram pieces keep reconfiguring, but in semi-abstract form: it's the changes in music and sound effects that act as extra cues to identification. As Alfie recognizes the rock star figure, he sways his body to the music and grins conspiratorially at me. And at the moment captured in Figure 33.2, Connie is using a Makaton sign to identify the dog that has just appeared barking and panting (their mother had taught them some Makaton signs some months earlier). As is often the case with twins, their language development was fairly limited, even at 24 months. Being able to identify things and share that knowledge with others is an exciting and pleasurable game for children of this age. *Laughing Moon* and many of the other movies they watched (mainly the children's TV channels) offered plenty of opportunities to do this.

Adults often mention focused attention of this kind in discussions of children's viewing, both in live contexts and on social media. Parents may express their pleasure at children's discoveries of movies they enjoy, remarking "he loves it" or "it's her favourite"; later on, they may make comments on the lines of "she's got bored with *Teletubbies*: it's all *Peppa Pig* now." These emotive terms contrast with the "medicalized" language they may use if they are anxious about children's viewing and worry that it may be bad for them, as in "he's absolutely addicted to *Frozen*" or "she's obsessed with funny cats on YouTube." These judgements are understandable in the hurly-burly and fast-changing world of toddler care. Carers don't often have the time to observe their children's viewing practices intensively. But close analysis of many instances of focused attention shows that two-year-olds can invest extraordinary levels of energy and thought in their movie-viewing. There can be several physical signs of this in addition to the fixed posture, open mouth, and deep breathing mentioned above. When children are viewing a large TV, proximity to the screen becomes important and they will often grip a nearby piece of furniture tightly. The child's gaze will flicker across the screen, following movement or switching to different points of interest; the body may be held rigid, for example, with shoulders hunched; a seated child may brace herself against the seat with clenched fists; a child whose mouth is open and is breathing deeply may need to lick his lips frequently; a child with a runny nose may quickly wipe it on her sleeve before resuming the same posture as before. There may be quick glances and comments to co-viewers, followed again by the resumption of the same posture. A child drinking from a bottle may hold it to one side so that he can maintain his gaze on the screen.

It is natural to wonder why children behave like this: what is attracting them to pay such close attention to movies and in many cases re-view them several times? The default interpretations do not square with what we know about children of this age: they do not have time to be "mesmerized." To get from babyhood to becoming a mobile, talkative, social being demands an enormous investment in learning. We have to assume that a toddler gazing at a screen is learning something, because that is what toddlers do. They bestow the same kind of attention on activities that are more generally approved of, such as working out the particularities of a new toy.

Making Sense

In her study of a two-year-old making drawings with her father, Lesley Lancaster makes the important point that "physical and bodily actions are visible indicators of the course of abstract reasoning used whilst engaging with the difficult business of finding out about how a system of symbolic representation works."[8] Although she is describing a child involved in a creative process, her analysis is equally salient for movie-viewing. In both cases, the issue of similitude is crucial—but as Lancaster says, "recognizing an image or an object as being like, in the sense of an accurate representation of, "the real thing," is not a simple matter of visual perception."[9] The two-year-old's environment of visual representations is extraordinarily diverse. It is a relatively unexamined "given" that pictures and movies for little children need to be simplified—but simplification take many different forms. So, both Dick Bruna's Miffy and Chuck Jones's Bugs Bunny, despite their differences, are intended to be—and are—identified as rabbits by two-year-olds, whether or not they have ever seen a real rabbit. Of course, this is not surprising, given that the ability to identify salient features at a glance confers an obvious evolutionary advantage (the ability to distinguish prey from predators, for example) so we would expect humans to be good at this from an early age. We know that neonates can recognize their mothers on the basis of visual clues alone.[10] And children's early drawings often focus entirely on what are, for them, salient features: a drawing of an adult may comprise just long legs and a head. Gunther Kress describes a three-year-old's drawing of a car that consists simply of "wheels"—a collection of circles.[11]

But multitudes of different graphic styles appear on children's clothing and on the packaging of child-oriented products, as well as in picture books, toys, and the material on mobile devices. Children do not have to make sense of them all by themselves: carers and older siblings constantly prompt their interpretations, exclaiming "look at the bunny-rabbit" or "here's a chicken." What very young children learn through these encounters is not just the salient features that distinguish one species from another. They also start to develop facility and confidence with a system within which there is a wide, but not infinite, range of variations, and enjoy playing with ideas about similitude and its boundaries: for example, claiming that a robot with two antennae on its head is a rabbit. At the same time, through exchanges with family members and friends, they are learning the values that their culture attaches to representations and to variance, and the pleasures to be derived from guessing and from recognition. At a deeper level, they are also developing what Lancaster calls "expectations of significance."[12] Their initial encounter with any cultural product that they may happen upon—a text on a smart phone, a book on economics, or a YouTube video, for example—can arouse their interest if they know that it is valued by the people close to them. If they can't read the text, or if the economics book doesn't have any interesting pictures in it, they will lose interest at once, but if they can latch on to anything recognizable, then they know it may be worth their while to pay more attention. Even if the YouTube video is definitely not for them, the figures, movement, and music may still hold their attention, if only for a while. They are likely to study it closely before either committing to it or swiping the screen in search of something they hope will reward their interest.

The Social Context of Viewing

The presence of co-viewers is clearly a key factor in arousing a child's expectations of significance. Of course, children do watch movies on their own: television, DVDs, and streamed movies on mobile devices are a godsend to busy parents trying to find a moment to cook dinner or get some housework done. But even the lone child viewer will be aware of the role of movies in her family's cultural behaviour and preferences. A big TV set in the living room conveys a message even when it is not being used: "movies are important in this household." The family's viewing practices will also be familiar to the two-year-old. These may be strictly limited and subject to rules about what can be watched, on what devices, and when, and by whom; or family members may be constantly watching and sharing movies on various devices. How decisions are made about what is watched, when, and where; what gets repeat-viewed or shared; whether the family gathers around to watch particular movies together on a big screen; whether they watch more casually and intermittently, alone on mobile devices or desktop computers; whether there are rules about watching and about how programmes, channels, streaming services, or DVDs are chosen and by whom; what kinds of talk and responses are heard during viewings; who gets frightened easily—all these are noticed and appear customary to all family members, including the youngest.

Children growing up in a family that doesn't watch movies will encounter other families, through friends, for example, or at a childminder's or babysitter's, who do watch them: this may be of intense interest to children for whom this is new and strange. And most children are at least aware that all kinds of movies are available on portable devices, from the latest funny video to full-length feature films, and, of course, recordings of people that they know. All of these phenomena communicate to the child the level of importance their family and friends ascribe to movies and how they expect them to be watched.

THE ATTRACTIONS OF MOVIES

Co-viewers' behaviour is an important factor in arousing children's expectations of significance, but it is not the only one. Movies themselves present compelling attractions: a child who never normally watches them may be just as attracted as regular viewers if they suddenly encounter a movie. Sound is significant here: Anderson and Levin noted in 1976 that children's voices, sound effects, and lively music were particularly likely to attract the attention of children aged between 12 and 48 months; I noted similar effects in my own research, with the addition of adult presenters' greetings (e.g., "Hallo!" being also likely to draw children towards a screen.[13]

Another crucial factor is, of course, movement: movies can offer the unique pleasure (unavailable in most of the other art forms that little children are familiar with) of being able to follow an action visually from beginning to end. In many cases this reveals motivation (e.g., reaching out to grab an object) or cause and effect (e.g., an extended foot tripping someone up) but even a very basic movement such as a forward-moving dolly shot, reproducing as it does the experience of revealing an environment as one walks, is carried, or pushed through it in a buggy, has an inherent interest for viewers. In the early days of cinema, "phantom ride" movies, shot from the top of a bus or the front of a train, were immensely popular with audiences, and many computer games offer the same pleasure, with the added advantage that one can control the point of view and explore the dimensions of an environment. In all of these cases, movies satisfy instinctive desires. All animals have to be able to respond to significant sounds and explore their environments: movies offer simple and accessible ways of experiencing what feels like exploratory movement.

But it can also be argued that many conventional narrative devices in movies can be seen as related to other instinctive behaviours. A point-of-view shot, in which a glance off-screen is followed by what viewers automatically assume is what that person is looking at, does not reproduce a live experience, but satisfies the basic instinct to follow another's gaze. A cut from a wide shot to close-up parallels the real-life experience of suddenly focusing our attention on a specific object (e.g., spotting a lost key on the floor). Parallel montage provides an equivalent to the real experience of being mentally preoccupied with something quite different from what we are actually doing at a given moment. And the convention of using camera angles to convey a character's strength or power (with a low angle) or weakness (with a high angle) "reproduces the structural features of real-life situations."[14] But interpreting these devices is not merely a matter of decoding. It is driven by the *desire* to discover significance, and to contextualize our interpretations within the wider environment—or within the story, in the case of narrative forms. Enjoyment of movies is thus closely bound up with the emotional satisfaction of being able to reward this desire through continually interpreting the stream of rhetorical devices. But the initial desire to discover significance can itself be seen as a form of emotion.

THE ROLE OF EMOTION
IN MOVIE-WATCHING

Most of us tend to identify a limited range of emotions—for example, joy, fear, anger, sadness, and disgust—and to see these as powerful feelings that are separate from, and need to be "managed" by, rational thought. The neuroscientist and psychobiologist Panksepp identifies a far wider range of emotions and uses the term to describe instinctive feelings that generate further thought and action. This offers us a very different model of humans' cognitive processes, contradicting the Cartesian belief that mind and body are separate entities. Panksepp also invites us to regard our evolutionary past as an important way in to understanding modern humans' thoughts and behaviours, rather than as primitive and long-abandoned stages of development. This is particularly helpful when we want to look at children in the phase between babyhood and pre-school. It is a developmental process that is largely self-driven: we can't teach one-year-olds to walk and we can't teach two-year-olds to talk. We can only encourage, facilitate and reward—while at the same time of course rushing to secure the knife drawer and the electric sockets, and to regret the early acquisition of that powerful word "No!" Because most children manage to do this, and because the process is full of mistakes and conflict with adults over seemingly unreasonable demands, public discourse tends to regard very young children as primarily "ruled by their emotions" and hence vulnerable to irrational—or even dangerous—ideas and beliefs. Their language-learning and their increased agility tend to be seen as "natural" developments rather than as "astonishing feats" of self-directed learning.[15] The curiosity of 2-year-olds' about everything new is often maddening to their modern carers, who may use the term "terrible twos," to describe them, but in the evolutionary time-scale, curiosity must have favoured survival.

Panksepp points out that all animals need to have innate, powerful systems of instinctive behaviours that help them to survive. Primates (including humans) retain these systems within their more developed brains, where they are experienced as basic emotions such as fear, anger, seeking, and sorrow. Their function is to "energise and guide organisms in their interactions with the world."[16] This echoes Vygotsky's claim that "action flows from bodily causes. It originates with a naturally essential force and is accomplished according to mechanical laws; its intensity contains the force of passions."[17] This is not a biologically deterministic model in which emotions mechanically "trigger" thought and action, but a more complex interrelationship between the physical and the psychological. Panksepp explains how emotional systems, centrally situated in the brain, "extensively interact, in strong and weak ways, with higher and lower brain functions"—that is, with cognitive perceptual processes *and* with autonomic processes.[18] These processes are complex, he says, and involve feedback loops that modulate the relationships between emotion, thought, and action in ways that are unpredictable and vary widely among individuals.

Panksepp's identification of "seeking" as one of the "primal emotional circuits" is of particular interest when we want to consider children's intense attention to movies that interest them, their huge investment of energy as they strive to understand them, and their desire to re-view some movies many times.[19] Panksepp links "seeking" with feelings of engagement and excitement and suggests that it generates anticipation and investigation, not only in doing things like foraging and finding shelter, but also in figuring out how things work and in developing plans and ideas.[20] "Seeking" thus offers us a different way of thinking about toddlers' fascination with movies; one that suggests the possibility of intellectual curiosity rather than passive absorption of content.

Antonio Damasio, another neuroscientist, describes a similar process but locates its origins in the much broader phenomenon of consciousness.[21] His account resonates with my observations of the twins' focused attention as they watched movies, and indicates how this could be seen as the physical evidence of learning processes under way:

> Consciousness results in *enhanced* wakefulness and *focused* attention, both of which improve image processing for certain contents and can thus help optimize immediate and planned responses. The organism's engagement with an object intensifies its ability to process that object sensorily and also increases the opportunity to be engaged by other objects—the organism gets ready for more encounters and for more-detailed interactions.[22]

To describe a 2-year-old's intense engagement with the screen as "passive viewing" is thus entirely wrong: an alert child must be thinking and observing.

SELF-DIRECTED LEARNING

Damasio's use of the term "organism" enables a helpfully wide sense of agency, releasing us from the preconceptions that accompany words such as "child" or "toddler" and encouraging us to recognize the common ground that exists between age-groups and indeed between species, when we are considering encounters with new phenomena and events. Even within the social viewing contexts that I described earlier, 2-year-olds' viewing is still largely self-directed. With access to a big TV screen, they are likely to try to get as close to it as they can, often standing right in front of it if they are interested in the movie, and sometimes touching its surface. Early attempts to "swipe" the image will quickly be abandoned. TV sets instead offer the opportunity to lay a finger or hand on the screen and watch as the images change beneath it. Children may touch the screen with a finger to point something out, or they may simply enjoy the warm silky feel of the surface under the palm of their hand.

They will constantly ask for repeat viewings of particular movies, but will also express decided preferences, either by simply dropping the phone, swiping the screen, or walking away; or by saying "no!" or "turn it off!" or "don't like this one!" In the context of shared viewing on a single screen, siblings are likely to argue about what to watch, and older co-viewers often have to try and arbitrate their viewing choices. It underestimates children to label these behaviours as short-lived idiosyncrasies. A 2-year-old's insistence on watching a *Peppa Pig* episode for the tenth time may be inconvenient, but it is not wilful: it is the result of a determination to understand and to learn. It is hard for older people to accept that there can possibly be anything to learn from a tenth re-viewing of *Peppa Pig*, but the 2-year-old is not the victim of mesmeric powers emanating from the screen. Her expectations of significance have not yet been satisfied: she knows that there is more for her to understand before she has "used up" the episode's potential for meaning.

I observed an unusual example of this just after the twins' second birthday. Connie became extremely upset by the "Sports Day" episode of *Peppa Pig* (2004–), in which there is a tug of war between the boys and the girls. The rope frays and breaks; both groups of children fall flat on their backs, and everybody laughs. Falling over and laughing is a standard end point in *Peppa Pig* episodes, but Connie found the rope-breaking unbearably shocking. Nevertheless, over subsequent days and weeks she watched and rewatched the episode, getting ready for the rope-breaking each time with growing tension, and when it happened, flinging herself to the floor in a storm of tears and screams. But gradually, as she continued to deliberately re-view it, she devised coping mechanisms. After about ten re-viewings, she could handle the key moment with nothing more than an irritated "tsk" and biting her own hand. There could be several theories about what it was that had upset her. Did she have a major emotional investment in wanting the girls to win? Did she hope for a happy and triumphant end to the episode's comic series of opportunities missed because Peppa had wasted time talking instead of competing? Did she keep hoping that maybe this time the rope wouldn't break?

UNDERSTANDING MOVIE NARRATIVES

We are all familiar with the experience of thinking that we know what is going to happen in a movie, and with the more interesting variant: wondering which of two or more possibilities the actual outcome is going to be. Our ability to predict what will happen next or even some time ahead is governed by our experience of narratives in different genres, our ability to spot clues in features such as dialogue, music and sound design, performance and mise-en-scène, and our experiences of many other narratives. We can take pleasure in being "fooled" by false clues and being made to rethink why we expected what we did.

Two-year-olds are in the process of acquiring enough experience to be able to share these pleasures. They can sometimes "misread" a scene in a movie, which may lead to distress (as in Connie's interpretation of the tug of war) or merely an interestingly aberrant reading. They can be shocked and upset by things that they do more or less understand, but are rarely encountered in children's movies, such as a sad event. The mother elephant's imprisonment in *Dumbo* (Ben Sharpsteen et al., 1941) was enough to stop the twins' watching it (aged 28 months) and to refuse to watch it again. When (aged 30 months) they viewed *Baboon on the Moon* (Christopher Duriez, 2002), they both picked up the signals of "sadness"—the baboon's tears as he gazes towards Earth; the slow, sad trumpet and piano music at the end—without understanding what the sadness is about. They did not want to watch it again: that particular search for significance was a step too far.

The ability to laugh at funny movies requires not only a familiarity with narrative devices but also a degree of social awareness: how it is thought that people ought to behave, for example. The twins' first completely spontaneous laughter at their first viewing of a movie gag (at age 32 months) was observed by their mother when they were watching the "Mind the Puddle" segment from the "Playing in the Rain" episode of *Teletubbies* (1997–) in which Tinky Winky manages to avoid stepping into the puddle by mistake as the other three Teletubbies have done, but then surprises everyone by stepping into it deliberately. Before this for example, at age 28 months, they had voluntarily re-viewed the crazy "Step in Time" dance sequence in *Mary Poppins* (Robert Stevenson, 1964) but maintained serious, deeply attentive expressions while their three adult co-viewers were in fits of laughter. But 5 months earlier they had been able to laugh at a few parts of *Monsters, Inc.* (Pete Docter, 2001). They watched it twice, in instalments, with their mother, who had told them that she loved the film and was enthusiastically commenting as they watched. They were also already familiar with a toy based on the green, one-eyed Mike character. But their main interest was in the human toddler character Boo, and they laughed knowingly with their mother at the sequence in which the big blue monster, Sully, tries to make Boo go to sleep.

Even after their second viewing, they were in floods of tears as the *Monsters, Inc.* credits slowly rolled and they had to accept that the movie was over. Connie learned relatively early on to accept the fact that eventually all movies must end; Alfie found this much more difficult. His dread of endings increased over the months, which simultaneously increased his skill in anticipating them: at the first signs of story resolution, he would be on his feet, ready to run from the room (at this stage, they were not watching movies on mobile devices: if they had been, he would have found another way to avoid the ending). In contrast with Connie's efforts to overcome her anguish about the rope-breaking moment in *Peppa Pig*, Alfie found it very hard to deal with his feelings about the non-negotiable finality of endings. He was 37 months old when, instead of offering him futile reassurances like "the ending's not really scary is it?" to help defuse his anxiety, we simply asked him, "Is it frightening to see the ending?" His answer, "Ye-a-a-h," surged out of his mouth, and he shuddered as though relaxing from extreme tension. It seemed that being asked for his opinion, being able to express it—and the adult recognition that an ending really could be frightening—had a cathartic effect. In all of us there is a natural tendency to be sad when something pleasurable is ending, but toddlers are well-known for throwing tantrums when it is time to stop playing and have dinner or to put coats on to go out. Alfie's horror of endings was more profound than this and was linked to similar issues, such as his dread of seeing the bathwater drain away; but sensible parental management eventually enabled him to manage and overcome these fears.

MISREADINGS

However, the "misreading" phenomenon, as illustrated by the tug-of-war episode that so upset Connie, is often mentioned by parents in social media discussions. It happens when very young children suddenly become inexplicably upset by innocuous events in a movie (often movies with which they are already familiar). If the children concerned are not yet fluent speakers, it can be hard for parents and carers to understand what the problem is. Before I began my research, I had observed the twins becoming terrified by an episode of *In the Night Garden* (2007–2009) when the little puppet character called Mr. Pontipine loses his big bushy moustache: it suddenly and inexplicably flies away, and great merriment ensues as the other characters try to catch it. Not so for Connie, who shrieked with terror, or for Alfie, who froze with fright. Responses to events like this (breaking ropes; fugitive, run-away moustaches) can be explained to some extent by separation anxiety, attachment theory, or, in somewhat simpler and probably more widely understood terms, by Jerome Kagan's account of how 18–24-month-olds can often be distressed by what they see as violations of states of affairs "which adults have indicated are proper." His examples include broken toys, damaged or dirty clothing, things missing from their usual places.[23] So what seems to be happening in these misreading episodes is that the emotional force of what children perceive as disturbingly significant overrides their more fragile ability to follow the narrative.

Wojciehowski's account of *diakresis*—the process through which, when we watch a moving image, we separate out what is (for us) salient enough to enter into our conscious awareness—is an interesting way of thinking about what goes on in these kinds of "misreadings," and could link them to our own mental processes rather than being merely as aberrant or quaint.[24] She draws on Dehaene's account of consciousness to describe how in daily life, let alone in movie-viewing, we cannot take everything in at once. Conscious access imposes a narrow bottleneck on our thoughts and perceptions: "what reaches our conscious mind is la crème de la crème, the outcome of the very complex sieve that we call attention."[25] She uses the word *diakesis* (i.e., "separating") to account for what does get through the bottleneck of consciousness: it is, unsurprisingly, what each viewer identifies as salient. This may be a conscious process, or it may be instinctive, but as viewers grow older, they become more adept at recognizing indicators of salience that movies provide, of what is meant to be significant, in other words. Adult viewers are, on the whole, better at identifying these features—although we can sometimes get things wrong. And certain genres—such as crime drama—specialize in concealing clues: a major pleasure in watching them is trying to spot the clues. Two-year-olds are less skilful, at least with movies that are new to them; but this does not merely mean that they "make mistakes" or "miss out" on features that "really are" important for the narrative. What two-year-olds are undoubtedly doing as they watch with focused attention is separating out what is salient *for them*.

EMPATHY AND UNDERSTANDING MOTIVATION

Much of the information about characters and their motivation is contained in dialogue, which presents a considerable challenge to children who are not yet very fluent verbally. However, they are extremely skilled at interpreting tone of voice, gestures, and expressions, even from early infancy. Again, it is easy to see how these skills could have conferred evolutionary advantages, and not only to humans.[26] A research programme at the University of Parma in the 1980s found "mirror neurons" in a macaque monkey's brain that discharged when the monkey performs a specific action also discharge when it hears the sound related to the action, and even when it simply observes the action performed by another.[27] Later research established similar functions in the human brain.[28] In 2014, *Philosophical Transactions of the Royal Society* published a special issue reviewing progress in mirror neuron research. The issue was edited by Pier Francesco Ferrari and Giacomo Rizzolatti, who discussed the "wide impact on cognitive disciplines" of these discoveries, and suggested two reasons for their significance:

> The first is that their discovery put the problem of how we understand others at the forefront of neuroscience. The second is that, by showing that mirror neurons were basically motor neurons, they suggested a rather unexpected solution to this problem: the motor system is involved in understanding the actions and intentions of others.[29]

In a series of papers published between 2001 and 2011, Vittorio Gallese, one of the Parma researchers, developed the concept of "embodied simulation" based on the mirror neuron discoveries to characterize the ways in which humans can identify and assess other people's emotions, intentions, and actions.[30] "Simulation" in this context does not mean pretence or imitation, but the process of modelling an event or activity in order to understand it better. This potentially casts new light on the ways in which all humans mimic other people's expressions and gestures, often unconsciously (as when two people talking at a party keep adopting the same positions) and leads to Gallese's argument that embodied simulation must be an essential basic requirement of empathy. This way of "trying out" the feelings that the bodily phenomena are expressing is certainly something that infants and toddlers also do, and it may be a significant element of children's learning to follow a narrative, when they recognize, relate to, and imitate, expressions, gestures, and postures of characters in movies, and sometimes also those

FIGURE 33.3. Connie imitates a supplicatory handclasp. Author's collection.

of the people watching with them. Figure 33.3 shows an example of this: here the children (aged 26 months are watching a short, animated movie based on the popular Eric Carle story, *Papa Please Get the Moon for Me* (2001). The central character in the film, Monica, pleads with her father to fetch the moon for her, clasping her hands as she does so. Connie is clearly intrigued by this somewhat archaic gesture, but she knows (having already seen the movie several times) that it must be effective in getting a parent to do something, even when the proposed task is extremely challenging. She immediately attempts to clasp her own hands, but she only succeeds in placing her fists together. Her mother then notices that she is doing this and says, "Is that how she does it, Connie?" clasping her own hands properly. Connie is distracted from the screen and studies her own hands, trying to work out how to lace her fingers.

This episode indicates the complex interrelationships that can exist between movie, viewer, and co-viewer, for which the embodied-simulation concept provides helpful insights, especially when the viewer is a two-year-old who cannot express her responses. It enables us to infer that a child's impulse to directly imitate a gesture made by a movie character reveals her desire to share the emotion (in this case, supplication expressed by the character). Gallese and Guerra, in reviewing the work of numerous scholars who have drawn attention to the embodied dimensions of responses to movies, confirm their insights with evidence from neuroscience and argue that embodied simulation is the foundation for "our identification with and connectedness to others."[31] When we observe preverbal children's self-directed engagements with movies, we can see this process at work. If further arguments are needed to make the case for the value of movies in children's earliest cultural experiences, then accounts of the role of movies in extending and enhancing children's intersubjective capacities could make a significant contribution. This, however, raises questions about what children watch and the extent to which adults should, or can, attempt to be selective about what children can see.

CHOICES AND PREFERENCES

It is impossible to force a toddler to sit still and watch a movie if they don't want to. The investment of energy in focused attention is always generated by the child's own emotions. They may initially be attracted to watch something new by particular sounds or movements, but they will not go on watching for long if the movie does not, in their view, reward their attention. And despite adult confidence (whether that of marketing executives, as in "all children will love this movie!" or of parents trying to share their own childhood favourites with their children, nobody can unfailingly predict what will appeal to any individual child. It is, of course, likely that most children across quite a wide age-range will enjoy popular movies, but this can never be guaranteed for every child. What is even less predictable is which movies, or parts of movies, children will select for repeated viewing. But it is reasonable to suppose that though children may re-view material two or three times simply because they enjoy it and want to relive that pleasure, numerous repeat viewings are likely to have a more substantial purpose. This may be to exorcise fears (as Connie did with the tug of war) or it may be to tease out further meaning.

The twins' re-viewing record was of a 5.5-minute animated film called *Animatou* (Claude Luyet, 2007) which consists of five sections, in each of which a cat chases a mouse. Each section is preceded by a live-action, speeded-up sequence showing an animator's hands creating a cat in a different medium—drawn, painted cel, sand, clay, and 3-D computer animation—after which the chase resumes and, needless to say, the cat never catches the mouse. Instead, the film ends when the computer version of the cat catches sight of the mouse, which has transmogrified into an actual computer mouse, but with ears and whiskers, and the cable attached to the computer's USB port doubling as a tail. The panic-stricken "mouse" detaches its "tail" from the computer as it tries to run away, and the movie ends abruptly as the screen immediately goes black.

The aim of *Animatou* is not to amuse children but to illustrate different animation techniques: the lack of resolution, and the apparently arbitrary alterations to the cat's appearance, seemed to present a conundrum to the twins that they could never quite solve; it took five months and more than twenty re-viewings before they decided that there really was nothing more to be got from it. In everything else the children wanted to re-view, they would eventually extract enough meaning to satisfy them. Their mother's phrase for this—"they've used it up"—is more appropriate than "they've got bored with it." On each re-viewing they would be attentive and serious during the parts they were still figuring out and would smile pleasurably during the parts that they anticipated and recognized. When they had "used up" a movie, they would move on—often to something that presented a bit more of a challenge.

To judge by the numerous comments and discussions in social media about children's movie re-viewing, it is a phenomenon that puzzles and irritates many parents and carers, often invoking anxious comments about "addiction" and "obsession." The *Teletubbies* TV series, aimed at toddlers, includes a live-action sequence in every episode, usually depicting children involved in some playful or exploratory activity, which is always shown twice. This is an effective device for appealing to the target age group. But to go further than that and argue that it is supporting an essential aspect of children's early learning can generate a good deal of scoffing and ridicule from older, bored co-viewers.

CONCLUSIONS

The key premise on which this chapter is based is that we all learned how to understand movies when we were very young. The fact that this learning happens so early in life does not diminish its significance. Unfortunately, dominant discourses on the cultural value of movies—particularly in Anglophone societies—tends to use the early acquisition of movie-watching competence as grounds for diminishing that value: if this is a medium that two-year-olds can learn to understand, without adult help, it is argued, clearly it must be worth less than reading and writing, which are much harder to learn. Underpinning this argument are the beliefs that learning is not pleasurable, that it is something that we have to be made to do; and that the only learning of value is what is defined, taught, and assessed by adults.

Teachers often discover that showing and discussing movies in the classroom with primary age children completely transforms their assumptions about the abilities of many of their pupils, who reveal themselves to be far more knowledgeable and articulate about topics such as narrative, genre, and character when they are talking about movies than when they are talking about books. But to acknowledge that children must therefore have learned all this already, without adult help, would be to undermine teachers' professional authority. Therefore, they tend to accept that movies may be "used" in teaching as a stimulus ("used" is a telling choice of word here—they see movies as having practical application but not as examples of a major art form, like poetry or the novel, worthy of study in their own right). The notion that educators might have a responsibility to extend children's experience of movies, introducing them to examples that they might not otherwise encounter, has a tiny foothold in formal education in the form of film studies courses for older teenagers and undergraduates, but is extremely rare in primary schools—even rarer than education about other, older art forms, which in any case are often marginalized, or might be.

To study the cultural experiences of very young children in their family settings is difficult and relatively unusual. But the period of life discussed in this chapter is extremely important in terms of the huge developments that happen during that period. Colwyn Trevarthen, in his important essay "The Child's Need to Learn a Culture," outlines the complexity of this learning and, by implication, indicates the challenges that researchers must face if they want to understand it:

> At this age [eighteen months], for most children, knowledge of what things mean, or what they communicate, greatly exceeds what can be said. Comprehension of what the mother says is much more evident than it was a few months before, but it is dependent on "the pragmatic and interpersonal context," which is to say that the child's grasp of the meaning of some names that others give to things, or some actions they describe verbally, depends on a richer mental grasp of what can be done with such things, and especially on how they, or things or actions like them, have been shared with others previously.[32]

The other key premise of this chapter, then, is that children's very early learning needs to be respected. We need to recognize that processes are underway that vary from child to child, from family to family, and from culture to culture but in every case forms the foundations of the child's social and cultural life, as well as her future learning.

This chapter's discussions of children's viewing indicate that to identify and explore these processes, it may be valuable to draw on theories from embodied cognition. This is a cross-disciplinary approach that draws upon philosophy of mind, cognitive neuroscience, and evolutionary biology, to suggest that many aspects of cognition are closely related to our physical bodies and to our bodily actions. A growing sector of scholarship has been developing this approach within film studies; using it to study toddlers' cultural learning, however, is relatively new.[33]

It is true that studying this age group presents many methodological challenges, for example, "practical and logistical considerations including gaining access, involving children as active research participants and negotiating consents."[34] Historically, the most influential studies of children under the age of three were done by family members in the home,[35] and it remains true that parents and grandparents can be the best placed to study the children they know so well.[36] Studies such as these may be challenged for lacking generalizability, but they can produce new perspectives that may, in turn, generate a different approach to research.

NOTES

1. Alan Hunt, *Governing Morals: A Social History of Moral Regulation* (Cambridge, UK: Cambridge University Press, 1999), p. 182.
2. *The Cinema: Its Present Position and Future Possibilities; being the Report and Chief Evidence Taken by the Cinema Commission of Inquiry Instituted by the National Council of Public Morals* (London: Williams and Norgate, 1917).
3. *Cinema: Its Present Position and Future Possibilities*, p. xxi.

4. David Buckingham, "A Special Audience? Children and Television," in Janet Wasko (ed.), *A Companion to Television* (London: Blackwell, 2005), pp. 468–469.

5. Martin Loiperdinger, "Lumiere's Arrival of the Train: Cinema's Founding Myth," *Journal of the Association of Moving Image Archivists* 4:1 (2004), pp. 89–118.

6. Jackie Marsh et al., *Exploring Play and Creativity in Pre-Schoolers' Use of Apps: Final Project Report*, University of Sheffield, 2015. http://www.techandplay.org/reports/TAP_Final_Report.pdf [accessed August 10, 2019].

7. The film is available on YouTube, https://www.youtube.com/watch?v=zKoPh98zkhc.

8. Lesley Lancaster, "Staring at the Page: The Functions of Gaze in a Young Child's Interpretation of Symbolic Forms," *Journal of Early Childhood Literacy* 1:2 (2001), pp. 131–152, at 132.

9. Lancaster, "Staring at the Page," p. 133.

10. See I. W. R. Bushneil, F. Sai, and J. T. Mullin, "Neonatal Recognition of the Mother's Face," *British Journal of Developmental Psychology* 7:1 (1989), pp. 3–15.

11. Gunther Kress, *Before Writing: Rethinking the Paths to Literacy* (London: Routledge, 1997), p. 11.

12. Lancaster, "Staring at the Page," p. 136.

13. Daniel R. Anderson and Stephen R. Levin, "Young Children's Attention to *Sesame Street*," *Child Development* 47 (1976), pp. 806–811.

14. Paul Messaris, *Visual Literacy: Image, Mind and Reality* (Boulder, CO: Westview Press, 1994), p. 9.

15. James Britton, *Language and Learning* (Harmondsworth, UK: Penguin Books, 1970), p. 37.

16. Jaak Panksepp, *Affective Neuroscience* (Oxford: Oxford University Press, 2004), p. 42.

17. L. S. Vygotsky, "The Teaching about Emotions," in Dorothy Robbins (ed.), *Collected Works of L. S. Vygotsky*, vol. 6 (London: Kluwer Academic, 1999), p. 165.

18. Panksepp, *Affective Neuroscience*, p. 44.

19. Ibid., p. 50.

20. Ibid., pp. 144–149.

21. See Antonio Damasio, *The Feeling of What Happens* (London: Vintage, 2000; Damasio, *Descartes' Error: Emotion, Reason and the Human Brain* (London: Vintage, 2006).

22. Damasio, *Feeling of What Happens*, pp. 182–183. Note that the "images" he refers to are not visual images, but "neural patterns or maps based on the momentary selection of neurons and circuits engaged by the interaction."

23. Jerome Kagan, *The Second Year: The Emergence of Self-Awareness* (Cambridge, MA: Harvard University Press, 1981), chap. 5.

24. Hannah Chapelle Wojciehowski, "The Floating World: Film Narrative and Viewer Diakresis," in Maarten Coegnarts and Peter Kravanja (eds.), *Embodied Cognition and Cinema* (Leuven: Leuven University Press, 2015), pp. 115–138.

25. Wojciechowski, "Floating World," p. 125.

26. Colwyn Trevarthen and Kenneth J. Aitken, "Infant Intersubjectivity: Research, Theory, and Clinical Applications," *Journal of Child Psychology and Psychiatry* 42 (2001), pp. 3–48.

27. G. di Pellegrino, L. Fadiga, L. Fogassi, V. Gallese, and G. Rizzolatti, "Understanding Motor Events: A Neurophysiological Study," *Experimental Brain Research* 91 (1992), pp. 176–180.

28. See, for instance, Maddalena Fabbri-Destro and Giacomo Rizzolatti, "Mirror Neurons and Mirror Systems in Monkeys and Humans," *Physiology* 23:3 (2008), pp. 171–179.

29. Pier Francesco Ferrari and Giacomo Rizzolatti, "Mirror Neuron Research: The Past and the Future," *Philosophical Transactions of the Royal Society B* 369 (2014), pp. 1–4, at 1.

30. Vittorio Gallese, "The 'Shared Manifold' Hypothesis: From Mirror Neurons to Empathy," *Journal of Consciousness Studies* 8:5–7 (2001), pp. 33–50; Vittorio Gallese and George Lakoff, "The Brain's Concepts: The Role of the Sensory-Motor System in Conceptual Knowledge," *Cognitive Neuropsychology* 22:3–4 (2005), pp. 455–479; Vittorio Gallese and Corrado Sinigaglia, "What Is so Special About Embodied Simulation?," *Trends in Cognitive Sciences* 15:11 (2011), pp. 512–519.

31. Vittorio Gallese and Michele Guerra, "Embodying Movies: Embodied Simulation and Film Studies," *Cinema: Journal of Philosophy and Film Studies* 3 (2012), pp. 183–210.

32. Colwyn Trevarthen, "The Child's Need to Learn a Culture," *Children and Society* 9:1 (1995), pp. 5–19.

33. See, for example, Maarten Coegnarts and Peter Kravanja (eds.), *Embodied Cognition and Cinema* (Leuven: University of Leuven Press, 2015; Gallese and Guerra, "Embodying Movies"; Torben Grodal, *Embodied Visions: Evolution, Emotion, Culture and Film* (Oxford: Oxford University Press, 2008

34. Lydia Plowman and Olivia Stevenson, "Exploring the Quotidian in Young Children's Lives at Home," *Home Cultures* 10:3 (2013), pp. 329–347.

35. See, for instance, Charles Darwin, "A Biographical Sketch of an Infant," *Mind* 2 (1877), pp. 285–294; Jean Piaget, *The Child's Conception of the World* (London: Routledge and Kegan Paul, 1928).

36. See, for instance, Matt Briggs, "Beyond the Audience: Teletubbies, Play and Parenthood," *European Journal of Cultural Studies* 9:4 (2006), pp. 441–460; Britton, *Language and Learning*; M. A. K. Halliday, *Learning How to Mean: Explorations in the Development of Language* (London: Arnold, 1975); Muriel Robinson and Bernardo Turnbull, "Veronica: An Asset Model of Becoming Literate," in Jackie Marsh (ed.), *Popular Culture, New Media and Digital Literacy in Early Childhood* (Abingdon, UK: Routledge, 2005), pp. 51–72.

BIBLIOGRAPHY

Briggs, Matt. "Beyond the Audience: Teletubbies, Play and Parenthood." *European Journal of Cultural Studies* 9:4 (2006), pp. 441–460.

Buckingham, David. "A Special Audience? Children and Television." In Janet Wasko (ed.), *A Companion to Television*. London: Blackwell, 2005, pp. 468–469.

Coegnarts, Maarten, and Peter Kravanja, eds. *Embodied Cognition and Cinema*. Leuven: University of Leuven Press, 2015.

Damasio, Antonio. *Descartes' Error: Emotion, Reason and the Human Brain*. London: Vintage, 2006.

Darwin, Charles. "A Biographical Sketch of an Infant," *Mind* 2 (1877), pp. 285–294.

Gallese, Vittorio, and Michele Guerra. "Embodying Movies: Embodied Simulation and Film Studies." *Cinema: Journal of Philosophy and Film Studies* 3 (2012), pp. 183–210.

Gallese, Vittorio, and Corrado Sinigaglia. "What Is So Special about Embodied Simulation?" *Trends in Cognitive Sciences* 15:11 (2011), pp. 512–519.

Grodal, Torben. *Embodied Visions: Evolution, Emotion, Culture and Film*. Oxford: Oxford University Press, 2008.

Lancaster, Lesley. "Staring at the Page: The Functions of Gaze in a Young Child's Interpretation of Symbolic Forms." *Journal of Early Childhood Literacy* 1:2 (2001), pp. 131–152.

Messaris, Paul. *Visual Literacy: Image, Mind and Reality*. Boulder, CO: Westview Press, 1994.

Panksepp, Jaak. *Affective Neuroscience*. Oxford: Oxford University Press, 2004.

Plowman, Lydia, and Olivia Stevenson. "Exploring the Quotidian in Young Children's Lives at Home." *Home Cultures* 10:3 (2013)), pp. 329–347.

Robinson, Muriel, and Bernardo Turnbull. "Veronica: An Asset Model of Becoming Literate." In Jackie Marsh (ed.), *Popular Culture, New Media and Digital Literacy in Early Childhood*. Abingdon, UK: Routledge, 2005, pp. 51–72.

Trevarthen, Colwyn. "The Child's Need to Learn a Culture." *Children and Society* 9:1 (1995)), pp. 5–19.

CHAPTER 34

STAR WARS, CHILDREN'S FILM CULTURE, AND FAN PARATEXTS

LINCOLN GERAGHTY

THE dominance of Hollywood in the international children's film market in many ways owes to the ebb and flow of Disney's cultural and popular appeal through history—its success in animated movie output in the 1930s and 1950s followed by television and music production in the 1980s and 1990s, and now its mega-franchise output like *Star Wars* (1977–) and the Marvel Cinematic Universe (2008–). Children's film—or more appropriately, the family film—is a form of entertainment created in Hollywood to target a general audience; it typically depicts scenarios and themes that are attractive to children (comedy, action, and adventure) and experienced by children alongside adult protagonists. It is a genre often considered to be mostly about profit. Hollywood maximizes income through a strategy of school holiday release dates backed up by aggressive marketing campaigns focused on toys, merchandise, and consumer product tie-ins. The family film really came to prominence in the 1980s following the emergence of the post-1970s blockbuster movie, which itself was the result of an increase in Hollywood output specifically targeting youthful audiences alongside a strategic shift in marketing and merchandising in which children were positioned as consumers. Scholars Noel Brown and Peter Krämer, however, have argued that we can identify the roots of the family film much earlier, and that they stretch back to the animated features of the 1920s and 1930s, as well as to Hollywood's attempt to make films for all ages that conformed to the Production Code (popularly referred to as the "Hays Code").[1] Officially known as the Motion Picture Production Code and published in 1930, it was an attempt to clean up Hollywood films—determining what content was appropriate and what was unacceptable for a public audience. Since there were no ratings for films at this time, all films conformed to the guidelines of taste and decency published in the Production Code and thus were considered suitable for general audiences. Whatever starting point we might agree on, it is evident that Hollywood has devoted much attention and funds to attracting a family audience of parents who can sit alongside their children and enjoy the movie in equal, but not necessarily the same, ways.

Cary Bazalgette and Terry Staples describe the early history of the family film in Hollywood as a reaction to the Great Depression, attracting adults and children to the cinema when financial times were tough.[2] Yet, following the argument that the family film was aimed at a general audience in order to circumvent the constraints of the Production Code, Krämer argues that, in the 1960s, Hollywood focused on younger audiences (young males in particular) because they were spending the most money going to the cinema. Although films for young children were potentially off-putting to teen audiences looking for more adult-themed movies containing sex and violence, Hollywood believed that getting kids accustomed to going to the movies early in life meant creating a loyal audience of filmgoers for the future. This, coupled with the fact that parents didn't want their children seeing violent movies and were more likely to go with them to the cinema, meant that the family film became an important part of Hollywood's strategy for increasing attendance and box office receipts.[3] As Hollywood increased production of family films that could be watched and enjoyed by children and adults on multiple levels, ancillary markets grew to surround both their distribution and reception. It is well-known that the success of George Lucas's Star Wars (1977), one of the first modern blockbusters, owed in large part to the mass merchandising push aimed at children and families—selling toys to the kids and a wholesome story of heroism and gallantry to older audiences. Since this chapter examines children's film and the surrounding paratexts that are created to support and extend it beyond the cinema screen, I will use Star Wars as my case study. Moreover, because the franchise has a large global fan-base, I will also consider how those children's paratexts, specifically the toys, have been transformed by adult fans into valuable symbols of identity and cultural capital.

Considering the reception of the blockbuster movie, Robin Wood has argued that Hollywood tends to construct the viewer as childlike and therefore receptive to the wonders of the cinematic illusion, a construction that is clearly related to the commercial success of Star Wars, its sequels The Empire Strikes Back (Irvin Kershner, 1980) and Return of the Jedi (Richard Marquand, 1983), and Steven Spielberg's Close Encounters (1977) and E.T. The Extra-Terrestrial (1982).[4] However, the prevalence and popularity of the family film also signals, according to Estella Tincknell, "one of the central concerns of the post-war moment" in that "the future of post-war society depended on the inclusion of children within its conception of the social."[5] Krämer alludes to this point in his analysis of Star Wars, arguing that it is a "family-adventure" movie that—by addressing children and parents and teens and young adults—portrays "childhood and family life in far from idealized terms."[6] Thus the film introduces children to adult themes of loneliness and longing, deceit, betrayal, and aggression, preparing them for the inevitable time when they will experience such things in adulthood. Krämer contends that because Star Wars combines action-adventure space opera with more mature messages of family life and responsibility, the film was aimed at what Time magazine called "the kid in everybody," and Lucas specifically marketed it as such almost as a counterpoint to the dystopic and bleak science-fiction movies of the 1960s and 1970s.[7] Modelled on the Disney approach, Lucas's film was a nostalgic return to the pulp sci-fi magazines of the Golden Age, radio, film, and Saturday afternoon TV serials, such as *Buck Rogers* (1939, 1950) and *Flash Gordon* (1936, 1959), and the westerns of his youth. For Adam Roberts, besides eulogizing its sci-fi heritage, *Star Wars* "translates it into something larger-scale, bigger-budget, more sophisticated and glossy," acting as an "intertextual force" looking backward "over the history of the genre itself."[8] These qualities were instrumental in making *Star Wars* appealing to children and adults on its first release, and they remain important reasons for the franchise's continued popularity and longevity with the fan community. With this in mind, I now turn to examine how the franchise has evolved from one film that was aimed at kids to become a transmedia narrative that spans cinema, television, video games, and merchandise that appeals not only to children, but also to adult fans that grew up with, and immersed themselves in, the fictional world created by George Lucas.

STAR WARS AS CHILDREN'S TRANSMEDIA FRANCHISE

Star Wars is a prime example of contemporary transmedia storytelling and a modern media franchise. The story and brand are both spread out across multiple media platforms and commodities, driven by the central narrative story arc of the ongoing battle between the forces of evil and good, for example, Sith versus Jedi, Rebellion versus Empire, and now Resistance versus First Order. *Star Wars* can be seen as a "commercial supersystem of transmedia intertextuality" as defined by Marsha Kinder.[9] Extending this, Henry Jenkins, Marc Steinberg, Colin B. Harvey, and others have described the phenomenon of transmedia storytelling, a strategy informing the creation and development of mega-media franchises like *Star Wars* through the dispersal of one story across multiple media outlets.[10] Both transmedia storytelling and media franchising contribute to how Hollywood builds on its filmic output, ensuring longevity and financial success well beyond the first iteration of a text. For Derek Johnson, "transmedia storytelling suggests cultural artistry and participatory culture, [while] 'franchising' calls equal if not more attention to corporate structure and the economic organization of that productive labor."[11] There is a clear relationship between transmedia storytelling and media franchising, and by examining how narrative develops within the *Star Wars* story world we can also see how important merchandise and other paratextual products are to the development and expansion of a fan culture.

To further the global spread and economic impact of *Star Wars*, George Lucas established the Expanded Universe (EU): an official, canonical story world that expanded the narrative beyond the films. Well-known, background, and even entirely new characters were depicted in novels and comics, starting with Alan Dean Foster's

Splinter of the Mind's Eye in 1978, then appearing continuously following Timothy Zahn's *Heir to the Empire* in 1991.[12] The EU grew as new technologies allowed Lucasfilm to develop video games and interactive experiences such as Disney's Star Tours that fitted into the wider transmedia story. Within the EU certain characters have been used as transmedia signposts, directing audiences of all ages to other media paratexts (such as the comics, novels, and film and television spin-offs) that surround the original movies (nine at the time of writing). These paratexts establish them as canon and, in turn, redirect audiences back to the movie universe. As a result, the characters that cross over are continually remade and reborn; they are signifiers of *Star Wars*'s transmedia history, carriers of inherent narrative meaning, and objects of fan cultural value. For example, Boba Fett started out as an animated character in the TV movie *Star Wars Holiday Special* (Steve Binder, 1977) and then made his first film appearance in *The Empire Strikes Back*, but then was added back into the re-release of *Star Wars*, under the modified title of *Star Wars: Episode IV—A New Hope* (George Lucas, 1997). Since then, his backstory has been fleshed out in books and comics, as well as in the prequels and animated series *Star Wars: The Clone Wars* (Dave Filoni, 2008–2014) and *Star Wars Rebels* (Dave Filoni, 2014–2018). Similar characters, such as Darth Maul, Ahsoka Tano, Grand Admiral Thrawn, and Saw Gerrera, have either started out in the original movies and moved to other paratextual platforms or were created as spin-off characters in books and television and have since been reintroduced into the movie cycle or subsequent animated series. The regular re-use and remediation of such characters, joining the different paratextual elements into one unified narrative, suggests that the *Star Wars* transmedia story is both flexible and reflexive. They have been transformed and reimagined to fit the transmedia narrative at different stages of its evolution over the last 40-plus years, but also act as catalysts for new stories and new franchise marketing opportunities.

Upon purchasing Lucasfilm in 2012, Disney's CEO Robert Iger was quoted saying that the thousands of planets and characters mapped out over thousands years of narrative history would provide the company with myriad ways of continuing the *Star Wars* story.[13] Following decades of EU material across books, comics, and games, Disney announced in 2014 that the canon would be reset in order to make the six original movies and *The Clone Wars* and *Rebels* television series "immoveable objects" in the narrative universe. New stories and texts would originate from this reset canon, underscoring Disney's strategy to rebuild *Star Wars* wholesale for a new generation.[14] In anticipation of the release of *Star Wars: Episode VII—The Force Awakens* (J. J. Abrams, 2015), this decision can be interpreted as a means of clearing the slate, deleting established characters, such as Luke and Leia's Jedi offspring, to introduce the likes of Rey and Kylo Ren (Ben Solo). But where Disney was originally criticized for abandoning the EU and antagonists like Thrawn, it is now re-using old fan favourites to attract and rebuild the universe for new audiences. As a corporate author of *Star Wars* after Lucas, Disney is keenly aware that it has to extend the franchise for future storytelling while playfully engaging with its past. New toys, associated merchandise like books and guides, and video games—in addition to the films and television series—all contribute to a complex narrative network of *Star Wars* texts. These work in tandem to underscore the pre-eminence of the new Disney strategy and recycle the mythic saga of the force. Yet at the heart of this textual network are well-established and iconic characters upon which Lucas and now Disney place tremendous narrative importance. These characters, when used strategically in marketing campaigns and in creating new backstories, are in effect the "immoveable objects" Iger had talked about. Characters become the texts, standing in as synecdochal signifiers of the *Star Wars* transmedia universe.

The transference of characters and narrative across different media platforms is emblematic of the transmedia storytelling I have already described. Henry Jenkins defines this as "stories that unfold across multiple media platforms, with each medium making distinctive contributions to our understanding of the world."[15] Each revisioning of the story adds another level of meaning, enhances the original, and makes a distinctive contribution to the *Star Wars* universe. For Jenkins, "The core aesthetic impulses behind good transmedia works are world building and seriality."[16] This statement describes *Star Wars* quite well, before and after Disney. But what has defined Disney's transmedia strategy since the acquisition is the effort to re-brand and re-establish the movie canon in the lead up to *The Force Awakens*. It recycled the world built by Lucas and added to it through the serialization of new spin-off novels and reference works. They even branded this strategy "Journey to *Star Wars: The Force Awakens*," labelling the front and back covers of new book titles with this tag line (Figure 34.1). This signalled to readers that the stories and characters contained within linked directly with what had come before and offered hints and clues about what was to come in the continuing narrative tendered by Disney. William Proctor and Matthew Freeman describe this as an example of the "transmedia economy" of *Star Wars*.[17] But even before Disney took over, Lucasfilm had manipulated and added to the *Star Wars* narrative, creating the potential for transmedia storytelling through the continual retelling and reordering of individual characters and their histories.

Merchandise and toys were important elements of the Lucasfilm EU, as they continued to be after Disney's takeover. Fans seek more content, wanting to read about the continuing adventures of Han, Luke, and Leia even though they have not appeared together in the films for a number of years. But the consumption of all kinds of physical objects and ephemera, such as toys and collectibles, also contributes to the expansion of the *Star Wars* story beyond film and television screens. Such was the popularity of the EU story world developed by Lucasfilm that both children and adult fans were able to buy action figures of characters that had never been seen on screen but were nonetheless vitally important to then-ongoing stories in the comics and novels. While Lucas himself concentrated on the three prequel films that intended to kick-start the original saga, the toys of the EU helped to keep *Star Wars* on toy store shelves and introduce the franchise to a whole new generation of children; filling the gaps for fans who had come to metaphorically inhabit the transmedia narrative of "a long time ago and in galaxy far, far away."

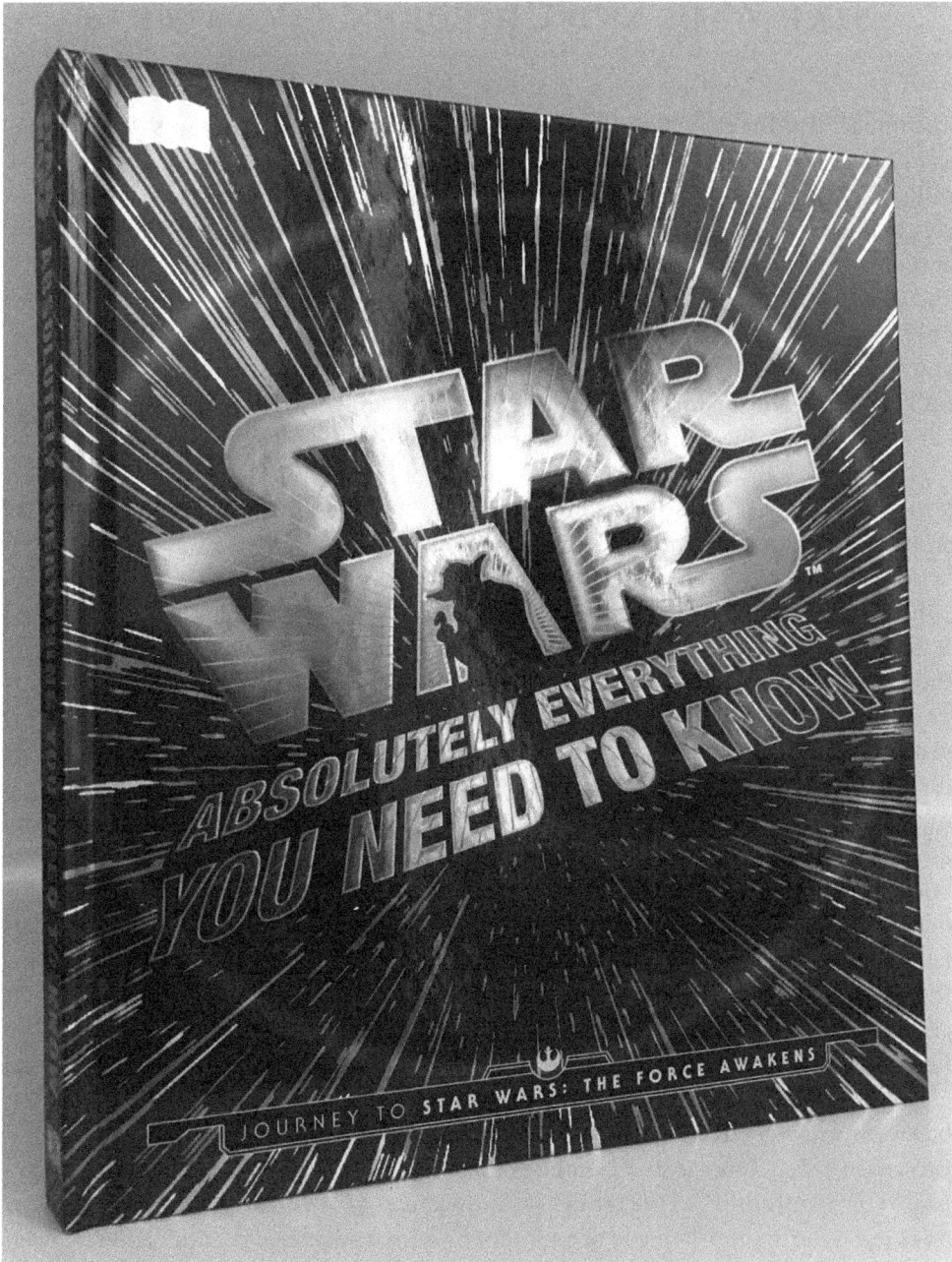

FIGURE 34.1. Disney developed the "Journey to" marketing strategy in the lead-up to the release of all three of the new trilogy movies. It was used for the books, comics, and other media. Author's collection.

STAR WARS AND CHILDREN'S PARATEXTS

The impact that the *Star Wars* action figures had on the toy industry was phenomenal, as evidenced by the fact that "in 1978 Kenner sold over 26 million figures; by 1985, 250 million." Profits from the toys, figures, lunchboxes, and video games eventually totalled $2.5 billion by the end of the first three films.[18] This was in addition to the huge takings at the box office, where *Star Wars* would follow Steven Spielberg's lead with *Jaws* (1975) and *Close Encounters of the Third Kind* and achieve blockbuster status. *Star Wars*, which only cost $11 million to make, "began as a summer movie, ran continuously into 1978, and was re-released in 1979." It earned "over $190 million in US rentals and about $250 million worldwide, on total ticket sales of over $500 million."[19] It is no secret that Lucas kept the rights to the merchandise in order to recover the investment in the film, and no doubt this is the reason Disney paid him $4 billion in 2012 for the intellectual property rights. The franchise helped to cement the summer blockbuster as part of North American film culture and made merchandising an integral part of Hollywood marketing strategy.

Justin Wyatt sees *Star Wars* as a *high-concept* franchise, the first really to approach toy merchandising with vigour, and, as a result, increase its market appeal. For Wyatt, the high-concept movie was an important part of the New Hollywood film industry. The term refers to films that are conceived as highly marketable and therefore highly profitable, as well as being visually striking and stylistically innovative. Such films are different through their "emphasis on style in production and through the integration of the film with its marketing."[20] In terms of the *Star Wars* films, we can describe them as "high concept" since they comprise what Wyatt labels "the look, the hook, and the book": "The look of the images, the marketing hooks, and the reduced narratives."[21] The fictional world of *Star Wars* that had kept children engrossed also had underlying marketing advantages: "The film's novel environment and characters have been so striking that Kenner Toys has been able to go beyond the figures in the film by adding new characters to the *Star Wars* line in keeping with the film's mythological world."[22] The infinite potential for expansion has kept the toys popular throughout the past forty years as children continued to watch and rewatch the movies and play within their own make-believe worlds. Wyatt's analysis of the high-concept blockbuster corresponds to Noel Brown's five-step, "non-textual," outline of the family film: (1) the film is marketed to appeal to the family unit; (2) the ratings system ascribes a viewing recommendation based on age and the appropriateness of a film for a young audience; (3) critics and reviewers help form the generic classification of the film with reference to its intended audience; (4) merchandising is seen as an integral part of the marketing pre- and post-release, targeting youthful audiences with toys, games, and other licensed ephemera; and (5) television helps to frame the film as family viewing by screening it at holidays and during the times of the day when children and adults tend to watch together, thus emphasizing notions of community and familial bonding.[23] The last three steps are particularly relevant to an understanding of how the non-textual elements of *Star Wars* (the toys, merchandise, and marketing campaign, including posters and adverts) work to promote and extend the story and create new arenas in which meaning and value are made. These non-textual elements are the *paratexts* of the franchise.

Therefore, the first step toward a wider consideration of *Star Wars* is to acknowledge the prominent position of what Jonathan Gray calls media *paratexts* as opposed to the centrality of specific *texts*. So, rather than study *Star Wars* as film text, we might study the related merchandise and physical ephemera that carry inherent meaning and significance in and of themselves. The peripheral texts—those associated with the commercialization of the franchise or brand such as the lunchboxes, toys, video games, and websites—are so much part of the meaning-making process that they become texts to study in their own right. Gray argues that "the paratexts may in time *become* the text, as the audience's members take their cues regarding what a text means from the paratext's images, signs, symbols, and words" rather than from the original.[24] This point helps us to understand the importance of the LEGO *Star Wars* toys and fan-made merchandise. As paratextual objects connected to *Star Wars* they serve to support the original text, but as collectible action figures how fans buy, remake, transform, and display them are often deemed more important than the movies and other related media paratexts. Therefore, they need to be analysed to fully understand the toys' appeal and fan nostalgia for the franchise: The "action figures underscore the plural in [*Star Wars*], declaring the central frame and theme to be that of a never-ending series of grand and cosmic battles of mythic proportions."[25] In this, we should also keep in mind the definition of "ancillary or paratextual materials" given in response to Gray by Martin Barker, where he argues that paratexts come into being "*because of* and *in relation to*" the original text, "*point towards the work* they relate to," are "*worth attending to*" separately from the original, and while existing "in a sea of others" have to be distinctive.[26] In the toys that fans collect and value, we see these qualities in their most physical and embodied form.

In the age of media convergence, "old and new media collide" and once-forgotten icons, symbols, images, sounds, and series from music, comics, film, and television are reborn and attract new fans to with which to share and indulge. As Jenkins asserts, convergence allows for the archiving of and searching for new forms of entertainment, where "the flow of content across multiple media platforms" links the web with older media forms, such as film and television.[27] *Star Wars*, as a long-standing movie franchise, is clearly subject to such flow across media, and through new owner Disney's own network of conglomerated outlets (television channels, movie studio, theme parks, etc.) its audience is potentially infinite. Yet Disney cannot do this alone. To spread its newly acquired intellectual property as far and wide as possible—in different forms and formats—it has undertaken a series of partnerships so as to benefit from the creative talent and energy offered by toy manufacturers. Franchises are built so as to reflect the corporate structure that bore them, but they are also influenced by changes in the wider media and entertainment industries. Johnson argues that the decline of mass production in Hollywood in the 1970s and 1980s meant that studios had to search for niche markets to promote their movies.[28] The blockbuster film-turned-franchise thus grew out of the need to stimulate renewed interest in film as a form of entertainment. As media conglomerates formed during the "merger movement" of the 1980s, due to the relaxing of anti-trust laws that prevented large-scale corporate ownership, synergy became one way of utilizing new networks of production and dissemination.[29] For Jennifer Holt, "integration" results in synergy which drives production, and thus we can see how the integrated strategies of Disney working with merchandising partners on *Star Wars* diversify potential markets and increase the dissemination and circulation of *Star Wars* as a media franchise.[30]

Modern media conglomerates seek to maintain their brands through strategies epitomized by the media franchise. Branded lines rely on corporate ownership, management, and protection of culture as intellectual property. In the case of *Star Wars*, this means that Disney protects its asset via copyright and manages it so as not to dilute the brand or risk alienating the target audience. The realignment of the *Star Wars* canon after 2014 signals its intention to assert its rights as owner of the franchise and protect the brand from alternative versions. Franchises exploit these strategies in service of consolidation and conglomeration, bringing the property under tighter control so as to prevent the brand from fading or its message from becoming confused. This affords the promise of synergy whereby the same content can dominate across markets and generate more income. For Kristin Thompson, synergy is about "selling the same narrative over and over in different media."[31] With Disney, this means continuing to produce new films and supporting television series, but also promoting *Star Wars* on its ABC network of channels, in its theme parks, and through its chain of high street stores. However, *Star Wars* is a mythic narrative, evidently very marketable, and therefore the story in its various incarnations and media-specific formats requires careful consideration and development. As a transmedia narrative, *Star Wars* forces Disney to look outside its own corporate structures to enlist creative talent, who can then drive and extend the property beyond Disney's established network reach.

In LEGO, Disney has the perfect partner to continue the merchandising machine. Since 1999, LEGO has been producing sets and mini-figures based on the *Star Wars* films and EU. Adapting well-known ships, characters, and scenarios into brick form might not have been the ultimate success it has since turned out to be. The Danish toy company has produced licensed sets based on established media franchises for some time with mixed results: LEGO sets based on other Disney films—such as *Toy Story*, *Pirates of the Caribbean*, and *The Lone Ranger*—have passed into obscurity. However, over time, LEGO has been instrumental in creating paratextual additions to the franchise, and now works with Disney to create animated shorts for the LEGO *Star Wars* website and Disney+. Following *The Force Awakens*, the series of shorts entitled *LEGO Star Wars: The Resistance Rises* (Lucasfilm, 2016) focuses on moments preceding the action of the movie, such as Poe Dameron rescuing Admiral Ackbar from Kylo Ren and the First Order. Shown on Disney's XD channel, this is an example of paratextuality: same characters, new scenarios.

Similarly, in a new series entitled *LEGO Star Wars: The Freemaker Adventures* (Lucasfilm, 2016–2017), also on XD, viewers are introduced to a new group of rebel heroes in LEGO form. Set between *The Empire Strikes Back* and *Return of the Jedi*, the series focuses on the Freemaker siblings, Rowan, Kordi, and Zander, who salvage wreckage for a living in their ship, the Star Scavenger. They become enmeshed in the struggle between the Empire and Rebellion, encountering old and new *Star Wars* characters along the way. The toys released to coincide with the series premiere combine traditional LEGO attributes such as mini-figures and movable parts, and fans of the franchise will recognize the inclusion of bounty hunter Dengar in the Eclipse Fighter set. LEGO *Star Wars* achieves balance through economy of design and the recognizability of salient features; it transforms important screen details into buildable and playable forms. According to Mark J. P. Wolf, "Instead of merely adapting a narrative, a playset will be designed to provide its user all the elements needed to re-enact a particular narrative, without requiring that the narrative be re-enacted."[32] The popularity of *Star Wars* LEGO—in toy, print, and video game form—is due in large part to "character abstraction," where the conflict inherent in the figure of the "doubled avatar" (the character in a video game compared to its source material original, for example) is alleviated through the "winsome, if somewhat mocking, representations of their cinematic selves."[33] Mini-figures represent important paratextual characters in the *Star Wars* narrative "built" from LEGO, but they are also "figurative" characters in their own right (Figure 34.2).

FIGURE 34.2. This set was released in 2019 as part of a series celebrating twenty years of *Star Wars* LEGO; a popular Hoth scene accompanied by an original Lando Calrissian 2003 collectible minifigure. Author's collection.

Star Wars has clearly affected the lives of millions of people, who not only believed as children in the make-believe world of a "galaxy far, far away," but also see the products of a multi-billion dollar merchandising campaign as integral components of the *Star Wars* experience. As Disney continues to work with companies such as LEGO in developing and expanding the fictional universe, the toys will continue to sell; they make the films, and now television series, more real. Where Robert Buerkle suggests that "LEGO acts as a signifier for childhood and toy play," creating nostalgia for past texts within a framework of "toydom," I would take this further and argue that LEGO's books, toys, and textual creations are very much part of Disney's strategy for *Star Wars* brand synergy: they reform the canon in order to create new audiences and to re-educate existing fans in preparation for new movies and spin-offs yet to come.[34] Over the years, including the run-up to the ninth instalment, *Star Wars: Episode IX—The Rise of Skywalker* (J. J. Abrams, 2019), there is no exception: merchandising and the toys have helped to make the franchise a household name. Lucas let the genie out of the bottle, and Disney is clearly capable of making the most from the potential crossover markets with partners such as LEGO. But perhaps the most important thing to consider is what the toys and associated merchandise allow fans to do: collect, make, and play.

Star Wars and Fandom

Dan Fleming sees the popular effect of playing with *Star Wars* toys as being part of what he calls "narrativization," whereby toy versions of TV and movie characters both represent the specific series and playing with the toy is informed by the familiar stories and relationships: "Throughout the 1960s the toy industry became increasingly dependent on cinema and, especially, on television for play-worthy objects that could borrow the popularity of a screen character or story. Such objects then came with a narrative attached."[35] Narrativization helps children interact with fictional reality, or make-believe, during play. This creates what Fleming terms "a semiotic space," where toys can act as transitional tools allowing children to experiment with their own developing identities and understand the adult world.[36] According to Kendall Walton, the appreciation of art, fiction, or music is similar to a child's devotion to playing in an imaginary world; paintings, novels, and plays are props in the relationship between the subject and the representational arts.[37] As children grow up, their props within their fictional world of make-believe—dolls, hobbyhorses, toy trucks, and teddy bears—are merely transformed as part of adult life: "The forms make-believe activities take do change significantly as we mature. They become more subtle, more sophisticated, less overt."[38] Although child play is described by Walton as less sophisticated, he acknowledges that examining the methods of creating imaginary worlds with the make-believe that children use during play is important in helping understand the relationships adults have with the real world, as well as with the various representations of reality seen in the visual and creative arts. For children who grow up imagining themselves as part of the

Star Wars universe, the toys are integral props in the make-believe relationship they have with that fictional world. Playing and collecting the toys affirms and brings the *Star Wars* story to life. Consequently, as Walton suggests about make-believe in adulthood, those adults who used to play with the figures begin to have a more complex relationship with the toys and figures they collected as children. They no longer see them as objects of play but as markers of personal identity, evoking memories of childhood, and as symbols of cultural capital that can be bought and traded within a fan community.

Art historian Michael Camille views collecting less as a pathology centred on economic consumption and more of "a socially creative and recuperative act," where the identity of the collector is self-fashioned through the accumulation of collectibles.[39] For Jeremy Beckett, a life-long *Star Wars* fan and toy enthusiast, adults collect the action figures for one of three reasons: they suffer from the Peter Pan Syndrome; they want to recapture their youth; or they want to get involved in a phenomenon that "has encompassed hundreds of millions of people around the world."[40] Whereas the first reason sees collectors returning to a nostalgic personal past when they played with toys and re-enacted scenes from the movies, the second reason hinges on the collector never having experienced the thrill of the original toys or movies because they neither could afford them nor had permission to buy them. Beckett's third reason for the popularity of *Star Wars* toys is largely a result of the renewed interest in the franchise created by the prequels. However, for Jonathan David Tankel and Keith Murphy, collecting "collectible" artefacts has become more than just trying to make money from the nostalgic yearnings of some die-hard fans: "For the fan, the potential for profit at some future date, while always present as in any economic transaction, is often overshadowed by the value created by the ownership of the artefact in the present."[41] John Fiske sees "the accumulation of both popular and official cultural capital," signalled through the fan collection (records, toys, books, etc.), as the "point where cultural and economic capital come together."[42] In other words, fans of popular culture such as *Star Wars*, and avid buffs of high culture such as opera, share the same desire both to know as much as they can about their subject and to collect as much physical material as they can by way of demonstrating their cultural capital.

In 2003, the official *Star Wars* fan club in Mexico held a convention to celebrate twenty-five years of *Star Wars* toy collecting. Fans and collectors from all over the world gathered in Mexico City to see, trade, and talk about the latest toys as well as the classics. It was what Dustin called in his diary of the conference, "*Star Wars* Collectors Convention in Mexico City" (2003), "pure heaven."[43] This convention attracted "celebrity" collectors, described as "Super Collectors" by Dustin, who even signed autographs for fans eager to hear their collecting and toy anecdotes. This particular revelation was interesting, since it is well documented that fans have great admiration for the stars of their favourite films and programmes, yet it slightly alters the fan-star relationship when the "star" is a collector like themselves. Quite clearly, toy-collecting fans have created their own hierarchy of esteem that not only includes the actors and producers of *Star Wars* but also members of their own community. Those, like Joseph Iglesias, who have collected toys since childhood, astounded Dustin, who was fascinated to hear about bootleg copies of his favourite figures: "From Brazilian figures made out of lead to the infamous Uzay 'Head Man; Joe [Joseph] seems to be on top of it all."[44] *Star Wars* toy collecting has become a real universe within the fictional universe created by the franchise: collector Joe can make his own Brazilian versions of famous figures, the Turkish company Uzay can make affordable bootleg figures to sell all over the world, and Kenner can produce an exclusive, members-only "*Star Wars* Convention Exclusive Silver Boba Fett with Star Case" that was distributed in Mexico City, yet all are in great demand (Figure 34.3).[45]

FIGURE 34.3. The Uzay series of bootleg *Star Wars* action figures are popular with toy collectors; attempts to get around copyright can be seen in the misspelling of *Star Wars* and Stormtrooper. Author's collection.

The fans at the Mexico City convention were working out a new identity in relation to their favourite collectibles, one based not on a particular political viewpoint but on postmodern concepts of self-identity and society. It is clearly ironic that collectors have chosen to use a licensed corporate product to define their identity; one might call it a form of surrender to the influences of US cultural hegemony. However, the fact that collectors also go beyond the boundaries set by Lucas and Kenner—creating their own versions of figures, buying and selling bootleg copies that are just as rare as official figures and revered in equal measure—signals that the hegemonic framework does not necessarily hold true when examined on a global scale. Recent scholarship on toys, action figures, and associated fan practices suggests that as multiply coded texts in their own right, they highlight the varied nature of both the fictional narrative from which they draw and emphasize the diversity of fans within and across the same fan communities. Philipp Dominik Keidl, for example, argues that while some fans may focus on the collecting and modification of action figures, others use them to make new media, such as fan videos and podcasts that spread the story across different media platforms: "In other words, those fans who belong to multiple communities of a franchise like *Star Wars* represent a form of inner-franchise trans-fandom."[46] In addition, Victoria Godwin's analysis of customized action figures used in videos, photo-stories, and fanfic suggests that the use of such toys from a range of franchises allows fans to display their "multi-dimensional fandom" creating "entirely original characters in habiting narrative worlds of their own devising."[47] In the case of the toy collectors discussed here, it is clear that the work some fans put into customizing an action figure places them and it above the mass-produced market. Such modification and customization "offer productive examples of how fans incorporate both pleasure and profit, use-value and exchange-value, into their fan practices, and how they explain or justify such practices to those within and outside their fan communities."[48] Fundamentally, modifying, playing with, and collecting paratexts like the toys allows fans to dip in and out of the imagined fantasy world of *Star Wars*, adding to and expanding the universe created by Lucas.

In his explorations of the dilemmas of modern selfhood, Anthony Giddens sees "what to do?," "how to act?," and "who to be?" as the "focal questions for everyone living in circumstances of late modernity [the here and now]."[49] Besides asking these questions, people try to answer them "either discursively or through day-to-day social behavior."[50] In what Giddens calls "the trajectory of the self," people are constantly trying to define themselves and their self-identity through reflexive examination of their "life-cycle."[51] In the *Star Wars* fantasy world, the collector-fan's self-identity is in a constant state of reflexive examination as new films are released, toys are produced, and conventions are organized. Dustin, Joe, and all the "star collectors" adapt and change their lives as they interact with each other and with the new toys they collect. Joe makes new bootleg copies to sell and display at conventions, people like Todd Chamberlain give lectures on the art of making vintage display cases, and Dustin himself feels he "can hold [his] own now after hearing these guys talk about" collecting "Lili-Ledy" collectibles.[52] *Star Wars* toys, and all their related packaging and display paraphernalia, carry intensely individualized personal meanings that define who these fan collectors are and help guide their own "trajectory of the self." Cornell Sandvoss's study of fandom suggests that "the more that approaches to fandom emphasize the element of the reader's self in the construction of meaning," or in terms of this study, their determination to collect all the figures and toys available, "the greater the degree of polysemy [multiple readings] they imply."[53] Self-reflection in fandom has often been taken to mean that texts become a blank screen on which fans reflect their own self-image; they "are *poly*semic to a degree that they become *neutro*semic—in other words, carry no inherent meaning."[54] Sandvoss asserts that "neutosemy" is the "semiotic condition in which a text allows for so many divergent readings that, intersubjectively, it does not have any meaning at all."[55] *Star Wars* toys, then, do not carry inherent meanings; rather, collecting and modifying them as part of being a fan creates the meaning.

For Jason Bainbridge, the possibility of children's entertainment becoming part of adult fan culture has always been present, but the fact that these toys are an integral part of the textual-paratextual world of the franchise brand means that they are points of "intersection for adult pleasures and childish fantasies, structured narratives and free-ranging play, material culture and digital culture—and through this breaking down of barriers, arguably become one of the most potent (if overlooked) symbols of media convergence."[56] Likewise, Bob Rehak, in an article on monster-movie merchandise, toys, and model kits, argues that such physical ephemera help map the history of fantastic media franchises, and that ignoring the material incarnations of film and television texts means we lose an understanding of their cultural persistence and commercial viability. Fan "object practices"—such as modelling, collecting, making, and modifying—bring to the fore "the physical artefacts and processes by which popular culture both remembers and recreates itself."[57] *Star Wars* collectors clearly see the toys and other merchandise ephemera as meaningful, and thus they "are not so much objects as they are congealed actions, passionate acts of seeking, selecting, and situating" the fan in an age of mass consumption and global media markets.[58] The acts of collecting, modifying, and curating show that the acquisition of commodities is not about consumption but "presents a metaphor of 'production.'"[59] Indeed, collecting *Star Wars* toys because they represent a connection to a childhood past might fit Jean Baudrillard's contention that "what you really collect is always yourself," but it also represents creativity and imagination that extends from the past and into a present and a future where joy comes from the new things that are created from the old (as in the re-modelled and bootleg action figures) and the opportunities to preserve artefacts for the wider fan community.[60]

CONCLUSION

In the examples of collecting *Star Wars* paratexts discussed here, popular children's film culture is made meaningful through memories. The fan culture built up around the franchise is not commodified, but personalized. Memories are essential to the production of subjectivity, and therefore the memories embedded within collections of toys, merchandise, and other collectibles are emblems of the self, markers of identity, and symbolic of the cultural capital that fans accumulate in their life-long engagement with a media text. Nostalgia is not so much about loss, but a romance of the self and a celebration of historical texts that no longer disappear thanks to new media technologies and spaces of fan interaction, like the convention or collectible store. Personal histories become embodied in the collected objects of children's film culture. The modifying and collecting of *Star Wars* toys today represents a new form of cultural capital because fans collect in order to possess and gain special access to the *Star Wars* movies and transmedia paratexts, making claims of ownership. Collecting the entire range of toys from the original movies up until the more modern releases becomes an important part of the competitive struggle within *Star Wars* fandom. *Star Wars* toy collecting can no longer be connected to debates over commodifying childhood; rather, it has to do with the cultural significance of international fandom and the influence of what is now a global media franchise. Fans bring their own life contexts to the toys and merchandise they collect; consequently, I would argue that a refocusing on the fans and their practices of collecting and remodelling existing toys inscribe new meanings to the paratexts of children's film, making them objects of cultural history.

Star Wars is a children's film franchise enhanced by its paratexts and made for a wide, multigenerational audience. George Lucas is the original content creator, originator of the brand, and author of a series of films and associated texts that speak to a family audience. Until Disney's takeover, the media strategy for marketing and producing new *Star Wars* films allowed for the production of parallel and multiple paratexts that opened up the Expanded Universe and helped to create and sustain a global fan community. Long gaps between film releases, particularly between the first and second sets of trilogies, and large gaps in the story world offered Lucas the opportunity to flesh out the narrative through paratextual production: from novels and comics in the Expanded Universe off-screen, the toys and collectible merchandise, to animated series and spin-offs on both film and television. Likewise, these spaces have encouraged fans to intervene and co-create their own fan paratexts—such as the remodelling action figures discussed in this chapter—that have become equally important in the continued popularity and success of the franchise. Even after Disney took control and started to re-order and police the boundaries between what was and wasn't canon, fans have continued to interact with *Star Wars* in unique and creative ways that prove the centrality and importance of paratexts to children's film culture. From unofficial memes and fan videos to official partnerships with licensed toy companies and theme parks, *Star Wars* post-Disney continues to target multiple audiences: children, adults, casual viewers, and dedicated fans. These audiences are long-standing, multigenerational, and able to engage with transmedia texts across convergent media platforms to access *Star Wars* content. How they relate to and interpret the franchise also highlights the contemporary appeal of children's film and the continuing effect of nostalgia on both general audiences and the global *Star Wars* fan community.

NOTES

1. See Noel Brown, *The Hollywood Family Film: A History, from Shirley Temple to Harry Potter* (London: I.B. Tauris, 2012); and Peter Krämer, "Would You Take Your Child to See This Film? The Cultural and Social Work of the Family-Adventure Movie," in Steve Neale and Murray Smith (eds.), *Contemporary Hollywood Cinema* (London: Routledge, 1998), pp. 294–311.

2. Cary Bazalgette and Terry Staples, "Unshrinking the Kids: Children's Cinema and the Family Film," in Cary Bazalgette and David Buckingham (eds.), *In Front of the Children: Screen Entertainment and Youth Audiences* (London: BFI Publishing, 1995), pp. 92–108, at 94.

3. See Peter Krämer, " 'It's Aimed at Kids—the Kid in Everybody': George Lucas, *Star Wars* and Children's Entertainment," in Yvonne Tasker (ed.), *Action and Adventure Cinema* (London: Routledge, 2004), pp. 358–370.

4. Robin Wood, *Hollywood from Vietnam to Reagan . . . and Beyond* (New York: Columbia University Press, 2003), p. 145.

5. Estella Tincknell, *Mediating the Family: Gender, Culture and Representation* (London: Hodder Arnold, 2005), p. 88.

6. Krämer, "It's Aimed at Kids—the Kid in Everybody."

7. Ibid.

8. Adam Roberts, *Science Fiction: The New Critical Idiom* (London: Routledge, 2000), pp. 85, 90.

9. Marsha Kinder, *Playing with Power in Movies, Television and Video Games: From Muppet Babies to Teenage Mutant Ninja Turtles* (Berkeley: University of California Press, 1991), p. 3.

10. See Henry Jenkins, *Convergence Culture: Where Old and New Media Collide* (New York: New York University Press, 2006); Marc Steinberg, *Anime's Media Mix: Franchising Toys and Characters in Japan* (Minneapolis: University of Minnesota Press, 2012); and Colin B. Harvey, *Fantastic Transmedia: Narrative Play and Memory across Science Fiction and Fantasy Storyworlds* (Basingstoke, UK: Palgrave MacMillan, 2015).

11. Derek Johnson, *Media Franchising: Creative License and Collaboration in the Culture Industries* (New York: New York University Press, 2013), p. 33.

12. Pablo Hidalgo, *Star Wars: The Essential Reader's Companion* (London: Titan Books, 2012), pp. 227–228, 303–308.

13. William Proctor and Richard McCulloch, "Introduction: From the House That George Built to the House of Mouse," in William Proctor and Richard McCulloch (eds.), *Disney's Star Wars: Forces of Production, Promotion, and Reception* (Iowa City: University of Iowa Press, 2019), pp. 6–11.

14. "The Legendary Star Wars Expanded Universe Turns a New Page," *Merchandise*, April 25, 2015, http://www.starwars.com/news/the-legendary-star-wars-expanded-universe-turns-a-new-page [accessed August 27, 2019].

15. Jenkins, *Convergence Culture*, p. 334.

16. Henry Jenkins, "The Aesthetics of Transmedia: In Response to David Bordwell (Part Two)," *Confessions of an Aca-Fan: The Official Weblog of Henry Jenkins*, 2009, http://henry jenkins.org/2009/09/the_aesthetics_of_transmedia_i_1.html [accessed August 27, 2019].

17. William Proctor and Matthew Freeman, " 'The First Step into a Smaller World': The Transmedia Economy of *Star Wars*" in Mark J. P. Wolf (ed.), *Revisiting Imaginary Worlds: A Subcreation Studies Anthology* (New York: Routledge, 2016), pp. 223–245.

18. Tom Engelhardt, *The End of Victory Culture: Cold War America and the Disillusioning of a Generation* (Amherst: University of Massachusetts Press, 1998), p. 269.

19. Kristin Thompson and David Bordwell, *Film History: An Introduction*, 2nd ed. (Boston: McGraw Hill, 2003), p. 522.

20. Justin Wyatt, *High Concept: Movies and Marketing in Hollywood* (Austin: University of Texas Press, 1994), p. 20.

21. Wyatt, *High Concept*, p. 22.

22. Ibid., p. 153.

23. Brown, *Hollywood Family Film*, pp. 6–8.

24. Jonathan Gray, *Show Sold Separately: Promos, Spoilers, and Other Media Paratexts* (New York: New York University Press, 2010), p. 46.

25. Gray, *Show Sold Separately*, p. 180.

26. Martin Barker, "Speaking of 'Paratexts': A Theoretical Revisitation," *Journal of Fandom Studies* 5:3 (2017), pp. 235–249, at 242–243. Italics in the original text.

27. Jenkins, *Convergence Culture*, p. 2.

28. Johnson, *Media Franchising*, pp. 68–69.

29. Tino Balio, "'A Major Presence in All the World's Important Markets': The Globalization of Hollywood in the 1990s," in Steve Neale and Murray Smith (eds.), *Contemporary Hollywood Cinema* (London: Routledge, 1998), pp. 58–71, at 61.

30. Jennifer Holt, *Empires of Entertainment: Media Industries and the Politics of Deregulation, 1980–1996* (New Brunswick, NJ: Rutgers University Press, 2011), p. 3.

31. Kristin Thompson, *Storytelling in Film and Television* (Cambridge, MA: Harvard University Press, 2003), p. 82.

32. Mark J. P. Wolf, "Adapting the Death Star into LEGO: The Case of LEGO Set #10188," in Mark J. P. Wolf (ed.), *LEGO Studies: Examining the Building Blocks of a Transmedial Phenomenon* (New York: Routledge, 2014), pp. 15–39, at 20.

33. Jessica Aldred, "(Un)Blocking the Transmedial Character: Digital Abstraction as Franchise Strategy in Traveller's Tales' LEGO Games," in Mark J. P. Wolf (ed.), *LEGO Studies: Examining the Building Blocks of a Transmedial Phenomenon* (New York: Routledge, 2014), pp. 105–117, at 106.

34. Robert Buerkle, "Playset Nostalgia: LEGO *Star Wars: The Video Game* and the Transgenerational Appeal of the LEGO Video Game Franchise," in Mark J. P. Wolf (ed.), *LEGO Studies: Examining the Building Blocks of a Transmedial Phenomenon* (New York: Routledge, 2014), pp. 118–152, at 148.

35. Dan Fleming, *Powerplay: Toys as Popular Culture* (Manchester, UK: Manchester University Press, 1996), p. 102.

36. Fleming, *Powerplay*, pp. 201–202.

37. Kendall L. Walton, *Mimesis as Make-Believe: On the Foundations of the Representational Arts* (Cambridge, MA: Harvard University Press, 1990), p. 11.

38. Walton, *Mimesis as Make-Believe*, p. 12.

39. Quoted in Janet Staiger, "Cabinets of Transgression: Collecting and Arranging Hollywood Images," *Particip@tions* 1:3 (2005).

40. Jeremy Beckett, *The Official Price Guide to Star Wars™ Memorabilia* (New York: House of Collectibles, 2005), p. 4.

41. Jonathan David Tankel and Keith Murphy, "Collecting Comic Books: A Study of the Fan and Curatorial Consumption," in Cheryl Harris and Alison Alexander (eds.), *Theorizing Fandom: Fans, Subculture and Identity* (Cresskill: Hampton Press, 1998), pp. 55–68, at 56.

42. John Fiske, "The Cultural Economy of Fandom," in Lisa A. Lewis (ed.), *The Adoring Audience: Fan Culture and Popular Media* (London: Routledge, 1992), pp. 30–49, 43.

43. Dustin, "*Star Wars* Collectors Convention in Mexico City," Rebelscum.com, July 14, 2003, http://www.rebelscum.com/story/actionfigure/Star_Wars_Collectors_Convention_In_Mexico_City_43924.asp [accessed November 25 2021].

44. Dustin, "*Star Wars* Collectors."

45. According to Jeremy Beckett, the "Turkish line of Uzay bootleg figures is without a doubt the most well-known line of *Star Wars* bootlegs in the world." The specific figure mentioned by Dustin, "Head Man," is an ultra-rare figure based on the official Emperor's Royal Guard figure from *Return of the Jedi* (1983) but with a chromed head and shield. The "*Star Wars* Convention Exclusive Silver Boba Fett with Star Case" was also available online from Amazon.com in the United States and Canada. Jeremy Beckett, *The Official Price Guide to Star Wars™ Memorabilia* (New York: House of Collectibles, 2005), p. 209.

46. Philipp Dominik Keidl, "Between Textuality and Materiality: Fandom and the Mediation of Action Figures," *Film Criticism* 42:2 (2018).

47. Victoria Godwin, "Customized Action Figures: Multi-dimensional Fandom and Fannish Fiction," *Journal of Fandom Studies* 2:2 (2014), pp. 111–125, 122–123.

48. Victoria Godwin, "Fan Pleasure and Profit: Use-Value, Exchange-Value, and One-Sixth Scale Action Figure Customization," *Journal of Fandom Studies* 4:1 (2016), pp. 37–54, at 40.

49. Anthony Giddens, *Modernity and Self-Identity: Self and Society in the Late Modern Age* (Cambridge, UK: Polity Press, 1991), p. 70.

50. Giddens, *Modernity and Self-Identity*, p. 70.

51. Ibid., p. 14.

52. Chamberlain is quoted by Dustin. See Dustin, "*Star Wars* Collectors Convention."

53. Cornel Sandvoss, *Fans: The Mirror of Consumption* (Cambridge, UK: Polity Press, 2005), p. 126.

54. Sandvoss, *Fans*, p. 126.

55. Ibid.

56. Jason Bainbridge, "Fully Articulated: The Rise of the Action Figure and the Changing Face of 'Children's' Entertainment," in Alan McKee, Christy Collis, and Ben Hamley (eds.), *Entertainment Industries: Entertainment as a Cultural System* (London: Routledge, 2012), pp. 31–44, at 41.

57. Bob Rehak, "Materializing Monsters: Aurora Models, Garage Kits and the Object Practices of Horror Fandom," *Journal of Fandom Studies* 1:1 (2013), pp. 27–45, at 43.

58. Bill Brown, *A Sense of Things: The Object Matter of American Literature* (Chicago: University of Chicago Press, 2003), p. 146.

59. Susan Stewart, *On Longing: Narratives of the Miniature, the Gigantic, the Souvenir, the Collection* (Durham, NC: Duke University Press), p. 164.

60. Jean Baudrillard, *The System of Objects*, trans. James Benedict (London: Verso, 2005), p. 97.

BIBLIOGRAPHY

Aldred, Jessica. "(Un)Blocking the Transmedial Character: Digital Abstraction as Franchise Strategy in Traveller's Tales" LEGO Games." In Mark J. P. Wolf (ed.), *LEGO Studies: Examining the Building Blocks of a Transmedial Phenomenon*. New York: Routledge, 2014, pp. 105–117.

Bainbridge, Jason. "Fully Articulated: The Rise of the Action Figure and the Changing Face of 'Children's' Entertainment." In Alan McKee, Christy Collis, and Ben Hamley (eds.), *Entertainment Industries: Entertainment as a Cultural System*. London: Routledge, 2012, pp. 31–44.

Balio, Tino. "'A Major Presence in All the World's Important Markets': The Globalization of Hollywood in the 1990s." In Steve Neale and Murray Smith (eds.), *Contemporary Hollywood Cinema*. London: Routledge, 1998, pp. 58–71.

Barker, Martin. "Speaking of 'Paratexts': A Theoretical Revisitation." *Journal of Fandom Studies* 5:3 (2017), pp. 235–249.

Bazalgette, Cary, and Terry Staples. "Unshrinking the Kids: Children's Cinema and the Family Film." In Cary Bazalgette and David Buckingham (eds.), *In Front of the Children: Screen Entertainment and Youth Audiences*. London: BFI Publishing, 1995, pp. 92–108.

Brown, Noel. *The Hollywood Family Film: A History, from Shirley Temple to Harry Potter*. London: I.B. Tauris, 2012.

Buerkle, Robert. "Playset Nostalgia: LEGO *Star Wars: The Video Game* and the Transgenerational Appeal of the LEGO Video Game Franchise." In Mark J. P. Wolf (ed.), *LEGO Studies: Examining the Building Blocks of a Transmedial Phenomenon*. New York: Routledge, 2014, pp. 118–152.

Fiske, John. "The Cultural Economy of Fandom." In Lisa A. Lewis (ed.), *The Adoring Audience: Fan Culture and Popular Media*. London: Routledge, 1992, pp. 30–49.

Fleming, Dan. *Powerplay: Toys as Popular Culture*. Manchester, UK: Manchester University Press, 1996.

Godwin, Victoria. "Customized Action Figures: Multi-dimensional Fandom and Fannish Fiction." *Journal of Fandom Studies* 2:2 (2014), pp. 111–125.

Godwin, Victoria. "Fan Pleasure and Profit: Use-Value, Exchange-Value, and One-Sixth Scale Action Figure Customization." *Journal of Fandom Studies* 4:1 (2016), pp. 37–54.

Gray, Jonathan. *Show Sold Separately: Promos, Spoilers, and Other Media Paratexts*. New York: New York University Press, 2010.

Harvey, Colin B. *Fantastic Transmedia: Narrative Play and Memory across Science Fiction and Fantasy Storyworlds*. Basingstoke, UK: Palgrave MacMillan, 2015.

Holt, Jennifer. *Empires of Entertainment: Media Industries and the Politics of Deregulation, 1980–1996*. New Brunswick, NJ: Rutgers University Press, 2011.

Jenkins, Henry. *Convergence Culture: Where Old and New Media Collide*. New York: New York University Press, 2006.

Johnson, Derek. *Media Franchising: Creative License and Collaboration in the Culture Industries*. New York: New York University Press, 2013.

Keidl, Philipp Dominik, "Between Textuality and Materiality: Fandom and the Mediation of Action Figures." *Film Criticism* 42:2 (2018).

Kinder, Marsha. *Playing with Power in Movies, Television and Video Games: From Muppet Babies to Teenage Mutant Ninja Turtles*. Berkeley: University of California Press, 1991.

Krämer, Peter. "Would You Take Your Child to See This Film? The Cultural and Social Work of the Family-Adventure Movie." In Steve Neale and Murray Smith (eds.), *Contemporary Hollywood Cinema*. London: Routledge, 1998, pp. 294–311.

Krämer, Peter. "'It's Aimed at Kids—the Kid in Everybody': George Lucas, *Star Wars* and Children's Entertainment." In Yvonne Tasker (ed.), *Action and Adventure Cinema*. London: Routledge, 2004, pp. 358–370.

Proctor, William, and Matthew Freeman. "'The First Step into a Smaller World': The Transmedia Economy of Star Wars." In Mark J. P. Wolf (ed.), *Revisiting Imaginary Worlds: A Subcreation Studies Anthology*. New York: Routledge, 2016, pp. 223–245.

Proctor, William, and Richard McCulloch. "Introduction: From the House That George Built to the House of Mouse." In William Proctor and Richard McCulloch (eds.), *Disney's Star Wars: Forces of Production, Promotion, and Reception*. Iowa City: University of Iowa Press, 2019, pp. 6–11.

Rehak, Bob. "Materializing Monsters: Aurora Models, Garage Kits and the Object Practices of Horror Fandom." *Journal of Fandom Studies* 1:1 (2013), pp. 27–45.

Sandvoss, Cornel. *Fans: The Mirror of Consumption*. Cambridge, UK: Polity Press, 2005.

Steinberg, Marc. *Anime's Media Mix: Franchising Toys and Characters in Japan*. Minneapolis: University of Minnesota Press, 2012.

Tankel, Jonathan David, and Keith Murphy. "Collecting Comic Books: A Study of the Fan and Curatorial Consumption." In Cheryl Harris and Alison Alexander (eds.), *Theorizing Fandom: Fans, Subculture and Identity*. Cresskill: Hampton Press, 1998, pp. 55–68.

Tincknell, Estella. *Mediating the Family: Gender, Culture and Representation*. London: Hodder Arnold, 2005.

Wolf, Mark J. P. "Adapting the Death Star into LEGO: The Case of LEGO Set #10188." In Mark J. P. Wolf (ed.), *LEGO Studies: Examining the Building Blocks of a Transmedial Phenomenon*. New York: Routledge, 2014, pp. 15–39.

Wood, Robin. *Hollywood from Vietnam to Reagan…and Beyond*. New York: Columbia University Press, 2003.

Wyatt, Justin. *High Concept: Movies and Marketing in Hollywood*. Austin: University of Texas Press, 1994.

CHAPTER 35

NORWEGIAN TWEEN GIRLS AND EVERYDAY LIFE THROUGH DISNEY TWEEN FRANCHISES

INGVILD KVALE SØRENSSEN

THE relationship between children and children's films is not an isolated one. Researchers have pointed out the medialization in children's lives, where ideas, characters, and plots from movies and television shows become integrated into children's play.[1] In addition, media and popular culture can act as a catalyst and as a ticket into peer-group culture.[2] After spending four months with girls in two after-school programmes in two schools in Norway in 2008, I observed that the Disney franchises *Hannah Montana* (2006–2011) and *High School Musical* (2006–2008) were highly visible actors in the schools.[3] They were visible by being included in online play, physical play, in discussions, and via merchandise. Disney's *Hannah Montana* and *High School Musical* are aimed at the tween audience.[4] *Tween* is a concept and a category encompassing those who are seen to reside in the space between childhood and adolescence, with an approximate age range of eight to twelve years.[5] Tweenness is configured, both by Disney and in research, as an ambivalent category in which children are thought to be moving forward into their teens and simultaneously looking back at childhood.[6] This prompted me to take a closer look at the phenomenon This chapter thus explores how Norwegian tween girls have domesticated the Disney tween franchises of *Hannah Montana* and *High School Musical* in their everyday lives in relation to age, gender, and daily practices.

DISNEY IN RESEARCH

Scholars have researched various aspects of the Walt Disney Company. A large body of this research is concerned with Disney content.[7] Another strand of research focuses on the "Disneyization" of society and how Disney influences and constructs culture and social life.[8] The *Hannah Montana* and *High School Musical* franchises have been the focus of some of these studies. Natalie Coulter, for example, explores how Disney becomes immersed in childhood histories, from toddlers to tweens, through different Disney franchises.[9] Some studies focus on how girls talk about love and friendship through *High School Musical* and *Hannah Montana*, while others focus on how gender and beauty are constructed through *Hannah Montana*.[10] This chapter looks at how the Disney tween franchises became part the everyday lives of Norwegian "tweenage" girls.

DISNEY IN NORWAY

Disney is part of Norwegian everyday life. In fact, Disney's place in Western society seems to be taken for granted, as Richard deCordova has argued: "Today something like a sacred connection exists between Mickey Mouse and the idealized childhood."[11] As in the rest of Scandinavia, Disney's products have an exceptional position in Norway. For example, Scandinavians have incorporated the *Donald Duck & Co* magazine into their culture in a way that is unique. Norway has one of the highest per-person consumption rates of the *Donald Duck & Co* magazine in the world.[12] With Disney Channel Scandinavia, which started broadcasting in 2003, Disney's presence in Norway has grown substantially: according to the public relations manager at Disney Channel Scandinavia, "Disney Channel is the most seen children's channel in Norway amongst children 3–14 as of the last 12 months (August 08–July 09)."[13] In addition to being the first choice of Norwegian children when watching television, the Disney market in Norway differed from that of other Scandinavian and European markets by being particularly strong.[14] Because a majority of Norwegian tweens at the time of the fieldwork were highly exposed to the Disney tween franchises, and because these franchises were highly visible in the fieldwork, there was a need to explore how the girls made sense of the media texts and how they incorporated them in their daily lives.

THEORETICAL UNDERPINNINGS: DOMESTICATING DISNEY

To explore Disney tween franchises *Hannah Montana* and *High School Musical* in the lived lives of Norwegian tween girls, I make use of domestication theory. *Domestication* as a concept was, according to Hartmann, Berker, Punie, and Ward, "developed to describe and analyze processes of (media) technology's acceptance, rejection and use."[15] Domestication theory seeks to make sense of people's perspectives on, and actions in relation to, media.[16] A useful aspect of domestication theory perspective is that instead of looking at how people are being influenced by media, the focus instead is on how people are domesticating and enacting the media within the household and in their daily lives.[17] Domestication can therefore be a tool to help us look beyond the dichotomous structure versus agency relationship between the audience and the media text, and instead examine the reciprocal constitutive enactment of both.

There are two strands of domestication theory: a media studies version that originated in the early 1990s, and a sciences and technology (STS) version.[18] The media studies version operates in four phases: appropriation, objectification, incorporation, and conversion.[19] The STS version focuses on three dimensions: (a) the construction of practices related to an artefact; (b) construction of the meaning of the artefact; and (c) the cognitive processes related to the learning of practices and meaning-making.[20] When examining my data, I looked at how the girls—through their talk of Disney Channel and its content—domesticated both the channel and the content within the three dimensions of the STS version—namely, the *praxis*, *meaning*, and *learning* dimensions. My emphasis is on how Disney tween media texts became part of Norwegian girls' everyday practices, how Norwegian girls' constructed meanings in their meeting with the media texts, and how they used Disney as part of their biographical narratives. These three dimensions together can inform how Disney—in both form and content—was domesticated in the daily lives of the girls in this study.

A main pillar in the STS version of domestication theory is a focus on action. Enabling this view is actor-network-theory (ANT). ANT is based on a co-constructionist perspective that does not favour humans but also scrutinizes non-human entities as taking part in the construction of what we can call reality. ANT, according to Jonathan Murdoch, seeks to "identify how relations and entities come into being together."[21] A strength of ANT in this study is its focus on understanding the social world, as far as possible, without a priori notions of what that world *is* and without imposing a priori assumptions on either the girls or the Disney tween franchises. An important aspect here is a focus on the doings, the enactment, and the meetings between actors, both human and non-human. A researcher should avoid placing actors in ready-made categories and should let them, as Bruno Latour suggests, "unfold their own differing cosmos, no matter how counter-intuitive they appear."[22] Knut Sørensen suggests we can draw on ANT as a theoretical resource in relation to domestication theory: "Domestication may be seen as the process through which an artefact becomes associated with practices, meanings, people and other artefacts in the construction of intersecting large and small networks."[23] Drawing on ANT, I am able to navigate away from a strictly social constructionist view and a strictly deterministic view, and look instead at how the Disney tween franchises, and the girls, were enacted and co-produced in the meeting between them.

The term *assemblages* is used as a means of conceptualizing how social actors affect one another in a particular context. As Jonathan Law and Annemarie Mol state, "An actor does not act alone. It acts in relation to other actors, linked up with them."[24] Actors together make up assemblages, which are composed of heterogeneous elements, both human and non-human (e.g., media texts) that enter into relations with one another.[25] By acknowledging that both human and non-human entities take part in constructing how everyday practices come into being, we can talk of a co-construction or co-production of the social and the artefacts. According to Latour, the social is not the glue that holds society together—rather, the artefacts and the material are the glue holding together what we call the social.[26] I will now explore what the assemblage of Disney's media texts *Hannah Montana* and *High School Musical* and the girls in this study produced.

METHODOLOGICAL AND ANALYTICAL APPROACH

This chapter is based on a larger study on tweens, consumption, and everyday life.[27] The research design consisted of an ethnographic-inspired observation in two after-school programmes in a large town in Norway, focus-group interviews in the after-school programmes, individual interviews with both girls and boys, and interviews with the parents of seven girls. The data used in this chapter are based on the individual in-depth and semi-structured interviews with seven girls recruited from the after-school programmes.[28] The focus in the interviews was on *High School Musical* and *Hannah Montana* and the everyday lives of the girls. The study was conducted in accordance with the ethical requirements of the Norwegian Ethical Board for Social Research. Informed consent was obtained from the girls, who were also told that they could withdraw at any time. The girls interviewed were all between nine and eleven years of age; because they were underage, I received written consent from their parents as well. The interviews were recorded and transcribed verbatim. To ensure anonymity, pseudonyms are used in the chapter excerpts.

My approach to analysis is an abductive one.[29] This means that what I ask, what I look for, and how I interpret my data are informed by the theoretical framework of the domestication theory and ANT, scrutinizing how Disney and the girls as human and non-human actors were enacted in the meeting between them. The transcribed interviews were indexed with numerous categories using the computer software NVivo.[30] This followed several readings of the interviews. Patterns emerge not by themselves, but as they are interpreted by the researchers and the theoretical framework. Because I was interested in the interrelationship and co-production of human and non-human entities, my focus in the coding process was on seeing how *High School Musical* and *Hannah Montana* and the girls were enacted in the different assemblages where they appeared.

Viewed through this analytical lens, it became clear that *High School Musical* and *Hannah Montana* were enacted differently depending on different assemblages. It was also clear in the data that *High School Musical* and *Hannah Montana* took part in the co-production of the girls' identity performances in one way or another. Making use of the three dimensions of the STS version of domestication theory, the chapter explores how the Disney Tween media texts were domesticated as part of a praxis dimension; how meaning was domesticated, with focus on gender; and the learning dimension, where the focus is on how the girls spoke about growing older through the Disney tween franchises.

THE PRAXIS DIMENSION: THE DISNEY CHANNEL AS EVERYDAY PRAXIS

In my data, the Disney Channel served as a common denominator and as praxis, and these girls seemed to view the presence of Disney in their everyday lives as a given. The girls I interviewed and observed would discuss the media texts, play with "dolls" on-line, act out scenes, dance and sing the songs, and talk about both the stars and what happened in the media texts. Several of the girls had *High School Musical* and *Hannah Montana* stationery and clothes.

In addition to the Disney Tween franchises being referenced to in social settings, in the interviews the girls would talk about the Disney Channel as *their channel*, as something that was a part of what they would do, or watch, daily, thus solidifying the Disney Channel as being domesticated as a praxis. The girls not only reported that they watched the Disney Channel for specific content; they also told me that they watched the channel even when what they wanted to see the channel wasn't on:

CATHY: *High School Musical* is boring. I've seen it so many times now, 'cause it's always on Disney Channel, and I can't do anything about that.
INGVILD: So then you have to watch?
CATHY: Yeah, if I don't have anything else to do.
INGVILD: So you've seen *High School Musical* several times even though you think it's boring?
CATHY: Yes.

The literature on tweens, such as that by Martin Lindstrom and Patricia Seybold and by James McNeal, often tends to portray the tween market as fickle and difficult to reach and hold on to.[31] My interviewees, however, claimed to like what was being served on the Disney Channel; but at the same time, they expressed a feeling of powerlessness in relation to what was being broadcast. On the one hand, the interviewees told a story of tweens watching what is being served to them as they might be an undeserved market, not having anything else to choose from in concurrence with how Disney Channel saw their tween audience.[32] On the other hand, this also says something about the activity of watching television. Watching television is not necessarily an all-encompassing, deliberate activity; it might just be engaged in to pass the time.[33] Hence, what the girls watched is not necessarily the main issue; rather, it is that they domesticated and incorporated Disney Channel into their daily lives.

Cindy White and Elizabeth Preston and Karen Lury have discussed the concepts of *place* and *space* in children's television channels.[34] By establishing a channel identity that the girls in this study seemed to relate to, the Disney Channel became such a place and space, as is evident in the girls' description of it "their" channel, even though its shows might not always be what they wanted to watch. Kristin expressed this notion of a channel aimed at her:

INGVILD: Why do you watch Disney Channel so much then?
KRISTIN: Because the others—we have like 600 channels—and there are only grown-up channels, so the only children's channels are Jetix, Boomerang and Toon Disney and Disney.

The question of *how* one watches surfaces here. That some of the tweens reported watching the Disney Channel despite not being pleased with what was being aired raises the questions: How attentive were they when they turned the television set on, and is this important? In line with the above quotations, I would suggest that the act of turning the Disney Channel on is itself the routine—not only *what* is being watched, or not watched—and therefore becomes part of the praxis dimension.

In contrast to the practice of turning on Disney Channel simply because of routine, several of the girls reported watching both the movies and episodes of the TV series several times *intentionally*, not simply because they were being aired. In fact, the girls reported having, and wishing for, the *Hannah Montana* and *High School Musical* DVDs of these shows that they had already watched repeatedly. Most of the girls told me that they really enjoyed watching the *High School Musical* movies over and over again so they could learn the dances and the songs. Such repeat watching of content has also been documented in previous research on tweens.[35] Thus, the mere act of watching television becomes an ambiguous and complex project, with variations in how attentive the audience is and how intentionally they have chosen the content. On the one hand, the girls I interviewed clearly considered the Disney Channel to be catering to them, as they domesticated it as "their channel." On the other hand, they actually had seen the content of *High School Musical* and *Hannah Montana* several times, whether they liked it or not. This begs the question: *Why* watch what you do not like?

In addition to it being "their channel," some of the girls described a motivation to keep up with the Disney Channel content as a social tool and as a means ensuring social inclusion. Kirsten Drotner argues that media today acts as a catalyst in the formation of social networks.[36] That the girls watched Disney tween content to gain social currency was evident in my interviews. The use of media and consumer goods as social currency and as a ticket into peer-group culture is a well-established research finding.[37] Gilles Brougere claims that "the sharing of common knowledge is crucial to children's peer groups"; and David Buckingham refers to the concept of "phatic speech."[38] Being able to engage in phatic speech—defined by Buckingham as "speech which serves simply to establish and maintain communication"—and using the tween content as social currency was emphasized in several of the interviews.[39] Katie articulated this quite explicitly when she told me that she wanted to see the premiere of the second *High School Musical* because she knew that her friends would be talking about it at school the following Monday:

KATIE: It's not really that important to me but it is fun when they talk about it at school and [to] be able to know about it so that I can talk about it.

This is part of what solidifies the Disney tween franchises as a cultural common denominator and an important cultural reference for these girls. When there is a feeling of needing, if not to watch the whole movie or series, then at least to have basic knowledge of the content, it becomes, in a way, a mandatory social cultural reference curriculum. Even the girls who resented the Disney tween media texts admitted to having seen parts of them. This is not to say that it generates normative pressure to obtain these social currencies. However, in my data, everyone, no matter how they felt about the content, knew about it and had seen at least parts of it. As David Morley and Roger Silverstone observe: "Television is part of our socialization just as we are socialized to television—in parlours, sitting rooms and kitchens. We learn from television; television provides the stuff of family talk and neighbourhood gossip."[40]

Not only did content figure as social currency, but it could also be a part of a social setting. Some of the girls reported having parties and watching the premieres of Disney Channel Original Movies as an activity they had participated in at one time or another. Thus, with regard to how the media content is viewed, there are different ways of watching. The interviewees reported watching alone before and after school. They would watch with a group of friends when visiting, and they would attend, or arrange, parties to watch the season premiere of the sitcom, and of the movies. How one watches Disney tween content is, in this way, context and content dependent. Therefore, in addition to using the media content as social currency, watching as a planned social activity also contributed to the Disney Channel's being a part of the girls' social and personal lives. Exposing themselves to the Disney tween franchises seems to figure as an identity trait of the interviewees. Hence, the Disney tween franchises were not only domesticated as part of their daily lives but also as an actor in what we can call a "friendship assemblage." The girls would expose themselves to media content for the sake of doing friendship and as a strategy to avoid being left out, as Katie explained.

There seem to be several reasons for watching the Disney tween content. And what accounted for the domestication of different Disney tween franchises into daily life appears to boil down to the varied reasons for watching. One reason is taste. The girls would watch it if they enjoyed it. Another factor has to do with social relationships and friendship, where the Disney Channel facilitated the doing of friendship and the avoidance of social exclusion. And yet another reason seems to be the place the Disney Channel had obtained with the interviewees as being domesticated as part of their daily lives.

Having established that the Disney Channel was domesticated as a daily routine for the girls in this study, I now turn to the meaning dimension. In other words, I examine how the girls described and divided the audience according to the type of television programme offered by Disney. Next, I will explore how the content was domesticated in relation to gender in the descriptions of the audience by the audience.

The Meaning Dimension: The Audience Constructing the Audience

This section concentrates on how the girls constructed the audience for *High School Musical* and *Hannah Montana* in relation to gender. The focus is on how the girls domesticated the meaning of the content as belonging to girl or boy practices (or both). Discussions of media and television shows can be a stage for the performance of gender.[41] Mirroring Joseph Jay Tobin's findings, my data indicated a clear construction of stereotypical girl and boy practices. Drawing from both Tobin's work and my own study, one could argue that things seen as stereotypically masculine and stereotypically feminine are domesticated and incorporated, not only as performances, but also as foundational understandings of what boy practices and girl practices consist of, thus reproducing gender stereotypes and gender boundaries.[42] Consequently, a co-interpretation of the content and of the self can be said to transpire. The content can be perceived as offering resources for the construction of gender practices while, simultaneously, these resources are the result of such interpretations of the content.

The girls, as well as the boys in the larger study, all seemed to agree on what content was considered to be for boys and what was intended for girls and subsequently domesticated that content correspondingly. To sum it up briefly: they reported that flirting and romance was for girls, and fighting and comedy was for boys. Since both Disney texts focus on romance and lack fighting, in my data they generated an understanding of being "typical" girl content; that is, there was an understanding—and subsequently a construction—of gender in relation to this content. Because the media texts were considered to be mainly for girls, boys tended to be excluded the from the content. Boys were constructed as a more homogenous group; whereas girls were also constructed through differentiation. This is not to suggest that all boys were constructed as being homogenous. However, as the topic of conversation was what is typically understood as a "girl thing," there was more room for different girl performances with respect to the content. According to Barry Thorne, children engage in *borderwork*, which is to differentiate one's self and one's gender by describing what one is not, and thus what the other gender is.[43] Erving Goffman coined the term *genderism* as a behavioural practice, referring to moments in life that evoke stereotypic beliefs as men and women "play out the differential human nature claimed for them."[44] In the quotations that follow, gender practices are constructed through this type of borderwork and genderism.

In my data the content's genre played a pivotal part in determining how it was domesticated. The *High School Musical* trilogy was domesticated as a girl-text and girl practice. The sitcom *Hannah Montana*, in contrast, could be incorporated in both girl and boy practices. Genre is the main difference between the two media texts, where we have (a) the sitcom, based on humour, and (b) the trilogy, which addresses the larger questions in life and focuses on self-growth through intra- and interpersonal relationships. The trilogy can also be said to belong in the genre of romantic movies, and several of the interviewees described romance and flirting as something for girls:

MARY: Like boys they don't usually like the romantic movies, and it's some love and kissing and then they get like, ew, and this it's gross, and it's for nine to fifteen-years old because like eight-year-olds don't really understand a lot of what's happening, at least not in English, they don't understand what they say and stuff.

Mary was ten years old at the time of the interview and, by her own account, belonged to the age category that enjoys the content. However, she stated that boys (in general and regardless of age, it seems) thought it was "gross." Therefore, when she talked about age, she implicitly referred to girls. Mary implicitly drew on an understanding of the maturity that girls are perceived to achieve before boys. Boys are, in Mary's statement, constructed as uninterested in romance, a belief that mirrors the findings of previous research.[45] Mary indicated that there are two different skills one needs to be able to understand the content—one needs to know English, and one needs to understand interpersonal relationships.

Generally, when the children talked about *High School Musical*, the trilogy appeared to generate a more typical girl-movie label and was domesticated as belonging to the girl realm. In contrast to this somewhat rigid perception that *High School Musical* is intended for girls, *Hannah Montana* was typically described as more flexible and versatile media content. In my data, it was possible for *Hannah Montana* to be domesticated as a boy practice as well. The girls would suggest that the sitcom had elements that both girls and boys could enjoy. In the segment below, Cathy talked about *Hannah Montana* and who she thought the sitcom was for:

CATHY: I think it's made mostly for girls because it's a girl's life we see, her; but it's also fun for boys to look more at Jackson and Rico who fight so it's, like, I think it's mostly girls because you see a girl's life how she lives, but also for boys because it's a little funny.

Cathy's response suggests that being able to identify with the main character is important to liking something. On a general note, it seems that Cathy thought that boys could only identify with boys. This is something that can be seen throughout the data. When the media content is mainly about a girl, then it is, by definition, more a girl thing than a boy thing. This is also well-established in earlier research.[46] The reflections of the children suggested that girls would connect with girl characters more than boys would connect with them. In addition to the point about identification, Cathy's statement also suggested that the sitcom was seen to be primarily for girls, because it is about a girl's life, but the comedy in the series was thought to open the media text up for boys as well. There is a suggestion here that boys are seen as more likely to watch and identify with boys on the screen. According to Cathy, there were several reasons boys might like the show. First, Rico and Jackson are boys who fight. Another reason, Cathy said, is that it is funny—in other words, in her view, boys appreciate humour. In the data, fighting was constructed as boy practices or typical boy interests. In *Hannah Montana*, the efforts to secure the continued secret life of Miley/Hannah led to slapstick-like situations when all the characters at one point or another appear to be clumsy. The clumsiness and the fighting were discussed as something that boys appreciated. Again, this echoes a stereotypical gender divide.

Flirting and romance were domesticated as "girl things," while action and humour were "boy things." The gendered clichés that were domesticated and articulated in my data may be reproductions of perceived "truths" about boys and girls, something Thorne also found in her study of how boys and girls play.[47] Children do not only reproduce gendered boundaries; they also produce them. And as Goffman suggests with his term *genderism*, people will express gender identity as it is presented to them via society, where media is thought to play a pivotal part.[48] As such, one could say that the interviewees domesticated the resources given in these media texts as scripts for how to *be* or *do* boy and girl, at least in principle:

KATIE: It's a typical girl series because she is in love with everybody, and then the boys get like, they will throw up, in my class anyway.

INGVILD: So being in love is a girl thing?

KATIE: *They* think so at least.

From what Katie said in her segment about *Hannah Montana* it is not she, as a girl, who defined what a girl thing is; rather, it was the boys who defined it as such. Being in love is a girl thing because it is not a boy thing; here, we have a case of boys being defined through negation. Girl things were defined by being anti-boy things. It is important to note that this does not mean that the girls were involuntarily forced to like things that they did not like; there was room for personal differences among the girls. But the boys were constructed in a more homogenous way, as being opposed to the trilogy but able to watch it because it had elements of comedy. However, there was, I suggested earlier, room for different girl interests within the girl practices, a diversity of domestication. Mary's statement below is as a good example of this. She claimed that kissing might be interesting for girls, but said that she did not care for it:

MARY: For example, boys, there are not that many boys who watch *Camp Rock* but they probably think that kissing, or, at least, they say that they don't like kissing, that it's gross and stuff.

INGVILD: How about girls?

MARY: Girls might think it's romantic and such. It really doesn't matter to me.

Here, Mary is demonstrating individual agency. By making room for differences within a category, Mary portrayed not the typical boy/girl binary but, rather, a continuum of gender within the girl category. Here, diverse practices were allowed. The act of distancing instead of conforming to perform one's identity thus seems clear. Mary also questioned the truth of boys not liking kissing and romance when she said that the boys "claimed" not to like kissing and romance. As Thorne suggests, when engaging in borderwork, gender becomes a pivotal matter.[49] However, borderwork or genderism only becomes a focus when gender needs to be asserted. In the same way that Katie over-suggested that *they* think that being in love is a girl thing ("they" being boys in that quotation), it could be that Katie did not necessarily believe that being in love is a girl thing but, rather, viewed it as something that is *not* a boy thing. Katie also indicated that she did not care for vain girls:

INGVILD: So if you were going to tell someone who had never heard of *Hannah Montana* . . .

KATIE: Then I would say that she is a pop star who is a teenager, and that there is a TV series. And then I would probably tell them that she is really good and stuff, because I like it more and more, but actually I like Lilly better, because she, she's like Lilly, she skates and she's not that vain.

When asked whom different Disney tween content was made for, the interviewees were clear about what was they considered to be made for boys and what was made for girls. Their domestication of the content corresponded with the scripts Disney was serving them.[50] They described romance as something that girls and older children would enjoy, excluding boys and younger girls. But they said that comedy, though it did not exclude girls, primarily targeted boys and younger girls. When one looks at how the girls in this data domesticated the content for girls and for boys, another question surfaces: How has Disney been domesticated as a means by which the girls understood their own age and as part of growing older.

THE LEARNING DIMENSION: GROWING OLDER THROUGH THE CO-INTERPRETATION OF DISNEY AND THE SELF

Moving from the meaning dimension of how the girls rationalized media content and its audience, I now focus on how the girls domesticated Disney content in light of their life trajectories. This can be viewed as a learning dimension of the domestication process. The reason for this focus is that several times in my data, the girls used Disney references to express their biographical narrative.[51] Disney was as used a tool to express their past and also their present. As such, Disney can be said to be domesticated to the point that it serves as part of the girls' experienced life trajectories, becoming an inextricable, taken-for-granted part of their lives. As Morley suggests, "Our personal memories—especially of childhood—are formulated around media experiences such as emblematic programs and TV characters."[52] Disney content became a symbol, and a tool through which the interviewees told their life stories. Below, I examine how the interviewees talked about the domestication of Disney as part of their biographical narratives.

In the data, the notion surfaced that one outgrew certain Disney content and moved on to other Disney content aimed at older children, as did the notion that one outgrew Disney altogether. To the extent that Disney content played a part in this trajectory, it was a part of the experience of growing up. Disney's marketing strategy for maximizing revenue was to segment its products age-wise.[53] Several of the girls used Disney as part of their biographical narrative:

IDA: But I would probably have been someone else if I didn't know about *High School Musical* and stuff.
INGVILD: How do you think you would have been different?
IDA: Um, I had been more like a smaller child than what I really am.
INGVILD: So *High School Musical* has given you something then?
IDA: Nyes, . . . sort of, in a way, yes.
INGVILD: Given you something that makes you not . . . be that little kid?
IDA: If not I would have gone outside and played in the snow every single day instead of, instead of sitting inside watching movies for example and I would have read Tom and Jerry and Donald Duck instead of reading Julia [girls' magazine] and Topp [teen magazine].

High School Musical can, in this segment, be seen as resource in the process of growing older, as an introduction to teen interests. Ida said that it had changed her or, at least, possibly help her develop faster, claiming that otherwise she would be "more like a smaller child than what I really am."

Tone also mentioned popular culture—and especially the Disney Channel—as an identifier when describing who she was:

INGVILD: If you were to explain, to someone who didn't know you who you are, would you say, "Well, Tone she's . . ." Who is Tone?
TONE: Well, I like *High School Musical* and Disney Channel.
INGVILD: Is that something that is sort of an important part of you?
TONE: When I was younger I used to copy Sleeping Beauty, and then I imitated Disney movies all the time. I had different dresses and crowns. I also had a magic wand that I cared a lot about. And of course I had the movie of *Sleeping Beauty*.
INGVILD: Was it the Disney movie?
TONE: Yes of course, all three-year-olds have to have that!

Although Tone knew that my primary interest was in the Disney tween franchise, "Who is she?" was rather an open question. She answered it by expressing her biographical narrative of her past through various Disney princesses and her present engagements with *High School Musical* and the Disney Channel as identity indicators of her current self. Tone was a self-proclaimed *High School Musical* fan. Throughout her interviews, she told me about acting out scenes from the movies and inventing homemade scenarios, reading all the books in the trilogy, and practicing the songs and dances. Thus, she expressed a domestication of the Disney content that had followed her as a young child and as an eleven-year-old, when there was different content for different ages, in a way that accorded with how representatives from Disney Channel Scandinavia and Disney Consumer Products Nordic defined their audiences.[54] We see in her statement how she moved through Disney content according to her age. Disney can be said to be domesticated by Tone as a resource in her life trajectory. Media texts seem to be taken-for-granted resources, put to use and domesticated to tell one's biographical narrative. Employing domestication theory and ANT enables us to incorporate non-human actors as elements in the construction of tweens.

The girls in this study seemed to have learned to domesticate media texts as parts of their life trajectories, and Ida can be said to domesticate the Disney tween content as a trajectory into becoming of age. There are two processes going on in both Ida's and Tone's quotes. On the one hand, the content is interpreted as belonging to different age groups (and as we saw in the previous section, gender); on the other hand, simultaneously, there is an interpretation of the self through the content. This co-interpretation of the self and the content can be seen as a parallel process. Disney franchises became part of a routine practice and resources used to define the self. In addition to drawing on Disney as a part of one's past and present, there also seemed to be a general rationale for children growing older and up through different Disney franchises.

Several of the interviewees talked about leaving Disney when get older; however, this did not mean they would denounce it completely. Tone said that having artefacts linked to media content could serve as a place of reminisces:

TONE: I used to think I was too big for it, but now I like Teletubbies again. I think they're cute. I like Winnie the Pooh as well. In kindergarten I used to collect Winnie the Pooh. I've collected things my whole life.

INGVILD: Why do you do that you think?

TONE: Because I probably want to have it with me when I get older, and then I can look at it and think, Oh, yes, now I remember why I liked it.

Tone did not reject her former interests. She regressed in old enthusiasms for characters like Teletubbies and Winnie the Pooh. She talked of them as keepsakes to remind her of her former self and anticipated that when she grows out of her current interest (for *High School Musical*) she would still keep everything to remind her. The merchandise becomes part of her life narrative, almost like a diary. Others have also found this tendency to grow out of liking things that they earlier were quite invested in.[55] My data suggests that Disney becomes a place to develop from Disney princesses and Winnie the Pooh to the tween franchises, possibly leading up to an end of the relationship with

Disney. However, as Tone claimed, having things to remind you of why you liked them can be seen as part of one's biographical narrative.

DOMESTICATING DISNEY IN EVERYDAY LIFE

This chapter has examined how Disney Channel and the Disney tween media texts *Hannah Montana* and *High School Musical* were domesticated as part of the daily practices of the girls in this study. There was a co-interpretation of the self and Disney as the content was domesticated as belonging to the girls' biographical narratives and incorporated as resources for interpreting the self both with regards to age and gender. There was a clear and coherent notion within the interviews when describing the audience.

My data show that there was indeed a domestication of the Disney tween media texts going on. Concerning the praxis dimension, the Disney Channel clearly was domesticated in these girls' practices. All the girls I talked to, no matter how much they liked or disliked the content, at one time or another had watched at least parts of it. It seemed as though Disney and the Disney Channel was established as "their channel." Knowledge of different Disney content was part of one's social currency or cultural curriculum. However, this curriculum did not come across as strictly mandatory. In none of the interviews with the girls, the focus-group interviews, and observations was there any evidence that any of the Disney Channel movies or series generated a normative pressure to have seen them in order to have an opinion about them. Neither did it seem to be necessary to even have a strong opinion about them: no side needed to be chosen. The content was merely there, and everybody seemed to know it. As such, Disney was domesticated as seemingly invisible, yet had a constant presence in the girls' daily lives. That said, being able to enjoy the content with friends was often mentioned as a benefit. Hence, social gratification could be achieved by watching with others, and also when using the content as social currency in contexts not related to watching television.

In my data, *High School Musical* was perceived as belonging to the girl realm, while *Hannah Montana* seemed to generate a boy audience as well. Thus, with respect to the meaning dimension, the interviewed girls had domesticated the classical gender binary Disney has been said to serve them.[56] In a sense, we can say that the girls' interviews and their domestication corresponded to how the Disney configured its audience.[57]

Media content can be seen as a tool for understanding oneself and the social world, and these tools form integrated aspects of everyday life.[58] In addition, Steve Woolgar's concept of consumption as ontological enactment prompts us to focus not on media as a secondary socialization form that is somehow isolated from the "real world," but rather as an interwoven factor, among many socialization factors, which in turn, resides in relational contexts.[59]

Disney can, paraphrasing Latour, be seen as the glue that holds the social together. I have shown that Disney was a part on the girls' daily lives. It served as a stable, overarching actor operating within different assemblages. Specifically, Disney seemed to be prominent in three different assemblages—namely, friendship, entertainment, and social currency. Disney could function as social currency to join conversations and take part in social relations. Disney was also an actor, used to perform friendship, where the girls reported watching things that they did not like in order to perform the part of a good friend. In addition, Disney was part of an entertainment assemblage. In this case, Disney was not used for any other purpose than to be entertained. Thus, not only was Disney part of the biographical narratives, but it was being used in social relations through its configuration in the friendship and social currency assemblages.

Notes

1. Pål Aarsand, "Young Boys Playing Digital Games," *Nordic Journal of Digital Literacy* 5:1 (2010), pp. 38–54; Stine Liv Johansen, "Everyday Media Play: Children's Playful Media Practices," *Conjunctions: Transdisciplinary Journal of Cultural Participation* 4:1 (2018).
2. Kirsten Drotner, "Difference and Diversity: Trends in Young Danes' Media Uses," *Media, Culture & Society* 22:2 (2000), pp. 149–166; Ingvild Kvale Sørenssen, "Consuming Disney Channel: An Actor-Network Perspective," *Young Consumers* 17:4 (2016), pp. 363–375.
3. *Hannah Montana*, created by Michael Poryes, Rich Correll, and Barry O'Brien, aired March 24, 2006–January 16, 2011, the Disney Channel; High School Musical, dir. Kenny Ortega, Salt Lake City: Disney Channel, 2006; High School Musical 2, dir. Kenny Ortega, Salt Lake City: Disney Channel, 2007; High School Musical 3, dir. Kenny Ortega, Salt Lake City: Disney Channel, 2008.
4. Ingvild Kvale Sørenssen, "Disney's *High School Musical* and the Construction of the Tween Audience," *Global Studies of Childhood* 8:3 (2018), pp. 213–224.
5. Daniel Thomas Cook and Susan B. Kaiser, "Betwixt and Be Tween," *Journal of Consumer Culture* 4:2 (2004), pp. 203–227; Ingvild Kvale Sørenssen, "Tweens as a Commercial Target Group," in Anna Sparrman, Bengt Sandin, and Johanna Sjöberg (eds.), *Situating Child Consumption: A Critical Approach to Childhood Consumption in the 21st Century* (Lund: Nordic Academic Press, 2012), p. 177.
6. Sørenssen, "Disney's High School Musical"; Kevin Cody, "'No Longer, but Not Yet': Tweens and the Mediating of Threshold Selves through Liminal Consumption," *Journal of Consumer Culture* 12:1 (2012), pp. 41–65; Cook, Thomas, and Kaiser, "Betwixt and Be Tween"; Ingvild Kvale Sørenssen, "The Social Construction of Everyday Concepts: Constructing the 'Tween,'" *BARN* 33:2 (2015), pp. 81–90.
7. Elizabeth Bell, Lynda Haas, and Laura Sells, *From Mouse to Mermaid: The Politics of Film, Gender, and Culture* (Bloomington: Indiana University Press, 1995); Douglas Brode, *Multiculturalism and the Mouse: Race and Sex in Disney Entertainment* (Austin: University of Texas Press, 2005); Eleanor Byrne and Martin McQuillan, *Deconstructing Disney* (London: Pluto Press, 1999); Henry A. Giroux and Grace Pollock, *The Mouse That Roared: Disney and the End of Innocence* (Lanham, MD: Rowman & Littlefield, 2010).
8. Alan Bryman, *The Disneyization of Society* (London: Sage, 2004); David Buckingham, "Disney Dialectics: Debating the Politics of Children's Media Culture," in Janet Wasko, Mark Phillips, and Eileen R. Meehan (eds.), *Dazzled by Disney? The Global Disney Audiences Project* (Leicester, UK: Leicester University Press, 2001), pp. 269–296; Ingunn

Hagen, "Norway: Norwegian Memories of the Disney Universe," in Wasko, Phillips, and Meehan, *Dazzled by Disney?*, pp. 222–256; Nicholas Sammond, *Babes in Tomorrowland: Walt Disney and the Making of the American Child, 1930–1960* (Durham, NC: Duke University Press, 2005); Janet Wasko, *Understanding Disney: The Manufacture of Fantasy* (Cambridge, UK: Polity Press, 2001).

9. Natalie Coulter, "From Toddlers to Teens: The Colonization of Childhood the Disney Way," *Jeunesse: Young People, Texts, Cultures* 4:1 (2012), pp. 146–158.

10. Shiri Reznik and Dafna Lemish, "Falling in Love with *High School Musical*: Girls' Talk about Romantic Perceptions," in Mary Celeste Kearney (ed.), *Mediated Girlhoods: New Explorations of Girls' Media Culture* (London: Peter Lang, 2011), pp. 151–170; Sørenssen, "Consuming Disney Channel"; Tyler Bickford, 'Tween Intimacy and the Problem of Public Life in Children's Media: 'Having It All' on the Disney Channel's 'Hannah Montana,'" *Women's Studies Quarterly* 43:1–2 (2015), pp. 66–82; Morgan Genevieve Blue, "The Best of Both Worlds? Youth, Gender, and a Post-Feminist Sensibility in Disney's Hannah Montana," *Feminist Media Studies* 13:4 (2013), pp. 670–675; Melanie Kennedy, "Hannah Montana and Miley Cyrus: 'Becoming' a Woman, 'Becoming' a Star," *Celebrity Studies* 5:3 (2014), pp. 225–241; Temple Northup and Carol M. Liebler, "The Good, the Bad, and the Beautiful: Beauty Ideals on the Disney and Nickelodeon Channels," *Journal of Children and Media* 4:3 (2010), pp. 265–282.

11. Richard deCordova, "The Mickey in Macy's Window: Childhood, Consumerism and Disney Animation," in Eric Smoodin (ed.), *Disney Discourse: Producing the Magic Kingdom* (London: Routledge, 1994), pp. 203–213.

12. Ingunn Hagen, "Norway: Norwegian Memories of the Disney Universe," in Wasko, Phillips, and Meehan, *Dazzled by Disney?*, pp. 222–256.

13. Ingvild Kvale Sørenssen, "Domesticating the Disney Tween Machine: Norwegian Tweens Enacting Age and Everyday Life" (unpublished PhD diss., Norwegian University of Science and Technology, 2014), p. 81.

14. Sørenssen, "Domesticating the Disney Tween," p. 81

15. Maren Hartmann, Thomas Berker, Yves Punie, and Katie Ward, introduction to Berker et al. (eds.), *Domestication of Media and Technology* (Glasgow: Open University Press, 2006), pp. 1–17, at 1.

16. Leslie Haddon, "Domestication and the Media," in Patrick Rössler, Cynthia A. Hoffner, and Liesbet van Zoonen (eds.), *The International Encyclopedia of Media Effects* (London: John Wiley & Sons, 2017), pp. 409–417.

17. Knut H. Sørensen, "Domestication: The Enactment of Technology," in Berker et al., *Domestication of Media and Technology*, pp. 40–61.

18. David Morley and Roger Silverstone, "Domestic Communication – Technologies and Meanings," *Media, Culture & Society* 12:1 (1990), pp. 31–55; Roger Silverstone, Eric Hirsch, and David Morley, "Information and Communication Technologies and the Moral Economy of the Household," in Roger Silverstone and Eric Hirsch (eds.), *Consuming Technologies: Media and Information in Domestic Spaces* (London: Routledge, 1992), pp. 15–31; Merete Lie and Knut Holtan Sørensen, "Making Technology Our Own? Domesticating Technology into Everyday Life." in Merete Lie and Knut H. Sørensen (eds.), *Making Technology Our Own? Domesticating Technology into Everyday Life* (Oslo: Scandinavian University Press, 1996), pp. 1–30.

19. Silverstone et al. "Information and Communication Technologies."

20. Sørensen, "Domestication: The Enactment of Technology."

21. Jonathan Murdoch, "Ecologising Sociology: Actor-Network Theory, Co-Construction and the Problem of Human Exemptionalism," *Sociology* 35:1 (2001), pp. 111–133, at 111.

22. Bruno Latour, *Reassembling the Social: An Introduction to Actor-Network-Theory* (Oxford: Oxford University Press, 2005), pp. 316; 23.

23. Sørensen, "Domestication: The Enactment of Technology."

24. John Law and Annemarie Mol, "The Actor-Enacted: Cumbrian Sheep in 2001," in Carl Knappett and Lambros Malafouris (eds.), *Material Agency: Towards a Non-anthropocentric Approach* (New York: Springer, 2008), pp. 57–78.

25. Martin Müller, "Assemblages and Actor-Networks: Rethinking Socio-Material Power, Politics and Space," *Geography Compass* 9:1 (2015), pp. 27–41.

26. Bruno Latour, "Where Are the Missing Masses? The Sociology of a Few Mundane Artifacts," in Wiebe E. Bijker and John Law (eds.), *Shaping Technology/Building Society: Studies in Sociotechnical Change* (Cambridge, MA: MIT Press, 1992), pp. 225–258.

27. Sørenssen, "Domesticating the Disney Tween Machine."

28. Steinar Kvale, *Interviews: An Introduction to Qualitative Research Interviewing* (Thousand Oaks: SAGE, 1996).

29. Mats Alvesson and Kaj Sköldberg, *Reflexive Methodology: New Vistas for Qualitative Research* (London: SAGE, 2009).

30. Patricia Bazeley, *Qualitative Data Analysis with Nvivo* (London: SAGE, 2007).

31. Martin Lindstrom and Patricia B. Seybold, *Brandchild: Remarkable Insights into the Minds of Today's Global Kids and Their Relationship with Brands* (London: Kogan Page, 2004); and James U. McNeal, *The Kids Market: Myths and Realities* (Paramount Market Publishing, 1999)

32. Sørenssen, "Domesticating the Disney Tween Machine"; Ingvild Kvale Sørenssen and Claudia Mitchell, "Tween-Method and the Politics of Studying Kinderculture," in Shirley R. Steinberg (ed.), *Kinderculture: The Corporate Construction of Childhood*, 3rd ed. (Boulder, CO: Westview Press, 2011), pp. 153–167.

33. David Buckingham, *Children Talking Television: The Making of Television Literacy* (London: Falmer Press, 1993).

34. Cindy L. White and Elizabeth H. Preston, "The Spaces of Children's Programming," *Critical Studies in Media Communication* 22:3 (2005), pp. 239–255; and Karen Lury, "A Time and Place for Everything: Children's Channels," in David Buckingham (ed.), *Small Screens: Television for Children* (Leicester, UK: Leicester University Press, 2002), pp. 15–37.

35. Lury, "Time and Place for Everything," pp. 15–37; Peggy Tally, "Re-Imagining Girlhood: Hollywood and the Tween Girl Film Market," in Claudia Mitchell and Jacqueline Reid-Walsh (eds.), *Seven Going on Seventeen: Tween Studies in the Culture of Girlhood* (New York: Peter Lang, 2005), pp. 311–329.

36. Kirsten Drotner, "Difference and Diversity: Trends in Young Danes' Media Uses," *Media, Culture & Society* 22:2 (2000), pp. 149–166.

37. Gilles Brougere, "How Much Is a Pokèmon Worth? Pokèmon in France," in Joseph Jay Tobin (ed.), *Pikachu's Global Adventure: The Rise and Fall of Pokémon* (Durham, NC: Duke University Press, 2004), pp. 187–210; Buckingham, *Children Talking Television*; Allison James, *Childhood Identities: Self and Social Relationships in the Experience of the Child* (Edinburgh: Edinburgh University Press, 1993); Randi Wærdahl, "Maybe I'll Need a Pair of Levi's before Junior High?," *Childhood* 12:2 (2005), pp. 201–219.

38. Brougere, "How Much Is a Pokèmon Worth?," p. 193.

39. Buckingham, *Children Talking Television*, p. 40.

40. Morley and Silverstone, "Domestic Communication," p. 33.
41. Joseph Jay Tobin, *"Good Guys Don't Wear Hats": Children's Talk about the Media* (New York: Teachers College Press, 2000), p. 33.
42. Barrie Thorne, *Gender Play: Girls and Boys in School* (New Brunswick, NJ: Rutgers University Press, 1993); Tobin, *"Good Guys Don't Wear Hats."*
43. Thorne, *Gender Play.*
44. Erving Goffman, "The Arrangement between the Sexes," *Theory and Society* 4:3 (1977), pp. 301–333, at 321.
45. Patricia A. Adler, Steven J. Kless, and Peter Adler, "Socialization to Gender Roles: Popularity among Elementary School Boys and Girls," *Sociology of Education* 65:3 (1992), pp. 169–187; Reznik and Lemish, "Falling in Love with *High School Musical*"; Tobin, *"Good Guys Don't Wear Hats."*
46. Dafna Lemish, *Children and Television: A Global Perspective* (London: Blackwell, 2007); Dafna Lemish and Linda-Renée Bloch, "Pokèmon in Israel," in Tobin, *Pikachu's Global Adventure*, pp. 165–186.
47. Thorne, *Gender Play.*
48. Goffman, "Arrangement between the Sexes."
49. Thorne, *Gender Play.*
50. Anthony Giddens, *Modernity and Self-Identity: Self and Society in the Late Modern Age* (Cambridge, UK: Polity Press, 1991).
51. Sørenssen, "Disney's High School Musical."
52. David Morley, "What's 'Home' Got to Do with It? Contradictory Dynamics in the Domestication of Technology and the Dislocation of Domesticity," *European Journal of Cultural Studies* 6:4 (2003), pp. 435–458, at 444.
53. Sørenssen, "Domesticating the Disney Tween Machine."
54. Sørenssen, "Tweens as a Commercial Target Group."
55. Brougere, "How Much Is a Pokèmon Worth?," p. 192.
56. Sørenssen, "Disney's High School Musical."
57. Sørenssen, "Domesticating the Disney Tween Machine."
58. Drotner, "Difference and Diversity"; Christopher Vogler, *The Writer's Journey: Mythic Structure for Storytellers and Screenwriters* (London: Pan Books, 1999); Annalee R. Ward, *Mouse Morality: The Rhetoric of Disney Animated Film* (Austin: University of Texas Press, 2002).
59. Steve Woolgar, "Ontological Child Consumption," in Sparrman, Sandin, and Sjöberg, *Situating Child Consumption*, pp. 33–51.

BIBLIOGRAPHY

Bell, Elizabeth, Lynda Haas, and Laura Sells, eds. *From Mouse to Mermaid: The Politics of Film, Gender, and Culture.* Bloomington: Indiana University Press, 1995.
Berker, Thomas, Maren Hartmann, Yves Punie, and Katie Ward, eds. *Domestication of Media and Technology.* Glasgow: Open University Press, 2006.
Bickford, Tyler. "Tween Intimacy and the Problem of Public Life in Children's Media: 'Having It All' on the Disney Channel's 'Hannah Montana.'" *Women's Studies Quarterly* 43:1–2 (2015), pp. 66–82.
Blue, Morgan G. "The Best of Both Worlds? Youth, Gender, and a Postfeminist Sensibility in Disney's Hannah Montana." *Feminist Media Studies* 13:4 (2013), pp. 660–675.

Brode, Douglas. *Multiculturalism and the Mouse: Race and Sex in Disney Entertainment*. Austin: University of Texas Press, 2005.

Bryman, Alan. *The Disneyization of Society*. London: Sage, 2004.

Budd, Mike, and Max H. Kirsch, eds. *Rethinking Disney: Private Control, Public Dimensions*. Middletown, CT: Wesleyan University Press, 2005.

Byrne, Eleanor, and Martin McQuillan. *Deconstructing Disney*. London: Pluto Press, 1999.

Giroux, Henry A., and Grace Pollock. *The Mouse That Roared: Disney and the End of Innocence*. Lanham, MD: Rowman & Littlefield, 2010.

Lemish, Dafna. *Children and Television: A Global Perspective*. London: Blackwell, 2007.

Reznik, Shiri, and Dafna Lemish. "Falling in Love with High School Musical: Girls' Talk about Romantic Perceptions." In Mary Celeste Kearney (ed.), *Mediated Girlhoods: New Explorations of Girls' Media Culture*. London: Peter Lang, 2011, pp. 151–170.

Sammond, Nicholas. *Babes in Tomorrowland: Walt Disney and the Making of the American Child, 1930–1960*. Durham, NC: Duke University Press, 2005.

Smoodin, Eric, ed. *Disney Discourse: Producing the Magic Kingdom*. New York: Routledge, 1994.

Sørenssen, Ingvild Kvale. "Domesticating the Disney Tween Machine: Norwegian Tweens Enacting Age and Everyday Life." Unpublished PhD diss., Norwegian University of Science and Technology, Trondheim, 2014, NTNU, 2014:263 https://ntnuopen.ntnu.no/ntnu-xmlui/handle/11250/244228.

Sørenssen, Ingvild Kvale. "Disney's *High School Musical* and the Construction of the Tween Audience," *Global Studies of Childhood* 8:3 (2018), pp. 213–224.

Telotte, J. P. *The Mouse Machine: Disney and Technology*. Urbana: University of Illinois Press, 2008.

Tobin, J. J. *"Good Guys Don't Wear Hats": Children's Talk about the Media*. New York: Teachers College Press, 2000.

Ward, Annalee R. *Mouse Morality: The Rhetoric of Disney Animated Film*. Austin: University of Texas Press, 2002.

Wasko, Janet. *Understanding Disney: The Manufacture of Fantasy*. Cambridge, UK: Polity Press, 2001.

Wasko, Janet, Mark Phillips, and Eileen. R. Meehan, eds. *Dazzled by Disney? The Global Disney Audiences Project*. Leicester, UK: Leicester University Press, 2001.

CHAPTER 36

A MULTIMETHOD STUDY ON CONTEMPORARY YOUNG AUDIENCES AND THEIR FILM/CINEMA DISCOURSES AND PRACTICES IN FLANDERS, BELGIUM

ALEIT VEENSTRA, PHILIPPE MEERS,
AND DANIËL BILTEREYST

AT the start of the new millennium, technological innovation heralded a new era in film and media consumption: the digital age! Within this context, Henry Jenkins introduced the concept of "convergence culture," which he developed based on studies of film and television audiences.[1] *Convergence culture* claimed a new position for contemporary and participating media audiences, who could be found across a wide range of media platforms. Jenkins noted "the migratory behavior of media audiences who will go almost anywhere in search of the kinds of entertainment experiences they want."[2] As such, audiences were to be in charge of shaping their personal media landscape.

The range of manifestations of convergence for media audiences is wide. This chapter focuses on one of these specifically: young film and cinema audiences. Youth today are often media savvy and able to adopt new technologies, and so they are central in efforts to analyse alleged changes in media practices.[3] By researching film consumption, we aim to map the contemporary preferences and practices of young audiences and, at the same time, to identify the limitations of convergence culture. The chapter draws on the large-scale audience project Screen(ing) Audiences (2014–2017) in Flanders, the northern, Dutch-speaking part of Belgium, and, more specifically, on a survey of a representative sample of 16- to 18-year-olds in high school that offers a clear and nuanced view of how young audiences talk about and experience film and cinema.

We ask two central questions. It has been common since the late 1990s to declare cinema dead, so our first question is, has film lost its central place in young people's media consumption patterns? That is, does cinema as a medium really belong to the past or is there continuity even after the major leap into the digital age? And second, if film remains relevant in young popular culture, what are the consequences for how it is consumed? In other words, are young people participating audiences, feeding and shaping their own media preferences and practices by making individual, informed selection choices? What kind of screens do young people prefer and use and for which kinds of films? Is the classical divide between Hollywood, European cinema, and national cinema reflected in their discourses and practices? And finally, how do they engage in participatory (fan?) activities beyond watching film?

On our first question, some prominent voices are quite optimistic. Francesco Casetti, in *The Lumière Galaxy* (2015), acknowledges that the cinematic experience is no longer tied to one technological apparatus or space. But this does not mean the end of cinema, in his view. Rather, there is a relocation "as we carry the idea of cinema into other locations, situations, and practices through a recognition of what the cinematic experience entails."[4] The possibilities of the digital are allowing cinema to define itself in the unlimited applications in which it is deployed. In other words, "The digital age is providing the conditions through which cinema is finding its true self: positive regeneration."[5]

On the second question, we take a sociological approach to film culture to identify the possibilities and limitations that inform contemporary media consumption, understanding young audiences' practices and preferences along a continuum between agency and structure.[6] This means that audiences both have agency (the power to act independently) and are constrained by structure (confined in the individual power to act). In understanding agency and structure as existing on a continuum, we avoid both the bias that often accompanies analyses of the possibilities associated with audience agency and the determinism embedded in analyses that solely focus on structure.[7] Exploring the tensions between agency and structure for young film audiences, we build a case for studying audiences grounded in the continuity of over a century of film-consumption research.[8]

In the first, theoretical, part of the chapter, we set the scene of the research on contemporary film audiences, looking at theories about active consumers in the digital age, whereby young people are portrayed as digital natives at the forefront of convergence culture. There are voices celebrating audiences' newfound agency through personalized media landscapes, in sync with individual tastes and preferences. We find this agency mainly in screen selection and participatory practices. Thereafter, we turn to the limits of the audience practices explored in theoretical and empirical studies. Authors such as Nick Couldry have pointed towards structure-informed limitations, corporate (discursive) strategies, and societal stratification.[9]

The second part of the chapter brings empirical results into the debate. The study shows that films are consumed on a multitude of screens, large and small; accessed through many channels; and enjoyed with varying company linked to different locations. We explore young people's discourses on the classical divide between Hollywood, European cinema, and national Flemish-Belgian cinema and how these discursive constructions impact their film consumption. Final reflections deal with the prominent place film, in all its platforms, technologies, and channels, continues to occupy with young audiences and problematize the celebratory emphasis on active audiences within the equilibrium between agency and structure in film consumption.

CONVERGENCE AND PARTICIPATORY AUDIENCES

On the cusp of a changing online environment—the moment when the platform-structured Web 2.0 allowed for non-expert participation online—Henry Jenkins wrote a highly influential book: *Convergence Culture: Where Old and New Media Collide.*[10] Jenkins described an active participatory culture that assumes audience agency, which he contrasts with "older notions of passive media spectatorship."[11] He proposed instead an (inter)active model, in which producers and consumers also interact beyond individual understanding and intention. Since then, convergence culture has been a prominent theme in communication studies.[12] This chapter explores the concept and its implications for contemporary young film audiences as "participating audiences" and "media users."

Jenkins defined "convergence culture" through three interconnected aspects: media platforms, media industries, and media audiences:

> By convergence, I mean the flow of content across multiple media platforms, the cooperation between multiple media industries, and the migratory behavior of media audiences who will go almost anywhere in search of the kinds of entertainment experiences they want.[13]

In addition, "convergence represents a cultural shift as consumers are encouraged to seek out new information and make connections among dispersed media content."[14] As such, audiences are found across platforms and content. Jenkins argues that the outcome of convergence is a "participatory culture," where producers and active audiences interact rather than exist side by side. Fans are considered the forerunners of what will eventually be widespread innovative and grass-roots participatory practices. Jenkins maintains that fans have a distinctive culture, but says that "more and more people are reading like fans as they move online."[15] As such, fan culture will eventually become the (online) norm. This approach assumes that all audiences are willing to participate, though not with the same capability or extent. By studying the practices related to large commercial film franchises, such as *Harry Potter* (2001–2011), *The Matrix* (1999–2003), and *Star Wars* (1977–), Jenkins emphasizes that convergence culture manifests itself in the realm of popular mainstream media.

Over the past two decades, other authors exploring contemporary media practices based on new technological developments have also leaned towards the notion of audience agency on an individual level. The premise is that, to fit their tastes, audiences "produse" their own (online) content[16] and "remix" existing materials.[17] In an "on-demand culture" audiences are "mobile," selecting whatever content they prefer, whenever they want it, and wherever they are.[18] "Home cinema cultures" make audiences less dependent on cinema programmes and broadcast schedules.[19] And "engaged audiences" are part of a new cinema culture in which the big screen loses its monopoly to other platforms[20]—even to the smallest smartphone screen.[21]

Having the ability to watch "anything, anywhere, anytime" implied a move away from the traditional linear television broadcast schedules and cinema programmes to a range of different screens. Initially, the possibilities of new technologies led to concern about how audiences would watch film: in a fragmented way, on a too-small screen. The classical argument that film is the most suitable for the cinema is raised again. Belton, for example, states: "Our experience of a motion picture will vary according to the size of the screen on which it is viewed"; film in the movie theatre is cinema, "everything else is movies."[22]

As screens multiplied, the debate evolved in the direction of the social experience of watching film with other people in the cinema versus watching individually on a home screen. In other words, there was a tension between the social and individual dimensions of watching film. Schenk, Tröhler, and Zimmermann, for example, propose an approach that constructs cinema as a social experience, in which "spectator activity" should be understood as a cultural practice.[23] Hanich makes a phenomenological attempt to move to a collective experience of individuals watching film in a "collective spectatorship."[24] He explores the social experience of the cinema by suggesting a socially informed analysis of watching film. Hanich draws a sharp distinction between the cinema and the "truly individualized and solitary experience" of watching film on any other screen (from television to the smartphone).[25] As such, going to the cinema is a collective event.[26] Watching film on any other screen is associated with the solitary experience of the individual. The social practice of watching in a home family context is often disregarded. In her work on "home cinema cultures," Klinger does bring cinema to the sphere of the home.[27] She uses the term "cinephile DVD cultures" to argue that viewers exist in different social contexts, and acknowledges diversity in audience practices. Klinger thus makes a strong case for the social context of film consumption, moving beyond the cinema in analysing film-watching practices. By contrast, Blake Hallinan and C. J. Reynolds bring the individualized experience from the home into the cinema, redefining the movie theatre in "new media" terms, as a "platform," where personalization, interaction, and on-demand access are available, as in online media experiences.[28] Here, the theatrical audience becomes another variation on the "digitized media user." The movie theatre ticket is reshaped as a gateway to a theatrical experience and, equally, a way to access alternative media formats. These authors differ in their approaches. Nonetheless, they arrive at similar conclusions: contemporary audiences benefit from personalized and individualized media consumption via new screens and platforms.

STRUCTURED PRACTICES
IN FILM CONSUMPTION

In response to praise of this notion of a digital era of quasi-autonomous audiences, two main bodies of critique have arisen. First, there are authors who question the extent of audience engagement when it comes to shaping their media consumption patterns. Bird, for example, questions the concept of the "produser," arguing that only relatively few will participate.[29] Van Dijck makes a similar argument in arguing that the agency practiced via user-generated content is limited. She warns us not to mistake non-participation for inactivity; *active audiences* and *participating audiences* are different entities.[30] Couldry's response is exemplary. He argues that the main issue is a simplification of social reality that results from generalizing specific practices to larger audiences. He proposes a more sociological approach. In doing so, Couldry questions who participates, who gets to participate, and how widespread participatory practices are.[31]

In the second body of critique are the authors who question the individualization of contemporary audiences. Couldry argues that social factors influence how audiences will consume media—regardless of the screens and platforms available.[32] In other words, audiences might watch media content by themselves, but the choice of content, and the way they access it, is not necessarily an individual one. A variety of recent quantitative audience studies illustrate this fundamental difference between the endless possibilities for film consumption in the digital era, and the actual practices audiences perform in daily life. In a study in the Czech Republic, Macek and Zahrádka challenged the concept of convergence culture (which they deemed "idealized" in focusing on specific audiences) by measuring general audience practices with a series of screens.[33] Macek and Zahrádka find that watching film is vastly popular among audiences. Moreover, most audiences watch film via a linear broadcast. When they looked at specific age groups, they found that audiences aged 18 to 29 also consume film via other channels, but that these practices were not a substitute for accessing film via linear broadcast Rather they overlapped: 79.6 per cent watched film on television; 68.1 per cent watched film via other channels. Macek and Zahrádka conclude that "TV broadcasting maintains its dominance as a source of content."[34] Greer and Ferguson argue that the tablet does not replace the television set in accessing television and film.[35] In a convenience sample among college colleagues and students retrieved in 2011 on the West Coast of the United States, they found that television remains popular. And among those who watch television on their tablets, they found that the content they accessed was similar to the content they would watch on television. In other words, though the screen may change, the repertoire of media consumption remains the same. An exception is Netflix; via this platform film and series are mostly accessed on tablets. In their study on young cinema audiences in Quito, Ecuador, Maria Hernandez-Herrera, Ariani Batista, and Daniel Gonzalez find that young people are avid cinemagoers and consume large amounts of film via subscription TV, which is their major mode of consumption, next to cable TV.[36] These recent studies point to a rather traditional use of screens, especially concerning film content.

When talking about constraints on film consumption, political economy perspectives should be brought into the discussion, as they combine both critiques of over-enthusiastic-audience studies. Scholars working within this paradigm traditionally identify constraints in media consumption starting from an analysis of media industries, including studies of distribution, circulation, and ownership structures.[37] Biltereyst and Meers underline the usefulness of studying audiences in understanding the politics of media—a research tradition not often associated with audience research.[38] They argue that political economy can simultaneously provide important contextualization and be better understood by studying audience composition. The politics in contemporary film consumption, then, are most tangible in relation to audience practices in focusing on the access to different platforms. Here, we find the sharpest political-economy-informed critiques of contemporary participating audiences: in the analysis of the infrastructures that restrict media platform use. Political economy has always situated film audiences within the international film industry, where Hollywood performs its global hegemony. The debate over national cinemas and European cinema vis-à-vis Hollywood is a classical trope of film studies, but it is seldom approached from an audience perspective.

HOLLYWOOD, NATIONAL, AND EUROPEAN CINEMA

The differentiation in a film's *origin*, which we understand as the country of production, is as old as the medium itself. Hollywood has been leading the Western film box office charts since the early twentieth century.[39] An important catalyst for its success is the blockbuster.[40] This popular, accessible, mainstream film genre relates to explanations for Hollywood's success in its "cultural proximity," as Straubhaar defends it,[41] or its "narrative transparency."[42] This means respectively either that a Hollywood film is appreciated when it is close to what one understands, or that one came to understand it because of its prominence or its universal accessibility. On the other end of the spectrum, from a political economy perspective, Miller et al. argue that Hollywood is not inherently better, but can maintain its prominence because of its dominant position in the global market.[43] As Scott concludes, Hollywood "is a central point of reference in the cultural economy of the modern world."[44] This hegemony has even resulted in a uniform filmic language.[45]

The popularity of Hollywood is reflected in the film-watching preferences of youth. In previous research, Meers concluded that Hollywood films are the most popular among youth in Flanders. National film (or Flemish films in this research, for we demarcate at the level of language) is acceptable for television but not for the cinema. With the occasional exception, European film is largely disregarded by youth in Flanders.[46] The resulting hierarchy is often ascribed to Hollywood's prevalence. It is surprising that similar findings emerge in a totally different cultural, economic, and geographical context. Hernandez-Herrera, Batista, and Gonzalez find that Hollywood entertainment rules in Quito, whereas there is a low appreciation of national cinema for the classical reasons: lack of special effects, tragic storylines, excess of social realism, poor visual quality, and genre.[47]

European cinema is not just an intellectual phantasy or a normative concept; it is now an economic and institutional reality, often present in the discourse of European media policymakers. The only problem is the reluctance of the actual, and extremely diverse, European audiences when it comes to watching European non-national fare. There is little circulation of national cinemas in Europe. Films aiming for the culturally specific are seen as more foreign than Hollywood to other countries, because European audiences are used to watching Hollywood film in great quantities of.

National cinema in Europe occupies a curious position, for it is simultaneously national (for its national audiences) and European (for other European national audiences).[48] We can build a conceptualization of national cinema in Europe on the by-now classical analysis wherein we focus on the "national" audience, in the sense defined by Higson, of a "national reception culture."[49] Here the focus is on the films national audiences watch, including foreign, mostly Hollywood films. Furthermore, a conceptualization of national cinema as relational and negotiating cultural transfers is in order. National cinema makes sense only as relation, not as an essence, being dependent of other kinds of film-making, such as commercial and international, to which its supplies the other side of the coin.[50]

It is important to highlight that in a federal, trilingual, culturally diverse state such as Belgium, the concept of national film is quite complex. As Willems suggests, speaking about Belgian cinema as a whole, without taking in to account these parameters, is too broad a concept.[51] The country has three different official languages: Dutch (spoken in Flanders and Brussels), French (spoken in Wallonia and Brussels), and German (spoken by a very small portion of the population living in the southeast). And language is a crucial factor in film consumption.[52] Therefore, here, we equate national film to Flemish film. With 6.4 million people, cinema made in Flanders fits the definition of small-nation cinema as used by Hjort and Petrie.[53] While small nations may be limited in terms of film budgets and number of productions, advantages such as local anchorage, cultural specificity, and similarity in potential audiences also apply.

In line with the limitations of audience agency mentioned earlier, audiences are likely to select a film within existing frames of preference. They know what type of films they like both in genre and origin. This again guides them in selecting film content from endless libraries. Now that the main concepts, debates, and results within the field have been summarized, the time has come to confront the concepts with the results of the empirical study.

STUDYING YOUNG FILM AUDIENCES
IN PRACTICE

To tackle studying young film audiences in practice, we designed a classical quantitative study that consists of a survey of young people. To construct a representative sample of youth aged 16 to 18 for the survey, we reached out to schools in 2015. The educational system in Flanders comprises three levels: primary education, secondary education, and higher education. Because we focused on youth aged 16 to 18, our research is concerned with the last two years of secondary education. We put together a stratified random sample based on statistics provided by the Flemish government. A stratified random sample "divides the sample into separate sub-groups and then selects random samples from within each group," making the sample representative for the specific youth population to be studied.[54] In other words, based on the information provided by the 1,015 respondents in our survey, we can make claims about the entire population of young people in that age group in Flanders, Belgium.

All the students in the sample filled out a paper questionnaire that contained 94 (mostly closed) questions, under the supervision of a researcher. Completion time was about 45 minutes. The questions were organized in ten different sections, each concerning a different aspect of film-watching: (1) how many times and in what way do you watch film; (2) at home; (3) watching television; (4) to the cinema; (5) favourite films, actors, and directors; (6) selecting a film; (7) related to film; (8) film and social media; and (9) knowledge of films, actors, and directors. The tenth section concerned demographics. All questionnaires were digitalized using Optical Mark Recognition software. We then used Statistical Package for the Social Sciences software to analyse our data.

Before we begin the detailed analysis of the results, a short description of the mediated home context is in order. High school students in Flanders have ample access to screens and platforms (see Figure 36.1). Only 1 out of 1,015 respondents indicated not having access to the internet in the home. With the exception of the projector screen, all screens are widely accessible in the home setting: 99.8 per cent of all students reported having at least one computer or laptop at home. A slightly lower number, 98.4 per cent, had at least one television set at home. A similar number of households have at least one smartphone, yet only 45.6 per cent of the students has a personal device. Access to tablets was slightly lower, both in household ownership (80.8 per cent) and personal ownership (18.8 per cent).

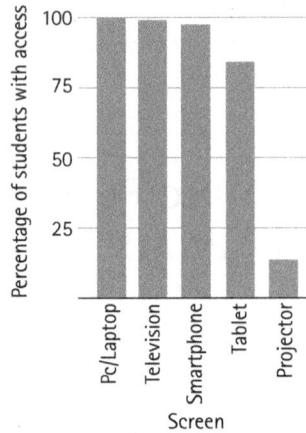

FIGURE 36.1. Access to screens in the home setting, in percentages.

Young Film Audiences and Their Screens: Practices and Discourses

The film and cinema world of young people in Flanders-Belgium turned out to be a fascinating media culture, and it delivered a rich variety of findings. First, we discuss the general results concerning preferences and the uses of film and cinema, various screens in diverse spaces, and their social contexts. Are young people truly convergence-culture audiences, feeding and shaping their own media preferences and practices through individually informed selection processes? And is the classical trope of the Hollywood, European cinema, and national cinema divide reflected in their discourses on and choices of film? Finally, we look at their practices beyond the screen, or the convergence-culture-engaging activities young people perform, besides watching film.

Young people's mediascape for film and cinema can be described at first level through a series of basic numbers, translating their discourses and practices. Returning to the first question asked at the start of the chapter, has film lost its central place in young people's media consumption patterns, it is crystal clear that film has not lost this central place at all. The digital age has not substantially altered young people's eagerness for the moving image. Young people in Flanders still thoroughly enjoy watching film. As Figure 36.2 shows, 84 per cent of youth like watching film; 13 per cent are neutral; and only 3 per cent do not like the watching film. Similarly, 77 per cent of youth like going to the cinema; 5 per cent do not; and 18 per cent are neutral.

A most striking result is that the cinema space is still the site par excellence to watch film; in other words, the attraction of the silver screen persists even for adolescents. Of course, young people use a wide range of screen types to watch various kinds of films. But the big screen is the most popular space to watch film. Figure 36.3 shows that half (52 per cent) of all youth prefer the cinema over all other means of watching film.

Film   Cinema

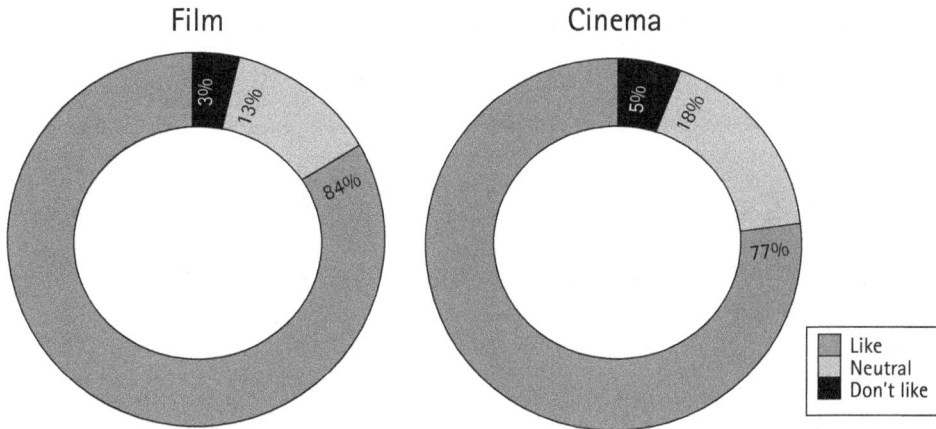

3%
13%
84%

5%
18%
77%

Like
Neutral
Don't like

FIGURE 36.2. Appreciation of watching film and going to the cinema, in percentages.

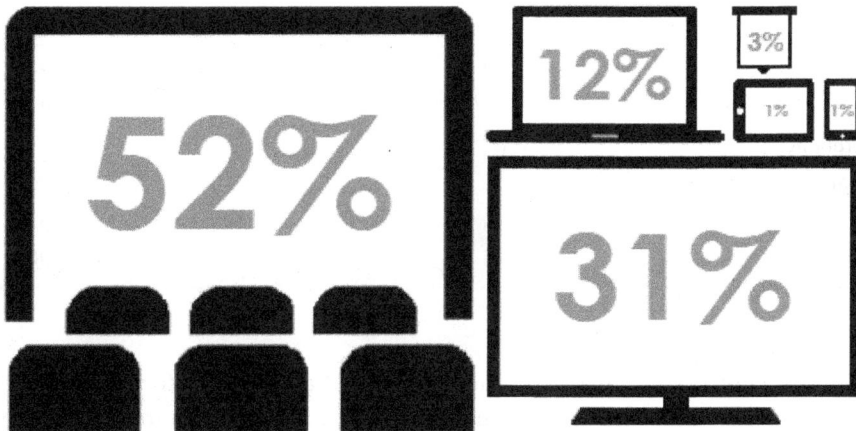

52%

12%

3%

1% 1%

31%

FIGURE 36.3. Preference for types of screens to watch film, in percentages.

Television comes in second, at almost one-third (31 per cent) of votes. Of the new screens, only the PC and laptop are somewhat popular, with a preference rate of 12 per cent. The projector (3 per cent), tablet (1 per cent), and smartphone (1 per cent) come in last. This means that traditional screens remain the most popular way of accessing film, and that the smallest screens come nowhere near to replacing the larger classical screens, as is often feared.

In the digital age, the possibilities for watching film on screens are almost infinite. Yet, as noted earlier, there is a wide gap between this array of screens and spaces and the actual kinds of screens young people use in their lived media practices. So again, caution is needed when equating preferences and practices. Although cinema stands out in preferences, the television screen is most common for watching film among high school students in Flanders (Table 36.1).[55] But surprisingly, as with preferences, film-watching practices revolve around traditional screens such as cinema and TV. The laptop is

Table 36.1. Most common ways to watch film, per screen type—in percentages

	Every day	Every other day	Every week	Every month	Every year	Never
Cinema						
Visiting the cinema	0	1	2	<u>49</u>	<u>45</u>	3
Television						
Linear television broadcast	5	7	<u>41</u>	<u>30</u>	10	7
Recorded from television	3	8	<u>39</u>	<u>30</u>	8	13
Owned DVD/Blu-ray	1	2	7	<u>22</u>	<u>32</u>	<u>37</u>
PC/laptop						
Not-paid-for streaming	3	7	<u>19</u>	<u>19</u>	11	<u>41</u>
Owned DVD/Blu-ray	0	1	4	13	<u>21</u>	<u>60</u>
Digitally stored	1	2	8	12	15	<u>62</u>
Tablet						
Linear television broadcast	1	1	3	5	5	<u>84</u>
Not-paid-for streaming	1	1	3	6	5	<u>84</u>
Recorded from television	1	1	3	5	4	<u>87</u>
Smartphone						
Not-paid-for-streaming	1	2	3	5	4	<u>86</u>
Linear television broadcast	1	1	2	4	4	<u>89</u>
Digitally stored	0	1	2	2	6	<u>90</u>

used occasionally, predominantly for not-paid-for streaming and for watching owned DVDs and/or Blu-rays. The smartphone and tablet, however, are rarely used to watch film—even with tailored (film) content available.[56] So both in preference and in use, the smaller screens lose the battle for attention.

A second observation is the surprising prominence of linear broadcasts on television. High school students thus do not necessarily make a choice between all (online and/or physical) available films. Rather, they regularly comply with choices made by others—such as the programmers, broadcasters, and cinemas—and choose from films offered to them at set times. They do occasionally record films to watch them later. This is not to say the small screens play any significant role. In particular, the PC and laptop are regularly used to watch film through (not paid for) streaming, as an individual viewing experience.

The issue of individual versus social viewing sheds light on the array of film-viewing experiences in space—from the semi-public space of the cinema to the private family environment to the intimate space of the bedroom—and sociality, from the solitary experience of family viewing to the social peer event (Table 36.2). The smaller the screen, the smaller the audience: on a PC or laptop, tablet, and smartphone film is mostly watched alone. An obvious explanation for this is the size of the screen: beyond a certain point, it

Table 36.2. Usual company when watching film—in percentages

Screen	N(use)	Company				
		alone	boyfriend/ girlfriend	friend(s)	brother(s)/ sister(s)	whole family
Cinema	945	1	<u>27</u>	<u>62</u>	4	6
Television	944	14	12	4	<u>16</u>	<u>54</u>
PC/laptop	848	<u>67</u>	19	7	6	0
Tablet	395	<u>82</u>	10	4	4	0
Smartphone	365	<u>92</u>	2	4	2	1

becomes too small to enjoy with multiple people. The alternative of watching on larger screen at home, the television, thus becomes more attractive, and opens up the possibility of a shared experience.[57] Film on television is mostly watched in a family context,[58] whereas film in the cinema is mostly enjoyed with a boyfriend, girlfriend, or friends.[59] In the digital age, cinema-going continues to be a social practice at large, even in the private sphere. This inherently social character of watching a film in the home context—that is, in the microcosm of the family, with the power dynamics among the young people and their parents—is often overlooked (or, at least, seldom conceptualized) in film studies.

Hollywood and National Cinema

Cinema and film practices do not only concern how and with whom young people consume film. Another crucial issue is what kind of films they watch. For example, we find a strong divide along genre lines.[60] The most popular genres among youth in Belgium are comedy and humour (liked by 81 per cent), action and adventure (liked by 73 per cent), and thriller and crime (liked by 63 per cent). The least popular are documentaries and biographies (disliked by 50 per cent), musicals and music (disliked by 53 per cent), westerns (57 per cent), and costume and historical dramas (64 per cent). Whereas girls aged 16 to 18 tend to prefer dramas, romances, musicals and music, and youth and family themes, boys mostly appreciate the action and adventure and war and disaster-film genres. This means that we can identify consumption patterns, with a strong relation between consumption patterns and social categories. The focus here, however, is on the classical divide between Hollywood, European cinema, and national cinema. Do we see this geographical but equally symbolic and even genre-infused division reflected in young people's discourses and practices (and if so, how)?

Indeed, films in English are the most popular, with North American (or Hollywood) films valued most and British film receiving positive evaluations as well. The results in Table 36.3 are quite explicit in reflecting the traditional divide. For national cinema, we

Table 36.3. Appreciation of film origin—in percentages.

Film origin	Appreciation		
	don't like	neutral	Like
American film	4	14	<u>82</u>
British film	20	34	<u>46</u>
Flemish film	24	<u>37</u>	<u>39</u>
French film	<u>60</u>	29	11
French-language Belgian film	<u>67</u>	24	8
Italian film	<u>73</u>	22	6
Spanish film	<u>74</u>	22	4
German film	<u>74</u>	22	4

made a distinction between Flemish cinema (in Dutch) and French-language Belgian film, because earlier research had showed that language is an important characteristic for film audiences.[61] Considering Flemish cinema as national cinema proved worthwhile: Flemish films are strongly preferred over French-language Belgian films. This language difference has an even stronger impact than the film's origin, as French films, for example, are valued over Belgian films in French. The harsh evaluation of French-language Belgian films is comparable with the low appreciation for films from other European countries. This means that the European film category is diverse in origin, yet quite coherent in its lack of appreciation.

Hollywood is still the reference point as a global cinema consumed in multiplexes and on all other platforms. European cinema remains the "disliked other," whereas Flemish cinema climbed a few rungs on the ladder of appreciation. This hierarchy of Hollywood, Flemish, and European film among young people in Flanders is in line with results found in the early 2000s, though Flemish film has grown in popularity since the start of the millennium. Moreover, this hierarchy is maintained with respect to the use of screens: Hollywood films are cinema material; Flemish films are mostly watched on television; and European films are accessed via the laptop.[62] This might imply that the European film, because it is less available in cinemas and on television, is accessed online through means that have only recently become available recently. As such, individual selection of media content enters the picture.

ACTIVE USERS BEYOND WATCHING FILM

In the theoretical part of the chapter, we discussed how contemporary digital film cultures are supposed to extend themselves through a range of participation practices surrounding film. In the contemporary media environment, the potential for participation seems unlimited, especially through Web 2.0 platforms. In this context, we explored how young people engage in film-related practices, such as visiting film locations, visiting online forums, and writing stories. First, a rather limited number of high school students in Flanders engage in some kind of film-related practice (Table 36.4). Again, possibilities for participation do not equal participation practices. For example, almost a third play a film-related video game at least once a year, and 17.5 per cent visit a film location at least once a year. One out of every ten high school students write a film-related story at least once a year. These film-related activities not only underline the popularity

Table 36.4. Frequency of film–related practices—in percentages from most (*top*) to least (*bottom*)

	every day	every other day	every week	every month	every year	at least once a year	never
playing videogames	1	1	5	7	14	28	72
finding additional information	1	0	2	7	15	26	74
visiting film locations	0	0	1	2	15	18	82
roleplaying	1	0	2	4	8	15	85
playing alternate reality games	1	1	2	4	7	15	85
making something artistic	0	1	1	2	7	11	89
visiting online forums	0	0	1	3	6	10	90
writing stories	0	0	1	2	7	10	90
making film	1	0	1	1	5	8	92
writing blogs	0	0	1	2	4	7	93

of film, but also its prominence in everyday (teenage) life. Nonetheless, the frequency of their involvement is highly limited, which endorses the caution Bird, Van Dijck, and Couldry have advised regarding the claim of widespread participation and their emphasis on the niche or fan aspects of these practices.[63]

Second, offline film-related practices are no less popular than online practices. Playing film-related video games, for example, was possible long before the internet came to be.[64] And third, when playing a film-related video game, people engage in a practice the industry designed to be interactive as a means to attract (potential) film audiences.[65] Similar mechanisms are found in alternate-reality games surrounding film.[66] In other words, film-related practices are more steered and structured than the concept of convergence culture implies. As such, observing participation without contextualizing these practices may result in a distorted image. The of limiting structures through (corporate) regulation should therefore be included in further analyses of practices surrounding film.

CONCLUSION

The main objective of this chapter was to put the concept of "convergence culture" to the test with young film audiences. It questioned the overestimation of audience agency in the individuality ascribed to contemporary media practices, based on an original large-scale audience study. In the first part, contemporary theories about the audiences for film in the digital age were reconsidered, and young people were situated at the forefront of participation in new technologies. Voices celebrating audiences' newfound agency through personalized media channels for individual preferences were contrasted with arguments about structured limitations and corporate strategies. The strong focus on change in media consumption through a rise in audience participation was found problematic. It assumes that participating audiences represent all audiences—or at least, eventually will. However, such participation is limited and only found among small audience sections. Audience participation is mainly found and analysed in the realm of fandom. However, there are many practices and degrees of immersion within fandom . As such, those specific practices are not generalizable to wider audiences. Furthermore, participation is often assumed to be a contemporary phenomenon. Active audience participation has, however, been observed all throughout the twentieth century, in many shapes and forms.

So, does the rather laudatory view of participating film and cinema audiences still stand when confronted with the lived experiences of young people in Flanders-Belgium? The answer cannot be a clear-cut yes or no. Cinema is, without a doubt, still relevant in popular youth culture, as it is highly appreciated and often consumed. Equally, the leap into the digital age shows large waves of continuity with the pre-digital era. Film is still consumed mainly through the traditional channels of cinema and TV. The prominent place film occupies with young people is thus not under scrutiny; the emphasis on young people as active and participating audiences is. Young audiences are not mere victims of the global film industry epitomized by Hollywood, of course. But neither are they free-wheeling, autonomous individuals who cherry-pick whatever film they desire. Probably the most widely used argument for participatory convergence culture is the active engagement in activities beyond the mere watching of film. Here again, the social reality of young people is complex and diverse. Our findings question the premise of widespread participation as characteristic of contemporary (converged) media consumption. Some do engage in these activities, but most do not. Young people are social beings, living within their social, cultural, and economic contexts, which come with constraints and structures. Their cinema cultures are no different.

In an age of unlimited access to global media, it is striking how film consumption preferences remain shaped along traditional lines of origin. The classical hierarchy between Hollywood and national cinemas definitely survived the change to the digital. Furthermore, Hollywood films are deemed suitable for all screens and show the strongest connection to cinema, whereas Flemish films are predominantly watched on television. These strong hierarchies in screen and origin point to structured media consumption in an age of convergence culture and its alleged migratory audiences. There are important implications in line with the political economy of audiences: if audiences stay put, rather than migrate, media industries remain crucial in shaping media consumption. In short, young audiences do not select just any screen, or just any film. Rather, they consume film in patterns similar to an offline, pre-convergence culture era.

Differentiating too strictly between former (passive) and contemporary (active) audiences results in further dichotomizing classifications (e.g., participating versus non-participating) of audiences. An analysis that situates audience research along a continuum between agency and structure guarantees a focus on continuity and, at the same time, avoids the celebratory notion of agency embedded in many analyses of contemporary media practices.

We make a case for an analysis of individually and socially informed practices and preferences. Contemporary film consumption is socially, culturally, and commercially informed. As such, these structures call for further attention, for they imply socially rather than individually shaped media consumption. Thus, while possibilities may be endless in a contemporary media landscape, audience practices are limited because they reflect social and commercial patterns.

Notes

1. Henry Jenkins, "The Cultural Logic of Media Convergence," *International Journal of Cultural Studies* 7:1 (2004), pp. 33–43; and Jenkins, *Convergence Culture: Where Old and New Media Collide* (New York: New York University Press, 2006).
2. Jenkins, *Convergence Culture*, p. 2.
3. Andy Bennett and Brady Robards, "Introduction: Youth, Cultural Practice and Media Technologies," in Andy Bennett and Brady Robards (eds.), *Mediated Youth Cultures: The Internet, Belonging and New Cultural Configurations* (Basingstoke, UK: Palgrave Macmillan, 2014), pp. 1–7.
4. Francesco Casetti, *The Lumière Galaxy Seven Key Words for the Cinema to Come* (New York: Columbia University Press, 2015).
5. Casetti, *Lumière Galaxy*.
6. Emile Durkheim, *The Elementary Forms of Religious Life* (1912; repr. New York: Free Press, 1965); Pierre Bourdieu, *Distinction: A Social Critique of the Judgment of Taste* (1979; repr. London: Routledge, 2009); Anthony Giddens, *The Constitution of Society: Outline of the Structuration Theory* (Cambridge, UK: Polity, 1984).
7. Nicholas Abercrombie and Brian J. Longhurst, *Audiences: A Sociological Theory of Performance and Imagination* (London: SAGE, 1998); Jostein Gripsrud and Erlend Lavik, "Film Audiences," in James Donald and Michael Renoc (eds.), *The Sage Handbook of Film Studies* (London: SAGE, 2008), pp. 454–470; Pertti Alasuutari, "Introduction: Three Phases of Reception Studies," in Pertti Alasuutari (ed.), *Rethinking the Media Audience: The New Agenda* (London: SAGE, 1999), pp. 1–21; David Morley, "'To Boldly Go...': The

'Third Generation' of Reception Studies," in Alasuutari, *Rethinking the Media Audience*, pp. 195–206.

8. For more comprehensive historical overviews on film audience research, see, for example, Richard Butsch, *The Making of American Audiences: From Stage to Television, 1750–1990* (Cambridge, UK: Cambridge University Press, 2000); Janet Staiger, *Media Reception Studies* (New York: New York University Press, 2005).

9. Nick Couldry, "More Sociology, More Culture, More Politics; or, a Modest Proposal for 'Convergence' Studies," *Cultural Studies* 25:4–5 (2011), pp. 487–501.

10. Tim O'Reilly, "What Is Web 2.0? Design Patterns and Business Models for the Next Generation of Software," 2005, http://www.oreilly.com/pub/a/oreilly/tim/news/2005/09/30/what-is-web-20.html [accessed August 3, 2020].

11. Jenkins, *Convergence Culture*.

12. Graeme Turner, "Convergence and Divergence: The International Experience of Digital Television," in James Bennett and Niki Strange (eds.), *Television as Digital Media* (Durham, NC: Duke University Press, 2011), pp. 31–51.

13. Jenkins, *Convergence Culture*, p. 2.

14. Ibid., p. 3.

15. Henry Jenkins, "Why Fiske Still Matters," in *Understanding Popular Culture* (London: Routledge Classics, 2010), pp. xii–xxxviii.

16. "In the social software, 'Web2.0' environment, the production of ideas takes place in a collaborative, participatory mode which breaks down the boundaries between producers and consumers and instead enables all participants to be users as much as producers of information and knowledge, or what can be described as produsers." Axel Bruns, "The Future Is User-Led: The Path towards Widespread Produsage," *Fibreculture Journal* 11 (2008), https://www.researchgate.net/publication/27472557_The_Future_Is_User-Led_The_Path_towards_Widespread_Produsage [accessed November 19, 2021]; and Bruns, "Reconfiguring Television for a Networked, Produsage Context," *Media International Australia* 126 (Feb. 2008), pp. 82–94.

17. Lawrence Lessig, *Remix: Making Art and Commerce Thrive in the Hybrid Economy* (London: Bloomsbury Academic, 2008).

18. Chuck Tryon, *On-Demand Culture: Digital Delivery and the Future of Movies* (New Brunswick, NJ: Rutgers University Press, 2013); and Tryon, *Reinventing Cinema: Movies in the Age of Media Convergence* (New Brunswick, NJ: Rutgers University Press, 2009).

19. Barbara Klinger, *Beyond the Multiplex: Cinema, New Technologies, and the Home* (Berkeley: University of California Press, 2006).

20. Sarah Atkinson, *Beyond the Screen: Emerging Cinema and Engaging Audiences* (New York: Bloomsbury Academic, 2014).

21. Roger Odin, "Spectator, Film, and the Mobile Phone," in Ian Christie (ed.), *Audiences* (Amsterdam: Amsterdam University Press, 2012), pp. 155–169.

22. John Belton, "If Film Is Dead, What Is Cinema?," *Screen* 55:4 (2014), pp. 460–470.

23. Irmbert Schenk, Margrit Tröhler, and Yvonne Zimmermann, "From the Ideal Spectator to the Social Practice of Reception: An Introduction," in Irmbert Schenk, Margrit Tröhler, and Yvonne Zimmermann (eds.), *Film-Kino-Zuschauer: Filmrezeption: Film-Cinema-Spectator: Film Reception* (Marburg: Schüren, 2010), pp. 17–26.

24. Julian Hanich, "Watching a Film with Others: Towards a Theory of Collective Spectatorship," *Screen* 55:3 (2014), pp. 338–359.

25. Hanich, "Watching a Film with Others," p. 359.

26. Going to the cinema as a social event is explored in empirical research on the audience practices of contemporary audiences. See Philippe Meers and Daniël Biltereyst, "Film Audiences in Perspective: The Social Practices of Cinema-Going," in Helena Bilandzic, Geoffroy Patriarche, and Paul J. Traudt (eds.), *The Social Use of Media: Cultural and Social Scientific Perspectives on Audience Research* (Bristol, UK: Intellect, 2012), pp. 123–140. On film festival audiences, see Marijke De Valck, "Drowning in Popcorn at the International Film Festival Rotterdam? The Festival as a Multiplex of Cinephilia," in Marijke De Valck and Malte Hagener (eds.), *Cinephilia: Movies, Love and Memory* (Amsterdam: Amsterdam University Press, 2005), pp. 97–110. On historical audiences in a "new cinema history" perspective, see Robert Allen, "Relocating American Film History," *Cultural Studies* 20:1 (2006), pp. 48–88; Richard Maltby, "New Cinema Histories," in Richard Maltby, Daniël Biltereyst, and Philippe Meers (eds.), *Explorations in New Cinema History* (Malden, MA: Wiley-Blackwell, 2011), pp. 3–40.

27. Klinger, *Beyond the Multiplex.*

28. Blake Hallinan and C. J. Reynolds, "New Media Goes to the Movies: Digitizing the Theatrical Audience," *Television and New Media* (2019), pp. 1–21, https://doi.org/10.1177/1527476419863131 [accessed August 3, 2020].

29. Elizabeth S. Bird, "Are We All Produsers Now? Convergence and Media Audience Practices," *Cultural Studies* 25:4–5 (2011), pp. 502–516.

30. José Van Dijck, "Users Like You? Theorizing Agency in User-Generated Content," *Media, Culture & Society* 31:1 (2009), pp. 41–58.

31. Couldry, "More Sociology, More Culture, More Politics."

32. Ibid.

33. Jakub Macek and Pavel Zahrádka, "Online Piracy and the Transformation of the Audiences' Practices: The Case of the Czech Republic," in Darren Hudson Hick and Reinold Schmücker (eds.), *The Aesthetics and Ethics of Copying* (New York: Bloomsbury, 2016), pp. 335–358.

34. Macek and Zahrádka, "Online Piracy," p. 354.

35. Clark F. Greer and Douglas A. Ferguson, "Tablet Computers and Traditional Television (TV) Viewing: Is the Ipad Replacing TV?," *Convergence: The International Journal of Research into New Media Technologies* 21:2 (2015), pp. 244–256.

36. Maria Hernandez-Herrera, Ariana Batista, and Daniel Gonzalez, "From Digital Cinema to Cloud Computing in the Film Consumption of Young Ecuadorians," *Cuadernos* 44 (2019), pp. 195–208.

37. Vincent Mosco, "Overview of the Political Economy of Communication," in *The Political Economy of Communication* (London: SAGE, 2009), pp. 1–20.

38. Daniël Biltereyst and Philippe Meers, "The Political Economy of Audiences," in Janet Wasko, Graham Murdock, and Helena Sousa (eds.), *The Handbook of Political Economy of Communications* (Malden, MA: Wiley-Blackwell, 2011), pp. 415–435.

39. Peter Decherney, *Hollywood's Copyright Wars: From Edison to the Internet* (New York: Columbia University Press, 2013); Andrew Higson and Richard Maltby, "'Film Europe' and 'Film America': An Introduction," in Andrew Higson and Richard Maltby (eds.), *"Film Europe" and "Film America": Cinema, Commerce and Cultural Exchange, 1920–1939* (Exeter, UK: University of Exeter Press, 1999), pp. 1–31.

40. Marco Cucco, "The Promise Is Great: The Blockbuster and the Hollywood Economy," *Media, Culture & Society* 31:2 (2009), pp. 215–230; Thomas Elsaesser, *The Persistence of Hollywood* (New York: Routledge, 2012).

41. Joseph D. Straubhaar, "Beyond Media Imperialism: Assymetrical Interdependence and Cultural Proximity," *Critical Studies in Media Communication* 8:1 (1991), pp. 39–59.

42. Scott R. Olsen, *Hollywood Planet: Global Media and the Competitive Advantage of Narrative Transparency* (Mahwah, NJ: Lawrence Erlbaum, 1999).

43. Toby Miller, et al., *Global Hollywood* (London: BFI Publishing, 2001).

44. Allen John Scott, "Cinema, Culture, Globalization," in *On Hollywood: The Place, the Industry* (Princeton, NJ: Princeton University Press, 2005), pp. 159–175.

45. Elsaesser, *Persistence of Hollywood*.

46. Philippe Meers, " 'It's the Language of Film!': Young Film Audiences on Hollywood and Europe," in Richard Maltby and Melvyn Stokes (eds.), *Hollywood Abroad: Audiences and Cultural Exchange* (London: BFI Publishing, 2004), pp. 158–175.

47. Hernandez-Herrera et al., "From Digital Cinema to Cloud Computing."

48. Jasmijn Van Gorp, "Wat Is Nationaal Aan Nationale Cinema?," *Tijdschrift voor Communicatiewetenschap* 38:1 (2010), pp. 49–62.

49. Andrew Higson, "The Concept of National Cinema," *Screen* 30:4 (1989), pp. 36–46.

50. Thomas Elsaesser, "Putting on a Show: The European Art Movie," *Sight and Sound* 4:4 (1994), pp. 22–27.

51. Gertjan Willems, "A Comparative Analysis of Contemporary Film Policy in Flanders and Denmark," *Tijdschrift Voor Communicatiewetenschap* 38:2 (2010), pp. 172–186.

52. Tim Bergfelder, "National, Transnational or Supranational Cinema? Rethinking European Film Studies," *Media, Culture & Society* 27:3 (2005), pp. 315–331; Meers, "It's the Language of Film!"

53. Mette Hjort and Duncan Petrie, introduction to Mette Hjort and Duncan Petrie (eds.), *The Cinema of Small Nations* (Edinburgh: Edinburgh University Press, 2007), pp. 1–22.

54. Patrick Sturgis, "Designing Samples," in Nigel Gilbert (ed.), *Researching Social Life* (Los Angeles: SAGE, 2008), pp. 165–181.

55. It should be noted that the popular streaming service Netflix, available through a number of television sets, was available in Belgium at the time of the survey. However, it was still rather new, and only 20 per cent of the high school students indicating having Netflix at home. Today, access is definitely more widespread.

56. Cf. Atkinson, *Beyond the Screen*; Odin, "Spectator, Film, and the Mobile Phone."

57. Klinger, *Beyond the Multiplex*.

58. More than two decades ago, Allen described the invention of the family film, especially catered to this audience composition; Robert C. Allen, "Home Alone Together: Hollywood and the 'Family Film,' " in Richard Maltby and Melvyn Stokes (eds.), *Identifying Hollywood's Audiences: Cultural Identity and the Movies* (London: BFI Publishing, 1999), pp. 109–134.

59. The practice of cinema visits in the company of a girlfriend, boyfriend or friend(s) is observed all throughout the twentieth century. See Daniël Biltereyst, Philippe Meers, and Lies Van de Vijver, "Social Class, Experiences of Distinction and Cinema in Postwar Ghent," in Richard Maltby, Daniël Biltereyst and Philippe Meers (eds.), *Explorations in New Cinema History* (Malden, MA: Wiley-Blackwell, 2011), pp. 101–124.

60. For a thorough discussion of film genre preferences, see Aleit Veenstra, Philippe Meers, and Daniël Biltereyst, "Exploring Film Genre Preferences through Taste Cultures: A Survey on Contemporary Film Consumption amongst Youth in Flanders (Belgium)," *Communications: The European Journal of Communication Research* 45:2 (2020), pp.

240–251. Here, we touch upon the complexities that come with the concept of genre and further elaborate on (methodological) choices made to measure film genre preferences.

61. Meers, "It's the Language of Film!"

62. For a detailed analysis of the relation between screen preferences and origin, see Aleit Veenstra, Philippe Meers, and Daniël Biltereyst, "Structured Film Viewing Preferences and Practices: A Quantitative Analysis of Hierarchies in Screen and Content Selection amongst Young People in Flanders (Belgium)," in Petr Szczepanik, Pavel Zahrádka, Jakub Macek, and Paul Stepan (eds.), *Digital Peripheries The Online Circulation of Audiovisual Content from the Small Market Perspective* (Cham, Switzerland: Springer, 2020), pp. 227–244.

63. Bird, "Are We All Produsers Now?"; Van Dijck, "Users Like You?"; Couldry, "More Sociology, More Culture, More Politics."

64. Jonathan Gray, *Show Sold Separately: Promos, Spoilers and Other Media Paratexts* (New York: New York University Press, 2010); Jesper Juul, "Games Telling Stories? A Brief Note on Games and Narratives," *Game Studies* 1:1 (2001), pp. 40–62.

65. CarrieLynn D. Reinhard, "Gameplay Marketing Strategies as Audience Cooptation: The Story of the Dark Knight, the Cloverfield Monster, and Their Brethren," *International Journal of Communication* 5 (2011), pp. 51–77.

66. Henrik Örnebring, "Alternate Reality Gaming and Convergence Culture: The Case of Alias," *International Journal of Cultural Studies* 10:4 (2007), pp. 445–462.

BIBLIOGRAPHY

Allen, Robert C. "Home Alone Together: Hollywood and the 'Family Film.'" In Richard Maltby and Melvyn Stokes (eds.), *Identifying Hollywood's Audiences: Cultural Identity and the Movies*. London: BFI Publishing, 1999, pp. 109–134.

Biltereyst, Daniël, and Philippe Meers. "The Political Economy of Audiences." In Janet Wasko, Graham Murdock, and Helena Sousa (eds.), *The Handbook of Political Economy of Communications*. Malden, MA: Wiley-Blackwell, 2011, pp. 415–435.

Couldry, Nick. "More Sociology, More Culture, More Politics; or, a Modest Proposal for 'Convergence' Studies." *Cultural Studies* 25:4–5 (2011), pp. 487–501.

Elsaesser, Thomas. *The Persistence of Hollywood*. New York: Routledge, 2012.

Giddens, Anthony. *The Constitution of Society: Outline of the Structuration Theory*. Cambridge, UK: Polity, 1984.

Gripsrud, Jostein, and Erlend Lavik. "Film Audiences." In James Donald and Michael Renoc (eds.), *The Sage Handbook of Film Studies*. London: SAGE, 2008, pp. 454–470.

Hallinan, Blake, and C. J. Reynolds. "New Media Goes to the Movies: Digitizing the Theatrical Audience." *Television and New Media* (2019), pp. 1–21. https://doi.org/10.1177/1527476419863 131 [accessed August 3, 2020].

Higson, Andrew. "The Concept of National Cinema." *Screen* 30:4 (1989), pp. 36–46.

Hjort, Mette, and Duncan Petrie. Introduction to Mette Hjort and Duncan Petrie (eds.), *The Cinema of Small Nations*. Edinburgh: Edinburgh University Press, 2007, pp. 1–22.

Jenkins, Henry. *Convergence Culture: Where Old and New Media Collide*. New York: New York University Press, 2006.

Klinger, Barbara. *Beyond the Multiplex: Cinema, New Technologies, and the Home*. Berkeley: University of California Press, 2006.

Macek, Jakub, and Pavel Zahrádka. "Online Piracy and the Transformation of the Audiences' Practices: The Case of the Czech Republic." In Darren Hudson Hick and Reinold Schmücker (eds.), *The Aesthetics and Ethics of Copying*. New York: Bloomsbury, 2016, pp. 335–358.

Maltby, Richard. "New Cinema Histories." In Richard Maltby, Daniël Biltereyst, and Philippe Meers (eds.), *Explorations in New Cinema History*. Malden, MA: Wiley-Blackwell, 2011, pp. 3–40.

Meers, Philippe. "'It's the Language of Film!': Young Film Audiences on Hollywood and Europe." In Richard Maltby and Melvyn Stokes (eds.), *Hollywood Abroad: Audiences and Cultural Exchange*. London: British Film Institute, 2004, pp. 158–175.

Meers, Philippe, and Daniël Biltereyst. "Film Audiences in Perspective: The Social Practices of Cinema-Going." In Helena Bilandzic, Geoffroy Patriarche, and Paul J. Traudt (eds.), *The Social Use of Media: Cultural and Social Scientific Perspectives on Audience Research*. Bristol, UK: Intellect, 2012, pp. 123–140.

Miller, Toby, Nitin Govil, John McMurria, and Richard Maxwell. *Global Hollywood*. London: BFI Publishing, 2001.

Morley, David. "'To Boldly Go…': The 'Third Generation' of Reception Studies." In Pertti Alasuutari (ed.), *Rethinking the Media Audience: The New Agenda*. London: SAGE, 1999, pp. 195–206.

Mosco, Vincent. "Overview of the Political Economy of Communication." In *The Political Economy of Communication*. London: SAGE, 2009, pp. 1–20.

Staiger, Janet. *Media Reception Studies*. New York: New York University Press, 2005.

Tryon, Chuck. *On-Demand Culture: Digital Delivery and the Future of Movies*. New Brunswick, NJ: Rutgers University Press, 2013.

Veenstra, Aleit, Philippe Meers, and Daniël Biltereyst. "Structured Film Viewing Preferences and Practices: A Quantitative Analysis of Hierarchies in Screen and Content Selection Among Young People in Flanders (Belgium)." In Szczepanik et al. (eds.), *Digital Peripheries: The Online Circulation of Audiovisual Content from the Small Market Perspective*. Cham, Switzerland: Springer, 2020, pp. 227–244.

Veenstra, Aleit, Philippe Meers, and Daniël Biltereyst. "Exploring Film Genre Preferences through Taste Cultures: A Survey on Contemporary Film Consumption amongst Youth in Flanders (Belgium)." *Communications: The European Journal of Communication Research* 45:2 (2020), pp. 240–251.

Willems, Gertjan. "A Comparative Analysis of Contemporary Film Policy in Flanders and Denmark." *Tijdschrift Voor Communicatiewetenschap* 38:2 (2010), pp. 172–186.

CHAPTER 37

AN EMPIRICAL REPORT ON YOUNG PEOPLE'S RESPONSES TO ADULT FANTASY FILMS

MARTIN BARKER

Have just been to see The Twin Towers—absolute magic...would happily sit through it again immediately. However, when the lights went up and everyone started leaving I was gobsmacked to see families with kids who can't have been more than four or five years old. I know the film has a 12A certificate—basically any responsible adult over the age of 18 can take a child under the age of 12—but how any adult taking such young children to see such a supremely bloody film can be classed as responsible is beyond me. Maybe I'm being overly protective, but I found it obscene that an adult could sit alongside a small kid through three hours of murder and mayhem (albeit beautifully done)....I'm sorry to rant but some people shouldn't be allowed gerbils let alone kids.[1]

FOR more than a century now, many different kinds of people—parents, politicians, educators, moralists, religious folk, researchers (and, of course, people combining these roles)—have thought and argued and written about young people and films/cinema. Particularly strong, and never really going away, has been a current of protective concern. Is this film, or are films in general and cinema as a whole "bad" for the young? Should we be worried about the potential impact of big-screened images on "impressionable" minds?

Academic researchers have been more than happy (not least since, often, money could be found to back such initiatives) to explore a host of particular and general cases, ranging across the possible impacts of advertising, violence, sex, homosexuality, smoking, eating habits, suicide, and many more. The record of such research is not good, by any means, ranging from the weak to the tainted to the virtually fraudulent. But it has depended heavily and repeatedly on a model implicit in that word *impressionable*.

Young people's minds and value systems are only part-formed, so the holes in their heads might get "filled up" with images, stories, stereotypes, representations, of a kind to worry decent folk.

This is, of course, not the only kind of work that has been done on young people and films/cinema (although it is arguably still the dominant one—or at least, one that is perpetually in waiting, ready to be reawakened in the next public scare).[2] But there is also, as other chapters in this volume demonstrate, a body of work on films made specifically for children and young people and on the representations of children themselves within films. Less often, but still occasionally, there is research on young people as audiences—asking in what ways their responses to films (whether child- or adult-oriented), their pleasures in film and cinema, may be like or unlike those of more adult viewers.[3] This chapter tries to add a dimension of new and specific knowledge to this last kind of work.

I draw on two very large resources. These are the databases from two international research projects, respectively conducted in 2002–2003 and 2013–2014, into the reception of Peter Jackson's film trilogies of *The Lord of the Rings* (2001–2003) and *The Hobbit* (2012–2014).[4] Both projects succeeded in gathering large numbers of responses from many countries: in the case of *The Lord of the Rings* (henceforth, *LOTR*) just under 25,000 responses, and over 36,000 for *The Hobbit*. The responses were garnered using a distinctive kind of questionnaire that combined a range of multiple-choice questions with open questions inviting people to tell us in their own words what they liked or disliked, and how they understood and related to the films. Because, unsurprisingly, we asked people to tell us their ages, we are able to separate out young people's responses, examine them in their own right, and compare them with those of older audiences.

For *LOTR*, people were asked to indicate the age-group they belonged to, beginning with "under 16," thence rising in ten-year spans. This gave us a total of 2,486 under-16s from our 24,738 total. (In addition, we had the opportunity to conduct a small number of follow-up interviews with young participants who exemplified emergent patterns that we had identified.) With *The Hobbit*, we took the different route of asking people to indicate their birth year (but had no opportunity to do follow-up interviews). This allowed us still to see the overall total of under-16 participants (2,060), but also showed us their precise age breakdown at that time (Table 37.1).

Albeit the figures for the youngest viewers are very low indeed, we will see that there are some striking indicators of changes in response by age.

Table 37.1. Numbers by age of young *Hobbit* respondents.

15	14	13	12	11	10	9	8
925	644	302	124	38	13	10	4

CRITICAL CONTEXTS

Noel Brown's wide-ranging study of the state of research and thinking about children's films declines simple definitions.[5] Instead, in a study which considers the history of such films in countries as diverse as India, Iran, Denmark, Brazil, and the United States, he positions "children's film" at the intersection of several forces:

- What children want and seek out: primarily commercial, this aspect strongly couples with non-cinematic leisure traditions (toys, games, merchandise, and the like).
- What "children" want: essentially driven by sentimental conceptions of a "childhood era," here there is emphasis on animals, cuteness, small adventures, and the safety of returning home.
- What children "need": pedagogic and ideological, this tends to be either state-driven or moralistically promoted, balancing the instructional and the protective.

The running tensions between these in different places and times shape what becomes available. In the course of these, *actual* children and their responses tend to be circumscribed or written out, as timeless conceptions overwrite them—and, of course, they only rarely and exceptionally get opportunities to voice their views publicly. But as Brown succinctly puts it, "The point is that, in spite of changes in culture and society, children's films continue to be measured against a widely-accepted generic framework—linked to social constructions of childhood—that delineates what they are, and what they are not"—and young people can be very aware of this.[6] Their responses to films and other media materials are formed against the backdrop of evolving definitions and debates about what they can/can't, should/shouldn't watch. In a related way, this chapter aims to demonstrate that, while the backdrop of adult definitions is undoubtedly important, young people's *actual filmic encounters* are not simply reducible to this. Indeed, a driving force can be a strong *will to transcend the sphere of childhood*, and to establish a foothold in current adult cultures, their materials, issues, and possibilities.

The problem is that children are rarely given opportunities to express these engagements in their own words. In a bravura overview of the state of this area of research, Martens et al. argued that too much of the agenda of research into children's cultural practices has been driven by a "production of consumption" approach, that sees consumption as effectively *forced* on consumers (seeing them as a "a homogeneous social group of apparently impressionable and pressurized individuals").[7] This has resulted, they say, in a "notable lack of interest in the symbolic meanings that people, whether adult or child, create around the goods and services they consume."[8] So, studies of children's choices of clothing, games, toys, stories, and media, for instance, have viewed them through a lens of *critique and protectiveness*. They also note that, despite the influence of Bourdieu's general theory of cultural reproduction, there is very little work on *how (far)* concretely children come to embrace and reproduce their parents' "habitus": that internalized patterning of everyday assumptions about tastes, the world, and oneself.

Curiously, what remains in place in this valuable critique is the very term that I want to query: "consumption." This term, while *appearing* descriptive, in fact carries a weight of connotations. One *consumes* (ingests, absorbs) food—and therefore, by analogy, one ingests and absorbs something from other kinds of cultural materials. This point has been forcefully made by others, notably Russell Belk and colleagues, and Richard Wilk, who have insisted that "consumption" operates as a powerful metaphor.[9] "Consumption" evokes heady questions about *amount* (too much?), *quality* ("junk"? "risky additives"?), and *cumulative dangers* ("addictive"?).[10]

This point has been forcefully made by, in particular, David Buckingham—whose research (along with a team of others at London's Institute of Education) into children's media cultures stands out as exemplary. Writing about the general impact of adult perceptions of the supposed impact of television, he concludes: "The children were very familiar with adult definitions of appropriateness, although they were inclined to displace any negative "effects" of television onto those younger than themselves, or onto "children" in general."[11] We will see that this exactly mirrors one aspect of young people's responses in our research.

LOVING *THE LORD OF THE RINGS* AND *THE HOBBIT*

In many respects young people's responses to *LOTR* map well on to those of older audiences—with small but revealing differences. Overall, the *LOTR* trilogy was very well received by all ages, but the youngest audiences were definitely the most enthusiastic. This remained the case with *The Hobbit*, although overall ratings were considerably lower, as Table 37.2 indicates.

Table 37.2. Proportions of "excellent" ratings by age groups

	Under-16	16–25	26–35	36–45	46–55	56–65
The Lord of the Rings						
Excellent	80.5	70.4	66.8	70.5	75.3	66.2
The Hobbit						
Excellent	67.1	36.8	25.2	30.7	37.6	39.9

Our younger viewers also attached higher levels of importance to their *LOTR* viewing (70 per cent judging them "extremely important," dropping to 58.2 per cent for the next age band). Unsurprisingly, fewer under-16s had read the books multiple times (41.5 per cent compared with over 60 per cent for those aged 36–55), but considerably more were still reading them (11.1 per cent vs. just 2.8 per cent for those aged 36–55). And in their "mentions" of favourite characters, there are strong commonalities with older viewers' choices.[12] So, for instance, attachment to central characters Aragorn and Frodo shows no signs of being age-related. But in other cases, there are some curious fluctuations. Mentions of Gandalf show a clear rising gradient by age, which may not be very surprising—but then less obviously, so do mentions of Sam (who rises steadily from under-16s' 15.5 per cent to 25.7 per cent for our oldest respondents). This hints, interestingly, that young people's involvement with *LOTR* may be significantly different than with *Harry Potter*, where Ranjana Das found that young viewers particularly attached value to the importance of friendship relations (loyalty, trust, intimacy)—qualities that Sam especially appears to embody.[13] An indication of the difference that might be at work here was given in one of the interviews we conducted as part of the *LOTR* project. Laura (#5933, 14 at the time of her interview) was asked to compare her feelings about *LOTR* and *Harry Potter*:

L: I think in some parts [*LOTR*] connects up with the real world, even though it isn't real and it is fantasy. But there's again, might be underlying messages, kind of comment to life, even now. It is…most of it is fantasy but some bits like…connect to the real world….

I: Do you find that that's the case with something say like Harry Potter as well?

L: Not really with *Harry Potter*, I just enjoy reading it cos they're fun books…I guess when they have problems at school you can kind of relate to that bit, but apart from that, it doesn't really relate to the rest of the world.

The implications of this distinction—that *LOTR* connects more widely than *Harry Potter* to "the rest of the world"—are considerable. (I return to our interview with Laura later.)

But the most evident age-dependent variable is in mentions of Legolas (dropping steadily from under-16s' 25.2 per cent to just 6.2 per cent for our oldest respondents). There is a strong gender dimension in here. Of the 627 who mentioned Legolas, 69 per cent are female—and, perhaps as revealingly, five times as many females as males name him "Orlando Bloom."[14] Clearly, the actor/character combination was a particular winner with young girls. This didn't stop some boys from choosing Legolas, even though they knew it was something different for girls, as here: "…[M]y sister who is twelve thinks Orlando Bloom is hot. I liked him because he has courage" [#23174]. The word "cool" recurs in the boys' talk. This delight in a combination of skill, courage, and heroic presence is not to be lightly dismissed—and surely connects with another most striking difference between younger and older viewers that I address next.

The Discursive Logic of "Amazement"

When it was first noticed, one small feature of young people's talk about *LOTR* and *The Hobbit* seemed interesting, but probably inconsequential.[15] But when we investigated further, it turned out to be of rich significance. This is their use of one word: "amazing." Clearly the word expresses intense pleasure, pleasure that went beyond previous experience (a passing example: "Emotional journey…amazing…exceeds my expectations" [#11768, *LOTR*, under-16]). When examined in the case of *LOTR*, the figures for uses of the word proved strongly age-related (Table 37.3).

With the exception of that small rise in the highest age group, there is a sizeable and steady decline across the ages. But in the *Hobbit* project it happened that we chose to ask for *year of birth*, with the result that it was possible to measure frequency of the word's use against people's exact ages. The results (here presented between ages 12–21) are striking (Table 37.4).

With caution (since the lowest-age totals are small), it does seem that the word "amazing" emerges as a serious option for use to describe the films at ages 13–14. Thereafter it slowly but steadily diminishes, to an eventual "steady state" of 5 to 6 per cent per year. It is of course possible—and not wrong—to wonder whether general vocabularies increase, enabling young people to choose from a wider range of words ("astonishing," "awesome," "astounding," etc.—although none of the obvious alternative candidates appear, upon checking, particularly age-influenced). But closer examination of how young people *use* the term does strongly suggest that it is carrying a range of connotations, hinting its connection to a wider emergent discourse about pleasure and its implications. First, consider some quotations from very young *Hobbit* respondents who *do not* use the term:

> I found the films very exciting, especially in the 3-D version, and I enthusiastically told my friends about the film. [#21497, *Hobbit*, age 11][16]
>
> I was excited because the films are cool, and I was curious to see what happens next. [#22511, *Hobbit*, age 10]
>
> The first two parts I liked very much, the third part I was a little disappointed, because they did not design it as well as in the book, the two first parts I found better implemented. [#22658, *Hobbit*, age 12]

Table 37.3: Use of "amazing" in evaluations of *LOTR* films, by age group (%)

Under-16	16–25	26–35	36–45	46–55	56–65
15.2	10.6	5.3	3.6	2.1	5.5

Table 37.4. Age by use of "amazing" (English–language *Hobbit* participants)

Birth	Age	Total	"Amazing"	%	Birth	Age	Total	"Amazing"	%
2002	12	17	1	5.9	1997	17	274	27	9.9
2001	13	47	10	21.3	1996	18	371	36	9.7
2000	14	112	24	21.4	1995	19	446	27	6.1
1999	15	189	30	15.9	1994	20	419	28	6.7
1998	16	223	32	14.3	1993	21	394	26	6.6

These responses are revealing. Capable—and perhaps proud—of using sophisticated language (in different ways "cool," "enthusiastically," and "implemented"), they suggest that the experience of the film was self-contained, except for the third for whom Tolkien's book has become the measure. The recurrent word "exciting/-ed" stresses the strength of reactions, but implies little beyond the films' ending, except reporting to friends that this was a "cool" (culturally appropriate and worthwhile) experience.

Compare these, then, with some uses of the term "amazing" in the peak age bracket, 13–14:

> The films have changed my life completely! I fell in love with them from the first 30 minutes of watching. They are truly amazing and have worked wonders on my mind and heart. I am very passionate about them. [#2083 *Hobbit*, age 14]
>
> It was amazing to see the book come to life, all the cast were perfect for the roles and the extra additions I did not mind as it was explaining the part of the story behind *Lord of the Rings*. [#7391 *Hobbit*, age 13]
>
> These three films were perhaps the most amazing cinematic experience ever. They introduced me to Middle-Earth, to Tolkien's world. They changed my life. [#9103 *Hobbit*, age 13]
>
> Simply amazing, all of the work and effort put into making all the sets and props and makeup etc. is extraordinary! The trilogy was fantastic even if it didn't stay exactly true to the books. [#14730 *Hobbit*, age 14]

The strength of responses is, of course, their first feature. For some, it is a qualified strength, coupled with specific criticisms. We should take seriously the expressed sense that for some this outruns their language. But to me, the most interesting feature of these responses is their reporting of *something that transcends simply being films*. For all that it is—or perhaps because it is—exceptional, consider this long response, from a 14-year-old girl:

> The most amazing trilogy of films that will ever be made. I believe they did a great job casting the actors and with the special effects. It is just fantastic! It has made my whole life seem different, like I live in a new world. There is so much to say and it also has a meaning to the films. There is something that will be left behind. And I

think that is all the loyalty that the fans will have over the years to come. There will be more fans as the years pass. No one will ever forget Middle Earth. Just the sense that there is more to this world than there is in our actual life. People would love to live the life of Middle Earth. It brings this strange feeling to all the fans, and it will stay with them, forever. I love it and I always think of it EVERYDAY of my life ever since I watched the films. Is it bad that I dream of it? Well, either way, all the fans are crazy in love with *The Hobbit*. For anyone who has not watched *The Hobbit* and/ or *The Lord of the Rings*, then I feel bad for them because they have no idea what on Middle Earth they are missing. My life would be incomplete if it were not for *The Hobbit* and *The Lord of the Rings*. And yes, I mean it. [#10091 *Hobbit*, age 14]

It does not matter if this may subsequently have changed. At the time of the experience, and in recollection to the point of responding to our questionnaire, this constituted a life-forming experience. The insistence in the answer is important—plus, her sense that this was a cumulative result from experiencing the two trilogies. This surely constitutes the formative end of what has become widely known as the "reminiscence bump": the widely-attested phenomenon that "public" memories laid down in the period of adolescence tend to be recalled with particular affection and significance in later life.[17] But research into this "bump" has tended to be focused on its operation in later life, rather than on the circumstances in which significant experiences might be laid down.

A similar situation occurs with young people's responses to the *Rings* trilogy, as these quotations illustrate:[18]

It was an amazing end to an incredible journey not just for the characters but also for the viewers. [#12286 *LOTR*, under-16]

Amazing, a real masterpiece!!!! The acting was superb (especially Elijah Wood and Sean Astin) and the visual and special effects were so good you couldn't tell they were there!!!! The best film ever made!!!! [#11090 *LOTR*, under-16]

My response to the film was very emotional. I felt a great connection with the Hobbits and the friendship theme that ran throughout the film. The film was amazing and I cried throughout it as well as for the last 20 minutes straight (approx.). This film means the world to me at the moment and it's helped me to figure out a lot in my life. I will always remember it and how it's helped me. [#12798 *LOTR*, under-16]

I thought this film was absolutely amazing. It made me realise how lucky I am to have such wonderful friends and I hope that if I ever need to take on a task such as Frodo had to, my friends will accompany me and support me. No goal is out of reach and no dream is too small. [#6501 *LOTR*, under-16]

As these examples show, not every "amazed" response is about extra-filmic associations. In quite a number of cases the amazement is at seeing the potential of film, and having one's measures and ideals of cinematic work stretched and solidified. But for a good number, this is again *more than a film*.

TWO CASE STUDIES

As illustrations of the full meaning of these findings, take two individuals: one boy and one girl. They are not presented as typical. Rather, I have picked them because they gave us such rich, extended responses to our questions, fleshing out what the categories mean, albeit each with some clearly distinctive individual characteristics.

"James"[19] (#13302) was a 15-year-old Australian boy, who rated both the *Hobbit* (and *LOTR*) films "excellent," and could think of nothing that disappointed him. He is clear about what pleased him:

> The films were beautiful and amazing. Words don't come close to how I feel. The movies have so much emotion, stories, virtues and so much more. The fantasy seems so real and it isn't a stupid fantasy that has nothing in it. This fantasy contains friend- ship, loyalty, love, people coming together and heaps more.

The clear demarcation of *this* fantasy from "stupid" ones is clearly important to him. He fleshes this out some more in answering our question as to whether he sees any "broader themes" in them: "It raises the theme of unity that we must put our differences aside to come together. It also raises the importance of friendship and being there for one an- other. The theme of greed and what greed can do to people is also evident." His chosen reasons for seeing the films were love of Tolkien's work as a whole, along with belonging to a community of people involved in them (which turns out to be an online one devoted to the films—he tells us that he is still reading the book), and enjoying the stunning locations.

James is one of the many who positively *reject* the idea that *The Hobbit* is a "children's story" (see the section below, "Keep Away from Children"), writing that "this movie is a whole lot more than a children's story. I believe that a child would not be able to com- pletely understand everything that's going on in all the moments of the film," adding that "I also feel that the movies are a whole lot more special than an average, generic Hollywood blockbuster or a star attraction." Instead, there is for him a sense of stored- up potential that makes them outrun standard Hollywood fare.

James is just discovering the wider world and reflecting on its importance to him. He records his three "favourite activities," as "going to Germany for the first time…speaking my second language (German) every day for 8 weeks…being able to explore a country I have never been to before." But his *attitude* to these comes through. Answering our question about who he thinks might share his views on *The Hobbit*, he writes that they will be "kind, generous, caring and loving people." And his account of what he sees as distinctive about himself is striking: "I am a curious person. I want to explore which I can relate to heavily in *The Hobbit*. A world like *The Hobbit*'s seems so interesting and vast. There are so many unknown things and so much still to explore. Whereas I feel today everything has been heavily touched by humanity. There's still places around the world to explore but it just doesn't feel the same as an open beautiful seemingly empty landscape." He is evidently threading together his fantasy experiences with his interest in locations (not yet visited but one of his chosen reasons for seeing the films) and with interest in the world beyond Australia. Without stretching things, we might say that he is on his way, in a very particular fashion, to *becoming a citizen of the world*, within which his rich delight in the films is playing a significant role. It is not difficult to see the connections with his choices for the *roles* he sees fantasy as playing now. They are "a way of experiencing and exploring emotions"; "a source of hopes and dreams for changing our world"; and they "allow us to explore different attitudes and ideas."

"Hannah," a 14-year-old American girl, also rated both film trilogies "excellent," with no disappointments. An important feature of her response was that she was "dragged along" to see them, not really knowing what to expect ("my best friend, it's his fault I'm into these movies now, anyway. I can't thank him enough for it"). Having seen them, her response crystallized:

> I was speechless, amazed, and I felt like I'd been on an adventure. I had never read the book or done any kind of research going into these movies, but I loved them re-gardless. They genuinely had a lot of work put into them, and the feeling I got after finishing the series in *Battle of the Five Armies* proved it.

Like James, Hannah rejected calling them "children's films" "because some kids can't un-derstand battle scenes or because they might have been scared by some of the creatures, like Gollum for example." Also, "I wouldn't consider this a coming-of-age story myself, because even though all the characters 'grew up' a bit during this movie, they didn't come across a huge realisation or epiphany that changed their lives forever."

But if the characters didn't have an epiphany, Hannah had something like one—her experiences *outran* those of the characters, leading her to perceive some important larger. "timeless" themes: "The themes regarding greed or want impacted me the most because it's something everyone deals with every single day of their lives. People are constantly talking about how you should want what you've got, that sort of thing, yet everyone always wants more. Thorin's character really showed the impact of that, which is really important in a society like today's. Or any society, in fact. It's really a timeless theme."

Hannah, interestingly, makes almost the same choices as James for the contemporary role of fantasy: they are "a way of experiencing and exploring emotions," a "source of hopes and dreams for changing our world," but also a "way of escaping." She is aware of being at a formative stage in her life, but not sure how she is coming out of it. This is how she answers our question about anything personal to her that might help us understand all her answers:

> I'm not sure how many of these things affected my opinions or not, but they all had some little impact: I'm in high school and I'm trying to figure out a lot of stuff

about myself and the world and what not, I have a friend I told you about that got me obsessed with these movies, I have two other friends that show a bit of interest in these movies but would rather talk about other things, and I went and saw *An Unexpected Journey* because of a school trip, but I came out wanting to see *Desolation of Smaug* at that very second.

Her sense being on the cusp of a change is further revealed by one small comment. Explaining what had most impressed her, she told us:

> The way the story was carried out made me feel like I'd been somewhere, which surprised me. You can become immersed in a movie, sure, but it takes a really good team of people to make you feel like you've been on an adventure within the span of about two and a half hours. I came out of the theater each time feeling like I'd been doing a lot of walking. I was on the edge of my seat as Smaug was shown for the first time, or for my first time seeing Rivendell. The character's deaths impacted me a lot more strongly than I would have ever expected them to. The way the characters were portrayed and their development really impressed me.

Note here her reference to her "first time seeing" Rivendell. Yet she has also told us that she had loved, and rated "excellent," the *Lord of the Rings* films, which contain long scenes in Rivendell. But she had obviously been too young when she saw these for them to have created this kind of impression. With the *Hobbit* films, Hannah was ready for something more formative, "new" in a distinctive way.

James and Hannah are, I stress, not "typical." They are what I might call emphatic examples. Their "amazement" at the films is a gateway to something wider. It is of course not possible to know what, of this, will remain as their lives go on. But there is every reason to think that, if nothing else, their transformative experiences from these films will constitute elements within their later "reminiscence bump." They are, I suggest, vividly joining world culture.

VERNACULAR ENGAGEMENTS

We can gain further insights into these things by considering some other surprising results to emerge from analysis of responses within the *LOTR* and *Hobbit* databases. The design of our questionnaires, in both cases, included a multiple-choice question asking participants to choose from a carefully constituted list up to three "vernacular" expressions which best captured their sense of the *kind* of films they had watched.[20] Table 37.5 displays the spread of choices for the two projects.

Although there are various interesting variations here, surely the stand-out result for *LOTR* relates to "War story," where young people's choices are well over double those of our overall population. But this figure becomes even more striking when linked with a

Table 37.5. Responses to "vernacular category" questions (overall vs. under 16s)

The Lord of the Rings			The Hobbit		
	All.	U-16		All.	U-16.
Allegory	10.5	7.3	Action-adventure	24.3	35.5
Epic	52.7	42.1	Children's story	2.7	1.0
Fairy tale	11.3	11.7	Coming-of-age movie	3.8	6.0
Fantasy	39.9	43.2	Digital novelty cinema	10.3	9.3
Game-world	2.4	4.4	Fairy tale	7.9	4.9
Good vs. evil	43.3	48.3	Family film	3.9	5.5
Myth/legend	36.0	30.8	Hollywood blockbuster	19.2	12.1
Quest	33.5	40.1	Literary adaptation	24.5	22.7
SFX film	22.5	21.9	Multimedia franchise	11.2	4.9
Spiritual journey	7.5	7.5	Part of Tolkien's legend world	61.6	70.5
Threatened homeland	6.8	14.5	Peter Jackson movie	22.4	24.8
War story	8.8	21.6	Prequel/sequel	24.3	25.1
			Star attraction	4.4	9.0
			Stunning locations	28.1	38.2
			World of fantasy	63.0	69.6

further discovery.[21] It was noticed that 134 of our youngest participants, asked to categorize their *occupation*, chose to label themselves "unemployed," even though because of their age they almost certainly counted as "students" of one kind or another.[22] This raised a question in our minds as to whether this was some kind of *disaffection* with education. And a cross-check of the responses of *this* subgroup to the vernacular categories question revealed a further rise in the proportion choosing "War story"—to almost 25 per cent (three times the overall proportion).

What, then, does "war" mean to these young people? There are absolutely no signs of this being a reference to the *genre* of war films, of any kind. Instead, what appears to be at the heart of their explanations is a combination of three things: the *seriousness* of the issues over which the war is fought; the *emotions* experienced by characters, or by viewers in response to their travails; and their *climactic* role in resolving the challenges people faced. The following answers to our "most memorable" question illustrate these tendencies:

> The charge of the Rohirrim into the battle at Pelennor Fields. Looking at the entire host of Rohan assemble and charge fearlessly into what seems to be their deaths was very moving. (#5092 *LOTR*)
>
> When Aragorn gives his speech to the remaining men at the battle of the Black Gate, it summed up the theme of the story. (#6039 *LOTR*)

Where Faramir is riding basically to his doom. That is where Denethor sends Faramir to retake the taken city. Pippin's song and the music and him charging on his horse was so powerful and overwhelming. (#8836 *LOTR*)

My favorite part was by far when all the men joined together (I love it when that happens, when everyone comes together to fight) and they charged the orc army and they just CRASHED into them and completely ploughed them down. It gave me chills. (#9630 *LOTR*)

"War" here is an occasion and opportunity for maximizing meaning and importance.

KEEP AWAY FROM CHILDREN

We couldn't include one of our intended questions in the *LOTR* questionnaire, for reasons of space.[23] It had been hoped to *pair* the vernacular category questions, asking both which choices participants would *positively make*, and which if any they would *definitely reject*. In the overall longer *Hobbit* questionnaire, this became possible. The most striking result to emerge from this concerned the category "Children's film." The category with the lowest positive choices (at 2.7 per cent), it was also decisively *rejected* by 60.8 per cent of all our participants. In a valuable essay, Lars Schmeink has used the *Hobbit* database to explore in detail the various kinds of reasons given for rejecting this label.[24] The reasons range across too much complexity in the story, the levels of violence displayed, and that they are too "scary" for children. But strikingly, the proportion of young people rejecting the category is *even higher* than the overall population, at 72.4 per cent. Reviewing young people's explanations of their refusals, some of the characteristics our young respondents displayed match Buckingham's account, mentioned earlier. The films are "too violent," "graphic," "dark," "scary," or "intense" for "small" or "young children." The self-distancing implied by the words "small" and "young" is important—"they" are not ready for these materials, whereas "we" are. A few go further. One reflects on his own younger brother's liking: "I do not believe it is for children, although my little brother is very fond of *The Hobbit* and *The Lord of the Rings* and he is 5 years old. People say it isn't good for little children to see it. Actually, if little kids see it, it wouldn't actually matter to me. I mean if they see it and like it, then they see it and like it. There is nothing you can do to make them not like it" [#10091 *Hobbit*].[25]

But a number of our young respondents hint at a further dimension not found among older participants: that these films *transcend* matters of age appropriateness. Sometimes age appropriateness is simply a sense that the films would be too "complicated" or "confusing" for younger children, but occasionally it is extended, as here: "*The Hobbit* is an action-packed movie with epic battles and deep meaning. It is definitely not a children's story" [#30699 *Hobbit*]. Or again: "I feel as though, even though *The Hobbit* was originally written as a children's story, it has become much more than that and should not be seen as JUST that" [#27769 *Hobbit*]. This extra is achieved by its becoming a "world of fantasy" in which you can "immerse yourself."[26]

To illustrate this, I return to the case of Laura, whom I quoted earlier on the differences between *LOTR* and *Harry Potter*. Laura is one of those who, though still in school, marked herself as "unemployed." Although the interview did not (unfortunately)[27] ask her directly about the meaning of this choice to her, there are a number of indications within the interview as to what it might signify. Laura got to see the first part of *LOTR* almost by accident—it was an opportunity to go to the cinema with her mum, and she had read generally good things about the film. But having seen it, it became something of an obsession ("I exited the cinema speechless," as she put it in her questionnaire). She immediately went and read and then re-read the books (although she insisted to us that the films were best and always came first in her interests). She had seen the final film nine times by the time of our interview.

What did she love about the film? Just about everything: its epic scale, the cinematography, the acting, the landscapes, and its very human dimensions, which engaged her emotions. Writing about her favourite moment, she declared she could have "killed Gollum, the git" because of his tricking of Frodo and Sam (her favourite character). She loved not only the films, but a lot of other things that accompanied it, the music, games, books, T-shirts, posters, etc., and bought whatever she could afford. They had their own influence on her. Howard Shore's film score for instance introduced her to classical music, which she hadn't previously appreciated.

An important part of the pleasure of the film for her was experiencing other peoples' positive reactions inside the cinema (clapping and cheering, for example), and knowing that around the world were loads of other enthusiasts—although not necessarily among her own circle of friends ("some of my friends said, oh, it's so boring"). Laura describes herself as "a bit anti-social," someone who didn't find talking easy—but she would happily talk for ages about *LOTR*. And her answer to our query about what kind of person would love *LOTR* in the way she did, was clear: they would be "broader-minded," with "more imagination," and not inclined to dismiss Tolkien as "just fantasy." There is an interesting moment in the interview when Laura touches on religion. Pointing to the importance of Tolkien's Christian beliefs, and declaring herself a Christian, she immediately surrounded this with hesitations, since she doesn't want it thought that this is the main reason for enjoying it—it is perhaps a small bonus for her, but she knows that for others this would be irrelevant: "I don't think it really makes a difference to many people because they just enjoy it anyway." The bigger point is that it is "more adult," and "you have to be pretty committed to read it." And in an interesting wording, she responds to her interviewer's question about whether she expects *LOTR* to remain important to her, with "I'd like to think it will"—it has a part within her envisioning of her future self and identity, as she reaches adulthood.

Another important feature of her pleasure was her sheer pleasure in *LOTR*'s *non-urbanized* world. Expressed as a long-ago "New Zealand," where in her imagination the story takes place, she also compared it with her experience of visiting the Brecon Beacons, the national park in Wales, where the housing was not concrete and ugly, but

natural within its landscape. Overall, Laura's encounters with *LOTR* were deeply important to her. Coming as a surprise, the film led her into a world of new emotions, ideas,
and images, which rubbed up against her tendency to be an outsider, and gave her one
avenue into a more adult range of engagements. Thinking of herself as a "student" didn't
quite fit with that for her.

IMPLICATIONS

What wider bodies or work, or debates, might these results connect with? Readers of
this chapter may well have their own thoughts on this, but I would particularly emphasize two topics.

The Intersection between Developmental Psychology and Generational Theory

There is a strong tradition within developmental psychology of work that breaks down
young people's development into relatively fixed stages. This is particularly true of work
influenced by Jean Piaget,[28] for whom cognitive growth was seen as closely linked to
biological growth; and Erik Erikson,[29] whose research into formations of identity led
him to separate a series of developmental stages—of which one in particular, Stage 5,
occurring between ages 12 and 18, captures young people's emergence as near-adults
with their own values and perspectives (but with the potential for role confusions if
subject to contradictory pressures from significant adults in their lives). The findings
presented here are broadly consonant with these theories—but with the addition that
a vital part of such transitions from childhood to adulthood is made possible by and
shaped by very particular culturally and historically located encounters. It is here that
the work of Karl Mannheim, and of those who have built on his ideas, becomes particularly valuable.

Mannheim argued that certain climactic events could shape a whole generation's experience, giving them a shared and distinctive sense of the nature of the opportunities,
tasks, and threats their society faces.[30] For Mannheim, this was likely to be cataclysmic
events such as world wars. But others accepting his framework have suggested that certain *cultural* events might perform similar functions, allowing us to speak of the "Beatles
generation," the "*Star Wars* generation," the "Nintendo generation." the *Harry Potter*
generation," the "digital generation," and so on. Some of this is loose and lazy talk, as
with a lot of discussions of "Generations X, Y, and Z." But Göran Bolin has developed a
thoughtful and critical version of this idea by emphasizing the specificity and localiza-
tion of people's senses of generational belonging (his main works in this area compare
Sweden and Estonia).[31] Curiously, I want to suggest that the evidence presented here

hints in the other direction: that among the impacts of mainstream "Hollywood" films may be to prompt a sense of "the world" as a common issue. If correct—and I am aware that the empirical evidence presented here can only tentatively point to this—it adds a curious reverse note to the overwhelmingly negative tone to the many approaches to "Hollywood," "globalization," and "cultural imperialism" debates.[32]

Rethinking the Politics of Fantasy

A recent, quite large body of work has been reconsidering the general nature and role of fantasy and, in particular, their relation to politics. This work began around 2000—and of course, the two projects that I have been drawing on here were very much part of the shift. In 2002, a special issue of the Marxist journal *Historical Materialism* was edited and introduced by China Miéville, who is himself a major fantasy author. The issue challenged the prevailing view that fantasy is in principle reactionary, and connected it instead with theories of *hope* and *utopia*. (Despite this, Miéville himself remained ambivalent towards Tolkien. As Patrick Curry noted recently,[33] he swung between critical rejection—citing Moorcock's smart rebuttal of Tolkien, that jailers don't hate escapism, they hate escape—and in 2009 being willing to acknowledge that Tolkien "rocked.") Until this point, with a few exceptions, the major theorizations of fantasy had come out of literary studies, and were particularly driven by a will to draw a line between The Fantastic (a proper literary genre) and "fantasy" (popular Tolkien pastiches, not worth studying).[34]

The rise of new theories of fantasy was in part a response to José Monleón's thesis that "fantasy" constituted the dark, repressed side of the Enlightenment's "dream of reason": the bursting out of the repressed, instinctual aspects of humans.[35] It is surely no accident that among those rethinking the field were writers, defending their field, including some involved in the emergence of "New Weird" fantasy in the 1990s.[36] On the back of this impulse came both new kinds of writing, and new theoretical approaches, addressing the general role of fantasy in political life.[37]

As so often, it is seen as enough to conclude, on formal grounds, whether the texts are "progressive" or "reactionary," without saying anything about what this might mean for audiences who enjoy and participate in them, let alone that exploring audience engagements might for one query such textual deductions. So, for instance, Dan Hassler-Forest explored a range of science fiction and fantasy story-worlds as part of a large thesis about social transformation. and contended that these worlds must be understood as expressions of the rise of "cognitive" or "fantastical" capitalism and associated with the rise of transmedia production systems, where audiences are involved in doing a lot of the work of building and sustaining media brands. Looking at HBO's mega-series *Game of Thrones*, for example, he argues that it proffers an apparently radical message—that the world is fundamentally unsafe, that ordinary strategies will not help with survival, and that to survive, one has to be flexible in a precarious world—but is virtually doomed to end with a solution that blunts this message by "solving" the problems of succession. Such series, he says, "operate as an expression of global capitalism," and that "popular fantasy is adopting the paradigm of cynical reason that appears increasingly hostile to the genre's traditional idealism," calling it even "ideology at its purest."[38]

As in most of these rethinkings, Hassler-Forrest has almost nothing to say about *actual* receptions, *real* audiences. It is apparently enough to postulate a *kind of audience* and impute reactions to them. And that is a real pity. What I hope this chapter has shown is that, in contemporary circumstances and for particular audiences, fantasy may provide certain opportunities for transformative experiences. Among the contemporary features that could be relevant to this is the very rise of the conception of "the world" as an interlocking set of systems. This has been strikingly demonstrated by Clark Miller, who traces the evolution of debates about climate policy, showing that "the *representation* of the Earth's climate in scientific and policy discourses changed dramatically between the mid-1960s and the late 1980s."[39] The change was away from an account in terms of national or regional weather systems, to "climate" as a world system:

> Only when the Earth's climate was reimagined as a *global* system, bringing views of the atmosphere in line with assumptions about the jurisdiction of international institutions, did claims about climate change begin to engage with debates about international politics.[40]

Equivalent shifts are surely evident in thinking about diseases and global health, economies, the environment, natural resources, habitat loss and loss of species. These areas of concern and intervention have then been paralleled by rises in attention within fantasy to "world-building": the search for coherent, persuasive, explorable narrative structures. The literature for this has recently grown substantially.[41] I want to propose very cautiously that the global rise of fantasy films and literature is making a small but signal contribution to young people's sense of the *importance* and the *potential mutability* of their world. It is perhaps fitting, then, to close with a quotation from a young participant in our project mentioning "world" in complicated ways in telling us why they rated *Lord of the Rings* so highly—and referencing "the world" in multiple ways:

> I think that every single movie in the trilogy is the best film ever made. These movies have changed my mindset for the world. I now respect nature and enjoy it much more than before I saw the movies or read the books. The books and movies are full of values that have been forgotten in the real world. I think the entire world could learn from this story. (#7834 *LOTR*)

In his recent study of Netflix, Ramon Lobato, among other things, examines the emergent conflicts between the company, whose preferences (embodied in its algorithms) are towards US-sourced materials, and various national regulatory agencies (most strongly within the European Union) which are pressing for mandatory and visible inclusion of a good proportion of locally produced materials.[42] Lobato asks astute questions about the evidential base behind claims and counterclaims as to "what people really want." But interestingly, he poses this as a choice between preferences for US-sourced, and nationally and linguistically local cultural provision. The evidence I have brought forward here offers a complicated amendment to this, suggesting that for at least *some* cultural materials, though their *source* may be America/Hollywood, at the point of reception they are taken as *concerning and addressing the world*. And that may particularly be the case with materials garnished with the imprimatur of "fantasy."

I close therefore with the responses of one young female participant (#12123) who—across three answers to our questions—enunciates almost perfectly the arguments I have been making here:

> *Response to the film?* To me the film gave me a feeling of pure satisfaction. It was more than a movie, it was a complete experience a mixture of fantasy and fun and life lessons. And somewhere within the experience was a spark of joy that I got from reading the books as much as from seeing the movie. It was pure intensity...*Favourite character?* Samwise Gamgee. This is because he has such an innocence about him when the journey begins and slowly the truth of the quest and of evil begins to overcome him. He sees Frodo who is as close to him as a brother fall into the corruption and dark world of evil power. And yet he continues amidst the words that must wrench at his heart, he goes after his master and beloved friend to the very last step of the quest. *Most memorable moment?* I would have to say the overwhelming emotions. Though the story was a fantasy I found myself taking the journey alongside the members crying my eyes out smiling like an idiot clenching my teeth in determination even laughing for pure joy. I fell headlong into the world of Middle-earth and forgot all about the movie theater. I will always remember those feelings and remember being completely sucked up into the movie.

Notes

1. Found at https://www.mumsnet.com/Talk/other_subjects/5291-lord-of-the-rings-would-you-let-a-five-year [posted December 30, 2002; accessed August 13, 2018].
2. The extent to which this history is dominated/distorted by moralizing influences is much debated, and I do not attempt to review it here. See, for instance, Ellen Wartella and Byron Reeves, "Historical Trends in Research on Children and the Media: 1900–1960," *Journal of Communication* 35:2 (1985), pp. 118–133; Chas Critcher, "Aspects of Public Debates about Children and Mass Media," in Kirsten Drotner and Sonia Livingstone (eds.), *International Handbook of Children, Media and Culture* (London: SAGE, 2008), pp. 91–105. See also, in particular, Jowett et al. on the Payne Fund Controversy, especially their essay on the "lost" work of Paul Cressey: Garth Jowett, Ian Jarvie, and Kathryn H. Fuller, *Children and the Movies: Media Influence and the Payne Fund Controversy* (Cambridge, UK: Cambridge University Press, 1996); Garth Jowett, Ian Jarvie, and Kathryn H. Fuller, "The Thirteenth Manuscript: The Case of the Missing Payne Fund Study," *Historical Journal of Film, Radio and Television* 13:4 (1993), pp. 387–402.

3. To my eye, one piece of work—now difficult to obtain—is particularly interesting. In 1954 Mary Field published the results of a study of pre-teenage children attending a Saturday matinee cinema screening. Using two infrared cameras, one pointing at the children and one at the screen, she was able to see which aspects of a western particularly caught their attention. Her book displays the two sets of images side by side. Perhaps most striking is the children's ability to switch at a moment's notice between running interactions with their neighbours and close, fascinated attention to the screen. See Mary Field, *Children and Films* (London: Carnegie, 1954).

4. The two projects were enabled by research grants: *The Lord of the Rings* from the Economic and Social Research Council (Grant No. 000-22-0323); and *The Hobbit* from the British Academy/Leverhulme (Small Research Grant No. SRG 2012-13).

5. Noel Brown, *The Children's Film: Genre, Nation and Narrative* (New York: Columbia University Press, 2017).

6. Brown, *Children's Film*, p. 19.

7. Lydia Martens, Dale Southerton, and Sue Scott, "Bringing Children (and Parents) into the Sociology of Consumption: Towards a Theoretical and Empirical Agenda," *Journal of Consumer Culture* 4:2 (2004), pp. 158–182, at 159.

8. Martens, Southerton, and Scott, "Bringing Children (and Parents)," p. 158.

9. Russell W. Belk, Gnliz Ger, and Søren Askegaard, "Metaphors of Consumer Desire," in Kim P. Corfman and John G. Lynch Jr. (eds.), *Advances in Consumer Research*, vol. 23 (1996), pp. 369–373; Richard Wilk, "Morals and Metaphors: The Meaning of Consumption," in Karin Ekström and Helene Brembeck (eds.), *Elusive Consumption* (Oxford: Berg, 2004), pp. 11–26.

10. As one illustration, take the American parental guidance website "MentalHelp.net," calling itself an "addiction centers resource." Its article "Managing Children's Media Consumption" extends the metaphor to talk of "healthy" vs. "unhealthy," "safe" vs. "addictive" vs. "proper media use." See Angela Oswalt, "Managing Children's Media Consumption." MentalHelp.net. https://www.mentalhelp.net/articles/managing-children-s-media-consumption/> [accessed December 10, 2018].

11. David Buckingham, "Children's Media Culture: An Orphan in the Academy?," 2006. http://www.sfu.ca/cmns/faculty/kline_s/320/06-spring/resources/course%20readings%20folder/Buckingham.doc [accessed February 10, 2019].

12. The idea of counting "mentions" carries certain risks and has complicated roots. The main risk is that it can pick up unintended references, as when a respondent writes "Sam because of the way he looks after Frodo"—thus generating a mention of both. The guiding principle is that such secondary mentions can be reasonably expected to be evenly spread. But counting "mentions" can be seen as simply an analytic tactic, a precursor to closer investigation of the *motives* for choosing different characters—or it can be based in wider theories of "cultural indicators." This chapter is not the place to address these issues in detail. For a valuable overview (although one that is surprisingly unaware of some of the theoretical conflicts involved here), see Gabriele Melischek, Karl Erik Rosengren, and J. Stappers (eds.), *Cultural Indicators: an International Symposium* (Vienna: Verlag der Osterreichischen Akademie der Wissenschaften, 1984).

13. Ranjana Das, "'To Be Number One in Someone's Eyes...': Children's Introspections about Close Relationships in Reading Harry Potter," *European Journal of Communication* 28:4 (2013), pp. 454–469.

14. I have previously addressed the issues this raises more extensively. See Martin Barker, "*The Lord of the Rings* and 'Identification': A Critical Encounter," *European Journal of Communication* 20:3 (2005), pp. 353–378.

15. I first noticed this while running an eye over a random sample of their responses to our first open question: What had led to their judgements about the overall quality of *Hobbit* films?

16. Throughout this chapter I follow the practice of correcting spelling errors and grammatical slips, where the intended meaning is clear, as a courtesy to all those who took the time and trouble to complete our long questionnaires.

17. See, for instance, Clare J. Rathbone, Chris J. A. Moulin, and Martin A. Conway, "Self-Centred Memories: The Reminiscence Bump and the Self," *Memory and Cognition* 38:8 (2008), pp. 1403–1414.

18. The following "touching" response could not be left out, even if it is not the most obviously relevant to my argument here: "It was a great movie! I went there with my girlfriend, and we hardly touched each other (like you would normally do when going to the cinema) because we were afraid we would miss something of the film. The special effects were amazing but were nothing compared to the superior story of Tolkien. It was a really long film but if you don't drink too much that doesn't matter." [#10951]

19. "James" and (for the next) "Hannah" are assigned names from among the most common for their national cohorts.

20. The lists were constructed out of careful examination of reports, discussions, and debates around the films, to offer the main range of circulating attitudes and positions. With *LOTR* the research team took the decision to limit the range to alternative summaries of *genre*. With *The Hobbit*, the decision was to widen the scope to broader debates about the *status* of the films.

21. My thanks go here to our then Research Assistant Kate Egan, who first identified this, and wrote an analysis of its workings. She has recently revisited this at my request and has given me invaluable further insight into its significance.

22. "Occupation" was again captured through a multiple-choice question, which asked participants to choose the label that came closest to their position from the following list: Administrative/Clerical; Creative; Executive; Home/child-care; Professional; Retired; Self-employed; Skilled manual; Service work; Student; Unemployed; Unskilled manual. This consciously encouraged an element of self-evaluation, hoping to evoke something of people's *attitudes* towards their position.

23. This was an odd side effect of the *LOTR* project being funded by a substantial grant from the Economic and Social Research Council, which enabled us to supplement online-gathered responses with ones collected outside cinemas. However, the practical price of this was that the questionnaire had to fit on two sides of an A4—necessitating the elimination of the second question. Paradoxically, the lower-funded *Hobbit* project, because it only gathered responses online, could afford to be longer, and thus include the second question.

24. Lars Schmeink, "How Bilbo Lost His Innocence: Media Audiences and the Evaluation of *The Hobbit* as a 'Children's Film,'" *Participations* 13:2 (2016), pp. 430–439.

25. In the other direction, one young participant apologizes to us for not being fully up to date with the state of research on potential harms to the young, saying, "Please be aware that these are based on what studies I have read and not all of my information may be accurate" [#20709]. There is such a commendable *seriousness* behind a response of this kind.

26. It is worth at this point comparing this with Peter Krämer's research into the changing fortunes and "naming" of Stanley Kubrick's *2001: A Space Odyssey*. See his "'A Film

Specially Suitable for Children': The Marketing and Reception of *2001: A Space Odyssey* (1968)," in Noel Brown and Bruce Babington (eds.), *Family Films in Global Cinema: The World beyond Disney* (London: I.B. Tauris, 2015), pp. 37–52). Krämer draws on extensive archival materials to show how *2001* shifted from being seen as a film for adults (with cautionary classification from the British Board of Film Classification, for example) to being a "children's film," and even—without the usual "low quality" judgements that go with this— a "family film," but with the complication that *2001* was adopted by many young people as grounds for deeper thought and hopes for personal and social futures. As Krämer says, "for many young viewers the experience of seeing *2001* resonated widely and deeply across their childhood and also their later lives" (p. 48).

27. The interview had been conducted before this issue was identified.

28. Jean Piaget, *The Language and Thought of the Child* (London: Routledge, 2001).

29. Erik Erikson, *Identity and the Life-Cycle* (New York: W. W. Norton, 1994).

30. Karl Mannheim, "The Problem of Generations," in Paul Kecskemeti (ed.), *Essays on the Sociology of Knowledge*, vol. 5 of *Karl Mannheim: Collected Works* (New York: Routledge, 1952), pp. 276–322.

31. Göran Bolin, *Media Generations* (London: Routledge, 2016); Göran Bolin, "Media Generations: Objective and Subjective Media Landscapes and Nostalgia among Generations of Media Users," *Participations* 11:2 (2014), pp. 108–131.

32. Since first drafting this chapter, another project—on the reception of the TV show *Game of Thrones*—has provided further rich evidence on the way fantasy series of these kinds may encourage and sustain ways of thinking and caring about the "world" as an overall consideration. See Martin Barker, Clarissa Smith, and Feona Attwood, *Watching "Game of Thrones": How Audiences Engage with Dark Television* (Manchester, UK: Manchester University Press, 2021), esp. chap. 6.

33. Patrick Curry, "The Critical Response to Tolkien's Fiction,'" in Stuart D. Lee (ed.), *A Companion to J. R. R. Tolkien* (Chichester, UK: Wiley Blackwell, 2014), pp. 369–388.

34. On this tendency, see Martin Barker, "Fantasy Audiences versus Fantasy Audiences," in Warren Buckland (ed.), *Film Theory and Contemporary Hollywood Movies* (London: Routledge, 2009), pp. 286–309.

35. José Monleón, *A Spectre Is Haunting Europe: A Sociohistorical Approach to the Fantastic* (Princeton, NJ: Princeton University Press, 1990).

36. Anne Vandermeer and Jeff Vandermeer, *The New Weird* (San Francisco: Tachyon, 2008).

37. See, for instance, Jeff Goodwin et al. (eds.), *Passionate Politics: Emotions and Social Movements* (Chicago: University of Chicago Press, 2001); Stephen Duncombe, *Dream: Reimagining Progressive Politics in an Age of Fantasy* (New York: New Press, 2007); and James Ormrod, *Fantasy and Social Movements* (Basingstoke, UK: Palgrave Macmillan, 2014). Sedlmayr and Waller's (2016) edited collection even asserts as a general criterion that *all* fantasy is of necessity political. See Gerold Sedlmayr and Nicole Waller (eds.), *Politics in Fantasy Media: Essays on Ideology and Gender in Fiction, Film, Television and Games* (Jefferson, NC: McFarland, 2014).

38. Dan Hassler-Forest, *Science Fiction, Fantasy and Politics: Transmedia Worldbuilding Beyond Capitalism* (London: Rowman & Littlefield, 2016), pp. 84, 74.

39. Clark A. Miller, "Climate Change and Global Political Order," in Sheila Jasanoff (ed.), *States of Knowledge: The Co-Production of Science and the Social Order* (New York: Routledge, 2006), pp. 46–66, at 53.

40. Miller, "Climate Change and Global Political Order," p. 51.

41. See, for instance, Mark J. P. Wolf, *Building Imaginary Worlds* (New York: Routledge, 2012); Stephen L. Gillett, *World-Building*, edited by Ben Bova (Colorado: ReAnimus Press, 2015); Berin Kinsman, *World-building Theory: The Second Pillar of Fantasy Adventure* (Dancing Lights Press, 2017); Justin Sirois, *RPG World Building for Beginners* (California, Ca: CreateSpace Independent Publishing Platform, 2017); Randy Ellefson, *Creating Life: The Art of World Building, Book 1* (Utah, Ut: Evermore Press, 2018); T. G. Franklin, *World Building Guide and Workbook* (PaperSteel Press, 2018); Mark Nelson, *Creative World-Building and Creature Design* (New York: Dover, 2019).

42. Ramon Lobato, *Netflix Nations: The Geography of Digital Distribution* (New York: New York University Press, 2019).

Bibliography

Barker, Martin. "Fantasy Audiences versus Fantasy Audiences." In Warren Buckland (ed.), *Film Theory and Contemporary Hollywood Movies.* London: Routledge, 2009, pp. 286–309.

Barker, Martin. "*The Lord of the Rings* and 'Identification': A Critical Encounter." *European Journal of Communication* 20:3 (2005), pp. 353–378.

Belk, Russell W., Gnliz Ger, and Søren Askegaard. "Metaphors of Consumer Desire." In Kim P. Corfman and John G. Lynch Jr. (eds.), *Advances in Consumer Research* 23, 1996, pp. 369–373.

Bolin, Göran. *Media Generations.* London: Routledge, 2016.

Bolin, Göran. "Media Generations: Objective and Subjective Media Landscapes and Nostalgia among Generations of Media Users." *Participations* 11:2 (2014), pp. 108–131.

Brown, Noel. *The Children's Film: Genre, Nation and Narrative.* New York: Columbia University Press, 2017.

Buckingham, David. "Children's Media Culture: An Orphan in the Academy?." 2006. "Studying children's media cultures: A new agenda for cultural studies". Found at: https://www.academia.edu/2748189/Studying_childrens_media_cultures_A_new_agenda_for_cultural_studies (accessed 9 November 2021).

Das, Ranjana. "'To Be Number One in Someone's Eyes ...': Children's Introspections about Close Relationships in Reading *Harry Potter*." *European Journal of Communication* 28:4 (2013), pp. 454–469.

Erikson, Erik. *Identity and the Life-Cycle.* New York: W. W. Norton, 1994.

Hassler-Forest, Dan. *Science Fiction, Fantasy and Politics: Transmedia Worldbuilding beyond Capitalism.* London: Rowman & Littlefield, 2016.

Jowett, Garth, Ian Jarvie, and Kathryn H. Fuller. "The Thirteenth Manuscript: The Case of the Missing Payne Fund Study." *Historical Journal of Film, Radio and Television* 13:4 (1993), pp. 387–402.

Krämer, Peter. "'A Film Specially Suitable for Children': The Marketing and Reception of *2001: A Space Odyssey* (1968)." In Noel Brown and Bruce Babington (eds.), *Family Films in Global Cinema: The World Beyond Disney.* London: I.B. Tauris, 2015, pp. 37–52.

Mannheim, Karl. "The Problem of Generations." In Paul Kecskemeti (ed.), in *Essays on the Sociology of Knowledge.* Vol. 5 of *Karl Mannheim: Collected Works.* New York: Routledge, 1952, pp. 276–322.

Martens, Lydia, Dale Southerton, and Sue Scott. "Bringing Children (and Parents) into the Sociology of Consumption: Towards a Theoretical and Empirical Agenda." *Journal of Consumer Culture* 4:2 (2004), pp. 158–182.

Miller, Clark A. "Climate Change and Global Political Order." In Sheila Jasanoff (ed.), *States of Knowledge: The Co-Production of Science and the Social Order*. New York: Routledge, 2006, pp. 46–66.

Monleón, José. *A Spectre Is Haunting Europe: A Sociohistorical Approach to the Fantastic*. Princeton, NJ: Princeton University Press, 1990.

Piaget, Jean. *The Language and Thought of the Child*. London: Routledge, 2001.

Rathbone, Clare J., Chris J. A. Moulin, and Martin A. Conway. "Self-Centred Memories: The Reminiscence Bump and the Self." *Memory and Cognition* 38:8 (2008), pp. 1403–1414.

Schmeink, Lars. "How Bilbo Lost His Innocence: Media Audiences and the Evaluation of *The Hobbit* as a 'Children's Film.'" *Participations* 13:2 (2016), pp. 430–439.

Wolf, Mark J. P. *Building Imaginary Worlds*. New York: Routledge, 2016.

CHAPTER 38

DISNEY'S ADULT AUDIENCES

JAMES R. MASON

IT may seem odd to find a chapter about adult audiences in a handbook of children's film, but children's films are not just watched by children: they are watched with parents, grandparents, and other adults; children grow up to be adults, and many adults choose to watch so-called children's films unburdened by the presence of their apparent target market. No studio is more closely associated with entertainment for the whole family than Disney.

Dozens of quotations have been attributed to Walt Disney about the audiences he tried to reach, with the following summing up his attitude succinctly:

> All my films are for grownups…Some people don't ever grow up and some are old the day they are born. But most of us retain a love for fantasy and heroic adventure to the longest day we live. These are the people we make movies for—and I don't care how old they are![1]

The studio's child-friendly output can be appreciated by the fact that not a single Disney-branded film has been released with an age restriction that prevents children from seeing it.[2] Although Disney says that its films are available for all ages, being an adult viewer can be problematic. David Buckingham has suggested that "to proclaim one's enjoyment of mindless pleasure, to profess an enthusiasm for all things American, or to celebrate one's infantile desires are simply untenable positions" if one wants to be taken seriously.[3] Janet Wasko has previously attempted to debunk the myth that "Disney is only for kids," recognizing that there are "many products and activities that Disney aims directly at adults."[4] In the years since Wasko's myth-busting endeavours, the Walt Disney Company has grown to include Pixar, Lucasfilm, Marvel, and 20th Century Studios (formerly 20th Century Fox). While the company's "underlying motive—the profit motive—endures,"[5] Disney's acquisitions have challenged the idea of what a Disney films is, and Disney is becoming an ever-more dominant part of the cultural landscape in a way that is unmatched by any other media company.

Through a large-scale piece of audience research, incorporating a survey completed by over 3,500 adults, I explored the relationships that adult audiences have with films produced by the Walt Disney Company. In addition, I conducted an output survey of 390 Disney films to determine the characteristics of the "typical" Disney film, potentially describing a "Disney genre," and discovering how this has adapted in the new millennium. This chapter draws upon this research to briefly consider the attributes of a Disney film based on the studio's output, and then explore how audiences perceive and enjoy Disney films as adults.

METHODS

When Disney scholars write about Disney films, they tend to single out the popular animated features that Disney designates as "Classics,"[6] or those described by Wasko as "Classic Disney," encompassing "the company's animated films, cartoons, and some live-action films."[7] Thus large numbers of Disney films are overlooked, possibly because they have not had the same cultural or historical impact as *Bambi* (David Hand et al., 1942) or *The Little Mermaid* (Ron Clements and John Musker, 1989)—not every Disney movie is created, marketed, or (re-)released equally.

Rather than use "Disney" as lazy shorthand for animation, the audience research and survey data that forms the basis of this chapter refers to the wider Disney film canon. To qualify as a "Disney film" for this research, a feature had to be over forty minutes in length, released theatrically in the United States, contain original content, and distributed and/or produced using the Disney name (distributed by Walt Disney Studios Motion Pictures or produced by Walt Disney Productions/Pictures or Disneynature).[8] The time span for this census began with Disney's first original feature-length film, *Snow White and the Seven Dwarfs* (David Hand et al., 1937), and ended with *Star Wars: The Force Awakens* (J. J. Abrams, 2015), the final Disney-released film of 2015, the most recent full year prior to the commencement of the research.

A total of 390 films were included in an output survey of Disney films that collected release dates, Motion Picture Association of America certificates, production companies, Academy Award nominations, availability on home media, box office performance, and details relating to genre through cross-checking of various sources, including *Disney A-Z: The Official Encyclopedia* (2006, 2016) and the Internet Movie Database (IMDb). This data was then analysed to identify historical trends and to compare with statistical data gathered from the audience research.

The audience research centred on an online survey in the form of a questionnaire, plus six focus groups. The questionnaire—consisting of seventeen questions and subquestions about Disney films and audience responses to them, plus a further six demographic questions about each participant—was shared online for six months, starting in January 2016. By its close, the questionnaire had generated 3,524 responses—almost triple that of the 1,252 responses gathered by the previous Global Disney Audiences

Project. Quantitative and qualitative data gathered from the questionnaire was combined with discussions held in six focus groups to better understand how audiences perceive and interact with Disney films.

WHAT IS A DISNEY FILM?

Disney films are regularly labelled as either family or children's fare, but it is not the purpose of this chapter to debate the definition of family films or children's films. Genre data drawn from IMDb ascribes "family" as a genre to 85 per cent of Disney films; that label, in itself, says nothing about the content of a film, except to indicate that it is considered suitable for all ages and therefore unlikely to offend (lacking explicit nudity, violence, and language, but not necessarily problems with representation).

According to IMDb, the "family film" genre label applies to all but two of the 150 Disney films released before 1982, as well as every animated film released from 1937 to 2015. However, since 2000, almost one-third of Disney's films have not been considered part of the family genre—this change occurred in tandem with Disney's acquisitions of Marvel and Lucasfilm, and the subsequent increase in PG-13/12A certificate releases is evidence of Disney's attempts to reach older audiences. "Adventure" and "comedy" are the next most popular genres in the Disney film canon, each accounting for almost 50 per cent of the films. Fully 96 per cent of Disney films considered to be comedies are also in the family genre—the first Disney family comedy after a string of historical dramas and adventure stories was *The Shaggy Dog* (Charles Barton, 1959), which "set the formula for many Disney movies to come: youngsters, animals, strange—sometimes magical—events, music, and a catchy title sequence."[9] That formula still exists in Disney movies today, particularly in the live-action remakes of animated films, but is not an all-encompassing description of the Disney film canon.

Of the 390 films, 104 are fully or part animated, whether traditionally hand-drawn, stop-motion, motion-capture, or CG animation. Animation is of course a medium, but it is commonly referred to as a genre, particularly when the word is used as (pejorative) shorthand for children's films. Unsurprisingly, the genre with least representation (1 per cent) in Disney films is horror, closely followed (2 per cent) by crime, biography, and war films, all of which are a little too adult for inclusion in a Disney film. In a turbulent world, it can be a comfort for audiences both young and old to know that a Disney film can be relied on to be free of horror, crime and war (which is not to say that Disney films do not have the potential to be upsetting).

However, Disney's Marvel and Star Wars films contain more violent content and added swearing, making them less appropriate for younger audience members, although they are catered for in the Disney Store and beyond with merchandise for every age group. An important aspect of the Star Wars films, particularly *The Force Awakens*, is their appeal to nostalgia among adult audiences who grew up watching the original films. In a similar vein, the live-action remakes of animated "Classics" appeal to adults

who are familiar with the originals, or who want to see how Disney has ruined childhood memories or adapted the original films to reflect modern filmmaking and political
sensibilities.

In recent years Disney, like other Hollywood studios, has begun tackling criticisms
of its films' representations of gender, race, and sexuality. Other scholars have written
about representation in Disney films,[10] and this chapter does not seek to engage with
such debates, but it is worth considering whether criticisms or celebrations of Disney's
record of representation are themselves representative of Disney's broader film output,
rather than a narrow examination of the animated canon.

Seventy-nine per cent of Disney films feature a human protagonist (as opposed to
animals or VW Beetles), and only 12 per cent feature a lead who is Black or minority
ethnic, and a similar percentage (15 per cent) feature a female lead. Without considering
how problematic or positive these representations are, they are clearly unrepresentative
of the films' international audiences. Disney does appear to have made some progress
since the census, and the box office success of films such as *Black Panther* (Ryan Coogler,
2018) and *Captain Marvel* (Anna Boden and Ryan Fleck, 2019) may contribute to further diversity in filmmaking, both in front of and behind the camera.

Disney's record on LGBT+ representation is worse. Although various characters,
particularly animated villains, have been read as queer,[11] it was not until 2017 that
audiences—those who did not blink—were witness to what *Beauty and the Beast*
(2017) director Bill Condon called an "exclusively gay moment in a Disney movie."[12]
LGBT+ content remained implicit until *Avengers: Endgame* (Anthony and Joe Russo,
2019) featured a brief scene with an (unnamed) gay character. How far Disney films
might go in terms of LGBT+ representation in the future may depend on international censorship, as well as a resistance to including positive LGBT+ content in
children's films.

The census of 390 Disney films from 1937 to 2015 demonstrated that an average Disney
film is suitable for all ages; likely to be live-action and contain humour, fantasy, and
adventure; with White, male, heterosexual lead characters, in an original or adapted
story. In the early 2000s, Disney films began a process of evolution, particularly after
the purchase of Lucasfilm and Marvel. The success of 12A- and PG-13-rated *Pirates of
the Caribbean: The Curse of the Black Pearl* (Gore Verbinski, 2003) could be considered
a turning point in Disney's pivot to seeking older audiences; thus, not every modern
Disney film is suitable for *all* ages.

The recent decade of Disney films has become more reliant on remakes and franchises
that garner ever greater box office results, which encourages the cycle to continue.
Whether this apparent lack of originality is seen as good or bad for Disney or Hollywood
more widely, the actors and filmmakers creating these films have begun to diversify in
terms of gender and race, and cracks are beginning to open in Hollywood's heteronormative hold.

Having briefly considered some of the key elements of a Disney film based on cinematic output, the next section explores audiences' understandings of Disney films and
the reasons they choose to watch or shun them.

ADULT AUDIENCES

Several of the edited collections dealing with Disney films include discussions of Disney's audiences, although these have generally been limited by a narrow focus on animation and theme parks, paying little heed to what audiences think about the subjects on a significant scale.[13] In 2001, Janet Wasko approached Disney's broader output and adult audiences from a holistic angle, recognizing that Disney encompasses an entertainment company that involves much more than animation. In *Understanding Disney*, Wasko drew on previous work in Disney Studies and her own research to describe seven Disney audience archetypes, ranging from Fanatics, Fans, and Consumers to Cynics, Uninteresteds, Resisters, and Antagonists, representing various levels of interest and commitment to Disney.[14] These broad audience categories are problematic in terms of (self-) identification with these archetypes—Fanatics may not self-identify as such, but they may be described in this way by a (self-confessed) Antagonist.

Having identified that "much more work is needed in analysing Disney audiences, especially in identifying examples of reinterpretation, resistance, and subversion,"[15] Wasko and her fellow authors took up the charge as part of the Global Disney Audiences Project (GDAP), as reported in *Dazzled by Disney?*[16] The GDAP carried out audience surveys and focus groups in eighteen countries, but the discussion relating specifically to the relationship of adult audiences with Disney was limited to David Buckingham's chapter on British audiences.[17] The survey employed by GDAP gathered 1,252 responses from participants representing fifty-three countries, and showed that 97.5 per cent of participants had "come into contact" with Disney films at some point in their lives, a much higher number than for any other Disney media.[18] The responses indicated a generally positive reception to most aspects of Disney, albeit with some dissenting voices, which could have been the result of selection bias. Respondents were not provided with a definition of Disney films, comics, or TV; thus their responses may well have been informed by a skewed perception of Disney media.

A similar result can be found in Paul Wells's audience research, which focused on Disney feature films, based on 435 respondents drawn from animation-focused festivals, lectures, and events.[19] Several respondents "confused the Disney style with that of another animated film—in this sample, chiefly, *Watership Down* (Martin Rosen, 1978)—or remembered a part live-action film,"[20] which shows that even those interested in animation cannot always correctly identify a Disney film. GDAP focus group participants also reported confusion "about whether Tom and Jerry, for example, was a Disney creation."[21] An inability to correctly identify a Disney film could occur because while Walt Disney did not invent animation, "one could say that he *defined* it,"[22] and Disney's output subsequently became defined *by* animation.

The research conducted for this chapter sought to address the gaps found in previous studies of Disney audiences by engaging with both Disney's audiences and the film texts they responded to.[23] Martin Barker has previously identified the tendency in academia to "either deconstruct the Disney corpus for its ideological operations…or undertake the difficult task…of looking at why and how people *enjoy* Disney films, theme parks, [and] merchandising,"[24] which sets the two approaches in opposition when they can be more effectively combined in a holistic approach. Barker demonstrated with the ambitious *Lord of the Rings* project[25] that *"through carefully structured audience research* [original emphasis] *it may be possible to derive a range of competing accounts of what the 'text' is,"* an approach echoed here.[26]

RESPONDENT DEMOGRAPHICS

Almost three-quarters of respondents identified as female. Although the demographic data on the respondents does not indicate who Disney's audiences are (it may say more about the type of people who are willing to spend time filling in a survey about Disney), it adds an interesting angle to the question "who are the target audiences for Disney films?" Ten per cent of the respondents selected women, and 4 per cent chose men, as the target audiences for Disney films, while 29 per cent selected girls and 20 per cent chose boys. The differences in the figures selected by respondents who said that they do not enjoy Disney films are revealing: 41 per cent of this group picked girls as Disney's target audience; just 22 per cent chose boys, and only 1 per cent believed that Disney films are aimed at men. The other discrepancy shown by those who do not enjoy Disney films is that 85 per cent of them believe that Disney films are for children under age 12, as opposed to just 55 per cent of respondents who do enjoy Disney films. One might conclude that those who perceive Disney films to be synonymous with animated princesses would choose children and girls as target audiences.

Almost half of respondents were aged 25 to 34. The prevalence of this age group is unsurprising, as statistics published by the British Film Institute have shown that the 25-to-34 share of cinema admissions has been greater than the share of any other age group since 2003.[27] It makes sense, therefore, that the age group most likely to visit the cinema is also most likely to complete a film-related survey. Representatives of seventy-one different countries completed the questionnaire, of whom almost half were from the United Kingdom and the Republic of Ireland; a third were from the United States; a tenth were European; and the rest ranged from Argentina to Zimbabwe. Few significant statistical differences were found when comparing data between the United Kingdom and Ireland and the rest of the world, which was reassuring because the attitudes expressed in the survey are more likely to be broadly generalizable.

Almost a quarter of respondents identified as LGBT+, reflecting data from a recent YouGov poll which found that "23 per cent of British people choose something other than 100 per cent heterosexual" when asked to place themselves on the Kinsey scale of sexuality.[28] The proportion of LGBT+ respondents in the Disney survey remains around a quarter for both genders (although men were more likely to identify as gay, and women were more likely to be bisexual). Of those who said that they enjoy Disney films, 25 per cent identified as LGBT+ compared to 33 per cent of those who do not enjoy Disney films who identified this way. Disney's poor record of LGBT+ representation may be to blame for this increased hostility towards Disney films from LGBT+ respondents.

Viewing Habits

As part of the survey, respondents were asked about their feelings about watching films in general: 91 per cent reported that they gained pleasure from this activity; and 17 per cent of respondents who do not enjoy Disney films also revealed that they do not like films in general, suggesting a correlation between the two attitudes. The overarching response about general film-viewing habits seemed to be that the majority enjoyed a good film, if they had the resources (time, money, and social) to spend on the activity. Although most respondents did not find time to regularly attend the cinema, a majority watched films at home on a weekly or monthly basis, whether on home media, streaming, or on TV.

To determine whether the survey had been hijacked by Disney fan communities, I asked participants to name the last film they had watched. Only two films were watched by over 200 respondents—*Deadpool* (Tim Miller, 2016) and *Star Wars: The Force Awakens*—the former an R/15 certificate Marvel superhero film from 20th Century Fox, and the latter, Disney's first Star Wars release (there was some confusion among respondents about whether *Deadpool* was a Disney movie; now that Disney owns Fox, it could be considered as such). The other answers to this question did not reveal a bias towards Disney films. Similarly, when Disney was provided as an option in a question asking about respondents' favourite film genre, only 3 per cent picked it, and just 1 per cent chose Disney as their least favourite genre, indicating that the survey had not been completed by scores of Disney fanatics or antagonists. A handful of respondents did later question the inclusion of Disney (and animation) as options on the favourite genre questions.

In fact, respondents' most popular choice of favourite genre turned out to be "no preference" (19 per cent), with only comedy (13 per cent), drama, and sci-fi (both 11 per cent) preferred by more than 10 per cent of respondents. In contrast, 38 per cent selected horror as their least favourite genre, and westerns were second, at 14 per cent. It seems that audiences are more confident identifying the films and genres they do *not* like than the ones they do, or perhaps horror and westerns are more easily definable genres and thus easier to single out.

Adult Relationships with Disney Films

Although only 3 per cent of respondents chose Disney as their favourite film genre, 90 per cent professed that they do generally enjoy Disney films as adults; and only 360 out of 3,524 people said that they do not. Broadly speaking, there are more people who enjoy

Disney films than not; however, the variety of responses indicates the many ways in which such enjoyment is manifested and negotiated by audiences.

Twenty per cent of respondents reported that they enjoyed Disney films more as adults, compared to 24 per cent who claimed to enjoy them less, and almost half remained constant in their feelings—just 3 per cent did not watch Disney films as adults. It is worth noting that respondents were deliberately *not* provided with a definition of Disney films, and so these responses are based on audiences' own perceptions of Disney films—some of those who claimed not to watch Disney films may well enjoy recent Star Wars or Marvel movies, for example, without realizing that Disney produced them. Only six respondents claimed to have never (knowingly) watched a Disney film, which either speaks to a restricted ability to access films generally, or ignorance of the range of films produced by Disney.

Only 84 per cent reported watching Disney films as children, with an unexplained disparity between the 82 per cent of British and Irish respondents and the 92 per cent of international audiences who had watched Disney films as children. Without a definition, 62 per cent said that they enjoyed watching "classic Disney films," and 51 per cent looked forward to watching new Disney films. Just 12 per cent reported that they only watch Disney films with their children or family, indicating that many adults are happy to admit to watching Disney films on their own.

When asked about what might encourage someone to watch a Disney film, over half of respondents were swayed by a film's marketing, while the least important factor was the film's director (13 per cent). It is not clear from this data whether film directors are generally less important factors for audiences when choosing a film, or whether this just applies to Disney films. It is worth noting that though the 390 Disney films in the output survey had collectively won fifty-three Academy Awards, none was in the category of Best Director. Today, as was the case in Walt's time, the Disney name appears to be the most important for capturing an audience—the film's cast were only important to 24 per cent of respondents.

Another question asked respondents to choose the Disney film-related activities that they had engaged in as adults. Sixty-four per cent admitted that they had watched Disney films at the cinema without being accompanied by children, while only 37 per cent had taken children with them. That the majority had been to the cinema without children is surprising given Disney's association with family and children's films. In terms of regional differences, 61 per cent of British and Irish respondents said that they had seen a Disney film at the cinema without children, compared with 71 per cent internationally. Perhaps attending a Disney film at the cinema without children is considered less socially acceptable by British and Irish audiences. The likelihood of watching a film at the cinema without children decreased with age: 76 per cent of 18- to 24-year-olds had done so, compared to 46 per cent of those aged over 45. Of those who professed not to enjoy Disney films, 20 per cent had still watched one at the cinema without children, perhaps being dragged there by friends or partners.

Over half of respondents had bought themselves or their partner Disney films on physical home media, and 29 per cent had also bought soundtrack albums for themselves or their partners. Just 10 per cent had created or shared fan fiction, cartoons, or artwork relating to Disney films, and 7 per cent had participated in online fan-site discussions of Disney films. Five per cent of respondents who enjoy Disney films had not participated in any of the provided Disney film related activities—this figure rose to 44 per cent among those who do not enjoy Disney films. For some of the respondents not enjoying Disney films, it seems that familial and social obligations rendered them unavoidable.

PERCEPTIONS OF DISNEY FILMS

Having established respondents' various adult relationships with Disney films, the survey sought to better understand what respondents understood by the term "Disney film," beginning by asking what genres they associated with Disney from an available list of options. Unsurprisingly, 92 per cent of respondents chose "animation" as a genre they associated with Disney; "family" was not far behind at 86 per cent; and "adventure," "fantasy," and "comedy" were all chosen by over 60 per cent of respondents; and half of respondents selected musicals and romance. Conversely, genres such as "crime," "horror," "thriller," "war," and "western" were associated with Disney films by fewer than 2 per cent of respondents. Evidently, Disney's animated output most strongly impacts audience perceptions of Disney films.

Comparing audience perceptions of Disney film genres with those found in the census of 390 films shows some disparities, particularly considering that only 27 per cent of the Disney films released between 1937 and 2015 were animated. Similarly, audiences have a much higher expectation of seeing the fantasy, musical, and romance genres in a Disney film than are represented in Disney's output. Audience expectations accord with actual output when it comes to the barely represented horror, war, western, and crime genres, as well as the more expected family genre—85 per cent of Disney films fit in this genre (according to IMDb classifications), and 86 per cent of survey respondents expect this.

The mismatch in audience expectations and actual output is most significant with animation: this is important, because animation is commonly understood as being for children. Animation historian Michael Barrier has identified television as the root of the connection between animation and children, noting that "while making cartoons more accessible, [television] has made them seem more a children's medium than ever before, by presenting them at times and in formats best suited to children's viewing."[29] Ironically, Barrier also identifies Disney as the first studio to produce animation for television.[30]

Disney has contributed to the association of its films with animation by prioritizing animated films over its live-action output. Disney's former director of corporate synergy, Lorraine Santoli, observed that "the films that worked the best with consumer products of course are the animated films."[31] Consumer products are a valuable source of income for Disney, and the ability to monetize and merchandize animated characters (who cannot demand a share of royalties for use of their likeness) is significant. A recently released chronicle of how every Disney film relates to other Disney products, such as the theme parks, TV series, and comics, demonstrates that Disney's animated films have been re-released and exploited across Disney's numerous media concerns more rigorously than their live-action counterparts.[32]

Beyond generic film categories, respondents were also asked to select from a given list the concepts they thought were most relevant to the term "Disney film." Although the majority of those who enjoy and do not enjoy Disney films both agreed that "entertainment" reflected Disney films, those who do not like the films were more likely to associate them with being simple, predictable, boring, and corrupting. Those who enjoy Disney films were more likely to consider them exciting, innocent, nostalgic, and a source of pleasure. Nostalgia proved to be an important association with Disney films for 68 per cent of total respondents, implying that perceptions of Disney are connected to memories of childhood.

Enjoyment of Disney Films: Quantitative Data

When the respondents were asked why they enjoy Disney films, the most popular answer (62 per cent) was that they were generally well made; this was closely followed by nostalgia, reported by 60 per cent of those who enjoy Disney films. It is possible that the 55 per cent of respondents who said that they enjoy animated films, and therefore enjoy Disney films, are also represented in the 62 per cent who think Disney films are well made, and that they interpret "well made" to mean animated to a high standard, or artistically worthy. Men were substantially more likely to point out the quality of Disney filmmaking (71 per cent) as important than women (59 per cent). A comparable disparity can be seen in the 20 per cent of women who think of Disney films as guilty pleasures, compared to just 12 per cent of men who said the same. Is referencing the craft of filmmaking rather than emotional responses to Disney films a more acceptable stance for men to take? Are women more familiar with the "pop-cultural epithet"[33] represented by the term "guilty pleasure" than men, since cultural experiences traditionally enjoyed by women, such as soaps[34] and reality television,[35] are often held in low regard? The data raise interesting questions, but it is outside the scope of this chapter to explore them further.

When asked why they do *not* enjoy Disney films, the most popular response (66 per cent) was Disney's treatment of gender, sexuality, race, or disability. Split demographically, 76 per cent of those who identified as LGBT+ found fault with Disney's record of representation, compared to 61 per cent of heterosexual respondents. Similarly, 69 per cent of women had problems with Disney's representation, compared to 56 per cent of men—these figures suggest that audience members are more likely to dislike Disney if they do not see themselves represented (positively) in Disney's films.

Over half of respondents were unimpressed by Disney's commercialism, and many others indicated that Disney films were not worth their time as discerning adults with more age-appropriate viewing choices available. This view reiterates the perception that Disney films are for children and thus somehow are less-worthy forms of entertainment, delivering pleasures too simple for mature adults to enjoy. Perceptions of over-commercialism could relate to Disney's prolific merchandising efforts, which as noted, are generally connected with their animated features.

Whether they enjoy Disney films or not, the adult respondents' reasons for taking either position indicate that there is a perception that Disney films are most significant for childhood viewing and now either enjoyed through a nostalgic lens or left firmly in the past with other childish pursuits. There are also strong indications from both the positive and negative perceptions of Disney films that they are assumed to be animated, and this perception likely helps to frame the films as being for children, following the equation: *cartoons = kids*. Although audiences may praise such films for their high-quality animation and production values, the stories that Disney represents on-screen are considered (too) safe and (too) easy to watch for adult audiences, as well as potentially problematic in terms of the conservative values they are perceived to promote.

At several points in the survey, respondents had the opportunity to freely write down their thoughts about Disney films, and many took the opportunity to declare their love or distaste for them, and to explain their quantitative answers. Over 1,000 written responses were reviewed and categorized, and then combined with focus-group discussions, from which three broad themes emerged relating to why adults enjoy Disney films, and a further three concerning reasons not to enjoy Disney films.

Enjoying Disney Films

Hidden Jokes

Of the 700 respondents who provided an answer to the question of why they enjoyed watching Disney films, more than half indicated an appreciation of jokes, references, or content that they had not understood or been aware of as children. These so-called hidden jokes involved wordplay and references that the respondents now had the cultural experience, education, and maturity to appreciate and understand. For many adult viewers, Disney films became suddenly more complex and layered, in ways that more mature audiences could appreciate.

Disney films are written, produced, and directed by adult filmmakers, so it stands to reason that they might contain cultural references that adults may find amusing or resonant, even if the primary audience for such films is children. Disney has always been in the business of trying to reach a wide range of audiences, though even Walt Disney once said: "I aim my work for adults. It's a success only if they like it. Sure, the children are important, but their parents pay for the tickets."[36] The importance of keeping parents and guardians interested has not lessened today, although 64 per cent of respondents watched Disney films at the cinema without children anyway.

The "hidden" jokes cited by respondents as reasons for enjoying Disney films have always been present in the films and could be said to have been hiding in plain sight. Many respondents explained that their appreciation of hidden jokes also extended to understanding more about character motivations, catching references to other Disney films, and spotting allusions to other cultural texts, such as echoes of Hamlet in *The Lion King* (Roger Allers and Rob Minkoff, 1994). One respondent observed: "There are a lot of great jokes for adults that go right over kid's heads. I enjoy finding what I missed when I was young, and I also enjoy that my kids don't understand yet" (F-US).[37]

Aside from the laughter these freshly understood jokes elicit, the adult audience member who spots the intertextual references or innuendoes can also take pride in their discovery, realising that they are in on a joke that children (including their younger selves) do not appreciate. Perhaps an adult audience member can also find pleasure in realising how much they have matured emotionally and intellectually, which offers a slightly different pleasure from nostalgia for lost childhood pursuits. Another respondent explained that Disney films are "magical, often with a secret language you'd only get once you reach your 18th Birthday" (F-GB). Of course, it is not reaching the age of 18 that magically awakens an audience to hidden jokes, but education and experiences. That is not to say that all audiences will be in on the jokes—humour that works for audiences in the United States may not translate, for example, to a Japanese audience.

One respondent made it clear that the hidden content that brings her pleasure is confined to animated films: "Rewatching Disney films (by which [I] mostly mean cartoons) makes me realise that there is nuance in them which is for adults and that I did not grasp as a child" (F-IT). Widely shared BuzzFeed and Tumblr lists of the in-jokes and self-referencing in Disney films are also almost exclusively devoted to the animated films; as usual, live-action Disney films are overlooked. The preference adult audiences express for hidden jokes and references therefore emphasizes the importance of animation to the perception of Disney films.

The need to justify taking pleasure in an animated feature may be what leads 18 per cent of respondents to describe enjoying Disney films as a "guilty pleasure." It is surprising that so few respondents defined their interest in Disney films as a guilty pleasure—and only one of these referred directly to the concept of Disney films as a guilty pleasure when invited to provide further comment, but to dismiss the idea: "Watching Disney films are just a pleasure, not a guilty pleasure :) [*sic*]" (F-GB).

While most respondents did not consider Disney films guilty pleasures, repeated references to the importance of hidden jokes as part of the pleasurable Disney film experience come freighted with implicit judgement. There is an implication that adult audiences are generally uncomfortable to admit taking pleasure from something as simple as the animation, songs or stories in Disney films. Thus, audiences must find more intellectual and adult-appropriate features within Disney films on which to hang their pleasure, and the identification of "hidden jokes" fulfils this brief.

Quality and Artistry

Over 100 respondents commented on the quality and artistry of Disney films, implying that their perception of Disney relates to animation rather than live action. Many of the comments about the craft of animation and filmmaking came from artists or animators, and a large proportion of respondents who appreciated Disney's artistic merits were male. For several respondents, it was only their admirable production quality that made Disney films, begrudgingly, acceptable: "I recently completed my university degree in animation, and because of that, I have developed [a] clear understanding of the amount of time and effort it takes to create a single Disney film, and I have a newfound respect for Disney because of it" (M-GB).

Just as the enjoyment of animated Disney films can be rendered acceptable when couched in terms of the craft of animation, the films of Pixar Animation Studios seem to represent the acceptable face of animation for the discerning adult film fan. Pixar films are commonly held to a higher standard than films from Disney's other studios, with over 50 respondents making particularly positive references to Pixar in their comments, such as "They usually have nuance that goes over kid's heads but that I now catch as an adult, especially the Disney Pixar films" (M-US).

One respondent credited Pixar with bringing filmmaking kudos to Disney, which it had apparently lacked before: "Since they bought Pixar they have started producing actually great films, instead of churning out obvious predictable stories" (M-GB). Pixar's status as the animation studio that it is acceptable to admit enjoying is particularly noticeable among male audience members, perhaps because Pixar is not associated with the princesses, romance, and musicals that audiences perceive to be typical of Disney animation. Instead, Pixar tends to produce male-dominated buddy movies; only two of the sixteen Pixar films in the census feature female leads—*Brave* (Brenda Chapman and Mark Andrews, 2012) and *Inside Out* (Pete Docter, 2015), both produced while Pixar was under Disney ownership—a poor record for a studio that was lauded by respondents for being more progressive and less conservative than Disney generally.

Many respondents enjoy Disney films because they expect them to be well made, and the pushing of technological and artistic boundaries begun by Walt Disney has continued into the modern day. Disney films represent a solid, reliable source of entertainment, which is an important consideration in a crowded film marketplace with high ticket prices. Many respondents even lauded Disney for the way it continues to improve its slow turn away from conservative social values, thereby improving the quality of Disney films overall.

Comfort and Nostalgia

Disney films can provide a source of comfort in a variety of ways, and the concept of nostalgia is closely linked with such comforts, especially for those who grew up watching the films. Respondents talked not just about their nostalgia for watching Disney films, but also the comfort of feeling like a child again, and of watching as part of a family: "Sense of comfort—of being a child and getting lost in the film away from stresses and strains of adult life" (F-GB); "Nostalgia of when I used to watch and catching all the little things I missed as a kid. I also love seeing the way my kids react to my faves and new movies as well" (F-US). The importance of the shared experience of Disney was echoed by many participants.

Disney films can act as a common cultural currency, bridging gaps between geography and generations: adults can share the films and their memories of them with their children and grandchildren: "I love sharing the films I loved as a child with my own children as well as enjoying the new films with them. The first film I ever took my son to cinema to see was *Wreck It Ralph*, the 2nd was *Planes*" (F-GB); "I am probably more excited to share Disney with my grandchildren than I was with my children—more time and money now" (F-US). Since "Disney's success means everyone, worldwide, has watched these films [they are] a great equalizer,"[38] the cultural currency crosses international borders: "I feel nostalgia when I watch the Disney movie, and the movie is usually well known over the world. It is good start to make the communication with international friend" (F-JP).[39]

Music is an important part of Disney films' cultural currency, and the songs of the animated "Classics," in particular, have become important reference points. Music and songs are therefore important to many audience members as a source of comfort and familiarity, and foster feelings of happiness, nostalgia, and social connection: "Also if you grow up with them it becomes a part of your culture. E.g. who can't sing along with the beginning of *Lion King*??" (F-GB).

Respondents often referred to the simplicity of Disney films, as well as a perceived innocence—qualities valued by audiences seeking respite from the violence and hypersexualization of other Hollywood films, or desiring escape from real world worries. The following respondents point to Disney films as a balm for adults: "In a world full of depression and hate it's a form of escapism. They're fun easy and can normally sing along which makes me happy" (F-GB); "I used them as a cheer up/anti-depressant which [I] suspect is a subconscious link to happier childhood memories" (F-GB).

Disney films are also perceived to be safe choices for parents who want films to watch with their children that can be enjoyed by both generations. The social bond that Disney films can foster between family members can last long after the children are grown too: "Myself and all my family love everything about Disney, so much so that my daughters 30th birthday is going to be Disney fancy dress!" (F-GB).

Other respondents reported that they take comfort and strength from Disney films regarding sexuality, despite Disney's poor track record with representation: "*Frozen* is an iconic gay extravaganza and Elsa helped me come out. YAAAAAAAAAAAAAAA AAAAAAAAAAAAAAAAS QWEEEEEEEN" (M-BG). Another respondent similarly did not require gay representation on screen to identify with Disney's characters: "It is nostalgic and has a special place in my heart because they were the first movies that I latched onto and saw myself in as a gay man, I related to the princesses" (M-GB).

Similarly, though some criticize the perceived overabundance of orphaned characters and dead parents in animated Disney films, these characters can offer comfort to people who have suffered loss: "I think as an adult, Disney films can be a great stress reliever, and have personally helped me through highly emotional issues such as coping with death" (F-GB). The perceived simplicity and safety of a Disney film can help an audience member to escape at a time of emotional distress but can also help them to process their feelings of grief, confusion, or trauma. Watching how a Disney character experiences the pain of losing a parent may provide strength and inspiration to both children and adults who find themselves in the same situation.

Aside from contentious matters of representation, Disney films also offer simpler comforts that are easier to identify. Familiarity combined with a perception of light-heartedness and simplicity means that adults often turn to Disney films in times of illness, particularly of the self-inflicted kind: "Perfect to watch on a Saturday afternoon if you have a hangover!" (M-GB).

NOT ENJOYING DISNEY FILMS

Problems with Representation

The number one concern of those who do not enjoy Disney films involves issues with representation, including race, gender, sexuality, disability, and body image. The perception that Disney films are all unrepresentative of modern social attitudes appears to be based on either hearsay or acquaintance with a handful of (admittedly potentially problematic) animated films. This perception does have some basis in truth, as the census of 390 Disney films has shown, and some respondents provided examples to support their positions, although most stated as fact that Disney films are bad for children, without evidence.

Feeling that Disney films are harmful to children, some parents ban them, but such censorship has the potential to make Disney films more attractive. A Disney ban may also be counter-productive if it causes children to feel excluded, unable to trade in the cultural currency that fosters communication across generational and national boundaries. Parents who perceive Disney films to be corrupting and problematic may pass their attitudes on to their children, perpetuating the negative perceptions.

That is not to suggest that such parental fears are completely unfounded. One respondent complained: "The classic films are so heteronormative and sexist that it makes my skin crawl" (F-US), although a *lack* of positive LGBT+ representation may not be at the top of a list of concerns for many parents. Issues with representations of race and an overabundance of White characters in Disney films can cause resentment: "My daughter is biracial, and [wants] to be a princess, which to her means blonde hair and White skin, so the racial issue is also a problem" (F-US).

Many female respondents attacked Disney for the lack of agency, unrealistic body image, and heteronormative relationship goals of its princesses: "I am a mother of two girls and I think their depiction of idealized feminine beauty can be a bit damaging to them. The stories often rely on outdated gender roles which grates on me" (F-GB). Concerns about the portrayal of women did not just affect mothers and daughters; some worried about the effect Disney's princesses might have on little boys and the men they will become. And it is not just the content of the films that respondents found problematic, but their marketing, particularly across Disney's subsidiary studios: "I'm very dissatisfied with the extremely gender-segregated marketing i.e. Marvel and Star Wars for boys and princesses for girls" (F-US).

Much of the criticism based on problems with representation raises questions about whether such attitudes are based on the respondent's own experiences or simply parrot opinions expected of responsible liberal audiences. The language used by respondents—"I now realise," "I now see," or "I can see"—implies that adulthood has led to an epiphany about Disney films that has removed the blinkers of childhood ignorance: "Because they have lost their innocence. Now I can see the underlying racism, sexism etc." (F-DE).

Just as many audience members like Disney films for the "hidden" humour, those who do not like Disney often refer to the "hidden" racism and sexism, which they can see as adults. There is sometimes an element of pride (even smugness) in the way that some respondents talk about Disney's problematic elements. Being able to point out the problematic elements in Disney films seems to be as rewarding to those who do not like them as discovering the hidden adult humour is to those who do like them.

Growing Up and Changing Tastes

Many respondents reported that they had outgrown Disney films, either because they had found other interests that they considered more suitable for adult consumption, or because they have had the metaphorical wool lifted from their eyes and become aware of Disney's problems with representation. Occasionally, such comments had a condescending tone, implying that those who persist in liking Disney as adults have failed to grow up. For example, when asked why they enjoy watching Disney films less as adults, some respondents replied: "Because I'm an adult" (M-GB); "They're aimed primarily at children and it shows" (F-US); "Less tolerance for bullshit" (US). Such remarks clearly position the respondents as aware of the audience boundaries of Disney films, and their place outside them. Other respondents explained that being older and more mature has affected their film tastes and choices using less pejorative language: "When I was a kid I could get completely lost in the story, no matter how trite/overly simplified it was. I still enjoy them as an adult but through a nostalgic filter. It'll never be the all-encompassing experience it once was" (F-US). Such comments imply that children are the more appreciative audiences of Disney films, because they can devote more time to their enjoyment.

Besides respondents claiming they do not have time to enjoy Disney films in the same way, several respondents pointed to their own adult cynicism as a barrier to their enjoyment: "I think I've become more cynical as an adult, and I've become more critical. I do appreciate the quality, even though I have issues with certain elements" (F-US). The claim of cynicism implies that Disney films are something to be cynical about, suggesting that the fantasy Disney films are perceived to trade in is not acceptable for mature audiences.

Not all adult audience members are cynical; some just gravitate to alternative interests, which were not necessarily available to them as children, when their worlds were shaped and influenced by parents and other adults: "My taste in films has grown and broadened so Disney now needs to contend with all film genres whereas as I child I liked Disney alongside other children's films" (F-GB). Such opinions are not critical of Disney films per se, although they do suggest that Disney films are particularly popular childhood viewing choices compared to other animated films, or more traditionally adult genres.

In contrast to those who value the simplicity and formulaic nature of Disney films as a way of escaping the complexities of daily life, some respondents crave complexity in their film choices. Simple stories no longer satisfy the needs of some adult audience members with their greater levels of education and experience, but perhaps a better description of unsatisfactory stories is that they are banal rather than simple, since Disney films are as narratively complex as any others. Some accuse Disney films of either being childish or making audiences feel childish for watching them: "Although Disney films are typically well-made, they're produced for families with children. When I watch them on my own I feel childish. This diminishes my enjoyment" (M-CA).

Walt Disney once observed that "it is the conventions, the expected staid behaviour of adults, the embarrassment at being thought 'childish,' which finally cramps down our imaginative flight and inventive curiosity."[40] Charges of sentimentality, simplicity, and childishness point to the differing perceptions of what is appropriate viewing for adult audiences. Respondents who differentiated between childhood and adulthood were critical and judgemental of both Disney films and those who enjoy them. Other respondents reported their tastes in film had developed and described the changing nature of their relationship with Disney films as a question of degree or shifted values rather than an outright dislike of Disney.

Commercialism

Responses of those citing issues with commercialism often had a vitriolic tone: "I have become aware of the consumerism and aspirationalism [associated] with the films and the brand....I dislike Disney as a brand, they represent a global oppression to me" (F-GB); "I recognize the over-commercialization of them and it disgusts me" (M-US).

These objections relate to the Disney brand more widely, which particularly irks parents dealing with the pester power of their children: "I suspect this might be off point but the merchandising is my only objection to Disney films, it's just obscene" (F-GB); "I have daughters. I think the horrendous merchandising is scandalous" (F-GB). The language used is emotive and demonstrates that Disney films do not exist in a vacuum—attitudes to the films are informed by Disney's wider commercial activity.

Several respondents' dislike of Disney stemmed from what they thought they knew about Walt Disney: "I've learned more about Walt Disney and his political ideology, particularly anti-Semitism, which is detestable" (F-US). Douglas Brode has observed that "all across the world, people know only a few things about Walt Disney: that he was a terrible Jew-hater, and that his head…remains cryogenically frozen."[41] Brode cites evidence from Walt Disney's life to refute claims of anti-Semitism, but as the handful of comments from respondents makes clear, this myth about Walt Disney continues to circulate and influences audience attitudes towards Disney films, over fifty years after his death. Another popular refrain was: "I am conflicted as Disney was a Nazi sympathizer" (F-GB). Considering the work that Walt Disney and his studio did during World War II to assist the Allied cause, this claim is problematic.[42]

Criticisms relating to commercialism and the activities of the wider Walt Disney Company are not necessarily baseless, but such views tend to be reported as accepted facts, and place ethical and moral concerns about Disney and its founder at the heart of Disney criticism. For those who hold these views, there is an implication that those who do enjoy Disney are colluding in and perpetuating Disney's transgressions. Again, these criticisms are not based on a perception of the films, but rather a perception of the wider Disney brand.

A smaller number of respondents found Disney films to be too readily available, either saturating the cinematic marketplace, particularly since Disney's acquisition of Marvel and Lucasfilm, or no longer having the novelty value of the periodically withdrawn and re-released theatrical and home media releases of earlier decades: "By owning Pixar, Marvel, Lucasfilm—Disney is so pervasive in pop culture that [seeing] films is just needed to keep up with everyone else" (M-US).

CONCLUSION

Walt Disney Productions was the only Hollywood studio with name recognition [in 1977]. It signified a wholesome and—equally important—predictable brand of family entertainment. People went to see Disney movies for no other reason than that they were Disney movies. Any film that was not identifiably Disney in tone or content might as well be *Deep Throat*; it would destroy the audience's preconception of a Disney movie.[43]

Disney is still arguably the only Hollywood studio whose films are identifiable to general audiences. When asked to name the attributes of films released by Paramount or Sony, focus groups were unable to answer. Although audiences share common perceptions of Disney films—animation, simplicity, high production values—how these perceptions manifest themselves depends on whether the audience already possesses a positive or negative attitude toward Disney and its films.

It is possible for audiences to hold conflicting opinions about Disney films: enjoying their comforting balm of nostalgia does not preclude finding them overly commercial or problematic in their presentation of gender roles. Data gathered for this research showed such conflicted responses to be quite common. The common perceptions described in the present research accord with the findings of the Global Disney Audiences Project (GDAP), which found that "whether or not respondents liked Disney, they generally agreed on the core values represented in the company's products."[44] The present audience research, with its larger dataset (3,500-plus versus 1,250-plus participants), agrees with this GDAP conclusion as far as it applies to Disney films. Focusing on the Disney film as a distinct part of the Walt Disney Company yields a more nuanced picture of the understandings and perceptions that audiences share. The data collected for this research do not prove the GDAP wrong when it concluded that "our respondents are strongly disposed to read Disney texts in these terms, regardless of an individual's particular feelings about the company."[45] However, the present data suggest that a consideration of positive and negative attitudes is an important aspect of the perception of Disney films, especially when it comes to adult audiences' renegotiation of their relationships with Disney films.

While one individual may consider the accessibility of Disney films to be a positive attribute, because it means that there is a shared language to communicate with their children, others may consider the accessibility of Disney films to be a negative because of the way they crowd out independent animation from the multiplex. The perceived predictability of a Disney film may be a great comfort to those who enjoy the films, but a sign of banality to those who do not. It is apparent that an individual's perception of Disney films is dependent on their existing attitude towards Disney more generally.

Several respondents claimed that as adults, the "magic" of Disney was no longer available to them: "I have become cynical and think more about the 'real' story behind the film" (M-GB). This respondent's claim to have "become cynical" is a common one and indicates that his response to Disney films has become less emotional and more intellectual or rational. The implication is that adult fans of Disney films respond with their hearts, whereas adult detractors respond with their heads.

The GDAP conclusion that respondents "pointed to differences between the traditional Disney and the 'new Disney' [and that the latter] is seen as the 'merchandisation of culture' and is rejected" is challenged in the present research.[46] The difference between traditional or classic Disney and "new Disney" identified by the GDAP in 2001 is slight compared to the changes that have occurred in the last 20 years. Pixar, Marvel, and Lucasfilm now form a large part of twenty-first-century Disney filmmaking, allowing for bigger franchises and grander opportunities for synergy across more platforms and channels than were previously available, but shared audience perceptions of Disney films continue to conjure up the same images of animation, high production values, predictability, and accessibility. Perceptions of Disney have not caught up with the actuality of Disney output as identified through an analysis of Disney's films.

The Walt Disney Company has changed significantly since GDAP's investigation of Disney audiences in 2001. It is impossible to predict how Disney might change in another decade, or how its acquisition of 20th Century Fox and launch of the Disney+ streaming service will impact audience understandings of Disney films. Whatever Disney does, decades of association with animation and children's films are unlikely to disappear, and the bigger it becomes, the more resentment it is likely to foster among its detractors. But adults who need an escape from the world, who wish to share in the simple pleasures of viewing films fit for children of all ages, will no doubt carry on watching Disney films, enjoying the nostalgia, and buying into the magic.

Notes

1. Cited in John G. West Jr., *The Disney Live-Action Productions* (Milton, WA: Hawthorne & Peabody, 1994), p. 192.
2. At the time of writing, no film produced and distributed under the Disney name has carried a 15, 18 (UK) or R, NC-17 (US) rating, but Disney-owned studios Touchstone, Hollywood Pictures, Miramax and 20th Century Studios have.
3. David Buckingham, "Disney Dialectics: Debating the Politics of Children's Media Culture," in Janet Wasko, Mark Phillips, and Eileen R. Meehan (eds.), *Dazzled by Disney? The Global Disney Audiences Project* (London: Leicester University Press, 2001), pp. 269–296.
4. Janet Wasko, "Challenging Disney Myths," *Journal of Communication Inquiry* 25 (2001), pp. 237–257.
5. Wasko, "Challenging Disney Myths," p. 246.
6. See Amy Davis, *Good Girls and Wicked Witches: Women in Disney's Feature Animation* (Eastleigh, UK: John Libbey, 2006); and Davis, *Handsome Heroes and Vile Villains: Men in Disney's Feature Animation* (New Barnet, UK: John Libbey, 2013).
7. Janet Wasko, *Understanding Disney: The Manufacture of Fantasy* (Cambridge, UK: Polity Press, 2001), p. 110.
8. These criteria excluded over 1,000 features that were made-for-TV and direct-to-video, as well as films by Touchstone, Hollywood, and Miramax Pictures, which were not released under a Disney name.
9. Dave Smith, *Disney A to Z: The Official Encyclopedia*, 5th ed. (Los Angeles: Disney Editions, 2016), p. 671.
10. See Elizabeth Bell, Lynda Haas, and Laura Sells (eds.), *From Mouse to Mermaid: The Politics of Film, Gender, and Culture* (Bloomington: Indiana University Press, 1995); and Douglas Brode, *Multiculturalism and the Mouse: Race and Sex in Disney Entertainment* (Austin: University of Texas Press, 2005).
11. See Sean Griffin, *Tinker Belles and Evil Queens: The Walt Disney Company from the Inside Out* (New York: New York University Press, 2000).
12. Quoted in Matt Cain, "The Nature of the Beast," *Attitude* (London, UK: Stream Publishing, 2017), p. 114.
13. See the Bibliography.
14. Wasko, *Understanding Disney*, pp. 195–218.

15. Ibid., p. 217.

16. Wasko, Phillips, and Meehan, *Dazzled by Disney?*

17. Buckingham, "Disney Dialectics."

18. Wasko et al., "Appendix 4: Worldwide Response to Disney Questionnaire," in Wasko, Phillips, and Meehan, *Dazzled by Disney?*, pp. 357–359.

19. Paul Wells, *Understanding Animation* (Abingdon, UK: Routledge, 1998), pp. 222–243.

20. Wells, *Understanding Animation*, p. 233.

21. Buckingham, "Disney Dialectics," p. 273.

22. Leonard Maltin, *Of Mice and Magic: A History of Animated Cartoons* (New York: Plume, 1987), p. 29.

23. The full PhD thesis this chapter is based on can be found online at the website White Rose eTheses Online, http://etheses.whiterose.ac.uk/19239/.

24. Martin Barker, *From Antz to Titanic: Reinventing Film Analysis* (London: Pluto, 2000), p. 189.

25. Martin Barker and E. Mathijs, *Watching "The Lord of the Rings": Tolkien's World Audiences* (New York: Peter Lang, 2007).

26. Martin Barker, "Changing Lives, Challenging Concepts; Some Findings and Lessons from the Lord of the Rings Project," *International Journal of Cultural Studies* 12 (2009), pp. 375–393, at 386.

27. British Film Institute, *Statistical Yearbook 2016* (London: British Film Institute, 2016), p. 178. Also available at BFI.org.uk.

28. Will Dahlgreen and Anna-Elizabeth Shakespeare, "1 in 2 Young People Say They Are Not 100 Per Cent Heterosexual," YouGov, August 16, 2015. https://yougov.co.uk/news/2015/08/16/half-young-not-heterosexual/ [accessed June 11, 2019].

29. Michael Barrier, *Hollywood Cartoons: American Animation in Its Golden Age* (Oxford: Oxford University Press, 2003), p. ix.

30. Barrier, *Hollywood Cartoons*, p. 559.

31. Interview with the author, conducted July 15, 2016.

32. James R. Mason, *Disney Connections and Collections*, vol.1: *Movies* (USA: Theme Park Press, 2018).

33. Jennifer Szalai, "Against 'Guilty Pleasure,'" *New Yorker*, December 9, 2013, https://www.newyorker.com/books/page-turner/against-guilty-pleasure [accessed June 11, 2019].

34. Ien Ang, *Watching Dallas: Soap Opera and the Melodramatic Imagination* (London: Routledge, 1989).

35. Brenda R. Weber (ed.), *Reality Gendervision: Sexuality and Gender on Transatlantic Reality Television* (London: Duke University Press, 2014).

36. Quoted in Jim Korkis, *Walt's Words: Quotations of Walt Disney with Sources!* (USA: Theme Park Press, 2016), p. 84.

37. The codes for respondents included letters to identify self-reported gender (F, M, or O), plus a two-digit identifier indicating their nationality.

38. Ron Suskind, *Life, Animated: A Story of Sidekicks, Heroes, and Autism* (Glendale, CA: Kingswell, 2014), p. 250.

39. Suskind, *Life, Animated*, p. 250.

40. Quoted in Korkis, *Walt's Words*, p. 81.

41. Douglas Brode, "Anti-Semitism American-Style and a Man Named Disney," in Douglas Brode and Shea T. Brode (eds.), *Debating Disney: Pedagogical Perspectives on Commercial Cinema* (Lanham, MD: Rowman & Littlefield, 2016), p. 222.

42. See Richard Shale, *Donald Duck Joins Up: The Walt Disney Studio during World War II* (Ann Arbor, MI: UMI Research Press, 1982).
43. John Taylor, *Storming the Magic Kingdom: Wall Street, the Raiders, and the Battle for Disney* (New York: A. A. Knopf, 1987), p. 15.
44. Janet Wasko and Eileen R. Meehan, "Dazzled by Disney? Ambiguity in Ubiquity," in Wasko, Phillips, and Meehan, *Dazzled by Disney?*, pp. 329–343.
45. Wasko and Meehan, "Dazzled by Disney?," p. 334.
46. Ibid., p. 335.

BIBLIOGRAPHY

Barker, Martin. *From Antz to Titanic: Reinventing Film Analysis*. London: Pluto, 2000.

Mason, James R. "Disney Film Genres and Adult Audiences: A Tale of Renegotiated Relationships." Unpublished PhD thesis. University of Leeds, September 2017.

Pallant, Chris. *Demystifying Disney: A History of Disney Feature Animation*. New York: Bloomsbury, 2013.

Wasko, Janet. "Challenging Disney Myths." *Journal of Communication Inquiry* 25 (2001), pp. 237–257.

Wasko, Janet. *Understanding Disney: The Manufacture of Fantasy*. Cambridge, UK: Polity Press, 2001.

Wasko, Janet, Mark Phillips, and Eileen R. Meehan. *Dazzled by Disney? The Global Disney Audiences Project*. London: Leicester University Press, 2001.

Wells, Paul. *Understanding Animation*. Abingdon, UK: Routledge, 1998.

Index